MAKING
A
NATION

The United States and Its People

Volume I

Jeanne Boydston
University of Wisconsin

Nick Cullather
Indiana University

Jan Ellen Lewis
Rutgers University, Newark

Michael McGerr
Indiana University

James Oakes
The Graduate Center, The City University of New York

Prentice
Hall

Upper Saddle River, New Jersey 07458

Library of Congress Cataloging-in-Publication Data

Making a nation : the United States and its people / Jeanne Boydston . . . [et al.].
    p. cm.
    Includes bibliographical references and index.
    ISBN 0-13-033771-4
    1. United States—History. 2. United States—Economic conditions. I. Boydston, Jeanne.
E178.1 .M22 2001
973—dc21

2001034375

Use the Internet and eliminate mail time and postage costs
http://cip.loc. gov/cip

Editorial Director: Charlyce Jones Owen
Senior Acquisitions Editor: Charles Cavaliere
AVP, Director of Production and Manufacturing:
    Barbara Kittle
Editor in Chief of Development: Susanna Lesan
Development Editors: Barbara Muller, Robert Weiss
Senior Production Editor: Barbara DeVries
Prepress and Manufacturing Manager: Nick Sklitsis
Prepress and Manufacturing Buyer: Tricia Kenny
Marketing Manager: Claire Rehwinkel
Creative Design Director: Leslie Osher
Interior and Cover Design: Maria Lange
Chapter Opener Art Creation: Bruce Killmer

Line Art Supervisor: Gary Ruggiero
Electronic Art Coordinator: Mirella Signoretto
Copy Editor: Martha Francis
Editorial Assistant: Adrienne Paul
Photo Research: Linda Sykes
Photo Permission Manager: Kay Dellosa
Photo Permission Specialist: Tara Gardner
Cartographer: CartaGraphics
Cover Photos: Scott Barrow/International Stock
    Photography Ltd.; Bob Firth/International Stock
    Photography Ltd.; Ransohoff Collection, Cincinnati
    Museum Center; James Darell/Stone; Tim Jahns/The
    Image Bank

This book was set in 10/12 Stempel Garamond Regular by Carlisle
Communications and was printed and bound by Courier Companies, Inc.
The cover was printed by Phoenix Color Corporation.

© 2002 by Pearson Education
Upper Saddle River, New Jersey 07458

Printed in the United States of America
10 9 8 7 6 5 4

ISBN 0-13-033992-X

PEARSON EDUCATION LTD., London
PEARSON EDUCATION AUSTRALIA PTY. Limited, Sydney
PEARSON EDUCATION SINGAPORE, Pte. Ltd.
PEARSON EDUCATION NORTH ASIA LTD, Hong Kong
PEARSON EDUCATION CANADA, LTD., Toronto
PEARSON EDUCATION DE MEXICO, S.A. de C.V.
PEARSON EDUCATION—Japan, Tokyo
PEARSON EDUCATION MALAYSIA, Pte. Ltd.
PEARSON EDUCATION, Upper Saddle River, New Jersey

BRIEF CONTENTS

1 Worlds in Motion, 1450–1550 2

2 Colonial Outposts, 1550–1650 32

3 The English Come to Stay, 1600–1660 60

4 Creating the Empire, 1660–1720 90

5 The Eighteenth-Century World, 1700–1775 122

6 Conflict on the Edge of the Empire, 1713–1774 154

7 Creating a New Nation, 1775–1788 184

8 The Experiment Undertaken, 1789–1800 220

9 Liberty and Empire, 1800–1815 248

10 The Market Revolution, 1815–1824 278

11 Securing Democracy, 1820–1832 308

12 Reform and Conflict, 1828–1836 334

13 Manifest Destiny, 1836–1848 362

14 The Politics of Slavery, 1848–1860 388

15 A War for Union and Emancipation, 1861–1865 416

16 Reconstructing a Nation, 1865–1877 448

CONTENTS

Maps   xii
Figures and Tables   xiv
Special Features   xv
Preface   xvi
About the Authors   xxi
Student Tool Kit   xxii

1

Worlds in Motion, 1450–1550   2

Christopher Columbus: World Traveler   3

The Worlds of Christopher Columbus   5
  European Nations in the Age of Discovery   5
  The Political Economy of Europe   5
  The World of the West African Peoples   7
  Slavery Before 1500   9
  The Golden Age of Spain   9

The World of the Indian Peoples   11
  The Archaic Indians   11
  The Indians of the Eastern Woodlands   13
  The Indians of the Plains   14
  The Indians of the Deserts   14
  The Indians of the Pacific Coast   15
  The Great Civilizations of the Americas   15

Worlds in Collision   15
  Christopher Columbus Finds a Patron   16
  Columbus Finds a New World   17
  Tainos and Caribs   17
  The Origins of a New World Political
    Economy   18
  The *Requerimiento* and the Morality of
    Conquest   19
ON TRIAL: Las Casas and Sepúlveda Debate the Morality
  of Conquest   20

The Biological Consequences of Conquest   21
  Demographic Decline   21
  The Columbian Exchange   22

Onto the Mainland   23
  The First Florida Ventures   23
  The Conquest of Mexico   25
  The Establishment of a Spanish Empire   26
  The Return to Florida   27
  Coronado and the Pueblo Indians   28

Web connection
America and the Horse   28

Conclusion   29
Chronology   30
Review Questions   31
Further Readings   31
History on the Internet   31

2

Colonial Outposts, 1550–1650   32

Don Luís de Velasco Finds His Way Home   33

**Pursuing Wealth and Glory Along the North
  American Shore   35**
  European Objectives   35
  The Huge Geographical Barrier   36

Spanish Outposts   38

**New France: An Outpost in the Global Political
  Economy   40**
  The Indian Background to French
    Settlement   40
  Champlain Encounters the Hurons   40
  Creating a Middle Ground in New France   43
WHERE THEY LIVED, WHERE THEY WORKED: Huronia   44
  An Outpost in a Global Political Economy   46

Web connection
Exploitation of the Americas   46

**New Netherland: The Empire of a Trading
  Nation   47**
  Colonization by a Private Company   47

Slavery and Freedom in the Dutch Political
 Economy 49
The Dutch-Indian Trading Partnership 50
The Beaver Wars 51

England Attempts an Empire 52
The Origins of English Nationalism 52
Raiding Other Empires 52
Rehearsal in Ireland 53
The Roanoke Venture 54
The Abandoned Colony 56
Conclusion 57
Chronology 58
Review Questions 58
Further Readings 59
History on the Internet 59

Changing the Land to Fit the Political
 Economy 80
The Puritan Family 81

Dissension in the Puritan Ranks 82
GROWING UP IN AMERICA: Childhood in Puritan
 New England 83
Roger Williams and Toleration 83
Anne Hutchinson and the Equality of
 Believers 84
Puritan Indian Policy and the Pequot
 War 85
Chronology 87
Conclusion 88
Review Questions 88
Further Readings 88
History on the Internet 89

3
The English Come to Stay,
1600–1660 60

The Adventures of John Rolfe 61

The First Chesapeake Colonies 63
Planning Virginia 63

Web connection
Folklore, Heritage, and National Character 64
Starving Times 65
Troubled Relations With the Powhatans 66
Toward a New Political Economy 68
Toward the Destruction of the
 Powhatans 68
A New Colony in Maryland 70

The Political Economy of Slavery Emerges 70
The Problem of a Labor Supply 71
The Origins of Slavery in the Chesapeake 71
Gender and the Social Order in the
 Chesapeake 72

**A Bible Commonwealth in the New England
 Wilderness 73**
The English Origins of the Puritan
 Movement 74
What Did the Puritans Believe? 74
The Pilgrim Colony at Plymouth 75
The Puritan Colony at Massachusetts Bay 77
The New England Way 78

4
Creating the Empire, 1660–1720 90

Tituba Shapes Her World and Saves Herself 91

The Plan of Empire 93
Turmoil in England 93
The Political Economy of Mercantilism 94

New Colonies, New Patterns 94
New Netherland Becomes New York 94
Diversity and Prosperity in Pennsylvania 95
Indians and Africans in the Political Economy
 of Carolina 96
The Barbados Connection 98

The Transformation of Virginia 100
Social Change in Virginia 101
Bacon's Rebellion and the Abandonment of the
 Middle Ground 101
Virginia Becomes a Slave Society 102

New England Under Assault 104
Social Prosperity and the Fear of Religious
 Decline 104
King Philip's War 105
Indians and the Empire 106

The Empire Strikes 107
The Dominion of New England 107
The Glorious Revolution—in Britain and
 America 107

The Rights of Englishmen   108
Conflict in the Empire   109

Massachusetts in Crisis   110
The Social and Cultural Contexts of
Witchcraft   110
Witchcraft at Salem   111

Web connection
Witches in the American Imagination   III

ON TRIAL: The Supernatural on Trial—Witchcraft at
Salem   112
The End of Witchcraft   112

French and Spanish Outposts   113
France Attempts an Empire   114
The Spanish Outpost in Florida   116

**Conquest, Revolt, and Reconquest in
New Mexico   116**
The Conquest of Pueblo Society   116
The Pueblo Revolt   118
Reconquest and the Creation of Spanish
Colonial Society   118
Conclusion   119
Chronology   120
Review Questions   121
Further Readings   121
History on the Internet   121

5

The Eighteenth-Century World, 1700–1775   122

*George Whitefield: Evangelist for a Consumer
Society   123*

**The Population Explosion of the Eighteenth
Century   125**
The Dimensions of Population Growth   125
Bound for America: European Immigrants   125
Bound for America: African Slaves   128
"The Great Increase of Offspring"   129

**The Transatlantic Political Economy: Producing and
Consuming   130**
The Nature of Colonial Economic
Growth   130
The Transformation of the Family
Economy   130
Sources of Regional Prosperity   132

Merchants and Dependent Laborers in the
Transatlantic Economy   134
Consumer Choices and the Creation of
Gentility   135

The Varieties of Colonial Experience   138
Creating an Urban Public Sphere   138
The Diversity of Urban Life   141
The Maturing of Rural Society   142
The World That Slavery Made   142
WHERE THEY LIVED, WHERE THEY WORKED: The
Chesapeake Plantation Village   144
Georgia: From Frontier Outpost to Plantation
Society   145

**The Head and the Heart in America: The
Enlightenment and Religious Awakening   145**
The Ideas of the Enlightenment   146
The Enlightenment and the Study of Political
Economy   146
Enlightened Institutions   147
Origins of the Great Awakening   147

Web connection
The Origins of The Great Awakening   148

The Grand Itinerant   148
Cultural Conflict and Challenges to
Authority   148
What the Awakening Wrought   151
Conclusion   151
Review Questions   152
Chronology   152
Further Readings   153
History on the Internet   153

6

Conflict on the Edge of the Empire, 1713–1774   154

Susannah Willard Johnson Experiences the Empire   155

The Wars for Empire   157
An Uneasy Peace   157
New War, Old Pattern   158
War and Political Economy   158

The Victory of the British Empire   160
The French Empire Crumbles From
Within   160
The Virginians Ignite a War   161

GROWING UP IN AMERICA: Youth in Captivity   162
    From Local to Imperial War   163
    Problems with British-Colonial Cooperation   165
    The British Gain the Advantage   167

Enforcing the Empire   169
    Pontiac's Rebellion and Its Aftermath   170
    Paying for the Empire: Sugar and Stamps   171

Web connection
Stamping Out Stamps   172

Rejecting the Empire   172
    An Argument About Rights and Obligations
       173
    The Imperial Crisis in Local Context   173
    Contesting the Townshend Duties   176

A Revolution in the Empire   177
    "Massacre" in Boston   178
    The Empire Comes Apart   178
    The First Continental Congress   181
Conclusion   181
Chronology   182
Review Questions   182
Further Readings   183
History on the Internet   183

7

Creating a New Nation, 1775–1788   184

James Madison Helps Make a Nation   185

The War Begins   187
    The First Battles   187
    Congress Takes the Lead   188
    Military Ardor   189
    Declaring Independence   189
    Creating a National Government   191
    Creating State Governments   191

Winning the Revolution   192
    Competing Strategies   192
    The British on the Offensive: 1776   193
    A Slow War: 1777–1781   194
WHERE THEY LIVED, WHERE THEY WORKED: The Winter
    at Jockey Hollow   196
    Securing a Place in the World   199

The Challenge of the Revolution   202
    The Departure of the Loyalists   203

    The Challenge of the Economy   203
    Contesting the New Political Economy   206
    Can Women Be Citizens?   206
    The Challenge of Slavery   208

A New Policy in the West   208
    The Indians' Revolution   208
    The End of the Middle Ground   209
    Settling the West   209

Creating a New National Government   211
    A Crippled Congress   213

Web connection
The Contest for Ratification   213

    Writing a New Constitution   214
    Ratifying the Constitution: Politics   215
    Ratifying the Constitution: Ideas   216
Chronology   218
Conclusion   218
Review Questions   219
Further Readings   219
History on the Internet   219

8

The Experiment Undertaken, 1789–1800   220

Washington's Inauguration   221

Conceptions of Political Economy in the New
  Republic   223
    Labor, Property, and Independence   223
GROWING UP IN AMERICA: Sally Brant   226
    The Status of Slaves, Women, and Native
      Americans   227

Factions and Order in the New Government   231
    The States and the Bill of Rights   231
    Congress Begins Its Work   232
    Political Economy and Political Parties   232
    Making a Civic Culture   234

Web connection
Hear Ye! Hear Ye! The Power of the Pen   235

A State and Its Boundaries   236
    The Problem of Authority in the
      Backcountry   237
    Taking the Land: Washington's Indian
      Policy   238

Western Lands and Eastern Politics: The
    Whiskey Rebellion   240

America in the Transatlantic Community   241
    Between France and England   241
    To the Brink of War   242
    The Administration of John Adams   243
Chronology   245
Conclusion   246
Review Questions   246
Further Readings   247
History on the Internet   247

9

Liberty and Empire, 1800–1815   248
Gabriel's Conspiracy for Freedom   249

Voluntary Communities in the Age of Jefferson   251
    Communities of Faith   251
    African Americans in the Early Republic   252
    Communities of Masters and Journeymen   255
GROWING UP IN AMERICA: Jarena Lee   256

Jeffersonian Republicanism: Politics of Transition   257
    A New Capital, A New President   257
    Jeffersonian Republicans in Power   259
    Protecting Commerce   259

Liberty and an Expanding Commerce   260
    The Political Economy of Cotton   260
    The Golden Age of Shipping   261
    Invention and Exploration   262

Web connection
For Better or For Worse?   263
    The Rule of Law and Lawyers   264

**The Political Economy of an "Empire
    of Liberty"   264**
    The Louisiana Purchase   265
    Surveying Louisiana   266
    The Burr Conspiracy   267
    Indian Resistance to Republican Empire   267

The Second War With England   269
    Neutrality and Isolation   270
    Democratic Republican Power and
        Disunity   271
    The War of 1812   271
    The Making of Heroes and Knaves   274
Conclusion   275
Chronology   275

Review Questions   276
Further Readings   276
History on the Internet   277

10

The Market Revolution, 1815–1824   278
Cincinnati: Queen of the West   279

New Lands, New Markets   281
    Westward to the Mississippi   281
    The Transportation Revolution   283
    The Waltham System of Manufacturing   286
WHERE THEY LIVED, WHERE THEY WORKED:
    The Lowell Mills   288

A New Nationalism   290
    A New Republican Political Economy   291

Web connection
Art Imitates Life   292
    The United States in the Americas   292
    Judicial Nationalism   293

Firebells in the Night   295
    The Panic of 1819   295
    The Missouri Compromise   296

The Political Economy of Regionalism   297
    Cities, Markets, and Commercial Farms in the
        Northeast   297
    Planters, Yeomen, and Slaves
        in the South   300
    The River and the West   303
Chronology   306
Conclusion   306
Review Questions   306
Further Readings   307
History on the Internet   307

11

Securing Democracy, 1820–1832   308
Jackson's Election   309

**Perfectionism and the Theology of Human
    Striving   311**
    Millenialism and Communitarians   311

Urban Revivals   313
Social Reform in the Benevolent Empire   314

Web connection
The Times They Are a Changin'   316

The Common Man and the Political Economy of Democracy   316
The Political Economy of Free Labor   316
Suffrage Reform   317
Opposition to Special Privilege and Secret Societies   319
Workingmen's Parties   320

The Democratic Impulse in Presidential Politics   321
Jackson's Rise to National Prominence   321
The Election of 1824 and the "Corrupt Bargain"   321
The Adams Presidency and the Gathering Forces of Democracy   323
The Election of 1828   323

President Jackson: Vindicating the Common Man   324
Jacksonian Democrats in Office   325
A Policy of Indian Removal   325
WHERE THEY LIVED, WHERE THEY WORKED:
Surviving Removal   328
The Bank War   330
Chronology   332
Conclusion   332
Review Questions   332
Further Readings   333
History on the Internet   333

12
Reform and Conflict, 1828–1836   334
Free Labor Under Attack   335

The Growth of Sectional Tension   337
The Political Economy of Southern Discontent   337
The Nullification Crisis   339
WHERE THEY LIVED, WHERE THEY WORKED: Gowrie   340
Antislavery Becomes Abolition   341
Abolitionism and Antiabolition Violence   343

Web connection
The Philadelphia Riot of 1838   345

The Political Economy of Early Industrial Society   347
Wage Dependency   347

Labor Organizing and Protest   348
A New Urban Middle Class   350
Immigration and Nativism   351
Internal Migration   353

Self-Reform and Social Regulation   354
A Culture of Self-Improvement   354
Temperance   356
The Common School Movement   357
Penal Reform   359
Conclusion   360
Chronology   360
Review Questions   361
Further Readings   361
History on the Internet   361

13
Manifest Destiny, 1836–1848   362
Mah-i-ti-wo-nee-ni Remembers Life on the Great Plains   363

The Setting of the Jacksonian Sun   365
Political Parties in Crisis   365
Van Buren and the Legacy of Jackson   366
Electoral Politics and Moral Reform   367
An Independent Woman's Rights Movement   369

The Political Economy of the Trans-Mississippi West   370
Texas   371

Web connection
The Un-Welcome Mat   371

Pacific-Bound   373
Nations of the Trans-Mississippi West   375

Slavery and the Political Economy of Expansion   378
Log Cabins and Hard Cider: The Election of 1840   378
And Tyler, Too   380
Occupy Oregon, Annex Texas   381
War With Mexico   382
GROWING UP IN AMERICA: Rankin Dilworth in the War With Mexico   385
Chronology   386
Conclusion   386
Review Questions   387
Further Readings   387
History on the Internet   387

14
The Politics of Slavery, 1848–1860   388

Frederick Douglass   389

The Political Economy of Freedom and Slavery   391
A Changing Economy in the North   391
Strengths and Weaknesses of the Southern
Economy   392
The Importance of the West   393

Slavery Becomes a Political Issue   396
Wilmot Introduces His Proviso   396
A Compromise Without Compromises   397
The Fugitive Slave Act Provokes
a Crisis   398

Web connection
The Return of Anthony Burns   398
The Election of 1852 and the Decline of the
Whig Party   399

**Nativism and the Origins of the Republican
Party**   400
The Nativist Attack on Immigration   400
The Kansas-Nebraska Act Revives the Slavery
Issue   401
The Expansion of Slavery as a Foreign
Policy   402
Kansas Begins to Bleed   403

A New Political Party Takes Shape   404
The First Sectional Election   404
The Labor Problem and the Politics of
Slavery   405

An "Irrepressible" Conflict?   406
The Slavery Issue Persists   406
The Lecompton Constitution Splits the
Democratic Party   407
Lincoln and Douglas Debate   408

The Retreat From Union   409
John Brown's War Against Slavery   410
ON TRIAL: John Brown   411
Northerners Elect a President   412
Conclusion   413
Chronology   414
Review Questions   414
Further Readings   414
History on the Internet   415

15
A War for Union and Emancipation, 1861–1865   416

Edmund Ruffin   417

From Union to Emancipation   419
The South Secedes   419
Civilians Demand a Total War   420
Slaves Take Advantage of the War   422
First Bull Run and the Shift in War
Aims   423

Mobilizing for War   424
Southern Political Weaknesses   425
Union Naval Supremacy   425
Southern Military Advantages   426
The Political Economy of Slavery Inhibits the
Confederacy   426
What Were Soldiers Fighting For?   427

The Civil War Becomes a Social Revolution   428
Union Victories in the West   429
Southern Military Strength in the
East   430
Emancipation as a "Military Necessity"   432
The Moment of Truth   433

Web connection
Whatever Happened at Fort Pillow?   434

The War at Home   434
The Care of Casualties   435
Northern Reverses and Antiwar
Sentiment   436
Gettysburg and the Justification of the
War   437
GROWING UP IN AMERICA: Litt Young   438
Discontent in the Confederacy   439

The War Comes to a Bloody End   440
Grant Takes Command   441
The Theory and Practice of Hard War   441
Sherman Marches, and Lee
Surrenders   443
The Meaning of the Civil War   444
Conclusion   446
Chronology   446
Review Questions   447
Further Readings   447
History on the Internet   447

16
Reconstructing a Nation,
1865–1877   448

John Dennett Visits a Freedmen's Bureau Court   449

Wartime Reconstruction   451
    Experiments With Free Labor   451
    Lincoln's Ten-Percent Plan *Versus* the Wade-
        Davis Bill   452
    The Freed People's Dream of Owning
        Land   454

Presidential Reconstruction, 1865–1867   455
    The Political Economy of Contract Labor   456
    Resistance to Presidential Reconstruction   457
    Congress Clashes With the President   458
    Origins of the Fourteenth Amendment   458
    Race Riots and the Election of 1866   459

Congressional Reconstruction   459
    Origins of the African-American Vote   459
    Radical Reconstruction in the South   460
    Achievements and Failures of Radical
        Government   461
    The Political Economy of Sharecropping   462

Web connection
**Did Reconstruction Work for the Freed
People?   463**

The Retreat From Republican Radicalism   465
    The Impeachment and Trial of Andrew
        Johnson   465

ON TRIAL: Andrew Johnson   466
    Republicans Become the Party of
        Moderation   468
    The Grant Administration and Moderate
        Republicanism   469

Reconstruction in the North   469
    The Fifteenth Amendment and Nationwide
        African-American Suffrage   470
    Women and Suffrage   470
    The Rise and Fall of the National Labor
        Union   471

The End of Reconstruction   472
    Corruption as a National Problem   472
    Liberal Republicans Revolt   474
    A Depression and a Deal "Redeem" the
        South   474
Conclusion   476
Chronology   477
Review Questions   478
Further Readings   478
History on the Internet   479

Appendix   A-1
Glossary   G-1
Bibliography   B-1
Credits   C-1
Index   I-1

MAPS

1

1-1 World Trade on the Eve of Discovery 6
1-2 Africa in the Age of Discovery 8
1-3 The Indian Peoples of North America and Their Languages, c.1500 12
1-4 The Columbian Exchange 22
1-5 The Spanish Exploration 24
1-6 A New Global Economy 29

2

2-1 North Atlantic Trade Routes at the End of the Sixteenth Century 36
2-2 Voyages of Exploration 37
2-3 European Colonization of the Southeast 39
2-4 The Iroquois Region in the Middle of the Seventeenth Century 41
2-5 French Exploration and Settlement, 1603–1616 42
2-6 The Wampum Trade 51

3

3-1 English Encroachments on Indian Land, 1613–1652 69
3-2 The English Colonies, 1660 78
3-3 New England in the 1640s 86

4

4-1 Trade Routes in the Southeast 98
4-2 Frontier Warfare During King William's and Queen Anne's Wars 109
4-3 Colonial North America, East of the Mississippi, 1713 113
4-4 Region of Spanish Reconquest of New Mexico, 1692–1696 118

5

5-1 Expansion of Settlement, 1720–1760 126
5-2 Exports of the Thirteen Colonies, c.1770 132
5-3 Commerce and Culture in Philadelphia, c.1760 139
5-4 Printing Presses and Newspapers, 1760–1775 140
5-5 George Whitefield's Itinerary 149

6

6-1 The Ohio River Valley, 1747–1758 167
6-2 The Second Phase of the French and Indian War, 1758–1763 168
6-3 The North American Colonies Before and After the French and Indian War 169
6-4 Pontiac's Rebellion, 1763 170

7

7-1 Battles of Lexington, Concord, and Breed's Hill 188
7-2 New York and New Jersey Campaigns, 1776–1777 194
7-3 The Battle for New York 198
7-4 The War of the South, 1779–1781 199
7-5 The Treaty of Paris 200
7-6 Sites of Revolutionary War Battles Involving Indians 210
7-7 Western Land Cessions 212

8

8-1 Distribution of Black Population 227
8-2 Extension of United States National Territories, 1783 and 1795 237
8-3 Western Expansion, 1785–1805 238
8-4 Major Indian Villages and Indian-U.S. Battle Sites, 1789–1800 240

9

9-1 Exploring the Trans-Mississippi West 265
9-2 Mounting Land Pressure, 1784–1812, and the Rise of Tecumseh's Confederation 268
9-3 Battles and Campaigns of the War of 1812 273

10

10-1 Frontier and Settled Sections, 1800–1810–1820 282
10-2 The Development of Regions and of Roads and Canals 287
10-3 Westward Expansion and Slavery, 1820 296

11

11-1 Revival and Reform 314
11-2 Toward Universal White Male Suffrage 318
11-3 The Election of 1824 322
11-4 The Election of 1828 324
11-5 Population Density Westward, 1790 and 1820 326
11-6 Indian Removals 327

12

12-1 Primary Sites of Antiabolition Violence 344
12-2 Slave, Free Black, and White Populations, 1830 346

13

13-1   Republic of Texas   373
13-2   Major Overland Trails   374
13-3   Major Trans-Mississippi Indian Communities,
       c.1850   376
13-4   Mexican War   384

14

14-1   Slavery's Expansion   394
14-2   Railroad Expansion   395
14-3   Stephen Douglas' Kansas-Nebraska Act of 1854
       Carved the Kansas Territory out of the larger
       Nebraska Territory   401
14-4   Mexican Cession   403
14-5   The Election of 1856   406
14-6   The Election of 1860   413

15

15-1   The Secession of the Southern States   421
15-2   The Virginia Campaigns of 1861–1862   423

15-3   The War in the West in 1862   428
15-4   The Battle of Antietam   431
15-5   The Battle of Gettysburg, July 1-3, 1863   437
15-6   The Siege of Vicksburg, 1862–1863   439
15-7   The Virginia Theater, 1864–1865   442
15-8   The Atlanta Campaign and Sherman's March,
       1864–1865   443

16

16-1   Reconstruciton and Redemption   456
16-2   Sharecropping   464
16-3   Effect of Sharecropping in the South: The
       Barrow Plantation in Oglethorpe County,
       Georgia   465
16-4   The Presidential Election, 1876   475

FIGURES and TABLES

FIGURES

1-1 World Population, 1650–2000 23

3-1 Disappearance of New England's Forests 81

5-1 The Importation of Servants from Europe into British America, 1580–1775 127

5-2 The Importation of Slaves into the Colonies, 1620–1810 128

5-3 Population of the Thirteen Colonies, 1610–1780 129

6-1 Tax Rates in Boston, 1645–1774 158

6-2 New England Captives, 1675–1763 159

6-3 Trade Between England and the Colonies 175

7-1 Inflation at Philadelphia, 1770–1790 204

7-2 Depreciation of Continental Currency, January 1770–April 1781 205

8-1 Revival of Exports to Great Britain 225

9-1 Volume of Cotton Exports, 1791–1815 260

9-2 Value of Exports and Re-exports From the United States, 1790–1815 261

12-1 Customs and Federal Revenue, 1815–1860 338

12-2 Increase in Irish Immigration, 1820–1850 351

14-1 The Decline of the Whig Party 400

15-1 The Productive Capacities of the Union and Confederacy 425

15-2 Casualties of War 435

16-1 Occupations of African-American Officeholders During Reconstruction 461

TABLES

3-1 English Population of Virginia, 1607–1640 65

3-2 Distribution of Land in Rowley, Massachusetts, 1639–1642 80

4-1 Population of British Colonies in America, 1660–1710 99

5-1 How Wealthy Were Colonial Amercans? 131

6-1 Major Events Leading to the Revolutionary War, 1763–1774 179

7-1 Key Provisions of the Articles of Confederation, The Virginia Plan, The New Jersey Plan, and the Constitution 215

8-1 Americans in 1790 223

8-2 Principle Exports From the United States, 1791 225

8-3 Sources of Federal Revenue, 1790–1799 233

9-1 Growth in the Black Population in Cities, 1800–1850 (Slave and Free) 254

9-2 Population of the Western States and Territories 264

13-1 The Liberty Party Swings an Election 379

13-2 Personal Income Per Capita by Region: Percentages of United States Average 382

16-1 Cotton Prices in New York 457

16-2 Reconstruction Amendments, 1865–1870 460

SPECIAL FEATURES

WHERE THEY LIVED, WHERE THEY WORKED

Huronia **44**
The Chesapeake Plantation Village **144**
The Winter at Jockey Hollow **196**

The Lowell Mills **288**
Surviving Removal **328**
Gowrie **340**

ON TRIAL

Las Casas and Sepúlveda Debate the Morality of Conquest **20**

The Supernatural on Trial—Witchcraft at Salem **112**
John Brown **411**

GROWING UP IN AMERICA

Childhood in Puritan New England **83**
Youth in Captivity **162**
Sally Brandt **226**

Jarena Lee **256**
Rankin Dilworth in the War With Mexico **385**
Litt Young **438**

PREFACE

Every human life is shaped by a variety of different relationships. Cultural relations, diplomatic relations, race, gender, and class relations, all contribute to how an individual interacts with the larger global community. This was as true in the past as it is today. *Making a Nation* retells the history of the United States by emphasizing the relationships that have shaped and defined the identities of the American people. For example, to disentangle the identity of a Mexican American woman working in a factory in Los Angeles in the year 2000 is to confront the multiple and overlapping "identities" that define a single American life. *Making a Nation* assumes that the multiplicity of cultures, classes, and regions, the vast changes as well as the enduring elements of our past, can nonetheless be told as the story of a single nation, always in the making. There are many ways to explore these relationships. *Making a Nation* views them through the lens of political economy. This is an especially appropriate way to approach American history.

In March of 1776, Adam Smith published his masterpiece, *The Wealth of Nations,* a few months before American colonists declared their independence from Great Britain. The imperial crisis had been building for some time and was a topic of international discussion. Smith delayed publication of his work for a year so that he could perfect a lengthy chapter on Anglo-American relations. Thus *The Wealth of Nations,* one of the most important documents in a new branch of knowledge known as *political economy,* was written with a close eye to events in the British colonies of North America, the colonies that were soon to become the United States. The fact that a large portion of Smith's book was framed as a history of England is equally important. Smith believed that history was one of the best ways to approach the study of political economy. *Making a Nation* shares that assumption; it takes political economy as an organizing theme for the history of the United States.

What did Smith and his many American followers mean by "political economy?" They meant, firstly, that the economy itself is much broader than the gross national product, the unemployment rate, or the twists and turns of the stock market. They understood that economies are tightly bound to politics, that they are therefore the products of history rather than nature or accident. And just as men and women make history, so to do they make economies—in the way they work and organize their families as much as in their fiscal policies and tax structures.

The term "political economy" is not commonly used any more, yet it is a way of thinking that is deeply embedded in American history. To this day we casually assume that different government policies create different "incentives" shaping everything from the way capital gains are invested to how parents raise their children, from how unmarried mothers on welfare can escape from poverty to how automobile manufacturers design cars for fuel efficiency and pollution control. This connection between government, the economy, and the relationships that shape the daily lives of ordinary men and women is the essence of political economy. But that connection points in different directions. Politics and the economy do not simply shape, but are in turn shaped by, the lives and cultural values of ordinary men and women.

In short, political economy establishes a context that allows students to see the links between the particular and the general, between large and seemingly abstract forces such as "globalization" and the struggles of working parents who find they need two incomes to provide for their children. *Making a Nation* shows that such relationships were as important in the seventeenth and eighteenth centuries as they are today.

So, for example, we begin this history of our nation by stepping back to view an early modern "world in motion." Every chapter in the book opens with a vignette that captures the chapter's theme, but each of the first six vignettes focuses on a different traveler whose life was set in motion by the European expansion across the Atlantic: an explorer, a settler, a young mother, a slave, a Native American. In a sense, globalization has been a theme in American history from its earliest beginnings. Europe, Africa, and the Americas were linked to each other in an Atlantic world across which everything was exchanged, deadly diseases along with diplomatic formalities, political structures and cultural assumptions, African slaves and European servants, colonists and commodities.

In subsequent chapters *Making a Nation* traces the development of the newly formed United States by once again stressing the link between the lives of ordinary men and women to the grand political struggles between Alexander Hamilton and Thomas Jefferson, between Andrew Jackson's Democrats and Henry Clay's Whigs. Should the federal government create a centralized bank? Should it promote economic development by sponsoring the construction of railroads, turnpikes, and canals? At one level, such questions exposed competing ideas about what American capitalism should look like and what the implications of those ideas were for American democracy. But a closer look suggests that those same political quarrels were propelled by the concerns that farmers, workers, and businessmen were expressing about the pace and direction of economic change. A newly democratic politics had given many ordinary Americans a voice, and they immediately began speaking about the way the policies of the government affected the basic elements of their daily lives. They have been speaking the same way ever since.

Similarly, the great struggle over slavery and freedom—a struggle that literally tore the nation apart in the middle of the nineteenth century—is told as the story of dramatic political maneuvers and courageous military exploits, as well as the story of women who created the modern profession of nursing by caring for civil war soldiers and of runaway slaves who helped push the United States government into a policy of emancipation. The insights of political economy frame the way *Making a Nation* presents the transition from slave to free labor in the South after the Civil War. A new labor system meant an entirely new pattern of gender relations between freedmen and freedwomen whose marriages were legalized for the first time.

In the twentieth century, as America became a global power, the demands of the new political economy of urban and industrial America inform our examination of both U.S. diplomacy and domestic affairs. It was no accident, for example, that the civil rights leader A. Philip Randolph took advantage of the crisis of the Second World War to threaten Franklin Roosevelt's administration with a march on Washington. For Randolph, the demand for racial equality was inseparable from the struggle for a more equitable distribution of the rewards of a capitalist economy.

The United States victory in World War II, coupled with the extraordinary burst of prosperity in the war's aftermath, gave rise to fantasies of omnipotence that were tested and shattered by the American experience in Vietnam. Presidents, generals, and ordinary soldiers alike shared in the illusion of invulnerability. America's was the greatest democracy and the most powerful economy on earth. Thus did Americans in Southeast Asia in the late twentieth century find themselves in much the same place that Christopher Columbus had found himself centuries before: halfway around the world, face to face with a people whose culture he did not fully understand.

Student Learning Aids

To assist students in their appreciation of this history, we have added several distinctive features.

Chapter Opening Vignettes

The vignettes that open each chapter have already been mentioned; they are intended to give specificity as well as humanity to the themes that follow. From the witchcraft trials in Salem to the Trumps' American dream, students are drawn into each chapter with interesting stories that illustrate the organizing factor of political economy.

"Where They Lived, Where They Worked" sections, such as the story of the company-owned town of Pullman, Illinois, featured in Chapter 20 help students see the connections between home and work that are obscured in most accounts of American history.

"Growing Up In America" includes the history of young people in a systematic way. Instead of just concentrating on famous people in history, these sections look particularly at one or a group of younger people and relate their experiences to the larger movements of their day. By providing students insights into the lives of ordinary people like themselves, such as Jarena Lee presented in Chapter 9, this special feature makes the text inherently more interesting .

"On Trial" highlights a series of cases, such as the Scottsboro trial in Chapter 24, that show how personal, social, and even political struggles are often played out as dramatic and illuminating courtroom battles.

Web Connection

Making a Nation is the first text to integrate Web-based activities into each of its chapters. Tied closely to the themes of the text, each Web Connection combines text, audio, and visuals to explore provocative topics in depth.

Maps

The study of history has always been enhanced by maps. To help students understand the relationships between places and events, *Making a Nation* provides extensive map coverage. With over 120 full color maps devoted to such topics as "Exploring the Trans-Mississippi West," "Patterns of Global Migration," and "The Globalization of the U.S. Economy," students can more readily place events in their geographic context. To capture the element of globalization, almost every chapter contains at least one map dedicated to that theme.

Pedagogical Aids

Each chapter has numerous aids to help students read and review the information. Chapter outlines, listing of key topics, chapter chronologies, review questions, further readings and a collection of related Internet sites are found in every chapter.

Additional Study Aids

In addition to providing several key documents in United States history, the Appendix presents demographic data reflecting the 2000 census figures. A Glossary explains important terms highlighted in the book, and an extended Bibliography offers an expanded compilation of literature, arranged by chapter.

Themes and Coverage

Because *Making a Nation* was written from the very beginning with an organizing theme in mind, we have been able to incorporate many topics relatively smoothly within the larger narrative. For example, this textbook includes some of the most extensive coverage of Indian and western history available, but because our coverage is integrated into the larger narrative, there is no need to provide a separate chapter on either topic. At the same time, the theme of political economy allows us to cover subjects that are often missed in standard texts. For example, *Making a Nation* includes more than the usual coverage of environmental history, as well as more complete coverage of the social and cultural history of the late twentieth century than is available elsewhere. And in every case the *politics* of globalization and environmentalism, of capitalist development and democratic reform, of family values and social inequality are never far from view. *Making a Nation* also provides full coverage of the most recent American history, from the end of the Cold War to the rise of a new information economy and on to the terrorist attacks against the World Trade Center and the Pentagon in September 2001. Here, again, the organizing theme of political economy provides a strong but supple interpretive framework that helps students understand developments that are making a nation in a new century.

Supplementary Instructional Materials

Making a Nation comes with an extensive package of supplementary print and multimedia materials for both instructors and students.

PRINT SUPPLEMENTS

Instructor's Resource Manual

Prepared by Laura Graves, South Plains College
Contains introduction to instructors, chapter outlines, detailed chapter overviews, discussion questions, lecture strategies, essay topics, suggestions for working with Web resources, and tips on incorporating Penguin titles in American history into lectures.

Test Item File

Prepared by Bruce Caskey, Herkimer County Community College
Includes over 1000 multiple-choice, true-false, essay, and map questions, organized by chapter. A collection of blank maps can be photocopied and used for map testing or other class exercises.

Study Guide *(Volumes I and II)*

Prepared by Laura Graves, South Plains College
Contains introduction to students, chapter overviews, chapter outlines, map questions, sample exam questions,

analytical reading exercises, collaborative exercises, and essay questions.

Documents in United States History *(Volumes I and II)*

Prepared by Paula Stathakis, University of North Carolina, Charlotte, and Alan Downs, Georgia Southern University
Edited specifically for *Making a Nation,* the Documents Set brings together over 200 primary sources and scholarly articles in American history. Headnotes and review questions contextualize the documents and prompt critical inquiry.

Transparencies

This collection of over 150 full-color transparencies provides the maps, charts, and graphs from the text for classroom presentations.

Retrieving the American Past 2001 Edition (RTAP)

RTAP enables instructors to tailor a custom reader whose content, organization, and price exactly match their course syllabi. Edited by historians and educators at The Ohio State University and other respected schools, RTAP offers instructors the freedom and flexibility to choose selections of primary and secondary source readings—or both—from 73 (14 new) chapters. Contact your local Prentice Hall representative for details about RTAP. Discounts apply when copies of RTAP are bundled with *Making a Nation.*

Themes of the Times

 This special newspaper supplement is prepared jointly for students by Prentice Hall and the premier news publication, the *New York Times.* Issued twice a year, it contains recent articles pertinent to American history, which connect the classroom to the world. Contact your Prentice Hall representative for details.

Reading Critically about History

Prepared by Rose Wassman and Lee Rinsky, DeAnza College, this brief guide provides students with helpful strategies for reading a history textbook and is available free when packaged with *Making a Nation.*

Understanding and Answering Essay Question

Prepared by Mary L. Kelley, San Antonio College, this helpful guide provides analytical tools for understanding different types of essay questions and for preparing well-crafted essay answers. It is available free when packaged with *Making a Nation.*

MULTIMEDIA SUPPLEMENTS

Companion Website™

The access code protected *Companion Website™* for *Making a Nation* is available at *www.prenhall.com/boydston* and offers students one of the most comprehensive Internet resources available. Organized around the primary subtopics of each chapter, the *Companion Website*™ provides detailed summaries, multiple-choice, true-false, essay, identification, map labeling, and document questions and Web Connection activities based on the text. Overview tables in each chapter facilitate quick review. Hyperlinks to other Web resources provide students with access to screened sites. Chat rooms and message boards allow students to share their ideas about American history with their own class or with colleges across the country.

The *Faculty Module* contains a wealth of material for instructors, including Microsoft PowerPoint™ presentations with maps, charts, and graphs that can be downloaded.

History on the Internet
This guide focuses on developing the critical-thinking skills necessary to evaluate and use online resources. It provides a brief introduction to navigating the Internet and outlines the many references to history Websites. Available free when packaged with *Making a Nation*.

PowerPoint™ Images CD-ROM
Available in Windows and Mac formats for use with Microsoft PowerPoint™, this CD-ROM includes the maps, charts, tables, and graphs from *Making a Nation*. These resources can be used in lectures, for slide shows, and printed as transparencies.

COURSE MANAGEMENT SYSTEMS
As the leader in course-management solutions for teachers and students of history, Prentice Hall provides a variety of online tools. Contact your local Prentice Hall representative for a demonstration, or visit *www.prenhall. com/demo*

Acknowledgements
We would like to express our express our thanks to the reviewers whose thoughtful comments and insights were of great value in finalizing *Making a Nation:*

Tyler Anbinder, George Washington University
Debra Barth, San Jose City College
James M. Bergquist, Villanova University
Robert Brandfon, College of the Holy Cross
Stephanie Camp, University of Washington
Mark T. Carleton, Louisiana State University
Jean Choate, Northern Michigan University
Martin B. Cohen, George Mason University
Samuel Crompton, Holyoke Community College
George Daniels, University of South Alabama
James B. Dressler, Cumberland University
Elizabeth Dunn, Baylor University
Mark Fernandez, Loyola University of New Orleans
Willard B. Gatewood, University of Arkansas

James Gilbert, University of Maryland at College Park
Richard L. Hume, Washington State University
Frederic Jaher, University of Illinois at Urbana-Champaign
Glen Jeansonne, University of Wisconsin-Milwaukee
Constance Jones, Tidewater Community College
Laylon Wayne Jordan, University of Charleston
Peter Kirstein, St. Xavier University
John D. Krugler, Marquette University
Mark V. Kwasny, Ohio State University-Newark
Gene D. Lewis, University of Cincinnati
Glenn Linden, Southern Methodist University
Robert McCarthy, Providence College
Andrew McMichael, Vanderbilt University
Dennis N. Mihelich, Creighton University
Patricia Hagler Minter, Western Kentucky University
Joseph Mitchell, Howard Community College
Reid Mitchell, University of Maryland Baltimore County
Carl Moneyhon, University of Arkansas at Little Rock
James M. Morris, Christopher Newport University
Earl Mulderink III, Southern Utah University
Alexandra Nickliss, City College of San Francisco
Chris S. O'Brien, University of Kansas
Peter Onuf, University of Virginia
Annelise Orleck, Dartmouth College
Richard H. Peterson, San Diego State University
Leo R. Ribuffo, George Washington University
Kenneth Scherzer, Middle Tennessee State University
Sheila Skemp, University of Mississippi
Kevin Smith, Ball State University
Michael Topp, University of Texas at El Paso
Gregory J. W. Urwin, University of Central Arkansas
Paul K. Van der Slice, Montgomery College
Jessica Weiss, California State University of Hayward
James A. Wilson, Southwest Texas State University
John Wiseman, Frostburg State University

The authors would like first to acknowledge their co-authors: Without the patience, tenacity, and intellectual support we received from each other, we could scarcely have continued to the end. And we are grateful of course to our families, friends, and colleagues who encouraged us during the planning and writing of *Making A Nation*.

Jeanne Boydston would like to thank Joy P. Newmann for her enduring patience. I dedicate my work here to my father, Donnell B Boydston, who probably would have quarreled with much of what I've written, but would have loved reading it.

Jan Lewis expresses special thanks to Andy Achenbaum, James Grimmelmann, Warren F. Kimball, Ken Lockridge, and Peter Onuf, who either read portions of the manuscript or discussed it with me. And I am grateful to Barry Bienstock for his enormous library, his vast knowledge, and his endless patience.

Michael McGerr: This is for Frances Asbach and Edward McGerr, Grace Sarli and Joseph Fanelli, and Pauline Tornay and Michael Tuoti, who helped make a nation, and for Katie and Patrick McGerr who will help remake it.

The authors would like to thank Bruce Nichols for helping launch this textbook many years ago, and the editors and staff at Prentice Hall, especially our acquisitions editor, Charles Cavaliere, editorial director and vice president, Charlyce Jones Owen, development editor Barbara Muller, Susanna Lesan, editor in chief of development, senior production editor, Barbara DeVries, marketing manager, Claire Rehwinkel, and designer, Maria Lange. We have benefited at each stage from their patience, their experience, and their commitment to this project. Thanks also to Linda Sykes who managed the photo research, Mirella Signoretto who formatted the line art, Nick Sklitsis, manufacturing manager, Tricia Kenny, manufacturing buyer, and Jan Stephan, managing editor, and many other people behind the scenes at Prentice Hall, for helping make the book happen.

ABOUT the AUTHORS

Jeanne Boydston is Professor of History at the University of Wisconsin-Madison. She is the author of *Home and Work: Housework, Wages, and the Ideology of Labor in the Early American Republic,* coauthor of *The Limits of Sisterhood: The Beecher Sisters on Women's Rights and Woman's Sphere,* co-editor of *The Root of Bitterness: Documents of the Social History of American Women* (second edition), as well as author of articles on the labor history of women in the early republic. Professor Boydston teaches in the areas of early republic and antebellum United States history and United States women's history to 1870. Her BA and MA are from the University of Tennessee, and her PhD is from Yale University.

Nick Cullather is Associate Professor at Indiana University, where he teaches courses on the history of United States foreign relations. He is on the editorial boards of *Diplomatic History* and the *Encyclopedia of American Foreign Policy,* and is the author of *Illusions of Influence* (1994), a study of the political economy of United States-Philippines relations, and *Secret History* (1999), which describes a CIA covert operation against the government of Guatemala in 1954. He received his AB from Indiana University and his MA and PhD from the University of Virginia.

Jan Ellen Lewis is Professor of History and Director of the Graduate Program at Rutgers University, Newark. She also teaches in the history PhD program at Rutgers, New Brunswick and was a Visiting Professor at Princeton University. A specialist in colonial and early national history, she is the author of *The Pursuit of Happiness: Family and Values in Jefferson's Virginia* (1983), and co-editor of *An Emotional History of the United States* (1998) and *Sally Hemings and Thomas Jefferson: History, Memory, and*

Civic Culture (1999). She is currently completing an examination of the way the Founding generation grappled with the challenge presented to an egalitarian society by women and slaves and a second volume of the Penguin History of the United States. She received her AB from Bryn Mawr College, and MAs and PhD from the University of Michigan.

Michael McGerr is Associate Professor of History and Associate Dean for Graduate Education in the College of Arts and Sciences at Indiana University-Bloomington. He is the author of *The Decline of Popular Politics: The American North, 1865–1928* (1986). With the aid of a fellowship from the National Endowment for the Humanities, he is currently writing a book on the rise and fall of Progressive America. Professor McGerr teaches a wide range of courses on modern American history, including the Vietnam War, race and gender in American business, John D. Rockefeller, Bill Gates, and the politics of American popular music. He received his BA, MA, and PhD degrees from Yale University.

James Oakes is Graduate School Humanities Professor and Professor of History at the Graduate Center of the City University of New York, and has taught at Purdue, Princeton, and Northwestern. He is author of *The Ruling Race: A History of American Slaveholders* (1982) and *Slavery and Freedom: An Interpretation of the Old South* (1990). In addition to a year-long research grant from the National Endowment for the Humanities, he was a fellow at the Center for Advanced Study in the Behavioral Sciences in 1989–90. His areas of specialization are slavery, the Civil War and Reconstruction, and the history of American political thought. He received his PhD from Berkeley.

MAKING A NATION
THE UNITED STATES AND ITS PEOPLE

Just as men and women make histories, so do they make nations. By showing the links between the specific and the general, and between large and seemingly abstract forces such as globalization and political conflict with the daily struggles of ordinary women and men, *Making a Nation* provides students with a rich and compelling perspective on American history. Carefully crafted by a team of leading scholars and experienced teachers, *Making a Nation* gets behind the facts to reveal the many stories that made—and continually remake—American history.

A focus on the relationships that shape and define human identity.
Making a Nation returns again and again to the concept that everyone's life is formed by many different relationships. Whether it be Indians negotiating with colonists in the 18th century, newly-freed slaves in the 19th century, or immigrant garment workers in the present century, *Making a Nation* confronts the multiple and overlapping identities that define American life.

The Varieties of Colonial Experience

Although the eighteenth-century industrial and consumer revolutions tied the peoples of the North Atlantic world together and gave them many common experiences, factors such as climate, geography, immigration, patterns of economic development, and population density made for considerable variety. Although the vast majority of Americans lived in small communities or on farms, an increasing number lived in cities, and urban centers played a critical role in shaping colonial life. At the same time, farming regions, both slave and free, were maturing, changing the character of rural life. The growing colonial population continued to push at the frontiers of settlement, leading to the founding of a new colony in Georgia.

Political economy approach establishes a context for seeing the links between the particular and the general.

Making a Nation traces the development of the United States to show the connections between government, the economy, and the relationships that shape daily life. The insights of political economy allow students to understand that economies and politics are the products of history rather than nature or accident.

Conceptions of Political Economy in the New Republic

Most free Americans believed that the success of the republic depended ultimately on the political virtue of its citizens. By "political virtue," they meant the essential characteristics of good republican citizens. In an age of breathtaking economic expansion, it is unsurprising that Americans associated those qualities with economic life. When people grew too wealthy and accustomed to luxury, many Americans believed, they grew lazy

A global perspective on American history.

More than any other text, *Making a Nation* highlights the ties between seemingly abstract forces and the struggles of ordinary men and women. It shows that globalization has been a theme of American history from its earliest beginnings—profoundly affecting human relationships on many different levels.

The Political Economy of Global Capitalism

The economic history of the late nineteenth century was sandwiched between two great financial panics, one in 1873 and the other in 1893. Both were followed by prolonged periods of high unemployment. Both led directly to tremendous labor unrest. The years between the two panics were marked by a general decline in prices that placed a terrible burden on producers. Farmers found that their crops were worth less at harvest time than they had been during planting season. They responded by expanding their enterprises to meet the worldwide demand for American agriculture.

xxiv

OUTLINE

Anthony Comstock's Crusade Against Vice

The Varieties of Urban Culture

Minstrel Shows as Cultural Nostalgia

The Origins of Vaudeville

Sports Become Professional

World's Fairs: The Celebration of the City

The Elusive Boundaries of Male and Female

The Victorian Construction of Male and Female

Victorians Who Questioned Traditional Sexual Boundaries

Immigration as a Cultural Problem

Josiah Strong Attacks Immigration

From Immigrants to Ethnic Americans

The Catholic Church and

Chapter outlines at the beginning of each chapter list primary topics that follow.

Opening vignettes capture each chapter's theme. Each chapter in *Making a Nation* briefly narrates the experiences of a person whose life embodies the key themes of the chapter.

Tituba Shapes Her World and Saves Herself

Her name was Tituba. Some say she was African, a Yoruba. Others believe that she was an Arawak Indian from Guyana. Had she not been accused of practicing witchcraft in Salem, Massachusetts, in 1692, she surely would have been forgotten by history. Now, more than three centuries later, the record is dim. Her name appears on a list of slave children owned by a Barbados planter in 1677. Whether she came from South America or Africa, she had been torn away from her home and sent to work on a sugar plantation on the Caribbean Island that the English had colonized almost fifty years before. In those years, the English were enslaving small numbers of Arawaks from the northern coast of South America. The peaceful habits of the Arawaks and their domestic skills made them good house servants, while their alliance with the Dutch, who were at war with the English, made them vulnerable to English raiders. Sugar planters preferred African slaves, however, and by the

1670s they were importing 1,300 of them each year onto the tiny island in order to feed Europe's insatiable appetite for sugar. By 1680, the African population of Barbados, at 37,000, was more than twice that of the European. Whatever her origins, Tituba lived in an African-majority society and absorbed African customs.

Tituba was still young, probably a teenager, when she was taken, once again as a slave, to a new home in Massachusetts in 1680. She had been purchased by a young, Harvard-educated Barbadian, Samuel Parris. Parris' father had failed as a planter, and now his son was about to meet the same fate as a merchant in Boston. Both planting and commerce were risky ventures, at the mercy of both the market and luck. Tituba found herself in Salem because of the market: Barbados planters wanted field hands and house servants, and now a failed merchant, Samuel Parris, abandoned commerce for the ministry. In 1689 Parris moved his

The Wonders of the Invisible World:

Being an Account of the

TRYALS

OF

Several Witches,

Lately Executed in

NEW-ENGLAND:

And of several remarkable Curiosities therein Occurring.

Together with,

I. Observations upon the Nature, the Number, and the Operations of the Devils.
II. A short Narrative of a late outrage committed by a knot of Witches in Swede-Land, very much resembling, and so far explaining, that under which New-England has laboured.
III. Some Councels directing a due Improvement of the Terrible things lately done by the unusual and amazing Range of Evil-Spirits in New-England.
IV. A brief Discourse upon those Temptations which are the more ordinary Devices of Satan.

By COTTON MATHER.

Published by the Special Command of his EXCELLENCY the Governor of the Province of the Massachusets-Bay in New-England.

Printed first, at Boston in New-England; and Reprinted at London, for John Dunton, at the Raven in the Poultry. 1693.

Where They Lived, Where They Worked sections help students see the connections between home and work, which are obscured in most accounts of American history.

WHERE THEY LIVED, WHERE THEY WORKED

The Chesapeake Plantation Village

The eighteenth-century Chesapeake plantation village linked the worlds of Europe, Africa, and North America. The plantation itself was a hub of production, producing tobacco to sell in the markets of Europe, as well as many of the manufactured goods used on the plantation, such as nails, bricks, and cloth. All were produced by slave labor.

The plantation's architecture combined English and African elements. After about 1720, the most affluent planters began building large brick homes, copying Georgian styles then popular in England. The wooden buildings on the plantation, however, including the homes of less prosperous planters, slave cabins, and other "out" buildings, were constructed with African techniques. Their frames were much lighter, more like those of central African houses than of contemporary English

ones. Winding paths that followed the natural contours of the land and raised burial plots also reflected African influences. Plantation villages themselves bore an uncanny resemblance to an African king's village, in which smaller homes were arrayed behind the chieftain's main house.

Whites borrowed from African culture in other ways. The barbecue at which "a great number of young people met together with a Fiddle and Banjo played by two Negroes" represented a melding of European (the fiddle) and African (the banjo) music. The ecstatic shouting and visions of African worship services also made their way into Baptist and Methodist church services. These borrowings were usually silent. Black influences quietly made their way into white culture, in the process creating a culture that was neither fully African nor fully European.

Notice the similarities in construction between the Zaire home (top) and the Virginia cabin (bottom left). Although the photo of the Zaire home is from c. 1910 and the Virginia cabin from 1897, they suggest how African homes and Virginia slave cabins looked in the late eighteenth century. The planter's "big house" and the slave cabins and other out buildings made a small village, similar in layout to that of an African chieftain's. The photo (bottom right) is of the plantation community at Green Hill Plantation, built in the late eighteenth century.

Growing Up in America features spotlight the history of young people, showing how American youth have always been part of a larger political economy.

GROWING UP IN AMERICA

Jane Addams at College

Jane Addams became a successful activist while still in school, long before she became famous for her social work among Chicago's poor. In 1877, at the age of 17, Addams enrolled in a seminary at Rockford, Illinois, to begin her college education. The fact that the school still called itself a seminary rather than a college was one indication that it had yet to transform its curriculum along the lines of Johns Hopkins, Cornell, or Harvard. Nevertheless, over the next several years, Jane and her contemporaries brought the struggle over the modern curriculum to Rockford. "So much of our time is spent in preparation, so much in routine . . . ," Addams complained while at the seminary. She and her companions therefore made "various and restless attempts" to challenge the "dull obtuseness" of the college curriculum.

In one of those "various attempts" Jane and her friends took opium in an effort to stimulate their imaginations; it didn't work. They fell in love with the grand themes of Greek philosophy and Romantic literature, but in the end they yearned for a more practical course of study in history and economics. More than the others in her group, Jane resisted the "evangelical" pressure to become a missionary. Instead, she threw herself into the movement to upgrade Rockford's curriculum so that it could join the growing number of colleges that awarded bachelor's degrees to women. She and her friends studied mathematics. They represented Rockford at the state intercollegiate oratory competition, the first time a women's college in Illinois was represented at such an event.

Above all, Jane and her colleagues were fascinated by science. In it they saw the unvarnished search for truth, freed from all dogmatism. They were inspired by the example of Charles Darwin. They were frustrated by those teachers who had yet to accept the theory of natural selection and also by the meager scientific holdings in the school's library. "I used to bring back in my handbag books belonging to an advanced brother-in-law who had studied medicine in Germany," Addams wrote some years later, "and who was therefore quite emancipated."

By studying mathematics, science, history, and economics, Addams had taken it upon herself to step outside the

A young Jane Addams was one of a new generation of college-educated women who committed themselves to social reforms.

boundaries of the traditional seminary curriculum. In so doing she and her friends transformed Rockford. A year after she had left college, Addams and a classmate returned "to receive the degree we had so eagerly anticipated." Together with two new graduates, they "were dubbed B.A. on the very day that Rockford Seminary was declared a college in the midst of tumultuous anticipations."

ON TRIAL

The Supernatural on Trial—Witchcraft at Salem

The eruption of accusations had begun in the household of Salem Village's minister, Samuel Parris, a dissatisfied and bitter man, often at odds with the members of his congregation, when his daughter Betty and her cousin Abigail Williams tried to foresee their future husbands. These young women and the others who became accusers were among the most powerless segment of New England's white population, and they must have enjoyed these outbursts against order and authority and the attention they drew to themselves.

When questioned by those in authority, curses and shouts

guilty by at least two witnesses who had observed a particular act of malice. As Tituba discovered when she confessed and pointed the finger at others, in Salem all those who confessed were ultimately released, while all those who were executed maintained their innocence, even when they were tortured. Richard Carrier, age 28, and his brother Andrew, 16, confessed only when they were "tyed ... Neck and Heels till the Blood was ready to come out of their Noses." They said their mother had recruited them. Their lives were spared; their mother, Martha Carrier, however, was executed.

Although it soon became evident that a confession was the

On Trial sidebars illuminate courtroom battles that profoundly affected the political, social, and cultural issues of the day.

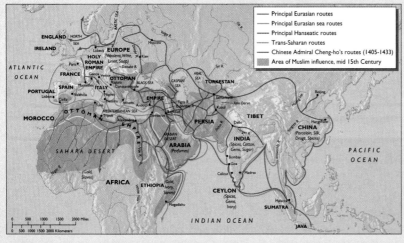

Global Maps vividly illustrate the global context of American history.

Map 1-1 World Trade on the Eve of Discovery.
For a thousand years, world trade centered on the Mediterranean. European, Arab, and Asian traders criss-crossed much of the Eastern Hemisphere, carrying spices, silks, and cottons from Asia; linens, woolens, and wine from Europe; and gold and slaves from Africa.

web connection

Stamping out Stamps

www.prenhall.com/boydston/stampact

In 1765, in the wake of its great victory in the Seven Years' War (known as the French and Indian War in the American colonies), Great Britain set about putting its imperial house in order. Retiring the debt was a major priority, and the Stamp Act was one of several revenue measures designed to force the colonies to pay a greater share of the costs of empire. Colonists refused to pay the new stamp tax. Instead they organized a boycott of British goods and proclaimed that Parliament lacked the power to tax them, something only their own colonial legislatures could legitimately do. Use the materials here to explore how Americans forged their own peculiar notions of representation.

Web Connection boxes in each chapter, prepared by John McClymer of Assumption College and Eileen Walsh of Bemidji State University, provide a direct link to Web-based learning activities that drill down to explore the impact of key episodes in American history. Combining primary sources, visuals, graphs, audio clips, and interactive maps, Web Connections provide opportunities for further exploration of important topics presented in *Making a Nation.*

Conclusions tie together the chapter's themes, review main topics, and set the stage for developments ahead.

Conclusion

At the middle of the seventeenth century, the New England and Chesapeake colonies could hardly have appeared more different. Although the forces of capitalism shaped each region, other factors left their distinctive imprint: the objectives of the founders, disease environment, demographic patterns, and relations with local Indians. In 1660, both regions had about 35,000 inhabitants, but the colonies of New England were much more settled. As much as anything else, the early history of New England was shaped by the extraordinary energy and cohesiveness of Puritan society. In fact, the cohesiveness of the New England colonies, their early success, and their great economic and social stability make them almost unique in the history of colonial ventures throughout the world. If New England achieved settlement within a few years, unsettlement was the norm. That surely was the case in New Spain, New France, and New Netherland, which all bore the marks of rough, frontier societies for many decades. It was particularly true of the Chesapeake colonies, which were still raw colonial outposts, disproportionately populated by aggressive young men long after New England had achieved a secure and gratifying order.

All of the North American colonies were outposts in the global political economy, created to enrich their mother countries and enhance their power. The New England colonies were the striking exceptions. Indeed, had the Virginia Company known that the founders of Massachusetts wanted to create a religious refuge rather

Review Questions in each chapter ask students to consider the central problems of each chapter.

Review Questions

1. What were the objectives of the founders of Virginia? Why did the colony survive, in spite of poor planning?

2. What were the objectives of the founders of the Puritan colonies at Plymouth and Massachusetts Bay? Compare the early years of these colonies to those of the Virginia colony?

3. What place did gender play in the social order of the Chesapeake and New England colonies? Compare and contrast family life in the two regions.

4. Compare and contrast relations with the Indians in the Chesapeake and New England.

Chronologies found at the end of each chapter provide a review of key events.

CHRONOLOGY

1838	Frederick Douglass escapes from slavery	1848	Zachary Taylor elected president
1844	Samuel F. B. Morse invents the telegraph	1851	The "Maine Law" enacts temperance reform
1846	David Wilmot introduces his "proviso"	1852	Uncle Tom's Cabin published in book form Franklin Pierce elected president
1847	Treaty of Guadalupe Hidalgo	1854	Gadsden Purchase Ratified Kansas-Nebraska Act

Further Readings and **History on the Internet** sections at the end of each chapter provide annotated lists of suggested print and Web resources.

Further Readings

Kathleen M. Brown, *Good Wives, Nasty Wenches, and Anxious Patriarchs* (1996). A provocative interpretation of Colonial Virginia that puts gender at the center.

William Cronon, *Changes in the Land: Indians, Colonists, and the Ecology of New England* (1983). A comparison of the ways that Indians and New Englanders used, lived off, and changed the land.

John Demos, *A Little Commonwealth: Family Life in Plymouth Colony* (1970). Brief and beautifully written, this book helped revolutionize the writing of American social history by showing how much could be learned about ordinary people from a sensitive reading of a wide variety of sources.

Jack P. Greene, *Pursuits of Happiness: The Social Development of Early Modern British Colonies and the Formation of American Culture* (1988). An interpretive overview of Colonial development that argues that the Chesapeake was the most American region of all.

Ivor Noël Hume, *The Virginia Adventure: Roanoke to James Towne: An Archaeological and Historical Odyssey* (1994). A detailed and well-written history of the early Chesapeake settlements with a focus on archaeology.

History on the Internet

"Religion and the Founding of the American Republic. America as a Religious Refuge: The Seventeenth Century"
http://lcweb.loc.gov/exhibits/religion/rel01.html

Through this Library of Congress website, discover the role of religion in the founding of the New England colonies. This site details the religious persecution religious "nonconformists" experienced in their European homelands and the promise of religious freedom the New World held out to these men and women.

"From Indentured Servitude to Racial Slavery"
http://www.pbs.org/wgbh/aia/part1/1narr3.html

Read about Virginia's recognition of slavery, slave codes, and the need for African slave labor. The site also contains scholarly commentary on the earliest African Americans and their experiences.

SUPPLEMENTS THAT MAKE A DIFFERENCE

Making a Nation comes with an extensive package of supplementary print and multimedia materials for both instructors and students.

PRINT SUPPLEMENTS

Instructor's Resource Manual

Prepared by Laura Graves, South Plains College

Contains introduction to instructors, chapter outlines, detailed chapter overviews, discussion questions, lecture strategies, essay topics, suggestions for working with Web resources, and tips on incorporating Penguin titles in American history into lectures.

Test Item File

Prepared by Bruce Caskey, Herkimer County Community College

Includes over 1000 multiple-choice, true-false, essay, and map questions, organized by chapter. A collection of blank maps can be photocopied and used for map testing or other class exercises.

Study Guide (Volumes I and II)

Prepared by Laura Graves, South Plains College

Contains introduction to students, chapter overviews, chapter outlines, map questions, sample exam questions, analytical reading exercises, collaborative exercises, and essay questions.

Documents in United States History (Volumes I and II)

Prepared by Paula Stathakis, University of North Carolina, Charlotte, and Alan Downs, Georgia Southern University

Edited specifically for *Making a Nation*, the Documents Set brings together over 200 primary sources and scholarly articles in American history. Headnotes and review questions contextualize the documents and prompt critical inquiry.

Transparencies

This collection of over 150 full-color transparencies provides the maps, charts, and graphs from the text for classroom presentations.

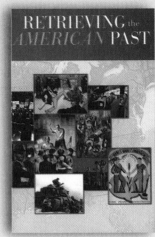

Retrieving the American Past 2001 Edition (RTAP) gives instructors the opportunity to tailor a custom reader whose content, organization, and price exactly match the their course syllabi. Edited by historians and educators at The Ohio State University and other respected schools, RTAP offers instructors the freedom and flexibility to choose selections of primary and secondary source readings—or both—from 73 (14 new) chapters. Contact your local Prentice Hall representative for details about RTAP. Discounts apply when copies of RTAP are bundled with *Making a Nation*.

Themes of the Times

This special newspaper supplement is prepared jointly for students by Prentice Hall and the premier news publication, the *New York Times*. Issued twice a year, it contains recent articles pertinent to American history, which connect the classroom to the world. Contact your Prentice Hall representative for details.

Reading Critically about History

Prepared by Rose Wassman and Lee Rinsky, DeAnza College, this brief guide provides students with helpful strategies for reading a history textbook and is available free when packaged with *Making a Nation*.

Understanding and Answering Essay Question

Prepared by Mary L. Kelley, San Antonio College, this helpful guide provides analytical tools for understanding different types of essay questions and for preparing well-crafted essay answers. It is available free when packaged with *Making a Nation*.

MULTIMEDIA SUPPLEMENTS

Companion Website

The access code protected *Companion Website*™ for *Making a Nation* is available at www.prenhall.com/boydston and offers students and instructors of American history one of the most comprehensive Internet resources available. The passcode to access the site is included with all new copies of the text. Organized around the primary subtopics of each chapter, the *Companion Website*™ provides detailed summaries, multiple choice, true-false, essay, identification, map labeling, and document questions and Web Connection activities based on the text. Overview tables in each chapter facilitate quick review. Hyperlinks to other Web resources provide students with access to screened sites. Chat rooms and message boards allow students to share their ideas about American history with their own class or with colleges across the country.

The *Faculty Module* contains a wealth of material for instructors, including a downloadable Microsoft PowerPoint™ presentation with maps, charts, and graphs that can be customized to an instructor's specific needs, and easy-to-follow directions for creating, posting, and revising a syllabus online.

History on the Internet — This guide focuses on developing the critical-thinking skills necessary to evaluate and use online resources. It provides a brief introduction to navigating the Internet and outlines the many references to history Websites. Available free when packaged with *Making a Nation*.

PowerPoint™ Images CD-ROM — Available in Windows and Mac formats for use with Microsoft PowerPoint™, this CD-ROM includes the maps, charts, tables, and graphs from *Making a Nation*. These resources can be used in lectures, for slide shows, and printed as transparencies.

COURSE MANAGEMENT SYSTEMS

As the leader in course-management solutions for teachers and students of history, Prentice Hall provides a variety of online tools. Contact your local Prentice Hall representative for a demonstration, or visit www.prenhall.com/demo

Powered by Blackboard 5, CourseCompass fuses the content of *Making a Nation* with Blackboard's powerful course-management tools to provide pre-loaded content, refined navigation, and national hosting to make it easier for instructors and students to create their own customized learning environments.

With a powerful menu of communication tools, testing options, and design tools, Blackboard makes creating, managing, and using online materials easy.

With such robust course-management tools as page tracking, progress tracking, and reporting tools, WebCT saves instructors valuable time in managing their courses.

For qualified adopters, Prentice Hall is proud to introduce Instructors 1st—the first integrated service program committed to meeting customization, support, and training needs. Contact your local Prentice Hall representative for details.

PRENTICE HALL AND PENGUIN BUNDLE PROGRAM: MAKING AN IMPACT ON HISTORY

Prentice Hall and PenguinPutnam are pleased to provide adopters of *Making a Nation* with an opportunity for their students to receive significant discounts when orders for *Making a Nation* are bundled together with Penguin titles in American history.

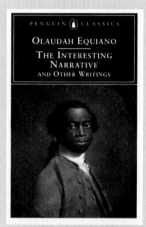

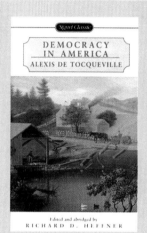

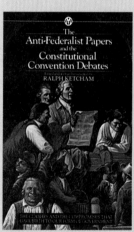

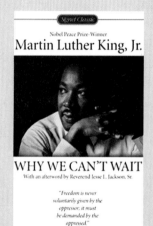

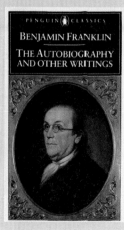

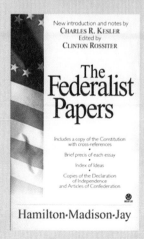

MAKING

A

NATION

The United States and Its People

1

WORLDS IN MOTION
1450-1550

OUTLINE

Christopher Columbus: World Traveler

The Worlds of Christopher Columbus
European Nations in the Age of Discovery
The Political Economy of Europe
The World of the West African Peoples
Slavery Before 1500
The Golden Age of Spain

The World of the Indian Peoples
The Archaic Indians
The Indians of the Eastern Woodlands
The Indians of the Plains
The Indians of the Deserts
The Indians of the Pacific Coast
The Great Civilizations of the Americas

Worlds in Collision
Christopher Columbus Finds a Patron

Columbus Finds a New World
Tainos and Caribs
The Origins of a New World Political Economy
The *Requerimiento* and the Morality of Conquest

The Biological Consequences of Conquest
Demographic Decline
The Columbian Exchange

Onto the Mainland
The First Florida Ventures
The Conquest of Mexico
The Establishment of a Spanish Empire
The Return to Florida
Coronado and the Pueblo Indians

Conclusion

Christopher Columbus: World Traveler

Christopher Columbus had been preparing all his adult life for his journey across the Atlantic to find a western route to Asia. When he arrived at the island in the Bahamas that the native Taino people called Guanahaní, and which Columbus gave the Spanish name of San Salvador, Columbus stayed barely long enough to scribble a few entries in his diary before moving on. Columbus and his crew of 89 men—divided among three ships: the *Santa María*, the *Niña*, and the *Pinta*—had departed the Spanish port of Palos on August 3, 1492. After a stopover at the Canary Islands they reached what he mistakenly thought was an island off the coast of China on October 12. Over the course of his four voyages to the region, he continued to believe it was Asia; hence he called the island the *Indies* and the inhabitants *Indios* (Indians). In a pattern he would repeat again and again, Columbus and his crew disembarked, gave the island a Spanish name, and

claimed it for the king and queen of Spain. When some of the residents gathered to see the strangers, he gave them gifts of red caps and glass beads, and they reciprocated with parrots, balls of cotton thread, and javelins. Columbus described these men and women as generous but poor. "All of them go around as naked as their mothers bore them," he wrote in his diary. "They are very well formed, with handsome bodies, and good faces. Their hair [is] coarse—almost like the tail of a horse—and short." In color they resembled the people of the Canary Islands, "neither black nor white," and some of them wore paint on their faces and bodies. Columbus concluded that these peaceful and intelligent people would make good servants and easy converts to Christianity, and he decided to bring a few of them back to Spain with him. Two days later, at dawn, Columbus and his crew set sail once again.

3

What had brought this long-faced man with prematurely white hair so far around the globe? He had been born in the independent Italian republic of Genoa forty-one years earlier, but he sailed for the queen and king of Spain. No European state had sponsored a visit to the Western Hemisphere since the Vikings had crossed the North Atlantic five hundred years earlier. And although occasional sailors from Europe or Africa may have crossed the Atlantic, before Columbus the last colonists to come to the Americas had walked across or paddled small boats alongside the land bridge that connected Siberia and Alaska.

Columbus' arrival in the Western Hemisphere dramatically and irreversibly changed the worlds into which he and the descendants of the Indians had been born. The encounter in effect fused their two worlds into one Atlantic world that Europeans and Indians—as well as Africans, most of whom were brought forcibly to the Caribbean as early as 1500—would inhabit and transform together.

In many ways, Columbus was an unlikely character to inaugurate such profound changes in the history of the world. With neither privilege nor education, his opportunities were sharply limited. Moreover, he shared fully in the prejudices of his age, but he was well-read and remarkably well-traveled for a man who lived at a time when most people spent their entire lives without journeying more than a few miles from the village in which they were born. By the time Columbus sailed to the New World for Spain, he had explored much of the Mediterranean world, as well as Portugal and her Atlantic colonies.

Christopher Columbus, shown here in the prow of his ship, arrives in the West Indies. This is the earliest known picture of Columbus.

Columbus had traveled even further through his reading. He had read a number of geography books as well as Marco Polo's thirteenth-century account of his travels to Asia. He knew that Polo had mentioned at least 1378 islands off the coast of Asia. He was also evidently entranced by Polo's description of the empire of the great Kublai Khan and a magnificent island called Cipango (Japan), 1500 miles off the coast of China. When Columbus left the island of Guanahaní, it was to search for gold and "to see if I can find the island of Cipango." Everywhere he went among the islands inhabited by the Tainos, Columbus asked where he could find spices and gold, and so he sailed on, convinced that the large island that the natives called Cuba, which was filled with "many and very large ships and many traders," was really Cipango and that its king "was at war with the Grand Khan." Columbus was filled with "the greatest sorrow in the world" because he could not learn the names of the thousands of trees and plants and flowers on islands that, in late October, were as green as Andalusia in the spring, but he had to push on, looking for commerce and gold mines.

Columbus was bold and restless in a world that suddenly valued such qualities. Dramatic changes in the political economy of Europe, in particular the expansion of trade and the consolidations of small principalities into powerful nation-states, set men such as Columbus out in search of trade and the wealth it would bring. In the process they helped create a truly global economy, one that transformed the worlds of all the peoples of the globe and continues to transform them still. ∎

KEY TOPICS

- European trade patterns on the eve of discovery.

- Portuguese and Spanish objectives in exploration and colonization.

- Native American civilizations and the development of Native American social and political organizations.

- Initial encounters: violence, the *encomienda,* and the enslavement of Indians.

- The biological consequences of conquest.

- The conquest of Mexico.

- Spanish settlements on the mainland United States as frontier outposts.

The Worlds of Christopher Columbus

Imagine a world in motion. Imagine a world in which most people live in small villages where they eat the food that they hunt or raise themselves and where most people die without ever having traveled more than a few miles from home. At the same time, other people are on the move, especially the traders, the warriors, and men and women displaced by war and famine. The traders push at the boundaries of the known world, looking for better goods and new markets. Often the warriors aim at conquest. They seize the land that others inhabit, pushing them aside, so that their own people may move in. The traders and the warriors set the world in motion and the population of the world shifts. Imagine a world on the eve of the greatest movement of peoples the world has ever known, and you will have a picture of the world in 1492, the year of Christopher Columbus' voyage to the New World. Of course, Columbus did not discover this world, nor was it truly new; it had been there from time immemorial. Columbus came as a trader and became a conqueror. In the process he introduced the ways of the Old World into the New, changing both of them forever. Yet the New World was not so very different from the old one. It too had its traders and warriors who set its many peoples in motion. The modern history of America begins in 1492 with the movement of all of these peoples, from the Old World and the New, on American terrain.

European Nations in the Age of Discovery

In 1492, Europe as we now picture it did not yet exist. Many of what later became major European nations—Spain, Italy, Germany—were merely collections of small principalities, each owing its allegiance to a local ruler. Indeed, Spain and Portugal had only recently been liberated from the Moors, a North African people who practiced the Muslim religion and who had invaded the Iberian peninsula in 711. France and England were led by a single ruler, but the power of that leader was still limited, as the ruler struggled with local feudal lords for control of the nation. It was at this time in history that European nation-states were being consolidated, each under the rule of a single leader, a hereditary monarch. In fact, not until a nation was unified under a strong leader could it turn away from internal struggles and focus on the world beyond. As the first nations to be unified, Portugal and Spain were the first also to begin to explore and conquer foreign lands. Holland, France, and England, unified about a century later, then followed the Spanish and Portuguese lead. Germany and Italy, not unified until the nineteenth century, lagged far behind in the race for foreign territory. The consolidation of the European nations unleashed enormous energy, which put the peoples of Europe in motion. The traders charted a way, first to China by an overland route and then to Africa, by sea.

The Political Economy of Europe

The world's peoples have always traded their goods with one another. However, the period between 1450 and 1750 witnessed the establishment of new trade patterns that changed the face of the world. In the preceding centuries, powerful empires had dominated trade in their regions of the world (see Map 1-1). In the middle of the fifteenth century, Islamic traders, for example, linked parts of Europe, Africa, and Asia. Because trade was a relatively minor part of the world economy compared to agriculture, trade had a relatively minor effect upon the political and social structure of the world.

Once Western Europe began to dominate world trade after 1450, it began to shape not only the world economy, but global, social, and political structures as well. The nations of Western Europe established truly global trade networks, linking Europe, Africa, Asia, and the Americas. These networks were so large, and the wealth extracted from Africa and the Americas so great, that the shape of the world was fundamentally changed. The inequalities between nations were heightened as wealth flowed first to Spain and Portugal and then England, France, and Holland.

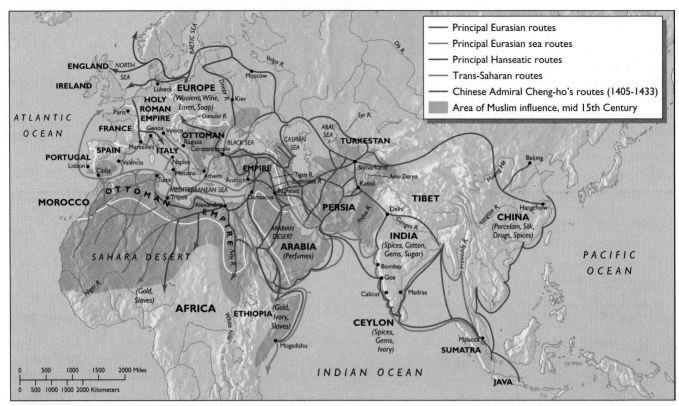

Map 1-1   World Trade on the Eve of Discovery.
For a thousand years, world trade centered on the Mediterranean. European, Arab, and Asian traders criss-crossed much of the Eastern Hemisphere, carrying spices, silks, and cottons from Asia; linens, woolens, and wine from Europe; and gold and slaves from Africa.

As Western European nations were becoming wealthier and their economies more complex, those areas of America, Africa, and (to a lesser extent) Asia that were conquered or colonized in the next centuries became economically dependent upon western trade. They supplied the raw materials that made Europe wealthy. Increasingly, their own populations were exploited and even enslaved, to turn out the gold and silver, sugar, and tobacco to quench the insatiable appetites of Europe.

When Christopher Columbus sailed west looking for Asia, he was trying to re-establish a European trade that had been disrupted by the Black Death. The bubonic plague had arrived in Europe in 1347, brought by a trade caravan from Asia. Until that time, the Italians in particular had engaged in commerce as far east as the Mongol empire in China. Marco Polo, the son of an Italian merchant, had written a book that described his stay in China and India between 1275 and 1292. In the middle of the fifteenth century, as Europe began to recover from the plague, its population began to grow, and the economy began to expand. With all of Western Europe united by the Roman Catholic faith, Christianity became more aggressive in its search for converts. Meanwhile merchants, especially along the Mediterranean, began to look for new markets.

The vast majority of Europeans were peasants, many living so close to the edge of destitution that they were at risk of starvation or serious malnutrition in years when the harvest was poor. Still, an increasingly prosperous elite (which included both the nobility and the affluent members of the urban middle classes) developed a taste for luxury items such as sugar, spices, soft fabrics, and precious metals. Marco Polo's descriptions of Asian temples roofed in gold had dazzled Italian readers since the end of the thirteenth century. It was the desire for these sorts of luxury goods that sent European explorers off in search of new routes to Asia.

By the middle of the fifteenth century, new technologies made it possible for Europeans to travel far from home. Some of these innovations were actually adaptations from other regions of the world—for example, gun powder from China and the navigational compass from the Arabs. Other improvements were developed in Europe, including better maps, stronger metal that could be turned into guns and cannons, and the caravel, a light, swift ship that was well suited for navigating along the coast of Africa. All of these innovations made it possible for Europeans to travel further in search of trade and eventually to subjugate peoples who did not have these modern technologies.

Europe was on the move by the end of the fifteenth century. The Portuguese had begun exploring along the Atlantic coast of Africa, searching for a water route to Asia. Portugal had recently driven out its Muslim conquerors. It was a small nation (about 1.5 million inhabitants, compared to almost 10 million for Spain), but it had achieved political unification under a strong king almost a century earlier. This combination of political unity, a strong monarchy interested in extending its power and wealth, and an aggressive merchant class looking for new markets enabled Portugal to become the first of the modern European imperial nations. By 1475, Portuguese explorers had reached the thriving kingdom of Benin on the lower Guinea coast (the modern country of Nigeria) and had established a series of trading posts all along the northwestern coast of the continent. In exchange for European goods such as horses, cloth, and wheat, the Portuguese traded for African luxury products such as ivory, and especially gold, that could be sold in the cities of Europe (see Map 1-2).

Earlier in the fifteenth century, the Portuguese had begun raiding the Sahara coast for slaves. Once they opened up the new trade with sub-Saharan Africa, however, they discovered that they could exchange European goods directly with African kings and be provided with slaves. The Portuguese then resold the slaves, primarily for use as servants, either in other regions of Africa or in Europe. Initially, the commerce in gold and ivory was much more important to the Portuguese than the slave trade. Until 1500, in fact, the Portuguese were shipping only between 500 and 1,000 slaves a year, most of whom were resold in Africa. However, with the opening of plantations (first in the Canary Islands, whose conquest the Spanish completed in 1496), the slave trade became an important part of the Portuguese economy.

The World of the West African Peoples

Starting with the Portuguese, European traders reached the west coast of Africa in the fifteenth century. There they found much of the population living in powerful and well-organized kingdoms, much like the European states. Some of those states, especially those just south of the Sahara such as Mali and Songhay, had been deeply influenced by Islam and had adopted its written language. Others, such as the central African Yoruba kingdoms, had developed into complex city-states that produced glorious works of art in bronze and ivory. The population density in the Lower Guinea region was higher than that of Europe at the time.

Not all African peoples lived in states, however. Many were members of villages or family groupings without rulers or bureaucracies. Despite this political diversity, there were only three basically different cultures. Moreover, religious beliefs were similar among the cultures, with Africans recognizing a supreme creator and numerous lesser deities. Gender relations among the African peoples were similar, too, with most people living in extended, male-led families and clans, which were the basis for the social order. Although men performed most of the heavy labor and women attended to domestic chores and child-rearing, both men and women engaged in farming. Men dominated government and commerce, but on occasion women from prominent families exercised power. Women were active as merchants as well.

Powerful kingdoms dominated trade and commerce in Africa. Their rulers welcomed trade with Europe, which supplied them with a wider array of prestigious goods. Although Africans themselves manufactured cloth, for example, European textiles in different colors and designs found a ready market in Africa. In fact, it was precisely those regions of Africa that already had thriving markets that were most eager to trade with Europeans. Soon African nations were drawn into a global market, one they entered willingly and on their own terms.

As in Europe, at any given moment some kingdoms were increasing their dominance while others were in eclipse. The once-magnificent kingdom of Ghana, for example, had been defeated by invaders in 1076. But such normal political developments as the rise and fall of nations took on new meaning after the appearance of Europeans. In 1591 the defeat of the Songhay empire by Moroccan invaders created instability in the region because no other kingdom could take its place. The warfare between competing states offered unique opportunities for Europeans to profit.

Yoruba sculpture, thirteenth century or earlier.

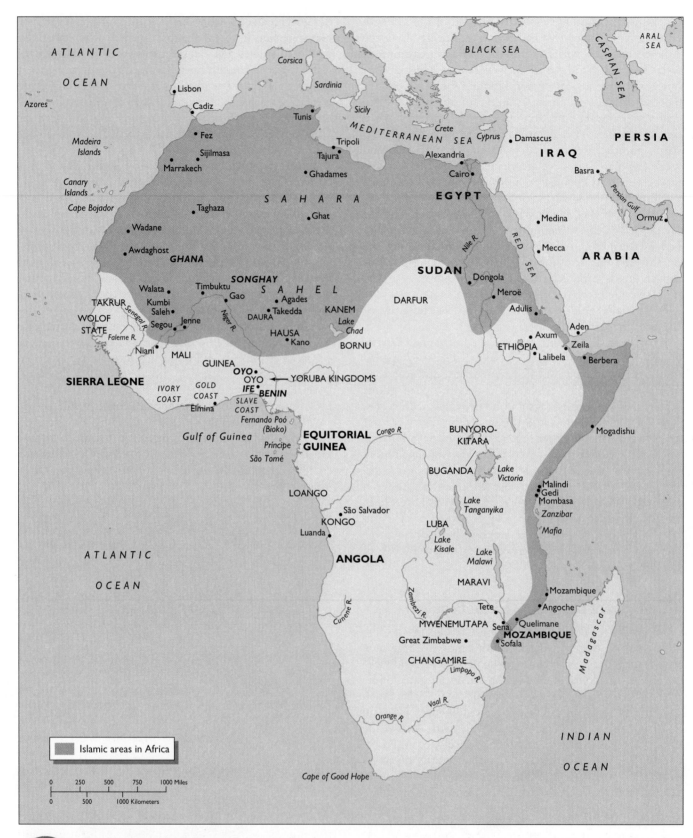

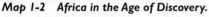
Map 1-2   Africa in the Age of Discovery.
Before 1450, Europeans knew little of Africa. Until that time, trade between Africa and Europe was controlled by Islamic traders, whose empire extended across North Africa. In the middle of the fifteenth century, the Portuguese reached the western coast of Africa and began importing both trade goods and a small number of slaves.

Source: Mark Kishlansky et al., Societies and Cultures in World History (New York: Harper Collins, 1995), 414.

Slavery Before 1500

The institution of slavery had a long history in both Europe and Africa. In each of these regions slavery was far different from what it would become after 1500, when the Atlantic slave trade was opened and Europeans transported African slaves to the Western Hemisphere. In general, slavery was an institution of limited importance in Europe. An exception was ancient Rome. There, as the Roman Empire expanded, it enslaved a number of the peoples it conquered, using them to raise food for the densely populated center of the empire in Italy. At the height of the Roman Empire, as many as 35 or 40 percent of its people were enslaved, a total of two or three million men and women. Unlike modern slavery, Roman slavery was not based on race, and Roman slaves came from a great variety of ethnic groups. The Roman form of slavery withered away with the decline of the Roman Empire.

By the time Portugal opened its trade with West Africa, slavery had disappeared altogether from northwestern Europe, including the British Isles. Some slaves were still being used in parts of Christian Europe along the Mediterranean, however. Moreover, the Muslims who inhabited northern Africa and the Middle East practiced slavery, and they brought their form of the institution with them when they invaded Spain and other regions along the Mediterranean in the eighth century. In addition to working as domestic servants, these slaves were used in the production of sugar.

Several centuries later, when European merchants expanded their trade into regions controlled by the Muslims, they also began plying the trade in human beings. Slavery had been a relatively minor institution in Portugal, Spain, Sicily, Cyprus, and other regions of Europe that touched the Mediterranean. However, once Portugal took over the Atlantic island of Madeira and Spain controlled the Canary Islands, the cultivation of sugar brought into being the much larger systems of plantation slavery. At first they enslaved native islanders, and soon after, they imported Africans to labor for European masters. Hence, although slavery had disappeared from northwestern Europe, Europeans such as Columbus who lived and sailed along the Mediterranean would have been familiar with the slave trade and would have associated slavery with plantation agriculture.

As in Europe, slavery had been practiced in Africa from ancient times, although its character was different because of Africa's different political economy. In Europe, land was the primary form of private, wealth-creating property. In Africa, however, land was owned collectively, and the primary form of private, wealth-creating property was slaves. European law entitled the land owner to everything that was produced on the land, while African law entitled the slave owner to everything that the slave pro-

duced. The way to wealth in Africa was to acquire slaves, and in Europe, to acquire land.

In other ways, however, European and African slavery were similar. African slaves generally worked as domestic laborers, both in Africa and in other regions of the world where they were sold. Similar to European slavery, the status of the slave was not fixed securely by law, and the children of slaves might move into freedom. The African continent was divided among a number of different states that sustained a vigorous internal slave trade. In addition, as the Islamic empire spread in the eighth century, Muslim merchants bought slaves in Africa, usually women and children, for export to other regions of the empire. The African slave trade thus had two components, an internal trade within the continent and an external trade, run primarily by the Muslims. When the Portuguese entered the slave trade, they participated in both components.

West and Central Africans were accustomed to selling slaves, and they entered willingly into the global slave trade. By the seventeenth century, the high prices that Europeans were willing to pay for slaves stimulated the African slave trade and stripped the continent of much of its population.

The Golden Age of Spain

Portugal was the first nation in western Europe to achieve political unity, and hence it was the first to embark upon exploration in search of trade. Spain was the second. Until the end of the fifteenth century, Spain as we now know it did not exist. The Iberian Peninsula was divided into five independent kingdoms. At one time, the entire Iberian Peninsula had been dominated by Muslims, who had invaded the region from North Africa in 711 and established an uneasy reign. Although the native Spanish and Portuguese rulers had resisted Muslim dominion from the outset, Islamic culture exerted a powerful influence in the region. Many Spanish people intermarried with the Muslims, adopting their religion and customs such as the seclusion of women.

At the time of the invasion, Arab civilization was considerably more sophisticated than that of the people they conquered. In fact, it was through the Muslims that Greek science was reintroduced into a region that had lost touch with much ancient learning after the fall of the Roman Empire. Although Muslim, Christian, and Jewish communities generally did not develop any great affection for one another, they were able to co-exist. Local leaders, however, for reasons that were political and economic as often as they were cultural or religious, contested the rule of the Muslims and entered into a seven-hundred-year period of intermittent warfare that is known as the *reconquista* or "reconquest."

Warfare became a normal and expected part of life on the Iberian Peninsula, and it shaped society accordingly.

The priests who proclaimed the *reconquista* a holy war against the Moorish infidel and the soldiers who carried on the conflict were elevated to positions of prestige. The surest path to wealth and honor appeared to lie in plunder and conquest, and a *hidalgo's* (gentleman's) honor was defined by his capacity to vanquish the Muslims and seize their land and wealth. Ordinary people participated with enthusiasm in what they believed was another crusade against non-Christians. The Crusades of the Middle Ages had failed to regain the Holy Land permanently for European Christians, but the Spanish hoped that the *reconquista* would be able to evict from their country those they considered infidels.

By the time Christopher Columbus arrived in Spain in 1485, the Muslims had been ousted from all of Spain except Granada. Castile and Aragon had recently been joined by the marriage of Isabel, princess of Castile, and her cousin Fernando, prince of Aragon. Although Isabel, half-sister of the king of Castile, was only 18 at the time of her marriage (and her husband a year younger), she had already demonstrated herself to be a woman of boldness and determination. She had rejected two suitors, the king of Portugal and the brother of the king of France, deciding that the alliance with Aragon would be both politically and personally more desirable than a connection with Portugal or France. Because the match was more in Aragon's interest than in Castile's, Isabel was able to dictate the terms of the marriage contract, making it clear that she would play the leading role in governing. Having consolidated their power and asserted their authority over their territories, Isabel and Fernando were able to turn their attention to the Moors and the final stage of the *reconquista.*

Uniting their subjects in a holy war against the Muslims proved a shrewd move politically for the young queen and king. By focusing the attention and energy of their nobles against a non-Christian opponent, Isabel and Fernando were able to forge a Spanish national identity for Christians, one that transcended their regional loyalties. Herself an exceedingly devout Christian, Isabel had earlier inaugurated an Inquisition, a Church tribunal authorized by the Pope, in order to root out converted Jews and others who seemed insufficiently sincere Christians. By the time it had completed its work, several hundred Spanish people had been burned at the stake and several thousand more imprisoned. All of Spain was put on notice that lapses from adherence to the official state religion would not be tolerated.

Spain finally conquered the Moorish province of Granada in the spring of 1492. Spain originally permitted the Moors to continue practicing their religion, but militant Christians soon insisted upon a forcible conversion and baptism of those Moors who chose to remain in the region. The Christian conquest of the Moors led swiftly to the eviction of another religious minority, the Jews. Less than three months after the fall of Granada, Isabel and Fernando signed an edict calling for the expulsion of the 150,000 or so Jews who resided in their kingdom, even though both of them had Jews among their ancestors. The Spanish colonization of the Americas and the subjugation of their native peoples were simply the next chapters in the reign of Isabel and Fernando, the rulers of a nation whose very identity was defined by its ability to vanquish those they defined as infidels.

It would be a mistake, however, to conclude that Spain was shaped by the forces of militarism and intolerance alone. In 1492, Spain was in the middle of its golden age. It was the most dynamic nation in Europe at the time, and it soon became the most powerful. Yet Spain welcomed and absorbed foreign influences, including Moorish art, science, and customs, as well as Flemish art and architecture and Italian **humanism.** Under the patronage of Queen Isabel, Spain became a center of this Renaissance intellectual movement, which, as its name implies, focused upon the intellectual and artistic capacities and achievements of humankind.

The interior of Cordoba, Spain's Mosque-Cathedral reveals a curious mixture of Moorish architecture (begun in the eighth century) and Christian art (in the statues above the arch) of the sixteenth century.

Spain's foray into the New World was both a commercial venture and a religious crusade. It was also fueled by the humanist spirit of discovery. As Isabel was told when she was handed a copy of the first book of Castilian grammar, printed in 1492 and written by one of the scholars she had brought to her court, "Your Majesty, language is the perfect instrument of empire." In establishing colonies in the New World, Spain spread her religion, her language, and her culture with equal vigor, in the process creating a new political economy.

The World of the Indian Peoples

At the end of the fifteenth century, the Americas comprised several large and powerful states, as well as a number of peoples, especially in North America, who lived in smaller and less complex social organizations, each with different political economies, traditions, cultures, and values. This diversity had its origins at least 12,000 years earlier when people known as the Archaic or Paleo-Indians had crossed from Siberia into Alaska. They were the ancestors of all the Indian peoples of the Americas. By the time of Columbus' voyage, there were hundreds of separate Indian cultures—speaking 375 different languages—that traced their origin to the Paleo-Indians (see Map 1-3). The total native population of America north of the Rio Grande may have been as high as 18,000,000 (with that of Europe perhaps five or six times higher). As in Europe and Africa, peoples were in movement as some civilizations were on the rise and others in decline.

The Archaic Indians

The first Americans were hunter-gatherers who followed the mammoth and other huge animals across the land bridge from Asia. These people were modern human beings who stood erect, wore clothing, and made tools. Once they had dispersed throughout America, they lived in small bands of perhaps two dozen people who occasionally interacted with another twenty or so bands. Each Paleo-Indian, then, had face-to-face contacts with about 500 people, which seems to be about as many names and faces as any person can remember. With strict bans on incest, men selected their marriage partners from the women in one of the local bands. Social and political relations among the Paleo-Indians were probably highly egalitarian, except for differences that were based on age or gender. Work, for example, was assigned by gender, with men hunting the large game and women gathering nuts, berries, and other foods. Each of these groups of Paleo-Indians

ranged over a territory about the size of West Virginia. The Paleo-Indians did not plant or store food, and hence they lived close to the edge of extinction. The death of a band's male hunter or a dearth of food could lead to the demise of the entire band.

With the end of the Ice Age, around 10,000 B.C.E., America's Paleo-Indians had to adapt to a world without the huge animals that had been their prey. As the earth warmed, three dozen classes of animals died, not only mammoths, but also mastodons, twenty-foot sloths, beavers the size of today's bear, and saber-toothed cats with eight-inch-long teeth. In order to survive, the Archaic Indians learned to hunt smaller game. Because these animals ranged over a much smaller region than their huge ancestors, the Archaic Indians became less nomadic and more settled. They established base camps, like the one discovered by archaeologists at Poverty Point, Louisiana, to which they returned periodically. Their tools became more sophisticated, and they began storing some food, which gave them the ability to survive shortages.

As the Archaic Indians became more efficient in their hunting and gathering of food, they also began to adapt the environment to their needs, for example by periodically burning meadows, to create an ideal environment for deer. By 3,000 B.C.E., some groups were beginning to cultivate native plants. The population in North America grew perhaps tenfold, to a million or so. Although the Archaic Indians still lived in small groups of probably no more than five hundred, they became less egalitarian. Those who represented the group to outsiders probably ranked above the rest. At this time, groups of Indians began to distinguish themselves from others, developing their own ceremonies and languages.

Changes in the North American climate during the Archaic period led to other, more significant differences among American Indians and their political economies. While the Eastern Woodlands area (generally, east of the Mississippi) was moist and hence hospitable to agriculture, the Plains region (between the Mississippi and the Rocky Mountains) was much more arid. Indians in the Plains region still lived in small, highly mobile bands and pursued the game that had survived global warming at the end of the Ice Age: bison, elk, bear, and deer.

Further west, in the desert-like Great Basin and Southwest regions, Indians subsisted on a combination of small game and seeds. Slowly, these peoples began to learn how to use the little moisture available to them, and they domesticated several crops, including maize (corn) and chiles. Some groups became sedentary, building pueblos and cliff dwellings as permanent homes.

On the California coast and in the Pacific Northwest, Archaic hunter-gatherers made use of the abundant natural resources, particularly fish. They also began to develop the striking artwork for which those regions are still known. Another regional culture began to develop south of the

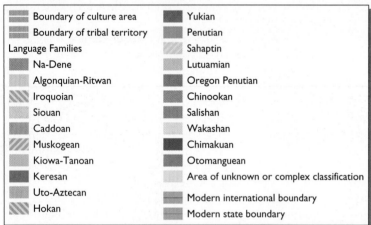

▦ Boundary of culture area	◼ Yukian
▦ Boundary of tribal territory	◼ Penutian
Language Families	▨ Sahaptin
◼ Na-Dene	▦ Lutuamian
▨ Algonquian-Ritwan	◼ Oregon Penutian
▨ Iroquoian	◼ Chinookan
▦ Siouan	◼ Salishan
◼ Caddoan	▦ Wakashan
▨ Muskogean	◼ Chimakuan
▦ Kiowa-Tanoan	◼ Otomanguean
◼ Keresan	▦ Area of unknown or complex classification
◼ Uto-Aztecan	▦ Modern international boundary
▨ Hokan	▦ Modern state boundary

Map 1-3   The Indian Peoples of North America and Their Languages, c. 1500.
When Europeans first arrived in America, there were hundreds of separate cultures, speaking 375 different languages. Boundaries between the groups were constantly shifting, as disease, conflict, and environmental changes caused some groups to prosper and others to decline. Much of the Eastern Woodlands region had lost its population to epidemics and emigration.
Source: Michael Coe, et al., Atlas of Ancient North America (New York: Facts on File, 1986), 44–45.

Arctic Circle, where Native Americans began to develop the boats, weapons, and tools necessary to hunt and live off whales and seals. Out of these regional environments—Eastern Woodlands, Plains, Great Basin and Southwest, California and Pacific Coast, and Subarctic—developed the distinctive Indian cultures that European explorers encountered in the years after 1492. Although American Indians are sometimes thought of as all being similar, by the time of Columbus' voyage, these Indian peoples were as different from one another as the peoples of Europe.

The Indians of the Eastern Woodlands

A distinctive Eastern Woodlands Indian culture had developed by 700 B.C.E., when Indians in this area had moved from hunting and gathering to cultivation of crops. Archaeologists have identified a succession of Indian cultures that inhabited the Mississippi and Ohio River valley areas and the southeastern quadrant of the United States between 700 B.C.E. and about 1500 C.E.—the Adena culture, the Hopewell culture, and the Mississippian cultures. These groups are distinguished by the areas in which they lived, the increasing complexity of their crafts, the extent

of their trade networks, and their increasing capacity to support large populations from their agriculture. All of them built mounds in which to bury their dead. Mississippian peoples used these mounds also as platforms for temples and other public structures; the mounds can still be seen today at places like Cahokia, in East St. Louis, Illinois, although the structures themselves and the people who worshiped in them have long since disappeared.

These Indian societies were increasingly hierarchical in their political and social organizations. By the Mississippian period, some offices were probably hereditary, and large cities such as Cahokia (with a population of between 10,000 and 30,000) and Moundville dominated smaller ones in the region. When powerful people died, they were buried with huge stores of luxury goods. In order to obtain these exotic goods, Woodlands Indians traveled throughout much of the continent, trading for bear teeth in Wyoming, silver in Ontario, shells and shark teeth along the Gulf Coast, and rare minerals in Minnesota, the Dakotas, and the Appalachians. Because Woodlands Indians buried these goods with the dead, rather than hoarding them and passing them on from generation to generation, they had to keep trading for new

The community at Cahokia, as reconstructed by an artist. The town was surrounded by a stockade, which enclosed the mounds, plazas, temples, and homes.

supplies in order to fill the graves of the dead. By the Hopewell period, Indians were crafting exquisite objects out of metal and stone to bury with their dead and to trade to distant tribes.

Before the arrival of Europeans, Indian cultures flourished and also disappeared for reasons that are not fully known. Spanish explorers encountered mound-building Indians in the Southeast in the sixteenth century, but by the time the English arrived a century later, the mound builders had disappeared from the Ohio River and Mississippi valleys. Archaeologists have theories about the disappearance of the Mississippians. Although these tribes were aggressive, their collapse does not seem to have been caused by warfare. Instead, pre-industrial cities were probably "population sinks" in which densely packed populations without effective sanitation systems served as breeding grounds for lethal diseases. Pre-industrial populations in all parts of the world always lived close to the edge of extinction, and a serious drought or epidemic disease could wipe out an entire population.

At about the time the Mississippian cities were collapsing, other Indian cultures were rising to prominence in the Eastern Woodlands. The Iroquois occupied the southern Great Lakes region, and the Algonquians covered much of eastern Canada and northeastern United States, as far south as Virginia. These two groups spoke different languages, and the Iroquois were matrilineal (tracing descent through the woman) and matrilocal (with husbands moving into their wives' clans), but in many other ways, these two cultures were similar. The Iroquois and Algonquians south of Canada were agriculturalists who practiced a slash-and-burn method of clearing fields for corn and other vegetables, planting them intensively, exhausting the soil, and then moving on to more fertile regions, where clearings once again were burned. This method of agriculture could not sustain as large a population as could the fertile river-valley cultivation of the mound builders; the population of the largest known Iroquois city was only between 2,000 and 3,000. Nonetheless, this method of farming became increasingly efficient, making hunting less important. Because almost all agriculture was the work of women, their prestige in their villages increased.

The Iroquois and Algonquians were fierce people, more violent than the Mississippians, although scholars are not certain why. One theory suggests that as agriculture became more efficient and women's prestige increased, men resorted to warfare in order to maintain their own prestige. Then, in order to protect themselves from their enemies, small groups of Indians began to band together in larger villages, which they surrounded with palisades (tall, wooden fences). As villages grew larger, there were fewer opportunities for intermarriage with outsiders, which might have acted as a brake upon warfare. As the population in these villages increased and they depended upon women's farming for survival, the prestige of the women grew, sending men into warfare to demonstrate their own prowess.

By the eve of European settlement, many Iroquois tribes had banded together in a confederacy in order to limit infighting—and to make them more effective in struggles against external enemies. Political influence within these cultures depended almost entirely upon persuasion, rather than force. The requirement of the consent of all concerned, women included, made the Iroquois in particular highly cohesive; by the time the Europeans arrived, the Iroquois were able to subdue internal violence and direct it outward at the interlopers and keep them at bay for over two centuries.

The Indians of the Plains

The popular image of the American Indian comes from Westerns: the brave on horseback, hunting bison. Plains Indians, however, did not become nomadic hunters on horseback until after the Spanish reintroduced horses to the Great Plains in the sixteenth century (they had died out at the end of the Pleistocene era). Like Indians east of the Mississippi, Plains Indians became agriculturalists after the end of the Archaic era. As was the Indian custom, women were responsible for raising maize and other crops, while men traveled periodically to buffalo corrals and "jumps." Hunters stampeded buffalo into enclosures, where they ambushed them, or forced them to jump over steep cliffs. One such jump, Head-Smashed-In in western Alberta, was in use for more than 7,000 years.

After the Spanish brought horses to the Plains Indians, these Indians became nomadic, abandoning their multi-family earth and wood lodges for tipis that could be carried from one campsite to the next. Buffalo then became a more important part of their diet than food that they had raised. With this shift, women's prestige decreased and that of men grew; some tribes may have shifted from matrilocal to patrilocal residence, with married couples living with the husband's kin rather than the wife's.

The Indians of the Deserts

The arid landscape of the desert West and Southwest shaped the development of Indian cultures in those regions. Slowly over the centuries, Indians learned to make maximum use of plants such as the piñon that grew in the dry climate and to cultivate increasingly productive strains of maize. In the Great Basin and desert regions, the population remained relatively small, but by about 200 C.E. villages began to appear in the Southwest. At that time, southwestern Indians began to construct pithouses, round dwellings carved about a foot and a half into the ground with walls and roofs constructed out of mud-covered wooden frameworks.

In the three centuries after 700 C.E., as the population grew, southwestern Indians moved out of these pit homes into multi-room adobe pueblos, such as the ones built on the surface at Chaco Canyon (in present-day New Mexico) and those carved into the cliffs at Mesa Verde (in present-day Colorado). These huge complexes were carefully designed and must have required the labor of well-organized work forces. Abandoned pithouses were turned into *kivas,* chambers for the practice of religious ceremonies, sometimes reserved exclusively for the men of the tribe. The inhabitants of Chaco Canyon engaged in trade with distant regions, and roads radiated out from the canyon in straight lines, like the spokes of a wheel.

Like the cities of the eastern mound builders, the Anasazi Indian communities at Chaco Canyon, Mesa Verde, and several other sites simply disappeared, Chaco sometime after 1100 C.E. and Mesa Verde in the last quarter of the thirteenth century. Archaeologists are not certain why these magnificent structures were abandoned. The most recent theories for the abandonment of Mesa Verde suggest a combination of pushes and pulls: Prolonged drought may have led to increased efforts to alter the landscape by dams and irrigation systems. Those who invested in their landscape in this way may have had to fight off outsiders who desired their improved land. At the same time, a new and attractive religion seems to have appeared in the south and acted as a magnet to pull people from the north, which was beset by a dry climate and hostile neighbors. Although climate was always a critical factor in the shaping of pre-industrial civilizations, these communities adapted to their resources in a wide variety of ways, creating elaborate religions and belief systems to give meaning to their worlds.

The Indians of the Pacific Coast

Along the California and Northwest coasts, the abundance of the environment led to the development of distinctive cultures. In both regions, the plentiful fish, game, and edible plants permitted the population to grow even in the absence of agriculture. In California, the amazing variety of local environments meant that each of 500 local cultures could concentrate upon its own specialties, which it traded with its neighbors. The Northwest Coast environment was more uniform, but no less lush, and it enjoyed a surplus of food. With so little work needed to supply the food needs of the community, Northwest Coast Indians were able to build up surpluses and create magnificent works of art such as totem poles and masks. Periodically, these Indians held "potlatch" ceremonies in which they gave away or even destroyed all their possessions. When Europeans first encountered this practice, they found it bizarre and even dangerous, so contrary was it to the doctrines of capitalism, which encouraged them to accumulate and hold onto their wealth.

The Great Civilizations of the Americas

Although the Indian peoples north of the Rio Grande were primarily agriculturalists or hunter-gatherers, several of those to the south developed much more complex political economies, technologies, and urban cultures. The splendid Maya civilization, which had developed both a writing system and mathematics, had dominated southern Mexico and Central America from the fourth to the tenth centuries. Historians do not know for certain why the great Maya cultural centers declined, but they suppose that the causes may have been "natural." Perhaps a change in climate or ecology made it impossible for Maya agriculture to support so large a population.

The next great empire in the region was that of the Toltecs, whose influence extended from central Mexico as far north perhaps as the cliff-dwelling Anasazi of the American Southwest. After the Toltec empire was destroyed in the middle of the twelfth century by invaders from the north, a number of different peoples struggled for dominion. The Aztec prevailed in this contest, and they dominated the region and the peoples in it until their own defeat at the hands of a Spanish and Indian alliance. Elsewhere in the Americas, other peoples were on the move, sometimes engaging in peaceful trade and other times attempting to wrest control of a region from those who inhabited it. The powerful and complex Inca empire in Peru had just reached its high point when the Spanish arrived.

Worlds in Collision

Columbus' voyages to the Americas marked the end of one era and the beginning of a new one. In a little over a quarter of a century, the world was made immeasurably smaller, and peoples who had lived in isolation from one another were brought into close contact. In this great age of European exploration, Bartolomeo Dias rounded the African cape in 1488, Vasco da Gama reached India in 1498, and an expedition led by Ferdinand Magellan (Fernão Magalhães in Portuguese) sailed around the world between 1519 and 1522. These explorers were seeking not to discover new lands but to find faster routes to old ones. They were propelled by an expanding Europe's desire for trade and for spreading the Christian religion. Within a few short years, for the first time in human history, all of the world's great urban civilizations, from Tenochtitlan to Cathay had become aware of one another's existence. Moreover, despite the obvious differences in language, dress, architecture, art, and customs, the Europeans who traveled to Africa and the Americas encountered people who lived in political and economic organizations enough like their own to make trade and diplomacy possible. Because of their compatible political economies, it was not at all difficult for Europeans to draw Africans and Native Americans into a huge new global economy. From one perspective, Europeans achieved their objectives as the entire world was drawn into their trade network, and the Christian religion was spread, by both force and persuasion. Yet the world was transformed more dramatically than anyone ever could have imagined, not only in the lands where European ships landed, but in Europe itself.

Christopher Columbus Finds a Patron

Between 1492 and 1504, Columbus made four voyages to America, sailing for Isabel and Fernando's Spain. But before he sailed across the Atlantic, he had already seen a considerable portion of the world known to Europeans. Born in 1451 into a family of weavers in the Italian city-state of Genoa, Columbus first went to sea on merchant ships that sailed the Mediterranean. In the middle of the 1470s, he moved to Portugal, where he began sailing to Portuguese outposts such as the Madeiras. Within a decade, Columbus had decided to seek support for a voyage to China and Japan, which he had read about in Marco Polo's book.

Although we do not know precisely how Columbus arrived at his decision, it seems that his ambitions were shaped by his reading and his extensive experience as a mariner, which had already taken him thousands of miles from the place of his birth. By the end of the fifteenth century, new methods of typesetting had decreased the price and increased the availability of books, and Columbus was familiar with a number of works of geography. By Columbus' time, it was generally known that the world was round, but the precise dimensions of the globe had not yet been determined. Nor were Europeans certain about the size and configuration of the lands to the east. There was,

however, great curiosity about them, which was fueled, of course, by the search for wealth and national power. It was only a matter of time until one European or another headed west and bumped into America while attempting to circumnavigate the globe. Perhaps Columbus was the first simply because he made a serious mistake in his calculations. His optimism was based upon the mistaken belief that Japan was only 2,400 miles away from the Canary Islands, when in fact, it was more than four times that distance away.

No private individual had the resources to finance such an expedition, so Columbus sought support from the most likely sponsors, first the king of Portugal and then the queen of Spain. The king of Portugal turned him down for reasons that are unclear, as Portugal would soon sponsor several other voyages to the west. Columbus then departed for Spain, where he sought patronage for his ambitious plan from Isabel and Fernando. Even though two scientific commissions appointed by Isabel and Fernando cast doubt upon Columbus' geographical assumptions and calculations, the monarchs were intrigued by his vision of a western route to Asia. Whatever their doubts, the possibility of finding new sources of gold and more infidels to vanquish was too attractive, and the likelihood that Columbus would seek sponsorship from a rival nation was too great.

The terms that Columbus received reveal what was most important to an ambitious man at the end of the fifteenth century. The monarchy agreed to finance most of his trip (paying for it not, as legend has it, by pawning Isabel's jewels, but by the much more modern method of deficit spending). The king and queen also granted him a number of powers and privileges. Columbus would realize his lifelong ambition of being made a member of the nobility. Columbus was to be named admiral, viceroy, and

Although some thought he had prematurely white hair and a long face, no one knows exactly what Christopher Columbus looked like. These are some of the ways that artists have imagined he might have appeared, with a thin face or a broad one, in a small hat or large one, with or without a beard.

governor general of all the lands that he might find. After deducting for expenses, Columbus would get to keep one-tenth of the income from the enterprise, with the monarchy retaining the rest. Considering the profits that Spain eventually reaped from her American colonies, the small amount spent on Columbus' voyages proved in time to be one of the shrewdest investments in the history of nations.

Columbus Finds a New World

Spanish dreams of wealth and Christian mission were inextricable. Columbus, for example, hoped that Spain could use the sought-after riches to finance a new crusade to reclaim Jerusalem for Christians. It was this dream, of mixed national and personal glory, that propelled Columbus when he and his crew departed the Spanish port of Palos on August 3, 1492. That was why they moved so rapidly from island to island in the Caribbean and finally to the mainland, searching for the lands described by Marco Polo.

This quest for wealth took Columbus back and forth across the Atlantic four times between 1492 and 1504. In those voyages he planted the Spanish flag throughout the Caribbean region, on the islands of Cuba, Hispaniola, and Puerto Rico, as well as on the mainland at Honduras and Venezuela. Ten years later Columbus was still as obsessed by gold as ever. "O, most excellent gold! Who has gold has a treasure with which he gets what he wants, imposes his will on the world, and even helps souls to paradise." Although he himself found only small quantities of gold, the Spaniards who followed him onto the mainland eventually found among the Aztec of Mexico and the Inca of Peru riches to match their most fantastic dreams. By the time these explorers finally found what they had been seeking, the patterns that shaped the next century of Spanish-Indian interaction in the Americas had been established.

Late-medieval Europeans tended to view the world in terms of opposites, which led them to exaggerate differences rather than see similarities or complexities. Columbus and subsequent explorers assumed that gold would be found somewhere, and they typically described the lands they visited as an earthly Paradise, even in the face of contrary evidence. By the time Columbus returned to Hispaniola on his second voyage, accompanied by 1500 Spaniards, it was clear that his hopes of easy wealth and harmonious relations with the natives were not to be realized. Columbus had left 39 men on the island among the Taino Indian inhabitants, whom he believed to be a gentle people. Columbus returned to find that they were all dead, the first of many casualties to the European colonial experience. According to the Taino chieftain, Columbus' sailors had set off on a spree of gold-seeking and debauchery, each of them "taking as many women and as much gold as he could," until they were fighting among themselves and became easy victims for a rival Indian chieftain.

The Spanish could not see the death of their sailors as a predictable response to their behavior. Instead, they fit it into the Europeans' growing perception that all Indians could be divided into two groups: friendly, peace-loving, unsophisticated, "good" Indians, such as the Tainos, and fierce, savage, "bad," man-eating Indians, for whom they used the Taino term "Caribs."

Tainos and Caribs

Although the Spanish saw the Indians of the Americas through the lens of the preconceptions they brought with them, there was often an element of accuracy in their perceptions. Historians and anthropologists have identified the Tainos and Caribs as two separate tribes of people, each with different histories and customs. The Tainos, who inhabited the islands of Cuba and Hispaniola, were a sedentary tribe of farmers whose agriculture could sustain a population as dense as that of Spain. It has been estimated that, before the arrival of Columbus, between 60,000 and several million Tainos inhabited the island of Hispaniola. The Tainos were successful farmers who were accustomed to taking direction from their *cacique;* hence it was not long before the Spanish coerced the Tainos into working for them. Although the Tainos sometimes fought among themselves, the Spanish perception that they were a peace-loving people is generally accurate.

In comparison, the Caribs were more aggressive. At the time of Columbus' arrival, the Caribs were in the process of moving north from the South American coast into the island chains of the Atlantic. If the energies of the Tainos were directed toward agriculture and the practice of religion, the Caribs focused upon trade and warfare, and their society was organized for that purpose. Men and women lived separately, and because Carib men often obtained their wives by raiding other villages, over time they came to treat their own women as if they were captives of war. The Carib *cacique* was always a male. Because the Caribs were a maritime people, able to travel long distances for trade and warfare, and because their men were skilled warriors, it is not surprising that they came into conflict with another maritime people practiced in the arts of war, the Spanish.

Although the Spanish, like all the Europeans who followed them into the Americas, depicted themselves as civilized and the Indians they encountered as either gentle but primitive or savage and inhuman, it would be a mistake to exaggerate the differences between Europeans and natives. Seven centuries of warfare with the Moors had made the Spanish, for example, a fierce people as well, and they believed that practices that later generations would condemn as cruel were justified for people at war. Once the Spanish decided that the Caribs were an enemy people, they began to treat them harshly. Columbus made a gift to one of his lieutenants of "a most beautiful cannibal

Taino customs. (left) A young man introducing himself to the family of the young woman he wants to marry. (right) The Taino raising their crops in small, carefully-kept gardens. These illustrations come from a manuscript thought to have been written by a Frenchman who traveled to the West Indies with Sir Francis Drake in the sixteenth century.

woman," but she resisted his sexual advances. "She scratched me with her fingernails to such a degree that I would not have wished then that I had begun," he later reported. "I grabbed a leather strap and gave her a good chastisement of lashes, so that she hurled such unheard of shouts that you could not believe. Finally, we reached an agreement in such a manner that I can tell you that in fact she seemed to have been taught in the school for whores." This account illustrates that at the same time that the Spanish saw themselves as the protectors of "good" Indian women, they justified the beating and rape of Carib women by claiming that they were willing prostitutes, no matter how fiercely they resisted.

The Origins of a New World Political Economy

As early as Columbus' second voyage of 1493, it became clear that the vast treasures he had anticipated finding were not readily at hand. Those who accompanied him to the Caribbean, however, expected to be rewarded for their services, and the queen and king who had financed his expedition were eager to reap profits on it. When Columbus found himself unable to send back shiploads of gold and pearls, he packed off more than five hundred Indians to be sold as slaves. He distributed another six hundred or so among the Spanish settlers on the island of Hispaniola, for them to use as they wished.

Once again a pattern of New World development had been established. The European quest for wealth led quickly to the subjugation of native peoples. Each European nation reacted somewhat differently to this movement toward enslavement. Generally, the Spanish rulers tried to

restrain their New World colonizers and protect their new Indian subjects. Although slavery was practiced both on the Spanish mainland and in the Canary Islands (and Isabel's court was served by Muslims enslaved in the *reconquista*), the institution was governed by a rather strict set of principles developed by the Church. No Christian was to be enslaved. In 1493, Pope Alexander VI confirmed Spanish dominion over all the lands that Columbus had explored, and he commanded the Spanish "to lead the peoples dwelling in those islands and countries to embrace the Christian religion." A subsequent treaty between Spain and Portugal, the Treaty of Tordesillas of 1494, divided all lands already discovered or to be discovered between Spain and Portugal, along an imaginary line 370 leagues west of the Azores. This Treaty formed the basis for Portugal's subsequent claim to Brazil, which her explorers reached in 1500. At the same time the Papal Bull secured the Spanish claim to the Indians' land, it also established the Church's interest in the spiritual welfare of the Native Americans.

As the monarch who had driven the Muslims out of Spain, Isabel took seriously her responsibilities to evangelize her Indian subjects. Isabel and her successors also had earthly political and economic goals, all of which they attempted to reconcile by insisting that the Indians who inhabited the islands seized by the Spanish were vassals, subjects of the Spanish Crown. When as late as 1499 Columbus was still sending slaves back to Spain, Isabel exploded, "What power of mine has the Admiral to give anyone my vassals?" In this way, Isabel attempted to fit the Indians into the Spanish political economy.

Like other vassals in Spain and its growing empire, the Indians were technically free, although they could be required both to work and to pay tribute to the Crown.

Isabel instructed the Governor to impose upon them a European-style civilization. They were to be "made to serve us through work, and be paid a just salary," and in order to assure their salvation, "they must live in villages, each in a house with a wife, a family, and possessions, as do the people of our kingdoms, and dress and behave like reasonable beings." Humane treatment, and with it freedom from slavery, thus became dependent upon the willingness of Native Americans to abandon their religion and customs and adopt those of the Spanish. It is easy to be cynical about Isabel's motives, but she considered the Native Americans as moral beings, rather than instruments of the devil. Her approach was considerably more benevolent than that of many others at her court and most of those who were engaged in the colonizing process.

With the Spanish monarchy refusing to sanction the enslavement of friendly Indians, the Spanish settlers had to devise an alternate means of getting labor from the Native Americans. Out of this struggle a New World political economy emerged. For the first several years, the Spanish simply demanded tribute from the Tainos. Many of the Spanish found this arrangement insufficiently lucrative, however, and they began to spread themselves out across the island, subduing individual *caciques* and compelling their villages to work for the Spanish. The Spanish settlers owned neither the land, which had to be obtained through separate grants from Spanish officials, nor the Indians who worked for them. They possessed only the unlimited right to compel a particular group of Indians to work. This system, called the **encomienda,** was unique to the New World; nothing precisely like it had existed in Spain or elsewhere in Europe. It was a new system of labor, imposed by Spanish settlers eager for wealth and looking for a means to get others to work for them. Technically it complied with Isabel's insistence that friendly Indians be made vassals of the Crown, rather than slaves.

We do not know precisely how the system developed, although there is some evidence that Spanish men first seized native women as their concubines, and that the village men subsequently rendered their services to the Spanish, either in the belief that their women had been legitimately incorporated into Spanish society or simply to remain close to them. We often picture the encounter between Indians and Europeans as a series of armed conflicts between groups of men. In truth, women often played a critical role in establishing the shape that a bi-racial society would take, whether as captives, as was the case on Hispaniola, or as willing participants in a European way of life, as was the case at other times.

Columbus appears to have sanctioned this new system of labor after it developed in the late 1490s, and it eventually received begrudging support from the monarchs in Spain. Under the guise of a system that paid due regard to the Indians' legal rights and spiritual requirements, Native Americans were subjected to overwork and abuse, even if they could not legally be bought and sold as slaves. Once

again a pattern that would shape the development of Euro-American society had been established within the first several years of contact. In this case, Spanish settlers' desire to realize a profit in the New World led to a new political economy and with it a form of exploitation unknown in Europe.

The *Requerimiento* and the Morality of Conquest

Throughout the period that Spain maintained a New World empire, there were tensions between the colonizers, who wished to increase their wealth and enhance their power unimpeded by the Crown, and the Crown, which wanted to limit the autonomy of New World settlers. Moreover, both the Spanish Crown and the clergy continued to be troubled by the enslavement of apparently friendly Indians and the maltreatment of those who worked on *encomiendas.* In order to clarify the legal basis for the enslavement of hostile Indians, in 1513 the Spanish Crown issued the **Requerimiento** or "Requirement," a document drafted by a committee of legal scholars and theologians. The *Requerimiento* promised the Indians that if they accepted the authority of Christianity, the Pope, and the monarchs of Spain, the *conquistadores* "shall receive you in all love and charity, and shall leave you, your wives, and your children, and your lands, free without servitude, and you may do with them and with yourselves freely that which you like and think best." If, however, the Indians resisted the peaceful imposition of Spanish rule, "we shall forcibly enter into your country and shall make war against you in all ways and manners that we can. . . . we shall take you and your wives and your children, and shall make slaves of them. . . . and we shall take away your goods, and shall do all the harm and damage that we can. . . . and that the deaths and losses which shall accrue from this are your fault, and not that of their Highnesses, or ours, nor of these gentlemen who come with us." Henceforth, each *conquistador* (conqueror) was required to carry a copy of this document with him and to read it to every new group of Indians he encountered. As befitting a legal document, each reading of the *Requerimiento* was supposed to be notarized and signed by witnesses.

As with the *encomienda,* there is evidence that the *conquistadores* complied with the letter, but not the spirit, of the *Requerimiento,* by mumbling it in Spanish to groups of uncomprehending Indians or reading it from the decks of ships, far from hearing distance. Moreover, the Crown provided no means of enforcement other than the good faith of the *conquistador* or *encomendero* (owner of an *encomienda*)—a very frail reed on which to rest the freedom and fate of the Indians. Considering the profits that might be reaped by the subjugation of a strange and seemingly uncivilized population, perhaps what is most amazing is not the failure of the Spanish Crown to protect the Indians but that it kept trying.

ON TRIAL

Las Casas and Sepúlveda Debate the Morality of Conquest

It was not actually a trial, but rather an audience before the highest tribunal in Spain. The king, Charles V, had summoned to his court at Valladolid two of the most important Catholic clerics in the nation, Bartolomé de las Casas and Juan Ginés de Sepúlveda, to debate the morality of conquest before the Council of the Indies. These two priests were the leading spokesmen for two sharply different points of view. Las Casas, whose father sailed with Columbus on his second voyage and who himself later became an *encomendero,* was convinced by personal experience that "everything which has been done to the Indians is unjust and tyrannical." Sepúlveda was an eminent scholar and committed nationalist whose defense of conquest had already won him the thanks of the municipal council of Mexico City.

The two adversaries did not meet face-to-face in Valladolid. Sepúlveda spoke first, resting his case on the innate barbarism of the Indians. Some people, he said, were born to be masters and others, slaves. Sepúlveda ridiculed the argument that the Aztec were "civilized" because they built cities and engaged in commerce. So what if they built houses? This "merely proves that they are neither bears nor monkeys and that they are not totally irrational." Not even the Aztec were anything more than "barbarous, uncultivated, and inhumane little men." War against them could be justified "not only on the basis of their paganism but even more so because of their abominable licentiousness, their prodigious sacrifice of human victims . . . their horrible banquets of human flesh." Subjecting them to Spanish rule would be the most "beneficial" thing that the Spanish could do for them.

Then Las Casas was summoned for his rebuttal. He spoke for five days until the exhausted Council told him they had heard enough. Warfare against the Indians was not justified, Las Casas argued. Instead, they could be won over by peaceful means, for they were "prudent and rational beings, of as good ability and judgment as other men and more able, discreet, and of better understanding than the people of many other nations." Again and again, Las Casas denounced Sepúlveda's "deadly poison" and the greed of the Spanish, which "has led to such crimes. . . as have never been committed by any other nation, no matter how fierce it may have been." He feared that Sepúlveda's course would, in the end, provoke God to "pour forth the fury of his anger and lay hold of all of Spain sooner than he had decreed." The Spanish must convert the Indians, not conquer them.

Although the judges who heard these presentations departed Valladolid without rendering a verdict, Las Casas' ideas seemed to prevail in Spain. As Las Casas asked, Sepúlveda was not allowed to publish the book he had been writing. Las Casas had already helped shape The Laws of Burgos (1513) and the New Laws of 1542, which attempted to regulate the working conditions of the Indians and finally forbade any further enslavement of the native population. His influence can be seen in the next set of regulations, issued in 1573, written to govern Spain's future colonial ventures, which were to be called "pacifications" rather than "conquests." Henceforth, Indians were to be treated gently "so as not to scandalize them or prejudice them against Christianity." But by that time, Spain's New World empire was essentially complete; there were relatively few Indians left to conquer or to pacify.

Sepúlveda argued for unlimited governmental power, but it was actually Las Casas' views that were most useful to the powerful monarchy. When Spain commenced her overseas ventures, it was not even a nation itself. The century that would witness Spanish expansion into most of present South and Central America also saw the growth of state power in Spain itself. Las Casas' efforts on behalf of the Indians meshed nicely with the political plans of the Spanish monarchy, which aimed at centralized state power. Like the *hidalgos,* who had claimed as their own the land they wrested away from the Moors, the *conquistadores* attempted to set themselves up as feudal lords, with almost unlimited control over the land in their possession and the Indians who inhabited it and with only limited obligations to the monarch. In insisting upon humane treatment of the Indians, the Spanish monarchs were undercutting the authority of the local *encomenderos.* In this way, as well as by forbidding the establishment of local representative governments, the Spanish monarchs prevented the development not only of a New World feudal aristocracy, which might challenge its power, but also of habits of self-government and local autonomy—all in the name of humanity.

The Biological Consequences of Conquest

Some of the most important changes produced by contact between Europeans and Native Americans were wholly unintentional. Because there had been almost no contact between the peoples of these continents for thousands of years, they had developed distinctive ecologies. Each continent had its own diseases, its own plants, and its own animals, all of which lived in their own balance. The arrival of Europeans wrenched people out of their environments, tipping a delicate pre-industrial balance in which everyone's effort was often needed to provide a food supply. They also introduced new diseases that spread like wildfire. If the biological effects of human contact were felt immediately, however, the consequences of plant and animal exchange took much longer. New breeds of animals were introduced from Europe into the Americas, and plants were exchanged between the continents. The face of the American landscape was changed, as domestic animals trampled meadows and increasing acreage was turned over to the cultivation of Old World crops. This environmental transformation ultimately made possible the dramatic growth of the world's population, as new crops were cultivated.

Demographic Decline

Although the *encomienda* system satisfied Spanish settlers, it proved a disaster for the Indians who were made to participate in it. The Spanish imposed harsh working conditions on the natives, but the agricultural methods of sedentary Indians such as the Taino could not produce the surplus that was necessary to support the Spanish. As soon happened to Indian communities throughout the Americas, the dislocation of their normal way of life proved deeply demoralizing. The birth rate began to fall, but the food supply was inadequate even for the smaller numbers.

Within a few years after the appearance of Europeans, the Native American population began to decline, and with the introduction of the smallpox virus to Hispaniola in 1518, the deadly process was hastened. By the time the first New World epidemic of this Old World disease had run its course, perhaps no more than a thousand of the island's original inhabitants survived. Disease soon worked the same terrible destruction on the nearby islands of Cuba, Puerto Rico, and Jamaica, almost completely destroying the native populations. Disease followed the Spanish and other Europeans every place they went in the Americas, making the work of conquest that much easier.

The diseases that Europeans brought with them proved far more deadly to the Indians than acts of warfare or cruelty. Europeans did not set out to kill off the native inhabitants of the Americas, if only because they always seemed to need more laborers than they had, but that is exactly what the diseases they brought with them did. The isolation of the native peoples had protected them from the diseases of the Old World. Although life expectancy in Europe was still quite low by modern standards (perhaps the mid-thirties), many Europeans built up some resistance to the most common diseases. Moreover, several centuries of trade with Asia and Africa had enabled people from the three continents to share and acquire some natural biological defenses against diseases from the other regions. (The most striking exception was the Black Death, which in 1347 had been carried on an Asian caravan to the shores of the Black Sea, and from there throughout Europe.) Without such natural immunities, Indians were overcome by wave after wave of European disease. After smallpox came typhus and influenza, which destroyed entire communities and left the survivors weak and demoralized.

These terrible European diseases challenged Native American belief systems. The Cakchiquel Indian Hernández Arana described the spread of a plague in his native Guatemala in 1521 that, by the time it had run its course, had killed a substantial proportion of the community: "Great was the stench of the dead. After our fathers and grandfathers succumbed, half of the people fled to the fields. The dogs and the vultures devoured the bodies. The mortality was terrible. Your grandfathers died, and with them died the son of the king and his brothers and kinsmen. So it was that we became orphans, oh, my sons! . . . We were born to die!" The shock of this dreadful plague turned Indians such as Arana against their traditional gods and prepared them to accept the God of the Spaniards.

The transmission of disease was by no means one way, although most diseases seemed to spread from Old World to New. Because syphilis, or at least a particularly virulent strain of the disease, first appeared in Europe shortly after Columbus and his crew made their first return voyage in 1493, historians have suggested that Europeans might have also carried a New World disease back to the Old. The disease spread rapidly through the world in the late fifteenth and early sixteenth centuries, with each nation naming the illness after the nation that seemed to carry it. The Italians called it the French disease, a term that has stuck; the English called it the disease of France or Spain; the Poles said it came from Germany, and the Russians blamed it on the Poles. Those in India and the Middle East called it a European disease; the Chinese identified it with the port of Canton, and the Japanese identified it with the

Chinese and the Portuguese. The spread of the disease, which killed millions and incapacitated many more, became a legacy of the European age of exploration as it followed traders and armies as they worked their way through the world.

The Columbian Exchange

Not only diseases and peoples were transported back and forth across the Atlantic. In what historians have called "the Columbian exchange," plants and animals, as well as human beings and their diseases, were shared between the two worlds that were connected in 1492, eventually transforming the environments of the Old World and the New (see Map 1-4). Along with the 1,500 Spaniards that Columbus brought with him on his second voyage, he also carried a collection of Spanish plants and animals: pigs, cattle, horses, sheep, and goats, as well as sugar cane, wheat, and the seeds for fruits and vegetables. European animals reproduced rapidly in the hospitable environments of the Americas, overrunning the lands that had

once been farmed by now-dead Indians. According to one Spanish report, by 1514, there were 30,000 pigs on the island of Cuba.

Just as Europeans brought their religion and their culture with them to the Americas, so they brought their own culinary habits. They did not develop a taste for native agricultural products and instead imported and planted familiar crops, such as wheat. They also introduced some of the plants such as sugar, rice, and bananas that later formed the basis for New World plantation economies. The addition of Old World plants doubled or tripled the number of plants in the New World, making it in some ways a land of plenty, so great were the variety of indigenous and newly introduced plants and so great their productivity. The combination of Old and New World plants and animals in the Americas after the fifteenth century has made the inhabitants of the Western Hemisphere the best fed people in the world. This food supply made possible the remarkable immigration (the transfer of peoples from the Old World to the New) of the past five centuries.

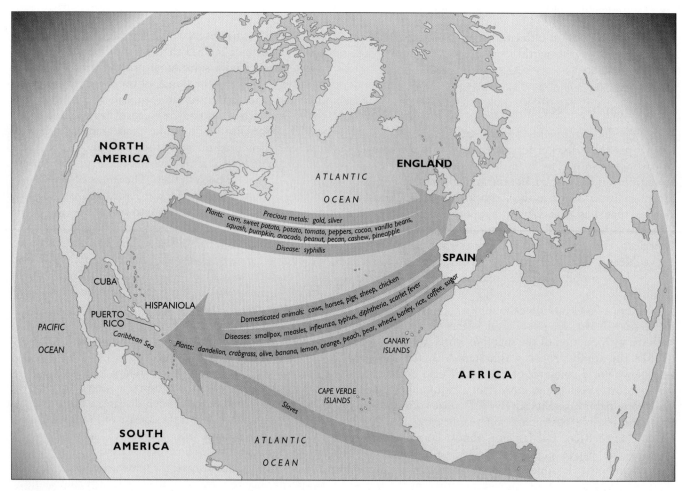

 Map 1-4 The Columbian Exchange.
The exchanges of plants, animals, and diseases dramatically changed both the Old World and the New.

The introduction of these new plants and animals also dramatically transformed the American landscape. Lands once farmed by native agriculturalists were overrun by herds of Old World animals, which trampled old farmlands and grassy regions, leading to their replacement by scrub plants. Indians adapted Old World life forms to their own purposes. American Southwestern and Plains Indian tribes took readily to the horse, which the Navajo and Apache acquired in the last half of the sixteenth century and the Sioux and Comanche somewhat later. The horse changed these Indians' way of life, making them more productive as hunters and more mobile and hence more dangerous as enemies, to both other Indian tribes and, eventually, the U.S. Army. Mounted Indians could easily kill more buffalo than they needed for their own subsistence, providing them with a surplus that they could trade with Europeans for European goods.

The Old World also was transformed as plants were introduced from the Americas. Just as some of the crops that we think of as most typical of the Western Hemisphere were actually carried there from the Old World, so also some plants that we associate with Europe came from the Americas. We may identify potatoes with Ireland, tomatoes with Italy, and paprika with Hungary, but none of these foods was produced in Europe before the sixteenth century. Moreover, it was not simply European (or African) cuisine that was altered by the introduction of plants from the Americas. In fact, the cultivation of Amer-

ican foods in the New World, particularly potatoes, both white and sweet, and maize (corn), which Europeans have generally used as fodder for their livestock, may well have made possible the dramatic growth in world population of the past five centuries (see Figure 1-1).

Onto the Mainland

Most of the early Spanish explorers and settlers were driven by dreams of wealth and glory. When they could not find riches, they turned to agriculture by forced labor, but that was usually a second choice. In a little more than a quarter of a century, the islands inhabited by the Taino had been virtually emptied of their native populations. In order to find workers to raise crops for them, the Spanish began raiding the islands of the Lesser Antilles and seizing Caribs, transporting them back to the Spanish colonies as slaves. At the same time that the Spanish were creating a new political economy based on forced labor in the Caribbean, other *conquistadores* pushed onto the mainland of America in search of gold, pearls, and other treasures. Indians who could not provide such booty soon learned to tantalize the Spanish with accounts of glittering empires just a little further on down the trail or up the river, just far enough away to get the Spanish out of their neighborhoods. Eventually, the Spanish found the empires dripping with gold and splendor of which they had only dreamed. The Aztec empire in Mexico and the Inca empire in Peru rivaled the most fantastic images from literature and legend.

The First Florida Ventures

Ambitious Spaniards continued the search for paths to the Orient and cities of gold (see Map 1-5). The early expeditions served as a training ground for a generation of young *conquistadores*. Indians who resisted were treated brutally. As the Spanish moved rapidly through a region in quest of wealth, they disrupted local political economies by spreading disease and undermining political structures.

Juan Ponce de León, the first European explorer to set foot on the mainland later to be called the United States, had accompanied Columbus on his second voyage and later directed the conquest of Puerto Rico in 1508. As governor, he had become wealthy, but when a political power struggle threw him out of office, he obtained permission from King Fernando to conquer lands to the north. In March of 1513 Ponce de León reached the Atlantic shore of the land he named Florida, which he mistakenly thought was an island. He and his men sailed around Florida to its gulf coast, landing and several times encountering hostile Indians, who evidently had already met with or heard about Spanish slave traders. On the

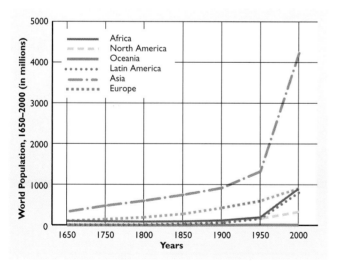

Figure 1-1   World Population, 1650–2000.
These rough estimates of world population suggest the way that the colonization of the New World affected world population. The introduction of Old World diseases led to population decline in the Americas, while the enslavement of millions of Africans led to population decline in Africa. At the same time, foods from the New World made possible the population increase of Europe and Asia.

Source: based on Alfred W. Crosby, Jr., The Columbian Exchange: biological and cultural consequences of 1492 (Westport, CT: Greenwood Pub. Co., 1972), 166.

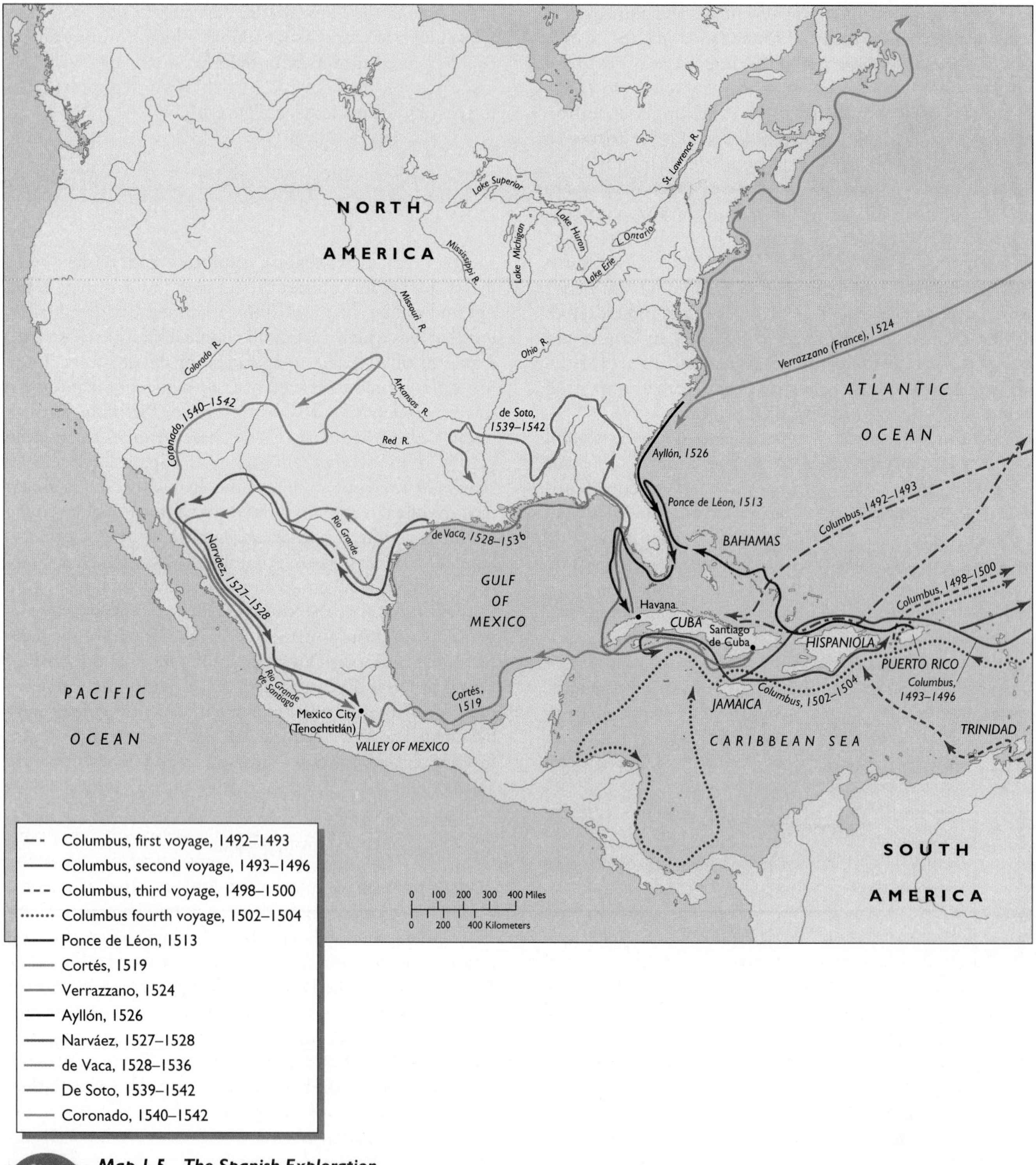

Map 1-5   The Spanish Exploration.
In the fifty years after Columbus' first voyage, Spanish explorers traveled across most of the southern half of the United States.

Map legend:
- Columbus, first voyage, 1492–1493
- Columbus, second voyage, 1493–1496
- Columbus, third voyage, 1498–1500
- Columbus fourth voyage, 1502–1504
- Ponce de Léon, 1513
- Cortés, 1519
- Verrazzano, 1524
- Ayllón, 1526
- Narváez, 1527–1528
- de Vaca, 1528–1536
- De Soto, 1539–1542
- Coronado, 1540–1542

west coast of Florida, he encountered the Calusa, who had become the most powerful tribe in the region. Ponce de León returned to Florida in 1521. He made the mistake of coming back to the same spot where the Calusa had at-tacked his men six years earlier, and this time he attempted to establish a village. The Calusa attacked; Ponce de León was wounded by an arrow, and he returned to Cuba to die.

As the Spanish entered Florida, they came into contact with a number of different Indian tribes. Nothing of these tribes remains except the names that the Spanish recorded. The diseases that the Spanish brought with them struck the densely settled agriculturalists particularly hard, and subsequent explorers routinely pillaged local villages and enslaved male Indians to carry their goods and females to provide them with sexual favors, thereby destroying native populations in another way. There were hundreds of small tribes, each with its own history, culture, and political and economic relationships with their neighbors. In this setting, the Spanish at first appeared to be either another enemy or a potential ally in their struggles with Indian adversaries.

The Conquest of Mexico

Before Spanish explorers returned to Florida, Hernando Cortés completed the conquest of the great Aztec civilization in Mexico, changing dramatically the shape of the Spanish empire in the Americas. Although the Spanish had continued to believe that vast and wealthy civilizations were to be found in the New World, until 1519 the only peoples they had encountered were small sedentary or semi-sedentary tribes, who lived in villages of what the Spanish described as huts. They heard tales, however, of the glittering Aztec empire of central Mexico.

The Aztec people had moved into the valley of Mexico only two centuries earlier, but by the time the Spanish appeared, their empire encompassed perhaps ten or twenty million people, making its population possibly twice as large as Spain's. In several ways, the Aztec resembled the Spanish: They were fierce and warlike and at the same time deeply religious. The two most revered persons in their society were the warrior and the priest. Despite many differences in culture, the Spanish were able to recognize in the Aztec signs of a complex civilization and distinctive political economy. The Aztec had built as many as 40,000 temples, and many of these buildings, like the palaces of the nobility, were quite splendid. Aztec society was rigidly hierarchical, with a nobility of warriors and priests at the top and slaves (usually captives of war or debtors) at the bottom. Sex roles were rigid as well, with women of all classes expected to remain in the home, bear children, and be silent in the presence of men. Boys and girls attended separate schools, with the boys learning the arts of war and the girls practicing the skills of the homemaker. The Aztec were literate, writing in a form of hieroglyphics on folded animal hide. Only a few of these codices, as the inscribed hides are called, have survived the Conquest, for Spanish priests destroyed what they considered pagan manuscripts.

The capital city of Tenochtitlan was built upon a lake, and it was traversed with canals; well-traveled Spaniards said that it reminded them of Venice. With a population of

An Aztec priest performing human sacrifice atop a pyramid at Tenochtitlan.

200,000, it was more than three times the size of Spain's largest city of Seville. Its whitewashed stone pyramids, temples glittering in the sunlight and reflected water, and clean straight avenues, made this city a stark contrast to the cramped and dirty streets of a typical Spanish town. The city's great marketplace was so impressive that soldiers who "had been in many parts of the world, in Constantinople, in Rome, and all over Italy said that they had never seen a market so well laid out, so large, so orderly, and so full of people."

The Aztec believed that the universe was dangerous and unpredictable and that their gods must always be appeased. In the midst of a serious drought about 1450, the Aztec feared that their god Huitzilopochtli was angry with them. When they offered him human hearts, cut out of the living with obsidian knives, the drought lifted. From that point on, the pace of human sacrifice quickened, until obtaining victims for sacrifice and offering them to the god became one of the primary activities of their society. The more victims the Aztec sacrificed, the greater their empire seemed to become, and so they made war against neighboring peoples. The Aztec derived their wealth by extracting tribute from those they conquered. These conquered peoples both feared and resented the Aztec, and they became eager allies for the Spanish in their assault.

There is no question that Cortés came with conquest in mind. He landed on the Yucatán coast with five hundred men in February of 1519. After the Tabasco Indians were defeated, they gave him all their gold and twenty slave women, one of whom, Malinche, became Cortés' translator and mistress. As Cortés marched toward Tenochtitlan, he picked up so many Indian allies that they soon greatly outnumbered Cortés' own troops. When they reached the Aztec capital, the Aztec ruler, Moctezuma, welcomed them in, probably because it was the Aztec custom to

The first meeting of Cortés and his translator and mistress, Malinche, whom the Spanish called Marina. When Europeans encountered Native Americans, women often acted as cultural brokers, negotiating between the two peoples.

offer hospitality to visiting emissaries. Unfortunately for his people, Moctezuma did not understand Spanish customs, and the foreigners soon placed him under a form of house arrest. When the Aztec repulsed a Spanish attack, Cortés laid Tenochtitlan under siege. After three months, in August 1521, the victorious Spanish entered the city, but the proud Aztec refused either to fight or to submit to the Spanish who had starved them. Frustrated, angry, unable to understand these now-gaunt people, Cortés and his troops killed twelve thousand and let their Indian allies slaughter forty thousand more. Then Cortés turned his cannons on the huddled masses of starving Aztec. By the time they surrendered, the city was in ruins. Cortés had promised his king a great prize in Tenochtitlan and its glittering civilization. Instead he had destroyed it.

The Establishment of a Spanish Empire

The ruined city became the center of the new Spanish empire, with a new political economy based upon the extraction of silver and gold and the production of plantation crops. In the next decades, the Spanish defeated another rich and complex civilization, the Inca of Peru, as well as many other tribes of Indians, each with its own history and traditions. Spanish rule now extended from the southernmost tip of South America to halfway up what is now the United States, excepting only the Portuguese colony of Brazil and some of the Caribbean islands. Finally the

Spanish had found the precious metals they craved, and when the Indians' stores ran out, the Spanish began using slave labor to mine more. After silver and gold, sugar was the next most important product of the New World, and as its cultivation spread, so did the demand for labor. The original *conquistadores* had brought their own African slaves with them (as well as some free blacks), and at first they used Africans to supervise Indian laborers. By the second half of the sixteenth century, as more and more Indians succumbed to disease and as the Spanish came to question the legitimacy of enslaving them, the Indians were replaced as laborers by African slaves. In this way, Africans became yet another good to be transported across the seas, transforming the New World, robbing Africa of its population, and making the European Old World rich.

In this context, the Spanish outposts in the present-day United States were simply borderlands, a frontier of much greater importance to Spain from a military standpoint than an economic one. Once other European nations saw the great wealth the Spanish were extracting from their colonies, they too were attracted to the New World, where they established their own colonies that came into conflict with the Spanish. The permanent settlements that the Spanish established in the north (St. Augustine, San Antonio, Santa Fe, San Francisco, for example) were relatively small communities, although the Spanish influence in some of these regions has been profound. In 1522, as the Spanish completed the conquest of Mexico, this territory was still unexplored, and no European yet knew whether another awe-inspiring civilization might yet be found.

The Return to Florida

When the Spanish resumed their exploration of Florida, then, it was with heightened expectations. There were several ventures, but the two most significant were led by Lucas Vázquez de Ayllón and Hernando de Soto. Ayllón sailed from Hispaniola in 1526, accompanied by an Indian slave the Spanish had captured on an earlier raid on the South Carolina coast. After the slave deserted him, presumably to return to his own people, Ayllón's expedition explored the South Carolina coast and established a short-lived town on the coast of Georgia.

Over the next several decades, the Spanish continued to explore the southern portions of North America. In 1528, Pánfilo de Narváez landed near Tampa Bay with 400 men and the king's commission to explore, conquer, and colonize Florida. He never found the great wealth that the local Indians, in what had already become a common defense tactic, insisted could be found in some territory beyond their own. Eight years later, a Spanish slaving expedition working in northwest Mexico found the only four survivors of the failed expedition.

The Spaniard who left the greatest mark on the southeastern part of the United States was a *conquistador* of the classic style. Hernando de Soto had participated in the assault upon the Inca empire in Peru, which provided him with a small fortune and the belief that more wealth could be found in Florida. He and his forces landed near Tampa Bay in 1539, authorized by the Crown to explore and settle the region. His party spent four full years exploring the southeastern part of the continent, and they traveled through almost the entire Southeast. They were the first Europeans to see the Mississippi, and de Soto's expedition crossed regions inhabited by Mississippian tribes. We may get a sense of how densely some regions of the

This illustration of Timucua Indians of Florida carrying his wife to the chief of their village suggests how these Indians looked at the time of the de Soto expedition.

Southeast were populated by measuring de Soto's movements. He and his men traveled between twelve and twenty miles a day, the distance between Indian maize plots, which were then plundered for food, along with stores of dried corn and beans.

Hernando de Soto came equipped for conquest. He brought with him six hundred young soldiers, a few women and priests, horses, mules, attack dogs, and a walking food supply of hundreds of pigs. He took whatever food, treasure, and people he wanted as he proceeded on his journey. Some Indian communities fought the Spanish fiercely, while others attempted to placate the invaders. At Mavila, the Spanish were welcomed inside the town's palisades by Tascaluzan Indians and entertained by twenty or so dancing women. But when a Spanish nobleman slashed off the arm of an Indian male who was resisting capture, five thousand Indians attacked. Although the Spanish escaped and the Tascaluzans closed the gates behind them, when de Soto saw them opening and displaying the trunks of treasure he had left behind, he decided to attack. The Spanish set fire to the town and engaged in hand-to-hand combat with those Indians who came outside. The day's battle left about 3,000 Indians and 20 Spanish dead. The 250 Spanish who were wounded used the fat of their Indian victims as an ointment to treat their wounds. When de Soto's forces finally left the destroyed village nearly a month later, they took with them the surviving dancing women "and divided them among the most seriously wounded, in order that they might serve them."

In this way de Soto made his way through the Southeast, plundering and battling, his forces slowly diminishing. In May of 1542, de Soto himself took sick and died. It was almost a year and a half, however, before the remnants of the expedition, three hundred men and one female servant, made their way down the Mississippi back to Mexico. As the small Spanish fleet neared the mouth of the Mississippi, they saw an Indian standing in his canoe and shouting at them in a language they could not understand. One of their Indian slaves translated for them: "If we possessed such large canoes as yours. . . . we would follow you to your land and conquer it, for we too are men like yourselves."

The Spanish had not found the great sought-after treasure, and because the land did not seem suitable for the large-scale agriculture of the *encomienda*, Spain never colonized most of the territory that de Soto had explored. Instead, military outposts, such as the one at St. Augustine, were established to protect the more valuable Spanish territories to the south. In order not to attract rivals to the northern reaches of its empire, Spain withheld from the rest of the world much of the geographical information it had secured by such expeditions. In the process Spain weakened its claim to the region, which depended upon right of prior exploration.

The impact of the expedition upon the Mississippian Indians is harder to reckon precisely. The Mississippian towns had begun to decline in the middle of the fifteenth century, even before the arrival of Europeans. The diseases they carried, however, certainly hastened the process. Perhaps as significant, the Spanish seriously disrupted the Mississippian political economy. Hernando de Soto's custom of capturing chieftains effectively undermined their leadership, and the losses incurred in battles made it impossible for the ruling elite to command lower-status tribe members to produce the food surplus and build the huge mounds that sustained the elite social order. Although other tribes such as the Creek and Choctaw filled the geographic void left by the collapse of the Mississippians, after the appearance of the Spanish no Indian civilizations would be able to match the power and sophistication of the Mississippians.

Coronado and the Pueblo Indians

At the same time that de Soto was attempting to conquer the Southeast, another group of Spaniards was setting out for the Southwest. They had heard tales of a city of Cíbola, supposedly larger than Tenochtitlan, and whose temples were decorated with gems. In May 1539, a party led by the Moorish slave Estevanico, one of the four survivors of the Narváez expedition, reached the city, which was actually the pueblo of Zuni in western New Mexico, near the Arizona border. In what was now a familiar pattern, the inhabitants recognized him as hostile and killed him. The survivors of the party did not contradict the popular belief that Cíbola was filled with treasure, however. As a result, just a little over a year later, another aspiring *conquistador*, Francisco Vázquez de Coronado, arrived at Zuni, with 300 Spanish, 1,000 Indian allies from Mexico, and 1,500 horses and pack animals. They took the Pueblo by force, and over

web connection

America and the Horse

www.prenhall.com/boydston/horse

One of the most enduring images of the American Indian is of a mounted warrior masterfully commanding his steed in battle. However, the horse is a recent import to America. In 1539, thousands of horses were brought to North America from Europe by Spanish *conquistadores* de Soto and Coronado. De Soto spent four years exploring the southeastern area of today's United States, while Coronado spent years in the Southwest. How did the addition of the horse to the ecosystem change the ways that American Indians lived?

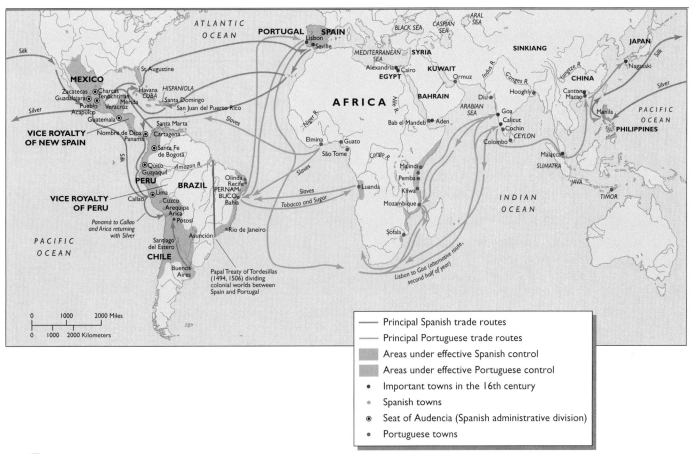

Map 1-6   A New Global Economy.
By 1600, both Spain and Portugal had established empires that reached from one end of the globe to the other.

the next two years, portions of the expedition traveled as far west as the Grand Canyon and as far east as Wichita, Kansas, coming within 300 miles of de Soto's expedition. One unfortunate Indian woman escaped enslavement by Coronado only to fall captive to de Soto.

Unprepared for the cold winter of 1540–1541, Coronado's men and animals depleted the food supplies of the Indians in the region of the winter camp near Bernalillo.

Some Spaniards literally took the clothes off the backs of their Indian hosts; when one Spaniard raped an Indian woman, the Pueblos rebelled. By the time the uprising was put down, 100 Indians had been burned at the stake, and 13 or so villages had been destroyed. This was the first of a number of revolts among the Indians of the region; they continued intermittently until the Apache leader Geronimo surrendered to the United States Army in 1886.

Conclusion

Within a half century after Columbus' arrival in the New World, both the world he had come from and the one he had reached had been transformed, as both were drawn into a new, global political economy (see Map 1-6). Spain, the first of the major European states to achieve unity, dominated exploration, colonization, and exploitation of the New World during this period and the decades that followed. The wealth that Spain extracted from her New World colonies would stimulate rival nations to enter into overseas ventures as well. Eventually France, England, the

Netherlands, Sweden, and Russia also established New World colonies, but because Spain (along with Portugal, which claimed Brazil) had such a head start, certain patterns had already been established. Perhaps most obviously, rival nations, if they did not want to challenge Spain directly, would have to settle for the lands she had left unclaimed. Spain had demonstrated that great wealth could be obtained from the New World by expropriation, and, along with Portugal, would soon show that fortunes could be made by plantation agriculture, as well.

CHRONOLOGY

c. 12,000 B.C.E.	Indian peoples arrive in North America
711 C.E.	Moors invade Iberian peninsula
1275–1292	Marco Polo travels in Asia
1347	Black Death (bubonic plague) arrives in Europe
1434	Portuguese arrive at West Coast of Africa
1488	Bartolomeo Dias rounds Cape Horn
1492	Spanish complete the *reconquista*, evicting Moors from Spain Jews expelled from Spain Columbus' first voyage to America
1493	Columbus' second voyage
1494	Treaty of Tordesillas divides New World between Spain and Portugal
1496	Spanish complete conquest of Canary Islands
1498	Vasco da Gama reaches India Columbus' third voyage to America, reaches South American coast
1500	Portuguese arrive in Brazil
1504	Columbus' fourth voyage to America ends
1508	Spanish conquer Puerto Rico
1513	Spanish *Requerimiento* promises freedom to all Indians who accept Spanish authority Spanish conquer Cuba Ponce de Léon reaches Florida The Laws of Burgos attempt to regulate working conditions of Indians
1518	Spanish introduce smallpox to New World
1521	Ponce de León returns to Florida Cortés lands on Yucatán coast
1519–1522	Ferdinand Magellan's crew sails around the world
1521	Tenochtitlan falls to the Spanish
1526	Ayllón explores South Carolina coast and establishes fort in Georgia
1528	De Narváez explores Florida
1539	Estevanico arrives at Zuni
1539–1543	De Soto and his party explore Southeast, arriving at Mississippi, devastating the Indians and their land
1540–1542	Coronado explores Southwest
1542	The New Laws ban further enslavement of Indians
1550	Las Casas and Sepúlveda debate the morality of slavery before the Council of the Indies

In the shadow of this dream of great and unprecedented wealth, a new global economy was established, linking the Old and the New Worlds. The gold and silver extracted from the Spanish empire sustained that nation's rise to power, and the plantation crops of the New World would make many Europeans wealthy. Once the Aztec and Inca civilizations were stripped of their wealth, however, all subsequent fortunes would depend upon human labor, to mine the precious metals and raise the crops. From the beginning, the Spanish enslaved native Indians to work the mines and work on farms and plantations. As the native populations were depleted and as the morality of enslaving native populations was questioned, the Spanish turned to African slaves. New World wealth always depended upon a ready supply of cheap labor, and those who would become wealthy had little concern about enslaving others and working them literally to death.

Review Questions

1. What were the forces that led Europeans to explore the New World?

2. Describe the development of Indian civilizations in North America from Archaic times until 1500. What were the major similarities among European, Native American, and African civilizations? The major differences?

3. What did the Spanish expect to find in the New World? How did their experiences alter their expectations?

4. What was the impact of European conquest on the population and environment of the New World?

Further Readings

Inga Clendinnen, *Aztecs* (1991). A remarkable description of the Aztec world, written from the Aztec point of view.

Alfred Crosby, Jr., *The Columbian Exchange: Biological and Cultural Consequences of 1492* (1972). An eye-opening introduction to environmental and biological history.

J.H. Elliot, *Imperial Spain, 1469–1716* (1963). The definitive history of Spain in this period.

Stuart J. Fiedel, *Prehistory of the Americas,* 2nd ed. (1992). A comprehensive and authoritative survey of the development of Native American civilizations in the Americas.

William D. Phillips, Jr., and Carla Rahn Phillips, *The Worlds of Christopher Columbus, 1400–1680* (1992). A short, readable introduction to Christopher Columbus and his world.

John Thornton, *Africa and Africans in the Making of the Atlantic World, 1400–1680* (1998). A provocative interpretation that places West Africa within an Atlantic context and emphasizes its active participation in the Atlantic world.

David Weber, *The Spanish Frontier in North America* (1992). Both a comprehensive survey of the history of Spanish North America and an interpretation, which shifts the focus of colonial history to the Spanish frontier.

History on the Internet

"Spanish Exploration and Conquest of Native America"
http://www.floridahistory.com
Containing text and analysis of conquest records, maps, and illustrations, this site explores the movements and experiences of the Spanish *conquistadors.* It also offers an in-depth look at the impact Spanish exploration had on the Native-American population.

"Hippocrates on the Web: Plagues and Peoples: The Columbian Exchange"
http://www.umanitoba.ca/faculties/medicine/history/ histories/plagues.html
Read the words of sixteenth- and seventeenth-century Europeans and Native Americans describing the devastating impact of disease.

2

COLONIAL OUTPOSTS

1550-1650

OUTLINE

Don Luís de Velasco Finds His Way Home

Pursuing Wealth and Glory Along the North American Shore
European Objectives
The Huge Geographical Barrier

Spanish Outposts

New France: An Outpost in the Global Political Economy
The Indian Background to French Settlement
Champlain Encounters the Hurons
Creating a Middle Ground in New France
An Outpost in a Global Political Economy

New Netherland: The Empire of a Trading Nation
Colonization by a Private Company
Slavery and Freedom in the Dutch Political Economy
The Dutch-Indian Trading Partnership
The Beaver Wars

England Attempts an Empire
The Origins of English Nationalism
Raiding Other Empires
Rehearsal in Ireland
The Roanoke Venture
The Abandoned Colony

Conclusion

Don Luís de Velasco Finds His Way Home

The Spanish gave him the name of Don Luís de Velasco. His own people, the Powhatan Indians of the Virginia coast, knew him as Paquiquineo. There is no record of what he looked like, although like most of his tribe he was probably tall and muscular, with skin a shade of copper. His hair was black, shaved on the right side of his head so that it would not get tangled in the strings of his bow, and tied into a long knot on the left. The son of a chieftain, he was a young man, perhaps still a teenager, when the Spanish picked him up in 1561 somewhere south of his home. The Europeans often abducted young Indians and took them back to their own nations where they were taught Spanish or English or French so that they could serve as translators and guides on subsequent expeditions. Sometimes the process worked the other way around, and Europeans who were members of trading or exploring expeditions were accidentally left behind. In order to survive, they learned the Native Americans' language and customs. If and when they were ever reunited with their countrymen, they were valuable as interpreters. In the early years of colonization, those men and women who had learned the ways of another culture gained influence far out of proportion to their actual numbers.

Don Luís did not see his own people again for ten years. First the Spanish took him to Mexico, where he must have seen the new city that the Spanish were building out of the ruins of the old Aztec civilization. What Don Luís saw most likely must have seemed more foreign to him than it had even to Cortés and his men, who had been in the cities of Europe. In Mexico, Dominican friars baptized and educated the young man. Later, Jesuit priests in Havana pronounced Don Luís "well educated," quite a compliment coming from a religious order known for its intellectual achievements.

The young convert was taken to Spain, where he was received royally by King Felipe II, and then back across the Atlantic to Havana, where he persuaded the priests to let him establish a Christian mission among his own people on the North American mainland. In 1566 Don Luís set sail on a Spanish ship with two priests and thirty-seven soldiers, but he was unable to find the Chesapeake. Four years later, when there were only priests and no soldiers on the voyage, Don Luís had no trouble locating his homeland.

Less than a week after the Jesuits and their Indian convert had settled in Virginia, Don Luís went back to his people. Soon he had returned to the customs of the Powhatans. He scandalized the Jesuits by taking several wives, which was one of the privileges of Indian men of high social standing. The Jesuits had expected Don Luís to act as an intermediary with his people, securing them supplies and favorable treatment. They had misjudged both him and their situation. Soon they had exhausted their own supply of food and had to go begging to Don Luís. But Don Luís was being pressured by his own people to prove his loyalty. They were suspicious of someone who had been away so long and returned wearing strange clothing and a peculiar haircut and bringing with him these arrogant foreigners who dared demand food during a drought.

Don Luís had to make a choice, and he chose his own people. Powhatans killed eight of the nine missionaries. According to Indian custom, one of the victims, a young Spaniard named Alonso, was spared, although Don Luís argued for his death also. Knowing that the Spanish would some day return, he wanted no witnesses. As Don Luís predicted, the Spanish, led by the governor of Cuba himself, came back a year and a half later. They retrieved Alonso, ordered Don Luís to appear for an inquest, and began trying and executing other Indians when he failed to appear. At these proceedings, Alonso acted as an interpreter. Don Luís never came back to the Spanish. They eventually left, never to attempt another settlement that far north on the North American coast.

In 1607 the English planted their first permanent colony on the mainland at Jamestown, among Don Luís' people. Don Luís, who was very young when he had been abducted by the Spanish, might well have been alive to greet these new foreigners. Throughout the seventeenth century, the English heard rumors about a Powhatan Indian who had spent time in the Spanish colonies.

Powhatan Indian fishermen.

Whether or not Don Luís, who had managed to hold off the Spanish, lived to see the English take their place, it is clear that the memory of the Europeans lived on among the Powhatans. Even before the English arrived on the North American mainland, the local Indians had encountered Europeans. Before they established permanent settlements, the English, French, and Spanish all explored along the North American coastline. In the process, Indians and Europeans such as Don Luís and Alonso met each other and learned each other's languages and customs. During this period of early American history, no sharp geographic or cultural line separated the Indians and Europeans. In fact, Indians and Europeans moved back and forth into each other's territories. Indians such as Don Luís lived among the Europeans, and Europeans such as Alonso spent time with the Indians. As a result, even before permanent colonies were established, each group knew the other moderately well. Although the customs and practices of the other group often seemed odd and even ungodly, they were never fully foreign. Like languages, customs and practices could be learned well enough for one to navigate through a strange land.

After the middle of the sixteenth century, Spain, France, the Netherlands, and England all established outposts in the United States. These early colonies were small and precarious, vulnerable to foreign or Indian attack. In these early years, success depended more upon the ability to come to an accommodation with the Indians than upon any other factor. When the number of Europeans settling north of the Rio Grande was small, Indian tribes saw the Europeans as potential allies, as well as enemies. Relations between Indians and Europeans were amazingly fluid. Those individuals such as Don Luís and Alonso, world travelers who had lived in other cultures and learned their ways, left their mark upon their world. Rarely did they abandon their own cultures. Instead, they became cultural brokers, working out the accommodations from which an entirely new world was born. These accommodations were critical if Europeans and Indians were to achieve their larger political economic objectives.∎

KEY TOPICS

- European objectives in exploring the North American coast

- French, Dutch, and English encounters with Indians

- Colonial settlements as outposts in a global economy

- The creation of a "middle ground" between French traders and Huron Indians in Canada

- The connection among trade, religious toleration, and slavery in New Netherland

- England's approach to colonization

- Why England failed to establish a permanent colony at Roanoke

Pursuing Wealth and Glory Along the North American Shore

The forces that propelled the Spanish across the Atlantic soon sent other European nations to the Americas in search of wealth and national prestige. As the English explorer Sir Walter Raleigh explained the principles of political economy, "Whosoever commands the sea commands the trade; whosoever commands the trade of the world commands the riches of the world, and consequently the world itself." Once the news of Columbus' voyage spread through Europe, other adventurous and ambitious sailors tried to enlist different nations in new voyages of exploration. In the process, they awakened the imaginations of national rulers, whose notions of their own nations' interests began to include overseas ventures. Most of the North American colonies established by European nations in the first half of the seventeenth century were outposts in the global economy. There were significant differences among these colonies, reflecting the different political economies of their parent nations, but all had certain factors in common: First, they were intended to bring in the greatest amount of revenue at the lowest cost. Second, success depended upon harmonious relations with—or elimination of—local Indians. Third, colonial societies slowly developed their own distinctive patterns, depending upon which route they followed to prosperity.

European Objectives

At first Europeans believed that Columbus had reached Asia by an Atlantic route. By the time they understood that he had discovered a land previously unknown to them, the Spanish were well on their way to conquering native peoples and stripping them of their wealth. The success of the Spanish inspired other European nations to mount their own ventures in the hope of discovering new sources of gold and silver in the regions Spain had not yet claimed. They also continued to seek a path through the Americas to the rich trading nations of Asia. Colonization of the New World was not a significant goal for almost a century, and even then colonies were designed to provide a quick return on investment, not to transplant Europeans onto foreign soil.

For many years the nations of northern Europe were unwilling to make the investment necessary for a permanent settlement. A foreign colony was a phenomenally costly proposition. It involved procuring a ship, provisioning it with a crew and supplies, providing a settlement with food and equipment—and reoutfitting more ships to resupply it until it could turn a profit. Spain had been lucky: Isabel and Fernando had been willing to take a considerable risk, which paid off relatively soon. By and large, the northern European nations could not afford such expeditions, and they were not willing to finance them until they were relatively certain of a good return on their investments. Except for the most adventurous souls, exploration for the sake of exploration had very little appeal.

Tales of wealth and adventure in New Spain spread throughout Europe, however. Would-be explorers and *conquistadores* who hoped to win fortune and fame began to sell their services to the highest bidder. John Cabot, who sailed for England, was, like Columbus, actually born in Genoa, Italy. Before coming to England, he had spent time in Muslim Arabia, Spain, and Portugal, apparently looking for sponsors for a voyage to Asia. He found them in the English port city of Bristol, from whence he sailed in 1497. He landed somewhere in North America, possibly at Newfoundland, and claimed the territory for England.

Although England was slow to follow up this claim to American territory, and Cabot himself drowned at sea on his next attempt at an ocean crossing, soon both England and France were sending fishing expeditions to the waters off Newfoundland (see Map 2-1). The population of northwestern Europe exploded in the sixteenth and seventeenth centuries, creating a demand for North American fish. Fishing expeditions to the Newfoundland coast came in the spring and left before winter and were relatively inexpensive to sustain. As already mentioned, neither England nor France was yet willing to make a substantial investment in North America.

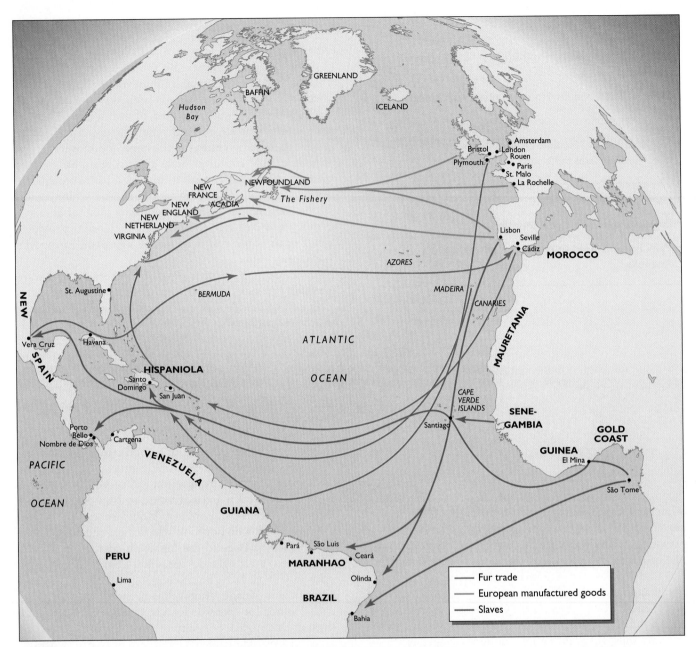

Map 2-1   North Atlantic Trade Routes at the End of the Sixteenth Century.
Hundreds of entrepreneurs from England, France, and Portugal sent ships to fish off the coast of Newfoundland to feed the growing population of Europe. The fur trade grew out of the Newfoundland fishing enterprise when fishermen who built winter shelters on the shore began trading with local Algonquian Indians (blue lines). At the same time, European cities sent foods, cloth, and manufactured goods to New Spain, in return for gold and silver (green lines). After 1580, the Portuguese began transporting slaves from Africa to sell in Brazil and New Spain (orange lines).

Source: D.W. Meinig, The Shaping of America (New Haven, Yale University Press, 1986), vol. 1, p. 56.

The French colony of New France, planted in the St. Lawrence River region of Canada, grew out of the French fishing venture off Newfoundland. Early French explorers discovered neither glimmering treasure nor a Northwest Passage to Asia. French fishermen, however, found that the Indians along the Canadian shore were willing to trade magnificent beaver pelts at prices so low that a man could make a fortune in a few months' time.

The Huge Geographical Barrier

In 1522 Ferdinand Magellan's expedition completed the first round-the-world voyage for Spain, proving finally that one could get to the East by heading west. Other nations then became interested in finding a way through, rather than around, the North American continent. Each of the exploring ventures they financed was also an en-

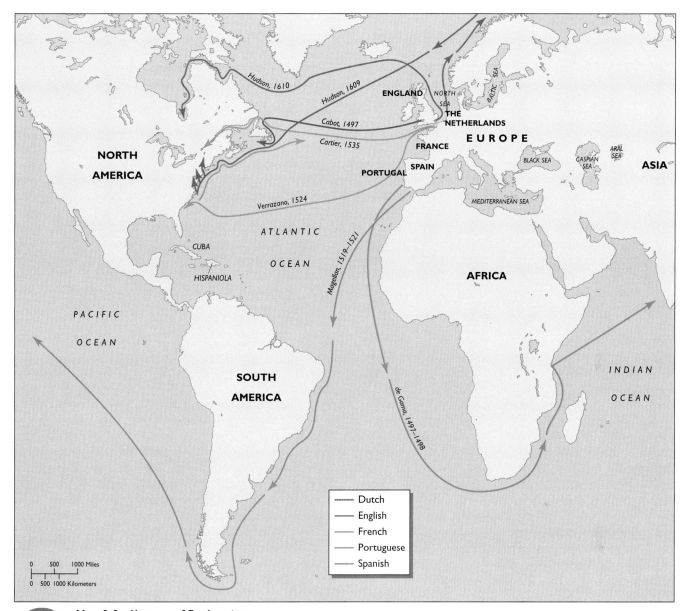

Map 2-2   *Voyages of Exploration.*
In a little over a century after Columbus' first voyage, European explorers had circled the world and charted most of the North American coastline.

counter between European and Indian peoples. Yet these experiences mattered little to the rulers of Europe, each of whom was struggling to advance his or her own nation's political and economic interests. Two years after Magellan's voyage, another Italian, Giovanni da Verrazano, sailed for France. He explored along the North American coast from South Carolina to Maine, and he and his crew were the first Europeans to see the New York harbor. As far as the rulers of Europe were concerned, however, all that Verrazano had discovered was that North America was, as one historian has put it, a geographical nuisance, a huge barrier between Europe and the rich trade lands of Asia (see Map 2-2).

That "huge barrier" of the North American continent was populated by Indians, some wary and some friendly. Unfamiliar with Indian customs, Europeans often could not distinguish hospitality from malice. When Algonquian Indians attempted to dry out one of Verrazano's sailors, who had almost drowned, by setting him near a campfire, the Europeans misunderstood this act of charity. According to Verrazano, they "were filled with terror, as always when something new occurs, and thought the people wanted to roast him for food." In the early years of exploration, the survival of a venture often depended upon local Indians, yet because the French were looking either for treasure or a Northwest Passage, they tended to focus on cultural differences rather than similarities. Europeans noticed similarities only when political economic objectives such as trade or alliance were in the forefront.

Between 1534 and 1542, King Francis I of France financed Jacques Cartier to make three expeditions to seek a route through North America and to look out for any riches he might find along the way. All three came to naught. On the first trip, the French only explored the coastline, but on their second, they made their way up the St. Lawrence River as far as the town of Hochelaga (near present-day Montreal), where their way was blocked by rapids. The Iroquois who lived there spoke of a wealthy land to the west whose inhabitants wore woolen clothes just like the French. Although the Iroquois may well have been trying to deceive the French so that they would race on in search of imaginary riches, it is possible that the shiny metal they spoke of was the copper that the Hurons to the west mined and traded. Likewise, the "woolen" clothing may have been the tailored fur outfits of the Eskimos (Inuit) who lived to the north and were members of the extensive Huron trade network. The winter was brutal; from November to April, the snow remained four feet deep, and the river was frozen solid. Even with food and attentive nursing from the Indians, at the end of the winter almost a quarter of the party was dead and less than a tenth of the people were in good health. Strangers in a strange land, the French found that their very survival depended upon the willingness of the native peoples to sustain them.

The subsequent expeditions failed as badly. The French quarreled with their Indian hosts, and they fought among themselves. Moreover, the region that they were exploring was so remote that no one could yet fathom why they were even bothering. The emperor of Spain, who feared that the French would intrude upon his nation's claims, was unimpressed by the French venture up the St. Lawrence: "It is of no value, and if the French take it, necessity will compel them to abandon it." Although all these early attempts at colonization failed, the French were making a point. European claims to the Americas would rest not upon decrees by the Pope, such as the one that divided the Western Hemisphere between Spain and Portugal, or abstract claims, but upon exploration, conquest of the natives, and colonization. Needless to say, this principle of European colonialism was established without the consent of the Indians who inhabited the land that was being claimed by European nations.

Spanish Outposts

Throughout the sixteenth century (and, indeed, as long as European nations claimed portions of North America), the European nations jockeyed for power on the continent, each attempting to secure the greatest advantage at the least cost. Because most of these nations were at war with each other for much of this period, exploring and colonizing North America was often a low priority. But at times when the fighting in Europe abated, the Europeans looked again across the Atlantic in the hope of gaining some advantage over a rival nation or finding a new source of wealth.

Soon the French and English, who were unable to find gold or jewels when they explored along the coastline, discovered an easier route to wealth—stealing from the Spanish. Every season, Spanish ships loaded the treasure that they had seized in Mexico and South America and made their way through the Caribbean, out into the Atlantic south of Florida, and up along the coast until they caught the trade winds to take them east across the Atlantic. The route was as unvarying as that cut by a superhighway. By the middle of the sixteenth century, French ships were lying in wait off the coast of Florida or the Carolinas. Because it was cheaper than exploration, preying upon Spanish ships became a national policy.

In order to put a stop to these costly acts of piracy, King Felipe II decided to establish a series of forts along the western and eastern shores of Florida. These outposts could also serve as rescue stations for the many Spaniards who were shipwrecked in the treacherous seas off the Florida coast. So many of the ships carrying American treasure were lost that the Ais and Calusa Indians of Florida grew rich from salvaging them. Almost at the very moment that King Felipe II was planning for his forts, a group of Huguenots (French Protestants) had established a colony in Florida called Fort Caroline, near present-day Georgia. For the new Spanish commander, Pedro Menéndez de Avilés, the first order of business was to destroy the French settlement, which was doubly threatening to the Spanish for being both French and Protestant. At dawn on a rainy September morning in 1565, 500 Spanish soldiers surprised the French at Fort Caroline, many of whom were still in their nightclothes. Although the French surrendered and begged for mercy, Menéndez ordered their slaughter. In this way, the religious and nationalist conflicts of Europe were transplanted to North America (see Map 2-3).

Menéndez indeed established his string of forts. One of them, St. Augustine, settled in 1565, is the oldest continuously inhabited city of European origin on the mainland of the United States. At the time, Santa Elena, just over the border in present-day South Carolina, was the more important settlement, but it, and all the other forts except St. Augustine, were eventually abandoned. As was true of many ambitious European explorers and conquerors, Menéndez' aspirations exceeded those of his nation. Menéndez even attempted to establish a settlement on Chesapeake Bay. That plan failed because Menéndez had staked its success on an Indian convert, one Don Luís de Velasco, who had his own ideas. In fact, most of Menéndez' plans for Spanish settlements were undermined by local Indians whom the Spanish alienated. Menéndez himself

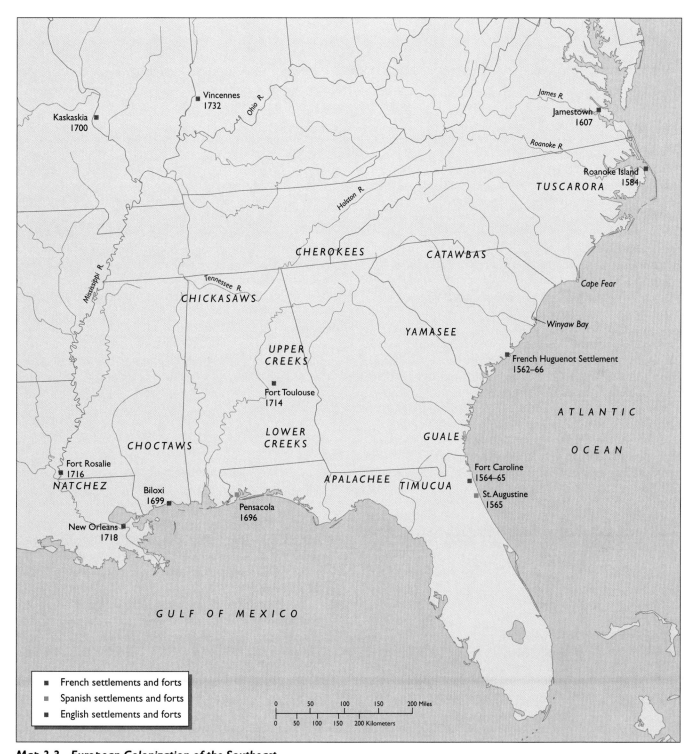

Map 2-3   *European Colonization of the Southeast.*
Beginning in the second half of the sixteenth century, the French, Spanish, and English established settlements in the Southeast.
Source: Charles Hudson, The Southeastern Indians (Knoxville: University of Tennessee Press, 1976), pp. 430–431.

seemed to realize that he needed the local inhabitants' good will. Although he was already married, he agreed to take as his wife the middle-aged and "not at all beautiful" sister of a local Calusa chieftain. In the short run, however, the Indians, aided by the English, prevailed. After attacks by the Orista Indians in 1576 and England's Francis Drake a decade later, the Spanish finally abandoned all of their Florida forts except St. Augustine. Spanish dreams of an empire in this region of North America had been reduced to a small garrison on the Atlantic coast.

New France: An Outpost in the Global Political Economy

The Spanish had given up hopes of an empire along the Atlantic coast of North America, but they had succeeded in scaring off the French. After the massacre at Fort Caroline, the French focused their interest on the region along the St. Lawrence that Cartier had explored and later on several of the islands in the Caribbean. Although dreams of a Northwest Passage through the American continent to Asia persisted until well into the nineteenth century, by the beginning of the seventeenth century the French had discovered a new way to make a profit in North America. French fishing crews, working off the coast of Newfoundland, struck up a trade for beaver pelts with the coastal Abenaki Indians. These pelts found a ready market in Europe, where they were turned into felt hats. A trade that began almost as an accident soon became the basis for the French empire in Canada, as the French traded metal tools and implements to the Abenakis, Hurons, and other local tribes for pelts. Maintaining the trade required friendly relations with the Indians and also a great deal of diplomacy. The French were drawing the Indians into a global economy, a process that dramatically changed not only the political economy of the Indians, but the European political economy as well.

The Indian Background to French Settlement

The French intruded upon a region where warfare among Indian tribes had been common. It was a widespread and prevalent practice, but limited in its scope. Eastern Woodlands clans and tribes of both the Algonquian and Iroquois culture groups were almost always at war, but the total casualties, unlike those in the European wars raging at the same time, were generally quite light. These fights were blood feuds called "mourning wars." When a member of a clan was lost in battle, his tribesmen, often aided and encouraged by his tribeswomen, sought revenge upon the enemy clan, either killing a warrior in return or seizing one who was then adopted into the tribe to replace the dead clan member. The mourning war sought to fill the space in tribal society that was caused by the loss, either actual or emotional, of a member. If the clan's grief was particularly great, many captives might be necessary to repair the emotional loss. Such warfare was surrounded by numerous rituals, which mourned the loss of the clan member, prepared warriors for battle, and integrated captives into their new clan. It also focused violence outward. The cruelty that Indians practiced upon their enemies shocked Europeans, whose own societies were quite brutal. Unlike in European society, violence and even crime within the clan were almost unknown.

By the fifteenth century, the mourning war was taking too great a toll among the Iroquois who lived in northern New York. Sometime after 1400 (and perhaps as late as 1600), the five tribes that lived south of the St. Lawrence and east of Lake Ontario, primarily in what is now upper New York State, created an alliance called the Five Nations or Great League of Peace (see Map 2-4). The establishment of this alliance was memorialized in the Iroquois Deganawidah Epic, which was retold from generation to generation. "Everywhere there was peril and everywhere mourning. Feuds with outer nations, feuds with brother nations, feuds of sister towns and feuds of families and clans made every warrior a stealthy man who liked to kill." According to tradition, Deganawidah the Peacemaker, a supernatural being, trained the Iroquois warrior Hiawatha in the gospel of peace, which together they brought to the Iroquois. The league strengthened the Iroquois when they encountered their traditional enemies such as the Algonquians and Hurons, a powerful Iroquoian tribe that was not a member of the league, and their new adversary, the French.

Champlain Encounters the Hurons

After Cartier's last voyage in 1541, the French waited more than half a century before again attempting to plant a settlement in Canada. Between 1562 and 1598, the French were preoccupied with a brutal civil war. In 1594, Henry of Navarre, a Huguenot, emerged the victor, converted to Catholicism, and in 1598 issued the Edict of Nantes, which granted limited religious toleration to the Huguenots. The bloodshed was over, and France could now look outward to North America.

The French had continued to fish off Newfoundland, and entrepreneurs began sending ships to the mainland to trade for beaver pelts. The profits were so high that a trader could grow rich in a single season. The French Crown now realized that commerce with the Indians could increase its power and wealth. Several early ventures to establish a permanent settlement failed, but in 1608, Samuel de Champlain and a small band retraced Cartier's route up the St. Lawrence and established a post at Quebec. Champlain, who made several voyages to New France over the next decades, finally established the first French foothold in Canada, created a trading network along the St. Lawrence River, and learned how to live among people with a culture different from his own (see Map 2-5).

Like many of the early European explorers of the Americas, Samuel de Champlain was a world traveler. He had spent most of his early life in the military. By the time he reached New France at the age of 38, he had fought for

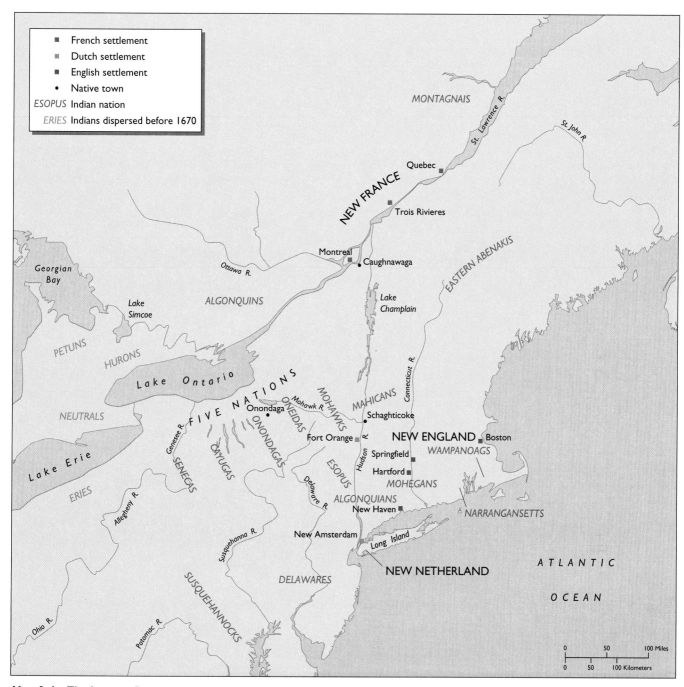

Map 2-4   The Iroquois Region in the Middle of the Seventeenth Century.
By the middle of the seventeenth century, the French, Dutch, and English had all established trading posts on the fringe of the Iroquois homeland. In the Beaver Wars (c.1648–1660), discussed later in the chapter, the Iroquois lashed out at their neighbors, dispersing several Huron tribes.
Source: Matthew Dennis, Cultivating a Landscape of Peace *(New York: Cornell University Press, 1993), p. 16.*

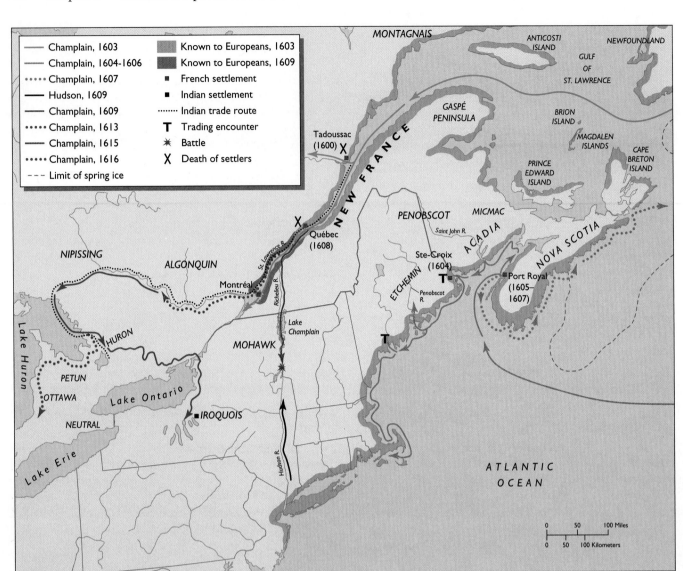

Map 2-5   French Exploration and Settlement, 1603–1616
Between 1603 and 1616, Samuel de Champlain and other French explorers made numerous trips up the St. Lawrence River and along the New England coast as far south as Cape Cod. They established several settlements, and they traded with local Indians and fought with them as well.

France on the continent of Europe and had signed on with the Spanish to help transport the annual treasure from the Americas to Spain. In this way he saw much of Spanish America, even crossing the Isthmus of Panama, which he suggested needed a canal.

The French government provided little support for Champlain's expedition to New France beyond a guarantee of a temporary monopoly on trade with the Indians. Without significant support from France, Champlain's party was dependent upon their Montagnais Indian (an Algonquian tribe) hosts. The price they had to pay in order to survive in New France was adapting to Indian custom. They had to assist their Indian benefactors in wars against their enemy, adjust to their food, and join their families.

Some of these accommodations were easier to make than others. Killing the enemy in warfare was relatively easy for an experienced soldier such as Champlain. Indian forms of torture, however, seemed barbaric, not because Europeans did not engage in torture, but because Europeans did not practice it against other soldiers, one's supposed equals. When his allies invited him to take part in the torture of a captive Mohawk, Champlain "pointed out to them that we did not commit such cruelties, but that we killed people outright, and that if they wished me to shoot him with the arquebus [a form of musket], I should be glad to do so." Champlain must have been remarkably persistent, for finally he was allowed to fire his gun. In Indian warfare, the purpose of torture was not death, but inflicting pain. The bravery that a man displayed as he was being slowly burned at the stake earned both him and his tribe the respect of his adversaries.

Over the next several years, Champlain succeeded in establishing a fur trade in the St. Lawrence region. He and other Frenchmen established a trade network that linked the French and the Indians in a transformed global political economy. Peasants were transplanted to New France in 1614 to raise food for the traders; Catholic priests were sent to convert the Native Americans. The missionaries, the first of whom had arrived in 1615, were more successful than the peasants. The persistence of the Catholic missionaries, their willingness to accommodate to a strange environment, and their ability to translate their religion into terms that were meaningful to Native Americans eventually gained them numerous converts.

After Champlain's original monopoly expired, his group had to compete with other bands of Frenchmen who were working the fur trade. The French government was too busy with conflicts at home and abroad to support any of these outposts. Nor could French merchants be persuaded to invest in these fledgling enterprises. In order to maintain a competitive edge, each summer Champlain pushed further up the St. Lawrence from his base at Quebec in order to intercept the northern and western Indian tribes who were bringing pelts to the east. Each winter he also sent some of his men to live among the western Hurons and Algonquians, to learn their languages and customs and to strengthen the trading partnerships that had been established. These Indians already engaged in an extensive trade in corn, fish, nets, wampum, and other items. As French traders and Huron and Algonquian hunters created a trade network, however, each group became dependent upon the other. They had to accommodate to each other's ways in order to obtain the goods that they craved.

Creating a Middle Ground in New France

Indians proved able to adapt French culture to their own purposes, and the French traders who lived among the Native Americans came to accommodate to Indian practices as well. Together Indians and French traders on the frontier created a **middle ground** that was neither fully European nor fully Indian, but rather a new world created out of two different traditions. The middle ground came into being every time Europeans and Indians met, needed each other, and could not (or would not) achieve what they wanted through the use of force.

The French drew Native Americans into a vast global trade network. The Indi-

ans began to hunt more beaver than they needed for their own purposes, eventually depleting the beaver population. Some historians have suggested that the introduction of European goods and commercial values into Native-American cultures destroyed them from within by making them dependent on those goods and inducing them to abandon their own crafts. Others have pointed out that the trade had different meanings for the French and for the Indians. For the French, trade was important for its cash value, but for the Indians, trade goods were important both for the uses to which they could be put and for their symbolic value in religious ceremonies. To be sure, iron tips for their arrows and metal knives made the Indians who possessed them more effective warriors. Yet Indians also integrated European goods into their traditional practices, breaking up brass pots, for example, into small pieces that could be made into jewelry. Iron tools enabled Indian craftspeople to create more detail in their decorative arts. Many of the new French trade goods found their way into Indian graves, to accompany the dead on their journey to the world beyond.

Just as the Indians were pulled into an international trade network centered in Europe, the French in North America were drawn into both the Indians' style of life and the Indians' political and economic concerns. Traders and priests learned to sleep on the cold ground without complaint and to eat Indian foods such as sagamité, a sort of cornmeal mush in which a small bird or animal was often boiled whole, with only the fur or feathers seared off. Many French traders came to Canada without their wives, and they found it convenient, both personally and professionally, to find Indian wives. Indians such as the

This drawing depicts the torture of a war captive. The French thought that Indian forms of warfare, including torture, were barbaric, not because Europeans did not practice torture, but because they did not torture other soldiers.

WHERE THEY LIVED, WHERE THEY WORKED

Huronia

In the middle of the sixteenth century, over 20,000 Huron Indians lived in Huronia, a huge region bounded by Georgian Bay and Lakes Huron, Erie, Ontario, and Simcoe. Most Hurons inhabited triple-palisaded villages of 2,000 or so people. The palisades were sometimes as tall as twenty feet high, in order to protect the Hurons from their Iroquois enemy.

The Hurons, like most of the northern Woodlands tribes, lived in longhouses constructed out of bent tree branches covered with bark. These houses, sometimes as large as 25 by 100 feet, housed several families, all members of the same clan. Inside the longhouse, two sets of racks extended along each side, upon which members of the clan slept at night: Children slept in the upper "bunks," and adults in the lower ones. Fires for cooking and warmth were built in the middle of the floor. Europeans found the thick smoke oppressive, but it drove the insects away. With each clan sharing a longhouse, there was no privacy; nor was there a concept of private property. In this way, living arrangements reflected the Hurons' political economy.

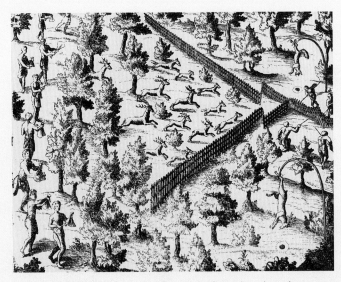

Huron deer hunt. This drawing, by Samuel de Champlain, shows how Huron men funneled deer into enclosures, where they could be trapped and easily killed.

A drawing of a Huron village, 1657, showing women at work, pounding corn.

Hurons accepted **polygyny,** that is, taking more than one wife, so they were not troubled if the French men who moved in to trade with them had French wives at home. Moreover, the Hurons were accustomed to adopting members of different ethnic groups and the French did not seem to have any aversion to racial mixing. Both the Indians and the French believed that mixed marriages provided a strong foundation for trading and military alliances. In fact, later in the seventeenth century, French officials com-plained that not *enough* Huron women were taking French husbands: "Your daughters have married with all neighbouring nations but not with ours. . . . Not that we have need of your daughters. . . . But we would like to see only one people in all the land."

The French were drawn into their Huron and Algonquian allies' political economy as well. In order to keep the furs flowing east, they had to take part in war parties, usually against the Iroquois, and eventually to finance their al-

There were other structures in a Huron village: sweat houses, where one went in the hope of sweating out an illness; small huts in which meat and fish were dried; and elevated racks upon which the dead were placed prior to burial. The ground between the longhouses and other village structures was covered with garbage, including the carcasses of dead animals. The stench must have been familiar to Europeans who came from crowded cities, where offal and human waste were likewise tossed onto the streets. On the perimeter of each village were the fields where the women raised vegetables, primarily corn, squash, and beans.

The Hurons, like the other northern Woodlands tribes, were matrilineal and matrilocal. Shortly after puberty, Huron men and women entered into sexual relations, which either party might initiate. The relationship might lead to marriage, or either party might move on to another partner. When a couple married, the man moved in with his wife's clan, in her family's longhouse, but when the marriage dissolved, which was commonly the case, he would return to the longhouse of

A reconstructed Huron village at Midland, Ontario, Canada.

his mother and sisters. Thereupon, his wife's brothers assumed the role of male teachers of the children. Each longhouse was supervised by a clan matron, who saw to the domestic and economic needs of her group; she also chose two men to lead the clan. Because the men of the clan spent much of their time away from the village, hunting, trading, or engaging in warfare, most of the day-to-day responsibilities, including raising crops, making clothing, and rearing the children, were performed by the women of the clan.

Huron children, like other Indian children of the Northeast, were brought up to participate in the world of the mourning war. Their parents trained them for "autonomous responsibility," to be independent men and women who were loyal to their clan. Babies were indulged by their parents, breastfed by their mothers until the age of three or four, and allowed to "toilet train" themselves. These parents did not believe in punishing their children and instead attempted reason or teasing when their children's behavior got out of hand. One Frenchman observed, "There is nothing for which these peoples have a greater horror than restraint. The very children cannot endure it, and live as they please in the houses of their parents, without fear of reprimand or chastisement." Another observed, "The mothers love their children with an extreme passion." Brought up in such a way, Indian children prized their liberty and felt great loyalty to the group that had nurtured them.

Parents taught their children skills that they would need as adults. The girls stayed close to their mothers, performing the easier household tasks, while the boys formed gangs that played competitive games and learned to hunt and make war. Sometimes the boys' gang went off on its own, leaving the village for days at a time. In this way, the boys learned to be independent of their parents and loyal to their group.

lies' battles with their enemies and purchase their loyalty with annual payments. The Hurons and Algonquians considered these payments as "presents," gifts from Onontio, the name they gave to their French "father," the king. The French considered these presents the cost of diplomacy. As long as the French maintained a presence in this region of North America (until 1763, when they were defeated by the British in the French and Indian War), they attempted to manipulate their Indian allies for their own benefit, just

as those tribes tried to maneuver the French to serve their own needs. There were costs and benefits on both sides.

The arrival of the French in the sixteenth century stimulated competition among the regional tribes for the positions of middlemen or brokers between the French and the other Indian tribes who had furs to trade in return for European trade goods. The pace and nature of Indian warfare, which had always been fierce, now changed dramatically, for a new motive for fighting had been introduced, control of the lucrative fur trade. Although the French had inadvertently stimulated this conflict, they were called upon to mediate it. With a combination of honed diplomatic skill and liberal dispensing of presents, French officials were usually able to quell the infighting among their allies. Once the Dutch and English established colonies to the south and made alliances with the Iroquois, maintaining the loyalty of their Huron and Algonquian allies became the major objective of French diplomacy in North America in the seventeenth and eighteenth centuries. Because they were attentive to Indian customs and willing to accommodate them, the French were the best diplomats in North America, and their Indian allies were the most loyal.

An Outpost in a Global Political Economy

New France began as a tiny outpost in a global economy. By the end of the seventeenth century, it had increased in both size and importance. The French population in North America grew slowly (356 in 1640, 2,000 in 1650, 19,000 in 1714), and the primary focus of New France remained the fur trade. In the 1630s, missionaries began to arrive in significant numbers, making the conversion of Indians to Catholicism the second most important endeavor in the colony. At the same time, the Huron population decreased dramatically. A series of epidemics—smallpox in 1634, smallpox or measles the next year, influenza the year after that, and then smallpox again in 1639—cut the population in half, carrying off many of Huronia's leaders. Some of the survivors, especially those who engaged in trade, converted to Christianity, while others blamed the priests for the diseases. The result was internal conflict and political instability that left the Hurons vulnerable to their Indian enemies and increasingly dependent on their French allies. At the same time, the French depended upon their allies, the Hurons (and the Hurons' allies, the Algonquians) to keep bringing them furs. The Hurons, in fact, operated as middlemen, not trapping beaver themselves, but acquiring beaver pelts from other tribes further to the west.

At some point in the middle of the seventeenth century, the supply of beaver in the regions closest to European settlements began to diminish. Before the arrival of the French, the Indians had trapped only enough for their own use. The huge European demand for beaver, however, led Indians to overtrapping, killing more beaver than could be replaced by natural reproduction. As a result, Europeans (or to be more precise, the Indians who acted as middlemen) extended their trade routes farther and farther north and west, where the supply of beaver was more plentiful. This expansion involved increasing numbers of Indians in the global economy.

The European demand for warm beaver coats and stylish beaver hats was almost insatiable. In order to trade for the pelts from which they were made, the French increased domestic manufacturing of cloth, metal imple-

ments, guns, and other goods that were attractive to the Indians. This pattern, in which the mother country produced goods to be sold or traded in foreign colonies for raw materials, was not unique to France. It was replicated in England and Holland as well. None of these nations found the treasures in the Americas that Spain had located in (and taken out of) Mexico and Peru. Nor did they ever find a passage to Asia and its lucrative trade. Instead, they found new products, such as beaver pelts, for which there was a growing demand in Europe.

A new economic theory called **mercantilism** soon developed to explain and guide the growth of European nation-states and the New World colonies they created. Mercantilism's objective was to strengthen the nation-state by making the economy serve its interests. According to the theory of mercantilism, the world's wealth, measured in gold and silver, was fixed; that is, it could never be increased. As a result, each nation's chief economic objective must be to secure as much of the world's wealth as possible. One nation's gain was necessarily another's loss. Colonies played an important part in the theory of mercantilism. Their role was to serve as sources of raw materials and markets for manufactured goods for the mother country alone. Hence national competition for colonies and markets, such as that on the North American continent among the French, British, and Dutch, was not only about economics, but about politics and diplomacy as well. The strength and survival of the nation was thought to depend upon its ability to dominate international trade.

New Netherland: The Empire of a Trading Nation

In many ways, the Dutch venture into North America resembled that of France. It began with an intrepid explorer in quest of a Northwest Passage to Asia and a government that was unwilling to make a significant investment in a North American colony. If profits were to be made, they would have to come from the fur trade and commercial alliances with local Indians. But unlike the French and the Spanish, however, the Dutch government assigned the task of establishing a trading settlement almost entirely to a private company. And unlike New France and New Spain, because Holland was a Protestant nation, there were no activist Catholic priests in New Netherland to spread their religion and oppose the excesses of a commercial economy. Even more than the French and Spanish colonies, then, the Dutch colony of New Netherland was shaped by the forces of commerce.

Colonization by a Private Company

Much like England, the other major commercial power at the time, the Netherlands was beginning its rise to power as a great merchant nation. The nation had once been under Spanish rule, but it had secured its independence after a long and bloody war, which finally ended in 1648. By the time that the Netherlands had achieved its independence and emerged as a major commercial power, Spain, which had overextended its empire, was going into decline.

Much like England, the Netherlands was Protestant, committed to a market economy, and sustained by a thriving middle class. Indeed, Amsterdam was the center of the world's economy. The Netherlands had a distinctive political economy, with neither a powerful aristocracy nor an oppressed peasantry. Its government and economy were dominated by a group of prosperous merchants.

Holland was the home of the Renaissance humanist Erasmus, and his values of toleration and moderation permeated the society. Jews who had been expelled from Spain found a new home in the Netherlands alongside strict Calvinists (Protestants who believed in predestination). The spirit of toleration enabled the Dutch to put aside religious and political conflict and turn their attentions to trade. As the English essayist Daniel Defoe later put it, "the Dutch must be understood as they really are, The Middle Persons in Trade, the Factors and Brokers of Europe. . . . They *buy* to *sell* again, *take* in to *send* out, and the greatest Part of their vast Commerce consist in being supply'd from All Parts of the World, that they may supply All the World again." In fact, wherever the English went, they seemed to find that someone from the Netherlands had arrived there first. When the British arrived in New England, ready to trade with the Iroquois, they found that the Dutch were already there.

It was really an accident that the Dutch and not the British claimed the Hudson River valley. Henry Hudson, an English explorer with eccentric but deeply held geographic notions, had already sailed twice for a group of English merchants, and he would sail for them again. Each of the three times he sailed for the English, Hudson tested his theory that a Northwest Passage to Asia could be found by sailing over the North Pole, where, he thought, the climate grew warmer the closer one got to the Pole. On his fourth and final voyage in 1610, Hudson and his crew were frozen into Hudson Bay for the winter. When spring came, the crew mutinied, casting Hudson and the weakest members of the party onto a small boat. They probably did not survive long. When the survivors arrived back in England, they reported that they had found the Northwest Passage, and so Hudson's geographical theory lived on, to tantalize Europeans for centuries to come.

If Hudson's legacy to the English was the claim to Hudson Bay and a durable geographic myth, he provided the Dutch with a claim to the Hudson River valley. In 1609 he had persuaded a group of Dutch merchants who traded in Asia, the Dutch East India Company, to finance another venture. Sailing on the *Halve Maen* ("Half Moon" in English), Hudson and his crew headed toward the Chesapeake, which he believed offered a passage to the Pacific. He and his crew sailed along the North American coast, anchoring in the New York harbor and trading with the local Algonquian Indians. They pushed up the Hudson as far as Albany, where they discovered that the river narrowed, apparently disproving Hudson's theory about a water passage through North America.

The opportunity to profit from the fur trade soon drew investors and traders to New Netherland. Within two years of Hudson's "discovery" of the river that still bears his name, Dutch merchants had returned to the region, and in 1614 a group of merchants calling themselves the New Netherland Company persuaded the government to grant them a temporary monopoly for trade in North America between the Delaware and Connecticut Rivers. The trade was so profitable that other merchant groups were attracted to the region. In 1621 the Dutch West India Company secured a monopoly for trade with both the Americas and Africa that also entitled it to establish colonies in "fruitful and unsettled parts." The Company aimed to increase the Netherlands' wealth by exploiting the most prosperous and promising lands it could find. Ultimately, the plantation regions in South America and the Caribbean and the regions of the African coast that could supply them with slaves were much more lucrative (and hence more important to Holland) than New Netherland. The profits from fur and timber could never rival those from plantation agriculture.

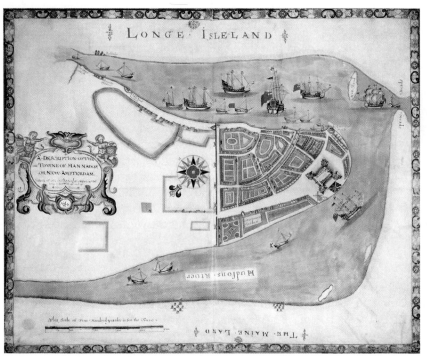

This early map of Manhattan (1661) shows the extent of Dutch settlement of Manhattan three years before the British takeover.

offered huge plots of land (eighteen miles along the Hudson River) and extensive governing powers to "patroons," men who would bring fifty settlers to the new colony. It also offered smaller grants of land to individuals who would farm the land and return to the Company one-tenth of what they produced. Both approaches placed restrictions on land ownership and self-government, and neither was very successful. In 1640, a new policy was introduced. Greater rights of self-government and 200 acres were offered to anyone who brought over five adult immigrants. This policy worked better, although the religious and ethnic diversity of New Netherland suggests that the "pull" of relative toleration was greater than the limited "push" of immigrants out of the prosperous Netherlands. The priest who said that as many as eighteen different languages were spoken in the new colony probably exaggerated, but only a few decades into its existence New Netherland had become a magnet for peoples from the widest variety of cultures and nations.

As the colony grew in population, it expanded up the Hudson, out from the island of Manhattan into New Jersey and Long Island, and as far south as the Delaware River.

The ethnic diversity of the colony was increased even further when in 1655 it absorbed the small colony of New Sweden, which had been established on the Delaware less than twenty years earlier. In some ways the history of New Sweden was like that of New Netherland writ small. It was a privately financed but government-encouraged trading outpost that failed when it was unable to return a quick profit on minimal investment.

The diverse population of New Netherland was united by no single religion or culture that could have established social order. In most European nations at the time, social order was maintained by a combination of state authority and cohesive religious structures and values. Where the religious or government order was fractured, as in France, bloody civil war was the result. In New Netherland, however, not only religious structure, but also the force of government was relatively weak. Only the governors of the colony saw the necessity of maintaining a degree of civil order and harmony. The governors were caught between the company, which expected them to help it profit, and the settlers, who wanted to prosper themselves. Peter Stuyvesant, who governed the colony from 1647 until the English takeover in 1664, was the most successful of the governors, but even he could not fully control New Netherland's disorder.

In one year alone, at a time when the population numbered less than 1,000, there had been 50 civil suits

In theory, the Company was supposed to operate in the public interest. But both the wealthy merchants who were appointed its commissioners and the more ordinary Netherlanders they enticed to migrate to the new colony pursued their private interest above all else. The only way investors or settlers could be attracted to so remote a colony was by the promise of profits, which they eagerly began to pursue. Within a few years' time, the company had established settlements at Fort Orange (present-day Albany) and New Amsterdam (present-day New York) and purchased the entire island of Manhattan from local Algonquian Indians for a meager sixty florins' worth of merchandise. The first thirty families arrived in 1624. All of these settlers, as well as the ones who came in the following years, were supposed to serve the fur trade, either by engaging in the trade with the regional Indians (the Iroquois to the north and the Delaware to the south) or by providing support for the traders. All the profits were reserved for the Company, with the settlers given small salaries.

Until the Company was willing to offer better terms to settlers, the colony grew very slowly. There were only 270 inhabitants in 1628, 300 in 1630, 500 in 1640, and fewer than 9,000 in 1664. It was difficult to attract settlers from a prosperous nation that, while by no means a modern democracy, permitted its people greater religious and political freedom than was customary in most European countries.

The Company experimented with a number of policies in order to draw colonists to New Netherland. In 1629, it and almost as many criminal prosecutions for crimes ranging from slander and theft to adultery and even murder. Good water was in short supply, but rum was not, and the rate of alcohol consumption seems to have been higher in New Netherland than in any of the other colonies on the North American mainland. In 1645, there were between 150 and 200 houses in New Amsterdam—and 35 taverns! One of the prominent ministers was often so drunk that he could not serve the communion wine without spilling it. As a consequence, one of Stuyvesant's first acts as governor was to shut the bars at nine o'clock at night. There were also complaints of sexual promiscuity, especially between European men and Indian women, bar brawls, and mischief caused by sailors on shore leave. In other words, New Amsterdam was well on its way to becoming the bustling, disorderly port city it has remained to this day.

Stuyvesant met with no more success in regulating the economy. He attempted to set prices on such commodities as beer and bread, but he was overruled by the Company. Considerations of political economy prevailed, for the Company feared that such controls upon the economic activities of the colonists would thwart further immigration. In a pattern that would eventually prevail in all of the North American colonies settled by the Netherlands and England, commerce triumphed. "It is better to proceed in this matter with modesty," the authorities in the mother country insisted, "that commerce, just at present threatened by many dangers, may not be discouraged and people disgusted with it, which apparently would cause a depopulation of the country and deprive us of the means to bring emigrants over there."

Slavery and Freedom in the Dutch Political Economy

The desire to enrich by commerce the colony, the Company, and the nation that chartered it led eventually to the introduction of African slavery into New Netherland. The fur trade did not prove as lucrative as investors had hoped, and the Company had found that European agricultural workers "sooner or later apply themselves to trade, and neglect agriculture altogether." In an attempt to make the colony serve the Dutch political economy and its imperial interests, the Company decided that the primary function of New Netherland should be to provide food for its more lucrative plantation colonies in Brazil and the Caribbean. Earlier in the century, the Dutch had seized a portion of northern Brazil from Portugal, had introduced a sugar-plantation slave economy, and from there had transplanted that economy to islands in the Caribbean. By that time they had also entered the transatlantic slave trade. In fact, a Dutch warship dropped off the first twenty Africans at the English colony of Jamestown in 1619 in return for

food. With its own plantation colonies to supply with slave labor, the Netherlands became a major player in the slave trade, ultimately transporting Africans to the colonies of other nations as well.

In the context of the Netherlands' lucrative trade in sugar and slaves, the colony at New Netherland was only a sideshow. Hoping to make the colony profitable, the Company turned to enslaved Africans, who cost about a year's wages for a European worker. By 1664, there were perhaps 700 slaves in the colony, a minuscule portion of the more than half million Africans the Dutch ultimately seized from their homelands. Slaves soon made up a considerable portion (about 8 percent) of New Netherland's total population. By 1680, after the English takeover, that proportion grew to 12 percent and by 1720, more than 15 percent.

Holland was perhaps the most tolerant nation of its day, and the Dutch Reformed Church, the official church of the Netherlands and its colonies, accepted Africans as well as Indians as converts, provided they could demonstrate their knowledge of the Dutch religion. The Dutch Reformed Church did not oppose the institution of slavery, however. Moreover, the nature of Dutch Calvinism placed limits to the Church's toleration. Protestantism, especially the Calvinist version practiced by the Dutch Reformed Church, appealed to the mind more than the emotions. It insisted that its followers be able to read and understand the Bible and the doctrines of the Church. In abandoning Roman Catholicism, Calvinist Protestantism had dispensed with the elaborate rituals and music of the Catholic Church.

In contrast, Catholicism required only that converts accept Jesus Christ, without demonstrating a detailed understanding of Christian theology. Catholic rituals were also similar enough to those practiced by both Africans and Indians that they could integrate them into their own belief systems, creating in the process new versions of Christianity, ones that contained Indian and African elements.

The primary force for tolerance in New Netherland, in fact, was the Dutch West India Company, which saw religious toleration as necessary to commercial prosperity. When the head of the Dutch Reformed Church in New Netherland and Governor Stuyvesant attempted to prevent the entry of a band of twenty-three Dutch Jews whom the Portuguese had expelled when they recaptured northern Brazil from the Netherlands in 1654, they were reversed by the Company. The directors, some of whom were Jews, clarified the relationship between religious toleration and commercial prosperity. Although they might have preferred to keep religious "sectarians" out of their colony, they doubted "whether we can proceed against them rigorously without diminishing the population and stopping immigration. . . . You may . . . allow everyone to have his own belief, as long as he behaves quietly and legally, gives no offence to his neighbors and does not oppose the government."

The Company also advocated a policy of fairness to the local Indian tribes. They insisted that land must be purchased from its original owners before Europeans could settle on it. Because some individual settlers were coercing Indians to sell their land cheap, in 1652 Stuyvesant forbade purchases of land without governmental approval.

It may appear puzzling that the Dutch officials and merchants who devised such policies of toleration of religious minorities and justice toward Native Americans would also introduce and encourage slavery in North America. The Dutch were not motivated, however, by abstract ideals of toleration or ethnic equality. The primary goal of the founders of New Netherland was profit through trade. Toleration of religious and cultural diversity, amicable relations with local Indians, and African slavery all served that end. For the Dutch, trade was everything.

The Dutch-Indian Trading Partnership

Despite the efforts of the Company to turn New Netherland into a breadbasket for its plantation colonies, in the forty years that the Dutch maintained their colony of New Netherland its most profitable activity was the fur trade. As the French already had in the North, the Dutch now disrupted the balance among regional Indian tribes. Just as European nations were competing to obtain pelts from the Indians, so the regional Indian tribes struggled for access to European trade goods. The arrival of the Europeans, rather than uniting the Indians, heightened long-standing local animosities among Native Americans. Tribes came to rely upon their European allies not only for goods, but also for weapons and even soldiers to fight their enemies.

Both the Indians and Europeans were playing a very dangerous game, one that required a constant low level of violence to prevent outsiders from moving in on an established trade. Yet if the violence escalated into full-fledged warfare, it then disrupted the very trade it was designed to protect. As a result, the trade frontier between Indians and Europeans was always filled with peril.

The Dutch began trading in the Albany region around 1614 and built Fort Orange there a decade later. This small outpost was in the middle of a region inhabited by between 5,000 and 8,000 members of the Mahican tribe, who were Algonquians and hence gave the Dutch access to the furs trapped by other Algonquian tribes to the north. The Dutch promptly began assisting the Mahicans in their trade rivalry with the Mohawks (one of the five Iroquois nations) only to find themselves attacked—and defeated—by the Mohawks. The Mohawks asked for peace, explaining that "they had never set themselves against the whites, and asked the reason why the latter had meddled with

them; otherwise they would not have shot them." Their objective was not to eliminate the Dutch, but to secure them as trade partners.

By 1628 the Mohawks had defeated the Mahicans and forced them to move east, into Connecticut. Their victory established the Mohawks as the most powerful force in the region, and as a consequence, they—not the Dutch—were able to set the terms of the regional trade. Kiliaen van Rensselaer, the patroon of a vast estate next to Fort Orange, complained that "the savages, who are now stronger than ourselves, will not allow others who are hostile and live farther away and have many furs to pass through their territory." The Dutch and the Mohawks quickly abandoned their former hostility for a generally peaceful trading partnership.

By and large the Dutch did what was necessary to maintain their lucrative trade. Sometimes that meant giving the Indians gifts, including liquor. At other times, it meant cutting off enterprising individuals who set out on their own, attempting to intercept Indian traders. Despite such efforts, by the 1660s New Netherland was in serious economic trouble. The underlying problem was an oversupply of wampum, beads made from the shells of whelk and quahog clams (see Map 2-6). Indians had placed a high value on wampum well before the arrival of Europeans, and it was mentioned in the Deganawidah, their creation epic. The Dutch introduced iron tools to their Indian trading partners and taught them how to mass-produce wampum in uniform, small tubular beads that could be strung together into ropes and belts. They also helped the Indians establish a trade in wampum itself, in which southern New England Algonquians manufactured wampum and traded it to the Dutch for European goods. The Dutch then exchanged the wampum for furs from the Mohawks and other Indian trade partners near Fort Orange. The Dutch then conveyed the furs to the Netherlands for more European goods. By the middle of the seventeenth century, perhaps as many as three million pieces of wampum were in circulation in the area dominated by the Iroquois. In the early years of the European colonies, wampum had served as currency for Europeans too.

By the 1640s English traders in New England had cornered the market in the beads, just at a time when New Englanders were ceasing to use them as money. The traders then dumped them into the Dutch market by buying up huge quantities of European goods. Almost instantaneously, the price of trade goods skyrocketed and the value of wampum fell, leaving the Dutch with too few of the former and too much of the latter. Competition among Dutch traders increased, the pressure upon Iroquois trade partners mounted, and profits fell. The economic crisis tipped the delicate balance of violence on the frontier and precipitated a major war with serious consequences.

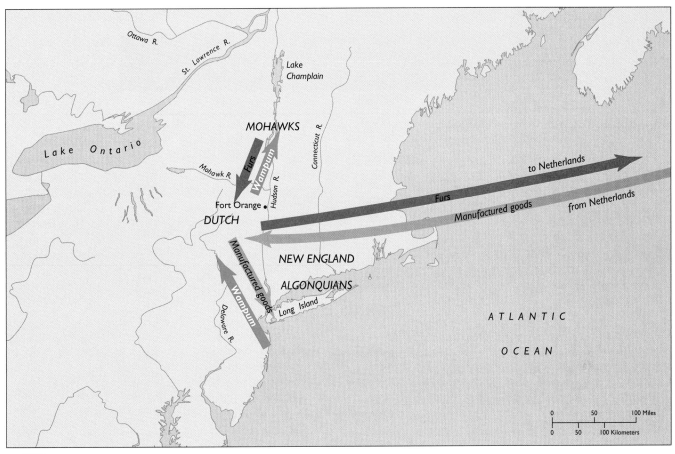

Map 2-6   The Wampum Trade
In the wampum trade, southern New England Algonquians manufactured wampum, which they traded to the Dutch for European goods. The Dutch then exchanged the wampum for furs from the Mohawks and other Indian trade partners near Fort Orange. The Dutch conveyed the furs to the Netherlands for more European goods, which they traded to the New England Algonquians for more wampum.

The Beaver Wars

As the economic position of the Dutch faltered, the balance among a welter of northeastern tribes collapsed. The Iroquois allies of the Dutch, who had come to depend on the Dutch for a steady supply of guns with which to fight their enemies, were now vulnerable. The Iroquois tribes in the West came under assault from the Susquehannocks, an enemy tribe to the south, while the Mohawks faced renewed pressure from the Mahicans to the east. Simultaneously, the Hurons had cut the Iroquois off from trade with the French to the north. Faced with these pressures, the Iroquois lashed out in hostilities that are known as the Beaver Wars and raged between 1648 and the 1660s. In these conflicts, the Iroquois attacked almost all of their Indian neighbors. With a series of assaults that fell like hammer blows, they succeeded in pushing the few surviving French-allied Hurons to the west.

This warfare was horrendous, not only for the enemies of the Iroquois, but also for the Iroquois themselves. So many had died in battle and been replaced by enemy captives that the tribes were as much collections of adopted enemy tribespeople as they were native Iroquois. In this way the traditional practice of the mourning war was adapted in another way to the New World. Raiding parties now went out to seize both captives and plunder that could be used to purchase European goods.

As Indian fought Indian, Europeans gained the upper hand. The Iroquois were the technical winners in the Beaver Wars, but their victory was only temporary. Although the Huron had been pushed west and dispersed, the Iroquois were not able to secure the French as trade partners. Once the Huron were gone, the French began trading with other Algonquian tribes who lived to the east. Although the Iroquois remained a powerful force in North America until almost the end of the eighteenth century, the Beaver Wars marked an important turning point. The Indians were never able to replace the population they lost to warfare, even by raiding other tribes. By the middle of the seventeenth century, however, the pace of European colonization was increasing. Waves of Europeans came to North America to fill the land once hunted by Indians.

Even before the English conquered New Netherland in 1664, the Iroquois were looking for new trade partners. They found them in the English. The transition in New Netherland from Dutch rule to English was relatively quiet. The Dutch had established the colony hoping to make money through trade. In the end, having failed in that objective, they had very little incentive to fight for control of the North American colony.

England Attempts an Empire

England came late to the business of empire building, but by the time the process was completed, that nation dominated not only North America, but much of the world as well. Eventually, the English would boast that "the sun never sets on the British empire." Although England's search for an overseas empire was motivated primarily by a search for wealth and power, it is impossible to separate these drives from the religious impulse. All of the great imperial nations of this era—Portugal, Spain, France, and England—believed that they conquered for God and country both, and hence nationalism was always tinged with religious fervor. But as a Protestant nation with a sense of its own mission, England soon came into conflict with the leading Catholic nations, first Spain and later France. In England, nationalism fused with a sense of religious mission so intense (and outrageous) that the English would insist that "God is English."

The Origins of English Nationalism

England did not achieve the political unity that was a precondition for empire-building until the second half of the sixteenth century. Between 1455 and 1485, England was torn by a dynastic struggle, the War of the Roses. King Henry VII and his son, Henry VIII, spent their reigns consolidating the power of the state by crushing recalcitrant nobles. When the Pope refused to let Henry VIII terminate his son-less marriage to Catherine of Aragon, the king made Protestantism the official religion of the nation. (This branch of Protestantism is known as the Anglican religion.) Henry banned Catholicism and confiscated all the land and wealth of the Catholic Church in his country, filling the coffers of the state treasury without having to tax the English people. Henry's daughter Mary, who reigned from 1553–1558, took the nation back to the Catholic religion, burning Protestants at the stake and throwing the nation into turmoil. Order was finally established under the rule of Henry's other daughter, Elizabeth I (reigning from 1558–1603), who re-established the Anglican Church and

presided over England's accession as an imperial power. She was able to subdue internal dissent and build upon the strong state that her grandfather and father had consolidated.

Queen Elizabeth, although the most ardent of nationalists, was unwilling to risk her treasury on North American adventures. Other English nationalists, however, were convinced that a New World empire could lead to both wealth and glory for the nation. By the end of the sixteenth century nationalist propagandists, such as two cousins both named Richard Hakluyt, were setting out the case for an overseas empire. The Hakluyts united nationalism, mercantilism, and militant Protestantism. They argued that if England had colonies to supply it with raw materials and provide markets for manufactured goods, it could free itself from economic dependency on France and Spain. Moreover, colonies could drain off the growing numbers of the unemployed. A long period of population growth combined with falling wages had created an English underclass, "a superfluous multitude of fruitless and idle people (here at home daily increasing)." The Hakluyts also believed that North American Indians could be relatively easily converted to English trade and religion, which they would much prefer to Spanish "pride and tyranie." The English could simultaneously strike a blow against the Spanish and advance "the glory of God." Although the Hakluyts' dream of converting the Indians was never realized, their plans for an English mercantile empire eventually provided a blueprint for overseas colonization.

Raiding Other Empires

England's first move was not to establish colonies but to try stealing from the Spanish. The English government had neither the wealth nor the vision to found a colonial empire, and Elizabeth I was unpersuaded by the arguments of the Hakluyts and other colonial propagandists. Like most European monarchs, Elizabeth was most concerned about international power politics in Europe, so she was quite willing to let individual Englishmen try to poach on the Spanish. Her goal was to weaken Spain more than it was to establish a North American empire. As early as 1562, John Hawkins tried to break into the slave trade. With a force of both private and royal ships, he intervened in a tribal war in West Africa, picked up a load of slaves, and sold them in the Spanish Caribbean. Before the Spanish forced him out of the slave trade a few years later, in the process killing 300 of his 400 sailors at San Juan de Ulúa (near Veracruz, Mexico), Hawkins had paid a visit to the French Huguenot colony at Fort Caroline to see if he could give the Protestants there some assistance.

Unable to make a killing in the slave trade, the English moved on to privateering, that is, state-sanctioned piracy. In 1570 Sir Francis Drake set off for the Isthmus of Panama

One of England's greatest adventurers, Sir Francis Drake sailed around the globe, defeated the Spanish Armada, and made a fortune stealing from the Spaniards.

on a raiding expedition. A west country seaman from a modest background, Drake was motivated equally by dreams of glory and a conviction that his Protestant religion was superior to all others. He had his start in Hawkins' slaving expedition, surviving the disastrous defeat at San Juan de Ulúa from which he had acquired a hatred of the Spanish.

In years to come, Drake led the second expedition ever to sail around the world, crossed the Atlantic many times, helped defeat a huge Spanish fleet, the Armada, and became both an architect and instrument of England's colonial strategies. Wherever he sailed, he took with him George Foxe's *Book of Martyrs,* and he read to Spanish prisoners passages that described the persecution of Protestants under England's Catholic Queen Mary. Personally brave and militantly Protestant, Drake was the English version of the *conquistador.* His venture into Panama failed to produce the hoped-for treasure, but it inspired a group of professional seamen, aggressive Protestants and members of Elizabeth's court, who were beginning to formulate plans for an English colonial empire. This group successfully pressured the cautious queen for support.

The success of Drake's round-the-world expedition (1577–1580) spurred further privateering ventures. He brought back to England not only enough treasure to pay for the voyage, but also proof that the Spanish empire was vulnerable. From 1585 to 1604, the English government issued licenses to privateers, sometimes as many as 100 per year. Each venture was financed by a **joint-stock company,** a relatively new form of business organization that was the forerunner to the modern corporation. These companies brought together merchants who saw privateering as a logical extension of their efforts to broaden their trade and gentlemen who saw it as a glamorous way to increase their incomes. Increasingly, the merchants played a dominant role, running privateering as much like a business as possible.

Rehearsal in Ireland

At the end of the sixteenth century, England embarked on a campaign to bring Ireland, which had long been in its possession, under its full control. The conquest of Ireland between 1565 and 1576 became the model for England's subsequent colonial ventures. Ireland presented the English monarchy with the same sort of political problem that all early-modern rulers faced, that is, a set of powerful nobles who put their own interests ahead of those of the nation. Consolidation of the nation meant bringing these nobles into line. That was what Elizabeth's grandfather and father had done in England, and now she was ready to extend that process to Ireland.

England not only subdued the Irish leaders and their people, but also forcibly removed some of them to make way for loyal Englishmen who were given grants of land as a reward for their service to the queen. Paying her followers with someone else's land made the conquest of Ireland relatively cheap. Elizabeth also allowed her followers to finance their military expeditions from joint-stock companies. These methods of colonization provided useful precedents to a queen who was never convinced that the establishment of colonies on the edge of the known world was in England's national interest. If, however, these ventures could be paid for privately (by privateering, charters to individuals, or joint-stock companies), she was willing to permit them.

The English conquest of Ireland provided not only practical experience in how to organize and finance a colonial venture, but also a set of attitudes about cultural difference that were transferred to North America and applied to the Indians. Although the Irish were technically Catholics and hence Christians, the English thought that people who behaved as the Irish did could not possibly be Christian. According to the English, the Irish "blaspheme, they murder, commit whoredome, hold no wedlocke, ravish, steal, and commit all abomination without scruple of conscience."

Having decided that the Irish were barbarians, the English tried to fit them to that mold. For example, because many of the Irish left their homes in the summer to follow their flocks to their pasture lands, the English decided that they were nomads and hence uncivilized. Civilized people, they insisted, lived in one place without moving around. Likewise, the English, without a shred of evidence to back them up, accused the Irish of cannibalism, another mark of the barbarian.

These attitudes became the justification for an official English state policy of terrorism. In two grisly massacres, one in the middle of a Christmas feast, hundreds of people—men, women, and children—were slaughtered. The English Governor, Sir Humphrey Gilbert, ordered that the heads of all those killed resisting the conquest be chopped off and placed along the path leading to his tent so that anyone coming to see him "must pass through a lane of heads." According to Gilbert, the dead would feel "nothing," but it would bring "terror to the people when they saw the heads of their dead fathers, brothers, children, kinsfolk, and friends." The English justified such harsh policies by the supposed "barbarism" of the Irish people. These ideas, which were quite similar to early Spanish depictions of the Indians of the Americas, were carried over to the New World, England's next stop in the expansion of its empire.

The Roanoke Venture

Roanoke, England's first colony in what became the United States, was a military venture, designed and implemented by military men. The colony was supposed to be a resupply base for privateers raiding in the Caribbean. With such a base, the ships would not have to recross the Atlantic each time they completed a raid. In 1584 Walter Raleigh received a charter to establish a colony in North America. Only thirty years old at the time, Raleigh was the half-brother of the late Sir Humphrey Gilbert. Hot-tempered and arrogant, Raleigh had been a soldier since the age of fourteen. Although Elizabeth was still not persuaded of the wisdom or necessity of colonies, she agreed to let Raleigh establish a combination colony-privateering base north of Spain's northernmost settlement at St. Augustine. Raleigh's scouting party had already found a potential site, at Roanoke Island, on the Outer Banks of North Carolina and brought back to England two Indians, Manteo and Wanchese. Elizabeth gave the enterprise some modest support, even investing in it herself. She knighted Raleigh, but refused to let the hotheaded young soldier lead the expedition himself.

The Roanoke expedition left Plymouth in early April 1585, under the command of Sir Richard Grenville, an aristocrat and soldier who had fought in wars in Hungary and Ireland. Half of the crew of 600 were probably recruited or impressed (that is, forcibly seized) from the unemployed poor of Britain. One commander referred to them as "wild men of mine own nation." Little value was attached to the lives of such poor men. When one of the ships in the original expedition became separated from the fleet and found its supplies running low, twenty men were dropped off at Jamaica, only two of whom were ever heard from again, and another thirty-two were deposited at an island in the Outer Banks. Such men were expendable, and so ultimately would be the entire population of Roanoke.

It turned out that Roanoke was a very poor port indeed, dangerous for small ships and totally inadequate for larger ones. When the primary ship in the fleet was almost wrecked and a major portion of the food supply lost, Grenville and the fleet departed for England and fresh supplies. Colonel Ralph Lane, another veteran of the war in Ireland, was left in charge as governor. He was supposed to look for a better port, start building a fort, and find food for the 100 men who were left under his command. Perhaps 100 men had already died on the voyage. On the way back to England, Grenville captured a Span-

John White's watercolor of an Algonquian village. Much of what we know about Algonquian life at the time of the Roanoke expedition comes from the paintings of John White, who was a member of the Roanoke expedition. Here we see a small village, surrounded by a tall stockade.

ish treasure ship almost twice the size of his own vessel. Privateering still appeared the surest route to quick profits.

Roanoke was established to gain an advantage over the treasure-filled Spanish ships traveling back to Spain. The men who were left on the island prepared for war—with Spain. When the fort was complete, its guns pointed out to sea, toward any Spanish ships that might approach. Raleigh intended to send another supply ship that summer, but the queen insisted that he sail instead to Newfoundland to warn the English there about the beginnings of a sea war with Spain.

The first settlers of Roanoke were ill-equipped to build a self-sustaining colony. Half soldiers and gentlemen, and half undisciplined and impoverished young men, no one knew how to work. The aristocrats searched half-heartedly for gold and silver and when none was found, spent the remainder of their time complaining about the lack of "their old accustomed dainty food" and "soft beds of down or feathers." Unable to provide for themselves, the colonists turned to the local Roanoke Indians (an Algonquian tribe), whom they soon alienated.

The Roanokes were evidently familiar with Europeans and ready to trade with them. The English tendency to resort to force and their need for more food than the natives could easily supply led, however, to conflict. Thinking that one of the Indians had stolen a silver cup, the English retaliated by burning an empty village and the surrounding cornfields, which were necessary to feed both Indians and English. In the light of such actions, the Indians had to balance the benefits brought by trade against the costs of English hostility. After an attempted ambush failed, the Roanokes decided to withdraw from Roanoke Island, leaving the English to starve. When Lane learned of this plan, he attacked the Roanokes, beheading their chieftain Wingina. Thomas Hariot, one of the colonists, later placed most of the blame for the deterioration of Indian-English relations on his countrymen: "Some of our company towards the end of the year, showed themselves openly too fierce, in slaying some of the people, in some towns, upon causes that on our part, might easily enough have been borne." Such was the result of leaving colonization in the hands of military men such as Lane, veterans of the wars in Ireland.

Not all the colonists, however, treated the Roanokes as an enemy to be conquered. Much of what we know about not only the Roanoke colony but its Indian neighbors is due to the work of two sympathetic colonists. John White, a painter, and Thomas Hariot, who later became the greatest mathematician of his age, were sent to survey the region and its inhabitants, its plants, its animals, and its natural features. Hariot mastered the Roanokes' dialect, and White's sketches and watercolors demonstrated an equal curiosity about and respect for local customs. Their illustrations, maps, and descriptions provide the most accurate

Portrait of an Algonquian mother by John White. This beautiful picture illustrates the indulgence of Algonquian mothers and the sensitivity of the English artist who painted her.

information about this region and its inhabitants before the arrival of large numbers of Europeans. Most of the party, however, lacked White and Hariot's ability to appreciate and adopt native customs, which proved most unfortunate for a group of men who had been deposited on a foreign shore with an inadequate food supply.

By June of 1585, it was clear that Roanoke had failed in its mission, and Lane and his men had had quite enough of colonizing. The resupply ship, promised by Grenville, was almost two months late. When Sir Francis Drake and his fleet appeared, on their way back from a year-long looting party in the Caribbean, the colonists decided to hitch a ride back to England. So great was their haste to clear out that they left behind three men who were out on an expedition into the interior. They were never heard from again. Apparently, Drake also dropped off several hundred Caribbean Indian and African slaves that he had liberated while picking up booty. Freeing slaves was one of his ways to hurt the Spanish. For the same reason, he had burned the outpost at St. Augustine as he passed by on his way up the East Coast. Probably all of these abandoned people (the three Englishmen and Drake's liberated Indians and Africans) melted into the Native Indian population, according to the Indian tradition of adoption. When Raleigh's supply ship arrived at Roanoke shortly thereafter, and then Grenville two weeks after that, the colonists had sailed with Drake and the others had already disappeared. Grenville dropped off fifteen men, and he returned to England.

The English advocates of colonization were not yet ready to give up. The original plan for a military-style privateering base that would commandeer local Indians had failed, and a new vision of colonization would now be tried. Raleigh's commitment to the colony was only lukewarm by this point, for Roanoke had already cost £30,000 without returning a cent. John White, the painter, remained enthusiastic, and he assembled a group of settlers that was the forerunner of all future successful English colonies. It included 110 people—men, women, and children who were prepared to raise their own crops—and the ever-loyal Manteo. (Wanchese had remained with his own people, and was now an enemy to the English.) In return for their investment in the enterprise, Raleigh granted each man 500 acres of land. The new expedition arrived at Roanoke in July 1587. The plan was to pick up the men Grenville had left and proceed north to the Chesapeake, for a superior harbor. The pilot of the fleet, who was more interested in privateering than colony-making, refused to take the colonists any further, however.

The second attempt to establish a colony at Roanoke was probably doomed by the poisoned relations with the Indians. White soon found that Grenville's men had been attacked by Roanokes. The colonists found themselves in a difficult situation. Despite the best of intentions, they were estranged from their Indian hosts. The survival of the colony now depended upon continued support from England. Hence the colonists, who included White's own daughter and granddaughter, decided to send White back with the fleet to act as their agent in England. No European ever saw any of these colonists again.

The Abandoned Colony

No one had planned to abandon the little colony. It was mostly a matter of priorities. Raleigh assembled a supply fleet the next spring. A sea war with the Spanish Armada was looming, however, and Elizabeth did not let the ships leave. Raleigh himself became busy, first with the war against the Spanish and then with sending colonists to his plantations in Ireland. White put together a two-ship party, but the crews set off in search of treasure instead of Roanoke. That took care of 1588. In 1589, the supply mission never got beyond the planning stage. In 1590, White arranged with a privateering fleet to drop him at Roanoke. For months White cruised about the Caribbean as the privateers went about their business. In mid-August White finally arrived in Roanoke, only to find that everyone was gone. There were signs of an orderly departure, and the word CROATOAN, Manteo's home island, was carved in a post. White assumed that was where the entire group had gone. Short of water and with a storm brewing, the fleet decided to return to the Caribbean for the winter and not to proceed on to Croatoan until the next spring. They never traveled there.

The colony of Roanoke was not "lost," as legend usually puts it; it was abandoned. Serving no useful economic or military purpose, the men and women of Roanoke were entirely expendable. Because Raleigh's claim to the land depended upon his sustaining a colony, he was better off maintaining the fiction that the colonists were alive than discovering that in fact they were dead or missing. In 1602, Raleigh finally sent out a search party that never quite made it to Roanoke. A year later Queen Elizabeth was dead, and her successor, James I, had Raleigh arrested as a traitor.

What happened to the abandoned colonists? Twenty years after White had last seen them, the English returned to the region, this time establishing a permanent colony at Jamestown, on the Chesapeake.

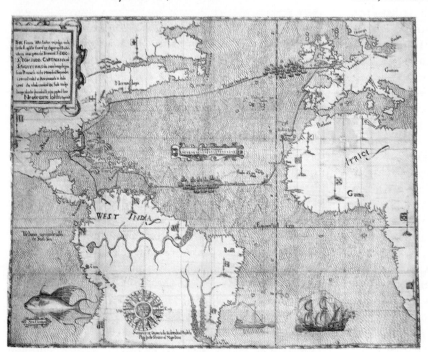

Contemporary map of Francis Drake's West Indian voyage, 1585–1586. On this voyage, Drake picked up Roanoke colonists and returned them to England.

One year later, in 1608, English men began to hear a story that Roanoke colonists had made their way up to Virginia and settled among the friendly Chesapeake Indians, who lived south of the bay. Indeed, the main body of the colonists that White had left at Roanoke had intended to seek out the Chesapeake. Perhaps the remainder went to Croatoan, leaving White the message carved into the post.

Those who moved north seem to have become victims of the Powhatans, a powerful and expansionist tribe. At just about the time that the English were arriving, their chief, also named Powhatan, ordered the slaughter of the Chesapeakes and the English who lived among them. There were reports that seven English people had escaped, and for years additional accounts came in from local Indians about people who lived in two-story stone houses and domesticated turkeys. At one point, a ten-year-old boy with "perfect yellow hair" and "white skin" was sighted among one tribe. The English at Jamestown eventually came to believe that the survivors of Roanoke were living fifty miles away, but no effort was made to find them. Perhaps they preferred to think that they all had been slaughtered or were being held prisoners against their will rather than to discover that they had intermarried with their hosts and adopted their ways. If anyone cared about the fate of the abandoned colonists of Roanoke, it was only the Indians, among whom they found a new home.

Almost twenty years after the abandonment of Roanoke, the English came back, finally establishing a permanent North American colony. By that time the Armada had been soundly defeated, and the Spanish Empire was sinking into its slow decline. In theory at least, the English would be able to provide better support for subsequent New World colonies. As their willingness to abandon the colonists at Roanoke demonstrated, however, they had limited interest in colonies that did not return a fast and reliable profit. Moreover, because the English settlers, with very few exceptions, antagonized their Indian hosts, the English could not rely upon the Indians for a food supply. As a result, the success of the English colonies would depend upon their capacity to grow their own food. In addition, although the focus of English colonization was trade, the architects of English imperial policy concentrated more upon trade with the English inhabitants of the New World than with Native Americans. Consequently, the history of the English in North America is by and large that of the growth of the English population (augmented by immigrants from other European nations and of course Africa) and the steady decline of the original Indian inhabitants.

Conclusion

European nations established colonies to achieve a political or economic advantage over their rivals. Most of the nations that established colonies had only recently been unified by force. This experience gave them both the energy to establish colonies in the rest of the world and a military model that they could use for colonization. The distinctive experience and political economy of each nation, however, shaped its relations with the Indians it encountered (just as the distinctive experience of the Indian nations shaped their interactions with Europeans). The Spanish came prepared for a new *reconquista* and poured huge and well-armed forces into the New World. They compared their Indian adversaries to the Moors, a powerful and sophisticated people. The French sent small numbers of military officers who quickly found Indian allies and became entangled in the Indians' own conflicts. The English used another military model, that of the pacification of Ireland. Most Europeans assumed that Native Americans were uncivilized and barbaric and that if they resisted European rule they would have to be crushed. Some nations, in particular France and Spain, were comparatively willing to reach out to alien cultures by sending missionaries to convert the Indians. Though more ethnocentric than the French or Spanish, the Dutch also recognized that the good will of the Indians was vital if a flourishing trade were to be maintained. The English proved the least interested in accommodating Indian cultures and the most interested in transplanting their own. Out of these different experiences, a North Atlantic political economy began to emerge. It was shaped by the forces of trade and the quest for national power, as Europeans, Indians, and Africans were drawn into a global economy in which the nations of the world competed for advantage.

The early years of American colonial history were shaped by the forces of political economy, vast impersonal forces that built empires and subjugated peoples. But they were also given a lasting imprint by individuals, many of them world travelers. Some set out to find new worlds, while others were forced into them by those with imperial ambitions. Captives such as Don Luís, Wanchese, and Manteo; intrepid explorers such as Jacques Cartier and Henry Hudson; ruthless soldiers such as Sir Francis Drake and Samuel de Champlain; the poor who were dragooned into sailing for Roanoke and left there to die; Africans liberated from the Spanish only to be abandoned on the North Carolina shore, perhaps melting into the Indian population; Huron women who took French traders as their husbands: All of them left their mark on the New World.

CHRONOLOGY

1275–1292	Marco Polo travels in Asia
1400–1600	Five Iroquois Nations create the Great League of Peace
1455–1485	War of the Roses in England
1497	John Cabot arrives in North America
1519–1522	Magellan expedition sails around the world for Spain
1522	Giovanni da Verrazano explores North American coast for France
1534–1542	Jacques Cartier makes three trips to Canada for France
1561	Spanish abduct Don Luís de Velasco
1562	John Hawkins tries to break into the slave trade
1565	Spanish establish settlement at St. Augustine
	Spanish destroy French settlement at Fort Caroline
1565–1576	The English conquer Ireland
1570	Don Luís de Velasco returns home to Virginia
1577–1580	Francis Drake sails around the world for England
1584	Walter Raleigh receives charter to establish colony at Roanoke
1585	First settlement at Roanoke established
1587	Second attempt to found colony at Roanoke
1590	English settlers at Roanoke have disappeared
1607	English establish permanent colony at Jamestown
1608	Samuel de Champlain establishes a fort at Quebec
1609	Henry Hudson arrives at New York, sailing for the Netherlands
1614	Dutch begin trading in Albany region
	French settlers arrive in New France
1621	Dutch West India Company established
1624	First Dutch families arrive at Manhattan
1648–1660s	Beaver Wars fought
1664	English take over New Amsterdam

Review Questions

1. What were the key European objectives for exploring North America in this period? To what extent did England, Spain, France, and Holland achieve their objectives?

2. What was the "mourning war"? What function did it serve in Iroquois culture? How was it adapted to new circumstances in the seventeenth century?

3. Compare the early encounters with Native Americans of the English, French, and Dutch.

4. Compare the approaches to colonization of the English, French, and Dutch governments.

5. What was the "middle ground," and how was it created?

6. Why was the colony at Roanoke established, and why was it abandoned?

Further Readings

W. J. Eccles, *France in America* (1990). The standard introduction to the history of New France, succinct and authoritative.

Michael Kammen, *colonial New York: A History* (1975). A readable survey of colonial New York's history.

Karen Ordahl Kupperman, *Roanoke: The Abandoned Colony* (1984), and David Beers Quinn, *Set Fair for Roanoke: Voyages and Colonies, 1584–1606* (1985). Two excellent histories of the Roanoke colony. Kupperman expertly places the colony in its fullest context, while Quinn offers a more comprehensive narrative.

David Beers Quinn, ed., *New American World: A Documentary History of North America to 1612* (1979). A five-volume collection of documents, indispensable for the study of early explorations of North America.

Daniel K. Richter, *The Ordeal of the Longhouse: The Peoples of the Iroquois League in the Era of European Colonization* (1992). An extraordinary introduction to the history of the Iroquois peoples that shows what early American history looks like when the focus is shifted from European settlers to the original inhabitants.

Helen C. Rountree, *Pocahontas's People: The Powhatan Indians of Virginia Through Four Centuries* (1990). A superb introduction to the history of this southeastern tribe, written by an anthropologist.

History on the Internet

"Canadian Museum of Civilization"

http://www.civilization.ca/cmc/cmceng/ca12beng.html

Read about trade between the Native Americans and the French that fostered cultural exchange. At this site, also view actual artifacts of the fur trade, both Indian and European wares. The site also contains a link to the Manitoba Museum of Man and Nature, which features more artifacts of the fur trade.

"Thomas Harriot's A Brief and True Report of the New Found Land of Virginia"

http://www.nps.gov/for/a/harriotreport.htm

http://www.nps.gov/fora/raleigh.html

This primary account describes the first English colony, including the natural environment, provisions for the colonists, and their experiences with Native Americans.

3
THE ENGLISH COME TO STAY
1600-1660

O U T L I N E

The Adventures of John Rolfe

The First Chesapeake Colonies
Planning Virginia
Starving Times
Troubled Relations With the Powhatans
Toward a New Political Economy
Toward the Destruction of the Powhatans
A New Colony in Maryland

The Political Economy of Slavery Emerges
The Problem of a Labor Supply
The Origins of Slavery in the Chesapeake
Gender and the Social Order in the Chesapeake

A Bible Commonwealth in the New England Wilderness
The English Origins of the Puritan Movement

What Did the Puritans Believe?
The Pilgrim Colony at Plymouth
The Puritan Colony at Massachusetts Bay
The New England Way
Changing the Land to Fit the Political Economy
The Puritan Family

Dissension in the Puritan Ranks
Roger Williams and Toleration
Anne Hutchinson and the Equality of Believers
Puritan Indian Policy and the Pequot War

Conclusion

The Adventures of John Rolfe

John Rolfe was an adventurer. His father had worked his way up in the world, achieving both economic success and an English gentleman's status in international trade. John Rolfe seems to have inherited some of his father's enterprising spirit, for in 1609, at the age of 25, he and his young wife set sail for the two-year-old English colony at Jamestown. Their ship was blown off course, however, by a storm more violent than any they had ever seen and was wrecked on a reef off the shore of the Atlantic island of Bermuda. It was not until a year later that Rolfe would make it to Virginia. By that time, he had survived a mutiny and the death of his infant daughter, whom he and his wife had named Bermuda, in honor of her place of birth. Rolfe's wife herself died shortly after their arrival at Jamestown, not only the date and cause of her death, but even her name, lost to history.

Soon Rolfe was experimenting with tobacco, trying to find a strain that would produce a fragrant leaf in Virginia's soil. Walter Raleigh's men had introduced tobacco into England, where the addictive pleasures of smoking soon created a market for the product. The English imported their tobacco from the Spanish West Indies, at 18 shillings per pound. With the founding of their colony at Jamestown in 1607, the English hoped for their own source of tobacco. Unfortunately, the variety grown by Virginia's Indians was "poore, weake, and of a byting taste." Rolfe tried planting West Indian tobacco seeds, and, using a process of trial and error, was able to produce a successful crop. By 1617, Virginians were exporting Rolfe's variety of tobacco to England. It was not quite as sweet as the West Indian product, but at 3 shillings per pound, it was a great deal cheaper. Tobacco proved the economic salvation of Virginia, in the process making many men and women rich and robbing others of their freedom. Like other foreign colonies, Virginia achieved its prosperity by feeding European cravings. Tobacco was no more a necessity than other plantation crops such as sugar, coffee, and tea. Like them, it was merely a pleasurable and habit-forming taste.

Relations with the local Powhatan Indians had been tense from the moment of the colonists' arrival. From time to time, the tension spilled over into warfare, making the region a dangerous place for English and Indian both. In the spring of 1613, the English captured Pocahontas, the favorite daughter of the chieftain Powhatan, and brought her back to Jamestown as a captive. By summer, John Rolfe had fallen deeply in love with the 18-year-old Indian princess. He asked permission of the English authorities to marry her, realizing that his countrymen would disapprove of his attachment to "one whose education hath been rude, her manners barbarous, her generation accursed." He thought people would gossip that he was marrying her just to satisfy his lust, but if that were the case, he reasoned, he "might satisfy such desire . . . with Christians more pleasing to the eye." He even feared that his love for Pocahontas was the work of the devil, and so he resolved to convert her to Christianity. In John Rolfe, the traditional ethnocentrism of the English was at war with love. In this case, love won out. Only two other English colonists married Powhatan Indians during the entire seventeenth century. Yet the marriage was more than a triumph of two people in love. It also established an alliance between their peoples that brought an end to years of warfare.

Two years later, in 1616, Rolfe took his wife and their young son to England, where Pocahontas adopted the dress of an English lady and even met King James and Queen Anne. The Virginia Company used her as a sort of walking advertisement for their colony. Her

John Rolfe's marriage to the Powhatan Indian princess, Pocahantas, depicted here in the painting "Marriage of Pocahantas" by artist Sidney King, established an alliance between English colonists and the Powhatans that brought an end to years of warfare.

transformation suggested to the English that Indians could easily be Europeanized. When Rolfe said it was time to return to Virginia, Pocahontas said she wanted to remain in her new home. She prepared to depart, but before the ship set sail she took ill and died, as a Christian. Only 31, John Rolfe had already buried two wives.

By the time that Rolfe returned to Virginia in 1617, tobacco had come to dominate the economy. The English population grew, and tobacco-planting settlers encroached on the Powhatans' land. Finally, on the morning of March 22, 1622, the new leader of the Powhatan Confederacy, Opechancanough, the brother of the recently deceased Chief Powhatan, orchestrated attacks upon all the plantations along the James River. By the time they were finished, nearly one-third of all the Virginia colonists—women and children, as well as men—had been killed. John Rolfe was one of the victims.

John Rolfe had imagined that English and Indian could live together in harmony. He was wrong. Once he developed a marketable strain of tobacco, the English could not be stopped from spreading onto Powhatan lands, turning them into tobacco fields. European demand for tobacco doomed not only the Indians who were driven from their homeland, but also generations of European indentured servants and, eventually, African slaves. A new kind of society, one based upon the political economy of plantation slavery, was beginning to take shape. Rarely in history is one person so directly responsible for the demise of his own dreams. ▮

KEY TOPICS

• Why the colony at Jamestown succeeded—and why it almost failed.

• The effect of the tobacco economy on society in the Chesapeake.

• Gender, family, and the social order in the Chesapeake and New England.

• Relations—and conflict—with the Indians in the Chesapeake and New England.

• The English Reformation and the origins of Puritanism in England.

• How Puritanism shaped New England's social order.

• How New England Puritans handled dissent.

The First Chesapeake Colonies

In 1607, twenty years after the abandonment of the Roanoke colony, the English had returned to North America. Their nation was strong and unified, at the beginning of a rise to wealth and power that would carry it well into the twentieth century. The English, however, had learned almost nothing from their failure in Roanoke, and although their colony at Jamestown (named after the king) was better financed, it was poorly planned. A combination of unrealistic expectations, flawed leadership, troubled relations with the local Powhatan Indians, and lack of economic viability almost doomed the colony. The difference between survival as a colony and extinction was tobacco. With the development of this cash crop, for which there was demand in Europe, Virginia began to prosper. But an economy based upon tobacco made for a strange sort of prosperity. Once John Rolfe had developed a palatable strain of tobacco, the primary requirements were land and labor. The English settlers' desire for land led them into warfare with the Powhatans; their desire for cheap labor led them to import indentured servants, white and black, and African slaves.

Planning Virginia

When Queen Elizabeth died in 1603, she was succeeded by King James I, who quickly signed a treaty with Spain,

ending decades of warfare. With peace established between the English and Spanish, all those who had lived off privateering and warfare had to look for another source of income, from legitimate trade. They joined with old advocates of colonization such as Richard Hakluyt to establish new colonies in North America. In 1606, James granted charters to two groups of English merchants and military men, one in London and the other in Plymouth. The Plymouth group was permitted to colonize New England, and the Londoners the Chesapeake region. Each operation was chartered as a private company, which would raise money from shareholders and finance, populate, and regulate each **charter colony** that it established. British merchants had begun to use such joint-stock companies, forerunners of the modern corporation, to finance shipping ventures. The Virginia Company used this structure to finance its colony, raising more money from wealthy London merchants than for any other colonial venture. Although both the Virginia and Plymouth Companies reported to a newly appointed Royal Council, these new ventures were fundamentally private operations, subject to very little governmental control.

Both the Virginia and Plymouth Companies eventually founded North American colonies, but the Virginia Company (named in honor of the nation's late, supposedly virginal queen) met with success first. Just before Christmas 1606 the Virginia Company of London sent out three ships under the leadership of Captain Christopher Newport, a one-legged veteran Atlantic explorer. When the ships arrived at Virginia on April 26, 1607, and the sealed orders from the company were opened, the 104 colonists learned that they were to be governed by a council of seven men. Unfortunately, two of them, Edward Maria Wingfield, one of the original investors in the Company but "an arrogant man of no special capacity," and Captain John Smith, a 27-year-old equally arrogant but considerably more capable soldier of fortune, had already grown to despise each other, and Smith had been put under arrest early in the voyage. As a result, the early years of the new colony at Jamestown, on the James River (both named after England's king) were marked by wrangling among the leaders. Soon external conflict developed as well, as the colonists antagonized their Indian hosts. Indeed, almost everything that could go wrong, did.

The English, who had indeed learned little from their experience with Roanoke, continued to hope for a land like Mexico that would provide them with gold and less glamorous raw materials. Whatever limited manufacturing was needed could be performed either by English criminals, who were sent over to work as their punishment, or by English men and women who agreed to work for a set period of time to pay off their transportation to the colony. These indentured servants were drawn from the lowest ranks of English society, and Virginia soon became known as a place for "parents to disburden themselves of lascivious sonnes, masters of bad servants and wives of ill husbands." The colonists were expected to strike up a trade with the local Indians, who were to be the primary suppliers of food.

The Company figured it could get the colony up and running within seven years. During that period all the colonists would work for the Company, which would give them food and shelter. At the end of that period, all of the colonists would receive grants of land. The Company evidently thought that such a colony would need a great deal of direction, for more than a third of the original settlers were "gentlemen," that is, members of the elite. Moreover, the Company continued to send over gentlemen (56 out of the next 190 colonists). In its first years, the proportion of elite in Jamestown's population was six times as great as it was in England, and each of these gentlemen brought with him several personal servants.

The Company also sent skilled laborers. Unfortunately, many of them had skills for which there was little use in the new colony. There were bricklayers, masons, tailors, goldsmiths, refiners, a jeweler, a tobacco pipe maker, and a perfumer. Some of these men, such as the tailors and the perfumer, were thought necessary for the upkeep of the gentlemen. Others were supposed to be on hand to work with the gold and precious gems the colonists hoped to find. Farmers and ordinary laborers, on the other hand, were in short supply. Nonetheless, when the Company put

web connection

Folklore, Heritage, and National Character

www.prenhall.com/boydston/jamestown

American society historically has been marked by a youthful brashness and physicality that seemed at odds with the nation's growing status as a world power. Historians have suggested that early and long-lasting frontier struggles for survival left an imprint on American folklore, heritage, and national character that distinguishes the United States from older nations. What was the frontier struggle that left such a legacy? One example is the settlement of Jamestown, which almost failed, for a variety of reasons ranging from environmental to political, and including relations with Indians. Why did the settlement at Jamestown almost fail, and why do we remember it?

out a call for additional colonists, it asked for ten ironworkers, four caviar preservers, two mineral men, two silk dressers, two pearl-drillers, and two brewers. The Com-

The Fort at Jamestown, as it may have appeared in 1607. The settlement at Jamestown was surrounded by a palisade, a high wooden fence. Some colonists lived in tents and others in wooden cabins.

pany somehow expected to set up in Virginia a highly complex and diversified economy.

Starving Times

Poor planning and bad luck placed the colonists on swampy ground with a bad water supply. The concentrations of salt in the James River were high enough to poison those who drank it. In addition, in summer the water around Jamestown became a breeding ground for the micro-organisms that caused typhoid and dysentery. Some historians have argued that these diseases left the survivors too weak to plant food, while others note that many of the healthy seemed to prefer prospecting for gold. Whatever the reason, the colonists were unable to raise crops in the first few years, making them dependent upon the resentful Powhatans for food. Malnutrition and even starvation made the effects of disease worse. This combination of factors, along with conflicts with the Powhatan Indians, led to appallingly high mortality rates. A majority of the settlers died in the first three years. As late as 1616, the English population was only 350, although more than five times that number had emigrated from England (see Table 3-1).

The first few years were particularly brutal. By September of 1607, half of the 104 Jamestown colonists were dead, and by the next spring only 38 were still alive. Although the Company sent over more colonists, women as well as men, they continued to die off at extraordinary rates. Immigration swelled Jamestown's population to 350 in the fall of 1609, but no more than a hundred survived to the next spring. Most who died at Jamestown were victims of malnutrition and disease. The lack of food was so great that over the winter of 1609–1610, the inhabitants were reduced to eating roots, acorns, and even human excrement. The rich boiled the ruffles on their clothing, to drain out the starch that had made them stiff and cook it into a porridge. The poor dug up an Indian who had been killed and buried some time earlier and "boiled and stewed him with roots and herbs." One man killed his pregnant wife, ripped the fetus from her womb, then salted his wife's corpse and had it half eaten before his crime was discovered.

For centuries this starvation has perplexed historians. The land around Jamestown was fertile and abounded with game, and the James River was teeming with fish. The colonists had had several growing seasons and should have been able to raise enough to keep themselves alive. Indeed, when Captain John Smith served as president of the Council from 1608 to 1609 (after all six of the other councilors had either died or returned to England), only a handful of colonists died. He imposed a military-style discipline and required all the colonists to work four hours a day. He bullied the Powhatans into giving the English some food,

TABLE 3-1

English Population of Virginia, 1607–1640	
Population in Virginia Colony	**Immigration to Virginia Colony**
104 (April 1607)	104 (April 1607)
38 (Jan. 1608)	
	120 (Jan. 1608, 1st supply)
130 (Sept. 1608)	
	70 (Sept. 1608, 2nd supply)
200 (late Sept. 1608)	
100 (spring 1609)	
	300 (Fall 1609, 3rd supply)
	540 (1610)
450 (April 1611)	
	660 (1611)
682 (Jan. 1612)	
350 (Jan. 1613)	
	45 (1613–1616)
351 (1616)	
600 (Dec. 1618)	
	900 (1618–1620)
887 (Mar. 1620)	
	1051 (1620–1621)
843 (Mar. 1621)	
	1580 (1621–1622)
1240 (Mar. 1622)	
	1935 (1622–1623)
1241 (April 1623)	
	1646 (1623–1624)
1275 (Feb. 1624)	
1210 (1625)	
	9000 (1625–1634)
4914 (1634)	
	6000 (1635–1640)
8100 (1640)	total: 23,951

Although about 24,000 men and women immigrated to Virginia between 1607 and 1640, in 1640 the population stood at only 8,100. Most of the inhabitants fell victim to disease, although the Indian uprising of 1622 took 347 lives.
Source: Data from Earle, Geographical Inquiry and American Historical Problems (1992) and Bernhard, "Men, Women, and Children at Jamestown: Population and Gender in Early Virginia, 1607–1610," Journal of Southern History, LVIII (1992).

and he also moved some of the colonists away from Jamestown's lethal water supply. Smith blamed the starvation on the laziness of the colonists, who preferred searching for riches to planting grain. Disease and malnutrition, however, were probably more to blame. Moreover, seeing so many die around them only increased survivors' sense of despair. They suffered from what can only be described as depression.

Decisions by the leadership only made the plight worse. John Smith, an effective but widely disliked disciplinarian, had returned to England in 1609 after a gunpowder injury, possibly an assassination attempt. The new rulers unwisely split up the settlement, sending a group of men down the James River to establish a fort and two other parties to establish settlements in spots already inhabited by Indians. In both cases the English were attacked and suffered heavy losses. The contemptuous Indians stuffed bread in the mouths of their hungry victims. Three thousand miles from home, literally starving to death, and surrounded by strange and sometimes hostile native peoples, the colonists who survived the winter were "distracted and forlorn," in many ways resembling modern prisoners of war. They had already begun to abandon the colony, when they were stopped by the arrival of Lord De La Warr, the new governor who had come to impose martial law.

In accordance with the military model of colonization, until 1618 Jamestown was ruled by military governors who imposed the "Lawes Divine, Morall and Martiall."

These harsh laws prescribed the death penalty not only for murder, but also for rape, adultery, theft, blasphemy, and even killing a chicken or stealing food while weeding a garden. At the same time, the colony struggled to find a way to earn a return for its investors.

Troubled Relations With the Powhatans

In Virginia, the English encountered one of the most powerful Indian tribes on the continent, the Powhatans, a confederacy of Algonquian tribes who, under their *werowance* or chieftain Powhatan, were also establishing themselves as leaders in their region, bringing less powerful Virginia Algonquians under their control. At the time of the English arrival, Powhatan's confederacy included about 20,000 Indians, divided into around three dozen tribes. Both groups tried at first to get the other to accept the status of an allied but subordinate tribe, but neither was prepared to accept the other as a diplomatic equal. At one point, the English pushed the aging Indian chieftain Powhatan, "a tall well proportioned man, with a sower look," down to the ground and put a fake crown on his head, imitating the ceremonies in which feudal princes pledged allegiance to a king. For his part, Powhatan held Captain John Smith temporarily captive and tried to bully him and other members of the English leadership into acknowledging his supremacy. In the context of these complex political maneuverings, both

Powhatan and English Dwellings
These are reconstructions of typical English and Powhatan Indian homes, c. 1607. Both are dark and low to the ground.

upon an Indian village. The English killed about seventy-five of the inhabitants, burned the town and its cornfields, and took as captives the wife of a chieftain and her children. As the English sailed back to Jamestown, they threw the children overboard and shot them as they swam in the water. When the party arrived back at Jamestown, De La Warr wanted the Indian queen burned, but one of his lieutenants interceded on her behalf, protesting that he had already "seene so muche Bloodshedd that day." Instead, she was taken into the woods and put to the sword.

These attacks upon the Indian villages were the opening battles of the First Anglo-Powhatan War, the first in a series of three debilitating conflicts between the English and the Powhatans that took place between 1610 and 1646. The first was ended in 1614, when the marriage between Pocahontas and John Rolfe cemented a truce between their peoples. The English objective, never fully implemented, was to kill the Powhatan religious and political leaders and kidnap their children. Pocahontas was one of these captives when Rolfe fell in love with her. She married Rolfe willingly, as previously described, accepted baptism as a Christian, and took the English name Rebecca.

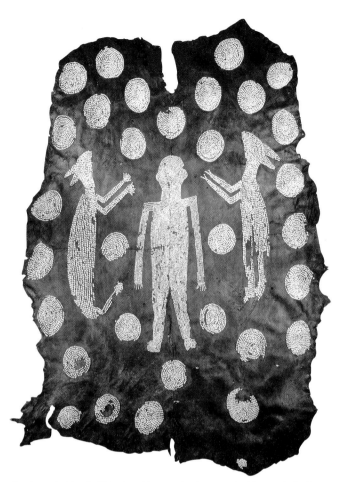

Powhatan's Mantle. This deerskin mantle, decorated with sea shells, is supposed to have belonged to Powhatan.

Powhatan and his enemies were sometimes willing to give the colonists food in the hope of winning them as allies. Although English bullying sometimes yielded food from the Indians, it also led to increased animosity, as did English settlement on Indian land.

English leadership also made the tensions between the two peoples worse. Some of the early English leaders had hoped for a bi-racial society in which the Indians would become the loyal subjects and trading partners of the English. No doubt frustrated by their inability either to produce their own food or get it from the Indians, and finding that they could survive only by subordinating themselves to military discipline, Jamestown's leaders came increasingly to think of all Indians as an enemy to be dealt with by military means.

No sooner had Lord De La Warr arrived than he set out to subjugate the Indians who had killed so many settlers the previous year. He reminded Powhatan of his "coronation" two years earlier as a prince subject to King James and ordered him to return English captives and equipment. When Powhatan refused, De La Warr ordered an attack

Pocahontas, also known to the Powhatans as Matoaka and to the English as Rebecca, in English dress, as she appeared when she accompanied her English husband John Rolfe to England.

In permitting his daughter to marry one of the English, Powhatan was adapting one of the means he had used to establish his powerful confederacy. He himself had an unusually large number of wives, perhaps as many as a hundred. He selected his brides from throughout his realm as a means of tightening his dominion. Among Algonquian tribes, intermarriage was used to cement ties to other kinship groups. Each of Powhatan's wives thus represented an important link between Powhatan's tribe and her own. After each of his wives had borne him a child, she and the child were sent back to her home village. In this way Powhatan could maintain a presence in each of the villages under his control. Sometimes, Powhatan also appointed his own son or son-in-law as *werowance* of a village. This strategic move brought that village more tightly under his control and at the same time undermined the customary power of Algonquian women to participate in the selection of the tribal leader. By tradition, *werowances* were supposed to be the kinsmen of *werowansqua* (tribal queens). At the same time that Powhatan was consolidating his own personal leadership, he was enhancing patriarchal authority in the tribes he controlled as well.

The marriage of John Rolfe and Pocahontas ushered in a brief period of peace, one that served the English better than the Powhatans. The English were so pleased with the new alliance that they soon asked for another one of Powhatan's daughters as a bride for one of their councilors, who happened already to have a spouse, as did the eleven-year-old girl he sought to marry. Powhatan refused, fearing that, as with Pocahontas, he would lose a daughter rather than gain a powerful and loyal English son-in-law. Powhatan had failed in his objective of turning the English into his vassals.

Toward a New Political Economy

The tide finally turned against the Powhatans, not so much because of diplomacy or the politics of marriage but because the English had finally found a way to make money in Virginia. John Rolfe's improved strain of tobacco had found a ready market in England, and that market stimulated the Virginia economy, transforming it almost overnight. The result was a very different sort of society than the one the Virginia Company had planned. Within three years of Rolfe's first cargo, Virginia was shipping 50,000 pounds of tobacco to England. By 1626, that figure had increased more than five times. Suddenly Virginia experienced an economic boom. By 1619, a man working by himself was reported making £200 in one crop, and a man with six indentured servants, £1000. Only the nobility was accustomed to seeing that kind of money. Once fortunes this large could be made, the race to Virginia was on.

All that was needed to make money in Virginia was land and people to work it. The methods that were used to attract colonists and distribute land changed the shape of the colony dramatically. In 1616 the Virginia Company, which had plenty of land but no money, offered land as dividends to its stockholders. Moreover, those already living in Virginia were given land, and anyone who came over (or brought another person over) was to be granted fifty acres a head (called a *headright*). The Company was taking an important step in the direction of private enterprise, away from the corporate, company-directed economy of the early years. The leadership of the colony was also generous in its grants to itself, laying the basis for its own wealth and power. Soon, it was far easier to obtain land in Virginia than in England.

As another means of attracting settlers, the Company scrapped its martial law and replaced it with the English common law, which guaranteed the colonists all the rights of the English people. The colonists were also granted far greater rights to self-government than were enjoyed by those who lived in England at the same time. The first elected representative government in the New World, the Virginia General Assembly, met in Jamestown on July 30, 1619.

These inducements attracted 3,500 settlers to Virginia in three years, three times as many as had come in the past ten. By accident more than planning, Virginia had found the formula for a successful English colony. It was a model that all the other colonies generally followed. In order for colonists to be attracted 3,000 miles across the ocean, they would have to be offered greater opportunities to make money and greater rights of self-government than they would have had at home. These changes came too late, however, to rescue the Virginia Company, which went bankrupt in 1624. King James I dissolved the Company and turned Virginia into a **royal colony**, under direct royal control.

Toward the Destruction of the Powhatans

As the new colonists spread out in the region around Jamestown, establishing private plantations, it became clear to the Powhatans that the English colony was both permanent and growing (see Map 3-1). Soon English settlers had claimed all the Indians' prime farmland on both sides of the James River and were beginning to move up the river's tributaries too. At the same time, the Powhatans were becoming increasingly dependent upon English goods such as metal tools. Moreover, as the English population increased and began to grow its own food, it had less need of Indian food, which was the only commodity these Indians had to trade. The Indians were slowly accumulating a debt to the English and losing their economic independence.

After Powhatan died, his more militant brother, Opechancanough, the new leader of the Powhatan Confederacy, decided that if the Indians were going to get rid

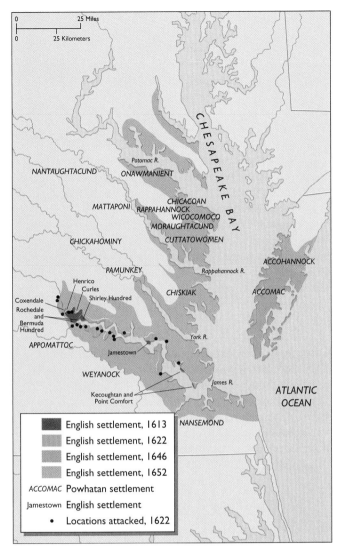

Map 3-1   English Encroachments on Indian Land, 1613–1652.
After John Rolfe's development of a marketable strain of tobacco, the English spread out through the Chesapeake region, encroaching steadily on Indian land. Tobacco planters preferred land along the rivers, for casks filled with tobacco bound for England were more easily transported by ship.

Source: Frederic Gleach, Powhatan's World and Colonial Virginia (Lincoln: University of Nebraska Press, 1997), and James Horn, Adapting to a New World: English Society in the Seventeenth-Century Chesapeake (Chapel Hill: University of North Carolina Press), 1994.

This reconstruction shows Jamestown as it may have looked during the 1622 uprising.

of the English interlopers, it was now or never. On the morning of March 22, 1622, the Indians struck at all the plantations along the James River. By the time they were finished, one-third of all the Virginia colonists had been killed. John Rolfe was among the casualties. The Second Anglo-Powhatan War, which continued for another ten years, had begun.

This war marked a turning point in English policy. Although some of the English recognized that the Indian attack had been caused by "our own perfidiouse dealing with them," most decided that the Indians were by their nature untrustworthy and incapable of being converted to the English way of life. Therefore, a policy of extermination was justified. Some were almost happy that the Indians had attacked; John Smith concluded that the massacre "will be good for the Plantation, because now we have just cause to destroy them by all meanes possible." Until this point, the English had claimed only land the Indians were not farming. Now they justified seizing territory the Indians had cleared and planted. In only 15 years' time, the English and Indians in Virginia had become implacable enemies.

Indian resistance only made the English more determined to stay, and with the tobacco economy booming, settlers continued to pour into Virginia. They spread across the Chesapeake to the Eastern Shore and as far north as the Potomac. The aged Opechancanough determined to make one final drive to push the English out of his native land. On April 18, 1644, his warriors struck again, killing 400 English people and taking many prisoners.

The Third Anglo-Powhatan War ended, however, in the Indians' total defeat two years later. Opechancanough was seized and taken back to Jamestown, where he was killed. The English took complete possession of the land between the James and York Rivers. Henceforth, no Indian was allowed to enter this territory without wearing a special jacket indicating that he was bringing a message from the chief *werowance*. Any English person who gave shelter to an Indian without permission was put to death. All English prisoners were to be returned by the Indians, but the English were to keep Indian prisoners as servants. The land north of the York was to be reserved for the Indians, making it the first American Indian reservation. In a few years' time, English settlers were moving into that region, too, and it was not the last time that the English settlers would break a treaty with the Indians.

A New Colony in Maryland

Virginia's original plan, to make money from trading with the local Indians, was not entirely forgotten. When the tobacco boom began, colonists became more interested in the Indians' land than in their trade. As tobacco prices dipped in the 1620s, however, trade with regional Indians became more attractive. By the late 1620s, an outpost had been established at the northern end of Chesapeake Bay in order to obtain beaver furs from the Susquehannocks, a tribe living further to the north. Sir George Calvert, the first Lord Baltimore and a Catholic, saw the commercial potential of this region and in 1632 persuaded King Charles I, a Catholic-sympathizer, to grant him the land north of the Potomac and south of the Delaware that was "not yet cultivated and planted." This territory became Maryland, the first **proprietary colony**, that is, a colony that was, literally, owned by an individual and his heirs. (Virginia was originally a **charter colony**, that is, one that was held by a group of private shareholders, but in 1624 it was made into a royal colony. In charter and proprietary colonies, the English Crown turned over both financing and managing the colony to the shareholders or proprietors.) Maryland, named after the Catholic queen of England, remained the hereditary possession of the Calvert family until the American Revolution.

As the first of the proprietary colonies, Maryland established the pattern for subsequent proprietorships. While looking for a proper legal precedent for the sort of grant he wanted, Calvert had come across the patent given to the Bishop of Durham in the fourteenth century. To enable him to maintain order on the border of England and Scotland, the wild frontier of its day, the Bishop received extensive *feudal* powers to grant land, build cities, create churches, and regulate trade. (**Feudalism** was a social and political system that had developed in Europe in the Middle Ages under which powerful lords offered less powerful noblemen protection in return for their loyalty. The English kings centralized the feudal system by giving the great lords huge estates in return for their loyalty and military service.) Charles' willingness to give Calvert a similar patent demonstrates that as far as he was concerned, North America was the end of the earth, so remote from civilization that it could be almost completely given away and its owner endowed with the power of a feudal lord.

Although the gift of Maryland was in form thus a feudal grant, the new colony quickly developed aspects of a more modern government. The proprietor had extensive powers to grant land and make laws by himself, but perhaps because he knew he would have to compete for settlers with Virginia, which already had a representative government, he agreed to the establishment of a representative assembly. In 1649 that assembly passed the Act of Toleration, which said that no one would be "compelled to the beliefe or exercise of any other Religion against his or her consent." Even though religious toleration was extended only to those who professed a belief in Jesus Christ, Maryland was still among the most tolerant places in the world at that time. It was far more welcoming of diverse religious beliefs than England itself, where Catholics, Quakers, and other Christian dissenters were still subject to persecution. Moreover, the extension of this right explicitly to women, as well as men, was also novel.

Although it would be a number of decades before Maryland's population increased substantially, the familiar political economy was already emerging. As was true when Virginia was forming, in order for colonists to be attracted to the New World, they would have to be offered greater opportunities and freedoms—of self-government and of religion—than were enjoyed by those who stayed at home. Ironically, the feudal form of Maryland's grant made it easier for the local government to develop in a more modern way. Once the king had transferred his authority to a proprietor, the proprietor was free to allow his colonists considerable liberties.

Throughout the period of conflict with the Powhatan Confederacy, the booming tobacco economy continued to draw settlers to Virginia and, after about 1650, to Maryland as well. Although they had separate governments, which often came into conflict with each other, Virginia and Maryland had similar political economies, based upon tobacco. The defeat of the Indians made more land in the Chesapeake region available for cultivation and needing only people to work it.

The Political Economy of Slavery Emerges

Chesapeake society in the first half of the seventeenth century was shaped by four forces: weak government, the market for tobacco, the availability of land, and the need for labor. The Chesapeake was shaped by the tobacco boom, and even when the glorious prices of the early years fell off, the imprint of the boom was still strong. Because government was weak, the forces of plantation agriculture were unchecked, and the profit motive operated without restraint. Those who could take advantage of these opportunities—male and female both—profited wildly, while the poor, both white and African, were without defense. Artificial distinctions such as social status in the Old World counted for little in comparison to willpower, physical strength, and often sheer ruthlessness. Even gender roles were undermined as women worked in the fields instead of churning butter, and wealthy widows controlled large estates. Those who were not in a position to take advantage of these opportunities because they were weak or because they lacked the initial capital found themselves at the mercy of those who had money and consequently power. It was in this environment that the political economy of slavery took root.

The Problem of a Labor Supply

Once the crises of the early years had passed, the Chesapeake's greatest problem was securing laborers to produce tobacco. As soon as John Rolfe had brought in his first successful crop, the Virginia governor began pressing England to send him its poor. The Virginia Company also encouraged the emigration of women, for the young colony was primarily male. No matter how many colonists came over, however, the demand for labor always outstripped the supply. By 1660 50,000 Britons, most of them single men in their 20s, had migrated to the Chesapeake, but the population was still only a little over 35,000. Because of the poor water supply and the disease environment, the death rate remained extraordinarily high. In some years, the mortality rate was as high as 30 percent.

The profits from tobacco were so great, and the likelihood of death from disease or other causes so high, that those who owned land and had servants to work it tried to squeeze out every penny of profit as quickly as they could. Those who were sharp enough to get land and servants to work it could become rich overnight. Colonial officials, including members of the legislature, took advantage of their positions and discovered a variety of ways to make themselves wealthy, from claiming vast tracts of land to assessing high fees for all sorts of transactions. The men and occasionally women who rose to the top during the boom years often came from humble backgrounds. Adam Thoroughgood had started out in Virginia as a servant at age 14.

This decorative section from a map of early Virginia shows shippers, planters, and slaves on a dock with barrels of tobacco waiting for shipment.

When he died at age 38 in 1640, he left his widow Sarah a wealthy and powerful woman.

Great wealth, however, could be achieved only by the labor of others. The demand for labor was almost insatiable. Perhaps 90 percent of those who migrated to the Chesapeake in the seventeenth century came as servants, and half of them died before completing their term of service. Servants were worked to the point of death. In England, custom and law both had afforded servants some basic protections. Three thousand miles across the ocean in Virginia, with the government in the hands of those who were profiting from the labor of servants, working conditions were brutal. In 1623, Richard Frethorne, a young servant, wrote back to his parents in England complaining about life in Virginia. "With weeping tears," he begged them to send food. "We must work early and late for a mess of water gruel and a mouthful of bread and beef." His cloak had been stolen by a fellow servant, who sold it for beef and butter. Servants might be beaten so severely that they died, or they might find their indentures (the contract that bound them to service for a period of usually seven years) sold from one master to another, almost as if they were slaves. In some ways, the position of servants resembled that of slaves. Their treatment was brutal, and they found very little protection from the Virginia or Maryland courts. They were not, in fact, slaves. They would become free if they outlived their period of indenture; they retained all of the rights of English people (on paper at least), and their position was not hereditary. But they were far worse off than servants in England.

The Origins of Slavery in the Chesapeake

Other New World plantation societies where labor was in short supply had already turned to slavery, so it was probably only a matter of time until the Chesapeake did so as well. Historians do not know precisely when slavery was first practiced in the Chesapeake colonies, but Africans first arrived in Virginia in 1619, when a Dutch ship sailing off its course sold its cargo of "twenty Negars" to the Virginians. It has never been clear, however, if these Africans were treated as indentured servants or as lifelong slaves. As long as life expectancy in the region was low, it was more profitable for a planter to purchase an indentured servant for a period of seven years than a slave for life, as the slave was much more expensive. Not until life expectancy improved toward the end of the seventeenth century were significant numbers of African slaves imported into the Chesapeake.

All of the English plantation colonies followed the same pattern in making the transition from white servitude to African slavery as the primary source of labor. African slavery had been introduced into the region a century earlier by the Spanish, and Africans were present from the beginning in all the English plantation colonies, such as

Barbados and Providence Island in the West Indies. The shift toward African slavery was quick in some places and slow in others. Providence Island moved from servitude to slavery in less than ten years during the 1630s, while Virginia took about three-quarters of a century. This transition was made without debate everywhere. The primary factors dictating how quickly English colonists adopted African slavery were the need for plantation laborers and the availability of African slaves at a good price. By the time the English began to import African slaves into their colonies in the seventeenth century, the Spanish and Portuguese had been using enslaved Africans as plantation laborers for well over a century. The English were entering into a global economy that had already come to rely upon slave labor.

To the extent that there was any discussion at all about the justice of slavery, the English claimed that slavery was an appropriate punishment for certain crimes and for prisoners taken in just wars. No white people were ever enslaved in the English colonies, however. It was a practice reserved for "strangers," primarily foreigners of a non-Christian religion. In addition, the association between slavery and plantation economies was very strong. Still, all the British colonies eventually practiced slavery, and it became critical to plantation economies. African slaves were even brought back to the British Islands, and by the middle of the eighteenth century, 2 percent of London's population was African.

Even before there was substantial contact with African people, there seems to have been some prejudice among the English and other northern Europeans against Africans and other dark-skinned people. By the second half of the sixteenth century, the English were depicting Africans in almost wholly derogatory terms. They said that Africans were unattractive, with "dispositions most savage and brutish." Northern Europeans considered African women particularly monstrous, sexually promiscuous, and neglectful of their children. Africans' communities, their religions, and their governments were all, it was said, primitive. Although these views were not used to justify slavery, they formed the basis for the racism that would develop as slavery grew.

During the seventeenth century, African slavery and white and African servitude existed side by side, and laws to enforce slavery appeared slowly and in a piecemeal fashion. The Chesapeake was a society with slaves, but it was still not a slave society. The first clear evidence of enslavement of Africans in the Chesapeake dates to 1639, when the Maryland Assembly passed a law guaranteeing "all the Inhabitants of this Province being Christians (Slaves excepted)" all the rights and liberties of "any naturall born subject of England." A year later, there are signs that slavery was being practiced in Virginia, when "a negro named John Punch" who had run away from his master was sentenced to serve "for the time of his natural life." The first Virginia law recognizing slavery, passed in 1661, said that

any English servant who ran away with an African would have to serve additional time not only for himself, but for the African as well. Historians presume that such Africans were already slaves for life and hence were incapable of serving any additional time.

Such laws and legal proceedings show not only the piecemeal way in which laws enforcing slavery were put together but also the great familiarity that existed between white and black servants. Slaves and white servants worked together, enjoyed their leisure together, had sexual relations with each other, and broke the law together by running away. As late as 1680, Africans made up less than 7 percent of Virginia's population and less than 10 percent of Maryland's. Most of the labor on plantations was still being performed by white indentured servants. There is no evidence that they were kept separate from Africans by law or inclination.

As long as the black population remained small, the color line was rather blurry. Not until very late in the seventeenth century were laws passed that placed restrictions upon those African Americans who remained free. In fact, there is evidence that Africans who lived in Virginia in the seventeenth century themselves owned slaves. By 1660, Anthony Johnson, an African who had arrived in Virginia as a servant in 1621 and survived the Indian uprising of 1622, owned both land and African slaves. In the 40 years that he had been in Virginia, the institution of slavery had developed and become recognized by the law, but the laws separating the races had yet to be enacted.

Gender and the Social Order in the Chesapeake

The founders of England's New World colonies hoped to replicate the social order that they had known at home. For that reason, as early as 1619, the Virginia Company began to pay for the transportation of single women to the colony. These women were forbidden to marry servants. Instead, they were supposed to become brides for the unmarried planters who were beginning to make fortunes in the tobacco boom. As in England, it was expected that men would perform all the "outside" labor, including planting, farming, and taking care of the large farm animals. Women would do all the "inside" work, including preserving and preparing food, spinning thread and weaving cloth, making and repairing clothing, and tending the garden. In English society, a farmer's wife thus was not simply a man's sexual partner and companion, she was also the mistress of the household economy, performing work vital to its success. "In a new plantation," the Virginia Assembly noted in 1619, "it is not known whether man or woman be more necessary." Both men and women were vital to the social and economic order that the English wanted to create in the Chesapeake.

This is a reconstruction of a settler's cabin, showing a woman at work cooking in a small, dark one-room dwelling.

Once again, the powerful tobacco economy demonstrated its ability to transform dramatically both the economy and society of the New World. In the first place, with profits from tobacco so high, women went right into the tobacco fields instead of the kitchen. When children were born, as soon as they could work, they were in the fields too. Only when a man became rather wealthy did he hire a servant—often a woman—to replace his wife in the fields so that she could churn butter and spin yarn. As a result, for many years, Virginia society lacked the "comforts of home" that women produced such as prepared food, homemade clothing, and even soap (which women made from boiling animal fat and lye). Nor were planters and their wives able to buy and sell household products at local markets. Tobacco was everything.

The circumstances of colonial society weakened patriarchal controls, making it very hard to get women to marry and remain obedient wives to the leading planters. Local governments worked in vain to reimpose patriarchal authority. Far from their own fathers, living in a remote part of the world where the government was relatively weak, women in the Chesapeake found themselves unexpectedly liberated from some of the harshest traditional restrictions. Chesapeake governments attempted to control immigrant women, insisting, for example, that a woman receive government permission before marrying, and prosecuting for slander women who spoke out against the government or their neighbors.

Although women without the protection of fathers were certainly vulnerable to exploitation in seventeenth-century plantation societies, where men outnumbered women three or four to one, women often found themselves in a position of relative power. Local governments struggled to impose order by prosecuting women for adul-

tery, fornication, and giving birth to bastard children. The public, however, was more tolerant of sexual misconduct than government officials. When the widow Alice Boise and Captain William Epes kept a roomful of drunken partygoers awake most of the night with their "great bussleing and juggling" on the bed, they were not prosecuted for fornication. Instead, the man who gossiped about their nighttime activities was tried for slander. Similarly, when a ship's captain was executed for having sex with a boy on his ship (one of five executions for homosexual activity in the colonial period), the protests were so widespread that the protesters themselves were punished.

The first generation of women to immigrate to the Chesapeake in the seventeenth century married relatively late—in their mid twenties—to men at least as old. Many had to wait out their periods of service until they could marry. As a result, they had relatively few children, having already passed through a portion of their childbearing years. With disproportionately few women, having on average only several children each, it was many decades before Chesapeake society reproduced itself naturally. With the disease environment taking a huge toll, perhaps half of all children born in the colony died in infancy, and one or the other marriage partner was also likely to die within seven years of marriage. At least until 1680 or so, to be a widow, widower, or orphan was the normal state of affairs, rather than the exception. In such a society, women who survived their husbands and inherited their possessions were unusually powerful and were much in demand on the marriage market. Children, however, were especially vulnerable, often losing their inheritances to a stepparent. In the raw, new society, there were no grandparents or aunts and uncles to look out for the children's interests.

A Bible Commonwealth in the New England Wilderness

Only thirteen years after the founding of the Virginia colony at Jamestown in 1607, England planted another permanent North American colony at Plymouth, and nine years after that, one at Massachusetts Bay. In many ways the Virginia and Massachusetts colonies could not have been more different. The primary impetus behind the Massachusetts settlement was religious. Both the Pilgrims at Plymouth and the much more numerous Puritans at Massachusetts Bay moved, as families and communities both, to New England in order to escape persecution and to establish new communities, based upon God's law as they understood it. The Puritans and Pilgrims were almost entirely middle class in their origins, and their ventures were well-financed and capably planned. Their colonies prospered almost immediately. The environment was much healthier than that of the Chesapeake, or even that of England, and because the number of men and women was roughly equal, the population reproduced itself rapidly. In addition, relations with the local Indians were considerably better than in the Chesapeake. Nonetheless, the Puritan movement was a product of the same developing political economy that led to the European exploration of the New World. Both grew out of the consolidation and growth of national states in Europe and the expansion of commerce. As the newly developed printing press spread knowledge and increased literacy, especially among the growing urban middle classes of Europe, dissatisfaction with the powerful and authoritarian Catholic Church increased.

The English Origins of the Puritan Movement

By the time that England's King Henry VIII decided to replace his wife, the Protestant Reformation had already taken hold in much of northern Europe. Ordinary people and powerful monarchs had vastly different reasons for abandoning the Roman Catholic Church in favor of one of the new Protestant churches. In England, these differing motives led to 130 years of conflict, including a revolution and massive religious persecution. Henry's reasons for establishing his own state religion in England, the Church of England, in place of Catholicism, were political more than pious. After ten years of marriage to Catherine of Aragon, Henry still did not have a male heir. With one of Catherine's ladies-in-waiting, Anne Boleyn, already pregnant, Henry pressed the Pope for an annulment of his marriage to Catherine. The Pope was caught in an awkward position, between Henry, on the one hand, and the continental Catholic monarchs on the other, for Catherine was the daughter of Isabel and Fernando and the aunt of Charles V, the Holy Roman Emperor. In 1533, the Pope refused Henry an annulment. Henry responded by removing the Catholic Church as the established religion of England and replacing it with his own Church of England (whose adherents are known as Anglicans in Britain and Episcopalians in the United States). An added bonus for Henry came from the confiscation of Catholic Church lands, which he redistributed to members of the English nobility in return for their loyalty. In one move, Henry eliminated a powerful political rival, the Roman Catholic Church, from his domain, and he consolidated his rule over his nobility.

Henry's replacement of the Catholic Church with the Anglican one, however, did not bring stability. His successors alternated between adherence to Protestantism and persecution of Catholics, and support of Catholicism and persecution of Protestants. Under the reign of Catherine's

daughter Mary, hundreds of Protestants left the country to avoid being burned at the stake.

When Mary's Protestant sister, Elizabeth I, ascended to the throne, these exiles returned, having picked up the Calvinist doctrine of predestination on the Continent. John Calvin, the Swiss Protestant reformer, insisted that even before people were born, God foreordained "to some eternal life and to some eternal damnation." Although the Church of England during Elizabeth's reign adopted Calvin's doctrine of predestination, it never held to it thoroughly enough or followed through on other reforms well enough to please the "Puritans," those who desired further purifications of the Church of England. And because the monarchs viewed challenges to the state religion as challenges to the state itself, Catholics, Puritans, and other religious dissenters were frequently persecuted for their beliefs.

What Did the Puritans Believe?

The political conflicts between ambitious European rulers created the opportunities for religious dissenters to develop their own religious practices and beliefs. Until the reign of Elizabeth's successor, James I (1603–1625), Puritans in Britain often had the freedom to work within the Church for reform and to establish their own congregations. Their version of Protestantism spread rapidly, fulfilling spiritual needs that had been unmet by the established Church of England.

Like all Christians, Puritans believed that all of humanity was guilty of the original sin committed by Adam and Eve when they disobeyed God in the Garden of Eden. They believed that God's son, Jesus Christ, had given his life to pay (or "atone") for the original sin, and that as a consequence, all faithful Christians would be forgiven their sins and admitted to heaven after they died, there to enjoy eternal life. **Calvinism** differed from other Christian religions primarily in the Calvinists' insistence that there was nothing that men or women could do to guarantee that God would give them the faith, by an act of "grace," that would save them from eternal punishment in hell.

Protestants rejected much of the hierarchy of the Catholic Church. Most of them maintained that the relationship between God and humanity was direct, "unmediated." Every person had direct access to the inspired word of God through the Bible. Hence Protestants placed more emphasis on literacy and on translating the Bible into the vernacular. King James I, for example, ordered a translation of the Bible into English, while the Puritans used an English translation of John Calvin's Geneva Bible.

As Calvinists, Puritans carried certain features of Protestant belief to their logical conclusions. Unlike Anglicans, they wanted to "purify" the Church of England of all the remnants of Catholicism. Anglicans had reduced the number of sacraments; Puritans wanted to eliminate them all. Anglicans retained some church rituals and a church

Richard Mather was a Puritan minister in England who had been banned from the pulpit for refusing to follow Anglican rituals. In 1635 he fled with his family to Massachusetts, where he became a prominent minister. Four of his sons followed him into the ministry.

hierarchy (but not the Pope); Puritans rejected all rituals and all priestly hierarchy.

Finally, Anglicans had increasingly come to think that believing Christians could earn their way to heaven by good works, a doctrine that the Puritans labelled **Arminianism** (after the Dutch theologian, Arminius, who developed it). Puritans, in contrast, believed that saving grace was the free gift of an all-knowing and all-powerful God, and that human beings could not force His hand. All that individuals could do was to prepare for grace, should it come, by reading and studying the Bible, so that they understood God's plan, and by attempting to live as good and decent a life as they could in the meantime. Individuals could also look for signs of God's grace, although they could never know for certain whether they had been saved. Hence, Puritans always lived with a certain amount of anxiety.

Puritanism contained a powerful tension between intellect and emotion. On the one hand, Puritanism was a highly rational religion. Its ministers were highly learned, and it required all of its followers to read and study the Bible, as well as to listen to and understand long sermons that explored fine points of theology. As a result, Puritanism led to high rates of literacy among its followers,

male and female both. On the other hand, Puritans believed that no amount of book learning could get a person into heaven and that saving grace was as much a matter of the heart as of the mind. The feeling of salvation was profoundly emotional and overpowering, a sort of euphoria that had to be disciplined by the intellect. Throughout its history, the Puritan movement struggled to contain this tension, as some of its believers moved toward a more fully rational religion and others abandoned book learning for emotion.

Under state religions, such as the Roman Catholic Church or the Church of England, all residents of the nation were required to attend the church dictated by the government. Puritans, however, believed that church membership was only for those who could demonstrate that they were saved. As they were persecuted for their faith, they came to believe that, like the Israelites of old, they were God's chosen people, that they had a *covenant* or agreement with God, that if they did His will, He would make them prosper.

Some of what displeased the Puritans was simply the chaos of Elizabethan England. The population grew too rapidly for a changing economy and state to contain; between 1520 and 1640, the population of England doubled. It appeared to the Puritans that the entire society had been thrown into disorder. There were just too many unemployed or underemployed people, too poor to marry and establish orderly families, wandering about. The Puritans called them "masterless men." At the same time, the rich seemed increasingly given to excessive display and lax morals. As the Puritans looked around, they saw a land filled with sinners, being led by a Church whose leadership itself was mired in sin. At a time when most parish priests were so poorly paid that they had to perform extra work on the side, the Archbishop of Canterbury was surrounded by a thousand retainers, half of them gentlemen dressed in gold.

The first order of business for the Puritans was to reform the Church of England. Once it became evident to them that the Church of England would resist further reformation and would continue moving away from the Calvinist principle of predestination, some of the Puritans began to make other plans.

The Pilgrim Colony at Plymouth

The first Puritan colony in North America was established in 1620 at Plymouth, by a group of Puritans known as the *Pilgrims.* While most Puritans hoped to reform the Church of England from within, the Pilgrims were *Separatists* who had given up all hope of changing the Church and instead were prepared to separate from it. The Pilgrims had already moved to Holland, thinking its Calvinist religion would offer them a better home. It was hard for the Pilgrims to fit themselves into Holland's highly structured economy, however, and they found their children seduced from strict religion by "the manifold temptations of the place."

By 1620 the Pilgrims were ready to accept the Virginia Company of London's offer to subsidize land it controlled to any English people who were willing to pay their own way to America. With the colony at Jamestown floundering, the Company was looking for other opportunities for profit. As far as the Company was concerned, the Pilgrims were just a group of settlers whose mission was to work for the Company and return a profit quickly. To that end, the Company filled out the two ships in the expedition, the *Mayflower* and the *Speedwell,* with non-Pilgrims who were willing to pay their own way, Separatists who had not gone to Holland, and the Pilgrims.

The *Speedwell* leaked so badly it had to turn back, but the *Mayflower* arrived at Plymouth, Massachusetts, in November 1620, far north of its destination, outside the jurisdiction of the Virginia Company. (Plymouth was actually within the jurisdiction of the Plymouth Company, which had financed voyages to North America in 1607 and 1608 and established a short-lived outpost at the mouth of the Kennebec River in Maine.) Because the Pilgrims had landed in territory to which the Virginia Company had no legal claim and hence no lawful government, all the adult men on board signed a document known as the *Mayflower Compact* before disembarking. The men thus bound themselves into a "Civil Body Politic" to make laws and govern the colony and also to recognize the authority of the governor.

Only one of the 102 passengers on the *Mayflower* had died *en route,* but only half of the party survived the harsh first winter. Years later the second governor, William Bradford, remembered the Pilgrims' arrival in a strange land and their early ordeals. The Indians, he claimed, were "savage barbarians . . . readier to fill their sides full of arrows than otherwise." And their new home was "a hideous and desolate wilderness, full of wild beasts and wild men."

In fact, the Plymouth Colony would never have survived had it not been for the assistance of several friendly Indians. Like the French in New France and in contrast to the English at Jamestown, the Pilgrims were able to establish effective diplomatic relations both because the Pilgrims were better diplomats and because the local Indians needed foreign allies more than the Powhatans had. Until perhaps a year or so before the Pilgrims' arrival, Plymouth Bay had been inhabited by as many as 2,000 Indians, with ten times as many in the surrounding region. Then European fishermen and traders introduced some fatal disease for which the Indians had no resistance, and it was carried as far as the trading network reached. In 1615, there had been between 20,000 and 25,000 Indians in the region between Penobscot Bay and Cape Cod. By the time the Pilgrims arrived, perhaps as few as one-tenth of them were still living, and one-time villages were filled with the skulls and bones of the unburied dead. So recently had Patuxet and Pokanoket Indians inhabited the region settled by the Pilgrims that the Pilgrims were able to supplement their meager supplies by rummaging Indian graves, homes, and hidden stores of grain.

The world was vastly changed for those Indians who survived. Squanto, a Patuxet warrior, had spent the plague years in Europe, having been kidnapped by an English ship's captain and taken to Spain to be sold as a slave. Rescued by Spanish priests, Squanto made it to London, where he began praising the virtues of his native land in the hopes that the English would take him home. Once back in Massachusetts, Squanto abandoned the English exploring party that had returned him. He found that the plague had sharply altered political relations in his native land. His own tribe, the Patuxet, had almost entirely disappeared. The once-powerful Pokanoket, led by Massasoit, were now paying tribute to the Narragansett, who had escaped the deadly disease. Squanto cast his lot with Massasoit, and they in turn decided that the English who arrived at Plymouth in November of 1620 might prove

Bartholomew Gosnold trading with the Indians of Martha's Vineyard, 1602. It was from trading encounters such as these that New England's Indians caught European diseases such as smallpox.

effective allies against the Narragansett. At least the Pilgrims demanded less corn in tribute. Thus in the spring of 1621, Squanto and Samoset, a member of another local band, turned up to offer the Pilgrims their assistance and showed them how to grow corn, using fish as fertilizer.

From the Indian perspective, this assistance was not so much an act of charity as a careful diplomatic initiative. The two Indians helped negotiate a treaty between the Pokanoket and the Pilgrims. Unlike the powerful Powhatan in Virginia, Massasoit agreed to submit himself to the English. By the time Squanto died of a fever in 1622, he had helped secure the future of the Plymouth Colony. On his deathbed, he asked Governor Bradford to "pray for him that he might go to the Englishman's God in heaven." It is impossible to know whether this was a sincere conversion or simply the last in a long series of brilliantly calculated acts of diplomacy.

Although the Pilgrim Colony at Plymouth survived, it grew slowly and proved a great disappointment to its investors, who eventually sold their shares to the Pilgrims. Plymouth remained a separate colony until 1691, when it was absorbed into Massachusetts, which was much larger and more influential. Socially much like the Massachusetts Bay Colony, Plymouth was economically somewhat less diverse, and religiously it was more alike than different. Plymouth, however, was politically insignificant because it was so much smaller. Yet its early success demonstrated that New England could be inhabited by Europeans. It also demonstrated that effective diplomatic relations with local Indians were critical for a colony's survival.

The Puritan Colony at Massachusetts Bay

Throughout the 1620s, other groups of English people attempted to found colonies in the region around Massachusetts. Most of them failed on their own, although one, Thomas Morton's community at Merry Mount, was actually crushed by other Englishmen, the Pilgrims at Plymouth. Morton and a handful of English servants had adopted Indian custom, drinking, "dancing and frisking" with the local Indian men and women. Having come 3,000 miles across an ocean to distance themselves from sin, the Pilgrims were not willing to tolerate such "licentiousness" in their back yard.

In 1629, the Massachusetts Bay Company, a group of London merchants, received a charter from King Charles I to establish a colony. The plan was similar to that on which Virginia had been founded. The investors in the joint-stock company would have full rights to a swath of land reaching from Massachusetts Bay west across the entire continent. Along with a number of Puritans who were looking for a new home, the company included some who still hoped, in the face of abundant evidence that it was impossible, to turn a profit from trade. Taking advantage of a loophole in the Company's charter, which failed to specify where its headquarters were to be, the Puritans plotted to take over the Company and move it to Massachusetts. Their objective was to make the colony entirely self-governing, with the directors of the Company and the governors of the colony being one and the same.

The expedition began in 1630, and by the end of that year Boston and ten other towns had been founded. By the early 1640s, between 20,000 and 25,000 Britons had migrated to the Puritan colonies of Plymouth, Massachusetts Bay, Connecticut, Rhode Island, and New Hampshire. Although fewer than half as many people migrated to New England as went to the Chesapeake, by 1660 both had populations of a similar size—around 35,000 (see Map 3-2).

New England was able to catch up and keep pace with the Chesapeake because of two factors. First, New England was, quite simply, a much healthier region than the Chesapeake, or England for that matter. The long, cold winters killed the mosquitoes that carried fatal diseases

A late-nineteenth-century sculpture of the Patuxet warrior, Squanto, who acted as an intermediary between the Indians and the Pilgrims.

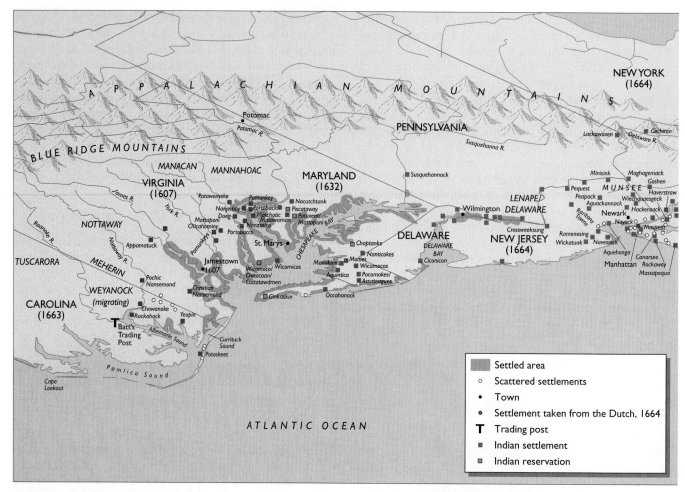

Map 3-2   The English Colonies, 1660.
By 1660, English settlements dotted the East Coast, but most of the population was concentrated in two regions: New England and the Chesapeake.
Source: Helen Hornbeck Tanner, ed., Settling North America (New York: Macmillan, 1995), 46–47.

such as malaria and yellow fever, the water supply was good, and food was plentiful. In fact, New Englanders, especially in the seventeenth century, proved remarkably long-lived. Men born in New England could expect to live into their early sixties, and women, their late fifties. Second, Puritans migrated as families. Ninety percent came as part of a family group, typically a nuclear family with the parents in their thirties. This pattern was almost exactly the reverse of that in the Chesapeake. In the healthy environment of New England, the population soon reproduced itself.

The Puritans had come to stay. Before leaving England, they had sold their property, never expecting to return. Most were prosperous members of the middle range of society. Many of the men were professionals—doctors, lawyers, and an extraordinary number of ministers (200 before 1660). Others were craftsmen of one sort or another. Generally, they came from one of two regions, either large cities or farming regions that encouraged individual initiative. By and large, the Puritans who migrated were people who were profiting from the changes in the

English economy of the late sixteenth and early seventeenth centuries. Once again, the contrast with the Chesapeake was dramatic. There, the vast majority of migrants were people with few skills and dim prospects. By no means were the Puritans forced to migrate by economic circumstances. By moving to Massachusetts, many of them traded a relatively high standard of living for one that was much lower.

The New England Way

The Puritans were men and women with a mission. Their first governor, John Winthrop, set out the vision of a Bible commonwealth in a lay sermon he preached aboard the *Arbella* in the spring of 1630, even before the ship carrying the Puritans to their new home docked at Boston. God, Winthrop said, had entered into a *covenant* with the Puritans, just as they had entered into a covenant with one another. Together they had taken enormous risks and entered into an extraordinary experiment to see whether they could establish a society based upon the word of God.

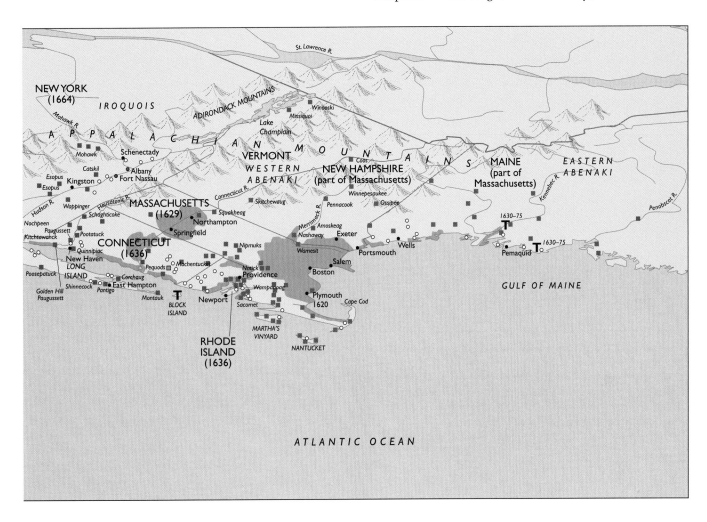

God—and the world—would judge them as a group. "We shall be as a city upon a hill, the eyes of all people are upon us. So that if we shall deal falsely with our God in this work we have undertaken, and so cause Him to withdraw his present help from us, we shall be made a story and a by-word through the world." If the Puritans failed, they would be the laughingstock of the entire world, but if they succeeded, God "shall make us a praise and glory, [so] that men shall say of other plantations: 'The Lord make it like that of New England.' " Although not all those who migrated to New England were Puritans, and there were significant variations among the Puritans themselves, this vision shaped the development of New England society and its political economy.

This communal vision made early New Englanders exceptionally cohesive. Each town was created by a grant of land by the Massachusetts General Court (the name given to the legislature) to a group of citizens. Typically, the settlers, in turn, entered into a covenant with one another to establish a government and distribute the land that they held collectively.

At first, the newly established towns divided up only a portion of the land that they held, reserving the rest for newcomers and the children of the original founders. The land was distributed unequally, according to social status and family size. Although in absolute terms New England society was relatively egalitarian with only a small gap between the richest and poorest, the Puritans set out to create a social hierarchy. As Winthrop explained, "God Almighty in His most holy and wise providence hath so disposed of the condition of mankind as in all times some must be rich, some poor; some high and eminent in power and dignity, others mean and in subjection." Social order required inequality, or, to be more precise, demanded that the Puritans recreate the hierarchy that they believed God had ordained. The rich and powerful were supposed to take care of those who were poor and powerless, and, indeed, Puritan towns developed mechanisms for assisting all those who could not care for themselves, such as the disabled, widows, and orphans. They were either given aid at home or placed in the homes of those who were more prosperous.

TABLE 3-2

Distribution of Land in Rowley, Massachusetts, 1639–1642

	Rowley, 1639-c. 1642
Acres	**No. of Grants**
over 400	
351–400	
301–350	
251–300	
201–250	1
151–200	1
101–150	
51–100	7
21–50	22
20 or less	63
no record	1
Total	95

Between 1639 and 1642, the town of Rowley, Massachusetts, distributed a little over 2,000 acres to 95 families—an average of just 23 acres per family, even though the grant to the town was for many thousand acres. Although most grants were for under 20 acres, some families received considerably more. The founders of Rowley wanted to recreate the hierarchical social order they had known in England.

Source: David Grayson Allen, In English Ways: The Movement of Societies and the Transferal of English Local Law and Custom to Massachusetts Bay in the Seventeenth Century (Chapel Hill: University of North Carolina Press, 1981), p. 32.

Each town administered itself through a town meeting, a gathering of the adult male property holders who met at least once and as many as a dozen times a year to attend to the town's business. In the interim, the town was governed by a small group of *selectmen* elected at the town meeting. In the past historians pointed to the democratic elements in the town meeting, finding in it the source of American democracy. More recently, historians have recognized the elements that remained undemocratic. Participation was restricted to adult male property holders, who were perhaps 70 percent of the men, but only 35 percent of the adult residents, once women are considered. (Many of the adult men who could not vote, however, were still living in the homes of their voting fathers.)

At least as significant as this statutory restriction upon participation were the customary ones. The habit of deference to those who were more powerful, prosperous, and educated was so strong that a small group of influential men tended to govern the towns year after year, and decade after decade. Moreover, Puritans abhorred conflict, which they thought was a symptom of the disorder that Adam and Eve brought into paradise with their original sin. It also reminded them of the England they had just left. Great social pressure was brought to bear to assure harmony and limit dissent.

If democracy means the right to disagree and majority rule in open elections, then the New England town meeting was not fully democratic, for it squelched dissent in order to achieve harmony. However, even with its formal restrictions on participation and informal ones on dissent, the New England town meeting was far more democratic than any form of government in England at the time. In England, the vast majority of men, not to mention women, were excluded from any form of participation in self-government.

Changing the Land to Fit the Political Economy

The Puritans' corporate social vision was generally compatible with a capitalist political economy. Although land was distributed to covenanted towns, once those towns transferred parcels of the land to individual farmers, the farmers were free to leave it to their heirs, to sell it to whomever they pleased, or to buy more land from others. Any improvements that people made on their land (from clearing away trees to building homes, fences, dams, or mills) remained the property of the owners. These practices were not exclusive to Puritans; they followed English law.

The contrast with Indian patterns of land use was dramatic. Local Indians held their land communally, not individually. When it was sold, the entire group had to consent to its transfer. Moreover, when Indians "sold" land to the Puritans, they thought that they were giving them the right to use the land only and to share the land with them. Hence the Puritans would be allowed to build a village, to plant, and to hunt, while the Indians retained their own village, fields, and hunting rights. In fact, Indians believed that they could sell their land (that is, the right to use the land) to several groups of Europeans at once.

The Puritans' notion of exclusive land rights was one of the cornerstones of their political economy. Because a man could profit from the improvements he and his family made on his land and because he could pass those on to his heirs, he had every incentive to make improvements that would increase the value of his land. Moreover, not only the land but its products became commodities to be sold. As in other areas where Europeans settled, the Puritans of New England turned their Indian neighbors into commercial hunters. For centuries, the Indians had taken only as many beaver as they needed, but soon they were overhunting, which led to the disappearance of beaver in the region. The Puritans themselves cleared the forests of trees. They found a ready market for timber in England, as New England's trees were much taller and straighter than any known in Europe at the time. The English navy came to depend on New England for its masts (see Figure 3-1).

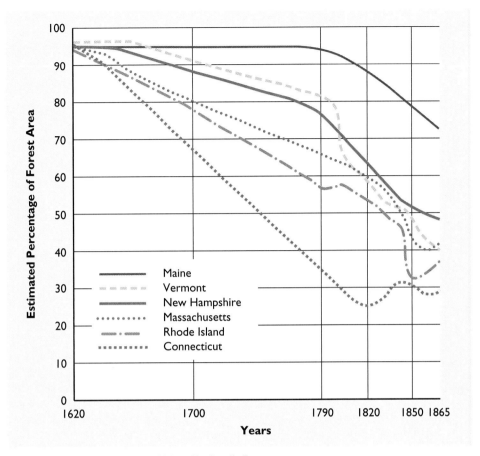

Figure 3-1 Disappearance of New England's Forests.

As the rate of settlement increased, the percentage of the land that was forested decreased.

Source: Carolyn Merchant, Ecological Revolutions: Nature, Gender, and Science in New England *(Chapel Hill: University of North Carolina Press, 1989), p. 225.*

In these ways, both Indians and Puritans turned the environment into commodities that could be sold for a price. This *commodification* of the environment led rapidly to its depletion. Although the bounty of the land had seemed limitless, by 1800 much of southern New England had been stripped of its forests and native animals such as deer, beaver, and turkey.

Prosperity did not come to Massachusetts immediately. For the first decade, the colony maintained a favorable balance of trade with England only by sending back the money that new immigrants brought with them in return for the goods imported from the mother country. New England's rocky soil meant that it would never develop a cash crop such as tobacco. In the 1640s and 1650s, the government tried to shape the economy by encouraging local manufacturing (to cut down on imports) and exporting local raw materials. Through a combination of government policy and individual initiative, New England eventually found that it could make a profit from selling timber, wood products, and fish and by acting as merchants. While most New Englanders remained farmers, soon Boston and Salem developed a thriving merchant class.

The Puritan Family

The cohesiveness of Puritan society was nurtured in the family. Like most early modern western Europeans, Puritans thought of the family as the society in microcosm. As they put it, "a familie is a little Church, and a little commonwealth." There was no sharp distinction between home and the wider world, and in fact, most of the social services that are now provided outside the home were delivered within the confines of the Puritan household. Although Harvard College was founded in 1636 (to train ministers) and the General Court of Massachusetts established a system of public education in 1647, most early instruction and virtually all vocational teaching took place at home. Indeed, parents were required to teach their children to read the Bible. By the age of seven or so, girls began to learn how to perform household tasks from their mothers, and boys learned their fathers' crafts or occupations.

The family was also a place of business, as it was at the center of the Puritans' economy. Farmers, of course, worked at home, as did almost all craftsmen. Men had

New England's landscape, before and after. The illustration on the left shows what New England's forests looked like before the land was cleared for planting. The illustration on the right shows how it looked after the land had been cleared and planted.

responsibility for the exterior of the household, including the fields, livestock, and tools. Women also performed tasks critical to the economic survival of the family. They were in charge of the preservation and preparation of all food and clothing, from the brewing of beer to the slaughtering of pigs. Although tasks were assigned by gender, in the absence of her husband a woman could assume his responsibilities, selling the products he had made or even picking up a gun to fight off Indians. The family, like society, was a hierarchy, with the husband at the top, and his wife just below him as his "deputy."

Because the patterns of authority that prevailed in society were replicated, and nurtured, in the family, the family could perform a variety of functions for society. Those who had no other home or place in society, such as those too poor or weak to support themselves, orphans, and even criminals, were assigned to live in a family. Even Puritans who could afford to care for their own children sometimes sent them into other homes, perhaps because they believed that other parents might be better disciplinarians than they could be. Puritans considered excessive affection and particularly excessive maternal love a danger. Those children who remained in their parents' household were subjected to strict discipline not out of cruelty, but from the deepest and most sincere religious convictions. Puritans lived in fear of lawlessness, and they used the family as an instrument of order. Neither conflict nor disobedience was tolerated, and the Puritan household achieved an extraordinary harmony. Considering that Puritan women bore on average eight or nine children, almost all of whom survived infancy, and that families were confined in small houses over long New England winters, this harmony was probably necessary for survival.

Despite the premium placed on control, Puritan households were hardly prisons. If Puritans believed that

men were the natural heads of the household and that women bore particular responsibility for Eve's original sin, they also believed that both men and women were equally capable of preparing for and receiving God's grace. Puritans distrusted the passion of love, because they thought it could lead to impulsiveness and disorder. They had great respect, however, for the natural affection that grew between a man and a woman over the course of their marriage. The poems of Anne Bradstreet and the letters that John Winthrop exchanged with his wife give ample testimony to the Puritan capacity for love.

So successful were the early Puritans in establishing tight-knit communities organized around church and meeting that only two years after the Great Migration to America had begun, the Reverend Thomas Welde could write proudly back to England that "here I find three great blessings, peace, plenty, and health. . . . I profess if I might have my wish in what part of the world to dwell I know no other place on the whole globe of the earth where I would be rather than here. We say to our friends that doubt this, Come and see and taste."

Dissension in the Puritan Ranks

It is not surprising that a society that took its religious beliefs so seriously should have spawned dissent within and conflict with external enemies. The Puritan movement was itself a product of dissent. Moreover, it embodied tensions that inevitably made for individual and social turmoil. Puritans had difficulty finding a balance between emotion and intellect, between the individual and the community,

GROWING UP IN AMERICA

Childhood in Puritan New England

Puritans believed that children were little Adams and Eves, born sinners. As the poet Anne Bradstreet put it:

Stained from birth with *Adams* sinfull fact
Thence I began to sin as soon as act:
A perverse will, a love to what's forbid,
A serpent's sting in pleasing face lay hid.

It was the parents' job to break that will, and when a child began to assert its will, typically at the age we still recognize as "the terrible twos," parents believed that they were now entering into combat with Satan for the child's soul. A parent (and it could be either the mother or father) might let a child cry until she fell asleep or sternly refuse to hug a child until he became compliant. On occasion, food might even be withheld from a disobedient child until she was perfectly submissive. Likewise, even very small children were lectured about the fires of hell that awaited the disobedient.

When Betty Sewall was eight years old, her father asked her to read to the family a Bible passage that described in vivid detail God's punishment of sinners. She began sobbing, and her father cried with her. Seven years later, Betty showed signs of "dejection and sorrow," and one evening, after dinner, she burst into tears. She told her mother that she was "afraid she should go to Hell, her Sins were not pardon'd." Her mother asked her if she prayed, and she replied that she did, but that she "feared her prayers were not heard." For almost a year, Betty remained deeply dejected. She was convinced that she was a sinner who "Loved not God's people as she should." She told her father about "the various temptations she had." She no longer could read the comforting passages in the Bible, the ones that spoke of God's love, without weeping. Betty's dejection passed, and three years later at the age of eighteen she married. As she lay on her deathbed, at the age of 35, a mother with eight children, her father prayed with her, telling her that "when my flesh and my heart faileth me, God is the strength of my heart and my portion forever." She took comfort from his words, telling him, "I am just a-going."

---

between spiritual equality and social hierarchy, between the anxiety of not knowing for certain if you were saved and the self-satisfaction of thinking yourself one of a chosen people.

Furthermore, the Puritans had no mechanisms for channeling or accommodating dissent. For a Puritan, the greatest sin of all was disobedience. Any act of dissent was interpreted as a replay of Adam and Eve's original sin, further proof of humanity's inherent sinfulness. The migration to a new and strange land, populated by people they thought of as savages, as well as the pressure of thinking that the whole world was watching them, only increased the Puritans' desire to maintain a strict order.

Roger Williams and Toleration

The Massachusetts Bay Colony was only a year old when trouble appeared in the person of Roger Williams, a brilliant, sweet-tempered, and rather obstinate young minister. No sooner had he landed than he announced that he was really a Separatist and would not accept appointment at a church unless it repudiated its ties to the Church of England. Williams and his wife found even the Pilgrims at Plymouth insufficiently Separatist for their taste. Massachusetts Bay was already walking a fine line between outward obedience to the laws of England and inner rejection of the English way of life. The leaders of the colony considered an explicit repudiation of England's established church an act of political suicide.

Without a church of his own, Williams simply began preaching to those who would listen, finding a receptive audience especially among devout women. Saying that the king had no right to grant land owned by the Indians, he questioned the validity of the Massachusetts charter and even said he intended to raise the issue with the king. He also argued for a strict separation of church and state and a strict separation of the regenerate (those who had had a conversion experience) and the unconverted. Williams went so far as to advocate religious toleration, with each congregation or sect governing itself completely free from state interference.

These doctrines were heresy to the Puritan church and state both. Williams was summoned before the colonial magistrates a number of times. In 1635 when he violated an order to stop preaching his unorthodox views, the magistrates decided to ship him immediately to England, where

This house, built in Dedham, Massachusetts in 1636 (with several additions in the eighteenth century), had four rooms, two upstairs and two downstairs. Like most early New England homes, it was dark, both inside and out, with few windows to let cold air—or light—into the dwelling.

he might be imprisoned or executed for his religious notions. John Winthrop, who genuinely liked Williams, warned him of his impending fate, which gave Williams the opportunity to sneak away to Narragansett Bay, outside the jurisdiction of Massachusetts Bay. Some of Williams' followers joined him, and they established the new colony of Rhode Island, which received a charter in 1644. (By that time, the Puritan revolution, which had begun in England in 1642, had put into power officials who were more sympathetic to Williams than King Charles would have been.) The colony soon became a refuge for dissenters of all sorts, although the Puritans of Massachusetts referred to it as "the sewer of New England."

Anne Hutchinson and the Equality of Believers

No sooner had Williams been exiled than Massachusetts was ripped by another religious controversy, this one caused by an outspoken and brilliant woman. One of Puritanism's many tensions concerned the position of women. By insisting upon the equality of all true believers before God and the importance of marriage, Protestantism and especially its Puritan branch undermined the starkly negative image of women that prevailed in sixteenth-century Europe. When Puritan ministers preached that women and men were both "joynt Heirs of salvation" and that women, rather than being a "necessary evil," were in fact "a necessary good," they were directly criticizing both the Catholic legacy and common folk belief. According to

Catholic doctrine, it was better for a man to marry than burn eternally in hell for committing fornication, but it was better still to lead a celibate life as a priest. Even Queen Elizabeth's Anglican Bishop told her, in language that came directly from folk culture, that

> Women are of two sorts: some of them are wiser, better learned, discreeter, and more constant than a number of men; but another and worse sort of them are fond, foolish, wanton, flibbergibs, tattlers, triflers, wavering, witless, without council, feeble, careless, rash, proud, dainty, tale-bearers, eavesdroppers, rumour-raisers, evil-tongued, worse-minded, and in everyway doltified with the dregs of the devil's dunghill.

At the same time that Puritanism extended women respect, it also insisted that they must be subordinate to men. In Puritan society, every one and every thing had its place in the elaborate hierarchy, and woman's position, according to the Puritan ministry, was clearly beneath that of man. "Though she be . . . a Mistress, yet she owns that she has a Master." It was never easy, however, for Puritanism to find the balance between women's spiritual equality and their earthly subordination. Hence, although most Puritan women were deferential to male authority, others took advantage of the opportunity that Puritanism seemed to offer. Without exception, the Puritan authorities put them back in their place.

Anne Hutchinson was just over 40 when she, her husband, and their 12 surviving children followed the Reverend John Cotton to Massachusetts Bay. Cotton was an especially popular preacher who placed particular emphasis upon the doctrine of predestination. Hutchinson pushed that doctrine to its perhaps logical, if unsettling, conclusion. The daughter of an Anglican minister who had been imprisoned for his Puritan beliefs, Hutchinson claimed that she had experienced several direct revelations, one telling her to follow Cotton to Boston. John Winthrop, who despised her ideas, described her as "a woman of a ready wit and bold spirit." At informal Bible discussion meetings at her Boston home, which even the new governor, Henry Vane, attended, Hutchinson challenged the Puritan doctrine of "preparation." If God had truly chosen those whom He would save well before they were born, it was unnecessary for Puritans to prepare themselves for saving grace by leading sin-free lives. Nor was good behavior, which Puritans called *sanctification*, a reliable sign that a person had been saved. It was not that Hutchinson favored sin. She simply thought that her neighbors and especially some of the leading ministers were deluding themselves into thinking that good works would get them into heaven. Hence, she accused them of the heresy of Arminianism. For her part, by claiming that the Holy Spirit spoke directly to her, Hutchinson opened herself to charges of another heresy, *antinomianism.*

Hutchinson's views became extremely popular, especially among the more prosperous residents of Boston, who were beginning to resent communal control of their business practices. In fact, probably a majority of the colony's residents became Hutchinson followers. The orthodox leaders of the colony, however, were troubled by Hutchinson's doctrines, especially when she named particular ministers whom she considered unconverted.

Hutchinson's opponents mounted a careful campaign against her. In 1637 they moved the site of the election for governor outside Boston, where her strength was greatest, so that John Winthrop could win. Thereupon, both church and state moved against her and her allies. In November, after her most prominent ally among the ministers had already been banished, Hutchinson was put on trial for slandering the ministry. She almost surely would have been acquitted had she not asserted that God had revealed to her that He would punish her persecutors. This was heresy, and a dangerous one at that. The Puritans believed divine revelations had stopped in biblical times. Who knew what kinds of disorder lay ahead if men and especially women were claiming that they were getting direct messages from God? Hutchinson was convicted and ordered to leave the colony. Followed by 80 other families, Hutchinson and her family found refuge in Roger Williams' Rhode Island. A few years later, after the death of her husband, Hutchinson and six of her children pushed on to Westchester County, New York, then part of the New Netherland Colony. In 1643 all but the youngest child were killed by Indians, casualties in an Indian war.

Although any man who had challenged Puritan doctrine the way Anne Hutchinson did would have faced trial and exile also, the fact that these ideas came from a woman made them even more dangerous to the Massachusetts leadership. John Winthrop called her an "American Jesabel" and suggested that she might be a witch. Without any evidence at all of sexual misconduct, ministers such as John Cotton asserted that Hutchinson and her female followers were driven by lust and that unless they were punished, "That filthie sinne of the Communitie of Woemen and all promiscuous and filthie cominge togeather of men and Woemen without Distinction or Relation of Marriage, will necessarily follow." Puritan leaders simply assumed that whenever women challenged authority it must lead to communal living, open sex, and the repudiation of marriage.

It is sometimes asserted that Puritans came to New England in search of religious freedom, but they never would have made that claim themselves. They wanted the liberty to follow their own religion but actively denied that opportunity to others. As Nathaniel Ward put it in 1647, "All Familists, Antinomians, Anabaptists, and other Enthusiasts shall have free Liberty to keep away from us, and such as will come to be gone as soon as they can, the sooner the better." At the same time that Puritans felt a strong sense of obligation to their own, they insisted upon their right to keep out nonbelievers. "No man hath right to come into us," John Winthrop wrote, "without our consent."

Puritan Indian Policy and the Pequot War

Perhaps it was coincidence that all of the Puritan dissidents, despite the great diversity of their religious beliefs, were critical of the Puritans' Indian policy. Thomas Morton had been "frisking" with the Indians, Roger Williams insisted upon purchasing land from them instead of simply seizing it, and the men in the Hutchinson family refused to fight in the Pequot War of 1637. The Puritans had been extremely fortunate in beginning their settlement in a region whose Indian population had recently been decimated and in having the English-speaking Squanto walk into their camp offering his diplomatic services. The Puritan communities expanded so rapidly, however, that they were soon intruding upon land populated by Indians who had no intention of giving New Englanders exclusive rights to it.

Within a few years of the founding of the Massachusetts Bay Colony, small groups of Puritans were spreading out in all directions (see Map 3-3). The Reverend John Wheelwright, who had been Anne Hutchinson's brother-in-law and most ardent supporter, took a party into what is now New Hampshire. Others settled in Maine. Massachusetts claimed all of this land. In 1638, New Haven, Connecticut, was founded by the Reverend John Davenport and a London merchant, Theophilus Eaton, who had arrived in Boston in the middle of the antinomian controversy and decided to look for a more peaceful place to settle. The New Haven group purchased the land for their town from the local Indians. Four years earlier, the first Puritan settlers had reached the banks of the Connecticut River in western Massachusetts. In 1636 the Reverend

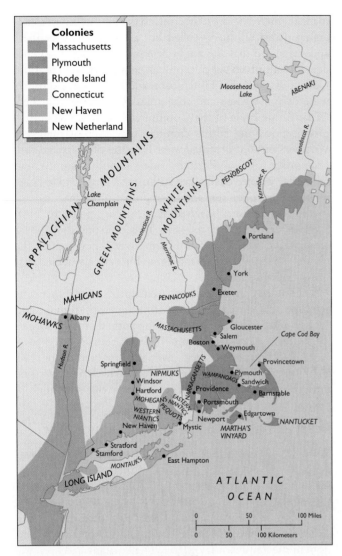

Map 3-3   New England in the 1640s.
This map shows the land settled by each of the New England colonies, the regions inhabited by Indian tribes, and the region of Dutch settlement.
Source: John Murrin et. al., Liberty, Equality, Power (Harcourt College Publishers, 1st ed., 1995), p. 73.

Thomas Hooker led his followers to Hartford. Many were drawn by the more fertile soil of the region, although Hooker himself had some religious differences with the leading ministers of Boston. Hooker made it easier to become a church member, while Davenport, down the river, was tightening up the requirements for membership. Puritan Congregationalism inevitably encouraged individual ministers and their followers to interpret church teachings in a variety of ways.

The Pequot War grew out of conflicts among Europeans about who would govern the Connecticut River valley and among Indians about who would trade with the Europeans. Until the arrival of the English in Massachusetts, the Dutch had controlled the trade along the Con-

necticut River. They had granted trading privileges to the Pequots, which frustrated all the other tribes who had access to the Dutch only through these middlemen. When the English appeared on the scene, the Pequots' enemies attempted to attract them to the valley, as trading rivals to the Dutch. The Pequots, afraid of losing their lock on the trade with Europeans, then made the mistake of inviting Massachusetts Bay to establish a trading post in the region. They were playing a dangerous game, counting on their ability to control not only their Indian enemies but the Dutch and English as well.

As hundreds of settlers led by Thomas Hooker, instead of just the few traders they expected, poured in, the Pequots became alarmed. They appealed to their one-time enemies, the Narragansetts, to join with them to get rid of the English because they were "strangers" who would soon deprive them of their land "if they were suffered to grow and increase." The Narragansetts, however, had already been approached by the Puritans at Massachusetts to join them in fighting the Pequots. That is where the Narragansetts calculated that their long-term advantage lay.

It was not, however, the Pequots who initiated the war. They were caught in a rivalry between the parent colony at Massachusetts and the new offshoot in Connecticut, both of which wanted to dominate the Pequots' land. The Connecticut group struck first, acting to avenge an attack by the Pequots, which in itself was in revenge for an attack upon their allies. At dawn on May 26, 1637, a party of 90 Connecticut men accompanied by 500 Narragansett allies attacked a Pequot village at Mystic. It was filled with women, children, and old men. As the raiders knew, most of the warriors were away from home. As his men

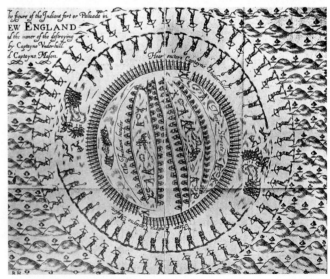

The Attack on Mystic Fort. *On the inner ring are the New Englanders, attacking the palisaded Indian village.*

encircled the village, the commander, Captain John Mason, set a torch to the wigwams, shouting, "We must burn them." Those Pequots who escaped the fire ran into the ring of waiting Englishmen. In an hour, all but seven of the Pequots were dead. Mason's party had killed between 300 and 700 Indians, while losing only two of their own men. The Narragansetts' allies were so horrified by the brutality of the attack that they refused to participate in it.

Deeply demoralized, the remainder of the Pequot tribe was easily defeated. Several hundred more were either killed or sold to the West Indies as slaves. By 1638, the Puritans could declare the Pequot tribe dissolved. Although Massachusetts Bay and Connecticut had joined forces to defeat the Pequots, and they read the victory as a sign of God's favor, by 1639 Connecticut had established its dominance over the Pequots' land. In that year Connecticut established its own government, modeled after that of Massachusetts. In 1662, after the restoration of the British monarchy, it became a royal colony.

CHRONOLOGY

1533	Henry VIII breaks with Roman Catholic Church, establishes Church of England
1603	Queen Elizabeth I dies, succeeded by James I
1606	James I grants two charters for North American settlement to Virginia Company
1607	English found Jamestown
1608	John Smith named President of Virginia's Council
1609	John Smith returns to England
1610–1614	First Anglo-Powhatan War
1612–1617	John Rolfe develops a marketable strain of tobacco
1614	John Rolfe and Pocahontas marry
1616	Virginia Company offers 50-acre headrights to each immigrant
1619	First meeting of Virginia General Assembly
	First Africans arrive in Virginia
	Virginia Company pays for transportation of women to Virginia
1620	Pilgrims found colony at Plymouth; Mayflower Compact signed
1622–1632	Second Anglo-Powhatan War
1624	Virginia Company dissolved; Virginia becomes a royal colony
1625	James I dies, succeeded by Charles I
1629	Massachusetts Bay Company receives charter to establish colony in North America
1630	Massachusetts Bay Colony founded
1632	George Calvert receives charter for Maryland
1636	Harvard College founded
	Roger Williams exiled from Massachusetts
1637	Anne Hutchinson and her followers exiled
	Pequot War
1638	New Haven founded
1639	First law mentioning slavery, in Maryland
	Connecticut establishes its government
1642–1647	English Revolution
1644	Rhode Island receives charter
1644–1646	Third Anglo-Powhatan War
1647	Massachusetts establishes system of public education
1649	Charles I beheaded
	Act of Toleration passed in Maryland
1660	Restoration of English monarchy; Charles II crowned king
1661	First Virginia law mentioning slavery
1662	Connecticut becomes a royal colony
1691	Plymouth Colony absorbed into Massachusetts

Conclusion

At the middle of the seventeenth century, the New England and Chesapeake colonies could hardly have appeared more different. Although the forces of capitalism shaped each region, other factors left their distinctive imprint: the objectives of the founders, disease environment, demographic patterns, and relations with local Indians. In 1660, both regions had about 35,000 inhabitants, but the colonies of New England were much more settled. As much as anything else, the early history of New England was shaped by the extraordinary energy and cohesiveness of Puritan society. In fact, the cohesiveness of the New England colonies, their early success, and their great economic and social stability make them almost unique in the history of colonial ventures throughout the world. If New England achieved settlement within a few years, unsettlement was the norm. That surely was the case in New Spain, New France, and New Netherland, which all bore the marks of rough, frontier societies for many decades. It was particularly true of the Chesapeake colonies, which were still raw colonial outposts, disproportionately populated by aggressive young men long after New England had achieved a secure and gratifying order.

All of the North American colonies were outposts in the global political economy, created to enrich their mother countries and enhance their power. The New England colonies were the striking exceptions. Indeed, had the Virginia Company known that the founders of Massachusetts wanted to create a religious refuge rather than a money-making venture, it probably would not have given them a charter. So successful was New England in achieving a stable society that we sometimes forget that it was the exception and not the rule.

Review Questions

1. What were the objectives of the founders of Virginia? Why did the colony survive, in spite of poor planning?

2. What were the objectives of the founders of the Puritan colonies at Plymouth and Massachusetts Bay? Compare the early years of these colonies to those of the Virginia colony?

3. What place did gender play in the social order of the Chesapeake and New England colonies? Compare and contrast family life in the two regions.

4. Compare and contrast relations with the Indians in the Chesapeake and New England.

5. Compare and contrast the social order in the Chesapeake and New England.

Further Readings

Kathleen M. Brown, *Good Wives, Nasty Wenches, and Anxious Patriarchs* (1996). A provocative interpretation of colonial Virginia that puts gender at the center.

William Cronon, *Changes in the Land: Indians, Colonists, and the Ecology of New England* (1983). A comparison of the ways that Indians and New Englanders used, lived off, and changed the land.

John Demos, *A Little Commonwealth: Family Life in Plymouth Colony* (1970). Brief and beautifully written, this book helped revolutionize the writing of American social history by showing how much could be learned about ordinary people from a sensitive reading of a wide variety of sources.

Jack P. Greene, *Pursuits of Happiness: The Social Development of Early Modern British Colonies and the Formation of American Culture* (1988). An interpretive overview of colonial development that argues that the Chesapeake was the most American region of all.

Ivor Noël Hume, *The Virginia Adventure: Roanoke to James Towne: An Archaeological and Historical Odyssey* (1994). A detailed and well-written history of the early Chesapeake settlements with a focus on archaeology.

Stephen Innes, *Creating the Commonwealth: The Economic Culture of Puritan New England* (1995). Argues that the Puritans were capitalists.

Francis Jennings, *The Invasion of America: Indians, Colonialism, and the Cant of Conquest* (1975). A highly critical history of Puritan Indian policy that may be read along with Alden T. Vaughan, *New England Frontier: Puritans and Indians, 1620–1675* (1979), which is more sympathetic to the Puritans.

Karen Ordahl Kupperman, *Indians and English: Facing Off in Early America* (2000). An insightful account of the encounter between Indians and English along the Atlantic coast in the seventeenth century, emphasizing mutual attempts—and failures—at understanding.

Edmund S. Morgan, *American Slavery, American Freedom: The Ordeal of Colonial Virginia* (1975). A powerful and magnificently written history of Virginia that argues that racism was intentionally cultivated by elites to keep poor blacks and whites from uniting.

Edmund S. Morgan, *Visible Saints: The History of a Puritan Idea* (1963). A brilliant explanation of one of Puritanism's key ideas.

History on the Internet

"Religion and the Founding of the American Republic. America as a Religious Refuge: The Seventeenth Century"

http://lcweb.loc.gov/exhibits/religion/rel01.html

Through this Library of Congress website, discover the role of religion in the founding of the New England colonies. This site details the religious persecution religious "nonconformists" experienced in their European homelands and the promise of religious freedom the New World held out to these men and women.

"From Indentured Servitude to Racial Slavery"

http://www.pbs.org/wgbh/aia/part1/1narr3.html

Read about Virginia's recognition of slavery, slave codes, and the need for African slave labor. The site also contains scholarly commentary on the earliest African Americans and their experiences.

CREATING THE EMPIRE

1660-1720

OUTLINE

Tituba Shapes Her World and Saves Herself

The Plan of Empire
Turmoil in England
The Political Economy of Mercantilism

New Colonies, New Patterns
New Netherland Becomes New York
Diversity and Prosperity in Pennsylvania
Indians and Africans in the Political Economy of Carolina
The Barbados Connection

The Transformation of Virginia
Social Change in Virginia
Bacon's Rebellion and the Abandonment of the Middle Ground
Virginia Becomes a Slave Society

New England Under Assault
Social Prosperity and the Fear of Religious Decline
King Philip's War
Indians and the Empire

The Empire Strikes
The Dominion of New England
The Glorious Revolution— in Britain and America
The Rights of Englishmen
Conflict in the Empire

Massachusetts in Crisis
The Social and Cultural Contexts of Witchcraft
Witchcraft at Salem
The End of Witchcraft

French and Spanish Outposts
France Attempts an Empire
The Spanish Outpost in Florida

Conquest, Revolt, and Reconquest in New Mexico
The Conquest of Pueblo Society
The Pueblo Revolt
Reconquest and the Creation of Spanish Colonial Society

Conclusion

Tituba Shapes Her World and Saves Herself

Her name was Tituba. Some say she was African, a Yoruba. Others believe that she was an Arawak Indian from Guyana. Had she not been accused of practicing witchcraft in Salem, Massachusetts, in 1692, she surely would have been forgotten by history. Now, more than three centuries later, the record is dim. Her name appears on a list of slave children owned by a Barbados planter in 1677. Whether she came from South America or Africa, she had been torn away from her home and sent to work on a sugar plantation on the Caribbean Island that the English had colonized almost fifty years before. In those years, the English were enslaving small numbers of Arawaks from the northern coast of South America. The peaceful habits of the Arawaks and their domestic skills made them good house servants, while their alliance with the Dutch, who were at war with the English, made them vulnerable to English raiders. Sugar planters preferred African slaves, however, and by the 1670s they were importing 1,300 of them each year onto the tiny island in order to feed Europe's insatiable appetite for sugar. By 1680, the African population of Barbados, at 37,000, was more than twice that of the European. Whatever her origins, Tituba lived in an African-majority society and absorbed African customs.

Tituba was still young, probably a teenager, when she was taken, once again as a slave, to a new home in Massachusetts in 1680. She had been purchased by a young, Harvard-educated Barbadian, Samuel Parris. Parris' father had failed as a planter, and now his son was about to meet the same fate as a merchant in Boston. Both planting and commerce were risky ventures, at the mercy of both the market and luck. Tituba found herself in Salem because of the market: Barbados planters wanted field hands and house servants, and now a failed merchant, Samuel Parris, abandoned commerce for the ministry. In 1689 Parris moved his wife, their three children, Tituba, and her slave husband John Indian to Salem Village, where he had been appointed minister.

Three years later, all of their lives changed forever when one of Parris' daughters, Betty, and her cousin Abigail followed the old folk custom of trying to see their futures in the white of an egg dropped into a glass of water. Soon several girls and young women were playing with magic. Then Betty began to experience strange and seemingly inexplicable pains, which soon spread to some of the others. When neither doctors nor ministers could make the pains go away, a neighbor woman asked Tituba, the family cook, to bake a "witchcake" out of rye flour and the girls' urine. This was a piece of "white magic," intended to uncover the identity of the witch who must have been bewitching Betty and the others. Their suffering, however, only got worse. Parris now questioned the girls closely: Who was bewitching them? This time the girls had an answer: two older, rather marginal white women—and Tituba.

The three women found themselves facing a panel of magistrates, charged with the capital offense of witchcraft. Under duress, the first woman, Sarah Good, reluctantly implicated the second, Sarah Osborne. When Osborne was examined, she steadfastly denied her guilt—and was promptly returned to jail. Finally, Tituba was summoned. As a slave, she was particularly vulnerable. Perhaps calculating the odds carefully, Tituba slowly began to embroider a story. She named only two names—Sarah Good and Sarah Osborne. She talked about a tall,

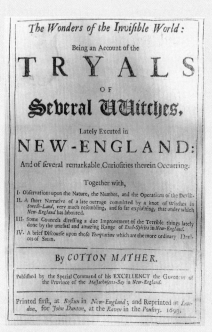

The Reverend Cotton Mather's account of Salem's witchcraft panic was published only a year after the events.

white-haired man in Boston who made her sign a mysterious book and of conspiring with other witches (unnamed) to afflict the girls.

For two days, Tituba answered the magistrates' questions. Evidently responding to the hints of her Puritan interrogators, Tituba confirmed that she had entered into a covenant with the Devil, the tall man in Boston. But she also added elements that, while foreign to English culture, were common in both African and Indian societies, such as a "thing all over hairy, all the face harye & a long nose . . . & is about two or three feet high." Tituba's elaborate tales of witches' meetings, of flying to Boston on a broomstick, of wolves and birds and hairy imps persuaded her interrogators that their colony was beset by witches. A children's game of fortune telling soon spiraled into a witchcraft panic. Tituba, however, escaped with her life. Having spent most of her life as a prisoner in other people's lands, she had combined their cultures with her own, crafting them into a strategy for survival.

Colonial America in the second half of the seventeenth century was still a world shaped by conflicting cultures and crossing economic currents. In some ways, Tituba was a victim of political economy. She found herself in Salem because Samuel Parris' father failed as a planter and Parris himself failed as a merchant. Neither was able to succeed in the global economy. Tituba's freedom was sacrificed so that other, more powerful people could become prosperous. But by melding her own culture and those of her captors, Tituba was able to save herself when the dislocations of the late-seventeenth century brought her to the Salem meetinghouse to face accusations of witchcraft. Though more dramatic, Tituba's story is like that of many late-seventeenth-century Americans. Caught in the cross-currents of culture and economic transformation, they adapted their cultural inheritances to new circumstances. ∎

The Plan of Empire

Trying to make sense out of the haphazard development of Britain's American colonies, the English political theorist Edmund Burke explained in 1757, "The settlement of *our* colonies was never pursued upon any regular plan; but they were formed, grew, and flourished, as accidents, the nature of the climate, or the dispositions of private men happened to operate." Although Burke exaggerated for effect, in comparison with the tight direction the Spanish and French governments gave their overseas colonies, the English government had comparatively little to do with the shape that the colonies ultimately took. "Nothing of an enlarged and legislative spirit appears in the planning of *our* colonies." As expressions of Britain's political economy, all of the colonies were private ventures, by individuals or groups, chartered by the British government but given very little supervision and virtually nothing in the way of material support. So long as the mainland colonies contributed little to the national wealth and cost the government less, the government was willing to exercise only the loosest of controls and permit each of the colonial societies to develop in its own way.

Turmoil in England

In the middle decades of the seventeenth century, the British government was thrown into turmoil as Parliament and the king struggled over the future direction of the nation. Two fundamental and overlapping issues were at stake, religion and royal power. The uneasy balance that Elizabeth I had established between Puritan religious reformers and more conservative Anglicans collapsed under her successors, James I (1603–1625) and Charles I (1625–1649). Archbishop of Canterbury William Laud moved the Church of England away from the Calvinist belief in predestination, brought back worship ceremonies that smacked of Catholicism, and persecuted Puritans. His imposition of these forms of worship on Presbyterian Scotland prompted a revolt in that part of the empire and led directly to political crisis.

All wars cost a great deal of money to wage, but Parliament refused to appropriate the funds that Charles requested. Instead, in 1628, Parliament passed the Petition of Right. It reasserted those freedoms that Britons had come to hold dear, including no taxation except by act of Parliament, no arbitrary arrest or imprisonment, and no quartering of soldiers in private homes. After years of stalemate, in 1642 Charles raised an army and moved against the recalcitrant members of Parliament, beginning the English Civil War, which concluded in 1647 with the victory of Parliament. Two years later, Charles was executed, by beheading. Oliver Cromwell, a Puritan, ruled as Lord Protector until his death in 1658. When his son and successor proved an inept leader, in 1660 Charles II was invited to reclaim the British Crown.

Oliver Cromwell, a Puritan and military leader of the English Revolution, ruled as Lord Protector until his death in 1658. Notice the Bible clutched in his hand.

Although the monarchy had been restored, its authority had been diminished. Britain had been transformed into a constitutional monarchy in which the power of the Crown was balanced by that of Parliament. In addition, Britain once again found a middle way between a Calvinist Protestantism and Catholicism. When the Catholic king James II (1685–1688) tried to fill the government with his Catholic supporters and attempted to rule without the consent of Parliament, he was removed in a bloodless revolution, known as the Glorious Revolution (1688). It brought Mary, James' Protestant daughter, and her equally Protestant husband, William of Orange (Holland) to the throne.

The Political Economy of Mercantilism

After the restoration of the British monarchy in 1660 and the reassertion of Parliament's authority in 1688, the British state became increasingly strong and centralized. Britain then embarked upon a course that would make it the world's most powerful nation by the early nineteenth century.

Throughout the political turmoil of the seventeenth century, Britain's economic policies were guided by a theory called **mercantilism.** This theory held that the chief object of a nation's economic policies was to serve the state, rather than, for example, particular interests within the nation or its inhabitants in general. Mercantilism developed just at the time that the European nation-states were consolidating, and it was designed to facilitate that process. The new nations required vast amounts of money to support their growing bureaucracies and the armies and navies. Mercantilism's theorists considered the economy and politics both as zero-sum games; one side's gain could come only by another's loss. Mercantilism defined wealth exclusively as hard money, that is, gold and silver. Since there was only a finite amount of gold and silver in the world, a nation could best improve its position by capturing a share of other nations' money. Mercantilism thus led naturally to rivalries with other nations. Its chief expression was the regulation of foreign trade.

Between 1651 and 1696, the British government, following mercantilist theories, passed a series of trade regulations known as the Navigation Acts. These acts required that all goods shipped to England and to her colonies be carried in ships owned and manned by Englishmen (including colonists). In addition, all foreign goods going to the colonies had to be shipped via Britain, where they could be taxed. Certain colonial products (tobacco, sugar, indigo, and cotton, with others added later) had to be sent first to England before they could be shipped elsewhere. According to mercantilist doctrine, the mother country was supposed to supply finished products, and the colonies were to supply raw materials. Hence, when the colonies began to manufacture items such as woolen cloth and hats, Parliament passed legislation to restrict those

industries. Historians disagree on how much these regulations helped or hurt the colonies. They probably stimulated the New England ship-building industry, while limiting the profits of Chesapeake tobacco planters.

New Colonies, New Patterns

In the absence of tight control by the English government, each colony developed in a different direction. In the second half of the seventeenth century, two important new colonies, Pennsylvania and South Carolina, were established, and New Netherland was seized from the Dutch. Each colony followed its own plan, and each developed in distinctive ways. As a rule, the most successful colonies were those that offered the most opportunity to free white people and the greatest amount of religious toleration.

New Netherland Becomes New York

By the middle of the seventeenth century, the British were ready to challenge their chief trade rival, the Dutch. The two nations fought three wars, the Anglo-Dutch Wars, between 1652 and 1674, and the English emerged victorious. The Navigation Acts had been designed to cut the Dutch out of international trade, and that is exactly what they did. Britain also began to challenge Dutch dominance of the slave trade. In 1663 King Charles II chartered the Royal Africa Company to carry slaves out of Africa to the British West Indies. At the same time, Britain made a move for New Netherland.

James, the Duke of York and King Charles II's younger brother, was an ambitious man who longed for an empire of his own. He persuaded Charles to grant him the territory between the Connecticut and Delaware Rivers (present-day Pennsylvania, New Jersey, New York, and part of Connecticut), which just happened to be occupied by the Netherlands. In 1664 James sent over a governor, 400 troops, and several warships that easily conquered the small colony. In 1665 James gave away what is now New Jersey to two of his royal cronies, Lords John Berkeley and George Carteret, and in 1667 New York's governor gave the territory on the western side of the Connecticut River to that colony. New Netherland had become New York.

The English confronted a colony that was part Dutch (in New York City and along the Hudson) and part English (on Long Island, where New England Puritans had migrated). The first governors attempted to satisfy both ethnic groups. On the one hand, the governors confirmed Dutch landholdings, including the huge estates along the Hudson, guaranteeing the Dutch the freedom to continue following their own religion. On the other, the governors gave out about two million more acres of land, most of it

A map of New Amsterdam (New York), as it appeared in 1660. Settlement was concentrated in the lower tip of what is now Manhattan.

in enormous chunks that, following feudal terminology, were called manors. Although the owners of these manors were not made members of the English nobility, like feudal lords they were allowed to rent out land to tenants and set up courts on their estates.

Yet if religious toleration served as a magnet to attract diverse peoples to the region, feudal land policies and England's failure to restore self-government no doubt kept others away. Without an elective legislature to raise taxes, the governors, following English mercantilist policy, used customs duties to raise the revenue necessary to run the colony and send back a profit to James. These attempts to regulate trade and direct the economy not only angered local merchants but actually harmed the colonial economy. For example, New York's fur production actually declined between 1660 and 1700. Eventually, James gave in to popular discontent, and in 1683 he allowed New York to have an elective assembly.

At its first meeting, this small group of English and Dutch men passed a "Charter of Libertyes and Priviledges," which, had the king approved it, would have guaranteed New Yorkers both a number of civil liberties and the continuing right to self-government by its elected assembly. New York's proposed charter was an expression of the principles of **liberalism** that were beginning to spread through both Britain and the Netherlands. Specifically, the charter would have guaranteed all freemen the right to vote and to be taxed only by their elective representatives. The charter also provided for trial by jury, due process, freedom of conscience for all peaceful Christians, and certain property rights for women, the latter two items reflecting Dutch practices. However, James, who in 1685 had become king, refused to approve the charter on the grounds that it would have given the New Yorkers more rights than any other colonists and that the privileges extended to the New York assembly might have undermined the power of Parliament.

Without a secure form of self-government, New Yorkers fell to fighting among themselves. Despite the attraction of religious toleration, European immigrants looking for a better life generally avoided New York. "What man will be such a fool as to become a base tenant to Mr. Delius, Colonel Schuyler, Mr. Livingston," it was asked, "when, for crossing Hudson's River that man can for a song purchase a good freehold in the Jerseys?" Political instability in combination with feudal land holdings retarded New York's population growth.

Diversity and Prosperity in Pennsylvania

Pennsylvania demonstrated the potential of a colony that offered both religious toleration and economic opportunity. The colony took its name from its founder, William Penn, a Quaker and the son of one of Charles II's leading supporters. After the Restoration of the English monarchy, Charles had a number of political debts to repay, and giving away vast chunks of North America seemed to be a rather cheap way of discharging the obligation. As a Quaker, Penn was eager to get out of England. In 1661 alone, 4,000 English Quakers were thrown in jail, and Penn himself was imprisoned four times. The Quakers were a radical sect of Protestants, considerably more extreme in their rejection of authority than the Puritans. They believed in the possibility of human perfection and that God offered salvation to all and placed an "inner light" inside each man and woman. Although some of the early Quakers were defiant and even reckless in their disregard for authority, generally they were a hard-working, serious, and moral people. They rejected violence as a means of resolving disputes and hence refused to serve in the military or even pay taxes for its support. Once they arrived in America, they endeavored to live peaceably with the Indians.

Penn received his charter in 1681. To raise money for his venture, Penn sold land to a group of wealthy Quaker merchants, the Free Society of Traders. In return for their investment, he promised them government positions, and he granted certain economic concessions. Penn also sought to attract ordinary settlers. He promised self-government (although one stacked in favor of the merchant elite), freedom of religion, and reasonably priced land.

In 1682, by the time Penn arrived at Philadelphia (Greek for the "city of brotherly love"), the new colony already had 4,000 inhabitants. Penn had very clear ideas about how he wanted his colony to develop. He expected the orderly growth of farming villages, neatly laid out along Pennsylvania's rivers and creeks. He mapped out the settlement of Philadelphia along a grid pattern, with each house set far enough from its neighbors to prevent the spread of fires. He sought and achieved orderly and harmonious relations with the local Indians, at least for the first several decades of Pennsylvania's history. Penn gave the Delaware tribe £1,500 for a portion of their land

William Penn concluding a treaty with the Delaware Indians, as depicted by Benjamin West. In this exchange, Penn presents the Indians with cloth, one of the European trade goods most in demand by Indians.

and issued several "letters" to them outlining his hopes for peaceful relations.

Penn's policies attracted a wide variety of Europeans to his colony. His policy of religious toleration was a magnet for religious eccentrics and visionaries such as the mystical astronomer Johann Kelpius, who thought that in America he would live forever, an error he acknowledged just before his death. Soon Pennsylvania was a multilingual colony, populated by self-contained communities, each speaking a different language or practicing a different religion. Although this diversity eventually led to a certain amount of factionalism in government, Pennsylvania's early history was characterized primarily by rapid growth and widespread prosperity. Europeans moved to Pennsylvania in families, and the healthy climate spurred natural population increase. Pennsylvania's fertile land made farming quite profitable. However, this growth and prosperity undermined Penn's plans for a cohesive, hierarchical society. People generally lived where and how they wanted, pursuing the economic activities they found most profitable.

While moving away from the inequalities of the old world, Pennsylvania replicated those of the new. A high proportion of the Europeans who came to the colony were indentured servants or *redemptioners,* people who worked for a brief period to pay back the ship's captain for the cost of transportation to the colony. And by 1700, the Pennsylvania Assembly had passed laws recognizing slavery. Penn himself owned African slaves. Although slavery took hold in the colony, it was not without some opposition. As early as 1688, four residents of Germantown questioned the "traffick of men-body," and by that time English Quakers had already registered their disapproval. That the institution could take root in a colony where some questioned its morality suggests both the force of its power in shaping early America and the weakness of the opposition. At a time when most Europeans still believed that society should be organized hierarchically, that some were born socially superior to others, and that servitude was a natural and necessary institution, it was almost impossible to develop a coherent assault upon the institution of human slavery.

Indians and Africans in the Political Economy of Carolina

King Charles I named Carolina after himself when he granted the region to one of his followers in 1629, but that

Chapter 4   Creating the Empire, 1660–1720   97

grant lapsed. The next king, Charles II, gave the region to a group of eight wealthy noblemen, many of whom already had experience in the colonies. Like Pennsylvania and Maryland, South Carolina was a proprietary colony. One of the proprietors, Anthony Ashley Cooper, the Earl of Shaftesbury, and his secretary John Locke drafted the Fundamental Constitutions for the new colony. Locke later became well known as a leading political philosopher in his own right, and the Constitutions reflect the liberal, rights-guaranteeing principles that he later developed more fully.

The Constitutions made provisions for a representative government and widespread toleration of religion, even those of Indians and Africans, although the Anglican Church was established in the colony. At the same time, the document embodied the traditional assumption that liberty could be guaranteed only in a society with a complete social hierarchy. Shaftesbury and Locke attempted to set up a complex hierarchy of landholders with a made-up nobility including made-up titles such as "proprietors," "landgraves," and "caciques" at the top and hereditary serfs at the bottom. The Fundamental Constitutions also recognized the New World form of inequality, African slavery. Carolina was the first colony that introduced slavery at the outset. The Constitutions never went into full effect, for the first Carolina representative assembly rejected many of their provisions. As might have been predicted, the attempt to transplant a British-style nobility failed. The only aristocracy that the Carolinas developed was one of wealth, supported by the labor of slaves.

The first settlers sent by the proprietors arrived at Charles Town (later moved and renamed Charleston) in 1670. They were moving into a semi-tropical climate, with wonderfully fertile soil, 50 inches of rain a year, and a growing season of up to 295 days. The region had once been explored by the Spanish, as well as occasional Englishmen, and was still claimed by the Spanish. It was inhabited by mission Indians, that is, Indians who had accepted Spanish Franciscan missionaries into their villages and had converted to Catholicism.

As happened so often when Europeans entered a region, Indian tribes competed to trade with them, and rival groups of Europeans struggled to dominate the trade. Carolina Indian traders quickly established their control over the entire Southeast (see Map 4-1). They moved in on the Spanish to the south, the Virginians to the north, and even, after 1699, the French to the west. (Beginning in 1699, the French established a series of forts and trading posts along the Gulf Coast between New Orleans and Mobile and north into the mainland. Although twenty years later there

The Trial of John Lawson. In 1711, while exploring present-day western North Carolina for South Carolina, John Lawson and his party were captured by Tuscarora Indians. Lawson was put on trial and then executed. Notice his African slave, also bound and facing the Tuscarora tribunal.

were still no more than 400 people in these settlements, the French were able to carry on a lucrative trade for deerskins.) In 1680, in the Westo War, the Carolina traders sent their allies, the Savannah Indians, out to destroy the Westos, who were the Virginians' link to the Indian trade of the Southeast. The Carolinians were able to vanquish the Spanish as well by sending in other Indian allies to destroy the mission towns, thus demonstrating the inability of the Spanish to protect them. In this way, the Carolina traders eliminated their European rivals and established their dominance over all the regional Indians.

In the colonial period, Indian wars were an expression of political economy. They usually pitted one group of Europeans and their Indian allies against another group of Europeans and their native allies, with the Indians doing most of the fighting and suffering most of the casualties. Such wars were an extension of Europe's market economy, for Indians fought for access to European goods, and Europeans fought to achieve a monopoly over Indian products. The English were particularly successful in achieving dominance, not simply because they knew how to turn one Indian tribe against another, but also because of their sophisticated market economy. London's banks had perfected the mechanisms of credit, which financed a fur trade in the forests half a world away.

At the same time that Carolina traders were exchanging European goods for southeastern deerskins, they had found an even more valuable commodity on the southeastern frontier, Indian slaves. In fact, until about 1690, slaves were the most valuable commodity produced by the Carolina colony. The traders and their native allies ranged through the Spanish missions carrying off the Indian inhabitants. In 1704, for example, 50 Carolinians and 1,000 Creek, Yamasee, and Apalachicola allies moved against the

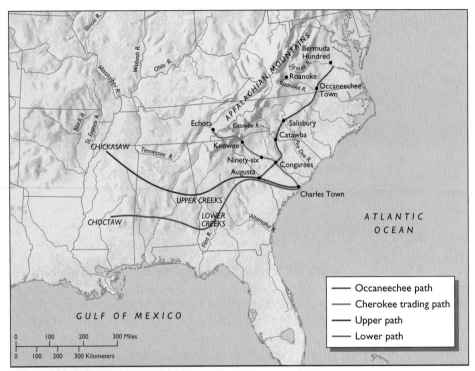

Map 4-1   *Trade Routes in the Southeast.*
Beginning in the seventeenth century, English traders from Virginia and later Carolina followed several paths to trade with Southeastern Indians as far west as the Mississippi.
Source: Adapted from W. Stitt Robinson, The Southern Colonial Frontier (Albuquerque: University of New Mexico Press, 1979), p. 103.

missions among Apalachee Indians (near present-day Tallahassee, Florida). They tortured the Franciscan missionaries and came back with approximately 5,000 slaves. It was the largest slave raid ever in the territory that became the United States, comparable to a slaving foray in Africa. Once in the traders' hands, the Indian slaves were sold either on the mainland or to the West Indies to work on sugar plantations alongside Africans. African slavers generally preferred men, but Carolina slave traders much preferred women and children. They thought they were less likely to run back to their communities or revolt. Of the 5,000 captured at Apalachee, 4,000 were women and children. Evidence about the trade in Indian slaves is very spotty, but it suggests that Carolina planters preferred Indian slaves, and when the supply ran out, they turned to Africans. The majority of Africans who were imported were male, and they found ready mates among the already-enslaved Indian women. Their children became members of the first generation of slaves born in the Carolinas.

The Barbados Connection

Slavery drew Carolina into a far-flung Atlantic political economy, one based upon trade, plantation agriculture, and slavery. Many of the early Carolina settlers already had substantial experience with African slavery. In fact, one of the reasons for the founding of the colony was to draw off

the extra European population of the English colony of Barbados. As Barbados became a slave society, the poorest white planters (such as Samuel Parris' father) were squeezed out.

Barbados, a small island in the Caribbean, had been settled in 1627 and within a decade had become a major source of the world's sugar. By that time, it also had an African majority, making it Britain's first slave society. (The Leeward Islands, colonized in the 1620s, Jamaica, seized from Spain in 1656, and the Bahamas, settled in 1718, essentially completed Britain's Caribbean empire.) By the end of the seventeenth century, Barbados was the most productive of all Britain's colonies. Moreover, its per capita exports—one measure of productivity—were higher than not only any place in the New World, but any in the Old World as well. As a result, the per person income was much higher in Barbados than in England.

This income was not shared equally among the inhabitants of the island, however. Those who owned the largest plantations became fabulously wealthy, and even lesser planters enjoyed a high standard of living. Conditions for African slaves, however, were brutal. As in their other slave societies, the British magnified the differences between Europeans and Africans in order to enhance the distinction between insiders, whites with an investment in the institution of slavery, and African outsiders, who were the slaves. Barbadians were the first to portray Africans as beasts. The slave code of 1661 described them as "a heathenish, brutish and uncertaine, dangerous kinde of people." The racism of Caribbean planters was intense, and the slave codes the harshest of any in the Atlantic world. The laws prescribed that male slaves convicted of crimes could be burned at the stake, beheaded, starved, or castrated. Unofficial punishments were similarly gruesome. One Jamaica planter punished his slaves by having another slave defecate into their mouths, which he gagged shut for several hours. When Caribbean slavery was imported into Carolina, these attitudes came with it. The Carolina slave code, enacted in the 1690s, was the harshest on the North American continent.

Unlike the mainland, neither Barbados nor Jamaica made sex between whites and blacks illegal. Not only single planters but married ones as well kept slave mistresses, and the law protected these coerced relationships.

At the same time that laws and attitudes separated whites from blacks, differences among Europeans were minimized. Despite early restrictions against Irish Catholics and Jews, after Barbados (and other West Indian islands) became slave societies, some of those restrictions were lifted. In 1650, the Council in Barbados allowed the immigration of Jews and other religious minorities, six years before similar legislation was passed in England (which had expelled its Jews in 1290). As in the Chesapeake, increasing freedom for those of European descent developed in tandem with the enslavement of Africans. Those Barbadians who emigrated to Carolina took with them their experience of a fully formed, African-majority slave society.

The sugar plantations of Barbados, and later Britain's other Caribbean islands, made their extraordinary profits from the labor of African slaves. Quite simply, British planters worked Africans harder than they would European indentured servants and harder than many other European planters were generally willing to work their slaves. Profits came from keeping labor costs down, in large part by compelling slaves to work in closely supervised gangs, under conditions so oppressive that no one would do so willingly. Profits also came from the growing demand for sugar. The European demand for plantation crops, many of which, like sugar, were either highly or slightly addictive, was insatiable. It is important to remember that the New World slave system would not have grown as it did without Europeans' demand for plantation products.

The Barbadians who came to Carolina drew upon their experience in a tropical plantation society in creating their new homes. In many ways, Carolina and later Georgia had more in common with the English Caribbean plantation societies than with the rest of the mainland colonies. Of the 400,000 Britons who migrated to America in the seventeenth century, 56 percent (225,000) headed for the Caribbean islands such as Barbados and Jamaica (see Table 4-1). But the tropical climate proved deadly for Europeans

TABLE 4-1

Population of British Colonies in America, 1660 and 1710						
		1660			1710	
Colony	White	Black	Total	White	Black	Total
Virginia	26,070	950	27,020	55,163	23,118	78,281
Maryland	7,668	758	8,426	34,796	7,945	42,741
Chesapeake	**33,738**	**1,708**	**35,446**	**89,959**	**31,063**	**121,022**
Massachusetts	22,062	422	22,484	61,080	1,310	62,390
Connecticut	7,955	25	7,980	38,700	750	39,450
Rhode Island	1,474	65	1,539	7,198	375	7,573
New Hampshire	1,515	50	1,565	5,531	150	5,681
New England	**33,006**	**562**	**33,568**	**112,509**	**2,585**	**115,094**
Bermuda	3,500	200	3,700	4,268	2,845	7,113
Barbados	26,200	27,100	53,300	13,000	52,300	65,300
Antigua	1,539	1,448	2,987	2,892	12,960	15,852
Montserrat	1,788	661	2,449	1,545	3,570	5,115
Nevis	2,347	2,566	4,913	1,104	3,676	4,780
St. Kitts	1,265	957	2,222	1,670	3,294	4,964
Jamaica				7,250	58,000	65,250
Caribbean	**36,639**	**32,932**	**69,571**	**31,729**	**136,645**	**168,374**
New York	4,336	600	4,936	18,814	2,811	21,625
New Jersey				18,540	1,332	19,872
Pennsylvania				22,875	1,575	24,450
Delaware	510	30	540	3,145	500	3,645
Middle Colonies	**4,846**	**630**	**5,476**	**63,374**	**6,218**	**69,592**
North Carolina	980	20	1,000	14,220	900	15,120
South Carolina				6,783	4,100	10,883
Lower South	**980**	**20**	**1,000**	**21,003**	**5,000**	**26,003**
Totals	109,209	35,852	145,061	318,574	181,511	500,085

Source: Jack P. Greene, Pursuits of Happiness *(Chapel Hill: University of North Carolina, 1988).*

Interior of a freedman's house and interior of a middling planter's house, mid-seventeenth century Chesapeake. By the middle of the seventeenth century, middling planters were able to furnish their homes with chairs, tables, pewter dishes, tablecloths, and candles and candlesticks (left). The standard of living for freedmen was much more stark. Without chairs, the family either sat on benches or storage chests at mealtime or ate leaning against a wall. Without candles, once the sun went down at night, the only light came from the fire in the fireplace (right).

and Africans alike. In 1700, only 30,000 whites were living in the Caribbean (12 percent of the total white population for British America). In that period even more Africans (about 264,000) had been sold into slavery in the Caribbean. Only about half were still living in 1700. A quarter of all slaves imported into the Caribbean were dead within three years. Carolina's climate was lethal also, and it took a steady influx of both whites and Africans simply to maintain population levels.

African slaves were imported into Carolina from the outset of the colony's existence, but it was not until sometime after 1690 that the colony developed a staple crop that increased the demand for slave labor. Sometime in the 1690s, Carolinians learned how to plant and harvest rice. Africans probably taught their masters how to cultivate the crop, for, unlike the English, they had raised the crop in their native lands. Soon rice became the region's major cash crop, and as it did, African slaves became more valuable. By 1720, Africans comprised more than 70 percent of Carolina's population. With a black majority and wealth concentrated in the hands of an elite, Carolina resembled the Caribbean islands to the south more than it did the other English colonies on the mainland. In only a few decades, Carolina had become a slave society, not simply a

society with slaves. Slavery stood at the center of the political economy and gave shape to the entire society.

The Transformation of Virginia

At the same time that a newly invigorated England was planting new colonies, those established earlier in the century were taking new shape. In the final quarter of the seventeenth century, all of the older colonies experienced a period of political and sometimes social instability, which was followed by the establishment of a lasting order. This period, then, was one of transition. In Virginia, the transition was marked by a violent insurrection known as Bacon's Rebellion. Significantly, the rebels sought not to overthrow the social and political order but to secure economic opportunity and a legitimate government that protected that opportunity. Although the rebellion attracted both slaves and indentured servants, in its aftermath Virginia became a slave society, as slavery became the center of the political economy. Economic opportunity for whites came at the expense of Indians, who inhabited fertile lands to the west, and Africans, who could be forced to labor for white people's benefit.

Social Change in Virginia

As Virginia entered its second half-century, the health of its population had finally begun to improve. Apple orchards had matured so that Virginians could drink cider instead of impure water. Ships bringing new servants were arriving in the fall, a much healthier time of year. Increasingly, these men and women served out their period of indenture and expected to set out on their own, planting tobacco. By that time, however, most of the best land in eastern Virginia had already been claimed, and the land to the west was occupied by Indian tribes, most of whom had entered into peace treaties with the English. To make matters worse for the freemen and poorer planters, the government was in the hands of a small clique of men who were using it as another means of getting rich. For example, Virginia's legislators voted themselves payments 200 times as high as representatives in New England were getting. Also, taxes, assessed in tobacco, were extraordinarily high. And just as taxes rose, the price of tobacco began to fall. Ordinary planters, and especially the freemen, were caught in a squeeze. Many could not afford their own plantations and had to work for others as tenants or overseers.

Despite these circumstances, servants kept coming to the colony. Most were from the lower ranks of British society. "Some are husbands who have abandoned their wives; others wives who have abandoned their husbands; some are children and apprentices who have run away from their parents and masters." A restless and unhappy set of men and women, these servants participated in a series of disturbances beginning in the middle of the century. The elite responded to this potential for mass unrest by lengthening the time of service and stiffening the penalties for running away.

Bacon's Rebellion and the Abandonment of the Middle Ground

When the revolt came, it was led, however, not by one of the poor or landless, but by a member of the elite. Nathaniel Bacon was only twenty-seven when he arrived in Virginia in 1674. Well-educated, wealthy, and a member of a prominent family, Bacon and his wife Elizabeth had left England after he disgraced himself by marrying without his father-in-law's consent and attempting to cheat a man out of his property. Tall, dark-haired, and brooding, Bacon made an immediate impression upon Virginia's ruling clique, and Governor Berkeley invited him into the colony's Council of State. For reasons that may never be entirely clear, however, Bacon decided to cast his lot with Berkeley's enemies among the elite. At that time, the instability of colonial elites in Britain's accidental empire gave rise to political factions in a number of colonies. When ruling elites, such as Berkeley's in Virginia, levied exorbitant taxes and ignored the needs of their constituents, they left themselves vulnerable to challenge.

The contest between Bacon and Berkeley might have remained an ordinary faction fight had not Bacon been able to capitalize on the discontent of the colony's freemen. The conflict that is known as Bacon's Rebellion was triggered by a routine episode of violence on the "middle ground" inhabited by Indians and Europeans. Seeking payment for goods they had delivered to a wealthy frontier planter, a band of Doeg Indians from Maryland crossed into Virginia, killed the planter's overseer, and tried to steal some of his hogs. Over the years, Europeans and Indians who shared the middle ground had adapted the Indian custom of providing restitution for crimes committed by one side or the other. Although this practice inevitably accepted sporadic violence, it also helped maintain order in regions inhabited by both groups. It also reflected the Indian concept of communal responsibility more than the European one of individual accountability. But this time, the conflict escalated, as Virginians sought revenge, prompting further Indian retaliation.

Soon an isolated incident had escalated into a joint Maryland and Virginia militia expedition with 1,000 militia men, an extraordinarily large force at a time when the entire population of the two colonies could not have been more than 50,000 Europeans. For six weeks this colonial war party laid siege to the reservation of the Susquehannocks, a tribe drawn unwillingly into the conflict. The Susquehannocks escaped and avenged themselves on settlers on the frontier.

When Berkeley refused to commission an expedition against the Susquehannocks and instead told Virginia settlers to stay out of Indian territory, the frontier planters were infuriated. Their belief that Berkeley's government was corrupt and oppressive fused with their resentment of his concern for his "protected and Darling Indians," with whom he was carrying on a lucrative trade in furs. They complained that their taxes went into the pockets of Berkeley's clique instead of being used to police the frontier. Planter women were particularly upset, and they used their gossip networks to tell "hundreds" that Berkeley was "a greater friend to the Indians than to the English."

With his wife's encouragement, Nathaniel Bacon agreed to become the leader in a wholesale war upon "all Indians whatsoever." Bacon's rebels went off in search of Susquehannocks and settled for massacring some hitherto friendly Occaneechees. Bacon then turned around and with 400 armed men marched on the government at Jamestown, demanding an immediate commission to fight "all Indians in general, for that they were all Enemies." Berkeley consented, then changed his mind, but it was too late. Bacon was effectively in control, and Berkeley fled to the eastern shore. He sent his wife Frances, a prominent member of the English elite, back to London to lobby for assistance.

By the time that a Royal Commission and 1,000 of the king's soldiers arrived in January 1677 to put down the disorder, Bacon had died and Berkeley had regained control. Twenty-three leaders of the rebellion were executed, and Berkeley himself was removed from office by the king. Support for Bacon's Rebellion had been amazingly broad, but equally shallow. Berkeley estimated that upwards of 14,000 Virginians had backed Bacon, but after his death, that support quickly dissipated.

After Bacon's Rebellion, the government remained in the hands of the planter elite, but the rebels had achieved their primary objective. The frontier Indians had been dispersed, and their land was now free for settlement. As the elite increasingly became native-born, those in power became more responsive to the needs of the white members of society. Other factors, not directly related to the revolt, also improved the economic condition of the colony's freemen. Tobacco prices began a slow climb, improving the economic condition of the planters. And soon, indentured servants began to be replaced by slaves.

Virginia Becomes a Slave Society

No one had planned for Virginia to become a slave society. With the new colonies like New York and Pennsylvania offering greater opportunity to poor whites, the supply of European indentured servants to the Chesapeake dried up just at the time that more Africans were becoming available. Britain entered the slave trade at the end of the seventeenth century, authorizing private merchants, in 1698, to carry slaves from Africa to North America. Planters soon could not get enough slaves to meet their needs. In 1680, only 7 percent of Virginia's population was African in origin, but by 1700 the proportion had increased to 28 percent, and half the labor force was enslaved. The proportion of slaves in the population climbed steadily until, on the eve of the American Revolution, it had reached 42 percent. Within two decades, Virginia had become a **slave society**, one in which slavery was central to the political economy and the social structure. With the bottom 40 percent of the social order enslaved, and hence unable to compete for land or wealth, opportunity for all whites necessarily improved. By 1705, one planter boasted that Virginia had become "the best poor Man's Country in the World." Increasing opportunity for whites came at the cost of decreasing freedom for Africans.

As the composition of Virginia's labor force changed, so did the laws to control it. Although all slave societies had certain features in common, the specifics varied from place to place. Everywhere, governments enacted particular pieces of legislation, called slave codes, to maintain and define the institution. By 1705, Virginia had a thorough slave code in place.

American slavery was different from both ancient slavery and Latin American plantation slavery. All forms of slavery, however, have had certain elements in common: perpetuity, kinlessness, violence, and the master's access to the slave's sexuality. First, slavery is a lifelong condition. Second, a slave has no legally recognized family relationships. Because kinship is the basis of most other social and political relationships in society, a slave is socially "dead," outside the bounds of the larger society. Third, slavery rests upon violence or its threat, including the master's sexual access to the slave.

American slavery added several other elements. First, slavery in all the Americas was hereditary, passed on from a mother to her children. Second, compared to other slave systems, including that of Latin America, *manumissions*—the freeing of slaves—in the American South were quite rare. Finally, southern slavery was racial. Slavery was reserved for Africans, some Indians, and their children, even if the father was white. As the Virginia planter Robert Beverley explained in 1722, "Slaves are the negroes and their posterity, following the condition of the mother." The line between slavery and freedom was one of color, and it was this line that the slave codes worked to define.

Slave codes also defined gender roles. Two of the earliest pieces of legislation denied African women the privileges of European women. A 1643 statute made all adult men and Negro women taxable, assuming that they (and not white women) were performing productive labor in the fields. As Robert Beverley explained, in Virginia "a white woman is rarely or never put to work in the ground, if she be good for anything else . . . whereas it is a common thing for to work a woman slave out of doors." Nineteen years later, another law specified that children were to inherit the status of their mother.

Later in the century, in the wake of Bacon's Rebellion, legislation was addressed directly at African men. The 1680 "Act for preventing Negroes Insurrections" forbade "any negroe or other slave" to carry a weapon. In 1705, slaves were denied the right to own livestock, and all Negroes, mulattoes, and Indians, whether slave or free, were denied the rights to hold government office and to testify in court. These acts denied African men the privileges most associated with manhood in the seventeenth century. Without a gun, a man could not hunt for food or protect his family, and without livestock, he could not provide them with meat or milk. And denied the right to hold office or testify in court, he was without the fundamental political rights that were becoming the birthright of all white men in British America.

The same set of laws that created and sustained racial slavery also began to increase the freedom of whites. New

TABLE 4-2

Codifying Race and Slavery

1640—Masters are required to arm everyone in their households except Africans (Virginia)

1643—All adult men and African women are taxable, on the assumption that they were working in the fields (Virginia)

1662—Children follow the condition of their mother (Virginia)

1662—Double fine charged for any Christian who commits fornication with an African (Virginia)

1664—All slaves serve for life; that is, slavery is defined as a lifelong condition (Maryland)

1664—Interracial marriage banned; any free woman who marries a slave will serve that slave's master until her husband dies, and their children will be enslaved (Maryland)

1667—Baptism as a Christian does not make a slave free (Virginia)

1669—No punishment is given if punished slave dies (Virginia)

1670—Free Blacks and Indians are not allowed to purchase Christian indentured servants (Virginia)

1670—Indians captured elsewhere and sold as slaves to Virginia are to serve for life; those captured in Virginia, until the age of 30, if children, or for 12 years, if grown (Virginia)

1680—In order to prevent "Negroes Insurrections": no slave may carry arms or weapons; no slave may leave his or her master without written permission; any slave who "lifts up his hand" against a Christian will receive thirty lashes; any slave who runs away and resists arrest may be killed lawfully (Virginia)

1682—Slaves may not gather for more than 4 hours at other than owner's plantation (Virginia)

1682—All servants who were "Negroes, Moors, Mollattoes or Indians" were to be considered slaves at the time of their purchase if neither their parents nor country were Christian (Virginia)

1691—Owners are to be compensated if "negroes, mulattoes or other slaves" are killed while resisting arrest (Virginia)

1691—Forbidden is all miscegenation as "that abominable mixture"; any English or "other white man or woman" who marries a "negroe, mulatto, or Indian" is to be banished; any free English woman who bears a "bastard child by any negro or mulatto" will be fined, and if she can't pay the fine, she will be indentured for five years and the child will be indentured until the age of 30 (Virginia)

1691—All slaves who are freed by their masters must be transported out of the state (Virginia)

1692—Special courts of "oyer and terminer" are established for trying slaves accused of crimes, creating a separate system of justice (Virginia)

1705—Mulatto is defined as "the child of an Indian, the child, grandchild, or great grandchild of a negro" (Virginia)

1705—Africans, mulattoes, and Indians are prohibited from holding office or giving grand jury testimony (Virginia)

1705—Slaves are forbidden to own livestock (Virginia)

1705—"Christian white" servants cannot be whipped naked (Virginia)

1723—Free Blacks explicitly excluded from militia (Virginia)

1723—Free Blacks explicitly denied the right to vote (Virginia)

Slavery is a creation of law, which defines what it means to be a slave and protects the master's rights in his slave property. Slave codes developed piecemeal in the Chesapeake, over the course of the seventeenth century. Legislators in the Chesapeake colonies defined slavery as a racial institution, appropriate only for Africans, and protected it with a series of laws, which, in the process, also created a privileged position for whites.

World plantation slavery was developed in a world in which the freedom of most Europeans also was limited in various ways. In fact, two-thirds of the Europeans who migrated to British America before the American Revolution were unfree—servants or redemptioners. (When Africans are added, virtually all of whom were enslaved, the total increases to 90 percent.) But at the same time that the freedom of Africans in British America was being restricted, the freedom of whites was being increased. The increase in freedom for whites was the product of several sorts of policies. First, it depended on the widespread availability of cheap land. As we have already seen, whites could obtain this land only by dispossessing the Indians who inhabited it. Second, it depended on policies of the British government, such as permitting self-government in the colonies. As we have seen, colonies offered this right as a means of attracting immigrants. Third, it depended on specific laws that improved the conditions of whites, while often at the same time limiting the freedom of blacks. For example, in 1705 Virginia made it illegal for white servants to be whipped without an order from a Justice of the Peace. It would be more than a century before indentured servitude was eliminated as a status for whites, but by the end of the seventeenth century, the first steps on that long route had been taken.

New England Under Assault

The Puritan movement had been born in adversity. It had grown through persecution. American Puritans believed that they could be a beacon to the world. At the beginning of the English Revolution in 1642, however, eyes turned from New England's city upon a hill back to England. England's Puritan revolutionaries followed their own path, which was more tolerant of other versions of Protestantism. Then, when the English monarchy was restored in 1660, New Englanders found that the new king, Charles II, was suspicious of them nonetheless. Rather than leading the way for the rest of the world, the world had passed them by. At the same time, the New England colonies prospered, and that prosperity led to problems, both internal and external. How would a religion that had been born in adversity cope with good fortune? A combination of conflicts among the New England colonies and a growing population that encroached on Indian lands led to the region's deadliest Indian war in 1675. At almost the same time as Bacon's Rebellion, the New England colonies were thrown into turmoil.

Social Prosperity and the Fear of Religious Decline

In many ways, the Puritan founders of the New England colonies saw their dreams come true. Although immigration came to a virtual halt as the English Revolution broke out, natural increase kept the population growing at a steady rate, from about 23,000 in 1650 to 50,000 in 1675 and more than 93,000 in 1700. Life expectancy was higher than in England, and families were larger. Men and women lived long enough to see their grandchildren, an experience that was relatively rare in both the Chesapeake and England.

Most New Englanders enjoyed a comfortable, if modest, standard of living. By the end of the century, the simple shacks that had been hastily erected by the first settlers had been replaced by two-story frame homes. Fireplaces were more efficient, making homes warmer in winter, and glass windows replaced heavy oiled paper, letting light into rooms on sunny days. By our standards, these homes would still have been almost unbearably cold in the winter, when indoor temperatures routinely dropped into the 40s, freezing laundry hung up to dry. Without any screening on doors or windows, swarms of insects were almost as common indoors as out in the summer. Still, if many New Englanders had seen their standard of living drop when they left their homeland, by the end of the century their children and grandchildren were beginning to enjoy the sort of prosperous village life they had once known.

For Puritans, such good fortune presented a problem. As the ministers looked around the society that they had created, its prosperity became a cause for worry. Too many people seemed to have turned their minds away from God to more worldly things. In the 1660s and 1670s, New England's ministers preached a series of *jeremiads,* lamentations about the spiritual decline of their people. They used these sermons as an opportunity to criticize troubling developments, ranging from public drunkenness and sexual license to land speculation and excessively high prices and wages. If New Englanders did not repent and change their ways, the ministers predicted, "Ruine upon Ruine, Destruction upon Destruction would come, until one stone were not left upon another."

Most of the churches were embroiled in a rather serious controversy in the 1660s concerning who could be church members and under what circumstances. New England Congregationalism had assumed that most people, sooner or later, would have the conversion experience that entitled them to full church membership. By the time of the third generation, however, it was clear that there were many children and grandchildren of full church members who simply had not had the deeply emotional experience of spiritual rebirth. In 1662 a group of New England ministers met and adopted the Half-Way Covenant, which set out terms for church membership and participation. Full church membership, which granted the privilege of receiving communion, was reserved for those who could demonstrate a conversion experience. Their offspring who had not been reborn could still be "halfway" members of the church, receiving its discipline and having their own children baptized. The ministers were attempting to expand church membership and the reach of their religion. They were resisted by those who wanted to maintain the purity and exclusivity of the church. Rather than settling this question, the Half-Way Covenant actually aggravated tensions that were always at the surface of the Puritan religion.

Turmoil broke out as well in the continuing persecution of Quakers, despite Charles II's having issued an order to stop their persecution. Only two years earlier, in 1660, Massachusetts had executed the Quaker Mary Dyer, who had returned to Boston after her banishment. As a female and one of Anne Hutchinson's supporters, Dyer appeared particularly dangerous. The Quakers had been brazen in their defiance of authority, not only returning to the colony when they knew it meant certain death, but even running naked through the streets or in church. Quakers found a refuge in Rhode Island, and although Massachusetts and Connecticut Puritans viewed that colony as the region's cesspool, it certainly survived.

King Philip's War

Although New England's colonies developed along a common path, until the end of the seventeenth century conflicts among the colonies were intense. In fact, the region's deadliest Indian war, for both Indians and colonists, grew out of one of these conflicts. As in Bacon's Rebellion, the underlying cause of the war was the steady encroachment of English settlers upon land inhabited by Native Americans. In the 1660s, Rhode Island, Massachusetts, and Plymouth all claimed the land occupied by the Wampanoags, Massasoit's old tribe, now under the rule of his son Metacom, known by the colonists as King Philip. By 1671, the New England colonies had resolved their dispute and ordered King Philip and his people to submit themselves to

the rule of Plymouth. No longer able to play one colony against another, King Philip began to prepare for war. The colonists of all the New England colonies prepared as well—except Rhode Island, which attempted in vain to mediate a resolution. In June 1675 King Philip's men attacked the Plymouth village of Swansea.

Over the course of the next year, Indians and colonists adopted each other's methods of war, making the war particularly brutal. The New Englanders began attacking entire villages of noncombatants, and the Indians retaliated in kind. From the Indians, New Englanders learned how to ambush. At the beginning of the war, New Englanders looked down upon their opponents' traditional methods as evidence of Indian depravity, saying they fought "more like wolves than men." By the end of the war, they too were practicing "the skulking way of war." Both sides committed brutalities, including scalpings and putting their victims' heads on stakes. That was the fate of King Philip himself. His wife and nine-year-old son, who in Puritan fashion was held literally liable for the sins of his father, were sold into slavery, along with hundreds of captives.

The New Englanders had won King Philip's War, but the cost was enormous for both sides. The casualty rate was the highest for any American war, before or since. About 4,000 Indians died, many of starvation, after the New Englanders destroyed their corn fields. The war eliminated any significant Indian presence in southeastern New England. All the Indians who remained were isolated in "praying villages," communities of Indian converts to the Puritan religion. In the conflict, 2,000 English settlers (one out of every twenty-five) were killed. At one point, the Indians had pushed to within twenty miles of Boston. They attacked more than half of New England's towns, burning 1,200 homes. Refugees from the outlying villages flooded into towns on the coast. Every man between the ages of fifteen and sixty was required to serve in the militia, and desertion and draft-dodging were rampant. Men who were willing to defend their own villages refused to go fight somewhere else. It took the region decades to rebuild from the demoralization, dislocation, and debt brought on by the war.

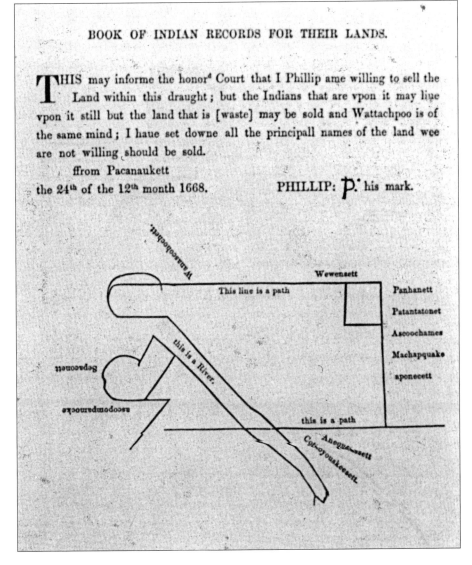

King Philip (Metacom's) Map, 1668. A map of the lands that Metacom (known by New Englanders as Philip) sold in 1668. Note that Metacom's understanding of what it meant to "sell" land differed from English conceptions of property ownership. He insisted that the Indians who were living on the land could continue to do so.

Massachusetts Soldiers Adopt the Indians "Skulking" Way of War. During King Philip's War, Massachusetts soldiers consciously imitated Indian tactics, such as taking cover behind rocks.

Sir Edmund Andros, Royal Governor of New York, named by James II as Governor of the Dominion of New England.

Moreover, the Puritans owed their victory to the Anglican colony of New York, its governor Edmund Andros, and his Mohawk allies. Andros worked effectively with local Indians, not because of any natural sympathy, but because he kept his eye on the big picture. In the long run, he believed, the British empire would be best served by maintaining peace among its various colonies and the regional Indians. The British would be in a better position to defend themselves against their true enemies, the French and the Dutch. Andros was also determined to secure his own colony's best interest, and in 1676 that meant putting an end to the warfare that was raging to the east in New England.

With Nathaniel Bacon's followers simultaneously fighting all the Indians they could find to the south, a huge alliance among Native Americans to evict the English from their continent seemed a distinct possibility. Over the protest of New England, Andros encouraged the Mohawks, one of the five Iroquois tribes who made their home in New York, to attack King Philip's forces. Once the Mohawk entered the war, the tide was turned.

Indians and the Empire

New England's relations with Indian tribes in the region were not simply a local concern. They were of deep interest to the British empire, as Andros' participation demonstrated. The British government always had to balance the desires of its colonists against the empire's larger geopolitical objectives. As the French expanded their presence in North America, using friendly Indians to check their advance became one of those objectives. In 1673 the French explorers Jacques Marquette and Louis Joliet had traveled down the Mississippi as far south as the Arkansas River, and nine years later LaSalle reached the mouth of the river

and named the surrounding territory Louisiana, in honor of his king, Louis XIV. Biloxi was founded in 1699, New Orleans in 1718, and the forts at Cahokia and Kaskaskia several years later. Except for Louisiana, which became a prosperous slave colony in the eighteenth century, the French presence in what would become the United States was minimal. Through their trade partnerships with regional Indians, however, the French and their Indian allies were able to maintain effective control of the Great Lakes region and the eastern shore of the Mississippi all the way to its mouth. The British were confined to the East Coast, although the border between British and French control was always in flux.

This geopolitical reality dictated Britain's Indian policy. Andros saw a role for Native Americans as trade partners and allies in Britain's continuing conflict with the French. His role in achieving victory over the Wampanoags and their allies enabled him to dictate the terms of the peace at the end of King Philip's War. He welcomed the Indian survivors of the conflict into New York and refused to send them back to New England for execution and enslavement. Adapting the royal model of government to the North American continent, the Governor of New York became the "father" who offered protection to his Indian "children." The British and the Iroquois, who dominated all the other tribes in the region, were joined in an alliance known as the Covenant Chain, which was so strong that "the very Thunder . . . would not break it in Sunder." The Covenant Chain enhanced the positions of both New York and the Iroquois. The Iroquois were allowed to become the middlemen between all the other tribes in the area and the merchants at Albany. With the British paying a third more for beaver pelts than the French, the Iroquois were in an enviable position. Moreover, with British support, they were allowed to push as far north and west against the French-allied tribes as they could.

New England played a relatively small role in Britain's political economy, and hence it had a very weak bargaining position. With New York exercising the dominant political role in the British-Indian alliance, the New England colonies were effectively hemmed in. New York used the Mohawk to make a claim to Maine. The colony also blocked New England's movement to the west. Moreover, Albany became the undisputed center of the Indian trade. In every way, King Philip's War had proved exceedingly costly for the New England colonies. As Andros put it, "The advantages thereby were none, the disadvantages very great and like to be more."

The Empire Strikes

As Britain regained political stability at the end of the seventeenth century, it tried to bring more order to its "accidental empire," not so much by interfering in colonial affairs as by making the colonies play a larger role in imperial geopolitics. In fact, Britain's attempt to intervene in the colonies during the reign of James II (1685–1688) was thwarted. While the Glorious Revolution that removed James from the throne secured constitutional government for Britain's subjects on both sides of the Atlantic, it also made Britain strong and stable enough to challenge France for world supremacy. Between 1689 and 1763, the Anglo-French rivalry drew the colonies into four international wars that shaped the colonies in important ways.

The Dominion of New England

When James II ascended to the throne, he decided to punish New England. His experience as proprietor of New York convinced him that his American empire, especially New England, needed to be reined in. The New Englanders had never been disciplined for their disloyalty to the Crown during the Puritan Revolution. Moreover, there were continuing reports that New Englanders were defying the Navigation Acts by smuggling. James looked across the English Channel to France, where Louis XIV had centralized his administration and brought both his nation and his empire under firm control. James decided to give it a try himself. In North America, he began unilaterally to revoke the charters of the colonies. Proceedings

were begun against Massachusetts, Plymouth, Connecticut, New York, and New Jersey, and by 1688 all these colonies, along with New Hampshire and Rhode Island, had been joined together into the Dominion of New England, and Edmund Andros named its governor.

Neither James nor Andros lasted very long, but before they had been evicted by the Glorious Revolution of 1688, considerable havoc had been wrought in New England, and Massachusetts, New York, and Maryland had all suffered revolts. James' attempt to centralize administration of the empire and tighten control over the colonies was a dismal failure. But it marked a turning point for most of the British North American colonies, their last period of significant political instability before the eve of the Revolution.

James' attempt to tighten his control over the colonies affected Massachusetts most seriously. He ordered it to tolerate religious dissenters. Some feared that the Catholic king would impose Catholicism on the colony. He took away liberties that the residents of Massachusetts had enjoyed for over half a century. For example, now juries were to be appointed by sheriffs, town meetings were limited to once a year, and town selectmen could serve no more than two two-year terms. All titles to land had to be reconfirmed, with the holder paying Andros himself a small fee for the privilege. Andros claimed the right to levy taxes on his own, and he began seizing all common lands, including the town common in Cambridge, and reassigning them to whomever he pleased. Some of the Boston merchants allied themselves with Andros, hoping to win his favor. This alliance revealed a growing rift in New England between those who welcomed commerce and a more secular way of life and those who wished to preserve the old ways. By and large, however, most people in Massachusetts and certainly the ministers despised Andros and feared the road he was leading them down. A group of Bostonians complained that New England was being "squeez'd by a Crew of abject Persons fetched from New York, to be the Tools of the Adversary," that is, Satan. Andros' opponents in Massachusetts sent the prominent minister Increase Mather to London in 1688 to plead on their behalf. Mather arrived just as the Glorious Revolution was beginning and James was about to depart, involuntarily.

The Glorious Revolution— in Britain and America

In Britain, the Glorious Revolution made it clear that Parliament, and not an autocratic monarch, would play the leading role in government. It also determined, after almost a century and a half of conflict, that the Anglican religion would prevail, and Catholics would continue to suffer discrimination. The Glorious Revolution ushered in a period of remarkable internal political stability that enabled Britain to become, for a period, the world's most powerful nation.

In the next century Britain's North American colonies idealized this moment in British history and looked to it for a model of Constitutional government. Their understanding of events in Britain was shaped by political philosopher John Locke's *Two Treatises of Government* (1690). Since the time that he and Shaftesbury had written Carolina's *Fundamental Constitutions* more than twenty years earlier, Locke had become increasingly radical. Gone were the vestiges of feudalism, with its peculiar social and political hierarchy of lords and caciques. In its place was a bold assertion of fundamental human equality and universal rights. The *Treatises* were written during the 1680s as Locke and other opponents of autocratic royal government developed the political theories that would justify a revolution.

The *Treatises* have become the founding documents of political liberalism and its theory of human rights. Locke argued that governments were created by people, not by God. Man was born "with a Title to perfect Freedom," or "natural rights." When people created governments, they gave up some of that freedom in exchange for the rights (called "civil rights") that they enjoyed in society. The purpose of government was to protect the "Lives, Liberties," and "Fortunes" of the people who created it, not to achieve glory or power for the nation or its king or even to serve God. Moreover, should a government by "Ambition, Fear, Folly or Corruption" take away the civil rights of its citizens, then they had a "right to resume their original Liberty." This right of revolution was Locke's boldest and most radical assertion.

John Locke is also considered the first theorist of *political economy*. That is, he argued that there was a systematic connection among social institutions such as the family, political institutions, and the rights of property.

Locke's position, of course, was not the official policy of the British government, even though it justified the Glorious Revolution. The British government certainly had not given up any of its control over its colonies. Once news of the Revolution reached Massachusetts, its inhabitants poured into the streets. To the steady beat of drums, they seized the government and threw the despised Andros in jail. They proclaimed loyalty to the new king, while Increase Mather lobbied in London for the return of their charter. Rhode Island and Connecticut, in fact, soon got their charters back, but Massachusetts, which was still perceived as too independent, in 1691 was made a royal colony, with a royal governor. Although Massachusetts lost some of its autonomy and was forced to tolerate dissenters, the town meeting was restored. In addition, Massachusetts was allowed to absorb both Maine and Plymouth. At the same time, New Hampshire became a royal colony.

As in Massachusetts, the citizens of Maryland and New York took the opportunity presented by the Glorious Revolution to evict their royal governors. In Maryland, tensions between the tobacco planters and the increasingly dictatorial proprietor, Charles Calvert, Lord Baltimore, had been building for several decades. Although the price of tobacco had fallen considerably, Baltimore refused to lower the export duty. Four-fifths of the population was Protestant, but the colony's government was dominated by Catholics, who used their positions to allocate themselves the best land. When the Protestant planters protested, Baltimore responded by imposing a property qualification for voting and by appointing increasingly dictatorial governors, one of whom insisted that his authority to rule "undoubtedly derived from God." These grievances combined with irrational fears of an impending attack by a Catholic-Indian alliance. When news of the Glorious Revolution reached Maryland in 1689, a group led by John Coode, a militia officer, took over the government in a bloodless coup, known as Coode's Rebellion. The rebels proclaimed their loyalty to William and Mary and were able to get the new government in Britain to take away Baltimore's right to govern the colony. In 1691, Maryland also became a royal colony.

New York's rebels were less successful in achieving their aims. There, a group of prosperous Dutch traders led by Jacob Leisler took over the government and ran it for almost two years. Unlike Coode in Maryland, Leisler was not willing to turn the reins of government over immediately to the new king's appointees. As a result, once the new governor had assumed power, he put the rebel leaders on trial. Leisler and his son-in-law were executed, their bodies decapitated and quartered.

This brutal conclusion to a bloodless revolt did not bring political stability to New York, however. The ethnic and regional divisions ran too deep. In the other colonies, by the end of the seventeenth century, the elite had managed to consolidate its position by accepting the authority of the British government, on the one hand, and providing opportunity and self-government for their fellow colonists, on the other. In New York, however, the mostly English top tier of the elite competed for leadership with the second, mostly Dutch tier, keeping the colony in political turmoil for years.

The Rights of Englishmen

Although the Glorious Revolution restored self-government to Britain's North American colonies, many questions were left unanswered. In the decades to come, it became evident that the American colonists and their British governors interpreted that event somewhat differently. In the minds of the colonists, it gave them all the rights of Englishmen. These rights were of two sorts. First was the full array of civil rights, from trial by jury to freedom from unreasonable searches. Equally important were the fundamental rights of self-government: to be taxed only by their own elected representatives, to legislate for themselves, and civilian rather than military rule. The colonists believed that their own legislatures were the local equivalent of Parliament, and that just as the citizens of Britain were governed by Parliament, so they should be governed by their own elective legislatures. These ideas were not fully spelled out until the American Revolution.

At the same time, the British government of the colonies was working on another and rather different set of assumptions. First, it believed that the colonies were like children of the mother country, dependents who needed a parent's protection and who owed that parent obedience. Second, the good of the empire as a whole was more important than that of any one of its parts. The worth of a colony was established by how much it contributed to "the gain or loss of *this* Kingdom." Third, just as the colonies were subordinate to the empire, the colonial governments were subordinate to the British government. Colonial legislatures were nothing more than "so many Incorporations at a Distance," set up for the convenience of but in no way interfering with the "Power of the Mother State." Finally, the British government had complete jurisdiction over every aspect of colonial life. Even if the government chose not to exercise this power, it was still its to use, should it ever decide to. In fact, for many decades, Britain decided that there was no point in asserting its authority simply for the sake of asserting it, especially if it might lead to colonial resistance. By the time events required the colonists to compare their idea of how the empire should operate with Britain's, they discovered how radically their viewpoints had diverged.

Conflict in the Empire

Between 1689 and 1713, Britain fought two wars against France and her allies, King William's War (1689–1697) and Queen Anne's War (1702–1713). At the same time, competition between the European powers for the allegiance of Indian tribes and the struggle of the individual colonies to gain the advantage in trade and territory made the borders between European and Indian settlement uncertain and dangerous.

King William's War and Queen Anne's War followed a similar pattern in North America. Each was produced by a European struggle for power, and each resulted in a stalemate in both Europe and North America. Although the population and wealth of the British North American colonies were much greater than those of the French colony of Canada, the British were unable to conquer Canada or wrest away much of its territory. The North American phase of each war began with a Canadian-Indian assault upon isolated British settlements on the northern frontier (see Map 4-2). King William's War commenced with the capture of the British fort at Pemaquid, Maine, and the burning of Schenectady, New York, and Falmouth, Maine. Queen Anne's War was announced in North America in 1704 by a horrific raid upon Deerfield, Massachusetts. Half the town was torched, almost one-fifth of its population of 300 was killed, and another third carried north as captives.

The British colonies responded to these raids with massive retaliation. Although they sent out their own raiding parties, they poured most of their resources into ambi-

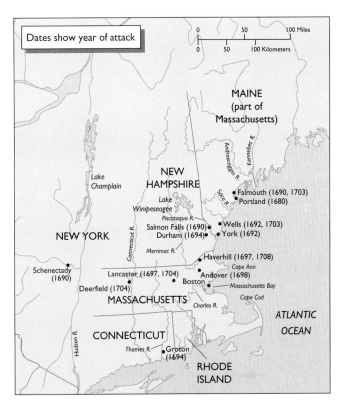

Map 4-2   Frontier Warfare During King William's and Queen Anne's Wars.

During these international conflicts, the New England frontier was exposed to attack by French Canadians and their Indian allies.

Source: Alan Gallay, ed., Colonial Wars of North America, 1512–1763 (New York: Garland, 1996), p. 247.

tious and ultimately unsuccessful attacks upon Quebec. In May 1690 Massachusetts governor Sir William Phips conquered the French privateering base at Port Royal, Acadia, then determined to seize Quebec in a two-pronged attack by land and sea. Unable to get British support for the venture, Phips appealed to Boston's merchants for financing. By the time he reached Quebec in October, many of his force of 2,300 had already succumbed to small pox. Unbeknownst to Phips, the troops that had been sent out from Albany to rendezvous in Quebec had turned back more than a month before. The failed expedition cost 1,000 lives and £40,000. Unable to defeat the French, the American colonies remained vulnerable on the northern frontier, and settlers retreated.

Queen Anne's War followed much the same course. Canadian-Indian attacks upon frontier villages such as Deerfield were met with raids upon Indian villages. Once again, New England decided upon a two-pronged attack upon Quebec. This time a force of 12,000 soldiers, sailors, Indians, and attendants sailed from Boston, while 2,300 marched north from Albany, a total that was almost half the population of Canada. When 900 troops (and 35 female camp followers) were killed as their ships ran aground in the foggy St. Lawrence, the commander canceled the expedition, judging it not worth the risk. Like King William's

War, Queen Anne's ended in disillusionment for New Englanders who had been eager to remove the twin threats of Catholicism and French-backed Indians to the north.

Finally, the imperial wars merged with and were survived by long-standing conflicts with Indian tribes. In fact, the European nations in North America almost never confronted each other directly but usually mobilized their own Indian allies and made war upon those of their adversary. Between the expansion of the colonial population into Indian territory on the one hand and the attempt of Indian tribes to secure trade monopolies on the other, colonists found themselves vying with regional Indians as well. As a result, conflict on the frontiers was endemic.

Massachusetts in Crisis

If the imperial wars provide a window onto a world of international tensions, the Salem witchcraft trials provide a window onto a society in crisis, one coping with economic development, the conflict between religious and scientific ways of understanding the world, and the threats presented by political instability, imperial war, and conflict with the Indians. In 1692 Massachusetts executed 20 people who had been convicted of witchcraft in Salem. Although this was the largest outbreak of witchcraft in the colonies, it was still a relatively minor episode in American history. After all, almost 100 times that number of colonists had been killed in King Philip's War. Still, even in a society that believed in witchcraft, the execution of so many people at once was an aberration, one that revealed deep tensions in Massachusetts.

The Social and Cultural Contexts of Witchcraft

Although the vast majority of New England's colonists were Puritan, many of them probably believed in magic as well. At the same time that they subscribed to such tenets of Puritanism as predestination, they also believed that they could make use of supernatural powers for their own purposes, such as predicting the future, protecting themselves from harm, and hurting their enemies. Although the ministry identified the use of magic with the Devil, ordinary people did not necessarily think of magic as antagonistic to their religion. Tituba's folk religion and that of New Englanders were not incompatible. Before the development of scientific modes of explanation for such catastrophes as epidemics, droughts, and the sudden deaths of humans and animals, people looked for supernatural causes.

New Englanders used the occult to explain the otherwise inexplicable. It was one of the tools they used to make sense of underlying social and political tensions. In 1692, the inhabitants of Massachusetts were unusually anxious. They

Frontispiece to Joseph Glanvill, Saducismus Triumphatus; or, Full and Plain Evidence Concerning Witches (1689). Books such as this combined folklore and Christian theology, providing graphic representations of Satan and witches alongside standard religious doctrine.

were without an effective government because they had not yet received their new charter. The opening battles of King William's War had just begun, with the French Catholics of Canada and their Algonquian Indian allies raiding settlements on the northern and eastern frontiers. The memories of King Philip's War were still vivid, and now New Englanders had to worry about a Catholic-Indian alliance. At the same time, several slaves reported that the French were planning to recruit New England's Africans to join a force of Indians and French soldiers. So certain were the New Englanders of the impending assault that in 1692 sixty armed men charged out into the woods around Gloucester searching for an enemy that no one could find.

These immediate sources of stress increased underlying tensions, many of which concerned gender. Although men and women both attempted to use magic, the vast majority of those who were accused of or tried for witchcraft in seventeenth-century New England were women. Almost 80 percent of the 355 persons officially accused of practicing witchcraft were women, and an even higher proportion of the 103 persons actually put on trial were female. Most of these women had neither sons nor other male heirs. They were thus an anomaly in Puritan society, women who controlled property. By the end of the seventeenth century, land was an increasingly scarce commodity in New England, and any woman who controlled it could be perceived as threatening to the men who wanted it.

In addition, declining opportunity also disrupted the social order that the Puritans had worked so hard to maintain. Because land was scarce, it became more difficult for young couples to start out. Consequently young people began to delay their marriages. The age of marriage began to increase, to early-to-mid-twenties for young women and mid-to-late twenties for men. Just because these men and women had to postpone marriage does not mean, however, that they waited to enter into sexual relations. The number of women who were pregnant on their wedding day began to climb steadily through the eighteenth century. The number of women who gave birth without marrying at all began to grow as well. As the number of out-of-wedlock births increased, courts less frequently insisted that the fathers be made to pay for the support of their babies. Instead, courts increasingly shifted responsibility to the young mothers, who were required to bear all the burden of their children's support. By the end of the seventeenth century, New Englanders were even more inclined than previously to hold women responsible for sin.

Witchcraft at Salem

It was in this context of social strain and political anxiety that on February 29, 1692, magistrates John Hathorne and Jonathan Corwin were called to Salem to investigate accusations of witchcraft. By the time the investigation and trials were finished that autumn, 156 people had been accused of witchcraft and jailed. Twenty of these were killed, nineteen executed by hanging and one crushed by heavy stones in an attempt to extract a confession. As in previous witchcraft scares, most of those who were accused were women past the age of forty, and most of the accusers were women in their late teens and twenties, although in Salem respectable members of the community and a four-year-old child were accused as well.

The witchcraft trials at Salem became the focus of New England's worst anxieties. Most of the accused fell into several categories, each of which revealed the stresses in Puritan society. Many, like Sarah Good, were the sorts of disagreeable women who had always attracted accusations

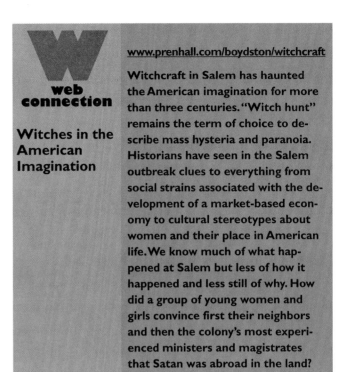

www.prenhall.com/boydston/witchcraft

web connection

Witches in the American Imagination

Witchcraft in Salem has haunted the American imagination for more than three centuries. "Witch hunt" remains the term of choice to describe mass hysteria and paranoia. Historians have seen in the Salem outbreak clues to everything from social strains associated with the development of a market-based economy to cultural stereotypes about women and their place in American life. We know much of what happened at Salem but less of how it happened and less still of why. How did a group of young women and girls convince first their neighbors and then the colony's most experienced ministers and magistrates that Satan was abroad in the land?

of witchcraft. Others had ties to Quakers, and some may have been suspected as Baptists. Several were suspiciously friendly with the Indians. Indeed, a significant number of the accusers had been orphaned or displaced by the recent Indian wars, and it is not surprising that they described the Devil as "a Tawney, or an Indian color." As a dark-skinned woman from an alien culture, Tituba (whose story is told in detail at the beginning of this chapter) was also vulnerable. In addition, most of the accusers lived in Salem Village, an economic backwater, while most of those accused lived in or had ties to Salem Town, a more prosperous merchant community several miles to the east. The pattern of accusations suggested resentment, perhaps unconscious, about the increasing commercialization of New England's economy.

By late September, the accusations were falling upon wealthy and well-connected men and women such as Lady Phips, the wife of the governor. The original accusing women were being taken from town to town to root out local witchcraft, while other people were drawn to Salem like medieval pilgrims, looking for explanations for their problems. At that point, the leading ministers of Boston, most of whom believed in witchcraft but had been skeptical of the Salem trials all along, stepped in. Increase Mather insisted that, "It were better that ten suspected witches shall escape, than that one innocent person should be condemned." Governor Phips, who had been fighting Indians on the frontier when the trials began, ordered the court adjourned. No one was ever convicted of witchcraft in New England again.

ON TRIAL

The Supernatural on Trial—Witchcraft at Salem

The eruption of accusations had begun in the household of Salem Village's minister, Samuel Parris, a dissatisfied and bitter man, often at odds with the members of his congregation, when his daughter Betty and her cousin Abigail Williams tried to foresee their future husbands. These young women and the others who became accusers were among the most powerless segment of New England's white population, and they must have enjoyed these outbursts against order and authority and the attention they drew to themselves.

When questioned by those in authority, curses and shouts poured out of the accusers' mouths, they were struck dumb, or they fell into strange contortions. Most of the convictions in Salem rested upon "spectral" evidence. That is, the accuser claimed that the specter of the accused witch, rather than the actual, physical person, had committed a particular act. It was almost impossible for an actual, physical person to prove that his or her specter had not been afflicting others and causing various sorts of harm.

The trials at Salem proceeded in a most unusual manner. Up until this time, those who were convicted and executed usually either had freely confessed to witchcraft or been "proven"

guilty by at least two witnesses who had observed a particular act of malice. As Tituba discovered when she confessed and pointed the finger at others, in Salem all those who confessed were ultimately released, while all those who were executed maintained their innocence, even when they were tortured. Richard Carrier, age 28, and his brother Andrew, 16, confessed only when they were "tyed . . . Neck and Heels till the Blood was ready to come out of their Noses." They said their mother had recruited them. Their lives were spared; their mother, Martha Carrier, however, was executed.

Although it soon became evident that a confession was the surest way to avoid execution, Giles Corey refused to admit guilt, even as heavy stones were piled upon his chest; his last words reportedly were "more weight." He had earlier accused his own wife of witchcraft, accusations of others being the second most reliable means of self-preservation. As a result, she was executed. In effect he committed suicide, perhaps overcome by guilt. Years later, in 1706, Ann Putnam, one of the original and most active accusers, asked God to forgive her for her role in the taking of "innocent blood." "It was a great delusion of Satan that deceived me in that sad time." A judge and a number of jurors later repented as well.

The End of Witchcraft

Although New Englanders and other colonists continued to believe in witchcraft, magic, and the occult, by the end of the seventeenth century they were no longer using them to explain unusual events. Increasingly, people came to believe that the universe was orderly and that events were caused by natural, and hence knowable forces. As one minister explained, "Many things have been dubbed witchcraft, and called the works of the devil, that were nothing more than the contrivance of the children of men."

By the eighteenth century, educated people took pride in their ability to use rational means of explaining weather and diseases, for example, and they disdained a belief in the occult as mere superstition. This change in thinking reflected a new faith not only in the powers of human reasoning but also in the capacity of ordinary men and women to shape their own lives. Witchcraft had offered a useful explanation for why bad things happened. By the beginning of the eighteenth century, more and more peo-

ple, especially those who were well-educated, prosperous, and lived in cities, believed that they could control their own destinies and that they were not at the mercy of invisible evil forces. The seed of individualism had been planted in New England's rocky soil.

As individualism slowly spread (it would not triumph for more than another century), the cohesion of Puritan communities necessarily waned. Communities became larger, and people began to go their own ways. Eccentrics could more easily be left alone. The eighteenth century brought new attitudes toward women that stripped them of their symbolic power to do harm. Eccentric women were soon considered more pathetic than dangerous.

The end of witchcraft trials also marked the conclusion of New England's belief in itself as a covenanted society, with a collective future. Until the end of the seventeenth century, Puritans had believed that God had chosen them for a special mission. As a result, they read a providential meaning into every event, from a sudden snowstorm to an Indian attack. Anything that had happened might have been a sign from God of His plans for the Puritan community. By the eighteenth century, however, people began to evaluate events separately, rather than as part of God's master plan.

French and Spanish Outposts

The imperial ambitions of the European powers brought them into conflict on the North American continent, but most of those battles were waged by the Europeans' Indian allies. At the end of the seventeenth century, however, in the territory that became the United States, Britain was the only European power that had established a substantial presence (see Map 4-3). The French and Spanish both had outposts on the American mainland north of the Rio Grande, but these European nations lacked the will, the need, and the resources to turn these outposts into thriving colonies. Their focus—and their resources—went to more valuable colonies, for the Spanish, Mexico and Latin America, and for the French, the West Indies. Largely irrelevant to the political economies of their parent nations and useful primarily as military outposts, Spanish settlements in Florida and New Mexico and French ones in Quebec and Louisiana developed slowly, each taking its own course.

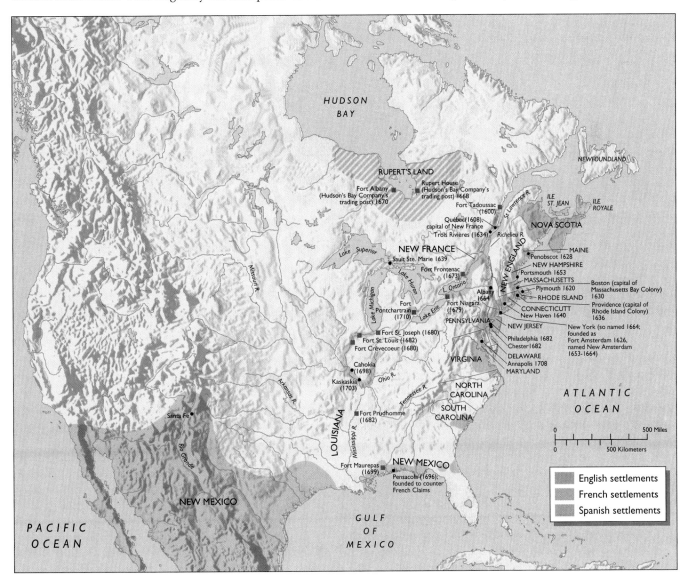

Map 4-3   Colonial North America, East of the Mississippi, 1713.
This map shows the expansion of European settlement. English settlement was concentrated in a strip down the east coast from Maine to North Carolina, with pockets of settlement in Canada and Carolina. French settlements formed a ring along the St. Lawrence, from the Great Lakes south along the Mississippi, and along the Gulf Coast. The Spanish had outposts along the Gulf and in Florida.
Source: Adapted from The Times Concise Atlas of World History, Geoffrey Barraclough, ed. (Maplewood, NJ: Hammond, 1994), p. 67.

France Attempts an Empire

Back at the beginning of the seventeenth century, France's civil wars of religion had ended, leaving France free to establish foreign colonies. Until the middle of the century, however, its efforts were haphazard. After 1664, France's minister Jean Baptiste Colbert tried to establish a coherent imperial policy, directed from Paris. He envisioned a series of settlements, each, in accordance with mercantilist principles, contributing to the wealth of the nation, through the fur trade and fishing in North America and plantation agriculture in the West Indies. Trade with Africa was supposed to supply slaves for the Caribbean plantations. France tried to direct the development of its New World empire into the eighteenth century. However, it lacked the resources and capacity to control small settlements so far away, particularly those on the mainland, which contributed little or nothing to the national wealth.

Colbert attempted to control every aspect of life in Quebec. Not only did he subsidize emigration, but he had the backgrounds of female migrants investigated to make sure that they were not only healthy but morally sound, too. Livestock was sent, in the hope of establishing a self-sustaining agricultural society. In order to encourage reproduction, dowries were offered to all men who married by the age of twenty—and men who married later, or women who married after the age of sixteen, were supposed to be fined. Lawyers, held in disrespect in France, were banned. Agriculture did develop and the population grew, more from natural increase than immigration. Most of the immigrants from France returned home after a brief stay in Quebec.

Colbert's hope to make Quebec a tightly run hierarchical society on the Old World model failed, however. Native Americans were more successful in shaping the fur trade, the mainstay of the Quebec economy, than was Colbert. The French depended upon their Indian trading partners to supply them with furs, and the British settlements of New York and New England only increased the Indians' leverage. The French came to need the Algonquian allies, not only as trading partners but also as military allies. By the end of the seventeenth century, there were no longer enough beaver to supply the French demand, due to overhunting. Northern Indians, including France's Algonquian allies, began replacing beaver pelts with less desirable deerskins and other furs, but the French had to accept them if they wanted to maintain the loyalty of those Indians. When Indians headed south and tried to trade their furs to the British, the French established—at considerable cost—forts to intercept them. At the same time, French traders smuggled beaver pelts to the British in return for British-made stroud, which the Indians much preferred to the inferior French fabric. The French complained that the Canadians were picking up the worst traits of the Indians, including lack of respect for authority. Canadians refused to let their children work as servants, and Canadian women were wearing short skirts like Indian women. Moreover, simply to maintain the allegiance of their Algonquian allies, the French had to supply them annually with gifts of ammunition, knives, cloth, tobacco, and brandy. When the declining revenues from the fur trade are balanced against the cost of these presents and the maintenance of forts and a military, it is questionable whether Canada was of any economic benefit to France. In fact, France maintained the fur trade more for political than for economic reasons.

It was for political reasons as well that France established a series of outposts in present-day Louisiana and Mississippi, including Fort Biloxi (1699), Fort Toulouse (1717), and New Orleans (1718), all in the territory named Louisiana. When the French explorer LaSalle reached the mouth of the Mississippi in 1682 and claimed it for France, the Spanish mainland empire was cut in two, and the British now faced a western rival. British traders in Carolina had pushed into the lower Mississippi region looking for deerskins and Indian slaves. They encouraged Natchez, Creek, and Chickasaw Indians to raid tribes to the west for slaves, and they gave them weapons and ammunition in return, thereby increasing the warfare among Indians in the Mississippi valley. By the time that the French arrived, tribes such as the Choctaws and Mobilians were looking for allies to help protect them from the British and their allies. In return for the customary "presents," even the Chickasaws, who had recently lost 800 men in warfare, were willing to ally themselves with the French. Within several decades, the French had developed an extensive trade and diplomacy network in the Mississippi valley and established trading posts as far north as Kaskaskia and Cahokia in the Illinois territory.

The early history of the Louisiana colony resembled that of the British settlement at Jamestown. The French shifted authority back and forth between the state and private investors, seeking a formula that would assure survival of the settlement. As in Virginia, the first settlers were ill-suited to the venture. The first group of settlers was top heavy with military personnel and Caribbean pirates. Louisiana was so unattractive a destination that it could not attract colonists wanting to better their lives. France began deporting criminals to the colony, including one woman who had been accused of fifteen murders. Debilitated by the unhealthy environment, colonists could not even grow their own food. Caught up in wars on the continent, the French could not or would not provide adequate support for the colony, and so its very survival depended upon the generosity of local Indians. Some of the settlers adopted the customs of the Indians and supported themselves by entering into trade with them and smuggling with the Spanish colony in Florida.

Without a secure economic base, the leaders of the Louisiana colony began clamoring for African slaves. In the century since Jamestown's founding, the French and British had both established plantation colonies in the

Drawing of the Savages of Several Nations, New Orleans, 1735, by Alexandre de Batz. Notice the array of foods, products, and crops produced by the Indians in the New Orleans area.

Caribbean and entered into the African slave trade, so now it was possible for a colony to make the conscious decision to try to become a slave society. As early as 1699, one of the founders of the colony asked for permission to import slaves from Africa. A few years later, another suggested trading Indian slaves, who routinely deserted back to their tribes, for Africans. When these requests were rejected, they began smuggling slaves in from the Caribbean. In 1719, France relented and permitted the importation of African slaves, but even as the African population grew, the colony still floundered.

Unlike the Chesapeake, colonial Louisiana never developed a significant cash crop. Because the colony was not very important to French economic interests, French mercantilist policies protected their Caribbean plantations at the expense of those in Louisiana. Deerskins purchased from the Indians often rotted in the steamy weather. Although Louisiana had a slave majority by 1727, the settlement was not a slave society. Many slaves worked at crafts in New Orleans, rather than on plantations, and in many ways, Louisiana's economy was one of frontier exchange, among Europeans, Indians, and Africans, rather than one of commercial agriculture. Many Africans enjoyed more

liberty than those who lived in slave societies, and that liberty sometimes made them a dangerous population for the French settlers. In an uprising reminiscent of the Second Anglo-Powhatan War, Natchez Indians who were unhappy with the settlers' encroachments on their land struck against the French in 1729, killing 10 percent of the French population. The Natchez were joined by African slaves, and the French armed other slaves to help put down the revolt. Two years later, the French foiled a conspiracy led by Bambaras, Africans from the upper Senegal River region, that was supposed to unite African slaves and several Indian tribes in a coordinated attack on the French. Although Africans and Indians never joined again in revolt, relations between the two groups remained good.

As it was marginal to France's political economy, Louisiana was largely left to itself. Europeans, Indians, and Africans all depended upon each other for survival. They intermarried and worked together to maintain an exchange economy. Despite Louisiana's leaders' hopes to create a hierarchical order based on plantation agriculture, social and economic relations in the colony remained fluid.

The center of France's New World political economy was in the Caribbean. By 1670, the islands of Martinique and Guadeloupe were producing significant amounts of sugar with African slave labor. At the same time, the French colonized the western half of the island of Santo Domingo, which they called Saint Domingue. By 1703 the African slave population outnumbered the French 45,000 to 8,000. Plantations were large—100 slaves on 200 acres— and lucrative for their owners. By the middle of the eighteenth century, Saint Domingue was producing more sugar than any colony in America and was soon to become the world's greatest producer of coffee as well.

The Spanish Outpost in Florida

Like France's colony at Louisiana, Spain's settlement at St. Augustine, Florida, was intended to be a self-supporting military outpost. Unable to attract settlers and costly to maintain, Florida, like Louisiana, grew slowly and unsteadily. As one Spanish official observed, "Only hoodlums and the mischievous go there from Cuba." At the beginning of the seventeenth century, the Spanish considered abandoning the colony altogether and moving the population to the West Indies. They relented only when Franciscan missionaries protested that it would be impracticable to relocate all of the Indians they had converted.

Once the British established their colony at Carolina, however, Florida once again became important to Spain— and it gained a new source of settlers, runaway slaves. The British and Spanish began attacking each other, usually using Indian and African surrogates. Spanish raiders seized slaves from Carolina plantations. The Spanish paid these Africans, many of whom were highly skilled, wages and introduced them to the Catholic religion. Soon, as Carolina's governor complained, slaves were "running dayly" to Florida. In 1693, Spain's king offered liberty to all British slaves who escaped to Florida.

Because Spain and England were often at war in the eighteenth century, the desertion of slaves to Florida had important military repercussions. Escaped slaves fought in Queen Anne's War, the Yamasee War, and King George's War in the first half of the eighteenth century and in raiding parties in times of peace.

The border between the two colonies was a place of violence—and also, for Africans, opportunity. Africans gained valuable military experience and, in 1738, about 100 former slaves established the free black town of Gracia Real de Santa Teresa de Mose (Mose, for short), two miles from St. Augustine. At the same time that Spain integrated free blacks into its New World colonies, it also established free black communities. Mose's leader was the Mandinga captain of the free black militia, Francisco Menéndez, one of the bold adventurers and world travelers the colonial Atlantic world seemed to spring forth. A former slave who had been re-enslaved, he persisted in petitioning for his freedom. Against the opposition of Florida officials, who had been paying off debts to their citizens with re-enslaved runaways from Carolina, Spain freed Menéndez and other Africans

like him and reiterated the policy that all British slaves who escaped to Florida should be free. Thus, the persistence of Menéndez and the other escaped slaves forced Spain to alter its policy and led to the establishment of the first free black community on the North American continent. Mose's exposed position left it vulnerable, and the town was evacuated during King George's War, resettled in 1752, and finally abandoned at the end of the French and Indian War, when Spain finally surrendered its Florida colony.

Conquest, Revolt, and Reconquest in New Mexico

In the western half of the continent, more than 2,000 miles from the Atlantic coast, the Spanish outpost in New Mexico developed into a colony. Like the settlements in Louisiana and Florida, it was an outpost on the edge of a world empire, far from the centers of power and largely irrelevant to Spain's political economy. Early in the seventeenth century, the Spanish considered abandoning the settlement, but, as in Florida, Franciscan missionaries persuaded Spain to maintain the colony so the priests could minister to the Native Americans. In the eastern half of the continent, regional Indians could play the European powers against each other, but in the western part, Spain was the only European nation with a presence, reducing the Pueblo Indians' leverage. Nor were there African slaves, either to perform work or to complicate local power structures. When the Pueblo Indians rose up against the Spanish at the end of the seventeenth century, the survival of New Mexico was in doubt.

The Conquest of Pueblo Society

Spain established its colony in New Mexico by conquest. Although Coronado's party had entered New Mexico and explored the Southwest from Arizona to Kansas (1541–1542), it had not planted a permanent settlement. In 1598, Juan de Oñate was appointed governor and authorized to establish a colony. Oñate was a Mexican-born aristocrat who had increased his wealth by marrying Isabel Cortès Moctezuma, the great-granddaughter of the great Aztec leader Moctezuma and the *conquistador* Hernán Cortès. Oñate consciously imitated Cortès, and he assumed that the Pueblo Indians he planned to conquer would have heard exactly how the Aztec empire had fallen. Everywhere he went, Oñate acted out scenes of the Aztec conquest. He even chose as his guide, interpreter, and mistress a young Indian woman by the name of Doña Inés, who he hoped would be "a second Malinche," the Tabasco Indian woman who had been Cortès' translator and mistress.

Much like Cortès, in some places Oñate was able to get the local Pueblos to accept him as their new ruler. In other places, he had to overcome them by force. His harsh means proved effective, and the Spanish soon dominated the entire Southwest. In 1610 they established their capital at Santa Fe, and the colony, called New Mexico, began to grow very slowly. In 1640, there were only about 800 Spanish in the colony and in 1680, no more than 2,000. The primary purpose of the New Mexico colony was to serve as an outpost of the Spanish Empire in North America, protecting its northern border from incursions by the French, just as St. Augustine was established to offer protection from the English along the Atlantic. The most important "business" in the colony was to convert the Pueblo Indians to Catholicism. Indeed, official Spanish policy held that "preaching the holy gospel . . . is the principal purpose for which we order new discoveries and settlements to be made."

Franciscan priests, members of a religious order founded by St. Francis of Assisi, established a series of missions in New Mexico. Although there were never more than fifty or so Franciscans in New Mexico at any one time, they would claim to have converted about 80,000 Indians in less than a century. Most of these conversions, however, were in name only. In hindsight it is clear that a profound religious and cultural gap separated the Indians from the Franciscan missionaries and that the Indians deeply resented the priests' attempts to change their most important customs and beliefs. The priests, who had taken vows of celibacy, considered the more relaxed sexual practices of the Indians sinful. In Pueblo culture, however, sexual intercourse had a sacred dimension, for it joined the male forces of the sky with the female forces of the earth. Cosmic harmony depended upon this union. When Pueblo women offered themselves to Spanish soldiers and priests, it was in order to harness an outside male force to re-establish harmony. However, the Spanish interpreted these actions as the most abject sort of subservience and an example of Indian immorality.

The Franciscans attempted to make the Pueblos follow Spanish sex roles. In Indian society, men were expected to hunt, weave, and protect the community, while women built and tended the household and cared for the children. The Franciscans insisted that men must now build and repair the homes, while women were to spin yarn and weave it. Once domestic animals such as cows and pigs were introduced, it was no longer necessary for men to hunt for food. The priests offered young men these animals and other gifts as a reward for conversion, undermining the traditional power of tribal elders to determine who should be rewarded. The Franciscans also insisted that the Indians practice monogamy. They objected to the positions in which Pueblo men and women engaged in sexual intercourse, and insisted that they use the so-called "missionary position" of man on top, woman on bottom. The priests were also deeply disturbed by Pueblo *berdaches*, men who dressed and adopted the mannerisms of women and had sex only with other men. In Pueblo culture, the *berdache*, half man and half woman, symbolized cosmic harmony. From the perspective of Spanish culture, however, he was simply a "male whore." By assuming the traditional roles of both fathers and mothers in Pueblo society and by forcing the Indians to adopt European sex roles and sexual mores, the Franciscans undermined not only Pueblo religion, but also their society.

The Pueblo at Acoma. The Acoma pueblo sits atop a mesa that rises 400 feet above ground. In January 1699, Spanish soldiers destroyed the pueblo and killed 800 of its inhabitants, in retaliation for the killing of a dozen soldiers. All the male survivors over the age of 12 and all female survivors were sentenced to 20 years of servitude to the Spanish, and the men over the age of 25 each had a foot cut off as well. The pueblo was rebuilt after its destruction.

The Pueblo Revolt

Spanish rule fell harshly upon the Pueblos. Although Spanish law now forbade enslavement of conquered Indians, some Spanish settlers openly defied that law by rounding up unconverted Indians and selling them into slavery. More common was the *encomienda* system. Oñate had rewarded a number of his lieutenants by naming them *encomenderos*, which entitled them to tribute from the Indians who lived on the land they had been awarded. Rather than accepting tribute in the form of grain or blankets, some *encomenderos* began to demand labor or personal service. Women working in Spanish households were vulnerable to sexual abuse by their masters. Suffering under such burdens, the Indian population declined from about 40,000 in 1638 to only 17,000 in 1670.

A combination of Spanish demands for labor and tribute and a long period of drought that began around 1660 left the Pueblos without the food surpluses that they had been selling to the nomadic Apache and Navajo to the west. As a consequence, the nomadic tribes began to raid the Pueblos, simply taking by force that which they could no longer get by trade. Under these pressures, hungry and frightened Pueblo Indians turned once again to their own tribal gods and religious leaders. It seemed clear to the Pueblos that Catholicism could not protect them from starvation or enemy attack.

When the Spanish punished the Indians who returned to the practice of their traditional religion, they pushed the already unhappy Pueblos over the edge and into revolt. From the northernmost Pueblo of Taos, a medicine man named Popé began to plan the eviction of the Spanish from New Mexico. He united the leaders of most of the region's pueblos, and he sent messengers out to carry his message. He promised that if the Indians threw out the Spanish and their gods and prayed once again to their ancient gods, then food would be plentiful once more. Popé promised that "who shall kill a Spaniard will get an Indian woman for a wife, and who kills four will get four women." Nor would the Indians ever have to work for the Spanish again, he said, and Indian customs would be restored.

Popé planned his revolt brilliantly. It began on August 10, 1680, just before the resupply caravan from Mexico arrived, and when the Spanish would be low on supplies. First, the Indians seized all the horses and mules, which prevented the Spanish both from reaching or notifying other settlements quickly and from engaging in mounted warfare. Next, they blocked all the roads to Santa Fe. Then they systematically destroyed all the Spanish settlements, one at a time. Just as the Spanish had destroyed the Indians' sacred katsina masks and ceremonial spaces (kivas), so the Indians took special care to desecrate the mission churches and images of Christ and the Virgin Mary, sometimes even covering them with manure and human feces. Twenty-one of the region's thirty-three Franciscans were killed, many by tor-

ture. By the end of the day, more than 400 Spanish had been killed, about a fifth of the colony's entire Spanish population. The survivors huddled in Santa Fe in the north and Isleta in the South. The Pueblos laid siege to Santa Fe, eventually forcing the Spanish to abandon the town and retreat to El Paso. Isleta was abandoned as well. In the most successful Indian revolt that North America would ever see, the Spanish had been driven from New Mexico.

Reconquest and the Creation of Spanish Colonial Society

The Pueblos held off the Spanish for thirteen years. Not until 1696 did Diego de Vargas reconquer New Mexico. The ongoing struggles had taken a heavy toll on the Pueblos. Contrary to Popé's promise, the eviction of the Spanish and their God had not ended the drought. Warfare with the Spanish took additional lives, and the population continued to drop, falling to 14,000 in 1700.

The revolt taught the Spanish several lessons. The new Franciscans who came to minister to the Indians were far less zealous than their predecessors. The *encomienda* was

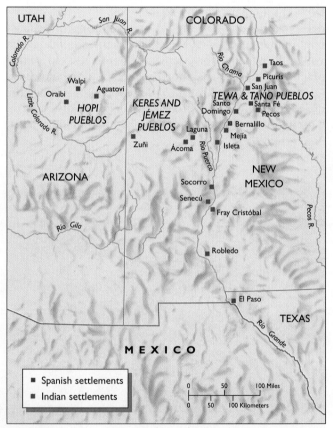

Map 4-4   Region of Spanish Reconquest of New Mexico, 1692–1696.
This map includes the pueblos reconquered by the Spanish, as well as Spanish settlements.
Source: Adapted from Oakah L. Jones, Jr., Pueblo Warriors and Spanish Conquest (Norman, OK: University of Oklahoma Press, 1966) p. 37.

not re-established, and levels of exploitation were significantly lower. Slowly the Spanish colony began rebuilding itself (see Map 4-4). The town of Santa Cruz was established in 1695 and Albuquerque in 1706. By 1746 the Spanish population had swelled to more than 4,000, while that of the Indians had dropped to about 5,500.

This population was divided into four social groupings, ranging from a small nobility at the top to enslaved Indians at the bottom. The Pueblo Indians continued to live in their pueblo villages, relatively isolated from the Spanish. The Spanish population lived primarily in the colony's three towns and in farms along the Rio Grande between the Taos and Isleta Pueblos.

At the top of society was the nobility, a hereditary aristocracy of about fifteen or twenty families, which included government officials. In all societies with hereditary aristocracies, those groups develop codes of honor to distinguish themselves from the lower orders. On the New Mexican frontier, without strong social or political institutions that might have moderated the behavior of the aristocrats, they developed a code of honor that was exaggerated in the extreme. This group prided itself on its racial purity, considering whiteness of skin a clear sign of superiority, and scorned those of mixed blood, many of whom, of course, were the illegitimate children of elite Spanish men and the Indian women they raped or seduced. Aristocratic men placed a high value on the personal qualities of courage, honesty, and loyalty, as well as sexual virility. Female honor consisted of extreme modesty, especially in the presence of men, and sexual purity. In this society, the reputation of a woman's entire family depended upon her retaining her virginity until marriage and strict modesty and sexual propriety afterwards. Love was considered dangerous, for it suggested an individualism that placed the desires of a man or woman ahead of the needs of the family. Elite parents usually arranged their children's marriages, sometimes when the children were still infants.

The second group in the Spanish society in New Mexico were landed peasants, most of them *mestizos,* half-Spanish and half-Indian. In this highly color-conscious society, the *mestizos* prized the Spanish part of their heritage and scorned the Indian. Next came the Pueblo Indians, living in their own communities.

Eighteenth-century Spanish Illustrations of New World Racial Mixture. In this case, the union of an Indian ("Yndio") and a "Mestiza" produces a "Coyote" child. The Spanish were much more attentive to color distinction than were the English, and they developed a large vocabulary so that they could make these distinctions with great precision.

At the bottom were the *genízaros,* conquered Indians who had been enslaved. After the reconquest of New Mexico, Apache Indians continued to raid the borders of the Spanish colony. They, as well as the Comanches and Pawnees, had been armed by the French, who hoped they would keep the Spanish colony weak and in a constant state of anxiety with their raids. The Spanish raided the Apaches and other nomadic tribes and seized members of these tribes as slaves. This lower class of slaves was joined by Indians who left their tribes and moved to Spanish settlements. Often these immigrants were outcasts from their own tribe, such as women who had been raped by Spanish men and were now shunned by their own society. A century after their first conquest, the Pueblo Indians had begun to adopt the values of their conquerors.

Conclusion

By the end of the seventeenth century, almost all of the British North American colonies had developed the political economies that they would maintain until the American Revolution. For the most part, the colonies were prosperous, with a large middle class. The efforts to replicate a European hierarchical order in New York, Maryland, and Carolina had largely failed. Each region had found a secure economic base, with a diversified economy, including farming and shipping in New England, mixed farming in the middle colonies, and single-crop planting in the

CHRONOLOGY

1598	Juan de Oñate colonizes New Mexico for Spain
1610	Santa Fe established
1627	Barbados settled
1628	Parliament passes Petition of Right
1642–1647	English Revolution
1649	King Charles I beheaded
1652–1674	Three Anglo-Dutch Wars
1656	Britain seizes Jamaica from Spain
1651–1696	Navigation Acts passed to regulate trade
1660	British monarchy restored, Charles II crowned king
1662	Half-Way Covenant
1664	British seize New Netherland, renaming it New York
1665	New Jersey established
1669	Fundamental Constitutions written for South Carolina
1670	Carolina settled
1673	Marquette and Joliet explore Mississippi for France
1675–1676	King Philip's War
1676–1677	Bacon's Rebellion
1680	Pueblo Revolt in New Mexico re-establishes Indian rule
	Westo War, Carolina defeats the Westos
1681	William Penn granted charter for Pennsylvania
1683	New York's assembly meets for first time
1685	King Charles II dies and James, Duke of York, becomes King James II
1686	Massachusetts, Plymouth, Connecticut, Rhode Island, and New Hampshire combined in Dominion of New England; New York and New Jersey added two years later
1688	Glorious Revolution
1689	Leisler's Rebellion in New York, Coode's Rebellion in Maryland
	William and Mary become King and Queen of Britain; Dominion of New England overthrown
1689–1697	King William's War
1690	Publication of John Locke's *Two Treatises of Government*
1691	Massachusetts is made a royal colony
	Maryland is made a royal colony
	New Hampshire is made a royal colony
1692	Salem witch trials
1696	Reconquest of New Mexico
1702–1713	Queen Anne's War
1706	Spanish establish settlement at Albuquerque
1718	French establish settlement at New Orleans

southern ones. The southern colonies had become slave societies, resting their prosperity and the freedom of white men on that institution, and slavery was practiced in every colony.

The contrast with New Mexico, which remained a frontier outpost without a secure economic base, was dramatic. Although the British colonies and New Mexico had all undergone a period of political turmoil in the final quarter of the century, that unrest led in different direc-

tions. New Mexico had succeeded in establishing an exaggerated version of a European feudal and hierarchical society, with a hereditary aristocracy at the top. The English colonies had failed to plant Old-World hierarchies and had struggled to achieve political order in their absence. Yet this failure was the source of their ultimate success. The new sorts of societies they had created were heading down a path that would lead to the American Revolution.

Review Questions

1. What was Britain's plan of empire? What role were the American colonies supposed to play in it?

2. Many of the American colonies experienced a period of political instability in the last quarter of the seventeenth century. Describe the rebellions and other examples of political instability and explain what caused them.

3. What effect did political turmoil and the change of leadership in Britain have upon the American colonies in the second half of the seventeenth century?

4. Describe Indian-white relations in the American colonies in the second half of the seventeenth century. What was the Covenant Chain, and how did Edmund Andros' vision of Indian-white relations differ from that of settlers in New England?

5. What were the primary causes of the witchcraft trials in Salem in 1692? What were the primary results?

6. Describe the causes and results of Popé's Rebellion of 1680, and describe New Mexican society in the early eighteenth century.

Further Readings

John Putnam Demos, *Entertaining Satan: Witchcraft and the Culture of Early New England* (1982). A fascinating exploration, from a variety of perspectives, of witchcraft in New England life.

Stephen Foster, *The Long Argument: English Puritanism and the Shaping of New England Culture, 1570–1700* (1991). A learned and insightful analysis of changing Puritan theology.

Richard Godbeer, *The Devil's Dominion: Magic and Religion in Early New England* (1992). Shows the ways in which occult and folk religion were an integral part of New England's culture.

Ramón A. Gutiérrez, *When Jesus Came the Corn Mothers Went Away: Marriage, Sexuality, and Power in New Mexico, 1500–1856* (1991). A brilliant analysis of the role of gender and sexuality in structuring colonial New Mexican society.

James Horn, *Adapting to a New World: English Society in the Seventeenth-Century Chesapeake* (1994). A bold new interpretation that argues for the influence of English patterns and values in colonial Chesapeake society.

Winthrop D. Jordan, *White Over Black: American Attitudes Toward the Negro, 1550–1812* (1968). Slightly dated, but still the most comprehensive account of the development of American racism.

Jill Lepore, *The Name of War: King Philip's War and the Origins of American Identity* (1998). A provocative new interpretation of King Philip's War that emphasizes the cultural distance between Puritans and Indians.

Wilcomb E. Washburn, *The Governor and the Rebel: A History of Bacon's Rebellion in Virginia* (1957). A highly readable account of Bacon's Rebellion.

History on the Internet

"William Penn: Visionary Proprietor"

http://xroads.virginia.edu~CAP/PENN/pnhome.html

By examining Penn's plans for the city of Philadelphia and his relationships with Native Americans, this site provides great insight into Penn's religious, political, and social ideology, both as a Quaker and a member of the elite class.

"Famous American Trials: Salem Witchcraft Trials, 1692"

http://www.law.umkc.edu/faculty/projects/ftrials/salem/SALEM.HTM

This comprehensive site contains various sources about this infamous incident in American history including excerpts from trial transcripts, biographies of key accusers and the accused, copies of arrest warrants for alleged witches, and illustrations. Also, read Cotton Mather's primary account of the events titled "Memorable Providences."

National Park Service's "Salina Pueblo Missions"

http://www.nps.gov/sapu/home.htm

Through this site of the National Park Service, learn about the Pueblo Indians prior to their cultural clash with Spaniards and the establishment of missions. Maps, narratives, and illustrations tell of the social, political, and religious ideologies of the Pueblos and how they differed from those of Europeans.

"Imperial Political and Economic Relationships: Colonial North America, 1492–1763"

http://www.ucalgary.ca/HIST/tutor/colony/18imp.html

Through this site, explore the meaning of mercantilism and the impact it had on all facets of life in the North American colonies of the eighteenth century.

5

THE EIGHTEENTH–CENTURY WORLD

1700–1775

OUTLINE

George Whitefield: Evangelist for a Consumer Society

The Population Explosion of the Eighteenth Century

The Dimensions of Population Growth

Bound for America: European Immigrants

Bound for America: African Slaves

"The Great Increase of Offspring"

The Transatlantic Political Economy: Producing and Consuming

The Nature of Colonial Economic Growth

The Transformation of the Family Economy

Sources of Regional Prosperity

Merchants and Dependent Laborers in the Transatlantic Economy

Consumer Choices and the Creation of Gentility

The Varieties of Colonial Experience

Creating an Urban Public Sphere

The Diversity of Urban Life

The Maturing of Rural Society

The World That Slavery Made

Georgia: From Frontier Outpost to Plantation Society

The Head and the Heart in America: The Enlightenment and Religious Awakening

The Ideas of the Enlightenment

The Enlightenment and the Study of Political Economy

Enlightened Institutions

Origins of the Great Awakening

The Grand Itinerant

Cultural Conflict and Challenges to Authority

What the Awakening Wrought

Conclusion

George Whitefield: Evangelist for a Consumer Society

In 1740 there were no more than 16,000 people living in Boston, but on October 12, some 20,000 men and women filled the Common to hear an English minister who had been preaching his way up the colonial coast. Everywhere he went the crowds were unprecedented—8,000 at least in Philadelphia, 3,000 in the little Pennsylvania village of Neshaminy. And those who could not see the evangelist in person read about him in their newspapers. If there was one binding experience for the American people in the decades before the Revolution, it was the ministry of George Whitefield.

When George Whitefield was born in Bristol, England, in 1714, no one would have guessed that he would become one of the most influential preachers in the

history of Christianity. Whitefield had trouble with his studies and much preferred the theater, romance novels, and fancy clothes. Because of the growth of the market economy, men and women on both sides of the Atlantic could now participate in a growing consumer culture that offered many more ways to spend both money and leisure time. To those schooled in a traditional Calvinist religion, the consumer society was both attractive and frightening. Could one serve God and oneself at the same time?

At the age of 17, when Whitefield discovered that he had no aptitude for trade, the career he had chosen, and his family was too poor to support him further, he faced a personal crisis. Then, one morning, as he was reading a play to his sister, he blurted out the words that had just come into his mind: "Sister, God intends something for me which we know not of." Whitefield then set out to prepare himself for the ministry. He enrolled at Oxford University, where he could pay his way by working as a servant to wealthy students. At Oxford he began to criticize the lax religious observance of the elite. He became friendly with the Methodists, a group of religious young men led by the brothers John and Charles Wesley, who were planning a mission to the new English colony of Georgia. Much like the Puritans, the Methodists insisted on a strict religious and personal discipline. Under their influence, Whitefield gave up the theater, fancy clothing, and rich food and drink. He turned his back on some of the attractions of consumer culture. Now, "whatsoever I did, I endeavoured to do all to the glory of God." George Whitefield's life now had meaning, and he was determined to share what he had learned with all who would hear.

George Whitefield, the great evangelist, was not afraid to show his feminine side, and he captivated men and women both with his heartfelt preaching.

Whitefield helped create a mass public that broke down the boundaries of small communities. Before Whitefield's ministry, each minister or priest typically addressed only his own congregation, within the walls of its church. The crowds Whitefield attracted were often too large for any building to hold, so he preached out of doors, with a voice so loud that Benjamin Franklin calculated that it could be heard by 25,000 people at a time. Although Whitefield spoke directly to the heart of each individual, he also drew together entire communities in a way no one had ever done before.

Again and again, Whitefield embodied the great contradictions of his age, without threatening the political or economic order that sustained them. He appealed to men as well as women, to the poor as well as the rich, to slaves as well as their masters, and to those who were suffering from capitalism's transformation of the economy as well as those who were spurring it. Whitefield's strategy was to criticize the individual without attacking the system. The religious leadership came under his censure, but not the church itself. Cruel slave masters were condemned, but not the institution of slavery. Perhaps most important of all, Whitefield showed men and women who were adrift in the new political economy how to acquire the personal self-discipline that would enable them either to succeed in a competitive and unpredictable market or to bear their failures with Christian resignation. He helped them not only to display their emotions but to understand religion and to experience it as an intense and personal feeling. He showed people how to find meaning for their lives in a time of rapid economic transformation.

A world traveler who came to call Georgia his home, Whitefield died in Newburyport, Massachusetts, in 1770, preaching to the end. Five years later, a band of Continental Army officers, on their way to fight the British in Quebec, dug up his corpse. The evangelist's body had decayed, but his clothing was still intact. The soldiers snipped pieces of it to take with them, to protect them on their perilous mission. ∎

KEY TOPICS

- The dramatic growth of the colonial population, both black and white, from both immigration and natural increase in the eighteenth century

- The maturing and diversification of the colonial capitalist economy as it produced for, and consumed from, the North Atlantic market

- The development of a public sphere in the cities and its relationship to new ideals of gentility and sociability

- The importance of slavery to the colonial economy and the contributions of Africans to the colonial world

- The Enlightenment and the Great Awakening as two different responses to the world created by the market economy and eighteenth-century consumer culture

The Population Explosion of the Eighteenth Century

George Whitefield could speak to the hearts of the American colonists because he understood their world. Increasingly, the American colonies were tied into a political economy that spread across the North Atlantic world, bringing dramatic changes everywhere it went. One of the most important changes was the increase in population. This population produced goods for the world economy and provided a market for them as well. This population boom was both the product of American prosperity and the precondition for its further growth.

The Dimensions of Population Growth

The population in the American colonies grew at a rate unprecedented in human history. In 1700 there were just over 250,000 people living in all of the colonies, but by 1750 the population had grown more than 300 percent to more than 1 million. The rate of growth was highest in the free population in the most prosperous farming regions. It grew rapidly everywhere, however, even among the slaves, in spite of the harsh conditions of their lives.

Much of the colonies' population growth was caused by their unquenchable thirst for labor. The colonies attracted an extraordinary number of immigrants, and when

free labor did not satisfy the demand, unfree labor (slaves, indentured servants, and redemptioners) filled the gap. In fact, when the number of Africans who came in chains is added to the Europeans who migrated as indentured servants and redemptioners, 90 percent of the immigrants to the British colonies between 1580 and 1775 were unfree at the time of their arrival.

Increasingly, these immigrants reflected the broad reach of the North Atlantic political economy. At the beginning of the eighteenth century, the population of the American colonies was primarily English in origin. By the beginning of the Revolution, the character of the population had changed significantly. Now there were small numbers of a large variety of nationalities and backgrounds, including those with Finnish, Swedish, French, Swiss, and Jewish heritage. There were also large numbers of other non-English peoples as well, including Welsh, Scotch-Irish, Germans, Dutch, and Africans. In fact, half the population south of New England was non-English. The foundation for the subsequent diversity of the American population had been laid.

Bound for America: European Immigrants

A significant portion of the colonies' population increase came from immigration. Almost all the European immigrants in the seventeenth century had come from England, but in the eighteenth century, substantial numbers came from Scotland, Northern Ireland, Wales, and Germany. All

In 1745, after the failure of the Jacobite rebellion, many Scots were evicted by their landlords. Although this painting is from the nineteenth century, it suggests the misery of Scottish tenants forced to leave their homes.

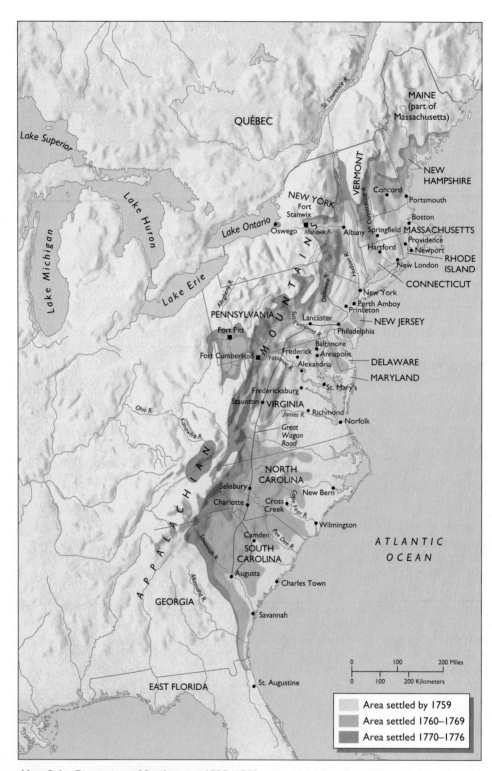

Map 5-1   Expansion of Settlement, 1720–1760.
By 1760, the colonial population made up an almost continuous line of settlement from Maine to Florida
and was pushing west over the Appalachian Mountains.

Source: Adapted from Bernard Bailyn, Voyagers to the West (Knopf, 1986), p. 9.

told, about 425,000 Europeans migrated to the colonies in the eighteenth century. The largest number of European immigrants were Scotch-Irish, that is, Scottish people who had moved to Northern Ireland to escape famine in their own country. A series of bad harvests in their new land, combined with the religious persecution they experienced as Presbyterians in an Anglican society, drove as many as 250,000 of them to seek a better life in the British colonies. At first, Massachusetts invited the Scotch-Irish to settle on their borders, as a buffer between the settled region of the colony and the Indians. Once the Scotch-Irish began to arrive in large numbers, however, the English inhabitants began to worry that they would have to provide relief for the impoverished newcomers. In 1729 a Boston mob turned away a shipload of Scotch-Irish would-be immigrants, and in 1738 the Puritan inhabitants of Worcester burned down a Presbyterian church recently erected by the town's Scotch-Irish. Henceforth the vast majority of Scotch-Irish immigrants headed for the middle colonies and the South, where they were more welcome.

Going where land was the cheapest, the Scotch-Irish settled in the region between the English settlements along the seaboard and the Indian communities on the west, from Pennsylvania south to Georgia (see Map 5-1). As the Scotch-Irish population increased, it pressed against the Indians, seizing, for example, a 15,000 acre tract that the Penn family had set aside for the Conestoga Indians. "It was against the laws of God and nature," they asserted, "that so much land should be idle when so many Christians wanted it to labor on and to raise their bread."

Like the Scotch-Irish, most of the German migrants settled in the back country from Pennsylvania to the Carolinas. Between 1700 and the outbreak of the Revolution, more than 100,000 Germans moved to the American colonies, and by 1775, a third of the population of Pennsylvania was German. The Germans were a diverse group, including not only Lutherans and Catholics, but a variety of other sects, including Quakers, Amish, and Mennonites. German immigrants established prosperous farming communities wherever they settled. Indeed, those colonies such as Pennsylvania that welcomed the widest variety of immigrants became not only the most prosperous, but also the ones in which that prosperity was most widely shared.

In contrast to the migration of the seventeenth century, an increasing proportion of the eighteenth-century migrants were skilled but relatively impoverished artisans. They were pushed from Europe by lack of work and

drawn to America by the colonies' demand for skilled labor. As African slaves began to fill the demand for agricultural workers, especially in the South, the colonists eagerly sought skilled workers, especially those who could build anything from houses to bridges and those who could repair whatever was broken. One Marylander who was trying to recruit laborers explained, "The more weavers, shoemakers, tailors, joiners, carpenters, bricklayers, and farmers, and the fewer women there are among them the better." Once the sex ratios in the colonies evened out and male colonists could find wives, there was little demand for female immigrants.

The majority of European migrants to the colonies were unfree, not only indentured servants and redemptioners but also the 50,000 British convicts whose sentences were commuted to a term of service in the colonies. Most of the English and Welsh migrants were single men between the ages of 19 and 23 who came as indentured servants. The Scotch-Irish migration included a larger number of families, and three-fourths of the Germans came in family groups. For all immigrants, the passage to America, which could take three months or more, was grueling. Gottlieb Mittelberger described the afflictions of the journey: "The ship is full of pitiful signs of distress—smells, fumes, horrors, vomiting, various kinds of sea sickness, fever, dysentery, headaches, heat, constipation, boils, scurvy, cancer, [and] mouth-rot." The lice were so thick that they had to be scraped off the passengers' bodies, and the food and water were filled with worms. Once the migrants arrived in the colonies the servants and convicts were sold for terms of service in auctions that resembled those held for African slaves. One man who witnessed such an auction in

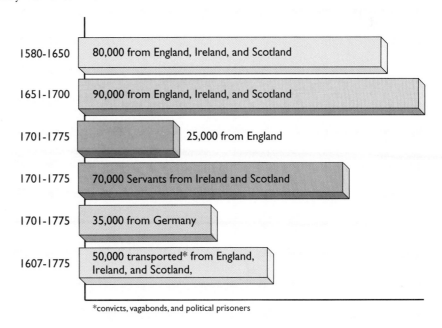

1580-1650   80,000 from England, Ireland, and Scotland
1651-1700   90,000 from England, Ireland, and Scotland
1701-1775   25,000 from England
1701-1775   70,000 Servants from Ireland and Scotland
1701-1775   35,000 from Germany
1607-1775   50,000 transported* from England, Ireland, and Scotland,

*convicts, vagabonds, and political prisoners

Figure 5-1   The Importation of Servants from Europe into British America, 1580–1775.
Source: Richard S. Dunn, "Servants and Slaves," in Jack P. Greene and J.R. Pole, Colonial British America (Baltimore: John Hopkins, 1984), p. 159.

A coffle of African slaves, being force marched by an African slave trader from the interior of Africa to a European trading post on the coast.

Williamsburg said that some of the men and women were almost "naked and what had cloths was as black as chimney swipers [sweepers], and all most starved."

Bound for America: African Slaves

The increase in the African population in the colonies was even more dramatic than that of Europeans (see Figure 5-1). In 1660 there were only 2,920 African or African-descended inhabitants of the mainland colonies. A century later they numbered more than 300,000, an increase of more than 10,000 percent. The proportion of Africans in the colonial population grew most rapidly in the southern colonies, where it stood at almost 40 percent on the eve of the Revolution. By 1720 South Carolina had an African majority. In 1770 the African portion of the American population peaked at 21 percent, and although the number of persons of African descent in the American population continued to grow, it never again made up as large a segment of the total population.

Most of the increase in the African population of the colonies came from the transatlantic slave trade. By 1808, when Congress closed off the traffic in human beings to Americans, about 523,000 African slaves had been imported into the nation (see Figure 5-2). Of this number, two-thirds had arrived before the Revolution, primarily during the eighteenth century. Americans entered the slave trade relatively late, about two centuries after it had begun, and they played a relatively small role in it. Less than 5 percent of the approximately 12,000,000 Africans who were sold into slavery in the Western Hemisphere arrived in the mainland British colonies, about the same number who were sent to the tiny island of Barbados.

The African slave trade was a profitable and well-organized segment of the world economy. As a rule, Euro-

pean and American traders depended on Africans to provide them with a steady supply of slaves. Until the eighteenth century, when increased demand from the New World changed its character, the transatlantic slave trade was controlled by Africans. That is, they set the terms, including the prices, of the trade. Generally, Europeans were not allowed into the interior of the continent of Africa, and instead slaves were brought to the coast for sale. Many African nations taxed the sale of slaves and regulated the trade in other ways. Each nation imposed its own restrictions. The kingdom of Benin forbade the export of male slaves from 1516 until the eighteenth century. Some nations supplied a steady stream of slaves, while others offered them intermittently, suggesting that participation in the trade was a matter of conscious policy. In the eighteenth century, the supply of slaves from the Senegambia region shrank because those Africans no longer found European trade goods attractive.

Because African slaves were unwilling and sometimes rebellious passengers on the ships that transported them across the Atlantic, European slave ships needed larger crews and heavier weapons than ordinary cargo required. This resistance on the part of the slaves increased the cost

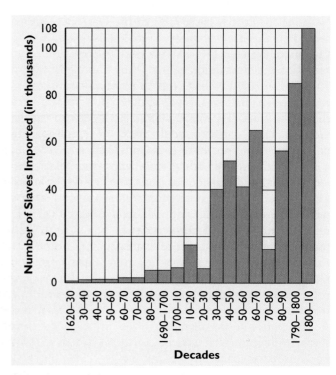

Figure 5-2   The Importation of Slaves into the Colonies, 1620–1810.

Source: Helen Hombeck Tanner, The Settling of North America (Macmillan, 1995), p. 51.

of transporting them so much that, according to a recent study, the higher prices may have spared half a million Africans enslavement.

Most slaves were captives of war, and as the New World demand for slaves increased in the eighteenth century, the tempo of warfare in Africa intensified in response. Sometimes slaves were captured by large raiding parties, for the most part led by other Africans, and on occasion small groups of Africans were kidnapped and sold into slavery. In times of famine and epidemic, sometimes brought on by the slave trade itself, desperate families might even sell their own children to a trader. The New World preferred male slaves, leaving most of the female captives to the African domestic slave market, where they became domestic slaves or plural wives to wealthier Africans.

As bad as the voyage to America was for indentured servants, the trip for enslaved Africans was worse. Perhaps 10 percent died even before reaching the African coast, a march for some of almost 400 miles. Until they arrived at the coast, many of them had never seen an ocean or a white man, and both sights terrified them. They were confined in pens or forts for as long as half a year while waiting for a ship to take them to the New World. Their heads were shaved, and sometimes they were branded with their owners' initials. They were stripped naked just prior to departure.

The voyage, or "middle passage" as it is often called, itself proved lethal to many more. Male slaves were shackled one to another and confined below deck for most of each day. Chained together and without enough room to stand up, many were unable to reach the large buckets that served as latrines. Some captains let the slaves lie in their own filth until the voyage's end. Heat and disease compounded the misery. One ship's doctor reported that the slaves' deck "was so covered with the blood and mucus which had proceeded from them in consequence of the flux, that it resembled a slaughterhouse." The women were left unshackled, but their relative freedom left them prey to the sailors' lust. As the slave trade became more efficient in the eighteenth century and ships were built to the specifications of the trade, the mortality rate in passage dropped, from perhaps 20 percent to half that amount. Those who survived were ready to begin their lives as New World slaves.

"The Great Increase of Offspring"

Most of the increase in the colonies' population came not from immigration or the slave trade but from natural increase, what Benjamin Franklin called "the great increase of offspring." The rate of population growth for both Europeans and Africans in the colonies was extraordinary (see Figure 5-3).

For European Americans the main source of population increase was a lower age of marriage for women and a higher proportion of women who married. In England, for example, as many as 20 percent of women did not marry by age 45, compared to only 5 percent in the colonies. The age of marriage for women in the colonies was also considerably lower, with women marrying in their late teens or early twenties, compared to late twenties in England. Because more women married, and married earlier, they bore more babies, on average seven or eight each, with six or seven surviving to adulthood. As a rule, the more economic opportunity, the earlier the age of marriage for women and men, and the more children. Likewise, the healthier the climate, the more children survived to adulthood, but compared to today, child mortality rates were high. A baby born today is as likely to survive to the age of 65 as a baby born in the colonies was to reach its first birthday. Still, the rate of population growth in the colonies was phenomenal, and as a result the American population was exceptionally young. In 1790 the median age was 16, compared to 35 in the year 2000.

In many ways, the history of the African-American population resembled that of European Americans, for both suffered from the dislocations of moving to a new land. Those slaves who were born in the colonies, however, married young and established families as stable as slavery permitted. By the time they were eighteen, most slave women usually had their first child. Following African custom, they might not form a lasting union with the father of their first child, but within a few years many settled into long-lasting relationships with the men who would father the rest of their children. When slave marriages were disrupted, it was most often by the death of one partner or by sale, rather than by the choice of the partners. Slave women bore between six and eight children, on average. With child mortality even higher

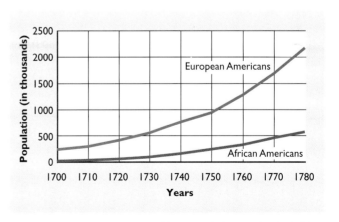

Figure 5-3   Population of the Thirteen Colonies, 1610–1780.

Source: Jacob Cooke, ed., Encyclopedia of North American Colonies (New York: Scribner's, 1993), I, 470.

for African Americans than for European Americans, however, between 25 percent and 50 percent of these slave children died before reaching adulthood. Even so, enough slave children survived that the slave population more than reproduced itself.

For Europeans and Africans both, the prosperity and healthy climate of North America sustained high rates of reproduction. By the middle of the eighteenth century the African-American population was growing more from natural increase than from the importation of slaves. Only a tiny fraction of the Africans sold into slavery ended up in mainland British colonies. Nonetheless, when slavery was abolished after the Civil War, the United States had the largest population of African descent in the New World.

The Transatlantic Political Economy: Producing and Consuming

The American colonial economy in the eighteenth century was built and sustained by trade. This economy, in turn, shaped the sort of societies the American colonies developed. In the eighteenth century, the American colonies became capitalist societies, tied increasingly into a trade network that spanned the Atlantic. Increasingly, labor was organized systematically for the market. That is, people began to produce for the market, so that they could buy the goods the market had to offer. Throughout the Atlantic world in this period, ordinary people were reorienting their economic lives so they could buy more goods. Historians talk about two economic revolutions in this period. The first was a **consumer revolution** that was really a slow and steady increase in the demand for, and purchase of, consumer goods. The second was an **industrious revolution** in which people simply worked harder and organized their households (that is, their families, their servants, and their slaves) to produce goods that could be sold, so that they would have money to pay for the items they wanted. Income went up only slightly in the eighteenth century, much less than it would in the next century, for example. Yet people were buying more, and buying particular sorts of items for particular reasons. In the process, they created a consumer society. With the consumer and industrious revolutions, the political economy of capitalism took shape.

The Nature of Colonial Economic Growth

Throughout human history, population growth has usually led to a decline in standard of living as more people compete for fewer resources. In the American colonies,

however, population growth led to an expansion of the economy, as more of the continent's abundant natural resources were brought under human control. Historians debate whether economic growth led to a rising standard of living for Americans or whether the increasing wealth was simply spread among the increasing population. Probably, the standard of living for most free Americans improved somewhat, although not dramatically. As the economy matured, a small segment of the economy, in particular urban merchants and owners of large plantations, became increasingly wealthy. At the same time, the urban poor and tenant farmers began to slip toward poverty.

All of these changes took place, however, without any significant changes in technology. Most wealth was made from shipping and agriculture. Eighty percent of the colonies' population worked on farms or plantations, and there were no major technological innovations in these areas. Virtually all gains in productivity came instead from labor. Quite simply, more people were working, and they were working more efficiently. That is, they were organizing themselves to produce for the market.

The economy of colonial America was shaped by three factors: abundance of land and shortages of labor and capital. The plantation regions of the South and the West Indies were best situated to take advantage of these circumstances, and the small-farm areas of New England, the least. Tobacco planters in the Chesapeake and rice and indigo planters in South Carolina sold their products, which were raised in only a small part of the world, on a huge world market. As a consequence, their profits were large enough to enable them to purchase more land and more slaves to work it.

Northern farmers, in contrast, raised crops and animals that were also produced in Europe. As a result, profits from agriculture alone were relatively low, too low to permit farmers to acquire large tracts of land or obtain much additional labor (see Table 5-1). Northerners who hoped to become wealthy had to look for other opportunities. They found them in trade. Although the leading southern planters diversified their economic activities, for example by speculating in land or lending money, northerners out of necessity had to expand the range of their business undertakings even more. By the time of the Revolution, the southern economy was more prosperous than the northern one. It was more dependent on the export trade but was still less diversified.

The Transformation of the Family Economy

In colonial America, the family was the basic economic unit, and all production was organized by the household. From the time they were able, all family members were expected to make a contribution to the family economy. Work was organized by gender. On farms, women were responsible for the preparation of food and clothing, child

TABLE 5-1

Property-Owning Class	New England	Mid-Atlantic Colonies	Southern Colonies	Thirteen Colonies
Men	£169	£194	£410	£260
Women	£42	£103	£215	£132
Adults 45 and older	£252	£274	£595	£361
Adults 44 and younger	£129	£185	£399	£237
Urban	£191	£287	£641	£233
Rural	£151	£173	£392	£255
Esquires, gentlemen	£313	£1,223	£1,281	£572
Merchants	£563	£858	£314	£497
Professions, sea captains	£271	£241	£512	£341
Farmers only, planters	£155	£180	£396	£263
Farmer-artisans, ship owners, fishermen	£144	£257	£801	£410
Shop and tavern keepers	£219	£222	£195	£204
Artisans, chandlers	£114	£144	£138	£122
Miners, laborers	£52	£67	£383	£62

Source: Alice Hanson Jones, Wealth of a Nation to Be: The American Colonies on the Eve of the Revolution *(New York: Columbia University Press, 1980), p. 224.*

Much of a colonial woman's work was done either at her kitchen hearth or in the garden outside her door.
Most of a farming man's work was done outside in the fields.

care, and care of the home. Women grew vegetables and herbs in their gardens; they provided dairy products; they smoked hams and bacon from the pigs they slaughtered themselves. They transformed flax and sheep's wool into linen shirts and wool pants. The daughters in the family worked under their mother's supervision, perhaps spinning extra yarn to be sold for a profit. Prosperous farm wives hired less affluent families' daughters as "helps" to alleviate some of the burden of domestic labor.

While women were responsible for the home and its vicinity, men performed the work on the rest of the farm. They raised grain and maintained the pastures. They

cleared the land, chopped wood for fuel, and built and maintained the house, barn, and all the other structures on the farm. They took their harvested crops to market. If they were prospering, they hired young men from the neighborhood to assist them.

Men's and women's work were complementary, and both were necessary for the family's economic survival and prosperity. For example, men grew the barley that women brewed into beer. Men planted the apple trees, children picked the apples, and women made them into cider. Men herded the sheep whose wool women sheared, carded, spun, and dyed. When a husband was disabled, ill, or away from home, his wife could, without any threat to her femininity, fill in for him, performing virtually all of his tasks as a sort of "deputy husband." Men almost never performed women's work, and men whose wives died remarried quickly in order to have someone to take care of household and children.

The industrious revolution transformed the family economy. Or to be more accurate, when people decided to produce goods to sell, they changed their family economies. Historians are just beginning to study this aspect of social change, but they believe that increased production in this period came primarily from the labor of women and children, who worked harder and longer than they had before.

Sources of Regional Prosperity

The South was the most productive region of all. It accounted for more than 60 percent of colonial exports (see Map 5-2). Even after tobacco prices fell after the 1720s,

tobacco remained the region's chief cash crop. Next came cereals such as rice, wheat, corn, and flour, and then indigo, a plant used to dye fabric. In the 1740s, Eliza Lucas Pinckney and other South Carolinians experimented with indigo and found it could grow on high, dry land not suitable for rice cultivation.

Slave labor accounted for most of the southern agricultural output, and the slave labor force was organized to produce for the market. When profits from tobacco began to slip (because of falling prices and the depletion of the soil), planters took steps to maintain their profits. They worked their slaves harder than they had been able to work European indentured servants. Planters in the Chesapeake also began to plant corn and wheat. While half the corn was used for food on the plantation, 90 percent of the wheat was sold. By diversifying their crops, planters were also able to find tasks to keep their slaves busy throughout the year. The male slaves on George Washington's plantation, for example, were assigned 57 different tasks, from plowing and digging ditches in the spring, to harvesting and

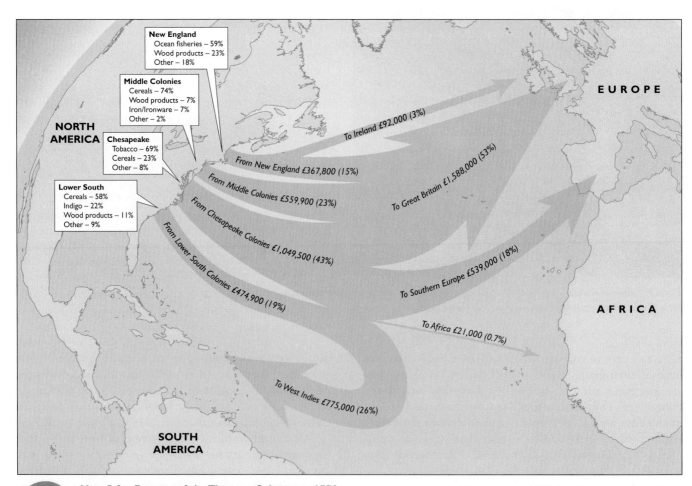

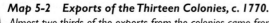
Map 5-2   Exports of the Thirteen Colonies, c. 1770.
Almost two-thirds of the exports from the colonies came from the South, and more than one-half went to Great Britain alone. Tobacco and grains were the most important exports of all.

Source: Jacob Cooke, ed., Encyclopedia of North American Colonies (New York: Scribner's, 1993), I, 514.

making livestock pens in the fall. Slave women were responsible for 67 tasks, many of which were reserved for women alone, such as spinning and weaving, as well as specific agricultural tasks. Slave boys and girls also had specific work assignments. Successful planters made maximum use of their slave labor force.

The work routine of slaves depended on the crops that they tended. On tobacco plantations, where careful attention to the plants was necessary in order to assure a high quality of tobacco, planters or their white overseers worked the slaves in small gangs. Each gang was carefully selected and arranged in order to maximize productivity. Thomas Jefferson thought of a slave gang as a "machine." The strongest field hand, for example, would be put at the head of a row of hoers, and all the other slaves would be made to work at his pace.

In the rice-growing regions of the lower South, however, slaves were usually assigned specific tasks, which they would work at until the job was completed. Rice growing required far less supervision than did tobacco planting. In addition, because many Africans had grown rice in Africa, it is more likely that they taught Europeans how to grow it in America than vice versa. Under these circumstances, rice planters were willing to let the slaves set their own pace. Once the slaves had finished their task for the day, they could use their time as they pleased. Many planted gardens to supplement their own diets or to earn a little income from selling their own crops. South Carolina law permitted slaves to sell to their masters, and many also carried on an illegal trade with other whites. Slaves trafficked in a wide range of products, not only rice, corn, chickens, hogs, and catfish, but also canoes, baskets, and wax. Slaves who worked under the task system generally had less contact with whites and more autonomy than those who worked in gangs.

The inhabitants of the middle colonies grew prosperous primarily by raising wheat and other grains to sell on the market. The ports of Baltimore, Philadelphia, Wilmington, and New York all became thriving commercial centers that collected grain from regional farmers, milled it into flour, and shipped it to the West Indies, Southern Europe, and the other American colonies. Farmers in the middle colonies relied on indentured servants, to a lesser extent cottagers, and slaves to supplement the labor of family members. Cottagers were families who rented out part of a farmer's land, which they worked for wages.

As long as land was cheap and easy to obtain, the middle colonies enjoyed the most evenly shared prosperity on the continent. Most inhabitants fell into the comfortable middle class, with the gap between the richest and the poorest relatively small. Pennsylvania, which offered both religious toleration and relatively simple procedures for the purchase of land, was particularly prosperous. The energy that elsewhere went into religious conflict here was freed for work and material accumulation. Gottfried Mittleberger, who had endured a horrendous journey to Pennsylvania, later described his new home as a sort of paradise: "Our Americans live more quietly and peacefully than the Europeans; and all this is the result of the liberty which they enjoy and which makes them all equal."

When land became expensive or local practices made it difficult to obtain, however, conflict might ensue. In the 1740s and 1750s, both New Jersey and New York experienced land riots when conflicting claims made land titles uncertain. In other regions, such as the Chesapeake and southeastern Pennsylvania, increasing land prices in the decades before the Revolution drove the poorest inhabitants into tenancy or to the urban centers. The widespread prosperity of the eighteenth century led Americans to expect that every family who wanted a farm would be able to own one. Unlike in Europe, land ownership was the rule, rather than the exception, and any deviation from this norm produced tension and anger.

Like the middle colonies, New England was primarily a farming region. However, indentured servants, cottagers, and slaves were far less common than in the other regions of the colonies. Instead, most farm labor was provided by the male members of the family. Although farms in some regions, such as the Connecticut River valley, produced considerable surpluses for the market, in most of New England farm families had to look for other sources of income to pay for all that they wished to buy.

Town governments in New England encouraged enterprise, sometimes providing their inhabitants with gristmills, sawmills, and fields on which cattle could graze. These capital investments paid off handsomely. As a result the region prospered, and New Englanders came to expect that government should act to enhance the economy. Agricultural exports from the region were relatively slight, although New Englanders sent both grain and livestock to the slave plantations of the West Indies. The primary exports of the region were fish, wood and wood products, and ships built from New England timbers. The chief customers for New England foods were the planters of the West Indies. With slave labor dedicated almost wholly to the production of sugar and other plantation crops, Caribbean planters imported most of their food. In fact, more than 25 percent of the American colonies' exports (and more than 70 percent of New England's exports) went to the West Indies. Most of the rest went to southern Europe. For example, Catholics, whose religion required them periodically to abstain from eating meat, provided a market for fish.

The other major exports of the American colonies in the eighteenth century were fur and hides. By the eve of the Revolution, 95 percent of the furs imported into England came from North America. As in the previous century, most of the furs were provided by Indians, who traded them to European middlemen. Most furs came from Canada,

Men landing and drying cod in Newfoundland. Increasingly, fishing became a form of dependent wage labor, as merchants supplied the boats and equipment and hired other men to fish for them.

New York, and Pennsylvania, and deerskins (also procured by Indians) came from the southern back country.

Merchants and Dependent Laborers in the Transatlantic Economy

Almost all regions of the colonies participated in a transatlantic economy. The exceptions were newly settled farming regions, where almost all the labor went into creating new farms, and subsistence farming regions, remote from the rivers or roads that could transport products to market. In each region those who were most involved in the market (and hence, most fully committed to a capitalist economy) were those with the most resources. These were large planters in the southern colonies, owners of the biggest farms in the middle colonies, and the merchants of the urban regions. The wealthiest colonists never made their fortunes from farming or planting alone but always enhanced their incomes from supplemental activities, such as speculating in land, practicing law, lending money to neighboring planters, and running a gristmill or sawmill. These supplemental activities developed the colonial economy. A speculator's land was worthless unless he could attract purchasers to it by selling it at affordable prices, building stores to sell provisions, and providing transportation to the region. Early American capitalists of necessity inspired their countrymen and women to orient their economic activities to the market.

If some economic development was spurred from above, by enterprising individuals or by governments (British mercantilist policy attempted to encourage some economic endeavors and retard others), much also developed from the aspirations of ordinary men and women. New England's mixed economy of grain, grazing, fishing, and lumbering required substantial capital improvements such as gristmills, sawmills, and tanneries if the inhabitants were to turn a profit. Within decades of the first settlements, the region had established a shipbuilding industry, and by the beginning of the eighteenth century, shipbuilding was a substantial part of the economy. In fact, by the early part of the century, London was the only place in the English-speaking world that built more ships than Massachusetts. By 1775, one-third of the English merchant fleet had been built in the colonies.

The shipbuilding industry, in turn, spurred further economic development. Economic historians call this process **linked economic development,** for it ties together a variety of enterprises. Shipbuilding stimulated lumbering, for the masts, planks, pitch, and tar needed to construct each ship, as well as a number of related crafts and occupations. The availability of ships also made possible a flourishing trade. The profits generated by shipbuilding and trade were reinvested in sawmills to produce more lumber, in gristmills to grind grain into flour, and, of course, in more trading voyages. As either workers or investors, the majority of men in centers of trade such as Boston were involved in shipbuilding or trading.

The growth of shipping in port cities such as Boston, Newport, New York, Philadelphia, and Charleston led to the emergence of an affluent merchant class. Trading was a risky business, and although many tried it, few rose to the top. It was relatively easy to start out; it took a little capital to buy goods or the contacts to persuade a British merchant to extend credit. With returns on investment at around 10 percent, only those who had thousands to invest could make substantial profits. Nonetheless, many enterprising people in towns such as Boston and Philadelphia tried their hand at trade, investing in a trading venture or purchasing dry goods from London to resell at home. As a result, competition was stiff, and the colonies were glutted with even more goods than acquisitive Americans could buy.

One ship lost to a storm could ruin a merchant, as could a sudden turn in the market. In 1759 two enterprising Philadelphians, Daniel Wister and Owen Jones, with just over £4,000 between them, persuaded English merchants to send them £94,000 worth of goods. This was a colossal venture, equaling 4 percent of Pennsylvania's imports from Britain at the time. For two years the partnership prospered, but when the market went sour in 1761, Wister was left bankrupt while Jones struggled to pick up the pieces. With an average of ten times the capital of even the leading colonial merchants, English merchants could weather such reverses. Because capital was scarce in the colonies, merchants found themselves taking great risks, seeking to turn a quick profit during wartime or gambling on a sudden spurt in the price of wheat. Bad choices or bad luck could ruin any merchant.

The seafaring trades were at the forefront of capitalist development in the colonial economy. Although this de-

"Commerce Moves All," according to this certificate of membership in a sailmakers' society. Here we see not only linked economic activities such as sailmaking (lower right-hand corner) and trade but also the moral benefits that were imagined to flow from commerce—charity (upper right-hand corner) and abolition of slavery (upper left-hand corner).

velopment led to the creation of a wealthy, risk-taking merchant class, it simultaneously created that other distinguishing mark of a capitalist economy, a wage-earning class. As long as there was a labor shortage in the colonies, workers had an advantage. By the beginning of the eighteenth century, however, rapid population increase led to a growing supply of labor in towns such as Salem and Marblehead. Merchants could get men to fish for them without extending credit as they had in the previous century, and those fishermen without the resources to buy their own boats and equipment were reduced to fishing for others for wages. Although they were free to shop around for the best wages, they had become part of a wage-earning working class, dependent on others for their employment and income.

This process of economic development had a profound impact on the kinds of lives that colonists could expect to lead. A more complex economy created greater opportunities for both success and failure, and whether one succeeded or suffered could be as much a matter of chance as of skill. Although only a small portion of the American population was working for wages on the eve of the Revolution, it was a sign of things to come.

Consumer Choices and the Creation of Gentility

By design of the British mercantilist system (see chapter 4), the colonies were supposed to export raw materials to the empire and import finished products from the empire. To a certain extent, the British Empire followed this pattern, with the colonies sending sugar (from the West Indies), tobacco, wheat, lumber, fish, and animal pelts to Britain. In return, the colonies imported primarily cloth and iron. Yet within these general patterns, which were encouraged by the Navigation Acts, individual men and women made choices about what to buy.

On both sides of the Atlantic, demand for both plantation products and consumer goods was almost insatiable. At first only the wealthy could afford such luxuries as sugar and tobacco. But as more and more labor was organized to produce for the market, ordinary men and women found themselves with added income. They used it to purchase products once considered luxuries. The colonists soon developed a taste for these items, consuming even more tobacco and sugar than the British. Tea, imported

James Balfour, the representative of an English mercantile firm, and his wife Jemima moved to Virginia, where they assumed the roles of proper members of the merchant elite. James is depicted with his business papers and his son, illustrating the two aspects of a gentleman's character, his acumen for business and his affection for his family, while his wife is pictured holding a book, demonstrating that she is a woman of education, with the leisure to pursue it.

into both Britain and the colonies from Asia, was well on its way to becoming, like tobacco and sugar, a mass-consumed luxury. By the time of the Revolution, annual sugar consumption in England had skyrocketed to 23 pounds per person, and tobacco consumption was about 2 pounds per person—enough for a pipeful a day. Demand for these plantation products led directly to the traffic in African slaves.

As most of the plantation products flowed east across the Atlantic, so manufactured goods came back to the colonies. Consumer behavior on both sides of the Atlantic was quite similar. Just as consumers on both sides were smoking tobacco and sweetening their tea with sugar, so also were they buying more clothing, more household goods, more books, and more of every sort of good that was being manufactured.

The consumer revolution was not a product of higher wages. Instead, people made choices about how hard they would work—they chose to work harder. They made choices about what kind of work they would do—they chose work that brought in money. They decided what they would do with that money—they chose to buy particular items. Increasingly, people bought items that their friends and neighbors could see and that

they could use in entertaining their friends and neighbors. In seventeenth-century America, extra income that was not invested in additional production (more land, more livestock, more slaves, farm equipment, barns, and so on) was spent on items of lasting value. For example, men and women purchased tablecloths and bed linens that they kept folded away in a chest, to be passed on to their children.

In the eighteenth century, men and women bought more clothing, made out of cheaper and less durable fabrics. Until the seventeenth or eighteenth century, most people had only a few outfits of clothing. What they were not wearing at the time, they hung on pegs in the wall. The wealthy, of course, always had large wardrobes, made from fine fabrics. In the eighteenth century, however, fabric prices fell, and new, cheaper fabrics were manufactured in order to satisfy growing consumer demand. Then people needed new pieces of furniture in which to store their garments. Chests of drawers, or dressers, first became available to wealthy Britons and Americans in the 1630s and 1640s. By 1760, they had become a standard item of furniture for the middle class.

People became increasingly interested in how they appeared to others. Hence, ordinary people began to pay attention to the latest fashions, which had once been a concern only of the truly wealthy and the nobility. An English traveler to the colonies reported in 1771 that "the quick importation of fashions from the mother country is really astonishing." By 1700, two new items appeared that made it easier for those who had the time and money to attend to their appearance, the dressing table and the full-length mirror. For the first time in human history, people could now see how they appeared to others, head to toe. Washing oneself, styling one's hair or periwig, arranging one's clothing so as to appear pleasing to others became standard rituals in the eighteenth century, not simply for the wealthiest fraction of society, but for all who hoped to appear "genteel."

In the eighteenth century, prospering people on both sides of the Atlantic created and tried to follow the standards of a new style of life, **gentility.** Gentility had no precise meaning, but it represented all that was polite, civilized, refined, and fashionable. It was everything that vulgarity, its opposite, was not. Gentility meant not only certain sorts of objects, such as a dressing table or a bone china teapot, but also the manners that were necessary to use such objects properly. The guests at Virginia planter Robert Carter's table later ridiculed the tobacco inspector who committed the social sin of holding his glass of liquor with two hands and then drinking it "like an Ox."

Standards of gentility established boundaries between the genteel and the vulgar, such as the social distance that separated Robert Carter and the guzzling tobacco inspector. Those who considered themselves genteel looked down on those whose style of living seemed unrefined, and they became uncomfortable when circumstances required them to associate with their social inferiors. Philip Fithian, a young Presbyterian minister, complained that when he lodged with a family on the Pennsylvania frontier in 1775, he had to sleep "in the same room with all the Family—It seems indelicate, at least new, to strip, surrounded by different Ages & Sexes, & Rise in the Morning, in the Blaze of Day, with the Eyes of, at least, one blinking Irish Female searching out Subjects for Remark."

Yet if gentility erected a barrier between the genteel and the vulgar, it also told the vulgar precisely what it took to become genteel. All that was necessary was to acquire the right goods and learn how to use them. Throughout the colonies, ordinary people began to purchase consumer goods that made their lives more pleasant and established their gentility. Travelers noticed that even relatively poor people often owned a mirror, a few pieces of china, or a teapot. In Charleston, slave women stood out for their "excessive and costly apparel." The slaves who were executed in New York City in 1741 were probably conspiring not to burn the city down, but to steal clothing and other fancy goods that could be resold to poor people in the underground economy. This mass consumption and widespread distribution of consumer goods created and sustained the consumer revolution.

The consumer revolution had another egalitarian dimension: It encouraged *sociability.* Throughout the Atlantic world, men and women, particularly those with a little leisure and money (perhaps half the white population) began to cultivate social life. Many believed that the purpose of life was the sort of society that men and women created in their parlors when they met with friends and family for an evening of dining and conversation. Thomas Paine explained this belief most succinctly in his revolutionary tract *Common Sense* (1776) when he said that "Society in every state is a blessing." Long before Paine and other political thinkers had found a place for society in their theories, ordinary men and women were creating it in their homes.

In order to put all of their guests on an equal footing, men and women began to purchase matching sets—of dinner plates, silverware, glasses, and chairs. Until the eighteenth century, the most important people at the table—the man of the house, his wife, and high-ranking men—got the best chairs, those with backs. Children, servants, and those of less social standing had sat on stools, benches, or boxes, or they stood. Even if there had been enough dishes, utensils, and mugs for all, they rarely matched. Often, diners in the seventeenth century would have simply poked their knives into common serving bowls, spearing pieces of meat, or sometimes even scooped the food up with their hands. Matched sets of tableware and chairs of equal height underscored the symbolic equality of all dinner guests.

The newest and most popular consumer goods made their way quickly to America. Inexpensive drinking glasses, which could be held in one hand, freeing the other for gesturing, appeared in England in the middle of the seventeenth century and in the colonies before 1700. Unknown in England before 1660, forks were available in the colonies by 1690. Such objects were brought to the colonies by merchants and sea captains, just the sort of widely traveled, cosmopolitan people who valued gentility most highly. Each new implement and style carried with it its own rules of usage, its etiquette. Such rules were daunting for the uneducated, such as the ridiculed tobacco inspector. But once the etiquette was mastered, a person could enter polite society anywhere in the Atlantic world and be accepted. For this reason, those people who were most deeply involved in the market eagerly adopted and spread the objects and values of the consumer revolution. Good manners became the ticket to a genteel world that spanned the Atlantic, reaching from London to the North Carolina cottage where a woman served her guests tea from a china pot. The eighteenth-century capitalist economy created a trade not only in goods and raw materials, but one in styles of life as well.

Historians debate the effects of the consumer revolution, but on balance it was a democratic force. Although the affluent were often outraged when ordinary men and women and even slaves wore clothing or used objects that

In 1750 in Charleston, South Carolina, Mr. Peter Manigault and his friends toasted each other, demonstrating their civility and their knowledge of the rules of polite behavior, including how to drink punch from a stem glass.

considerable variety. Although the vast majority of Americans lived in small communities or on farms, an increasing number lived in cities, and urban centers played a critical role in shaping colonial life. At the same time, farming regions, both slave and free, were maturing, changing the character of rural life. The growing colonial population continued to push at the frontiers of settlement, leading to the founding of a new colony in Georgia.

Creating an Urban Public Sphere

In the eighteenth century cities began to grow rapidly. At the end of the seventeenth century, none of the colonial towns—except Boston, with 7,000 people—was much more than a rural village. By 1720, Boston's population had grown to 12,000, Philadelphia had 10,000 inhabitants, New York had 7,000, and Newport and Charleston were home to almost 4,000 each. Forty years later, a number of other urban centers had sprung up, each with populations around 3,000—Salem, Marblehead, and Newburyport, Massachusetts; Portsmouth, New Hampshire; Providence, Rhode Island; New Haven and Hartford, Connecticut; Albany, New York; Lancaster, Pennsylvania; and in the South, Baltimore, Maryland; Norfolk, Virginia, and Savannah, Georgia.

By the eve of the Revolution, the largest cities were even larger. Philadelphia had 30,000 residents, New York had 25,000, and Boston had 16,000 (see Map 5-3). All of these cities were either ports or centers for the fur trade. Colonial cities were centers of commerce. That was their reason for being.

Social life in colonial cities was characterized by two somewhat contradictory trends. On the one hand, nowhere in the colonies was social stratification among free people more pronounced than in the cities. By the eve of the Revolution, each city had an affluent elite, made up of merchants, professionals, and government officials, who took the lead in establishing a refined style of life. Each city also developed a class of indigent poor, not only widows and orphans but also men who could not provide for themselves and who had to be supported at public expense. On the other hand, urban life itself brought all classes of society together in public at theaters, in taverns, and at religious revivals such as the one led by George Whitefield. All cities enjoyed a vibrant civic life, which became one of the seedbeds of the Revolution because it provided a forum for the exchange of ideas.

Affluent city dwellers created for themselves a life as much like that of London as they could. Not only did they

were "above their station," those men and women came to think it was their right to spend their money as they pleased. As one Bostonian put it in 1754, the poor should be allowed to buy "the *Conveniencies,* and *Comforts,* as well as *Necessaries* of Life . . . as freely as the Rich." After all, "I am sure we Work as hard as they do . . ; therefore, I cannot see why we have not as good a *natural Right* to them as they have."

At the same time, the consumer revolution rested on new systems of production that eventually led to the industrial revolution and the creation of a working class. Even before that time, men and women were working harder so that they could buy the new goods. Some made the choice voluntarily, but many did not. In the southern colonies, slavery expanded in order to produce the luxury goods that new consumers wanted to buy.

The Varieties of Colonial Experience

Although the eighteenth-century industrial and consumer revolutions tied the peoples of the North Atlantic world together and gave them many common experiences, factors such as climate, geography, immigration, patterns of economic development, and population density made for

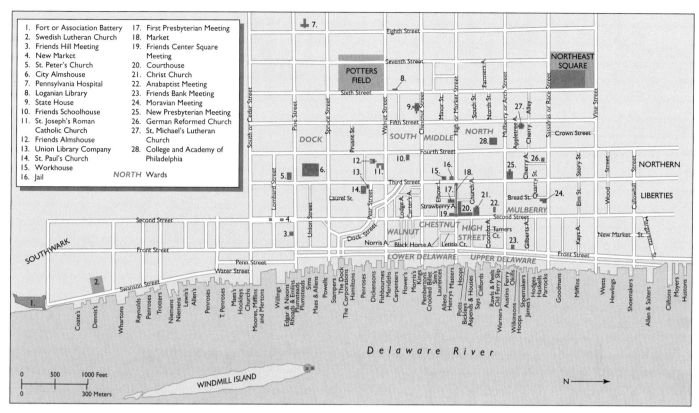

Map 5-3   Commerce and Culture in Philadelphia, c. 1760.
This map illustrates the close connection between commerce—note how many docks there are along the Delaware River—and culture. By 1760, Philadelphia was home to churches of many different denominations as well as an array of enlightened institutions—a hospital, a college, and two libraries.
Source: Lester Cappon, ed., The Atlas of Early American History (Princeton, 1976).

The photograph above depicts the city seen from the southeast, looking across Philadephia Harbor.

import European finery and housewares, but they established English-style institutions, seeking to replicate the life styles of their English counterparts. Elites in each of the cities founded social clubs, dancing assemblies, and fishing and hunting clubs where they could meet with members of their class. Although many of these associations were for men only, some, such as dancing assemblies, brought men and women together, and others periodically entertained ladies. Such organizations helped the elite function as a class. By the middle of the eighteenth century, half of Philadelphia's merchant families belonged to the Dancing Assembly.

Urban associations reflected the ideals of the Enlightenment (see pages 145-147). Some, such as the Masons, a European fraternal order that had branches in all the major colonial cities, espoused the ideal of **universalism,** that all people were by their nature fundamentally the same. Other institutions advocated self-improvement.

Whereas some urban institutions separated out the elite and others challenged the ruling hierarchy, still others brought together all members of society, creating a "public sphere." Some institutions created new public spaces that united men, and sometimes women, of all classes. City dwellers could see stage plays in Williamsburg by 1716,

Charleston and New York by the 1730s, and Philadelphia and Boston by the 1740s. Women and their beaux sat in the boxes, where they could be seen by the entire audience, while single gentlemen sat in the pit, near whose doors lurked prostitutes soliciting for customers. Working-class men and servants sat in the balcony, from which they hurled trash and insults if they were unhappy with the production.

Taverns brought all ranks into even closer proximity. Although the Puritan establishment had attempted to restrict the sale of liquor, by 1720 Boston's officials caved in to public pressure and began approving a majority of the applications for liquor licenses. By 1737, Boston had 177 taverns, one for every 99 inhabitants of the city. (Between 30 and 40 percent were owned by women, usually widows.) Taverns not only served food and drink, but they became true public institutions where people could meet and discuss the issues of the day. There, the illiterate listened while others read the newspaper aloud.

Newspapers also played a critical role in creating a public sphere and extending it beyond the cities. The first newspaper with more than one issue was not published in the colonies until 1704, when the *Boston News-Letter* appeared. By the time of the Revolution, thirty-nine newspapers were being published, and the chief town in each colony except Delaware had at least one newspaper (see Map 5-4).

Strict colonial libel laws prohibited the printing of opinions critical of public officials, or even the truth about them if it cast them in a bad light. Benjamin Franklin's brother James, editor of the *New-England Courant*, was jailed in 1727 for criticizing the clergy, and John Peter Zenger, editor of the *New-York Weekly Journal*, was put on trial in 1735 for criticizing the governor. Zenger's flamboyant attorney, Andrew Hamilton, persuaded the jury that they should rule not simply on the facts of the case (Zenger *had* criticized the governor) but on whether the law itself was just. When the jury ruled in Zenger's favor, cheers went up in the courtroom, and the overjoyed spectators carried Hamilton out into the street. Although the ruling established no precedents, and it would be many years before freedom of the press would be guaranteed by law, the Zenger case was a milestone in the developing relationship between the public and government officials. The verdict expressed the belief that in the contest between the people and government officials, the press spoke for the people, and hence it was the people themselves, not government, that would hold the press accountable.

City dwellers came to think of themselves as a "public." Not only successful artisans such as Benjamin Franklin and Paul Revere but less affluent craftsmen and mechanics all thought of themselves as part of a public that had certain rights or "liberties" such as making their views known and enjoying a fair price for their goods.

In keeping with Anglo-American tradition, public parades, celebrations, and even riots were an expected part of urban life. Sometimes the elite led such parades and even

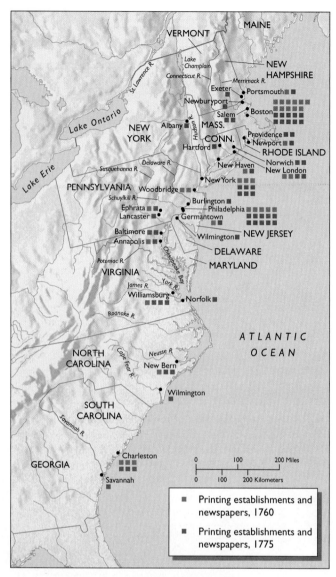

Map 5-4 Printing Presses and Newspapers, 1760–1775.
Between 1760 and 1775, the number of printing presses and newspapers in the colonies grew dramatically, as new cities acquired presses and major cities such as Boston, New York, and Philadelphia gained additional ones.
Source: Lester Cappon, ed., The Atlas of Early American History (Princeton, 1976).

provided alcoholic refreshments, for example to celebrate the king's birthday or an important military victory. At other times, working men and servants, both black and white, directed the public festivities, with the acquiescence of the elite. New Yorkers celebrated Pope Day every November 5 by drinking, dancing in the streets, and parading effigies of the Pope and the Devil. Pinkster Day offered slaves a similar opportunity to make merry (although without the anti-Catholic overtones). At other times, however, working people, acting as a "public," used mob action to assert their political views. Laborers in New York responded to a devaluation of the penny in 1754 by taking to the streets "armed with Clubs and Staves." Mobs in both New York and Boston reacted violently to press gangs that scoured the waterfront for additional hands for the Royal Navy. Although the success of a riot depended on the stance of the elite, and whether it chose to prosecute, by the time of the Revolution city dwellers had a long history of asserting their rights in public.

The Diversity of Urban Life

Periodic downturns in the urban economy, especially after the middle of the century, led to increased activism on the part of workers and the urban poor. Colonial politics had been premised on the deference of the less powerful to their social and economic "betters," but by the middle of the eighteenth century small cracks in this system began to appear. It was hard enough for prosperous artisans such as Benjamin Franklin to work their way into an elite populated by colonial officials and wealthy, well-educated merchants who scorned those who worked with their hands. It was more difficult for seamen and journeyman laborers to claim their right to be heard. The increasing wealth of those at the top and the appearance of a small class of permanently poor at the bottom of the economic hierarchy began to undermine the assumption that all city dwellers shared a common interest and that, consequently, the wealthy and well-educated could be trusted to govern for the benefit of everyone.

Although by today's standards the American colonial population, even in the cities, remained remarkably equal, in the eighteenth century it became much more stratified than it had been. At the beginning of the eighteenth century, none of the cities had a substantial number of poor people. In New York, in 1700, there were only 35 paupers, almost all of whom were aged or disabled. Over the course

of the eighteenth century, however, a series of colonial wars sent men home disabled and left many women widowed and their children orphaned. Facing competition from other port cities and without a staple to market, Boston suffered the most.

Each city responded to the growth in poverty by building almshouses for the poor who could not support themselves and workhouses for those, including women and children, who could be put to work. Even so, there were too many poor for the cities to support. By the eve of the Revolution, about 5 percent of the population was receiving poor relief in Boston, New York, and Philadelphia. In Philadelphia and New York about 25 percent of the population was at or below the poverty level for the time, while in Boston perhaps as much as 40 percent of the population was living at or near subsistence. Many colonists feared that colonial cities were coming to resemble London, with its mass of impoverished and desperate poor.

Popular unrest in the cities could take a distinctive form as well. All the major cities had slaves, and in some of these cities the black population was considerable. By 1746, 30 percent of New York City's working class consisted of slaves. A serious slave revolt in 1712 and a rumored revolt in 1741 did nothing to stop the importation of Africans into the city. Instead of halting slave importation, the white population responded to real and perceived slave revolts with harsh punishments. In the wake of the 1712 revolt, which had left nine white men dead, city officials executed thirteen convicted rebels on the gallows, burned three at the stake, let one starve to death in chains, and broke one on the wheel, a medieval instrument of torture. Six more committed suicide to escape this fate. The response to a rumored slave insurrection in 1741 resembled Salem's witchcraft trials. Although the evidence was flimsy, eighteen

As an affluent merchant class began to emerge in cities like Philadelphia, Boston, and Charleston, they built larger and more elegant homes (left), while working people lived in houses that were much smaller and significantly less comfortable (right).

slaves and four whites were hanged, and thirteen slaves were burned at the stake.

New York enacted a stringent slave code after the 1712 revolt, and Boston and Pennsylvania imposed significant import duties on slaves. Nonetheless, the importation of slaves continued into all the port cities, where they were in demand as house servants and as artisans. Almost all of Boston's elite owned at least one slave, as did many members of the middle class. Wealthy white artisans often purchased slaves instead of enlisting free whites as apprentices, splitting the white artisan class into those who could afford slaves and those who complained that slaves were taking the jobs that more properly belonged to them.

In Charleston, South Carolina, where more than half the population was enslaved, many masters let their slaves hire themselves out in return for a portion of their earnings. Such slaves enjoyed remarkable freedom to set their own hours, to engage in their own recreational and religious activities, and to participate in the growing consumer economy by selling their own products and purchasing what they wanted with their profits. Some whites complained about the fancy dresses of the black women at bi-racial dances attended by "many of the first gentlemen" of Charleston. Interracial sex in Charleston seems to have been common. Although white city dwellers were troubled by the impudence and relative freedom of urban slaves and worried about slave revolts, urban slavery flourished. Even in northern cities, the advantages of the institution outweighed its dangers, in the minds of most whites.

The Maturing of Rural Society

The population increases that made possible the development of an urban culture had a different impact in rural areas. Over the course of the eighteenth century, some of the longer-settled regions of the colonies became relatively overcrowded. Land that had once seemed so abundant had been carelessly farmed and had lost some of its fertility. Tobacco planters were notorious for their exploitation of the soil, while New England's soil had never been as productive as that of southern regions. This relative overcrowding, which historians call *land pressure,* led to a number of changes in colonial society. These were felt most acutely in New England. Population density increased, and all cultivable land was claimed. With no additional farm land available, the rate of migration from the farms to newly settled areas and cities increased. Both the concentration of wealth and social differentiation increased, dividing the farm community into rich and poor, as some were able to take advantage of these changes and others were forced off unproductive land.

Such broad economic changes had a direct impact on individual men and women. Families with numerous children to provide for were hard pressed if the original plot of land could not be divided into homesteads large enough

for each son. (Daughters were given movable property such as farm animals, household equipment, and slaves.) Facing such land pressures, children began to defer marriage. Some sons migrated to nearby cities, looking for employment there. Others worked on other men's farms for wages or, in the South in particular, became tenant farmers. Daughters became servants in other women's households. In such older-settled regions, the average age of marriage began to creep upward. In Middlesex County, Virginia, by 1740, women were marrying at age 22, two years older than earlier in the century. By the time of the Revolution, women in Andover, Massachusetts, were, on average, even older—24 before they married, a year or two older than in the previous century.

As young men and women in the long-settled regions of the colonies had to defer marriage, increasing numbers gave in to the temptation to enjoy sexual relations before marriage. In some towns, by the middle of the eighteenth century, between 30 and 50 percent of brides bore their first child within eight months of their wedding day. The growing belief that marriage should be based primarily on love probably encouraged some couples to become intimate even before they married, especially if their poverty required them to postpone their marriage for long. That appears to have been the case with Lucy Barnes of Concord, Massachusetts, whose father wanted her to marry a wealthy young farmer instead of the poor cabinet maker with whom she had fallen in love. Only when Lucy became pregnant by her lover did her father consent to the marriage. Lucy, and young women like her who engaged in sexual relations before marriage, took quite a risk. If their lovers declined to marry them they would be disgraced, and their futures would be bleak indeed.

The World That Slavery Made

The rural economy of the South depended on slave labor. As a consequence, rural society included whites and their black slaves, who worked together and formed two distinctive cultures, one in the black-majority lower South and the other in the Chesapeake region. In both regions, the most affluent slave masters sold their crops on the international market and used the profits to fill their plantations with elegant furniture and to dress themselves in the latest London fashions. Not only styles of decor and dress, but also music, religion, literature, and general cultural values came from Britain. Like their affluent English counterparts, prosperous southern planters aimed for moderation in all things—from the measured cadences of the minuets they liked to dance to and highly stylized love letters, to restrained mourning on the death of a loved one.

Chesapeake planters modeled themselves after English country gentlemen, while low country planters imitated the elite of London. Chesapeake planters designed their plantations to be self-sufficient villages, like English country estates. Because slaves produced most of the goods and services the plantation needed, planters such as William Byrd II imagined themselves living "in a kind of independence on everyone but Providence." But unlike English country gentlemen, southern slave owners were wholly dependent on both slave labor and the vagaries of the market for their fortunes.

South Carolina planters used their wealth to build elegant homes not on their plantations, but in Charleston and other coastal cities, where they spent as much of the year as possible and established a flourishing urban culture. By the eve of the Revolution, the area around Charleston was the most affluent in the mainland colonies. Per capita wealth, at £2,338, was four times as high as in the next richest area, the Chesapeake.

In spite of their affluence, the southern planter elite class never achieved the secure political power enjoyed by its English counterpart. In England the social elite dominated government. With noble rank inherited and voting rights so limited that the affluent were easily able to prevail, the English government was remarkably stable. The colonial elite, however (in the northern colonies as well as the southern ones), was cut off from the top levels of political power, which remained in England. The colonists were at the mercy of whichever officials the Crown happened to appoint.

Unable to count on support from above, the colonial elite needed to guarantee the loyalty of those below them. Nowhere was this venture more successful than in Virginia. The elite acted as middlemen for lesser planters, advancing them credit and marketing their tobacco for them. In general, they wielded their authority with a light hand, and punishments for crimes committed by whites were not particularly severe. Finally, they enhanced their authority by the use of ritual. Actions were calculated for the effect they would produce on both peers and social inferiors. Simply sitting astride his horse, dressed elegantly, and wearing a wig, a planter was an imposing figure on the landscape. Arriving at church *en masse,* some in coaches and some on horseback, the gentry impressed their superiority on ordinary people.

Because the cultivation of tobacco required careful supervision, Chesapeake planters came into close contact with their slaves. As a result, their culture was shaped not only by English influences but also by those of their African slaves.

Despite the close contact necessitated in tobacco cultivation, members of the gentry often tried to distance themselves from their slaves, whom they considered "vulgar." Eighteenth-century racial views notwithstanding, some whites were able to cross the color line, and some did it in a very dramatic way. Although there are no clear measures of how much racial mixing took place, some historians believe that sexual relations between whites and blacks were common. Several prominent Virginians acknowledged and supported their mulatto children. Some interracial relationships included affection; others were entirely coerced. All of the resulting offspring were in a vulnerable position; like all slaves they were dependent on the will of whites.

In the low country, the absenteeism of the planters combined with the task system to give plantation slaves an unusual degree of autonomy. In the early years of the colony, Indians often seemed a more serious threat than slaves, and during the Yamasee War (1715), planters armed their slaves to help them fight off attacks by the Yamasee Indians. Living in a region where they were in the majority, slaves were better able to retain their own religions, languages, and customs than Africans in the Chesapeake. The Gullah language, still spoken today on the Sea Islands off the coast of South Carolina and Georgia, combined English, Spanish, Portuguese, and African languages. African religious practices, which included visions and trances, shocked European Christians, who described them as "pagan" and "heathen."

The greater autonomy of low country slaves gave them greater opportunities to run away and to plot rebellions as well. Since the 1690s the Spanish colony at St. Augustine, Florida, had served as a refuge for runaway Carolina slaves. As mentioned previously, in 1733 the king of Spain issued an edict guaranteeing freedom to any English slaves who sought refuge in Florida, and a small colony of escaped slaves established the town of Gracia Real de Santa Teresa de Mose, a few miles north of St. Augustine along the Atlantic coast.

The mainland colonies' bloodiest slave revolt, the Stono Rebellion, took place in 1739, only a year after the founding of the Spanish free black outpost. The uprising was led by about 20 slaves born in Kongo (present-day Angola). The rebels were probably Catholics, for the king of Kongo had accepted conversion from the Portuguese and made Catholicism his nation's religion. Early in the morning of September 9, the rebels broke into a store near the Stono Bridge, taking the weapons and ammunition, killing the storekeepers, and leaving their heads on the front steps. The rebels moved south toward St. Augustine, killing more than 20 whites and gathering blacks into their fold. Although the main body of the rebels was dispersed that evening, and many were executed on the spot, skirmishes took place for another week, and the last of the ringleaders was not captured for another three years.

The authorities reacted with predictable severity, putting dozens of slave rebels "to the most cruel Death" and passing a strict slave code to revoke many of the liberties the slaves had enjoyed. A prohibitive duty was placed on the importation of slaves, and attempts were made to encourage the immigration of white Europeans instead. Although slave imports dropped significantly in the 1740s, by 1750 they were back to their pre-Stono levels. Although there were certainly periodic crackdowns on slave autonomy, during the colonial period slaveowners

WHERE THEY LIVED, WHERE THEY WORKED

The Chesapeake Plantation Village

The eighteenth-century Chesapeake plantation village linked the worlds of Europe, Africa, and North America. The plantation itself was a hub of production, producing tobacco to sell in the markets of Europe, as well as many of the manufactured goods used on the plantation, such as nails, bricks, and cloth. All were produced by slave labor.

The plantation's architecture combined English and African elements. After about 1720, the most affluent planters began building large brick homes, copying Georgian styles then popular in England. The wooden buildings on the plantation, however, including the homes of less prosperous planters, slave cabins, and other "out" buildings, were constructed with African techniques. Their frames were much lighter, more like those of central African houses than of contemporary English

ones. Winding paths that followed the natural contours of the land and raised burial plots also reflected African influences. Plantation villages themselves bore an uncanny resemblance to an African king's village, in which smaller homes were arrayed behind the chieftain's main house.

Whites borrowed from African culture in other ways. The barbecue at which "a great number of young people met together with a Fiddle and Banjo played by two Negroes" represented a melding of European (the fiddle) and African (the banjo) music. The ecstatic shouting and visions of African worship services also made their way into Baptist and Methodist church services. These borrowings were usually silent. Black influences quietly made their way into white culture, in the process creating a culture that was neither fully African nor fully European.

Notice the similarities in construction between the Zaire home (top) and the Virginia cabin (bottom left). Although the photo of the Zaire home is from c. 1910 and the Virginia cabin from 1897, they suggest how African homes and Virginia slave cabins looked in the late eighteenth century. The planter's "big house" and the slave cabins and other out buildings made a small village, similar in layout to that of an African chieftain's. The photo (bottom right) is of the plantation community at Green Hill Plantation, built in the late eighteenth century.

had neither the heart nor the inclination for the sort of systematic policing of their slaves that would have kept them completely under their control.

Georgia: From Frontier Outpost to Plantation Society

Nowhere was the white determination to create and maintain a slave society more clear than in Georgia. It is sometimes said that the introduction of slavery into the North American mainland was an unthinking decision, that the Africans who were brought to America's shores were already enslaved. Supposedly the colonies became slave societies slowly, as individual planters purchased slaves, but without the society as a whole ever committing itself to slavery. Although there is some truth to this analysis for the early colonies, it is not accurate for Georgia, where the introduction of slavery less than twenty years after the colony's founding was a conscious and purposeful decision.

The establishment of the English colony at South Carolina had, of course, made the Spanish nervous because of its proximity to their settlement at St. Augustine. With the French founding of New Orleans (1718) and Fort Toulouse (1717), Carolinians became increasingly concerned that their colony would be threatened by either Spain or France. The French were establishing their presence along the Gulf of Mexico and showing signs of monopolizing the Indian trade all the way from Louisiana to Canada. By the early part of the eighteenth century, Carolinians were eager for the English to establish a colony to the south, which would serve the double purpose of being a buffer between Florida and South Carolina and, if it extended far enough west, cutting the French colonial empire in two.

The British Crown issued a twenty-one-year charter to a group of trustees led by James Oglethorpe, a young philanthropist who had achieved some prominence in England by bringing about reforms in England's debtors' prisons. The colony, Georgia, was designed as a combination philanthropic venture and military-commercial outpost. Its colonists, who were to be drawn from Britain's "deserving poor," were supposed not only to protect South Carolina's borders but also make the new colony a sort of Italy-on-the-Atlantic, producing wine, olives, and silk.

Unfortunately, Oglethorpe's humanitarianism was not coupled with a practical understanding of the world political economy. By that time it was well known that excessive indulgence in alcohol was undermining the cohesion of many Indian tribes. Consequently, Oglethorpe had banned liquor from the colony, thinking that it weakened the colonists and their Indian neighbors both. However, without a product to sell to the world, the colony could not prosper. South Carolina's wharves, merchants, and willingness to sell rum to the Indians enabled it to domi-

nate the trade with the Creeks, Cherokees, and other local Indians. Oglethorpe had also banned slavery from the colony for humanitarian reasons (making it the only colony expressly to prohibit slavery). As a result, Georgia farmers looked enviously across the Savannah River at South Carolinians growing rich off slave labor. The settlers were angry too that, contrary to common practice in the colonies, women were not allowed to inherit property. Finally, and again, contrary to common practice in the colonies, the trustees made no provision for self-government. By 1738 "Malcontents" were objecting to these policies. Georgia, despite its founders' noble intentions, lacked everything that the thriving colonies enjoyed: a cash crop or product, large plots of land, slaves to work the land, and the right to bequeath that land to whomever one pleased, under laws of one's own devising.

Never able to realize their dream of a colony populated by small and contented farmers, the trustees surrendered Georgia back to the Crown a year early, in 1752. With Oglethorpe's idealistic laws repealed and slavery introduced, the colony soon resembled the plantation society of South Carolina, and Savannah became a little Charleston, with its robust civic and cultural life, and its slave markets as well.

The Head and the Heart in America: The Enlightenment and Religious Awakening

American religious, intellectual, and cultural life in the eighteenth century was shaped by two significant movements, the Enlightenment and a series of religious revivals known as the Great Awakening. In many ways, these movements were separate and distinct, even opposite, appealing to different groups of people with different principles. The Enlightenment was a transatlantic intellectual and philosophical movement that held that the universe could be understood and improved by the human mind. The Great Awakening was a transatlantic religious and social movement that held that all people were born sinners, that all could feel their own depravity without the assistance of ministers, and that all were equal in the eyes of God. On the face of it, the movements might seem fundamentally opposed to each other, with one emphasizing the power of the human mind and the other disparaging it. Both movements, however, criticized established authority and valued the experience of the individual. Both contributed to the humanitarianism that emerged at the end of the century, and both were products of the world that capitalism had created.

The Ideas of the Enlightenment

The roots of the Enlightenment can be traced to the the Renaissance and the spirit of inquiry and faith in science that led explorers like Columbus halfway around the globe. But the gloomy mysticism of Columbus and the belief in the supernatural of virtually all the early explorers and colonists disappeared in the bright light of possibility that the discoveries of the Renaissance ushered in. Men and women of the Enlightenment had seen the world become smaller, and it showed signs of becoming better. People contrasted the ignorance, oppression, and suffering of the middle or "dark" ages, as they called them, and their own enlightened time. Thomas Jefferson described the earlier period to Joseph Priestly, the English chemist who had discovered oxygen, as "the times of Vandalism, when ignorance put everything in the hands of power and priestcraft. All advances in science were proscribed as innovations. . . . We were to look backwards, not forwards, for improvement." Enlightened thinkers believed fervently in the power of rational thinking and scoffed at its opposite, superstition.

People of the Enlightenment believed that God and his world were knowable. "Your own reason," Jefferson told his nephew, "is the only oracle given you by heaven." Rejecting revelation as a guide, the Enlightenment looked instead to reason. Significantly, Jefferson's "trinity of the three greatest men the world had ever produced" included not Jesus Christ but Isaac Newton, the scientist responsible for modern mathematics and physics; Francis Bacon, the philosopher who outlined the scientific method; and John Locke, the political philosopher of democracy. The Enlightenment was interested in knowledge not for its own sake but for the improvements it could make in human happiness. "The rapid Progress *true* Science now makes," Benjamin Franklin told Priestly, "occasions my regretting sometimes that I was born so soon." He looked forward to the time when twice as much food could be produced by a fraction of the labor and "all Diseases may by sure means be prevented or cured, not excepting even that of Old Age."

Enlightenment thinkers such as Jefferson, Franklin, and Priestly were more interested in what all people had in common than in what differentiated them. No passage in the Bible was more important to the Enlightenment than Genesis 1:27: "So God created man in his *own* image." It was the basis not only for overcoming Calvinism's belief in humanity's innate depravity, but also for asserting the principle of human equality. All the people of the earth were the descendants of a single creation, and hence, there was a common human nature. The biblical account of Creation, according to Thomas Paine, demonstrated "the unity or equality of man." All people were fundamentally the same, equally created in God's image and with equal natural rights and duties.

Humanity's duties were both clear and simple. Chief among them, according to Franklin, was "doing good to [God's] other children." In fact, people served God best not by praying, which, as Paine put it, "can add nothing to eternity," but "by endeavouring to make his creatures happy." Scientific inquiry and experiments such as Franklin's with electricity all had as their object the improvement of human life.

Although the eighteenth century had seen a number of improvements in the quality of life, the world was still extremely violent and filled with pain. The Enlightenment responded to the pain and violence of its world in two ways. First, it attempted to alleviate and curtail them. Scientists eagerly sought cures for diseases. The Reverend Cotton Mather of Boston learned about the procedure of inoculating against small pox (using a small amount of the deadly disease) from an article in the *Philosophical Transactions of the Royal Society* in England and from his African slave Onesimus, who knew of its practice in Africa. An epidemic that began in 1721 gave Mather and Dr. Zabdiel Boylston an opportunity to try out the technique. The revulsion against pain and suffering also encouraged humanitarian reform, such as James Oglethorpe's reform of English debtors' prisons and, eventually, the antislavery movement. It would be many years, however, before such scientific and moral programs would have any substantial effect on the quality of life.

In the meantime, men and women of the Enlightenment cultivated a stoic resignation to the evils that they could not change, and a personal ideal of moderation, so that they would neither give nor receive pain. The gentility and politeness of the urban elite was another expression of this ideal of moderation. In fact, both gentility and the Enlightenment were espoused by the same set of people, the urban elite: professionals, merchants, and prosperous planters tied into the global economy. Affluence gave such people the leisure to study science and cultivate the arts, and their participation in the transatlantic community convinced them that life had already been improved and with their efforts could be made better still.

The Enlightenment and the Study of Political Economy

Enlightenment thinkers began to study the connections among society, politics, and the economy. John Locke was the first to link all of these together into a theory of *political economy*. He argued that there was a systematic connection between social institutions (such as the family), political institutions, and the rights of property. He began with the claim that each person has the right to life and, hence, the right to preserve that life. In order to sustain their lives, people form families, and in order to support themselves and their families, they labor. The basic right to life then, according to Locke, gives people the right to the product of their labor, that is, property. To protect their lives and their property, people create governments. They give up some of their liberty, but receive protection of their lives and property in return.

Locke also developed a new economic theory. He said that money has no intrinsic value. His idea was a departure from mercantilism, which said that the value of money was fixed. In the second half of the eighteenth century, Scottish philosophers such as Francis Hutchinson and Adam Smith carried Locke's ideas even further. They argued that human beings should be free to value the things that made them happy. Dazzled by the consumer revolution, they developed a full-scale defense of consumption.

Using *happiness* as their standard for human life, the Scots also argued that people should be free to produce. Adam Smith's influential *The Wealth of Nations* (1776) was both a critique of mercantilism and a defense of free markets and free labor. For Smith and other Enlightenment theorists of a free-market political economy, the best incentive to hard work was the prospect of increased wealth and the comforts it would bring. Human beings were happiest, they said, when they lived under free governments, which protected private property while leaving the market largely unregulated. These ideas became increasingly popular in the colonies around the time of the Revolution.

Enlightened Institutions

The Enlightenment spurred the creation of a number of institutions that embodied its principles. Humanitarianism led to the building of the Pennsylvania Hospital in 1751 and the Eastern State Mental Hospital at Williamsburg in 1773. Benjamin Franklin, a man of boundless energy, played a central role in organizing a number of institutions. In 1743 he proposed a society of learned men, modeled after the Royal Society of London and the Dublin Society in Ireland, to study and share information about "all philosophical Experiments that let Light into the Nature of Things, tend to increase the Power of Man over Matter, and multiply the Conveniencies or Pleasure of Life." He also helped establish the Library Company of Philadelphia in 1731, the first lending library in the colonies. Philadelphia acquired a second library in 1751 when the Quaker philosopher and book collector James Logan bequeathed his library, books and building both, to the city. By the time of the Revolution, Newport, New York, Charleston, and Savannah all had libraries.

The ideas of the Enlightenment were also spread in the social clubs formed in the eighteenth century. For example, the Masons, founded on the belief in a universal brotherhood of man that transcended religious sect and nationality, were the embodiment of its ideals.

The Enlightenment had a significant effect on organized religion as well. The Anglicans, in particular, were receptive to its ideals of moderation and rationalism. In England, John Tillotson, who was made Archbishop of

Benjamin Franklin, man of the Enlightenment and Philadelphia's first citizen. Here he is experimenting with electricity.

Canterbury at the end of the Glorious Revolution, began preaching a comforting and simple Christianity. God, he insisted, was "good and just" and required nothing "that is either unsuitable to our reason or prejudicial to our interest . . . nothing but what is easy to be understood, and is as easy to be practiced by an honest and willing mind."

This message became popular in the colonies, as well, even among some Congregationalist ministers, who abandoned the Calvinism of their forefathers. John Wise, the minister of Ipswich, Massachusetts, insisted that "to follow God and to obey Reason is the same thing." Once anathema in New England, Arminianism (the belief that salvation was partly a matter of individual effort rather than entirely God's will) was enjoying a new popularity. By the beginning of the eighteenth century, Harvard was a hotbed of liberal theology. In response, religious conservatives founded Yale in New Haven, Connecticut, in 1701, in order to guarantee that New England's ministers could get the proper Calvinist education Harvard no longer offered. Throughout the eighteenth century, rational religion was enormously influential, and Calvinists continued to fight it.

Origins of the Great Awakening

The problem with rational religion was that it was not particularly fulfilling emotionally. For the first decades of the eighteenth century, American colonists in every region could not get enough of the kind of religion that they craved. Although a minority of colonists were then formal church members or regularly took communion, probably a majority of free, white adults attended church and

web connection

The Origins of the Great Awakening

www.prenhall.com/boydston/
greatawakening

In the early 1740s British evangelist George Whitefield brought the "Methodist" message of John Wesley to the colonies. Thousands flocked to his sermons, became convinced of their own sinfulness, and eagerly accepted the grace of salvation Whitefield assured them was offered by their Savior. Whitefield was joined in the field by scores of lesser-known preachers who, nonetheless, enjoyed comparable success. Other ministers, dubbed "Old Lights," charged that the conversions owed less to grace than to hysteria. This was the "Great Awakening." What were the roots of this stirring, controversial, and influential event?

considered themselves church adherents. The population grew so rapidly, however, that there were never enough churches or ministers for those who wanted them. As a result, those who lived in outlying areas, as well as indentured servants and slaves, had very little contact with organized religion at all. In the middle colonies, for example, there was only one minister to attend to 27 German Lutheran congregations. Moreover, the ministers who were available were too often unable to provide real spiritual leadership to their congregations. By the beginning of the eighteenth century, ministers were berating their congregations for "sleeping at Sermon" and "carping at them." In all of the colonies, conflicts between congregations and their ministers were common.

Popular demand for more and better religion led to a series of revivals, known as the Great Awakening, that swept through the colonies between 1734 and 1745. Revivals increased church membership, especially on the frontiers. At first, church leaders looked with pleasure on the stirrings of spiritual renewal. In the winter of 1734–1735, some of the rowdiest young people in Northampton, Massachusetts, men and women who carried on parties for "the greater part of the night," began seeking religion at the church of a brilliant young minister, Jonathan Edwards. At about the same time, Gilbert Tennent, a young Presbyterian minister, converted 300 people in Basking Ridge, New Jersey. A "burly, salty, downright man," Tennent preached "like a Boatswain of a Ship, calling the Sailors to come to Prayers and be damned." Everyone rejoiced at these signs of spiritual awakening.

The Grand Itinerant

When George Whitefield arrived in Philadelphia in 1739, the local ministers, including officials of Whitefield's own Anglican church, welcomed him enthusiastically. Whitefield drew audiences in the thousands everywhere he spoke. In the 15 months of his grand tour, he visited every colony from Maine to Georgia, met all of the important ministers, and was heard at least once by most of the inhabitants of Massachusetts and Connecticut (see Map 5-5). He made the revival a true public event that took place not in a church on the Sabbath, but outdoors in public spaces during the week. He spoke to the entire community—rich, poor, slave, free, old, young, male, and female—which stood literally on an equal footing to hear him. The young evangelist acted out simple scripts based on biblical stories. The message was always the same, the sinfulness of man and the mercy of God.

In a calculated move, perhaps intended to increase his audiences, Whitefield began speaking out against some in the ministry, accusing them of being unconverted. He started with the deceased Archbishop of Canterbury, John Tillotson. From there, he went on to criticize some of the clergymen who were alive and preaching. Following his lead, Gilbert Tennent, who was now on a preaching tour of New England, warned about "The Danger of an Unconverted Ministry." Tennent compared some of the region's ministers to the "Pharisees" of biblical times who "look'd upon others that differed from them, and the common People with an Air of Disdain; and especially any who had a Respect for JESUS." He implied that such ministers were in it for the money and that true Christians should leave their churches for those of honest preachers.

Even ministers sympathetic to the revival were shocked by these accusations, which turned their congregations against them and split their churches. Those ministers such as Charleston's Anglican Commissary Alexander Garden and Boston's Congregationalist Charles Chauncy, who already had reservations about Whitefield and the other revivalists because of their emotional style, now condemned the revival as "the genuine source of infinite evil." Such accusations only made the revivalists more popular and attracted even larger crowds.

Cultural Conflict and Challenges to Authority

The Great Awakening walked a fine line between challenging authority and supporting it, which no doubt explains its widespread appeal. It was provocative enough to antagonize the top tier of the elite, the ones with the most power and arrogance, but not provocative enough to challenge the fundamental structures of colonial society. The revivalists' accusations against the ministry were especially shrewd. First, they turned upside down a familiar sermon theme, the *jeremiad* (see chapter 4), which ministers had

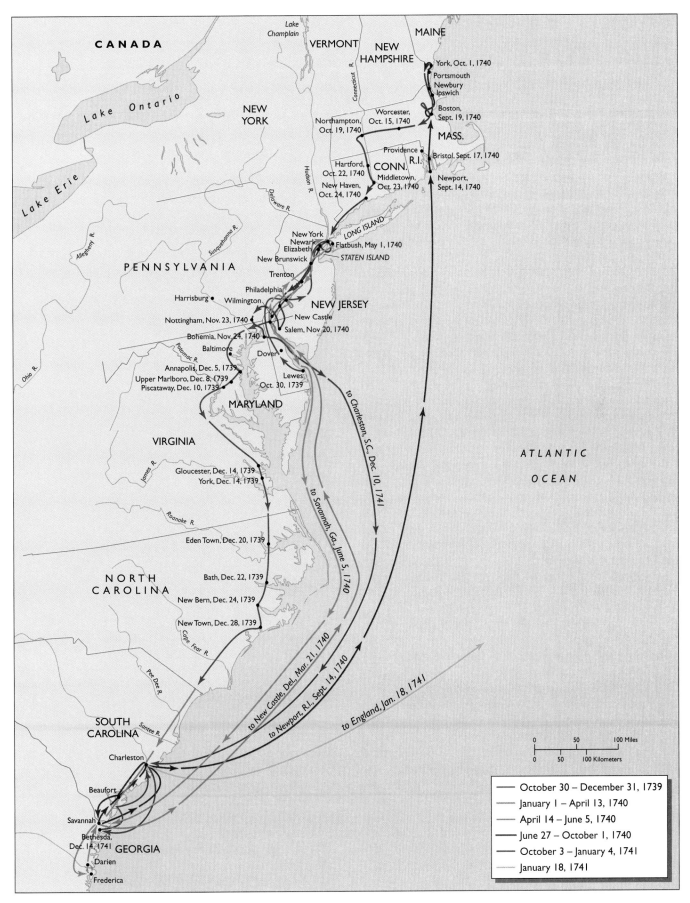

Map 5-5 George Whitefield's Itinerary

In the 15 months between October 30, 1739, and January 18, 1741, Whitefield covered thousands of miles, visiting every colony from New Hampshire to Georgia, and stopping in some states such as Pennsylvania, South Carolina, and Georgia several times.

Labels on the map:

CANADA

Lake Ontario

Lake Erie

Lake Champlain

VERMONT

NEW HAMPSHIRE

MAINE

York, Oct. 1, 1740
Portsmouth
Newbury
Ipswich
Boston, Sept. 19, 1740
MASS.
Worcester, Oct. 15, 1740
Northampton, Oct. 19, 1740
Providence
Bristol, Sept. 17, 1740
Hartford, Oct. 22, 1740
CONN.
R.I.
Middletown, Oct. 23, 1740
New Haven, Oct. 24, 1740
Newport, Sept. 14, 1740

NEW YORK

Connecticut R.
Hudson R.
Delaware R.

PENNSYLVANIA

Allegheny R.
Susquehanna R.

Harrisburg
Wilmington
Philadelphia
Nottingham, Nov. 23, 1740
New Castle
Bohemia, Nov. 24, 1740
Salem, Nov. 20, 1740
NEW JERSEY
New York
Newark
Elizabeth
New Brunswick
Trenton
Flatbush, May 1, 1740
LONG ISLAND
STATEN ISLAND

Potomac R.
Baltimore
Dover
Annapolis, Dec. 5, 1739
Upper Marlboro, Dec. 8, 1739
Piscataway, Dec. 10, 1739
Lewes, Oct. 30, 1739
MARYLAND

Ohio R.

VIRGINIA
James R.
Gloucester, Dec. 14, 1739
York, Dec. 14, 1739
Roanoke R.
Eden Town, Dec. 20, 1739

to Charleston, S.C., Dec. 10, 1741

NORTH CAROLINA
Bath, Dec. 22, 1739
New Bern, Dec. 24, 1739
New Town, Dec. 28, 1739
Cape Fear R.

to Savannah, Ga. June 5, 1740

ATLANTIC OCEAN

Pee Dee R.

SOUTH CAROLINA
Santee R.
Charleston
Beaufort
Savannah
Bethesda, Dec. 14, 1741
GEORGIA
Darien
Frederica

to New Castle, Del. Mar. 21, 1740
to Newport, R.I., Sept. 14, 1740
to England, Jan. 18, 1741

0   50   100 Miles
0   50   100 Kilometers

Legend:
October 30 – December 31, 1739
January 1 – April 13, 1740
April 14 – June 5, 1740
June 27 – October 1, 1740
October 3 – January 4, 1741
January 18, 1741

149

been using since the second half of the seventeenth century to blame the people for their failure to live up to God's expectations. Now, if the people were in danger of suffering God's wrath, it was the fault of the ministers, not the people. Second, by attacking the ministers, but not government officials, the revivalists were able to criticize authority without suffering any real consequences.

The Great Awakening appealed to all classes of people throughout the colonies. Its greatest impact, however, was in those areas that had experienced the greatest change, in particular, cities (especially among the lower orders), the frontier, and those slightly older towns that were beginning to suffer from overcrowding. In these places lived the people who had been most poorly served by the churches and whose lives were most disrupted by changes in the economy. Disturbed by the increasing competitiveness of their society, men and women were attracted to the democratic fellowship of the revivalist congregation.

Yet while criticizing the materialism and competitiveness of eighteenth-century society, the revival told men and women to look inside themselves for change, not to the structures of society. For example, Sarah Osborn, a young widow who heard both Whitefield and Tennent preach at Newport, Rhode Island, blamed herself for her woes, which she thought were her punishment for her sinful singing and dancing. After her spiritual rebirth, she trusted in God and reconciled herself to her poverty with Scripture: "Let your conversation be without covetousness, and be content with such things as ye have." Spiritual rebirth provided such men and women with a sense of joy and fulfillment that their competitive and changing world had been unable to supply.

The revival also walked the same fine line in its treatment of slavery. Early in his travels to the colonies, Whitefield spoke out against the cruelties of slavery and harangued slaveholders, telling them that his blood had "frequently almost run cold within me" when he compared their luxury to the misery of their slaves. And only a few months after the Stono Rebellion, he shocked southerners when he said that he was surprised that there had not been even more slave revolts. At the same time, however, Whitefield maintained a slave plantation in South Carolina and pestered the trustees to permit the institution in Georgia. Like many slaveowners after him, Whitefield argued that while it was immoral to enslave Africans, it was not immoral to own them provided that one treated them well and Christianized them. In fact, Whitefield preached to slaves wherever he went, and he continued to insist that masters must provide their slaves with Christian instruction. By linking humanitarianism, Christianity, and slavery, the Awakening anchored slavery in the South, at least for the time being.

Although it is hard to say if slaves actually were treated more humanely on the plantations of evangelicals, it is clear that beginning in the 1740s large numbers of

This satirical cartoon of the Evangelist George Whitefield makes fun of his crossed eyes ("His poor Eye Sparkles with Holy Zeal") and his sexual appeal ("I wish his Spirit was in my Flesh").

slaves were converted to Christianity and that by some point in the nineteenth century virtually all slaves had become Christians. Although some slaves may have converted to Christianity just to please their masters and to get Sundays off, as a rule blacks were attracted to evangelical religion for the same reason that so many whites were. It offered them the means to order their lives and believe that their lives were meaningful.

To a great extent, poor whites and slaves, especially in the South, had been left out of the society that more prosperous people had created. Evangelical religion placed the individual in a community of believers. It not only offered slaves the opportunity for church discipline and personal responsibility on almost the same terms as whites, it even gave some blacks the possibility of leadership in a bi-racial community. With the encouragement of his master (but the opposition of local authorities) Georgia slave Andrew Bryan began preaching to fellow slaves, eventually founding the first Baptist church in Georgia. Africans grafted some of their religious practices, such as shouting and ecstatic visions, onto the Christian revival, so that worship in southern Baptist and Methodist churches became a truly Afro-American phenomenon.

What the Awakening Wrought

The opponents of the Great Awakening feared that it would turn the world upside down. The Awakening did, in fact, release the antinomian impulse that Calvinism had pretty much held in check since the days of Anne Hutchinson (see chapter 3), but the leaders of the revival movement disciplined their own wildest members, such as New London's James Davenport. Davenport had led his flock through the streets late at night, singing at the tops of their lungs. They also made a bonfire so that they could rid themselves of heresy by burning the books of their opponents and idolatry by burning the clothes they were wearing. The stripping party was stopped by several evangelicals in the crowd, and Davenport was brought back to his senses by his fellow revivalist ministers.

In general, the Awakening took colonial society in the direction that it was already heading. Rather than restoring the unity of early seventeenth-century New England communities or the hierarchical stability of the Chesapeake, the revival encouraged individualism. Church after church split into evangelical and traditional factions. In New England, there were now New Lights and Old Lights; in the Middle Colonies, New Side and Old Side Presbyterians; and throughout the colonies, new denominations altogether, such as the Baptists. (A Baptist revival swept through Virginia in the 1760s and early 1770s.) Which religion to follow became a matter of personal choice, and even those colonies with established churches tolerated

dissenters. Inadvertently, the Awakening increased religious toleration in the colonies. Religion itself, as a general force, was strengthened, making the colonies simultaneously the most Protestant and the most religiously diverse culture in the world.

Just as the Enlightenment spurred the establishment of educational institutions (for example, Philadelphia College, the forerunner of the University of Pennsylvania, 1755), so also did the Awakening. Princeton, chartered in 1748 as the College of New Jersey, grew out of the evangelical seminary run by Gilbert Tennent's minister father. Next came Dartmouth, Brown, and Rutgers, chartered in 1766, to advance "true religion and useful knowledge." Columbia, chartered in 1754, represented the Anglicans' response, although the board of trustees included representatives of other denominations. William and Mary, established in 1693, was still the only college in the South, but groups were working to charter colleges in both Georgia and South Carolina. The focus of higher education was slowly shifting from the preparation of the ministry to the training of leaders more generally. The Great Awakening diminished the power of ministers while increasing the influence of personal religion. All the colonial colleges reflected this trend.

At the height of the Awakening, opponents lined up on either side, defending and attacking religious enthusiasm. Yet it was hardly a battle of the pious against the godless or the well-educated against the uninformed. Although opponents of the revival such as Charles Chauncy were certainly devoted to Enlightenment rationalism, Jonathan Edwards, one of the greatest minds of his age, drew from the Enlightenment as well. He praised both Locke and "the incomparable Mr. Newton." For Edwards, however, reason and good habits were not enough. Reason must be supplemented by emotion, in particular the emotion of God's grace. Like all Calvinists, Edwards insisted that natural (unsaved) man was corrupt, as loathsome as a spider or worm. However, once Edwards said that religious salvation and virtue were more matters of the heart than the head, he opened the way for a popular religion that was democratic, intensely personal, and humanitarian.

Conclusion

Eighteenth-century America was part of an expanding world market economy and a capitalist political economy. A growing colonial population sustained a vigorous economy, one that produced for a world market and purchased from the world market. As participants in an "industrious revolution," white Americans worked themselves and their slaves harder and harder in order to purchase the goods increasingly available to consumers. These new goods enabled people to live more genteely, to cultivate a social life.

Especially in the cities, this new emphasis on social life spawned an array of institutions where people could acquire and display learning and gentility. The maturing of the colonial market economy and the spread of consumer culture were not without cost, however. The benefits of the economy were not shared equally. Slaves produced for the market economy but were denied its rewards. The increasing stratification of urban society and land pressures in rural regions meant that a growing segment of the population would be too poor to profit from the expanding economy. At the same time, there emerged a new elite of merchants and planters who had taken advantage of the market economy and avidly purchased its products.

The eighteenth-century world spawned two different but related intellectual responses, the Enlightenment and the Great Awakening. Both were critical in shaping the eighteenth-century colonial world, and both paved the way for the Revolution. The Enlightenment stimulated colonial optimism, leading some to believe that rational thought and the scientific method would someday conquer even death itself. At the same time, the revivals of Calvinist religion reminded men and women that life was still short and ultimately beyond their control. The Awakening told them to look inward and scrutinize their own hearts. In different ways, then, the Enlightenment and the Great Awakening both encouraged the individualism that would become a distinguishing characteristic of American life.

Review Questions

1.   What were the primary sources of population increase in the eighteenth century? Compare the patterns of population growth of Europeans and Africans.

2.   What was the "industrious revolution"? How did it shape the development of the colonial economy? What were the other key factors shaping the development of the colonial economy? What effect did this development have on the lives of ordinary men and women?

3.   What were the primary changes in urban and rural life in the eighteenth century?

4.   Describe the development of the eighteenth-century consumer culture and discuss how it affected everyday life.

5.   What were the chief ideas of the Enlightenment? Why did some men and women find them attractive?

6.   What were the sources of the Great Awakening? Why were some men and women drawn to it?

CHRONOLOGY

1693	College of William and Mary founded
1701	Yale founded
1704	First newspaper, *Boston News-Letter*, published in colonies
1712	Slave revolt in New York City
1715	Yamasee War
1716	First theater built in Williamsburg
1717	French build Fort Toulouse
1718	French found New Orleans
1731	Library Company, first lending library in colonies, erected in Philadelphia
1733	Georgia founded
	King of Spain guarantees freedom to English slaves who run away
1734	Great Awakening begins
1735	John Peter Zenger acquitted of libeling New York's governor
1739	Stono Rebellion
	George Whitefield begins his American tour
1741	35 executed in New York City after slave revolt scare
1748	College of New Jersey (Princeton) founded
1751	Pennsylvania Hospital built in Philadelphia
1752	Georgia becomes a Crown colony
1754	Columbia College founded
1755	Philadelphia College (University of Pennsylvania) founded
1766	Queens College (Rutgers) founded
1773	Eastern State Mental Hospital built in Williamsburg

Further Readings

Richard Bushman, ed., *The Great Awakening: Documents on the Revival of Religion, 1740–1745* (1989). There is no better introduction to the Great Awakening than this collection of sermons and first-person accounts.

Cary Carson, et al., *Of Consuming Interests: The Style of Life in the Eighteenth Century* (1994). An important introduction to the material culture of eighteenth-century consumer culture.

Cornelia Hughes Dayton, *Women Before the Bar: Gender, Law, and Society in Connecticut, 1639–1789* (1995). Uses court records to reveal the lives of ordinary women and their deteriorating position in the eighteenth century.

Thomas M. Doeflinger, *A Vigorous Spirit of Enterprise: Merchants and Economic Development in Revolutionary Philadelphia* (1986). Describes the lives and aspirations of this important segment of the colonial population while providing an excellent introduction to the period's economic history.

David Eltis, *The Rise of African Slavery in the Americas* (2000). A bold new interpretation of the development of slavery that places it in a global context and emphasizes the role of Africans in shaping the slave trade.

Richard Hofstadter, *America at 1750: A Social Portrait* (1971). A beautifully written description of America's peoples and regions that suggests that the Great Awakening made a middle-class society even more so.

Rhys Isaac, *The Transformation of Virginia, 1740–1790* (1982). A magnificent description of the different cultures of Virginia's elite and poor, showing how religious revivals changed them forever.

Philip D. Morgan, *Slave Counterpoint: Black Culture in the Eighteenth-Century Chesapeake and Low Country* (1998). A learned and comprehensive study of slave life in the colonial South.

Gary B. Nash, *The Urban Crucible: Social Change, Political Consciousness, and the Origins of the American Revolution* (1979). Detailed, comprehensive, and indispensable for understanding the social and political world of urban working men.

History on the Internet

"The Exercise of a School Boy"

http://www.history.org/life/manners/rules2.htm

This site lists the text of the etiquette book entitled *Rules of Civility and Decent Behavior in Company and Conversation.* As a youth, George Washington transcribed these rules as a lesson of colonial gentility.

"Immigrant Communities in Maryland"

http://www.clis.umd.edu/~mddlmddl/791/communities/html/index.html#jewish

In addition to exploring the origins of Maryland and its social, political, and cultural characteristics, this site offers a detailed look into the colonial immigrants from Germany and enslaved Africans. Of special interest is the story of a slave named Job who tells of his capture in Africa and his enslavement in Maryland.

"The European Enlightenment"

http://www.wsu.edu/%7Edee/ENLIGHT/ENLIGHT.HTM

On this comprehensive site, read about the general tenets of Enlightenment philosophy, excerpts from the works of Enlightenment thinkers, and a glossary of terms and concepts. This site links to several others on the subject.

"Religion and the Founding of the American Republic"

http://lcweb.loc.gov/exhibits/religion/re102.html

This Library of Congress site explores religion in eighteenth-century America and chronicles the coming of the religious movement known as the Great Awakening. It features many of the best-known religious leaders of this movement, including Johnathan Edwards and George Whitefield. The site also offers the views of critics of this movement.

CONFLICT ON THE EDGE
OF THE EMPIRE

1713-1774

6

OUTLINE

Susannah Willard Johnson Experiences the Empire

The Wars for Empire
An Uneasy Peace
New War, Old Pattern
War and Political Economy

The Victory of the British Empire
The French Empire Crumbles From Within
The Virginians Ignite a War
From Local to Imperial War
Problems With British-Colonial Cooperation
The British Gain the Advantage

Enforcing the Empire
Pontiac's Rebellion and Its Aftermath
Paying for the Empire: Sugar and Stamps

Rejecting the Empire
An Argument About Rights and Obligations
The Imperial Crisis in Local Context
Contesting the Townshend Duties

A Revolution in the Empire
"Massacre" in Boston
The Empire Comes Apart
The First Continental Congress

Conclusion

Susannah Willard Johnson Experiences the Empire

Today the town is called Charlestown, New Hampshire, but then it was known simply as "No. 4," another small farming village on the northern frontier of Massachusetts. In 1754 Susannah Willard Johnson and her husband James had lived there for four years, having taken advantage of a break in the near-constant struggle between Britain and France for North America by moving up to the frontier from Lunenburg, Massachusetts. At 24, Susannah was still a young woman, but she had been married for seven years and already had three children, Sylvanus (6), Susanna (4), and Polly (2), with another due any day. James was ten years older than his wife. A native of Ireland, he had commenced his life in America as a servant indentured to Susannah's uncle Josiah. After working for Josiah for ten years, he purchased the remainder of his time, married Susannah, and set out to make his way by a combination of farming and shopkeeping. James had also become a lieutenant in the militia.

The region's Abenaki Indians—a branch of the Algonquians who were allied with the French and had their own set of grievances against the encroaching settlers—presented both danger and opportunity. At first the settlers at No. 4 were so frightened that they stayed in the fort. Within a few years, however, Susannah later reported, "every appearance of hostility at length vanished—the Indians expressed a wish to traffick, the inhabitants laid by their fears, and thought no more of tomahawks, nor scalping knives." As a farmer and shopkeeper, James Johnson was part of the consumer revolution, selling goods to his fellow settlers and to the Abenakis, who gave him furs in return.

Susannah Johnson and her family led a good life. She described it as "harmony and safety," and "boasted with exaltation that I should with husband, friends, and luxuries, live happy in spite of the fear of savages." By the summer of 1754, however, there were rumors of impending warfare with France, which would make the frontier village a target, not of the French soldiers, but of their Abenaki allies.

On the night of August 29, 1754, the Johnsons, Susannah's sister, and some friends stayed up until midnight, eating watermelon and drinking flip, an eggnog spiked with liquor. The next morning, just before daybreak, a neighbor who was coming to work for the Johnsons appeared at the door with his ax in hand. As the Johnsons opened the door for him, they saw what Susannah later recalled as "a scene—terrible to describe!! Indians! Indians were the first words I heard." As the neighbor rushed through the door, eleven Abenaki men followed him, and soon, Susannah said, they were "all over the house, some upstairs, some haling my sister out of bed, another had ahold of me, and one was approaching Mr. Johnson, who stood in the middle of the floor, to offer himself up."

The Abenakis tied up the men and gathered the women and children around them. They took a little plunder and then marched the party off, to the north. None of the settlers from the village pursued, for it was believed that when trapped, Indians would kill their captives. They marched hard, even though Susannah, who had lost her shoes, had bloody feet. Then, on the second day of her captivity, Susannah went into labor. Her captors took the party to a brook where, attended by her sister and husband, Susannah gave birth to a daughter, whom she named "Captive."

This late nineteenth-century illustration of Hannah Duston's 1697 escape from the Mohawks who had taken her captive shows how Americans at that time imagined Indian captivity.

The French and Indian War had begun on the northern frontier, and the Indians were manipulating it to their advantage. In peacetime they traded furs for manufactured goods, but in time of war, they seized British settlers, took them to Canada, and sold them to the French, who in turn either ransomed them back to the British or traded them for prisoners of war. Although Susannah Johnson realized that she was worth more to her captors alive than dead, she was in no position to take the long view. What to others might look like an imperial struggle, Susannah Johnson experienced as a terrifying assault of Indians at dawn that took her from her home and eventually her family. The consumer revolution that gave settlers such as the Johnsons the opportunity to live a good life on the frontier took place in the context of an imperial struggle rooted in the political economy. France and England were competing to decide who would dominate both the markets the consumer revolution was creating and the lands it was populating. As families such as the Johnsons pushed at the frontiers, they became actors on a vast global stage. ∎

KEY TOPICS

- The imperial wars of the eighteenth century and their impact on colonial society.

- Relationships among the French, English, Spanish, and various Indian tribes and how those relationships affected imperial conflicts in North America.

- The sources of the French and Indian War in the Ohio River valley, why the French empire crumbled from within, and how the British achieved dominance.

- British attempts to reorganize the colonial empire at the end of the French and Indian War.

- The basis for growing colonial resistance to British regulation, its origins in British political and constitutional thought, and the development of new theories of government.

- The series of British acts and colonial responses that brought Britain and the colonies to the brink of war.

The Wars for Empire

The war that tore the Johnsons from their home was the fourth of the wars for empire between Britain and France that had taken place in 65 years. Indeed, in the years between 1689 and 1763, Britain and France were at war more than half of the time. All of these wars had their roots in a struggle for world dominance between the two most powerful nations. To a great extent, colonial and imperial objectives coincided. Both Britain and the colonies would benefit from securing the empire's borders and from expanding British markets by increasing the size and power of the British Empire. Yet the imperial wars also exposed the growing divergence between the political economy of the colonies and that of the mother country. The costs of international war were staggering, and they required an increasingly centralized state with a substantial bureaucracy and an aggressive and focused leadership. In the American colonies, however, governments remained small, taxes were minuscule, and local volunteer militias provided defense. When the growing empire and the wars that created it threatened to increase the power of the consolidated British government over the colonists, raise their taxes to pay for the empire, and station among them a permanent army, the colonists resisted and finally rebelled.

An Uneasy Peace

After the conclusion of Queen Anne's War in 1713 (see chapter 4), England and France entered into a peace that lasted until 1739. It was an uneasy peace for the British North American colonies, however, because they were encircled by warfare on their northern, western, and southern borders. On the north, New Englanders continued to fight with the Abenakis, forcing that tribe into a closer alliance with the French. Massachusetts attempted government-organized campaigns and also turned the fighting over to bands of bounty hunters by offering the huge payment of £100 for the scalp of each male Abenaki over twelve years old. At the same time, the French attempted to stabilize alliances with their Algonquian allies. The most common method was by providing "gifts" of trade goods to allied tribes, which ultimately cost the French treasury more than it regained from the fur trade.

Worried about their ability to control their Indian allies and worried about the expansion of the British colonies, the French began building new forts: Fort Toulouse (1717), Louisbourg (1720), Fort Niagara (1720), Fort St. Frédéric (1731), and the town of New Orleans (1718). The French settlement of the lower Mississippi valley led to conflict with the Natchez Indians, who were conquered and sold into slavery in reprisal for a bloody attack on French settlers. Unsuccessful French attacks upon the Chickasaw drove that tribe into a closer alliance with its British trading partners.

The British, however, were unable to establish peaceful relations with their Indian neighbors in the Southeast. Encroachments on their land, enslavement of their women and children, and abuses by traders led first the Tuscaroras and then the Yamasees to rise up. In 1711, the Tuscarora Indians attacked settlers in western North Carolina. The short and brutal war ended in the defeat of the Tuscaroras. The survivors made their way north, where they joined the Iroquois confederacy. Although the Yamasees had been reliable trading partners for 40 years and had fought with the British in Queen Anne's War, as with the Tuscaroras, unscrupulous South Carolina traders cheated them out of their land and enslaved their women and children. In retaliation, the Yamasees attacked, picking up Indian allies along the way and getting within 12 miles of Charleston before they were stopped, not by the ineffectual South Carolina force of hired whites and armed slaves, but by the crumbling of the Indian alliance. The Yamasee War (1715–1716) claimed the lives of 400 white South Carolinians, a higher proportion of the population than was lost in King Philip's War in New England. The war also forced South Carolina to abandon frontier settlements, and revealed the precariousness of the entire South Carolina settlement. When international war commenced again in 1739, the frontier regions were much as they had been a quarter of a century earlier, dangerous and unstable, for settlers, traders, and Indians alike.

New War, Old Pattern

Another round of international warfare broke out in 1739 and continued for nine years. In the first phase of the War of Jenkins' Ear (1739–1744), Britain attempted to expand into Spanish territories and markets in the Americas. Urged on by the merchants, and with the hearty approval of colonists who wanted to eliminate Spain as a rival, the British found an excuse for declaring war against the Spanish when a ship's captain, Robert Jenkins, turned up in Parliament in 1738 with an ugly stump on one side of his head and holding in his hand what he claimed was his ear, severed by the Spanish seven years earlier in the Caribbean. Once again, colonists joined in what they hoped would be a glorious international endeavor, only to meet disillusionment. In 1741, 3,600 colonists, mostly poor young men lured by the king's promise that they could share in whatever was plundered from the Spanish, joined 5,000 Britons in a failed attack upon Cartagena, Colombia. Poor planning and a lethal environment led to the deaths of more than half the colonial contingent, primarily from disease.

Another ambitious attempt to seize part of the Spanish empire failed in 1740: James Oglethorpe and an inadequate force of settlers hired by South Carolina, accompanied by Cherokee and Creek allies, failed to seize the Spanish outpost at St. Augustine and left the southern border vulnerable. When Oglethorpe and his troops repulsed a Spanish attack in 1742, however, Spain's plans to demolish Georgia and South Carolina and arm their slaves were thwarted.

Just as the North American phase of the War of Jenkins' Ear ended in stalemate, so did King George's War (1744–1748), a conflict between Britain and Austria, on one side, and France and Prussia on the other, about the successor to the throne of Austria. In North America, a French raid on a fishing village in Nova Scotia was met with a huge retaliation on the part of the British. This time, the troops from Massachusetts, subsidized by Pennsylvania and New York and supported by the British Navy, met their objective, capturing the French fort at Louisbourg. Finally, a joint British-colonial venture had succeeded. But, true to the old form, a planned two-pronged attack on Quebec had to be called off when the British fleet failed to arrive. The war then resumed its usual pattern, with European-inspired Indian raids along the frontiers. At the end of the war, Britain returned Louisbourg to France and warned the colonists that they must maintain the peace. Events in North America, however, were out of European control. The British blockade of French ports cut off trade to Canada, including the all-important presents to Indian allies and trade partners. Without the glue of gifts, the French-Indian empire began to crumble, and the balance of power that three world wars in a half a century had been unable to budge suddenly started to come apart.

War and Political Economy

Successive rounds of warfare had a significant impact on politics and society in British North America. Although the colonists identified strongly with the British cause and shared in the intense patriotism that the increasing power of Britain inspired, decades of warfare were a constant drain on the colonial treasury and population.

Wars are always expensive propositions. Generally, rates of taxation in colonial America were amazingly low, except when wars had to be financed (see Figure 6-1, for example). In a rehearsal for the conflicts that would lead to the American Revolution, the British government complained that the colonists were never willing to contribute their fair share to the North American portion of the imperial wars. As a rule, colonial legislatures were jealous of their powers, and the legislatures used royal demands for men and money as a means to increase their own powers. Colonial legislatures were willing to go only so far in raising taxes to pay for imperial wars or expeditions against Indians. Then they simply issued paper money, and more money after that. Inevitably, the currency depreciated, making even worse the boom-and-bust cycles that war economies always produce.

No colony did more to support the imperial war efforts than Massachusetts, but the result was heightened political conflict at home. Under the leadership of several ambitious governors eager to ingratiate themselves with royal officials in London, the colony was pushed to contribute as much as it could to the imperial wars. As many as one-fifth of the men of that colony may have served in the mil-

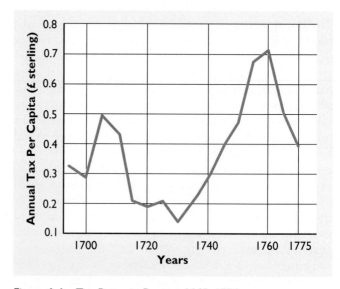

Figure 6-1   Tax Rates in Boston, 1645–1774.
The per capita tax rate in Boston followed the course of imperial war in 1713, increasing during the war of Jenkins' Ear (1739–1748) and rising to unprecedented heights to support the French and Indian War (1754–1763).

Source: Data from Gary B. Nash, The Urban Crucible (Cambridge: Harvard University Press, 1974), p. 403.

itary in the middle of the eighteenth century. Meeting the military's needs for money and manpower also required an unprecedented centralization of government, which in turn inspired a vigorous popular opposition, especially when the immediate demands of war had passed. Mobs in Boston resisted the royal Navy's attempt to "impress" (or force) men into service. When in 1747 Admiral Charles Knowles attempted to fill out his fleet by impressments, Bostonians rioted for three days, and the local militia refused to restore order. For the first time, Bostonians began to speak about a right to resist tyranny.

Much more than in Europe, civilians in America became victims of war. By the eighteenth century, conventions of "civilized" warfare held that civilians should be spared, but this belief broke down in America for two reasons. First, without Europe's sophisticated transportation system to bring supplies efficiently to the Army, troops in America often relied on plundering for their daily food. As New England soldiers marched north through Canada to Louisbourg in 1745, they stole chickens, wine, and livestock from French farmers along the way, as "everyone did what was right in his own eyes." Second, frontier Indians, adapting their traditional mourning war (see chapter 2), routinely attacked frontier villages to seize captives to re-

plenish their own populations and to ransom to the French. In the century between 1675 and 1763, with war on the frontier more common than peace, frontier settlers such as Susannah Johnson were often at risk. With few exceptions, however, Indians attacked only when wars were taking place. During that period, Indians took more than 1,600 New England settlers as captives, more than 90 percent taken during times of war (see Figure 6-2).

Almost half the colonists who were seized eventually returned home. Others died during the arduous march north to Canada. Sometimes Indians killed those they thought were too weak to survive the long journey, and they might quickly dispatch those who faltered along the way. Many died of disease, and a few, typically girls between 7 and 15, remained with their captors for the remainder of their lives. On occasion, a captive escaped. With the assistance of another middle-aged woman and a boy, Hannah Duston killed the Abenaki family that was holding them captive and returned to Massachusetts carrying ten scalps, six of them children's. Acclaimed a heroine, she was praised by the leading ministers and public officials and was given a scalp bounty of £25. The gentility that city dwellers increasingly cultivated was a luxury that had not yet reached the frontier.

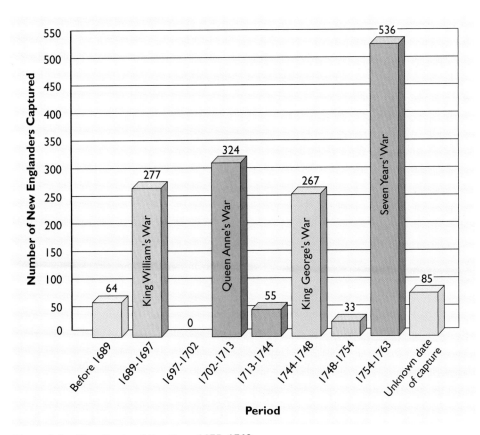

Figure 6-2   New England Captives, 1675–1763.
During periods of war, the number of New Englanders taken capture by northern Indians and the French increased dramatically, with more than 90 perent of the captives being taken during times of war.
Source: Alden Vaughan, Roots of American Racism (New York: Oxford University Press, 1990), p. 31.

The Victory of the British Empire

Each of the imperial wars was ignited by a political episode, but the fundamental issues were economic and imperial, matters of political economy, as Europe's great powers contended to dominate markets and assure themselves a steady supply of food and raw materials. Hence, another war between Britain and France was probably inevitable, given prevailing mercantilist assumptions. The period between the conclusion of King George's War in 1748 and the beginning of the French and Indian War in 1754 in North America was one of considerable tension, especially on the frontier. As a result, Britain and France were drawn into a war because of events that no one in London or Paris could control.

The French Empire Crumbles From Within

Like Europeans, Indians in North America looked for opportunities to advance their own interests. In the years after King George's War, a change in French policy offered a small band of Miamis the chance to gain an advantage over rival Indians. In the process, they started a chain of events that led to the French and Indian War.

Although King George's War had ended in a stalemate, the French position in North America was weaker at the war's conclusion than it had been at the beginning. The combination of the British blockade and the French need to divert resources to the military effort had required the French to cut back on their presents to allied Algonquian tribes, especially those who inhabited the Ohio River valley behind the British colonies. In addition, in order to raise revenue, the French sharply increased the charges for the lease of trading posts so that the traders in turn had to raise the prices that they charged the Indians for trade goods. These changes significantly weakened the hold of the French over their Indian allies, creating a political instability that was the underlying North American cause of the French and Indian War.

Unlike northern New York, where the Iroquois Federation held sway, the Ohio River valley was inhabited by a number of small, refugee tribes (Miamis, Weas, Kickapoos, Delawares, and many others) (see Map 6-1). As long as the French were liberal with their presents and trade goods were cheap, they were able to maintain a loose control over these many small tribes. Once that control ended, however, the French dominance disintegrated as each tribe sought to increase its advantage over the others. Moreover, at just this moment the British recognized the strategic and economic importance of the region.

The temporary power vacuum afforded a small group of Miamis led by a chieftain called La Demoiselle an op-

A member of the Shawnee nation, one of the Indian tribes that inhabited the Ohio River valley in the eighteenth century.

portunity to improve their situation by playing one group of colonists off another. It was this power play that led to the French and Indian War. The chain of events began in 1748 when La Demoiselle's group moved east from their home, near present-day Fort Wayne, Indiana, to establish a new village, Pickawillany, near the head of the Miami River, in present-day Ohio. La Demoiselle welcomed traders from Pennsylvania, because their trade goods were both better and cheaper. He also knew that as a rule the English were less demanding of their Indian allies than were the French. Hence he hoped for an advantageous trade with the British, unencumbered by any reciprocal political or military obligations.

La Demoiselle's move was bold and dangerous, for it threatened not only the balance of power between Britain and France, but that between the colonies of Pennsylvania and Virginia as well. The Pennsylvanians welcomed a trade alliance with La Demoiselle's Miamis, for it gave them a claim to western lands that Virginians also sought. At the same time, La Demoiselle was challenging a number of rival chieftains who wished to establish dominance in the area as well. He used his access to British traders to attract small bands to his village, and within a year his following had grown from 50 warriors to 400 families.

Alarmed, the French set out to re-establish their control of this region. In 1749, the French sent a small expedition out to cow their former Indian allies back into submission; it failed. With Indian tribes slipping out from under their control, the French shifted their policy away from trade to force. They began to raid dissident Indian encampments and to make plans to establish a fort in the Ohio River valley.

With this change in French policy, Indians in the region seemed to have two options, either to gather up Indian allies, which was what La Demoiselle was attempting, or to make alliances with the British, which was what a refugee Iroquois chieftain named Tanacharison tried. Neither route offered the Indians any security in the end, but the chaos these bids for advantage created ultimately drew the French and British into their fourth war in less than a century. In 1752, Tanacharison agreed to cede to Virginia not only the 200,000 acres claimed by the Ohio Company, a group of Virginia speculators, but also all the land between the Susquehannah and Allegheny Rivers (that is, present-day Kentucky, West Virginia, and the western half of Pennsylvania). In return, Virginia promised Tanacharison's people trade and protection from their enemies.

Tanacharison recognized that La Demoiselle had miscalculated. With no European or Indian power dominant in the region, conflicts had begun to break out, encouraged by the French, who hoped to use still-loyal Indians to pry off segments of La Demoiselle's alliance, weakening it enough that it could be conquered, which is precisely what happened. In a raid upon Pickawillany, 250 pro-French Ottawas and Chippewas killed La Demoiselle and, with his followers watching, cooked and ate him and several British traders. The village was destroyed, and the demoralized Miamis returned to the French fold, asking for protection. For the moment, the French seemed to have regained the ascendancy, but by shifting their policy from trade to force, they had put themselves on a course that would lead to the loss of their North American empire. Those Indians such as the followers of La Demoiselle and Tanacharison, who put their faith in cheap British goods and glittering British promises, would soon learn that the British could offer no more security than the French.

The Virginians Ignite a War

Both France and Virginia now claimed the Ohio River valley, and they raced to establish forts that would secure their claims. Virginia entrusted the job to a well-connected 21-year old with almost no qualifications for the post: George Washington. Washington was tied to the powerful Fairfax clan, a British family that owned 5,000,000 acres on Virginia's Northern Neck and held a share in the Ohio Company. In the Anglo-American political and social world,

George Washington, painted in 1772, but wearing his uniform from the French and Indian War.

advancement came through such interlocking ties of family and patronage. By securing the favor of those more powerful, Washington was in a position to ascend to the top tier in the Virginia hierarchy. As Washington himself recognized, "It was deemed by some an extraordinary circumstance that so young and inexperienced a person should have been employed on a negotiation with which subjects of the greatest importance were involved."

In the spring of 1754, the French and Virginians scrambled to see who could build a fort first at the forks of the Ohio (present-day Pittsburgh). The previous year, the French had already constructed three forts somewhat to the north. The force that Virginia sent to the region, with Washington as second in command, was pathetically small. Not surprisingly, this young man doing the bidding of wealthy speculators had found it difficult to attract volunteers for his mission. Although the French Army numbering 1,000 was only 50 miles away, a combined Virginia-Indian band led by Washington recklessly attacked and defeated a small French reconnaissance party. The French and Indian War had begun.

The Virginians had bitten off more than they could chew. The small fort that Washington and his men built and aptly named Fort Necessity was reinforced by British regulars. It was quickly deserted by the Indian allies who

GROWING UP IN AMERICA

Youth in Captivity

When his family was seized by a band of Abenakis early one morning in 1754, Sylvanus Johnson was only six years old. Eunice Williams was seven when she and her family were abducted from Deerfield, Massachusetts, in the winter of 1704. Half the captives taken from New England by Indians in the century before 1763 were children under the age of 16.

In Canada Sylvanus Johnson was separated from his family and adopted into an Indian family as a young hunter. When his captor came to take him away, a tearful young Sylvanus threw his arms around his mother and begged her to keep him. The last words she heard him say were, "I shall never see you again." They were reunited, however, four years later, in October 1758. At first he could not remember his mother, but after a few minutes' conversation, slowly some vague and confused memories came back to him; he could not remember at all his father, who had died in battle a few months earlier. Sylvanus had forgotten English completely and knew only a little broken French. According to his mother, "his habits were somewhat Indian." He had become a hunter and could now use a tomahawk and bow and arrow like a native, but, his mother said, those habits "wore off by degree."

Like Sylvanus Johnson, Eunice Williams also was adopted into an Indian family, a band of Mohawks who lived near Montreal. By that time she had lost two of her six siblings, killed by the Indians in their raid upon Deerfield, and her mother, who was killed along the march north when her strength gave out. At first Eunice's new Indian family refused to ransom Eunice back to her father, resisting the strongest of pleas by the governors of Canada and Massachusetts. Later, the choice seemed to be wholly Eunice's. By the time she was 16, she had converted to Catholicism, taking the new name of Marguerite, and had married a Mohawk by the name of Arosen. Shortly after her marriage, a New York trader met with her and her husband and tried every argument he knew

to persuade her to return to Massachusetts. He said that her family loved her, that they missed her, and that if she was unhappy in Massachusetts she could return to Canada. Eunice sat for several hours in stony silence. Finally, under pressure by both the desperate trader and a French priest, she replied, "Jaghte oghte," Mohawk for "no." The only explanation she ever gave for her unwillingness to return home was that her father had remarried, but surely there was more behind her decision. She had become a Catholic and a Mohawk and married a Mohawk man, with whom she lived for more than 50 years, until his death in 1765. Her daughters married Indians too. Although she visited her brother in Massachusetts several times and corresponded with him (using a translator), she refused his pleas to move back. She was a Mohawk now.

Individuals who had lived in two cultures, Sylvanus Johnson and Eunice Williams also illustrate broader patterns. Only one out of ten male captives from New England refused to return, but a third of the females chose to remain. Younger captives were far more likely to remain in Canada than were those who were adults at the time that they were carried north, for they were more malleable than adults, quicker to forget their homes and to adapt to Indian customs. Those most likely to make the transition from one culture to the other were girls, like Eunice Williams, between the ages of 7 and 15. More than half chose to remain with their captors.

Historians are not entirely certain why more girls than boys ultimately chose to make their homes among those who had captured them. Perhaps it was because Puritan culture had trained girls to be especially pliant, responding without question to those in authority. Or perhaps it was because, after the rigors of a Puritan upbringing, the relative freedom of Indian culture was inviting. Or it may have been that young girls resented the parents who could not protect them from the terrors of abduction at dawn and slowly shifted their loyalties to those who offered them new homes.

recognized that it was indefensible. The French overwhelmed the small fort, sending Washington and his troops scrambling back over the mountains to Virginia.

Although war was not officially declared in Europe until May 1756, the French and Indian War (known in Eu-

rope as the Seven Years' War) soon spread on the frontier, leading to raids such as the Abenaki one that seized Susannah Johnson and her family. Indeed, in Montreal she would soon meet two of Washington's captains who had been captured at Fort Necessity.

From Local to Imperial War

At the beginning of the war, the advantage was with the French. Not only was that nation's population three times as great as Britain's, but its Army was ten times the size, even though Canada's population was only one-twentieth of that of the British colonies. Even more important, the French state was more centralized and hence better prepared to speak with one voice to regional Indians and to coordinate the massive effort that deploying troops in an international war required. The British government knew that lack of coordination among its North American colonies could cripple the war effort. Hence, as early as the summer of 1754, even before Washington's defeat at Fort Necessity, it instructed all the colonies north of Virginia to meet together to plan for a collective defense and to shore up the alliance with the Six (Iroquois) Nations. Pennsylvania's Benjamin Franklin offered the delegates in Albany a plan, known as the Albany Plan of Union, which every colony rejected.

The characteristic localism of the American colonies made cooperation difficult if not impossible. To a certain extent this localism was the product of shortsightedness and squabbling between one colony and another and between colonial assemblies and their governors. But it also represented a deeply ingrained value, one that was profoundly suspicious of the centralized European state and its army of professionals.

Britain was now engaged in its fourth war with the French in less than a century. This was the first of these contests to break out in North America, however, and both Britain and France initially hoped that it could be confined to that continent. The British government had authorized Virginia's foray into the Ohio Valley and was prepared, after some debate in Parliament, to support it with troops. Two regiments under the command of General Edward Braddock were sent to Virginia in late 1754. Britain hoped that just as the colonists had begun the war, they could end it with only a little British assistance. But the disarray at Albany was only repeated in the months to come. Moreover, as in the previous imperial wars, colonial soldiers were reluctant to obey an officer from another colony, let alone one from the British Army.

With four times as many troops as the British had stationed in North America, superior leadership, and the lack of intercolonial rivalries, the French dominated the first phase of the war, from 1754 through 1757. At the outset of this period, the British and colonial governments decided on a four-pronged attack, with armies made up of British regulars and colonials. The plan was to besiege, in standard European fashion, four French forts in territory the British claimed as their own: Fort Duquesne (Pittsburgh), Fort Niagara (Niagara Falls), Fort St. Frédéric (Crown Point, at the southern end of Lake Champlain), and Fort Beauséjour (Nova Scotia).

Braddock was to lead the attack on Fort Duquesne, with a combined force of British regulars and colonial troops. No Indians, however, accompanied the expedition. Saying that "No Savage Should Inherit the Land," Braddock had alienated the regional Indians. Hence they moved back into the French alliance, fearing the colonists' land hunger more than any French danger. After a grueling two-month march in which they built their own roads ahead of them, on July 9, 1755, Braddock's forces were surprised just a few miles from their objective by a French and Indian force that was more than 80 percent Indian. Almost a thousand of the British and colonial troops were killed or wounded, including Braddock himself. One of the survivors was George Washington, who had been serving as an unsalaried adjutant to Braddock. He had apprenticed himself to the older general to learn the art of war.

Two of the other three planned assaults ended in disappointment as well. William Shirley, who had become

This detail depicting Braddock's Defeat is from a drawing by an engineer with the British Army.

Iroquois Indians were frequent guests at the home of trader and British official William Johnson. He took an Iroquois woman, Molly Brant, as his common-law wife. Johnson's Iroquois allies followed him into battle in the French and Indian War.

commander in chief of the British forces after Braddock's defeat, decided to lead the attack on Fort Niagara himself, and he assigned leadership of the attack upon Fort St. Frédéric to William Johnson, a Mohawk Valley Indian trader who had recently been assigned to supervise relations between the Six Nations and the colonies. In 1756 the assignment was extended with Johnson's appointment as superintendent of Indian affairs for the northern colonies. He was also made a baronet, only the second American to be given this rank of nobility.

Johnson was eminently well suited for leading Iroquois forays against the French, such as the one that the French had used to defeat Braddock on his way to Fort Duquesne. Shirley, however, sent Johnson to besiege Fort St. Frédéric, a four-story stone tower surrounded by thick, black limestone walls. Johnson led a force of about 3,500, including 300 of his Iroquois confederates, building their road ahead of them. Their advance was stopped by an ambush from the French and their Indian allies. But with equal casualties on both sides and the capture of the French commander, the British declared it a victory and elevated Johnson to the nobility. The British settled in for the winter of 1755–1756 to build Fort William Henry, and the French, Fort Carillon (which the British renamed Ticonderoga). Johnson tried to appease his Mohawk allies, who

had suffered heavy casualties, by following the custom of the mourning war and sending them several French prisoners to take their kinsmen's place. However, the Mohawk understood how weak the British were, and their women elders refused to let their men rejoin the fight.

Hampered by a rough terrain and intercolonial political wrangling, Shirley's force never made it to Fort Niagara. Like Johnson, Shirley had to settle in for the winter, at Fort Oswego, short of his objective. The only outright success was at Fort Beauséjour, across an isthmus from the British colony at Nova Scotia. It was also the only one of the four campaigns that did not require an arduous march across the wilderness. A British-financed expedition of New England volunteers easily seized the fort. Thereupon the British evicted all the Acadians (French residents of Nova Scotia) who would not take an oath of loyalty. More than half the 20,000 Acadians were sent unwanted to the various colonies. About 300 ended up in French Louisiana, where their name was abbreviated into "Cajuns."

War was not officially declared until May 1756. Like the British, the French had been reluctantly increasing their expenditures on the war, but both nations still expected their colonists to carry most of the load themselves. The British defeats and continued intercolonial rivalries left the British vulnerable and the frontier exposed. The

French began a cautious but highly successful offensive. First, they encouraged Indian raids along the frontier from Maine to South Carolina. Indians in the region swung back to the French because the French appeared the lesser of two evils. They concluded that they had nothing to gain from the land-hungry British. Once they had helped dispose of the British, they calculated that "we can drive away the French when we please." The price for French friendship, however, was participation in the war against the British. Indians attacked all along the frontier. By the fall of 1756, some 3,000 settlers had been killed, and the line of settlement had been pushed back 150 miles in some places. Such attacks upon the civilian population were a calculated part of French policy.

In the more conventional part of their offensive, the French and their Indian allies seized Fort Bull in March 1756, attacking on snowshoe, and Fort Oswego several months later. A little over a year later, the French assembled a massive force to attack Fort William Henry, a story that has been dramatized, with a certain amount of poetic license, in fiction and film. This loosely organized army of 8,000, under the leadership of Louis-Joseph de Montcalm-Gozon de Saint-Véran, included a thousand Indian warriors from as far as 1,500 miles away and another 800 converted Algonquians accompanied by their Catholic priests.

After a seven-day siege and heavy bombardment, the British commander surrendered on August 9, 1757. Montcalm offered them European-style terms: If the British would return their French and Indian prisoners, they could keep their personal weapons and belongings if they marched back to Fort Edward and promised not to fight the French for another eighteen months. Historians still debate whether Montcalm knew what was about to take place. The Indians had expected, as was their custom, to be allowed to take plunder and captives to replace their dead. As one explained:

> I make war for plunder, scalps, and prisoners.
> You are satisfied with a fort, and you let your
> enemy and mine live. I do not want to keep such
> bad meat for tomorrow. When I kill it, it can no
> longer attack me.

Denied this opportunity by Montcalm, they fell upon the British, including the sick, women, and children, as they were evacuating the fort the next morning. They killed anyone who resisted, perhaps as many as 200. Montcalm later commented that "what would be an infraction in Europe, cannot be so regarded in America."

The massacre at Fort William Henry had significant repercussions. Still angry at having been denied the spoils of war, Montcalm's Indian allies returned home, taking small pox with them. The French would never again have the assistance of such a significant number of Indian allies;

The new British commander, Lord Jeffrey Amherst, used germ warfare against the Delaware Indians who were fighting with the French. He invited them to a "peace talk" and gave them blankets infected with small pox.

the British were outraged. The new British commander, Lord Jeffrey Amherst, declared the surrender terms null and void, and the British subsequently denied the "honors of war" to the French they defeated in battle. Amherst took a particular disliking to Indians. Later, under his order, Delaware Indians who had been invited to a peace talk were given, ostensibly as presents, blankets that had been infected with small pox. "I hope it will have the desired effect," one officer commented. Indeed it did, leading to an epidemic among the Delawares.

Problems with British-Colonial Cooperation

The British blamed the colonists and the colonists blamed the British for their collective inability to defeat the French. There was some truth in each side's accusations:

unwillingness to sacrifice and disastrous infighting among the colonists, and extraordinary arrogance among the British. These recriminations, more than any particular failing on the part of either the colonists or the British military, created the greatest problems. The colonists and the British had very different expectations about how each should contribute to the war effort, grounded in diverging political economies. The colonists were not prepared for the high taxes or sacrifice of liberty that waging an international war required. Until these differences were overcome, victory would be impossible. There were two chief areas of conflict between the British and the colonists, one over raising money and troops, and one over discipline and direction in the Army.

The British were dismayed by what they perceived as the selfishness of the colonists. One British officer hoped that "for once in their lives, they will forget jealousies, and their petty provincial interests, for the general good of their fatherland." Instead, the British encountered massive profiteering and trading with the enemy. In Albany, colonists were selling boards to the army at prices inflated 66 percent. British warships that docked at Hampton Roads, Virginia, after a long ocean crossing, found that all water was in privately owned wells and that those who owned it demanded payment. Colonial governments were no more generous. Braddock's expedition to Fort Duquesne was delayed and hampered by the unwillingness of the colonies to provide his Army with supplies.

After Braddock's defeat, it was not only supplies the Army needed, it was troops, too, as colonials deserted *en masse*. The British began recruiting servants and apprentices, much to the anger of their masters. As one Massachusetts lawyer sympathetic to the Army put it, "If any native of the Province inlists, the Inlistment is critically examined, every imaginary flaw is made a real one, and the Desertion of such a person is encouraged." Moreover, local officials supported their countrymen, not the Army.

Another serious problem was that of quartering soldiers in the winter as they waited to begin their spring campaigns. Under the provisions of the Mutiny Act, which did not extend specifically to the colonies, troops on the move in England could call upon local communities for shelter, wood, and candles. Also, they were lodged in public buildings rather than private homes. In the colonies, however, there simply weren't enough buildings in which to house soldiers without resorting to private homes. The residents of Albany took in soldiers only under threat of force. Philadelphians faced the same threats but were rescued by the ever-resourceful Franklin, who opened a newly built hospital to the British troops. In Charleston, the residents adamantly refused, and soldiers had to camp outdoors, where they fell victim to disease. Their commander commented that "I shall always prefer to make two Campaigns than to settle the Quarters in any of our American Towns."

A second set of problems arose from joint operations, where conflict was probably inevitable. The British Army was a highly trained, highly disciplined professional fighting force, led by members of the upper classes; service in it was a career. In contrast, colonial soldiers were primarily civilian amateurs, led by the members of the middle class from their home towns. Loyalty extended no further than the colony and was deepest for men and officers from home. Colonial soldiers believed that they were fighting under contracts, limiting them to service under a particular officer, for a set period of time, for a specific objective, and a set rate of pay. If any of the terms of that agreement were violated, the soldier considered himself free to go home.

The British, however, expected the same adherence to military discipline from the colonists as they did from their professional army. Parliament made all colonial soldiers operating with regular forces subject to British martial law, which was cruel and uncompromising. One regular soldier, for example, was sentenced to 1,000 lashes for stealing a keg of beer, which a merciful officer reduced to a mere 900! General Amherst sentenced two Rhode Islanders to be executed by a firing squad for desertion. He gave instructions that after the first had been executed, the second, after having seen his friend killed, was to be taken to the place of execution "there to be told that in hopes that one Example may be sufficient to put a Stop to any further desertion in the Regiment [,] I pardon him."

The British officers neither understood nor forgave the colonists' different expectations. The British officers were almost unanimous in their condemnation of the colonial soldiers. According to Brigadier General James Wolfe, "The Americans are in general the dirtiest most contemptible cowardly dogs that you can conceive. There is no depending upon them in action. They fall down dead in their own dirt and desert by battalions, officers and all." General John Forbes called the colonists "an extreme bad collection of broken Innkeepers, Horse Jockeys, and Indian traders."

Yet the colonists certainly believed that they were doing their share. Taxes were raised dramatically. In Virginia, the tax rate tripled in three years, while in Massachusetts it went up to about £20 per adult man, which was a considerable sum where the average wealth was £38 per capita. The human contribution was even more impressive. At the height of the war, Massachusetts was raising 7,000 soldiers a year, out of a colony with only 50,000 men. The British were frustrated that these soldiers insisted upon returning home after the summer's campaign was finished, but they were not professional soldiers; most of them had other occupations. Perhaps as many as three out of ten adult men served in the military at some point during the war, and only the Civil War and the Revolution had higher casualty rates.

The British Gain the Advantage

Montcalm's victory at Fort William Henry marked the French high-water mark. Although his abandonment by the Indian allies represented an important turning point, the decisive step was the decision of the British government to commit more troops to the effort.

With a change of British government in 1757 came a new resolve to win the war, as William Pitt became head of the cabinet. His rise to power represented the triumph as well of the commercial classes and their vision of the empire. It was under his ministry that Brittania came to rule the waves. Pitt was the first British leader who was as committed to a victory in the Americas as in Europe, believing that the future of the British Empire lay not in Europe but in the extended empire and its trade. Consequently, Britain's war aim in North America shifted from simply regaining territory it had already claimed to seizing New France itself. Pitt immediately sent 2,000 additional troops, promised 6,000 more, and asked the colonies to raise 20,000 of their own, essentially to support campaigns of the British regular forces. So large an army, of course, required huge expenditures. Not only did Pitt raise taxes on the already heavily taxed British, but he borrowed heavily, doubling the size of the British debt. He won the cooperation of the colonies by promising their colonial legislatures that Britain would pay up to half of their costs for fighting the war. As all of this money poured into the colonies, it improved their economies dramatically. Pitt integrated colonial officers into the chain of command so that they could give orders to British regulars of a lower rank. And, finally, he sought out better generals and took a direct role in planning their campaigns.

Now the British were prepared to take the offensive. In a series of great victories, they won the prizes that had eluded them in 1755: First Louisbourg on Cape Breton Island in July 1758; then Fort Frontenac in August; and finally, in November, Fort Duquesne, which the British renamed Fort Pitt. The only defeat was at Fort Carillon (called Ticonderoga by the British) in a siege that failed; Pitt promptly replaced the losing general. Once the British seized Fort Frontenac, disrupting the supply lines from the French to the Ohio Valley Indians, those Indians were willing to shift their allegiance. At the same time, the British moved from a policy of confrontation to one of accommodation, partly under the influence of Sir William Johnson, who combined an understanding of Indian objectives with his own ambition to preside over an expanded Anglo-Indian empire in the West (see Map 6-1). In the Treaty of Easton (1758), more than 500 representatives of 13 Ohio Valley tribes agreed to remain neutral in return for a promise to keep the territory west of the Alleghenies free of settlers. At the same time, gifts to the Iroquois brought them back into the fold.

The British were now ready for the final offensive (see Map 6-2). Historians always argue about when and why a war is "lost." The answer is always debatable, for unless an army has been annihilated and the population entirely subjugated, which is a rare occurrence, when to surrender is always a subjective decision. Those who wield political and military power must decide when the loss in lives and resources can no longer be justified, and the population must agree that further fighting is pointless. By 1759, some of the French believed that the war was essentially over. Casualties were extremely high (20 percent a year), food was in short supply, and inflation was rampant. Most of the Indian allies had deserted the cause, and the French government was neither willing nor able to match Pitt's spending on the war. The army in North America was still large, however, and it would take two more years of fighting and the loss of thousands more lives before the French were willing to surrender.

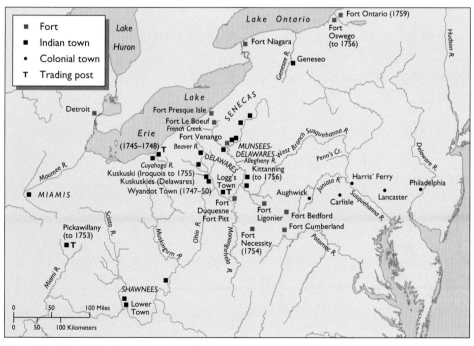

Map 6-1   The Ohio River Valley, 1747–1758.
This territory, inhabited by a number of small bands of Indians, was coveted by both the French and the British, not to mention several competing groups of colonial land speculators. The rivalries between the imperial powers, among the Indian bands and between rival groups of speculators, made this region a powder keg.
Source: Adapted from Michael McConnell, A Country Between *(Lincoln: University of Nebraska, 1992), pp. 116–117.*

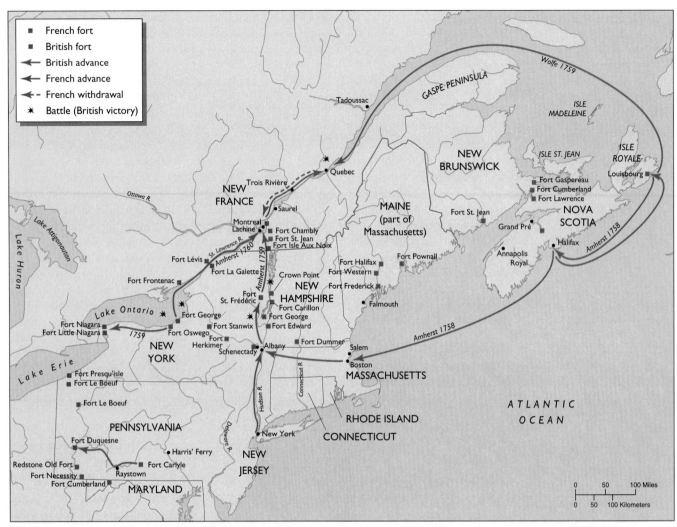

Map 6-2   The Second Phase of the French and Indian War, 1758–1763.
This map shows British advances in Pennsylvania, New York, and Canada.

In the summer of 1759, General James Wolfe took the struggle for North America into the heart of Canada, laying siege to Quebec, a city that sits on a bluff high above the St. Lawrence River. French defenses made the city almost impregnable, so for two-and-a-half months Wolfe bombarded the city and tried to wear down the will of its citizens, terrorizing those who lived on its outskirts by burning crops and houses. Anyone who resisted was shot and scalped. Finally, in mid-September, Wolfe ordered an assault up the 175-foot cliff. When, and if, the British reached the top, there would be no retreat. Hauling two cannons up with them, Wolfe's well-trained soldiers reached the top, and in a battle that lasted only half an hour, they claimed victory on the Plains of Abraham. Each side suffered casualties of 15 percent, and both Wolfe and his French opponent, Montcalm, were killed. Four days later, New France's oldest permanent settlement surrendered to the British. The war continued into the next year.

By the time the British reached Montreal, the French Army numbered fewer than 3,000 men.

The Treaty of Paris, which concluded the war, was not signed until 1763. By that time, Britain had also seized the French sugar islands in the Caribbean, and after Spain entered the war on the French side in 1762, Havana and the Philippines. Pitt would have continued to fight, but the British public had reached the limits of what it was willing to pay to increase the size of the Empire. The French too were thoroughly tired of war and Canada's drain on the national treasury. Hence, France surrendered all of Canada except for two small fishing islands off the coast of Newfoundland in return for the right to hold onto the most valuable of the sugar islands. France even gave New Orleans and all of its territory west of the Mississippi to Spain as a sort of compensation for losing Florida, which the British claimed (see Map 6-3). (Britain let Spain keep Havana and the Philippines.) Britain decided to stake its

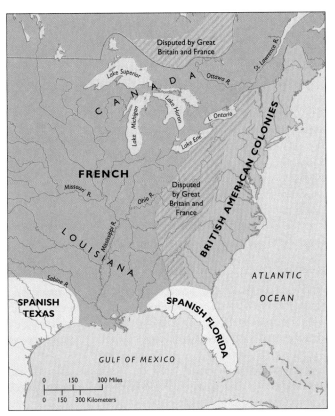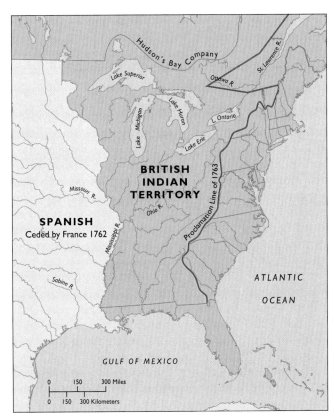

Map 6-3   The North American Colonies Before and After the French and Indian War.
In The Treaty of Paris in 1763, more American territory was transferred than at any time before or since.
Source: Helen Hornbeck Tanner, Atlas of Great Lakes Indian History (Norman: University of Oklahoma Press, 1987), p. 54.

future on the mainland of North America, believing correctly that it would ultimately be more valuable than the sugar islands of the Caribbean. A war that had been started in the remote woods of the Ohio Valley concluded with the transfer of more American territory than has changed hands at any time before or since.

Enforcing the Empire

Even before the French and Indian War had begun, some members of the British government believed that tighter control had to be exercised over the American colonies. What British officials stationed in the colonies saw during the war only reinforced that view. Despite their protestations of patriotism, colonists continued to smuggle and even trade with the enemy throughout the war, while the colonial Assemblies sometimes seemed to impede the war effort as much as they helped it. Pitt had finally increased Britain's national debt to pay for the war, rather than waiting for the colonial Assemblies. Now, with the war over, Britain faced a staggering debt of £122,603,336. The annual interest, at almost £4.5 million, was more than half the usual peacetime budget. Moreover, there was a huge new

territory to govern, a territory that was coveted by speculators and settlers and inhabited by a number of Indian tribes determined to resist encroachment.

The American Revolution grew out of British attempts to draw their American colonies more closely into the imperial system. Although from time to time various master plans for reorganizing the empire had been circulated, there was never an overarching design or a clear set of guidelines. What was new in 1763, then, was not a blueprint for empire but a combination of necessity and new resolve to enforce a set of assumptions about how an empire should function and what the role of colonies in it should be. In 1760 a new king, the twenty-two-year-old George III, ascended to the throne upon the death of his grandfather. Reasonably well-educated, though decidedly lacking in genius, the young king was determined to play a role in government, much to the distress of certain members of the House of Commons. Unable to find a minister to his satisfaction, he changed ministers frequently, which rendered the British government somewhat chaotic for a number of years. Some historians suggest that this turnover was one of the sources of the Revolution. It is not clear, however, that more enlightened leadership would have prevented the war, for George's ministers pursued a rather consistent, if imperfectly executed, policy toward the colonies. In resisting that policy, the American colonists developed a new and different idea of the purpose of government, one that propelled them to revolution.

Pontiac's Rebellion and Its Aftermath

Because the British had defeated the French in war and had entered into alliances with both the Iroquois and the Ohio Valley Indians, peace in the West should have been easy to secure. The British, however, soon made the same mistake that the French had made when they discontinued presents to their Indian allies 15 years earlier. The British thought that they could impose their will on the Indians rather than following the diplomacy of the middle ground. As a consequence the British soon found themselves embroiled in another war.

At the conclusion of the French and Indian War, the western Algonquian tribes hoped that the British would simply replace the French and follow the practices of the middle ground by mediating their disputes, trading with them at advantageous prices, and giving them "presents." Lord Jeffrey Amherst, who commanded the British forces in North America, cut off the presents, believing them too expensive. He thought that threats of an Indian revolt were exaggerated, "Meer Bugbears," and he was willing to take the risk of war.

The war that resulted in 1763 is commonly known as "Pontiac's Rebellion," named after the Ottawa chieftain who played a prominent role in it. It is probably more accurate to call it the "Western Indians' Defensive War." It was the first battle in a long, and ultimately unsuccessful, attempt by Indians to keep the region between the Mississippi and the Alleghenies free of European settlers. The Indians seized every fort except for Pitt, Niagara, and Detroit, and Detroit was under siege for six months (see Map 6-4).

The war spawned violence all along the frontier. Casualties were high, about 2,000 civilians, 400 soldiers, and an unknown number of Indians. Tortures by both sides were horrific. Pontiac himself was a notoriously violent man, especially when drunk. Once, he ordered a French man to drown a seven-year-old English girl, a captive, who, cold, sick, and naked, had dared to try to warm herself by Pontiac's fire. For their part, American colonists took out their aggressions on peaceful or defenseless Indians living in their midst. In December 1763, a party of 50 armed men from the small Pennsylvania village of Paxton descended on a tiny community of Christian Indians living at Conestoga Manor, eight miles west of Lancaster. They killed and scalped the six people they found—2 men, 3 women, and a child—and burned their houses. Two weeks later, another group of these "Paxton Boys" broke into the county

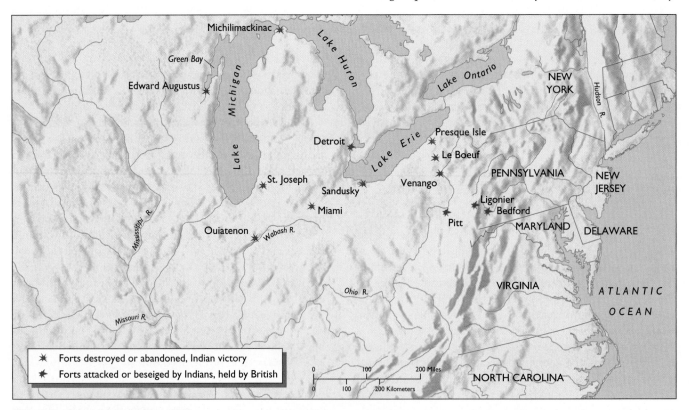

Map 6-4   Pontiac's Rebellion, 1763.
The war began when the British abandoned the policy of the middle ground and cut off presents to the western Indians. In their uprising, the Indians destroyed nine British forts and attacked another four before the war ended in a draw.
Source: Tanner, Atlas of Great Lakes Indian History, p. 49.

Chapter 6 Conflict on the Edge of the Empire, 1713–1774 171

workhouse, where the remainder of the small tribe had been put for their own protection, and killed them too.

Although colonial leaders decried such acts of violence and vigilantism, they did very little to prevent or punish them. As a man of the Enlightenment, Benjamin Franklin was revolted by the viciousness of the Paxton Boys. He denounced them as "cruel Men . . . . barbarous Men. . . . This is done by no civilized Nation in *Europe*. Do we come to *America* to learn and practice the manners of *Barbarians?*" Nonetheless, he arranged for their amnesty. British officials saw the inability of the colonists to maintain order on the frontier and protect innocent Indians from violence as further evidence of the fecklessness of colonial governments. King George himself ordered the colonial governors "to remedy and prevent those Evils, which are as contrary to the Rules of good Policy as of Justice and Equity."

Even before Pontiac's Rebellion ended in a draw, the British had decided that peace with the western Indians could be preserved only by keeping colonial settlers and speculators away from the Indians. The Proclamation of 1763 confined the colonists to the east of an imaginary line running down the spine of the Alleghenies. George Washington called the proclamation "a temporary expedient to quiet the minds of the Indians." Washington and other speculators simply ignored the proclamation, much as merchants had been ignoring customs regulations. Washington instructed his surveyor to "secure some of the most valuable lands. . . . under the pretense of hunting [game]."

The Proclamation fell harder on speculators than on settlers. Settlers could move west, squat on a piece of land, and hope that eventually Britain would validate their claim. Speculators could not sell land, however, without a legal claim to it, and so Virginia speculators tried a variety of stratagems to lay claim to the rich lands of Kentucky. A 1768 treaty between Britain's southern Indian agent and the Cherokee reserved that region for the Cherokee. Only a few weeks later, in the Treaty of Fort Stanwix, the Iroquois sold the same territory to Sir William Johnson, Britain's northern Indian agent. The territory was not the Iroquois' to sell, but they hoped to divert settlers away from their own lands. On the basis of this dubious claim, Virginia's speculators claimed land in the Kentucky region, but these claims were denied by Britain, which understood that the Cherokee, Shawnee, and other regional tribes would not give up the land. Virginia speculators looked for a pretext for taking the territory by force, and it came in 1774, when several settlers killed several Indians, and John Logan, a Mingo Indian, sought vengeance for his slain relatives. Rather than resolving this conflict in the time-tested ways of the middle ground, Virginia's royal governor, Lord Dunmore, did the bidding of the colony's speculators and sent a force of 2,000 Virginians to vanquish the Indians. Although the Virginians' success in Lord Dunmore's War extinguished Indian claims to Kentucky, Britain was still not ready to permit speculators or settlers to claim the land.

Paying for the Empire: Sugar and Stamps

On the edge of the British Empire, the colonies were important, but not nearly as important as Britain's domestic concerns. The shape that the new empire would take necessarily reflected higher priorities, ones that were central to the British political economy. One of George III's highest priorities was to maintain the size of the army. During the French and Indian War, the size of the British army had doubled, and it was filled with officers who were loyal to the king. The stability of the British government rested on just this sort of patronage, and the king did not want to disappoint his supporters. Responding to the king's wishes, Parliament in 1763 voted to maintain a huge peacetime army; 20 regiments (typically 1,000 men each) would be stationed in the colonies and West Indies. Colonists feared that the British intended to use the army to enforce customs regulations rather than to police the Indians.

This large army, of course, was going to strain the British budget, already burdened by a huge war debt. Although there was no attempt to saddle the colonists with this debt, George Grenville, the new prime minister, believed that the colonists should pay a portion of the £225,000 a year that the standing army would cost.

Under Grenville's leadership, Parliament passed four pieces of legislation to force the colonies to contribute to their own upkeep. Grenville noticed, for example, that Britain was spending £8,000 every year to collect customs duties in the colonies, and collecting only £2,000. The Molasses Act of 1733 had established a duty of 6¢ per gallon, but it was commonly understood that smugglers paid off customs officials at the rate of 1½¢ a gallon. At Grenville's urging, Parliament passed the Sugar Act (1764), which dropped the duty to 3¢ but established procedures to make certain it was collected. In order to discourage smuggling, all shippers were required to file elaborate sets of papers each time an item was loaded onto a ship. In addition, accused violators were to be tried in admiralty courts, the closest of which was in Halifax, Nova Scotia. There, the burden of proof would be on the defendant, and the judgment would be rendered by judges rather than a jury.

In order to regulate the colonial economies so that they served the interest of British creditors, the second piece of legislation, the Currency Act (1764), forbade the issuing of any colonial currency. The immediate cause was the complaint of some British merchants that Virginia's paper money was depreciating too rapidly. These merchants wanted to prevent the colonists from discharging their debts in a depreciated paper money. Moreover, the Sugar Act and the Stamp Act (passed the following year) required that duties and taxes both be paid in specie, that is, hard money. The colonists complained, however, that there simply was not enough specie to go around.

The third and most important piece of imperial legislation enacted in this flurry was the Stamp Act (1765). Its

web connection

Stamping out Stamps

www.prenhall.com/boydston/stampact

In 1765, in the wake of its great victory in the Seven Years' War (known as the French and Indian War in the American colonies), Great Britain set about putting its imperial house in order. Retiring the debt was a major priority, and the Stamp Act was one of several revenue measures designed to force the colonies to pay a greater share of the costs of empire. Colonists refused to pay the new stamp tax. Instead they organized a boycott of British goods and proclaimed that Parliament lacked the power to tax them, something only their own colonial legislatures could legitimately do. Use the materials here to explore how Americans forged their own peculiar notions of representation.

objective, clearly and forthrightly, was to raise revenue. This was unarguably the first direct tax on the American people. Hitherto, all taxes upon them had been indirect, and in a sense not taxes at all. For example, customs duties were used, in theory, as much to regulate trade as to bring in income. The Stamp Act placed a tax on 15 classes of documents used in court proceedings; papers used in clearing ships from harbors; college diplomas; appointments to public office; bonds, grants, and deeds for land mortgages; indentures, leases, contracts, and bills of sale; articles of apprenticeship and liquor licenses; playing cards; dice; pamphlets, newspapers (and the ads in them), and almanacs.

The final piece of legislation, the Quartering Act (1765), required the colonies to provide housing for troops in public buildings and to provide them with firewood, candles, and drink. New York was the first colony to confront the implications of this act, when it called on the British troops to put down uprisings of tenants on Hudson River estates in 1766 but refused to pay for provisions for the troops.

Although the colonists objected to all of these pieces of legislation, the Stamp Act was the most troubling. The reaction to it was immediate and loud. If one were to think of a tax that would anger the most powerful colonists, in the most irritating way, the Stamp Act was it. By taxing newspapers and pamphlets, it angered the printers and editors. This was a foolish group to alienate at a time when newspapers were taking the lead in criticizing the government and were perhaps the most significant public institu-

tion in the colonies. They were where political ideas were formulated and debated; they were the voice of the public, and they were where criticism of the government was nurtured. In addition, by taxing legal documents, the Stamp Act angered lawyers, for every time a lawyer performed the simplest task of his trade, he would have to buy a stamp.

Collectively, these laws fell hardest on the most affluent and politically active of the colonists, the merchants, the lawyers, and the printers. By way of contrast, when Parliament wanted to raise money in Britain to pay for the army and the national debt, it levied a tax on cider, the drink of the common man. In addition, tax collectors in the colonies were given the right to enter into any home in the nation to search the premises and seize anything that appeared suspect.

The purpose of this battery of acts was not to deny the colonists their liberties, to burden them with taxes, to stifle their economy, or even to make them pay for their share of the empire. Instead, all of these pieces of legislation were an extension of the British government and its political economy, an attempt to tie the colonies into a modern, centralized state. As the colonists framed their response to the new imperial legislation, they struggled with a question that has been central to American history. Could the people share in the benefits of the modern state, in particular a trade protected by its navy and borders secured by its army, without the state itself?

Rejecting the Empire

Colonial resistance to the imperial legislation of 1763–1765, especially the Stamp Act, was swift and forceful. A coalition of elite leaders and common people, primarily in the cities, worked together to overturn the most objectionable aspects of the new regulations. In 1765, there was no thought of revolution, nor would there be for almost ten years. Instead, the colonists rested their case on the British Constitution. All they wanted, they claimed, were the rights of Englishmen. Although in theory the colonists, as British subjects, were entitled to all of those rights, precisely *how* the British Constitution applied to colonies on the edge of the empire had never been clarified. The first phase of colonial opposition, then, took the form of a debate about the British Constitution, with the colonists insisting on their rights *within* the empire, and the British government's focusing on the colonists' obligations. Yet this was no argument about abstractions. The colonists interpreted British attempts to enforce the empire in the context of many years of strife with British officials in the colonies. It was these local circumstances, different in every colony, that made the new legislation appear so frightening.

An Argument About Rights and Obligations

All along, Britain had maintained its right to regulate the colonies. Precisely what this meant became a matter of dispute in the years after 1763. Did it mean regulation of trade? taxation? legislation? When Parliament under George Grenville's leadership passed these pieces of legislation, it represented a change in British *practices,* not in how Britons thought about the empire. The empire was a whole, the parts existed for the benefit of the whole, and Parliament had the authority to govern for the whole.

Britons were justifiably proud of their Parliament, which was one of the premier institutions of self-government in the world at the time. Indeed, American colonists agreed that Parliament "comes nearest the idea of perfection" of any government yet seen. In principle Parliament represented all the elements in society: the king, the aristocrats (in the House of Lords), and the common people (in the House of Commons). Applying the terms used by the Greek philosopher Aristotle, this was a mixed or balanced form of government. It mixed and balanced these three elements of society, which also represented the three possible forms of government: monarchy, rule by the king; aristocracy, rule by the hereditary aristocrats; and democracy, rule by the people. Each of these three possible forms of government had advantages. Monarchy produced order and energy; aristocracy, wisdom; and democracy, honesty or goodness. But each of these three forms of government had its disadvantages. Monarchy could deteriorate into tyranny; aristocracy into oligarchy, rule by the few; and democracy could descend into anarchy, the war of all against all. Britons believed, however, that theirs combined all these forms of government, thereby assuring liberty.

The British believed, and American colonists agreed, that their superb government was the product of centuries of struggle. English history told the story of how first the aristocrats struggled with the king for more freedom for themselves, gaining it in the Magna Carta of 1215, and how then the people themselves had struggled and won liberty, most recently in the Glorious Revolution of 1688. In this view, liberty was a collective right held by the people against the rulers. Liberty, thus, was thought of as a limitation on the power of the monarch. A chief example of public or civil liberty was the right to be taxed only by one's own representatives. The English had fought a revolution and King Charles I had been beheaded over this very issue. After the Glorious Revolution, this principle was firmly established. Taxes were a free gift of the people that they might yield up but that no monarch could demand.

These ideas about the British government can be described as **constitutionalism.** Constitutionalism comprised two elements: One was the rule of law; the other, the principle of consent, that one could not be subjected to laws or taxation except by duly elected representatives. Both were rights that had been won through struggle with the monarch.

In the decade between the first round of imperial legislation and the outbreak of the American Revolution, the colonists worked out their own theory of the place of the colonies in the empire. Opinion varied on certain issues, for example, whether the colonies could or should be represented in Parliament and whether Parliament could legislate for the colonies even if it could not tax them. However, there was consistency on two major points: the importance of the rule of law and the principle of consent. Those colonists who became revolutionaries never wavered on these two points. What the colonists debated in the decade between the Stamp Act and the beginning of the American Revolution was whether particular pieces of legislation violated these principles and how far the colonists should go in resisting those that did.

British officials never denied that the colonists should enjoy the rights of Englishmen. They merely asserted that as it was, the colonists were as well represented in Parliament as the majority of Britons. In fact, only one out of ten British men could vote, compared to about 70 percent of American white men. Yet British officials said that all Britons were represented in Parliament, if not "actually," by their choosing their own representatives, then by **virtual representation,** because each member of Parliament was supposed to act on behalf of the entire empire, not only his constituents or even those who had voted for him. In Britons' minds, Parliament reigned supreme, and it had full and indivisible authority over the colonists. In the decade between the Stamp Act and the beginning of the American Revolution, the controversy turned on only two questions: How forcefully would the British government insist upon the supremacy of Parliament? And could colonial radicals put together a broad enough coalition to resist Britain's force when it came?

The Imperial Crisis in Local Context

At the same time that colonial political thinkers were filling the newspapers and printing presses with denunciations of the new imperial legislation, Americans in every colony were taking their protests to the streets and to the halls of the colonial legislatures. Everywhere, a remarkable cross-class alliance of prosperous merchants and planters who had been the chief beneficiaries of the consumer revolution and poor people who had not yet enjoyed its benefits joined to protect what they perceived as their rights from encroachment by an arrogant British officialdom.

By the day that the Stamp Act was supposed to be put into effect, November 1, 1765, every colony except Georgia had taken steps to make certain that the tax could not be collected. Word arrived in April 1765 that the Stamp Act had been passed, but it was not until May that any of the colonial legislatures were willing to act. In Virginia, the House of Burgesses took the lead in protesting the act. An alliance of elite planters and less affluent evangelicals joined to protest the Stamp Act on constitutional grounds, but they shied away from any talk of revolution. A young and barely literate lawyer, Patrick Henry, played a key role in the debate on the Virginia Resolves, the four resolutions protesting the Stamp Act that were passed by the Burgesses. All four resolutions were standard constitutionalism. They asserted that the inhabitants of Virginia brought with them from England the rights of Englishmen, that Virginia's royal charters confirmed these rights, that taxation by one's own representatives was the only logical and constitutional policy, and that the people of Virginia had never given up their rights including the right to be taxed only by their own representatives. Henry came close to treason when he asserted that "in former times Tarquin and Jul[i]us had their Brutus, Charles had his Cromwell, and he Did not Doubt but some good American would stand up, in favour of his Country." Henry was shouted down and forced to retract his words. Although in agreement about the constitutional issues, Virginia's representatives were not yet ready to contemplate disloyalty.

In Boston, as in the other colonies, the protest against Britain united the elite with poorer colonists, and it built upon long-standing tensions between colonists and royal officials. Massachusetts was still reeling from the loss of life and extraordinary expense of contributing to the French and Indian War. Now that the war was over, imperialists such as Lieutenant Governor Thomas Hutchinson, who had engineered Massachusetts' war effort, wanted to tie Massachusetts more tightly to the empire. Hutchinson wanted to lead the colonies in the direction that the English political economy was already heading. He advocated a consolidation of power, a diminution of popular government (for example, by reducing the power of the town meeting), making offices that were elective appointive instead, and limiting the freedom of the press.

Moreover, Hutchinson had become involved in a sort of personal faction fight with the Otis family. When Massachusetts' royal governor appointed Hutchinson to the supreme court, a post that James Otis, Sr., believed he deserved, Otis and his son, the young lawyer James Otis, Jr., smelled corruption. Not only did Hutchinson already hold the post of lieutenant governor, but he was also a member of the Council (upper house), probate judge, and the captain of Castle William in the harbor. Such multiple office holding was an established pattern of British patronage politics, enabling loyalists to rack up the fees and salaries of a number of jobs. Finding the patronage route into the elite blocked by powerful and better-connected families such as the Hutchinsons, ambitious colonists such as the Otises and John Adams turned against the monarchy altogether. They joined with poorer people, who disliked the high taxes that the empire required, to oppose the Stamp Act.

The groundwork for opposition in Massachusetts had been laid by the Writs of Assistance case in 1761. In that case, James Otis, Jr., had argued on behalf of 63 Boston merchants who challenged the customs office's use of writs

of assistance. These were general search warrants that allowed customs officials to enter any building in Boston, during daylight, to look for illegal goods, even without "probable cause." Although Otis lost the case, his eloquent and abstract argument based on the British Constitution made him popular with other radical opponents of monarchy. John Adams later recalled that "the child independence was then and there born, [for] every man of an immense crowded audience appeared to go away as I did, ready to take up arms against writs of assistance."

With this recent history of radicalism, Boston's public was prepared for a much stronger response to the Stamp Act than the Massachusetts House of Representatives seemed prepared to make. The *Boston Gazette* criticized the House's resolution as a "tame, pusillanimous, daubed, insipid thing." Once word of the more radical Virginia Resolves arrived, the *Gazette* rebuked the weak political leaders of Massachusetts again, calling them "frozen politicians." Thawed by such heated language, a group of artisans and printers who called themselves the Loyal Nine and later changed their name to the Sons of Liberty began organizing the opposition, probably in concert with more prominent men who would emerge as leaders of the revolutionary movement such as James Otis, John Adams, and his cousin Samuel Adams, the Harvard-educated son of a brewer.

In a carefully orchestrated series of mob actions led by a shoemaker, Ebenezer MacIntosh, Bostonians made certain that the Stamp Act would not be enforced. When the

Sam Adams, one of Boston's most effective political agitators in the years leading to the Revolution.

Stamp Act Riots.
A crowd in New Hampshire stones an effigy of a stamp distributor.

militia refused to come out to protect royal officials in-cluding Andrew Oliver, a Hutchinson family relative and the collector of the stamp tax, the officials took refuge in Castle William in the harbor. Over a period of several days, the mob slowly and systematically targeted the homes of Oliver, Hutchinson, and several other wealthy govern-ment loyalists. They completely wrecked Hutchinson's home, removing the slates from the roof, destroying the windows, doors, furniture, paintings, and partitions be-tween the rooms, chopping down the trees in the garden,

and stealing £900 in cash, clothing, and silverware. Al-though the mob consisted mostly of artisans and poor peo-ple, clearly it had the support of Boston's merchant elite, for no one was ever punished for these actions. The protest succeeded, and the Stamp Act was never enforced.

Not only did each colony mount its own protest against the Stamp Act, but a majority of the colonies were now ready to act together. In October 1765, delegates from nine colonies met in New York in the Stamp Act Congress to ratify a series of fourteen resolutions protesting the Stamp Act on constitutional grounds. The congress as-serted, for example, "that it is inseparably essential to the freedom of a people, and the undoubted rights of English-men, that no taxes should be imposed on them, but with their own consent, given personally, or by their represen-tatives." At the same time, bands of activists shut down colonial courts so that no stamps could be used. As a fur-ther means of protest, merchants agreed not to import any British goods until the act was repealed. With 37 percent of British exports going to the colonies at this time, this was no idle threat (see Figure 6-3).

In the face of this opposition, the British were willing to back down, partially. George Grenville had been re-placed by the 35-year-old Marquess of Rockingham, a wealthy and inexperienced man who preferred race horses

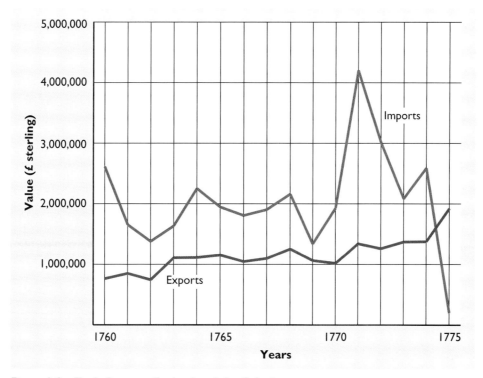

Figure 6-3   Trade Between England and the Colonies.
In the years between 1760 and 1775, colonial exports to England grew slowly, but steadily, only dropping off after the beginning of the Revolution. On the other hand, imports from England—which always exceeded exports—rose and fell in response to political conditions. Colonial nonimportation agreements forced drops in imports after the imposition of the Stamp Act and Townshend Duties. But in both cases, imports increased after repeal, and the growth of imports after repeal of the Townshend Duties was dramatic and unprecedented.

This cartoon shows the repeal of the Stamp Act, with George Grenville and other British officials carrying a coffin containing the Act. In the background, languishing on the dock, is cargo that could not be shipped to America during the colonial boycott.

to politics. He remained in office just long enough for Parliament to repeal the Stamp Act. Parliament was not prepared to concede the constitutional point, however, and in the Declaratory Act of 1766 it asserted ominously that Parliament "had, hath, and of right ought to have, full power and authority to make laws and statutes of sufficient force and validity to bind the colonies and people of *America*, subjects of the crown of *Great Britain*, in all cases whatsoever."

Contesting the Townshend Duties

Britain gave up on trying to tax the colonies directly, for even some prominent Britons such as William Pitt sided with the colonists on that point. But those in power were still determined to tighten the bonds of empire. Between 1767 and 1774, a succession of British ministries tried one means after another to force their vision of empire on the colonies. In response, radical activists and thinkers from throughout the colonies began to coalesce into a national, colonial opposition. Together these radicals took constitutionalism in new directions, grafting onto it different strands of Anglo-American opposition thought. By the time of the American Revolution, they had turned it into something radical and new, a new theory of government to support a new political economy.

Britain was still determined to impose its will on the colonies. After a brief return to power by the sick and deeply depressed William Pitt, Charles Townshend, a brilliant but erratic man nicknamed "Champagne Charlie," became the third prime minister in as many years. His first act was to punish New York's Assembly, which intentionally violated the Quartering Act asserting that in requiring the colony to provision British soldiers stationed there, Britain was engaging in taxation without representation. The Assembly was denied the right to pass any legislation

until it complied with the Quartering Act. The Assembly quickly backed down. The colonies refused, however, to comply with Parliament's next piece of legislation, the Townshend Revenue Act of 1767. Townshend believed that the colonists objected only to taxes within the colonies, "internal taxes," but that they would accept an "external tax," such as an import duty. Parliament had just reduced the tax on land in Britain, leading to a £500,000 deficit, and with the still-angry Grenville provoking him, Townshend decided it was time to get some money out of the colonies, about £40,000 worth. The revenues would be used to support colonial officials, making them independent of the colonial assemblies that had paid their salaries. The Revenue Act levied import duties on lead, paint, glass, paper, and tea.

Resistance to the Townshend Duties was somewhat slow to build. Even though standard constitutional arguments were used, it was a bit hard for colonists to make a case against all duties. Merchants were now complying with the new Revenue Act of 1766, which reduced the duty on molasses to 1¢ per gallon, which was below the going rate of bribes. Those colonists who had been most troubled by the first round of imperial legislation, however, were convinced that the Townshend Duties were part of a pattern of British oppression that would lead to tyranny. These radical thinkers believed that even a relatively inoffensive act of Parliament such as the Townshend Duties was really part of a larger plot to deprive the colonists of their liberties. A body of thought known as **republicanism** helped the colonists make sense of British actions. According to republicanism, these actions were not simply acts of debatable constitutionality, but rather a carefully orchestrated plot to deprive the colonists of their liberty.

Republicanism was a set of doctrines rooted in the Renaissance that held that power is always grasping, always dangerous, for "it is natural for Power to be striving to enlarge itself, and to be encroaching upon those that have none." Republicanism supplied constitutionalism with a motive. It explained how a balanced constitution could be transformed into tyranny. "Power" was not a vague abstraction that ate silently away at liberty. Instead it was manipulated purposefully by grasping men whose motive was to increase their power at the expense of the liberty of the people. Such would-be tyrants had at their disposal a variety of tools, all of which were in use in eighteenth-century Britain and were now being exported into the colonies. One of the chief tools of tyrants was a standing army, whose ultimate purpose was not the protection of the people but their subjection. Tyrants also engaged in corruption, in particular by securing loyalty to the government by dispensing patronage positions. They increased the number of government officials and the fees they could charge for their services, so that they grew rich at the expense of the people, and they encouraged multiple office holding.

So inexorable was the course of power that it took extraordinary character or *virtue* for an individual to resist the seductions of corruption. Consequently, republican citizens, it was thought, had to be economically independent. The poor were dangerous because their great need meant that they could easily be bought off by would-be tyrants. A secular theory with connections to Puritanism, republicanism asserted that people were naturally weak, and that exceptional human effort was required to protect both liberty and virtue.

Republicanism helped colonial political thinkers discern a pattern in the series of imperial acts after 1763. In his "Letters from a Farmer in Pennsylvania," John Dickinson, a wealthy, English-born Philadelphia lawyer, combined constitutional and republican arguments to tell his fellow colonists why the British no longer could be trusted. While they called the Townshend Duties simply "regulations of trade," Dickinson explained that "names will not change the nature of things." Once the colonists became aware of the true nature of British imperial legislation, they would recognize "an undoubted truth, confirmed by the unhappy experience of many states heretofore free, that unless the most watchful attention be exerted, a new servitude may be slipped upon us, under the sanction of usual and respectable terms."

Not only did people have to keep a close eye on power-hungry tyrants, they also had to look inside themselves. According to republican thought, history demonstrated that republics fell from within, when their citizens lost their virtue. The greatest threats to virtue were presented by luxury, an excessive attachment to the fruits of the consumer revolution. When colonists worried that they saw luxury and corruption "everywhere . . . everyday," they were thinking in terms of political economy and obviously criticizing the world that the consumer revolution of the eighteenth century had created. Although it is understandable why poor people, who saw others getting rich while they were squeezed, embraced republicanism, it may seem perplexing that wealthy merchants and planters were among the most vocal in their denunciations of "malice, covetousness, and other lusts of man." Yet the legacy of Puritanism was powerful, and even those who were profiting most from the new order could feel a deep ambivalence about the direction of change in their society. Joining with poorer people in criticizing those who were even more arrogant and more opulent than the colonial elite and accusing them of attempting to undermine colonial liberties helped forge a cross-class alliance in the decade before the American Revolution. Although the critique of luxury certainly had its purposes, the generation of colonists who entered into the Revolution had grown up in a world transformed by new consumer goods, and they did not want to turn back the clock.

Spurred by Dickinson's articles, which were published in newspapers throughout the colonies, the colonial legislatures slowly began to protest the duties. Massachusetts' House of Representatives, led by Sam Adams, sent a circular letter to each of the other lower houses in the colonies, asking them to join with Massachusetts in resisting the duties that were "infringements of their natural & constitutional Rights because they are not represented in the British Parliament. . . ." When Lord Hillsborough, a hardliner recently appointed to the new post of secretary of state for the colonies, received the letter, he responded with his own circular letter to the colonial governors in April 1768, instructing them to dissolve any colonial assembly that received the petition from Massachusetts. Hillsborough's circular letter angered the colonial legislators in a way that Massachusetts' never could. Massachusetts refused to rescind its letter, so Governor Francis Bernard promptly dissolved the legislature. With representative government threatened, those colonial legislatures that had not already approved the Massachusetts circular letter did so now, and were then dissolved. In response, many of the colonial legislatures met on their own, as extralegal representative bodies.

Not only did legislators assert their own authority, but ordinary people did so as well. In each colony, the radicals who called themselves Sons of Liberty organized a nonimportation movement. Perfecting techniques that would be used during the Revolution, they used both coercion and patriotic appeal to the entire community. In Boston, the appeal was made to "Persons of All Ranks," while in Annapolis, Maryland, the nonimportation movement drew in people of "every Degree." Women were actively recruited into the movement, both to encourage household manufacture (an economic activity redefined as a political one) and to refuse British imports. In 1769 women in little Middletown, Massachusetts, wove 20,522 yards of cloth, and in towns and cities throughout the colonies women added their names to the nonimportation agreements. This politicization of ordinary men and women horrified conservative British observers. One scoffed that it was "highly diverting to see the names & marks, to such Subscriptions, of Porters & Washing Women." Although there were pockets of defiance, the movement succeeded in cutting imports dramatically. By the time that the Townshend Duties were repealed in 1770, Britain had collected only £21,000, and lost £786,000 in trade.

A Revolution in the Empire

The resistance to the Townshend Duties established a pattern that would be repeated again and again in the years before the Revolution. Each attempt to enforce the empire was met with an organized colonial opposition, to which the British government responded with a punitive measure. Ostensibly economic regulations such as the Sugar Act, the

Townshend Duties, and the subsequent Tea Act, when rejected by the colonies, led to clearly political responses from Britain. Economics and politics became inseparable, as two visions of political economy came into conflict. Britain saw the colonies as a small, but integral part of a large and interdependent empire held together by an increasingly centralized and powerful government. The goal of the empire was to enhance its collective wealth and power, albeit under a system of constitutional government. While not rejecting the notion of a larger empire outright, increasingly the colonists equated representative government and prosperity, not just for the empire as a whole, but for its citizens in the colonies as well. Each round of colonial protest mobilized a larger segment of the population, eventually reaching out into the countryside and even to women.

"Massacre" in Boston

Years of conflict with royal officials, combined with a growing population of poor and underemployed, had made Boston the most radical and united spot in all the colonies. There were equally radical groups in other colonies, but nowhere was there more unity. The popular political leadership, especially the Otises and Sam Adams, had learned how to win popular favor in their ongoing strife with the governor and those who were loyal to him, such as the Hutchinsons. Although no colony had better supported the French and Indian War than Massachusetts, that colony's history of contention with royal officials and the brazenness of its smugglers made it a particular object of British attention. The repeated attempts of the British government to enforce its legislation, exerting increasing pressure upon Boston, led finally to revolution.

In an attempt to tighten up the collection of customs duties, the British government, now led by Lord North, decided to make an example of John Hancock, Boston's wealthiest merchant. Hancock valued popularity more than wealth, and over the course of his lifetime he sacrificed much of his fortune in the quest for popularity in the revolutionary movement. In June 1768, Boston's customs commissioners seized Hancock's sloop, the *Liberty,* on a technical violation of the Sugar Act. Hancock and several of his associates were threatened with fines totaling £54,000 (most of which would go into the pockets of the governor and the informer). All charges were dropped, however, after a riot of 2,000 "sturdy boys and men" sent the customs officials once again scuttling off to Castle William for protection. Had there been any doubt before, Hancock was now a confirmed radical.

In the wake of the *Liberty* riot, Governor Bernard asked for troops to be sent to Boston to support the customs commissioners, and several regiments arrived. Rather than restoring order, the arrival of the troops led to further conflict. British soldiers scoured the city, searching people's homes and looking for deserters. For a year and a half there was tension, as might be expected with so many sol-

diers stationed in a city of 15,000. Because of an economic depression, the cost of liquor in Boston was cheap, and off-duty soldiers regularly became drunk and offensive. Prostitution increased, women were assaulted, and every citizen, when walking through the city, had to be prepared to stop and identify him- or herself, at the point of a bayonet. Most important, moonlighting soldiers were willing to work cheaper than Bostonians. The Boston Massacre grew out of these tensions.

What angry colonists called a "massacre" was really the result of several months of scuffling between young men and adolescents and soldiers, perhaps inevitable in a town with so many men competing for so little work. Most of the participants knew one another from previous conflicts. On March 5, 1770, a fracas between a young apprentice and an Army officer escalated as a crowd surrounded the officer, calling him "you Centinel, damned rascally Scoundrel Lobster Son of a Bitch" and pelting him with snowballs and ice. Someone shouted "fire," and the crowd grew. Seven soldiers were sent to rescue their terrified colleague, and they too were hit with snow and ice balls and taunts of "kill them." When one was knocked down, he lost his temper, screaming, "Damn you, fire!" The soldiers then fired on the crowd. Eleven men were wounded, five killed. One victim was Crispus Attucks, a free black sailor. Subsequently the soldiers were tried, but the only two who were convicted were later pardoned. The British withdrew their troops from Boston.

As long as the British were willing to back down, however, more serious conflicts could be avoided. The Boston Massacre was followed by a three-year period of peace. The Townshend Duties had been repealed, except the one on tea, which the colonists could not manufacture themselves, and the nonimportation movement had collapsed. Colonial trade soon resumed its previous pace, and then, in 1772, imports from England and Scotland doubled. Colonists were not prepared to deny themselves consumer goods for long. The Quartering Act had expired, and the Currency Act was repealed, in bits and pieces. Troops were eventually removed from Boston and sent to the West Indies to head off possible slave revolts. As long as Britain allowed the colonists to trade relatively unimpeded, permitted them to govern themselves, and kept the Army out of their cities, all could be, if not forgotten, at least silenced by the clink of coins in the shopkeeper's till.

The Empire Comes Apart

Although the British government was under the control of conservative hardliners who believed that sooner or later the colonists would need to acknowledge that Parliament reigned supreme, the move that led directly to revolution was more accidental than calculated. The North American colonies were only part of Britain's extended empire. There were powerful British interests in India, where the British East India Company was on the verge of bankruptcy. Parliament decided to bail out the company, both to rescue its empire in India and also to help out the influential stockholders. The duty for importing tea into Britain was canceled, although the one for tea to America was continued. Moreover, Parliament allowed the company to sell directly to Americans, through a small number of American agents, cutting out all the middlemen. With the duty removed and the middlemen cut out, the price of tea could be dropped so that it would now be less expensive than smuggled Dutch tea, even with the Townshend Duties taken into consideration. In all of Massachusetts, only five men would be allowed to sell British tea,—two sons, a nephew, and two good friends of Thomas Hutchinson. The designated agents in the other colonies were men of a similar stripe, administration loyalists who gained their appointments by their connections more than by merit.

Radicals faced a real challenge, for they realized that once the tea was unloaded and the duty paid, colonists would be unable to resist the cheap tea. In each port city, activists warned their fellow colonists that the Tea Act (1773) was a trick intended to con them into accepting the principle of taxation without representation. According to the New York Sons of Liberty, the purpose of the Tea Act was "to make an important trial of our virtue. If they succeed in the sale of that tea, we shall have no property that we can call our own, and then we may bid adieu to American liberty." In Philadelphia, a mass meeting pronounced anyone who imported the tea "an enemy to his country." In

Charleston, the governor managed to get the tea off the ship and moved into a warehouse. It remained there until the Revolution, when the state sold it to help finance the war.

As might be expected, the most spirited resistance came in Boston, where Thomas Hutchinson, now governor, decided the tea would be unloaded and sold. He absolutely refused to let the first ship coming into port return without paying the duty. Sam Adams led extralegal town meetings attended by 5,000 people each (almost one-third of the population of Boston) to pressure Hutchinson to let the ship return. When Hutchinson refused, Adams reported back to the town meeting, on December 16, 1773, "This meeting can do nothing more to save the country!" (see Table 6-1). Almost as if it were a prearranged signal, the crowd let out a whoop and poured out of the meetinghouse for the wharf. There, about 50 men, with their faces darkened and wearing blankets to make themselves look like Indians, went onto the *Dartmouth* and two other tea-bearing ships that had recently docked, carefully escorted the customs officials ashore, and went about the business of opening 340 chests of tea and dumping their contents into Boston Harbor, 90,000 pounds, worth £9,000. The water was coated with tea; by morning, some of it had floated as far as Dorchester. The whole job was over by 9:00 P.M. Perhaps as many as 8,000 Bostonians had observed the "tea party." John Adams, never much for riots, was in awe. "There is," he said, "a Dignity, a Majesty, a Sublimity in this last Effort of the Patriots that I greatly admire."

TABLE 6-1

Major Events Leading to the Revolutionary War, 1763–1774

1763	Proclamation of 1763	Confines colonists to the east of an imaginary line running down the spine of the Allegheny Mountains.
1764	Sugar Act	Drops duty on molasses to 3¢/gallon, but institutes procedures to make sure it is collected, such as trial at Admiralty Court (closest is in Nova Scotia), where burden of proof is on defendant and verdict is rendered by judge rather than jury.
1764	Currency Act	Forbids issuing of any colonial currency.
1765	Stamp Act	Places a tax on 15 classes of documents, including newspapers and legal documents; clear objective is to raise revenue.
1765	Quartering Act	Requires colonies to provide housing in public buildings and certain provisions for troops.
1766	Declaratory Act	Repeals Stamp Act, but insists that Parliament retains the right to legislate for the colonies "in all cases whatsoever."
1767	Townshend Revenue Act	Places import duty on lead, paint, glass, paper, and tea; objective is to raise money from the colonies.
1770	Boston Massacre	Several citizens killed by British soldiers whom they had pelted with snowballs; grew out of tensions caused by quartering of four army regiments in Boston to enforce customs regulations.
1773	Tea Act	After Townshend duties on all items other than tea are removed, British East India Company is given a monopoly on the sale of tea, enabling it to drop price—and cut out middlemen.
1773	Boston Tea Party	To protest Tea Act, Bostonians dump 90,000 pounds of tea into Boston Harbor.
1774	Intolerable Acts	To punish Massachusetts in general and Boston in particular for the "Tea Party": 1). Port of Boston closed until East India Company repaid for dumped tea. 2). King to appoint Massachusetts' Council; town meetings to require written permission of Governor; Governor will appoint judges and sheriffs, and sheriffs will now select juries. 3). Governor can send officials and soldiers accused of capital crimes out of Massachusetts for their trials. 4). Troops may be quartered in private homes.
1774	Quebec Act	Gives Ohio River valley to Quebec; Britain allows Quebec to be governed by French tradition and tolerates Catholic religion there.
1774	First Continental Congress	Representatives of twelve colonies meet in Philadelphia and call for a boycott of trade with Britain, adopt a Declaration of Rights, and agree to meet in a year.

Summoned to appear before the Privy Council in 1774, Benjamin Franklin, the agent for Massachusetts, was humiliated—and turned into a radical.

Instead of dignity or patriotism, the British government saw defiance of the law and wanton destruction of property. Moreover, Britain concluded wrongly that all colonists were equally radical. The moderate Benjamin Franklin, in London as Massachusetts' agent, was summoned to appear before the Privy Council, where he was humiliated and thereby turned into a radical. Parliament passed five bills in the spring of 1774 to punish Boston and Massachusetts collectively for their misdeeds. First, the Boston Port Bill closed the port of Boston to all trade until the East India Company was repaid for the dumped tea. Second, the Massachusetts Government Act changed the Charter of 1691 in several important ways. From now on, the Council (upper house) would be appointed by the king, rather than elected by the House. Nor could town meetings be held without the prior written approval of the governor. Moreover, the governor would appoint all the provincial judges and sheriffs, and the sheriffs would select juries, who until then had been elected by the freeholders. Third, the Administration of Justice Act empowered the governor to send to Britain or another colony for trial any official or soldier accused of a capital crime who appeared

unlikely to get a fair trial in Massachusetts. Fourth, a new Quartering Act permitted the quartering of troops in private homes. Fifth, not directly related, but also odious to Protestant colonists, was the Quebec Act, for the administration of Quebec. It assigned to Quebec the Ohio River region, which the colonists coveted. Moreover, in Quebec, there was to be no representative government. Following the French tradition, civil cases would be tried without juries, and the Roman Catholic religion would be tolerated. Together, these acts were known in Britain as the Coercive Acts and in the colonies as the Intolerable Acts.

At the same time, General Thomas Gage was appointed governor of Massachusetts. Gage was authorized to bring as many troops to Boston as he thought he needed. As regiment after regiment arrived, Boston became an armed camp. The Port Act was easily enforced as Gage deployed troops to close the ports of Boston and Charlestown. The Government Act was another matter. Citizens who were summoned by the sheriff simply refused to serve on juries, and even some judges refused to preside. When Gage called for an election to the legislature, only some towns elected delegates. When Gage refused to meet with them, they joined the meeting of the shadow "Massachusetts Provincial Congress," which met in Concord in October 1774. Essentially, the citizens of Massachusetts had taken government into their own hands.

The British had thought that Massachusetts could be isolated. For years, hardliners had argued that clear and forceful measures would bring the colonists to their knees; they were wrong. Their chief miscalculation was in underestimating the colonists' attachment to their liberties. Although the colonists and the British both revered the same British Constitution and the liberties it assured, the different context of the colonial political economy gave them a different meaning. The widespread ownership of property, the relative economic equality (even as the gap between rich and poor was growing), the small size of government, and the widely shared right to participate in it gave a very different meaning to liberty in the colonies.

The threat to representative government presented by the Intolerable Acts was so clear that the other colonies soon rallied around Massachusetts. In June 1774, the Virginia Burgesses, who had been dissolved for calling a fast day, simply moved over to the Raleigh Tavern and sent out a circular letter suggesting a meeting of all the colonies. At about the same time, Massachusetts had issued a similar call for a meeting in Philadelphia. Spurred by the two most radical colonies, the others agreed to meet in early September.

The First Continental Congress

Every colony except Georgia sent delegates to the First Continental Congress, which convened on September 5, 1774. Only a few of the delegates had ever met any of their counterparts from the other colonies, an indication of just how provincial the colonies were. First impressions, however, were positive. Everyone admired the Virginians. "More sensible, fine fellows you never saw," according to Delaware's Caesar Rodney. For seven weeks these strangers met in formal sessions and got to know one another better at dinner parties and other social occasions.

Together they laid the foundation for the first national government.

With Massachusetts and Virginia almost ready to take up arms, and the middle colonies still favoring conciliation, the greatest challenge these new national leaders faced was how to achieve unity. That goal took precedence. Massachusetts needed the support of the other colonies, and hence it was prepared to abandon any discussion of offensive measures against the British. In return, the Congress ratified the Suffolk Resolves, a set of resolutions adopted by Massachusetts' Suffolk County that recommended passive resistance to the Intolerable Acts.

Having addressed Massachusetts' problem, the delegates could now consider national action. Congress issued a call for a boycott of all trade, both imports and exports, between the colonies and Britain and the West Indies, to be policed by committees elected "in every county, city, and town" in the colonies. Congress hoped to exert economic pressure on Britain. Then the delegates adopted a Declaration of Rights, which, once again, was more moderate than the most radical ideas in circulation, but not much. They reiterated, refined, and for the first time expressed as the collective determination, of every colony except Georgia, what had become standard constitutional arguments. The colonists were entitled to all the "rights, liberties, and immunities of free and natural-born subjects" of England. Parliament could regulate trade for the colonies, not by right, but only by the "consent" of the colonies. Otherwise, Parliament could neither tax nor legislate for the colonies. Again and again, the Declaration reiterated the twin principles on which resistance to imperial legislation had been waged: consent and the rule of law.

Finally, Congress agreed to reconvene in half a year, on March 10, 1775, unless the Intolerable Acts were repealed. Although the Congress was less radical than John Adams and Patrick Henry might have wished, the delegates had achieved consensus on the principles that would shortly form the basis for a new and independent national government.

Conclusion

Within a decade, the British empire had come apart on its westernmost edge. The ground had been prepared decades earlier when Britain had unintentionally allowed the colonies to develop in ways that assured more self-government and personal freedom than in Britain itself, without requiring them to pay a proportionate share of the costs of empire. As a result, the colonies developed their own political economy, one that linked self-government, limited government, and prosperity. Once Britain decided to knit the colonies more tightly into the empire and impose on them the controls of the centralized state

and its political economy, some conflict was almost inevitable. At the same time, both Britons and Americans revered the same Constitution, and Americans' protests invoked the values and protections of that political system. That those protests would culminate in revolution was by no means a foregone conclusion. Revolution would require both an unwillingness of Britain to compromise on issues of governance and the political skill of colonial radicals, who had to convince moderates that there was no other way. By the end of 1774 that point had almost been reached.

CHRONOLOGY

1715–1716	Yamasee War
1717	French build Fort Toulouse
1718	French build New Orleans
1720	French build Louisbourg and Fort Niagara
1731	French build Fort St. Frédéric
1733	Molasses Act
1739–1744	War of Jenkins' Ear
1741	Attack upon Cartagena fails
1744–1748	King George's War
1748	Village of Pickawillany established by La Demoiselle and his band of Miamis
1749	French military expedition fails to win back dissident Indians in Ohio Valley
1752	Tanacharison cedes huge chunk of Ohio Valley to Virginia
1753	French build small forts near forks of Ohio River
1754	Albany Plan of Union
1754–1763	French and Indian War
1755	Braddock's forces defeated
1757	British defeated at Fort William Henry, survivors massacred William Pitt accedes to power in Britain
1758	Treaty of Easton secures neutrality of Ohio Valley tribes in return for territory west of Alleghenies
1759	British seize Quebec
1761	Writs of Assistance Case
1763	Treaty of Paris, ending French and Indian War, signed Pontiac's Rebellion Proclamation of 1763 Parliament increases size of peacetime army to 20 regiments
1764	Sugar Act Currency Act
1765	Stamp Act Quartering Act Stamp Act Congress
1766	Declaratory Act
1767	Townshend Revenue Act
1768	Lord Hillsborough's circular letter John Hancock's sloop *Liberty* seized Treaty of Fort Stanwix
1770	Boston Massacre
1773	Tea Act Boston Tea Party
1774	Intolerable Acts (known as Coercive Acts in Britain) Lord Dunmore's War First Continental Congress

Review Questions

1. What effect did the imperial wars of the eighteenth century have on the American colonies? Which regions were affected most?

2. What were the bases for the conflicts among the British, French, Spanish, and various Indian tribes on the North American continent? Over the course of the century, who gained the most, and who lost the most? What role did the colonies play in these conflicts?

3. How and why did Britain attempt to reorganize its colonial empire at the end of the French and Indian War? Why did the colonists resist?

4. How did the colonists justify their resistance to British attempts to reorganize the empire and make them pay for their own defense? What was the source of those theories of resistance, and how did they change as tensions increased?

5. What was the series of events that brought Britain and the colonies to the brink of war by 1774? To what extent were they the product of poor leadership? differing theories of government? different social experiences?

Further Readings

Fred Anderson, *Crucible of War: The Seven Years' War and the Fate of Empire in British North America, 1754–1766* (2000). An engaging narrative that argues that the Seven Years' War was a critical episode in itself and not simply the prelude to the Revolution.

John Brewer, *The Sinews of Power: War, Money and the English State, 1688–1783* (1990). Brewer's book demonstrates how important war and its financing were in shaping the British state in the eighteenth century.

John Demos, *The Unredeemed Captive: A Family Story from Early America* (1994). A beautifully written and deeply moving narrative about what happened to the Williams family when they were captured in an Abenaki raid on their Deerfield, Massachusetts home in 1704.

Jack P. Greene, *Colonies to Nation, 1763–1789: A Documentary History of the American Revolution* (1975). A superb collection of political documents through which the development of an American political ideology can be traced.

Douglas Edward Leach, *Arms for Empire: A Military History of the British Colonies in North America* (1973). A comprehensive and readable account of colonial military history.

Ian K. Steele, *Betrayals: Fort William Henry and the "Massacre"* (1990). A brief but gripping account of the siege at Fort William Henry in 1757, later fictionalized in James Fenimore Cooper's *The Last of the Mohicans.*

Richard White, *The Middle Ground: Indians, Empires, and Republics in the Great Lakes Region, 1650–1815* (1991). A brilliant analysis of the conflict among the French, British, and Great Lakes Indian tribes for control of that region.

History on the Internet

"Two Divergent Accounts of the Boston Massacre"
http://odur.let.rug.nl/~usa/D/1751–1775/bostonmassacre/prest.htm

From both the British and colonists' perspectives, these two documents help to show the growing ideological rift between England and the colonies.

"Chief Pontiac's Siege of Detroit"
http://www.detnews.com/history/pontiac/pontiac.htm

This site contains the story of Pontiac, chief of the Ottawas, and chronicles his leadership in taking control of the Fort of Detroit. The site is enriched with illustrations, photos, and archival materials including a copy of Pontiac's surrender.

"Resolutions of the Stamp Act Congress"
http://odur.let.rug.nl/~usa/E/sugar_stamp/actxx.htm

With an introduction and background on colonial resistance, this site contains the full text of the resolutions of the Stamp Act.

"Declaration and Resolves"
http://www.ushistory.org/declaration/related/decres.htm

Read the Declaration and Resolves of the first Continental Congress. Under the "related information" link, read biographical sketches on colonial leaders and descriptions of events that led to the colonists' quest for freedom.

7

CREATING A NEW NATION

1775-1788

OUTLINE

James Madison Helps Make a Nation

The War Begins
The First Battles
Congress Takes the Lead
Military Ardor
Declaring Independence
Creating a National Government
Creating State Governments

Winning the Revolution
Competing Strategies
The British on the Offensive: 1776
A Slow War: 1777–1781
Securing a Place in the World

The Challenge of the Revolution
The Departure of the Loyalists

The Challenge of the Economy
Contesting the New Political Economy
Can Women Be Citizens?
The Challenge of Slavery

A New Policy in the West
The Indians' Revolution
The End of the Middle Ground
Settling the West

Creating a New National Government
A Crippled Congress
Writing a New Constitution
Ratifying the Constitution: Politics
Ratifying the Constitution: Ideas

Conclusion

James Madison Helps Make a Nation

Why do some people achieve greatness? Perhaps it is not as much a matter of personal qualities as a match between the person and the times, an ability to understand and respond to the needs of the age. There was nothing in James Madison's childhood to suggest that he would become a leader of a revolutionary nation in a revolutionary age. Madison grew up on the plantation his grandfather and his slaves had cleared out of the Virginia Piedmont forest in 1732. Only a few months later, Madison's grandfather was killed by several of those slaves. One of the slaves was executed, but another, a woman named Dido, was given twenty-nine lashes and sent home to work for the widow Madison. Although Madison's father, a child at the time, became a prosperous planter and slaveowner himself, perhaps James suffered from the knowledge that his grandfather had somehow brought on his own death.

Certainly, Madison was in no hurry to embark upon the life of a Virginia planter. He went north to college, attending Princeton in New Jersey. After his graduation in

1771 at the age of twenty, he just lingered around Princeton, finally suffering some sort of breakdown. Back in Virginia, Madison described himself as "too dull and infirm now to look out for any extraordinary things in this world for I think my sensations for many months past have intimated to me not to expect a long or healthy life." So short and slight of build that he was once described as "a mere shrimp of a man," Madison was convinced that his poor health would lead to an early death. Throughout his life, he periodically fell victim to attacks that he described as "somewhat resembling Epilepsy." He had a nervous stomach too, so bad that he never traveled to Europe, afraid that the seasickness would be more than he could bear. These illnesses kept him out of the military as well.

The event that drew this sickly, nervous young man out of his shell was the American Revolution. He became a leader, first in his county, then his state, and finally in the nation that he helped create and whose Constitution he helped write. James Madison committed himself to the principles of liberty and order, and he devoted his life to establishing a government that would assure both. Perhaps more than any other leader at the time, Madison understood how difficult reconciling these two principles would be.

Madison became a genius at managing conflict. He believed that the sources of strife and violence were deeply embedded in human nature, and he spent all his adult life trying to create a government that would assure peace without destroying liberty. He helped write the Constitution, in order to create a government that was secure and stable. Then he worked for the adoption of the Bill of Rights, to make certain that liberties were guaranteed. His first political battle in Virginia had been on behalf of the Baptists, a dissenting Protestant denomination that was demanding religious liberty. Although not a religious man himself, Madison was convinced that freedom of conscience was fundamental, and that religion must be kept absolutely free from governmental interference. As a political thinker and

leader, Madison came to advocate the great liberal principles of his age: the rights of conscience, consent, and property. Believing fervently in both the rights of property and human liberty, he could never reconcile himself either to slavery or its abolition. He put his faith in the new government he had helped to create and hoped that just as he had been able to live with his own mental and physical disabilities, so the nation itself would rise above its internal conflicts and inconsistencies.

Of the generation of men and women that fought the American Revolution and created the new national government, no one better understood the American political economy than Madison. Jefferson, perhaps, had a better appreciation for liberty, and Hamilton had a better understanding of the economy. Others more fully grasped the contradiction presented by slavery. But Madison understood Americans' twin commitments to liberty and to property, and he saw how they fit together in a system that rested on the principle of consent. ∎

KEY TOPICS

- How revolutionary ardor and early victories led Americans to think that the war would be short and relatively easy

- Revolutionary thought as an amalgam of republican, evangelical, and Enlightenment liberal ideas

- The politics of declaring independence and establishing new state governments

- American and British military strategies; the struggle to win the allegiance of the civilian population; why the British could have won the war, but not the peace; the role played by France and Spain

- The challenges presented to the economy and social order by the war itself and by revolutionary ideology

- The movement for a constitution: the problems with the Articles of Confederation, and which groups were most affected by them

- Why the Antifederalists opposed ratification of the Constitution, and how their objections were overcome

serted, had made the colonists "opulent." He believed that the merchants and lawyers of Boston were instigating the poor; hence, his objective always was to isolate the colonial revolutionary elite, by whatever means necessary, including the use of force.

By the fall of 1774, it was generally believed that conflict would come in Massachusetts, although both Gage and the colonial leaders were determined not to take the first step. In the spring of 1775, however, Gage received orders from England to take decisive action against the colonists, even if it would trigger hostilities. He determined to seize the colonists' military supplies, stored at Concord, but the alert Bostonians worked out a system to signal the patriot leaders once British troops began to march. On the night of April 18, the silversmith Paul Revere and the tanner William Dawes slipped out of Boston on horseback to carry the message that British troops were on the move. Warned in advance, militia men from several towns began to gather.

The British soldiers arrived at Lexington at daybreak, and they ordered the militia to surrender, which they refused to do. Exactly what happened next remains unclear.

The War Begins

By the end of 1774, conflict between the colonists and Britain seemed unavoidable. The British government, stabilized under the leadership of Lord North and with King George III firmly in command, seemed unwilling to make any significant concessions. In the colonies, the radical opponents of British rule dominated politics. The new British governor in Massachusetts, General Thomas Gage, was fortifying Boston. Colonial militias were preparing for battle. Despite these signs of impending conflict, no one anticipated eight years of warfare that would plunge the British government even deeper into debt and make of the colonies a single nation, under a centralized government.

The First Battles

By the time he became governor of Massachusetts in 1774, General Thomas Gage already had a long record of advocating force. He had called for the stationing of troops in Boston in 1768, which led to the "Boston Massacre." Even before the Boston Tea Party and Britain's retaliation with the Coercive Acts, he recommended limiting democratic government in Massachusetts. Also, he was convinced that Americans were too wealthy. Britain's protection, he as-

Members of the Massachusetts militia engaged British soldiers at Lexington at daybreak, April 18, 1775. It is unclear who started firing first, but in half an hour, eight colonists had been killed and the first battle of the American Revolution, the Battle of Lexington, had been fought.

The colonists later swore that British soldiers opened fire, saying, "Ye villans, ye Rebels, disperse; Damn you, disperse." The British major insisted that the first shot came from behind a tree. It is clear that the British soldiers then lost control and fired all about, and the colonists returned fire. When order was restored, eight Americans were dead, most killed while attempting to flee. The entire battle of Lexington was over in half an hour.

The second battle of the Revolution took even less time. At the same time that the militia in Lexington was gathering, the Concord militia assembled atop a ridge behind the meetinghouse. When the British marched up the road toward the North Bridge, the militia pulled back about a mile, allowing the British to enter an almost-deserted town. Fighting broke out when a fire that the British troops had set to the Concord liberty pole spread to the courthouse. Determined to protect their town, the militia began marching upon the British. When the Americans got near, the British fired. In the ensuing exchange, three British soldiers were killed, and several more were injured. The British were forced back across the bridge. The entire battle took two or three minutes, although skirmishes continued as the Redcoats made their way back to Boston, through hordes of angry colonists. These encounters were the first battles of the war for independence (see Map 7-1).

In the next year, popular enthusiasm for war drove the colonial leadership. Once news of the fighting at Lexington and Concord spread, militias began converging upon

Boston to evict Gage and his troops. Within a short time, more than 20,000 New England men were encamped in Boston. All were ready for a fight and just as eager to get back home to tend to their crops. Gage responded to this siege by declaring that all the inhabitants of Massachusetts who bore arms were rebels and traitors, although he was willing to pardon everyone but John Hancock and Samuel Adams, two leaders of the Provincial Congress that was meeting in defiance of the law. Rather than backing down, the colonists fortified Breed's Hill (next to the more famous Bunker Hill) in Charlestown, overlooking Boston. On June 17, Gage sent out one-fifth of his garrison, some 2,400 soldiers, to take the hill and to demonstrate that the army was stronger than civilian forces. The British proved their point but at an enormous cost. A thousand soldiers and 92 officers were casualties (compared to 370 casualties among the colonists). However, the British learned an important lesson: not to make frontal assaults against fortified positions.

At about the same time, other New Englanders were taking matters into their own hands, well in advance of any declaration of war or independence. A group of New Englanders under the leadership of Benedict Arnold, an ambitious, thirty-four-year old New Haven merchant, and Ethan Allen—the leader of the Green Mountain Boys, who had been engaged in a violent struggle with New York settlers for what is now Vermont—seized the crumbling fort at Ticonderoga on Lake Champlain. The fort fell quickly and with no bloodshed. The Green Mountain boys celebrated by getting drunk. Several other small posts were captured just as easily in these heady days early in the Revolution. Too many colonists thought that this would be a quick and relatively painless war.

Congress Takes the Lead

When the Second Continental Congress convened in Philadelphia on May 10, its greatest challenge, once again, was to maintain consensus. Although the previous Congress had insisted that all colonial military activity was to be purely defensive, colonists in New England had demonstrated their willingness to act aggressively. The most radical leaders, such as Samuel and John Adams from Massachusetts and Richard Henry Lee from Virginia, were ready for war. However, much of the rest of

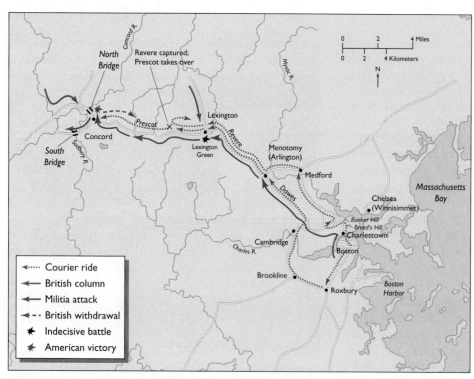

Map 7-1   Battles of Lexington, Concord, and Breed's Hill.
This map shows the sites of the first battles of the Revolution in and around Boston, along with the routes taken by Paul Revere and William Dawes to warn the colonists of the approach of British troops.

the leadership, especially in the middle colonies, still hoped that conflict could be avoided.

Colonists looked to Congress for leadership as Loyalists (colonists who remained loyal to the British government) fumed and royal officials looked on in disbelief. Because Congress was an extralegal body, the duly elected colonial Assemblies might easily have rejected its authority. But one after another, they transferred their allegiance from the British government to Congress.

Although some moderates in Congress hoped for a negotiated settlement with Britain, they were caught between a public and a British government both of which anticipated war. The British ministry refused even to acknowledge the petition sent by the First Congress. That refusal, combined with Gage's attack upon Breed's Hill, convinced the moderates that military preparations were necessary and that any backing away from colonial demands would appear to the British as a sign of weakness. Congress voted to create a Continental Army and put it under the leadership of Virginia's George Washington. Not only was Washington experienced in military matters and widely respected, but his selection helped solidify the alliance between New England and the South. Congress decided to attack Canada in the hope that a significant defeat of the British would force them to accede to American demands. To justify all of these actions, Congress also adopted the "Declaration of the Causes and Necessities of Taking up Arms," a rousing indictment of British "despotism," "perfidy," and "cruel aggression" drafted by Virginia's Thomas Jefferson.

At the same time, in order to preserve unity with the moderates, the radicals agreed to petition the king one more time. While not making any concessions, the Olive Branch Petition struck a different tone by appealing to George's "magnanimity and benevolence." The king, however, was not in any mood to be flattered. On August 23, 1775, he declared the colonists to be in "an open and avowed Rebellion." He called upon those loyal to Britain to suppress the rebellion and to punish the "divers wicked and desperate Persons" who had started it. Although Congress had neither declared war nor asserted independence, the Revolution had begun.

Military Ardor

Military ardor in the colonies reached its high point in the fall of 1775 and the spring of 1776, before independence had even been declared. Colonists expected war, and they thought it would be quick and glorious. They sincerely believed that "native Courage warmed with Patriotism" would easily overcome the decided advantage of the British in experience, discipline, preparation, and weaponry. As a consequence, the first enlistments were for a term of only a year. Even if the war was not over by then, Revolutionaries were fearful of creating a permanent,

standing Army. Better to rely on citizen-soldiers who could return to their farms and shops at the end of the campaign.

It was when this military fervor was at its height, in the summer of 1775, that the Continental Army marched on Canada, hoping to seize it from the British. Such a victory would have either forced the British to the bargaining table or, if the British had not been ready to capitulate, at least protected New York and New England from assault by British and Indian forces from the north. The contingent of the Continental Army under General Benedict Arnold's command sailed from Newburyport, Massachusetts, to Maine and then marched 350 miles to Quebec. Forty-five days later, in early November, after a grueling march, Arnold's forces prepared to assault Quebec. They were joined there by troops under the leadership of General Richard Montgomery, who had just seized Montreal. The generals decided to attack on December 31 because the terms of enlistment were running out and their troops would soon be going home. The battle was a disaster. Half of the 900 soldiers were killed, captured, or wounded, including Montgomery, who was killed almost instantly by a bullet through his head. By the time the Americans gave up on their hopes of capturing Canada and the expedition retreated back to New York in the spring, 5,000 men had been lost, most of them to disease and desertion. The suffering was extraordinary, but it only increased American resolve.

Declaring Independence

By the beginning of 1776, moderates in Congress who still hoped for a peaceful settlement with Britain found themselves squeezed from both directions. The king and Parliament were unyielding, and popular opinion increasingly favored independence. Early in the year, word arrived from Britain that all American commerce was to be cut off and the British Navy was to be empowered to seize American ships and their cargoes. Britain also began hiring German mercenaries known as Hessians. Virginia's Governor Dunmore made use of the troops he had on hand. When they were unable to hold Norfolk after skirmishing with patriot soldiers, he shelled the town from warships off shore. In the previous year, he had infuriated white colonists by offering freedom to any slaves who would abandon their masters to fight for the British. It seemed that every frightening prediction that the radicals had made was coming true.

Public opinion also pushed Congress toward a declaration of independence. In January 1776, Thomas Paine, an expatriate English radical who had moved to Philadelphia only two years earlier, electrified the public with his pamphlet *Common Sense.* At the age of thirty-nine, Paine had failed at almost everything he had ever done. *Common Sense* was his first and greatest success, selling more than

Thomas Paine, whose Common Sense *sold more than one hundred thousand copies in just a few weeks.*

100,000 copies in only a few weeks. In it, he liberated Americans from their ties to the British past so that they could start their government fresh. The idea of the balanced constitution, that combined king, nobles, and the common people in one government, was "farcical," and monarchy was "exceedingly ridiculous." Why should Americans have any respect for an aristocracy that traced its origins to William the Conqueror, "a French bastard landing with an armed banditti"? Paine had a message for Congress too: "The period of debate is closed."

With most members of Congress either desiring a declaration of independence or thinking it inevitable, the most important question was not "What?" but "When?" Most delegates agreed that unanimity was more important than speed, and so they waited through the spring of 1776 as one by one, the state delegations received instructions in favor of independence. Then, under instructions from his colony, on June 7, 1776, Virginia's Richard Henry Lee asked Congress to vote on the resolution that "these United Colonies are, and of right ought to be, free and independent States." The decision was put off until July 1 to accommodate moderates from the middle colonies, but a committee of five, including Thomas Jefferson, Benjamin Franklin, and John Adams, was appointed to draft a decla-

ration of independence. Adams asked Jefferson, a 33-year-old Virginia radical who had already demonstrated his ability to write stirring prose, to write the first draft. For four days, the delegates debated Jefferson's draft and took preliminary votes. A long clause that accused King George of forcing African slaves upon the colonies was deleted. On July 2, the delegates voted unanimously to declare independence from Britain. It was a remarkable display of unity. By delaying action until all hope of reconciliation with Britain had evaporated and public pressure upon the moderates had become insurmountable, the radicals were able to win the consent of more moderate delegates.

Many years later Thomas Jefferson insisted that there was nothing original about the Declaration of Independence, and he was not entirely wrong. The long list of accusations against King George, which formed the bulk of the Declaration, contained little that was new, and even some of the stirring words in the preamble had been used by the radicals time and again. Moreover, the revolutionaries borrowed ideas from a number of British and European sources, including constitutionalism, republicanism, Enlightenment thought (see chapter 6), and millenial Christian thought. The millenial strain in evangelical Protestantism suggested that the thousand-year reign of Christ might begin soon in America. If Americans would repent their sins, seek a spiritual rebirth, and defend their liberties, then they might find "a more perfect and happy state," not only in the next world, but here on earth. When **millenialism** was fused with these other strands of revolutionary thought, it gave Americans a sense of optimism and mission. If the colonists could throw off the shackles of despotic government, then they had it "in their power," as Thomas Paine put it, "to begin the world over again."

Although it drew from many sources, the Declaration of Independence was truly original. Nowhere else, except in Paine's *Common Sense,* had any American set out so clearly and explicitly a vision not only of government but also of society. These two documents offered blueprints for the new world that American revolutionaries hoped to create. Jefferson's achievement was to reformulate familiar principles in a way that made them simple, clear, and applicable to the American situation.

The most important idea of these principles was human equality, that all people were born with certain fundamental rights. Second, and closely related, was the belief in a universal, common human nature. If all people were the same and all had the same rights, then the purpose of government was to protect those rights. Just as people created government to protect their rights, they could abolish any government that became despotic. Third, government should represent the people.

It was many years, however, before the radical implications of the Declaration or its application to political economy became fully evident to the American people. At the moment more attention was focused upon immediate

Destruction of Statue of King George in New York City. Here, a small crowd in New York City pulls down the statue of King George on July 9, 1776, a few days after independence had been declared.

political struggles than upon the underlying philosophy of the Declaration. The revolution succeeded because at both the national and state levels moderates and radicals were able to create effective alliances, reversing the prerevolutionary trend toward class and political conflict. In the decades preceding the Revolution, colonial legislators had been transforming themselves into a self-conscious elite. In order to prevail, they had to forge alliances with poorer artisans and farmers. To maintain their positions as leaders of the opposition to Britain, elite revolutionaries like John Hancock continually had to appeal to their poorer and often more radical countrymen and women and to look out for their countryfolks' interests as well as their own.

The result at both the national and state levels was a revolution that was more moderate than it might otherwise have been, not to mention a revolution that succeeded. But it also meant continuing struggles between radicals and moderates over the meaning of the Revolution they had just embarked on together. Just as military fervor reached its high point in the spring of 1776, so also did political unity.

Creating a National Government

Although both the public and the state governments acted as if Congress were a legitimate national government, it really was not. It had no more authority over the states than they were willing to give it, and it had none whatsoever over the people. At the same time that Richard Henry Lee presented Congress with his proposal for independence, he also suggested that Congress should create a permanent national government, a confederation of the states with a written constitution. John Dickinson, a moderate,

was assigned to draft the Articles of Confederation. He sketched out a remarkably weak central government. It had the authority to make treaties, to carry on military and foreign affairs, to request the states to pay its expenses, and very little else. There was no chief executive, only a Congress in which each state would have one vote. Term limits were imposed on representatives, who could be recalled by their states at any time. Any act of Congress would require nine votes (of thirteen), and the Articles would not go into effect until all thirteen states had approved them. It was a measure of Americans' commitment to limited government that this was the strongest central government that anyone could design in 1776.

As weak as Dickinson's plan was, it was still too strong for many members of Congress. Moreover, with Congress functioning adequately at the moment and state jealousies strong, it took Congress more than a year to revise and accept a watered-down version of the Articles of Confederation. Establishing a permanent national government was not a very high priority. Sovereignty (ultimate authority) was assigned to the states, rather than to the Congress. Not until March 1781, with the end of the war only a few months away, had the final state ratified the Articles of Confederation, thereby putting the Articles into effect. By then, the weaknesses in a national government with no means of enforcing its regulations were becoming evident.

Creating State Governments

As explained previously, in 1776 there was very little interest in a national government. America's leading political theorists barely gave it a thought. Instead, all attention was focused on state governments, where the new ideas about liberty, equality, and government were put into practice. Americans were exhilarated by the prospect of creating their own governments. As John Jay marveled, they were "the first people whom heaven has favoured with an opportunity of deliberating upon, and choosing the forms of government under which they should live." Between 1775 and 1780, each of the thirteen states adopted a new, written constitution.

The new state governments were the products of both theory and experience. Because the Revolutionaries feared concentrations of power, the powers of governors were sharply limited. In two states, Pennsylvania and Georgia, the position of governor was abolished and replaced with a council. Governors were given term limits or required to run for re-election every year, and some states wrote in provisions for impeachment. Governors could no longer control when the legislatures met. Because the colonists had seen royal governors appoint their cronies to powerful positions and prominent families like the Hutchinsons monopolize public offices, governors also were stripped of their power of appointment.

The new state constitutions made the legislatures more democratic. The number of representatives was doubled in South Carolina and New Hampshire and more than tripled in Massachusetts, to 350, for a ratio of about one representative for every thousand people. As with governors, many constitutions imposed either term limits or frequent elections for representatives. As the property qualifications for holding office were lowered, the number of representatives increased, and poorer men came to sit in legislatures alongside richer ones. Wealthy men still held a disproportionate share of elective positions, but they no longer monopolized the positions of power. This was one of the greatest changes brought about by the Revolution, not the replacement of the wealthy by less affluent men, but the admission of more ordinary men into government. Now the elite had to learn to share power, and in order for them to stay in power they had to learn how to win the votes of men they had once scorned.

The new state constitutions accelerated a political process that had begun in the years before the Revolution. Protesting the actions of the British government had drawn ordinary men, and sometimes women, into politics. The new governments made it easier for ordinary people to participate in government. The result was an increase in the percent of white adult men who were entitled to vote, from about 50 to 80 percent before the Revolution to 60 to 90 percent after the state constitutions were written. The number of men taking advantage of this opportunity increased also, from only 10 to 15 percent voting at the beginning of the Revolution to 20 to 30 percent by its conclusion. This was still a low level of political participation, but it was nonetheless a revolution, compared to only a few years earlier.

Winning the Revolution

The British entered the war with clear advantages in population, wealth, and power, but with a flawed premise about how the war could be won. Britain was arguably the most powerful nation in the world, with a population in England alone more than three times that of the colonies. It had already entered the industrial revolution, produced all the armaments necessary for a modern war, and had the world's largest navy. It entered the war with the mistaken idea that the colonists could be made to submit by a swift and effective application of force. It also assumed that Americans loyal to the Crown would rally around the British troops. The actions of Britain's troops, however,

only alienated those Americans they encountered, turning them into reluctant patriots. Probably no more than one-fifth of the population remained loyal to Britain, but there were many more who shifted loyalties depending upon local circumstances. The war in America ultimately became a struggle for the support of this unpoliticized, local-minded population.

Competing Strategies

British political objectives shifted during the war. The first goal, based upon the belief that colonial resistance was being led by a handful of radical New Englanders, was to punish and isolate Boston. This was the strategy of 1774 and 1775, with the Intolerable Acts, and the battles of Lexington, Concord, and Breed's (Bunker) Hill. This strategy failed miserably. The early failures derived from the faulty assumption that well-trained British regular soldiers were necessarily superior to untrained colonial rustics. If the British had a misplaced faith in the invincibility of their regulars, so also did the Americans have a misplaced faith in their moral superiority—or to be more precise, faith that their supposed moral superiority was somehow relevant in military encounters. Over the course of the war, those who were capable of learning from past mistakes would realize that neither British professionalism nor American moral superiority could guarantee victory.

The result was a very long war, as both sides tried to avoid decisive major engagements that might prove fatal. For seven years, the two armies chased each other across the eastern seaboard. Neither side had masses of men to pour onto the battlefield. Moreover, there was no consensus in Britain about the strategic or economic value of the colonies, and hence there was always an opposition to the war. As a result, there was always a limit to the investment in troops and materiel that the British were prepared to commit to the war effort. The war required the British to double their debt, to £245,000,000. Beyond this expense, they would not go. Consequently, every battle presented a significant risk that troops who were lost could not be replaced. Moreover, desertions from the British Army were high, and they rose after every battle. Some deserters reenlisted, on the American side, in order to obtain the bonuses that were given to new recruits.

Manpower was also a serious problem for the Americans. It was always difficult to recruit enough soldiers into the Continental Army. After a defeat in battle or near the end of the year when terms of enlistment were almost up, men left the Army to return to their homes and farms. Militia strength rose and fell depending upon the prospects for success. Hence, one of the goals of the American war effort was *not* to do anything that would so demoralize the colonists that the armies would shrink to a dangerously small size. In other words, there was limited incentive to risk all in battle.

Early in the war, however, both sides hoped for a decisive victory that would bring the war to a speedy conclusion. The Americans had failed in their assault upon Quebec. The British pursued the Americans all the way back to Ticonderoga on Lake Champlain, but Benedict Arnold's leadership prevented the British from pushing the Americans any farther. The theater of action then shifted to southern New York and the middle colonies. The British objective was to cut off New England entirely. Having given up hopes of crushing New England directly, the British planned to isolate the region and defeat the Continental Army under George Washington's leadership. The British believed that such a loss would force an American surrender by undermining morale. The British also aimed at seizing all the major American cities. Indeed, at one point or another during the war, the British captured Boston (which was subsequently abandoned in 1776), Newport, New York, Philadelphia, Charleston, and Savannah. The capture of American cities, however, did not bring about an American surrender. On the eve of the capture of Philadelphia, for example, the Continental Congress merely moved itself out to Lancaster. With 90 percent of the American population living in the countryside, the British found that the seizure of a major city did not strike the hoped-for psychological or economic blow.

The British on the Offensive: 1776

In preparation for a British offensive in 1776, the new commander, General William Howe, assembled a huge force on Staten Island: 32,000 soldiers and 13,000 seamen, carried by 73 warships and several hundred transports. Some of these British soldiers were actually German mercenaries. Although some of the Hessians were war-hardened professionals who were merciless in their treatment of civilians, others were hapless German citizens, rounded up by patrols to enable their princes to meet their quotas for the troops they had promised the British. As a result, thousands deserted, finding homes among prosperous German farmers in the colonies.

In anticipation of battle and hoping to protect New York, Washington moved his army south to New York. He had about 19,000 soldiers, far too few to hold up to the British in a pitched battle. Washington kept about half his troops in Manhattan and sent the other half to Brooklyn Heights, where they dug in, in hopes of protecting Long Island. Rather than repeating the mistake of a frontal assault, as at Breed's Hill, the British sneaked up behind the Americans, inflicting 1,500 casualties, compared to 400 for the British. On August 27, 1776, Washington pulled the remainder of his Brooklyn forces back into Manhattan. Had the British pursued rapidly, they probably could have crushed Washington's army, but Howe may have been more concerned with winning a peace than a war. After

Washington had retreated to Manhattan, Howe invited members of the Continental Congress to meet with him privately on Staten Island. He was unable to recognize American independence, which was what the representatives insisted upon, and thus the first move in his peace strategy failed.

Still hoping for peace, Howe then began pushing Washington backwards, first out of lower Manhattan, then out of the northern part of the island. Simultaneously, he offered peace to any colonists in the region who would declare their loyalty. Seeing Washington on the run, thousands accepted the offer. On November 16, the British succeeded in forcing the Americans out of Manhattan when they captured the garrison at Fort Washington on the northern end of the island. Although British casualties were high (300 dead), the American losses were much worse: 54 dead, 100 wounded, and almost 3,000 captured along with precious weapons and supplies. Howe pursued the remainder of the Army out of Manhattan to White Plains and then through New Jersey to New Brunswick, where, on November 30, 2,000 militia men from New Jersey and Maryland simply departed, their terms of service having expired. The British almost caught Washington twice in New Jersey, but on December 8 the Americans crossed the Delaware at Trenton, taking every boat in the area with them to prevent a British pursuit. By Christmas Eve, Washington had only 3,000 soldiers with him, and General Charles Lee, the commander of the other half of the Continental Army, which Washington had left in New York, had just been captured by the British. As Thomas Paine wrote, "These are the times that try men's souls."

Howe had captured New York and had taken possession of New Jersey, where even a signer of the Declaration of Independence had taken a loyalty oath. He was poised to seize Philadelphia (which fell in September 1777). At the end of 1776, the British were very close to achieving their objective. Then, on Christmas night, with morale in the Continental Army dangerously low, Washington took his army across the ice-clogged Delaware and surprised the British garrison at Trenton at dawn. A thousand Hessian soldiers, sleeping off a Christmas celebration, were quickly captured. About a week later, Washington evaded a British trap and sneaked behind their lines to capture their outpost at Princeton (see Map 7-2).

These American successes were enough to bring another 1,000 troops into the American Army. Even more significant, the British decided to concentrate their troops near New Brunswick, fearing the loss of any more garrisons. This strategic decision on the part of the British revealed the weakness in their position and demonstrated why, at the moment when victory seemed closest, it was very far away. Never able to raise enough troops to overcome the Americans' home advantage, the British required the support not only of 30,000 Hessians, but also

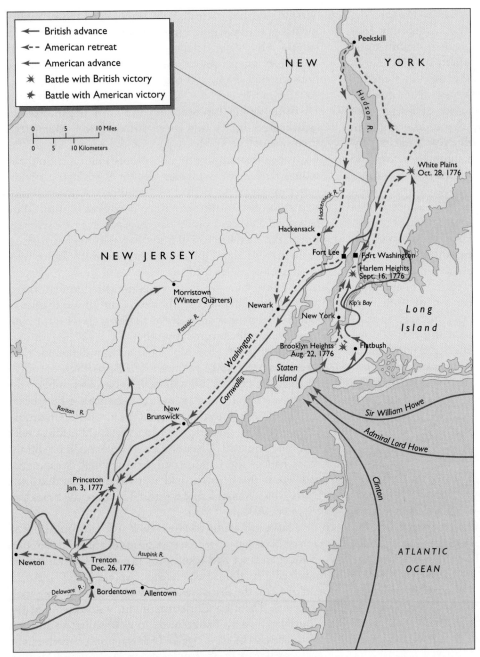

Map 7-2   New York and New Jersey Campaigns, 1776–1777.
In the second half of 1776, British troops chased Washington out of New York and across New Jersey. As he would for the remainder of the war, Washington took care never to let the British capture him and his troops, leaving him free to attack at Trenton and Princeton.

of a comparable number of Loyalist soldiers. They also needed to make certain that Americans did not aid the revolutionary war effort. Far from home, the British could get food only from Americans, sometimes only by seizing it. Thus, in order to assure the allegiance of Loyalists, the British had to offer them protection from American reprisals. However, the British were seizing the Americans' goods and property for the war effort. Then, once the garrisons were withdrawn, those who had declared

loyalty to the British were left alone and vulnerable to the reprisals of the patriots.

This was the British dilemma. They could control the American countryside only by maintaining troops there, but once the troops were withdrawn, civil warfare would break out. Thus, even though Washington's victories at Trenton and Princeton were rather small, they exposed the incapacity of the British to defeat the revolutionaries unless they were prepared to settle an army of occupation on the Americans. And although the British were willing to invest a great deal in winning the war, they were not prepared to establish martial law throughout the colonies.

A Slow War: 1777–1781

With the British held off and a major defeat avoided, Washington settled in for a long war, enlisting soldiers for an extended period. He never had as many soldiers as he would have needed to confront the British head-on, so he and the other American commanders mostly led the British on chases across the American countryside, trying to wear them down without getting trounced. As a result, the war dragged on for five more years. Maintaining such an army for year after year was expensive, but the American population was unwilling to be taxed at high rates to support it. Most soldiers in the Continental Army were from the bottom tier of society and signed up partly for the bonuses. They suffered grievously; at Jockey Hollow, New Jersey, in the winter of 1779–1780, men roasted their own shoes to eat, and even devoured their pet dogs. The local militia (generally members of the middle class) continued to come out as needed or as the fortunes of the war dictated.

In 1777, the British political objective was still the same; to isolate New England. The British planned to achieve this objective by seizing the middle colonies by taking the capital at Philadelphia and by marching down

New York, from Lake Champlain to Manhattan. American troops had the advantage in upstate New York by 3 to 1, however, and they defeated the British under General John Burgoyne at Saratoga, stopping the British advance (see Map 7-3).

The victory at Saratoga convinced the French to enter into a formal alliance, negotiated by Benjamin Franklin, the American envoy to France. Winning French support was perhaps the major accomplishment of the middle phase of the war. Not only did the entry of the French tie down the British in other parts of the world, but it also brought America more than $8 million in aid. In return, the Americans promised not to negotiate separately with Britain and to remain France's ally forever. Now the Americans could no longer pretend that they had freed themselves from the old-style power politics and international intrigue of the Old World.

The British strategy of isolating New England had failed, and it proved impossible to pacify the countryside of the middle colonies. As a result, the focus shifted away from the least loyal section of America, New England, to the most, the South. Stated British war aims shifted, too, in response to political realities at home. The new justification was to protect the Loyalists, who otherwise would be victimized at the hands of vengeful patriots. Indeed there was plenty of evidence that the patriots could be extraordinarily violent. In some heavily contested regions such as New Jersey and South Carolina, where neither side could maintain control, violence became endemic.

Seeking to capitalize on these internal conflicts and to rally the substantial number of southern Loyalists, the British invaded first Georgia in 1778 and then South Carolina in 1780. After seizing Charleston and trapping the American commander and thousands of troops, the British under General Sir Henry Clinton ranged out into the countryside, trying to rally the Loyalists and live off the land. That was the same contradictory strategy that had failed in New Jersey. One upcountry resident complained that "no sooner we had yielded to them but [they] set to Rob us taking all our livings, horses, Cows, Sheep, Clothing, of all Sorts, money, pewter, tins, knives, in fine Everything . . . until we were Stript Naked." As in New Jersey, the only way that the British could have maintained their control would have been to occupy a region.

In the meantime, the Continental Army and the militia worked together to wear down the British. The Continental Army in the lower South was never large enough to risk everything on a major battle with the British. When the Continental Army actually engaged the British, as at

George Washington, as he appeared at the beginning of the Revolution.

Revolutionary War soldiers, in uniform. Note the range, from full military regalia to the buckskin of a rifleman.

WHERE THEY LIVED, WHERE THEY WORKED

The Winter at Jockey Hollow

It was the worst winter in a century. It snowed twenty-eight times, and the drifts were so high that they covered the fences in the hollow of land tucked between Long Hill and the Watchung Mountains. It was snowing again on December 1, 1779, the day that General George Washington moved the Continental Army into its winter quarters, four miles outside the little New Jersey village of Morristown.

Washington chose Jockey Hollow because the low mountains and surrounding swamps offered it protection from sudden attack. The hilly terrain was covered with trees, which his soldiers, almost 11,000 of them, could chop down to build themselves cabins. The water supply was good, and the many farms in the region could provide food.

The first order of business was to build cabins, but the winter was so harsh that the work proceeded slowly. Until

cabins were built, the soldiers and the line officers had to sleep in their tents. The storm that raged for three days in early January was "one of the most tremendous snow-storms ever remembered; no man could endure its violence many minutes without danger of his life," Dr. James Thatcher reported. "Some of the soldiers were actually covered while in their tents and buried like sheep under the snow."

Not until February were most men in the "Log-house city" of more than 1,000 cabins. They were all the same size, and design, about fourteen feet wide by fifteen or sixteen feet long, and six and one-half feet high at the eaves. They were constructed out of notched logs, cut from the woods of Jockey Hollow, with the cracks filled in with clay. Each cabin had a fireplace, made out of stones, and twelve bunks for the

An Illustration of the Encampment at Morristown.

Soldiers wintered in small log cabins that offered imperfect protection from the cold winter.

Camden, South Carolina, in August 1780, it was defeated. As the British marched through South and North Carolina, they were harassed by bands of irregulars and militia. Each hit by the irregulars depleted the British forces, and each small victory brought more men into the American ranks. This, in fact, became the American strategy as the Continental forces, now commanded in the South by Nathanael Greene, drew the British, led by Lord Corn-

wallis, on a wild chase, exhausting them and depleting their ranks, almost always avoiding a direct conflict (see Map 7-4). Finally, with the British near exhaustion, Greene met the British at Guilford Court House in March 1781, inflicting heavy losses on them. Although the battle was a draw, Cornwallis, with his forces depleted, retreated and moved on to Virginia. Greene and the Continental Army retook almost all of the deep South. Once again, there were dozen soldiers who would call it home. Often, the soldiers did not cut windows until the spring.

Both food and clothing were in short supply. Joseph Plumb Martin, a nineteen-year-old private from Connecticut who had been in the Army for three years, complained bitterly, "We were absolutely, literally starved.... I did not put a single morsel of victuals into my mouth for four days and as many nights." Some officers gave their soldiers their own small rations of meat. Washington's requests to the Continental Congress for food and supplies had gone unanswered, but local farmers brought their produce to camp to sell at extortionate prices. Hungry soldiers, who had gone unpaid for five months, began foraging for themselves in the neighborhood. Washington threatened that unless the surrounding counties quickly sent supplies to his camp (for which he would issue IOUs to be paid at some future date), he would organize a

systematic forage of New Jersey. The problem was solved for the moment; but the large army quickly went through the new supplies, and by spring it was hungry again.

Some men began talking mutiny, "venting our spleen at our country and government, then at our officers, and then at ourselves for our imbecility in staying there and starving ... for an ungrateful people who did not care what became of us, so they could enjoy themselves while we were keeping a cruel enemy from them." Officers were able to appeal to the troops' patriotism, telling them that they had "won immortal honor to yourselves ... by your perseverance, patience, and bravery...." Cold, hungry, half-naked, most of the soldiers stayed on. "We were unwilling," Private Martin said, "to desert the cause of our country, when in distress ... we knew her cause involved our own."

The interiors of the cabins were dark, crowded, and uncomfortable.

The interior of the Ford Mansion, where the Ford family lived after they had been forced downstairs by the military occupation upstairs.

no stunning victories, just a war of attrition that depended on the Continental Army and the militia and on winning the allegiance of the civilian population.

The cost to South Carolina, however, was enormous. Most of the upcountry was criss-crossed by troops and stripped bare of anything of worth. As first one side then the other took control, neighbors attacked each other, plundered each other's farms, and carried away each

other's slaves. Over the course of the Revolution, one-fourth of South Carolina's slaves simply disappeared. Some ran away, some died of disease, some were stolen by whites, and some followed the British when in June 1780 their commander promised freedom to all rebel-owned slaves who agreed to fight with the British for the remainder of the war. Some of these were actually shipped off to slavery in the West Indies, but a good number fought on

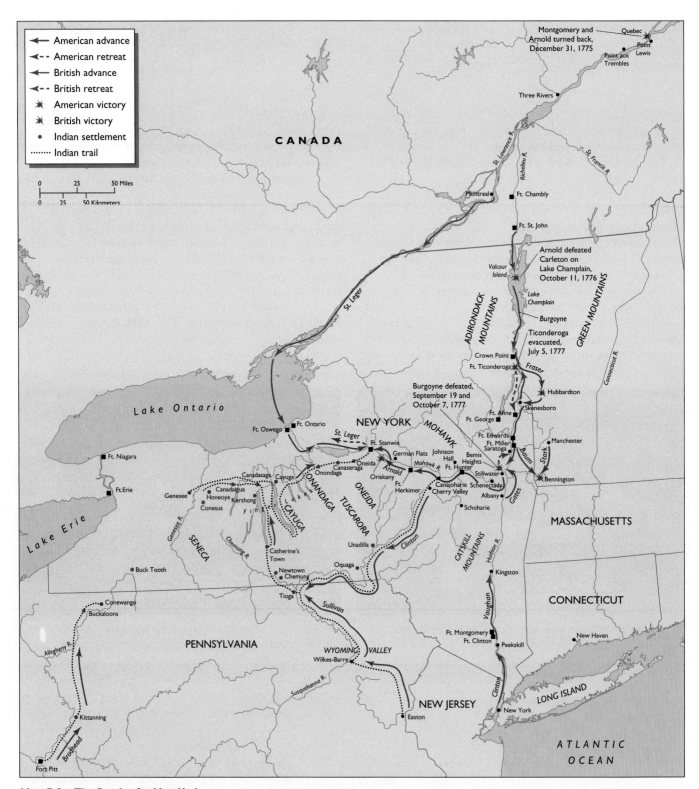

Map 7-3   The Battles for New York.
The war for New York was waged on two fronts. North of the Hudson River, the Americans failed in their attempt in 1775 to seize Quebec, were forced to abandon Fort Ticonderoga in July 1777, but defeated the British at Saratoga that fall. In 1778 and 1779, west of the Hudson, Sullivan and his troops succeeded in their goal of destroying the Iroquois and bringing devastation to their land.

the British side. This use of slaves as soldiers, of course, outraged white patriots, but it hardly pleased the Loyalists either. Loyalist slaveholders did not want their way of life undermined. Once again, the nature of the war imposed limits on the British. Had they been willing to wage a war of liberation, freeing all the southern slaves and using them to fight the war, they might have come closer to winning the war. But the British were fighting to preserve social and political order, not to overturn it. The British nonetheless disrupted the slave system significantly, and this disruption was another aspect to the civil war that beset the region for most of the revolutionary period.

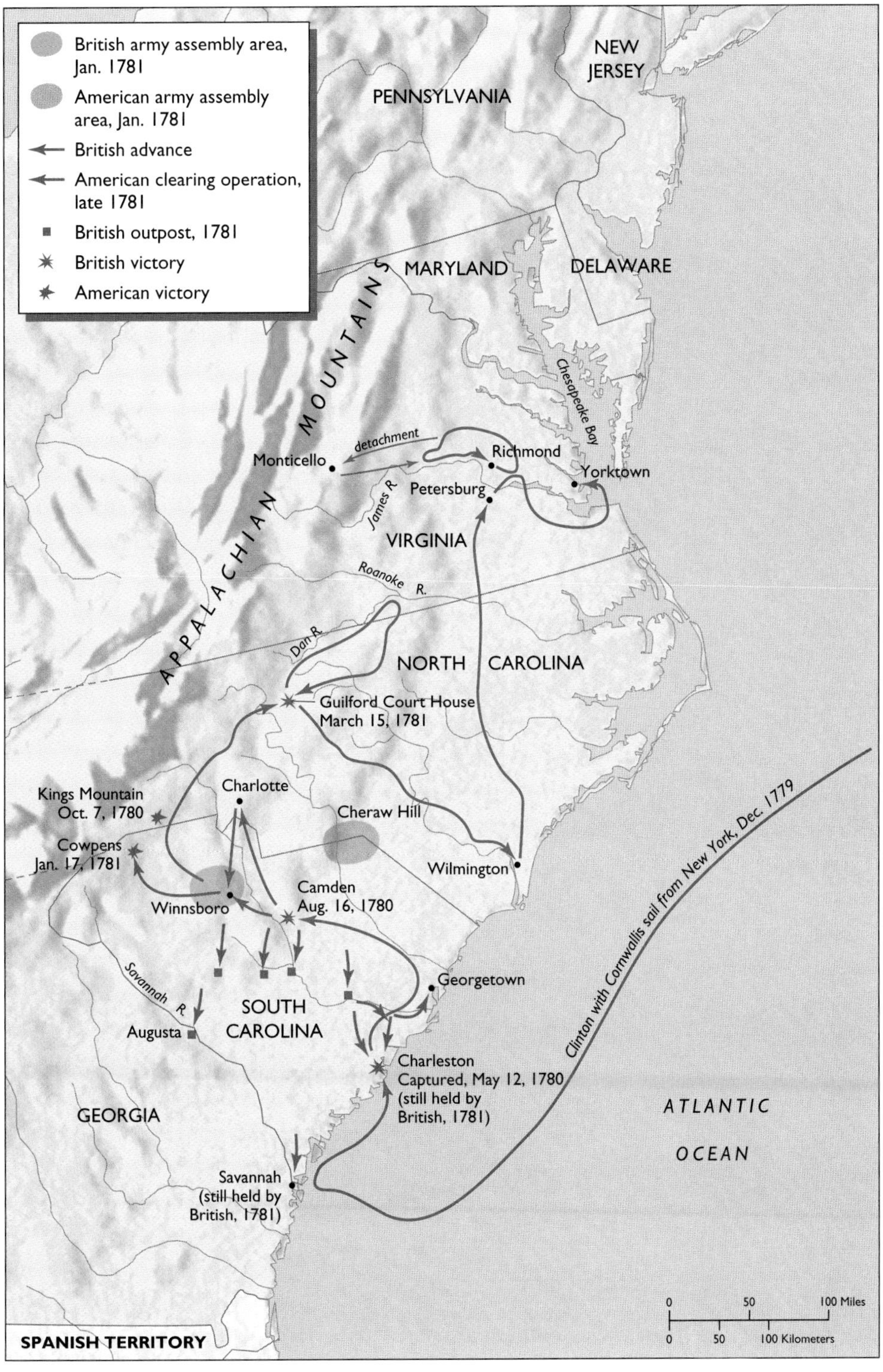

The British southern strategy had failed, but the Americans were not yet in a position to win the war. When Cornwallis moved on to Virginia in 1781, his troops went where they wanted, capturing Richmond, the new capital, and Charlottesville, there coming within a few minutes of capturing Thomas Jefferson. Yet the British had been seriously weakened by the war of attrition. George Washington, working closely with the French who sent a fleet into the Chesapeake across from Cornwallis' quarters at Yorktown, drew most of his forces to Virginia and laid siege. Trapped, Cornwallis surrendered on October 19, 1781. Although the Treaty of Paris (see Map 7-5) ending the war was not signed for two more years, the war was effectively over.

Securing a Place in the World

The United States revolted to escape from the British Empire and turn its back on European power politics. However, in order to win the war, the new nation had to strike bargains with those same European powers. These alliances and treaties set the stage for national and international struggle well into the nineteenth century as Americans tried to establish a place for themselves in the new world political and economic order. Successful diplomatic relations were critical to the success of the American political economy, for they would make possible the new nation's survival and its prosperity.

Map 7-4   The War in the South, 1779–1781.
In 1779, the theater of action shifted to the South. Washington's objective was to wear the British down, avoiding decisive battles in which his outmanned troops might be defeated. With the help of the French, his strategy succeeded, leading to the British surrender at Yorktown in October 1781.

Map 7-5   The Treaty of Paris.
The Treaty of Paris confirmed the boundaries of the new United States, north to the Great Lakes, south to Spanish Florida, and west to the Mississippi.
But it left the British in several forts west of the Appalachians, which they did not abandon until 1797.

Source: Walter LaFeber, The American Age, 2nd Ed. (1994), 29.

The new nation lacked the resources to win the war without assistance. Early in the war the United States had to call upon Britain's continental enemies—France, Spain, and Holland— for support, and it played these new allies off against Britain with as much intrigue and cunning as any Old World diplomat practiced. Benjamin Franklin, Congress' envoy to France, now 70, arrived at Court in 1776 as if he were a country rustic, refusing to wear the elegant silks and powdered wig expected of men of quality. His unfashionable appearance, however, was a ruse, intended to make the French think that he was more innocent and less calculating than he was. France entered the war as America's ally in the hope of breaking up the British Empire and reestablishing itself as the world's most powerful nation. France wanted the United States to be independent but small and weak. France was also willing to draw Britain's other great rival, Spain, into the fray in order to gain the use of the powerful Spanish Navy. Spain had a similar objective, keeping the United States small and too weak to challenge it. The United States wanted to secure its own independence, first and foremost, but it had no intention of remaining small or feeble. Americans hoped to obtain the territory between the Appalachians and the Mississippi and a sizeable chunk of Canada, as well as the right to navigate the Mississippi. In return for French and Spanish assistance, the United States at first was willing to offer only the right to trade, vastly overrating the value of the American trade to European heads of state.

With America wanting France and Spain to fight for an expanded American territory, and those two nations wanting instead to keep the new nation small and tangled up in European alliances, it took three years, until 1778, to negotiate formal treaties with France and for France then to draw Spain into the war a few months later. Franklin pushed the French along by holding secret truce discussions with a British agent late in 1777 and then leaking reports to several well-placed French friends. Although the alliance was an impressive accomplishment for the new nation, in order to secure French support it had to make several concessions. The Americans had promised not to negotiate separately with Britain and to remain France's ally "forever."

The United States broke both promises: the first within a few years and the second in the 1790s. In April 1782, after Cornwallis' surrender at Yorktown but before France and Spain had gained their military objectives, Franklin began discussions with a British representative, sent to Paris to commence peace negotiations. By

Surrender of British Army Led by Cornwallis at Yorktown, Virginia.

A loyalist encampment at Johnstown (now Cornwall) on the St. Lawrence River in Canada. Many Loyalists fled to Canada or England, abandoning their property, for which they later asked the British government for compensation.

November, a draft of the treaty had been completed, although Franklin assured the French that nothing would be signed without their consent. It was clear, however, that the agreement served British and American interests much more than those of France and Spain. Under the terms of the Treaty of Paris, signed in 1783, Britain recognized American independence, and the United States acquired the territory between the Appalachians and the Mississippi and south of the Great Lakes.

In the long run Britain probably struck the shrewder bargain. The land it ceded was of little use to them. The Americans failed to press for commercial concessions, and by the mid-1780s, the British had forbidden them to trade directly with either Britain or the West Indies. These restrictions seriously damaged the new nation's economy. Securing international markets for American goods became the most critical diplomatic issue confronting the new nation, an issue that divided the nation along political and sectional lines.

Neither France nor Spain gained much through the war. Although Spain won Florida, neither country achieved its other territorial objectives, and as was always the case after international wars, France was left with a large debt.

If America's allies France and Spain were relative losers, so also were Britain's allies, the American Loyalists and those Indian tribes that had entered into treaties with the British and fought by their side. The best the British could do for the Loyalists was to secure a commitment of no further reprisals against them and Congress' promise to get the states to consider making restitution. Rather than attempting to protect their Indian allies, the British sold them out by transferring their land (the territory between the Appalachians and the Mississippi) to the United States.

Once again the British had sown the seeds of further strife. Almost as if to make certain that the Americans and the western Indians would come into conflict, the British remained in their nine Great Lakes forts, supposedly to guarantee the rights of the Loyalists. Although in many ways a stunning achievement, the Treaty of Paris also set the stage for future conflicts.

The Challenge of the Revolution

During the Revolution and in the years that immediately followed, Americans experienced all the usual upheavals of war: death, profiteering, and inflation followed by economic depression. There were other challenges as well, those presented by the ideology of the Revolution itself, which sought to make the United States into a new nation based upon novel ideas about liberty and equality. Because the American Revolution was waged by a successful alliance of moderates and radicals, less social turmoil resulted than in many revolutions.

Radicals and moderates had compromised in order to begin and win the Revolution, yet there were significant disagreements between them. Although conflict was kept in check during the war, once the fighting had terminated, philosophical and practical differences surfaced. One of the greatest challenges that Americans faced was endeavoring to design and preserve political structures that could contain these conflicts and prevent the eruption of violence. The other great challenge came from the philosophy of revolution itself. The idea of human equality implied a transformed political economy. Followed to its natural conclusion, not only would the transformation lead to widespread prosperity, it would necessarily challenge slavery, as well as the subordination of women. If these inequalities were not overthrown, they would at the very least have to be reconciled with the ideals of the Revolution.

The Departure of the Loyalists

About 15 to 20 percent of the white population had remained loyal to the Crown during the Revolution, along with a majority of the Indians and a minority of slaves. Although this was a sizeable number of people (almost half a million whites), the Loyalists were never well-organized enough to present a real danger to the success of the Revolution. People became Loyalists for different reasons, and those reasons kept them from uniting into a single movement.

During the war, partisan fighting was fierce in those regions where neither side could maintain control, such as the Carolinas and New Jersey, but there was relatively little retribution after the war. There were no trials of Loyalists for treason, no mass executions, no significant mob actions directed against whites. Nor was there any significant resistance from the Loyalists. Perhaps as many as 80,000 left the country, seeking refuge in Canada, Great Britain, and the West Indies. Although moderates and radicals continued arguing about how best to fulfill the goals of the Revolution, there was virtually no one left in America who wanted to overturn the Revolution.

The loyalist exiles came disproportionately from the top tier of American society, and their departure left a void that less prominent Americans scrambled to fill. Although in relative terms, confiscated loyalist property represented only a small proportion of the nation's economy (about 4 percent), in absolute terms that was a great deal of property to be redistributed. Most often, it was people just below the now-empty top rung of society who took the Loyalists' places. The departure of the Loyalists thus enhanced the democratizing tendencies of the Revolution in two ways. First, it removed the most conservative element in American society. As a result, all subsequent discussions about American politics accepted the fundamental premises of the Revolution. Second, it created an opportunity for many Americans to rise to power.

The Challenge of the Economy

Wars disrupt the economy in two ways. First, they interfere with ordinary processes of production and exchange, hurting some people and creating great opportunity for others. Second, because wars are always expensive, they require some combination of increased taxation and deficit spending. During and after the Revolution, the American economy was disrupted in both of these ways, although the costs of war and the new nation's attempts to meet them had the most important effects.

Those who suffered the greatest economic hardships and enjoyed the greatest opportunities were those most deeply involved in the market. During the war, trade with Britain and the British West Indies was, of course, cut off; the British Navy seized American ships headed for Europe and destroyed the New England fishing industry. After the war, Britain continued to exclude American ships from the West Indies. Congress, operating under the Articles of Confederation, was too weak to negotiate a more advantageous trade relationship with Britain. As a result, merchants who had depended solely on trade with Britain and the West Indies were ruined.

At the same time, other opportunities opened up. Those merchants who were willing to risk seizure of their ships continued the trade with Europe and sold the goods they imported at astronomical prices. Privateering made other daring merchants rich. Provisioning the Continental Army with food and clothing during the war offered another avenue for profit. In 1779 alone, the Army spent $109 million on provisions, fueling a wartime economic boom. In addition, the Army's demand for supplies drove prices sky high. Prices for grain increased 200 to 600 percent in some regions, while those for wheat in Maryland skyrocketed 5,000 percent. In the Philadelphia region, the price of pork increased 80 percent between January and April 1777 (see Figure 7-1). Enterprising Americans with a little capital to invest could rise quickly.

Americans were shocked to see rough and uneducated men become a new elite. A disgusted Loyalist complained that "those who five years ago were the 'meaner people,' are now, by a strange Revolution, become almost the only men of power, riches, and influence." In fact, this was precisely the sort of revolution that men on the make had wanted, one that would permit them to rise into the positions of wealth and power that had been the exclusive preserve of elite families. Not everyone could take advantage of the dislocations of the revolutionary economy. In fact, although the Revolution eliminated a portion of the ruling elite, the Loyalists, it did not level the social classes. Most urban working people, farmers, and inhabitants of the countryside suffered from the economy's dislocations. Those who could not profit from the war economy had to work harder and struggle with rising prices. In order to meet the Army's demand for cloth and make up for the lack of imports, women increased the pace of home production. It was women who kept up the production of cloth, meat, and grain while the men in their families fought in the militia or the army. Because cities and states set prices for cloth, however, women were unable to reap exorbitant profits for their work. Skyrocketing prices fell hardest on those with limited incomes.

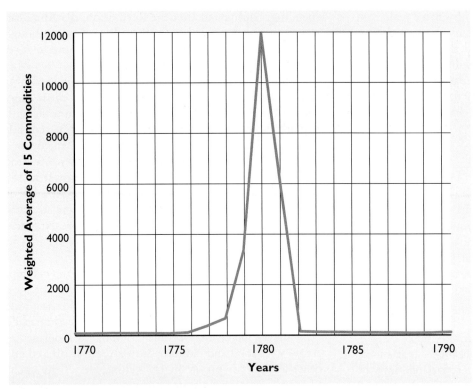

Figure 7–1   Inflation at Philadelphia. 1770–1790.
Beginning in 1776, wartime shortages caused prices for basic commodities—beef, chocolate, coffee, corn, flour, molasses, pepper, pork, rum, sugar, tea, wheat, iron, and tar—to skyrocket. By 1781, prices were 12,000% higher than a decade earlier. They began to fall the next year, finally reaching prewar levels by late in the decade.

alizing rapidly and displaying the rigid class stratifications that characterized European industrial economies. At the same time, slavery expanded into new territories in the South, assuring the persistence of inequalities based on race.

Even more than the dislocations of the revolutionary economy, the financing of the Revolution challenged the American economy. America entered the Revolution without any way to pay for it. Taxing the population was out of the question, not only because Americans had begun the Revolution precisely to avoid the high taxes that modern warfare required, but also because Congress had no authority to tax. Instead it simply printed money and more money after that. Then it spent what it had printed. There was no increase in underlying wealth to back up this currency, and the more Congress printed, the less it was worth. By 1780, Congress had printed more than $241,000,000. In addition it paid for supplies it requisitioned from the public with certificates that circulated like money; similar certificates were used to pay soldiers. These certificates put another $95,000,000 in circulation.

The plan was for each of the colonies to tax its own inhabitants to raise money to buy up the Continental currency and remove it from circulation. For a variety of

After the war, opportunities for profit and prosperity for some increased, while a postwar deflation pushed others to the brink of misery. Speculation in land and currency offered the fastest ways to become rich. Entrepreneurs bought up paper currency and land patents at a fraction of their worth, counting on the day when they would be redeemed at their face value. Even before the war ended, America's growing population was clamoring for land.

Between 1776 and 1790, America's population grew by almost 70 percent, from 2.3 million to 3.9 million, almost all of it from natural increase. Since before the Revolution, colonists had been pushing against the Indians to the west. By 1783, the Wilderness Road had taken thousands of settlers through the Cumberland Gap into Kentucky; seven years later, 100,000 people were living in Kentucky and Tennessee.

All along the western frontier, farmers rushed in to take up new lands. Speculators who had cornered huge tracts grew rich in the process, as they sold the land at extraordinary profits. This rush into newly opened farming regions reversed the trend that was taking place before the Revolution, when the growing population had sought employment in the cities. With the opening of new farming regions to the west, America would remain a farming nation for decades more, rather than industri-

Currency issued by the Continental Congress depreciated so rapidly that by the end of 1779 this Continental note, with a face value of five dollars, probably was worth no more than nineteen cents.

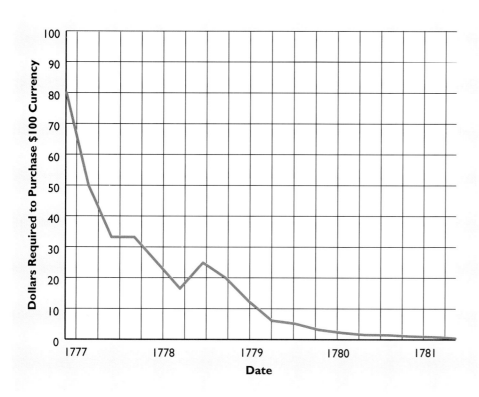

Figure 7-2   *Depreciation of Continental Currency, January 1770–April 1781.*
At the same time that prices were rising, the value of Continental currency was falling dramatically. Between 1777 and 1781, it lost almost all of its value, becoming close to worthless.

This picture of Col. Daniel Shays and his associate Job Shattuck is from a 1787 almanac. Shays and Shattuck are depicted wearing the clothing appropriate to their rank in the insurrection, with both wearing the clothing of gentlemen and carrying swords.

fore. Before the Revolution, Rhode Island had run its government on about £4,000 a year. By the end of 1779, it had levied half a million dollars in taxes. Levying taxes was one thing; collecting them was another. People simply could not pay in hard money, and the Continental currency was depreciating so rapidly that it was almost worthless to state tax collectors (see Figure 7-2).

With so much paper money in circulation, its value dropped and dropped. By April 1777, Continental currency was worth only half its face value; by April 1781, only half a percent of its face value. Even then it had not reached bottom. As always, inflation favored debtors, who were able to pay back their debts in depreciated paper money. By the end of the war, some creditors were refusing to accept paper money for the debts owed to them and insisted on hard money instead. Then, when the war ended and trade with Britain resumed, imports increased sharply (because of pent-up demand for consumer goods), while exports fell below prewar levels (because trade restrictions kept them out of British markets). The result was severe deflation, as America was flooded with cheap imports.

The weak central government was almost powerless to address these economic upheavals. In 1780 it simply stopped paying the army, which almost led to a mutiny at the encampment at Newburgh, New York. Congress looked to the states, hoping that if they retired their war debts, the economy would stabilize. The states addressed their economic problems in different ways. Each state had to decide what to do about its debt and which element of its population to serve. Many showed mercy to their debtors. Virginia paid off its debt at its depreciated value by giving out new certificates (to be backed up by tax revenues) in return for the old currency, sometimes at a ratio of only 1 to 1,000. Massachusetts, on the other hand, decided to pay off its debt at full face value, which required extremely high taxes, payable only in specie. Everywhere that taxes rose in order to pay off the state debts (at just the time when the postwar depression hit), hard-pressed debtors clamored for tax relief. In 1786, a group of armed men in New Hampshire imprisoned the state legislature, while in Maryland men attacked tax collectors and creditors. In western Massachusetts, a group of farmers led by

reasons, the states were either unable or unwilling to buy up enough currency for it to maintain its value. Moreover, the states issued their own paper money. Eventually, the states had to start taxing their inhabitants to pay off their debts at rates far higher than had ever been seen be-the revolutionary war captain Daniel Shays shut down the courts to prevent them from collecting debts. This is known as Shays' Rebellion.

Contesting the New Political Economy

As long as Americans focused on an external enemy, they did not have to argue among themselves about the shape of the new American political economy. Dramatic changes in the economy then forced Americans to consider what kind of government they were creating and what kind of economy and society the new government would sustain.

Economic upheaval and popular uprisings against state governments led many Americans to question whether democratic government could survive. The process of rebellion that had begun in 1765 seemed to be beginning again, although this time it was directed not against the British government but against the new republican state governments. Americans now had to face the same issue that had led to conflict with Britain. Were they willing to pay the costs of waging a huge war? Could they construct governments that could manage conflict without letting it break into armed rebellion? Could they avoid the perils of tyranny, on the one hand, and anarchy, on the other? Could they, in short, maintain democratic forms of government? This was one of the greatest challenges of the aftermath of the Revolution.

Shays' Rebellion was simply a more extreme form of the protest that had occurred in many of the states (against high taxes in a deflationary economy). Shays' Rebellion, in the winter of 1786–1787, was an attempt by debtors from western Massachusetts to force the government to alleviate their economic distress, primarily by shutting down the courts so that their debts could not be collected, but also by passing legislation for the relief of debtors. By 1786, many of the western Massachusetts farmers had become accustomed to the absence of government. Courts had been shut down in the region pretty much since 1774, and this area often declined to send representatives to any provincial bodies. It had not, for example, sent representatives to the convention that wrote the Massachusetts Constitution of 1780, which it now found too aristocratic for its taste. Those who put down Shays' Rebellion did so in republican terms, faulting the Shaysites for inadequate virtue. How could the gains of the Revolution be preserved in the face of hostility to all government?

Popular uprisings of this sort raised serious questions about whether the democratic governments created after the Revolution could contain anarchy. Every state that faced such uprisings learned that peace could best be preserved by going easy on the rebels. After Shays' Rebellion was put down, John Hancock was elected governor with the support of the Shaysites on a platform of amnesty for the rebels and relief for debtors. Reflecting upon the rebellion, Thomas Jefferson said, "I hold it, that a little rebellion, now and then is a good thing, and as necessary in the political world as storms in the physical." As a rule, popular uprisings by economically independent men (as distinguished from those by dependent laborers or slaves) have been punished very lightly in America, which may be one of the sources of American political stability.

Yet if both the relatively light punishments meted out to debtor insurgents and the generally inflationary policies of state governments quelled popular unrest, they did little to satisfy those who wished for political order and a growing economy. The postwar depression and the inability of Congress to negotiate trade agreements with Britain devastated commerce. The huge national debt was, by and large, simply going unpaid, leaving numerous creditors holding worthless pieces of paper. Popular unrest in the states had helped debtors, but not those to whom they owed money. The nationalists, a group of commercial-minded political leaders centered in Congress and including James Madison, Gouverneur Morris, Robert Morris, and Alexander Hamilton, were beginning to advocate a political economy based on a strong national government that would actively advance commerce and protect private property. These nationalists were, in general, the moderates of the revolutionary era, men who had fought vigorously for the Revolution but moderated its radicalism. Radicals envisioned a different political economy, based on a weaker central government, a more localized democracy, and a hands-off approach to the economy. The dispute about how best to preserve the gains of the Revolution was between the uneasy allies of the Revolution, its moderates and its radicals. Whether their different visions of the American political economy could be reconciled was one of the greatest challenges presented by the Revolution.

Can Women Be Citizens?

The American Revolution began as a political revolution, but it raised questions that threatened and in some cases changed the social order. A revolution based on beliefs in human equality and a common human nature brought into question all social relations, including the role of women.

Many women were drawn into the Revolution as consumers. They had been actively recruited into the boycott movements of the 1760s and 1770s, and they had eagerly participated both in boycotts and in increased production at home to make up for declining imports. During the Revolution women not only took part in riots directed against merchants who were hoarding or charging excessively high prices for food, they also directed one-third of such actions. Many women identified with the goals of the Revolution and participated actively in one of its engines of enforcement. They could turn their efforts against the revolutionary governments, as well, when they thought that the governments were interfering with their rights as consumers and duties as homemakers. Early in the war, the women of Kingston, New York, mobbed the town's revolutionary committee and threatened that unless the committee turned over the tea it held, "their husbands and sons shall fight no more."

If it was generally agreed that women could extend their traditional economic roles as producers and consumers to support or even challenge the war effort, there was no consensus on how greatly women's political roles should be expanded. Following the logic of revolutionary thought, some women pointed out that the right to be taxed only by one's own representatives should apply to them too. Married women were generally denied the right to own property in their own names, but what was the basis for denying the vote to unmarried women who owned property? This was the question that the widowed Hannah Lee Corbin asked her patriot brother Richard Henry Lee. Obviously squirming, Lee admitted that neither "wisdom" nor "policy" would "forbid Widows having property from voting." In a famous letter, Abigail Adams asked her husband, John, who was in Congress on the eve of the Revolution, to see to it that Congress would "remember the Ladies." In 1776, New Jersey extended the vote to unmarried women who met the property qualification (although this right was rescinded in 1807). Few revolutionaries were willing to go this far. Conservatives such as John Adams argued to exclude from full participation in government those whom they deemed "too little acquainted with public Affairs to form a Right Judgment," not only women but poor men as well. Unprepared to accept the full implications of revolutionary thought, they wanted to maintain old inequalities.

Although American revolutionaries were not prepared to let women vote, except in New Jersey, they began to expand their views about women's intellectual and political capabilities in other ways. The state laws that confiscated Loyalists' property, for example, often presumed that married women were capable of making their own political choices. This notion was a radical break with the past, which had always asserted that married women in particular had no political will separate from their husbands.

It was this idea that the Revolution challenged, that women had no independent minds and could not be expected to think for themselves. The Enlightenment belief that all human beings were endowed with the capacity to reason and that all differences were the product of environment led to significant improvements in women's education in the decades just after the war. Reformers, many of them women, argued that if women appeared ignorant or inca-

Liberty Displaying the Arts and Sciences. So powerful was the revolutionary idea of human equality that many came to believe in the liberating potential of education for both women and blacks.

pable, it was only because of their inferior education. Massachusetts writer Judith Sargent (Stevens) Murray asked, "Will it be said that the judgment of a male of two years old, is more sage than that of a female's of the same age?"

Enlightenment ideas about women's intellectual abilities meshed neatly with republican ideas about the need for virtue and liberal ideas about the necessity of consent. If the fate of the nation depended upon the character of its citizens, then both men and women should be able to choose as their partners intelligent, upright patriots. Likewise, the Revolution's rejection of arbitrary power accelerated a trend that had begun before the war, a belief that people should choose their own marriage partners and marry for love rather than for crass material interest. If women were to be able to make such choices wisely, then they must be educated well.

Yet once again the revolutionary impulse had its limits. Discussions about women's citizenship and intellectual capacities implicitly applied only to prosperous white women. Moreover, almost no one advocated professional education or even knowledge for its own sake for women. Overly intellectual women were ridiculed as "women of masculine minds." The family was still the bedrock of the nation, and women's education was supposed to make them better wives and better mothers, to enable them to perform their domestic roles better, not to challenge them.

The ideas of the Revolution presented a powerful challenge to the subordination of women, one that the revolutionary generation was only partially prepared to meet. Women were recognized as intelligent beings who could make important choices in the market, about their families, and even about their political loyalties. They were partial citizens, and in their halfway citizenship they revealed the limits of revolutionary doctrines of equality.

The Challenge of Slavery

No institution in America received a greater challenge from the egalitarian ideals of the Revolution than slavery. White revolutionaries and slaves both recognized the inconsistency between revolutionary ideals and the institution of human slavery. The world's first antislavery movement began in America before the Revolution with the Pennsylvania Quaker John Woolman, who in 1754 condemned slavery in humanitarian and religious terms. Within a few years of Woolman's first critique of slavery, political radicals in the North and South both recognized that the institution was inconsistent with the ideals of freedom that they were beginning to espouse. This realization is striking evidence of the profound radicalism of revolutionary thought.

African-American slaves immediately saw that the Revolution offered opportunities for freedom. The combination of egalitarian ideas and wartime disruption enabled thousands of slaves to claim their freedom. Some used a combination of Christian and revolutionary principles of liberty to petition for "the natural rights and privileges of freeborn men." Others fought for their liberty, some by joining the revolutionary forces and even more by taking advantage of British offers of freedom to slaves who deserted their masters.

Even more slaves ran away, especially in areas occupied by the British or torn by war. Thomas Jefferson estimated that in 1781, 30,000 slaves left their masters. In South Carolina, one-fourth of the slave population disappeared, while Georgia lost about two-thirds. Runaway rates were also high in the region around New York and New Jersey.

This combination of revolutionary ideals of freedom and African-American activism presented a significant challenge to white Americans, and they were able to meet it in part. Every state north of Delaware eliminated slavery. Some states did it in their constitutions, and others passed gradual emancipation laws. In Massachusetts, courts ruled slavery a violation of the state's new constitution, declaring "there can be no such thing as perpetual servitude of a rational creature." Although slavery was not entirely eliminated from New York and New Jersey until just before the Civil War, these states freed perhaps as many as 40,000 slaves. In addition, the Northwest Ordinance of 1787 prohibited slavery in the Northwest Territory (the future states of Ohio, Indiana, Illinois, Michigan, and Wisconsin). In the states of the upper South (Virginia, Maryland, and Delaware) legislatures passed

laws making it easier to emancipate slaves. Like many of the slaves who ran away during the Revolution, many of the freed slaves made their way to cities like New York and Philadelphia, creating substantial communities of free blacks, one of the Revolution's most dramatic social consequences.

If slavery was eliminated in the North and questioned in the upper South, it still survived in every state south of New Jersey, even in the absence of a coherent or positive defense. Revolutionary ideals of freedom made slaveholders uncomfortable with the institution. Unwilling to eliminate it, they offered excuses, instead of a justification for the institution. They protested that abolishing slavery was just too difficult, or that it was too inconvenient to live without slaves. Slavery was an enormously powerful institution, with African-American slaves making up 22 percent of the nation's population at the end of the Revolution, the highest proportion of both slaves and African Americans in the population at any time in American history. The wealth of the South rested upon slavery. Historians still debate vigorously whether the inroads revolutionary thought made against slavery, under these circumstances, were one of the Revolution's greatest successes—or whether its inability to curtail the institution was its greatest failure.

A New Policy in the West

The new nation faced a major challenge in the West. It had to devise a policy that would be consistent with its political economy. The old model for colonies that had been established by Britain, France, and Spain would no longer work. As these nations had appropriated new lands, they had created colonies that were permanently politically subordinated to the mother country. Moreover, because all of these empires were created in the age of mercantilism, the colonies were subordinated economically as well; their role was to provide raw materials and to purchase finished products. When the United States revolted against the British Empire, it rejected these models for organizing an empire. But how would it organize the new territory acquired through the war? There was at the time no useful model for an expanding, democratic nation, one that would enable new territories and their citizens to become equal members of the new nation.

The Indians' Revolution

At the beginning of the Revolution, most Indians tried to stay out of the conflict. They regarded it as a fight among Englishmen that did not concern them. At the end of the war, all Indians were losers, as land-hungry Americans poured into the region beyond the Appalachians, space that had been the homeland of Indians who fought against the revolutionaries and with them, as well.

By 1776, both the British and the Americans were recruiting Indians into their causes, fearing that if they did not the other side would. Within a few years Indians all along the frontier had been drawn into the struggle, most often on the British side. Not only were these Indians fearful of American encroachments onto their land, but they found that only the British were able to provide the customary "presents" that cemented alliances. Indians struck at American communities all along the frontier. American settlements in the Wyoming and Susquehanna Valleys in Pennsylvania were completely destroyed by parties of Indians and British soldiers, making refugees of the survivors. By 1782, Shawnees and other Ohio Indians had killed 860 settlers in the Bluegrass region of the new settlement of Kentucky (see Map 7-6).

In retaliation for the Wyoming and Susquehanna attacks, Washington ordered General John Sullivan to accomplish "the total destruction and devastation" of Iroquois settlements in New York and western Pennsylvania and the capture of "as many prisoners of every age and sex as possible." In the fall of 1778, Sullivan's expedition burned down forty Iroquois towns, 160,000 bushels of corn, and all the crops that were ready for harvest. As some soldiers systematically chopped down orchards, others plundered Indian graves and skinned corpses to make boots. Such brutality understandably undermined American efforts to keep Indian allies.

The End of the Middle Ground

The end of the Revolution brought neither peace nor order. The Indians who had won victories on the frontier in the waning years of the war were amazed when word came that the British had surrendered and turned over all of the Indians' land to the Americans. Needing land for settlers more than it needed diplomatic allies, the United States soon abandoned the "middle ground" (see chapter 2). No longer able to play one group of Europeans against another, Indian tribes had little leverage left.

Western Indians soon found themselves in the midst of a competition among whites for their land. Congress wanted to establish a national claim to Indian lands so it could sell them to pay off the war debt, while New York, Pennsylvania, North Carolina, and Virginia all attempted to seize land that lay within their borders. Speculators moved in too, knowing that they could sell subdivided plots to land-hungry settlers at an immense profit. At the end of the Revolution, one-third of the men in western Pennsylvania were landless; they believed that the Revolution's promise of equality entitled them to cheap land. Some of the poorest settlers did not wait to purchase land

from state or national governments or wealthy speculators. Instead, they poured across the Appalachians into Kentucky and Ohio, even as the Revolution was being fought, squatting on Indian-owned lands.

Those who had already lived on the frontier and both suffered from and inflicted frontier violence maintained a visceral hatred of Indians, sometimes advocating their extermination. George Rogers Clark, an American Army officer who led the fight against the British in Kentucky during the Revolution, once commented that he would like to see all Indians eliminated, and "for his part he would never spare Man woman or child of them on whom he could lay his hands." These settlers expected government to secure frontier lands for them and to protect them from the Indians who still believed it was theirs. They met widespread resistance from Indians who refused to surrender their land without a fight. Both Congress and the states moved quickly to force Indians, some of whom had no authority to speak for their tribes, to sign treaties ceding their land.

Such treaties (fifteen were signed between 1784 and 1796) were close to meaningless. Indians refused to honor any agreements made under duress and that did not include the customary exchange of gifts and wampum belts, while the states would not recognize another state's claims or those of the national government. Indian leaders who attempted to rally their communities were encouraged by the British and the Spanish, both of whom hoped that the new American nation would fail. The Mohawk leader Joseph Brant (the brother of Sir William Johnson's common-law wife Molly Brant) took his followers to Ontario, where they were welcomed by the British. Alexander McGillivray united the Creeks and secured military support from the Spanish in Florida. Years of struggle ensued, and it was not until well into the nineteenth century that American claims to Indian land east of the Mississippi were secured and Indian resistance was put down.

Settling the West

Establishing effective government in the West was one of the biggest problems that the new nation faced. Many of the frontier regions (in particular Kentucky and the area north of the Ohio River, as well as portions of Vermont and Maine) were claimed by competing groups of speculators from different states. Although the Articles of Confederation gave Congress very limited powers of government in the West, it soon became clear that some sort of effective national policy was necessary. Guerilla warfare had broken out between competing groups of speculators both in Vermont and in Pennsylvania's Wyoming Valley. Many of the new settlers were resentful of all authority and were receptive to separatist movements. In the years just

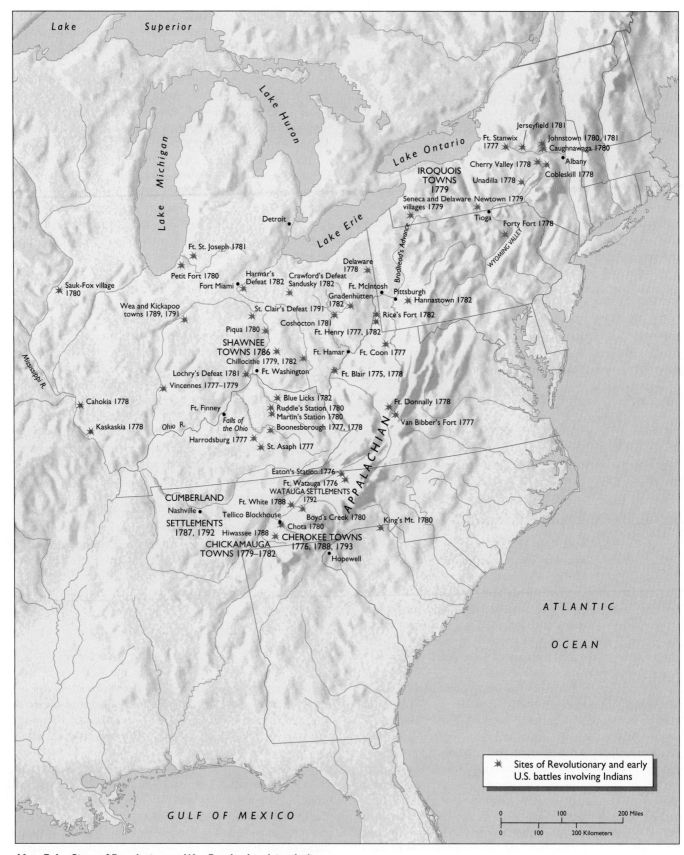

Map 7-6   Sites of Revolutionary War Battles Involving Indians.

Indians were active participants in the Revolution, fighting on both sides and making the West a significant site of conflict.

Source: Wilcomb Washburn, *Handbook of North American Indians (Washington, D.C.: Smithsonian, 1988)*, p.115.

After the Revolution, the Mohawk leader Joseph Brant took his followers into exile in Canada.

after the Revolution, groups of dissident settlers in New York, Pennsylvania, Kentucky (then part of Virginia), and Tennessee (then part of North Carolina) all hatched plans to create their own states.

Both state governments and nationalists in Congress believed that the union was in peril. Yet it was very difficult to reach a compromise among the competing interests. Those states with significant western claims (Massachusetts, Connecticut, New York, Virginia, North Carolina, and Georgia) wanted Congress to recognize their claims and protect them from interlopers, while those states without any western lands wanted all of the western lands to be turned over to Congress. Also at issue was which speculators' land claims would be upheld. In several regions, groups of speculators with dubious claims to the land—secured, for instance, by plying cooperative Indians with liquor—were selling it to settlers at bargain prices. These were the men who were fomenting separatist movements, fearful that state legislatures would invalidate their claims.

The Northwest Ordinance, ratified by Congress on July 13, 1787, was a compromise among these competing interests. Finally realizing that they could not manage vast areas of territory, the large states yielded their claims to Congress. Virginia insisted, however, that dubious

claims by private speculators must not be validated. The losers in the compromise were unscrupulous speculators, as well as the unfortunate people who had obtained land from them at cheap prices. Congress, however, was willing to tolerate respectable speculators, gentlemen who bought directly from Congress. The Land Ordinance of 1785, upon which the Northwest Ordinance was built, set out a system for surveying and selling the Northwest Territory (see Map 7-7).

The Northwest Ordinance did more than resolve jurisdictional disputes among the states and claims among speculators: It set out a model of government for the western territories, one that reflected the liberal political philosophy of nationalists in Congress, and established a process for the admission of new states into the nation on "an equal footing with the original States, in all respects whatever." This was a clear rejection of Britain's colonial model of territorial expansion. Territories would be eligible to apply for statehood once they had 60,000 free inhabitants. There were other important breaks with the past as well. Slavery was now forbidden north of the Ohio River; this was the first time in America that a line had been drawn saying that henceforth no slaves could be taken into a particular region. There was also a provision forbidding any laws that impaired contracts. Trial by jury and *habeas corpus* were guaranteed as well as the right to bail. Cruel and unusual punishments were barred. The first article guaranteed freedom of religion. These were such important principles that, except for the provision excluding slavery, they would all appear again in the Constitution and Bill of Rights.

The Northwest Ordinance was designed to create an orderly world of middle-class farmers who obeyed the law, paid their debts, worshiped as they pleased, and were protected from despotic government and the unruly poor. The ordinance represented the triumph of the moderate revolutionaries' vision of government.

Creating a New National Government

At the beginning of the Revolution, radicals and moderates had been able to work together to accomplish their common goals. With Britain's oppressive government right before them, almost everyone had agreed that a strongly centralized government was not simply unnecessary, but also downright dangerous. The years of war, however, slowly pulled the radicals and moderates apart. During this period, many of the moderates, particularly those who served in Congress or as officers in the Continental Army, became nationalists. They had worked with

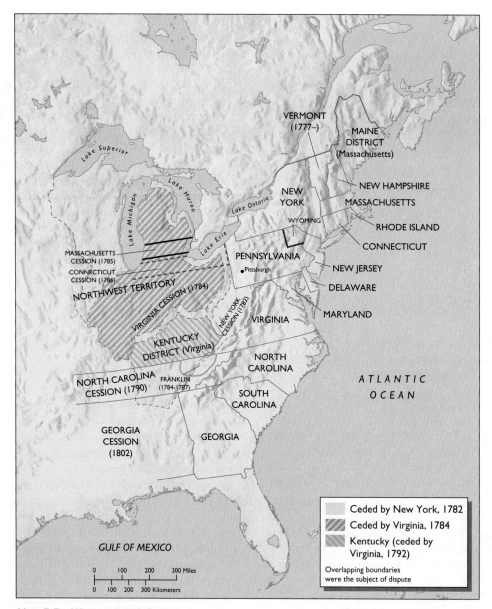

Map 7-7 Western Land Cessions.
Between 1782 and 1802, eastern states ceded to the national government the territory they claimed in the west. Under the principle established by the Northwest Ordinance, new states were carved out of this territory. Never before had a nation developed such a procedure for bringing in new regions not as colonies but as fully equal states.

men from other states on national projects, and they had come to think of the states as a threat to the success of the Revolution. States refused to pay their share of the war costs or provide supplies for the Army, and states passed laws for the relief of debtors. Many of the radicals, meanwhile, retained a local perspective. Still influenced by republican political thought, they continued to fear a centralized government, and they were afraid that the Continental Army would become a standing army that might take away their liberties. Their sympathies remained with the poor farmers and ordinary craftsmen,

and they criticized as "aristocrats" those nationalists who wanted a stronger central government.

This split between moderate nationalists and radical localists culminated in the battle over the Constitution, written by the nationalists to create a stronger central government and resisted by the localists who feared that it would subvert liberty. This conflict was not simply about political beliefs; it also represented a profound disagreement about the future of the American political economy. The nationalists were deeply involved in the market economy, as merchants, as financiers, as farmers and planters who wished to sell abroad or even to regional markets. The localists, as a rule, were much less involved in the market and very suspicious of those who were. As long as taxes were low and their creditors did not harass them to pay their debts, they were satisfied. From their perspective, the Articles of Confederation provided all the national government and national economy that was needed.

A Crippled Congress

It soon became evident to nationalists in Congress that the national government was almost powerless to address the most pressing questions, almost all of which concerned the economy. Congress tried its best to grapple with these problems, eventually pushing them back upon the states, which were equally ill-suited for the task. By 1779 Congress had already printed $200,000,000 worth of paper money whose value was dropping by the day, and it had shut down its printing presses. It then told the states that it was their responsibility to provision the Army. State legislatures, however, dithered while the Army went unclothed and unfed. By the time the war was finished, the unpaid Army was threatening mutiny. Congress gave up on trying to pay its war debt and passed that back to the states as well. Some states refused or were unable, leaving their portion of the debt unpaid. States such as Massachusetts that raised taxes in order to pay off their portion faced armed upheavals such as Shays' Rebellion.

Congress was powerless to alleviate the economic distress. At the end of the war, British goods flooded into a nation that had been starved for them, and consumer demand seemed insatiable. There was no comparable British demand for American farm products or other exports. In fact, Britain closed off its ports to American trade. In theory, America should have retaliated by closing its ports to British ships and then letting the two nations' diplomats work out a compromise, but the Articles of Confederation denied Congress and its diplomats the authority to regulate interstate or foreign commerce. Each state was on its own, designing a set of competing commercial regulations. Additional foreign loans, which had kept the nation afloat during the Revolution, were out of the question. Congress could not pay back the loans it had already taken out from France and Spain, and by 1786, it was about to default on the loans it had received from Holland as well.

Even western policy, the area of Congress' greatest triumph, presented problems. The states had ceded western territory to Congress because they recognized their lack of resources to manage such vast tracts of land. Yet once those lands came under Congress' jurisdiction (leading to the passage of the Northwest Ordinance), Congress discovered what the British government had learned at the end of the French and Indian War: It takes an army and a great deal of money to police a territory inhabited by Indians and cov-

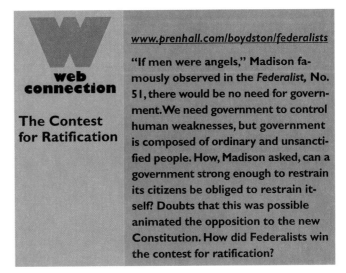

web connection

The Contest for Ratification

www.prenhall.com/boydston/federalists

"If men were angels," Madison famously observed in the *Federalist*, No. 51, there would be no need for government. We need government to control human weaknesses, but government is composed of ordinary and unsanctified people. How, Madison asked, can a government strong enough to restrain its citizens be obliged to restrain itself? Doubts that this was possible animated the opposition to the new Constitution. How did Federalists win the contest for ratification?

eted by land-hungry settlers. Congress did not have that money, and it could not even pay the army that it had. Worse, the British were still occupying a string of forts in the Northwest Territory because the United States had not yet complied with the provision in the Treaty of Paris that guaranteed Loyalists and other Britons the right to collect debts contracted before the war. Congress had no power to compel the states to make their citizens honor those debts; it could only recommend that they do so.

By the beginning of the 1780s, nationalists were attempting to strengthen Congress, but these attempts at reform failed, as they could not gain the approval of the states. By the middle of the decade, several of the boldest nationalists had decided that reform was not only impossible but undesirable. They were convinced that a new and stronger form of government should be created. Alexander Hamilton had been contemplating this issue since the early 1780s. When James Madison returned to Virginia at the end of 1783 (a victim of term limits, having served the maximum of three consecutive years in Congress), he began an exhaustive study of history to learn what he could about the principles of effective government. Other nationalists began talking about calling a constitutional convention. But the challenge they faced was how to effect changes that the states themselves did not seem to want.

The road that led to the Constitutional Convention in Philadelphia in 1787 ran through two smaller meetings that were called earlier to address questions of trade. Their larger agenda was to create a groundswell for a convention at which nationalists could create a new and stronger form of national government. First, in 1785, at Madison's suggestion, commissioners from Virginia and Maryland met at Washington's home, Mount Vernon, to resolve disputes about navigating the Potomac. Madison suggested a further meeting of representatives from all the states in

Annapolis, Maryland, to build upon the accomplishments at Mount Vernon. When only twelve men, representing just five states, arrived for the three-day meeting, they issued a call for another meeting, in Philadelphia, nine months later. In those nine months, Shays' Rebellion and the continued stalemate in Congress persuaded nationalists in seven other states that strengthening the national government should at least be considered. So, over the summer of 1787, 55 men from twelve states met in Philadelphia to write one of the most influential documents in the history of the world.

Writing a New Constitution

The men who assembled in Philadelphia were primarily moderate nationalists. It is a measure of their commitment to the goals of the Revolution that they did not turn their backs on self-government and democratic principles but rather sought, in James Madison's words, "republican remedies" for the problems of republican government. The 55 delegates met for almost four months during the summer of 1787, finally ratifying the federal Constitution on September 17. They conducted their deliberations in secret; this privacy enabled them to talk freely and achieve compromises. Hence, the shutters to the 40 foot × 40 foot room were closed and nailed shut, and precautions were taken to make sure that the talkative Benjamin Franklin did not spill any secrets to his friends and acquaintances. The heat and stench of human sweat in the room must have been almost unbearable. Although there were sharp differences of opinion on specific issues, there were wide areas of agreement. Most of the delegates had considerable experience in state and national government. George Washington came as a member of Virginia's delegation. He was the most widely respected man in the nation, and his presence reassured skeptics. He was elected the presiding officer of the convention.

Although veterans such as Washington gave the convention as much tradition as America could muster at that point, collectively the delegates were an amazingly young group, with most in their thirties and forties. Although among the best-educated and most thoughtful men in their nation, they were really provincials, the leaders of a small upstart nation on the western edge of the Atlantic. No one played a more important role in the convention than James Madison, who had just turned 36.

Madison came to the Constitutional Convention with a design for the new government already worked out. Known as the Virginia Plan, it was presented by Edmund Randolph of Virginia on May 29, four days after the proceedings began. It was the outline from which the Constitution was created. The most heated debates were between the small states, which feared being overwhelmed, and larger ones, which wanted fair representation for their constituents; and between the slave and nonslave states. With most of the delegates believing in the need for a federal constitution, the greatest challenge was to find grounds for compromise that would leave each state believing that it had struck the best bargain it could.

The Virginia Plan was clearly a blueprint for radical and substantial change. Although the delegates made numerous changes, they preserved many of its elements: a strong central government divided into three branches, executive, legislative (itself with two branches), and judicial, that would check and balance one another; a system of federalism that guaranteed every state a republican government; and proposals for admitting new states and amending the Constitution. The only alternative, the New Jersey plan, offered on June 15, was rejected three days later. This was the idea of the small states, which were worried that if representation in both houses was based upon population, then they would be at a disadvantage. The New Jersey Plan proposed a single-house legislature, with all states having an equal vote, and also a plural executive, chosen by the legislature (see Table 7-1).

The delegates were in basic agreement that the new national government would have to be much stronger. Consequently, there was relatively little debate about most of the new powers that the delegates gave Congress in Article I, Section 8 of the Constitution. Congress would now have the power to collect taxes and duties, to pay the country's debts, to regulate foreign commerce, and to raise armies and pay for them. Once the delegates compromised on a method for choosing the president (by electors chosen in each state) and the length of his term (four years, eligible for re-election), they readily agreed to grant him considerable powers. The president could propose legislation, veto bills of Congress (subject to congressional override), conduct diplomacy, and command the armed forces. The delegates vested judicial authority in the Supreme Court and inferior federal courts and granted them authority over the state constitutions as well. The Constitution left a number of issues, as well as the structure of the federal court system, up to subsequent Congresses and the courts themselves.

Although the delegates were able to reach agreement rather easily on the structure and powers of the new government, they argued bitterly, and with revealing candor, any time the interests of their states seemed in jeopardy. The most difficult issues related to the question of representation: Would the numbers of senators and representatives be based upon population or wealth, or would each state have equal numbers? If based on population or wealth, would slaves be counted, either as people or as property? Large states generally wanted representation to be based upon either population or wealth, (they had more of both), while northern states did not want slaves to be counted, either as population or as property (wealth). The conflict between the large and small states was resolved by Roger Sherman's Connecticut (or Great) Compromise.

TABLE 7-1

	Articles of Confederation	Virginia Plan	New Jersey Plan	Constitution
Executive	None	Chosen by Congress	Plural; chosen by Congress	President chosen by electoral college
Congress	One house; one vote per state	Two houses	One house	Two houses
Judiciary	None	Yes	Yes	Yes
Federalism	Limited; each state retains full sovereignty	Yes; Congress can veto state laws	Yes; acts of Congress the "supreme law of the states"	Yes; Constitution the "supreme law of the land"; states guaranteed a republican form of government; Supreme Court to adjudicate disputes between states
Powers of Congress	Conduct diplomacy and wage war; cannot levy taxes or raise army	All powers of Articles of Confederation, plus power to make laws for nation	All powers of Articles of Confederation, plus power to regulate commerce and make states pay taxes	Numerous powers, such as levy taxes, declare war, raise army, regulate commerce, and "make all laws which shall be necessary and proper" for carrying out those powers

Key Provisions of the Articles of Confederation, the Virginia Plan, the New Jersey Plan, and the Constitution

Each state would have an equal number of senators, satisfying the small states. And the number of representatives would be based upon either population or wealth, satisfying the large states.

The Connecticut Compromise solved the conflict between small and large states, but only by creating another between slave and free states. The South Carolinians were adamant. Whether slavery was called population or wealth, the institution must be protected. The argument was fierce, with several delegates threatening to walk out. Finally the convention compromised. Representation in the House would be based upon the entire free population (including women and children, but not Indians) plus three-fifths of the slaves, thus increasing the South's representation by 20 percent and providing it with additional political "security." The delegates recognized that the Three-Fifths Compromise was fundamentally illogical, but only when it had been accepted could the delegates agree to the Connecticut Compromise. The Three-Fifths Clause was the foundation that made the Connecticut Compromise possible.

The Three-Fifths Clause became the most notorious provision in the Constitution. Although the delegates were careful not to use the word "slave" anywhere in the Constitution (instead using bland phrases such as "other persons"), clearly they were establishing a racial line. The Convention made two other concessions to slavery. First,

it agreed that Congress could not ban the slave trade until 1808 at the earliest. Interestingly, this debate split the South, with representatives of the upper South speaking against slavery and delegates from the lower South insisting that their region could not "do without slaves." In addition, the Constitution included a fugitive slave clause, which required states to return runaway slaves.

The nationalists were determined not to leave Philadelphia until they had a constitution. They were willing to enter into whatever compromises seemed necessary in order to gain the consent of their fellow delegates. Despite occasional impasses and heated debates, those compromises were achieved, and the convention adjourned on September 17. The delegates' work was not over, however. Now the Constitution had to be ratified.

Ratifying the Constitution: Politics

There was nothing inevitable about the nation, the Constitution, or the particular form either would take. That the Constitution would be ratified was by no means a given. The sense of nationhood at the time was very weak, while the attachment to states was quite strong. The Constitution was the creation of a small group of men who thought nationally. The Federalists, as these advocates of a federal government are known, had the difficult task of getting the

Constitution ratified by a nation that still thought about government in almost wholly local terms.

The Philadelphia Convention decided that the Constitution would go into effect once nine states, rather than all of them, had ratified it. Of course, they could not bind any states that had not ratified, but the nine signatories could go ahead. Then, in another clever strategic decision, the convention sent the Constitution back to Congress, asking *it* to send it along to the state legislatures, requesting them to convene ratifying conventions.

One of the ironies of the ratifying process was that after all the small-states/big-states debate in the Convention, small states were the first to ratify. These states were the ones that most needed the union. For example, Georgia, the fourth state to ratify, was still in many ways a frontier region, vulnerable to Indian assault; its capital at Augusta was an armed camp, ringed by a wooden palisade. The most serious opposition came from the large, powerful states of Massachusetts, New York, and Virginia, which were closer to being capable of surviving without a union.

The convention had concluded on September 17, and by December 7, Delaware had already ratified the Constitution. By January 9, 1788, New Jersey, Georgia, and Connecticut had ratified it, with barely any dispute. The Federalists in Pennsylvania forced ratification by using strong-arm tactics. The Federalists in other states learned from these mistakes and more willingly made concessions to their Antifederalist opponents.

The next state to meet was Massachusetts, where, as in Pennsylvania, there was considerable opposition from the western part of the state, among those sympathetic to Shays' Rebellion. In an inspired move that would be used also in Virginia, the Federalists were able to make certain that the Constitution was debated section by section, en-

abling the better-informed Federalists to win, point by point. And in another critical strategic decision, the Federalists agreed that the convention in Massachusetts should propose amendments. Equally important was the form that these amendments would take, not as a condition for ratification, but as part of a package that recommended ratification. This concession, which ultimately made the Constitution both stronger and more democratic, was critical in winning ratification.

Only three more states were necessary for the Constitution to go into effect. The more politically adept Federalists postponed or stalled the debate until those states that were more favorable to the Constitution had ratified it. The Virginia ratifying convention was one of the most dramatic, with leaders of the Revolution divided over the issue. Patrick Henry, who had refused to attend the Philadelphia Convention, saying that he "smelt a rat," spoke in opposition. Each of Henry's impassioned speeches was rebutted by James Madison's careful and knowledgeable remarks. Having worn down the Antifederalists (as the opponents of the Constitution were called) with logic, the Federalists carried the day, and the Constitution was ratified. As in Massachusetts, the Antifederalists agreed to abide by the result, even though there had earlier been threats of armed rebellion. The decision of Antifederalists to accept the Constitution and to participate in the government it created was one of the most important choices made in this era.

In New York, the Federalists stalled the debate until news of Virginia's ratification. Then they posed the inevitable question. The Constitution had been ratified, and would New York join in or not? Even then, the vote was close. Once nine states ratified the Constitution, it went into effect. Eventually it was ratified by all the states. As a condition for ratification, several states had insisted that the first Congress consider a number of amendments. These amendments became the Bill of Rights.

Ratifying the Constitution: Ideas

Even the Federalists did not understand exactly what kind of government they had created until they finished their work and had to explain it to the public. The final document was the product of many compromises, and it did not precisely fit anyone's previous ideas. As the Federalists had to explain the benefits of the Constitution in terms that would make sense to skeptical Americans, and as the Antifederalists tried to explain what they thought was wrong with the Constitution, a new understanding of what American government should be was crafted. Although there were still significant disagreements, particularly about the shape of the American political economy, this new understanding (which incorporated the Bill of Rights) was sufficiently broad that Antifederalists could accept

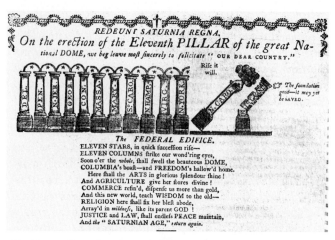

This Progress Toward Ratification. When New York ratified the Constitution in June 1788, it became the eleventh "pillar" of the new republic.

their defeat and join the new government by running for office and hoping to shape the government from within.

Nonetheless, the differences between the Federalists and Antifederalists were profound. As a rule, the Antifederalists were more rural and less involved in the market than the Federalists. They generally came from the western or backwoods regions in contrast to the eastern and urban Federalists, and they were more likely to be veterans of the militia than of the Continental Army. The Antifederalists were, above all, old-line republicans, who continued to use the language of corruption, tyranny, and enslavement to discuss government, although now it was the Federalists, not the British government, who appeared to present the danger to liberty.

The Antifederalists were localists who believed passionately in the local community. They continued to assert that republics could survive only in homogeneous, organic communities, where all people had the same interests and values. They believed that too much diversity, whether economic, cultural, ethnic, or religious, destroyed a republic. One Massachusetts Antifederalist criticized the Constitution because it would not allow states to cut off the flow of immigrants so as "to keep their blood pure." Although Antifederalists generally, like Federalists, supported freedom of religion, they also favored the spread of Protestantism as a means for assuring morality.

At the same time, the Antifederalists were committed to individual rights, and it is to them that the nation is indebted for the Bill of Rights. They retained the republican fear of power, especially if it were remote. They did not trust the person they could not see. If government were remote, then it would become oppressive. It would deprive the people of their liberties, and it would tax them. One of the most consistent complaints of the Antifederalists was not so much that taxation would be enacted without representation as that it would be enacted at all. Patrick Henry was passionate on this issue. If the national government needed money, let it ask the states for it (although this was the same system that had been tried and had failed under the Articles of Confederation). "If money be the vitals to Congress, is it not precious for those individuals from whom it is to be taken? Must I give my soul—my lungs, to Congress. Congress must have our souls. . . . I tell you, they shall not have the soul of Virginia." The Antifederalists turned against the new government out of the same fear of centralized government and hatred of taxation that had led them to revolt against Britain. The Antifederalist contribution to American political thought was a continuing critique of government itself.

Federalists shared many of the beliefs of the Antifederalists. In fact, had there not been significant overlap, there would have been no Revolution and no Constitution. Like the Antifederalists, the Federalists were firmly committed to the rights of individuals, which was why they so readily accepted the Antifederalist proposal to list and protect those rights as amendments to the Constitution. The second area of overlap was a suspicion of government. Most Federalists still agreed with Paine that "government even in its best state is but a necessary evil." The **separation of powers** and elaborate series of checks and balances that the Constitution created, as well as the system of federalism itself, reflects their fear of unchecked government. The Federalists divided power; unlike the Antifederalists, they did not deny it.

Their experience in the market economy of the eighteenth century, as officers in the Continental Army, and as members of the national government during the Revolution provided the Federalists with a different perspective on political economy. They had come to believe that all people were motivated by self-interest. While the Antifederalists hoped to reform people out of their self-interest, the Federalists were willing to accept self-interest and build a government around it.

The experience of the 1780s had convinced the Federalists that no government could rest itself entirely upon the virtue of its people. The challenge was to construct a government out of imperfect human materials that would preserve liberty instead of destroying it. In *The Federalist* No. 10 (one of a series of 85 essays written by Madison, Hamilton, and John Jay and published anonymously in New York newspapers to influence the ratification debates in that state), Madison explained how the new Constitution would work. He noted that the causes of conflict "are sown into the nature of man." The only way of eliminating them would be either by "giving to every citizen the same opinions, the same passions, and the same interests" (the Antifederalist solution) or by destroying liberty itself. But "as long as the reason of man continues fallible, and he is at liberty to exercise it, different opinions will be formed." Toleration was the price of liberty and the necessary result of human imperfection.

The debate between the Federalists and Antifederalists completed the Constitution. In the Philadelphia Convention, the Federalists had been so intent upon working out compromises and reconciling their own states' competing interests that they had not had time to develop a philosophy to explain the profound changes they were proposing. That philosophy emerged from the ratification debates, where it was met by an alternate philosophy, drawing heavily from republican thought, crafted by the Antifederalists. Both these bodies of thought, sometimes in harmony, sometimes in deep disagreement, constitute the legacy of the Revolution. This dialogue has continued to frame American government from their day until ours.

CHRONOLOGY

1775	Battles of Lexington and Concord
	Fort Ticonderoga seized
	Battle of Breed's Hill
	Second Continental Congress convenes
	Continental Army created, with George Washington in charge
	Congress adopts "Declaration of the Causes and Necessities of Taking up Arms"
	George III declares colonists in rebellion
	Governor Dunmore offers freedom to Virginia slaves who fight for the British
	Continental Army attacks Canada
1776	Thomas Paine writes *Common Sense*
	Declaration of Independence
	Articles of Confederation drafted
	British capture Manhattan
	Washington captures Trenton and Princeton
	New Jersey Constitution allows unmarried, property-owning women to vote
	Washington captures Princeton
1777	British capture Philadelphia
	American victory at Saratoga
1778	French enter into treaty with United States
	British conquer Georgia
	Sullivan expedition into New York and Pennsylvania
1779	Continental troops winter at Jockey Hollow
1780	British conquer South Carolina
1781	Articles of Confederation ratified
	Battle of Guilford Court House
	Cornwallis surrenders
1782	Franklin begins peace discussions with British
1783	Newburgh Conspiracy
	Treaty of Paris
1785	Land Ordinance of 1785
	Virginia and Maryland commissioners meet at Mt. Vernon
1786–1787	Shays' Rebellion
	Meeting at Annapolis
1787	Northwest Ordinance
	Constitutional Convention
1787–1788	Federalist Papers published
	Constitution ratified

Conclusion

With the ratification of the Constitution, the United States entered a new phase of its history. In rejecting the increasingly centralized British state, the revolutionaries were clear about what they did not want. Over the course of the Revolution, they began to envision the kind of society and kind of nation that they hoped to create. It would assure individual liberty and economic opportunity. But this was a vague vision for the future. As the first modern nation created by revolution, the United States was entering uncharted territory. The United States weathered the crises of the revolutionary era. Winning independence from the world's most powerful nation, ratifying the federal Constitution, and planning for the admission of new territories into the federal union were all extraordinary accomplishments, unique in world history.

Yet there were many problems left unresolved, some of which were barely grasped at the time. Not only was Britain still occupying forts in the Northwest Territory, but the European nations were skeptical that the new nation would survive. Although the United States had more than doubled its size, much of the new territory could not be settled because it was still inhabited by Indians who refused to recognize America's sovereignty. There were disagreements among the Americans themselves, particularly about political economy. How could a nation founded on the principle of liberty practice slavery? How would individual rights be reconciled with the general welfare? Whose economic interests would be served? The American people had embarked upon a great experiment whose outcome was far from assured.

Review Questions

1. Why was revolutionary ardor highest at the beginning of the war? What were American and British expectations in 1775? Why was independence not declared for another year?

2. What were American and British strategies for winning the war? What were the chief challenges the Americans faced in mounting the war, and how did they affect military strategy? What were the constraints upon the British in waging a war on American soil?

3. What was the effect of the war on American society? What challenges did the war present, and how were these challenges met?

4. Which Americans believed a stronger central government was necessary, and what did they do to create it? What were the compromises they made in writing the Constitution? How did they secure its ratification? What political strategies did they use, and how did they attempt to persuade other Americans? Why did the Antifederalists oppose the Constitution, and why were they defeated?

Further Readings

David Brion Davis, *The Problem of Slavery in the Age of Revolution, 1770–1823* (1975). A brilliant analysis that places the first debates about slavery in America in the context of the first worldwide abolition movement.

Linda K. Kerber, *Women of the Republic: Intellect and Ideology in Revolutionary America* (1980). Demonstrates the centrality of gender to revolutionary ideology and the importance of revolutionary ideology in thinking about gender.

Adrienne Koch, ed., *Notes of Debates in the Federal Convention of 1787 Reported by James Madison* (1987). A remarkable record, which shows history being created as a roomful of men attempted to reconcile principal and interest in the writing of the Constitution.

Jack N. Rakove, *Original Meanings: Politics and Ideas in the Making of the Constitution* (1996). A new and compelling account of the writing of the Constitution.

Charles Royster, *A Revolutionary People at War: The Continental Army and American Character, 1775–1783* (1979). A dazzling and beautifully written analysis of conflict between ideology and military necessity in the winning of the Revolution.

John Shy, *A People Numerous and Armed: Reflections on the Military Struggle for American Independence* (1990). A provocative series of essays that places the war for American independence in the wider context of military history.

Gordon S. Wood, *The Creation of the American Republic, 1776–1787* (1969). One of the most important books ever written on the American Revolution, it makes a powerful case for a profound change in the way some Americans thought about the nature and purpose of government over the course of the Revolution.

History on the Internet

"The History Place American Revolution"

http://www.historyplace.com/unitedstates/revolution/index.html

This website provides a chronology of the American Revolution that is linked to copies of full text documents such as the Articles of Confederation, the Declaration of Independence, and Thomas Paine's *Common Sense.* It also contains a portrait gallery featuring paintings of revolutionary actors.

"Essays on the Revolution"

http://revolution.h-net.msu.edu

Under the icon "essays," discover numerous scholarly articles that discuss the negotiation and controversy over the U. S. Constitution.

"Chronicling the Revolution"

www.pbs.org/ktca/liberty/chronicle/related-topics.html

This site addresses a wide range of topics concerning the American Revolution, including songs of the revolutionaries, details of women's and Native Americans' involvement, and revolutionary events that took place in the urban landscape.

8

THE EXPERIMENT UNDERTAKEN

1789-1800

OUTLINE

Washington's Inauguration

Conceptions of Political Economy in the New Republic

Labor, Property, and Independence

The Status of Slaves, Women, and Native Americans

Factions and Order in the New Government

The States and the Bill of Rights

Congress Begins Its Work

Political Economy and Political Parties

Making a Civic Culture

A State and Its Boundaries

The Problem of Authority in the Backcountry

Taking the Land: Washington's Indian Policy

Western Lands and Eastern Politics: The Whiskey Rebellion

America in the Transatlantic Community

Between France and England

To the Brink of War

The Administration of John Adams

Conclusion

Washington's Inauguration

The procession assembled on Cherry Street just after noon on April 30, 1789. Slowly, it wound through lower New York City, down Queen and Great-Dock Streets to Broad and then on to the Federal State House, where the new U. S. Congress had been meeting since the beginning of the month. At the head of the file came the military guard, almost 500 men strong, including horse artillery, grenadiers, light infantry, and an entire company of Scottish Highland bagpipers. The formal escort committees of the new Senate and the new House of Representatives came next, followed by local officials, merchants, wealthy artisans, and other "gentlemen of distinction." At their heels pressed an eager crowd of on-lookers.

In the middle of it all, dressed in a simple brown cloth suit and (according to some) markedly ill-at-ease, was the man they had come to see: the president-elect of the United States of America, George Washington.

As the procession approached its destination, the military escort divided into two columns, forming a corridor through which Washington, the official committees of Congress, and a small group of special guests entered Federal Hall. After a few moments, during which the president-elect was formally introduced to the full assembled houses of Congress, Washington stepped out onto the gallery overlooking Broad Street. There, in the presence of Congress and a now-hushed "multitude of citizens," he took the oath of office prescribed by the Constitution of the United States.

The silence was abruptly shattered. "Long Live George Washington!" someone shouted. As thirteen cannons boomed a salute, the entire crowd took up the cry. "LONG LIVE GEORGE WASHINGTON!" they chanted, over and over, in the loudest ovation, one reporter claimed, "that love and veneration ever inspired." That evening brilliant fireworks lighted the harbor sky, and the houses of the French and Spanish ministers were dazzlingly illuminated in celebration. Parties, official and spontaneous, went on deep into the night.

For George Washington, April 30, 1789, was a day of sober reflection. At every stop along his journey to New York, he had been feted as none before him, with banquets, toasts, parades, pageants, and military reviews. Nevertheless, as he later wrote, every step of the way he had felt like a culprit skulking to his punishment. Quieting the crowd, his first words after taking the oath of office were to confess that "Among all the vicissitudes incident to life, no event could have filled me with greater anxieties" than the news that he had been elected president of the United States. The "magnitude and difficulty of the trust" humbled him. "The preservation of the sacred fire of liberty, and the destiny of the republican model of government," he said simply, "are justly considered as deeply, perhaps as finally, staked on the experiment entrusted to the hands of the American people."

Washington's anxiety was well-founded. Even as he took office, the new nation was beset with problems. The requisite nine states had ratified the Constitution, but not without serious reservations. Many of the representatives gathering in New York believed that the government's first order of business ought to be amending the document that had brought it into existence. In the major cities, large groups of craftsmen put on elaborate parades, ostensibly to celebrate the inauguration, but also to remind politicians that their success depended as much on the nation's artisans as on its wealthy merchants. Farmers also complained that rich eastern elites sought to dominate the new government. In the territories, would-be settlers and large proprietors fought with each other over rights to the land, even as both groups occupied Native American homelands and howled for national intervention when the Indians struck back. On the edges of the nation, France, Spain, and especially Great Britain bade their time until the republic faltered.

These were the immediate problems, but they implied larger, long-term challenges for the nation. The "experiment," as Washington had astutely observed, was entrusted to the American people, not simply to their government. But who were "the American people"? Were free women included? Were "the people" only the nation's partisans, or did the experiment somehow include political critics, newcomers, disfranchised inhabitants, slaves and even the Native Americans from whose lands the nation was constructed? In his inaugural address, Washington asserted that an "indissoluble" correspondence existed between the ends of an orderly government and the "characteristic rights of freemen" in a republic. But what were those rights? What types of institutions and political safeguards were necessary to protect those rights, and what type of society and economy could produce citizens willing and able to insist upon such a government? The new Constitution structured a government and recognized the general importance of certain social and economic values, but it left most of these larger questions unresolved. For good and for ill, sometimes nobly, sometimes not, in the turmoil of time Americans would answer those questions and constantly revise their answers.

In the meantime, Washington found himself equipped with a handful of advisors (some of whom, like Jefferson, were not yet in the country), the ragtag remnants of an army, no judiciary system, a Congress that was still straggling into town, a staggering war debt, and his personal reputation. Before the end of Washington's first term, the backcountry careened near civil war and competing philosophies of government and visions of political economy gelled into bitterly antagonistic political parties. By the end of his second term, one foreign war had been narrowly averted and another loomed on the horizon. ∎

This rendering of Washington's reception by the ladies at Trenton, New Jersey, en route to his inauguration, suggests both Washington's great personal popularity and the way in which political themes were often depicted in terms of gender. Here, women approach Washington in a supplicatory manner, while men observe from horseback or standing.

KEY TOPICS

- The relationship of property and citizenship in the new republic
- The sources of conflict in the new government
- The impact of land hunger on Indian policy
- Hamilton's policies as secretary of the Treasury
- The dilemmas of international neutrality
- The first American party system

Conceptions of Political Economy in the New Republic

Most free Americans believed that the success of the republic depended ultimately on the political virtue of its citizens. By **political virtue,** they meant the essential characteristics of good republican citizens, characteristics they associated with economic life. When people grew too wealthy and accustomed to luxury, many Americans believed, they grew lazy and domineering and were willing to support corrupt governments for their own selfish purposes. Poverty, on the other hand (as the example of European urban mobs taught), led to desperation, riots, and anarchy. The question was, what kind of economic life supported a middle course, encouraging both personal ambition and an abiding interest in the common good? What kinds of work, what kinds of property, and what levels of commerce expressed the balance of interests that seemed so necessary to the success of the republic?

Labor, Property, and Independence

The answers that individual Americans gave to these questions tended to reflect the circumstances and aspirations of their own lives. In 1790, 97 percent of free Americans lived in nuclear households (parents and children) on farms or in rural villages, where they depended on access to the land to produce much of their own food and many of their own clothes, tools, and furnishings. Only five percent of the free population lived in cities (see Table 8-1). Most of those rented their dwellings and depended on wages or sales for a substantial part of their living. A tiny fraction made up the large merchant families and great landed proprietors whose livelihoods depended on extensive and elaborate commercial transactions.

For most citizens, then, republican virtue was rooted in the land, and particularly in the land as transformed into a working farm. This rural way of life fostered an emphasis on the private ownership of property and on an ideal of personal labor and self-reliance. In *Letters from an American Farmer* (1782), J. Hector St. John de Crevecoeur had identified the new nation as "a people of cultivators scattered over an immense territory . . . animated with the spirit of an industry that is unfettered and unrestrained, because each person works for himself." Jefferson had echoed this view in his *Notes on the State of Virginia* (1785). "Those who labor in the earth are the chosen people of God, if ever he had a chosen people, whose breasts He has made His peculiar deposit for substantial and genuine virtue," Jefferson had declared. "Corruption of morals . . . is the mark set on those, who, not looking up to heaven, to their own soil and industry, as does the husbandman, for their subsistence, depend for it on casualties

TABLE 8-1

Americans in 1790					
Population 1790: 3,929,000					
Northeast		**Northcentral**		**South**	
Whites	1,901,000	Whites	50,000	Whites	1,271,000
African Americans	67,000	African Americans	1,000	African Americans	690,000
Urban	160,000	Urban	0	Urban	42,000
Rural	1,807,000	Rural	51,000	Rural	1,919,000
Free African Americans	58,000				
African-American Slaves	700,000				

In 1789, most Americans lived in the countryside and considered farming the activity most likely to produce political virtue in the new republic. As this illustration suggests, by "farming" Americans meant not simple subsistence, but a division of the land into cultivated, privately owned (and at least partly commercial) property.

and caprice of customers." Farming allowed one to feed, clothe, and house one's self, and therefore to remain free of the whims and corruptions of an employer or master.

The ideal of self-sufficiency resided not simply in the labor of farming, but more specifically in *owning* the property one farmed. As Hudson Valley land proprietor William Cooper insisted, the farmer who worked someone else's land "is unable to soar above the idea of perpetual poverty" to seize "the bright view of independence." The ownership of land not only enabled people to achieve self-sufficiency in the present, but it also opened the prospect of self-sufficiency for future generations, enlivening the spirit and encouraging ambition.

This emphasis on labor and the private ownership of land did not mean that rural Americans disparaged all forms of manufacturing and trade. Although (as author Samuel Goodrich later recalled of his rural Connecticut boyhood) "every family lived as much as possible within itself," most rural households were tied to villages where farming families bought, sold, and bartered among themselves and with independent craftspeople for what they could not produce. The Goodrich family (which grew much of its own food and made "its own bread . . . soap, candles, butter, cheese, [and] cloth") traded in a general store and hired the services of a butcher, a shoemaker, a carpenter, a seamstress, and a spinner, among others. In the backcountry village of Hallowell (in the later state of

Maine), neighbors depended on midwife Martha Ballard to birth their children and on her husband to survey their land and saw their trees into lumber. Even Jefferson, far away to the south, who loathed the "workshops" of Europe, conceded that "carpenters, masons, smiths" were essential to an agrarian way of life.

American citizens embraced international as well as local commerce as a component of republican political economy. Jefferson considered overseas trade essential to rural virtue, because it gave Americans access to manufactured goods without having to bear the scourge of industrialization. Especially in the late 1780s, as trade with Britain began to improve and European demand for American agricultural products climbed, rural Americans grew convinced that the success of the new nation required a booming free international commerce (see Figure 8-1). In 1791, Americans exported more than $7,500,000 worth of grain to Europe, more than $4,000,000 worth of tobacco, and more than $1,250,000 worth of lumber, all of them products of the countryside (see Table 8-2).

Even though most farmers viewed commerce and profit making as honorable elements of a good republican economy, they were suspicious of the vast revenues enjoyed by some large merchants and landowners. This suspicion had many origins. Many of the great landed proprietors and large merchants had laid the foundations of their fortunes before the Revolution, and with

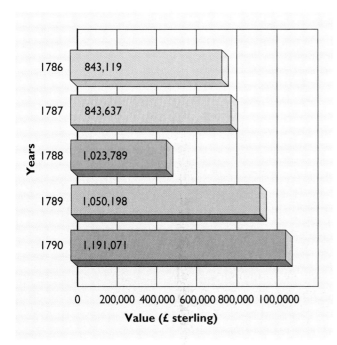

Figure 8-1   *Revival of Exports to Great Britain.*
Source: Douglass C. North, The Economic Growth of the United States, 1790–1860 (New York, 1961), p. 19.

TABLE 8-2

Principal Exports from the United States, 1791	
Commodity	**Value**
Grain, meals, bread	$7,649,887
Tobacco	4,349,567
Rice	1,753,796
Wood	1,263,534
Salted fish	941,696
Pot- and pear ash	839,093
Salted meats	599,130
Indigo	537,379

Source: Curtis P. Nettels, The Emergence of a National Economy, 1775–1815 (White Plains, NY: 1962), p. 221.

the help of the Crown. In the years after the war, the revival of the American re-export trade (foreign goods carried by American ships through American ports but destined for sale elsewhere) created a windfall for merchants without doing much to help country producers or city laborers. In Boston, the wealthy merchant families who made up 10 percent of the population controlled 65 percent of the wealth of the city, while the poorest one-third of the population owned less than one percent of the wealth.

Now, at the birth of the republic, urban elites continued to exert an iron grip on the rural economy. Through trade and loans, eastern merchants controlled lines of credit that extended far into the countryside. Great proprietors controlled the most precious commodity of the countryside, land. They hired surveyors to stake their claims, they often refused to sell homesteads in favor of charging high rents that kept small farmers economically dependent, and they sent out the sheriff to throw squatters off the land. Both large landowners and merchants tended to support strong governments, which meant higher taxes.

Farmers, small shopkeepers, landless settlers, and craftworkers saw these sources of income ("rents, money at interest, salaries, and fees") as the moral equivalent of theft. "Labor is the sole parent of all property," Massachusetts farmer and tavern keeper William Manning argued in 1799. "The land yieldeth nothing without it, and there is no food, clothing, shelter, vessel, or any necessary of life but what costs labor." For most rural Americans (and many urban workers as well), the act of labor was the central act of independence and the only authentic claim to the ownership of physical property. "[N]o person can possess property without laboring," Manning emphasized, "unless he get it by force or craft, fraud or fortune, out of the earnings of others." Rabble-rouser and backcountry preacher Samuel Ely complained that common folks like him were being "persecuted . . . by a systematic junto of luxurious sons [and] patentee land jobbers . . . who are striveing [sic] to be independent Lords in a glorious Republic." "Instead of applying themselves to labor," the wealthy proprietors were "continually prowling for the hard earnings" of someone else's "industry," stolen in the form of high rents and taxes. Rural philosophers like Ely and Manning viewed this distinction between "those that labor for a living and those who get one without laboring—or, as they are generally termed, the Few and the Many"—as "the great dividing line" of society.

Unsurprisingly, the "independent Lords" saw matters differently. Merchants and landed proprietors agreed with farmers, planters, and squatters that republican virtue resided in labor, but they meant commercial labor, labor that opened markets and expanded trade. It was commerce, they believed, especially large-scale commerce, that nurtured ambition and daring, taught discipline, and contributed genuinely new wealth to the community as a whole. In their eyes, subsistence labor scarcely counted as labor at all.

Alexander Hamilton, the first secretary of the Treasury of the new nation, was a chief proponent of this view. Born in the West Indies, he was raised by his mother Rachel, a shopkeeper, who died when he was 13. Alexander then entered the merchant firm of Beekman and Cruger as a clerk, eventually proving himself so valuable that Cruger raised the money to send him to New York for a college education. These experiences taught Hamilton that it was the merchant class (traders, investors, and financiers who risked their private means to generate new

GROWING UP IN AMERICA

Sally Brant

By 1794, George Washington's government had moved from New York City to Philadelphia, the first permanent capital of the United States. While the president tried to quiet conflict within his own cabinet and remained alert to the potential for disorder on the northwestern frontier, Philadelphians Henry and Elizabeth Drinker (members of the city's merchant class) worried about the lack of discipline and social authority in the young republic. In 1794, the Drinkers' concerns focused on young Sally Brant, one of several teenagers indentured as a maid to their household.

The practice of indenturing remained common in the early United States. Poor families indentured children to wealthier households as a means of supporting them and as a way of providing them with occupational training. (Masters and mistresses were supposed to provide indentured servants with a skill.) Municipal authorities occasionally imposed indentures on individuals they considered unruly, using it especially as a way of controlling free black Americans.

The circumstances under which Sally Brant had been indentured to the Drinkers at age ten are unclear. What is clear is that by the summer of 1794 Sally was exhibiting an independence of spirit her employers considered utterly unacceptable for a person of her sex, station, and age.

That summer, like virtually every other summer, Elizabeth Drinker adjourned with her household staff and children to the Drinkers' country estate, fleeing from the heat and recurrent fevers of the city. Henry commuted back and forth between the city and the country as business permitted. Sally's responsibilities were not onerous. Some days she helped make jelly, mend socks, or bake breads and puddings. Other days she turned the hay in the barn or weeded the garden. In her off-hours, she was free to relax with the family or to walk to the nearby rural village of Miles Town.

It was in August that Elizabeth Drinker first began to suspect that her "little maid" was pregnant. "Tis possible I may be mistaken," Drinker wrote in her diary, "'tho I greatly fear the reverse." A few days later, Drinker's fears were confirmed.

For Elizabeth and Henry Drinker, Sally's pregnancy was a "melancholy occasion," but (much to the Drinkers' dismay) Sally herself remained "as full of Glee, as if nothing ail'd her."

Elizabeth Drinker was confounded that "a girl brought up from her 10th year, with the care and kindness that SB has experienced from our family, could be so thoughtless and hardened."

Sally may have been disguising her true feelings, or she may in fact have been less distressed by the pregnancy than were her employers. Much to the alarm of the new nation's more staid citizens, the economic and social disruption of war and the heady atmosphere of liberty had eroded older constraints on social behavior. These developments were especially visible among the young urban laboring classes in a soaring premarital pregnancy rate. For young women, this new liberty was double-edged. On the one hand, it signaled a growing independence from paternal households and constant supervision. On the other hand, few young women were able to provide themselves with a secure livelihood. Premarital pregnancies may have reflected their poverty and recourse to casual prostitution for economic survival, as well as their new-claimed autonomy. Meanwhile climbing premarital pregnancy rates earned poor women the special censure of wealthier citizens.

Sally's child was born, a month premature and jaundiced, in December, by which time the Drinker household was back in Philadelphia. Fulfilling what they saw as their responsibility for the period of indentures, Henry and Elizabeth kept Brant on their staff, but they remained displeased with her apparent lack of remorse. "S.B. very well, and in rather too good spirits, everything considered," Elizabeth Drinker complained to her diary on December 23, 1794. When Sally named her daughter Hannah, Elizabeth Drinker unilaterally "disapprov[e]d it, and chang'd it to Catharine Clearfield." Although angry, Brant was in no position to contravene Drinker's assertion of authority. Poor, female, and indentured, Brant could not raise Hannah herself, and her mother had already refused to take the child. Elizabeth Drinker's diary suggests that she and her husband placed the baby out in an institution or private home, where Sally seldom saw her. On July 1, 1795, Hannah died, an event that Sally did not learn about until four days later. Sally Brant remained in the Drinker household for another year after the death of her child. In mid-June, 1796, her indentures up, she left, disappearing from the historical record.

wealth, new markets, and new ideas) who best embodied the qualities needed in republican citizens and whose interests should be encouraged by a republican government. Hamilton agreed with William Manning that there would always be a "division of [society] into the few & the many" and that these divisions would represent the creditors and the debtors. Unlike Manning, Hamilton saw this division as desirable in a "community where industry is encouraged," because the emergence of a creditor class would signal the existence of the commercial energy on which the republic depended.

Just as farmers viewed merchants and financiers with distrust, so wealthy merchants and proprietors often regarded Americans of the middling and laboring ranks as their inferiors. The mass of the people were undisciplined and gullible, Hamilton believed, "reasoning, rather than reasonable." Vulnerable to the deceptions of fanatics and demagogues, they required proper leadership. George Washington held similar views. "I am sure," he observed, "the mass of Citizens in the United States mean well—and I firmly believe they will always act well whenever they can obtain a right understanding of matters. . . ." But giving them that right understanding was the responsibility of their betters.

Large merchants and great proprietors were especially contemptuous of their backcountry compatriots, whom they tagged "yahoos" and "clodpoles." In the eyes of more affluent citizens, the rude huts of homesteaders, their barefoot children, and their diets of beans, potatoes, and coarse bread all signaled not the hardships of settlement, but rather the laziness of the settlers, who, one agent concluded, wanted "to gain much by little labor." Proprietors were particularly impatient with squatters' disregard of legal formalities and their constant complaints about rents and taxes.

The merchants and proprietors also disliked the casualness with which country people (including more prosperous farmers, craft workers, and shopkeepers) treated debt. Rural people conducted trade in a combination of barter, cash, and promissory notes. Accounts ran on for years, now tipping one way, now the other, with payments constantly renegotiated in terms of the goods, services, or whatever paper money might be at hand. As their creditors (suppliers, landlords, and mortgage holders), merchants and proprietors could not tolerate such arrangements. They needed timely payment, preferably in hard currency, to pay off their own debts, make new investments, or arrange with long-distance business partners for new shipments.

The Status of Slaves, Women, and Native Americans

In his comments on the virtue of farming, Thomas Jefferson had observed that "Dependence begets subservience and venality, suffocates the germ of virtue, and prepares fit

tools for the design of ambition." At the republic's founding, nevertheless, most of its inhabitants (slaves, married free women, children) were legal "dependents" who owned neither their own labor nor the products of that labor. Moreover, most citizens viewed Native Americans, who inhabited the territories and large parts of many states, as incapable of the industry required for republican virtue.

Slavery was a thriving institution in the United States in 1789. Of a population of 3.9 million, an estimated 700,000 (or roughly 18 percent) of the inhabitants of the new nation were enslaved. In large areas of Virginia and South Carolina, slaves made up at least half of the population. Moreover, although slavery was a predominantly southern institution, it was not yet unique to the South (see Map 8-1). In 1789 northerners still owned more than 30,000 slaves and many northern merchants remained active in the overseas slave trade. In addition, many shippers, merchants, and artisans in the North relied on business ties to the South.

White Americans did not deny that slaves could, and should, labor, but most white Americans did deny that hard work produced republican virtue in slaves. They argued that since slaves could not own the property they

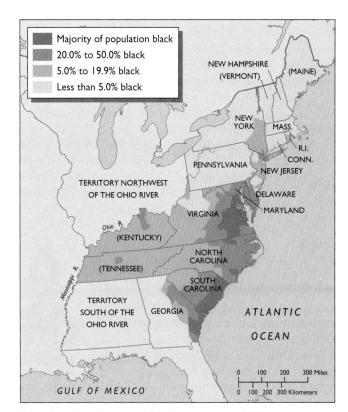

Map 8-1 Distribution of Black Population, 1775.
At the founding of the nation, the overwhelming majority of African Americans lived in the South and were enslaved. In parts of the south Atlantic states, African Americans had long outnumbered whites. (Future states are here identified in parentheses.)
Source: Lester J. Cappon et al., eds., Atlas of Early American History: The Revolutionary Era, 1760-1790 (Princeton: Princeton University Press).

produced, slaves' labor could never lead to the self-reliance or the stake in the public order essential to citizenship. Indeed, slaves were themselves property, symbols of the independence and stake in society of other Americans.

This view was rife with contradictions. As Thomas Jefferson, himself a slaveowner, pointed out in *Notes on the State of Virginia,* it was the ambition of slave owners that was most undermined by slavery. "[I]n a warm climate, no man will labor for himself who can make another labor for him," Jefferson wrote. "This is so true, that of the proprietors of slaves a very small proportion indeed are ever seen to labor." Even more fundamentally, if slaves were incapable of virtue, not on the basis of their character, but simply because of their status as slaves, then surely the institution of slavery was itself unrepublican.

For years, white Americans had blurred the differences between the legal restrictions on slaves and the character of the people enslaved, suggesting that it was something in the character of African Americans (rather than something in the attitudes of white citizens) that excluded slaves from the rights of citizenship. Even Jefferson, who noted the corrosive effects of slavery on slaveowners, pronounced African Americans (free or enslaved) inferior to whites in reason and incapable of independent, purposeful enterprise. "It is not their condition...," Jefferson insisted, "but nature, which has produced the distinction."

By 1789, many northerners had come to oppose the institution of slavery. Vermont banned it outright in its 1777 state constitution, and the Massachusetts Supreme Court ruled in the early 1780s that slavery was contrary to its state constitution. In the 1780s, Pennsylvania, Connecticut, and Rhode Island all instituted measures for gradual abolition. Free property-owning African-American males enjoyed the right to vote in some northern states in the first years of the republic.

Even in the North, however, slavery died slowly. New York did not pass an emancipation act until 1799 (permitting slavery to exist in the state in some form until 1827), and New Jersey did not officially act against slavery until 1804. Meanwhile, regional opposition to slavery was not strong enough to prevent northern states from ratifying a constitution that permitted slavery elsewhere in the nation and protected the international slave trade until 1808. In 1793, Congress passed a national Fugitive Slave Act, requiring that Americans everywhere return escaped slaves to their owners.

For most white northerners, moreover, opposition to the institution of slavery did not amount to a belief in the equality of African Americans, free or enslaved. White New Yorkers objected to what they perceived as a "deluge" of free African Americans into the city from the South and complained that free African Americans were "flippant" and did not know their place. All across the northern states, white craftsmen refused to work in shops that employed free African Americans, white passengers refused to ride in stagecoaches alongside them, and landlords refused to rent them any but the worst housing.

Scattered early antislavery societies challenged these attitudes and behaviors. To illustrate "the genius, capacity and talents of our ill fated black brethren," the Pennsylvania Society for the Abolition of Slavery published profiles of African Americans of exceptional ability, like the "African calculator" Thomas Fuller, a Virginia slave who solved difficult mathematical problems in his head in a matter of seconds. Society members charged that the institution of slavery constituted "an atrocious debasement of human nature." A 1789 petition signed by society president Benjamin Franklin called on Philadelphians to oppose slavery and to join to help free African Americans obtain employment and education.

Still, even many white opponents of slavery doubted that emancipated slaves could survive in American society. The anonymous author of the antislavery tract *Tyrannical Libertymen: A Discourse on Negro-Slavery in the United States* (published in New Hampshire in 1795) argued that slaves were "habituated, not to reason, but to obey" and were "not fit to be their own guides." During the transition to freedom, younger slaves should be held in "a state of dependence and discipline," the author insisted, after which they should be resettled in the territories. Older slaves should be shipped to Africa.

Although most Americans believed free white women to be citizens in some general sense, even free women labored under legal disabilities that rendered independence difficult and under social prejudices that limited or obscured that independence even when they did achieve it. Under the English common law principle of coverture, a married woman subsumed her separate legal identity under that of her husband. Although some individual women (usually wealthy women who had access to special legal measures) did own property in their own names, as a category married women could not own property or wages, could not enter into contracts, and were not the legal guardians of their own children. Thus the law simultaneously proclaimed women a dependent social class and created the conditions within which they remained that way. The abolition of primogeniture and of the practice of giving eldest sons a double portion did improve daughters' inheritance prospects, and reformed divorce laws enabled women to seek and obtain legal separations more easily. Still, most women lost control of their own property upon marriage and took little property other than their own clothing in divorce.

Legal status aside, social prejudice made it difficult for most women to earn an independent living. Women had always provided an important part of the livelihood of their households, and that contribution was even more essential in the hard economic years after the war. Rural women sold eggs, butter, cheese, herbs, and clothing items. City streets were filled with female vendors. Women opened prominent politicians, viewed women as a group as incapable of "substantial and genuine virtue" and given to timid and irrational behavior. Most late eighteenth-century writers insisted that, for women as a group (as for African Americans), these qualities were "natural" and unchangeable. "Male and female," Tom Paine had written in *Common Sense* in 1776, "are the distinctions of nature."

Somewhat contradictorily, Americans believed that the condition of women could vary. American authors of the late eighteenth century were fond of claiming that societies could be evaluated based on the status of (white) women, which reflected the progress of "civilization." This belief helped provoke a lively discussion of whether the new nation could really consider itself free and enlightened if women were excluded from the polity. The debate was punctuated in 1792 by the publication of Englishwoman Mary Wollstonecraft's controversial *Vindication of the Rights of Woman*, which was widely read in the United States. Wollstonecraft insisted that women were systematically educated to be vain and frivolous. Their inability to function as good citizens, she argued, was thus a construction of society, not an expression of their natures, and could be ended when women received a more equitable education. Also in 1792, essayist Judith Sargent (Stevens) Murray, of Gloucester, Massachusetts, began to publish a series of essays entitled "The Gleaner." Murray put women at the center of republican theory by arguing that the best model of republican citizenship was found in the relations of the family, not in the relations of government. In 1798, Philadelphian Charles Brockden Brown published *Alcuin*, a fictional dialogue between a man and woman in which Brown argued directly for female suffrage. That goal was a long way off, however. Even New Jersey, the only state originally to permit propertied females to vote (under a provision that also included property-owning free African Americans), reversed this position in 1807.

Although slaves (and, by extension, African Americans generally) and most free women were viewed as incapable of fulfilling the demands of republican citizenship, they were nonetheless perceived as a part of republican society and as important participants in the economy. In contrast, most white Americans viewed Native Americans as the quintessential outsiders to the republic, who occupied land the white settlers wanted for themselves and embodied a way of life white Americans saw as the exact opposite of the political economy required for a republic. White Americans saw Indians as "spontaneous products of nature" who survived (as Thomas Jefferson wrote to James Madison in 1787) altogether "without government" and subsisted instinctively through simple hunting and gathering. This view imagined Native Americans as naïve "noble savages," untouched creatures of the pristine wilderness. White Americans sometimes adopted this image for themselves in political conflict with authorities they considered corrupt. The marauders in the Boston Tea Party had

The frontispiece of the September, 1792, Philadelphia Lady's Magazine reflected the importance of Wollstonecraft's Vindication of the Rights of Women in the United States. Here, "The Genius of the Ladies Magazine, accompanied by the Genius of Emulation [Ambition] ... approaches Liberty, and ... presents her with a copy of the Rights of Woman."

small businesses as tavern-keepers, boardinghouse operators, and seamstresses and sought work in the needle trades, the rope yards, as day laborers, and as domestic servants, among other occupations. But the more lucrative male crafts and professions were closed to them, and most working women struggled to make ends meet.

Women also faced a broad social bias against the very idea of female autonomy. Most Americans believed woman was intended to be man's "help-mate" and dependent. Ambition in a woman was, by definition, a dishonorable quality. As the *Apollo Magazine* put it in 1795, the exemplary woman married and asked no more than that "Her good man [was] happy and her Infants clean." Many Americans, including many of the nation's most

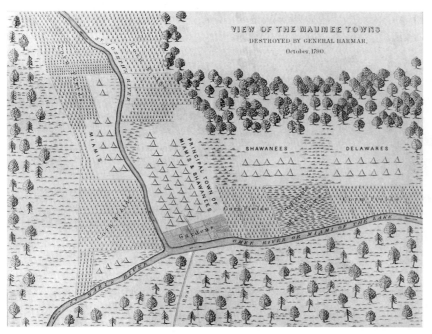

This 1790 drawing suggests the complex economic arrangement of the Maumee River Indian towns and the diverse groups that occupied the towns.

disguised themselves as Indians, and backcountry squatters dressed as Indians in their attacks on land surveyors and tax collectors. Yet, white Americans remained contemptuous of Indian economies and social practices. They pronounced Native Americans wasteful, "lazy," and hostile to "civilization" (defined as the practice of laboring regularly on privately owned property to "improve" the land and make it yield a profit).

In fact, Indians did "improve" the land (and in much the same ways that white farmers improved theirs) and did engage in commerce. The fur trade with Native Americans had provided Europeans with their first economic foothold in eastern North America, and most of the eastern Indians lived in fairly settled agricultural communities. The Indian town of Kekionga ("Miami Town") illustrated the vibrancy of Indian economies in the late eighteenth century. The most important of a string of Indian villages, Kekionga was strategically located at a crossroad of trade east of Lake Erie on the portage of the Maumee and Wabash Rivers, near a British fort. The village was surrounded by huge cornfields and luxurious vegetable gardens, supported large herds of cattle, and accommodated guests of all backgrounds and purposes. Traders and explorers mingled with soldiers, Europeans with Indians, Miamis with Shawnees, Piankashaws, Weas, Wabash, and Kickapoos, women with men, and children with adults. Residents and visitors bargained furs, tools, quills, beads, animals, food, and services. Singing, dancing, feasting, and gift giving were almost constant, as the plaintive sounds of the Indian flute co-mingled with the music of the minuet.

Contrary to Jefferson's characterization, Native Americans did live under systematic forms of governance, although those systems were generally far less centralized than the new government of the United States. Most Indian communities identified their leaders through processes of consensus, rather than through formal balloting. Councils met as needed, rather than according to a designated calendar, and policy was implemented not through a bureaucracy, but through the personal authority of leaders and the willingness of others to follow them. These systems were no less effective for being more flexible than those ratified in the new United States Constitution. Over the years, Native Americans had shared land and resources, reconciled differences, sustained elaborate and sometimes very long-distance intertribal trade relations, and supported powerful intertribal confederacies. They developed and preserved complex societies, sophisticated cultures, and highly efficient economies.

Where native people differed from Americans of European descent was not in the fact of civilization, but rather in the political economy that supported and constituted civilization. Eastern Woodland and Great Lakes Indians did not share Euro-American views on the importance of privately owned property. Although native peoples generally considered an individual's personal possessions as his or her own, and some communities prized display as an indicator of skill and status, few Indian societies valued material accumulation for its own sake. Instead, they encouraged practices of gift giving as marks of rank. Far from virtuous, white American society seemed to native people to be driven by an "insatiable avarice" that clouded the heart and distorted the mind.

Native Americans were especially offended at the European idea that the land itself could constitute property, to be bought, sold, and possessed by individuals. In 1799, American agent Benjamin Hawkins reported that the mere mention of selling land to settle a debt "excites very disagreeable emotions" among the Creeks. "I have explained the mode among civilized people, of taking property of every description, even land, to satisfy just claims," Hawkins wrote to the fur company president. "They are pleased with the mode, so far as it respects personal property, but land they say should not be touched." Indians understood that their very way of life depended on preserving the land uncolonized. As the Hallowing King of the Lower Creek village Cowetas put it in 1789: "These last strides tell us they [white settlers] never mean to let their foot rest; our lands are our life and breath; if we part with them, we part with our blood. We must fight for them."

Factions and Order in the New Government

Concerns about the political economy of the new nation focused not only on the character of citizens, but also on the character and operation of government, state and federal alike. Here, too, questions of property loomed large. In the *Federalist*, No. 10, James Madison had argued that the most common cause of internal conflict in a nation was "the various and unequal distribution of property." Madison viewed this unequal distribution of property as arising from selfish interests on the state and local level, and he recommended that one of the most important benefits of the new more-powerful central government would be its capacity "to break and control" these provincial interests. Most of the ratifying conventions had expressed just the opposite worry, however: that a strong central government would become the tool of the wealthy for personal gain.

The States and the Bill of Rights

Although they had ratified the Constitution, the state conventions had formally suggested more than 200 changes in the document, possibly to be added as a bill of rights. Many Federalists considered bills of rights superfluous lists of "aphorisms" (as Alexander Hamilton put it in *Federalist*, No. 84). If the Constitution itself did not protect liberty and property, Hamilton believed, no appended list of rights was going to help. Originally James Madison had agreed with Hamilton, but by the time he ran for and was elected to the House of Representatives, he had changed his mind. He pledged that his first priority would be to secure additional safeguards.

Within a month of Washington's inauguration, Madison set about making good on his promise. By no means did all of the state proposals deal directly with questions of property. For example, the ratifying conventions were adamant about the need for freedom of religion and freedom of the press. The proposals did, however, betray a fear that the new federal government could easily itself become a self-interested faction, seeking to amass power against the interests and freedom of individual citizens, and many of the proposed amendments rested upon assumptions that tyrannical governments sought to deprive citizens of their rightful property. To prevent this, states proposed amendments to limit the power of Congress to levy taxes and to protect the right to bear arms, the right to trial by a jury of one's peers, and the right against unreasonable search and seizure.

Madison never expected to incorporate all 200 of the proposals in a bill of rights (not even in distilled and summary form), and he never imagined that he could placate all of the groups critical of the Constitution. But he did believe that, with a few minor changes to the Constitution, moderate Antifederalists could be brought into sympathy with the new order. This goal of broadening moderate support for the Constitution guided the sifting process through which Madison arrived at a body of proposed amendments. He tended to reject proposals that altered in any essential way the structure of the central government as delineated in the Constitution. He also rejected proposals that strengthened the powers of the states at the clear expense of the federal government (proposals generally intended to stem despotism). Among the ideas eliminated, for example, were a Massachusetts proposal restricting Congress' power to tax and a Virginia proposal denying the federal government the power to maintain a standing army in times of peace. Some of these proposals had been endorsed by the great majority of the ratifying states. For example, all eight states that proposed amendments wanted to see explicit restraints on Congress' power to interfere with elections and on the federal power to tax, and many shared Virginia's concern about a standing army. None of these sentiments found their way into Madison's package of proposed amendments (although the reference to a "well-regulated Militia" in the Second Amendment and the Third Amendment's restrictions on the quartering of soldiers reflected Americans' profound mistrust of standing national armies).

The Constitution gave the federal government the power to mint currency. These two coins (front and back of a 1795 $5 piece and front and back of a 1795 $1 piece) showed early official renderings of lasting United States icons: the female figure of "liberty" and the American eagle.

Instead, Madison favored amendments that affirmed human rights in broad and abstract terms, without conveying to the states the specific power to enforce those rights. The First Amendment protected the citizens against congressional interference in freedom of religion, speech, the press, the right of assembly, and the right of petition. The Fourth Amendment protected the rights of citizens "to be secure in their persons, houses, papers, and effects, against unreasonable [government] searches and seizures." The Fifth, Sixth, Seventh, and Eighth Amendments laid down the rights of citizens accused of crimes. The Ninth and Tenth Amendments addressed rights not specifically enumerated in the Constitution. The Ninth affirmed that the Constitution's silence on a specific right of the people "shall not be construed" as a denial of that right, and the Tenth ambiguously reserved all rights not delegated to the new government "to the States respectively, or to the people."

Congress eventually sent twelve amendments to the states for ratification. Of these, two were rejected: one addressing the process for changing the compensation of Congress (finally adopted in 1992 as the Twenty-Seventh Amendment) and one covering representation. The remaining ten amendments were declared in force on December 15, 1791. On March 1, 1792, Thomas Jefferson, secretary of state, transmitted an official text of the Bill of Rights to the governors of the thirteen states.

Congress Begins Its Work

Although George Washington did not take the oath of office until April 30, his term began on March 4, 1789. By the time Washington was inaugurated, then, Congress was already in session. It had not made a promising start: only thirteen elected members of the House of Representatives and eight elected senators were on hand when the first Congress was convened in New York City, the nation's temporary capital.

Among Congress' first tasks was the problem of what the president should be called, a purely symbolic matter that revealed the balance of sensibilities in the new republic. Some members of the Senate (including Vice President John Adams, president pro tem of the Senate) thought the executive officers of the republic should have impressive titles, to demonstrate to the entire world that the new nation was "civilized." A Senate committee recommended, "His Highness the President of the United States of America, and Protector of the Liberties." But the House balked at this language, arguing that the Senate's suggestion smacked of aristocratic pretension and would only inflame the already active suspicions of much of the citizenry. Moreover, in the structure of the early republic, the House of Representatives (directly elected by voters), not the president (elected by the Electoral College), stood as the protector of the people's liberties. In the end, the House insisted simply on "The President of the United States."

Meanwhile, the Congress approved a series of official advisors to the president (the cabinet), corresponding to the departments that had existed under the Articles of Confederation. Washington's first administration reflected both his own close circle of friends and the political clout of the large states. The president was from Virginia, the most populous state (including slaves by the three-fifths calculation), as were his secretary of state, Thomas Jefferson, and his attorney general, Edmund Randolph. For his secretary of the Treasury he chose former aide-de-camp Alexander Hamilton of New York. Washington's vice president (John Adams), his secretary of war (Henry Knox), and his postmaster general (Samuel Osgood) were from Massachusetts. Knox was also Washington's former chief of artillery.

The Constitution had specified the existence of a third branch of government, a judiciary, but had not offered much of a blueprint for its structure. It provided simply that "The judicial power of the United States shall be vested in one Supreme Court, and in such inferior courts as the Congress may from time to time ordain and establish." The Constitution also gave to the federal court system power over "all cases, in law and equity, arising under this Constitution, the laws of the United States, and treaties made." Given such a wide compass, Congress might have created a federal system that virtually dominated state courts. Recalling the highhandedness of British courts toward the colonials, however, Congress was loath to place great power in the least representative branch of government. In September, Congress passed the Judiciary Act of 1789, which created a federal court system with limited power. The law established a six-person Supreme Court, required each justice to ride two circuit courts a year (a slow and cumbersome process), and created federal districts so large that they were inaccessible to most people as a vehicle of appeals. Under its first chief justice, John Jay, the Supreme Court remained a minor branch of government.

Political Economy and Political Parties

As Congress deliberated the structure of government, Secretary of the Treasury Alexander Hamilton turned to the problem of financial solvency. His recommendations to Congress concerning the fiscal operation of the new nation soon polarized views on the political economy of a republic.

The first challenge was to raise money for the current expenses of the government. Hamilton proposed that Congress place a **tariff** on imported goods and the foreign ships carrying them, a plan that might also boost American shipping and the sale of American-made goods. The Tariff Act of 1789 passed easily. In the coming years the federal government would depend on tariffs for the vast majority of its funds (see Table 8-3).

TABLE 8-3

Sources of Federal Revenue, 1790–1799

	Tariffs	Internal Taxes	Other (Inc. Sale of Public Lands)
1790–1791	$4,399,000		$ 10,000
1792	3,443,000	$209,000	17,000
1793	4,255,000	338,000	59,000
1794	4,801,000	274,000	356,000
1795	5,588,000	338,000	188,000
1796	6,568,000	475,000	1,334,000
1797	7,550,000	575,000	563,000
1798	7,106,000	644,000	150,000
1799	6,610,000	779,000	157,000

Source: Curtis P. Nettels, The Emergence of a National Economy, 1775–1815 (White Plains, NY: 1962), p. 221.

Hamilton was also eager for the United States to pay off the enormous debt left over from the American Revolution. In his January 1790 *Report on the Public Credit*, he advised that the federal government should bolster its own international standing by guaranteeing the payment of all remaining state and national debts incurred in the Revolution. Those debts existed in the form of various types of certificates—script and paper money the states and Continental Congress had used to purchase goods and services during the war. Hamilton suggested that the new national government replace all of these obligations dollar-for-dollar at face value with new federal bonds. To fund the plan, he proposed that the government sell additional bonds to create a fund whose interest could be used only to pay off the interest and principal on the debt.

Madison and Jefferson were alarmed. Most southern states had paid their debts by 1790. Federal assumption would force them to help pay northern debts as well, in effect rewarding northern states for being slow to meet their financial obligations. In addition, Hamilton's plan would amount to a bonanza for speculators who had acquired certificates at discounted value from their original owners. (It was rumored that federal legislators were hurrying to buy up the old bonds left in circulation.) On March 14, 1790, a deeply shaken Madison confided to his friend Edward Carrington, "there must be something wrong, radically & morally & politically wrong, in a system which transfers the reward from those who paid the most valuable of considerations, to those who scarcely paid any consideration

at all." Madison suggested that the government find a way to channel some of the profits to the original owners.

Although many members of Congress shared Madison's dislike of Hamilton's proposal, other issues eventually led to its passage. Southerners were also unhappy about the possibility that the nation's capital (temporarily located in New York) might be moved permanently to Philadelphia. Southerners, including Washington, hoped to locate the capital on the Potomac River in Virginia. At last representatives struck a compromise: Hamilton got his debt plan, and southerners got the nation's capital. In July Congress passed an act to move the capital temporarily to Philadelphia until a permanent capital was erected on the Potomac by 1800. In August 1790, the Assumption Act became law. The following December, Hamilton asked for a series of new taxes, including one on spirits, to generate revenue. This excise tax became law in March of 1791.

In a second *Report on the Public Credit*, Hamilton next recommended the creation of a national bank to manage these fiscal functions. In addition to its practical purposes, Hamilton saw the bank as ensuring a stable currency and enabling the government to mobilize large amounts of capital for development, two activities he considered essential to an expanding commercial economy. The bank would be chartered by Congress for a specified number of years; would collect, hold, and pay out government receipts; would hold the new federal bonds and oversee their payment; would be empowered by Congress to issue currency; and would be backed up by government bonds.

The bank proposal passed Congress, but against the opposition of Madison, Jefferson, and other Virginians

The first Bank of the United States was authorized in 1791. This stately building was erected in Philadelphia in 1795.

who viewed the bank as an extralegal structure to support the interests of merchants and financiers against "the republican interest." When Washington asked his cabinet for guidance, Jefferson advised the president to veto the bill on the grounds that the Constitution gave the federal government no expressed authority to create such an institution, a position known as **strict constructionism.** Hamilton countered that every specified power in the Constitution implied "a right to employ all the means requisite . . . to the attainment" of that power. In granting the federal government the responsibility to coin and regulate money, pass and collect taxes, pay debts, and provide for the general welfare and to "make all laws which shall be necessary and proper" to these ends, the Constitution implied the power to create a bank as a means. Jefferson and Madison argued in vain that the bank bill actually did none of these things, but instead only set a dangerous precedent for exceeding the Tenth Amendment, which reserved powers to the states and to the people. In the end, Washington accepted Hamilton's position, and on February 25, 1791, he signed the bank bill.

By the time Hamilton made his final major recommendations to Congress, the *Report on the Encouragement of Manufactures*, in which he called on the federal government to subsidize domestic manufacturing, Jefferson and Madison were convinced that the republic was being sold out to the interests of speculators and financiers. Hamilton had been using a Philadelphia newspaper, John Fenno's *Gazette of the United States* (founded in 1789), to promote his views. In October 1791, Jefferson and Madison prevailed upon their friend Philip Freneau to come to Philadelphia to establish a newspaper favorable to their position.

Almost immediately, Madison began to use Freneau's *National Gazette* to publish a series of essays in which, over the course of a year, he framed the rationale for the permanent necessity of political parties in a republic. In the *Federalist*, No. 10, Madison had acknowledged the inevitability of differing interests in a republic, but he had hoped that they could be prevented from solidifying into permanent factions. Revising that view, he now declared parties "unavoidable." There would always be schemers who placed self-interest above the good of the whole, and true republicans would always be forced to organize against them. Parties, according to Madison, did not spring into existence to express a variety of equally worthy perspectives, but rather as a struggle of the true "republican interest" against dangerous conspirators, a struggle of "good" against "evil." He identified the two groups as "Republicans" and "Anti-Republicans."

In late 1792 and early 1793, sympathizers with Jefferson and Madison became known as **Democratic Republicans,** after the Democratic Republican Societies, into which some organized themselves. The societies opposed a strong central government and vowed to maintain vigilance against the "monied interests" who threatened "liberty

and equality." The societies included some common mechanics, but most of the known members were from middling and even quite prosperous families (for example, Philadelphian Benjamin Rush, a signer of the Declaration of Independence). Nevertheless, many of the societies kept at least part of their membership secret, insisting that this was necessary to protect them against their powerful opponents. This secrecy made the societies controversial. Some observers denounced them as dangerous "self-created" organizations trying to position themselves as "intermediary guides betwixt the people and the constituted authorities." Washington blamed the societies for stirring up trouble in the backcountry and labeled their members irresponsible men who "disseminated, from an ignorance or perversion of facts, suspicions, jealousies and accusations of the whole government."

Hamilton and his supporters were no more tolerant of disagreement than were the Democratic Republicans. In the election of 1792, Hamiltonians described their opponents as "demagogues, democrats, mobocrats, non-contents, dis-contents, mal-contents, enemies to the government, hostile to the constitution, friends of anarchy, haters of good order, promoters of confusion, exciters of mobs, and sowers of sedition." Rejecting Madison's formulation, allies of Hamilton identified themselves as supporters of Washington's administration, advocates of the policies of the secretary of the treasury, or, increasingly, as **Federalists,** retaining the older designation to suggest their abiding commitment to union and the new government.

Although partisans on both sides were more than happy to assail their opponents viciously in the public press, as late as the election of 1794 most candidates for national office resisted formal party alignment, and congressional voting patterns showed little sense of "party" discipline. There were several reasons for this, including the tendency of most citizens (including many of the partisans themselves) to associate political parties with corruption and a loss of independence. One Pennsylvanian lambasted a 1792 state law establishing party slates for national elections as the work of vile "Ticket Mongers" determined to foment "intrigue, favoritism, cabal" and, perhaps worst of all, "party."

By 1796, nonetheless, the lines had become clearly drawn. The jumble of labels had sorted itself out to "Democratic Republicans" and "Federalists," and congressional voting patterns revealed a distinct tendency to vote on one side or the other.

Making a Civic Culture

Through the young parties, Americans formed and debated their views of republican government and organized their political identities as citizens of a new nation. But the process of forming a civic culture, of clarifying their ideas about who they were as a people, how they should behave as citizens, and what they should expect from their new republic, was not restricted to overtly political settings. The process occurred simultaneously in numerous other social institutions, many of which had existed, in some form, before the Revolution.

America's mushrooming press not only communicated information from place to place, but it also bridged some differences in outlook between different parts of the new nation. Fewer than 20 newspapers were published in all the British North American colonies in 1760, but by 1790 the new republic claimed 106 newspapers and more than 200 by 1800. Much of the content of these newspapers was strictly local, but editors sought to fill out their pages (and satisfy their readers) by publishing official government documents and reprinting articles from other cities and states. In the process, they created within their sheets a reading experience of the nation as a coherent whole. The addition of numerous articles reprinted from European papers about specific European nations implied a corresponding American national identity.

In addition to newspapers, Americans purchased printed sermons and tracts, magazines, and novels like Brown's *Alcuin*. The magazines carried essays, poems, dramas, anecdotes, and articles on travel and the sciences. Many of these were reprinted from European sources, but some, like Murray's "The Gleaner" series, were original attempts to envision an ideal American society. The 1790s also saw the beginnings of an indigenous fictional literature. In 1789, William Hill Brown published *The Power of Sympathy*, often considered the first genuinely American novel because some of its content was based on contemporary events in Boston. Other novelists also tried to develop distinctly American stories and themes. Actress and author Susannah Rowson's historical novel *Rachel and Reuben* (1798) imagined the lives of the fictional heirs of Columbus, and Charles Brockden Brown chose the countryside outside of Philadelphia as the setting for *Weiland* (1798), a tale of religious zealotry and the fallibility of human reason. In Connecticut, a group of poets known collectively as the Hartford Wits (Federalist in sympathy) produced a series of political satires that celebrated New England as the model for national order and self-discipline.

Regional and national news was easiest to come by in the cities, but a variety of information sources linked city to backcountry and region to region. Copies of newspapers and periodicals found their way out into the countryside and comparatively high literacy rates produced a reading audience that went beyond urban elites. Even rural political philosopher William Manning, who had less than six months of formal education in his life, described himself as "a constant reader of public newspapers." Gathered in shops, taverns, and homes, those who could not read listened as a co-worker, family member, or friend read aloud. Where papers did not reach, travelers, itinerant peddlers, and preachers served as additional conduits of information and opinion. Among the peddlers was Mason Locke "Parson" Weems, an Anglican

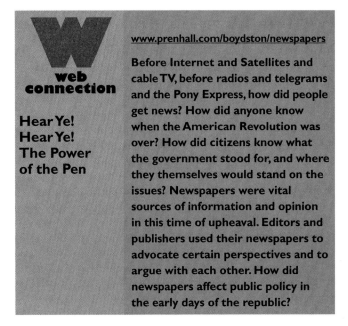

www.prenhall.com/boydston/newspapers

web connection

Hear Ye! Hear Ye! The Power of the Pen

Before Internet and Satellites and cable TV, before radios and telegrams and the Pony Express, how did people get news? How did anyone know when the American Revolution was over? How did citizens know what the government stood for, and where they themselves would stand on the issues? Newspapers were vital sources of information and opinion in this time of upheaval. Editors and publishers used their newspapers to advocate certain perspectives and to argue with each other. How did newspapers affect public policy in the early days of the republic?

minister who traveled through the countryside selling books. One of these was his own *The Life and Memorable Actions of George Washington*, into the fifth edition of which he inserted the fictional account of Washington's chopping down the cherry tree. In Virginia, peddlers organized mercantile fairs that attracted vendors from considerable distances and brought together large groups of people to swap news as well as make deals.

In cities, Americans established salons (where local luminaries gathered to discuss politics and culture), museums, libraries, and specialized societies of learning. Many of these reflected Americans' fascination with their place in the world and their keen sense of themselves as involved in a distinct historical undertaking. Charles Willson Peale's "Repository for National Curiosities" (a collection of paintings, fossils, mineral exhibitions, and preserved animals focusing on North American themes) took shape in Philadelphia in 1786 and remained popular well into the next century. In 1791, Bostonians founded the Massachusetts Historical Society, dedicated to finding and preserving the record of the new nation's past, with a particular emphasis on New England. The Philadelphia subscription library, founded in 1731 by Benjamin Franklin and others, became the *de facto* library of the new government until 1800, when the capital moved to Washington, and the Library of Congress was founded.

The early republic was also an era of school-building, primarily academies to prepare sons for professions or for university training and to prepare daughters to participate in the discussions (if not the formal electoral politics) of republican society. More than 350 academies for females opened between 1790 and 1830, most of them directed by women. The Philadelphia Young Ladies Academy, established in

Worried that the poor lacked the self-discipline to be good citizens, wealthy Philadelphians supported a public almshouse to feed and shelter the homeless, but also to reform them.

In the early years of the republic masters (presumably acting on behalf of their workers) organized associations intended to share information, lobby for favorable government policies, and protect the integrity of the craft. The members of this shop belonged to the Society of Master Sailmakers (1797).

1787, offered a complete academic curriculum. It became the model for the Litchfield (Connecticut) Academy, founded by Sarah Pierce in 1792, and the Young Ladies Academy in Boston, founded by Susanna Rowson in 1797.

Citizens also formed societies intended to provide immediate relief to the needy in their communities. A group of prosperous Philadelphians established an almshouse to improve the care and housing of the poor and to teach

them the values of industrious citizens and a new penitentiary to reform criminals by isolating them from one another's influence. African-American citizens in Philadelphia organized The Free African Society to assist destitute members of their community. During the 1793 yellow fever epidemic, members of the society volunteered their services in the deadly labor of nursing the sick, transporting bodies, and digging graves. Jewish organizations founded in New York in the late eighteenth century survived until after the War of 1812, providing aid for medical care, food, shelter, and burial costs for the city's small Jewish community.

To these associations were added a variety of occupational and manufacturing societies. Masters and journeymen formed craft associations to promote their interests. In 1791, as a means to promote his economic plans, Alexander Hamilton and his assistant secretary, Tench Coxe, formed the Society for Establishing Useful Manufacturers, a joint-stock corporation intended to demonstrate the economic virtues of investment cooperation between the private sector and the government.

The new associations proved to be instruments of continuity and of change. Through them, Americans continued to learn the everyday mechanics of self-governance. Most voluntary associations had written constitutions, held elections, and convened in regular meetings. Often organized on the basis of ethnicity, gender, or wealth, however, the societies revealed the distinctions of identity within the civic society.

A State and Its Boundaries

By transferring to the Confederation almost all of the area west of the Appalachians to the Mississippi River and south to the Gulf of Mexico, the Treaty of Paris had created not just a nation, but an empire with vast subject territories. The Northwest Territory, the region north of the Ohio River valley formed from the land cessions of Virginia, New York, and other states, was already organized for national settlement. South of the Ohio River valley were territories of more ambiguous status, where the western land claims of individual states had not yet been fully ceded in 1789 and where Spain still claimed large territories. Most white Americans viewed these lands (and the unsettled regions of the states) as the foundation of the political economy of the republic, an inexhaustible reservoir of land that would ensure propertied independence for future generations, preventing the great disparities of wealth and power that characterized European society.

But the West also posed one of the gravest challenges to the authority of the new administration.

The Problem of Authority in the Backcountry

For all of its symbolic importance as the reservoir of republican order, the backcountry had so far proven little more than a setting for constant conflict among owners and settlers and between Indians and Americans.

Americans fought over land prices and rights of ownership. Seeking quick revenue, the government sold large tracts of land to speculators and large proprietors, some of whom were luminaries of the new federal government. For example, Secretary of the Treasury Alexander Hamilton and Secretary of War Henry Knox were both silent partners in the huge Macomb Purchase in New York State, a grant of roughly 1,000 square miles fronting on the St. Lawrence River. Proprietors subdivided their tracts for sale, but the resulting prices were often too high for average settlers ("lawless fellows," according to easterners), who squatted on lands and claimed the rights of possession and improvement, much to the annoyance of the legal owners.

Despite their differences, squatters, proprietors, and governments shared the assumption that the land was theirs to fight over. The Treaty of Paris had contained no acknowledgement of Indian claims. The British had assured northern Indians that the 1768 Treaty of Fort Stanwix boundary was still in force north of the Ohio River, but the Americans, who believed that all the lands covered by the Treaty of Paris were theirs "by right of conquest," never agreed to such an interpretation. South of the Ohio River valley even the British made no pretense of protecting Indian rights. Treaty promises in the mid-1780s that southern Indians would be left in peace in exchange for large land cessions proved illusory. By the time Washington took office in 1789, the backcountries were in an uproar. Undisciplined federal troops and freebooting state militias criss-crossed western lands in search of a fight, often attacking neutral or even sympathetic Indian villages. Betrayed and angry, Indians banded together in loose confederations, retaliating against settlers and striking alliances with the British and Spanish.

By 1789, the lives and cultures of Eastern Woodland and Great Lakes nations had been deeply altered by the westward pressure of white settlement (see Map 8-2). In the

Map 8-2 Extension of United States National Territories, 1783.   *Extension of United States National Territories, 1795.*
The Treaty of Paris with Great Britain (1783) left the United States' borders with Spain (much of the western and southern boundaries) ambiguous. Those borders were clarified in the Pinckney Treaty with Spain (1795).

north, a group of Iroquoian villages, the battered remnants of a once-powerful confederation, traded large tracts of land for promises of security and called upon the great western tribes of the Northwest Territory to do the same. Having already experienced waves of white settlement and the constant arrival of dislocated eastern bands, the Shawnee, the Delaware, the Miami, the Wyandot, the Ottawa, the Potawatomi, and the Ojibwa nations absolutely refused to compromise with the whites and effectively shut down settlement north of the Ohio River valley. In the South the Creeks, trapped between oncoming white settlement and the Indian nations of the Mississippi River valley, allied with militant Cherokees to keep the Georgia, Tennessee, and Kentucky frontiers ablaze with war parties.

There were additional reasons for Washington to worry about order in the western territories (see Map 8-3). By 1789, Spain was actively luring United States settlers into New Spain at the foot of the Mississippi River, promising free land,

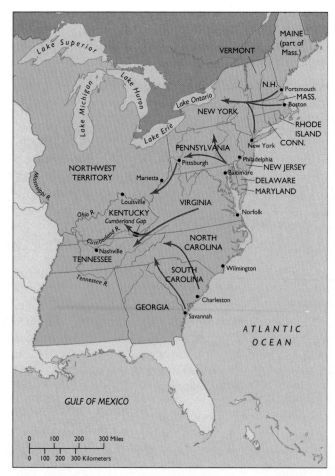

Map 8-3 Western Expansion, 1785–1805.
Between the Treaty of Paris (1783) and the Louisiana Purchase (1803), Americans flooded into the territories that lay between the Appalachians and the Mississippi River. Then (as later) migration often followed rivers and valleys into the interior of the continent.
Source: Data from Gregory Evans Dowd, A Spirited Resistance: The North American Indian Struggle for Unity, 1745–1815, p. 92.

political liberty, freedom of religion, and the use of Spanish storage and shipping facilities (closed to inhabitants of the United States). It was a strategy designed to weaken the loyalty of the West to the new United States government. In the Great Lakes region, meanwhile, Great Britain hung onto the string of forts it had promised to give up as a part of the Treaty of Paris. The United States complained that Britain used the forts to support Indians hostile to the new government. Britain countered that the United States had reneged on its treaty promises, permitting the states to harass former Loyalists and failing to pay debts owed to British subjects. Publicly, Britain assured the United States that it would meet its treaty obligations when the United States did likewise, but many Americans believed that Britain was biding its time to regain control of the lands south of the Great Lakes.

All of this turmoil took its toll in the East. The inability of the national government to control Native Americans angered states, would-be settlers, and the small business people who expected to make profits from the settlement process. Great proprietors complained that their property rights were not being protected, and small settlers complained of favoritism in land distribution. Easterners with little personal stake in the territories nevertheless viewed the behavior of the British and Spanish as threats to the integrity of the new nation. Understanding that not only external relations, but also the domestic authority of the federal government was at stake, Washington turned immediately to the problem of the backcountry. His policy was twofold. On the one hand, working with Secretary of War Henry Knox, Washington sought to bring consistency and a greater degree of fairness to Indian policy. On the other hand, he used the territories to demonstrate (and in demonstrating, to establish) the raw power of the federal government.

Taking the Land: Washington's Indian Policy

Less than a month after assuming office, Washington submitted to Congress a report on Indian affairs. Authored by Henry Knox, secretary of war in the Confederation government, the report called for substantive revisions in policy toward Native Americans. Knox argued that the United States should acknowledge a residual Indian "right in the soil" not affected by a treaty between Britain and the United States. That right could be extinguished, Knox insisted, only by some separate dealing with the Indians. Knox conceded that a military victory would accomplish this end, but he recommended that the United States instead meet its moral and legal obligation by purchasing Indian claims to the disputed lands. At Knox's suggestion, in 1789, Congress authorized the territorial governors to function as Indian superintendents and appropriated $20,000 for negotiations.

In part, Knox and Washington saw this policy shift as required by plain justice. In part, however, they were trying to avoid the expense of outfitting an expeditionary

Among the casualties in St. Clair's defeat was General Richard Butler, whose arrogance had earned him the special hatred of the Shawnees. Finding Butler wounded, Indians killed him and took his heart, leaving his body to be devoured by animals.

force necessary to take the Northwest Territory by conquest. A change in tactics did not constitute a change in ultimate goals, however. Although Knox undertook repeatedly to keep white settlers outside treaty boundaries, his policy did not recognize an ultimate right of Native Americans to refuse to negotiate. His approach wrote into American policy one of the enduring paradoxes of federal relations with Indians: the linkage of a rhetoric of negotiation with a reality of coercion.

Seeking to bolster the authority of the national government and to end the sometimes brutal involvement of individual states in Indian affairs, Knox argued that the Indian bands were not communities within state borders, but rather foreign entities, on the level of nations. Indian relations were therefore properly the business of the federal government. The impulse was toward greater consistency. In the process, however, Knox in effect declared Indians aliens on their own lands, lending the weight of federal policy to American inclinations to see the Indians as the ultimate outsiders.

By 1790 continuing troubles in the Northwest Territory convinced Washington that the federal government had to project a military presence into that region. His first two efforts were dismal failures. In 1790 a combined force of Miamis, Shawnees, Delawares, Fox, Sauk, and Ottawas led by the Miami war leader Little Turtle routed the United States Army, led by General Josiah Harmar. The next year a much smaller party of Miamis, Shawnees, Delawares, Ottawas, Chippewas, Wyandots, Mingos, Cherokees, and Potawatomis crushed the troops of territorial Governor General Arthur St. Clair (see Map 8-4). In the later encounter, more than 600

U. S. soldiers were killed, wounded, taken captive, or missing. Fewer than 500 survived unharmed. Harmar and St. Clair both resigned in disgrace, and settlers seethed at the ineptitude of the new government.

To stem the growing crisis of confidence in the new government, in 1792 Washington sought and received congressional authorization to build a "strong coercive force" (bigger, better paid, and better trained) in the Northwest Territory. To lead the army, Washington turned to a 47-year-old infantry officer noted for his aggressive tactics, his popularity with his troops, and his overwhelming vanity, Pennsylvanian Major General Anthony Wayne. By the time Wayne found the Indians in 1794 at Fallen Timbers, on the Maumee River near the west end of Lake Erie, his Army numbered more than 3,000 well-equipped and highly disciplined troops. They faced a force of only 400 warriors, weakened for battle by ritual fasting. Wayne claimed a decisive victory in the battle that followed. When escaping Indians were denied refuge in nearby British Fort Miami, the remnants of the confederacy surrendered.

According to the Treaty of Greenville, signed August 3, 1795, Indians ceded two-thirds of the later state of Ohio and a piece of present-day Indiana. In return, the Indians received annual federal payments, ranging from $1,000 to $500 per band. Paid out in lump sums to individuals for distribution, the annuities bought the United States influence within Indian communities and rendered the Indians more economically dependent on the U. S. government. In addition, the treaty tried to convert the Indians to white ideas of work and economy by offering to pay the annuities in the form of farm equipment, cows, and pigs.

Indian efforts at confederacy proved less successful in the South, where deep fractures existed within the Cherokee and Creek nations. Older leaders, wearied of constant warfare with settlers, and mixed-heritage populations, more familiar with white economic and social ways, sometimes favored accommodation over battle and entered into agreements they lacked the authority to make. At the Treaty of New York in 1790, Alexander McGillivray and twenty-three other Creek leaders agreed to exchange lands belonging to the entire Creek nation for annual payments from the federal government and promises of U. S. protection for their remaining lands in the western Carolinas and the territories beyond. A faction of the Cherokee nation entered into a similar pact at Holston in 1791.

These internal disputes weakened Indian military efforts. When the government proved unable to stem the tides of settlers flowing into the future state of Tennessee, younger Creeks, Chickamaugas, Cherokees, and Shawnees repudiated the treaties. Encouraged by events in the North, in 1792 they attacked the American community at Buchanan's Station, near Nashville, Tennessee, planning to proceed south to Nashville itself. Older Cherokee leaders, fearing reprisals, betrayed the plan, and the assault was

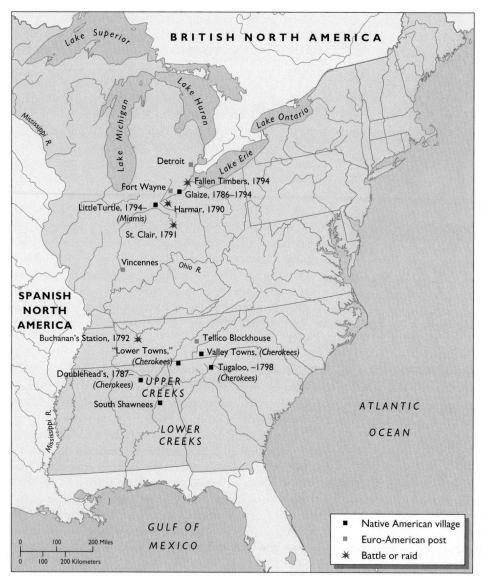

Map 8-4 *Major Indian Villages and Indian-United States Battle Sites, 1789–1800.*
During its first decade of existence, the new federal government struggled to assert control over the trans-Appalachian territories, claimed by Native Americans as their homelands and coveted by United States settlers and land speculators.

stymied, by both accommodation and loss in battle. They would be resurrected at the turn of the century by two Shawnees, already young men by the time of Wayne's victory, who watched as the confederacy came apart. One, Tenskwatawa, would later become an important prophet. The other, his half-brother, was named Tecumseh.

Western Lands and Eastern Politics: The Whiskey Rebellion

The West posed a domestic, as well as an external, threat to the authority of the federal government. By 1791 western settlers were deeply disenchanted with the seeming inability of the government to protect their interests and had fallen into the practice of simply disregarding federal policy when it did not suit their interests. In violation of federal treaties, they trespassed onto Indian lands, dispatched unorganized militias to enforce their claims, traded illegally with Indians, and simply ignored federal agents who inveighed upon them to stop these actions. In 1791, western Pennsylvanians took the step of repudiating the authority of the federal government explicitly, setting the stage for a direct confrontation between the government and its people.

The trouble began in earnest with the passage of Hamilton's excise tax (which was, ironically, intended in part to raise money to support military operations in the backcountry). Living in an area perfectly situated to function as a gateway to the Northwest Territory, residents of western Pennsylvania had long anticipated an economic bonanza from free-flowing westward migration and had long been frustrated with the failure of the government to secure safe passage into the Ohio River valley. Hamilton's tax gave their simmering anger another focus, the question of republican fairness. Many Americans regarded excise taxes (internal taxes on specific goods) as unfair in principle. This particular tax seemed targeted specifically at western farmers, who found it easier to transport their grain in liquid than in bushel form, and the tax was structured to benefit the wealthy over the humble. It was to

thrown back. Militant Creek and Chicamauga movements were further weakened by the gradual withdrawal of British and Spanish assistance, as those European nations decided it did not benefit them to add to the conflict on the U. S. borderlands. United States Indian commissioners used a series of military victories to coerce new land cessions from the southeastern nations and to insinuate white customs more deeply into Indian cultures, especially into that of the Cherokees. Threatening to withdraw federal annuities, agents forced the Cherokees to acknowledge certain jurisdictions of white courts and to create an internal police force. They also urged the Cherokees to adopt a more centralized system of government.

Resistance continued, in both the North and the South, but dreams of a pan-Indian confederation were temporarily be levied according to the capacity of the still, not its total annual output. Because big stills generally ran year-round while smaller stills operated only seasonally, the small producer was going to take a harder hit.

Popular protests had begun within months of the tax's passage, and they intensified at each new report of the Army's failure in the Northwest Territory (efforts the tax was supposed to fund). Western Pennsylvanians dug in their heels, vowing that they would not pay the tax and calling on citizens to treat the collectors with "contempt." At the high point of unrest, in July of 1794, some tax collectors were tarred and feathered.

Washington took the challenge seriously, and in August of 1794 he sent an intimidating contingent of 13,000 troops into western Pennsylvania. In the face of this show of force, the rebellion fizzled, but the government drove its point (and power) home. Remaining protestors were roughly rounded up and held in open pens exposed to the elements. Twenty men were returned to Philadelphia to face treason charges, and two were sentenced to death. Washington eventually pardoned both, but he had proven the authority of federal law in the new republic.

The citizens of western Pennsylvania were not without sympathizers, however. Most of the congressional elections of 1792 were fought as competition between the policies of Alexander Hamilton and those of the self-named "republican interest," many of whom (even if they lived in the East) identified the settlers as defenders of republican virtue, oppressed by the greed of eastern financiers. It was not the last time that the struggle for the West would reveal the divisions of the East.

America in the Transatlantic Community

Still reeling from internal conflicts, the United States was soon to be confronted by external challenges as well. On February 1, 1793, France (the sister republic of the new United States) and Spain declared war on Great Britain and Holland. Americans were divided over the proper response of the United States. Many Democratic Republicans (among them Jefferson and Madison) had been avid supporters of the French Revolution. Jefferson had spent years in France and had grown to love the people and the culture. Although the growing violence of the French Revolution had strained Franco-American relations, the Democratic Republicans viewed with horror the possibility that America might join with its former colonial master against a fellow republic. Hamiltonians, meanwhile, looked with equal disdain upon the social and political chaos of France and continued to believe that friendly relations with Great Britain best served American interests. Searching for

a middle ground, President Washington endorsed neutrality. Then, on May 16, Edmond Charles Genêt, citizen of France, arrived in Philadelphia, now the nation's capital.

Between France and England

Genêt came to America as the minister of a French republic that saw its destiny as inextricably joined to that of the United States. Not only was the United States still formally allied with France, but the American Revolution had served as the model for the French. Washington's inauguration had been followed within weeks by the storming of the Bastille, and Washington, Madison, and Hamilton had been given honorary French citizenship.

France had several hopes for the Genêt mission. The revolutionary government believed that it was the destiny of the French republic to free the oppressed people of Europe from their tyrannous monarchs. As a part of this undertaking, France was eager to incite the European colonies in the Americas to revolution, a goal Genêt's presence might help achieve. Genêt was also to press the United States for a new commercial treaty allowing French naval forces and privateers to rearm and provision themselves in American ports as they battled Great Britain on the seas. Finally, the French wished to interpret existing treaties as granting them favorable tonnage duties.

These hopes were not entirely fanciful. Many Americans had supported the early phases of the French Revolution. Impoverished as it was, the Washington administration advanced money to help the new French government, and Washington moved quickly to instruct the U. S. ambassador to France, Gouverneur Morris, to recognize the republic as the legitimate government of France. Also, many Americans would have been only too happy to see colonial rebellions throw Spain and England out of North America.

The French overestimated the lengths the American government would go to achieve that goal. Preferential treatment for French ships, either warships or commercial ships, could only strain already difficult relations between America and England. Barely able to muster a force to the Northwest, President Washington was not about to risk a foreign war. Neither was he willing to have tensions further inflamed on the nation's western borders. Washington considered Genêt's proposals reckless.

Many Americans, especially Jefferson, had welcomed Genêt warmly. As the agent of a nation that had renounced its own "executive" (the king was executed in January 1793), Genêt may have been only too ready to believe that Washington's views did not represent the sentiments of the Americans generally. Undeterred, he put into motion a series of actions that assumed essential American support for French goals. He authorized the renaming and refitting of a captured English ship, anchored in Philadelphia, which was intended for duty as a French privateer, and he encouraged efforts to organize American settlers in Kentucky to lead an attack on the Spanish.

Washington was furious. "Is the Minister of the French Republic to set the Acts of this Government at defiance, with impunity?" he fumed. "And then threaten the Executive with an appeal to the People!" It did not help Genêt's standing in Washington's eyes that the French minister had also encouraged the Democratic Republican Societies Washington so loathed. Issuing a formal Proclamation of Neutrality, Washington disavowed Genêt and in August of 1793 demanded that he be recalled. With his government quickly losing power in the onrushing events of the French Revolution, Genêt requested, and was given, asylum in the United States (probably saving him from the guillotine), but his influence was at an end. Disappointed by Washington's growing support of Federalist policies, Jefferson resigned as secretary of state in December.

To the Brink of War

Even without Genêt's provocations, by 1794 tensions with Great Britain were high. To the old issues of unsettled revolutionary war reparations and the British forts in the Northwest had been added new charges that the British Navy was harassing U. S. merchant ships. Trying to cut off France from American goods, by March the British had begun seizing American ships, cargoes, and sailors in the West Indies.

Still, Washington sought to avoid confrontation. In spite of restrictions on British ports, U. S. shipping had been steadily expanding from earnings of about $7.4 million in 1790 to almost $15 million in 1793, and from a total tonnage (of United States shipping to foreign ports) of about 355,000 in 1790 to almost 448,000 in 1793. Under these conditions, it was hard to argue that British policies were so injurious to American trading as to warrant the risk of an all-out trade war. Washington was saved from having to make that judgment by an unexpected moderation of British official policy. Hoping to take advantage of the shift, Washington dispatched Chief Justice of the Supreme Court John Jay as a special emissary to England to resolve outstanding issues between the two nations.

Although Great Britain at first had little interest in the mission, the heating up of French-British animosities eventually enabled Jay to negotiate a treaty that significantly reduced the immediate tensions between Britain and the United States. Britain agreed to open West Indies ports to U. S. ships of 70 tons or less, provided those ships' cargoes were intended for import into the United States. The two countries agreed that (except for tonnage restrictions) their ships would receive equal treatment in each other's ports and that neither country would permit prizes captured from the other to be sold in its ports. In the event of war, neither country would try to confiscate property of the other or to sequester debts. They also agreed to establish boards of arbitration to set the boundary between Canada and the United States, to address issues of compensation for U. S. merchants (hurt by British seizure of American ships), and to settle the claims of British citizens against the United States. Most important to the United States, Britain promised to evacuate its forts in the Northwest by June 1, 1796.

Most Americans did not know anything about the provisions of Jay's Treaty until after it was approved, for the Senate debated and ratified it in secret. When Democratic Republicans learned of its contents and its ratification, they were outraged. One irate essayist compared Washington to Caesar, wearing "the mask of hypocrisy" to conceal ambitions to despotism. Another critic insisted that the House of Representatives should either impeach Washington or resign themselves. Democratic Republican Societies protested the concealed character of the deliberations and objected that the treaty would benefit the merchant class while taxing everyone to pay for its provisions. Southerners were furious that merchants were to be compensated but not planters whose slaves had escaped behind British lines during the American Revolution.

But public protest soon fizzled. News of Anthony Wayne's victory against the Great Lakes tribes at the battle of Fallen Timbers overtook news of the treaty and cast its provisions for the evacuation of the British forts in a more positive light. Word followed that Thomas Pinckney had also concluded a treaty with Spain, opening the Mississippi River to U. S. navigation and permitting Americans to store goods duty-free in New Orleans. (Pinckney's Treaty also set the boundary between the United States and Florida at the 31st Parallel.) The treaty was a sign of Spanish weakness. Spain desperately needed the grain that western farmers produced and the flow of their trade through New Orleans, where shipping activity had fallen off sharply during the European wars. Seeing the United States make its peace with Britain, and fearful of an Anglo-American alliance, Spain resigned itself to the possibility of increased American encroachment across the river and sought peace with the new republic.

Taken together, Wayne's victory and Jay's and Pinckney's negotiations seemed at last to have opened the territories to settlement. Western land prices soared and the U. S. export trade boomed. Between 1792 and 1796, shipping profits tripled, boosting shipbuilding and, in turn, demand for more tar, lumber, and rope. Daily wages for shipbuilders and laborers in Philadelphia doubled between 1790 and 1796. By the time opponents in the House of Representatives tried a last ditch effort to scuttle Jay's Treaty by denying funds necessary to enforce it, popular sentiment had shifted to strong support for the treaty as an element of returning prosperity.

The Administration of John Adams

George Washington had been reluctant to serve a second term in office and had been convinced to do so only when both Jefferson and Hamilton argued that no one else could bring the young republic's fractious politics together. But Washington refused to run for a third term, and in 1796 the nation faced its first contested presidential election.

In his farewell address, published on September 19, 1796, George Washington made clear his own essentially Federalist concern with social order and personal discipline. Having acknowledged the right of the people to alter their Constitution, he stressed the "duty of every individual to obey the established Government," until it was changed "by an explicit and authentic act of the whole people." With Democratic Republican support for France in mind, he cautioned against "a passionate attachment of one nation for another." The address also sounded themes that would continue to echo through the first half-century of the republic. He warned against unlawful "combinations and associations" with designs upon the rightful "power of the people," an image that, 30 years later, would drive the emergence of Jacksonian democracy.

Led by Hamilton, Federalists put forward Vice President John Adams as their candidate. Adams had served in the Continental Congress, had been a part of the committee to draft the Declaration of Independence, had served as representative to France during the American Revolution, had helped negotiate the peace treaty, and had served two terms as vice president. The Federalists settled on Thomas Pinckney of South Carolina as their vice presidential choice. For president, Democratic Republicans supported former Secretary of State Thomas Jefferson, a man of impeccable political credentials and, along with Madison, the most visible opponent of Hamilton. New Yorker Aaron Burr was intended as vice president.

Although contested, the election of 1796 was not decided by popular majority. Two-fifths of the members of the Electoral College were chosen, not by popular state vote, but by state legislators. Moreover, procedures in the Electoral College did not permit a distinction between votes for the office of president and votes for the office of vice president. The person who received the most electoral votes became president. The person who received the second highest number of electoral votes became vice president.

Intended to ensure stability in the presidential election process, this procedure proved dangerously volatile in practice and yielded unexpected results. Fearful that Pinckney might receive more votes than Adams from southern electors, some New England Federalist electors refused to cast ballots for him, but Pinckney ran less well in the South than these electors had anticipated, and Thomas Jefferson ran better in the border states. As a result, while the Federalist Adams received a majority of electoral votes (71) and became president, the Democratic Republican Jefferson received the second highest count (68 to Pinckney's 59) and became vice president.

Benjamin Franklin once said of John Adams that he was "always an honest man, often a wise one, but sometimes, and in some things, absolutely out of his senses." Wise he may have been, and he was certainly honest, but he was also cranky, defensive, and plagued by self-doubt. He was not the man to negotiate growing party rifts successfully. Although opposed to the Federalist administration, Democratic Republicans considered Adams better than Hamilton and were consoled with their vice presidential victory. But many Federalists looked to Hamilton, rather than Adams, for direction. Any possibility for alliance between those two was dashed when Adams learned that Hamilton had toyed with the idea of supporting Pinckney for the presidency.

These intricate convolutions of party feeling formed the political landscape upon which Adams had to deal with an increasingly hostile relationship with France. Unsurprisingly, Franco-American relations had been harmed by the signing of Jay's Treaty, which had seemed to France to ally America with England, and by the French practice of plundering American ships. Claiming the ships were trading with Great Britain, France used its loot to support its ongoing war with England. Even before his inauguration on March 4, 1797, Adams began to entertain the

As the view of Philadelphia's busy Market Street shows, social, commercial and political—"public" and "private"—life all commingled on the streets of the early republic's cities.

The politics of the early republic were often rough. Here two congressmen (one of them later convicted under the Sedition Act) come to blows on the floor of the House of Representatives.

possibility of sending a special envoy to France, perhaps Madison himself, to try to resolve these issues. Whether Madison would have accepted the position is debatable, but when Adams' cabinet objected, the president temporarily abandoned the plan. At the end of March, he learned that newly arrived American ambassador Charles Cotesworth Pinckney had been unceremoniously kicked out of France. Until mutual grievances were resolved, the French foreign minister had informed Pinckney that the French government would "no longer recognize or receive" an ambassador from the United States. In this context, Adams returned to the idea of sending a mission to France. In the end, he appointed not Madison, but Elbridge Gerry, John Marshall, and Pinckney, who was still in Europe.

When the American mission arrived, French Foreign Minister Talleyrand let it be known that he expected a bribe for his willingness to talk, a quarter of a million dollars to him personally and a loan of several million dollars to his nation. Arrangements of this sort were not uncommon in eighteenth-century European politics, but to the starched and circumspect Adams, the very idea was abhorrent. He turned over the entire documentation of the affair to Congress, altering the papers only to the extent that he identified Talleyrand's agents by letters: W, X, Y, and Z.

The news of the so-called XYZ affair came to a largely Federalist Congress, which immediately suspended all commercial ties to France, empowered American

ships to seize armed French vessels, and embarked on an expansion of the nation's almost nonexistent military. But the Federalists also used the scandal to attack their political opponents. Insisting that pro-French influence was endangering the nation, in 1798 Congress passed four acts collectively known as The Alien and Sedition Acts, measures aimed at gagging the Democratic Republican opposition and intended to prevent it from organizing on the war issue to win the 1800 election. The acts required a 14-year naturalization period (targeted at immigrants, whom the Federalists presumed to be Democratic Republicans), empowered the president to deport any "suspicious" aliens, and established a broad definition of sedition, intended to stop all Democratic Republican criticism of the administration's policies.

The Alien and Sedition Acts backfired against the Federalists. Twenty-five prosecutions were eventually brought under the Sedition Act (all against Democratic Republicans) and ten men were convicted. The acts were so transparently partisan that the individuals convicted quickly became martyrs to the Democratic Republican cause. Their high "crimes" were laughable in their triviality. For example, one man was convicted of sedition for wishing out loud that the wad of a cannon salute might smack President Adams in the rear. Another man, a Vermont congressman who published criticisms of administration policies, was re-elected even as he served out his four-month jail term.

Although Democratic Republicans insisted that the acts were unconstitutional, they hesitated to challenge

Through a tumultuous quarter of a century, Washington had embodied order and stability to the nation. At his death in 1799, citizens in many cities staged elaborate funeral processions in his honor, like this one in Philadelphia.

them in the Supreme Court, both because the court was dominated by Federalists and because Democratic Republicans did not want to set a precedent for giving the Supreme Court the power to rule on constitutionality. Instead, Madison and Jefferson turned to the states, which they encouraged to pass resolutions denouncing the Alien and Sedition Acts. Madison, who had since retired from Congress, authored and engineered the passage of a set of resolutions in Virginia affirming the rights of states to judge the constitutionality of federal laws. Jefferson, still the vice president of the United States, framed a more militant set of resolutions for the Kentucky legislature, stating that states might declare federal laws they deemed unconstitutional to be "without force" within their state boundaries. In 1799, Jefferson wrote a second set of resolutions defending this principle of "nullification" as the proper course for the states under such circumstances.

Jefferson and Madison may have expected that other states would rally to the support of the Virginia and Kentucky Resolves, but they did not. Nor were the hated Alien and Sedition Acts ever renewed, for the Republicans were returned to power in the election of 1800. The acts expired in 1801.

Before retiring, the Federalist Congress got off one more shot at the Democratic Republicans. In January of 1801, just as the session expired, Congress passed the Judiciary Act of 1801, which gave John Adams the power to expand the federal judiciary by appointing sixteen new judges, forty-two new justices of the peace, and numerous attorneys, clerks, and marshals. Needless to say, he filled these positions with good Federalists, and then he left office.

CHRONOLOGY

1785	Thomas Jefferson's *Notes on the State of Virginia* is published
1789	George Washington inaugurated Congress approves the first cabinet Judiciary Act of 1789 Tariff Act of 1789 Henry Knox recommends new Indian policy ("rights in the soil") John Fenno founds *Gazette of the United States* William Hill Brown publishes *The Power of Sympathy*
1790	Alexander Hamilton's two-part *Report on the Public Credit* recommends federal assumption of debts and creation of national bank Assumption Act passes
1791	Excise Tax (including tax on whiskey) passes Washington signs bill creating first Bank of the United States Philip Freneau establishes *National Gazette* Hamilton's *Report on the Encouragement of Manufactures* recommends federal subsidies to manufacturing Bill of Rights ratified
1792	Whiskey Rebellion begins Judith Sargent Murray begins publication of "The Gleaner" essays in the *Massachusetts Magazine* (published as book 1798)
1793	Fugitive Slave Act Edmond Genêt arrives in the United States
1794	Battle of Fallen Timbers Washington sends 13,000 troops to end Whiskey Rebellion
1795	Jay's Treaty approved by Senate Treaty of Greenville Pinckney's Treaty
1796	John Adams elected president in the first contested election
1798	XYZ Affair Charles Brockden Brown publishes *Alcuin* Alien and Sedition Acts
1798–1799	Virginia and Kentucky Resolves
1800	Jefferson elected president
1801	Judiciary Act of 1801

Conclusion

George Washington died at Mount Vernon on December 14, 1799. In his retirement, as at the moment of his inauguration, he had continued to worry that Americans lacked the judgment, restraint, and generosity of spirit to "act the part of good citizens."

Indeed, the first decade of the federal government's existence had demonstrated that the love of liberty and the love of order sometimes led in different directions, and they gave rise to very different visions of what constituted "good" citizenship. Democratic Republicans fumed at what they saw as the liberties Federalists had taken with the Constitution and their willingness utterly to abrogate civil rights. Federalists were more convinced than ever that Democratic Republicanism was a dangerous scourge upon the land, tantamount to lawlessness and, itself, the greatest threat to the republic. The 1790s had witnessed a steady escalation of suspicion and distrust, of which the Whiskey Rebellion, the Alien and Sedition Acts, and the Virginia and Kentucky Resolves had been only the most striking illustrations. The political parties organized that fractious spirit, but they did little to defuse it. As Americans struggled to give shape to a republican political economy, Madison's deepest concerns about factionalism seemed justified. Liberty seemed to give rise to lawlessness and prosperity to greed.

Even in its quieter, less dramatic manifestations, the expanding presumptions of liberty were altering and recreating the republic. As they formed new congregations, experimented with the mechanisms of elections, gathered in taverns and shops to read the latest news, and pondered the seemingly never-ending wars in Europe, Americans were learning to worry less about order and to embrace with growing pleasure the possibilities of personal freedom and choice. In this spirit, voters elected Virginian Thomas Jefferson as the third president of the United States in 1800. Also in this spirit, another Virginian, a slave by the name of Gabriel, plotted his own road to freedom.

Review Questions

1. William Manning understood American society as divided into "the Few and the Many." Identify other individuals or groups discussed in this chapter who implicitly or explicitly understood the early republic in similar terms. Did they all mean the same thing? How did this view of society shape the early political parties?

2. Did Jefferson and Hamilton disagree on all aspects of commercial policy? What assumptions did they share, and where exactly did their views differ?

3. How did social clubs, political parties, newspapers, schools, museums, and libraries help stabilize the society of the early republic? Did these structures create conflict and instability in any way?

4. In what ways was free women's citizenship restricted? In what ways did free women participate in the political life of the early republic?

5 What views about land and property guided U.S. Indian policy during the years 1789–1800?

6. Did Federalist foreign policy (as represented in Jay's Treaty) represent the interests primarily of the wealthy eastern elites, as Democratic Republicans charged, or did it address concerns shared by large numbers of citizens?

Further Readings

Harriet B. Apple White and Darlene G. Levy, eds., *Women and Politics in the Age of the Democratic Revolution* (1993). This collection of essays by noted women's historians evaluates the impact of the eighteenth-century democratic revolutions on the political lives of women in Europe and North America.

Richard R. Beeman, *The Evolution of a Southern Backcountry: A Case Study of Lunenburg County, Virginia, 1746–1832* (1984). This history of a single county in Virginia offers a window into the ongoing social, economic, and political conflicts between wealthy planters and common farmers in revolutionary and postrevolutionary America, with a particular emphasis on the importance of religion in shaping ideas of authority and legitimacy in the South.

Michael Merrill and Sean Wilentz, eds., *The Key of Liberty: The Life and Democratic Writings of William Manning, "A Laborer," 1747–1814* (1993). This volume reprints writings of Massachusetts farmer, tavern owner, and political philosopher William Manning, along with a detailed and accessible introduction to Manning's life and the political culture of the early republic.

James Roger Sharp, *American Politics in the Early Republic: The New Nation in Crisis* (1993). An overview of the first decade of American politics, this study pays particular attention to the sharp conflicts that divided Republicans from Federalists and includes an especially insightful discussion of the election of 1800.

Wiley Sword, *President Washington's Indian War: The Struggle for the Old Northwest* (1985). Wiley traces the evolution of Washington and Knox's Indian policy in the Old Northwest from its origins in Confederation policies and practices to its eventual reliance upon armed warfare.

Alan Taylor, *Liberty Men and Great Proprietors: The Revolutionary Settlement on the Maine Frontier, 1760–1820* (1990). Using the Maine frontier as a microcosm of continuing conflicts over the meaning of liberty in the early republic (especially the tensions between individual freedom and social stability), Taylor describes the militant and often violent resistance of land-poor white settlers to the legal claims of wealthy proprietors.

History on the Internet

"The Federalist Papers"

http://www.yale.edu/lawweb/avalon/federal/fed.html

This site contains the text of the influential *Federalist Papers.*

"The Whiskey Rebellion"

http://www.earlyamerica.com/earlyamerica/milestones/whiskey/index.html

In addition to general reading about this uprising in the Pennsylvania backcountry, read George Washington's original instructions to the militia to reinstate order.

"Divergent Views of Slavery"

View these two websites to see divergent views of slavery—one based on property rights and citizenship and one on the desire for racial equality and freedom.

"Pro-Slavery Petitions in Virginia"

http://www.pbs.org/wgbh/aia/part2/2h65.html

"Banneker's Letter to Jefferson"

http://www.pbs.org/wgbh/aia/part2/2h71.html

1911
LIBERTY AND EMPIRE
1800 - 1815

OUTLINE

Gabriel's Conspiracy
for Freedom

Voluntary Communities
in the Age of Jefferson
Communities of Faith
African Americans in the Early Republic
Communities of Masters and Journeymen

Jeffersonian Republicanism:
Politics of Transition
A New Capital, A New President
Jeffersonian Republicans in Power
Protecting Commerce

Liberty and an Expanding
Commerce
The Political Economy of Cotton
The Golden Age of Shipping

Invention and Exploration
The Rule of Law and Lawyers

The Political Economy
of an "Empire of Liberty"
The Louisiana Purchase
Surveying Louisiana
The Burr Conspiracy
Indian Resistance to Republican Empire

The Second War With England
Neutrality and Isolation
Democratic Republican Power and
Disunity
The War of 1812
The Making of Heroes and Knaves

Conclusion

Gabriel's Conspiracy for Freedom

On the morning of October 10, 1800, Gabriel, a tall man, 24 years of age, with a bearing of "courage and intelligence," mounted the gallows in the town center of Richmond, Virginia. Gabriel was a slave and had been all of his life. On that day in October, Gabriel was about to pay with his life for leading a dangerous conspiracy for freedom.

The plot had been a bold one. Inspired by a recent slave revolt in Saint Domingue, the rebels planned to take control of Richmond and spread through the countryside, freeing slaves as they went. By some accounts, they intended to kill all the whites except those "friendly to liberty" and the "poor white women who had no slaves" and then (aided by the French or by Indians) to escape to freedom. By other accounts, Gabriel was willing to make his peace with white southerners, if they would free African Americans.

The conspiracy was discovered, but not before hundreds of slaves had been recruited to the cause. Twenty-seven African Americans, including Gabriel, were

eventually executed. According to white witnesses, all went to their deaths with "a sense of their rights and a contempt of danger." It was a determination, Congressman John Randolph later recorded grimly, "which, if it becomes general, must deluge the Southern country in blood."

It is impossible to know when Gabriel first dreamed of revolution. It may have been a legacy from his father, a blacksmith like Gabriel and a respected member of the black community. It may have been when he met and fell in love with Nanny. Because they were both slaves, their marriage had no legal standing. Surely Gabriel was angry that the American Revolution had left the institution of slavery intact. Perhaps he had heard stories of the successful slave revolution in Saint Domingue, 1791–1793, or met slaves from there carried to the United States by their refugee owners. Perhaps as he went about the daily business of hiring out his own labor in town (when he was not needed on the plantation), negotiating his own hours, handling his own pay, living and working side by side with free men, he raged against the society that kept him enslaved. At the end of the day, or the week, or the month, Gabriel was not free. His wages and his life belonged to Thomas Prosser.

In many respects, the conditions that led to Gabriel's conspiracy were unique to enslaved African Americans in the new republic. No white Americans faced the absolute tyranny of enslavement, and few white Americans were sympathetic to the black people who did. Most Americans did not consider liberty synonymous with universal equality. In 1800 as in 1776, most believed that some groups of people (females, African Americans, Indians) were naturally incapacitated for citizenship and equal liberties.

In other ways, however, Gabriel's yearnings for freedom reflected larger patterns in American society in 1800. The Revolution had promised greater liberty, yet most Americans, even most technically free adult Americans, still lived and worked in some form of legally sanctioned paternalistic relation (wife-to-husband, worker-to-master, or slave-to-owner) within which both their economic freedom and their legal rights were curtailed. By 1800, many of those Americans, enslaved as well as free, were pushing and pulling at old assumptions about order, subordination, and hierarchy, testing the promises of their new republican world. Some left home in search of new economic opportunities elsewhere. Some challenged the authority of their masters and mistresses by forming new trade guilds or self-help societies. Some came together in energetic philanthropic efforts, intended to strengthen the bonds of new or existing communities, and many joined (or formed) new religious organizations. In family life, religious life, and economic life, they were in fact, haltingly, trying out a new,

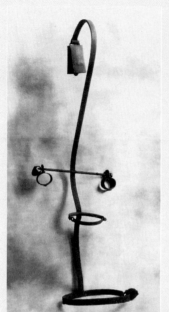

Slaves who attempted to escape were often put in an iron slave harness (shown at left) to punish them and prevent any future escape plans. Some slave owners also used hot irons (shown right) to brand slaves, as proof of ownership.

more democratic political economy, one based on opportunity rather than restraint and on liberty rather than deference. In 1800, in what Thomas Jefferson would later call "as real a revolution in the principles of our government as that of 1776 was in its form," voters extended their experiment to the national government, throwing out the Federalists, choosing instead Jefferson's Democratic Republican Party.

In some ways, the election of 1800 did mark a "revolution." The Federalists never regained the presidency and their pleas for a society based on rank and deference were soon drowned in a sea of democratic yearnings. And yet the ultimate meaning of the rising republican spirit in the United States was far more complex than Jefferson implied. Liberty expanded unevenly in the new republic. New freedoms for some spelled deepened bondage for others. The Democratic Republican political economy, meanwhile, did not always lead where Americans had intended to follow. As they had at the birth of the nation, most free Americans still associated personal liberty with property, and property with the kind of agrarian ideal propounded by Jefferson, Massachusetts political philosopher William Manning, and the "liberty men" of backcountry Maine. With enough land they expected not only to ward off pernicious dependencies, but also to enter successfully into trade, both local and overseas. Joining liberty to property, they thought, they could realize the full promise of the republic. But in their pell-mell rush for western lands, they not only brought catastrophe to the Native Americans living there and planted slavery deep in the soil of the new nation, but also laid the foundations for a political economy that would ultimately give rise to the very dependencies they sought to avoid. ▪

▌▌ KEY TOPICS

- Expanding expectations of liberty

- The decline of the Federalists and the rise of Democratic Republicanism

- The growth of commerce in the United States

- The cotton boom and the expansion of slavery

- The Louisiana Purchase

- Indian resistance and Tecumseh's Confederation

- The War of 1812

Voluntary Communities in the Age of Jefferson

From the Revolution on, free Americans had differed among themselves about the potential of individuals to conduct their own affairs. Federalists pointed to the French Revolution, the revolution in Saint Domingue, the Whiskey Rebellion, and later Gabriel's conspiracy, as examples of the dangers of too much liberty. By 1800, however, free Americans were taking a growing amount of personal liberty for granted in their everyday lives. One measure of that new freedom was the creation of new communities in the backcountry. The military and diplomatic successes of the 1790s reopened the West. By 1800 half a million southerners (some of them passing through Richmond, where Gabriel may have encountered them) had crossed the mountains into Kentucky and Tennessee and another half million northerners had pushed west into the Northwest Territory. Americans were also working through the meanings of liberty in other aspects of their lives.

Communities of Faith

One of the earliest ways in which Americans had begun to act on their changing conceptions of liberty was by forming new communities of faith. Members of the established clergy grumbled about the irreligion of the age, but it was religious freedom, not irreligion, that most citizens sought.

With political independence had come a demand for freedom from the state-supported Anglican and Congregational churches. Anglicanism had been disestablished in the South in the 1780s, replaced by the Protestant Episcopal Church. Even that change of status was insufficient to stem the growth of new evangelical faiths, especially the Methodists (who had formally seceded from the Anglican Church in 1784) and Baptists (who had migrated into the South from New England). In contrast to the more staid and ritual-based practices of the Episcopalians, these sects stressed the personal, emotional nature of religion and the ability of individuals to struggle actively for their own redemption. Methodists, for example, rejected what they deemed artificial differences among Christians, pronouncing "[o]ne condition, and only one" required for salvation: "a real desire." Their system of itinerant preaching (preachers traveled among congregations, rather than associating with a single church) enabled the clergy "to preach in many places," as minister Jesse Lee put it, and to reach out to the dispersed and the displaced. Emphasizing inner truth, a plain style, and congregational independence, the evangelical denominations offered a more egalitarian vision of the community of believers. This proved especially attractive to the poor and disfranchised, including both enslaved and free African Americans and white women. Some congregations went so far as to question the morality of slaveholding itself. Among the itinerant preachers were African Americans like Jarena Lee. Lee

Often held in the countryside in hastily constructed settings, the high emotionality of religious revivals provided drama for early nineteenth-century Americans, both for converts and for those who merely came to gawk.

began to preach in 1807. By the 1820s her extraordinary gifts as an exhorter had earned her a wide reputation up and down the coast.

Although Congregationalism was not fully disestablished in all states until 1834, it was plagued by breakaway movements from within as well as by competition from the evangelical sects. The most important of the splinter groups were the Unitarian and Universalist movements, which held generally positive views of human nature, embraced universal salvation, and were especially attractive to educated northerners seeking some relief from the harsh doctrines of Calvinism. Even in New England, however, the far greater threat to established religion came from Methodism and Baptism, which found willing converts among the country people and city workers.

This religious unrest led to a series of turn-of-the-century revivals, beginning in Virginia and western New England. The revivals first spread west, fed perhaps by the isolation of backcountry life. In 1800, religious pressure in Kentucky and Tennessee exploded, sending out a tidal wave that raced back through the Carolinas and Virginia, up through Pennsylvania into New York, and by 1802, to that bastion of Congregationalism, Connecticut.

The most famous of the turn-of-the-century revivals occurred in August of 1801, a year after Gabriel's ill-fated rebellion, in the tiny rural community of Cane Ridge, Kentucky. Worried about religious apathy, Minister Barton Stone had traveled to nearby Logan to investigate a series of small, intense prayer meetings. He was amazed by what he found. "Many, very many fell down . . . in an apparently breathless and motionless state," he recorded, their trances broken only "by a deep groan, or piercing shriek, or by a prayer for mercy most fervently uttered." When at last they regained their senses, they rose up "shouting deliverance . . . men, women and children declaring the wonderful works of God."

Much to Stone's dismay, the stories he carried back to Cane Ridge set off an even greater spiritual awakening there. "Scores" of residents joined spontaneous prayer meetings that continued day after day and deep into the night. News of the revival at Cane Ridge spread "like fire in dry stubble driven by a strong wind." Soon, the roads were jammed "with wagons, carriages, horsemen, and footmen," as "between twenty and thirty thousand" people (women, men, and children, whites and African Americans, anguished sinners, prodding family members, and the merely curious) hastened to the scene.

Eventually, the awakening spread to all parts of the country and to virtually all faiths, even, for a time, to the Congregationalists and Presbyterians, who joined in a Plan of Union to extend their influence in the West by settling joint congregations. Yet many members of these denominations were unhappy that revivals were led by unschooled preachers and encouraged unconventional beliefs and extravagant emotionalism. In 1803 to 1805 these misgivings led to schism, as the "Old Light" members of the Kentucky Synod purged "New Light" revivalists. In 1805, the national Presbyterian General Assembly reminded its members that "God is a God of order and not of confusion."

Where Congregationalists and Presbyterians saw confusion, Methodists and Baptists saw possibility. In the first years of the nineteenth century, the number of Baptist congregations increased from about 400 to about 2,700 and membership in Methodist churches more than doubled from 87,000 to 196,000. Eager to encourage prospective converts, Methodists founded the first denominational publishing house in the United States (the Methodist Book Concern). In 1817, they founded the national Sunday School Union.

Some observers thought religion and politics were directly linked. For example, Thomas Robbins, Congregational minister of Danbury, Connecticut, assumed that all evangelicals were Democratic Republican, and that the growing "infestations" of Democratic Republicans were all evangelical. The linkages were seldom so simple. Neither Jefferson nor Madison, the founding lights of the Democratic Republican Party, embraced evangelical faiths. Yet religion and politics did reflect and constantly modify one another. Americans tended to formulate visions of the ideal political community in religious and specifically Christian images and to suspect those who disagreed with them not only of bad politics but of moral weakness.

African Americans in the Early Republic

For no group of Americans had the promises of the Revolution proved emptier, or the dangers of the new society more palpable, than for African Americans. For no group were new communities of freedom more vital.

The failure to abolish slavery was the glaring contradiction of the American Revolution, but it was not the only sign that life in the new nation might become harder, rather than better, for African Americans. Although some slaves had escaped during the war and some had been freed after the Revolution, in most respects the struggle for independence harmed slave communities. The rhetoric of revolution had alarmed southern whites, who feared slave insurrection. News of the 1791–1793 Saint Domingue rebellion, followed by the arrival of large numbers of refugees, and reports of conspiracies among Saint Domingue slaves resettled in Louisiana, reawakened these fears. Southern legislatures moved to limit individual emancipations and to tighten legal surveillance over slaves, further restricting even the limited autonomy of enslaved individuals and creating an atmosphere in which abuse thrived. Slaveowner efforts to capitalize on new economic opportunities after the war often proved devastating to slave communities and slave families. When owners faltered, slaves paid the price with less food, poorer housing, and longer hours of work. When planters failed, slaves became the liquid capital through which they settled their debts. In some parts of the

Slaves hired out for wages were often forced to wear badges like the one above, identifying them as slaves and indicating their occupation and the place where they worked.

This painting of African American sawyers at work in a Philadelphia square suggests the mixing of races and classes in public spaces in the early nineteenth century. An African-American woman carrying a white child stops to chat. In the background, a carriage driver tends his horse. Note the racially caricatured features of the African Americans.

South, the sale of slaves as a result of death or insolvency in the 1780s and 1790s substantially increased the incidence of slave owning among whites, giving a larger part of the white community a personal stake in the institution. All of these changes fostered a reluctance to tolerate even minor criticism of the institution of slavery. By the turn of the century, both Baptists and the Methodists in the South were retreating from their earlier flirtations with abolition.

Meanwhile, a small, fragile free African-American community took shape, made up primarily of individuals and families who had escaped during the war or been freed after it. Because few free African Americans were able to afford land, most migrated to the cities in search of jobs and opportunity (see Table 9-1). By 1800, New York and Baltimore claimed free African-American communities of 3,500 and 2,700, respectively. Philadelphia, the gateway to the North, had the largest free African-American population, at almost 6,400 inhabitants. By 1820, New York would surpass Philadelphia with a free black population of over 10,000.

With abolition proceeding slowly even in the North, and racial prejudice growing, the making of free African-American communities was an act of defiance and of self-defense. In Philadelphia, as in other cities, African Americans created a range of institutions to ensure survival, foster growth, and project their presence into the larger community. By 1814, Philadelphia's African-American community had organized eleven **mutual aid societies** and four Masonic lodges. African-American Masons marched proudly in public processions, including the 1800 commemoration of George Washington's birthday. Led by teachers Absalom Jones, Amos White, and Ann Williams, in 1800 African-American Philadelphians took control of the education of their children. In 1807, Cyrus Bustill founded the Society of Free People of Color for Promoting the Instruction and School Education of Children of African Descent to guarantee the financial autonomy of the schools.

No institution was more important to the survival of these fragile, young communities than the church. African Americans responded warmly to the new evangelical religions, especially to Methodism, drawn by the communal character of revivals, their ecstatic tone (which echoed the dancing movements, calls, and spirit-visions of African religious practice), and the immediacy with which evangelical preaching dramatized the cataclysmic triumph of good over evil. Yet African-American members faced poor treatment in many white-dominated congregations, where they were restricted to segregated seating and excluded from offices. When African-American Philadelphians

TABLE 9-1

							Increase, 1800–1850	
Growth in the Black Population in Cities, 1800–1850 (Slave and Free)								
Cities	**1800**	**1810**	**1820**	**1830**	**1840**	**1850**	**Number**	**Percent**
Albany	680	n.a.	754	1,050	886	860	180	26.47
Baltimore	5,614	7,686	14,683	18,910	21,166	28,388	22,774	405.66
Boston	1,174	1,464	1,687	1,875	2,427	1,999	825	70.27
Brooklyn	641	n.a.	847	973	1,775	2,424	1,783	278.16
Buffalo	n.a.	n.a.	32	219	503	675		
Charleston	10,004	13,143	14,127	17,461	16,231	22,973	12,969	129.64
Cincinnati	20	82	433	1,090	2,240	3,237	3,217	>10,000.00
Louisville	77	495	1,124	2,638	4,049	6,970	6,893	8,951.95
New Orleans	3,000	10,911	13,592	26,038	33,280	26,916	23,916	797.20
New York	6,367	9,823	10,886	13,977	16,358	13,815	7,448	116.98
Philadelphia	4,265	6,354	7,582	9,806	10,507	10,736	6,471	151.72
Pittsburgh	102	185	286	473	710	1,959	1,857	1,820.59
Providence	656	871	979	1,213	1,302	1,499	843	128.51
St. Louis	371	n.a.	n.a.	1,232	2,062	4,054	3,683	992.72
Washington	746	2,304	3,641	5,459	6,521	10,271	9,525	1,276.81

Source: From Leonard P. Curry, The Free Black in Urban America, 1800–1850 *(University of Chicago Press, 1981).*

formed their own church, the African Church of Philadelphia, in 1794, the white Methodist minister threatened to expel any African-American Methodist who supported the new congregation. Offended, the new society voted to affiliate with the Episcopal Church, while individuals who wanted to remain Methodists organized a separate Methodist church, known as "Mother Bethel." By 1814, Philadelphia's African-American community had also organized an African Presbyterian church, an African Baptist church, and a second Methodist church.

A few members of Philadelphia's free African-American community achieved spectacular prosperity. For example, by 1807 Philadelphia sailmaker James Forten employed a workforce of thirty men and had amassed a fortune of more than $100,000. Richard Allen speculated in real estate and grew wealthy enough to keep servants and indentured workers.

But for most free African Americans, daily life remained a struggle. African-American women worked as tavern-keepers, bakers, seamstresses, chimney sweeps, street vendors, cooks, washerwomen, and garden women. They set up small groceries in their homes. They fished along the wharves and sold their catch in market stalls, or dug roots or oysters for sale on the city streets. African-American men worked as carpenters, shipbuilders, shopkeepers, blacksmiths, silversmiths, sailors, day laborers, brewers, as well as in a variety of personal service jobs. Mutual aid societies helped to spread meager resources, but families also took in relatives and neighbors down on their luck, and friends helped friends find jobs and cheap housing.

The obstacles free African Americans faced increased after the turn of the century, as white attitudes continued to harden into racial prejudice. Cities, states, and even the

This early nineteenth-century drawing of an African-American scrubwoman is interesting both because it individualizes the subject and because the subject, a worker, is presented in a style of almost classic reflection.

federal government began categorically to restrict African Americans from certain occupations. For example, as early as 1798 the secretaries of war and the navy had each tried to bar African Americans from the military. In 1810, the federal government excluded African Americans from delivering the mails. Meanwhile, northern states moved one by one to deny free African-American men the vote, defining suffrage as not only a male, but also a white privilege. In 1816, whites formed the American Colonization Society. Dedicated to removing free African Americans from their native land to Liberia, in Africa, the ACS signaled waning white support for a racially integrated republic. That year, in response to repeated attacks on African-American churches and churchgoers, African-American Methodists from Baltimore and Philadelphia founded the African Methodist Episcopal Church.

Communities of Masters and Journeymen

That the destruction of older, hierarchial institutions did not always result in increased equality was also suggested by the breakdown of the craft shop in these years.

In the late eighteenth century, most American manufacturing occurred either in individual households or in small craft shops. In the shops, a master presided over one or more journeymen and an apprentice or a helper or two. By custom the master paid at least part of workers' wages in food and lodging, and supervised them almost like a father.

By the mid-1790s there were signs that, under the strain of the volatile and changing economy, these older paternalistic relationships were disappearing, replaced by new alignments that cut across the institution of the shop. The shift was apparent in many crafts. Eager to increase sales to cotton planters in the South and rich sugar planters in the West

At the turn of the century, urban shoemakers worked in small shops where they made shoes both to custom order and, as suggested here, for some ready-made trade. Wives and daughters, working in their kitchens, often did part of the stitching.

In the early nineteenth century, most women made their own clothes in their homes, perhaps with the help of a hired seamstress. Dressmakers, like the one shown here, did custom sewing for wealthy women.

GROWING UP IN AMERICA

Jarena Lee

Jarena Lee was probably seventeen years old when Thomas Jefferson was elected, and when Gabriel was executed (see page 249 for Gabriel's story). Like Gabriel, she was of African descent. Unlike Gabriel, she had been born legally free, and she came to seek an expansion of her freedom not in rebellion, but rather in the religious awakenings sweeping the new nation.

Lee was born in Cape May, New Jersey, near Philadelphia, and spent most of her life working as a house servant. Unable to support their family, her parents were forced to send her out to work when she was only seven. Although Lee was able to return at great intervals to visit her home, she saw her mother only four more times in her life. She grew up as an orphan on her own and under the governance of the white people who employed her.

By her young adulthood, however, Lee felt drawn to the African-American religious communities forming in Philadelphia. In 1804 or 1805, when she was about 21 years old, Lee attended a service at which Methodist minister Richard Allen preached. Allen had helped to found Philadelphia's first separate African-American church. As he spoke that afternoon, Lee was overwhelmed by the feeling that she had at last found "the people to which my heart unites." Three weeks later, her spiritual awakening deepened into religious conversion, which she experienced as a call to forgive those who had harmed her. "[T]here appeared to my view, in the centre of the heart, one sin," she remembered, "and this was *malice* against one particular individual, who had strove deeply to injure me." But Lee's response went farther: "I said, *Lord* I forgive every creature."

For the next four or five years, Lee continued her religious meditations, but the day came "on a certain time, [when] an impressive silence fell upon me, and I stood as if someone was about to speak to me." "Go preach the Gospel," she was commanded, and when she protested that no one would listen to her, the voice spoke again: "Preach the Gospel; and I will put words in your mouth, and will turn your enemies to become your friends." Lee went to seek the advice of the Reverend Allen, but he told her that women were not permitted to preach in Methodist faith and that she should be satisfied with lay exhorting and leading prayer meetings. This she did for eight years, during which time she married and moved away from Philadelphia. Yet the conviction of her youth remained strong.

After the death of her husband, Lee returned to the Philadelphia area, where she continued to hold prayer meetings in her house and urge others to salvation. One day, she attended services at Bethel Church to hear Richard Williams preach. But Williams had barely gotten started when he suddenly announced that "he seemed to have lost the spirit" to preach and could not continue. "[A]s if altogether by supernatural force," Lee recalled, "I sprang . . . to my feet" and began to exhort, declaring that she was like Jonah and had for eight years ignored the work to which she was called. So powerful was her declaration, that Richard Allen, now a Bishop of the African Methodist Episcopal Church, stood up from the congregation and affirmed her calling and the rightness of her being permitted to preach.

For Gabriel, the African-American community was a community of slaves, whose salvation lay in the liberty of their bodies. For Jarena Lee, the African-American community was one of belief, where freedom lay in spiritual salvation. Lee spent the rest of her life as an itinerant preacher to that community. In 1827, as a woman in her 40s, she journeyed over two thousand miles and preached almost two hundred times.

Indies, for example, furniture makers sought to cut costs and improve efficiency. They achieved these ends by subdividing the tasks of production, which allowed them to employ cheaper, less-experienced workers whom they paid in cash and to whom they had a lessened sense of obligation. In this way, as early as 1795, one New York chairmaker was able to generate a shipment of 5,000 Windsor chairs. Master tailors (interested in boosting sales of low-cost clothing to sailors and laborers) and master shoemakers (seeking profit from the southern market for rough shoes for slaves) sought ways to cut costs and increase production, at the cost of quality, if necessary. Meanwhile, many large merchants and retailers branched out into production, creating new competition for existing shops. Prosperous masters were able to keep up and sometimes to expand their business. Smaller shops, already on a more precarious financial footing, often went under.

Workers paid for these changes in falling wages. Pressed to the edge of destitution, journeymen in Philadelphia, New York, and Baltimore formed mutual aid societies that provided emergency loans and sickness and death benefits to members. They soon began secretly to reorganize these mutual aid societies into trade associations. In 1805, in the first strike in United States history, associated Philadelphia journeyman shoemakers tried to demand a craft-wide bill of higher wages. In the eyes of the law, the new community of interest amounted to a conspiracy against the rights of trade. The stunned shoemakers were arrested, tried, convicted, and required to pay stiff fines.

Among workers, this conflict assumed an increasingly ethnic cast. On Christmas, 1806, for example, gangs of native-born and Irish workers, many of them employed as laborers or in occupations undergoing sharp reorganization, battled with clubs and stones in the streets of New York. One man was killed and many others were injured. The ostensible cause of the riot, national pride, masked deep occupational insecurities and growing competition for jobs and for decent wages.

By 1800 manufacturers were beginning to assert a new authority in the American economy. Lobbying for protective tariffs, they argued that investment in manufacturing was "more beneficial to the community, because its profits will be distributed among our own citizens; [and] more conducive to the prosperity of the Government, because the internal intercourse it will occasion will tend to assim-

ilate and strengthen the union." Some of the petitioners were craft masters who had ascended through the ranks, but a growing number were merchants who had only recently been converted to manufacturing. Initially, the traditional craft masters refused to associate with these new entrepreneurs. By the early 1800s, however, there were signs of erosion in the old master solidarity. Especially in New England, where wealthy merchants brought both cash and status to the craft, societies of masters began slowly to admit the newcomers and, reluctantly, to turn a blind eye to their hiring practices.

Jeffersonian Republicanism: Politics of Transition

This quiet revolution in Americans' ideas of personal freedom underlay the national political "revolution" of 1800. A government dominated by old elites and committed to federal activism was replaced by one devoted, as Jefferson's secretary of the Treasury put it, to "principles of limitation of power and public economy." In his inaugural address, Jefferson tried to capture the essential features of that new political economy. He called for "equal and exact justice to all men, of whatever state or persuasion, religious or political." To guard against "antirepublican tendencies" and to encourage the small merchants, tradesmen, mechanics, and especially farmers, Jefferson advocated "the support of state governments." He promised to replace a bloated federal administration with "a wise and frugal government" devoted to the "encouragement of agriculture and of commerce as its handmaid." Although Jefferson called for conciliation, announcing "We are all Republicans, we are all Federalists," both he and other Democratic Republicans resolutely set about reforming the policies of the Federalists, laying the groundwork for national economic independence through agriculture at home and unimpeded free trade abroad. Ironically, in the context of turn-of-the-century national and international politics, the Democratic Republican political economy proved a far less dramatic departure from the policies of the Federalists than partisans of either party expected.

In the election of 1800, Federalists attacked Thomas Jefferson as a dangerous free-thinker and social radical, incapable of providing the strong and virtuous leadership of a Washington.

A New Capital, A New President

The contingent character of Jefferson's presidency was captured concretely in the new national capital where he was inaugurated on March 4, 1801. The city (named Washington, District of Columbia, after the nation's first president) had been in the planning since Jefferson and Hamilton had struck their bargain on the assumption of state debts in 1790. George Washington had turned supervision of the project over to Jefferson who had, in turn, secured the services of French engineer Major Pierre Charles L'Enfant. Ironically, for the model of the capital of the world's first permanent republic, L'Enfant chose Versailles, the palace of French kings.

President and Abigail Adams moved into the new executive mansion in the fall of 1800, just in time for Adams to fail in his re-election bid. Abigail Adams did not mind the brevity of her stay in Washington. She found the city dirty, its inhabitants disreputable, and the executive mansion damp and cold. She eventually commandeered the "great, unfinished audience-room" as a "drying-room . . . to hang the clothes in." Visitors to the city agreed that it was "both melancholy and ludicrous." Like the executive mansion, the Capitol was not complete. Congress took up its duties under an unfinished roof, and the Supreme Court set to work in temporary chambers in the basement. The community, such as it was, consisted of mud-mired streets connecting clusters of boardinghouses, workers' shanties, and half-framed buildings. It gave the appearance, as one visitor put it, "of a considerable town, which had been destroyed by some unusual calamity."

It was in the unfinished Capitol that Thomas Jefferson took the oath of office. Few people better embodied the transitional state of the republic than the new president himself. Jefferson was born in 1743 and survived until July 4, 1826 (the fiftieth anniversary of the Declaration of Independence), a life span that witnessed the flowering and decline of the European Age of Reason and the birth of the American market revolution. Jefferson belonged to both. A "zealous amateur" of Newtonian physics and the new sciences of botany, zoology, and mathematics, Jefferson was nonetheless drawn to eighteenth-century ideals of order, a quality evident both in his political writings (most notably the Declaration of Independence) and in his personal habits. He shunned crowds and public controversy, preferring quiet discussions in private salons to the power-brokering of politics.

Jefferson's political and economic world-view was shaped by the experience of eighteenth-century mercantilism. Jefferson was a planter, producing raw materials for European markets and reliant upon those markets for the production of manufactured goods. This relation produced a constant friction with wealthy European merchants, who extended credit to planters and held their debts. As a man who lived most of his adult life in debt, Jefferson distrusted paper money and banks, which he saw as tools of privileged merchants to subjugate vulnerable producers. It was the influence of merchants over transatlantic politics in the late eighteenth century that convinced Jefferson of the importance of national commercial independence if the republic was to remain politically free and socially virtuous.

But Jefferson also was a Democrat, and he was drawn to the dynamics of an expansionist, fluid, and democratic society. He associated liberty with self-sufficient agriculture and with commerce unfettered by state-imposed restrictions. He was unreservedly optimistic about the future of the United States and unabashedly certain of the right of Americans to claim and exploit the vast natural resources of the continent. Like many Americans at the turn of the century, he was a "mechanic," always seeking pragmatic uses of abstract principles. Among his inventions were a ventilating system, a device for copying documents, and a moldboard plow, for which he was recognized by the Society of Agriculture in Paris. He was equally willing to experiment with social structures. His proposed 1778 Virginia educational reforms (not enacted) would have vastly expanded public access to education. In 1789, he suggested to Madison that the laws and constitutions of states should be renewed every nineteen years, to ensure that future generations would not be saddled with the ideas and institutions of earlier ones.

No issue of his personal or political life revealed these two worlds in conflict more dramatically than Jefferson's views on slavery. Like many other members of the eighteenth-century planter class, Jefferson was deeply dependent for his own comfort on the forced labor of others. Over the course of his lifetime he owned some 600 people, of whom he freed only five. But Jefferson was also the single person most directly responsible for the exclusion of slavery from the Northwest Territory, and as president he would sign the bill outlawing the foreign slave trade. The wholesale executions that followed the discovery of Gabriel's conspiracy sickened and frightened him. If the executions continued, he warned, "The other states and the world at large . . . will forever condemn us." Perhaps nothing in Jefferson's life so captured his ambivalence toward slavery than his intimate relationship with one of his own slaves, Sally Hemings. The connection may have lasted for several decades and (despite the racism of *Notes on the States of Virginia*) Jefferson may well have loved Hemings. Long-term liaisons between planters and female slaves were by no means unheard of in the South. However, they did not necessarily imply consent or mutual feeling on the part of the women. All of the five slaves Jefferson freed were Hemings, but his sense of moral obligation on this point never broadened beyond that family.

Jefferson's presidency traced a course like a tacking sailboat. He knew the direction in which he meant to take the republic, but often, in the press of circumstance, he had to take it on the slant, pragmatically. As a result, his policies often yielded paradoxical results. Although he lionized the self-sufficiency of farmers, Jefferson eventually found himself proposing an embargo that harmed farmers and benefited wealthy merchants. Although wary of large-scale manufacturing and wage-dependency, Jefferson made decisions that laid the foundations of America's industrial economy. Jefferson repeatedly criticized Hamilton for "subverting step by step the principles of the constitution," but given the chance to buy Louisiana, he willingly sacrificed strict constructionism.

Jeffersonian Republicans in Power

Upon gaining control of the national government, Democratic Republicans moved first to close a hole in the Constitution that had almost cost them the election. With 53 percent of the popular vote, Jefferson had clearly defeated Adams. But in the Electoral College, the practice of balloting by party (rather than by office) had spelled disaster. Both Jefferson and Aaron Burr, the Democratic Republican vice-presidential candidate, received 73 votes. In the House of Representatives, Federalists threatened to support Burr to block Jefferson. Only after 34 ballots was Jefferson elected. Stunned Democratic Republicans rushed to pass the legislation that would eventually become the Twelfth Amendment (1804), providing for party tickets in national elections.

Democratic Republicans turned next to the judiciary. Intending to weaken this least representative branch of government, they ended up strengthening it and setting the stage for a series of decisions by Chief Justice John Marshall that would expand the power of the federal government. Although some Democratic Republicans wished to excise every vestige of the hated Federalist regime, Jefferson settled for replacing only about half of the numerous patronage appointments. The most dramatic assault on the judiciary was the attack on Associate Supreme Court Justice Samuel Chase, whose case raised the question of standards for impeachment. Chase was notorious for his open partisanship during the Sedition Act prosecutions, but it was unclear that his behavior had met the constitutional standard of "Treason, Bribery, and high Crimes and Misdemeanors." Although Democratic Republicans were suddenly content with a loose reading of the Constitution, Federalists took up strict construction, arguing that the power to impeach had been narrowly drawn and should be used only in cases of clear criminal behavior. In the final vote, Chase was acquitted. The Supreme Court remained Federalist, 5 to 1. Jefferson's desire for a Democratic Republican court had to wait for unforced vacancies in 1804 and 1807 and the creation of a new western circuit in 1807.

Meanwhile, in a move that would ultimately produce a landmark Supreme Court decision, Jefferson went after the "midnight" appointments of the Judiciary Act of 1801. While Secretary of State James Madison refused to issue the necessary commissions for new justices, Congress repealed the Judiciary Act of 1801, reinstating the Judiciary

Act of 1789, with its smaller court system. The 1789 act had given the Supreme Court oversight over the delivery of new judicial commissions. Its reinstatement had the effect of making the Supreme Court (with its new chief justice, the Federalist John Marshall) the judge of Madison's actions. Sensing an opportunity, one of the rebuffed Adams appointees, William Marbury, sued. Although Marbury's suit arose from the Judiciary Act of 1801, Marshall's decision focused on the now-restored Judiciary Act of 1789 and on the question of whether the Supreme Court had a right even to hear Marbury's case. The Marshall Court ruled that it did not. In granting the court jurisdiction over the delivery of judicial commissions, Marshall reasoned, Congress had exceeded the Constitution, which gave the court no such authority. Declaring that portion of the Act of 1789 invalid, the court renounced any power to redress Marbury's grievances.

Marbury v. Madison established the **principle of judicial review.** Implicitly affirming the view that the Constitution did not have a self-evident meaning, the decision identified the Supreme Court as the final arbiter of constitutional intent and, thus, as the highest embodiment of "the people's will." Marbury's petition was denied, and Democratic Republicans carried the day, but federalism (as invoked by Justice Marshall) left a lasting imprint on the structure of power in the republic.

Protecting Commerce

Jefferson's wish to foster a "frugal government" based on the independence of "agriculture and of commerce its handmaid" was to prove more complicated than he imagined, and was, indeed, to rob his second administration of much of the luster of his first. The earliest hint of this came in 1801 from the tiny principalities of North Africa.

Jefferson entered his presidency determined to reduce the size of the federal government. Working with Secretary of the Treasury Albert Gallatin, he slashed the Army budget by half and the Navy budget by more than two-thirds. He also supported congressional efforts to reduce the $80 million national debt and to repeal internal taxes. By 1807 the Democratic Republicans had paid off all the debts they could legally call in.

These efforts at thrift were soon derailed by the politics of overseas commerce—not the politics of European merchants, but rather those of the monarchs of the North African nations of Tunis, Algeria, Morocco, and Tripoli. These principalities had long sought to dominate shipping on the Mediterranean, exacting tribute as the price of permitting ships to travel the Barbary coast unaccosted by pirates. As soon as the United States became a separate nation, it became separately liable for such payments. In 1794 the United States had responded by creating the Navy to protect American shipping in the Mediterranean, the very Navy whose budget Jefferson was now cutting.

Renewed demands for tribute in May of 1801 brought the crisis to a head. Democratic Republicans opposed war as expensive and tending to enlarge the powers of the federal government. Moreover, as Gallatin argued, even a successful war would not guarantee "the free use of the Mediterranean." Yet to pay tribute was to abandon the principle of free trade. Concluding that his only hope lay in a small, contained war, Jefferson supported a congressional appropriation of $146,000 for warships and gunboats (almost doubling the naval expenses of Adams' administration). He directed the squadron "to protect our commerce and chastise their insolence—by sinking, burning or destroying their ships and vessels wherever you shall find them."

Results were mixed. Democratic Republicans did manage to avoid new internal taxes, but only by financing the war from the large surplus inherited from the Federalists and from tariff increases. The consequence was a spectacular rise in the tariff, which averaged more than 15 percent by 1804 and ultimately nurtured a boom in domestic manufacturing and laid the foundation for post-War of 1812 industrialization. America's military intervention in the Mediterranean was not particularly successful, however. The warship *Philadelphia* ran aground off Tripoli and would have become loot of war had a raiding party led by Lieutenant Stephen Decatur not burned it before it could be taken. A treaty signed in 1805 required the United States to surrender $65,000 for prisoners. Payments continued until 1815.

Liberty and an Expanding Commerce

These military frustrations paled in the light of economic prosperity, however. Wars in Europe and new traffic to the Indian Ocean produced new and expanded markets for United States products (lumber and pitch for the military and fish, meat, rice, and grain to feed the war-ravaged civilian populations). Bolstered by the rise of cotton as an export crop, overseas commerce financed the import of manufactured items, preserving the republic free from large-scale domestic industrialization. The promise of agricultural profits drove up land prices. Farmers hired on extra workers; teamsters hurried goods to port; shipbuilders, sailmakers, ropemakers, caulkers, blacksmiths, and brass fitters turned out new ships at an astonishing rate; and captains hired crews to sail them around the world. Soon Americans would have reason to question the benefits of their dependence on foreign trade, but for a time Jefferson's advocacy of a political economy based on free international commerce seemed vindicated.

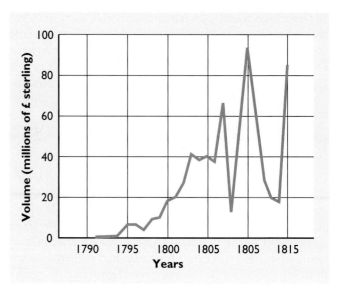

Figure 9-1   Volume of Cotton Exports, 1791–1815 (in millions of pounds).

Source: Douglass C. North, The Economic Growth of the United States; 1790–1860 (New York: W.W. Norton, 1966).

The Political Economy of Cotton

The most significant boost to American commercial agricultural arose from the late-eighteenth-century mechanization of the English textile mills and from the resulting sharply increased demand for raw cotton. The colonies had not been an important source of raw cotton, since the only variety that grew well in most parts of North America was a type (short-staple) that was extremely laborious to clean (the seeds clung tenaciously to the short, matted fibers). Spurred by the new English markets, in 1793 Eli Whitney invented a mechanism that reduced the cleaning time of short-staple cotton from a pound a day to fifty pounds a day. Although the initial design would later be improved, almost at a stroke Whitney's gin made cotton a viable cash crop for much of the South.

The invention occurred at a critical moment in transatlantic economic history. Important sectors of the southern American export economy were stagnant. American indigo was losing English market share to indigo from the East Indies. Sales and prices of tobacco were in decline. The market for rice was still strong, but rice cultivation required such large investments of land and labor as to exclude most farmers from production. Meanwhile, the gradual mechanization of the British textile mills at the end of the eighteenth century steadily increased the British demand for raw cotton. As markets for other exports deteriorated, planters and middling farmers turned to this crop. Between 1790 and 1810, American cotton production increased from 3,000 bales to 178,000 bales a year. After 1800, cotton was the United States' largest single export commodity (see Figure 9-1).

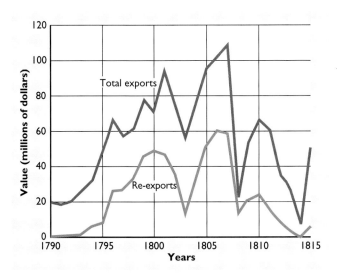

Figure 9-2   Value of Exports and Re-exports From the United States, 1790–1815.

Source: Douglass C. North, The Economic Growth of the United States; 1790–1860 (New York: W.W. Norton, 1966).

The profits available in cotton set off an explosion of migration into the southern tip of North Carolina, South Carolina, and Georgia and, later, into parts of Alabama, Mississippi, Louisiana, Arkansas, and Texas. Most of this land had become available to the United States as a result of successful turn-of-the-century diplomacy. The Pinckney Treaty (1795) had clarified United States claims to present-day Alabama and Mississippi. The Louisiana Purchase (1803) added the present state of Louisiana and part of present-day Mississippi. In 1814, Andrew Jackson would claim remaining lands in Mississippi, Alabama, and western Georgia in his war against the Creeks.

The cotton boom fatefully reinvigorated the institution of slavery. Planters scrambled to beat the 1807 constitutional deadline on the foreign slave trade, when Congress would first be able to pass legislation limiting the sale of slaves into the country. Between 1793 and 1808, South Carolinians imported as many as 36,000 slaves, primarily in ships that sailed out of New England, especially Rhode Island. In the two decades between ratification of the Constitution and 1807, the United States imported more slaves than in any other twenty-year period of its history, perhaps as many as 200,000 people.

The slave trade did not end in 1808 with its legal closure. Slavers smuggled their human cargo into the United States, either directly to the Georgia and South Carolina coasts or by land through Florida (still disputed territory) or Louisiana. By one estimate, as many as 50,000 slaves were smuggled into the United States after 1808.

Even among farmers who grew a single acre of cotton, the dizzying profits possible from the fiber encouraged wasteful economic practices. Lands were planted with a single cash crop and worked hard, year after year until they were exhausted, and then those settlers who were able moved onto fresh lands. For example, early migrants into Tennessee settled in the foothills of the Smoky Mountains and on the poor lands just beyond, raising cattle to sell to drivers, who moved them to the coast. When richer lands became available in the central plateau of the state, prosperous families migrated there, eventually establishing large flax, hemp, tobacco, and cotton farms.

The Golden Age of Shipping

American maritime prosperity between 1793 and 1805 seemed to affirm the wisdom of Jefferson's vision of a republic based on agriculture and international commerce. American shipping was of three types: export (primarily agricultural, including wheat, rice, indigo, tobacco, some sugar, and especially cotton), **re-export** (the shipping of goods between two foreign ports with an intermediate stop in the United States), and some simple carrying trade between two foreign ports (see Figure 9-2). Overall, American shipping tonnage tripled, reaching almost 11,000,000 tons annually by 1807. American ships increased their share

From the late eighteenth to the early nineteenth century, America's tall-masted oceangoing ships, like the ones shown here, dominated global trade.

of the traffic between England and the United States from 50 percent in 1790 to 95 percent by 1800, and American-owned vessels sailed on virtually every known ocean of the world. They carried goods from the West Indies to the United States and then to Europe, between ports in Europe, and from Europe and the United States to Asia.

This commercial prosperity rested in part on cotton and in part on the efficiency of the American shipping industry. New England turned out ships at half the cost of European builders and, according to Massachusetts merchant and Republican Jacob Crowninshield, "We sail our vessels cheaper," making shorter voyages and spending less time in port.

Prosperity was due, however, to the United States' success in steering clear of, and profiting from, European wars. War created demand in Europe and also hindered the ability of European shippers to meet that demand. England in particular benefited from letting American ships dominate the carrying trade, while it focused on the continental blockade of France. Although American shipping was not entirely free from harassment (notably the British seizure of American sailors to serve on British ships), the value of the re-export carrying trade increased from about $500,000 a year in the 1790s to about $60,000,000 a year in 1807.

Ironically, this flourishing commerce, so desired by Jefferson as the safeguard against American industrialization, strengthened both the attitudes and the institutions upon which industrialization would eventually be based. High commercial profits encouraged the development of business services in the new nation, especially in the middle and northern states. Banks, credit houses, retail stores, warehouses, and insurance companies prospered, as did the overseas slave trade. This commerce laid the foundation for fortunes that would later underwrite early industrialization, notably the Cabots and Lowells of Massachusetts. Shippers could lose everything in a single voyage, but they could also reap spectacular profits. Between 1800 and 1807, John Jacob Astor of New York, who began his career exporting furs, more than tripled his net worth to $900,000.

Shipping also produced catalysts for more democratic change. While settlers in the West expressed their new autonomy in religious revival, young adults on the coast (mostly men, but a few women) tried out the republic of the sea. Sailing was dangerous, with wages scarcely higher than those paid a common laborer, but the ship was known as a place where status, ethnicity, and nativity mattered less than skill and hard work. In the first years of the nineteenth century, as many as one-fifth of American seamen were foreign born, and another fifth were African American. African Americans and Indians were on board the *Beaver* in 1791 when it became the first Nantucket ship to sail for the Pacific fisheries, and African-American

sailors may have accounted for more than 40 percent of American whaling crews.

Invention and Exploration

The invention of the cotton gin illustrated the close reciprocal relationship between expanding economic opportunity and advances in science and technology. By the late 1790s, one northerner claimed that "every neighborhood had its mechanical genius." By the turn of the century, water-powered sawmills operated in the Allegheny River valley in Pennsylvania and near Savannah and Mobile in the South. On a plantation near New Orleans, horse-drawn rollers squeezed the juice from sugar cane, to be left in pans to crystallize in the open air. In Philadelphia and New York, steam-powered refineries turned imported sugar into neat, white loaves. In 1803, Philadelphian Oliver Evans nearly succeeded in mechanizing the process of milling flour. Evans' mill weighed, cleaned, ground, and partly packaged flour by machine. Workers were needed only to dump the grain down a chute at the beginning of the process and to close the barrels at the end.

Many of America's inventors were native born, but from the 1790s on, merchants also actively sought to lure mechanics from England. One of those emigrants was Samuel Slater, who had apprenticed in the textile industry in England. In America, Slater joined the merchant firm of Almy and Brown and, by 1793, had established a mechanized spinning factory in Pawtucket, Rhode Island. The firm employed children in the mill itself and their parents to weave yarn in their homes. Both the economic and the political circumstances of the late 1790s boded well for mills like Slater's. The expansion of cotton production in the South provided raw fiber for the mills. The expansion of slavery in the South and the federal military build-up during Adams' administration created a demand for the yarn the mill produced. By 1800 Slater's first mill had grown large enough to employ more than 100 workers, and a second mill was underway. In 1804, there were four cotton mills in New England. By 1809, there were 87.

The needs of the United States government provided other spurs to science and technology. The War Department had already established one armory (at Springfield, Massachusetts, 1794) and had purchased land for a second (at Harpers Ferry, Virginia, 1798) when the war fever that accompanied the XYZ affair encouraged an aggressive search for new technologies in arms production. Two proposals seemed promising—one from Simeon North of Berlin, Connecticut, and one from Eli Whitney—in Hamden, Connecticut. Both men proposed more efficient production through the use of water power and the subdivision of labor. Of greater importance to the military, both espoused the principle of interchangeable parts, so that "the component parts" of each weapon "may be fitted to any other." The principle of interchangeability promised enormously increased efficiency in both production and use. As it turned out, Whitney was preoccupied during these years fighting off creditors and trying to assert a patent right to the cotton gin. Although he sketched out innovative plans, most of his rifle components were made in the independent shops of subcontractors and were not in fact interchangeable. North came closer to success. An 1816 review of his contract concluded that he had achieved "a more rigid uniformity" of parts than the investigators (the superintendents of the Springfield and Harper's Ferry armories) "have heretofore known."

The military not only promoted technological change, but it became an important reservoir of scientific knowledge. In 1802, the federal government founded the U. S. Military Academy at West Point, New York, an institution whose initial curriculum emphasized science and technology. This focus reflected the actual day-to-day deployments of the U. S. Army. Mustered out to escort settlers, protect surveyors, punish Indians, and enforce treaties, the Army was the government's arm of continental discovery. It was to an Army officer, Meriwether Lewis, that Jefferson entrusted the task of exploring the Louisiana Purchase in 1804. Military men led many of the subsequent early scientific expeditions in-

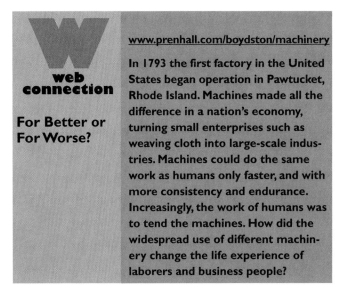

web connection

For Better or For Worse?

www.prenhall.com/boydston/machinery

In 1793 the first factory in the United States began operation in Pawtucket, Rhode Island. Machines made all the difference in a nation's economy, turning small enterprises such as weaving cloth into large-scale industries. Machines could do the same work as humans only faster, and with more consistency and endurance. Increasingly, the work of humans was to tend the machines. How did the widespread use of different machinery change the life experience of laborers and business people?

to the Trans-Mississippi West: Zebulon Pike in the Mississippi Valley and along the Arkansas River in 1805–1806 and 1806–1807, Stephen Long across the Great Plains in 1819, and John C. Frémont in the Pacific Northwest in 1843–1844.

Samuel Slater's water-powered Pawtucket mill, shown here in the early nineteenth century, lacked the power loom but showed that textile manufacturing could be a successful industry in the United States.

The Rule of Law and Lawyers

Americans had long emphasized the importance of the written and therefore *knowable* law to the preservation of the republic. By the turn of the century, however, it was apparent that the law of the republic lay only partly in written statutes. In a world of increasingly complex commercial contracts, patents, and land claims, law also existed in the skill of lawyers to argue cases and in the authority of judges to interpret them.

For workers, the social power of judicial interpretation became alarmingly clear in March of 1806, when the striking Philadelphia journeyman boot- and shoemakers were found guilty of common law conspiracy to restrain trade. Conservative Philadelphia newspapers applauded the verdict, but the Jeffersonian *Aurora* protested that there was nothing in the (written) Pennsylvania or U. S. Constitution to support such a decision. The paper condemned the use of (unwritten) English common law as a "curse entailed upon us by what has been called the '*parent country*'." The common law, the *Aurora* insisted, would soon "reduce the laboring whites to a condition still more despicable and abject" than "the unfortunate Africans."

New statutes echoed the common law bias against workers. All but four of the states passed laws that reinforced the power of masters over apprentices, in one case requiring runaways to serve double time for the labor lost. Such laws hinted at a growing restlessness of young workers, impatient with the authority of masters and the prolonged training required by the craft system, and at keen competition among employers for workers—problems faced even by Democratic Republican masters.

When the common law tradition clashed with economic development, however, judges tended to side with the interests of entrepreneurs. For example, English common law assumed the owners and users of waterways had a right to enjoy those waterways undisturbed by alterations upstream. As households and businesses experimented with the use of water power in manufacturing, they sought to erect dams and millraces that altered the flow of fish into lower streams. In 1805, in *Palmer v. Mulligan*, a New York court ruled in favor of the right of development, against customary common law rights. The bias toward economic development expressed in *Palmer v. Mulligan* would later be reflected in national judicial decisions.

The composition of Congress began to mirror the growing status and importance of lawyers in this culture of contracts and property rights. In the first Congress, only about one-third of the members were lawyers. By 1815 that proportion was more than half. From the ranks of the law would come the giants of the next generation: Henry Clay, Daniel Webster, John C. Calhoun, Andrew Jackson, and John Quincy Adams.

Although much of the work of lawyers occurred in the halls of Congress and the cities of the east coast, the power of the profession made itself felt even in the territories—as Daniel Boone learned, much to his chagrin. Well into the 1790s, Boone had been able to turn his knowledge of Kentucky into a thriving business as land hunter, enjoying fine commissions from speculators and accumulating a large land holding of his own. But by the turn of the century, the skills of the backwoodsman were giving way to the skills of the lawyer. "[N]ew claimants successfully contested our land titles," he recalled near the end of his life, "and once again we were thrown into poverty and despair." Many of the "new claimants" were the men who had once hired Boone's services, but who now hired lawyers against him.

The Political Economy of an "Empire of Liberty"

For Jefferson, the right of empire, like the right of free trade, was fundamental to the political economy of the republic. "By enlarging the empire of liberty," President Jefferson once observed, "we multiply its auxiliaries, and provide new sources of renovation, should its principles, at any time, degenerate, in those positions of our country which gave them birth." When Jefferson purchased the Louisiana Territory in 1803, he doubled the size of the United States. For many Americans, this did enlarge opportunities for freedom. The spatial growth of the nation had the opposite effect for other people, however. The cotton boom had already cemented slavery in the political economy of the South. The Louisiana Purchase supplied new territories for slavery's march west. In both the North and the South, the Louisiana Purchase ensured that the American assault on Native American lands, communities, and freedom would be projected across the Mississippi River (see Table 9-2).

TABLE 9-2

Population of the Western States and Territories			
State	**1790**	**1800**	**1810**
Kentucky	73,677	220,955	406,511
Tennessee	35,691	105,602	261,727
Ohio		45,365	230,760
Indiana		5,641	24,520
Illinois			12,282
Mississippi		8,850	40,352
Louisiana (Missouri)			20,845
Territory of Orleans (Louisiana)			76,556
Michigan			4,762

Source: E. R. Johnson and collaborators, History of Domestic and Foreign Commerce of the United States, *Table 12.*

The Louisiana Purchase

Whatever paradoxes of means and ends lay in the Tripoli War, they were eclipsed by Jefferson's purchase of Louisiana. Many citizens of the republic, including Jefferson himself, had long presumed that white Americans would eventually want lands west of the Mississippi for settlement, but Pinckney's 1795 treaty (which had improved American access to the Mississippi) had removed any need for immediate action.

Napoleon Bonaparte revived that urgency. By the turn of the century, American-French relations had chilled from the days when the two countries greeted each other as sister republics. Ambitious to establish his own empire in the Americas and determined to prevent further United States expansion, in 1800 Napoleon acquired Louisiana from Spain. Jefferson learned of the sale soon after coming into office. He worried that France would eventually send troops to occupy New Orleans, perhaps forcing the United States into a defensive alliance with Great Britain (an unsavory prospect to Jefferson). Hoping to block Napoleon, and perhaps to win West Florida (whose own-

ership had been left unclear in the sale) as an immediate consolation prize, Jefferson dispatched Robert Livingston to France.

Bonaparte had indeed intended to fortify New Orleans, but he first diverted his troops to Saint Domingue in an attempt to reverse the revolution there. His plan to reconquer the island fell victim to poor planning, yellow fever, and Domingian determination not to permit the restoration of slavery. Some 30,000 French troops died. Frustrated and in need of money, Bonaparte grew weary of the whole American enterprise.

Livingston saw his chance. Perhaps, he hinted, if West Florida were offered as a *gift*, the United States would take Louisiana off France's hands by purchase. As it turned out, Florida still belonged to Spain. Nevertheless, on April 12, 1803, the deal was struck. The United States paid France $11.25 million and agreed to take responsibility for satisfying American claims against France (from the Revolution) up to a value of an additional $3.75 million. For $15 million, or roughly three-and-a-half cents an acre, the United States obtained the Territory of Louisiana (see Map 9-1).

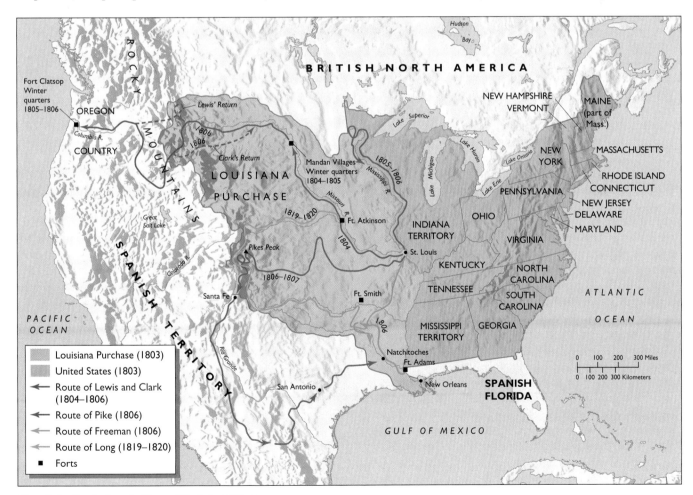

Map 9-1   Exploring the Trans-Mississippi West.
Although Lewis and Clark made the first exploration of the Louisiana Purchase, other explorers quickly followed. Among the most important were Zebulon Pike, who explored the Arkansas and Red Rivers, and Steven Long, who explored the Arkansas and Platte Rivers. Long described the plains as the "Great American Desert."

Jefferson's own "strict" reading of the Constitution indicated that the purchase required a constitutional amendment. He had implied as much to Albert Gallatin early in 1803, and he later repeated this conviction to John Dickinson of Pennsylvania: "The general government has no powers . . . of holding foreign territory, and still less of incorporating it into the Union." But Jefferson's Democratic Republican belief in explicit powers ran counter to his Democratic Republican belief that the nation required lands for future expansion and his fear that Napoleon might change his mind about the sale. The only serious constitutional objection raised by either party was whether the United States could grant citizenship to French and Spanish inhabitants simply by purchase, rather than by some process of naturalization. (In the end, it did. The status of the roughly 150,000 Indian inhabitants did not arise, and a congressional effort to outlaw slavery in the territory went nowhere.) Jefferson rationalized to himself "that the good sense of our country will correct the evil of [loose] construction when it shall produce ill effects."

Surveying Louisiana

When the United States had requested a statement of the exact boundaries of its purchase, French minister Talleyrand had declined: "You have made a noble bargain for yourselves, and I suppose you will make the most of it." That was exactly what Jefferson intended, and he was optimistic that there would be much to make.

At least three times before (twice in the 1780s and once in the 1790s), Jefferson had supported proposed expeditions to the West. Those American efforts had not materialized, but on July 22, 1793, a Scotsman by the name of Alexander Mackenzie had succeeded in traveling overland from Montreal to the Pacific. Published in London in 1801, Mackenzie's *Voyages* reached Jefferson in 1802. Long before Louisiana was in the hands of the United States, Jefferson began to plan its exploration.

To lead the expedition, Jefferson appointed his trusted secretary, Captain Meriwether Lewis, and another officer, William Clark. Lewis was an ambitious soldier with some experience in the old Northwest. He was familiar with Mackenzie's account, enjoyed Jefferson's complete confidence, and had received Jefferson's own tutoring in the natural sciences. Clark, who had commanded troops on the Mississippi, was a skilled surveyor and mapmaker. Their mission, as outlined in Jefferson's instructions, was "to explore the Missouri River, & such principal streams of it, as, by its course and communication with the waters of the Pacific Ocean, whether the Columbia, Oregon, Colorado or any other river may offer the most direct & practicable water communication across this continent for the purposes of commerce." The commerce Jefferson sought was not across the Pacific. His eyes were on the Indians liv-

ing along the northern Missouri and its tributaries, whose trade was now enjoyed chiefly by the British.

The expedition set out from St. Louis on May 14, 1804. It included three boats containing 45 men and a dog, firearms, medicines, scientific instruments, tools, twenty barrels of flour, and seven barrels of salt. They traveled first up the Missouri River, closely observed by the Mandans and the Minnetarees and later the Hidatsas, who visited their camps at night and sent ahead stories of these curious people. In early November, the white men stopped to make their winter camp near present-day Bismarck, North Dakota. When the expedition broke camp the following spring, a Shoshone woman, Sacagawea, her French-Canadian trapper husband, Charbonneau, and their newly born child left with them.

As a young girl, Sacagawea had been captured and adopted by the Minnetarees. Now, traveling with Lewis and Clark, she would return home. En route, her foraging and fishing skills added roots, berries, and fish to the party's diet. As the party moved up the Missouri into the land of the Shoshones, she became an invaluable guide and interpreter. At last, on August 17, 1805, Sacagawea met again a brother and a nephew, and the friend with whom she had been captured many years before.

Some of the expedition's encounters with Native Americans were less friendly. Far more dangerous than the Indians, however, were the waterfalls and rapids, the cliffs, the freezing temperatures and paralyzing snows, the inevitable accidents, diseases (especially dysentery), and dead-end trails. The final portage across the Rocky Mountains in the fall of 1805 proved longer and more difficult than Jefferson or Lewis had anticipated. Snow and hail brought the expedition's progress to a standstill. Even with a skilled guide, the party got lost. Exhausted and underfed animals wandered off. Supplies ran out. On the verge of slaughtering their pack animals, the expedition at last cleared the worst of the mountains and came to Indian villages where they were fed and sheltered. On November 7, 1805, Lewis and Clark finally reached the Pacific Ocean.

Throughout their journey, Lewis and Clark had represented themselves as the envoys of a great nation to whom the Native Americans should now direct their commerce. To cement these new trade relations, they presented medals of friendship to Native American leaders. But they also kept an eye out for the prospects of future settlement. What they found, according to Lewis, was "a most delightfull country . . . fertile in the extreem . . . covered with lofty and excellent timber." Game ran thick, and scores of varieties of fish filled the waterways. The plains gave way to the prairies, the prairies to the forested mountains, the mountains to the verdant Pacific coast. It was, Lewis wrote to his mother in March, 1804, "one of the fa[i]rest portions of the globe." After their return, in 1806, parts of their journals and letters, including detailed maps and drawings, slowly found their way into print, advertising to the thousands of settlers who would soon follow the full extent of America's new "empire of liberty."

The Burr Conspiracy

Even before Lewis and Clark had returned, other Americans had their eyes on the West. While Lewis and Clark traveled as national representatives and imagined national glory, men like Aaron Burr saw in the West the means to personal aggrandizement.

If any man was born to prominence, it was Aaron Burr. The scion of an old New England family (his grandfather was minister Jonathan Edwards), Burr had been elected to the Senate from New York at a young age and had been a presidential candidate in the 1796 election. By 1804, as vice president of the United States, he seemed destined for greatness.

There had always been nagging reservations about Burr. Even his supporters whispered that his "principles" were unclear and that he was "unsettled in his politics." Worried about Burr's periodic efforts to court Federalist support, Alexander Hamilton was particularly severe, declaring Burr a man of "extreme and irregular ambitions . . . far more cunning than wise, far more dextrous than able." When he heard of Hamilton's remarks in 1804, Burr challenged him to a duel. Hamilton was mortally wounded, and Burr's public career was ruined.

Burr refocused his ambitions on the West. In 1805, after leaving office, he made his way to New Orleans. He may have intended to foment rebellion in Louisiana, perhaps to assemble a corps of mercenaries to invade Mexico or Florida. In any event, by 1806 he had raised a force of several thousand men, setting off a wave of rumors that eventually reached Washington. Convinced that Burr intended treason, Jefferson ordered his arrest. Burr was captured trying to make his way to Pensacola and returned to Richmond to stand trial for treason before John Marshall, who happened to be riding the federal circuit. Prosecution proved difficult. Fearful of being compromised by publication of subpoenaed documents, Jefferson claimed executive privilege and refused to provide them. For his part, Marshall interpreted treason in the narrowest sense possible, as requiring two witnesses to an overt act of war against the United States (or of abetting the nation's declared enemies). No witnesses were forthcoming. Acquitted, Burr lived to a ripe old age practicing law in New York.

Indian Resistance to Republican Empire

In the world of the slave Gabriel, opportunities created by national expansion had heightened the agonies of slavery. In the world of the Eastern Woodlands, America's political economy of aggressive expansion collided violently with Native American practices.

In 1800, large areas of land remained under dispute in the trans-Appalachian region. Although the Treaty of Greenville had presumably established United States control of most of Ohio, Hurons, Delawares, Shawnees, and remnants of the Iroquois Confederation occupied reservations there. The newly created Indiana Territory (the later states of Indiana, Illinois, and Wisconsin) contained most of the remaining Indian lands in the Northwest, including the homes of the Sauk, Fox, Kickapoos, Menominees, Winnebagoes, and Ojibwas. To the south, Cherokees and Creeks still dwelled in the Carolinas, Georgia, and Tennessee; Seminoles controlled the Georgia-Florida border; and Choctaws and Chickasaws resided in Mississippi Territory.

As settlers occupied new lands, Indians lost their villages and fields. Thrown back increasingly on the fur trade, they over-hunted dwindling grounds. By the turn of the century, many of the pelts and skins brought to traders by Menominees, Sauks, and Ojibwas in the Northwest Territory had in fact been hunted west of the Mississippi, and the deer were all but gone in the Southeast. Protestant missionaries urged the Indians to adopt Euro-American religious and social practices, including male-headed households and the private ownership of property. Unscrupulous agents coaxed and bullied Indian nations into signing away their claims to the land. When the Indians resisted, the agents made deals with leaders they knew to be of doubtful legitimacy, promising bounties and annuities for territory. This crisis of cultural and economic survival virtually assured armed confrontation.

Although he expressed benevolence toward Indians (in *Notes on the State of Virginia*, he had described them as "in body and mind equal to the white man"), President Jefferson believed that Native Americans must give way to American settlement. Not only did the territories represent the supply of land necessary to nurture republican virtues and stabilize republican institutions internally, but they provided a buffer against the threats Britain, France, and Spain posed on the western borders. Jefferson much preferred that American westward expansion occur peacefully. He tried to enforce the boundaries between white and Indian lands designated in trade and intercourse acts and offered to relocate Indians to protected reserves where they could learn Euro-American ways. But he contentedly saw a cycle of growing dependency in which Indians would eventually have no choice but to turn to settled agriculture and sell off their lands (see Map 9-2).

Native Americans resisted these assaults on their autonomy. Seneca communities accepted missionary aid, but only selectively, refusing to abandon their community holdings, their gender division of labor, or their matrilineal households. The great southern nations declined Jefferson's promise of new lands in the West and focused on constructing the types of internal institutions that Americans might be forced to recognize as "civilized." For example, the Cherokees adopted a series of laws that functioned as a

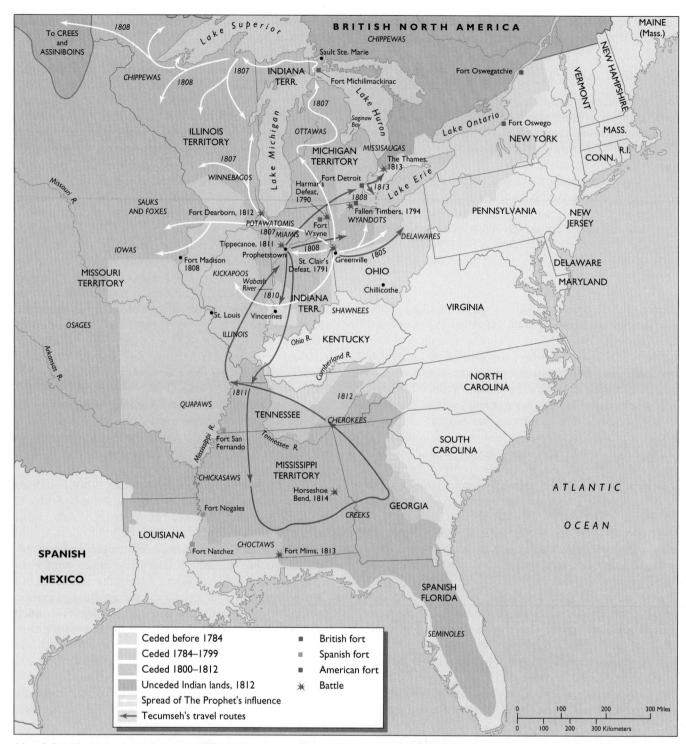

Map 9-2   Mounting Land Pressure, 1784–1812, and the Rise of Tecumseh's Confederation.
The pan-Indian movement led by Tecumseh and The Prophet was the culmination of years of United States incursions into Indian lands and pressure, official and unofficial, on Indians to cede territories to the United States. As this map suggests, the influence of Tecumseh and The Prophet was greatest in the regions most recently ceded or where ongoing pressure was greatest in 1800–1810.

constitution, established a congress, and executed individual land titles. Through their principal chiefs, Native Americans repudiated illegal treaties and the members of their own communities who had participated in those treaties, but they also disavowed raiding parties that drove

miners and settlers from lands promised them in earlier treaties.

Resistance to Euro-American culture also took the form of a broad movement for spiritual revitalization. Ganioda'yo (Handsome Lake), who rose to influence among the Senecas after 1799, preached revival through a synthesis of traditional beliefs and Christianity, but among other groups revitalization centered on cleansing themselves of Euro-American practices. As early as 1796, Munsee Delawares reported seeing an apparition that "reproached" them for abandoning their traditional values. A Seneca girl dreamed that the Quakers were "Devil[s]" come to destroy the Indians, and a Mohawk was warned in a vision that all Iroquois people should return to old forms of worship. In the South, Cherokees revived the Green Corn Ceremony, which celebrated the importance of personal bonds and repudiated material wealth. Federal agent Jonathan Meigs reported the growing influence of Cherokee shamans, who taught their people "that the great spirit is angry with them for adopting the manners, customs, and manners of the white people who they think are very wicked."

The rejection of Euro-American culture was not purely symbolic, however. As early as 1807, William Henry Harrison, governor of Indiana Territory, heard rumors that war belts were being passed among the northwestern tribes, with "a general combination of the Indians for a war against the United States" as the object. But it took two Shawnee leaders, Tecumseh and his half-brother, Tenskwatawa (known as The Prophet), to coalesce the diffuse anger into effective organized resistance. Tecumseh was respected as a warrior, an orator, and a judicious leader. Witnessing the repeated massacre of Shawnees and the invasion of their lands, he developed a fixed hatred of whites and fought against them both in the Northwest and with

the Cherokees and Creeks in the South, experiences that later helped him build a pan-Indian alliance. His brother Tenskwatawa became influential after 1805 as the leader of a movement that rejected white culture, including the use of woven cloth, individual ownership of land, and intermarriage with whites. About 1808, Tecumseh and Tenskwatawa founded a village in present-day Indiana on the banks of the Tippecanoe River. There The Prophet remained while Tecumseh traveled as far east as New York and as far south as Florida encouraging organized resistance to white settlement.

By 1811, Tecumseh's widespread success alarmed Harrison. That fall, as Tecumseh made his way to the villages of the Cherokees and the Creeks, Harrison marched an army toward Tecumseh's village on the Tippecanoe River in Indiana. Although cautioned by Tecumseh not to be drawn into battle in his absence, on November 7, 1811, The Prophet engaged Harrison's troops and was thoroughly defeated. The Prophet was discredited, but when war broke out between Britain and the United States the following year, Tecumseh retained sufficient influence to amass a huge force on the side of the British. He played a decisive role in the British victory over United States troops at Detroit but was killed in battle on Canadian soil in October 1813. His death marked the end of organized Indian resistance east of the Mississippi.

The Second War With England

In the fall of 1804, Jefferson's popularity was soaring. Internal taxes had been abolished, the national debt was falling, the United States had (seemingly) stood up to international coercion, and, most amazing, America had acquired a huge western empire. Choosing George Clinton of New York as his running mate, Jefferson won re-election handily (162 electoral votes to Federalist Charles C. Pinckney's 14), and the Democratic Republican Party took control of both houses of Congress. Faced with the prospect of federal surpluses, Jefferson began to contemplate a future role for the federal government encouraging "the great objects of public education, roads, rivers, canals, and such other objects of public improvement as may be thought proper." Jefferson acknowledged that such ventures would require a constitutional amendment. Nevertheless, that Jefferson even considered such initiatives illustrates the Democratic Republican drift toward a political economy based on federal activism. These reveries were soon overtaken by transatlantic politics. A "national road" from Washington through Cumberland, Maryland, to Wheeling, Virginia, was laid out, but that was all. Jefferson's second term had barely begun when his attention was riveted to developments in Europe.

Tecumseh, a sagacious Shawnee leader and skilled warrior, organized the last concerted resistance to white settlement east of the Mississippi River.

Neutrality and Isolation

In his first inaugural address, Jefferson had counseled "peace, commerce, and honest friendship with all nations, entangling alliances with none." He remained committed to American neutrality as he commenced his second term. But by 1805 Napoleon's rise to power in France and his expansionistic designs upon Europe had considerably complicated this policy. On the one hand, Jefferson was eager to settle the unresolved question of West Florida, still claimed by Spain, and knew he might yet need France's help. On the other hand, Napoleon's growing power and France's increasing indifference toward American shipping rights raised the possibility that the United States might need Britain as an ally. Napoleon's victory over Austria in 1805 made France the undisputed master of Western Europe. At the same time, English victories over the fleets of France and of France's sometimes-ally Spain had made England the undisputed master of the seas. The stalemate was to have dire consequences for American shipping.

Jefferson's early hopes that Britain might respect the neutrality of American ships were dashed in 1805 when Britain reasserted an old policy (suspended since 1800) to seize ships traveling between enemy ports. The revived practice was announced with the seizure of the American ship *Essex*, which was en route to Cuba from Spain after a brief stop in an American port, and the subsequent seizure of more than 200 American ships in that year alone. Not to be outdone, Napoleon declared a blockade of England and also began seizing American ships on the high seas, in coastal waters, and barely out of European ports. In June of 1807 the British ship *Leopold* raised the stakes, stopping the American frigate *Chesapeake* just as it left the port of Norfolk, Virginia. Insisting that the *Chesapeake* had recruited British deserters for its crew, the captain of the *Leopold* demanded the right to search the American ship. When he was denied, he disabled the ship with cannon fire, boarded it, and took four men prisoner, leaving the *Chesapeake* to limp home in ignominy.

Fortunately, Congress was not in session, for otherwise American outrage might have brought immediate war with England. As it was, Jefferson had the summer to try to discover "peaceable means of repressing injustice." He immediately ordered all British ships out of American waters and demanded reparation for the *Chesapeake*. By the time Congress returned, in the early fall, sentiment had quieted slightly. In secret sessions, Congress passed an act that permitted only those American ships with the president's express approval to sail into foreign ports and prohibiting foreign ships

from the American export trade. In effect, the United States had embargoed itself.

It was the most disastrous policy of Jefferson's career. Because enforcement was virtually impossible, the embargo had a highly uneven effect on Americans. Large and well-heeled merchants who could bear the risks enjoyed the large profits of smuggling. At the same time, small merchants, sailors, and shopkeepers who were dependent on a steady maritime trade were thrown into crisis, and farmers in the South and West, who needed regular markets, had trouble finding overseas trading outlets for their cotton and grain. As the economy settled into depression in 1808, the surviving elements of the Federalist Party charged that the embargo was actually helping Napoleon, whose weaker navy was free to concentrate on the British. Adding to American frustration, Napoleon now disingenuously claimed the right to attack U. S. ships in any continental port, since by the president's own order they could not be legal carriers.

The ironies of the embargo did not end there. Jefferson signed the first law on December 22, 1807, but as violations mounted, Congress passed, and the president signed, ever more repressive versions of the bill, versions that eventually endangered the liberties of Americans. The final, fifth Embargo Act (signed January 9, 1809) swept away protections against self-incrimination and the right to due process and trampled on the right to trial by jury. By comparison, even the hated Federalist Alien and Sedition Acts looked tame.

In this pro-Federalist cartoon, titled "An Old Philosopher Teaching His Mad Son Economical Projects, 1809," Jefferson and Madison pull a U.S. ship into harbor at the bidding of Napoleon, while a contentious Congress (its galleries closed to the public) debates the Embargo Act.

As he himself at last acknowledged, the Embargo Acts represented the final failure of Jefferson's agrarian political economy. His dream of a republic of farmers was dead, the victim of the very principles of territorial expansion and free trade upon which he had based it. Pinning America's need for manufactured goods solely on "this exuberant commerce," as Jefferson admitted in 1809, "brings us into collision with other powers in every sea, and will force us into every war of the European powers. The converting of this great agricultural country into a city of Amsterdam,—a mere headquarters for carrying on the commerce of all nations, is too absurd."

With American prestige turned into a joke, American commerce deteriorating, and American agriculture crying out for relief, on March 1, 1809, Jefferson signed a bill repealing the Embargo Act. Three days later, Jefferson left the office that he now described as a "splendid misery."

Democratic Republican Power and Disunity

Jefferson's was not the only misery. Although the great majority of Americans supported the president, the embargo nevertheless inflicted hardship on most average Americans. Sailors were stranded in port, artisans saw their markets dwindle and disappear, and farmers had no place to sell their export crops. Soon, the broad anguish caused by the Embargo Acts brought into the open long-simmering dissension within Democratic Republican ranks.

Cracks in party unity had become evident almost as soon as Jefferson took office. An early controversy concerned Georgia's western territories, ceded to the federal government in 1802. A history of shady dealings had confused the titles to some of the lands. When Jefferson offered to buy out claimants, a few fellow Democratic Republicans began to worry that he was winking at corruption.

A far more serious rupture came in the aftermath of the Louisiana Purchase. Although Jefferson insisted that he had obtained West Florida as a part of the Louisiana Purchase, Spain claimed that it had never ceded that land to France in the first place. Napoleon hedged, but his ministers let it be known that the right price might convince them to lobby the American cause with Spain. Jefferson approached Congress for the money.

To his critics, Jefferson's willingness to bribe France was the last straw. Loosely organized, Jefferson's congressional critics dubbed themselves the *Tertium Quid* (the "third something") as a way of distinguishing themselves from both the Federalists and the majority Democratic Republican caucus. Their most vocal spokesperson, John Randolph, broke publicly with the administration, explaining that he felt his choice was to "co-operate or be an honest man." But the renegade *Quids* were outnumbered by party stalwarts. When he publicly sided with Randolph, Speaker of the House Nathaniel Macon lost the speakership.

By 1808, the *Quids* were threatening open rebellion. Although Secretary of State James Madison seemed the logical heir to Jefferson's presidency, Quids talked of throwing their support to James Monroe of Virginia or even Vice President George Clinton of New York. To avoid the risk of public party brawling, in 1808 party loyalists met in closed caucus to select Jefferson's successor. They chose James Madison. In the election, Madison captured 122 electoral votes to Federalist Charles C. Pinckney's 47. Clinton, who ended up on the ballot, won only 6 electoral votes. The Democratic Republicans again won both houses of Congress.

"King Caucus" had inaugurated its reign. From 1801 until 1829, the federal government would remain under the control of a single party. In and of itself, that did not challenge Democratic Republican principles. Neither Madison nor Jefferson considered a two-party system a necessary feature of American political life. Both men, however, had warned against the day when a small cadre of like-minded men would meet together in secret to choose the nation's ruler. Democratic Republican ascendancy itself had now come to rest upon just such a closed institution.

The War of 1812

James Madison had stood side by side with Thomas Jefferson on virtually every important political and ideological issue since the founding of the nation. In 1809 Madison inherited his friend's presidential woes.

Madison's approach to the international trade crisis and to the growing tensions between the United States and England, on the one hand, and France, on the other, differed little from that pursued by Jefferson. Like Jefferson, Madison favored American neutrality and free trade. Like Jefferson, he favored defensive policies of commercial coercion over aggressive policies of alliance and armed conflict.

In 1809, with Madison's approval, Congress replaced the embargo with the Non-Intercourse Act, reopening trade with all Europe except England and France, but authorizing the president to reopen commercial ties with whichever of these countries dropped its restrictions and attacks on American shipping. The act set off a series of diplomatic feints on the part of England and France, as both pretended to be on the verge of altering their policies without making actual concessions.

In this game, France eventually came out ahead. In the summer of 1810, Napoleon's ministers officially communicated to Madison that, as of November of that year, France would reverse its policy toward American trade and stop seizing American ships on the condition that Britain would do likewise. Probably correctly, Britain did not believe France would follow through on this policy. But Madison did accept the French declarations, and he altered American non-intercourse policy to apply to Britain alone.

Still, war might have been averted. A quarter of a century of European wars and Napoleon's "Continental policy," which effectively closed continental markets to English goods, had taken its toll on Britain's economy. Although far more powerful militarily than the United States, Britain would have been happy to avoid the cost of an additional declared war with any nation. Unfortunately, on June 1, 1812, in light of a seeming change in French policy and continuing British attacks on American shipping, Madison had requested that Congress declare war on Great Britain. On June 4, the House voted a war bill. On June 18, the Senate concurred. Ironically, two days earlier, on June 1, unaware of events in the United States, England had announced that it was revoking its maritime policy against United States ships.

The war vote in Congress suggested that the young nation faced domestic as well as international troubles. The vote went largely along party, and regional, lines. New England shippers remained firmly opposed, protesting that shipping was just beginning to recover and that American prosperity was deeply dependent upon Britain (America's chief trading partner in pre-embargo days). Hurt by the embargo's restrictions on the markets for their produce, farmers and planters in the West and South were ready to fight to open up the seas. They suspected that the war might prove useful in other ways, too. Western migrants were convinced that Creek and Shawnee resistance was the work of the British, still hanging onto their forts along the Great Lakes. War with England could provide the excuse for an American invasion of Canada, which could, in turn, serve the dual purpose of grabbing more land for Americans and wiping out the Indians. Southern planters believed that the Spanish in Florida provided shelter and solace to interracial communities of Creeks and runaway slaves engaged in guerrilla resistance against the encroaching white settlers. Combat with England might also cover illegal American retaliatory missions in the Florida peninsula.

Even the Democratic Republicans were not fully unified, however. Led by Henry Clay of Kentucky and John C. Calhoun of South Carolina, the War Hawks (a group of fiercely nationalistic and resolutely expansionist young men who had come of age since the Revolution) were eager to respond to British insults. Democratic Moderate Republicans were more hesitant. Not only did they dread the cost of the war, but, after years of budget cuts, many doubted that the nation could gear up to take on such a formidable foe.

All of these tensions were reflected in the election of 1812. Maverick Republican De Witt Clinton, who doubted that the painfully shy Madison had the temperament to be an effective commander in chief, rallied the support of Federalists and ran as Madison's opposition. He did not win, but his 89 electoral votes (to Madison's 128) constituted a higher proportion than the Federalists had enjoyed since the election of 1800.

Doubts about America's war readiness were soon justified (see Map 9-3). An attempt in the summer of 1812 to invade Canada floundered in confusion and indecision. Two thousand American troops under a hesitant General William Hull surrendered at Detroit, and two overland advances (one up the Niagara River toward Queenston Heights and another along Lake Champlain toward Montreal) failed when state militiamen insisted that their military obligations did not include leaving the country to fight. Only Commodore Perry's dramatic victory on Lake Erie saved American honor in the North. On September 10, 1813, after having 21 men dead and 63 wounded on his flagship *Lawrence* and scrambling hastily onto the *Niagara,* Perry at last forced the surrender of the entire British Great Lakes squadron. "We have met the enemy," he relayed to a relieved General William Henry Harrison, "and they are ours—two ships, two brigs, one schooner, and a sloop."

A comparable victory eluded Americans in the Atlantic. After a few initial successes at sea, the tiny American Navy (consisting of seven frigates) was easily overwhelmed by superior British sea power and spent the rest of the war cowed in port. Americans turned to private schooners and sloops, highly maneuverable and jerry-rigged for war, and by the war's end managed to capture more than 1,300 British vessels. Nevertheless, by 1813 the British Navy had succeeded in blockading the American coast from the Chesapeake south through the Gulf of Mexico to New Orleans. The following year the blockade was extended to New England, cutting off the last dribbles of trade between America and Europe. Viewing the United States as pursuing a deliberate policy of destruction on the Canadian border, the British fleet pummeled the United States cities and villages along the coast, first bombarding them from sea and then sending parties on shore to fire the ruins and attack the fleeing refugees. On Wednesday, August 24, the British troops invaded Washington and laid waste the federal government, burning the Capitol, the White House, the Treasury Building, and the Naval Yard, and terrorizing the civilian population. The entire cabinet, including President James Madison, fled in confusion to a quickly devised hideout. Dolley Madison paused to save the Gilbert Stuart portrait of George Washington before making her way separately to the countryside. So unpopular was her husband's war policy that she had to travel in disguise in order to obtain food and shelter.

While Washington lay smoldering, the British turned their attention to Baltimore. All through the night of September 13–14 the ships fired on Fort McHenry, the island citadel that guarded Baltimore's harbor. Among the anguished observers in the harbor was a Washington lawyer by the name of Francis Scott Key, detained on a British ship as the bombardment continued. Elated when the rising sun revealed the United States flag still flying over the fort, Key quickly scribbled out the words that would in

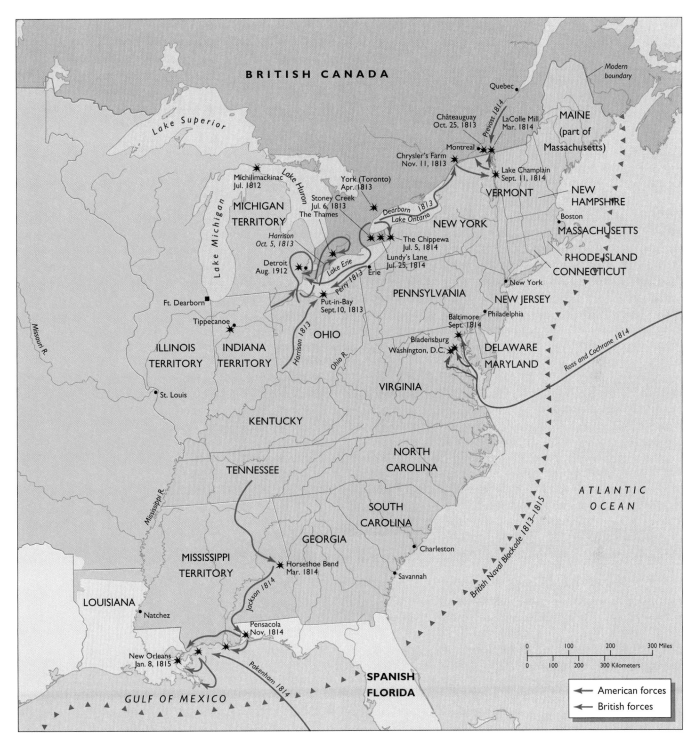

Map 9-3   Battles and Campaigns of the War of 1812.
The War of 1812 was largely a naval war, fought along the Atlantic coast, in the Gulf of Mexico, and on the Great Lakes. Several land campaigns proved important, however: the British ground attack that ended in the looting and burning of the capital, and Jackson's trek overland to New Orleans.

1931 be adopted as the lyrics of the national anthem, "The Star-Spangled Banner."

In the South, Andrew Jackson used the war to suppress Indian resistance to U. S. settlement, resistance he believed incited by British provocateurs operating in Spanish West Florida. When news reached Nashville that the militant Creek faction known as the "Red Sticks" had attacked a U. S. fort and settlers in Mississippi Territory, Jackson quickly assembled a volunteer militia, including a few free African Americans and Indians, and went in pursuit. In

March 1814, Jackson caught and defeated the insurgents at Horseshoe Bend, forcing them to sign a treaty whereby the Creek Nation ceded two-thirds of its remaining lands to the United States.

The Making of Heroes and Knaves

For a time the war worked in favor of the Federalists. Although they were not able to win the presidency in the election of 1812, they did capitalize on opposition to the war to double their numbers in Congress. Perhaps misled by those results and by the disunity within the Democratic Republican Party, some Federalists grew rash. Angry at declining profits and frustrated by Virginia's domination of the presidency, in October of 1814, Massachusetts Federalists called for a convention of the New England States "to lay the foundation for a radical reform in the National compact." They planned to meet on December 15 in Hartford, Connecticut.

The Federalists who convened in Hartford were divided. Extreme Federalists, arguing that the union could no longer be saved, lobbied for a separate New England confederacy that could immediately seek an end to the war. More moderate voices prevailed, however. In the end, the convention sought not secession, but rather amendments to the Constitution. They demanded restrictions on the power of Congress to declare war, an end to the "Three-Fifths Compromise" that allowed slaves to be counted for purposes of representation, exclusion of naturalized citizens from elective federal office, and restrictions on the admissions of new states. The Federalists also sought to limit the number of terms a president could serve and the frequency with which the candidate for president could be chosen from a given state. The resolutions expressed not only a hostility toward Democratic Republicans (in, for example, the restrictions on naturalized citizens and on new states) but also a developing identification of the Republicans as the party of the South.

Federalists misjudged their strength and mistimed their efforts. By 1814 the Napoleonic wars were ending. Weary of war, Great Britain was ready to end even the skirmish with its former colonies. Battering the United States in North America, however, and emerging as the dominant power in Europe, Britain had little incentive to offer the Americans more than simple peace. Signed in Ghent, Belgium, on December 24, 1814, the treaty that ended the War of 1812 was silent on the issues of free trade and impressment that had triggered the war and sidestepped boundary

disputes between Canada and the United States by referring them to commissions of arbitration. On only one point did the British negotiators give ground. They agreed to remove British troops from the Northwest and ended efforts to protect neutral Indians in the region, in effect acknowledging the failure of trans-Appalachian Indian resistance to white settlers and the state and federal governments that supported them. It was an important concession for white Americans, but it was a small victory to carry away from a devastating war.

Only Andrew Jackson's ragtag militia saved Americans from outright humiliation. After the victory at Horseshoe Bend, Jackson's troops had made their way south to Pensacola and west to New Orleans, where a British fleet of more than 50 ships prepared to attack the city and take control of the mouth of the Mississippi River. Unaware that a peace treaty had been signed, on January 8, 1815, a force of 7,500 British regulars stormed Jackson's position. Although less polished and trained, Jackson's men were scrappy and skilled, and in thirty minutes the battle was over. Miraculously, the Americans had won. Almost 300 British soldiers had died and another 1,700 had been wounded, compared to only 31 Americans dead and 40 wounded. Bringing Jackson into the national limelight and establishing him as a national hero, the Battle of New Orleans signaled the rise of a new star, a rise that would eventually spell the end of Democratic Republican domination of American national politics and the coming of the second two-party system.

This engraving portrays the surrender of Creek war leader Red Eagle to Andrew Jackson following the Battle of Horseshoe Bend in 1814.

But that day was still a decade away. In the early days of 1815, the chief political importance of Jackson's victory was the lift it gave to American nationalism and the light it cast on the Federalist Hartford Convention, still meeting in Connecticut. Threatening secession was one thing in the context of a failing war, quite another in a moment of national triumph. Suddenly, the proceedings at Hartford seemed downright traitorous.

Conclusion

It was more than the turn of a century that made the Age of Jefferson an age of transition. Between 1800 and 1815, both the people and the political leaders of the nation endeavored to understand the meaning of their experiment in republican government, economics, and society. As they built upon the institutions that had characterized the beginnings of that experiment (liberty of belief, voluntary citizenship, economic freedom), they also changed those institutions forever, gradually laying the foundation for the industrial political economy of nineteenth-century America. They embraced the continuing development of a market economy and free labor, but an economy of transatlantic commerce and nascent manufacturing relied on the institution of slavery. American settlers humbled themselves before their God, but the renewal of grace did not deter their proud march across the continent. Indeed, regeneration seemed simply to reconfirm their sense of national destiny. Buoyed by the end of the War of 1812, the market expanded and further loosened bonds of deference and rank. But many Americans worried about the communities that would be fostered in the new democracy.

CHRONOLOGY

1800 Gabriel's conspiracy
Thomas Jefferson elected president
American ships carry 95 percent of US-British trade
Samuel Slater's Pawtucket Spinning Mill employs 100 people

1801 Federalists pass Judiciary Act of 1801
Cane Ridge (Kentucky) Revival
Barbary War

1803 Louisiana Purchase
Marbury v. Madison establishes principle of judicial review

1804 Jefferson re-elected
Lewis and Clark begin exploration of Louisiana

1805 *Palmer v. Mulligan* (New York)
Essex Decision (British Admiralty Court)

1806 Philadelphia journeyman shoemakers convicted of conspiracy

1807 First Embargo Act

1808 External slave trade becomes illegal
(by 1807 act of Congress)
Democratic Republicans nominate James Madison in closed Congressional caucus
Madison elected president

1809 Non-Intercourse Act

1810 American cotton production reaches 178,000 bales a year

1811 Tecumseh at peak of influence
Battle of Tippecanoe River

1812 Congress declares war on Great Britain
Madison re-elected

1814 Federalists convene Hartford Convention
Treaty of Ghent ends War of 1812

1815 Battle of New Orleans

1816 American Colonization Society founded
African Methodist Episcopal Church founded

Review Questions

1. In what specific ways did Jefferson's philosophical emphasis on the importance of agriculture and commerce reflect everyday life in the United States in 1800?

2. What was the "empire of liberty"? What did it represent to Jefferson? To potential white settlers? To enslaved African Americans? To Indians?

3. Why did many westward migrants and members of new evangelical sects perceive the Jeffersonian Republi-cans as preferable to the Federalists? What aspects of Democratic Republican thought and/or style might have appealed to them?

4. In his first inaugural address, Jefferson said "We are all Republicans, we are all Federalists." In what ways was this an accurate statement?

5. Characterize the differences between Jefferson's first administration and his second.

Further Readings

Gregory Evans Dowd, *A Spirited Resistance: The North American Indian Struggle for Unity, 1745–1815* (1992). Dowd argues for the emergence, in Jeffersonian America, of a coordinated and militant resistance, led by prophets like Tenskwatawa and by his half brother, Tecumseh, and expressed through a pan-Indian spiritual revival.

Douglas R. Egerton, *Gabriel's Rebellion: The Virginia Slave Conspiracies* (1993). The source of much of the dis-cussion of Gabriel in this chapter, Egerton's book locates Gabriel's rebellion both within the political ferment be-tween Republicans and Federalists in late-eighteenth-century Virginia and within the history of slave resistance in the Americas.

Gary B. Nash, *Forging Freedom: The Formation of Philadelphia's Black Community, 1720–1840* (1988). This study of the struggles of Philadelphia's African-American population (both enslaved and free) to build a community in the early republic includes discussions of work, religion, class, and the responses of the African-American commu-nity to growing white hostility.

Curtis P. Nettels, *The Emergence of a National Econ-omy, 1775–1815* (1962). Although almost fifty years old, this remains one of the clearest and most comprehensive overviews of shipping, farming, business, and manufactur-ing in Jefferson's America and of the inventors, workers, and settlers who made those changes possible.

Howard B. Rock, *Artisans of the New Republic: The Tradesmen of New York City in the Age of Jefferson* (1984). Rock traces the experience of the craftworkers of New York City, 1800–1815, examining the legacy of pride and independence that mechanics and tradesmen carried with them from the Revolution and the dislocations and loss of status threatened by the changing marketplace and the expanding commercial economy.

Robert W. Tucker and David C. Hendrickson, *Empire of Liberty: The Statecraft of Thomas Jefferson* (1990). This exploration of Jefferson's political philosophy and foreign policy is an especially useful guide to the circumstances surrounding the Louisiana Purchase and the War of 1812.

Laurel Thatcher Ulrich, *A Midwife's Tale: The Life of Martha Ballard, Based on her Diary, 1785–1812* (1990). A 20-year-long diary provided the primary source for this careful examination of the work, family events, and daily social interactions of a midwife in rural Maine in the early republic.

History on the Internet

"Thomas Jefferson on Politics and Government"

http://etext.virginia.edu/jefferson/quotations/

Containing over 2,700 quotes from Thomas Jefferson, this site contains, in his own words, Jefferson's thoughts on the theory and structure of Republican government, citizens' rights, and judicial review. Also, this site offers numerous links to other resources that contain additional writings of Jefferson.

Technology and Change

Read about two men and the technology they implemented that changed the social, economic, and political landscapes of America.

"Eli Whitney"

http://eliwhitney.org.ew.htm

This site contains information about Whitney and his invention of the cotton gin, which made cotton and slavery even more viable staples in the southern economy.

"Samuel Slater: Father of the American Industrial Revolution"

http://www.geocities.com/~woon_heritage/slater.htm

Containing text and photos of Slater's Rhode Island mill operation and his mill villages, this site provides information on the textile workers, adult and children, and how early industrialization shaped their lives. You can also take a virtual tour of the Slaterville Mill and Industrial Villages.

The Expansion and Exploration of the West

"The Louisiana Purchase Treaty, April 30, 1803"

http://www.yale.edu/lawweb/avalon/diplomacy/louis1.htm

Read the full text of this historic treaty that greatly enlarged the nation and helped to fulfill the republican hopes for westward expansion of territory.

"Lewis and Clark: The Journey of the Corps of Discovery"

http://www.pbs.org/lewisandclark/inside/idx_cir.htm

Trace the discoveries of Lewis and Clark in what was the Jeffersonian West through this website. Timelines, maps, academics' assessments of their journey, and a question-and-answer section put Lewis and Clark's important trek in historical perspective. The site also contains portions of Lewis and Clark diaries that are searchable online.

"The American War of 1812"

http://www.hillsdale.edu/dept/history/documents/war/FR1812.htm

Providing links to over 50 primary-source documents concerning the War of 1812, especially newspaper articles and reports, this site addresses the debates among Americans on entering the war, militia campaigns in the Northwest, and eyewitness accounts of the Battle of New Orleans.

10

THE MARKET REVOLUTION

1815-1824

OUTLINE

Cincinnati: Queen of the West

New Lands, New Markets
Westward to the Mississippi
The Transportation Revolution
The Waltham System of Manufacturing

A New Nationalism
A New Republican Political Economy
The United States in the Americas
Judicial Nationalism

Firebells in the Night
The Panic of 1819
The Missouri Compromise

The Political Economy
of Regionalism
Cities, Markets, and Commercial
Farms in the Northeast
Planters, Yeomen, and Slaves
in the South
The River and the West

Conclusion

Cincinnati: Queen of the West

On February 13, 1815, after weeks of "distressing intelligence" on the war, the Cincinnati newspaper *The Western Spy* rushed to print with a special edition on the British defeat at New Orleans. A week later, a second *Spy* "extra" published the full text of Jackson's battle report to Secretary of War James Monroe. On February 23, the *Spy* was elated to announce "Peace Between England & America."

Coverage of the War of 1812—acclaim for Jackson, details of the Treaty of Ghent—lingered in the columns of the *Spy* through March, but by April the celebration of victory was giving way to jubilation at the return of business. Alongside a long poem "On the Ratification of Peace," the April 1 issue touted an equally long list of "New Goods, at Peace Prices." Samuel Kidd's dry goods store was pleased to offer fine cloth, satin ribbons, kid gloves, tea, and chocolate, all at dramatically reduced cost.

Subsequent issues of the *Spy* testified to Cincinnati's steadily expanding economy. Borrowing against their collateral, shopkeepers stocked groceries, drugs, and farming equipment to sell to local inhabitants and settlers moving west. For consumers with a little extra money to spend, merchant Robert Best offered eight-day clocks and mounted silver swords, while Rachel Gulick and her sisters opened a new dressmaking shop on the west side of Main Street. Foreseeing the revival of trade from the country-side, the owners of the Cincinnati Steam-Mill prepared to open a new mill "where *Fulling, Dyeing,* and *Finishing* [of cloth] will be carried on . . . on an improved plan." The Cove Ferry added flatboats and skiffs to accommodate traffic across the Ohio River. Best of all, there were new jobs. Richard Allen "Wanted Immediately" an experienced brickmaker for his brickyard. William Baley needed "5 or 6 coopers, to whom constant employment will be given." Other tradesmen sought coach makers, chair caners, blacksmiths, tailors, shoemakers, and bookbinders.

Like other towns in the Ohio and Mississippi River valleys, the settlement's prospects had been bright from the moment it was founded, in the winter of 1788–1789. Its location on the Ohio River positioned the town to become a thriving trade center, shipping wheat, corn, rye, and livestock overland to Pittsburgh and downriver to New Orleans, and merchandizing goods and services to local farmers. "There is hardly anything you can bring here but will sell," one New England migrant had observed in 1806.

The War of 1812 indelibly shaped the character and direction of Cincinnati's economy, however. Even before the war, Cincinnatians had begun to reorient their trade from overland routes across Pennsylvania to water routes down the Mississippi. The outcome of the war guaranteed the United States access to those routes all the way to the

279

A gateway to the Northwest and the South, by 1820 Cincinnati was a thriving city. This view of the Ohio River wharf suggests the complex economy that supported the city's prosperity: retail establishments, wagons carrying settlers west and bringing produce from the backcountry, and steamboats transporting goods and people up and down the Mississippi River system as far south as New Orleans.

Gulf of Mexico and opened the way for the steamboat, first tested on the Mississippi in 1811, to carry goods upriver, as well. As an economic region, a network of buyers and sellers and suppliers, the Mississippi River valley had been born. Soon, the eastern port cities felt the blow. "Never was the trade of Philadelphia exposed to greater danger than at present," one eastern newspaper complained in 1817. "Large portions of the western country, formerly dependent on Philadelphia, now derive their supplies from New Orleans." Civic leaders in the Ohio River valley regarded their growing reliance on the Mississippi River as both inevitable and desirable. "Already do we view the commerce of the west fast falling into that channel which nature and our interests so plainly point out," one author observed. By 1819, when it incorporated as a city, Cincinnati claimed a population of 10,000 residents and had earned the title "Queen of the West."

Like so many other cities, in 1819 Cincinnati plunged abruptly from prosperity into economic and political turmoil. When runaway post-War of 1812 speculation led to a collapse of credit and the panic in 1819, Cincinnati was hard hit. Loans were called in, prices fell, and farmers and businesses went bankrupt. At almost the same moment, Missouri's controversial application to enter the union as a slave state exposed wrenching contradictions between Cincinnati's economy (increasingly dependent on southern states downstream) and its political identity as a free state. Reflecting the ambivalence felt by many of their readers, the editors of the *Western Spy* assumed a hands-off, states' rights position, and heaved a sigh of relief when Congress

struck a compromise. By 1825, both crises had receded. Business was improving, and construction was about to begin on a canal linking Cincinnati to Lake Erie. Meanwhile, city leaders reaffirmed their solidarity with neighbors downriver by upholding a draconian "Black Code" to discourage the immigration of free African Americans or runaway slaves.

In many ways, the history of Cincinnati between 1815 and 1830 reflected the larger history of the republic during these years. The end of the War of 1812 ushered in an era of enormous spatial and economic expansion, based increasingly on the interdependency of commercial farmers and domestic manufacturers, linked by new internal cash markets. Settlers still sought Jefferson's republic of farmers, but these were farms linked to processing plants and textile mills and dependent on wholesalers and retailers. The new political economy seemed to capture the essential qualities the citizens of the republic had long sought: national self-sufficiency and the promise of personal opportunity. The growth of internal markets reinforced a pattern of regional economic specialization and interdependency and gave rise to a robust and optimistic nationalism based on constant westward expansion. These developments also heightened differences in the political economies of those regions, especially distinctions between a North increasingly identified economically and politically with wage labor and a South that based its identity and growth on enslaved labor. In every region, moreover, the market economy was a roller coaster ride, bringing bust as often as boom. ∎

KEY TOPICS

- Tensions between regionalism and nationalism in the republic
- The expansion of plantation slavery in the South
- The growth of wage labor and cities in the North
- Transcontinental politics in the United States
- The growth of National Republicanism

New Lands, New Markets

Americans had never been entirely self-sufficient. From the time of the earliest colonies, households had relied on goods manufactured in Europe as well as goods and services produced and exchanged locally. This pattern of economic activity seemed to vindicate Jefferson's faith in the power of international free trade to protect average Americans from deeper market dependence. Ironically, the War of 1812, the war fought to protect that political economy, ultimately helped to alter it forever. With Britain out of the picture, American settlement in the trans-Appalachian territories swelled. The communities they settled, the goods they produced, and the demands they created all fostered domestic markets for eastern goods. Merchants and local entrepreneurs alike were eager to meet these new demands. The foundation was laid for America's **market revolution**.

Westward to the Mississippi

The biggest market of all was the market in land. The Treaty of Paris ending the American Revolution had officially awarded the new nation all the territory beyond the Allegheny Mountains north to the Great Lakes, west to the Mississippi and south almost to the Gulf of Mexico. But it was the War of 1812 that secured practical control of this dominion.

The Treaty of Ghent called for the restoration of Indian lands taken in battle, but the federal government had little will to oppose the land hunger of its citizens and good reason to support it. Land sales promised a precious stream of revenue. For a time, the federal government tried to control the encroachment of white Americans into the territories. First, the federal government moved to shore up its control of trade with the Indian nations. Secretary of War William H. Crawford justified this policy on the grounds that it kept whites and Indians separate (thus reducing opportunities for armed hostility) while also extending both the influence of the federal government and the dependence of the Indian nations. But eager private traders opposed government control of commerce, and in 1822 the government trading houses were closed. Although the federal government continued to pass measures putatively to protect the Indian tribes from the depredations of civilization, the 1822 act threw the frontier open to settlers. As a result the question of obtaining Indian lands and selling them to settlers became the paramount issue of American policy.

Of course, the land first had to be acquired from its inhabitants. The model for using treaties to force land cessions had been set in the first years of the republic, but the sheer size of the territories in question after the War of 1812 meant that these practices were pursued on an unprecedented scale and with growing assertiveness.

In the South, years of forced cessions had left the Cherokees with only a fraction of their homelands in the Smoky Mountains. Struggling to avoid further cessions, in 1817 eastern Cherokees at last affirmed their willingness to "follow the pursuits of agriculture and civilization" (in other words, to live like Euro-Americans) if they could keep their remaining lands. To demonstrate good faith, they passed a program of extensive political reforms in the form of a six-part law (resembling a constitution) that specified in writing the governance structure and the land tenure and inheritance systems of the Cherokee nation. When the federal government threatened to terminate all annuities, other payments, and federal protections, however, members of the Cherokee National Council signed treaties in 1817 and 1819 ceding a total of some 4 million acres of land in Georgia, Tennessee, and the Carolinas. In signing the treaties, the Cherokees believed they had retained the right to remain on the remnants of their eastern lands. They soon discovered that the United States had no intention of honoring that option. In the years that followed, the United States continued to coerce additional parcels of land from Indian nations across the Northwest and Southwest, forcing communities onto smaller and smaller tracts and rendering them more dependent on federal annuity payments.

In the actual sale of the lands, however, the federal government had conflicting interests. On the one hand, making the land accessible to settlers of modest means would speed settlement, benefiting the economy of the nation as a whole by increasing agricultural production and stimulating new internal markets. On the other hand, the federal government needed the revenues from land sales for its own support. Selling the land at higher prices to wealthier investors would yield greater revenues.

Specific policies changed over time, tracing a compromise between the two goals. The Land Act of 1800 (passed at the urging of William Henry Harrison, delegate to Congress from the Northwest Territory) had reduced the size of the minimum parcel from 640 acres to 320 acres and for the first time permitted buyers to spread their payments over time. In 1804, the minimum size was decreased to 160 acres, and the price was reduced from $2.00 to $1.64 an acre. The cost of land and supplies for the journey was still beyond the reach of the poorest Americans, but lower minimums and the ability to buy on credit opened the West to tens of thousands of settlers who would not otherwise have been able to go. At the same time, however, wealthy investors were still able to purchase large tracts and hold them for later resale, and small buyers were sometimes lured by credit provisions to go into a debt that they could not repay in the allotted time.

The Treaty of Ghent set off an unprecedented fury of migration into the territories, a migration that soon changed the character of the national polity (see Map 10-1). The populations of the older western states swelled. Kentucky grew from 407,000 in 1810 to 688,000 in 1830, and Tennessee grew from 262,000 to 682,000. Even Ohio, ad-

mitted to statehood in 1803, increased its population from 231,000 to 938,000 inhabitants. Equally important, settlement led to the organization of new states. After Ohio in 1803, nine years passed before the next new state, Louisiana, entered in 1812. But then the admissions came rapid-fire. Indiana became a state in 1816, Mississippi in 1817, Illinois in 1818, and Alabama in 1819. By then both Missouri and Maine were also eager to join the union.

The backcountry roiled in "anxiety and confusion," one observer noted, as newcomers raced to claim their share of territorial lands. With the resumption of trade between the United States and Britain, cotton prices rebounded in the South. The old Northwest Territory lacked the lure of spectacular cotton profits, but it offered rich farming lands and (as settlers in Cincinnati had foreseen) favorable possibilities for transportation economies. Speculators were eager to seize the chance for huge returns on land investment, and migrants were eager to escape debt and taxes, oppressive jobs, and overworked soil.

As a result, American westward migration was a remarkably heterogeneous parade. The earliest arrivals were usually hunters, fur traders, explorers, and surveyors. Wealthy speculators (European as well as American)

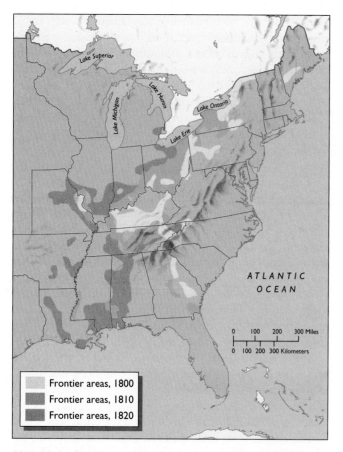
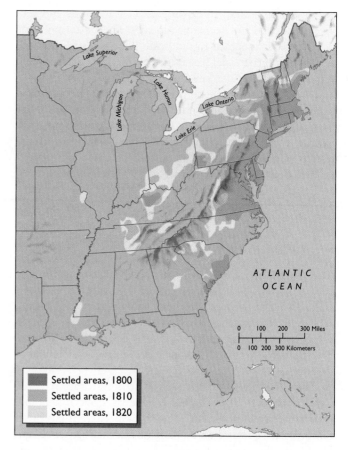

Map 10-1   Frontier and Settled Sections 1800–1810–1820.
Although by 1820 Americans were beginning to project a presence across the Mississippi River, settlement was still thin in much of the region between the Appalachians and the Mississippi.

sometimes traveled to the backcountry just long enough to buy up the best parcels of land, then scurried home to sell their tracts to other investors and would-be migrants. Single men (displaced mechanics, youngest sons of poor farmers, husbands sent ahead to purchase land) picked their more humble ways along dusty roads, sometimes on horseback, often on foot. Families soon followed. Experienced and well-off families packed food and seed, a few household items, an ax, and perhaps a gun into a small wagon and herded a cow or a few pigs alongside. Equally common was the sight of a "man, wife, and five children, with all their household goods thrown in a wheelbarrow . . . walking to Ohio."

However they traveled, the trek cross-country was seldom easy. Journeying into Alabama with his family in 1818, physician John Owen chronicled the daily fare of illness, discomfort, and petty disaster. "Started at 9[,]" he recorded on November 5. "Mother sick[.] bad roads[.] Cart turned over no damage of consequence only shaff Broke—Low spirited. . . ." Harriet Noble described her family's migration from Geneva, New York, to Michigan as consisting of three stages. First came a wagon trip over "bad roads" to Buffalo, followed by a "tedious" boat trip over Lake Erie to Detroit (spent "entirely prostrated with seasickness"), concluded by a four-day hike through mud and over "fallen timber, brush, &c." to Ann Arbor. For the Nobles, as for other families, the first attempt at homesteading proved a failure, and the whole process was repeated farther west. The Nobles moved again a mere year after their first arrival in Ann Arbor.

Not all of the migrants were white. Forced land cessions created homelessness for many Native Americans, who now wandered the territories as individuals or in small bands, returning periodically to government posts for the payment of annuities. Some individual and coordinated resistance continued, but most white migrants encountered Native Americans, not as war parties, but as transients entering settlements in search of trade goods or food. John Owen reported that an Indian took a shot at him one evening, but he recorded the incident more as a nuisance than a threat. And white women like Harriet Noble, engaged in the daily labors of laundry and cooking, eventually grew accustomed to finding unknown Indians staring in their doorways looking for food. In Illinois Territory, settlers overran and took possession of grazing lands, corn and squash fields, and sugar groves prepared and cultivated by Kickapoo, Potawatomi, Ojibwa, Fox, and Sauk villages, displacing the former inhabitants.

In the South, the migrants included slaves, for whom westward settlement meant forced migration. The trials of twenty-year-old Elizabeth Ramsey and her infant daughter, Louisa, were illustrative. Elizabeth and Louisa were sold from South Carolina to a Georgia cotton planter by the name of Cook. When cotton speculation and high living landed Cook in bankruptcy, he fled to Mobile, Alabama, where he hired out both Elizabeth and Louisa as domestic servants. His fortunes still failing, he eventually sold Elizabeth to a new owner in Texas and her daughter to a man in New Orleans.

Before 1808 most enslaved people were taken south and west as part of planter migrations. But by the 1820s, as many as one-third of all migrating slaves (a figure equal to about 15,000 people a year) went west as the property of traders. Although sometimes run by free-lancers, the internal slave trade was often a highly organized business, with firms employing ten or twenty employees (bosses, clerks, guards, agents) in fine offices in Charleston, Richmond, and Baltimore. Some slaves were shipped south on a boat, but they were often driven overland. It was a "singular spectacle," one English visitor to Tennessee remembered. "In the early gray of the morning, [coming upon] a camp of negro slave drivers, just packing up to start. They had about three hundred slaves with them, who had bivouacked the preceding night in chains in the woods." Leading the convoy was "a caravan of nine waggons and single horse carriages, for the purpose of conducting the white people."

Former slave Frederick Douglass, born in Maryland, later described the terror that the threat of being "sold South" struck in the hearts of enslaved African Americans. His owner died when Douglass was eight or nine years old. The enslaved workers were hustled together to be appraised and allotted—some to be retained by family members, some to be "sold at once to the Georgia traders." "I have no language to express the high excitement and deep anxiety which were felt among us poor slaves during this time," Douglass wrote. "Our fate for life was now to be decided. We had no more voice in that decision than the brutes among whom we were ranked. A single word from the white men was enough—against all our wishes, prayers, and entreaties—to sunder forever the dearest friends, dearest kindred, and strongest ties known to human beings." One in three enslaved children under 14 was separated from at least one parent as a result of westward migration. One in three slave marriages in the upper South was destroyed.

The Transportation Revolution

Westward migration created the potential for vastly enlarged domestic markets. Settlers were eager to get their tobacco, wheat, corn, hemp, and cotton to coastal and European customers, and merchants and manufacturers were impatient to get their buttons, shoes, pots, pans, and farm tools to rural stores. Making that connection was still a backbreaking task, as John Owen's 1818 journey to Alabama illustrated. In his diary, Owen classified the roads he and his family crossed on a simple scale: "tolerable," "intolerable," and "infernal."

Not all westward migration was voluntary. By the 1820s, the internal slave trade was a highly developed business. Traders purchased slaves in the upper South, drove them in large groups into the West and Southwest, and sold them off as labor for the new plantations there.

The first efforts at improving transportation came in a spate of largely locally sponsored toll-road building. Although states generally granted a special charter of incorporation for such projects (and occasionally purchased a few shares), most of the capital came from investors in the immediate neighborhood who expected to benefit from tolls. New York communities, the most aggressive in this respect, increased their road mileage from 1,000 miles in 1810 to more than 4,000 miles in 1820. In an effort to bolster the trade from cities like Cincinnati, Pennsylvania extended an older highway that ran from Philadelphia to Lancaster all the way to Pittsburgh. But the toll roads proved a poor investment. Only one (a short turnpike in Connecticut) paid profits of even 5 percent and many made no money at all. In the end, the most important consequence of road building in the post-War of 1812 era was the encouragement it gave to bridge building. Erected at critical points of passage, the new bridges (like one constructed over the Hudson River at Newburgh, New York) made a dramatic difference in the time and cost of transport. More heavily used than individual roads, the bridges usually turned a good profit.

Far more important, however, was the application of the steam engine to transportation. By the postwar era, the steam engine had reached a sufficient level of development to attract investors. A few hardy souls experimented with steam-powered overland rail carriers, but these lines remained fragmentary until the 1850s and conveyed only passengers, not cargo. The use of steam engines to power boats would prove more successful. As early as 1787, James Rumsey of Maryland built a boat propelled by a jet stream from the stern, and John Fitch of Connecticut designed a steam-driven paddle boat. By 1790 Fitch was running a passenger ferry on the Delaware River. In 1804 Philadelphian Oliver Evans demonstrated a steam-powered river dredger, fitted with a stern wheel.

This technology was at last brought together in August 1807 when Robert Fulton and his patron Robert Livingston (Jefferson's minister to France during the Louisiana negotiations) announced the Hudson River trial run of the *North River Steamboat of Clermont,* a 140-foot-long vessel with two steam-driven paddle wheels. Fulton wryly described the trip as "rather more favorable than I had calculated." "The distance from New York to Albany is one hundred and fifty miles," he explained. "I ran it up in thirty-two hours, and down in thirty. I had a light breeze against me the whole way, both going and coming, and the voyage has been performed wholly under the power of the steam engine. I overtook many sloops and schooners beating to windward, and parted with them as if they had been at anchor."

Although he had not invented the steamboat, Fulton had demonstrated its practicality for the transportation of people and goods. By 1817 steamboats were common in the coastal waters of the East and across the Great Lakes, but their most telling impact on American life occurred on the western rivers: the Ohio, the Wabash, the Monongahela, the Cumberland, and especially the Mississippi. In 1809 Livingston and Fulton hired Nicholas Roosevelt to survey the river waters from Pittsburgh to New Orleans, and in 1811 they sent the steamboat *New Orleans* downriver from Pittsburgh. Pressed into service carrying troops and supplies up and down the river during the War of 1812, in 1815 steamboats began to ply regular private routes upriver on the Mississippi.

The steamboat bolstered the market development of the Mississippi River valley and knitted its northern and southern regions together in an integrated economic system. Able not only to move export goods downstream efficiently but also to carry passengers and manufactured goods upstream, the steamboat helped spread the cotton boom to the southern Mississippi. In 1811 the Mississippi River valley produced some 5 million pounds of cotton. Within two decades it produced 40 times that much, virtually all of it carried downstream to market on steamboats. Meanwhile, higher up the Mississippi, the steamboat also opened the Ohio River valley to economic development, both by encouraging downriver markets for northern grain, livestock, and manufactured goods and by improving the access of the Ohio River valley to the Gulf of Mexico. In 1817 the overland route from Cincinnati through Pittsburgh to Philadelphia or New York took nearly two months. On steamboats, freight sent downriver from Cincinnati through New Orleans and on by packet to Philadelphia took about half the time.

The steamboat soon became a conspicuous symbol of American economic promise. Not only were steamboats fast, trim, and exciting, but they were relatively inexpensive to own and operate. Buying a small steamboat cost about as much as setting up a small store. Like land, steamboats were out of the question for America's poor, but they were well within the dreams (if not always the means) of small investors, who were eager to have a chance at making their fortunes. On the grounds of encouraging an orderly and reliable pace of development, however, state policy often tended to encourage large enterprises, awarding them monopoly rights to specific prime routes. The states sometimes further sweetened the pot by providing aid in the form of improved riverbeds. In 1798, for example,

Robert Livingston had gained exclusive rights for 20 years over the waters of the state of New York by vessels propelled by steam, a monopoly he revived and expanded to include Robert Fulton in 1803. Fulton and Livingston failed to obtain sole rights to the Mississippi, but in 1811 they succeeded temporarily in gaining a monopoly on steamboat transportation at the mouth of the river. Their success provoked a hailstorm of protest from would-be competitors, who saw government aligning itself with wealth at the expense of the small entrepreneur. In 1819 the monopoly was withdrawn, but many would-be operators remained convinced that the power of the state had been brought to bear in favor of the wealthy and against the average citizen. In fact, few operators got rich running steamboats on the Mississippi. The twists and hidden snags of the shallow river saw to that. Only in the East, where rivers were deeper and where steamboats became the fashionable means of transportation for wealthy travelers, did investors realize large fortunes.

Even steamboats were limited by the existing waterways. Since the turn of the century, various investors and inventors had sought ways to enlarge those water routes by linking them artificially with canals. As with the first experiments with steamboats, the early history of canals did not portend great success. By the end of the War of 1812, only about 100 miles of canals existed in the United States (the longest ran 27 miles between the Merrimack River and Boston Harbor). None earned much money.

Thus, when, at the end of the war, New York City Mayor De Witt Clinton proposed building a canal to connect Albany and Buffalo, many people thought he had taken leave of his senses. As recently as 1809, Thomas Jefferson had declared the whole idea "madness." Clinton's project was madness multiplied. The canal would run 364 miles, making it the longest canal in the world. It would require an elaborate system of aqueducts and locks to negotiate a 571-foot rise in elevation and (including a smaller canal running from Lake Champlain to the Hudson) would cost $7,000,000. It was a far larger investment than anything comparable in the history of America. Opponents derided the idea as "Clinton's Big Ditch."

Clinton was not deterred. He insisted that the canal would "create the greatest inland trade ever witnessed." It would, he claimed, tie the "most fertile and extensive regions of America" to the city of New York, making that city "the granary of the world, the emporium of commerce, the seat of manufactures, the focus of great moneyed operation." In 1817 he convinced the state legislature not only to authorize the project but also to pay for it entirely in state funds, a gamble that amounted to a $5 per capita levy for the entire population of New York.

Begun on July 4, 1817, the Erie Canal was completed in 1823 and officially opened two years later. At 10:30 on the morning of Wednesday, November 2, 1825, the first boats cleared the final locks and made their way into the

Canal construction was dirty, dangerous, and poorly paid work. Most of the laborers were recent Irish immigrants and free African Americans excluded from other occupations. Women traveled with the crews to cook and do laundry.

Albany basin. Bells pealed, bands played, a huge crowd cheered, and 24 cannons fired successively in a national salute. That night, downtown Albany was ablaze with torches, and from the Capitol hung a backlighted mural depicting scenes of internal trade and navigation, titled "Peace and Commerce!" Presiding over it all was *Governor* De Witt Clinton.

Clinton's gamble paid off spectacularly. Passenger boats and transport barges crowded each section as quickly as it was opened, producing revenues so high that the state was able to pay for later stages of construction from the profits of early ones. Transportation costs from Buffalo to New York City, $100 a ton before construction of the canal, fell to about $10 a ton when the canal opened and dropped even lower later on.

The Erie Canal set off an explosion of canal building that lasted up to the Civil War, but later canals seldom duplicated its success (see map 10-2). The federal government granted roughly 4 million acres of public domain to various canal companies, and states put up most of the money for construction. In the East, however, the terrain impeded construction, making canal building dangerous and costly. In the West, projects fell victim to local interests, overran their budgets, and were seldom able to make back their investments.

The Waltham System of Manufacturing

Road workers, canal builders, slaves, and free farmers migrating west all created large new markets for manufactured goods. In cities and in the countryside, laborers needed cheap clothing and shoes. Settlers needed seed,

building materials, and equipment. Although most of these needs continued to be met by individual artisans working in small shops with hand tools, by 1814 mechanics and investors had laid the foundations for industrial manufacturing in America.

Americans had been experimenting with industrial technologies since 1790, when Samuel Slater had replicated the English water-powered carding and spinning machines. Industrialization was advanced by Eli Whitney's invention of the cotton gin in 1793, by Whitney's and Simeon North's attempts to manufacture weapons with interchangeable parts at the turn of the century, and by the ongoing experiments with steam-powered engines.

The first full applications of these advances to manufacturing came to fruition only after the War of 1812, through the efforts of a wealthy Boston merchant named Francis Cabot Lowell. Along the northern Atlantic coast, the War of 1812 had disrupted profits from overseas trade and had accelerated a shift in investment to internal commerce. Some eastern merchants put money in transportation projects; others speculated in land.

Lowell had his eye on textile manufacturing. The success of Samuel Slater's mills had already demonstrated the feasibility of developing the textile industry in the United States. However, because Slater lacked the power loom (whose design was a jealously guarded industrial secret in England), the Rhode Island mills were unable to turn yarn into finished cloth. A graduate of Harvard with a mathematics major and a knack for machine design, Lowell traveled to England to see the loom for himself and to memorize its design. At home, he worked with mechanic Paul Moody to duplicate the English model. Armed with a special charter from the Massachusetts legislature, in 1814 Lowell and his Boston associates (now organized as the Boston Manufacturing Company) opened the United States' first fully mechanized textile mill, in Waltham, Massachusetts. Within three years the mill had expanded to two buildings, was paying 20 percent dividends, and was using all available water power.

Lowell died in 1817, but under Nathan Appleton's leadership the company (now the Merrimack Manufacturing Corporation) raised more than $8 million to finance a second group of mills in East Chelmsford, Massachusetts. The new mills turned out their first finished cloth in 1823. A sleepy rural village of 200 in 1820, by 1826 East Chelmsford had grown to 2,600, had become the site of a second set of mills, and had incorporated as the city of Lowell, America's first industrial town.

The **Waltham system,** as it was called, differed from earlier American manufacturing enterprises in several ways. Most impressive was its scale. Capitalized at $400,000, it was the largest industrial undertaking attempted in America up to that time. Waltham also represented a new approach to business organization. Detaching ownership from supervision, the Boston Company

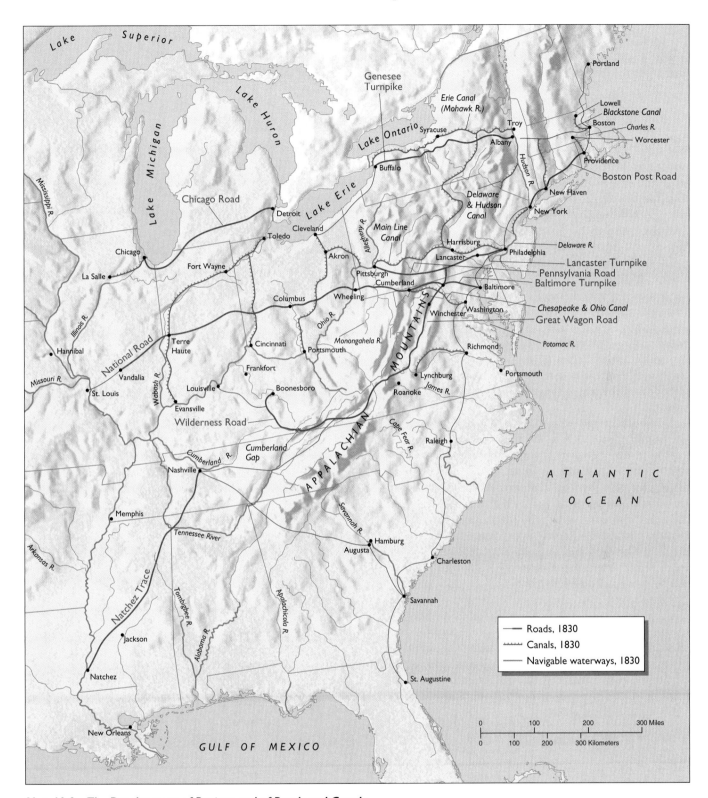

Map 10-2   The Development of Regions and of Roads and Canals.

By 1830 internal development had fostered a growing transportation infrastructure throughout the United States. That development was regional in character, however. In the southern states, where natural waterways ran from deep in the interior to the coast, citizens saw little need to build additional linkages. In the North, where natural waterways seldom ran directly to coastal outlets, investors were far more willing to spend money on internal development, especially canals.

WHERE THEY LIVED, WHERE THEY WORKED

The Lowell Mills

Most of the original Lowell operatives were neither girls nor settled, married women, but young adults in their late teens and early twenties, curious, playful, and eager to escape from the surveillance even of affectionate families. Some were recruited to Lowell by company agents, but many went (and received their parents' permission to go) because they had friends and relatives there already.

Sarah Hodgson left Rochester, New Hampshire, for Lowell, Massachusetts, in 1830, when she was sixteen. Her decision was prompted largely by the desire to earn her own way. Sarah's parents operated a prosperous 75-acre farm and did not need Sarah's wages to survive. She traveled to Lowell with two friends, Elizabeth and Wealthy, with whom she roomed in one of the company's boardinghouses. Older than Sarah and experienced at mill work, Wealthy acted as a watchful eye and wrote separate, reassuring letters to Sarah's parents.

By the time Sarah went to Lowell, three corporations were operating mills there: the Hamilton, the Appleton, and the Merrimack Companies. In four- and five-story buildings, the operatives labored at huge, noisy machines until the factory bell gave them permission to break. If Sarah was intimidated, she did not say so in her letters. Instead, she soon reported confidently to her parents that she had "gone into the mill and like [it] very well." She learned to operate one of the power looms, proudly earning a dollar a week, as much as her sister earned as a teacher. The work regimen was severe—12 hours a day, from bell to bell, 6 days a week, 309 days a year—but not longer or harder than the dawn-to-dusk routine of the farm. In return for hard work she had the pleasures of earning and keeping (and, when she liked, spending) her own money. In the early days of Lowell, too, the work pace retained a certain casualness, reminiscent of country life. Operatives told stories, teased one another, made up riddles and puzzles, and took turns tending each

By 1826 the sleepy Massachusetts village of East Chelmsford had become the city of Lowell—and the center of United States textile manufacturing.

other's looms, while one of them read aloud. In the company-owned boardinghouses, the female operatives developed strong and lasting friendships.

Still, independence was not an unabated pleasure. City life, even small-city life, sometimes brought unsettling experiences. Sarah was surprised to learn that the Lowell Baptists charged a pew fee, which she could not afford. Equally confusing, when she attended a Methodist service with her friend Wealthy, she discovered that she liked it! Disconcerted, Sarah rushed off a letter to her mother, asking that she "write to me what to do wether it is best to go to the babptist or to the methodist."

As time passed and competition grew in the textile industry, the freedom that Sarah enjoyed as an operative became rare. The pace of work increased. Operatives were assigned to more machines (a management tactic called the "stretch-out") running at a faster pace (the "speed-up"), and the company offered bonuses to supervisors who could drive

hired a manager to oversee the daily operation of the mill. Finally, the company devised a residential system in which its employees would live in subsidized and supervised housing at the mill site.

For their work force, the owners turned to the young women in the surrounding countryside of Vermont, New Hampshire, and western Massachusetts. The decision to

hire women was not altogether remarkable. Textiles were traditionally women's work. Since most observers assumed that water- or steam-powered equipment would only make that work easier, there was no reason to associate machinery with men. The chief precedent for mechanized textile production, the Rhode Island mills, employed children and whole families. Female workers were cheaper

Slater's early Rhode Island mills had lacked the power loom. Frances Cabot Lowell stole the design from England and replicated it first in Waltham and later in the Lowell Mills.

TIME TABLE OF THE LOWELL MILLS,

To take effect on and after Oct. 21st, 1851.

The Standard time being that of the meridian of Lowell, as shown by the regulator clock of JOSEPH RAYNES, 43 Central Street

	From 1st to 10th inclusive.				From 11th to 20th inclusive.				From 21st to last day of month.			
	1st Bell	2d Bell	3d Bell	Eve. Bell	1st Bell	2d Bell	3d Bell	Eve. Bell	1st Bell	2d Bell	3d Bell	Eve. Bell
January,	5.00	6.00	6.50	*7.30	5.00	6 00	6.50	*7.30	5.00	6.00	6.50	*7.30
February,	4.30	5.30	6.40	*7.30	4.30	5.30	6.25	*7.30	4.30	5.30	6.15	*7.30
March,	5.40	6.00		*7.30	5.20	5.40		*7.30	5.05	5.25		6.35
April,	4.45	5.05		6.45	4.30	4.50		6.55	4.30	4.50		7.00
May,	4 30	4.50		7·00	4.30	4.50		7.00	4.30	4.50		7 00
June,	"	"		"	"	"		"	"	"		"
July,	"	"		"	"	"		"	"	"		"
August,	"	"		"	"	"		"	"	"		"
September,	4.40	5.00		6.45	4.50	5.10		6.30	5.00	5.20		*7.30
October,	5.10	5.30		*7.30	5.20	5.40		*7.30	5.35	5.55		*7.30
November,	4.30	5.30	6.10	*7.30	4.30	5.30	6.20	*7.30	5.00	6.00	6.35	*7.30
December,	5.00	6.00	6.45	*7.30	5.00	6.00	6.50	*7.30	5.00	6·00	6.50	*7.30

* Excepting on Saturdays from Sept. 21st to March 23th inclusive, when it is rung at 20 minutes after sunset.

YARD GATES,

Will be opened at ringing of last morning bell, of meal bells, and of evening bells; and kept open Ten minutes.

MILL GATES.

Commence hoisting Mill Gates, Two minutes before commencing work.

WORK COMMENCES,

At Ten minutes after last morning bell, and at Ten minutes after bell which "rings in" from Meals.

BREAKFAST BELLS.

During March "Ring out"........at....7.30 a. m.........."Ring in" at 8:05 a. m.
April 1st to Sept. 20th inclusive....at....7 00 " " .... " " at 7.35 "
Sept. 21st to Oct. 31st inclusive.....at....7.30 " " .... " " at 8.05 " "
Remainder of year work commences after Breakfast.

DINNER BELLS.

"Ring out" ....12.30 p. m.........."Ring in".... 1.05 p. m.

In all cases, the *first* stroke of the bell is considered as marking the time.

This 1851 Timetable from the Lowell Mills illustrates the regimented schedules imposed on mill employees.

their workers to higher levels of production. The first American industrial labor force, in the 1830s Lowell women would become among the first American workers to walk off the job in large-scale strikes. Some 800 women in 1834 "turned out," and as many as 2,000 did so in 1836. By that time, Lowell had ceased to be a place where young, rural women could go to test their independence and had come, instead, to represent "the oppressing hand of avarice" of the industrial elite.

Signs of what lay ahead were present even before Sarah Hodgson arrived, however. The company housing that provided the foundation for worker camaraderie also gave the mill owners considerable oversight over their employees'

leisure-time behavior and increased worker dependency on the owners. By 1829, specific management practices, like the Lowell corporations' agreement to blacklist workers fired from the other Lowell companies, portended a coming era of company control over workers' lives.

than men, the result of their long exclusion from customary craft protections and their loss of the right to make contracts if they were married.

At least in the early years, parents and daughters both saw benefits in mill work for unmarried young women. Presumably, a daughter would leave home anyway when she married. Going into the mills before marriage could help out the family by reducing the number of mouths to be fed. The residential system put to rest any fears that a young woman was compromising her respectability. Matrons supervised company-owned boardinghouses, where operatives lived together in single-sex settings. Strict rules of behavior guided the workers' leisure time, and factory bells started and ended the

By the mid–1820s, the original Boston Manufacturing Company in Waltham, Massachusetts, the first fully integrated cotton textile mills in the United States, had become an imposing industrial complex. This painting shows the operatives' boardinghouses as well as the mills themselves. In emphasizing the pastoral quality of the surrounding landscape, the artist reflected the early optimism about industrialization and the belief that it was compatible with an agrarian way of life.

workday and announced lunch breaks. Meanwhile, the young women themselves enjoyed a financial and social independence unknown under the parental roof. They lived, ate, and played together and looked for much of their guidance to a female head-of-household. They returned home largely at their own discretion for periods of vacation. Although operatives sometimes sent some of their wages to their families, many of the young women kept all or most of their pay, enjoying (perhaps for the only time in their lives) a separate disposable income. Working in the mills may have had additional long-term effects on women's lives. Operatives were more likely to marry later than their stay-at-home sisters, to marry urban rather than rural men, and to live in town rather than on the farm.

Later, after employers had cut pay and intensified production, the Lowell operatives came to view their experiences in the mills far less favorably and organized to protest "the oppressing hand of avarice." But in the early years, the mills of Waltham and Lowell, like the new territories of the West, seemed to herald a new age of independence and opportunity.

A New Nationalism

Having snatched some victories from the frustrations of the war, Democratic Republicans remained in power after the Treaty of Ghent. In 1817, James Monroe, the heir apparent to caucus nomination and the third Virginian in a row to hold the office of president, succeeded James Madison. Monroe thoroughly defeated New Yorker Rufus King, the last Federalist to run for the presidency, receiving 183 electoral votes to King's 34. When Monroe ran for re-election in 1820, he was opposed not by a Federalist, but by a member of his own party, John Quincy Adams, who garnered a single electoral vote. Beneath this apparent calm, however, the Democratic Republican Party was continuing along the path of transformation glimpsed in the paradoxes of Jefferson's own policies. Democratic Republicans continued to clarify the boundaries of the nation, extending the territory and the influence of the "empire for liberty" whenever they could. Like Jefferson himself by the end of his presidency, they also gave up the hope that the republic could survive based on a political economy of limited government, free international trade, and domestic agrarianism. In the years after the War of 1812, under the influence of a new generation of leaders, the Democratic Republican Party came to embrace principles of governmental activism, entrepreneurialism, and the development of large-scale domestic manufacturing.

A New Republican Political Economy

Although the presidency continued to be occupied by individuals of the revolutionary generation, in the early nineteenth century the Democratic Republican Party fell increasingly under the influence of younger politicians. Having come of age during the troubled years of the Confederacy, and having witnessed the effects of poor transportation and a weak federal military in trying to prosecute the recent war, these men did not share Jefferson's fears of a strong national government. To the contrary, they believed that an activist central state might well be the nation's best protection against localism and dangerous fragmentation. By the election of 1824, they would identify themselves as **National Republicans.**

This new brand of Republicanism was epitomized by four men who dominated the party in the early nineteenth century: Henry Clay of Kentucky, John C. Calhoun of South Carolina, and Daniel Webster and John Quincy Adams of Massachusetts. Although they preached nationalism, these Republicans tended to bear the imprint of the local politics that produced them. Henry Clay (1777–1852) entered national politics as the champion of large planters and merchants of Kentucky, whose ambitions for internal development had been frustrated on the state level by subsistence-oriented farmers. Putting aside possible differences of interest among them, the Kentucky elites had turned to the federal government for support for projects (especially transportation improvements) they could not win at home. By the time of the War of 1812, Clay was the speaker of the House of Representatives. John C. Calhoun (1782–1850) was first a representative and later senator and vice president. Although both Calhoun and South Carolina later became symbols of states rights sentiment, in the postwar years South Carolinians believed that their export economy (based on rice, indigo, and cotton) was best served by a strong federal government able to ensure access to national and international markets.

Adams and Webster, both ardent New Englanders, illustrated the compatibility of the new National Republicanism with the old Federalist views. Webster, who came to national prominence as an impassioned defender of his alma mater (and the principle of contract) in *Dartmouth v. Woodward* (see page 294), steadfastly promoted the interests of New England's banking classes, even when that meant contradicting his own earlier positions. Initially an advocate of free trade, he became a strong supporter of protective tariffs after the War of 1812, as a growing number of Massachusetts merchants shifted from importing to domestic manufacturing. Born in 1767, John Quincy Adams was deeply influenced by his father's Federalist views, and he was first elected to the Senate in 1800 by the Federalist Massachusetts legislature. Adams broke rank with his party when it opposed the Louisiana Purchase, however. By the time Clay and Calhoun arrived in the House of Representatives on the eve of the War of 1812, Adams was a seasoned diplomat, serving as Madison's minister to Russia.

Led by Clay, the new nationalists fashioned a vision of a Republican political economy based on a general endorsement of individual entrepreneurial and market development (including domestic manufacturing) guided by the strong hand and active involvement of the federal government. Calhoun promised his colleagues that the private virtues of ambitious, self-promoting men would lead to the public virtue of the entire nation. Dismissing small government as "the old imbecile mode," Calhoun called on Americans to endorse a policy of "prosperity and greatness," but these broad principles concealed a number of differences among Republicans. Some emphasized geographic expansion; some stressed the importance of developing manufactures and a strong business infrastructure. Like the old Federalists, some Republicans feared that "ambitious, self-promoting men" were likely to be reckless and undisciplined and required the guidance of wiser men on the federal level. Others harbored reservations about the very development they advocated, embracing a strong central government as the only way to control the possible excesses of an expanding capitalist economy. Some viewed a strong central government as the best protection against northeastern financial elites, for whom they still harbored a distinctly Jeffersonian distrust.

Not surprisingly, their platform, the "American System," was less a clear plan than a patchwork of proposals devised to appeal to local interests and identities. In the West and South, where local politics had often blocked internal development, that meant promoting a national subsidy to improve transportation. For the Northeast, National Republicans called for a protective tariff to safeguard infant industries and a new national bank to keep currency and credit stable. (The 20-year charter of the First Bank of the United States had been allowed to expire in 1811.)

The various elements of the American System came before Congress in a series of separate bills, each of which commanded a somewhat different coalition of supporters. The bills to create the Second Bank of the United States and to increase the national tariffs passed with relative ease and were signed by President Madison. Authorized in 1816, the Second National Bank resembled the first. It was chartered for 20 years and located in Philadelphia, with the federal government providing one-fifth of its 35-million dollars capitalization and appointing one-fifth of its directors. Opposed by merchants in the North who still saw their best profits in free trade and by southerners who feared increases in the prices of manufactured goods, the tariff bill (passed soon after) was less aggressively protective than some nationalists wished. Rates on many imported goods, including cottons, iron, sugar, and hemp, were actually lower than the rates levied during the War of 1812. A particular beneficiary of the new tariff was the young Massachusetts textile industry. Francis Cabot Lowell lobbied successfully to have all imported cottons valued for tax purposes at a minimum of 25 cents a yard (even if they were in fact worth less), a provision that protected the cheap textiles produced in Waltham.

Transportation subsidies fared less well. Although Madison had reconciled himself to signing the bank and tariff bills, he remained skeptical about the constitutionality of this form of federal intervention. In his annual messages of both 1815 and 1816 he urged Congress to initiate a constitutional amendment to clarify federal power in this area before proceeding with legislation. Congress itself was deeply torn. Many legislators were unwilling to support projects that would directly benefit other regions of the nation rather than their own constituencies, and not until its second session was the Fourteenth Congress able to pass a bill creating a federal fund for internal improvements. On his last day in office, Madison vetoed it. His successor, James Monroe, made clear in his inaugural address that he could support such legislation only "with a constitutional sanction." In 1818, the federal government did at last succeed in opening a section of the National Road, a stone-based and gravel-topped highway that connected Baltimore to Wheeling, Virginia (later West Virginia). Otherwise, federal transportation initiatives fell victim to questions of constitutionality and to local and regional jealousies.

web connection

Art Imitates Life

www.prenhall.com/boydston/identity

Having survived its own creation, the United States developed or discovered its own national identity, with its own heritage and peculiarities. The U.S. was no longer a colony of England or Spain, and indeed had uneasy relations with Canada and Mexico, which maintained colonial ties to Europe. Technically, the U.S. reached from the Pacific to the Atlantic, but who really knew what lay between? This uncertainty led to distinctive forms and subjects in popular art that reveal American world-views.

The United States in the Americas

In the eyes of Clay and most other Americans, national "greatness" included achieving an undisputed stature in the world of transatlantic diplomacy and politics. The Treaty of Ghent, which had wrested control of the remaining contested tracts of the old Northwest Territory and the lower Mississippi Valley from Great Britain, had marked an important step toward this goal. Now the federal government turned its attention to clarifying its place on the American continent. By 1819 the United States would assert territorial claims that stretched all the way to the Pacific. By 1823 it would claim a diplomatic sovereignty that extended to the entire hemisphere.

The first initiatives in this direction were a series of agreements clarifying details of the country's relations with British colonies in North America. In 1817 acting Secretary of State Richard Rush and British Minister Charles Bagot agreed to limit British and American forces on the Great Lakes, establishing the precedent of an unmilitarized border. The next year, in the Convention of 1818, they extended that border along the forty-ninth parallel to the Rocky Mountains. The question of the occupation of the territory beyond the Rocky Mountains was left unsettled. Nevertheless, the convention established the longest unfortified national boundary in the world. It also formally acknowledged American fishing rights off the Labrador and Newfoundland coasts.

The following year, 1819, the United States at last negotiated clear southern and western boundaries for Jefferson's Louisiana Purchase. After the purchase, Jefferson had attempted unsuccessfully to buy Florida from Spain. Jefferson's successor, Madison, had taken a different approach, simply declaring that West Florida had been a part of the Louisiana Purchase all along. Emboldened by Jackson's victory at New Orleans, Madison had used his war powers to move the line of American sovereignty eastward from New Orleans to the Perdido River. Taking the Florida peninsula itself had been left for the first administration of James Monroe. With Spain too weak to fulfill its treaty obligations to prevent Seminole raids into Georgia and South Carolina, Monroe authorized the war hero Andrew Jackson to lead a raid into Florida, ostensibly to frighten the Seminoles into leaving white settlers alone. But Jackson wanted more. Without clear authorization, in 1818 Jackson's troops entered Florida, destroying Seminole settlements, summarily hanging two of their leaders, capturing a Spanish fort (contrary to explicit orders), and executing two British citizens whom Jackson held responsible for supporting Indian resistance. Jackson did not conquer all of Florida; there was no need. By May of 1818 it was plain that the United States could take the territory whenever it chose.

A year later, in the Transcontinental Treaty of 1819, Spain and the United States made the status quo official.

Spain ceded all of Florida to the United States in return for the U. S. government's agreement to assume private American claims against Spain in the amount of about $5 million. The Transcontinental Treaty also clarified the border between the United States and Spanish Mexico, which had been left vague in the Louisiana Purchase. The United States gave up claims not only to California (which few people considered part of the original purchase), but also to Texas (which many people did). In return, the United States gained a boundary that ran in a series of large ascending steps from Louisiana to the Pacific.

As well as claiming specific territories, the Transcontinental Treaty expressed an important shift in the nation's international identity. Having removed Britain from its Great Lakes forts, purchased Louisiana from France, and established by treaty with Spain its right to extend across the entire continent, the United States began in the 1820s to view itself as *American,* not quasi-European. Under Monroe, the U. S. government began to assert an identity as protector of the Americas against Europe.

Political turmoil in Europe and in other parts of the Americas encouraged United States assertiveness. Spain was in chaos, its own monarchy threatened by rebellion and its crumbling South American empire torn by independence movements. By 1815 a number of former Spanish colonies, including Argentina, Chile, and Venezuela, had revolted, and an independence movement was under way in Mexico. As these new republics struggled for and won their independence, they turned to the United States for recognition and support. Against this tide, the absolute monarchies in Europe sought to preserve and extend their territorial empires. In 1823 France supported the Spanish monarchy against an internal revolt and offered to help Spain regain its colonies in South America. At the same time, Russia reasserted and strengthened its long-standing claims in the Pacific Northwest.

More concerned about keeping markets stable than about establishing new colonies, Great Britain offered to make a joint declaration with the United States, disavowing future territorial ambitions in the Americas and warning any other nations against intruding into the internal affairs of Western Hemisphere countries. An alliance with Britain would have enhanced U. S. diplomatic credibility, but many Americans suspected that, once having established a right to have its Navy in the area, Britain would squeeze the United States out of South American markets.

Secretary of State John Quincy Adams saw an additional problem. By the early 1820s, Adams was getting ready for his second run for the presidency. He needed a strategy for enlarging his support beyond New England and for distinguishing himself from a formidable pack of potential candidates, which included both Clay and Calhoun. Adams saw his chance in convincing Monroe to refuse the British offer and, instead, to issue a unilateral state-

ment of support for the new republics. It would be far better, he argued, to act independently than to seem "to come in as a cockboat in the wake of the British man-of-war." Privately, Adams hoped that being identified with this policy would help him shed the pro-British tag that was associated with so many New Englanders.

At last Monroe agreed. In his annual message to Congress in 1823, he enunciated the policy that has since become known as "the Monroe Doctrine." Affirming American respect for the political integrity of its European neighbors, Madison asserted a special United States relationship with all parts of North and South America, with which, he insisted, "we are of necessity more immediately connected." "We owe it . . . to candor and to the amicable relations existing between the United States and those [European] powers," he continued "to declare that we should consider any attempt on their part to extend their system to any portion of this hemisphere as dangerous to our peace and safety." With "existing colonies," the United States had no quarrel. But with former colonies who had now "declared their independence and maintained it . . . we could not view any interposition . . . by any European power in any other light than as a manifestation of an unfriendly disposition towards the United States." In short, North and South America were closed to additional external colonization.

Although merely a statement of intended policy (a policy far beyond the capacity of the United States to enforce in 1823), the Monroe Doctrine marked an important milestone in the development of American nationalism and internationalism, completing the journey of identity hinted at in the Transcontinental Treaty. Declaring itself the adjudicator of North and South American interests, the United States not only asserted a new relation (as peer) to the European nations, but a new relation to the Americas as well. Whatever it did in the Americas, the United States would no longer consider itself the newcomer and an outsider, but rather the consummate insider, the "guarantor" of the Americas. Surveillance over the nations of North and South America would be the domestic right of the United States.

Judicial Nationalism

In the years immediately after the War of 1812, the new, nationally oriented Republicans found important support in the Supreme Court. The court was still guided by Jefferson's old nemesis, John Marshall. But by 1819 the similarities between the old Federalist policies and the new Republicanism were strong enough for Marshall to prove an ally to the Republican cause. Between 1819 and 1824, in a type of **judicial nationalism,** the Marshall court delivered three landmark decisions that strengthened the power of the federal government and legitimated the new Republican vision of an America of expansive economic growth.

John Marshall, shown here in 1830, was Chief Justice of the Supreme Court for 34 years and presided over a number of landmark cases supporting federal power and economic expansion.

The earliest of the three, *Dartmouth v. Woodward* (1819), explicitly reinforced the principle that the rights of people were best protected through the rights of contract. The case concerned an attempt by the state legislature of New Hampshire to alter the original charter of Dartmouth College, given to the college by King George III in 1769, when the nation was still a series of British colonies. New Hampshire argued that the original charter was not binding on the current state government, but Dartmouth insisted that the charter was in fact a contract, protected under Article VI of the U. S. Constitution, which protected debts and engagements entered into before the Revolution. Acting to ensure the stability of contract in the broadest sense, the court ruled in Dartmouth's favor.

The case of *McCulloch v. Maryland*, also decided in 1819, centered on the Second Bank of the United States. The creation of the bank had been one of the successes of the new Republicans, who had managed to overpower tra-

ditional Republican objections to national banks by attracting Federalist votes. Since its establishment, the Second Bank had created a number of branches, one of which was in Baltimore. Viewing the presence of the federal institution within its borders as a potential threat to its sovereignty, Maryland attempted to assert its authority over the Baltimore branch by taxing it. Specifically, Maryland required that the bank purchase and affix revenue stamps to its bank notes. Acting on behalf of the bank, James W. McCulloch, chief clerk of the branch, refused. Maryland appealed to the Supreme Court, arguing that because the federal government was a creation of the states, its branch institutions could be taxed in the states where they existed. Marshall's court unanimously rejected this position, finding instead that the federal government was the direct creation of the people acting through the special conventions that ratified the Constitution. The federal government was superior to the states, the Supreme Court concluded. Because the power to tax was potentially the power to destroy, the states could not have the power to tax the creations of the federal government, wherever they might be located.

Gibbons v. Ogden (1824), the last in Marshall's long line of landmark decisions, concerned a disputed ferryboat monopoly in New York. Having been awarded exclusive rights to operate steamboats in the state's waters, Robert Fulton and Robert Livingston had, in turn, "contracted" a part of this right out to Aaron Ogden, giving him a ferry monopoly across the Hudson River from New York to New Jersey. At the same time, however, a man by the name of Thomas Gibbons had obtained a federal license to operate a boat line along a coastal route that came into conflict with Ogden's line. The question was: Who controlled these waters and therefore had the right to grant licenses, New York or the federal government? Consistent with its national view of power and development, the Marshall court found in favor of the federal power. The decision noted that the Constitution had given to Congress (Article I, Section 8) the right "to regulate Commerce with foreign nations, and among the several States." Because the waterways under dispute did not fall clearly within the boundaries of a single state, the state power was in this case in conflict with the federal power. Where an action of a state conflicted with an action of the federal government, the Marshall court found, the federal power took precedence.

The decisions of the Marshall court supported rights of contract and private property fundamental to the economic expansion in which most white Americans were engaged. Nevertheless, the court's decisions ultimately supported a political economy that valued the activities of large investors like the Merrimack Manufacturing Corporation over those of workers and small entrepreneurs. Although the court had struck down a state-granted monopoly of the sort that many small investors deemed unfair, workers and Americans of middling means remained cautious about the concentration of power the national bank represented, especially about its ability to disrupt the credit arrangements of the fragile new market economy.

Firebells in the Night

Visitors to the new nation often praised the freedom of its citizens and marveled at its robust economy. Yet they noted discrepancies in the expanding democracy: the survival of slavery, the treatment of Native Americans, the deterioration of some city neighborhoods, the reckless mania for speculation. In 1819, even as the Supreme Court ratified the basic legal principles of market development and the Transcontinental Treaty assured continuing westward settlement, citizens of the republic themselves were forced to stop and take at least momentary account of the price of expansion. In that year, the bubble of speculation suddenly burst, casting the nation into the worst financial crisis of its young history. Also in 1819, Missouri applied for statehood, forcing the issue of slavery onto the national political agenda. Referring to Missouri, former President Thomas Jefferson wrote that "This momentous question, like a firebell in the night, awakened and filled me with terror. I considered it at once as the knell of the union." Both events awakened such anxieties.

The Panic of 1819

In 1819 Americans learned that the market revolution could produce dream-shattering plunges as well as exhilarating rises. Having signed the bill chartering the Second Bank of the United States in 1816, James Madison had promptly appointed an old political ally, Captain William Jones, as its director. Jones proved a poor choice; he speculated in bank stock and was willing to accept bribes to overlook reckless local practices. By the time Jones was replaced, bank stock was at an all-time low, and the state banks had glutted the economy with unsecured paper money.

Jones' successor, Langdon Cheves, moved quickly to cut the supply of paper money (too quickly, given that Great Britain was taking the same measures). Cheves began to call in loans and to redeem the bank's holdings of currency issued by the various state banks. Dangerously overextended, the state banks were forced to respond with their own programs of retrenchment. As credit dried up and the value of paper money plummeted, the nation was thrown into a sharp depression. Without credit or sufficient circulating money, commodity prices crashed throughout the Atlantic community. The market in cotton, which had propped up the growing American economy, fell by almost two-thirds. For three long years, the economy stalled. When they could not make their mortgages, farms and businesses failed. As businesses failed, tens of thousands of workers lost their jobs. Visitors to America warned potential immigrants not to come, as their chances of success would be "at best problematical."

Because the branches of the Second Bank of the United States reached far beyond the East Coast, so did the distress of the panic. When the branch in Cincinnati, Ohio, suddenly cashed in the paper money it held from local banks, for example, Cincinnati's booming economy felt the blow, as local banks scurried to collect enough debts to make good on the face value of their paper. In similar fashion, the shock waves rolled through Kentucky and Tennessee and into the states of the lower South.

Cheves had saved the monetary system of the United States, but he had not made many friends for the Second Bank. State legislators, who saw the national bank (not runaway speculation or wildcat state banks) as the villain, scrambled to reduce its power. Fourteen states passed laws preventing the bank from collecting its debts, Kentucky abolished imprisonment for debt, and six states levied heavy taxes on bank branches. After opening 18 branches in 1817 (including the one in Cincinnati), the Second Bank opened no additional new branches until 1826.

The Panic of 1819 only underscored more persistent weaknesses and inequities in the market economy. Although some people realized huge returns from investments and speculations during these years, even in the best of times it took money to make money. The original investors in the Boston Manufacturing Company enjoyed average annual dividends of 20 percent on the Waltham mills for over a decade, but on an initial investment of $400,000. Few people were in a position to buy into that kind of opportunity. On a somewhat smaller scale, the E. I. du Pont de Nemours gunpowder works, established in 1802 near Wilmington, Delaware, was capitalized at 18 shares of stock worth $2,000 each. Even $2,000 was several times more than the annual income of most professionals in America at the turn of the century and more money than most workers saw in a decade.

It was not only in the new manufacturing sector that it took money to make money. Much of the most profitable speculation was in land. Although the federal government had been slowly modifying its land sales policies since the turn of the century, in 1820 the minimum parcel was still 80 acres at $1.25 an acre. The $100 cash needed to purchase an 80-acre plot was more than half a year's wages for many journeymen in 1820, and most female workers would have had to save literally every penny they earned in an entire year to afford the purchase price. Few craft workers, male or female, possessed $100 in real property to be sold to stake a venture to the west. Most people had to wait for speculators to carve up large holdings into smaller lots for resale (and for substantial profit). In the late 1820s and the 1830s the frustrations created by these conditions would fuel the hatred of land barons and banks. In the meantime, land dealing was still an occupation of the rich and well connected.

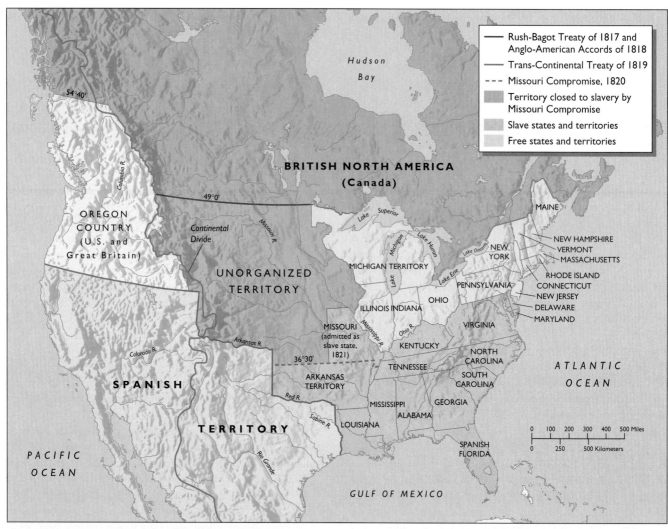

Map 10-3 Westward Expansion and Slavery, 1820.
As treaties signed with Great Britain and Spain in 1817, 1818, and 1819 began to outline a United States that would stretch from the Atlantic Ocean to the Pacific, Americans worried about the division of that territory into areas open to slavery and areas closed to slavery. Although in 1820 more acres were closed to slavery than not, the Missouri Compromise permitted slavery in territories where it had not existed before, reinforcing northerners' fears that planter interests dominated in national policy.

The Missouri Compromise

Land hunger had fueled the new American economy. By 1819, land had come to represent national as well as individual prosperity for many Americans. Only in 1819, when Missouri applied for permission to organize as a state, did Americans begin to perceive a new danger in the settlement of the West: its power, paradoxically, to tear the nation apart (see Map 10-3).

The question of Missouri was principally a question of political power on the federal level, but it was inextricably tied to the question of slavery. Northerners had long been unhappy with what they saw as the unfair advantage awarded to southern states by the Constitution's Three-Fifths Compromise, which allowed states to count slaves (on a three-fifths basis) toward representation in Congress. Admission of Missouri would extend that unfair pattern of representation in the House and create a new imbalance in the Senate, where each state had the same number of representatives regardless of population. In 1819 there were 22 states in the union, 11 free and 11 slave. Admission of Missouri would give the slave states domination in any purely sectional disputes. (Florida, certain to apply for admission as a slave state at some point in the future, would add to the disparity.) Meanwhile, the South continued to dominate the presidency.

There were other issues. Missouri was the first wholly new state to be organized from the Louisiana Purchase. (Louisiana had already entered as a slave state, but slavery had been established there before the territory became a part of the United States.) Missouri, northerners feared, would set a precedent for extending slavery into additional new states carved out of the territory. Moreover, by 1819 many northerners no longer believed that slavery would simply die out of its own accord. Far from withering away, the institution seemed to be thriving. Americans had imported only about 5 percent of the Africans forced into slavery in the hemisphere, but by 1819 slaves in the United States constituted one-third of all the people of African descent in the Americas. Slavery seemed to be making some headway even in free states. When Illinois had entered the union in 1818, for example, it had entered as a free state, but with a "Black Code" that limited the economic and civil rights of free African Americans and permitted the continuation of slavery where it existed in the southern parts of the state.

The trouble over Missouri began almost at once. In the course of the House debate, New York Representative James Tallmadge proposed that Missouri be admitted under two conditions. First, no more slaves were to be brought into the state, and second, slavery was to be gradually abolished after the state was admitted to the union. Southerners lined up unanimously against the amendment, while northerners voted unanimously in favor of it. The more populous North carried the vote. But when the House bill reached the Senate, the vote was reversed. The Tallmadge amendment died in committee, to be reintroduced in the next session.

By the time Congress reconvened, positions on both sides had hardened. Northern congressmen insisted that Congress had the power to prohibit slavery from the Louisiana Territory (the Congress of the Confederation had earlier prohibited slavery from the old Northwest Territory) and should do so. Southern congressmen responded that the Constitution provided no such power to Congress and that the states had carefully preserved their equality in joining the federal pact. In addition, they argued that in guaranteeing that no citizen could be deprived of life, liberty, or property without due process of law, the Fifth Amendment actually protected the right of slaveowners to carry slaves into new states.

Both in its general outlines and in its specific arguments, the struggle over Missouri foreshadowed with chilling accuracy subsequent congressional debates over slavery. It also foreshadowed the reluctance of the North to press the confrontation. Arguing for the continuation of slavery, Senator Nathaniel Macon of North Carolina cautioned his northern colleagues that in no place in the United States were free people of color truly welcome. No one rose to dispute him. Indeed, racism was codified in many northern state constitutions. Ohio and Connecticut excluded African-American men from voting. Vermont and New Hampshire barred African-American men from the militia. Rhode Island and Indiana prohibited African-American and white people from marrying, and Indiana also barred African Americans from appearing as witnesses against whites.

The firestorm over Missouri was finally resolved when Maine applied for statehood as a free state. Under Speaker of the House Clay's guidance, the two bills were linked, preserving the balance in the Senate. The compromise also contained a provision that slavery would be permitted in Arkansas Territory but excluded from the rest of the Louisiana Purchase. The compromise passed narrowly in March of 1820.

Almost immediately, another problem arose when Missouri submitted a state constitution that barred free African-American people and free persons of mixed heritage from the state. This ran contrary to Article IV of the Constitution, which provided that citizens of one state should enjoy the rights of citizens in all states. Struggling to put the deal back together, Clay engineered a second, ignominious compromise. Congress allowed Missouri to enter under the proposed constitution, but it demanded that the new state legislature promise never to interpret the clause to mean what it so obviously meant, that Missouri reserved the right to deny constitutional protection to free African Americans. The Missouri territorial legislature made the promise but added a disclaimer of any power to bind the people of the state to what it said. Finally, in August 1821, President James Monroe greeted Missouri as the twenty-fourth state of the union.

The Panic of 1819 and the controversy over the admission of Missouri underscored profound contradictions inherent in the emerging political economy of the nation. But within a few years, both crises seemed to have passed.

The Political Economy of Regionalism

Many Americans were caught up in the economic expansion of the postwar years, an expansion that rested on a rough regional specialization: a South built on plantation-style export agriculture, a North built on business and trade, and a raw backcountry in the West. No region was completely uniform; more important, none was autonomous. They had developed interdependently. Southerners relied on the North for shipping and business services, and some agricultural and manufactured goods. Northern merchants and bankers depended on southern customers. Both areas looked to the West for new lands and markets. As the Missouri controversy foreshadowed, however, the economic systems of the regions were fostering distinctive social and political systems that would, in time, prove incompatible.

Cities, Markets, and Commercial Farms in the Northeast

In the Northeast, port cities had developed in tandem with the agricultural hinterlands that surrounded them, supplying food for consumption and export and markets for imported goods. By 1820, the region radiated from the northern Atlantic seaports through a web of interior cities, towns, villages, and farms all the way to western New York and Pennsylvania. It was united by the density of cash markets, the growing importance of wage labor, and the steady spread of urban institutions.

The Northeast remained anchored in the cities of the north Atlantic coast. By 1820 New York claimed a population of 152,056, Philadelphia of 63,802, Boston of 43,738, and Baltimore (at the northern tip of the Chesapeake) of 62,738. These ports were still centers of overseas commerce, but by the 1820s their swelling populations (and federal tariff protections) had encouraged the growth of substantial urban manufacturing sectors as well. Old craft shops competed with larger retail manufactories to produce boots, shoes, furniture, clothing, coaches, tools, ships, and a host of other goods, some intended for the local trade, some shipped south, west, or overseas.

After 1820 this urban growth was fed by waves of immigration. The end of the Napoleonic Wars abruptly reduced jobs in war-related occupations in Europe. Coincidentally, a series of crop failures in Germany, parts of Scandinavia, and Ireland forced hundreds of thousands of peasants off the land. New immigrants who were able (especially Germans and Scandinavians) joined the trek west, often traveling across the Great Lakes to settle in Michigan and Wisconsin Territory. Poorer immigrants tended to remain in the Northeast, where they took jobs as laborers and factory workers.

City life was smelly, noisy, and fast. "By an early hour in the morning," a traveler recalled, "we have an abundance of discordant noises on the streets. Men squalling *milk*, and negro boys shrieking *sweep.* . . ." Merchant and match girl, butcher and banker, shopper and swindler all mingled in the rich sociability of the city streets, joined by draft horses, chickens, and the wild hogs that some householders raised for their own tables. Pickpockets, lotteries, and private individuals seeking donations for personal causes competed for the shopper's purse. At street level insurance companies and banks vied for space with confectioners, milliners, boardinghouses, bakeries, and private clubs, and basement doorways opened into taverns, oyster houses, and groceries.

Even beyond its largest cities, the Northeast was far more urbanized as a region than either the South or the West—the result of an intricate pattern of interdependent markets that tied farms to villages to towns to interior cities to the eastern ports. Smaller cities like Albany, New York (12,630), Providence, Rhode Island (11,767), and Salem, Massachusetts (11,346) served as manufacturing centers for their own districts and as shipping and receiving centers with the coast. Through these intermediate layers, commercial markets penetrated the countryside to an extent that sometimes surprised recent immigrants. " 'The whole world is set upon money &c.' Why do *you* say so?" Mary Ann Archbald wrote to her cousin in Scotland in 1816. "You ought to have left this observation for me to make on the west side of the Atlantic. It applies exactly to the people here!"

Women's market-oriented activities (butter and cheese making shown here) helped farm families accumulate the capital necessary to survive the market revolution by enlarging their acreage or specializing their operations.

Most households made the transition to greater cash dependency without much conscious thought. City wage workers had little choice. Fewer and fewer employers were willing to hire individuals "found" (that is, with room and board as part of their pay). Workers had to accept cash, which they needed in any event to purchase food and shelter. In the countryside, farmers responded to improved transportation by growing food for more distant markets. New York and Pennsylvania farmers plowed more acreage for corn and wheat to be shipped to the South, to coastal cities, or overseas. Vermont, New Hampshire, and upstate New York produced maple sugar, apples, strawberries, and lumber. Connecticut families cultivated onions and small patches of tobacco, which the women rolled into cigars. Some farmers continued to carry their own produce to market, but the need to ship longer distances promoted the rise of a variety of intermediate agents, attached at the other end of the transaction to merchants or buyers who did not have direct contact with the farmers. These conditions favored the rise of formal systems of payment and credit over personal systems of barter and trust. Some farming families struggled to preserve subsistence-oriented lives, but this became more difficult as even local shopkeepers and craftspeople required cash to meet their own obligations.

After 1810, in response to the demand in cities and in the South for domestically manufactured goods, rural workers oriented work they had previously done for their own families—making brooms, cheese, yarn, and, later, straw hats—toward the commercial market. At first, local stores functioned as collecting points, paying farm people in store credits while building up large inventories to be shipped east to wholesalers. By the 1830s, these forms of

Early nineteenth-century cities were churning cauldrons of human activity. This depiction of the Procession of Victuallers in Philadelphia suggests the swarms of people, the mingling of purposes, the crowded living conditions, and the crush of shops that characterized urban life in 1819.

household production had evolved into a system of rural "outwork." Family members worked directly for contractors who provided raw materials and paid them by the piece for items made in their own homes. The shift was most apparent in shoemaking. Wives of male shoemakers had for decades been involved in stitching together the leather their husbands cut and fashioned into shoes. After 1810, rural New England women also did this work in their own homes for piece wages from merchants.

Urbanization and the growing reliance on cash exchange and wages left a deep imprint on the society and culture of the Northeast. It altered the foundations of family and community life in several ways. With family holdings too small to provide land to all the male children, fathers lost their economic grip on sons. Ambitious young men took to the roads as peddlers, hired out as agricultural wage workers, moved to cities to get jobs in offices, or struck out for the West. Daughters took jobs in the mills or as schoolteachers or left for the city, hoping to find employment in shops or as domestic workers. These changes diminished the importance of patriarchy in the Northeast and eroded older notions of republican virtue based on community, or corporate, obligation. Increasingly, civic virtue consisted of individual achievement, especially as measured in cash terms.

In cities, family size decreased, beginning a century-long decline among native-born white families from six or seven children at the turn of the century to five by mid-century and four by 1900. The change may have reflected parents' worries about their ability to set sons up in occupations as well as a judgment that child labor was less useful in a wage-based economy than in a semi-subsistence household. The decreases were most marked in families where the women were educated, however. Perhaps these women were better informed about their own health, more attentive to prescriptive writing about child rearing, and more able to assert their own family-size preferences.

By bringing more people into closer proximity, urban life permitted and encouraged the growth of organizations of all kinds, from libraries and reform associations to charity groups. Elite women had long been involved in such groups, but in the early decades of the nineteenth century, northeastern urban women from more middling families also began joining in growing numbers, especially in response to what they perceived as the breakdown of old family bonds. Their interest in these societies initially followed along the lines of their customary family responsibilities: They organized maternal societies, prayer groups, and Bible societies. Made possible by their close geographic proximity to one another, these extrafamilial organizations would eventually draw northeastern middle-class women into much more extensive involvement in public life.

The cities offered opportunity. For Mrs. J. Cantelo, a New York seamstress, the 1820s were flush years. Her dressmaking establishment did so well that she moved to a new location, hired "a fashionable dressmaker" to "superintend" the new store and a milliner to work in it, and scheduled a lavish grand opening for May 1, 1826. Cantelo's timing was perfect. Having recovered from the slump of 1819, New York's economy was booming. Southern families were resuming their long shopping trips north, and middling and wealthy urban families once again had disposable income for new summer wardrobes. Cantelo had to hire apprentices, shirtmakers, and eventually another milliner to keep up with demand.

But there were troubling signs in the new political economy of the Northeast. The cities' small manufacturing shops relied increasingly on workers trained in only one aspect of a craft, employees who could be easily fired and replaced and could not command high wages. Also, good housing was hard to find. Builders focused on the needs of prosperous families, leaving the laboring classes to the mercy of landlords who divided up old two-story houses and charged high rents for cramped apartments. By 1826 two third-floor rooms in a house in lower Manhattan cost $425 a year, double the wages of most workers. As housing

deteriorated, families who could afford to do so moved uptown, creating economically segregated residential districts.

Planters, Yeomen, and Slaves in the South

In contrast to the network of towns and cities that crisscrossed even the farming districts of the Northeast, the South remained largely agricultural, preserved in that way of life by overseas and northern demand, a temperate climate, and the legality of slavery. At the founding of the nation the "South" had run from the Chesapeake down the

Cutting Sugarcane

The specific labor of plantation slaves, and the way that labor was organized, depended on where they lived and what crop the plantation grew. These drawings suggest three common forms of plantation labor: picking cotton in the deep South (left), cutting sugarcane in Louisiana (top right), and cultivating rice (considered by many the most dangerous of all plantation labor) in Georgia (bottom right).

Cultivating Rice

coast to Charleston. By 1820 the cotton boom had extended the political economy of slavery into virtually all of the territory south of Pennsylvania and the Ohio River valley and east of the Mississippi River, as well as into Missouri and Louisiana, across the Mississippi.

The symbol of the South was the plantation, a large farm of several hundred or more acres owned and operated by a single white family and worked under the supervision of various hired employees by a community of twenty or more enslaved laborers. Cotton plantations proliferated in the new western lands of the region, where speculators could accumulate large tracts of fresh soil. Meanwhile, the reopening of international markets in the postwar years gave new life to tobacco plantations in Virginia and North Carolina, rice plantations in parts of South Carolina and Georgia, and sugarcane plantations in Louisiana.

Some plantations were complex economic concerns, with dispersed fields, multiple barns and outbuildings, batteries of craft workers, an internal village of slave cabins, manicured grounds, and a "big house" with balconies and railings and furnished with European imports. Many were somewhat less noble, however. Northerner Emily Burke described the "big house" of a Georgia plantation as a mere husk of a building with unplastered walls, a plank floor she could see through to the ground, and a roof like a sieve. Many planter families lived part of the year in the nearest large city, which gave their lifestyle a quality of transience.

Of the 1,500,000 enslaved inhabitants of the South in 1820, probably three-quarters lived on plantations. The number of slaves on a given plantation varied widely. Sugar plantations averaged 30 or more workers, and the wealthiest families of the South (whatever their primary crop) sometimes owned hundreds of slaves. On plantations, most men and women worked in the fields, their days determined by the crop and the season. Tobacco workers were especially busy in the spring, carefully transplanting young plants and pruning off extra shoots. At harvest, cotton workers stooped all day, dragging their load as they pulled the sticky cotton fibers from their bolls and continuing by the light of torches long after sunset. Masters on sugar cane plantations reputedly drove their workers hardest, but it was rice cultivation (where workers stood ankle-deep in mud under the blazing sun in snake-infested, swamp-land fields) that was, as one man observed in 1828, "by far the most unhealthy work in which slaves are employed." The crop also influenced the organization of labor. Skilled rice cultivators commonly worked by the "task" system, under which workers were assigned a specific objective for the day's work (repairing a drainage ditch, for example) and were able to exercise some autonomy over the pace and process of their labor (see the story of Gowrie in Chapter 12, page 340). On large cotton plantations, slaves were more likely to be organized in "gangs," set at repetitive tasks (like hoeing or picking) with close supervision from hired overseers or appointed slave "drivers."

Not all plantation slaves worked regularly in the fields. On big plantations and on plantations in the older states, where soil was exhausted and planters made much of their income by selling and renting out slaves, as much as one-quarter of the work force was assigned either to domestic service or to crafts intended to make the plantation more self-sufficient. Although white observers tended to view household servants (butlers, maids, waiters, chefs, confectioners, bakers, valets, and nannies) as particularly fortunate in their work, the lot of house servants was not necessarily better than that of field workers. Constantly on call, their workday could last even longer than that of field workers. Subjected to close scrutiny for work that often lacked clear objective criteria, they were especially vulnerable to the caprices and violent outbursts of owners.

More independent were the five to eight percent of the work force trained to craft work. Men became carpenters, smiths, iron workers, and boatmen. A smaller number of women became spinners, weavers, seamstresses, and dairymaids. Because their work was often housed in separate shops, craft workers often enjoyed a degree of autonomy rare for most slaves.

Three-quarters of enslaved people lived on plantations, the cultural symbols of the South, but neither slave-owning nor plantation farming typified the experiences of most southern whites. While the wealthy had long since claimed the best and largest holdings, most white southerners lived on

Although southern law did not deem their marriages legal, enslaved African Americans constructed their own rituals, often adapted from African practices, to solemnize and celebrate marriage.

small holdings of several hundred acres or less. These "yeoman" households typically owned no slaves, although they sometimes hired slaves from nearby planters. Living in rough dwellings at some distance from one another, they produced as much of their own food as they could, put in a patch of cash-crop tobacco, cotton, or grain, and often relied on nearby planters as agents in selling their crops or purchasing new equipment. Beneath the yeoman households, economically and socially, was a white underclass of tenant farmers and day laborers and a precarious free black population.

Although most white people did not own slaves, the institution of slavery exerted a steady influence over their material lives and their personal values. Siphoning private investment away from transportation and manufacturing, slavery and plantation agriculture prevented the development of an internal market network comparable to that occurring in the Northeast. Small farmers could hire field slaves from larger planters at rates cheaper than they could hire free labor, and planters could put a slave to craft work for less money than it would cost to hire a free artisan. These circumstances discouraged the development of a free labor-wage market in the South. By 1820 the South did boast textile mills, iron foundries, lumber mills, mines, turpentine manufacturers, and tobacco processing plants, but most of the workers in these industries were slaves. Some white southerners supported transportation improvements (construction of the first railroad began in Maryland in 1828) and improved communication (the first two cities linked by telegraph in the 1840s were Washington, D. C. and Baltimore). But the South was favored with navigable rivers that flowed from deep in the interior all the way to the fall line and with a long coastline. Because enslaved labor could be employed in off-seasons to transport many commodities, improved speed had little effect on the ultimate cost of production. What highway building was done in the South was funded with state money.

Plantation slavery also stunted the growth of cities and of an urban working or middle class, whose livelihoods depended on wages and salaries. Even in the older seacoast states less than three percent of southerners lived in cities. This number included planters taking refuge during the malaria season, slaves hired out to domestic service for the urban professional class, and the South's free African-American population. In a long-standing practice, southern planters looked to Philadelphia and New York for the services to export their crops rather than to urban centers within their own regions. Where they borrowed and sold, they also bought, supporting New York retailers like Mrs. Cantelo over local dressmakers in Charleston or Mobile. When planters sought alternatives to this pattern of external dependence, they looked not to local villages or towns, but to their own plantations, reassigning field workers to produce the butter, cheese, and tools they might otherwise have purchased locally. With a few exceptions, the economies of southern cities (New Orleans,

Mobile, Savannah, and Charleston, for example) were based narrowly on the commerce of slaves and cotton.

Most white southerners continued to live in rural settings under the authority of fathers. Children had few options for autonomy and most free women were too widely separated to come together in the extrafamilial organizations that would provide the foundations for middle-class women's independent social activism in the North. In this environment, white southerners clung to an older understanding of republican virtue, one still based on the corporate interdependencies of rural life, increasingly romanticized to obscure the fact that most of those dependencies were coerced and violent. In this version of republicanism, the good citizen was the patriarchal father who protected his family, provided wise stewardship to his human and nonhuman resources, and was generous to his neighbors, not the self-striving wage-earner or entrepreneur of the North. The comparative sparseness of formal cash networks preserved the centrality of personal reputation in both economic and social relations, heightening the emphasis on unquestioned personal integrity as an aspect of southern republican manhood.

Depicting slaves merely as a type of dependent to be guided with wisdom and compassion, this version of republicanism obscured both the violence of the institution itself and the violent influence that slavery had on the culture of the South as a whole. "Guidance," in the master-slave relationship, could include beatings, torture, sexual assault, mutilation, and murder, all of which were rhetorically normalized in the discourse of republican stewardship. Even beyond that primary relationship, however, slavery required a legal system honed over time to the purpose of condoning violence, an extralegal system of vigilante groups ready to step in should the law falter, and a society of individuals (especially men) ready to react to even the smallest insubordination. Violence was not constant in the South, but it was potential in every interaction; when it occurred it was often both publicly witnessed and publicly approved.

In all its forms, slavery constituted a steady assault on the selfhood and the family and community life of slaves. The killing of a slave was only the most extreme example of this aggression. More common were the casual humiliations and the recurrent interference with daily life. The early life of Elizabeth Keckley (who later purchased her freedom and founded the Contraband Relief Organization to support freed slaves during the Civil War) illustrated common patterns of dislocation. Born in 1818, Keckley scarcely knew her father, who belonged to a different Virginia planter. When she was 18, Keckley was hired out to a man in North Carolina, by whom, cut off from the protection of family and friends, she conceived a child. She later returned to Virginia, but not to her master's plantation. Rather, she lived with her mother in the household of her owner's son-in-law and was taken west with him when he moved to St. Louis. There, faced with the threat of having her aging mother hired out for service, Keckley worked for wages as a seamstress, "ke[eping] bread in the mouths of seventeen persons."

It was not unusual for enslaved women to bear children whose fathers were free and white. Large bi-racial populations existed in all parts of the region, putting the lie to whites' claims of racial separatism and "purity." Undoubtedly, some intimate relations between enslaved women and free men were consensual, but most were not, and a woman's consent was always restricted by the fact of her enslavement. In *Incidents in the Life of a Slave Girl*, Harriet Jacobs described the limited choices available to female slaves. Jacobs' master began making sexual advances when she was only 15, finally trying to force her to become his mistress. "[S]hudder[ing] to think of being the mother of children who should be owned by my old tyrant," and hoping to make him so mad that he would sell her, Jacobs entered a sexual relationship with another white man, with whom she eventually bore two children.

Nevertheless, slaves constructed rich familial and community bonds. Whites denied legal recognition to slave marriages, but slaves sanctioned their own relationships, combining African ceremonies with European wedding rituals, and struggled to provide stability in their children's lives. Frederick Douglass did not recall ever having seen his mother by daylight (she was hired out to a neighboring farm), but he remembered all his life that, night after night, she risked capture by slave patrols to walk the 12 miles home to be with him as he fell asleep. White owners flattered themselves that they were the masters of all their chattel, but African-American parents made certain their children understood, as Jacobs remembered her father's words, "You are *my* child, and when I call you, you should come immediately, if you have to pass through fire and water."

Enslaved workers also found camaraderie and strength in labor. Field workers carved out implicit understandings with their masters about at least some of the terms of their labor. "Task" groups who finished early expected to be rewarded with free time. Individuals with particular expertise (in laying tobacco plants, cutting sugar cane, or picking cotton, for example) expected deference from drivers, overseers, and even owners. Throughout much of the South, a two-hour lunch break in the hottest part of the summer day was customary, and in virtually all parts of the South slaves had Sunday for their own work and families.

The power of whites over African Americans was never absolute. While whites used whippings, executions, sexual assault, and vigilante terrorism to intimidate slaves, slaves fought back with arson, poison, feigned illness, work slow-downs, and the threat of their own violence. Harriet Jacobs remembered that her grandmother delivered "scorching rebukes" to her master. In the pivotal moment of his struggle for autonomy, Frederick Douglass

rose up against an abusive overseer, seizing the white man by the throat and refusing to be beaten ever again.

As slaves built the economy of the South, they also left a lasting imprint on the emergent southern regional culture. Enslaved African Americans had begun converting to Christianity in the late eighteenth century, and many had embraced the religious revivals of the early nineteenth century. Yet as they accepted Christianity, they made it their own. Slave preachers made selective use of older Christian themes to suit the needs of their congregations, emphasizing the story of Moses and the escape from bondage, and other messages of freedom, over homilies on human depravity and the importance of absolute obedience. Newly arrived Africans (smuggled into the country even after the close of the legal slave trade in 1808) provided a constant infusion of American Christianity with African religious forms, such as dancing, spiritual singing, chanting, and clapping. They also introduced distinctly African and Afro-Caribbean religions, such as voodun. Slave religious practice became both the embodiment and the instrument of self-assertion. Circles of belief forged strong common bonds within which slaves relived African culture and created distinctly African-American practices and affirmed their determination to be free. The call to "cross over Jordan" that constituted the refrain of many slave songs symbolized the harshness of slave life, but on any given night, in any given service, it might also signal the singer's intention to escape.

The River and the West

Like the South and the Northeast, the trans-Appalachian West was not a uniform region with a single culture or perfectly homogeneous interests. Indeed, even more than the other regions, the West was an idea of freedom and opportunity and a rolling, ragged, ever-shifting place. Although the Mississippi River offered a rough western border for the region, soon after the War of 1812 settlers were pouring into Arkansas Territory beyond the river. Based on population density, the eastern boundary of the West was a broken line that curved southeast from Buffalo, New York, on Lake Erie, bisecting Pennsylvania, and following the western borders of present-day Virginia and North and South Carolina south into Georgia before cutting southeast to the Atlantic. By definition, however, this eastern edge was a vanishing line, ever less distinct as more and more settlers crossed the Appalachians and settled communities to the west of them.

The West overlapped both the South and the western reaches of the Northeast and reflected the economies and cultures of those two older regions. Settled largely by northeasterners, the Northwest (Ohio, Indiana, northern Illinois, and Michigan Territory) was characterized by family farming, small manufacturing, and wage labor. In contrast, the Southwest (western Georgia, Alabama,

Mississippi, Louisiana, southern Illinois, Florida and Arkansas Territories, Kentucky, and Tennessee) was settled by southerners, depended on slavery, and was oriented toward export farming.

These two disparate regions were bound together by the Ohio and Mississippi Rivers, flowing from the western border of Pennsylvania all the way to the Gulf of Mexico. For years this had been a one-way system. Indians, trappers, and fur traders had long used the Mississippi to float hides downstream to St. Louis and New Orleans. Farmers and merchants followed suit, building large flatboats (12 or 14 feet wide and up to 50 feet long) to carry salted or dried pork, corn (often distilled into whiskey), and wheat (ground into flour) downriver for sale or export. So long as goods could only move downstream, however, settlers in the Northwest divided their economic efforts between the river and overland routes east. They used the river to ship cargo downstream to New Orleans for sale, but they did their buying in the East, carrying purchases home overland. The development of the steamboat, which enabled goods to be moved efficiently upriver as well as down, boosted the value of New Orleans as a source of clothing, furniture, and equipment and drew transplanted New Englanders and transplanted Virginians and Carolinians into a web of common interests.

Western settlers up and down the Mississippi were also knit together by the politics of land. Most migrants to the West were small farmers, families looking for affordable land and access to eastern and foreign markets. They favored generous federal land policies and easy credit, but the land boom, and the particular ways that Congress structured land sales, encouraged corruption. Surveyors sometimes set aside choice parcels for themselves or for affluent benefactors. Like earlier acts, the Act of 1804 required that lands be bought at auction and required an immediate down payment, features that benefited wealthy buyers (usually speculators). Land office agents, who controlled the auction calendars, exacted bribes for setting auction dates favorable to particular bidders. Taking advantage of provisions for speedy foreclosure if settlers fell behind in their payments, land agents used their inside information to buy up cheap lands in danger of repossession. Largely unregulated state commercial banks offered sweetheart deals to friends and wealthy patrons, often with insufficient collateral. Worse yet, in the eyes of most settlers in the West, were the eastern banks, which were engaged in an unceasing battle to restrict credit.

Settlers fought back for fair access to the new lands. They lobbied Congress for a right of preemption that would allow settlers to claim land before it came up for auction, and for a guaranteed fair price for improvements on repossessed property. When the federal government (which needed the revenue from land sales) resisted these remedies as endangering overall receipts, settlers took

measures into their own hands. Some new arrivals simply "squatted" on the land they wanted and defied federal agents to push them off. Organized in loose vigilance associations, neighbors attended land auctions, using the threat of their presence and sometimes their fists to intimidate speculators and profiteers. But the line between "settlers" and "speculators" blurred. Andrew Jackson, who would later come to embody this distrust of special privilege, was himself a speculator in western lands in the postwar years.

The population of the trans-Appalachian West doubled during these years. In Ohio the number of people per square mile of land increased from about 4 in 1810 to about 24 in 1830, and in Indiana it increased from less than 1 to almost 10. By 1825 the trans-Appalachian West had developed a discernible regional political economy, based on commercial agriculture and trade and oriented toward the western riverways. Farmers produced corn, wheat, and livestock in the North and cotton, sugar cane, and some grain in the South. Villages and small towns functioned as collection points, where crops were channeled out toward the rivers. Larger cities on the waterways collected the inland produce, provided processing services, and channeled goods north or south to market. With New Orleans, gateway to the Gulf, at one end and Pittsburgh, gateway to the East, at the other, the Ohio-Mississippi system traced a chain of booming commercial centers, including Cincinnati, Louisville, St. Louis, and Memphis. Functioning initially as shipping hubs, the western cities (especially those on the northern part of the system, where plantation culture did not siphon off entrepreneurial investment) soon developed into regional manufacturing centers as well. By 1820, Cincinnati constituted its own "emporium" of the West, offering tailors, seamstresses, milliners, cabinet makers, saddlers, chandlers, iron manufacturers, a tannery, tin and copper workers, brickmakers and papermakers, a steam mill, and a gunpowder maker, among other manufacturers.

This relatively dense pattern of settlement in the Northwest permitted and encouraged the development of societies and civic groups reminiscent of the Northeast. Cincinnati supported a circulating library, a seminary for young ladies, a medical society, a saving society, a literary magazine, a chapter of the Bible and Tract Society, and a humane society for rescuing people who fell into the river. Still, the western cities claimed a flamboyant assortment of people and a rough-and-ready character that distinguished them from their eastern counterparts: gamblers looking for an easy mark, land agents looking for buyers, dispirited newcomers looking for supplies, Indians looking for food, and aging frontiersmen looking for a fight. On the rivers, flatboatmen and steamboat crews hurled obscenities at one another.

Settlement remained sparse in most places, and migrants could find themselves virtually isolated for the first

By the 1820s, the steamboat had become essential to the movement of cotton down southern and western rivers to the coast for transport north or overseas. Here, slaves load bails of cotton on a steamboat on the Alabama River.

several years of homesteading. Creating a new home called on all the resources that settlers could muster and some they did not know they had. In Dexter, Michigan, their second stop, Harriet Noble's family was fortunate to find the shell of a cabin already built, but it lacked a roof, a door, and a chimney. Noble described it as a "square log pen." By late November the roof was on, but the cabin still lacked a chimney. "I said to my husband, 'I think I can drive the oxen and draw the stones, while you dig them from the ground and load them'," she remembered. "He thought I could not, but consented to let me try. He loaded them on a kind of sled; I drove to the house, rolled them off, and drove back for another load. I succeeded so well that we got enough in this way to build our chimney." "I suppose most of my lady friends would think a woman quite out of 'her legitimate sphere' in turning mason," she reflected, "but I was not at all particular what kind of labor I performed, so we were only comfortable and provided with the necessaries of life."

Most new arrivals settled for caves or huts, however, or (like the young Abraham Lincoln, whose family migrated to Indiana from Kentucky in 1816) lived in "half-faced camps" (three-sided cabins with trees for corner posts and branches for a roof) and turned their immediate attention to getting a crop in. If they lived close enough to neighbors, they might get help in that first year or at least the offer of equipment. But settlers often staked their claims in isolated, wooded areas, where the presence of trees indicated fertile land and gave them protection from winter winds. The family cleared four or five acres to start: a small patch each for a kitchen garden and for flax, larger plots for wheat and corn. Men felled trees; women and children dragged them away for later use building barns or cabins or for use as winter firewood. As soon as possible, the settlers broke the ground, pulling the plow themselves if they had no animals. Women worked alongside men in planting and hoeing, and later in harvesting the crop.

The early stages of farming settlement seldom gave the appearance of being very settled or very prosperous. Hungry families crouched in dark clearings in rude huts, while their animals roamed free in search of food. Settlers slept on piles of leaves on dirt floors, got wet in rainstorms, shivered in the winter, ate food from a slab of wood, and wore clothing made of homespun flax. Many of the settlers were not skilled farmers, and their early yields were poor. One Ohio settler described her family's first crop as consisting mainly of "unsound corn" and "sick wheat." What she salvaged she had to grind by hand, for the nearest flour mill was seven miles away.

CHRONOLOGY

1807 First trip of Robert Fulton's *North River Steamboat of Clermont*

1814 Treaty of Ghent
Waltham mills open

1815 Steamboats begin regular two-way trips on the Mississippi

1816 Second Bank of the United States is created
Tariff is passed
James Monroe elected president

1817 Madison vetoes Federal Transportation Subsidies Bill
New York begins construction of Erie Canal (opened 1825)

1818 United States and Great Britain negotiate Convention of 1818

1819 *Dartmouth v. Woodward* and *McCulloch v. Maryland*
Missouri applies for statehood
United States and Spain negotiate Transcontinental Treaty
Panic of 1819

1820 Maine becomes a state

1821 Missouri becomes a state

1823 Monroe Doctrine
Merrimack Manufacturing Company mills produce first finished cloth

1824 *Gibbons v. Ogden*
John Quincy Adams elected president

1825 Erie Canal opens

Conclusion

In the summer of 1817, recently inaugurated President James Monroe made a triumphal tour of New England, celebrating the demise of old party animosities and the return of national prosperity. When Monroe arrived in Boston, so warm was the outpouring of sentiment that the editor of the *Columbian Centinel,* a Federalist newspaper, was moved to declare the dawning of an "Era of Good Feeling." In many respects, the years between 1815 and 1824 were years of political consolidation, diplomatic success, and heady economic growth. As the United States asserted breathtaking new national and international claims, it transformed itself internally into a land of expanding interdependent regional markets and well-oiled political institutions.

And yet there were "firebells" enough, for those who chose to hear them. The great improvements in transportation were undertaken on the state, not the federal, level. The American System had to be carefully negotiated in Congress, and it authorized a bank that helped bring about economic pandemonium. In some cases, nationalism and expansionism seemed to heighten fragmentation, suggesting that the national political economy was in fact a series of more discrete political economies, dependent upon different ways of organizing material life and promoting different personal values and national politics. The National Republicans chose not to hear the growing dissatisfactions of workers, family farmers, and small businessmen, who felt excluded from much of the promise of the market revolution. Most citizens decided that the lesson of Missouri was simply to avoid the issue of slavery altogether. Few took notice, in January of 1821, when, in the wake of the Missouri controversy, a newspaper writer by the name of Benjamin Lundy founded the first openly antislavery newspaper, the *Genius of Universal Emancipation.*

Review Questions

1. Was the "market revolution" really a revolution? Was it a phenomenon of local markets, regional markets, national markets—or all three? List five factors, occurring after 1800, that encouraged the growth of markets, 1815–1824.

2. In what ways did the development of regions and the development of a new sense of nationalism complement each other? In what ways did they conflict with each other?

3. Were the years between 1815 and 1824 an "Era of Good Feeling"?

4. Consider what was gained and/or lost for each of the following groups by the spread of internal markets: a farming family in western Massachusetts, a laboring-class family in New York, a wealthy merchant family in Philadelphia, a slave family in Virginia.

5. In what ways did the new, National Republicans represent an extension of Jeffersonian Republicanism? In what ways did the two political philosophies differ?

Further Readings

Frederic Bancroft, *Slave Trading in the Old South* (1931). This classic study of the internal slave trade (the first major examination of slavery to attack the mythology of slavery as a benevolent institution) details both the interregional movement of enslaved workers in the antebellum South and the institutions that facilitated the diaspora.

George Dangerfield, *The Awakening of American Nationalism, 1815–1828* (1965). Dangerfield remains one of the most readable overviews of United States life and politics in the wake of the enormous expansion of markets that followed the conclusion of the War of 1812.

Thomas Dublin, *Women at Work: The Transformation of Work and Community in Lowell, Massachusetts, 1826–1860* (1979). *Women at Work* traces the founding and early years of the textile industry in Lowell, Massachusetts, with particular attention to the family and economic backgrounds of the female operatives, the social relations of their work in the mills, early organizing as conditions of labor began to deteriorate in the 1830s, and the growth of an Irish work force.

John Mack Faragher, *Sugar Creek: Life on the Illinois Frontier* (1986). Faragher uses the history of a single Illinois community to examine the motivations that led early settlers west, the day-to-day hardships they faced in obtaining land, getting in a crop, and settling a family, and the circumstances that led some settlers to remain permanently in Sugar Creek while others soon moved on to other frontiers.

William G. McLoughlin, *Cherokee Renascence in the New Republic* (1986). McLoughlin examines the history of the Cherokees, 1789–1833, with emphasis on the destructive impact of United States Indian policy and the various military, diplomatic, and cultural strategies through which Cherokees sought to preserve their lands and autonomous society.

History on the Internet

"History of the Erie Canal"
http://www.history.rochester.edu/canal
See how, in the era of great internal improvements, the opening of the canal had an impact on New York and the country. The site contains a chronology of the building of the canal, the evolution of boats used, biographical sketches of key players in the canal's history, and a link to searching primary documents about the canal.

"The Great Migration to the Mississippi Territory"
http://mshistory.k12.ms.us/features/feature9/migrate.html
Through this site, trace the great migration of whites and slaves to the West through this feature story, *Mississippi History Now.*

"The Five Points Site"
http://r2.gsa.gov/fivept/fphome.htm
Through this site, which utilizes both urban archaeology and history, learn about the famous nineteenth-century New York neighborhood that was home to working-class Irish immigrants.

11
SECURING DEMOCRACY
1820-1832

OUTLINE

Jackson's Election

Perfectionism and the
Theology of Human Striving

Millennialism and Communitarians

Urban Revivals

Social Reform in the
Benevolent Empire

The Common Man and the
Political Economy
of Democracy

The Political Economy of Free Labor

Suffrage Reform

Opposition to Special Privilege
and Secret Societies

Workingmen's Parties

The Democratic Impulse in
Presidential Politics

Jackson's Rise to National
Prominence

The Election of 1824 and the
"Corrupt Bargain"

The Adams Presidency and the
Gathering Forces of Democracy

The Election of 1828

President Jackson: Vindicating
the Common Man

Jacksonian Democrats in Office

A Policy of Indian Removal

The Bank War

Conclusion

Jackson's Election

"If vigilance and exertion be the conditions upon which we hold our rights," the *United States Gazette* warned early in 1828, "there never was a moment when they were more imperiously called for than the present." Although the tone suggested that foreign invasion was imminent, the object of the *Gazette*'s fears was in fact much closer at hand. Indeed, it was none other than the American hero, General Andrew Jackson. For two years the editors of the *Gazette* had watched with growing apprehension as Jackson's men had moved across America, lobbying local politicians, flattering voters, funding newspapers, silently converting the electoral system into a network of pro-Jackson forces. To Jackson's opponents, like the editors of the *Gazette,* the mere idea of a Jacksonian presidency was abhorrent. The man was an infidel and a would-be "despot," they charged, who had already demonstrated his contempt for the Constitution and would institute a new "reign of terror" across the land.

Eight months later, the *Gazette*'s worst fears were realized. On March 4, 1829, Andrew Jackson became the seventh president of the United States.

For Jackson supporters, the general's election bore a very different meaning. It represented not the destruction of

the republic, but its rebirth, not cataclysm, but something far closer to national salvation. At long last, according to some observers, "the people in all their majesty" had defeated the last vestiges of European-style "Aristocracy." The nation had found its soul, and "the Democracy of the country" had swept from power the wealthy cabals and elites that had tainted the republic since its birth. Like ecstatic believers in the throes of conversion, Jackson supporters swarmed the nation's capital, jamming the halls of Congress and mobbing the White House. "I never saw such a crowd here before," Daniel Webster declared, "... *and they really seem to think that the country is rescued from some dreadful danger!*" They did, and nothing better measured just how dreadful they thought the danger had been than their elation in success. They had beaten back the corrupt insiders and championed the rights of the common man. They had saved the national experiment!

In truth, the election of 1828 was not Armageddon, and the conditions that led to it did not constitute a stark drama of good and evil. By the mid-1820s the United States had shed much of its earlier, more deferential republican character. Revivalists called upon Americans to assume responsibility for their own destinies, and the

Much to the dismay of conservative critics, the "common man"—and woman—were very much in evidence at Andrew Jackson's inauguration in 1829. This depiction of the official White House reception suggests the broad grass roots support for Jackson and his admirers' readiness to travel long distances to celebrate their hero.

robust economy and breathtaking geographical expansion offered the landscape upon which many free men of modest means did so. With gusto they embraced the rhetoric and the political economy of democracy.

Still, a quarter of a century after the Revolution, the results of the national experiment were not all good. Prosperity had come at the price of deepened commercial and industrial dependencies, single-party rule, a more activist government, and the beginnings of economic consolidation through special charter. By 1828 there was a wide strain of disaffection running through the ranks of small farmers and working people and a belief that evil conspirators were secretly arrayed against them.

Jackson did not create this paradox of surging optimism and brooding distrust, but he captured it perfectly in his life history and in his temperament. The archetypical individual of the Age of Jackson was the white, male westward migrant, ingenious, self-reliant, and scrappy. Especially after the Panic of 1819, many Americans feared this "common man" was being sacrificed to the interests of the eastern banks, merchants, and speculators who controlled his credit, his access to land, and his markets. Jackson himself had left the east coast a penniless boy and fought his way to wealth and fame in Tennessee. As president he lobbied Congress for and finally got an Indian Removal Act, which he expected to make more western land available to settlers. He attacked privileged eastern elites, corporations that gave special

advantages to the wealthy, and political parties that trampled on the needs of common folk. He destroyed the most hated bank in America, the Second Bank of the United States. In all of these policies, he embraced with vigor a new political economy of democracy: all men (at least, all white men) deserved the opportunity to make their place in the world and to be heard on political matters that affected that opportunity. It was a credo of raw and restless confidence.

However triumphal the rhetoric, Jacksonian democracy was both pessimistic and limited. Behind the celebration of the common man lurked the certainty that the common man was in fact losing power and dignity. The very rhetoric of the "common man," moreover, contained a kind of shrillness that hinted at its own falsities. Not only did the political economy of the Jacksonian era continue to exclude African Americans and women of all statuses and classes from the full enjoyment of economic, political, and social liberty, but it also failed to address directly the growing plight of wage-earning men. White male suffrage became virtually universal in these years, but Jackson himself had little use for the crowds of angry workers who filled city streets, as he had no patience for the increasing assertiveness of evangelicals, the growing public presence of women in reform, or the constant attacks on slavery. These internal contradictions of Jacksonianism were the fault lines along which the new political economy would eventually fracture. ∎

KEY TOPICS

- The sources of Jacksonian democracy

- Optimism and expansionism in Jacksonian America

- Opposition to special privilege during the Jacksonian era

- The expansion of white male suffrage

- Revivalism and the Benevolent Empire

- Jackson's policies of Indian removal

Perfectionism and the Theology of Human Striving

American religious life in the 1820s reflected the paradoxes of the age. Some Americans looked at the changes of the preceding decades (the growth of market relations and individual freedom and the decline of older, more corporate communities) and saw a nation on the verge of losing its moral compass. Convinced that the day of final reckoning grew near, they preached doom and often withdrew from society into covenanted communities to prepare themselves for the end of time. Other Americans regarded the changes in their world less pessimistically. Although they worried about American society, and especially about the mounting poverty and sin of the cities, they remained hopeful that the nation could yet be redeemed. Far from withdrawing from the world, these reformers believed that it was the responsibility of each individual to work actively for the perfecting of American society, a conviction that grew in the wake of a renewed period of revivalism in the 1820s. Where the reformers agreed with separatists, however, was in their conviction that social life should be modeled on the principles of religion, particularly the principles of Protestant Christianity. As much as anything else, this broad belief (sometimes optimistic, sometimes pessimistic) in the Christianizing of society bound together a national culture in the first 25 years of the nineteenth century.

Millennialism and Communitarians

Separatist communities were not new to the American spiritual landscape in the years after the War of 1812, and they never accounted for more than a minority of the American people. Nevertheless, they enjoyed renewed success in these years. As a group, these religious **communitarians** sought to prepare for the millennium by creating more perfect societies on earth, an effort they undertook by withdrawing from most forms of daily contact with their neighbors and instituting tightly controlled spiritual, social, and economic regimens within their own borders. Some of the largest and most enduring separatist communities embracing **millennialism** were products of Europe, based on agrarian models of a simple, orderly life.

One of the earliest of these religious communities was the United Society of Believers in Christ's Second Appearing, a radical branch of Quakerism that often called itself the Millennial Church. This group was soon dubbed "Shakers" by their critics, for the "[d]ancing, singing, leaping, clapping . . . , groans and sighs" that characterized its services. American Shakerism was rooted in the experiences of Ann Lee, a late eighteenth-century English factory worker and charismatic lay preacher who believed that she was the second, female embodiment of the Messiah. Lee preached that believers should return to the simplicity and purity of the early Christian Church, pooling all their worldly resources, withdrawing from the vanities of the society, and observing strict celibacy. The Shakers migrated to North America in 1774 and soon established their first community near Watervliet, New York. "Mother" Lee died in 1784, but the church flourished. By the turn of the century the Shakers had established a dozen communities in New England. Soon after the turn of the century they began to move west, establishing four more settlements in Ohio and Kentucky. By the 1830s membership approached 4,000 persons living in some 60 separate communities.

Shaker beliefs required the establishment of a particular kind of community. "A true church of Christ" could be founded only on the basis of a perfect "union of faith, of motives, and of interest" of all members. To ensure this perfect unity, Shakers organized their communities into "families" of 30 to 100 members, each of which was supervised by a panel of eight persons (two women and two men to oversee spiritual matters, and two men and two women to oversee temporal concerns). The various "families" within a given community were guided by a ministry (also composed equally of men and women), and the individual communities submitted to the authority of a head ministry at New Lebanon, New York.

Their search for perfection led the Shakers to repudiate many of the values of the increasingly market-driven economy in which they lived. Although Shakers were willing to sell goods to outsiders, they rejected the materialism and competitive individualism that were becoming hallmarks of American economic life, requiring new members to sign over their worldly goods to the society and allocating individual labor according to the needs of the

Outsiders labeled members of the United Society of Believers in Christ's Second Appearing "Shakers" after the active twirling and shaking movements that accompanied their services. Here Shakers engage in a ritual dance called "The Whirling Gift."

community. This alternative political economy resulted in prosperity and a high level of invention. A Shaker woman perfected the flat nail, and other members of the community invented fruit peelers, seed pitters, eggbeaters, and other household tools. Shaker gardeners developed the first American seed industry, and Shaker farmers produced bumper crops of grain and bred large and healthy herds of dairy cattle. Although many Americans of the 1820s viewed Shakers as dangerous cultists, others found in the orderliness of Shaker communities a refuge from the social and economic turmoil of early nineteenth-century American life.

Women appear to have been especially drawn to Shakerism, probably because of the Shaker emphasis on the separation of the sexes and formal equality between men and women. Labor was strictly organized by gender. Men and women even lived in separate quarters and entered and left buildings by separate doors. In addition, Shakers believed in the absolute spiritual equality of men and women. This was reflected in the authority structure of the communities, which called for mixed ministries of men and women at every level, with "sisters" and "female elders" supervising the women's lives and "brothers" and "male elders" supervising the men's. The Shaker practice of celibacy (explained, perhaps, by Ann Lee's history of painful pregnancies) afforded women freedom from the dangers of childbirth.

Separatist millennial communities shared a belief that the day of atonement was at hand, but their specific beliefs and organizational structures varied widely. Like the Shak-

ers, the followers of German farmer George Rapp rejected the private ownership of property (at least, through most of their history) and practiced celibacy. Unlike the highly evangelical Shakers, Rapp's followers did not actively seek converts or embrace the simple life. Believing that "[w]ithout a doubt, the kingdom of Jesus Christ is approaching near," they considered it the responsibility of the truly devout to amass great material wealth to put at the disposal of Jesus Christ upon his return to earth.

George Rapp and several hundred followers first arrived in North America in 1803 and migrated to western Pennsylvania, where they established the town of Harmony. In search of better soil and access to water, they moved on in 1815 to the banks of the Wabash River in Indiana Territory. There the Rappites enjoyed astonishing success. By 1824 their membership numbered 800, and their holdings had grown to over 20,000 acres, where they grew fruit, grain, and cotton, grazed sheep and erected a cotton and woolen mill and a distillery, as well as houses and community buildings. Unfortunately, the climate that made the Wabash hospitable to agriculture also made it hospitable to malaria. Weary of yearly scourges of the disease, in 1824 the Rappites sold New Harmony to the English social reformer Robert Owen and moved back to western Pennsylvania, founding their third community, Economy. After Rapp's death in 1847, membership flagged, perhaps from the lack of a charismatic leader, perhaps because members became more interested in personal prosperity and less concerned about the millennium.

In terms of numbers and longevity, the most important of the millennial communities of the early nineteenth century was the Church of Jesus Christ of the Latter-day Saints, also known as the Mormons. Founder Joseph Smith, Jr., born in upstate New York in 1805, was the child of poor, tenant-farming parents who were never quite able to pull themselves out of debt in the increasingly commercial agricultural environment. The family got by on rural wage labor and clung to a faith based on visions, mysticism, and divine intervention. In 1820, Smith had a vision in which he was informed that Catholicism and all existing forms of Protestantism were deluded faiths and that God was soon to establish his true church on earth. Three years later, Smith had a second vision in which an angel disclosed to him the existence and location of golden tablets that described God's intentions for the "latter days" of creation, now approaching. In 1830 Smith published the plates as the *Book of Mormon* and formally founded the Church of Christ.

At its founding, the church consisted of roughly 50 members, but Smith's preaching gradually attracted a body of rural followers, most of them people who had been displaced and were deeply troubled by the torrent of changes affecting the antebellum North. To these listeners, Smith preached that the Church of Christ was the successor of a long-lost tribe of Israelites who had made their way to America. It was God's will that they go forth into the wilderness, he insisted, to found the city of Zion, where they would reign over the coming millennium.

The opposition of their neighbors, who considered Mormon beliefs blasphemous, soon forced the Mormons to leave New York. Smith first moved his followers to Ohio, where they established the town of Kirkland and organized a communal economy run by the church, and then to Missouri. In 1839 a large group of Mormons moved on to Illinois, where they founded the city of Nauvoo. By the early 1840s, Smith had begun to preach the doctrine of plural marriage, permitting some Mormon men to take more than one wife. In the confusion ignited by these new teachings, the Mormon community split and anti-Mormon outrage flared anew. Although he was guaranteed protection, Smith was arrested and thrown in jail in Carthage, Illinois, where, on June 27, 1844, he was murdered by a mob (allegedly with the help of a jail guard and the support of leading citizens). In 1847, under the guidance of Smith's trusted associate Brigham Young, the Mormons uprooted once more, this time not stopping until they reached the Great Salt Lake in the West. There, at last, they founded their permanent community of believers. By 1850 hard work, irrigation, and careful cultivation had turned the desert into a garden paradise inhabited by more than 11,000 people.

Urban Revivals

Important as advocates of alternative models of religious, social, and economic practice, separatist millennialists nevertheless represented a relatively minor stream in the floods of religious organizing that characterized the post-War of 1812 era. Far more numerous were the Americans who sought to perfect society not by withdrawing from it, but by carrying the spirit of revival and reform deep into their own communities. As it had earlier, this massive evangelizing of America took many forms. Itinerant Methodists and Baptists like the Reverend Barton Stone continued to minister to the newly settled churches in the backcountry. By the 1820s, however, the revivals had also begun to assume an urban character, reflecting a growing sense on the part of religiously concerned Americans that the danger to the nation's soul lay in its cities as much as in its territories. Soon even the great metropolises like Boston, Philadelphia, and New York became hothouses of evangelism.

The career of the Presbyterian minister Ezra Stiles Ely reflects this shift in mainstream American religious life. From 1811 to 1813, Ely was employed as a chaplain by the Society for Supporting the Gospel, working with men and women who lived in public shelters. In that capacity, he led religious services, distributed Bibles, and prayed at the bedsides of the sick and dying. In the course of performing his duties, Ely observed firsthand the growing poverty of American cities and grew frustrated with the limited impact of his efforts. In the years after the War of 1812, he extended his work beyond the almshouse into the shanties and tenements of New York's poor neighborhoods. More important, he increasingly understood his mission to be not merely providing solace, but also converting souls. Neither Ely nor the other reformers who gradually took up city mission work believed that they had the power to save people who were not chosen by God, but they did believe that the elect were to be found even among the most vicious of the city's poor. As the Presbyterian Female Missionary Society for the Poor of the City of New York, founded in 1816, asked in its Second Annual Report: "Are there not some among the destitute of our own city for whom Christ died? Some elect who must yet be gathered in?"

The new urban-based missionary societies soon turned their attention to the boomtowns of the West. The New York Evangelical Missionary Society of Young Men, for example, raised money to fund missionaries to the teeming new settlements of western Pennsylvania, upstate New York, and Georgia. Of these missionaries to the West, none would be more successful or more controversial than Charles Grandison Finney, who would become one of the most influential advocates for a dynamic Protestantism based on personal responsibility and the power of the individual to change society.

Born in Connecticut, Finney had originally trained in the law. In 1821, however, at the age of 29, he had experienced a calling to the ministry. Although Finney's rejection of the Presbyterian belief in original sin worried his teachers, he soon developed into an effective and charismatic preacher, and at last, in March of 1824, he was licensed as a minister. That year, he moved to upstate New York to begin his work.

Finney had spent some time in upstate New York as a boy, but by the 1820s the world he had known there was quickly disappearing. Construction of the Erie Canal was well advanced, drawing even the most remote farmers closer to the markets of the East Coast and bringing the relations of cash and commerce to the lush western valleys of the state. Inhabitants of the towns and small cities of the region found themselves at the center of the rapidly developing market economy. Some of those inhabitants, like the people who eventually followed Joseph Smith, were troubled by the swirl of development around them. Others were more alert to the possibilities for success in the new economy and were attracted to the way in which it appeared to reward industry, hard work, and personal ambition (see Map 11-1).

To this latter audience, Finney preached a message of the power of human spiritual striving. In the place of the stern God of Calvinism, he offered a God of Justice, who, like an impartial advocate, laid his case before a humankind "just as free as a jury" to accept salvation or not. Jonathan Edwards, the most famous minister of the eighteenth-century Awakening, had terrified his congregation with descriptions of the utter helplessness of "Sinners in the Hands of an Angry God" (see chapter 5). In contrast, Finney admonished his listeners that they were "Sinners Bound to Change Their *Own* Hearts." This theology gave greater latitude than orthodox Presbyterianism to human effort, but it also placed a new burden on the sinner. If "a man that was praying week after week for the Holy Spirit . . . could get no answer," Finney insisted, it must be that the man "was praying from false motives," not that an indifferent God had abandoned him.

Finney enjoyed immediate and wide success in the Genesee Valley of New York. Especially drawn to his preaching were members of the groups most directly benefiting from the economic boom: the families of merchants and bankers, grain dealers and mill owners, and the young, ambitious employees in such businesses. Finneyite Presbyterianism set individual ambition in a new context. It was a part of the process of salvation, a sign not of human corruption, but of the potential for human good. Eventually, Finney repudiated the older Calvinism entirely, claiming for America a new and optimistic religion based on the power of the individual. If each person attended to his or her own soul and also reached out to others, urging them to take their spiritual destinies into their own hands, surely the millennium could not be far away!

If Finney's preaching excited many members of the growing western communities, it alarmed the Presbyterian establishment in the East. As the career of Lyman Beecher suggested, what made Finney so disturbing to more orthodox leaders was not merely the emotional style of the revivals and Finney's unconventional views, but also his presence and influence in the new western areas. Beecher had started out life as an orphan in Connecticut, but by 1826 he had advanced to become pastor of the prestigious Hanover Street Presbyterian Church in Boston. Although he employed some revival methods and admitted a greater element of free will in redemption than some orthodox ministers were prepared to acknowledge, Beecher deeply identified with the institution of the New England Presbyterian Church. Like many New Englanders of his generation, Beecher was convinced that the future greatness of the United States lay in transferring New England culture, and especially New England orthodoxy, westward. Finneyite unorthodoxy was by no means the greatest peril (Beecher would come to believe that the greatest threat lay

in Catholic immigrants), but it represented a dangerous first step. In time, Beecher made peace with Finney (whom he eventually invited to preach in Boston), but he was never reconciled to the idea of a culturally heterogeneous nation. In 1832, Beecher moved his family to the new boomtown of the West, Cincinnati, where he assumed the presidency of the Lane Theological Seminary. There, in 1835, he wrote *A Plea for the West*, in which he predicted that the final battle of the Christ and the Antichrist would take place in the American West.

Social Reform in the Benevolent Empire

"Every truly converted man turns from selfishness to benevolence," Charles Finney once said, "and benevolence surely leads him to do all he can to save the souls of his fellow man. This is the changeless law of benevolent action." In these words, Finney spoke for a whole generation. The new evangelical emphasis on personal agency soon assumed the character of a broad impulse for social reform, expressed in religious terms and organized through a loose network of charities and associations, often referred to as the Benevolent Empire. Initially, at least, reformers saw no bounds to the good that could be worked by benevolence. Only with time would the reformers recognize the obstacles, in their world and in themselves, to their dreams of a perfected society.

The **Benevolent Empire** was grounded in Americans' long-standing love of organizing, a tendency observed by Frenchman Alexis de Tocqueville when he visited the

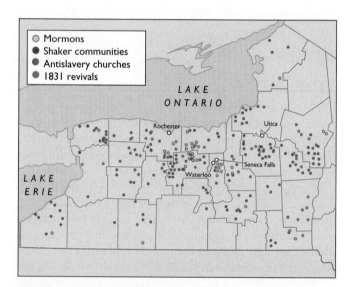

Map 11-1   Revival and Reform.
Social and economic tranformation, religious revival, and social reform movements often went hand in hand in the antebellum North. The so-called "burned over district" of New York (the region directly served by the Erie Canal) nurtured numerous millennial sects (including Mormons and Shakers), antimasonry, Finneyite revivals, and antislave activism, as well as the Seneca Falls woman's rights convention.

United States in 1831–1832. Americans, Tocqueville wrote, "are forever forming associations." Toqueville reported the curious mixture of evangelicalism and social perfection that characterized American associationism: "Americans combine to . . . found seminaries, build churches, distribute books, and send missionaries to the antipodes. Hospitals, prisons, and schools take shape in that way. Finally, if they want to proclaim a truth or propagate some feeling by the encouragement of a great example, they form an association."

The description was not far from the mark. Beginning in the early nineteenth century, but mushrooming in the 1820s and after, evangelical Americans turned their attention to building a network of organizations through which to propagate their religious beliefs (and especially evangelical Protestantism) throughout society. Charitable and missionary societies founded before the War of 1812 flourished and, drawn together by the ministers of the revivals, linked up into national umbrella groups. Among the largest of these were the American Bible Society (which distributed Bibles in cities and new settlements), the Female Moral Reform Society (devoted to reclaiming women from prostitution), and the American Board of Commissioners for Foreign Missions (which promoted missions in the West and the South Sea Islands). In addition, every major city fostered smaller, loosely affiliated efforts: Bible groups, asylums to help the poor, houses of industry, orphanages, and humane societies, among a host of others. By 1830 the broad influence of evangelical benevolence had also given rise to a Sunday school movement (originally aimed primarily at the children of church members)

Although this American Tract Magazine woodcut (1825) suggests that poor families were grateful to the wealthier neighbors who distributed Christian pamphlets among them, relations between benefactors and the objects of their charity were not always so amicable. The poor often resented what they felt as condescending intrusions into their lives.

and a movement against permitting the delivery of mail on the Christian Sabbath.

Benevolent societies represented a curious combination of emotional and rational approaches to reform. The method of the Benevolent Empire was **moral suasion.** Reformers (many of whom were volunteers) believed that social change came about not from external laws and rules, but rather through the gradual internal awakening of individual moral purpose, coaxed through personal contact, testimony, and (where needed) exhortation. Yet increasingly, the structure of benevolence became that of the bureaucratic corporation.

Founded in 1816 in New York by a group of relatively wealthy Christian men, the American Bible Society illustrates this paradox. The society consisted initially of a volunteer board of managers who had no offices of their own and hired out the printing and binding of Bibles to independent printing shops. By 1818, however, the board felt the need to hire a full-time salaried manager to oversee its increasingly complex business affairs. Between 1818 and 1832 the society added a corresponding secretary, an accountant, a recording secretary, and an assistant treasurer and built its own building in Manhattan. Even as the business operations became more rationalized, however, the society still depended on idealistic young ministers (hired temporarily before they received regular appointments elsewhere as pastors) as its traveling agents and local volunteer organizations as its community contacts.

As they pursued their good deeds, whether distributing Bibles, praying with the sick, or handing out religious tracts on street corners, evangelicals came into intimate contact with the nation's poor. Like Ely, almost inevitably, benevolent reformers began to minister to the material, as well as the spiritual, needs of the people they had come to convert. They arranged fuel deliveries and medical care, helped homeless families find lodgings, and organized soup kitchens to help feed the poor. In firsthand accounts of their work, the city missionaries published their experiences to a broader readership. They fashioned a distinctly American blend of philanthropy and religion that called upon wealthier Americans to acknowledge the inequities of American society.

Both men and women were engaged in the charitable associations of the early nineteenth century, but for women voluntary reform offered special opportunities. With the encouragement and approval of ministers and prominent laymen of their communities, women had already been active in organizing maternal societies to discuss and scrutinize their parenting habits and Bible societies to discuss their own moral failings. By the second decade of the nineteenth century, women were founding orphan asylums to care for the children who were not their own, becoming actively involved in the Sunday school movement, founding homes for wayward girls, and establishing asylums for "respectable" homeless adults. "The

Society for the Relief of Aged and Indigent Respectable Females" and "The Society for the Protection of Aged Seamen" sought to minister to the spiritual and the material needs of the poor. Lyman Beecher protested that "A greater evil, next to the loss of conscience or chastity, could not befall the female sex." Nevertheless, by the 1820s women had become the acknowledged volunteer backbone of the Benevolent Empire.

In the second and third decades of the nineteenth century, the Benevolent Empire provided one of the strongest cultural bonds among regions. Having fewer cities and a more dispersed population, the South claimed fewer associations overall, yet the impulse to organize society according to the principles of Christianity was as strong there as in the North—perhaps stronger among those whites who believed that Christianizing slaves would make them more docile. Charleston, South Carolina, for example, supported an Orphan House, a Society for the Advancement of Christianity in South Carolina, a Bible Society, a Unitarian Book and Tract Society, a Temperance Society, and a Sunday School Union, as well as miscellaneous other benevolent associations. County seats often had a charitable or a Bible society.

Yet the Benevolent Empire was not identical in the North and South. Unwilling to broach the subject of slavery itself, southern reformers seldom raised the sharp issues of social inequality that came to characterize some northern benevolent societies over time, instead remaining more purely focused on charity. Indeed, it was the growing importance of perfectionism in northern benevolence, with its emphasis on expunging all evil from society, that eventually drove a wedge between northern and southern reformers and rendered reform an instrument of division rather than of cross-regional bonding. Even in the North, however, the immediate beneficiaries of questions about social inequity were not African Americans, but rather white men who did not own property.

The Common Man and the Political Economy of Democracy

Americans had long associated republican virtue with labor, particularly with labor that created sufficient property to afford a level of economic independence. In the very early years of the republic, that virtue-producing labor was most often represented in the figure of the farmer and, to a lesser extent, that of the craftsman. Nineteenth-century Americans continued to praise the self-sufficient and industrious common citizen as the mainstay of the political economy of the nation, but with some changes. On the one hand, the celebration of labor became more democratic and the figures through which Americans evoked the virtues of work became more varied. On the other hand, discussions of the virtue of labor became more defensive and the embodiment of that virtue became more distinctly gendered and racialized.

The Political Economy of Free Labor

This shift toward a more generic, in some ways more democratic, idiom of work mirrored changes in the American economy, especially the growing political and economic importance of renewed westward migration and the growth of commerce and manufacturing. The "farmer" was likely to be depicted as a scrappy backwoods pioneer, rather than as the modest husbandman of Jeffersonian lore. "Everywhere," editor Hezekiah Niles proclaimed, "the sound of the axe is heard opening the forest to the sun." But more people were taking up nonfarm occupations, and the ways in which Americans talked about labor reflected that shift. Writers broadened the concept of virtuous worker to include the mass of "honest and industrious citizens who earn their daily bread by the sweat of their brow" and included in this definition the self-made shopkeeper, the clerk climbing the ladder of success, and the craft worker. It was the fact of gainful employment, not the specific occupation, that conferred dignity. Some commentators equated "labor" with simple "industriousness," which was in turn equated with "ambition." The distinguishing trait of the hard-working Americans, according to Niles, was simply the desire "to get forward."

Interlaced with this reaffirmation, even enlargement, of their commitment to individual opportunity, some Americans also expressed a lurking uneasiness that individual opportunity was somehow under assault in the new

web connection

The Times They Are a Changin'

www.prenhall.com/boydston/census

Who is an American, anyway? From the first United States census in 1790, the American population has been counted every ten years. And every ten years, the population has looked different. Each snapshot of this dynamic population revealed some things were changing—where most people were living, where they used to live, who they lived with, and what they did for a living, for instance. What can the census reveal about American society's composition and values?

political economy of the postwar years. Economic hard times before and during the War of 1812 revived an older critique of unearned profits and gave rise to a protest literature that focused on the dignity and importance of labor. In 1817 Cornelius Blatchly, a Quaker physician from New Jersey, published a pamphlet titled *Some Causes of Popular Poverty.* Blatchly argued that property owners had become the new tyrants of America, enabled by law to steal from laborers the value that they produced and which rightfully belonged to them. The Panic of 1819, which had occurred at a high tide of post-War of 1812 economic expansion when many Americans had been drawn more deeply into market relations than ever before, reawakened that skepticism. The sudden collapse of credit and agricultural prices and the consequent widespread business failures and unemployment reminded some Americans of just how precarious the new economy was. Although wealthy speculators were also hurt, the harshest lessons were dealt to small farmers and wage workers, who began to suspect that their interests were not being well served by the policies of the Republicans. Even in the improving economic climate of the 1820s, workers became more assertive about the value and dignity of their labor.

One of the most outspoken defenders of the dignity of labor was English industrialist Robert Owen, who arrived in the United States in 1824. A cotton manufacturer turned social critic, Owen did not denounce industrialization, but he did denounce a system of laws that awarded the profits produced by machine workers to the people wealthy enough to own the machines. "Manual labor, properly directed, is the source of all wealth," Owen flatly asserted, and, he felt, manual labor should receive its fair share of wealth. To demonstrate what a just society would look like, Owen purchased land from the Rappites in 1825 and established New Harmony, a utopian community designed to combine industrial efficiency with the equal provision of leisure, security, and personal cultivation for all its members.

Contrasted on one side with the parasitism of wealthy elites, the concept of "the dignity of labor" was defined on the other side by the existence of slavery. Although many free workers saw slavery as an immoral institution, they also perceived it as antirepublican and viewed slaves as the embodiment of a state of dependence against which free workers constantly struggled. By 1818, as one American lawyer noted, free hired workers refused to be referred to as "servants," because of the habit of "confounding the term *servant* with that of *slave*" in white southern culture.

The economic developments of the post-War of 1812 years gave force to the urgency with which white workers sought to distinguish themselves from slaves. The institution of slavery was in fact spreading in the United States, and although that growth affected free workers in the South far more directly than those in the North, slavery did still exist in some northern states in the early decades of the nineteenth century. No white male worker feared actually being enslaved, but the declining standard of living of many white workers (especially in 1819 and immediately thereafter) and the fact that some slaves were hired out for wages blurred the social and economic distinctions between free workers and slaves. White workers began to describe their employment not simply as labor, but rather as "free labor," in implied contrast to "unfree" enslaved labor. When they described their worsening condition, they portrayed bosses bent on reducing them to "a degrading vassalage" and rendering them "abject slaves."

In American culture, the symbol of virtue-producing labor had long been gendered male, but this association, too, may have been reinforced by westward migration and by the precariousness of the new market economy. Although American myth depicted the West as a place of manly independence, in the real West land was expensive, hard to get, and easily lost in the credit crunch of a recession. In the East, most laboring (and even middling) families required the income of wives. Perhaps most galling to working-class men, the city streets, and even their own homes, were becoming the haunts of assertive female reformers.

Suffrage Reform

At the founding of the nation, suffrage was restricted not only by gender and race, but even more universally on the basis of property ownership and tax payment. Urban mechanics, who often owned little more property than the tools of their trade and the clothes on their back, had objected to this state of affairs, demanding the vote on the basis of their military service, their loyalty, and their economic importance to the nation. Most of all, they had demanded the vote as the emblem of liberty. "Suffrage," as one editor insisted in 1801, "is the first right of a free people." As white workingmen felt their status eroding in the early nineteenth century, they returned to the issue of the vote as the battleground upon which to establish their credentials as free men.

The new political economy sharpened their challenge to property ownership or tax payment as the basis for suffrage. Although the United States remained a rural nation throughout the nineteenth century, the proportion of Americans who worked in agriculture peaked in 1810 and declined steadily thereafter. Improvements in transportation, the growth of manufacturing and banking, and westward expansion highlighted the regional and national economic importance of these growing nonfarm waged occupations, from hauling to dredging to figuring accounts. The geographical extension of the market and the growing interdependencies of its parts meant that fewer and fewer communities were insulated from the decisions made at the federal level. When Jefferson declared an embargo against England and France, not only teamsters, sailors, dock workers, rope makers and outworkers on the East Coast, but also traders, shippers, craft workers and peddlers inland felt the repercussions. Exposed to the consequences of government policies, they demanded the right to help select the policymakers.

The new, less-settled states (which were also the states where the Federalists were weakest) led the way in expanding white male suffrage. Vermont entered the union in 1791 (the first new state after the original 13) with virtually universal white manhood suffrage. White men had only to live in the state a year and maintain "quiet and peaceable behavior." The following year, neighboring New Hampshire dropped its last effective qualification (a tax-paying requirement), and Kentucky entered the union without significant restrictions on adult white males. Tennessee, which became a state in 1796, required that voters own property but did not set a minimum value. Ohio became a state in 1803 without property requirements for voting, and every one of the six states admitted to the union between 1812 and 1821 entered with virtually universal white male suffrage.

In 1817 Connecticut became the first of the older states to reform suffrage, abolishing all property qualifications for white men. By 1821 the demand for suffrage reform had reached the proportions of a "passion . . . pervading the union," according to one incredulous Federalist. Three years later, when Jackson made his first run for the presidency, only Virginia, Louisiana, and Rhode Island retained any significant restrictions on white male suffrage and only 6 of the (by then) 24 states of the union retained indirect selection of the delegates to the Electoral College (see Map 11-2 for details on the growth of white male suffrage).

The struggle for an expanded male suffrage was fought openly on the landscape of race. Opponents of suffrage reform offered lurid visions of politically energized African Americans taking advantage of loosened property restrictions, "debased and degraded . . . rush[ing] to the polls in senseless and unmeaning triumph." A Rhode Islander warned that universal male suffrage would add both Indians and African Americans to the electorate, creating unnamed "evils" entailed "upon our latest posterity without remedy."

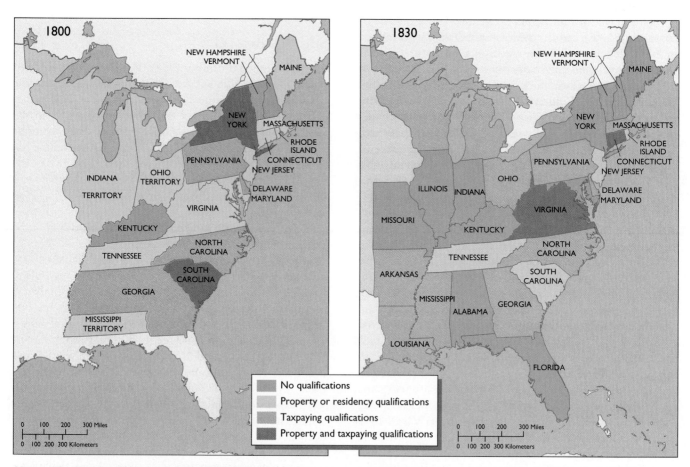

Map 11-2   Toward Universal White Male Suffrage.
As the western territories organized and entered the union, they formed a band of states in which there were no property qualifications on white male suffrage, and often minimal tax-paying qualifications. By 1830, Virginia and Connecticut were unusual in the nation for restricting white male suffrage based on both property and tax payment. At the same time, free black males and women lost the vote where they had enjoyed it.

Already defensive about the possible association of waged labor with enslaved labor, in state after state workers and suffrage advocates quickly abandoned any aim of universal male suffrage and argued instead for universal white male suffrage. Through suffrage reform, white Americans refashioned the vote as an emblem and right of white citizenship. Every new state admitted from 1819 on specifically excluded African Americans from the vote, and older states that had once permitted a few propertied African-American men to vote (New Jersey, Pennsylvania, and Connecticut, for example) revised suffrage laws to exclude them. "The people of this state are for . . . a political community of white persons," one Pennsylvanian asserted bluntly.

The partial exception to this pattern was Rhode Island, where elite forces were able to block universal white male suffrage throughout the 1830s. When in 1841, white working men rebelled, calling a People's Convention to demand universal white male suffrage, they also specifically rejected pleas from the African-American working-class community to include African-American men in their demands. (Ironically, the revolt was first led by Rhode Island attorney and abolitionist Thomas Dorr, whose name remained associated with the episode long after his followers abandoned his convictions.) Spurned by the white working men, African Americans supported the conservative opposition, helping to create an atmosphere in which the state militia was successfully mobilized against the white workers. When Rhode Island conservatives later reconsidered their position and broadened the franchise, they repaid African-American men for their earlier support by including them.

Opposition to Special Privilege and Secret Societies

Since the nation's founding, one strain of American political rhetoric had focused on the presumed presence in the republic of corrupt insiders who enjoyed opportunities not available to other citizens. In the early nineteenth century, the religious and economic emphasis on personal striving combined with the growing political assertiveness of white working men who felt excluded from the dignities of full citizenship to reinvigorate those older fears. Once again, politics became a symbolic battle of the virtuous "Many" against the corrupt "Few."

Early in the century, specially chartered corporations became visible symbols of affluence and the target of these suspicions. By 1812, for example, corporations already accounted for one-fifth of all of the wealth of New York City. That figure did not include the personal wealth of stockholders in the corporations. Created by special acts of state legislatures, these corporations were, theoretically, open to all Americans. Theoretically, anyone could organize a band of investors and apply for a special charter. In point of fact, however, the charters were granted on a highly personal basis to people known to individual legislators, people of wealth, power, and reputation. For this reason, they were always vulnerable to charges of insider advantage.

The movement to use special charters to promote development accelerated after the War of 1812. States chartered special companies to build roads, provide transportation over specified waterways, and establish banks. Meanwhile, the federal government had both chartered a second national bank to provide venture capital and passed tariff after tariff to protect American enterprise. Local reactions to specially chartered projects were mixed. Many ambitious persons of modest means shared journalist William Leggett's bitterness that "Not a road can be opened, not a bridge can be built, not a canal can be dug, but a charter of exclusive privileges must be granted for the purpose." Yet some of the specially chartered initiatives, especially banks, seemed to aid the endeavors of local farmers and workers by flooding the states with easy credit. Much to the delight of such groups, under the early leadership of Captain Jones (see chapter 10), the national bank had supported these goals. But Cheves' policies and the Panic of 1819 had ended that bubble of easy local credit. Devastated by the contraction, shopkeepers, farmers, and urban workers focused their anger on the power of eastern bankers, and especially of the Second Bank of the United States, and grew convinced that a small cadre of wealthy easterners was protecting its own interests at the direct expense of common citizens. Not for a moment did most of these groups waver in their fundamental support of expansionist policies. Rather, they wavered in their loyalty to the new Republican leadership, suspecting that the party had been taken over by an elite bent on increasing, rather than eliminating, preferential rules. The bitterness, like the misery, was widespread. By 1820 John C. Calhoun noticed the appearance, in "every part of the Union," of "a general mass of disaffection to the Government . . . looking out anywhere for a leader."

Corporations were not the only focus of these feelings. With so many people on the move, social relations were characterized by a certain paranoia, a fear that American society was riddled with con artists and counterfeiters, passers of bad notes, vendors of nonexistent western lands, and other schemers against the unwary. (One source of opposition to the Mormons arose from the belief that Joseph Smith's visions and tablets were all a hoax, perpetrated on desperate and gullible people.) In western New York, where the opening of the Erie Canal had ushered in an era of economic boom and widespread social instability, these feelings exploded in a virulent fear of Masons in the late 1820s.

The Masonic movement had originated as an organization to protect craft masons against encroachments on their trade. But in the eighteenth century a new Order of Freemasons emerged, made up of urban businessmen, shopkeepers, merchants, professionals, and politicians who pledged their political and economic support to one another. Accepting and inducting new members only by secret ritual and yet boasting publicly of their civic power, by the 1820s the Masons seemed to many working people to embody the dangerous antidemocratic spirit of the age. This vague, general distrust of Masonry was galvanized into concerted popular opposition in 1826 by the mysterious disappearance (and presumed murder) of New Yorker William Morgan, a disaffected Mason who had authored *Illustrations of Masonry*, an exposé of the order's purported rituals and secret designs on public power. Before the book could be published, Morgan had vanished, last seen when he was released from jail after being arrested on a small-debt charge. His friends later came to believe that the charge had been trumped up and that corrupt officials (bought off by the Masons) had held Morgan only long enough to release him into the waiting hands of his foes. The story spread that Morgan had been ferreted away to Niagara Falls, held for three days, and then drowned. The seriousness of this subversion of justice was magnified, in the popular outcry, by the fact that hundreds of local, state, and national officials, including both Andrew Jackson and the charismatic Henry Clay, were also Masons. By 1827 New Yorkers who opposed the Masons had organized a separate political party and pledged never again to vote for a Mason and to work for the defeat of any Masons already in office.

The Antimason Party spread from New York into other states, doing especially well in the late 1820s and early 1830s in local elections in Massachusetts, Pennsylvania, and Vermont. In 1831 Antimasons held the first open presidential nominating convention, choosing William

Wirt of Maryland as their candidate for the 1832 election. Wirt carried only one state, and the party remained a minor player in national politics. Nevertheless, their battle against secret cabals illustrated the reviving belief that American party politics amounted to a struggle of hardworking common people against the moneyed aristocracy who conspired to stand in their way. This would become a staple of Jacksonian political rhetoric.

Workingmen's Parties

Suffrage reform was a step toward political empowerment, but many workingmen wanted to do more than vote. They wanted to set the political agenda through the formation of their own political parties.

As the labor newspaper *The Working Men's Advocate* complained in 1830, too often none of the candidates for office reflected the interests of workers. No one talked about problems of chronic un- and underemployment, no one proposed reforms of debt and eviction laws, no one argued for better and cheaper housing, safer working conditions, or education for the children of workers. "Why then do you send these very men to your legislature and give them every office?" the *Advocate* asked. "Think ye they will legislate for you against themselves?"

By the late 1820s workers had begun to mobilize to make their votes more effective. In 1827 a group of workers in Philadelphia, primarily journeymen in crafts previously organized in separate societies, combined to form the Mechanics' Union of Trade Associations. Within a year they had dissolved that group into the Philadelphia Working Men's Party, a new political party dedicated to promoting "the interests and enlightenment of the working classes." Over the next five years, under various names (the "People's Party," the "Farmer and Mechanics' Society," the "Workingmen's Association"), the movement spread through most of the nation, becoming strongest in the cities from Philadelphia northward.

That such parties came into existence at all suggests that workers were at historic crossroads. On the one hand, the formation of the Working Men's Party implied that workers still remained optimistic that change was possible. That optimism was reflected in the party's demands. Although workers deplored the degraded working and living conditions that accompanied industrialization and attacked all forms of wealth that fed on *the labours of the working class,* they stopped short of indicting the entire system. Instead, they argued that the monopolizing greed of the commercial classes was made possible by

When former Mason William Morgan disappeared and was presumed murdered, many New Yorkers blamed a Masonic conspiracy. This antimason broadside shows the pillars of Masonry crushing Morgan to death.

the fiscal and land policies of a government grown too large and too distant to understand the common needs of the people. Those policies must be changed. Producers must restore the virtues of hard work, mutuality, and respect to the republic. Most tellingly, early workingmen's parties included a wide variety of workers and occupations in their compass, such as small masters, shopkeepers, petty entrepreneurs, farmers, professionals, ministers, and educators. Moreover, workingmen understood their concerns and themselves not simply as alienated labor power, but rather as citizens with the right and power to affect the entire social and cultural makeup of the republic. Their unwillingness to separate work from civic culture was evident in the variety of issues they advocated, including public education, broadened incorporation laws, an end to imprisonment for debt, and banking reform.

On the other hand, the organization of a separate political party indicates that workers remained deeply skeptical that the existing parties could or would be responsive to their concerns and that workers were moving toward a distinct identity within the new political economy.

The Democratic Impulse in Presidential Politics

Americans' homage to the principles of personal responsibility and the dignity of the common man revealed the strange paradox of national culture in the 1820s. Both concepts expressed a great faith in human nature and social life, a belief that citizens would conduct their affairs responsibly and deserved to live free from most restraint. Yet the very energy with which many Americans insisted upon these principles also suggested a certain suspicion that the republic was not living up to its highest purposes. That combination of confidence and mistrust described exactly the man who was elected to office in 1828, Andrew Jackson.

Jackson's Rise to National Prominence

In his person and in his life, Andrew Jackson embodied well the volatile mixture of confidence and defensiveness, expansiveness and intolerance that characterized the United States in the flush years of nationalism and economic growth following the War of 1812. Early in life, he had paid the price of the patriot. After his father vanished when he was very young, Jackson had lost the rest of his family in the American Revolution. He himself had received a gash with a sword across the forehead for refusing to clean the boots of a British officer.

After the war, Jackson had fitted himself for the new order. He had studied the law in North Carolina, but his rest-

Andrew Jackson in 1829, the year in which he first assumed the presidency.

lessness carried him west along with hundreds of thousands of other white Americans searching hungrily for property and prosperity in the territories. In what would later become the state of Tennessee, Jackson purchased land and settled down near the future city of Nashville. He was soon called on to serve as a district attorney and a judge. By the time he first ran for the presidency in 1824, he had also served briefly in the House of Representatives and the Senate.

Although the law gave Jackson his start, his popular reputation was made as a military man. Jackson first became a national figure during the War of 1812, first as commander of the devastating campaign against the Creek Nation and then, at war's end, as the hero of the Battle of New Orleans. His controversial but effective campaign against the Seminoles in 1818–1819 and his subsequent brief career as governor of the Territory of Florida completed his credentials as an unyielding champion of the western settler.

The Election of 1824 and the "Corrupt Bargain"

When the Tennessee legislature nominated Jackson for the presidency in 1822, few seasoned politicians took the candidacy seriously. Jackson was running against some of the most experienced and respected national leaders of the era: John Quincy Adams (Monroe's secretary of state),

John C. Calhoun (Monroe's secretary of war), Henry Clay (speaker of the House), and William H. Crawford of Georgia (Monroe's secretary of the Treasury). Jackson's detractors underestimated his great popularity as a war hero and the attractiveness of his humble background and character to an electorate inching its way toward a more democratic political culture. He did not share Adams' or Clay's ties to the new entrepreneurial elites, and he did not share their personal comfort with genteel society. As an orphan and a westerner, Jackson was temperamentally the outsider, a position with which many voters identified.

An early indication of how powerful a role this changing political sensibility would play in the election came with the Republican nomination. Because James Monroe had not designated a successor, the selection was thrown to the Republican congressional caucus, a circumstance expected to benefit Crawford, who was particularly well connected in Washington. But this time, unlike earlier nominations, the other candidates simply pulled out, loudly disowning the caucus as a corrupt and irregular institution, the "great whore of Babylon," as Jackson himself put it. To accept nomination from the caucus was to prostitute oneself to an undemocratic process. So effective was the repudiation that in the end only 66 of a possible 216 Republican members of Congress even attended the caucus. As expected, Crawford got the nod, while the other potential candidates relied on their own networks of supporters to organize their campaigns.

When the election itself was held, no candidate claimed a majority either of the popular vote or of the Electoral College. Jackson finished first, with 43 percent of the popular vote and 99 electoral votes. He had received all or a majority of the electoral votes of Louisiana, Alabama, North Carolina, Illinois, Pennsylvania, Maryland, Mississippi, South Carolina, Tennessee, Indiana, and New Jersey. Next was Adams, who had swept New England, tallying 31 percent of the popular vote and 84 electoral votes. Crawford, who had suffered a stroke during the campaign, managed only 41 electoral votes. Clay, who took only Ohio, Missouri, and Kentucky, came in last with 37 electoral votes. Calhoun had dropped out to run for the vice presidency (see Map 11-3).

The election was thus thrown to the House of Representatives, where members had to select from among the three candidates with the highest electoral count. Initially, Jackson, the highest vote-getter and the only candidate with anything like national appeal, was unperturbed, but by late December 1824 he had begun to hear rumors "that deep intrigue is on foot." He wrote a friend "that Mr. Clay is trying to wield his influence with [O]hio, Kentucky, Missouri & Elonois [Illinois] in favor of Adams." Rumors were correct. Although Adams did not receive a single popular vote in Kentucky, and although the Kentucky state legislature had directed its delegation to vote for Jackson, Clay used his prestige to override those instructions

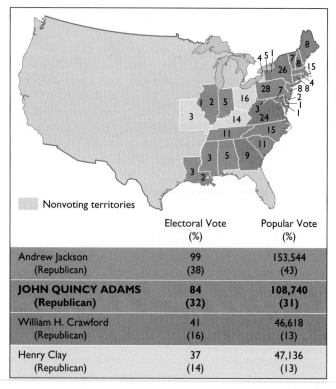

	Electoral Vote (%)	Popular Vote (%)
Andrew Jackson (Republican)	99 (38)	153,544 (43)
JOHN QUINCY ADAMS (Republican)	84 (32)	108,740 (31)
William H. Crawford (Republican)	41 (16)	46,618 (13)
Henry Clay (Republican)	37 (14)	47,136 (13)

Nonvoting territories

Map 11-3   The Election of 1824.

and to marshal enough additional support for Adams to deny Jackson the election. With Clay behind him, Adams received the votes of 13 out of the 24 state delegations. Jackson received 7 and Crawford 4.

Jackson later charged that Adams had bought Clay's support with the promise of the post of secretary of state. In fact, Adams did quickly offer Clay that job. Even without a reward, however, Clay had good reasons for allying himself with Adams. Clay and Adams shared similar National Republican political philosophies. In addition, Jackson and Clay vied for the same regional vote. Supporting Jackson in 1824 would have helped the Tennessean build a stronger western base for 1828. All Clay would say was that he worried about "the unfitness of Gen. Jackson for the Presidency," an allusion to Jackson's alleged arrogance and inflexibility.

Jackson was furious. "Intrigue, corruption, and sale of public office is the rumor of the day," he roared. "How humiliating to the American character that its high functionaries should conduct themselves as to become liable to the interpretation of bargain & sale of the constitutional rights of the people!" His supporters charged that the election had been stolen in a "corrupt bargain" brokered by insiders who debased the virtue of the republic and flagrantly disregarded the clear will of the electorate. In the place of the man of the people, the House had selected the man of old Boston, that preserve of elitism and privilege.

The Adams Presidency and the Gathering Forces of Democracy

John Quincy Adams was a wise and principled statesman, but he was never able to set an independent agenda for his presidency. His every act was shadowed by the political battle that began with his election and in which his regional identification with banking and mercantile interests constantly hurt him. Defensive and prickly in public, he was not good at creating strong political alliances. Not a particularly canny politician, he misread the times and underestimated the gulf developing within the American electorate.

Adams' first mistake was to offer the State Department to Clay. Although Adams may have assumed that the election produced a mandate for National Republicanism, the selection of Clay not only looked like a payoff but also sent Vice President Calhoun's supporters into the Jackson camp in an effort to block Clay's ascendancy. Opposition to Clay and Adams grew so strong in Congress that later, when the president and secretary of state urged the United States to participate in a congress of American nations in Panama, Congress delayed the appointment of a delegation long enough for the conference to be over before the delegation arrived.

Adams also provoked fiscal conservatives and even some moderate supporters into the opposition camp by using his first annual message to Congress, in 1825, to lay out a grand vision for federal involvement in the nation's political economy. He called not only for economic projects, like transportation improvements, but also for the creation of a national university, a national observatory, and a naval academy comparable to the Army's West Point, as well as an elaborate system of roads and canals, all supported by federal expenditures. In a particularly ill-chosen phrase, Adams urged a potentially hesitant Congress not to be "palsied by the will of our constituents." His opponents objected that this was clear evidence of his intention to benefit the wealthy at the expense of the common people.

Jackson's supporters attempted to discredit Adams further (and build support for Jackson) on the issue of the tariff. The tariff was a regional issue, unpopular in the South and much of the West, but increasingly popular in the manufacturing Northeast. Sly Jackson supporters in the North wished to associate themselves with the tariff without implicating Jacksonians elsewhere in the country. Thus Jackson might be able to increase his support in the mid-Atlantic, Northwest, and Northeast. The plan was to propose a tariff so outrageously high on raw materials (some of the rates went as high as 40 percent and 50 percent) that the East and West would eventually join with the South to defeat it. Vice President John Calhoun, who now opposed tariffs as providing special advantages to the Northeast, nevertheless helped to author the bill, which was officially proposed by northern Jackson supporters.

It was a risky plan, and it backfired. In their eagerness to force New Englanders to oppose the bill, southerners insisted that every outrageous provision, and especially some that fell hard on raw materials imported into New England, be preserved. In the end, New Englanders did win a few modifications and concluded that bad protectionism was better than none at all. Their manufacturing revolution well under way, representatives from New York and New England abandoned their earlier free trade positions and were willing to absorb higher prices for raw materials. The Northeast swallowed the bitter pill and voted "yes," and the Tariff of 1828 became the law of the land.

The Election of 1828

The congressional fight over the tariff provided the stage on which the early phases of the election of 1828 were fought, but the underlying issue was the deep and lasting conflict over the power of the federal government. This was not a simple question of nationalism versus localism. Although Jackson loathed the power of eastern elites, he was a nationalist who was willing to support some level of protective tariff, who had even conceded at one point in the 1824 campaign that "It is time we became a little more *Americanized.*" The difference between Adams and Jackson was the question of the *basis* of federal legitimacy. In what actions could the federal government claim the authority of the American people? And in what actions did it overstep that authority? That conflict, which had raged since the founding of the nation, was now infused with all the energy of a rising democratic spirit.

The question of federal power was at times hard to make out in the flood of personal invective that characterized the campaign. Both camps sought to manipulate the heightened religious sensibilities of the age, and both used racialized images to charge their attacks. Adams' supporters tarred Jackson as a liar and a blasphemer incapable of self-restraint. They accused Jackson of having "prevailed upon the wife of Lewis Robards of Mercer County, Kentucky, to desert her husband, and live with himself, in the character of a wife" and they claimed that "General Jackson's mother was a COMMON PROSTITUTE" who "married a MULATTO MAN, with whom she had several children, of which number General JACKSON IS ONE!!!"

Jackson supporters retorted that Adams was a Sabbath breaker, a closet Federalist, and an unprincipled hypocrite who had been willing to buy the presidency and whose long residence in Europe had taught him disdain for popular government. Without the strong leadership of Jackson, they predicted, within 25 years the American people would become "the slaves . . . of such ambitious demagogues as Henry Clay." To make the point, Jacksonians began to refer to themselves as Jacksonian Democrats.

The Democratic campaign of 1828 ushered in a new era of national political campaigning. Whereas earlier campaigns had been fought primarily on the local level and among a far smaller group of potential voters, in 1828 Martin Van Buren coordinated a national campaign designed to appeal to a mass electorate. Van Buren (known as the "Little Magician" for his political skill) oversaw the creation of an intricate, highly controlled party hierarchy structured along lines similar to the structure of the Benevolent Empire, with local societies linked to state societies linked to the national organization. Van Buren closely coordinated the various levels of the campaign. He pioneered the use of carefully choreographed "spontaneous" grass-roots demonstrations and converted nonpartisan occasions (like Fourth of July celebrations) into Democratic rallies by sending out armies of Jackson supporters armed with American flags and placards calling for "Jackson and Reform." Van Buren also engineered the use of political imagery to evoke campaign themes. Taking advantage of Jackson's nickname, "Old Hickory" (for the hardest wood in the United States), Jackson committees were called "Old Hickory Clubs" and campaign workers handed out hickory canes to crowds at political events. At the same time, supporters used editorials and campaign tracts to describe Jackson in terms that identified him as the very embodiment of the common man. Turning Jackson's obstinacy and lack of formal education into strengths, they argued that he was nature's product, "artificial in nothing" with a "native strength of mind" and "practical common sense."

Finally, Van Buren urged Jackson himself to become more visible in the campaign. In the past, candidates for the presidency had remained discreetly in the background, professing great unworthiness even to be considered for such a high honor. Jackson himself had pursued this course in 1824, but when the Louisiana Democrats invited him to a celebration marking his victory over the British in the Battle of New Orleans, he accepted. As Jackson approached New Orleans by the Mississippi River, huge crowds (some people had traveled from as far as New Hampshire) lined the wharves and clung to the rigging of ships in the harbor. The event turned out to be, as one reporter proclaimed, "the most stupendous thing of the kind that had ever occurred in the United States."

When the votes were counted in 1828, Jackson had won a clear majority: 56 percent of the popular vote and 178 electoral votes to Adams's 83 (see Map 11-4). Although Adams had retained New England, New Jersey, Delaware, and northern Maryland, Jackson had solidly taken the South and the West, as well as Pennsylvania, most of New York, and even the northern tip of Maine.

Jackson was elected by a strong cross-section of voters who identified (albeit in differing ways) with his stance as an outsider to, and victim of, established eastern elites. He was most notably the candidate of westerners, migrants, settlers, and landowners who opposed eastern banks and

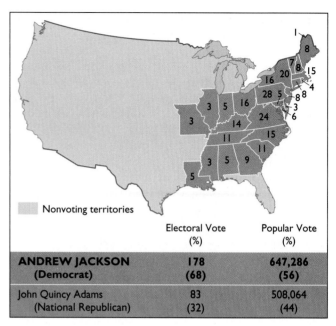

Map 11-4   The Election of 1828.

	Electoral Vote (%)	Popular Vote (%)
ANDREW JACKSON (Democrat)	178 (68)	647,286 (56)
John Quincy Adams (National Republican)	83 (32)	508,064 (44)

Nonvoting territories

congressional land policies, but Jackson also drew support from urban professionals and shopkeepers, as well as laborers and craftsmen who believed that special privilege was denying them their fair chance at prosperity. A planter and a southerner, Jackson could claim the mantle of Jefferson and cloak his new "Democratic" Party with the legacy of true Republicanism. Reflecting that older political economy, he favored limited government, feared growing concentrations of economic and political power, and seemed to share Jefferson's emphasis on the individual. A slave owner, he drew the support of southerners who, despite his stand on the tariff, saw Jackson as vastly preferable to the New Englander Adams.

President Jackson: Vindicating the Common Man

Even in the pandemonium of the inauguration, the message of the new presidency was clear. "As the instrument of the Federal Constitution . . . ," Jackson declared, "I shall keep steadily in view the limitations as well as the extent of the Executive power, trusting to discharge the functions of my office without transcending its authority." Lest anyone miss his meaning, Jackson recited the details of Adams' transgressions, contrasted with his own policies. He advocated fiscal restraint, an end to government patronage, the appointment only of men of "diligence and talent," and a constitutional amendment to remove "all intermediary agency in the election of President and Vice-President." In a direct slap at Henry Clay, he suggested that members of Congress voting to break a presidential deadlock be disqualified from running for the presidency themselves. The task of his administration, Jackson announced, must be "the task of reform."

Jacksonian Democrats in Office

The Jacksonians were vague about exactly where political virtue resided. Structurally, they believed that it evolved from the states. In his inaugural address Jackson pledged "not to confound the powers [the states] have reserved to themselves with those they have granted to the Confederacy." This endorsement of federal restraint was confused, however, by Jackson's equally strong conviction that he *was* the people and that his will was indistinguishable from theirs. The ironic result was a continuous migration of power from the states to the executive during the presidency of the man elected to protect the common man.

A tendency to personalize political struggle characterized Jackson's presidency. He never forgave the National Republicans for publicly questioning the legitimacy of his marriage or, by implication, his wife Rachel's virtue. In 1829, when some members of his cabinet publicly opposed the marriage of Secretary of War John Eaton to Margaret O'Neale Timberlake (the high-spirited daughter of a tavernkeeper), Jackson made her defense a litmus test of loyalty to him and his administration. Later, he viewed his battle against the Second Bank of the United States in the same highly personal terms: "The Bank," he informed Van Buren, "is trying to kill me, *but I will kill it.*"

If Jackson understood himself as the embodiment of the people's will, he understood the new Democratic Party as its direct instrument. The premier "voluntary association" of American politics, over time the Democratic Party emerged as a parallel structure to the states. After personal loyalty to Jackson, party loyalty became the avenue to appointment and the justification for an unprecedented turnover in officeholders. Replacing social status, party loyalty permitted the Democrats to appoint men of humble origins to high office. For example, Martin Van Buren, the architect of Jackson's victory and his first appointee to the important position of secretary of state, was the son of a Kinderhook, New York, tavernkeeper. Unfortunately, party loyalty did not guarantee competence or honesty. Jackson's choice for New York customs collector, Samuel Swartwout, used his position to embezzle over a million dollars before he fled the country to escape prosecution in the 1830s.

The overall results were mixed. Invigorated by his confidence that he spoke for the nation, Jackson expanded the powers of the presidency, facing down challenges from the states, from Congress, and from the Supreme Court, but Jackson's conviction that he alone embodied the true virtue of the republic also led to personal pettiness, widespread patronage in the name of reform, and constant turmoil within his cabinet. His efforts to abolish the National Bank finally wreaked serious material hardship for tens of thousands of average Americans, and his hostility to Native Americans resulted in widespread death and impoverishment.

A Policy of Indian Removal

For Andrew Jackson, the quintessential "common man" was the western settler, struggling to bring new lands under cultivation and new institutions to life. Pioneers confronted various obstacles (tight credit, eastern speculators, corrupt land office agents, and federal land policies), but no barrier loomed larger than the resistance of Indian peoples. The War of 1812 had effectively brought an end to intertribal resistance east of the Mississippi. By 1828, most of the Great Lakes nations had been pushed out of Ohio, southern Indiana, and Illinois, but the Ojibwa, Winnebago, Sauk, Mesquakie, Kickapoo, and Menominee retained sizeable homelands in the Northwest. In the South, in spite of repeated forced cessions, the Chickasaw, Choctaw, Creek, and Cherokee nations retained ancestral territories, and the Seminoles still controlled parts of Florida.

Jackson's views concerning Native Americans had been settled many years earlier, in the crucible of the Indian wars of the 1790s. "Does not experience teach us that treaties answer no other Purpose than opening an Easy door for the Indians to pass [through to] Butcher our citizens?" he wrote in 1794, from his first home on the Cumberland River. Congress should "Punish the Barbarians."

Despite recurrent wars and federal treaties, western settlers were no happier with federal initiatives in the 1820s than they had been in the 1790s. Tension ran especially high in the South, where the uneven distribution of land among whites was dramatic, especially in Georgia. There officials complained that the federal government had never kept its promise to remove all Indians from the state, a condition of Georgia's agreement to cede its western land claims to the federal government in 1802. A few Creeks and most of the Cherokee nation remained, unwilling to cede additional lands. In 1826 the federal government pressured the Creeks to give up all but a small strip of their remaining lands in Georgia, but white Georgians were not satisfied. Encouraged no doubt by former President Monroe's repeated calls for large-scale Indian removal, Georgia Governor George Michael Troup sent surveyors onto that last piece of Creek land. When President Adams objected to this encroachment on federal treaty powers, Troup threatened to call up the state militia.

The election of Andrew Jackson only a few months later emboldened the Georgians to go after Cherokee land.

By state law they invalidated the constitution of the Cherokee nation within Georgia and proclaimed that the Cherokees were subject to the authority of the state of Georgia. When discoveries of gold sent white prospectors surging onto Cherokee land, Georgia refused either to stop the trespassers or to protect the Indians. Jackson quickly made his position clear, notifying his Cherokee "children" that "their father cannot prevent them from being subject to the laws of the state" and that it was his duty, as president, to "sustain the States in the exercise of their rights."

In fact, the states were not exercising their rights, as Chief Justice John Marshall would later make clear in a series of decisions arising from the Cherokee appeal to the Supreme Court (see Map 11-5). In 1831, in *Cherokee Nation v. Georgia*, Marshall agreed that the Cherokee nation had the status of a foreign nation and enjoyed certain claims as a result of treaties with the federal government. Yet the Cherokee nation belonged to a distinct class of foreign governments, Marshall reasoned. It was not really a *foreign* power at all, but rather a "domestic dependent nation." As

such, it was beyond the jurisdiction of the Supreme Court. The following year, Marshall revised that decision. In *Worcester v. Georgia*, the court identified the Cherokees as "a distinct community" within the United States (not as a part of a specific state) and ruled that the Cherokee nation came under the direct protection of the federal government. Georgia had thus acted unconstitutionally.

Court rulings must be implemented by action of the executive branch, and this Jackson was not prepared to do. Upon being informed of the decision, Jackson is alleged to have responded: "John Marshall has made his decision; *now let him enforce it.*" By the time the Cherokee cases had found their way to the United States Supreme Court, Jackson had already successfully forced a different solution: removal.

Jackson had long insisted to Congress that the best policy, "not only liberal, but generous," would be to remove the Indians entirely from the lands sought by the settlers and to relocate them elsewhere until such time as they "cast off their savage habits." The place he had in mind was across the Mississippi River. Because full-scale removal of the Indians involved shifting populations across state lines and into federal territories, however, the policy required congressional consent. In Congress the Native Americans found unexpected allies. To the old Adams men, now led by Henry Clay, "removal" was the policy of states, forced on the federal government. For Congress to pass an act authorizing the policy would have been the same as encouraging states to trample on federal powers. Clay was supported by numerous foot soldiers of the urban-based Benevolent Empire. Led by the American Board of Commissioners for Foreign Missions, city and foreign missionaries, Sunday school workers, members of religious tract and Bible societies, and others (women as well as men) lobbied hard against the bill. Van Buren responded on behalf of Jackson by forming a counter lobby, the Board for the Emigration, Preservation, and Improvement of the Aborigines of America, which argued that Indians were ill equipped for contact with white civilization and that removing them to the lands west of the Mississippi was only humane.

Map 11-5 Population Density Westward, 1790 and 1820.

The Trail of Tears, depicted here by Brummett Echohawk, shows Cherokees being forced marched from their homelands in eastern states to Indian territory in what is now Oklahoma.

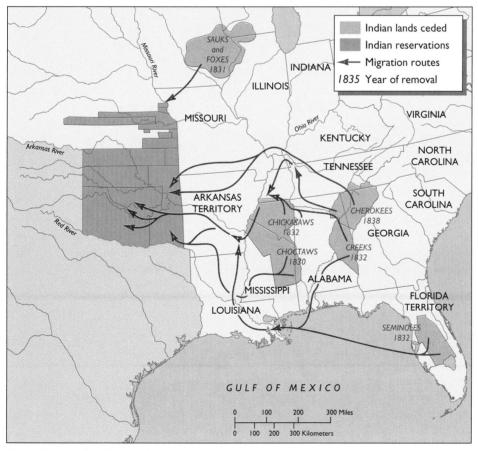

Map 11-6   Indian Removals.
Jackson's policy of Indian removal required Native American peoples to leave their homelands east of the Mississippi River for government-designated lands west of the Mississippi. Some Indian groups signed treaties ceding their lands, but these groups often lacked authority to do so. Some groups (like the Cherokee) fought removal in court. Others (like the Seminoles, Sauk, and Fox) fought the policy in open combat.

Passed in 1830 by a margin of five votes, the Removal Act empowered the president to purchase Indian homelands in the East in exchange for lands west of the Mississippi, and it authorized $500,000 to begin the work. In one sense, the act only made official a policy that Americans had pursued steadily since the founding of the nation, but official approval of the policy accelerated the process and increased the opportunities for graft. In 1830 the Choctaws were forced from their lands in Mississippi to a location in present-day Oklahoma. The Chickasaws (also Mississippi Indians) and the Creeks (now crowded into Alabama) followed in 1832.

Three years later, after their unsuccessful appeals to the Supreme Court and after several years of continued resistance, the Cherokees were removed from northern Georgia, western North Carolina, and eastern Tennessee. In a forced march that became known as the "Trail of Tears," they were driven off their homelands to Indian Territory in what is now eastern Oklahoma. Although perhaps 2,000 Cherokees had already left, most people had delayed leaving until the last possible moment and had made few preparations for the journey. Hustled off their lands by the Army, they went with few supplies and little planning. Some Cherokees died in stockades where they were held before the march began. Others died of disease, malnutrition, dehydration, and exhaustion along the way (see Map 11-6).

Indians did not accept removal willingly. The Cherokees had struggled in vain to make white Americans accountable to their own republican ideals. The Sauk and Fox resorted to arms. In 1831, the Sauk and Fox (a loose, ethnically diverse population descended from Indians who had earlier been pushed across the Great Lakes region) were forced to relocate once

WHERE THEY LIVED, WHERE THEY WORKED

Surviving Removal

In his State of the Union address in 1830, President Andrew Jackson congratulated Congress on the passage of the Removal Act. Jackson praised the law as an act of "Philanthropy." He reminded Congress that for generations Euro-Americans had been "leav[ing] the land of their birth to seek new homes in distant regions." New lands meant opportunity and liberty, the chance to "range unconstrained in body or in mind, developing the power and faculties of man in their highest perfection." "Doubtless it will be painful to leave the graves of their fathers," he acknowledged of the eastern Indians, "but what do they more than our ancestors did or than our children are now doing?" In fact, leaving "the land of their birth" was a very different act for Native Americans than it was for the white western settlers—not an act of opportunity, but rather an eviction from their very identity as a people.

The Cherokees, one of the largest Indian nations the United States sought to displace, had lived on the rocky slopes and in the pocket coves of the southern Appalachians since long before the arrival of the Europeans, and their understanding of themselves as a people was intimately tied to the mountains. Their ancestors, Kana'ti and Selu, the first man and the first woman of the Real People, had migrated into this land when the land itself was newly created. They had been fed from game Kana'ti found in a deep cave and from the corn and beans Selu had produced by rubbing her stomach and armpits.

These beginnings were preserved in the social and economic life of the Cherokees in the early nineteenth century. They lived in settled agricultural communities in the Smoky Mountains, where their communities were anchored by the fields women cultivated. Men traveled long distances and sometimes for years at a time to find game, but they always returned to the villages of the mountains. Although the Cherokee diet included rabbits and other small game as well as melons and squash and other produce, corn and deer remained at the center of the culture. Men and women still ritualized marriages by exchanging corn and deer, and each year communities celebrated the Green Corn Festival, when their elders recited the stories of their origin and migration into the mountains. Social and political life were governed by the principle of harmony and balance. Each village had a council hall large enough to hold the entire community, and decisions were achieved by consensus. For the Cherokees, where they lived and where they worked was who they were. They had become Cherokee by entering the land of the

Sequoyah devised the Cherokee syllabary (similiar to an alphabet), one of the ways in which Cherokees attempted to accommodate white cultural practices while retaining their own customs and homelands.

mountains, and they remained Cherokee because they remained in the mountains.

Two centuries of contact altered that way of life. Some Cherokees embraced racial slavery. Most grew more dependent on farming. Trying to accommodate white practices, Cherokees adopted a written alphabet. Yet they clung to their diminishing lands. Only in 1836 did a small splinter group (claiming to speak for the whole nation) at last agree to removal. The Treaty of New Echota provided that within two years the Cherokees would leave their homelands for Indian Territory, in return for safe passage, $5 million, and food, shelter, equipment, and medicine for a year after their arrival. The Senate ratified the treaty in the spring of 1836 and considered that the clock had begun to tick on Cherokee removal. The pro-treaty Cherokees began to leave almost immediately. The overwhelming majority of Cherokees, who considered the treaty fraudulent, remained in the East.

Two years later, in late spring 1838, the U. S. Army (under General Winfield Scott) arrived to enforce the provisions of the treaty. They found a settled people unwilling and unprepared to move. They had not gathered their families

This watercolor of a Cherokee was done in 1820, as pressures for the removal of Southeastern Indians began to build.

together for a journey or set aside blankets and food for the trip. Their fields were newly planted, and their cattle were at spring pasture. Often at the point of a bayonet, they were rounded up and herded into stockades, where they were held for weeks. Corrupt land dealers took advantage of the circumstances to buy Cherokee lands cheap, and thieves stripped houses and outbuildings of furniture and equipment.

Gathered at three points (two in Tennessee, one in Alabama) for embarkation, the Cherokees went west in two waves. Under the supervision of the Army, three groups totaling nearly 3,000 Cherokees started almost immediately, in the hottest part of the summer ("the sickly season," the Cherokees called it). According to one missionary present at the events, the agent shipped the Cherokees "by multitudes," "[n]ine hundred in one detachment, and seven hundred in another . . . driven onto boats" to carry them up the Tennessee and Ohio Rivers to the Mississippi. "It will be a miracle of mercy if one-fourth escape the exposure to that sickly climate." Hundreds did not.

With the death count mounting, the Cherokees requested authority to manage their own removals and to delay them until the end of summer. Getting permission, they used every means at their disposal to survive the journey. Those who were permitted to return to their homes before leaving salvaged whatever bedding, food, and equipment remained. By one account, some of the contingents included hundreds of wagons and thousands of horses, but others were far less well supplied. The wagons sometimes began as family vehicles but soon became the equipment of the entire caravan, carrying

whoever could not walk, usually the sick and the aged. Those who lacked wagons or ponies and could still walk bundled their goods in blankets on their backs or made pallets.

All of the contingents were escorted by soldiers, sometimes making them look like "the march of an army, regiment after regiment, the wagons in the center, the officers along the line and the horsemen on the flanks and at the rear." At least for the removals they organized, however, the Cherokees established their own internal police, "whose duties are to seize & promptly punish any offences against good order," according to an army lieutenant. To the meager stocks of salt pork and often moldy corn and wheat flour provided them by military suppliers, the Cherokees added whatever they could hunt or forage along the way: turkeys, small game, occasionally deer, and berries. Those who had pots shared them with those who did not.

The later removals avoided the season of greatest disease, summer, but they faced the cold weather, winds, and ice storms of winter. Many of the migrants had only thin clothing and few blankets, and the cold was especially hard on elders, children, and the sick. To protect their members, caravans "sent on a company every morning, to make fires along the road, at short intervals," so their poorly dressed comrades could warm themselves periodically.

Removal did not annihilate the Cherokees, but it did indeed inflict deep gashes in the fabric of Cherokee society and identity. The entire process claimed 4,000 (perhaps as many as 8,000) of the roughly 17,000 Cherokees who were initially rounded up. Those who arrived in Indian Territory found a land very different from the one they had known, drier and flatter. The United States government had promised to support the migrants during their first year in the West, but government subcontractors lined their own pockets by supplying insufficient and substandard goods. As deaths mounted and poverty, illness, and alcoholism increased, the hatred between pro-removal and anti-removal parties within the Cherokee nation ignited into civil war, leaving Cherokees to begin a long process of rediscovering the principle of harmony that lay at the center of their world.

In his 1830 address, Jackson compared the Indians in removal (unfavorably) to American settlers. The latter, he contended, "remove hundreds of and almost thousands of miles at their own expense, purchase the lands they occupy, and support themselves at their new homes from the moment of their arrival." Such praise of the settlers not only overlooked the lawlessness and discontent of white migrants, but missed the central element of Indian removal: the meaning of where they lived and how they worked there.

again, from Illinois into the eastern part of the future state of Iowa. No sooner did they reach their new lands, however, than they began to hear rumors that whites were desecrating their former burying grounds. When Indians recrossed the Mississippi to rebury their dead and harvest produce from their old fields, white farmers and Illinois militia attacked them.

The Sauk and Fox turned for leadership to a revered old fighter, Black Hawk, who raised a band of several thousand followers (including perhaps 500 warriors), crossed the Mississippi moving east, and then traveled north to the village of the prophet White Cloud whom they asked for guidance. Attacked by state militiamen, they spent the summer fighting in a series of wasting skirmishes, called Black Hawk's War. Finally, on August 2, 1832, low on food and exhausted, the remnants of Black Hawk's band were cornered and massacred by the Army.

Far more successful were the Florida Seminoles, also a diverse community including militant Creek warriors, known as Red Sticks, and runaway slaves. When federal troops arrived to remove the Seminoles in 1832, the Indians resisted with skill and determination, using the swamps and marshes to good tactical advantage. Unfamiliar with the terrain and vulnerable to malaria, the American troops were picked off by both disease and Indian and African-American snipers. The war dragged on for seven years. Not until 1842 could President John Tyler proclaim victory.

Sporadic fighting continued, but by 1842, for all intents and purposes, the Great Lakes and Woodland Indian nations had been removed from the land east of the Mississippi River. The trans-Appalachian West was at last fully opened up for white settlement.

The Bank War

Jacksonians saw the Indians as the western barrier to their progress, but when they looked eastward, they saw a different obstacle: the aggregate of special privileges and unfair advantages available to the rich and well-connected. In his career, Jackson had associated this obstacle with a long series of people and institutions, including Henry Clay, John Adams, John Calhoun, and the Republican caucus. By 1828 Jackson had focused his anger on the Second Bank of the United States.

Jackson hated the bank for all the reasons common among southerners and westerners. He hated its power. He hated the fact that the government had, in effect, received $1.5 million for granting the charter. He hated its privilege, especially after the Marshall Court ruled that states could not tax the bank's branches. And he hated that most of the private bank stock was held by wealthy easterners and the rest by foreign investors.

Jackson nurtured some personal and idiosyncratic reasons for hating the bank, however. In 1795 Jackson had accepted promissory notes in payment for land, notes he had

subsequently spent. When the man who signed the notes went bankrupt, Jackson himself was held accountable for their full value. The matter dragged on for years, more than once threatening Jackson with complete financial ruin. For the remainder of his life, Jackson opposed debt and speculation in all forms, including paper money. "I do not dislike your bank more than all banks," Jackson commented to the president of the Second Bank. The truth was, he hated all banks. Few of his credit-hungry fellow westerners would have gone so far.

Jackson also specifically hated this bank. Soon after his first election, he had heard rumors that the Second Bank of the United States had used its power to buy votes for Adams in 1828. Declaring that the bank threatened "the purity of the right of suffrage," Jackson vowed to oppose it.

Nicholas Biddle, the bank's brilliant but impolitic president, refused to take Jackson's criticisms seriously. "All this stir about monopolies will blow off like the vapor from a Steam Boat as soon as the question gets fairly under way," he insisted. Confident that the bank enjoyed the support of most Americans (which it probably did), Biddle decided to force the issue before the next presidential election. Although the bank's authorization ran until 1836, on January 6, 1832, Biddle requested Congress to take up renewal early. Jackson may have felt Biddle's behavior to be a personal challenge, for when the act reached him in July 1832, he vetoed it, explaining that he was compelled to do so "to preserve the republic from its thralldom and corrupting influence."

The Democrats carried the bank veto proudly into the 1832 election. It was, they insisted, a contest of "the Democracy and the people, against a corrupt and abandoned aristocracy." The Republicans responded that Jackson's veto showed once again his tendency toward despotism. The Supreme Court had ruled the national bank constitutional, they pointed out, and Congress had voted to recharter it. They stated that Jackson, the would-be "dictator," had trammeled the authority of both of the other branches of government, taking upon himself the sole right to determine the future of the bank.

Jackson won re-election handily in 1832, although by a smaller majority than in his first election. By 1833 he was ready to move ahead with his plans to disassemble the Second Bank of the United States. He asked Secretary of the Treasury Louis McLane to begin to select other banks into which the federal government could move its deposits. McLane balked, worried that the selection process would be compromised by politics and that the state banks would lose all fiscal restraint in view of such windfall deposits. Impatient, Jackson replaced McLane with William J. Duane, and then replaced Duane with political crony Amos Kendall. On October 1, 1833, the federal government began to distribute its deposits to 22 state banks, called Jackson's "pet banks" by his critics. By the close of the year, the government deposits had been largely removed.

The deposits in question did not exist as cash on hand, but had been used to make loans to individuals and corporations around the country. In order to make them available, the Second Bank set furiously about calling in loans and foreclosing on debts, requiring payment from state banks in specie. In effect, and no doubt with a certain grim relish, Biddle was repeating the process that triggered the Panic of 1819. In the first two months he took over $5 million of credit out of the economy. In six months he took out more than $15 million.

As recession gripped the nation, the Senate passed an unprecedented resolution censuring Jackson for assuming "authority and power not conferred by the constitution and laws." Jackson's response, utterly unrepentant, underscored the new "democratic" politics of the times: "The President," he maintained (and no other branch of government), "is the direct representative of the American people." Earlier presidents had claimed to represent the interests of the American people as a whole, but the nature of representation in the federal government had been assumed by most politicians to be indirect, certain filters having been purposely put in place to sift out the greatest excesses of "the people." The expansion of white male suffrage (and the spreading practice of electing members of the Electoral College directly) made Jackson the first president who could claim to be the single individual in the federal government selected directly by the voters. The presidency had now become the symbolic head of "the democracy." Congress, on the other hand, would soon become the symbolic repository of "republicanism" and the power base of transregional elites who considered themselves the heirs of the "leading characters" of the revolutionary era. This distinction would later underlie the naming of a new party, the Whigs, a designation chosen to remind Americans of the eighteenth-century English politicians who had opposed the British monarchy. The American Whig Party would not take shape until the late 1830s, but the term was probably first used in Congress by Henry Clay in April of 1834 in an attempt to associate Jackson's bank war with despotism.

The first recession passed quickly as state banks receiving the deposits began to churn out loans (in the form of paper money) and wildcat banks sprang up to take advantage of the glut of paper money. Much of the borrowing went for land sales, which increased from 4 million acres in 1834 to 15 million only a year later.

Correctly, Jackson believed that the excess of paper money in circulation had caused the recession. As soon as conditions began to improve, he began to implement a hard money policy. Late in 1833 he had announced that the federal government would no longer accept drafts on the Second Bank in payment of taxes, a move that sharply curtailed the value of the bank's notes. In 1834 Jackson declared that the "deposit" banks receiving federal monies could not issue paper drafts for amounts under $5 (later raised to $20), an act that curtailed the small-denomination paper in circulation. In July of 1836 he had the Treasury Department issue the Specie Circular, which directed land offices to accept only specie in payment for western lands. (Jackson thought this would discourage large-scale speculators. In fact, it effectively shut out actual settlers, who were seldom able to get together enough gold or silver for their purchases.) Meanwhile, the Deposit Act, passed in June of 1836, expanded the number of "pet banks" to nearly 100 and provided that all federal depository banks must redeem all notes in specie. It also provided for the distribution of a federal surplus of more than $5 million to the states. The distribution was to be carried out using a formula proportional to the states' representation in Congress, in four installments through the year 1837. This money was on top of the over $22,000,000 already deposited in the state banks as a result of funds shifted from the Second Bank of the United States. Underregulated and susceptible to local pressure, the state banks were incapable of absorbing this flood of funds wisely. They issued loans and printed money that vastly exceeded their assets. When the bubble burst in 1837, the nation was thrown into the worst financial disaster of its young history.

This cartoon portrays the unemployment and poverty of the Panic of 1837. The Panic brought about the formation of Loco Focos (a radical workers wing of the Democratic Party). Note the entrance of troops from the street middle left, presumably to enforce order.

CHRONOLOGY

1816	American Bible Society founded
1824	John Quincy Adams elected president (the "Corrupt Bargain")
	Rappites sell New Harmony to Robert Owen and return to Pennsylvania, establishing third community, Economy
	Charles Grandison Finney begins preaching in upstate New York
1825	Owen establishes New Harmony labor reform community
1827	Antimason party organized
1828	Andrew Jackson elected president
	Virtually universal white male suffrage
	Philadelphia workers organize the Philadelphia Working Men's Party
	Protective Tariff of 1828 passes
1830	Shakers support 60 communities
	Removal Act passes
	Joseph Smith organizes the Church of Jesus Christ of Latter-day Saints
1831	Antimason Party holds first open presidential nominating convention
	Cherokee Nation v. Georgia
1831–1832	Alexis de Tocqueville visits United States
1832	*Worcester v. Georgia*
	Black Hawk's War
	Jackson vetoes act rechartering Second Bank of the United States
	Jackson re-elected
1834	Female Moral Reform Society formed
1836	Deposit Act expands number of Jackson's "pet banks" and provides for distribution of federal surplus

Conclusion

The political economy of the Jacksonian consensus was forged from a fervent belief in the efficacy of the individual, a distrust of unfair privilege, and a commitment to expansionism (understood both geographically and as an expansion in the rights of citizens to pursue individual economic improvement). Few of these elements were new to the theories of American political economy of the 1820s, but their meanings had undergone important shifts since 1776. The republic was becoming a democracy.

The harmony that seemed to be expressed in the Jacksonian celebration of democracy and individualism was misleading. Consensus was always partial and contingent, and conflict was always present and growing. If the republic was expanding geographically and politically, it was also contracting. African-American men were being excluded from suffrage; workers were being excluded from opportunity; Indians were being excluded from their homelands. If Jackson the southerner, the settler, and the son of common parents was able to draw support from across a wide variety of constituencies, he was not without his detractors. These included southerners who hated the tariff, reformers who opposed his policies, and merchants and entrepreneurs who wanted a more stable currency. Within 25 years of Jackson's election, workers were in the streets, hundreds of thousands of Americans were petitioning to end slavery, the political parties had dissolved into chaos, and the nation stood on the brink of civil war.

Review Questions

1. What did Jacksonians mean by "special privilege"? What economic and social conditions of the 1820s made the charge of "special privilege" so successful politically?

2. In what respects did the rise of the rhetoric of the "common man" express an enlarged democracy in the years after the War of 1812? In what respects did this rhetoric reflect the narrowing of opportunity?

3. In what ways did the religious and political organizing of the 1820s and 1830s arise from similar impulses?

4. Identify three potential sources of conflict among Americans who would identify themselves as "Jacksonians."

5. Identify ways in which both the National Republicans and the Jacksonian Democrats were products of the market revolution. In what ways did the two parties share

views of market expansion, and in what respects did their views of the market differ?

6. In what ways did Jackson's views of the republic echo those of Thomas Jefferson?

7. Did the Indian Removal Act of 1830 represent a continuation or a shift in U. S. Indian policy?

Further Readings

Paul E. Johnson and Sean Wilentz, *The Kingdom of Matthias: The Story of Sex and Salvation in Nineteenth-Century America* (1994). Focusing on the role of urbanization, gender, and class in nineteenth-century popular religious movements, this study of lay preacher and cult-leader Matthias the Prophet captures the drama of the urban religious revivals of the 1820s and 1830s and touches upon the careers of a number of other famous reformers of the era, including Isabella Van Wagenen (later Sojourner Truth) and Joseph Smith, founder of the Church of Jesus Christ of the Latter-day Saints.

Donald Jackson, ed., *Black Hawk: An Autobiography* (1955). This volume reprints an 1833 publication alleged to be the autobiography of the influential Sauk leader Black Hawk, along with a critical introduction examining the authenticity of the document (which was written down by a French interpreter and edited and published by an American journalist) and raising important questions about how students and historians should read and use such evidence.

Mary P. Ryan, *Cradle of the Middle Class: The Family in Oneida County, New York, 1790–1865* (1981). Ryan examines the impact of the market revolution on household structure and patterns of family authority in upstate New York, arguing that the breakdown of older community structures encouraged the enlarged participation of women in social affairs, especially through the mechanism of the Finneyite revivals.

John William Ward, *Andrew Jackson—Symbol for an Age* (1953). Half a century old, Ward's study remains highly provocative in suggesting the qualities of background and personality that underlay Jackson's popularity and his ability to embody the broad democratic-movement impulses of his times.

Harry L. Watson, *Liberty and Power: The Politics of Jacksonian America* (1990). Although its primary focus is on politics and parties, *Liberty and Power* grounds the party politics of the Jacksonian era securely in broad social and economic currents of the age, including slavery, westward expansion, and Indian removal.

Deborah Gray White, *Ar'n't I a Woman? Female Slaves in the Plantation South* (1985). This path-breaking study of the experiences of enslaved women examines the work that female slaves performed in the plantation economy, the experiences of female slaves as family members, the important community roles that enslaved African-American women played, and the networks of friendships that female slaves constructed with each other.

History on the Internet

"Andrew Jackson and the Bank War"
http://odur.let.rug.nl/~usa/E/bankwar/bankwarxx.htm
Through this site, investigate every aspect of the debate over the power and privileges of the Second Bank of the United States, including key political actors and their points of view.

"The Shakers—Another America"
http://www.shakerworkshops.com/shakers.htm#
This richly detailed article describes the Shakers' beliefs, daily reflections, and rules and ordinances governing their lives.

"Hope of Reclaiming the Abandoned"
http://womhist.binghamton.edu/fmrs/doc1.htm
An excerpt from a report of the Female Moral Reform Society of New York, this document illustrates how reformers used ideas about female "purity" to argue for an activist social role for women.

"Indian Removal and its Aftermath"
http://www.synaptic.bc.ca/ejournal/jackson.htm
Read Andrew Jackson's messages to Congress addressing Native Americans and his policies toward them. This site contains the full text of the Indian Removal Act of 1830.

12

REFORM AND CONFLICT

1828-1836

OUTLINE

Free Labor Under Attack

The Growth of Sectional Tension
The Political Economy of
Southern Discontent
The Nullification Crisis
Abolitionism and Antiabolition Violence

**The Political Economy
of Early Industrial Society**
Wage Dependency
Labor Organizing and Protest

A New Urban Middle Class
Immigration and Nativism
Internal Migration

**Self-Reform and Social
Regulation**
A Culture of Self-Improvement
Temperance
The Common School Movement
Penal Reform

Conclusion

Free Labor Under Attack

In the summer of 1832, only months before Andrew Jackson was elected for his second term as president, former Rhode Island carpenter Seth Luther traveled across New England denouncing the political economy of Jacksonian America. Journeying from city to city, through Maine, New Hampshire, and Massachusetts, Luther condemned the "tyranny," "avarice," and "exclusive privilege" that drove "AMERICAN MANUFACTURE" and laid before his sympathetic audiences a chilling catalogue of the havoc wrought in the lives of the "producing classes." He reminded his listeners of the 15-hour days, driven by the despotism of the clock and "the well seasoned strap" of the boss—all for a mere 75 cents a day. He described adults exhausted and brutalized and children made "pale, sickly, haggard . . . from the worse than slavish confinement of the cotton mill." Luther lingered especially over the stories of the children. He spoke of one 11-year-old girl whose leg was shattered by an impatient supervisor wielding a stick of wood, and another child who had a board split over her head by "a heartless monster in the shape of an overseer of a cotton mill 'paradise.' " Early industrialization was turning out vast quantities of cottons and woolens. But here, in these changes in the lives of workers, was the true product of "the AMERICAN SYSTEM," he jeered. It created a social order in which "manufactures must be sustained by

injustice, cruelty, ignorance, vice, and misery," a system in which "the poor must work or starve" while "the rich . . . take care of themselves." It was a bleak description of the political economy of an industrializing democracy.

In some respects, Luther's harangue was simply the labor counterpart of a standard Jacksonian political stump speech. It rang with denunciations of wealth and special privilege, praised the worth and dignity of common people, demanded reform, and flamed with images of the impending Armageddon. However, Luther was speaking in 1832, not 1828, and he was addressing a nation in which the common man had presumably reigned triumphant for four years. Luther's closing exhortation that workers were free men in name only and must now rededicate their lives to "LIVE FREEMEN and DIE FREEMEN" hinted at deep failures in Jacksonian democracy.

In some respects, Luther's indictment seems unaccountable. Jackson's landslide 1828 election had represented the successful coming together of a remarkably diverse coalition, including southern planters and northern manufacturers, wage workers and entrepreneurs, and political pragmatists and at least some social and religious perfectionists. These groups represented very different interests, but in 1824 and 1828 they had found enough common ground to produce a clear majority behind the Jacksonian Democrats. By 1832, moreover, Jackson had

335

done a good deal to reward the expectations of the voters. He had cleaned house of National Republican appointees. He had supported white claims to Indian lands in the West, opening hundreds of thousands of acres to new settlement. He was preparing to take on that behemoth of elite privilege, the Second Bank of the United States. In national presidential politics, the consensus held. Jackson was re-elected in 1832 and his vice president succeeded him to the presidency in 1836.

Workers printing calico in a cotton mill, 1834.

But Jackson's first four years in office had also revealed disturbing, unreconciled tensions within the new democratic political economy. These tensions arose in part from the very strengths of democracy and economic growth. The expansion of personal liberties created a society in which persisting inequities were all the more obvious, their persistence underscored by Americans' very commitment to perfectibility. Slavery was the glaring exception to democracy. Continuing slave resistance served as a constant reminder to whites in the South and the North that the institution was neither benign nor stable. Free African-American communities offered a model of African-American liberty and provided a launch pad for antislavery activism. Hurt by the vagaries of market growth and disappointed in the policies of Andrew Jackson, white southerners began to fight back the tides of democratic discourse by asserting the distinc-tive character of the South and claiming a unique kinship to the more hierarchical republicanism of the founding generation. Only a small group of white northerners organized to confront slavery directly. However, the disappearance from the North of slavery and other systems of external restraint (for example, indenturing) led even northerners who did not care about slaves to view the South as a region of peculiar, even alien, customs.

Economic expansion and the widening rhetoric of democracy also exposed problems in the political economy of free labor. Of all groups in the United States, white workingmen had experienced the most dramatic expansion of their political rights (and, in some respects, their economic independence) in the early nineteenth century. Yet, as Luther's criticisms made clear, by 1832 many American workers (female as well as male) felt threatened by the new industrial order. By the early 1830s, worker protests had become common in the cities and manufacturing centers of the nation, and workingmen's

parties had begun to assume a more clearly oppositional stance toward the major political parties. "The dignity of common labor" had become the rallying cry of protest.

Rather than turning out into the streets, Americans of more middling means responded to the volatility of indus-trial society by attempting to withdraw from it and especially attempting to distance themselves from the struggles of workers. They elaborated a distinc-tive style of living, based on a belief in the individual household as the last sanctuary of morality and sanity in an increasingly dangerous world. Although this new American middle class continued to insist upon the dignity of labor, it grew less certain that the laboring classes could claim this dignity. If workers were poor, perhaps they lacked ambition, were negligent, drank too much, or were irreli-gious. Criticisms of workers soon focused especially on Irish immigrants, whose growing numbers brought to the surface the virulent anti-Catholicism of many native-born Americans, middle-class and working-class alike.

Not all Americans gave up on their search for social perfection, but in this atmosphere of dislocation and division, reform itself became an object of controversy. The increasingly vocal struggle against slavery aroused deep hostility in the North as well as the South. The visi-bility of women in abolition and other reform movements, always criticized by some sectors of American society, was especially offensive to the new middle-class domestic sensibility. Some reform women began to challenge their critics directly, wondering why they should not also enjoy full citizenship in the new political order. That discontent would not result in an independent women's rights movement for another decade. In the meantime, most reform women, like most reform men, shunned controversy and focused their efforts on the need for control in a democratic society. Some extolled the importance of self-control, through education and temperate personal habits. Others called for new external controls (laws and institutions) to save those who would not save themselves. Ironically, as the common ground slipped away, the rhetoric of democracy grew more shrill. Whatever their own goals, political leaders denounced their enemies as the foes of a demo-cratic political economy itself. ∎

■■ KEY TOPICS

• The controversy surrounding nullification

• The birth of the abolition movement

• Class formation during the 1830s

• The wage system and class conflict

• Immigration and nativism and their effect on U.S. politics

• A culture of self-improvement

The Growth of Sectional Tension

The strains in Jacksonian America became apparent almost immediately after Jackson's first inauguration, not in the form of the economic plight of industrial workers, but in the form of growing sectional conflict. Americans had not always viewed the differences in the political economies of the North and South as bad. Potential disagreements had been deferred (although not resolved) through various political compromises. Meanwhile, those very regional differences had powered American nationalism after the War of 1812. But economic growth eventually matured old differences into open conflict. The immediate catalyst was the tariff, but by 1832 the tariff question seemed ready to ignite a far broader debate over the institution of slavery itself.

The Political Economy of Southern Discontent

Although they had apparently won the struggle, many white southerners had felt betrayed by northern criticisms of slavery during the Missouri controversy. A series of economic and political frustrations in the 1820s nurtured that sense of mistreatment, creating the context within which the planter class, which had so far dominated the nation's presidency, could see itself as the victim of dishonorable conspiracies in the nation's capital.

Most important was the economy. By 1828 cotton prices were only about one-third of their 1815 levels. Many planters and farmers tried to compensate for declining profits by planting more acres, but worn-out fields

kept production low. Large eastern planters rode out the hard times with difficulty, often having to sell off slaves, lands, and city houses to meet their obligations. Many smaller farmers, dependent on cotton as their cash crop to pay off debts, were forced to sell out. Conditions were not much better in the cities, where small businesses failed, property values plummeted (by 50 percent in Charleston), and beggars became more numerous on the streets. Although the Panic of 1819 hurt northern farms and businesses, too, many white southerners experienced their own hard times as a contrast to the northerners, whom they were increasingly inclined to view as unsympathetic to their plight. Most of the Northeast did bounce back from the panic more quickly than the South.

Probably more important in framing the way southerners saw the North, however, was the impact of the Missouri debates in coalescing antislavery sentiment in individual northern states. Pro-slavery advocates in Illinois (where many African Americans were already held in indentures comparable to slavery) were unable to elect a pro-slavery congressman in 1820. In 1824 Ohio asked Congress to consider a plan for the gradual abolition of slavery throughout the United States. On July 4, 1827, New York completed its long process of gradual emancipation, an occasion celebrated by free African Americans as far south as Virginia. Peddlers and manufacturers' agents from the North were blunt about their "great aversion to the . . . Slaveholding States," even as they made their living from southern sales, and northern farmers migrating into the upper South were outspoken in their criticisms of slavery, suffrage restrictions, and the political power of planters. On top of this, news from England had it that abolitionist William Wilberforce was likely to succeed in his effort to get slavery outlawed in the British West Indies.

The tariff of 1828 helped give focus to these southern insecurities, but even before 1828 southerners had complained that tariff policy was unnaturally driving up the prices of European imports, forcing already hard-up southerners to purchase expensive northern-made products. "We have no objection to the North being enriched by our riches," one Charleston *Mercury* reporter wrote in 1827, "but not from our poverty." The new tariff hurt the South in two ways. First, although some southern products benefited from protection (for example, hemp producers in Henry Clay's Kentucky profited from decreased foreign competition), as an export-oriented economy the South as a whole depended for its sales on open markets with other nations. But these nations reacted to reduced American sales with reduced purchases from America. In addition, by raising the costs of imported goods, the tariff further concentrated southern buying in the North while allowing northern prices to rise (see Figure 12-1).

Among the slaveholding states, South Carolina was particularly sensitive to perceived interference from beyond its state borders. In addition to other anxieties,

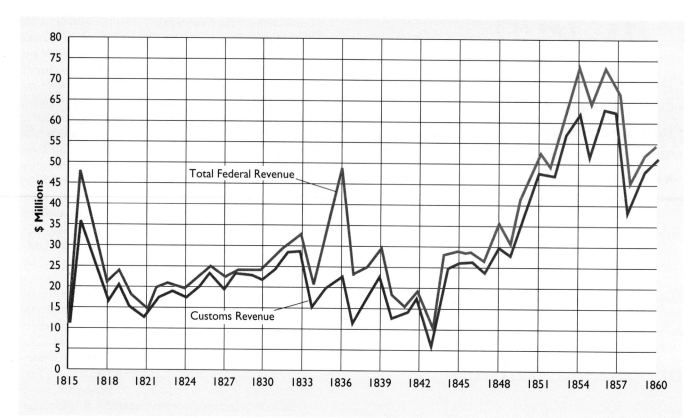

Figure 12-1   Customs and Federal Revenue, 1815–1860.

white South Carolinians were faced with a growing African-American majority (the result of white migration west), a demographic condition that heightened their fears of slave insurrection. Those fears were triggered in 1822, when at the very last moment white authorities exposed a plot to launch a statewide slave rebellion. Devised by free carpenter Denmark Vesey, the conspiracy had been shaped (among other influences) by Vesey's familiarity with Toussaint L'Ouverture's earlier successful revolution in Saint Domingue. Although the conspiracy was betrayed and Vesey and 34 others were executed, the white racial regime of South Carolina was deeply shaken.

The events surrounding Vesey's conspiracy helped revive interest among white South Carolinians in theories of nullification (the right of states to disregard laws they considered repugnant to their interests). In response to rumors that Vesey had used free African-American sailors to communicate with the Saint Domingan government, from which he allegedly expected support, the state legislature mandated that free African-American sailors arriving in Charleston be held in jail until their ships left port. Under pressure from an extralegal organization of planters known as the South Carolina Association, the sheriff of Charleston duly imprisoned free Jamaican sailor Harry Elkinson. When Elkinson's case came to court, lawyers for the Association argued that any treaty that interfered with the power of the state to guard against internal revolution

must itself be unconstitutional. The court rejected this position (agreeing with Secretary of State Adams that the law violated international treaties), but South Carolina continued to enforce the act.

Passage of the tariff of 1828, the "tariff of abominations," again revived nullification talk in South Carolina and gave the position a new defender, John C. Calhoun. Like other South Carolinians, Calhoun had been disenchanted by the experiences of the 1820s and was a far less-enthusiastic nationalist than he had once been. Yet he retained enough faith in the Democratic Party to believe that Democrats would lower the tariff, once in office, and could be made to see the injury that such national laws were inflicting upon southern states. Hoping to encourage both results, in 1828 Calhoun wrote the *South Carolina Exposition and Protest,* in which he laid out the historical, legal, and social justification for the theory of nullification. Although Calhoun published the pamphlet anonymously (still aspiring to the presidency, he was reluctant to associate himself too openly with the South Carolina Association), he let his authorship be widely known, hoping thereby to gain standing among the Radicals within his home state. In the *Exposition,* Calhoun argued that the federal government was the creation of the states, "distinct political communities . . . acting in their separate and sovereign capacity," not of "the people" as a whole. In agreeing to create a federal government, Calhoun argued, the states had ceded some of their powers, but only conditionally. They had always reserved whatever powers were necessary to their survival as distinct entities. Should the policies of the federal government threaten the distinctive character of a state, he declared, that state had the right to assert its reserved sovereignty in defiance of the policies. It was at such a juncture, Calhoun argued, that the states of the South had arrived in 1828. They had become the "minority" culture, their interests and institutions endangered by "the unrestrained will of a majority." The "tariff of abominations" would gradually drain away the money and the independence of the South, subjecting it to northern tyranny.

There was much in America's history to support Calhoun's view. The states had existed before the federal constitution. Representation at the Constitutional Convention and ratification of the Constitution had been by state, and representation in the federal government continued to be on the basis of states. Moreover, among the defenders of the theory were no less personages than Thomas Jefferson and James Madison, in their resolutions opposing the Alien and Sedition Acts.

On the other hand, the Constitution's status as the supreme law of the land rested on the fact that it had been ratified by the people, acting through special conventions, not by the state governments, and subsequent suffrage reform had increased white male participation in the government. Moreover, the Hartford Convention (see Chapter 10) had associated states' rights arguments with a lack of patriotism. The *Exposition* went a good deal farther than the convention resolutions: Calhoun argued explicitly what the Federalists had dared only hint, that if all else failed, states always retained the right to withdraw from the compact.

By 1828, however, many Americans viewed the federal government as the creation of "the people," not the states. Among these was President Jackson.

The Nullification Crisis

Other southern states, less economically pressed than South Carolina and more optimistic that the differences in the political economies of the various regions might yet be fine tuned into harmony, did not rush to endorse the *Exposition*. Late in the year, however, the question of slavery once again intruded into the houses of Congress. As with so many issues of antebellum American life, the immediate subject was western migration.

Eager to attract population, the territories and western states had long lobbied for a reduction in the price of federal lands. Southern representatives now offered to support such a measure provided that the western states would join in opposing the tariff. For New Englanders, western migration continued to create a labor shortage and to strengthen fears of becoming the political backwater of the nation. In December 1829 Senator Samuel A. Foot of Connecticut advocated limiting land sales in the West. Seeking a South-West alliance, Senator Robert Y. Hayne of South

Carolina charged that the idea was little more than a conspiracy to pool cheap labor in the East. He insinuated that the government was keeping land prices artificially high to build a slush fund "for corruption—fatal to the sovereignty and independence of the states."

When Massachusetts Senator Daniel Webster rose to defend the patriotism of his region, Hayne made the serious tactical error of bringing up the Hartford Convention. Webster responded that it was South Carolina, not the Northeast, that posed a threat to national unity, and he pointed for evidence to the South Carolina *Exposition*. Hayne protested that the *Exposition* was in the long, honored tradition of American political protest and petition, but Webster was contemptuous. The Revolution had been fought by the American people, Webster thundered, and the American people had created the federal government. What Webster said next was uncannily prescient of later events in American history. "When my eyes shall be turned to behold, for the last time, the sun in heaven," he implored, "may I not see him shining on the broken and dishonored fragments of a once glorious union . . . on a land rent with civil feuds, or drenched, it may be, in fraternal blood!" No, he insisted: "Let their last feeble and lingering glance rather behold the gorgeous ensign of the republic . . . its arms and trophies streaming in their original lustre, not a stripe erased or polluted, not a single star obscured." And let that ensign not bear that motto of southern malcontents, " 'Liberty first and Union afterwards'; but . . . that other sentiment, dear to every true American heart,—Liberty and Union, now and forever, one and inseparable."

Although Daniel Webster's address was widely reported and enthusiastically received in the North, Calhoun and the South Carolinians remained convinced that all true Americans, certainly all true southerners, must agree with them. The following April, at a banquet commemorating Jefferson's birthday, they made the mistake of putting that assumption to the test. With President Jackson, the entire cabinet, more than 100 congressmen, and various other federal officials present, southern congressmen rolled through a series of prepared toasts celebrating the principle of state sovereignty. Called on to propose the first voluntary toast, a mortified Jackson reputedly stared hard at John Calhoun and lifted his glass: "Our Federal Union," he declared. "It must be preserved."

Although he supported the federal union, Jackson sympathized with southern complaints that tariff levels were too high and unfair to some sections of the country, and he advocated tariff reform. Ironically, the resulting tariff only confirmed South Carolinian fears and set off the most serious constitutional crisis of Jackson's presidency. The Tariff of 1832 lowered duties on many goods to 1816 levels, but it did not lower protection on textiles and iron. In this continued protection for the largest northern industries, South Carolinians saw a defiant reaffirmation of a special relationship between northern interests and the federal government.

WHERE THEY LIVED, WHERE THEY WORKED

Gowrie

"Gowrie" was a plantation, 265 acres of fertile rice fields spread across a large island in the middle of the Savannah River, just upstream from Augusta, Georgia, and just over the border from the South Carolina lowlands.

In 1833, Gowrie's land and enslaved labor force of 50 people became the property of Charles Manigault. Manigault had lost half of his paternal inheritance in merchant ventures in the volatile markets of the early 1820s. By the late 1820s, he was eager not simply to restore his earlier wealth, but also to establish his family among the ruling dynasties of the South.

For Manigault, Gowrie was the means to that end—an investment and a profit-center, but never his "home." He never lived full time at Gowrie and never built a family seat there, preferring to live in the elaborate mansion at Marshlands, his plantation seven miles outside of Charleston. Manigault ran Gowrie from afar, directing affairs through periodic visits and regular letters of instruction to his resident overseer, while he traveled abroad and enjoyed more cosmopolitan living.

For the enslaved workers who lived there, Gowrie held more complicated meanings. It was, above all, a place of hard, forced labor. Rice cultivation began in the winter months, when slaves burned off the old stubble in Gowrie's 15 fields and leveled and plowed the land. Women seeded the rice between mid-March and early June. As soon as the seed was in, "trunk-minders" (aided by the tides of the Savannah River) opened the elaborate irrigation systems to flood the fields, protecting the seeds from birds and the sprouts from too much sun. As

the seeds grew into young plants, the slaves periodically partially drained the fields (to allow for weeding and hoeing) and then reflooded them, until the final flooding in mid-July.

The flooding and draining reduced (but did not eliminate) the work of cultivation. However, it created the additional labor of building, repairing, and cleaning ditches and canals to channel the water, traps to close it off, and drains to carry it away. Men constructed the systems, while women were put to work hauling in the mud to construct earthworks and hauling away the muck that collected in drains and clogged ditches and canals.

But for its laborers, Gowrie was also home. Life at Gowrie offered slaves a few advantages over life on other types of farms. Because rice was most profitably grown on a large scale, rice plantations were among the largest in the South and had unusually large slave populations—119 at Gowrie at its largest in 1849. The size of the work force created a community of kin and friends unknown to slaves on smaller holdings. Moreover, the complexity of the labor led most overseers to employ the task system—which provided slaves with a degree of autonomy in the organization and execution of their labor. The periodic breaks in the rhythms of cultivation (first while the seeds sprouted and then during the main growing season) allowed slaves time to plant their own gardens, yielding produce to improve their diets and perhaps some to sell. Perhaps because families provided effective means of transferring the complicated skills of rice cultivation from one generation to the next, owners like Manigault appear to have felt some reluctance to break up families.

By the time South Carolina responded, the South had been the scene of another slave insurrection. In the summer of 1831 an African-American driver and preacher by the name of Nat Turner launched a slave rebellion in Virginia. The rebellion was put down and Turner and other conspirators were executed, but unlike earlier plots, this revolt had actually taken place. Inspired by a millennialist fervor, for two days Turner and his followers had effectively controlled parts of the southern Virginia countryside, recruiting new allies as they went from plantation to plantation executing whites and freeing slaves. Although the number of active insurrectionists probably never exceeded 70 or so, before the uprising was put down 57 whites had died. The number of white fatalities was higher than in any previous slave rebellion. Southern whites took their revenge, instituting a month-long reign of vigilantism in

which many African Americans who had no part in the revolt were summarily executed.

But the insurrection had left its mark. Southern whites lived in a state of constant apprehension for a long time and felt certain that northerners and southern slaves were in a deep conspiracy against them. In November 1832 South Carolina Radicals called a statewide convention whose delegates voted 136 to 26 that the tariffs of both 1828 and 1832 were null and void in the state. The acts of the convention forbade the collection of the tariffs within South Carolina.

For Jackson, the act of nullification transformed the crisis from a question of regional interests to a question of national union. In December he issued a proclamation asserting his conviction that the union was a creation of the people, not the states. "The laws of the United States must be executed," he declared, "I have no discretionary power

Yet if Gowrie was home to the slaves who lived there, it was a harsh home. Tending the muddy or flooded fields was dangerous as well as exhausting labor, and accidents were common. Because embankments regularly washed away, and ditches filled with silt, rice plantations required more cold, wet winter labor than other kinds of plantations. Constantly wading in the waters, rice workers were particularly subject to snakebites and to malaria. Gowrie's location on a river and near the ocean, which made it easier to flood, made the plantation an especially dangerous place for slaves. Being forced out in the unpredictably high tides, hurricanes, and floods to mend dikes

and clear canals was part of everyday labor on rice plantations. Manigault evidently did little to reduce these dangers. Health decisions were often left up to the overseer (who virtually never called in a doctor) and to a single elderly slave woman (who was hard pressed to care for such a large community).

While Manigault grew spectacularly wealthy, the ultimate price of rice production to enslaved workers was a staggeringly high mortality rate, especially among children. None of the six infants present at Gowrie when Manigault purchased the estate lived to see adulthood. By January 1835, only half of the original labor force remained alive.

The labor of children and women was essential to rice production. Women (shown in the right drawing loading rice onto flat boats) were especially skilled at preparing and sowing the seed and tending the irrigation systems. Children (like the little girl in the left picture, helping to carry in the harvest) were employed in various jobs that exposed them to the accidents and disease of the flooded fields.

on the subject; my duty is emphatically pronounced in the Constitution." Jackson soon asked Congress for a law specifically affirming his responsibility to compel the collection of the tax in South Carolina, by force of arms if necessary.

Congress rushed to find a compromise. In early 1833 it passed a tariff that gradually reduced duties over the next decade, but Congress also passed the law Jackson had requested, known as the Force Bill. On March 2, 1833, Jackson signed both the new tariff law and the Force Bill, a pointed reminder to South Carolina that nullification and secession would not be tolerated.

In 1832 South Carolina stood virtually alone even among southern states. The supporters of nullification had no choice but to withdraw their ordinance. At the same time, however, they voted to nullify the Force Bill within the boundaries of the state of South Carolina. Jackson let

the gesture pass, and at least for the time being, the constitutional crisis was over.

Antislavery Becomes Abolition

By 1832, nevertheless, the growing sectional crisis had escaped its strictly federal moorings and was no longer a question exclusively for politicians to debate. Most white Americans had long finessed the question of slavery. By the time Jackson left office, however, a small but dynamic social movement against slavery had taken shape in the North, and slavery had become a nationally divisive issue.

By the late 1820s, the movement for African-American self-sufficiency, founded out of necessity at the beginning of the republic, had yielded a rich harvest of African-American mutual aid and benevolent associations. Organizing was most lively in Philadelphia, where free African-Americans established more than 40 new societies between 1820 and 1835, but (propelled by the growth of the free African-American community) the self-help impulse extended south to Baltimore and Charleston and north to New York and Boston. Although some societies were clearly limited in membership to relatively prosperous free African Americans, self-help organizing was vigorous across economic lines: coachmen, porters, barbers, brickmakers, sailors, cooks, and washerwomen all formed associations.

In the 1820s, in the wake of the Missouri debates and the steady erosion of African-American male suffrage, African-American organizing became more explicitly political and more antislavery. At first, African-American associations protested the efforts of the American Colonization Society to deport emancipated slaves. By 1826, however, with the formation of the first all African-American antislavery organization, the General Colored Association of Massachusetts, African Americans had taken the institution of slavery itself as its target. In New York in 1827 John Russwurm and Samuel E. Cornish founded the first African American newspaper, *Freedom's Journal,* devoted to exposing the evils of slavery.

African-American protests of the late 1820s reflected the expectation that African Americans could not and *should not* count on white allies and would have to help themselves. "Too long have others spoken for us," Russwurm and Cornish declared in the first issue of *Freedom's Journal.* In 1829 David Walker, a second-hand clothes dealer in Boston, published a pamphlet titled *An Appeal to the Colored Citizens of the World,* calling on African Americans to take resistance to slavery into their own hands by armed insurrection, if necessary. In 1832 Maria Stewart, a free African-American woman in Boston, urged African Americans gathered at Boston's Franklin Hall to take their destinies into their own hands. "If they kill us," she said simply, "we shall but die." As she spoke, Stewart became the first American-born woman to address publicly a mixed audience of men and women in the United States.

These entreaties found responsive audiences. From 1830 until 1835 (and less regularly thereafter), free African Americans met annually in a series of conventions intended to coordinate African-American antislavery efforts and secure to free African-American men "a voice in the disposition of those public resources which we ourselves have helped to earn." This National Negro Convention movement consistently framed its goals in the idiom of "manhood," calling for "the speedy elevation of ourselves and brethren to the scale and standing of men." Nevertheless, African-American women, so central to the self-improvement societies, also were deeply engaged in antislavery politics. They worked to raise funds for the antislavery press and to raise awareness by inviting antislavery speakers to address their societies. In 1832 African-American women formed female antislavery societies in Salem, Massachusetts and Rochester, New York, that became the model for the formation of white female antislavery societies.

Although many whites in the North disliked the institution of slavery and had been alarmed by the South's aggressive defense of slavery during the Missouri controversy, most were reluctant to confront an issue that had such obvious power to ignite social violence and political division. Few white northerners thought of African Americans as their equals. Many based their livelihoods directly or indirectly on the southern economy. For all of these reasons, white antislavery activism took root only slowly in the North. In 1821 Ohio newspaperman Benjamin Lundy began publication of *The Genius of Universal Emancipation,* the first white abolitionist paper. In the years that followed, popular clamor prompted a few northern states to pass laws making it more difficult for masters to recapture runaway slaves. Nevertheless, in the mid-1820s the American Colonization Society remained one of the largest benevolent organizations in the nation and was the primary focus of northern efforts at improving the conditions of slaves.

It took the growth of the perfectionist impulse associated with Finneyite revivalism to begin to dislodge northern complacency. The most dramatic break came in the person of William Lloyd Garrison, Lundy's co-editor, whose commitment to perfectionism led him eventually to conclude that even Lundy was too tolerant of slaveowners. Garrison left *The Genius of Universal Emancipation* and, on January 1, 1831, in Boston, founded his own abolitionist newspaper, the *Liberator.* In the first issue Garrison announced not only his determined opposition to slavery

Through drawings like this one, published in Garrison's Liberator on May 3, 1834, abolitionists in the United States tried to convince Americans to put aside their complacency about slavery by emphasizing the brutality of the owner or overseer and the helplessness of the enslaved worker.

but also his absolute break with all forms of antislavery sentiment that compromised with the institution: "I will not equivocate—I will not excuse—I will not retreat a single inch—and I will be heard." Garrison's approach, known as **immediatism,** called upon antislavery reformers not only to work for the immediate abolition of slavery and to struggle for the immediate conversion of all individuals to antislavery activism, but also to confront all forms of compromise with slavery, public or personal, wherever they encountered them.

"Immediatist" antislavery activism centered in Boston and tended to attract individuals, like Garrison, who had been only peripherally linked to the mainstream Benevolent Empire, a fact that no doubt made it easier for them to criticize the accommodationist tactics of the Colonization Society. Most were urban professionals from liberal Protestant backgrounds, people like the author Lydia Maria Child, wealthy lawyer Samuel Sewall, Wendell Phillips (scion of an old Massachusetts family), and Henry and Maria Weston Chapman (he a merchant, she the principal of a young ladies' high school before her marriage). In 1831, under Garrison's leadership, the "Boston Clique" formed the New England Anti-Slavery Society.

Other antislavery workers, equally committed to the cause, were more willing than the Garrisonians to risk contact with the imperfect world. One of these was Theodore Dwight Weld. Born in Connecticut, Weld was an early supporter of the Colonization Society. After his conversion in the Finneyite revivals of 1825 and 1826, however, he came to feel morally compromised by the presence of slaveowners in the society and began to doubt that the society would ever risk alienating its southern constituency. By the 1830s Weld was a committed abolitionist. As a student at Lane Seminary in Cincinnati, Ohio, he organized 18 days of antislavery discussions and led a group of students out of Lane to Oberlin College when Lane President Lyman Beecher moved to squelch the controversial activities. In 1834, Weld became a full-time antislavery organizer. Although he had himself come to antislavery work through religious perfectionism, Weld never broke entirely from contact with more moderate groups, and he was willing to remain engaged in politics. In the early 1840s he returned briefly to active antislavery organizing to head a reference bureau for an insurgent group of Whigs seeking congressional consideration of abolition in the District of Columbus. Among Weld's recruits to abolition was later Liberty Party presidential candidate James Birney.

There were some quick converts to the new, energized antislavery movement, especially in the urban areas of the Northeast, upstate New York, and Pennsylvania and in those western states most heavily settled by New Englanders, especially Ohio. Quakers and liberal Congregationalists were particularly active in the early movement. Local antislavery societies formed throughout New England by 1832. Although Garrison envisioned a gender- and racially integrated abolition movement, local societies generally

formed on a sex-segregated and often a racially segregated basis. Maria Weston Chapman helped organize the Boston Female Anti-Slavery Society in 1832. In 1833 Quaker Lucretia Mott helped to found the Philadelphia Female Anti-Slavery Society. By the end of 1833, local and state organizations had grown numerous and strong enough to support a national society, the American Anti-Slavery Society, which included six African Americans on its original board.

Abolitionism and Antiabolition Violence

The American Anti-Slavery Society dedicated itself to the total abolition of slavery without compensation for owners and to the admission of African Americans to full, free citizenship. Society members pledged to pursue their goals through nonviolent moral suasion, that is, by exhorting individuals to undertake self-reform and the reform of society voluntarily.

Although nonviolent, moral suasion was not necessarily nonconfrontational. In 1835 the Society decided to flood the United States mails with abolitionist literature.

Pro-slavery apologists tried to convince white Americans that abolition would result, not in a racially equal society, but in a racial inversion of the conditions of slavery, a society in which African Americans would dominate whites.

The campaign was intended to support recruitment and organizing in the North, but its central purpose was to take the antislavery fight directly into the South.

Abolitionists had relied on the press to spread their views since the early 1820s. Yet in the early 1830s even Garrison's *Liberator* remained largely unknown. The postal campaign of 1835 was made possible by the fact that the movement's center of gravity had shifted from Massachusetts to New York, where wealthy New York merchants Lewis and Arthur Tappan were able to bankroll its publishing, and by a sudden decline in the cost of printing. In 1835 the Society dramatically increased its publication of antislavery pamphlets from approximately 100,000 pieces to 1,000,000 pieces. Roughly 20,000 tracts, fliers, and periodicals, many of them emblazoned with vivid graphics of the effects of slavery, were mailed to southern destinations. Meanwhile, a contingent of agents and lecturers spread out across the North.

The response, in the North as well as the South, was immediate and fierce (see Map 12-1). In the South, anger and panic soon turned violent. With the memory of Nat Turner still fresh, slaveowners denounced the campaign as incendiary and pointed to hundreds of alleged slave conspiracies as the direct handiwork of the northern abolitionists. Southern communities offered large rewards for prominent abolition leaders, dead or alive. Local authorities appointed vigilante committees to patrol free African-American neighborhoods (presumed hotbeds of insurrection), to patrol coastal boats for runaway slaves, and to search post offices for offending materials. In Charleston,

South Carolina, a mob broke into the post office, ransacked the mail, stole the abolitionist literature, and burned it publicly. In Washington, D. C., a mob several hundred strong destroyed the business of a free African-American man rumored to support the abolitionist campaign and then rampaged through the African-American community.

Even before the 1835 campaign, northerners, too, had begun to express their disapproval of abolitionists. In 1833, for example, whites had boycotted a local school for young women when its principal, Prudence Crandall, admitted two African-American scholars from out of state. When Crandall admitted an entirely African-American student body, white citizens lobbied for laws to prevent African-American students from entering Connecticut to get an education, threatened Crandall personally, and eventually burned the school to the ground. In 1834 mobs surged through the African-American communities of both Philadelphia and New York, attacking churches and destroying homes.

The magnitude of the postal campaign unleashed a new fury in the North. Anti-African American and anti-abolitionist riots tore through St. Louis, Pittsburgh, Cincinnati, and Philadelphia. From Boston to Utica, New York, to Granville, Ohio, abolitionist meetings were broken up by mobs. In Boston in 1835, a crowd captured William Lloyd Garrison and dragged him through the streets on a rope. English abolitionist George Thompson was hounded by mobs everywhere he went on his American tour. Attacks on Thompson were so notorious that President Jackson referred to him in a December 1835 address, praising northerners for their repudiation of "emissaries from foreign parts who have dared to interfere" in the question of slavery.

Responding to the abolitionists' use of the press, antiabolitionist mobs targeted newspapers especially. In 1836, an antiabolitionist mob in Cincinnati made "the destruction of their Press on the night of the 12th instant," the symbolic warning of greater violence to come. Rioters in Alton, Illinois, destroyed abolitionist newspaper editor Elija Lovejoy's press four times in 1837. In the last attack, they murdered Lovejoy himself. Prominent in most of these disturbances were "gentlemen of property and standing," pillars of their communities who were convinced that the abolitionists meant to destroy the union and force a racially integrated society (see Map 12-2 for a population breakdown).

Many white northerners who opposed slavery were nonetheless distressed by the violence, which seemed to threaten a complete breakdown in civil society. A few northern state legislatures admonished radical abolitionists for their extreme measures, although none went so far as to pass laws restricting abolitionist activity. Some antislavery activists rushed to assure southerners that true abolitionists would always "entreat [slaves] to wait in patience ever so

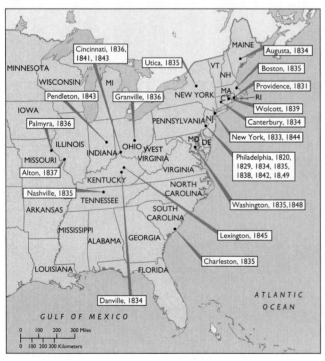

Map 12-1   Primary Sites of Antiabolition Violence.

Titled "New Method of Assorting the Mail," this antislavery cartoon depicted southern white workingmen breaking into the Charleston, South Carolina Post Office in an effort to destroy abolition materials entering the state through the federal mail. Note the posted reward for Tappan (who led the propaganda campaign) and the well-dressed citizens in the background, presumably goading the marauders on.

long rather than [take] recourse to insurrection." A larger number chastised what they saw as the extreme fringe of their own movement, criticizing them for a too-zealous approach. Catharine Beecher, eldest child of the Presbyterian minister Lyman Beecher, complained that abolitionist tactics of using "reproaches" and "rebukes . . . to convince the whites that their prejudices were sinful" were misguided and divisive. Writers for the Boston *Courier* worried that the abolitionists would dangerously *"inflame the passions of the multitude,* including the women and children." "Who among us," one critic cried, "can calculate the amount of trouble and calamity which will ensue, upon the perseverance of the antislavery society?"

Abolitionists were undeterred and even began to find a wider range of converts. Antiabolition violence suggested to some moderates that pro-slavery forces would stop at nothing to protect their peculiar institution—even the flagrant violation of civil rights, the destruction of property, and murder. They were the more distressed when, in his annual address to Congress in 1835, President

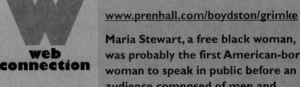

web connection

The Philadelphia Riot of 1838

www.prenhall.com/boydston/grimke

Maria Stewart, a free black woman, was probably the first American-born woman to speak in public before an audience composed of men and women. Although she called for a racially just society, she was severely criticized even by Boston's black community. White abolitionist Angelina Grimké also faced censure—from the white clergy, the white middle class, and white antiabolitionist rioters. How did these two women's views of fighting racism differ? How did each react to the opposition she faced?

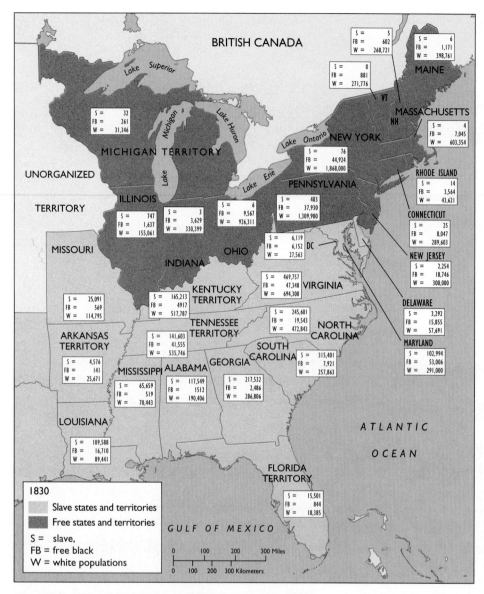

Map 12-2 *Slave, Free Black, and White Populations, 1830.*
In 1830, the North was virtually a white society and most white northerners—whatever their views on slavery—preferred to keep it that way. In many southern states, meanwhile, African Americans and specifically slaves constituted the majority of the population.

Seeking to mollify southerners, in June 1836 the House of Representatives resolved that antislavery petitions to Congress be automatically tabled. The resolution, known as the "gag rule," was renewed by succeeding Congresses until 1844.

The American Anti-Slavery Society was quick to capitalize on the passage of the gag rule. In July the society published *An Appeal to the People of the United States,* charging that the gag rule was a flagrant violation of the constitutional rights of all Americans, and especially the cherished right of petition. "Let no one think for a moment that because he is not an abolitionist," the tract read, "his liberties are not and will not be invaded." That same summer, female antislavery leaders from across the North began organizing a systematic, widespread drive to obtain signatures on antislavery petitions. Female abolitionists traveled across the North, speaking in private parlors and in public halls, often exposing themselves to harsh public censure. Within two years, they collected some 2 million signatures, more than two-thirds of which were women's.

The petition campaign served many ends. It called attention to the gag rule, to the implied congressional support of slavery, and to the ways in which pro-slavery forces could abridge the rights of all Americans. It also provided moderate northerners with a relatively nonconfrontational, discreet avenue of protest. Benefiting from a growing public discussion of the evils of slavery, the American Anti-Slavery Society grew from 225 local auxiliaries in 1835 to more than 1,500 by the end of the decade.

Immediatist sentiment often contained a critique of the North as well as of the South. The critique did not originate in the discovery of slavery, but rather in disillusionment with northern reformers who were willing to compromise with slavery. The direct target of immediatist organizing was not the South, but the North, which had to be shaken from its deep and complacent dependence on slave-produced products. Perhaps, "besotted by the influence of the institution of slavery," as Garrisonian

Jackson asked for measures curtailing antislavery organizing, including closing the mails to abolitionist literature. Congress refused, but northerners were shocked by the very idea that the president would propose to restrict freedom of the mails to protect southern interests.

If antislavery advocates took heart from Congress' refusal to interfere with the federal mails, they were less happy with other decisions. Opponents of slavery had long petitioned Congress to end slavery in the nation's capital. The petitions provoked especially heated responses from southern congressmen, including a series of resolutions by John C. Calhoun asserting that it was the absolute responsibility of the federal government to protect slavery wherever it existed in the states or territories.

Samuel J. May would later put it, the North had already lost its moral bearing in the headlong rush to industrial prosperity.

The Political Economy of Early Industrial Society

Abolitionists were not the only Americans to criticize the political economy of the industrializing North. Seth Luther's indictment of the "American system of manufacturing" focused on the "57,000 persons, male and female, employed in cotton and woollen mills, and other establishments connected with them" across the 12 nonslave states of the union, but by 1832 the wage dependency Luther deplored extended far beyond the textile mills. Shoemaking, the nation's second-largest industry, employed tens of thousands of men and women, a diminishing number of them self-employed in independent shops. Another 10,000 women in Boston, New York, Philadelphia, and Baltimore labored as underpaid seamstresses in the garment industry, stitching shirts, collars, skirts, and ladies' cloaks. In Seth Luther's eyes, by 1828 the artisans and craft workers once presumed to be the repository of American virtue were being crushed in "a cruel system of exaction" that destroyed their bodies and minds for the benefit of the rich. Luther had a name for what they had become. He called them "the Working Classes."

Wage Dependency

The reorganization of manufacturing labor had proceeded slowly and unevenly, but by 1830 a general outline of changes was becoming visible through much of the Northeast. In response to growing regional and local markets, master craftsmen sought ways to increase production and decrease costs. They subdivided the production process into smaller discrete tasks. When possible, they distributed aspects of the production to outworkers, an amorphous group including men, women, boys, and girls, who sometimes lived in the same city, sometimes in villages miles from the manufacturer. They worked part of the shoe, or hat, or shirt, returning it to the manufacturer (or a subcontractor) for piece wages. In house, employers relied more and more on the labor of apprentices or poorly trained helpers, whose labor came cheaper than that of journeymen. As the work was subdivided, requiring a small body of knowledge and skills from each worker, workers became more interchangeable, and their wages dropped.

The Panic of 1819 had thrown thousands of people out of work, driving wages down and prices up. The reviving economy of the 1820s did not reverse those trends, which were deepened by recurrent cycles of depression in 1829

and 1837. Seth Luther was not alone in his indictment of the "American system of manufacturing." In an 1833 "Appeal of the Working People of Manayunk [Pennsylvania] to the Public," workers protested fourteen-and-a-half-hour days in "overheated" rooms "thick with the dust and small particles of cotton, which we are constantly inhaling to the destruction of our health, our appetite, and strength." "Our wages," they declared, "are barely sufficient to supply us with the necessaries of life. We cannot provide against sickness or difficulties of any kind, by laying down a single dollar, for our present wants consume the little we receive." They cited the larger system of market relations that gripped them in its vice: "It requires the wages of all the family who are able to work (save only one small girl to take care of the house and provide meals)," they explained. "[C]onsequently the females have no time either to make their own dresses or those of the children, but have of course to apply to trades for every article that is wanted."

The lives of outwork seamstresses, of whom there were tens of thousands in the largest eastern metropolises, were even more harrowing. In his "Address to the Wealthy of the Land" (1831), Philadelphia philanthropist Mathew Carey estimated the wages of Philadelphia seamstresses at $1.25 a week. That amounted to a meager $65 a year if they were able to secure regular year-round work, which, as Carey noted, none did. As it turned out, Carey was overly optimistic. A committee of seamstresses quickly informed

Seamstresses were among the most exploited and impoverished workers of the early industrial Northeast. In this picture, exhausted women sew by bad lighting in an overcrowded central shop under the tyranny of the clock. Seamstresses were generally paid by the piece.

him that they were lucky to earn $1.12 1/2 a week. After rent, they were left with a little more than a nickel a day for food, clothing, heat, and anything else they needed.

Although many workers continued to thrive, by 1830 the urban northeastern corridor was bearing witness to the damages of wage dependency and the subdivision of labor. In the largest cities of the North, neighborhoods had become visibly class stratified, with workers living in the poorest housing. The New York neighborhood of Five Points had once been a thriving community of master craftsmen and trade shops. By 1829, it was the home of prostitutes, beggars, public drunks, thieves, and confidence men engaged, respectable New Yorkers insisted, in "horrors too awful to mention." In working-class neighborhoods, high rents crowded whole families into single unventilated rooms. Many people went homeless or threw up makeshift shanties at the edges of the city. For breathing space, adults and children were forced out onto the streets where "the air was foul, and, in the hot weather, sickening, with putrefying garbage. . . ."

New York was not unique. The industrial housing of Lawrence, Massachusetts, a new textile center, consisted mainly of sod-insulated "shacks" built from "slabs and unfinished lumber with over-lapping boards for roofs." In New Haven in the 1820s and 1830s, some white workers were able to live in individual frame dwellings, but many poorer whites lived in tenement houses erected specifically for the working class, and African Americans and immigrants occupied housing that reminded one observer most of all of "barracks." Their diet was confined largely to potatoes, corn, peas, beans, cabbage, and tomatoes. Increasingly dependent on the market for their most basic subsistence needs, workers were able to afford only the bare minimum, the cheapest, and the poorest quality goods. The exotic new commodities of the market, like ice and fresh berries out of season, were far beyond working-class budgets.

Labor Organizing and Protest

By the mid-1820s, poor working and living conditions produced a clamor of protest, as workers formed unions and took to both the printing presses and the streets to air their grievances. Employing an older model of complaint, some workers (like the textile workers of Manayunk) drew up public appeals—in effect, petitions to the citizenry to help them secure relief. Other workers wrote letters to editors of newspapers or, like Seth Luther, published full tracts exposing the conditions of the laboring classes.

In 1826 New Yorker Langton Byllesby, a journeyman printer, published *Observations on the Sources and Effects*

By 1827 Five Points in New York City, once the site of a thriving community of craft shops and small retailers, had become one of New York City's poorest neighborhoods and, as this drawing suggests, a symbol of urban poverty, immorality, and crime.

of Unequal Wealth. In this tract, Byllesby examined the impact of the "machine age" on manual labor and called for producers' cooperatives to return to workers some control of the products of their labor. A correspondent to the New York *Daily Sentinel* in 1831 protested the dangers to pottery workers, who were being slowly poisoned by the lead in the glazes with which they worked, producing "enlarged spleen . . . loss of their teeth . . . [p]alsy of the limbs . . . [and] [c]onsumption of the lungs. . . ." Stonecutters were subject to "sundry diseases of the lungs," the writer added, and gilders to mercury poisoning.

Workers also turned out in huge numbers to hear labor organizers and social critics denounce the growing greed and inequities of American life. Scotswoman Frances Wright, one of the most flamboyant and popular of these speakers, focused especially on education and religion, charging that the clergy conspired to keep workers shackled to superstition. Wright, who lived for a time at Owen's New Harmony and attempted her own utopian community of Nashoba in Tennessee, also inveighed against slavery and advocated for women's rights. The explosive combination earned her the title "the red harlot of Infidelity" from more conservative citizens.

In addition to using these older forms of protest and redress, workers turned to labor unions. Earlier workers had formed numerous craft societies and some more militant labor combinations. The most famous of the early associations led the 1805 strike of Philadelphia journeyman boot- and shoemakers. The unions of the 1820s and 1830s combined craft society with militant association. They came into existence chiefly to oppose the overwhelming power of employers in early industrial society to control wages and hours. The unions' weapon was the strike.

Among the earliest of the new trade unions was one formed by New Orleans printers in 1823 to fight for the regular payment of agreed-upon wages. Over the remainder of the decade weavers, carpenters, tailors, cabinet makers, masons, stevedores, and workers in other crafts turned out on strike throughout the major cities of the nation. In 1825 Boston carpenters struck for the ten-hour workday. At issue in this strike was not only the status of workers, but also the meaning of labor in the republic. Strikers argued that the shorter day was essential if they were to have time to refresh themselves, to spend with their families, and to obtain the education necessary for newly enfranchised voters. Paternalistic employers countered that the 10-hour day would undermine "industry and economy of time" and would "expose the Journeymen themselves to many improvident temptations."

Cross-trade demands for the ten-hour day and the repeated failures of individual strikes helped bring about the formation of the earliest citywide and regional labor organizations, most of which were devoted to political action. The first, the Mechanics' Union, was established in Philadelphia in 1827. It grew out of earlier successful efforts to found the Mechanics' Library Company and a labor newspaper, the *Mechanics' Free Press,* both to promote worker self-education. Pledged to the ten-hour day, the Mechanics' Union protested the mental and spiritual exhaustion associated with industrialization and the larger "desolating evils which must inevitably arise from a depreciation of the intrinsic value of human labor."

When the Philadelphia Mechanics' Union dissolved, leadership of the ten-hour movement passed to the New England Association of Farmers, Mechanics, and Other Workingmen, founded in 1831 by, among others, Seth Luther. Convened in Boston, the New England Association invited "every citizen whose daily *exertions* . . . are his means of subsistence" to participate in its efforts to police conditions of labor and compile evidence to present to state legislatures. The association also used its newspaper, the *New England Artisan,* for worker self-education and organizing and published Luther's *Address to the Workingmen*—a pamphlet that ran through three editions. Luther's assault on the greed and power of employers touched the nerve of an economy in which the cost of living was quickly outstripping workers' pay.

Strikes multiplied throughout the 1830s. In February 1831, with wages in sharp decline, over 1,800 tailoresses (women who worked in specific aspects of the tailoring craft) struck the central shops and retail establishments of the New York garment industry. The tailoresses had been advised not to strike, that striking would only expose them to harsh public censure, that they should wait patiently for times to improve. "We have been told, my friends," declared Sarah Monroe, the secretary of the union, "that it is impossible for us to do anything at present to improve our miserable condition." But, Monroe asked, who would do so, if not the women themselves? She answered her own question: "Long have the poor tailoresses of this city borne their oppression in silence, until patience is no longer a virtue—and in my opinion to be silent longer would be a crime." The women drew up a constitution, elected officers, and stayed out on strike for five months.

At last, deteriorating conditions of labor led to protest even in that industrial paradise, Lowell (see chapter 10). After a decade of rapid expansion in which the owners had grown accustomed to dividends of up to 25 percent, the market stalled in 1834. In response to falling prices, the owners cut wages by 12 1/2 percent. In response, some 800 female operatives walked off their jobs in Lowell. The protest failed (owners used the break in production to lower their inventories), but two years later, when the owners tried to enforce an increase in the price of company housing, the operatives were ready. Two thousand went out on strike, forcing the owners to rescind the increases. The 1836 victory was fleeting, however. Business was booming, and the owners had a vested interest in keeping the mills open. As the failed strike of 1834 suggested, when business was slow or inventories high, workers would have far less power to assert their interests.

Workers attempted to strengthen their position by forming regional and national associations. Such linkages were now a possibility thanks to improved transportation and the greater interdependence of markets. Throughout the mid-1830s, carpenters, weavers, and cordwainers, among other workers in trades, tried in vain to form national trade associations. The most successful national association of the period was the National Trades' Union, formed in 1834 when the New York General Trades Union convened a conference for organizations from other cities. The NTU survived for a number of years, but it was unable to effect the type of statewide coordinated actions its organizers envisioned. Too many labor organizations remained local, and cross-city solidarity had little effect on a strike. In the end, much of the energy of the national union went into lobbying for currency reform, worker access to education, free land for workers, and the ten-hour day.

A New Urban Middle Class

Seth Luther framed his criticisms of American industrial society in terms of a struggle between "the producing classes" and the "rich," language inherited from the late eighteenth century. It was clear, however, that this bipartite division did not adequately capture the composition of American industrial society. Certainly, there were still rich Americans, the sources of their wealth now firmly grounded in business, manufacturing, transportation, and real estate. The concept of the "producing classes," however, was an ambiguous one, encompassing Americans of many different standards of living and levels of wealth. When Luther used the term he meant primarily urban-based households heavily dependent on wage labor. Luther sometimes fell into a more complex way of analyzing American society, distinguishing among the "poor," the "rich," and American's "middling classes." The idea of a middle group was not new. Americans had long taken pride in their great "middling" ranks of solid farmers and artisans. But the composition of the category had changed dramatically by the 1830s, as had its relation to the group Luther now called the "working classes."

These new "middling classes" were difficult to define exactly. They seldom identified themselves in economic terms, preferring designations that suggested qualities of character and reputation, like "respectable," "frugal," "useful" and "hard-working." Like the new "working classes," the "middling classes" were primarily urban based. Unlike those of industrial workers, however, middle-class households tended to receive their income in the form of fees and salaries, rather than wages, and their paid workers were employed in jobs that required mental, rather than physical, labor. These included doctors, lawyers, ministers, middle managers, agents, supervisors, tellers, clerks, shopkeepers, editors, writers, and schoolteachers.

The relationship of these urban households of moderate means to the new industrial economy was complicated. On the one hand, even families of moderate means were not immune to catastrophic economic reversal, in the form of sudden unemployment, business failure, or bad speculation. Popular essayist Lydia Maria Child underscored this point in her 1829 *The American Frugal Housewife*. Addressing "persons of moderate fortune," Child nevertheless concluded the book with a sobering chapter titled "How to Endure Poverty." In their letters and diaries, businessmen and professionals kept obsessive track of friends whose firms had gone under and whose jobs had been lost. Women, like Martha Coffin Wright of Auburn, New York, recorded their fears of "the mania for speculation, the reckless endorsing for others and the thousands of unprofitable schemes that are hurrying [their husbands] to ruin." Moreover, even middle-class workers understood that the world of paid work had become a brutalizing place where workers were driven to "exhausting labor" and corrupted by "coldness, jealousy, and slander," "frauds and corruptions."

At the same time, the new middle class was created by and benefited from the industrial transformation. The paid occupations on which middle-class families depended (the professions, supervisory positions, and office work) had all expanded enormously as a result of the growth of commerce and industrialization. These jobs brought annual salaries ranging roughly from $1,000 to $1,500, compared to the $300 to $400 an average workingman might earn, and enabled middle-class families to endure hard times with somewhat more security than working-class families could. In addition, middle-class families tended to have access to a variety of other resources, through family, friends, and business connections.

This contradictory relation to the market produced contradictory responses among the new middle class to the changes ongoing in American society in the antebellum years. On the one hand, they celebrated the new political economy that had produced their class. They generally commended the expansion of democracy, were unrestrained in their praise for the growth of individual opportunity, deplored lingering evidence of the special privilege of the wealthy, and congratulated themselves for aspiring merely to be "content" and not "longing after social notoriety." Few members of the urban middle class joined the most radical of the religious and reform movements, but as a group the new urban middle class was profoundly religiously oriented. Embracing with gusto the doctrines of personal agency, they were churchgoers who both donated to and participated in the causes of the Benevolent Empire. At the same time, the new middle class took great pains to insist that its success had come through hard work and steady habits, not through any good fortune of family or opportunity, and to seclude itself from the turmoil and economic struggles of early American industrial society.

In daily practice, however, individuals who aspired to urban middle-class status took far greater pains to distinguish themselves from the swelling ranks of the urban poor than from the exclusive ranks of the rich. This was especially evident in their understanding of personal responsibility and material success. In sermons and tracts, children's books and novels, members of the new middle class described the new industrial economy as a test of personal character. Success demonstrated not privilege or good luck, but rather superior individual industriousness and self-discipline; failure signified the opposite. It was a formulation that took its toll on the middle class itself, since middle-class families did fail, bringing on themselves all the social and psychological censure contained in their own philosophy of success. Nevertheless, middle-class writers continued to hone the broad idiom of the "common man" into the more class-based language of the "self-made man" of business. From this point of view, the middle class had become the repository of moderation in the changing political economy, the rhetorical equivalent of Jefferson's idealized "husbandmen" and of workers' "producers."

Meanwhile, middle-class families struggled in other ways to distinguish themselves from the working class. Middle-class parents recoiled from the "ungentility" of manual labor and urged their sons to become "a rich merchant, or a popular lawyer, or a broker." They expressed a new value for education, even for their daughters, both as a means to financial security and as a sign of social respectability. While workers crowded into smaller and smaller living areas, the emerging middle class expressed itself in terms of growing, separated, and increasingly elaborate residential space and sentimentalized its highly privatized household as the icon of American virtue. The ideal home of the emerging middle class, the "cottage," offered a private sitting room for the family (a refuge from the hazards of social life) and a separate "public" parlor for receiving guests. The parlor also provided a stage where the family could present tangible evidence of their successful arrival in the world of business: tables, Bibles, pictures, dishware, vases, sofas, ottomans, and a variety of other objects.

To emphasize their desired distance from the industrial world, members of the new urban middle class insisted upon a "natural" division of temperament and capability between men and women. Although men were required to expose themselves to the degradations of labor, they insisted, women were of a gentler disposition, intended by nature to remain at home, where their sweet influences and sustaining love could revive the hardened sensibilities of husbands and raise children protected from the ravages of industrialization.

This view of women as the primary influence on children represented a dramatic change from colonial opinions, which presumed that fathers were better fitted to form the moral character of children. Moreover, it was largely inaccurate when measured by the daily lives of most families of the new middle class. Many middle-class women pursued paid labor of some variety. Lydia Maria Child supported her hapless lawyer-husband with her writing. The earnings from Harriet Beecher Stowe's novels and stories were essential to her family's support. Other middle-class women took in boarders, did fancy sewing, opened schools, and worked in family-owned businesses, among other occupations. All women of the new middle classes worked unpaid at the daily labor of family health and well-being: cooking, cleaning, washing, ironing, preserving food, sewing, and caring for the children. Gradually, nonetheless, the new middle class asserted a view that associated women with the home and identified the home as the antithesis of labor. Respectable women affected not to work. Indeed, visible labor was a sign of probable immorality in a woman. Domestic womanhood became the primary symbol of middle-class respectability and a bulwark against the many contradictions of the new industrial political economy.

Immigration and Nativism

Swept up in enormous changes in the way they lived and worked, even those Americans who seemed to be benefiting from early industrial society were wary and alert for sources of potential danger (real or imagined) to their lives and families. Many labor leaders and utopianists felt that industrialists were posing that danger. More common, however, was the tendency of Americans to focus their anxieties on the poor, whom they deemed incapable of achieving republican virtue and liable to fall under the influence of demagogues or tyrants. For members of the new middle class, but also for many native-born working-class Americans, the new targets of such **nativism** were the immigrants, and especially the Catholic Irish (see Figure 12-2).

In spite of the difficulties encountered by wage workers, the robust economy of the United States proved a

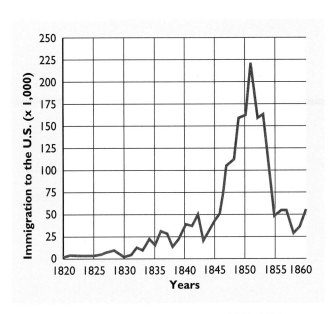

Figure 12-2 Increase of Irish Immigration, 1820–1850.

magnet for increasing numbers of immigrants from Europe, where economic turmoil continued to drive the poor from their livelihoods. Ninety percent of the immigrants came from England, Germany, or Ireland. The largest group by far was Irish (see Figure 12-2). Plagued by recurrent poverty and dominated by British rule, almost 60,000 Irish citizens migrated to the United States in the 1820s, 235,000 in the 1830s, and 845,000 during the potato famines of the 1840s. Through most of the period, Irish immigrants accounted for more than one-third of all immigrants. As early as the mid 1820s, however, in some years Irish immigrants accounted for more than half of all arrivals.

Even in the teeming streets of New York City, their customs and their poverty made Irish immigrants conspicuous. Unable to afford land that would permit them to resume their occupations as farmers, they remained crowded in the seaports where they arrived. Unfamiliar with urban life, they were the prey of city con artists who stole immigrants' luggage while pretending to haul it to a nearby boardinghouse or demanded finders' fees for jobs that never materialized. Desperate, they often had to accept jobs and conditions that native-born workers scorned. Because they had no other place to go, one boss observed, the Irish could "be relied on at the mill all year round." The employer of a largely Irish work force in Fall River, Massachusetts, declared coolly: "I regard [my] people just as I regard my machinery. . . . When my machines get old and useless, I reject them and get new, and these people are part of my machinery."

Not all of the Irish went into mills. Many of them took jobs with the construction companies, improving roadways, dredging river bottoms, and building new canals. The men dug and hauled, earning perhaps $10 a month plus their keep. Irish women cooked and did laundry for the camps or hired out as domestic workers in middle-class households.

Most of all, the Irish were distinguished by their Catholic religion. By 1830, immigration had virtually doubled the number of Catholics in the country. Not all Catholics were Irish, but many were—leaving the Irish particularly visible as targets of long-standing American anti-Catholic prejudices. In fact, anti-Irish sentiment was fed by all the insecurities of the new industrial society, but it often took the form of stereotypes that represented Catholics as given to superstition and unthinking obedience. Funded by members of the new middle class and supported by Protestant ministers, anti-Catholic newspapers had been on the increase in the United States since just after the War of 1812, when immigration began to resume. Numbering some 30 by 1827, these periodicals charged the Catholic hierarchy with "tyrannical and unchristian" acts "repugnant to our republican institutions." The American Bible Society also assumed an aggressive, if tacit, anti-Catholic stance, emphasizing its intention to "encourage a wider circulation of the Holy Scriptures without note or comment," a direct swipe at the Catholic Church's claims to authority over Christian scripture.

By the early 1830s, growing anti-Catholicism spilled over into street violence. Anti-Catholic organizations such as the New York Protestant Association, founded in 1831, sponsored "public discussions" on the immorality of monks, the greed of priests, and the Pope's alleged designs on the American West. The public debates soon deteriorated into small riots, which Protestant newspaper editors described as Papist attacks on "the liberty of free discussion." Anti-Catholicism took an especially dangerous turn in Massachusetts. The state had been the scene of a series of minor nativist incidents since the late 1820s. In 1834, on the defensive from the growth of new Protestant denominations, the associated Congregational Clergy of Massachusetts issued a frantic challenge to all Protestants to rescue the republic from "the degrading influence of Popery." In the weeks that followed, sermons from pulpits (including the pulpit of Lyman Beecher) and editorials from newspapers whipped up a frenzy of anti-Catholic fear. The hysteria was aimed especially at an Ursaline Convent in Charleston, which operated a public school in which, purportedly, nuns were

In 1834 unemployed native-born workers in Charlestown, Massachusetts, blamed their troubles on competition from Irish immigrants. Incited by a series of local anti-Catholic addresses, on August 11 they burned an Ursaline Convent to the ground, charging that the teaching sisters of the order were brainwashing their Protestant students.

brainwashing their innocent Protestant students. On the night of August 11, 1834, a mob of workers (perhaps joined by members of the community) burst into and eventually torched the convent, cheering as it burned to the ground. Anti-Catholicism was beginning to serve as a bond among Americans who otherwise had less and less in common with one another.

Internal Migration

The constant stream of internal migrants also heightened the sense of antebellum America as a society in turmoil. Like immigration, the swirl of internal migration held mixed and contradictory implications. It was evidence of growth and new opportunity. But it also produced a constant stream of individuals who seemed to have no settled stake in American society, people who were always on the move.

Many of these travelers were westward settlers, but many were rural folks losing out in the industrial revolution and migrating to the cities in search of employment. They were mainly unmarried young adults, leaving the family farm in search of better opportunities, and most were male. There was both a push and a pull to this internal movement. Children were pushed out from farming families whose land could no longer support them or be subdivided for inheritance. They were pulled to the cities by the very conditions that spelled disaster for the artisan tradition: the breakdown of the apprenticeship system and the subdivision of skills, which created new jobs for young workers from the farms.

In the cities, these young people sometimes roomed with family friends or relatives, but they often lived in rented rooms, apart from adult guidance. Young men joined neighborhood fire companies that served as gathering places for fun and sport. Young women navigated the city unescorted and dated young men disapproved of by parents. Young men and women used their earnings to buy the things unavailable in the countryside: new shoes, jackets, trousers, dresses of the latest cut, hats, and canes. Perhaps most unsettling of all, these young people moved almost too fast to be counted. In Rochester, New York, one newspaper editor estimated that 120 people left town every day, and another 130 arrived. Probably 75 percent of these people were under 30 years of age.

Migrants did not usually move very far in any single trek, traveling the fairly short distances to the nearest large towns and cities. Nonetheless, they swelled the populations of the midsized cities in which most American manufacturing took place. About 50 miles up the Schuylkill River from Philadelphia, Reading, Pennsylvania, sat in the middle of a prosperous agricultural and manufacturing region and was a hub for regional transportation and trading. In the 1840s alone, Reading's population doubled to 15,000 people. Nearly half of the unskilled laborers in

Reading had not been born in the city but had come from within 25 miles, mainly from areas with poor land and big families.

Although the West was the bright emblem of American opportunity, the constant, restless migration of Americans westward also provoked alarm among the eastern, urban middle class. Moralistic urban observers worried that this migration west was sapping ambitious, upright citizens away from the East Coast, exposing them to the dangers of the wilderness, and leaving the dregs of society behind. Most of the westward migrants were native born. They were not irresponsible and rootless young adults, moreover, but rather married couples beginning families. They were not people without other options; the very expense of outfitting a trip westward ensured that most settlers were from at least the lower margins of the middling classes.

Observers like Lyman Beecher (author of *A Plea for the West*) worried about the influence of the West on future American citizens. The West lacked all those institutions that easterners (especially New Englanders) associated with civilization and civic responsibility. There were few schools and churches and too many unattached young men, saloons, and brothels. Moreover, in some respects the process of westward migration canonized the very materialism and greed that easterners were beginning to worry about in their own communities. On the trail and in the new western settlements, the ambition for money was very strong, driving some families on and on in an almost endless migration. One family, the Shelbys, had made at least four major moves by 1850, when they ended up in Oregon. The father had been born in Kentucky, the mother in Tennessee, three children in Illinois, three in Iowa, and the youngest in Oregon. By 1860, over 350,000 of those born in the Old Northwest had already left for the new frontiers of Minnesota, Iowa, Kansas, and Oregon.

Into this land of apparently very unsteady habits were being born more and more of the nation's young. Once the frontier had passed the stage of initial exploration and families had begun to pour in, fertility rates in the newly settled areas became far higher than they were in the older, coastal regions. In New England in 1830, there were about 800 children under 5 years of age for every 1,000 women. In the Old Northwest, there were about 1,700 children under 5 for every 1,000 women. Easterners were alarmed by the specter of a generation of children growing up in the wilderness, without the proper social constraints. Especially for native-born observers on the East Coast, the times seemed precarious indeed. The values of self-reliance, industry, and civic virtues, values that only a decade before had seemed to capture the essence of American nationalism, appeared to be in danger of being trampled under the stampeding feet of change. By the 1820s, these observers had begun to focus their fears on the growing waves of European immigrants.

Self-Reform and Social Regulation

Acknowledging a tone of "decided hostility" in his address to workingmen in 1832, Seth Luther explained that he rose to uncover "principles and practices which will, if not immediately eradicated and forsaken, destroy all the rights, benefits, and privileges intended for our enjoyment, as a free people." Luther's combativeness stood in contrast to the approach of earlier reformers, who had adopted a far more optimistic tone. Faced with the deep divisions and seemingly insurmountable obstacles to perfecting industrial society, American reformers began to refocus their efforts, from broad programs of social perfection to endeavors that centered on self-control and, when necessary, strengthened external restraint. The shift clearly reflected the sensibilities of the new middle class, but it was often endorsed by members of the laboring classes, who despaired of meaningful improvement from the benevolence of others.

A Culture of Self-Improvement

Answering criticisms from fellow senators that only the rich and well-connected enjoyed the benefits of the new American industrial order, in 1832 Henry Clay rose to the defense of the new American entrepreneurial class. "In Kentucky," he asserted, "almost every manufactory known to me is in the hands of enterprising and self-made men, who have acquired whatever wealth they possess by patient and diligent labor." Clay's emphasis on personal enterprise in business life echoed Charles Finney's emphasis on personal agency in spiritual life and captured a perspective that was increasingly common among ambitious Americans by the 1830s. Success or failure in the new industrial order was less a matter of external injustice and constraint than of individual striving. Those who truly worked hard—who were industrious and clever and frugal—would of course succeed. Those who did not, would not. This celebration of personal ambition and self-improvement, often to the exclusion of recognizing external barriers to success, amounted to a profound reframing of that key tenet of Jacksonian democracy, the assault on unfair privilege. In the culture of the self-made man, there was no unfair privilege. There were only those who strove and those who did not.

The new emphasis on self-improvement was not limited to the privileged. Poor Americans, African American and white, had long pooled their resources in self-help societies. They were quick to perceive the importance of self-reliance. In a rapid changing society, workers were especially eager for access to information. Much of the popularity of radical labor lecturers like Fanny Wright resided in their attacks on the cultural controls of "professional aristocrats."

Frances Wright, a Scotswoman who spent much of her time in the United States between 1824 and her death in 1852, was a charismatic advocate of labor unions, workers' education, women's rights, religious free thought and abolition, and a fervent support of Andrew Jackson.

As well as denouncing the efforts of organized religion to enchain the minds of the working classes, Wright decried workers' dependence on wealthy individuals (whose interests had little in common with the interests of workers) for everything workers knew about their bodies and their world. Wright founded a "Hall of Science" in the Bowery in New York where workers could educate themselves about a variety of subjects (including health matters).

The teachings of health reformer Samuel Thomson sprang from a similar desire to democratize education. Thomson was a New Hampshire farmer who believed that both his mother and his wife had been victimized by the brutal techniques of professional physicians. Convinced that doctors cared more about their fees than their patients' health, Thomson resolved to resurrect the herbal treatments he had received as a youth—treatments families could administer themselves at low cost. Thomson popularized his methods through repeated tours across the North and then, after 1822, in his *New Guide to Health*. By 1839 the book had sold over 100,000 copies.

Yet, as Clay's words had implied, the culture of self-improvement enjoyed a particular popularity among members of the new middle class, who eagerly endorsed the theology of industry and personal enterprise and considered themselves entirely "self-made." The emphasis on self-creation also reflected the reclusive character of middle-class life and helped to resolve middle-class ambivalence about industrial society: middle-class families had escaped the worst ravages of wage labor, not because they were lucky or because they had some special advantage, but because they worked harder.

Americans' enormous interest in self-improvement in the antebellum years was reflected in their enthusiasm for public lectures, known as the lyceum movement. This cartoon gently spoofed a lecture by James Pollard Espy, a meteorologist. As the drawing suggests, women were prominent in lyceum audiences.

The culture of self-improvement was not limited to lessons for the mind and spirit, however. It embraced the body as well. As early as 1822, when a group of prominent Philadelphia physicians organized the American Phrenological Association, Americans had demonstrated a growing fascination with the study of the skull and the structure of the face as maps to physiological and character traits. Although many phrenologists did not believe that skull type determined social status, phrenology provided a framework within which prospering Americans could justify both their good fortune and the misfortunes of others, especially immigrants, Native Americans, and African Americans.

Over the 1820s, 1830s, and 1840s, health reform became a national obsession, as Americans experimented with new diets, new ways of dressing, vastly increased programs of exercise, abstinence in various forms, and hydropathy, the cleansing of the body through frequent bathing and the drinking of water. Particularly influential among the health reformers were Samuel Thompson and, slightly later, Sylvester Graham.

Sylvester Graham came to prominence in 1832 as Americans braced themselves for a return of cholera. In a highly successful series of lectures, Graham argued that Americans were especially susceptible to illness because they ate too much meat and spicy food and drank too much alcohol, coffee, and tea. Graham recommended a diet of fruits, vegetables, and coarsely ground wheat (the origin of the Graham cracker), combined with regular bathing and the wearing of loose clothing. By 1834, Graham had extended his regimen of self-discipline to include sexual appetites, warning that sexual excess in any form (certainly masturbation, but also including too frequent

sexual relations between spouses) "cannot fail to produce the most terrible effects."

Hungry for this message, men and women of the new middle class crowded lectures and devoured written materials that espoused the philosophy of self-culture. In the mid-1820s, this rush for information became more formal. In 1826 New Englander Josiah Holbrook published *Associations of Adults for Mutual Education,* which proposed a network of lectures and libraries focused on dispersing "rational and useful information through the community," with the ultimate goal of "raising the moral and intellectual taste" of Americans. By 1831 the resulting lyceum movement claimed several thousand local organizations and a national umbrella association and sponsored such speakers as the writer Ralph Waldo Emerson, Daniel Webster, and later Abraham Lincoln himself. Meanwhile, middle-class readers supported a publishing bonanza in novels, periodicals, and tracts devoted to themes of self-improvement.

These publications promoted a variety of images of the self-made American. In his *Leatherstocking Tales,* James Fenimore Cooper celebrated the pioneer, escaping from urban blight and moneyed decadence to test his true mettle on the American frontier. Novels like Catharine Sedgwick's *Rich Man, Poor Man* romanticized urban poverty and suggested that "true wealth" (virtue, not necessarily material prosperity) lay easily within the reach of even the most humble family, if only they worked hard and shunned aristocratic pretensions.

Although in most of its manifestations, the myth of the self-made American was decidedly male, focusing on the self-reliance of backwoodsmen or the self-discipline of young men preparing for business, it also implied a new emphasis on childrearing and therefore on women. Prescriptive writers certainly directed their attention to fathers, but their primary audience was mothers. Periodicals like the *Ladies Magazine* and *Godey's Lady's Book* (both edited by popular author Sarah Josepha Hale) and advice books like Lydia Maria Child's *The Mother at Home* and William Alcott's *The Young Mother* instructed women on the development of proper mental and moral habits in the young. Writers like Catharine Beecher launched long careers as advisors on the management of safe, well-regulated households, both teaching about female self-reliance and modeling that behavior in their own lives.

A generation of female novelists also appropriated the themes of self-culture (especially as they applied to women) for their fiction. Catharine Maria Sedgwick was the daughter of a self-made lawyer. In her 1827 novel, *A New-England Tale,* she told the story of a young orphan, left penniless and alone by an improvident wealthy father and an ineffectual, pampered mother. Jane, the protagonist of the tale, learns through her trials that hard work builds both economic independence and strength of character and is appropriately rewarded at the end of the story with a prosperous husband, children, and a safe middle-class home.

Some writers mounted a determined (if contradictory) assault on the new American political economy. American Transcendentalists like Ralph Waldo Emerson, Margaret Fuller, and William Ellery Channing believed in the power of the independent mind not only to understand the material environment, but also to transcend sensory perceptions and achieve a perfect spiritual wholeness with the world. They also saw that in contemporary America self-improvement was often cultivated only for immediate material gain. In his essay "Self-Reliance" (published in 1841) Emerson tried to distinguish true independence of mind from slavish rushing after preferment and celebrity. "Society is a joint-stock company," he wrote, "in which the members agree, for the better securing of his bread to each shareholder, to surrender the liberty and culture of the eater. The virtue in most request is conformity. Self-reliance is its aversion." Although Emerson was a professional man, not a laborer, in many respects his attack on the political economy of antebellum America echoed the themes of Seth Luther's.

Temperance

Of the many movements for regulating the body, the largest by far—and the longest lived—was the temperance movement. By the 1840s hundreds of thousands of Americans had taken the pledge to swear off demon rum.

Prior to the nineteenth century, liquor played a traditional, central role in the work and social lives of Americans. The Puritans (even the ministers) had insisted on having their good supply of wine, beer, and hard cider. In craft shops, workers took rum breaks from their labor. The construction boss or ship's captain who did not supply the customary barrel of rum (albeit watered down) was in for trouble from his workers. As one visitor from England complained: "You cannot go into hardly any man's house without being asked to drink wine, or spirits, even in the morning." Well into the 1840s advice-manual writers felt they needed to convince mothers that it was safe to forego the occasional dollop of hard spirits to the children.

Some religious groups, especially the Quakers and the Methodists, had opposed the drinking of hard liquor in the eighteenth century, but it was only in the early nineteenth century, in Saratoga, New York, in 1808, that the first temperance society was formed. Within the next five years, at least four more temperance societies were established in New England. The founders were generally ministers and professional men, and the "temperance" for which they called concerned only hard liquor, and even that was permitted "for medicinal purposes."

In the 1820s, the temperance movement was taken over by evangelicals who understood demon rum as the enemy, not just of piety, but of that self-control so central to the broad perfecting of society. Working through the camp meetings and revivals of the teens and twenties, evangelists began to depict drinking as one of the signs of social

The cover of this almanac revealed the association of alcohol with the working classes and with sin. Notice the devil figure lurking in the background, tending the still, and the neglected children in the foreground.

disorder in democratic America. Propounding this new view, in a series of six sermons preached through the fall of 1825, Lyman Beecher effectively changed the debate over alcohol. He called not for moderation, but rather for absolute abstinence from hard liquor, and he inveighed upon his followers to form voluntary associations all across the land to drive the demon rum from American society. The following February saw the formation of the American Society for the Promotion of Temperance. ASPT workers asked a new convert to sobriety to sign a pledge, placing a "T" beside the signature to indicate "Total Abstinence" (shortened to "teetotaler"). Using the structure of the Benevolent Empire, the ASPT quickly set about organizing local chapters across the country. By 1834 there were at least 5,000 state and local temperance societies. Most of these were in the North, but there were also many in the West and the South.

By no means were all of the advocates of temperance Protestant, middle-class reformers. In April of 1840 a group of six mechanics and artisans met in a Baltimore tavern, swore off liquor, and founded the Washingtonian society (named in honor of the first president, who *did* in fact drink). Within three years, some 600,000 men, many of them working class, had joined the Washingtonians. Unlike the primarily male American Society for the Promotion of Temperance, the Washingtonian movement encouraged the development of separate female societies, called "Martha Washington Temperance Societies." Women brought their own perspective to the critique of alcohol. Protestant evangelicals had attacked drink as sin, or as undermining self-discipline. Increasingly, Washingtonians concentrated on drunkenness as the destroyer of families. It was in this form that the temperance movement would, in the 1840s and after, become a major issue of women's movements.

The Common School Movement

By the 1830s workers, members of the new middle class, and elite philanthropists all identified education as a critical arena for reform. In this as in other reform movements, however, the motives of different groups varied widely.

Since the founding of the nation, educational opportunities for the sons and daughters of more prosperous parents had steadily increased—especially in the middle and northern states. Children from the wealthiest urban families had private tutors, followed (for boys) by formal training in private seminaries and academies. Opportunities for daughters had also gradually improved. A host of transient "adventure" schools offered education for young women in the South. By the 1820s young women from prosperous northern families could choose from a growing number of formal seminaries, such as Emma Willard's Troy (New York) Female Academy (founded in 1821), Catharine Beecher's Hartford (Connecticut)

Female Seminary (founded in 1823), or Mary Lyon's Mount Holyoke Female Seminary (founded in 1837 in South Hadley, Massachusetts). Meanwhile, subscription schools offered basic education to rural children.

These schools were out of reach for working-class children, whose parents could not afford tuition and sometimes could not afford to release their children from wage-earning labor. Labor reformers linked this lack of schooling directly to the larger process of industrial oppression and to workers' diminishing status as free and equal citizens of the republic. In their 1831 constitution, the Working Men's Association of New York placed the demand for "a system of equal, republican education" above every other goal, convinced, as they explained, that education "secures and perpetuates every political right we possess." Seth Luther elaborated the theme in his 1832 "Address to the Working Men of New England," blasting industrialization as "a cruel system of exaction on the bodies and the minds of the producing classes," preventing "the producing classes from a participation in the fountains of knowledge." Luther pointed to Pawtucket, Rhode Island, birthplace of the American textile industry, where the necessity for long hours of labor had resulted in "at least five hundred children who scarcely know what a school is." Benevolent reformers had founded charity schools in many eastern cities, but workers saw these as inferior—an "odious system...the bare idea of which impresses a consciousness of degradation," as Stephen Simpson declared in his 1831 *A Working Man's Manual.* Only free public education, workers argued, could defy "the siege of aristocracy."

Many middle-class parents were also unable to afford the costs of private academies, a circumstance that mattered more and more as they contemplated the treacherousness of the new economy and their own inability to provide appropriate occupational training. Master craftsmen and farmers did not have the skills to prepare their sons for jobs as insurance clerks and bank tellers, and insurance clerks and bank tellers did not work in their residences, where earlier generations of sons had learned their fathers' callings at their knees. In 1830, worried fathers in Utica, New York, called for a public-school system that would permit children to "keep pace with the age in its improvements" and "calculate their own profits in the world."

Middle-class parents were anxious about daughters as well as sons. They worried about the new burdens on mothers, and they worried that traditional skills of housewifery would be of little use to daughters who faced the demands of increasingly complex market relations and new domestic technologies, including furnaces and the cast iron stove. Most of all, they worried that their daughters might not marry or might marry into families that would face financial ruin. These conditions suggested that daughters, as well as sons, should be educated.

Emma Willard, on the left, and Catharine E. Beecher, on the right, were two pioneers in women's education. Willard's Troy Female Seminary opened in September 1821 with public funding. Its curriculum included science, mathematics, and social studies. Beecher founded a number of schools for girls and young women, the earliest of which was the Hartford Female Seminary, founded in 1823. Both schools offered academically rigorous curricula.

Reformers often also supported expanded public education out of anxieties that the expanded suffrage would introduce volatility into the American electoral process. "The great bulwark of republican government is the cultivation of education," Governor Clinton urged the New York legislature in 1827, "for the right of suffrage cannot be exercised in a salutary manner without intelligence." If white workingmen and their sons were to vote, it was important that they first be educated.

This convergence of interests led to a growing demand for expanded common schools in the late 1820s and throughout the 1830s. Nevertheless, broad segments of the American public resisted the idea. In Cincinnati, wealthy property owners opposed paying taxes to send poor children to school. In Rhode Island, ministers' organized and vocal support for free schools awakened fears of a religious takeover of education and galvanized a backlash among citizens. Other skeptics considered the whole idea an invasion of their basic rights as free citizens. In the 1820s and early 1830s, states were often reduced to passing simple enabling legislation, like Pennsylvania's 1834 act, that made public schools a local option. In Pennsylvania, fewer than

half the possible districts actually established local public schools at the time.

In 1837 the Massachusetts legislature at last ventured further, creating a state Board of Education and appointing long-time educational reformer Horace Mann as its first secretary. Mann proved a great success, in large part because he was able to frame the common school debate in language that reflected the anxieties of more prosperous Americans—about their own children and about the children of workers. On the one hand, he reassured middle-class parents that relying on an extrafamilial institution was both right and natural, given the vast changes of the previous half century. On the other hand, he assured them that nothing else need change about the industrial society on which they depended. Poverty, he later wrote, was "no part of the eternal ordinances of Heaven." It was not decreed by God or required by American society, which had the potential to produce wealth "more than sufficient to supply all the rational wants of every individual." Only the lack of education barred the poor from prosperity. "When we have spread competence through all the abodes of poverty," Mann reassured his fellow citizens, "when we

Mary Lyon opened Mount Holyoke Female Seminary (later Mount Holyoke College) in 1837 in South Hadley, Massachusetts. Lyon made a superb academic education available, even to girls of moderate means, by requiring that the students do part of the domestic work of the school.

have substituted knowledge for ignorance," then America would realize its long-deferred potential as the treasury of human virtue. Reframing the question from one of class antagonism to one of class uplift, Mann provided a comforting vision of a world in which benevolence and education would "disarm the poor of their hostility toward the rich."

Whites were less concerned about the potential hostility of the small free African-American community. Until the 1850s, free African-American children were excluded from public common schools, and public-school tax monies were not used to establish schools for African Americans. Meanwhile, improvements in education for free African-American children came almost entirely from the work of the free African-American community, where benevolent foundations, churches, and mutual aid societies all struggled to raise money for better schools. In the North, the efforts bore fruit, but in the South hardening opposition to the education of slaves severely blocked efforts of free African-American students. In fact, many enslaved and free African-American southerners did learn to read and write, but usually surreptitiously in secret schools held in private homes.

Penal Reform

In the first years of the republic, when memories of British injustice were still fresh, Americans tended to think of crime as a problem of bad laws, not flawed individual character. Fair laws would nurture good republican character, and good republican citizens would respect laws they had a hand in passing. In a series of state constitutional conventions at the opening of the nineteenth century, citizens had presumably clarified and rationalized their laws, even as they had broadened the franchise.

Yet by the 1820s eastern cities were incarcerating thousands of their citizens—some for debt (which a growing number of people considered inappropriate in a republican government) but many for robbery, larceny, fraud, vagrancy, and disorderly conduct. To many Americans—especially members of the wary new middle class—it seemed that the early approaches had failed. Good laws were not sufficient to create a good citizenry. Like salvation, law-abiding behavior was in part a function of the efforts of the individual, regardless of the fairness of the law. Where individuals failed to make the necessary effort to obey the law, the community must devise some mechanism for its own protection.

The solution that enjoyed the greatest popularity from the 1820s on was the establishment of state prison systems, where deviant individuals could be kept apart from the striving community but where inmates might also be subjected to a regimen of rehabilitation. State and city prisons soon began to replace older charity institutions, especially almshouses. Connecticut, Massachusetts, Ohio, Maryland, and New Jersey all experimented in new designs, but all of these were variants of the two primary competing models, devised by New York and Pennsylvania. These two were actually variants on a single principle: that the first step in making prisons places of genuine reform was to prevent inmates from influencing one another.

The New York version was first tried at Auburn State Prison in the second decade of the century, but it later became most widely associated with the new New York penitentiary at Ossining, New York, known as Sing-Sing. At Sing-Sing, prisoners worked side by side all day but were prevented from talking or even looking at one another. They slept in separate cells. The Pennsylvania model, put into execution in Pittsburgh and Philadelphia in the later 1820s, called for absolute isolation of the prisoners.

Visitors to the United States often toured these prisons and frequently applauded them, but they also commented on the exaggerated hopes that Americans seemed to have invested in them. Famous French visitor Alexis de Tocqueville and his secretary and companion, Gustave Beaumont, observed of American reformers: "Philanthropy has become for them a kind of profession, and they have caught the monomanie of the penitentiary system, which to them seems to remedy for all the evils of society."

But as de Tocqueville foresaw, even prisons did not answer the need for greater surveillance and social control felt by prosperous urban Americans. In the 1840s, American reformers enlarged their "monomanie" to include urban police forces. Replacing the older, more casual system of night "watches," the new urban police forces' main work was scarcely reformatory at all. Their goal was to keep the city safe for wealthy citizens and the new middle class—not to save the poor, but simply to keep them off the streets.

Conclusion

By the time Andrew Jackson left office in 1837, the coalition that had elected him and given character and vibrancy to the promise of Jacksonian democracy was deeply divided. Conflict and confrontation were time-honored instruments of American political culture, and they had sometimes served the purposes of unification, but the ruptures of the 1830s seemed both more volatile and more permanent. In the wake of increasing social and economic differentiation in the American political economy, it was hard to say just who the American "common man" was. Jackson himself always associated the image with tough-minded western settlers, but angry urban wage workers pointed out that it was *their* labor that was fueling the new industrial system, while anxious members of the new middle class insisted that they best embodied republican industriousness and virtue. As the decade wore on, these differences produced sharper and sharper conflicts.

In this context, the impulse for reform, once the source of so much optimism, now became the tool of division. Middle-class reformers took refuge in new mechanisms of control—of themselves and of others—and a small but growing number of Americans, weary with a history of compromises with slavery, began to demand that the first item of reform be to purify the nation of the moral stain of slavery. In the nation's short history, the West had always functioned as the republic's social and cultural release. Soon that symbol of national reconciliation and prosperity would itself become the site and the symbol of America's insoluble conflicts.

CHRONOLOGY

1822 Denmark Vesey conspiracy
Samuel Thomson publishes *New Guide to Health*

1826 General Colored Association of Massachusetts formed
American Society for the Promotion of Temperance formed

1827 Russwurm and Cornish found *Freedom's Journal*

1828 Andrew Jackson elected president
Tariff of 1828
Calhoun writes *South Carolina Exposition and Protest*

1829 David Walker publishes *An Appeal to the Colored Citizens of the World*

1830 National Negro Convention Movement begins

1831 Nat Turner leads rebellion in Virginia
William Lloyd Garrison begins publication of *The Liberator*
New England Anti-Slavery Society founded
New England Association of Farmers, Mechanics, and Other Workingmen founded

New York Protestant Association founded
Lyceum movement begins

1832 Tariff of 1832
Jackson re-elected
South Carolina passes Nullification Resolution
Maria Stewart lectures in Boston

1833 Congress passes Force Bill
American Anti-Slavery Society founded

1834 Anti-African American riots in major cities
Anti-Catholic mob burns Ursaline Convent in Charleston, Massachusetts
Lowell operatives go on strike
National Trades' Union formed

1835 American Anti-Slavery Society begins postal campaign
Lyman Beecher publishes *A Plea for the West*

1836 Congress passes "Gag Rule"

1837 Abolitionist editor Elija Lovejoy murdered in Alton, Illinois
Bread riots in New York City
Massachusetts creates first State Board of Education; Horace Mann appointed secretary

Review Questions

1. Although workers had organized and struck in earlier periods, the late 1820s and the 1830s witnessed unprecedented surge of worker protest. What changing conditions help account for the timing of this activity?

2. Why did the reform impulse, once the very cement of the Jacksonian coalition, become a source of conflict in the 1830s?

3. Explain the difference between "immediatism" and other forms of antislavery sentiment.

4. The Nullification Crisis was not the first time Americans had threatened to withdraw from the union. List precedents since 1789, and explain the similarities and differences between those earlier episodes and the Nullification Crisis.

5. Was the culture of self-reform and self-regulation entirely a movement of the new urban middle class? Provide specific examples to support your conclusion. Explain why Americans might have become especially concerned about matters of self-control in the 1820s and 1830s.

6. Why did some white northerners violently oppose abolition?

Further Readings

Lawrence J. Friedman, *Gregarious Saints: Self and Community in American Abolitionism, 1830–1870* (1982). Friedman provides a compelling overview of the immediatist wing of the United States abolition movement, from its origins in early nineteenth-century millennialism to victory in the Civil War, and offers detailed discussions of such leaders as Garrison, Arthur and Lewis Tappan, Marie Weston Chapman, Gerrit Smith, and Lucretia Mott.

Carl F. Kaestle, *Pillars of the Republic: Common Schools and American Society, 1780–1860* (1983). This fine survey traces Americans' views of education and education policy from the founding of the nation to the eve of the Civil War, grounding the common school movement in the broad social and cultural currents of the early republic.

Leon F. Litwack, *North of Slavery: The Negro in the Free States, 1790–1860* (1961). Litwack provides a thorough and illuminating depiction of the restrictions on African Americans' civil, legal, and economic rights in the "free" antebellum North.

David R. Roediger, *The Wages of Whiteness: Race and the Making of the American Working Class* (1991). This collection of essays explores the importance of racialized thinking in the emergence of the wage system in the North, with particular attention to the importance of the institution of slavery in shaping Northern "free labor" ideology.

Christine Stansell, *City of Women: Sex and Class in New York, 1789–1860* (1986). In one of the very few studies of the impact of urbanization, the industrial reorganization of labor, and early class formation on laboring women, Stansell explores the ways in which working-class women's experiences differed both from those of men in their class and from more prosperous women.

David Walker, *David Walker's Appeal to the Coloured Citizens of the World* (1995). Calling upon Africans in all nations to unite against racial injustice and urging African Americans in the United States to take control of their own destinies by whatever means were available, including armed rebellion, Walker's 1829 *Appeal* illuminates the growing assertiveness of free African Americans organizing in the 1820s.

History on the Internet

"John C. Calhoun: A Brief Introduction"
http://xroads.virginia.edu/~CAP/CALHOUN/jcc1.html
This site offers an excellent introduction to the world and mind of Calhoun. It also provides instructive information on the Nullification Crisis and the growing sectionalism that gripped the nation.

"Free Blacks in the Antebellum Period"
http://lcweb2.loc.gov/ammem/aaohtml/exhibit/aopart2.html
Read about the struggles and accomplishments of free African Americans during this era. Rare books and pamphlets illustrate the free African-American press and their own quest for nationwide freedom.

"A Treatise on Domestic Economy—A Mission"
http://xroads.virginia.edu/~CAP/UTC/bchaps.html
Known as an authority on middle-class domesticity, Catharine Beecher explains, in her 1841 volume, the areas that were proper and suitable pursuits for middle-class women of the era—domestic issues ranging from home care to cooking to childcare. Here, read one chapter of her guidebook for women titled "Peculiar Responsibilities of American Women."

"Men and Women in the Early Industrial Era"
http://www.albany.edu/history/history316/history316f2000.html
This site provides excellent links to numerous primary-source documents that address the early struggle for labor reform and life on the shop floor.

13

MANIFEST DESTINY

1836-1848

OUTLINE

Mah-i-ti-wo-nee-ni Remembers Life on the Great Plains

The Setting of the Jacksonian Sun
Political Parties in Crisis
Van Buren and the Legacy of Jackson
Electoral Politics and Moral Reform
An Independent Woman's Rights Movement

The Political Economy of the Trans-Mississippi West
Texas

Pacific-Bound
Nations of the Trans-Mississippi West

Slavery and the Political Economy of Expansion
Log Cabins and Hard Cider: The Election of 1840
And Tyler, Too
Occupy Oregon, Annex Texas
War With Mexico

Conclusion

Mah-i-ti-wo-nee-ni Remembers Life on the Great Plains

As recorded when she was interviewed years later, Mah-i-ti-wo-nee-ni was born sometime in the mid-1830s in the Black Hills. Her homelands had been a part of Jefferson's Louisiana Purchase from France in 1803, and they would later become the states of South Dakota and Wyoming. In the 1830s, however, the Great Plains were still Indian country.

Mah-i-ti-wo-nee-ni's father was Cheyenne, and her mother was Lakota (or Sioux). The Lakota had long been respected as a raiding society, known for their prowess in war. The Cheyennes had once been a semiagricultural people who "planted corn every year . . ., then went hunting all summer," pursuing buffalo, elk, and smaller game on foot and returning in the fall to gather the crops. The horse changed all that. First introduced to the southern plains by the invading Spanish armies, horses were probably common throughout the region by the early eighteenth century. They made the Plains Indians faster and better hunters and more effective raiders, and they created a highly specialized nomadic way of life. By the time Mah-i-ti-wo-nee-ni was born, the Cheyennes had long since given up settled farming, organizing their life around the hunt and foraging "wild turnips, wild sweet potatoes and other root foods" and berries as they went.

The horse made the Plains a place of constant movement. Whole villages migrated to seasonal hunting grounds. Competing for game, villages sent out war parties against one another or fast-moving raiders to steal horses or take captives for later exchange. Individuals and small groups criss-crossed the landscape in search of trade. Mah-i-ti-wo-nee-ni recalled a time in her childhood (probably in 1840) when the Cheyennes and the Arapahoes traveled south to meet in a great peace council with their traditional enemies, the Kiowas, Comanches, and Apaches. The

northern Indians traded guns and blankets for horses, returning home, Mah-i-ti-wo-nee-ni remembered, with "more horses than we had ever owned before."

Although Mah-i-ti-wo-nee-ni did not remember much contact with white people during this tranquil period of her life, the signs of white encroachment were already evident at the time of the great southern peace council. In part, the horse's growing importance to the Cheyennes reflected the U.S. policies of removing eastern Indians to the Plains region. As eastern Indians were forced across the Mississippi, competition for food increased on the Plains. At the very moment of the great southern peace council, moreover, massive white overland migration to the Pacific was getting under way. Between 1840 and 1860 more than a quarter of a million people migrated from the eastern United States into the trans-Mississippi West. Some of them settled in the new republic of Texas or wound their way into northern Mexico, but many headed straight into the northern Plains, bound for Oregon and, after rumors of gold filtered north and east, the valleys of northern California. As they went, the migrants not only uprooted their own lives, but they uprooted as well the lives of the peoples whose lands they crossed and claimed. Missionaries exhorted Indians to convert to Christianity. Settlers trampled Indian plantings, destroyed Indian settlements, spread disease, decimated the buffalo upon which the western Indians depended, and demanded the lands upon which Indian communities lived.

For the white settlers, migration across the Mississippi was simply another act in the personal search for liberty and opportunity and in the political process of nation building. The Jeffersonians of the early 1800s, the National Republicans of the 1820s, and the Jacksonians of the 1830s had all viewed territorial expansion as essential to the maintenance of a

363

republican political economy. It was in the West, many Americans had long believed, that the nation renewed its virtues and purified the republican model of government. In the mid-1840s Americans coined a lasting phrase for this association of land and liberty. Taking the continent was simply their "manifest destiny."

The United States settlement of the trans-Mississippi West implied a different manifest destiny for Mah-i-ti-wo-nee-ni and her people. Although she recalled virtually no contact with whites when she was very young, Mah-i-ti-wo-nee-ni did remember that after a while federal representatives began to appear among the Cheyennes. They offered gifts of brass kettles, coffeepots, knives, and wonderful striped blankets in return for Indian promises to recognize white land claims and to permit settlers to cross through Cheyenne lands unharmed. She also remembered the time when the U.S. government abandoned these efforts to coax the Cheyennes into giving up their lands voluntarily. In 1877, after years of struggle and compromise, Mah-i-ti-wo-nee-ni and her people were forcibly displaced from their homelands in the Black Hills and conveyed south into Indian Territory. Eventually, the other nations of the Great Plains were also forced onto reservations as the U.S. government continued, across the Mississippi, the policies it had developed in the eastern regions.

Because much of the land Americans sought for settlement lay within the boundaries of the nation of Mexico, the trans-Mississippi "manifest destiny" of white Americans also implied a destiny for Mexicans in the northern provinces of Mexico and, ultimately, for the Mexican nation itself. Claiming that they were mistreated by the Mexican government, white American settlers in the Mexican province of Coahuila y Tejas rebelled in 1836, formed the Republic of Texas, and immediately sought entry into the United States. Some American expansionists wanted more. In 1846 the United States provoked a war with Mexico to claim large portions of that nation's northern territories.

The costs of America's belief in its "manifest destiny" were not limited to the people whose lands Americans wanted, however. Those costs were also visited on the nation itself and its citizens. Since the 1790s, the protection of the

Most Native American cultures celebrated the arrival of boys and girls at adulthood. This painting portrays a Cheyenne coming-of-age ceremony—similar to one Mah-i-ti-wo-nee-ni may have experienced.

West (both slave and free) had been among the most important duties of the federal government, but by the 1840s questions of territorial expansion had become laden with controversy. Each stage of geographical expansion had required that the federal government reaffirm its commitment to the preservation of slavery in at least some part of the new territories. Thus, each step west forced the nation to revisit not only questions about the existence of the institution of slavery in a republic and growing sectional differences, but also the question of the morality of a government that was slavery's guarantor.

By the late 1830s those questions were both the source and focus of a wide range of internal conflicts. Free workers saw the extension of slavery as a threat to their already precarious standard of living. A vocal minority of northern reformers demanded the end of slavery as evidence of national morality. Fearing national discord, a second group of equally vehement white northerners arrayed itself against the abolitionists. Some white southerners made it clear that they were prepared to violate any law to protect slavery, and many white southerners were increasingly convinced that the federal government was conspiring against their way of life.

National in character and implication, these controversies flared within a national political system ill equipped to respond effectively to them or to defuse them. American politicians would continue to try to forge compromises to sidestep potentially explosive differences, but the party system was in disarray, and no strong leader arose to hold it together. To the contrary, in a number of ways Jackson's own charismatic leadership had helped weaken that system. His highly charged rhetoric encouraged Americans to conceive of politics as a righteous crusade against corruption. His uncompromising policies had contributed to broad social discontent, to the sharpening of sectional animosities, and ultimately to the weakening of his own party. His popularity had rendered the once-mighty Republican Party ineffective as an opposition or alternative. By 1848, in the face of a war in the West some viewed as being fought to protect slavery, some Americans were prepared to give up on their government altogether. ∎

KEY TOPICS

- The decline of moral suasion
- Pressures on the party system
- A woman's rights movement
- The annexation of Texas
- Expansion to the Pacific
- War with Mexico

The Setting of the Jacksonian Sun

In his 1837 inaugural address, Martin Van Buren announced emphatically that the nation had arrived at a "singularly happy!" condition. Less optimistic, Missouri Democrat Thomas Hart Benton observed that in Van Buren's ascendancy to office, and Jackson's departure, "the rising was eclipsed by the setting sun." Both views underestimated the difficult times ahead. By 1837, both the material and the moral costs of America's expansionist political economy and the flaws in Jackson's own policies were becoming dramatically apparent. Jackson had undermined the old Republican dynasty, but his own Democrat Party contained too many diverging interests to remain stable. Democrats were soon torn apart by the apparently irreconcilable differences between the nation's competing systems of political economy, one based on slavery and the other on wage labor. These party troubles were heightened by the fiscal consequences of the bank war. Elected in 1836, Martin Van Buren would lose re-election on the Democratic ticket by a landslide in 1840, and he would fail again when he ran on a third-party ticket in 1848.

Political Parties in Crisis

The expansion of white male suffrage and the translation of moral-reform agendas into electoral politics clearly energized American politics in the 1830s and 1840s. In 1840, 66 percent of the electorate voted in Massachusetts, 75 percent in Connecticut, and 77 percent in Pennsylvania. Yet the capacity of major political parties to accommodate a wide range of conflicting interests and beliefs, and remain effective, was limited.

Increasingly fractured since the election of 1824, the Republican Party struggled to reorganize on the basis of a shared hatred of Andrew Jackson. Jackson's war on the national bank offered the immediate occasion. Although unable to save the bank, Henry Clay and the anti-Jacksonians were able to pass (by a narrow 26 to 20 vote) a Senate resolution censuring Jackson for assuming "authority and power not conferred by the Constitution and the laws, but in derogation of both." It was in that debate that Clay identified the anti-Jackson position as "Whiggish" (opposed to executive tyranny, as had been the Whigs of seventeenth- and eighteenth-century England), a label that would stick to identify the new **Whig Party** Clay led.

Former National Republicans centered in the urban Northeast and upper West made up the bulk of the new party and defined its essential policies. Some of these were beginning to doubt the wisdom of uncontrolled geographic expansion, which seemed to promote political corruption and sectional conflict and implied the ongoing extension of slavery. Nevertheless, they continued to embrace market expansion and the elements of the American Plan: a new national bank, the enactment of a strong protective tariff to promote developing industries, and aggressive internal improvements. Fearing the power of wildcat settlers, wage workers, the faceless urban poor, and immigrants to subvert orderly economic relations, former National Republicans redoubled their commitment to a strong, interventionist government as necessary to ensure a stable market.

By 1834, some former Democrats were also disenchanted with the party of Jackson. Prospering urban shopkeepers and middling merchants were beginning to understand their own interests as distinct from those of the urban laboring classes. Uneasy with the turmoil of the streets, they were attracted by the Whig emphasis on personal and political discipline and order. Some southerners were still angry over the tariff and refused to forgive Jackson for his handling of the Nullification Crisis. Some small farmers and shopkeepers who had been wiped out by the Depression of 1837 blamed Jackson for their hard times. Workers, who had little trust for the merchant classes that made up the core of the new Whig Party, tended to form splinter parties or to stay with the Democrats.

With this assortment of interests, through most of the 1830s the Whigs remained an amorphous and disorganized opposition. Unable to decide on a single candidate, in 1836 the Whigs ran four regional challengers, hoping to deny Van Buren a majority in the Electoral College and throw the election to the House of Representatives. The Whig field included William Henry Harrison (Indiana, but nominated by an Antimason convention in Pennsylvania), Senator Hugh Lawson White (nominated by unhappy Democrats in Tennessee), Daniel Webster (nominated by the Massachusetts legislature), and Willie P. Mangum (a protest candidate of the South Carolina Nullifiers).

Jackson's vice president, Martin Van Buren, seemed exactly the candidate to withstand the Whig onslaught. To Van Buren went much of the credit for melding the competing constituencies into a successful Democrat coalition in the first place. In Washington, Van Buren had been constantly at Jackson's side, first as secretary of state and then as vice president. What's more, there was at least a chance that Van Buren could skirt rising sectionalism. His power in New York gave him a sufficient base in the North to risk publicly declaring himself "the inflexible and uncompromising opponent of any attempt on the part of Congress to abolish slavery in the District of Columbia" or to interfere with slavery "in the states where it exists." Van Buren was hopeful that this position, and the fact that he had supported William Crawford of Georgia for the presidency in 1824, would solidify southern support and allow him to "go into the presidential chair" (as he once put it) a *national* choice.

The results of the election of 1836 suggested otherwise. Not only was Van Buren unable to draw the nation together, but he almost did not "go into the presidential chair" at all. Van Buren did well in New York, New England (with the exception of Massachusetts), and the mid-Atlantic states, but he lost Ohio and Indiana in the Northwest and almost lost Pennsylvania. Unable to convince southerners that a northerner could head "the party of Jefferson," he lost Georgia (Crawford country), Tennessee, and South Carolina and barely captured Mississippi and Louisiana. Not only did Van Buren manage only a 26,000-vote popular majority (the combined Whig candidates took 49.1 percent of the vote), but his Electoral College majority of 170 votes was far closer than the numbers indicated. A shift of fewer than 2,000 votes in Pennsylvania would have deprived Van Buren of an Electoral College majority and thrown the election to the House of Representatives.

Van Buren and the Legacy of Jackson

Despite Van Buren's optimism, the signs of upcoming hard economic times were already visible when he was inaugurated in March of 1837. His first legacy from his mentor was the Panic of 1837.

The Panic was the direct result of the politics of the bank war, in combination with economic troubles in Europe. Jackson's various hard money measures, culminating in the Specie Circular (see chapter 11), had effectively drained the nation of specie, leaving American prosperity to float on the bubble of credit flowing from European financiers and the largely unregulated "pet banks." When conditions in England suddenly produced a demand for hard currency there, strapped European capitalists pulled back from American investments and called in loans.

As credit evaporated, interest rates rose, paper money depreciated, and debt mounted. Against a background of declining land sales and growing foreclosures in the West, by February the credit-dependent cotton market had begun to collapse, taking with it several large import-export firms in New York and New Orleans. Especially in the context of years of hardship from the high prices of inflation, the failures ignited a run on the over-extended banks, as depositors tried to hoard their savings before the hard currency was paid out for mercantile debts. Perhaps a strong federal hand could have stemmed the damage, but Van Buren shared Jackson's view that (as the new president put it in September 1837) "it was not designed by the Constitution that the Government should assume the management of domestic or foreign exchange." In the end, Van Buren's efforts at philosophical consistency probably deepened the crisis. His announcement on May 4 that he intended to maintain the Specie Circular in force ensured that the pressure on banks would continue. On May 10, 1837, fearing collapse after frightened depositors drained $650,000 from their reserves, New York City banks closed. Only a show of force by the military prevented a riot.

Coinciding with large waves of German and Irish immigration, the depression fell with special severity upon the East Coast. Wages declined faster than prices did. Unemployment was widespread, and the losses from speculative failures touched even the prosperous middle classes. Hopeful signs of economic improvement in 1839 soon vanished, as hard times remained obstinately upon the land

This political cartoon, "Weighed and Found Wanting or The Effects of a Summer's Ramble," referred to the 1836 election contest between Clay and Van Buren.

until 1843. While Democrats scrambled to avoid political responsibility and bombarded Van Buren with contradictory advice, the new Whig Party began to look ahead optimistically to 1840.

Although an additional distribution of federal funds to state banks in 1837 might only have fed the frenzy, Van Buren's decision to delay the distribution (on the grounds that the windfalls had unintentionally amounted to a federal influence over banking practice) added a new confusion to an already volatile situation. In an effort to return stability to the nation's monetary system, Van Buren laid plans to separate the federal treasury entirely from the banks, proposing that the Treasury Department establish its own financial institutions to receive, hold, and pay out all government funds. The institutions would be entirely government operated (no private directors) and would exist for the sole purpose of managing government accounts. They would not issue paper currency and would not be involved in loans to business.

The proposal for an independent treasury met with substantial opposition. Predictably, Whigs objected that removing government holdings from circulation in the economy would have the effect of reducing credit in all forms. But many Democrats also opposed the independent treasury for the brake it would put on growth. In his original message, Van Buren conceded that the treasury might be permitted to receive and pay out some paper currency on a short-term basis, a modest association with commerce that nevertheless went too far for Jacksonian purists. The independent treasury did not pass until 1840, when it was enacted as an entirely separate, specie-based system, empowered neither to receive nor to pay out paper currency.

Two disputes on the Canadian border, both of them seemingly of minor importance, underscored the volatile mood of the American electorate in the late 1830s. The first occurred in northern Maine, where by 1838 Americans and Canadians were ready to come to blows over who owned the rich timber reserves of the Aroostook River valley. Believing that Canadian lumberjacks had been setting up new camps in the region, frustrated, down-on-their luck Maine Democrats demanded federal protection. Van Buren responded by sending in the Army under General Winfield Scott. Aware that the economy was in no condition to support a war, however, he also chided Maine Governor Fairfield for helping to precipitate the crisis and instructed Scott to offer terms for a truce. If Canada would acknowledge Maine's predominant interest in the valley, the United States would pledge to respect existing Canadian settlements pending final disposition of the area.

Late in 1840, just as Scott seemed to be succeeding, the United States became entangled in a second potentially dangerous clash on the Canadian border. Three years earlier a small group of Canadians had launched a rebellion against Great Britain. Although the United States had remained neutral, some sympathetic Americans on the northern New York border had raised funds for the rebels and had offered their ships to transport men and arms to Canada. In 1837 Canadian pro-British troops had secretly crossed into the United States, captured one of the American ships (the *Caroline*), towed it out into the river, and burned it. Within a few months Americans retaliated by seizing and sinking a British ship. There matters tensely stood, until 1840, when a Canadian deputy sheriff by the name of Alexander McLeod was overheard in an American tavern bragging that he had killed an American during the *Caroline* incident. Claiming state jurisdiction, New York authorities immediately arrested him. Although Great Britain took full responsibility for ordering the attack on the *Caroline* and insisted that McLeod's status was an international matter, angry New York mobs clamored for a trial. Only when McLeod was shown in court to be a liar who had in fact been miles away at the time of the incident did emotions at last subside.

Electoral Politics and Moral Reform

Andrew Jackson himself had never had much use for moral reformers, most of whom he considered arrogant and condescending. Yet in marshaling his political support almost as a sacred calling to cleanse the nation of evildoers, Jackson inadvertently helped mobilize electoral politics as the avenue to moral reform. As reformers grew frustrated with the seeming resistance of social problems to techniques of moral suasion and became alarmed by what they saw as the rise of extremism in their movements, they followed Jackson's lead and turned increasingly to electoral politics for solutions. The effect was to fragment and weaken party organization rather than to consolidate it. Workingmen's parties and the Antimason Party had come into existence before 1828. After 1828 the political landscape was littered with a series of specialized and often largely local parties whose very existence testified to the inability of the major parties to address and harness fundamental areas of social conflict.

Nowhere did possession of the vote assume a more central practical role than among newly enfranchised white male workers. Over the course of the struggles of the 1820s and 1830s, laboring people had concluded that many of their problems would be remedied only through electoral action. As long as the economic power of employers was backed up by laws that directly oppressed workers (debt laws that imprisoned them, bankruptcy laws that took their property, conspiracy laws that made union organizing illegal), the moral suasion of strikes and petitions would never be enough.

Workers had been involved in electoral politics throughout the 1820s, but in the winter of 1835–1836 anger at the legal system came to a head. With inflation and unemployment running high, New York City journeymen tailors went out on strike. The leaders of the union were promptly arrested, tried, convicted on conspiracy charges, and fined between $50 and $150 each, a staggering amount for workers. The labor press denounced the courts as "the tool of the aristocracy, against the people!" At a rally a week later, nearly 30,000 people (the largest crowd in American history to that date) turned out to protest the convictions. Among songs and diatribes, the protesters resolved to meet the following fall in Utica, New York, where they would take steps to organize a "separate and distinct" political party to represent workers' interests. The 93 "workers, farmers, and mechanics" who met in Utica six months later demanded laws protecting the right to organize and to reform the judiciary, and they voted to form the Equal Rights Party.

Separate electoral organizing was strongest in New York, but labor movements in other states also began to focus their efforts on legislative reform. The ten-hour day, a long-standing labor demand, re-emerged in the late 1840s as a central point of labor organizing. Throughout New England workers supported candidates friendly to the ten-hour movement, petitioned legislatures for state laws setting the hours of labor, and testified before legislative committees investigating labor conditions. Much to the shock

A Voice from the People!

Great Meeting in the Park!!

The General Trades' Union of New York used this symbol on signs encouraging workers to participate in the 1836 meeting to protest the conviction and fines of striking journeymen tailors. 30,000 supporters turned out for the rally. Note the distinctly masculine (and white) portrayal of workers in the image.

of their middle-class detractors, female workers sometimes testified before legislative committees, using their life stories to create sympathy for the cause; it was male workers, however, who had the power to threaten representatives by voting them out of office.

Other reform movements also began to focus their energies on electoral strategies, although their motives for doing so varied. The Female Moral Reform Society had commenced its work against prostitution with little knowledge or understanding of the lives of poor urban women, but the cross-class contact brought about through the reform work soon awakened among some bourgeois females a new appreciation of the legal obstacles faced by laboring women and a heightened sense of shared social and economic disabilities based on gender. They began advocating and lobbying for the passage of rent laws and property protections for women. This growing emphasis on legal reform during the 1830s and 1840s grew out of an enhanced sense of connection between the reformer and the recipient of her aid.

Although the first state law prohibiting the sale or manufacture of liquor was not passed until 1851 (in Maine), throughout the 1840s temperance workers focused their efforts increasingly toward state legislators and the passing of laws. Among some temperance advocates (especially females) the shift was motivated by a heightened concern for legal protections for the wives and families of alcoholic men, but an increasing emphasis on legal strategies among temperance workers also expressed a growing skepticism that alcoholics could be reformed merely by moral suasion. Millions of Americans had signed the pledge for total abstinence, yet the use of alcohol remained widespread, a state of affairs that middle-class, native-born reformers blamed on the working classes and especially on Irish immigrants.

In fact, there was little evidence that alcoholism was confined to the working classes, native born or immigrant. Nevertheless, by the 1840s temperance workers were inclined to depict alcoholics, not as fellow strugglers gone temporarily astray from the path to perfection, but as members of an alien and inferior class. "You might as well persuade the chained maniac to leave off howling, as to persuade him to leave off drinking," asserted one minister in a particularly revealing comparison. As they identified drinkers as fundamentally different from themselves, temperance workers grew less interested in working directly with drinkers and less optimistic about the success of moral suasion, which, they assumed, required self-discipline beyond the reach of immigrants. Instead, they were more willing to take recourse to legal controls.

The new interest in electoral politics soon created major divisions in some reform movements, most notably in abolitionism. Among moderate abolitionists, the passage of the congressional "gag rule" had raised questions about the effectiveness of Garrison's antipolitical stance (see chapter

12). They also flinched at the increasingly aggressive tactics of the Garrisonian-led movement and at the very visible participation of women and African Americans.

These tensions were palpable in 1840 as the American Anti-Slavery Society met for its national convention in New York. Participants quickly divided over questions of whether women should participate in deliberations and whether the organization should work to elect abolitionist candidates to office. The Garrisonian branch, centered in New York, took control of the convention. But when Abby Kelley (a controversial abolitionist lecturer whom one Connecticut minister had decried as a "Jezebel") was elected to the previously all-male business committee of the association, anti-Garrisonians walked out. A stark repudiation of Garrison and of female activism, the exodus also freed the renegades, led by wealthy New York philanthropists Arthur and Lewis Tappan, to help launch an abolitionist political party. By the end of the year, the new Liberty Party, formed on the platform that the Constitution recognized slavery where it existed in 1787 but barred the federal government from creating it in any new states or territories, had nominated abolitionist James Birney for the presidency.

By definition, recourse to electoral reform excluded females. Nevertheless, some women were among the earliest advocates of the new electoral strategies. Laboring women, as well as men, worked for bankruptcy reform, ten-hour laws, and an end to conspiracy trials. Middle-class women, as well as men, advocated temperance laws and supported antislavery candidates for office. In the 1830s few of those women intended by their actions to claim electoral rights for themselves.

An Independent Woman's Rights Movement

For other women, however, the experience of social activism and, by the 1840s, the growing importance of suffrage and electoral tactics to reform movements gave rise to a new consciousness of their precarious status. Reform work permitted women to participate actively in shaping the new democratic order and to perfect skills useful in civic culture. They ran meetings, kept track of money, took notes, maintained records, and honed their skills at public speaking. For elite women involved in charities, there were also lessons in making use of the new institutions of the market revolution. Because married women could not hold property or make contracts in their own names, most women would have had trouble accumulating the money to fund asylums and schools. But *these* married women, the wives and daughters of wealthy and influential men, could use their social position to obtain donations, endorsements, and even special charters (comparable to the charters granted to male entrepreneurs) that permitted a group of married women to function legally as a male.

Reform women soon learned that there were limits to the authority that religion or domesticity could confer upon females, however. Even those women who were involved in the mildest of reform activities (for example, as members of the American Bible Society) were rebuked for "acting out of their appropriate sphere." Women engaged in more controversial activities like labor reform or abolition work found themselves hounded by mobs and decried as freaks of nature. Catharine Beecher blasted Fanny Wright as a sexual monstrosity for her labor activism. "Who can look without disgust and abhorrence upon such an one as Fanny Wright," Beecher wrote in 1836, "with her great masculine person, her loud voice, her untasteful attire . . . mingling with men in stormy debate, and standing up with bare-faced impudence, to lecture to a public assembly."

In 1837, in her *Essay on Slavery and Abolitionism*, Catharine Beecher attacked female abolitionists for violating the bounds of "rectitude and propriety" and accused them of being motivated by unwomanly "ambition" and "the thirst for power." The same year, the Massachusetts clergy issued a pastoral letter attacking Sarah and Angelina Grimké (members of the southern planter class who were touring the North in the abolitionist cause) for daring to take "the place and tone of man as public reformer."

As if that were not enough, by the late 1830s women involved in abolition work found themselves subjected to growing criticism from within their own ranks. Although Garrison remained a staunch ally, other leaders like the influential Tappan brothers believed that outspoken, assertive women were embarrassing and distracting the movement. For women who had not only given years of their labor but had directly endangered their lives in the cause of abolition, these attacks were especially galling. Disappointing, too, was the growing willingness of such men to abandon the old moral reform strategies. In moral reform, women were men's peers. Even if they were often organized in gender-segregated societies, women did essentially the same kinds of work that men did. Over time they had become increasingly visible in positions of public authority—serving on committees, delivering public lectures, and even taking paying jobs as agents. Perhaps most important, the central act of moral suasion, personal conversion, was not limited to either gender. But the turn toward electoral reform categorically reduced women to second-class status in reform. They could still raise money and lobby and speak, but they could not perform the new essential act of reform, voting.

In the wake of the 1840 split of the American Anti-Slavery Society, in which controversies over political strategies and women's rights figured so centrally, abolitionist women began to spearhead a drive for an organized **woman's rights movement.** Early efforts came to fruition in Seneca Falls, New York, in July of 1848. On July 14, five women (including the seasoned Quaker abolitionist Lucretia Mott, and the much younger Elizabeth Cady

These images show Lucretia Mott (1793–1880) and Elizabeth Cady Stanton (1815–1902) in the 1840s, when they helped launch the woman's rights movement. Mott was already a seasoned and widely respected activist. At that time, Stanton, twenty-two years her junior, was a young mother, much newer to reform causes. Like Mott, she would end up devoting her life to social change.

Stanton) placed an advertisement in the *Seneca County Courier* under the heading. "Woman's Rights Convention." The announcement stated: "A convention to discuss the social, civil and religious condition and rights of woman will be held in the Wesleyan Chapel, Seneca Falls, New York, on Wednesday and Thursday, the 19th and 20th of July current, commencing at 10 A.M." The organizers clearly expected some women to be timid. "During the first day the meeting will be held exclusively for women," they promised. But they also added a special attraction for the second day, when "The public generally are invited to be present . . . [and] Lucretia Mott of Philadelphia and other ladies and gentlemen will address the convention."

The response was overwhelming. On July 19, some 300 people (including perhaps 40 men, among them the famous abolitionist Frederick Douglass) showed up at Wesleyan Chapel. By the end of the second day, the group had debated, voted on, and passed a Declaration of Sentiments (modeled after the Declaration of Independence) and a list of resolutions. Many of the resolutions demanded specific social and legal changes, including a role in lawmaking, improved property rights, equity in divorce, and access to education and the professions. But several of the resolutions addressed broader social conditions, such as the systematic destruction of women's self-confidence and the existence of a pervasive sexual double standard. All of the resolutions passed unanimously but one: a demand for the vote.

Even as American reform became ever-more deeply embedded in electoral strategies, some of the assembled reformers considered suffrage too radical for women.

The Political Economy of the Trans-Mississippi West

As their political interests fragmented, Americans sought reconciliation where they had so often found it before, in geographical expansion. **Manifest destiny,** the belief that white Americans had a providential right to as much of the land of North America as they might care to claim, had been part of the beliefs of American citizens and of official U.S. policy since the founding of the republic. It was implicit in the Northwest Ordinance, in scores of Indian treaties, in the Louisiana Purchase, in the Transcontinental Treaty, in the 1824 Monroe Doctrine, and in the Removal Act of 1830. But it was only in 1845 that the phrase itself entered the American vocabulary, when journalist John O'Sullivan proclaimed grandiosely that it is "Our manifest destiny . . . to overspread the continent allotted by Providence for the free development of our yearly multiplying millions." O'Sullivan was referring explicitly to the vast migration of Americans across the Mississippi River, into

Texas and the Southwest, across the Great Plains into Oregon, and by ship and overland to California. But, as the United States' treatment of Native Americans had long made clear, manifest destiny was also a statement about the relative worth of different peoples in the Americas, and especially about the superiority of people identified as of European descent. As New England minister Horace Bushnell put it, "Out of all the inhabitants of the world . . . a select stock, the Saxon, and out of this the British family, the noblest of the stock, was chosen to people our country." The manifest destiny of America, according to observers like Bushnell, was racial as well as territorial.

Texas

By the terms of the 1819 Transcontinental Treaty the United States had given up claims to Spanish lands south of the Forty-second Parallel. Nevertheless, within a few short years individual Americans began to enter the region in growing numbers.

Many of these immigrants were specifically invited; some were not. The Spanish had conceived of their northern region as a buffer zone against the Lipan Apaches and Comanche Indians, on the one hand, and between New Spain and the United States, on the other. They had created a string of missions to try to control the Indians, erected a system of military garrisons, and attempted to attract settlers into the area. After independence, the new Mexican government expanded those policies by offering land grants to Americans. In return for the promise to bring settlers, the Mexican government granted individual U.S. citizens (called *empresarios*) large tracts of land. The first American to take full advantage of the invitation was Stephen F. Austin, who inherited a grant from his father and began settling a colony on the banks of the Brazos and Colorado Rivers in 1821. By 1830 there were upwards of 20,000 Americans (including 1,000 slaves) living in the northeastern province of Mexico, adjacent to the state of Louisiana.

Conflict between immigrant Americans and resident Tejanos was inevitable. Already feeling ignored and mistreated by politicians of the more central provinces, where power was concentrated, Tejano residents in the region resented the influx of Americans. The national government was often careless in drawing the new grants and awarded to Americans lands that already belonged to Tejanos or that included long-standing Tejano communities. Tejanos complained that the *empresarios* had no respect for existing claims and made little attempt to control their settlers or other, illegal squatters who used the American colonies to hide stolen livestock. "The foreign empresarios are nothing more than money-changing speculators who care only for their own well-being," Tejanos protested. When local Tejano officials confronted them, Americans scorned

web connection

The Un-Welcome Mat

www.prenhall.com/boydston/irish

American expansion required large numbers of settlers who held individual land claims, and immigrants from elsewhere were those settlers. The U.S. has long prided itself on being the chosen land of adventurous people from other continents, those who took the initiative to go to the U.S. and make new lives. Yet American society did not welcome newcomers warmly at the time of entry; often, immigrants were mistreated as individuals and discriminated against as a social group. What did immigrants from China and Ireland encounter in the U.S. in the 1840s? How did they make places for themselves despite a hostile environment?

their authority or complained that they were being unfairly picked on.

In fact, although they were happy to take advantage of the cheap prices Mexico offered, many Americans had never fully acknowledged the right of Mexico to these lands. Viewing the region as the natural next frontier for American plantation agriculture, southerners had denounced the 1819 treaty as a "give away" of American rights, and they lobbied first John Quincy Adams and then Andrew Jackson to purchase the tract free and clear. By 1839 some Americans were convinced that Texas was destined to become the "land of refuge for the American slaveholders." In much of their rhetoric, the immigrants framed and justified their criticisms of the Mexican government in the standard language of free men and republicanism. They objected to high taxes; they protested efforts to get them to convert to Catholicism and adopt the Spanish language; they protested Mexican naming customs and inheritance practices (which tended to pass land through the female line, although not to give control of land to females).

Beneath the Anglos' objections to policies of the Mexican government were two other, more fundamental issues: slavery and the immigrants' disdain for Mexican culture. There had been African-American slaves in the region for at least 300 years, but they were in such small numbers that the institution had little social or economic importance before the early nineteenth century. The number of slaves increased after 1800, when the weakening of the central government had made it possible for slave traders to use Texas as an entry to the U.S. market. Especially after Mexico gained its independence, Mexicans condemned the trade as antirepublican. Ironically, this was just as the central government was encouraging slave-owning immigrants from the southern United States to settle in the region.

The new Mexican government faced much the same dilemma the new U.S. government had faced 30 years earlier. Should they act to strengthen the economy by protecting property rights (including the right to own slaves), or should they act to enforce the republican ideal of liberty by banning slavery? Like the United States, Mexico pursued a paradoxical course, now banning slavery altogether, now allowing slaves and their owners to enter the nation (although providing for mandatory gradual abolition).

By the mid-1820s, however, the immigrants had developed a cotton economy dependent on slave labor and were determined to preserve the institution. Although they continued to seek an exception to the official Mexican policy on slavery, they regarded Mexican inconsistency and resistance as evidence of betrayal. Even Stephen Austin who had never been a particularly devoted supporter of slavery, by 1824 devised a set of regulations for his colony that included harsh provisions for slaves who tried to escape or free people who abetted runaways. By 1830 Austin had come to the conclusion that "Texas must be a slave country. Circumstances and unavoidable necessity compels it. It is the wish of the people there. . . ." "The people," in Austin's view, included only the white U.S. immigrants and others who agreed with their goals.

The same immigrants who defended slavery simultaneously claimed a vast cultural superiority over the Mexicans who were their hosts. The Americans' fault finding focused on anxieties over miscegenation and, in characteristic Jacksonian fashion, associated "civilization" with a particularly aggressive and entrepreneurial notion of manhood. Mexicans were lazy and unmanly, the immigrants declared, a "mixed race" in which European descent had been diluted by intermarriage with Indians and African Americans. Mexicans were incapable of taking full advantage of the lands they owned. Although the most common forms of anti-Mexican rhetoric emphasized ancestry, anti-Mexican feeling in the immigrant community also focused on religion. Mexicans were Catholic, while the U.S. immigrants were predominantly Protestant. Relying on the growing anti-Catholicism of the United States, the immigrants identified Mexican Catholicism with superstition, dependence, and antirepublican attitudes.

Tension between the immigrants and the Mexican government increased. Although the northern borderlands continued to be of less pressing interest to Mexican authorities than were other parts of the nation, after 1830 the government took some steps to stem the tide of immigration. They also sought to project a more forceful presence in the region by locating troops on the United States-Mexican border. Immigrants interpreted these measures as outrageous efforts at intimidation and obstructions to their

rightful claims. In 1832 the Anglos demanded the right to organize their own separate state within Mexico.

The rise of General Antonio Lopez de Santa Anna provided the occasion for acting on that ambition. When Santa Anna dissolved the Mexican Congress in 1834, abolishing the federal system of states and making himself dictator, Anglo-Texans sharpened their criticisms of Mexican government. Casting themselves as the quintessential republicans, they vowed to fight for the old Mexican constitution, and they drew up a new state constitution. The clear goal of immigrant unrest was complete independence, however, not reformation, and on March 2, 1836, Texas declared itself a free and sovereign republic.

Armed conflict broke out on March 6, 1836, when the huge Mexican Army, led by Santa Anna, wiped out 187 Texas patriots barricaded in a mission called the Alamo. It was a costly and fleeting victory. Santa Anna's Army suffered 1,544 casualties and unintentionally created martyrs for the rebels' cause. Under the leadership of Sam Houston (a protégé of Andrew Jackson), the rebels retreated east, gathering recruits as they went. On April 21 the Texans surprised an encampment of Mexican troops on the San Jacinto River. Attacking at dawn from the east, the Texans scored a huge victory, crowned by the capture of Santa Anna himself. Bargaining to save his life and purchase his freedom, Santa Anna declared Texas a free nation, a declaration the reinstated Mexican republican Congress later repudiated. Ecstatic Texans immediately drew up a constitution, made Army commander in chief Sam Houston their first president, and called for annexation to the United States as soon as possible (see Map 13-1). Many Americans greeted the event as the inevitable product of manifest destiny. The Texas rebellion, according to Thomas Hart Benton, "has illustrated the anglo-Saxon character, and . . . shows that liberty, justice, valour—moral, physical, and intellectual power—discriminate that race wherever it goes."

But Houston's mentor, Andrew Jackson, hesitated. In the years of struggle with Mexico, told and retold in the U.S. press, Texas had come to embody the highly charged issue of slavery. Raising that controversy in 1836 would have endangered the election hopes of Martin Van Buren, Jackson's loyal supporter and vice president, then waiting in the wings for his chance at the presidency. Moreover, Mexico would certainly have fought to keep Texas, and the cost of a war would have undermined Jackson's program of distributing the federal surplus to the states.

With the nation in economic crisis and his own party already bickering over who was responsible, the last thing Van Buren wanted as president was a bitter battle over Texas and slavery. He doubted that a "strict adherence to the letter and spirit of the Constitution" permitted annexation, and he feared that annexation would be construed as meddling in Mexico's internal affairs. He was also worried about the impact of annexation on American domestic politics and the fortunes of his own party. Anticipating Texas'

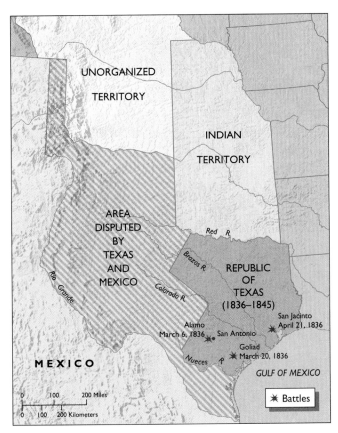

Map 13-1   Republic of Texas.
After the decisive American victory at San Jacinto that resulted in the independence of Texas, the border dispute between Texas and Mexico continued until it was resolved by the Mexican War a decade later.

application for admission, abolitionists had made opposition to annexation a central issue in their massive petition campaign of 1837–1838, giving the controversy a wide popular foundation in the North. John Quincy Adams had already delivered a powerful and stirring speech against annexation in the House, and some senators were publicly denouncing slavery in general and especially in Texas. Southerners had responded with their own petitions, affirming states' rights and insisting that slaves were citizens' property in Texas and could not be taken away without due process. In the end, Van Buren did not submit to Congress Texas' request for statehood.

Pacific-Bound

The question of Texas was in many ways the question of the West and of whether America had a right to expand to the Pacific. That larger question could not be indefinitely tabled. The lands beyond the Mississippi had long been home to white explorers, fur traders, and trappers. By the early 1840s they had become the scene of a massive migration of settlers, bent on making new and permanent homes across the Great Plains.

The migration began modestly enough, as a trickle of missionaries in the 1830s. In 1831 rumors reached the East Coast of four young Indians who had (so the stories went) abruptly appeared in St. Louis, exhausted and sick, imploring the white clergy there to carry Christianity to their people. Two years later, in 1833, the Methodist *Christian Advocate and Herald* published a letter from a Wyandot Indian who claimed that the western tribes hungered for instruction in Christianity. Whether true or not, such stories enabled missionaries to claim that they had been invited into Indian communities. In 1834 the Methodist Missionary Society sent the Reverend Jason Lee west to found a mission in the Willamette Valley of Oregon Territory. Two years later, in January of 1836, the Board of Commissioners for Foreign Missions voted to send a party of six people (including the first two women to go in this capacity) to settle permanent missions in Oregon.

For their first mission, the board selected Marcus and Narcissa Prentiss Whitman. He was a doctor and she a Sunday school teacher who had been converted during the New York revivals of 1818–1819. In September of 1836, after a three-month-long trip west with a fur train, the Whitmans established their mission among the Cayuse Indians near Fort Walla Walla on the Columbia River. Their fellow missionaries, Henry and Eliza Hart Spalding, founded a mission some 125 miles away among the Nez Percés.

At first, the Whitmans seemed to thrive. Marcus Whitman preached and doctored among the Cayuse and taught the men agriculture, and Narcissa taught school and oversaw the domestic operation of the large mission. Over the following decade, however, as white immigration into the region swelled, the Cayuse came to view the missionaries as the cause of the constant influx of white people and new diseases into the Pacific Northwest. In 1847, in response to a measles epidemic that killed large numbers of Cayuse children (who had no immunities to the disease), a Cayuse band attacked the growing missionary settlement, killing Marcus and Narcissa Prentiss Whitman and a number of other white people.

By then, overland migrants to the West Coast were so numerous that travelers could see (and taste) the columns of dust churned up by other wagon trains near them (see Map 13-2). According to one observer, the roads of Iowa "were literally lined with long blue wagons . . . slowly wending their way over the broad prairies," leaving deep, rutted, virtually permanent tracks. In the years of heaviest migration, watering holes were so overused and sanitary conditions so poor that the road west became a breeding ground for typhoid, malaria, dysentery, and cholera.

Most of the migrants were farming families of moderate means, pushed out of the Midwest by the hard times of 1837. Men often made the initial decision to leave, sometimes seemingly out of the blue. For example, in Illinois, Sarah Cummins returned home from school one day to

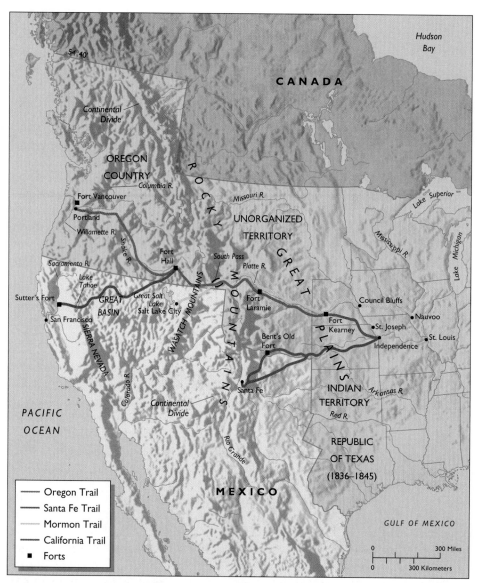

Map 13-2 Major Overland Trails.
The overland trails to the west started at the Missouri River. The Santa Fe Trail was a conduit for traders and goods to Mexico. The Oregon Trail traveled through Wyoming, and branched off to California and Oregon.

less choice. Moreover, women appear often to have felt more keenly than men the wrenching separation from family, church, and community and the hardship of having to give up whatever domestic comforts the family enjoyed for the dangers of the trail. Nevertheless, the excitement of moving west was not limited to men and the sorrow of leaving family and friends was not limited to women. Narcissa Whitman pronounced herself healthier and in better spirits than ever, as she faced the Overland Trail. Catherine Haun, an emigrant in 1849, recorded the congenial visits women paid to one another's wagons, "talking over our home life back in 'the states,'" but also "voicing our hopes for the future . . . and even whispering a little friendly gossip of emigrant life." Migrants kept their spirits up by singing, telling stories, playing games, and picking wild flowers. When they could, men sometimes tried (usually unsuccessfully) to hunt buffalo.

Travelers funneled through St. Louis (where they picked up supplies for the trip), eased across Missouri to rendezvous with their wagon trains near St. Joseph or Independence, Missouri, and then followed one of two main routes west. The northern route, known as the Oregon Trail, zigzagged northwest at roughly the Forty-second Parallel to the Rocky Mountains. At that point, the trail split. The northern branch followed the Snake River up into the beautiful Willamette Valley near the Columbia River. The southern branch veered southwest into the Mexican province of California. Another line of settlers journeyed southwest out of Independence on the Santa Fe Trail, which led along the Arkansas River through what would later become the state of Kansas before heading directly into Mexican lands. At the Mexican city of Santa Fe, the trail divided, feeding immigrants west along the Old Spanish Trail (mapped by Franciscan missionaries) or south to Chihuahua, Mexico.

The overland migrants traveled in families, in groups of families from the same neighborhood in Ohio, or Indiana, or Illinois, and occasionally in entire communities. Most of the migrants were from farming families and were

discover that her father had sold the farm and that "as soon as school closes we are to move." Preparations for the trip took up to half a year. Men arranged to sell the land and farm equipment and whatever stock was not to go with them, repaired harnesses and traces, and purchased wagons for the trip. Women prepared the clothing, bedding, soap, food, containers, medicine, and utensils the family would need. As Kit Belknap recorded in her diary in October 1848, "Now, I will begin to work and plan to make everything with an eye to starting out on a six month trip" the following April.

Not everyone cherished those dreams with equal pleasure. Men who dreaded, or feared, the West usually simply did not go, or if they did, they drifted westward only at the prompting of hard times. Most women and children had

Although many overland pioneers traveled west in large caravans that included wagons, most individuals within those caravans walked and some migrations—notably the Mormon migration to the Great Salt Lake—consisted almost entirely of people walking and pulling handcarts.

used to hard work and deprivation, but the trail supplied much more. If they did not have team animals, families pulled their possessions in two-wheeled handcarts. Mormon Mary Ann Hafen, whose family traveled to Utah in 1860, recalled a party of "126 persons with twenty-two handcarts and three provision wagons drawn by oxen." Wagons and team animals did not ensure an easy trip. Even with wagons, which were needed for supplies, most migrants walked west. Wagons broke down, were washed away in river crossings, or had to be emptied to ease the burden on the animals. After they left the plains, wagon trains sometimes went days without finding water or game. Some work remained gender-defined. Women did the cooking and laundry, while men usually did the hunting for large game. However, women as well as men drove the wagons and herded the cattle, collected firewood, and caught small animals for food. When broken equipment or sickness slowed individual families, the trains were often forced to leave them behind, lest the others not clear the Rocky Mountains before winter.

The harrowing dangers of that possibility were immortalized in the experiences of the ill-fated "Donner Party," caught by an early winter trying to clear the Sierra Nevada Mountains en route to California. For four months the party was trapped by snow in the mountains, without sufficient fuel, blankets, or food, slowly starving. When relief finally arrived in mid-February 1847, "the dead were lying about on the snow, some even unburied, since the living had not strength to bury their dead," according to one survivor. Of the 87 persons snowed in at Donner Lake, 42 died.

For migrants who survived the journey west, the rewards were not always apparent at once. "My most vivid recollection of that first winter in Oregon," one woman recalled, "is of the weeping skies and of Mother and me also weeping." Another settler was equally glum: "We may now call ourselves through, they say; and here we are in Oregon making our camp in an ugly bottom, with no home, except our wagons and tent, it is drizzling and the weather looks dark and gloomy."

As soon as their homes were built and their fields plowed, though, many of the newcomers were ready to declare Oregon "this best country in the world." Settlers kept hogs and cattle, and the weather was hospitable to crops of wheat, flax, and corn and to apple and pear orchards. Lumber was plentiful, and the streams ran full of fish. Farther south was the "mild and delightful climate of California," an even greater attraction after 1848, when rumors of "inexhaustible" gold strikes began to filter north and east.

Nations of the Trans-Mississippi West

The territories through which the migrants traveled, and the lands to which they eventually laid claim, were neither uninhabited nor unclaimed. Most wagon trains west departed from one of the settlements along the Mississippi in Missouri, which meant that settlers first crossed through Indian Territory, where growing numbers of Native Americans had been guaranteed safe refuge from white intrusion. Between Independence, Missouri, and the Rocky Mountains lay the Indian nations of the American prairies and Great Plains: the Blackfoot and the Crow to the northwest; the Sioux, the Pawnee, the Arapaho, the Shoshone, and the Cheyenne through the northern and central Plains; and the Kiowa, the Apache, the Comanche, and the Navajo in the Southwest. Along the Pacific were the Yakima, the Chinook, the Cayuse, and the Nez Percés, and to the south, in California, Pomo, Chumash, Yuma, and many other groups (see Map 13-3). Most of this vast territory was also part of the nation of Mexico, and Great Britain laid claim to the northwestern region known as Oregon. Crossing to utopia meant transgressing the boundaries of all of these nations and the homes of the people who lived there.

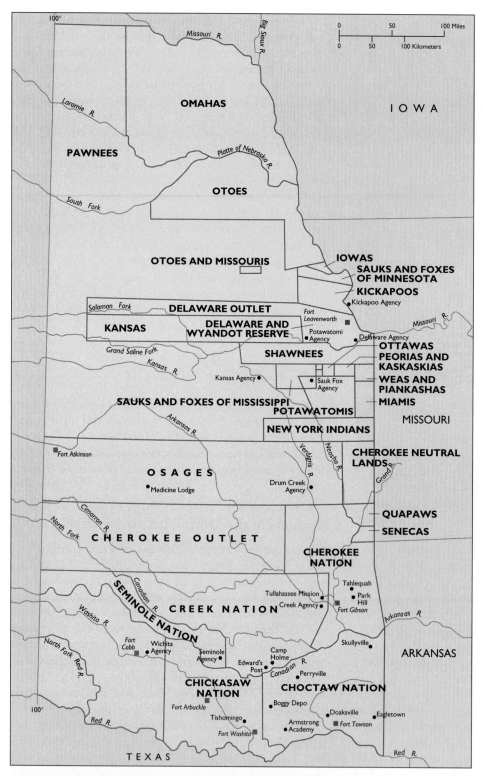

Map 13-3 Major Trans-Mississippi Indian Communities, c. 1850.
Most of the Indians living in the Indian Territory in the 1830s and 1840s had been "removed" from areas east of the Mississippi River. The territory was located west of Arkansas, Missouri, and Iowa. The section to the South (now Oklahoma) was home to Cherokees, Choctaws, Creeks, and Seminoles from the Old Southwest. The northern part (now Kansas and Nebraska), was inhabited by Indians from the Old Northwest.

American penny novelists would depict this contact of peoples as a violent confrontation, in which cunning and bellicose Indians again and again swooped down to massacre naïve and well-meaning migrants. In fact, of the more than 250,000 settlers who crossed the plains between 1840 and 1860, fewer than 400 were killed by Native Americans protecting their homes, about the same number of deaths as those inflicted by white migrants seeking to take the Indian lands for themselves. More often, during the 1840s, white migrants and Indians merely passed each other silently on the trail or relied upon one another for food and other supplies. Edwin Bryant described such a meeting in 1846. "Circles of white-tented wagons may now be seen in every direction," he wrote. "An immense number of oxen and horses are scattered over the entire vally [sic], grazing upon the green grass," and "parties of Indians, hunters, and emigrants . . . galloping to and from" in "a scene . . . of almost holiday liveliness."

Prior to the massive migration of the 1840s, official U.S. policy toward the Indians had been one of removal (by force, if necessary, often by pressured sale of lands and physical relocation). It was a policy that assumed an eventual limit to white aspirations west. But even in the 1830s observers saw no evidence that Americans recognized a boundary short of the Pacific Ocean. Alexis de Tocqueville commented on the contradiction, noting that "when it promises these unlucky people a permanent asylum in the West," the U.S. government "is well aware of its inability to guarantee this." The trans-Mississippi migrations of the middle of the nineteenth century proved the wisdom of de Tocqueville's observation. If it was the purpose of Americans, as Walt Whitman said with specific reference to Mexico, to people "the New World with a noble race," then where exactly were other "races" to go? What was to be left for them after white Americans had overrun the entire continent?

By the late 1830s, as the last of the great eastern "removals" were being accomplished, federal policy toward Indians had begun to reveal a subtle shift. Removal and resettlement continued to be the primary stated goal of U.S. Indian policy. Many of the western tribes were confined to reservations in the West or moved to lands in Indian Territory. But whereas earlier removals had contained as their official goal the relocation of Indian communities to new *tribally* owned reservations, later removals aimed more overtly at relocation culminating in *individual* ownership of reservation lands. An 1839 treaty gave the Brotherton Indians of Wisconsin a tract of land to be individually owned. Such interference with the land customs of Indians was, of course, what many Americans (including Andrew Jackson most notably) had sought for decades, believing that Native Americans had to be brought into the "civilized" political economy of the United States through individual ownership of property. The Brotherton Treaty gave formal explicit expression to that belief. Citizenship was awarded to individual Indians who received and accepted private allotments of lands. Although through much of the next three decades the treatment of the Plains Indians continued to emphasize the earlier reservation policy, allotment would become the official U.S. policy toward all Indians by the end of the century.

By the mid-1830s, when white Americans started making the trans-Mississippi crossing in huge numbers, most of these nations had already tasted the effects of expansionism. The Comanches (the largest of the southwestern nations) and the Apaches, for example, had been at war with Euro-Americans for several centuries. They had first fought the Spanish who came up from New Spain, then the Mexicans who overthrew Spanish rule, and since the 1820s both the Mexican settlers and garrisons in the northern provinces of Mexico and the U.S. settlers who migrated into Texas. In addition to these intrusions, all of the Plains Indians, but perhaps especially the Sioux, the Kiowa, and the Comanches, had already felt the impact of eastern Indians who had been displaced or officially relocated west. The Sioux, for example, had been at war off and on for decades with the Indians of the old Northwest Territory, who were being slowly shoved across the Mississippi River by white settlers and their guards, the militias and the U.S. Army.

For the Indians of the plains and prairies, the effects of the migration of the 1840s were social, cultural, and economic. Although the number of Indians' deaths that resulted from actual warfare with Americans remained surprisingly low, the number that resulted from disease was far higher. The experience of the Cayuse was all too common. Epidemics took especially high tolls on the children and older members of Indian villages, wiping out both the elders who carried a community's history and collective wisdom and the young people who represented its future. Under demographic stress, Native communities were confronted with missionaries preaching Christianity, new forms of medicine, new codes of behavior, and new forms of knowledge. Traders brought guns and alcohol. Federal agents introduced new textiles and metal goods.

Among other effects, these forms of contact gradually altered the social organization and gender division of labor of the Indians of the plains and prairies. As it became harder to claim and protect planting grounds, tribes shifted from semiagricultural to more nomadic ways of life. The relative importance of women's foraging and planting diminished, and the relative importance of men's skills as hunters and warriors increased. The growing reliance on the horse altered even the social rituals of hunting. Among some Indians the hunt had previously been on foot with large numbers of people, women as well as men, working together to trap animals where they could be caught and killed. Now, all-male groups hunted on horseback.

By 1840, the great northern grasslands and southern plains of central North America supported a complex economy of hunting and foraging. The Indians consumed corn, melons, berries, wild sweet potatoes, turnips, and an abundant array of fowl and small game, harvested in a seminomadic way of life and traded through the overlapping networks that ran north to south. At the center of this economy stood the buffalo, supplying not only food but also material for clothing, for shelter, and for trade. The way of life that had evolved on the plains by 1840s could survive unchanged only as long as the buffalo survived.

That way of life was already endangered. As early as 1829, Congressman Lewis Cass had observed that "The herds of bison are constantly retreating." "[S]everal years ago they were approaching the foot of the Alleghenies," Cass predicted in a report to Congress that "in a few years it will perhaps be difficult to see any of them in the immense plains that stretch the length of the Rocky Mountains." Settlers' need for food had only a minor impact on the buffalo. More deadly was their fascination simply with hunting and killing such a huge creature, regardless of whether they needed its meat and hides. Fortunately, many of the migrants were indifferent hunters, but over time recreational hunting parties, as well as bands of hunters intent upon wiping out the buffalo specifically to deprive Indian communities of their support, took their toll. By 1848, Thomas A. Harvey, western superintendent of Indian Affairs, was warning of the inevitable effects of "the immense traveling of emigrant companies over the prairies, and the consequent increased destruction of buffalo."

What worried Harvey had in fact already come to pass. Western tribes found their hunting grounds depleted.

In 1834–1835, western artist George Catlin observed the importance of the buffalo to Plains Indians. Here he depicted Comanche women dressing buffalo robes and drying buffalo meat. Notice the presence of horses in the village, a sign of European influence on western Indian life.

The paths home to their winter settlements were marked by the bodies of their starved members. As early as 1842 and 1843 the Teton Sioux had complained to federal Indian agents that the heavy migrations were harming their hunting grounds. By 1846 the Sioux were demanding that the U.S. government do something to stem the migrations and to prevent the migrants from killing animals indiscriminately and beyond their needs. When the government ignored the complaints, the Sioux devised their own remedy, preventing wagon trains from making passage until migrants had paid a toll in money, tobacco, or supplies. Enraged by this request for "tribute," the indignant overland travelers criticized the federal government for coddling the Indians and demanded that the trails be reopened.

In the mid-1840s the energies of the federal government were primarily engaged in the southwestern borderlands, where American nationalists were demanding action against Mexico. In the northern plains, the government made some efforts at conciliation but settled for the construction of a chain of forts across the West. These forts were intended as quarters for armed rifle units called "dragoons," who would, theoretically, drive the Indians back from intimidating the overland migrants. The strategy was not very effective. During the late 1840s, as the U.S. government laid its claim to the southern plains, the Indians continued to exert a level of control over white migration through northern Indian country.

Slavery and the Political Economy of Expansion

Even as individual Americans poured west in search of opportunity, the question of expansion became a source of controversy within the collective politics of the nation. The problem was not the principle of manifest destiny itself. Few politicians questioned that territorial expansion was the clear right of the nation if its people so chose, but by the late 1830s the subject of expansion was linked in the public debate with the subject of the extension of slavery. That subject, controversial enough in itself, raised other festering grudges. Southerners viewed northerners as unfaithful to a fifty-year-old deal ratified in the Constitution. Northerners looked with envy upon the high per capita income of the new Southwest (Louisiana, Mississippi, Alabama, and Arkansas) and worried about the political leverage of a new slave state the size of Texas.

Log Cabins and Hard Cider: The Election of 1840

As they approached the election of 1840, both of the major political parties found themselves engaged in a delicate balancing act. Both hoped to exploit certain aspects of regional difference, but both hoped to do so without raising the most divisive issues associated with slavery. Whigs considered Van Buren vulnerable, in large measure because the nation still languished under the effects of the Depression of 1837, but also because he was a northerner (bad enough in the eyes of many southern Democrats) who (worse yet) seemed to be blocking the annexation of Texas. Henry Clay, leader of the Whig Party, opposed the annexation of Texas, but he calculated that southern Democrats would choose a Kentuckian over a New Yorker. Well aware of Van Buren's liabilities in the South, Democrats too were eager to keep slavery out of the debates, although Van Buren was willing to have northerners see him as the alternative to a southern president. A number of northern Whigs were vaguely suspicious of Clay's ties to the South.

There were ominous signs that slavery would nonetheless haunt the election. In June of 1839 the U.S.S. *Washington* had intercepted the ship *Amistad* in American coastal waters. Although the ship was Spanish-owned and sailing out of Cuba, it was under the control of its cargo of kidnapped Africans, who were attempting to sail it home to Sierra Leone. Tricked by the ship's pilot, they had sailed instead into Long Island Sound. Almost immediately the case drew widespread news coverage and became the center of heated controversy, as pro- and antislavery forces argued over whether the Africans should be returned to the ship's owners and to slavery. Ultimately the case reached the U.S. Supreme Court, where former president John Quincy Adams argued successfully that because the international slave trade was illegal in the United States, the Africans must be returned to their homes. The *Amistad* quickly became a *cause célebre* among abolitionists, who implicitly accepted the violence of the mutiny in their arguments that the Africans must be set free, but the impact of the case went beyond activist circles. Heavy newspaper coverage (and the fact that the case did not raise questions about race and slavery *within* the United States) aroused the sympathy even of moderate opponents of slavery, again broadening the antislavery debate and increasing interest in the new Liberty Party (see Table 13-1).

As anticipated, Van Buren received the Democrat nomination, but Henry Clay was again disappointed in his search for the presidency. In an effort to skirt the explosive issues that confronted the nation, the Whigs turned to William Henry Harrison, an outspoken advocate of cheap western land and the hero of the battle of Tippecanoe (see chapter 9). Whigs hoped Harrison might attract disaffected Democrats, as well as party loyalists.

Equally important from the point of view of Whigs, Harrison was the candidate, out of the full 1836 Whig field, who had run strongest against Van Buren. Harrison had taken 36.7 percent of the vote compared to Van Buren's 50.9 percent. To bolster the broad appeal of their slate, for their vice presidential candidate the Whigs chose the recent refugee from the Democrat Party, John Tyler of Virginia, a southerner, a strong advocate of states' rights, and (at the time) a Clay supporter.

Harrison was a "sentimental" candidate. Through him, the Whigs hoped to evoke untroubled feelings of national military glory and westward expansion, not unlike the appeal launched by the Democrats in Jackson's first campaign. Studiously avoiding tough issues, they threw their energy instead into crafting a Jackson-like campaign for "Tippecanoe and Tyler, too." When a newspaper editor derided Harrison as a country bumpkin whose highest aspiration in life consisted of sitting on his porch drinking cider, the Whigs took up the image with gusto. In what came to be known as the "Log Cabin and Hard Cider Campaign," the Whigs celebrated Harrison as a simple man of the people (like Jackson). They made signs with log cabins, buttons with log cabins, flags and drapes depicting log cabins, and even hastily threw together full-sized log cabins when Harrison was coming to town. In point of fact, Harrison was from a quite wealthy, old Virginia family. But he could be linked to the West, an incalculable advantage in a depression year in which many Americans sought renewal and unity. As Daniel Webster observed, Harrison's main appeal was the vague "hope of a better time."

The popular turnout was large (80 percent of eligible voters went to the polls), and the popular results were close. In the end, Harrison received 1,275,000 votes and Van Buren 1,128,000, but the Electoral College was a different story. Harrison, who had taken every large state but Virginia, triumphed with 234 electoral votes to Van Buren's 60. The anti-Harrison vote was suggestive, however. The Democrats held New Hampshire, Illinois, Missouri, Arkansas, Alabama, Virginia, and South Carolina. With

TABLE 13-1

The Liberty Party Swings an Election					
Candidate	Party	Actual Vote in New York	National Electoral Vote	If Liberty Voters Had Voted Whig	Projected Electoral Vote
Polk	Democratic	237,588	170	237,588	134
Clay	Whig	232,482	105	248,294	141
Birney	Liberty	15,812	0	—	—

When Democrats ridiculed William Henry Harrison as a backwoods oaf who lacked both intelligence and ambition, Whigs turned the criticism into praise. This 1841 almanac celebrated Harrison's candidacy in what came to be called the "Hard Cider and Log Cabin" campaign.

the exception of New Hampshire, they were all (including Illinois) states with deeply pro-slavery sentiments.

And Tyler, Too

Whig jubilation was short lived. Sixty-eight-year-old William Henry Harrison became ill shortly after his inauguration and died of pneumonia on April 4, 1841, the first president to die in office. As prescribed by the Constitution, Harrison was followed in office by his vice president, John Tyler. Most observers assumed that Tyler (quickly dubbed "His Accidency") would function as a caretaker president until the next general election. He soon proved them wrong, setting the precedent for vice presidents to succeed to the full stature and authority of the office of president.

Tyler's ascendancy threw the Whig Party into chaos, for once in office the southerner reverted to his Democrat roots. Although he had often opposed Jackson on specific issues, there was much about Tyler that was reminiscent of the earlier president. Not only did Tyler, like Jackson, oppose every element of the National Republican Ameri-

can System (see chapter 10) and favor slavery and the annexation of Texas, but also like Jackson Tyler was willing to use the full power of the executive to enforce those views. (As president, Tyler threatened to use federal troops to quell the Dorr "People's Constitution" movement in Rhode Island, where universal white male suffrage had been blocked.) Unlike Jackson in office, Tyler was an enthusiastic advocate of southern states' rights positions.

Tyler's attention was first drawn to continuing diplomatic troubles with Britain. Echoing the earlier *Amistad* mutiny, in 1841 the slave crew of the U.S. ship *Creole*, en route from Virginia to New Orleans, had seized control of the vessel and forced it into the port of Nassau where, by British law, the crew was freed. To no avail, white southerners demanded the return of the crew. Meanwhile, northern anti-British feeling flared over the question of Oregon Territory, a vaguely defined expanse between northern California and Alaska that Britain and the United States had agreed in 1818 to occupy jointly. As late as 1840 there were only about 40 Americans in the entire area. By 1842, however, Captain Charles Wilkes' Great United States Exploring Expedition (around Antarctica and along the Pacific Coast from Alaska to California) had returned with descriptions of the North American Pacific Coast as a veritable "storehouse of wealth in all its forests, furs, and fisheries." The reports had both stimulated immigration and stirred American sentiment to claim the Oregon Territory all the way to Alaska at the Fifty-fourth Parallel.

In 1842 U.S. Secretary of State Webster and British emissary Ashburton concluded delicate negotiations intended to resolve these issues. The Webster-Ashburton Treaty drew a northern boundary between the United States and Canada from Maine to the Rocky Mountains (Oregon was left undivided), established the terms of extradition between the two nations, and created a joint American-British effort to restrict the international slave trade off the coast of Africa. In a separate exchange of letters, Great Britain agreed to instruct its colonial governors not to interfere with foreign vessels.

Tyler's success in foreign relations was overshadowed by his 1841 break with his own party. Led by Henry Clay, Whigs in Congress succeeded in passing a number of pieces of legislation that embodied the Whig platform, including various tariff bills, a national bank bill, and a bill to distribute federal surpluses to states in order that they might fund internal improvements. Tyler vetoed almost every initiative. Although he had earlier supported federal distribution, he now denounced it as inappropriate in an era when the federal government was in deficit. He vetoed tariff bill after tariff bill until at last, in 1842, the Whigs in Congress offered lower increases than Clay wished and detached the tariff from the question of distribution. Citing the need for federal funds, Tyler signed the bill. Tyler did support the repeal of the independent treasury, a Whig goal, but this, too, proved a bitter victory for Clay and the Whig Party, because Tyler vetoed the national bank with which the Whigs wanted to replace the independent treasury.

Tyler soon found himself a president without a party. Clay threatened that "Tyler dare not resist me." As early as January 1843, there were calls in the House of Representatives for his impeachment. (Investigations and censures of the president would continue through the rest of his term.) That year, when Tyler vetoed the bill rechartering the national bank, his entire cabinet resigned, save only Webster.

"His Accidency" proved more resilient than Clay anticipated. Tyler was encouraged by Democrat gains in the 1842 elections, which he interpreted as evidence of support for his positions, particularly on the national bank. Wielding the power of patronage to surround himself with friends, Tyler also began to search for more lasting means to bolster his political fortunes. Urged on by the extreme states' rights advocates in Virginia and South Carolina, he took up the cause of the annexation of Texas. After Daniel Webster resigned from the cabinet in the spring of 1843 Tyler fell almost entirely under the influence of southerners (including new Secretary of State Abel Upshur) who were committed to Texas.

Texas did everything in its power to make annexation an urgent issue for Americans. It allowed Great Britain to serve as an intermediary between Texas and Mexico in Texas' efforts to win official recognition from Mexico and hinted that, if Mexico would recognize the independent Republic of Texas, Texas might abolish slavery. The idea of an alliance between Texas and Great Britain reawakened old anti-British sentiments in the United States. In addition, the prospect of a nonslave republic so close to their borders and so squarely in the path of westward migration filled southerners with dread.

Seeking to capitalize on these anxieties, in 1843 President Tyler secretly opened negotiations with Texas for admission to the union, expecting that he would justify the completed treaty as necessary to protect the United States against British influence in the hemisphere. In the spring of 1844, Tyler submitted a treaty of annexation to Congress. He evidently hoped that the potential for controversy would be buried in larger American expansionist interests. He was wrong. Even before the treaty was submitted, John Quincy Adams and 12 other Whig members of Congress denounced it as constitutionally unauthorized and warned that it would bring the nation to "dissolution." Abolitionists, who had been petitioning against annexation since 1837, labeled the move a naked power grab by slaveowners, bent on the "perpetuation of Slavery and the political power of the Slave States." Even more moderate northerners worried that annexing Texas would bring about an expensive war with Mexico, consuming northern taxes and killing northern soldiers without yielding the North any tangible gains. Some southerners worried that the fresh soils of Texas would offer economic competition to the more depleted lands of the South, harming cotton and sugar profits.

By then, other election-year dramas were afoot. John Calhoun, who had succeeded Upshur as secretary of state, still longed for the presidency. He believed that he had a reasonable chance against Tyler, another southerner, if he could deny Van Buren the Democrat nomination. To that end, Calhoun authored a note to the British minister that the U.S. goal in Texas was to protect slavery against British abolitionists. As Calhoun hoped, the note became public. The impact of the explicit association of Texas and slavery was to drive Van Buren away from endorsing the treaty, an act that might have made him a stronger candidate in the South. An overwhelmingly sectional vote defeated the treaty, but Calhoun believed a Democrat victory in 1844 would revive it.

Occupy Oregon, Annex Texas

By the fall of 1844 the American political party system was in serious disarray. Neither party had been able to discover whatever consensus existed in the American electorate. Harrison's rather impressive victory in 1840 had not signaled a broad endorsement of Clay or the American System, any more than Van Buren's victory in 1836 had signaled the persistence of a strong and clear hard money, anti-bank sentiment. To the contrary, between 1836 and 1844 the party system seemed more successful at polarizing than at uniting American interests.

Nowhere was that state of affairs more evident than in the 1844 Democrat convention in Baltimore, Maryland. Martin Van Buren still considered himself the head of the party, and his supporters believed that the party owed him the nomination. And yet by 1842 his liabilities were legion. In the South, pro-slavery, pro-annexation Democrats led by John C. Calhoun were vowing to make "a slave-holder for President next time regardless of the man." Andrew Jackson was disappointed with Van Buren's refusal to endorse annexation and was encouraging former Tennessee governor James K. Polk to run. In the North, workers and entrepreneurs who had been hard hit by years of deflation had no stomach for more of the "Little Magician's" magic. When the convention opened, Van Burenites were unable to block a rule requiring a candidate to receive the votes of two-thirds of the convention delegates to secure the nomination. Van Buren could not marshal that level of support. Neither, as it turned out, could Tyler or Calhoun or Lewis Cass, the first "compromise" candidate to whom the convention turned. Finally, on the eighth ballot the deadlocked convention fell back on Jackson's choice, James Polk. (Indeed, so close were the two in political outlook that Polk's supporters liked to refer to him as "the Young Hickory.") Tyler accepted renomination by a renegade group of supporters, also meeting in Baltimore, who styled themselves Democratic Republicans.

The 1844 Democrat Party ran on the platform of manifest destiny. Solidly in favor of the annexation of Texas, but also eager to capitalize on northern interest in Oregon

Territory, the 1844 Democrat platform called for "the reoccupation of Oregon and the reannexation of Texas." It was an odd formulation, given that the United States had several times officially denied possession of Texas and had yet to occupy Oregon very fully. The platform went even further on the Oregon issue. Although the official U.S. government claim to Oregon had never extended beyond the Forty-ninth Parallel, the Democrats now declared their willingness to go to war to gain the entire disputed region. ("Fifty-four forty or fight!" was their slogan.) Their bellicose strategy incorporated war fears over Texas into a broader assertion of national destiny. For his running mate, Polk chose former Pennsylvania senator George Mifflin Dallas.

Meanwhile, in 1844 Henry Clay at long last secured the Whig nomination for himself. Clay was certain that opposition to the extension of slavery was now too strong to tolerate a Texas-Oregon compromise and that Americans, at last enjoying a revived economy, would not support a war with Mexico (see Table 13-2). As a candidate Clay moderated his opposition to annexation, but he ran primarily as a supporter of the American System as the necessary means for stabilizing the economic and social processes of national growth.

Although both parties approached the election with confidence, the results suggested a nation teetering on the edge of serious political division. Polk, annexation, and manifest destiny won, but by only 38,000 of more than 2.5 million votes cast. More striking, James G. Birney of Ohio, the candidate of the new, explicitly antislavery Liberty Party, drew 62,000 votes, most of them from Clay. Had Birney not run, the election might have been a dead heat.

Nevertheless, both John Tyler and Congress read the election as a referendum on the Democratic platform and specifically on Texas. Early in 1845, with Tyler still in office, a bill approving annexation passed the House. To move it through the Whig-dominated Senate, Senator Robert Walker of Mississippi suggested the Senate version be amended to include the *option* of negotiating a whole new treaty. Only days away from the presidency, Polk was said to favor this approach, and Whigs liked the idea because they thought a revised treaty might better address

some of their objections and get them out of a difficult and politically costly position. With the appended option, the Senate approved the treaty. The Whigs fully expected Tyler to concede the decision to the incoming president. They were wrong. In the last hours of his presidency he dispatched formal notice to Texas that (contingent only on its own agreement) the republic was forthwith annexed to the United States of America. Mexico immediately severed relations with the United States.

War With Mexico

The annexation of Texas would be the ostensible cause of the outbreak of war with Mexico in April of 1846, a year into Polk's term, but Texas was only a partial explanation for the war. In Polk's eyes, the annexation of Texas was a piece of a larger acquisition, to include not only Oregon, but also, perhaps most important, present-day New Mexico, Arizona, and California. In 1845 Polk confided to then-Senator Thomas Hart Benton from Missouri that, in making expansionism the centerpiece of his campaign, "I had California and the fine bay of San Francisco as much in view as Oregon." Certainly, Polk would have been happy to make these acquisitions peacefully. In the end, he was willing to go to war, if war was what it took.

Polk's two-track approach to foreign relations became evident early in his administration. In his first annual message in December of 1845, he announced his decision to withdraw from negotiations with Great Britain over Oregon, and he called on Congress to terminate the United States-Great Britain Convention of Joint Occupancy. Compromise on British terms would constitute an abandonment of American "territorial rights . . . self respect, and the national honour," he insisted, and could never be entertained. Polk's rhetoric was in fact more threatening than his intentions. He simultaneously informed his advisors that he was prepared to hear an offer of compromise from England. When one came, proposing a boundary at the Forty-ninth Parallel, Polk was pleased to submit it to Congress. By June 1846 the deal had been struck.

In the case of Oregon, Polk threatened war but quickly accepted peace. Thomas Hart Benton later suggested that appearance and intent were reversed in the Mexican borderlands. What Polk really wanted in that region, Benton claimed, was "a little war," big enough to justify grabbing the Southwest but not so big as to break the budget or create war-hero challengers for the presidency. Texas provided the excuse.

As a condition of his surrender and release, the Mexican General Santa Anna had agreed to the Rio Grande as the boundary between Texas and Mexico, a boundary that would have run northward to include present-day New Mexico, as well as western Texas. The Mexican government had never approved this line and had instead drawn the border at the Nueces River, recognizing only about half the territory claimed by Texans. Polk intended to set

TABLE 13-2

Personal Income Per Capita by Region: Percentages of United States Average			
	1840	1860	1880
United States	100	100	100
Northeast	135	139	141
North Central	68	68	98
South	76	72	51
West	—	—	190

Source: Richard A. Easterlin, "Regional Income Trends, 1840–1950," in Seymour E. Harris (ed.), American Economic History (New York: McGraw-Hill, 1961), p. 528.

After taking Monterrey, Taylor's army engaged the army of Santa Anna on February 21, 1847, at La Angostura, where a pass cut between two ranges of mountains. Although Taylor's force was far smaller (fewer than 5,000 troops to Santa Anna's 14,000) and although Taylor permitted his communications lines to be cut and failed to fortify the eastern side of the pass, U.S. artillery finally turned back the Mexicans. Having lost roughly 1,500 troops to Taylor's 500, that night the Mexican army left their campfires burning and retreated. Taylor did not pursue.

the boundary at the Rio Grande, and he may from early on have intended to secure not only the disputed Texas territory, but also additional large portions of northern Mexico.

To achieve these aims, he once again played a double game. As late as September, Polk was still appealing for a peaceful resolution of the Texas matter. That month, he dispatched former Louisiana Congressman John Slidell to Mexico to offer to purchase New Mexico and Texas for $30 million. The Mexican government refused even to receive Slidell.

Meanwhile, Polk prepared for war. As early as the spring of 1845 he sent in 1,500 soldiers under the command of General Zachary Taylor allegedly to protect Texas against a possible invasion by Mexico. When Texas approved union with the United States, Polk reinforced Taylor's troops and ordered them to approach the Rio Grande as closely as they dared, while also sending an American force under General Stephen Kearny into the northern part of the disputed territory. In August of 1846, Kearny occupied Santa Fe and set up a new government. At the

same time, Polk brought the rest of northern Mexico into play. In 1845 he ordered the U.S. squadron in the Pacific closer to the California coast and directed the U.S. consul in California, Thomas Larkin, to do what he could to encourage local disaffection with the Mexican government. When a small group of American settlers in the Sonoma Valley staged a rebellion in June and July, the representatives of the United States (now including John C. Frémont's scientific expedition, diverted to California for the purpose) used the occasion to claim California for the United States. Kearny later crossed into California to solidify the claim.

By that time, Polk's brinkmanship on the Rio Grande had produced results. Mexican troops had crossed the river to drive out Taylor's force. In the fighting that ensued, American soldiers had been killed and wounded. In May 1846, the United States Congress declared that "by the act of the Republic of Mexico, a state of war exists" between the two nations (see Map 13-4).

The United States entered the war sorely unprepared. Although 100,000 volunteers would eventually sign up, at the outbreak of hostilities the United States claimed an army of only 7,500 troops. Perhaps Polk was willing to move so incautiously because he shared the widely held expansionist view that Mexico was a "miserable, inefficient" nation. More likely, he simply believed that the United States could win the war. Mexico (and New Spain before it) had always been less interested in its northern provinces than in other parts of the nation that yielded greater economic resources. Moreover, the Mexican government had recently undergone a coup and remained extremely unstable. Indeed, for a time the United States hoped to sponsor Santa Anna's return to power, assuming that he would show his gratitude by coming to terms over the Southwest. Even when that failed, Polk knew that he was dealing with a central government whose effective power did not extend far beyond Mexico City. With California guarded by Frémont and the naval squadron, the United States could bring its military power to bear on Mexico City.

Finding the right leader for such a campaign proved tricky. Taylor, the obvious choice, was a Whig of growing popularity. Polk finally settled on Winfield Scott, not an altogether satisfactory alternative, since he, too, harbored Whig political ambitions. In the late winter of 1847, a naval squadron of 200 ships conveyed Scott's army through the Gulf of Mexico to Matamoros, Mexico, and then to Tampico and finally to Veracruz, where his army of 10,000 soldiers forced that city to surrender in April of 1847. In a series of difficult campaigns, Scott's troops fought their way to the outskirts of Mexico City. After delaying most of the summer, Scott began his final assault on September 8, and on September 14 Mexico City fell.

For all the military brilliance of the American campaign across Mexico, the prosecution of the war brought with it the steady erosion of support. From the beginning,

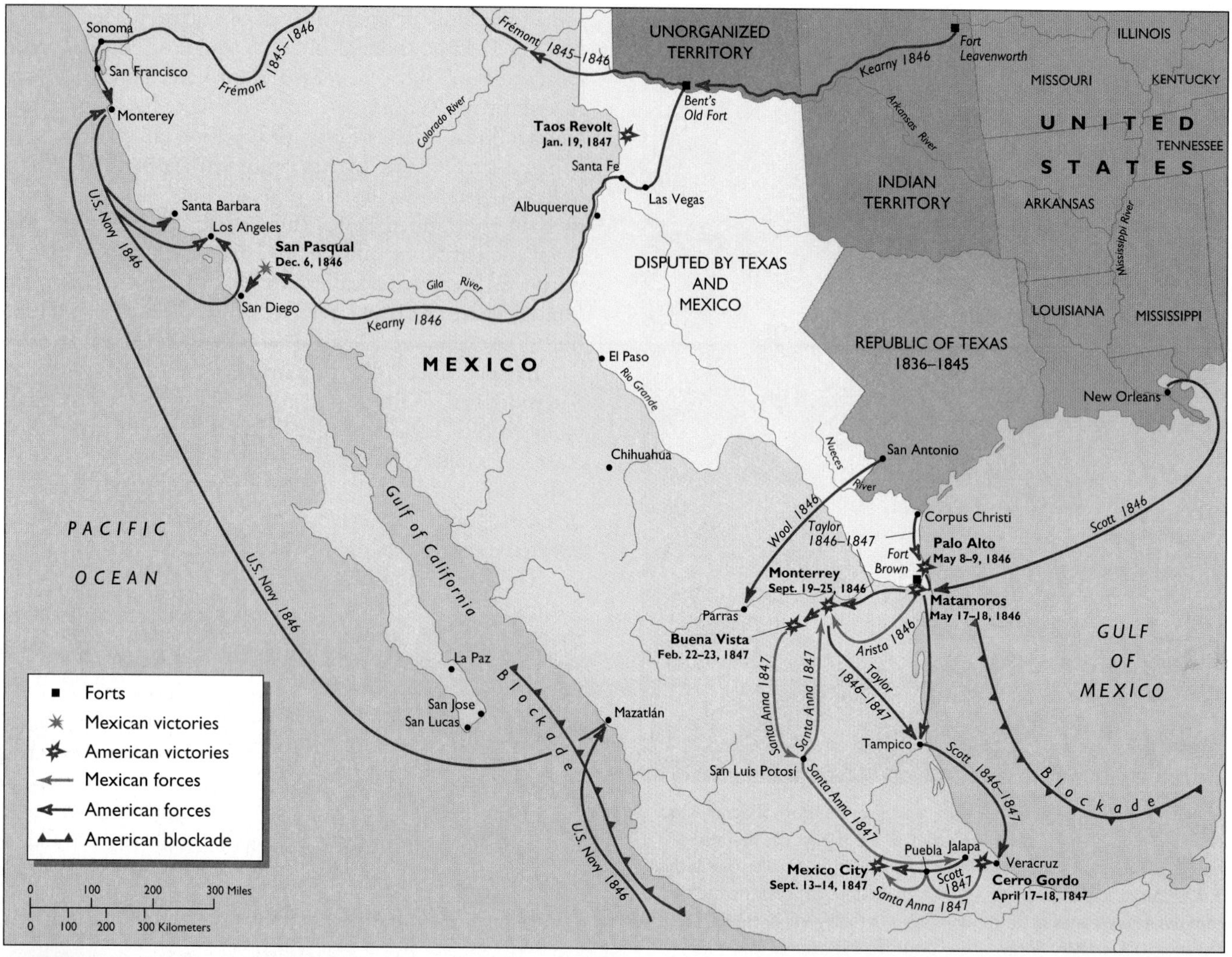

Map 13-4 Mexican War.
General Zachary Taylor's victories in northern Mexico established the Rio Grande as the boundary between Texas and Mexico. Colonel Stephen Kearny's expedition secured control of New Mexico. General Winfield Scott's invasion by sea at Veracruz and his occupation of Mexico City ended the war.

the war raised the question of slavery. Already feeling betrayed by Polk's willingness to compromise on Oregon, northern Democrats saw the war with Mexico as a transparent ploy to extend slavery. Northern antislavery activists spoke out against the war, and soon others, not previously known for their abolitionism, were catalyzed to declare themselves. Opposition to the war grew as stories of U.S. military atrocities began to filter back east. Even General Scott testified to acts of rape and murder sufficient, he stated, "to make Heaven weep and every American of Christian morals blush."

In spite of the unpopularity of the war, the end of hostilities found Mexico so weakened as to give Polk and some of his advisors momentary thoughts of extracting an even greater concession. His minister in Mexico, John Trist, opposed this proposal, however. When Polk recalled Trist, Trist refused to leave. In 1848 Trist negotiated the Treaty of Guadalupe Hidalgo, recognizing the Rio Grande as the border of Texas and granting the United States the terri-

tory encompassed in the present states of New Mexico, Arizona, Colorado, Utah, and Wyoming, as well as California. In return, the United States paid Mexico 15 million dollars and assumed war claims of American citizens against Mexico. Although outraged that Trist had not pushed for grander claims, Polk had little choice but to submit the treaty to the Senate, which approved it on March 10, 1848. The following May 25, Mexico concurred.

The story of John Trist marked a sad postscript to the War with Mexico. Trist was arrested and fired from his job in the State Department. Not until 1870, when he lay dying, did Congress award Trist the back pay due for his service to the United States in Mexico.

Although Polk's presidency was dominated by the War with Mexico, other familiar issues, notably the tariff and the independent treasury, continued to haunt domestic politics. In each case, Polk was victorious, dominating politics with a success not seen since Andrew Jackson. Like Jackson, Polk opposed protective tariffs, which he saw as

GROWING UP IN AMERICA

Rankin Dilworth in the War With Mexico

Rankin Dilworth was only 18 years old when he entered the United States Military Academy at West Point. Dilworth's father had died some time earlier. Although his mother had remarried, she was apparently a widow again by the time her son applied to the academy. Dilworth described himself as having to "depend upon my own resources," and he may well have seen the Army as his one opportunity to get ahead in life. Dilworth was apparently an average cadet, graduating in the middle of his class in 1844, one year behind Ulysses S. Grant, future general of the Union Army and president of the United States. But in 1844 neither Grant nor Dilworth was contemplating duty in a civil war. If young Dilworth had his sights fixed on any particular arena of service, it was surely the West, where American territorial ambitions were creating countless opportunities for military advancement.

By the spring of 1846, those opportunities were near at hand. Barracked outside of St. Louis, in April Dilworth's company was ordered to southern Texas, where hostilities had already broken out between United States troops and the Mexican Army. During the coming weeks they traveled by boat down the Mississippi and by steamer across the Gulf of Mexico to Matamoros, Mexico. From there, they marched up the Rio Grande to Carmargo, Texas, where Dilworth's unit joined with the American expeditionary force under General Zachary Taylor. From Carmargo, the combined force proceeded to Monterey. From April 28 to September 19, 1846, Dilworth kept an almost daily record of that journey.

The diary suggests that, officer or not, Dilworth was shadowed by nostalgia for home. Viewing the beautiful church in Renosa made him wonder "if I will ever go to church again where I hear the English language spoken." That night, he dreamed he was in church at home "without a thought of camps or bivouacs, with smiling happy faces around me." Suddenly awakened by the call to guard duty, "in an instant," he wrote, "I found myself on the hot sandy plaza of Reynosa, many, many miles from those I love."

Still, 24 years old and as interested in adventure as in military exploits, Dilworth found much to occupy his attention in the journey south. Especially early in the trip, there were cotillions and elaborate officers' messes. Dilworth also took a keen interest in Mexico. Often waxing romantic, he compared Mexico to "a magnificent flower garden" dotted with plots of "limes, oranges, lemons, [and] pomegranates." He admired young Mexican women, one of whom he declared "the handsomest female that I have seen since I parted with E. M. M."

(his sweetheart back East). Dilworth's descriptions of Mexico were not all flattering, however, and he sometimes betrayed the flippant cultural superiority that was so much a part of American expansionism of the 1840s. "The inhabitants present all shades from pure Indian to the white person," he wrote on one occasion. "Their intelligence is in the same scale."

Although Rankin Dilworth enjoyed aspects of the journey south, his diary also recorded the daily, and sometimes needless, hardships that plagued the campaign and would eventually make it infamous in Army annals. Swollen with untrained volunteers and newly trained officers (like Dilworth himself), the Mexican campaign was a tutorial in bad luck and bad judgment. Dilworth wrote about tents that collapsed in violent rainstorms, marches through mud so thick that it added ten pounds to the weight of each boot, and temperatures so hot that soldiers died of heat prostration. He wrote of arrogant and inept officers who could not even march their troops in the right direction. "Some persons occasionally make blunders," he noted, "but others are constantly making them."

On September 19, as his company approached Monterrey, Dilworth encountered an old friend in a different unit. The friend asked Dilworth if he had "heard the 'Elephant' groan," an expression that had by that time become common among the troops to express their bitterness and disappointment. Dilworth did not record his reply. Nor did he add any further entries in the diary. On September 21, General Taylor ordered a dangerous assault on Monterrey, dividing his small band of volunteers and inexperienced professionals into two groups to attack the city from opposite sides. The western troops gained their goals with relative ease, but the eastern forces lost their way in thick cane fields, arriving at the city on heavily fortressed roads where they were caught in deadly Mexican crossfire. Once in the city's narrow streets, they were easy targets for sharpshooters stationed in houses and along rooftops. Remarkably, inch by inch, house by house (often blasting their way through common walls by cannon rather than exposing themselves to sure death on the streets), Taylor's troops carried the day. On September 24, 1846, Mexican General Ampudia offered surrender.

None of this mattered to Rankin Dilworth. During the first day's assault a "twelve-pounder cannon ball" had torn off one of his legs. On September 27, at 24 years of age, he died. His family was unable to pay the costs of having his body returned to Ohio. Lieutenant Rankin Dilworth was buried in Monterrey, Mexico.

benefiting industrialists at the expense of farmers and republican values. Although Whigs in Congress continued to push for higher tariffs to support domestic manufacturing, the 1846 tariff eliminated flat duties and revised overall levels downward. Also like Jackson, Polk opposed the national bank. In 1846 he persuaded Congress to reinstate Van Buren's independent treasury as an institution to handle the federal government's necessary financial transactions. Meanwhile, he vetoed attempt after attempt on the part of the Whigs to enact legislation supporting internal improvements.

The similarities between Jackson and Polk extended to their broader understanding of politics in antebellum America and to the way in which they used the political machinery. Like Jackson, Polk framed battles of policy as battles between good and evil, as "a fierce and mighty struggle" between the champions of individual opportunity and the henchmen of finance and capital. At the same time, also like Jackson, Polk was willing to exercise the enormous power of the executive as the tool of the people's will. In that battle, he was convinced that it was the president, and not the legislature (Whig-controlled by his final years in office) that represented the people's will, and he wielded the power of the presidency with astonishing success. Before he left office, virtually every important item on his political agenda had been accomplished. Lost for the moment in that flush of victory was the steady erosion of popular support for the Democratic Party.

CHRONOLOGY

1834	First Missionaries arrive in Oregon Territory
1836	Martin Van Buren elected president
	Equal Rights Party formed
	Whig Party runs candidates for president
	Texas declares independence
1837	Sarah and Angelina Grimké tour North opposing slavery
	Pastoral Letter of Massachusetts Clergy
1838	"Aroostook" War
	Anti-Slavery Petition campaign at height
1839	Amistad Mutiny
1840	Independent Treasury Bill
	Anti-Slavery Society splits
	Liberty Party nominates James Birney for the presidency

	Large-scale overland migration to West Coast begins
	Whig candidate William Henry Harrison elected president
1841	John Tyler succeeds Harrison in office
	Creole Mutiny
1842	Webster-Ashburton Treaty
1844	James Polk is elected president
1845	The United States annexes Texas
1846	The United States declares war on Mexico
1848	Independent woman's rights movement begins at Seneca Falls, New York
	Treaty of Guadalupe Hidalgo
	Teton Sioux tax white settlers passing through their lands

Conclusion

In 1820, Fanny Wright had noted that many observers worried about the differences between the American North and South, but Wright had been buoyantly optimistic. If all else failed, she declared, the western states, settled by migrants from both North and South, would always be "powerful cementers of the Union."

By the end of the 1840s, it was clear that Wright's confidence had been misplaced. The War with Mexico revealed just how far apart the North and South had grown. By 1848, the northern tier of states was deeply implicated in a political economy of free labor. The southern states, meanwhile, had grown ever more committed to the political economy of slavery. The Mexican War signaled the end of an era in which North-South tensions could be displaced onto East-West ambitions, and the arrival of an era in which differences between the North and South would seem undeniable and intractable—and symbolized in the West.

In 1848, a young man by the name of Henry David Thoreau mounted a lecture platform in Concord, Massachusetts. Thoreau intended his lecture, later published as the essay "Civil Disobedience," as an explanation of his refusal to pay poll taxes, which he considered money paid both to support the institution of slavery and its expansion in the War with Mexico. Echoing the perfectionism of Jacksonian America, Thoreau declared himself ready to separate from his government—indeed, to see the union itself destroyed—rather than support one more initiative of the United States in the West. Thoreau's words were fateful: "How does it become a man to behave toward this American government today?" he asked. "I answer, that he cannot without disgrace be associated with it. I cannot for an instant recognize that political organization as *my* government which is the *slave's* government also."

Review Questions

1. List three policies or political practices of the Jackson administration that ultimately weakened Van Buren's success as president.

2. Account for the specific timing of the emergence of a demand for women's suffrage.

3. Democrats and Whigs both embraced market expansion. What distinguished their views on this subject?

4. List three reasons that the question of the annexation of Texas proved so divisive in terms of North-South relations?

5. Compare Polk's effort to balance North-South territorial acquisitions with earlier, similar efforts—for example, the Missouri Compromise.

Further Readings

John Mack Faragher, *Women and Men on the Overland Trail* (1979). Faragher describes the migration of white Americans into Oregon Territory in the 1840s–1860s, including discussions of motivations that prompted families to undertake the trek, the preparations required for the journey, the routes taken, the obstacles faced, and the ways in which the experience of westering differed for women and men.

Lacey K. Ford, Jr., *Origins of Southern Radicalism: The South Carolina Upcountry, 1800–1860* (1988). Ford offers an examination of society and economy in South Carolina as a case study in the rise of white secessionist thought in the South, from the Nullification Crisis through the regional politics that characterized South Carolina in the late 1830s, the 1840s, and the 1850s.

Reginald Horsman, *Race and Manifest Destiny: The Origins of American Racial Anglo-Saxonism* (1981). Horsman traces the ascendancy of ideas of racial superiority throughout the antebellum years, examining both the presence of racial thinking in broad currents of American culture and the ways in which those intellectual perspectives shaped the politics of westward expansion.

Gerda Lerner, "The Political Activities of Antislavery Women," in *The Majority Finds Its Past: Placing Women in History* (1979). Lerner traces the process through which antislavery activities in general (including the petition campaigns) and the antislavery work of the Grimké sisters in particular created new forms of public power for women, creating one of the avenues through which women came to the demand for the vote.

James M. McCaffrey, *Army of Manifest Destiny: The American Soldier in the Mexican War, 1846–1848* (1992). This brief study of the largely volunteer American Army of the Mexican War furnishes useful insights into the high politics, the broad military strategies, and the daily experience of common soldiers in Polk's war of expansion against Mexico in 1846.

History on the Internet

"The Seneca Falls Convention"

http://www.npg.si.edu/col/seneca/senfalls1.htm

In addition to a general overview of the Seneca Falls convention, this site features from the National Portrait Gallery portraits of the key women involved in the quest for equal rights. To read the full text of the Seneca Falls Convention and Declarations of Sentiment/Report of the Women's Rights Convention, consult http://www.luminet.net/~tgort/convent.htm. Choose the link for the date of July 19, 20, 1848.

"The End of the Oregon Trail Interpretive Center"

http://endoftheoregontrail.org/index.html

Read about the plight of men and women on the Oregon Trail. At this site, learn about the logistics of wagon travel and settling the countryside. Short sketches give specifics about the lives of settlers. A site link explores the syncretic jargon that white settlers and Native Americans developed to communicate with one another.

"The American Whig Party"

http://odur.let.rug.nl/~usa/E/uswhig/whigsxx.htm

This site offers information on the founding of the party and its subsequent demise. The site also provides numerous links to pages that discuss Democrat Andrew Jackson's politics, presidency, and policies.

"The U.S.-Mexican War"

http://www.pbs.org/kera/usmexicanwar/mainframe.html

The text of this website, in both English and Spanish, offers varied perspectives on the war, commentary from historians about the importance of the conflict, and valuable chronologies.

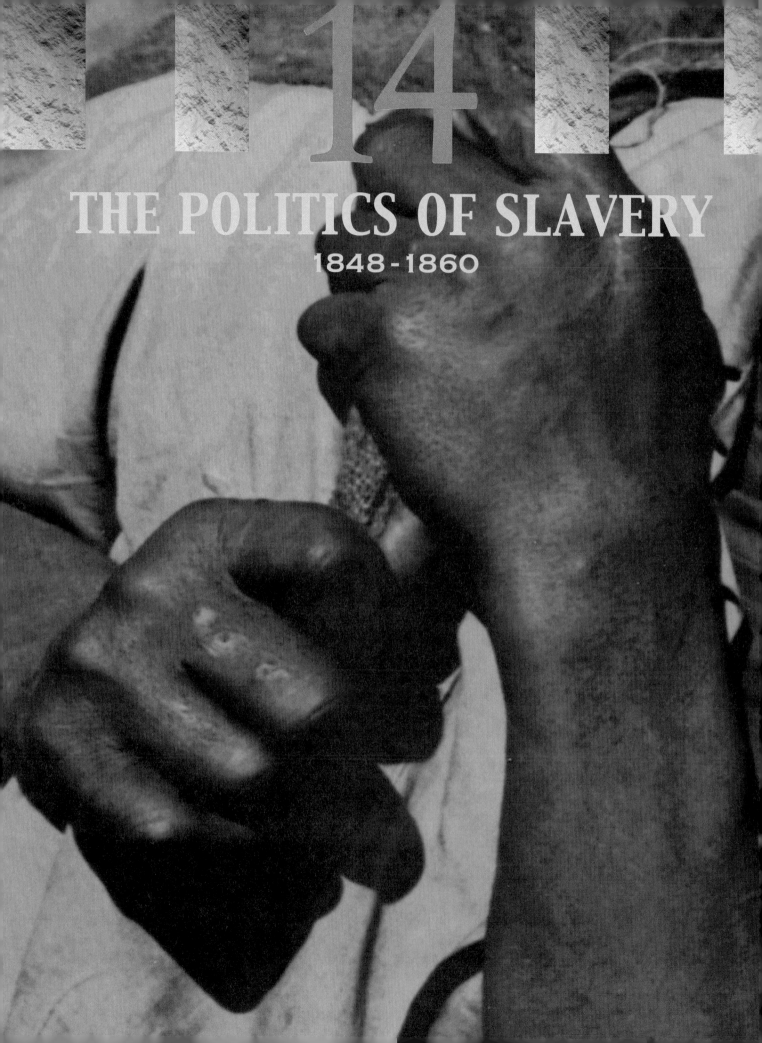

14

THE POLITICS OF SLAVERY

1848-1860

OUTLINE

Frederick Douglass

The Political Economy of Freedom and Slavery

A Changing Economy in the North

Strengths and Weaknesses of the Southern Economy

The Importance of the West

Slavery Becomes a Political Issue

Wilmot Introduces His Proviso

A Compromise Without Compromises

The Fugitive Slave Act Provokes a Crisis

The Election of 1852 and the Decline of the Whig Party

Nativism and the Origins of the Republican Party

The Nativist Attack on Immigration

The Kansas-Nebraska Act Revives the Slavery Issue

The Expansion of Slavery as a Foreign Policy

Kansas Begins to Bleed

A New Political Party Takes Shape

The First Sectional Election

The Labor Problem and the Politics of Slavery

An "Irrepressible" Conflict?

The Slavery Issue Persists

The Lecompton Constitution Splits the Democratic Party

Lincoln and Douglas Debates

The Retreat from Union

John Brown's War Against Slavery

Northerners Elect a President

Conclusion

Frederick Douglass

Frederick Douglass denounced the war with Mexico as "disgraceful, cruel, and iniquitous." It was, he believed, an act of piracy fought primarily to increase the number of slave states in the Union. Douglass expected such aggressive tactics from the slaveholders. What outraged him most was the support for the war in New England, even in Massachusetts, even among Whigs. Northern support for what he saw as a slaveholders' war only proved Douglass' conviction that the U.S. Constitution had created an unholy and unnatural union of liberty and slavery. The only solution was for New England to secede. "The Union must be dissolved," Douglass wrote during the war, "or New England is lost and swallowed up by the slave-power of the country."

Douglass had been urging disunion for several years, ever since he leaped from obscurity to become the most compelling antislavery voice in America. His authority derived from his extraordinary intelligence, his exceptional skill as a public speaker, and above all from the fact that he spoke of slavery from personal experience. For Frederick Douglass was not simply an abolitionist. He was also the most famous runaway slave in America.

He was born Frederick Augustus Washington Bailey, in Talbot County, Maryland, in 1818. He never knew who his father was, and his mother died when he was a young boy. In his earliest years Frederick was raised by his grandmother, but at the age of seven he was sent to Baltimore. There he became a skilled caulker working in the shipyards. He learned to hire out his labor, paying his master three dollars each week and keeping the rest himself. And there, in Baltimore, he grew to resent the arrangement. Why, the slave wondered, should one man claim the fruits of another man's labor? For the rest of his life he would associate freedom with the right to earn a living. When Frederick's master revoked their arrangement and demanded that the slave hand over all his earnings, Frederick began planning his escape.

389

On May 3, 1838, Frederick Bailey dressed up as a sailor and boarded a northbound train using the papers of a friend as identification. By September he had changed his last name to Douglass and was living and working in New Bedford, Massachusetts. Douglass saw New Bedford as a perfect example of the difference between a political economy based on free labor and the political economy of slavery. Compared to the docks he had worked on in Baltimore, New Bedford's wharf struck Douglass as a model of efficient and contented labor.

In New Bedford Douglass began attending antislavery meetings. He subscribed to William Lloyd Garrison's fiery abolitionist newspaper, the *Liberator*. In 1841 he was invited to speak during an abolitionist convention on Nantucket island, where he stunned his listeners with an eloquent recital of his own experience as a slave. William Lloyd Garrison himself was in the audience, and he immediately invited Douglass to become a speaker for the American Anti-Slavery Society. For the next several years Douglass was a leading spokesman for the Garrisonian wing of the abolitionist movement.

Frederick Douglass, the most famous fugitive slave in American history, in an 1855 engraving. After his 1838 escape from slavery, Douglass went on to become a lifelong, articulate champion of racial equality.

The Garrisonians were different from other abolitionists. They believed that the Constitution was hopelessly corrupted by its compromises with slavery. They saw no point in pursuing political reforms and criticized other abolitionists for working within a system tainted by a pro-slavery Constitution. Instead they advocated the political separation of the North from the South. Because they were pacifists, Garrison and his followers rejected all violent efforts to overthrow slavery, including rebellion by slaves themselves. Their preferred solution to the problem of slavery was moral persuasion of their opponents. Frederick Douglass initially believed all of these things.

The Mexican War was a turning point in Douglass' thinking, and by the late 1840s he began to question several aspects of Garrison's approach to abolition. He saw growing numbers of northerners join the Free Soil Party dedicated to halting the expansion of slavery, and he wondered why this could not become the basis for a potent political coalition against slavery itself. Over the course of the 1850s Douglass moved still further from the Garrisonians: he openly supported slave rebellion; he came to believe that political action was necessary to bring the institution of slavery down; and he also began to doubt the wisdom of dismissing the Constitution as a pro-slavery document.

Douglass was able to move closer to the mainstream of northern politics because antislavery sentiment had suddenly entered the mainstream. For more than half a century the major parties had studiously avoided the problem of slavery. At the center of American politics was an unspoken agreement not to discuss the issue. After the war with Mexico the agreement fell apart.

During the 1850s the slavery issue pushed all others aside and a third "party system" emerged in American politics. The first party system had divided the Republicans from the Federalists in the earliest decades of the century. During the 1830s and 1840s the Democrats and the Whigs formed a second party system, and both parties appealed to northerners and southerners alike. But in the 1850s the Whig Party collapsed entirely. In its place emerged the new Republican Party, openly hostile to slavery and sworn to restricting its expansion. Shortly thereafter the Democratic Party was captured by pro-slavery extremists. This was the third party system, and in its earliest years it was defined by sharp ideological differences over slavery. For the first time in American history the political mainstream could accommodate a radical abolitionist like Frederick Douglass, so Douglass moved to the mainstream. In 1848 he thought New England should free itself from the Constitution by withdrawing from the union. By 1861 he was urging the president to uphold the Constitution by suppressing the South's attempt to secede.∎

▌▌ K E Y   T O P I C S

- The social and economic differences between North and South

- The increasing significance of slavery as a political issue during the 1850s

- The decline of the Whig Party and the emergence of a Republican Party

- The role of the West in the sectional crisis

- The split within the Democratic Party

The Political Economy of Freedom and Slavery

The politics of slavery erupted at a moment of tremendous economic growth. As the depression of the 1840s lifted, the American zeal for internal improvements revived. The canals that had been constructed with such fanfare between 1800 and 1830 were systematically widened during the 1840s and 1850s so that they could accommodate a new technological development, the steamboat. Railroad construction exploded in the 1830s, collapsed during the depressed 1840s, and then came back stronger than ever in the 1850s. On the eve of the Civil War, the United States boasted more miles of railroad track than the rest of the world combined. No less spectacular was the rapid adoption of the telegraph. Invented by Samuel F. B. Morse in 1844, the telegraph made it possible, for the first time in history, for two human beings separated by oceans and continents to sustain virtually instantaneous communication. By 1860, there were 50,000 miles of telegraph wire connecting different parts of America. The first transcontinental line, connecting the west and east coasts, was completed in 1861.

In many ways these were national developments that tied all Americans together and so might have inhibited the growth of sectionalism. A sophisticated and efficient transportation network, together with a reliable system of long-distance communication, helped integrate the entire United States into a single national market. But market integration only succeeded in tying together two different political economies based on two very different systems of labor. By the 1850s the differences between North and South overwhelmed the connections that bound them together.

A Changing Economy in the North

The 1850s were booming years for northern farmers. Between 1845 and 1860 the market for agricultural commodities exploded and prices remained strong, in spite of a sharp recession in 1857. By mid-century few farm communities in the North were untouched by the national market. Railroads and telegraphs brought timely news of commodity prices and reliable means of sending crops to market. By the 1850s, it took less than a week to transport meat and grains from midwestern cities like Cincinnati to the major east coast metropolises. The result was a dramatic reduction in the price of western commodities in eastern markets. Northern farmers were therefore able to devote more of their time and effort to producing crops for sale rather than for consumption at home. Impressive new inventions like the steel plow, seed drills, and the McCormick reaper made it easier than ever for northern farmers to increase their production of goods for market. The resulting growth of northern agricultural output was quite dramatic. Between 1820 and 1860 northern farmers quadrupled their productivity.

Farmers could grow more crops for sale because more and more Americans were living in cities and working entirely for wages. Unlike farmers, wage earners produced little of their own food, clothing, or shelter. Yet so productive was American agriculture that as the number of Americans who lived off their wages increased, the proportion of farmers declined. In 1820, 75 percent of the labor force was devoted to agriculture. By 1860 the figure had dropped to 57 percent.

Wage labor was rapidly replacing independent labor as the most common way to make a living in the North. For decades wage earners had been scattered along the docks of the seaports or hidden in homes doing piece work. A large proportion of these earliest wage laborers were women and African Americans. In the first New England textile mills wage laborers were women more often than men, but in the second quarter of the nineteenth century this began to change. For the first time large numbers of white men earned their living not by independent labor but by selling their labor power in return for wages.

The growth of wage labor in the North was so rapid that native-born workers could not fill the growing demand for labor in the cities and factories. America had always been a nation of immigrants, but in the mid-1840s the number of Europeans coming to the United States jumped sharply. Of the five million immigrants who arrived between 1820 and 1860, about three million came in the single decade of 1845–1854. More than two-thirds of them were Irish or German, a substantial proportion of whom were Roman Catholic. Two successive failures of Ireland's potato crop in 1845 and 1846 left 1 million Irish dead and sent another 1.5 million emigrating, two-thirds of them to the United States. By 1855 a larger proportion of

Americans was foreign born than at any other time in the nation's history.

The most successful immigrants were those who came with the means to buy land or establish a business. They often relied on a network of other immigrants to provide material as well as moral assistance. Many immigrants, especially the Irish, came to America impoverished. Arriving penniless at east coast ports, they were rarely in a position to continue traveling in hopes of buying farmland on the western frontier. Instead they congregated in the growing cities and factory towns of the North. By 1860 immigrants made up more than one-third of the residents in northern cities with populations of at least 10,000.

Lacking the funds that would have allowed them to establish their economic independence, impoverished immigrants became wage laborers in numbers that far outstripped their proportions in the population. In New York City, for example, immigrants accounted for 48 percent of the 1860 population but 69 percent of the city's labor force. Men worked in unskilled jobs on the docks, at construction sites, or on the railroads and canals that were crisscrossing America. They were conspicuous in the coal mines and iron foundries of Pennsylvania. Women often worked as seamstresses, laundresses, or in other forms of domestic service. In the textile mills and shoe factories of New England, Irish families often worked together, husbands and wives alongside sons and daughters.

Industrialization was not the only reason for the growth of wage labor. By the 1850s a small but growing middle class of white-collar employees also worked for wages. This trend became noticeable in the 1840s, as businesses expanded beyond the confines of the traditional small shop. White-collar employees kept the increasingly complex accounting records, maintained the expanding files, and kept track of the growing volume of sales. As the scale of industrial production increased, individual businesses opened large downtown stores to sell their goods, sometimes hundreds of miles from where they were produced. Between 1859 and 1862, for example, A. T. Stewart built a huge dry goods store covering a full square block in lower Manhattan. Lord & Taylor and Brooks Brothers would shortly build similar stores of their own. The financial needs of these large-scale enterprises were met by an expanding number of banks, insurance companies, and accounting firms. All these enterprises employed armies of sales clerks, record keepers, and other white-collar workers.

Thus, economic growth in the North during the 1850s was a symptom of important social changes. A rural society was becoming more urban. Industry was replacing agriculture as the driving economic force. Wage labor was replacing independent labor. A Protestant nation encountered the first great wave of Catholic immigrants. And even back on the farm, machines were making it possible for one person to cultivate more acres than ever before. All

of this signaled the birth of a political economy based on new sources of wealth and new forms of work.

Strengths and Weaknesses of the Southern Economy

"You dare not make war on cotton," James Henry Hammond warned his fellow senators in 1858. "No power on earth dares make war upon it. Cotton *is* king." This was a plausible argument for a South Carolinian like Hammond to make in the 1850s, for they were among the most prosperous years in the South's history. The price of cotton rose steadily over the course of the decade, as did the price of slaves. Recovering from the economic doldrums of the 1840s, southern states threw themselves into the business of railroad construction with unprecedented vigor. By 1860 the South could claim a fairly large railroad network of its own, smaller than the North's but impressive by

In this 1854 caricature, an impoverished Irishman on the Dublin docks contemplates booking passage to America, in hopes of economic prosperity.

world standards. Steamboats plied the South's rivers. Telegraph wires sped news of cotton prices from the Mississippi River to the Atlantic coast. Southerners commonly boasted of their region's successful commitment to progress and prosperity. This was the context in which Senator Hammond, one of the wealthiest cotton planters in the South, so openly defied slavery's critics.

But no matter how efficient and profitable slavery was, it could not transform the South the way wage labor was transforming the North. The South had changed in many ways during the previous century. It had expanded across half the continent. Cotton had become the region's most profitable crop. The Atlantic slave trade was closed off to the South, and a native-born, largely Christian slave population had grown up. And yet, the southern social structure that was in place by 1750 was largely unchanged a century later. Slaveholders still occupied the top of the southern social pyramid, and slaves were still unambiguously located at the bottom. Most of those in between were called "nonslaveholders," another indication of slavery's pervasive influence on southern society.

Even in prosperous times slavery's critics pointed to what they saw as weaknesses in the southern economy. Prosperity in the North meant more factories and bigger cities, but a prosperous slave economy meant the opposite. During the 1850s the rising price of cotton sucked slaves out of the cities and back into the countryside. Under King Cotton's reign, urban life stagnated while the rural economy boomed. In the North, prosperity rested on a growing number of wage earners in business and industry. In the South, especially the lower South, good times reinforced the wealth of the long-established slave-owning class.

To be sure, there were important signs of social change, especially in the upper South. The immigrant workers Frederick Douglass met on the Baltimore docks were caught up in the same process of economic development as the dockworkers of New Bedford, Massachusetts. The steady sale of slaves from the upper to the lower South reduced the political influence of slaveholders in states like Maryland and even Virginia. Indeed, among whites across the entire South the proportion of slaveholders had been declining since 1830. As the price of slaves rose to new highs after 1850, it became harder than ever for small southern farmers to rise into the slave-holding class. In 1830 one-third of southern white families held slaves. By 1860 the proportion had dropped to one in four.

Leading southerners began to worry that small farmers would not remain loyal to slavery if they had no chance of becoming slaveholders themselves, and politicians devised a number of reforms aimed at increasing the proportion of slaveholders in the South. Some proposed legislation that would exempt an owner's first slave from all property taxes. Others argued that the African slave trade should be reopened so that the price of slaves would decline, making it easier for small farmers to purchase their first slaves. None of these proposals went very far. But all were prompted by the fear that small farmers, unable to enter the slave-holding class, could not be counted on to defend southern slave society in the face of an increasingly hostile North.

The Importance of the West

Despite the growing economic differences between the North and the South, both sections coveted western lands. By 1850 many northerners had come to believe that slavery degraded free labor and undermined economic opportunity. If slavery were allowed to expand into the West it would deprive free laborers of an important source of prosperity and independence. But the slaveholders had come to believe that their own prosperity depended on the diffusion of the slave economy into the West. The disposition of the huge land mass acquired in the War with Mexico therefore forced Americans into a sustained public debate over the future of slavery and freedom in the United States.

At the outbreak of the American Revolution most slaves were concentrated in a relatively narrow band along the east coast. By 1825 the slave economy had leaped beyond the mountains, covering Kentucky and Tennessee in the upper South, and Georgia, Alabama, and Mississippi in the lower South. Slavery was crossing the Mississippi River into Missouri, northern Louisiana, Arkansas, and Texas. Thwarted in California, slavery in the 1850s was threatening to move into the mines of New Mexico and onto the plains of Kansas. "The history of the United States shows there is a tendency in slave society to diffusion," Daniel R. Goodloe of North Carolina explained. "In fact, **diffusion,** or extension of area, is one of the necessities of slavery." Whether it was a necessity or not, slavery had expanded more than halfway across the continent of North America in about half a century (see Map 14-1).

The diffusion of the slave economy required a vigorous slave trade across the South. (The Atlantic slave trade had been closed to Americans in 1808.) By the 1850s some 20,000 slaves a year were being bought and sold on slave markets from Richmond, Virginia, to New Orleans, Louisiana. Thousands more were transported by individual masters who hoped to build a prosperous future on land in the West. For the slaves, westward expansion could be a painful experience. Inevitably it separated husbands from wives and parents from children. The ability to buy and sell human beings was a defining feature of slavery; without a slave market, the westward expansion of the slave economy would have been substantially hindered.

White southerners grew accustomed to viewing territorial expansion as a sign of progress. Critics of slavery were showered with statistics showing the upward curves of cotton production, southern population growth, and

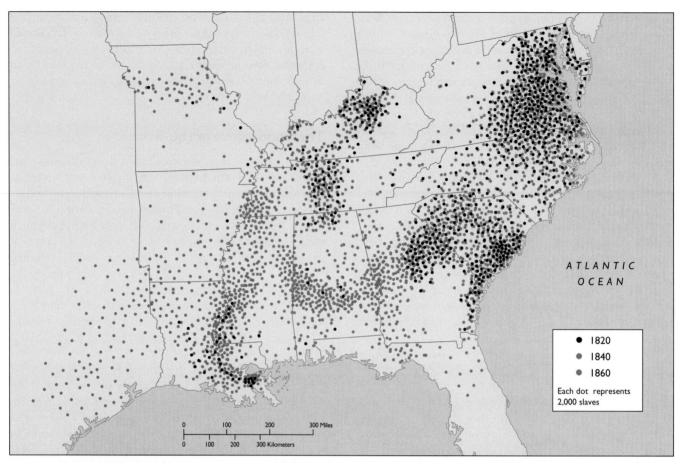

Map 14-1 Slavery's Expansion.
The westward expansion of the slave economy created political turmoil from 1820 until the Civil War. Sustained by an extensive internal slave trade that sold thousands of humans each year, slavery's expansion represented one of the greatest forced migrations in history.

above all the territorial expansion of the slave economy. The westward movement of the southern frontier demonstrated as nothing else could the continued strength of the political economy of slavery. To call a halt to that movement was to dam up the wellsprings of southern prosperity. It was an insult to the moral decency of white southerners, an obstacle to their economic vitality, and an unconstitutional infringement on their right to carry their property with them wherever they saw fit. So argued slavery's defenders, with increasing vehemence in the 1850s, for by then the West had captured the South's imagination, much as it had the North's.

But the economic growth of the North created equally strong ties between the East and the West. Mountains and rivers generally ran north and south, but turnpikes, canals, and especially railroads tended to compensate for nature's proclivities by running east and west. Of the approximately 20,000 miles of railroads built in the 1850s, few crossed the Mason-Dixon line to link the northern and southern economies (see Map 14-2). The transportation

revolution thus strengthened the ties between northeastern cities and the western frontier.

Under the circumstances, northerners came to view the West as essential to their prosperity. So long as there was room enough in the West for people in the East to settle, eastern workers could never be degraded to levels comparable to their European counterparts. The public lands of the West "are the great regulator of the relations of Labor and Capital," Horace Greeley explained, "the safety valve of our industrial and social engine." This **safety valve** theory was repeated over and over again in the North, even though there was not much truth in it. To move west, buy land, and establish a farm required resources far beyond the means of many, perhaps most, wage laborers at the time. Nevertheless, by 1860 the North and the West had clearly become economically interdependent. In the eyes of many northerners westward expansion was critical to the stability and prosperity of their entire social order. It was no wonder that the westward expansion of slavery caused so much anxiety in the North.

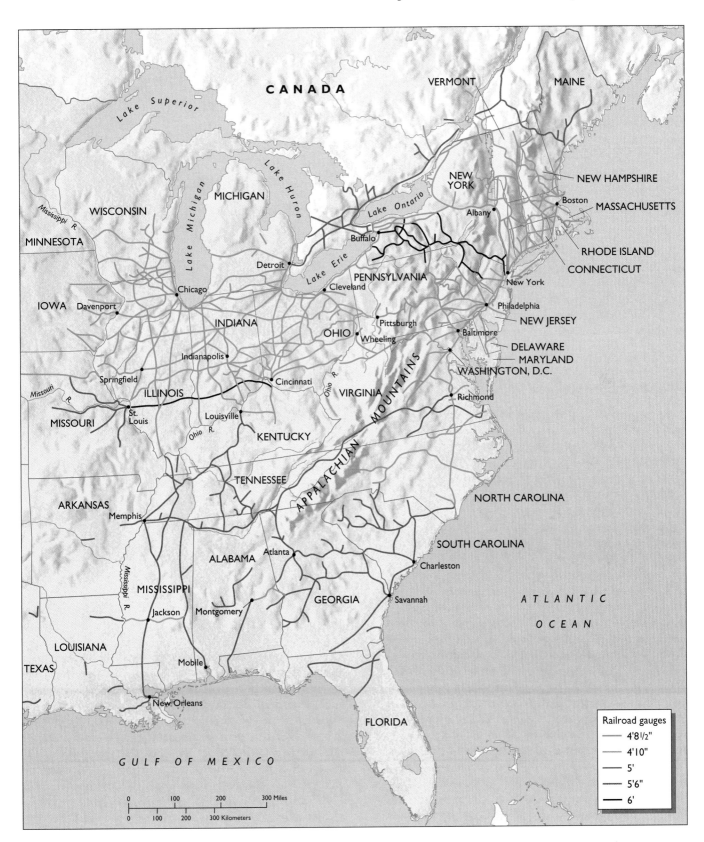

Map 14-2 Railroad Expansion.
This map shows that there were two distinct patterns of railroad development in the United States. In the North, rail lines connected the western states to the eastern seaboard. In the South, railroads tied the inland plantation districts to the coastal ports. Few lines connected the North to the South.

Slavery Becomes a Political Issue

Westward expansion forced the issue of slavery into the political mainstream. As far back as the 1780s opponents of slavery believed that halting its expansion was an important step on the path to abolition. In 1820 congressional efforts to restrict the westward expansion of slavery provoked a sharp political controversy that was resolved only by the Missouri Compromise (see chapter 10). The controversy erupted again in the 1830s, when abolitionists launched a campaign to mail antislavery propaganda to the South. Congress tried desperately to suppress the slavery issue by imposing a "gag rule" against antislavery petitions, but the huge land mass acquired by the United States during the War with Mexico revived the troublesome issue of slavery's expansion. For the next 15 years national politics would return over and over to one crucial question: Should Congress restrict the movement of slavery into the West?

Wilmot Introduces His Proviso

On August 8, 1846, David Wilmot, a Democratic congressman from Pennsylvania, attached to an appropriations bill an amendment banning slavery from all the territories acquired in the war with Mexico. This was the famous "Wilmot Proviso." Wilmot himself was hardly an abolitionist. He was not motivated, he said, by any "squeamish sensitiveness upon the subject of slavery, [or] morbid sympathy for the slave." Rather, he wanted western lands preserved for the settlement of whites. "I plead the cause and rights of the free white man," Wilmot insisted.

Initially, Whigs and Democrats from the North joined in support of the proviso, while their southern counterparts opposed it. When it was reintroduced in the next session of Congress, however, the administration lobbied the northern Democrats intensively, and the proviso went down to defeat. Nevertheless, it paralyzed Congress for several years in the late 1840s. Conditions in the West demanded federal legislation that Congress proved unable to enact. Mormon settlers had been pouring into the basin of the Great Salt Lake, and they required some form of government, but governmental authority in Utah could not be secured until Congress organized the New Mexican Territory. The discovery of gold in California brought a rush of settlers and a good deal of disorder to the mining camps of the Sierra foothills and the boomtown of San Francisco. A territorial government could not be established without congressional action. Every time such issues came up in Washington, D. C., Congress was frozen by sectional differences.

By 1850 four positions had hardened into place. At one extreme were those northern congressmen who still

Following the discovery of gold in California, prospectors from around the world headed for the mining camps that sprang up along the foothills of the Sierra Nevada mountains.

favored a Wilmot-like solution that would have banned slavery in all the territories. At the other extreme were the southern followers of John C. Calhoun who argued that Congress had no right whatsoever to regulate slavery in the territories. In between there were two different positions. Some wanted to extend the Missouri Compromise line, which would have pushed the North/South division all the way to the Pacific Ocean. Finally there was something called **popular sovereignty,** the position advocated early on by Michigan Democrat Lewis Cass and later supported by Stephen A. Douglas of Illinois. Popular sovereignty meant different things to different people, but in principle it gave settlers the right to decide for themselves whether they would have slavery in their territory.

The four conflicting positions that led to congressional gridlock also disrupted the major parties. In the presidential elections of 1848 antislavery men bolted both the Democrats and the Whigs and threw their support to the Free-Soil Party. With the Wilmot Proviso as their platform, the Free-Soilers won 14 percent of the northern vote. Meanwhile, proslavery **fire-eaters** threatened to walk out of the Democratic convention. The Whigs survived this turmoil to elect to the presidency Zachary Taylor, a hero of the war with Mexico. The Whig triumph was short lived, however. In 1849 President Taylor urged New Mexico and California to apply directly for admission to the Union without going through the usual territorial stage. California's application for statehood arrived with a constitution that prohibited slavery. This inevitably provoked a fight over whether any new slave states should be admitted to the Union. The House of Representatives, with a strong northern majority, reaffirmed the Wilmot Proviso. For good measure, it condemned the slave trade in Washington, D. C., and almost abolished slavery in the District of Columbia. The Senate, which had a strong southern wing, blocked all such measures.

This was no ordinary congressional stalemate. The president's proposal threw the nation's capital into turmoil. Fistfights broke out in the halls of Congress. Elected representatives traded insults and challenged each other to duels. Threatening secession, pro-slavery partisans called for a southern rights convention to meet at Nashville in June 1850. With passions running red hot, the stage was set for one of the most dramatic debates in congressional history.

A Compromise Without Compromises

Into this stalemate marched the "great triumvirate" of distinguished old senators, Henry Clay of Kentucky, Daniel Webster of Massachusetts, and John C. Calhoun of South Carolina. This was to be their final act in national politics. Clay, who had been instrumental in securing the Missouri Compromise of 1820 and resolving the Nullification Crisis of 1833, tried one last time to save the Union from collapse. He devised a series of eight resolutions, six of them paired in three measures designed to balance the conflicting interests of North and South. Under the first pair of measures, California would be admitted as a free state, but the rest of the Mexican territories would have no conditions regarding slavery attached to their applications for statehood. The second pair limited the number of slave states that could be carved out of Texas Territory, but in return the federal government would assume Texas' debt. The third pair abolished the slave trade in Washington, D. C., but protected slavery itself from federal interference. In addition Clay's compromise package included two more provisions that were partial to the South. One was a formal congressional promise not to interfere in the interstate slave trade. The other was a new fugitive slave law.

Clay gathered all eight provisions of his compromise into a single package, dubbed the "Omnibus Bill" by President Taylor. The senator's goal was simple. By coupling the pro-slavery and antislavery provisions, he hoped to gain enough support from centrists in each party to override both southern fire-eaters and northern Free-Soilers.

The congressional debate over Clay's package took place in the spring and summer of 1850 and left in its wake a series of extraordinary speeches. Daniel Webster con-

founded his antislavery admirers by eloquently supporting the compromise measures. Appealing for sectional harmony in his famous Seventh of March Address, Webster claimed to speak "not as a Massachusetts man, nor as a Northern man, but as an American." Calhoun, by contrast, spoke very much as a southern man. Deathly ill and unable to deliver his own speech, Calhoun listened as a colleague read his somber warning that the bonds tying the sections together had been snapped by the North's continued agitation of the slavery question. If constitutional protection of slavery were not enforced, Calhoun declared, the union of North and South would be severed. In response, New York's William H. Seward argued that the Constitution gave Congress every right to restrict slavery in the territories. In any case, Seward added, there was a "higher law than the Constitution" that compelled Congress to put slavery on the road to extinction. Seward's reference to a "higher law" had revolutionary implications that scandalized southerners and even shocked many of his fellow northerners.

The sectional hostilities exposed in the debate suggest why Clay's legislative maneuver was doomed from the start. Antislavery senators voted against the Omnibus Bill for its various provisions protecting slavery. Pro-slavery senators opposed Clay's measure for its restrictions on slavery. On July 31, after months of wrangling, the Senate killed the package. Exhausted and angry, Henry Clay gave up and left Washington. The old generation, led by the great triumvirate, had failed to resolve the crisis.

From that moment on national politics would be dominated by a new generation of congressional leaders. One of them was William Seward. Another was Senator Stephen A. Douglas, the "Little Giant" from Illinois. While Clay was recuperating in Newport, Douglas used his adroit parliamentary skills to rescue the compromise. He broke the omnibus package up into a series of five separate bills, each designed to win different majorities. Antislavery and moderate congressmen joined to secure the admission of California as a free state. Pro-slavery congressmen voted with moderates to win passage of a fugitive slave law. By similar means, Congress settled the Texas border, determined that New Mexico and Utah would apply for statehood under the principle of popular sovereignty, and abolished the slave trade in the District of Columbia. Douglas' legislative maneuvering was masterful. Although proslavery and antislavery forces in Congress never once compromised on a single issue, the five bills that Douglas and his allies steered through both houses came to be known as the "Compromise of 1850."

Douglas' efforts were aided by the untimely death of the president. Zachary Taylor's replacement, Millard Fillmore, was more sympathetic to sectional reconciliation. Fillmore pronounced the Compromise of 1850 the "final settlement" of the slavery question. For the next few years

Anthony Burns was a fugitive slave whose owners were attempting to return him to the South. His 1854 trial created an uproar across the North, but especially in Boston where the trial was held.

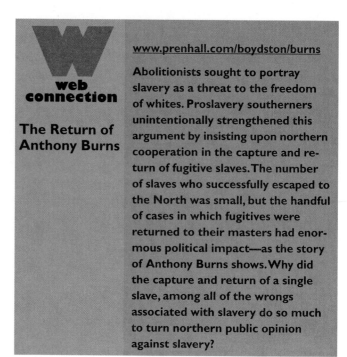

www.prenhall.com/boydston/burns

web connection

The Return of Anthony Burns

Abolitionists sought to portray slavery as a threat to the freedom of whites. Proslavery southerners unintentionally strengthened this argument by insisting upon northern cooperation in the capture and return of fugitive slaves. The number of slaves who successfully escaped to the North was small, but the handful of cases in which fugitives were returned to their masters had enormous political impact—as the story of Anthony Burns shows. Why did the capture and return of a single slave, among all of the wrongs associated with slavery do so much to turn northern public opinion against slavery?

moderate politicians across the country demonstrated a similar devotion to the compromise by swearing off all discussion of slavery. In the short run, the compromise apparently worked. The southern rights convention at Nashville fizzled. Its leader, Calhoun, was dead. The radical edge of the southern rights movement was blunted. But militant fire-eaters in the South and committed Free-Soilers in the North insisted that the day of reckoning had only been postponed. And in the North opposition to one feature of the compromise, the fugitive slave law, came swiftly and with unanticipated intensity.

The Fugitive Slave Act Provokes a Crisis

At first glance it is unclear why the Fugitive Slave Act of 1850 caused so much trouble. It was one of the least debated features of the compromise. The Constitution always had a fugitive slave clause, and a congressional law enforcing the clause had been in place since 1793. Why, then, did the new Fugitive Slave Act provoke such an uproar? The reason was that many northern states had passed laws to restrain fugitive slave catchers by guaranteeing the rights of due process to accused runaways. The 1850 statute was designed to thwart those northern efforts; it took jurisdiction over fugitive slave cases away from northern courts and gave it to a newly established cadre of

U.S. commissioners. These commissioners were paid 10 dollars if they ruled that a black captive should be returned to slavery but only 5 dollars if they ruled that the captive was legitimately free. Abolitionists naturally charged that this amounted to a bribe to send captives into slavery. Even more galling, the Fugitive Slave Act allowed commissioners to draft local citizens to assist slave catchers, thereby forcing northerners against their wills to send their neighbors into slavery.

The Fugitive Slave Act sent waves of terror through northern African-American communities. Slaves who had run away decades earlier, many of whom had established families and were long-settled in the North, now faced the prospect of being captured and sent back to the South. Even freeborn African Americans feared the prospect of being kidnapped into slavery without being able to prove their freedom in a court of law. Across the North vulnerable African Americans hurriedly packed their belongings and moved to the far West or the upper North, hoping to distance themselves from fugitive slave hunters. Thousands more migrated to Canada. A convention of African Americans meeting in Rochester, New York, denounced the Fugitive Slave Act as "the most cruel, unconstitutional, and scandalous outrage of modern times."

White abolitionists were no less vehement. The Reverend Charles Beecher denounced the Fugitive Slave Act as "the vilest monument of infamy of the nineteenth century." Even white northerners who cared little about the fate of African Americans were upset by the Fugitive Slave Act. The South seemed to be imposing its own laws and

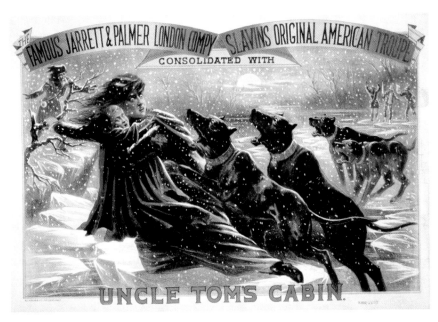

The tremendous popularity of Harriet Beecher Stowe's novel, Uncle Tom's Cabin, *reflected the surprisingly intense northern concern about the Fugitive Slave Act of 1850.*

institutions onto the North, forcing northerners into complicity with the slave regime. Appalled by the act, Harriet Beecher Stowe began serializing a story in a northern newspaper that was published as *Uncle Tom's Cabin* in 1852. The astonishing success of Stowe's novel is one measure of northern anxiety about the Fugitive Slave Act. *Uncle Tom's Cabin* quickly established itself as the most popular American novel published in the nineteenth century. In vivid, melodramatic prose Stowe drew a sentimental portrait of a slave mother and her infant child as they fled from a master who had contracted to sell them apart. In one of the book's most dramatic scenes, Eliza the slave clings to her daughter as she leaps across the ice-clogged Ohio River while being closely pursued by howling dogs. Few readers missed the point. Anyone who helped Eliza save her child stood in violation of the Fugitive Slave Act of 1850.

A surprising number of northerners tolerated violations of the Fugitive Slave Act. Antislavery crowds in Boston repeatedly defied slave catchers by harboring fugitives until they could be sent to safety in Canada or England. President Fillmore vowed to enforce the law with federal marshals if necessary. But Frederick Douglass, revealing how far he had moved from his earlier pacifism, advocated violent resistance. "A half dozen or more dead kidnappers carried down South," he suggested, "would cool the ardor of Southern gentlemen, and keep their rapacity in check." Violence did break out in Christiana, Pennsylvania, in September 1851. Attempting to recover two fugitives, a Maryland slaveholder, two of his sons, and three federal marshals were met with gunfire. In the ensuing "Battle of Christiana" the slave-

holder was killed and five others were wounded. The fugitives fled successfully to Canada.

The Election of 1852 and the Decline of the Whig Party

White southerners were outraged by evidence of the North's unwillingness to obey the Fugitive Slave Act. In the North and the South the Democratic Party made enforcement of the Compromise of 1850 its rallying cry in 1852. To be sure, the Democrats were torn by sectional divisions. But they managed to patch up their differences long enough to nominate Franklin Pierce, a dark horse candidate from New Hampshire thought to be sympathetic to southern interests. Pierce and the Democrats ran on a platform pledged to silencing discussion of the slavery issue by strict federal enforcement of the Compromise of 1850, "the act for reclaiming fugitives included."

The Whigs found no such unifying principle. White southerners abandoned the party because it harbored so many antislavery advocates. Northern voters punished the Whigs for their association with the Compromise of 1850. Henry Clay wrote the Fugitive Slave Act. Daniel Webster supported it. Millard Fillmore signed and aggressively enforced it as well. All were Whigs. The Whig Party convention met in Baltimore a month after the Democrats, but it produced no comparable show of sectional unity. Northern Whigs were determined to prevent the renomination of Millard Fillmore, and they succeeded. After 52 ballots, the convention nominated Winfield Scott of Virginia, despite nearly unanimous southern opposition. The southern delegates did secure a platform that reaffirmed the party's commitment to the Compromise of 1850. But this only meant that the Whigs would run a candidate who was objectionable in the South on a platform that was objectionable in the North. "We accept the candidate," Whigs in the North declared, "but we spit on the platform." Scott himself refused to endorse his own party's platform, thereby prompting the defection of several prominent southern Whigs.

Southern defections all but assured a major Whig defeat in the November election (see Figure 14-1). Pierce won 254 electoral votes. Scott won only 42. The Democratic candidate won 27 out of 31 states. The Whigs could not overcome the division between the northern and southern wings of the party. Severely weakened by the 1852 election results, the Whigs found themselves unable to meet another challenge that burst into American politics in the early 1850s, hostility to immigrants, otherwise known as nativism.

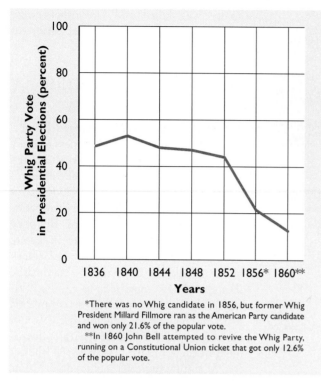

Figure 14-1   The Decline of the Whig Party.

Nativism and the Origins of the Republican Party

The politics of **nativism,** directed at restricting the flow of immigration to the United States, finally destroyed a Whig Party already weakened by sectionalism. From 1852 through 1854 the nativist American Party gained surprising strength. Hostility to immigrants, however, was not enough to rally northerners concerned about slavery, especially in the face of a Democratic Party that was more than ever the defender of southern slavery. What, then, would replace the Whig Party in the North? As usual, the question was decided in the West. After a brief but powerful outburst of nativist politics, the expansion of slavery returned to the center of national politics thanks to events in Nebraska Territory. As the dust of the western prairie reached Washington, D. C., nativism receded into obscurity. In its place was a new and powerful political force, the Republican Party, dedicated to halting slavery's westward expansion.

The Nativist Attack on Immigration

For a time the arrival of large numbers of Catholic immigrants stirred nearly as much animosity among Yankee Protestants as did slavery. In the early 1850s the Catholic

Church was widely known for its conservatism. The Pope himself expressed an abiding contempt for "progress." The Vatican had roundly condemned a series of liberal revolutions that swept across Europe in 1848, revolutions that were widely supported by most Americans.

There was more to Protestant contempt for Catholicism than a titanic struggle between the modern world and its critics. Anti-Catholicism had about it a strong odor of middle-class condescension as well. Nativism appealed to a broad range of shopkeepers, independent craftsmen, and white-collar clerks. These were people for whom the Protestant ethic of steadiness and sobriety amounted to a scriptural injunction. They looked with disdain upon a working class of Irish and German immigrants who drank heavily, lived in squalor, and seemingly lacked the dignity that native-born Protestants associated with economic independence. Nativist reformers took special aim at immigrant drinking habits by passing a series of temperance laws, beginning in Maine in 1851. But it was immigrant voting, particularly among Irish Catholics, that most unsettled the nativist soul. It was bad enough that the Irish were registering to vote so quickly after their arrival in America. Still worse was the fact that they voted Democratic.

The Democrats' appeal to Irish Catholics was double-edged. On the one hand, the party's populist rhetoric attracted working-class immigrants who were stung by the snobbery of Yankee Whigs. At the same time, Democrats stepped up their racist invective. Irish Americans began to identify themselves as "white," something they had not done in Ireland. They heaped contempt upon African Americans with whom they competed for jobs and housing. Democrats cultivated this sentiment, using racism to assimilate Irish working-class voters into the mainstream of American politics at a time when many Americans were organizing to keep immigrants out. The consequences for sectional politics were significant. The Democrats argued that abolition would force white workers into economic competition with an inferior race. Northern Democrats increasingly played this brand of racially inflected class politics. With the critical support of the Irish voting bloc, the Democratic Party sponsored a wave of new restrictions on the civil rights of free African Americans in many northern states.

In the elections of 1854 those voters who believed that immigration was the greatest threat to the American way of life cast their ballots for the American Party. (They were often called "Know-Nothings" because of their origins in a secret organization whose members insisted, when questioned, that they "know nothing" about it.) Voters who cared more about the threat of slavery voted for the Free Soil Party. Although both parties appealed to many of the same constituents, the American Party fared far better in 1854. Nativist candidates took 25 percent of the vote in New York and 40 percent in Pennsylvania. In Massachusetts the American Party won 63 percent of the vote and took control of the state legislature.

In 1854 it seemed as though nativism would eclipse slavery as the great issue of American politics. The Democrats were sworn to silence about slavery and the nativists were more upset by immigrants than by slaves. But slavery and nativism were never entirely separate issues, even within the American Party. Middle-class Yankees often viewed the struggle against Catholicism as inseparable from the struggle against slavery. Both were said to represent authoritarianism, ignorance, and a rejection of the "modern" values of individualism and progress. "Slavery and Priestcraft" have a common purpose, declared a nativist petition from Massachusetts in 1854. "One denies the right of a man to his body, and the other the right of a man to his soul. The one denies his right to think for himself, the other the right to act for himself." Given the close ties between nativism and antislavery sentiments, it was unclear which issue would eventually prevail. The question was decided not in the immigrant-crowded cities of Boston and New York, but rather on the sparsely settled plains of Kansas and Nebraska (see Map 14-3).

The Kansas-Nebraska Act Revives the Slavery Issue

The long struggle over what to do with Nebraska began in 1853. That was when the House of Representatives passed a bill banning slavery in Nebraska Territory on the grounds that it fell north of the Missouri Compromise line. Southerners killed the Nebraska Bill in the Senate. The following year Stephen Douglas reintroduced it, this time organizing the territory on the principle of popular sovereignty. In theory the Douglas Bill left Nebraskans free to decide whether slavery would be allowed in their territory.

No one was satisfied with Douglas' proposal. Northerners were outraged that the 1850 agreement to extend the Missouri Compromise line was so quickly scuttled. Militant southerners, having grown suspicious of all congressional attempts to regulate slavery in the territories, now rejected popular sovereignty in principle. So Douglas withdrew the bill and reintroduced it in January 1854, but with a new twist. He split Nebraska Territory in two, placing Kansas to the west of the slave state of Missouri and Nebraska to the north of Kansas. Both were to be

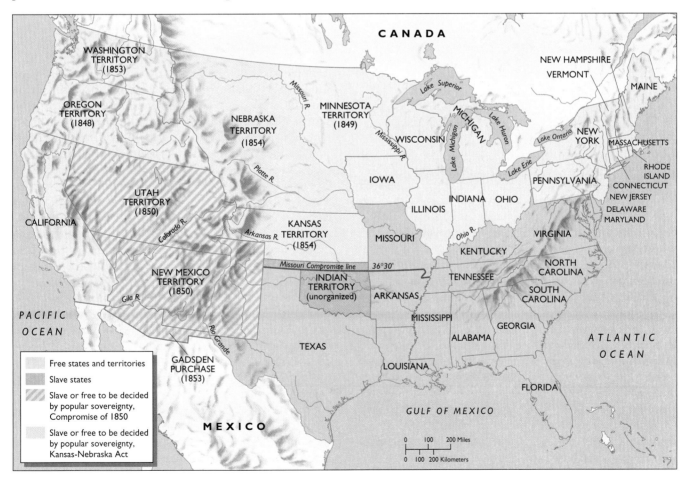

Map 14-3   Stephen Douglas' Kansas-Nebraska Act of 1854 Carved the Kansas Territory out of the Larger Nebraska Territory.
Because Missouri was already a slave state, the map indicates that slaveholders could move west and settle in Kansas. But because Kansas lay north of the 1820 Missouri Compromise line, many northerners wanted slavery restricted from the territory.

Senator Stephen A. Douglas, the "Little Giant" from Illinois, became the leading advocate of "popular sovereignty" as a solution to the crisis over slavery in the 1850s.

organized on the principle of popular sovereignty, but the inference everyone drew was that Kansas would become a slave state and Nebraska a free state. To win the support of southern congressmen, the final version of Douglas' bill explicitly repealed the Missouri Compromise of 1820.

Douglas correctly predicted that his Kansas-Nebraska Act would provoke "a hell of a storm." The debate was ferocious: Southerners denied that Congress had the right to regulate slavery in the territories, through popular sovereignty or any other means. Northerners pointed out that the federal government had been regulating slavery in the territories since the 1780s. In one memorable exchange, George Badger of North Carolina declared, "If some Southern gentleman wishes to take the . . . old woman who nursed him in childhood and whom he called 'Mammy' . . . into one of these new Territories for the betterment of the fortunes of his whole family—why, in the name of God, should anybody prevent it?" To which Benjamin Wade of Ohio answered, "We have not the least objection . . . to the

senator's migrating to Kansas and taking his old 'Mammy' along with him. We only insist that he shall not be empowered to sell her after taking her there."

In the end, Douglas succeeded in winning passage of the Kansas-Nebraska Act. Yet as with other southern victories in the recent past, especially the defeat of the Wilmot Proviso and the passage of the Fugitive Slave Act, the Kansas-Nebraska Act only increased support for antislavery politicians in the North. It persuaded many northerners that popular sovereignty was a proslavery swindle, even though Douglas sincerely believed that it would produce mostly free states. Yet for that very reason southerners no longer trusted popular sovereignty either. Douglas had paid a heavy price for his victory. In the 1852 elections the Whig Party suffered from its association with the Fugitive Slave Act. Two years later northern voters punished the Democrats for sponsoring the Kansas-Nebraska Act. In the elections of 1854 the number of northern Democrats in Congress fell dramatically, from 91 to 25. The Kansas-Nebraska Act had split the Democratic Party in two and destroyed the credibility of popular sovereignty as a solution to the slavery problem. It also seriously damaged expansionism as a political program.

The Expansion of Slavery as a Foreign Policy

The Pierce administration's disastrous support for the Kansas-Nebraska Act undermined its ability to pursue the expansionist policies of its Democratic predecessors. To be sure, Pierce tried. His presidential addresses were filled with bluster about America's right to more Mexican territory and to various parts of the Caribbean, particularly Cuba. But all of Pierce's expansionist efforts were southward, and that meant they all promised the further expansion of slavery. This was hardly an accident. Pierce filled his cabinet with southerners and southern sympathizers. He appointed slaveholders to crucial diplomatic posts. Pierce himself had no objections to the expansion of slavery. In 1844 hardly anyone would have questioned such a foreign policy. In 1854 it generated tremendous opposition.

Pierce sent a South Carolinian, James Gadsden, to Mexico with instructions to spend up to $50 million to acquire a substantial portion of northern Mexico for the United States. Mexico's leader, Santa Anna, resisted Gadsden's extravagant requests. The American diplomat returned to Washington, D. C. with a treaty giving the United States just enough Mexican territory to build a transcontinental railroad across the southern tier of the nation. But even this was too much for most northern senators. For the first time in American history, the Congress rejected land ceded to the United States. With northern Senators unwilling to add any more potential slave territory to the Union, the Gadsden Purchase ended up securing only a small piece of land to even out the southern border of the United States (see Map 14-4).

Map 14-4   Mexican Cession.
The huge Mexican Cession opened the door to the further expansion of slavery, and in so doing provoked a political crisis that was resolved only by the Civil War.

Pierce's expansionist designs fared even worse in Cuba. The president appointed Pierre Soulé, a reckless and flamboyant Louisianan, as minister to Spain. Soulé was instructed to negotiate the purchase of Cuba, but with the understanding that if Spain refused to sell he should encourage the Cubans to rise in rebellion. To Soulé's presumptuous behavior the Spanish government offered an extraordinary response. It proposed to free millions of Cuban slaves, form them into a militia, and arm them for the defense of the island against a possible American invasion.

The Pierce administration professed to be shocked by Spain's audacity, but it was in no position to object. For years the U.S. government had encouraged private expeditions into Latin American countries for the purpose of adding more territory to the United States. These semiprivate adventurers were known as filibusters, and in 1853 the most famous filibuster in America was a Mississippi slaveholder named John A. Quitman. With friends in the cabinet and financial backing from prominent Americans, Quitman developed elaborate plans to invade Cuba and spark a rebellion against Spanish authority. Quitman made no secret of his plans, and the administration did little to thwart him. This was the context in which Spain made its bold suggestion to defend Cuba with freed slaves.

The United States responded by encouraging its English, French, and Spanish envoys to meet in Europe for a

"full and free interchange of views" on Cuba. The meeting took place at Ostend, Belgium, where Pierre Soulé succeeded in encouraging his two fellow envoys to sign and publish a shockingly aggressive declaration of American intentions. The 1854 Ostend Manifesto, as it was called, declared that Cuba was "naturally" a part of the United States. It urged Spain to accept an offer of $120 million for the island, promising wealth, power, and contentment for the Spanish people in return. But if Spain refused the offer, the manifesto darkly warned, the United States would use all of its power to "wrest" the island of Cuba by force.

The Ostend Manifesto reached the United States at the height of northern reaction against the Kansas-Nebraska Act. It was immediately denounced as yet another example of slavery's insatiable hunger for expansion. The Pierce administration, already thwarted in Mexico, quickly withdrew its support for Quitman's filibustering designs against Cuba. Expansionism, long one of the most popular political programs in America, was now hopelessly tainted by its association with slavery. As Pierce's secretary of state, William L. Marcy, admitted, "the Nebraska question" had shattered the Democratic Party in the North "and deprived it of that strength which was needed and could have been more profitably used for the acquisition of Cuba." Even after the Cuban crisis subsided and the Pierce administration backed away from its expansionism, the "Kansas question" burned hotter than ever.

Kansas Begins to Bleed

Under the terms of the Kansas-Nebraska Act, it was up to the people in Kansas to determine whether their territory would enter the Union as a slave or free state. Elections for the territorial legislature were set for March 1855. Hoping to secure victory for the antislavery forces, the New England Emigrant Aid Company was organized to support settlers opposed to slavery. By the time election day came, however, proslavery settlers were probably in the majority and would have won a fair election, but on the day the polls opened proslavery partisans from neighboring Missouri crossed the border and cast thousands of phony ballots. This action inevitably cast doubt on the legitimacy of the newly-elected proslavery legislature meeting in Lecompton that probably would have been elected anyway. To make matters worse, the new legislature went out of its way to torment those who opposed slavery. It made it a crime to question slavery in Kansas and a capital crime to protect fugitive slaves. To top it off, proslavery representatives expelled the few antislavery members who had been elected.

Free-state settlers responded by repudiating the proslavery government in Lecompton. In January 1856 free-staters elected a governor and legislature of their own. In March this shadow government met in Topeka, adopted its own statutes, and named its own senators. By the spring of 1856 Kansas found itself with two competing governments, a proslavery one in Lecompton and an antislavery one in Topeka. By then the number of free-state settlers had swollen, and they were now the majority. Nevertheless, proslavery Senator David Atchison vowed "to kill every God-damned abolitionist in the district." Local sheriffs and federal marshals, backed up by more "border ruffians" from Missouri, tried several times to enter the town of Lawrence to arrest free-staters and close down their presses. They tried again May 21, 1856, only to discover that most of the free-staters had fled. The frustrated Missourians promptly destroyed two printing presses and burned the Free State Hotel to the ground. The only person killed in the "sack of Lawrence" was a proslavery rioter caught beneath the collapsing hotel. Although little blood had been shed, the eastern press blasted this latest example of proslavery violence. Kansas, they said, was bleeding.

Three days after the sack of Lawrence, Kansas really did begin to bleed when John Brown launched his famous raid on proslavery settlers at Pottawatomie Creek. Brown was an awesome and in many ways a frightening man. Where most abolitionists believed that human beings could be perfected, John Brown was an unusually fierce Calvinist who saw human degradation everywhere he looked. The wrath of God, not moral persuasion or political organization, was Brown's preferred solution to the problem of slavery. A miserable failure as a businessman, Brown was remarkably successful at persuading others to invest in his hair-brained schemes or to join his own personal holy war against slavery.

In May 1856, the day after he learned of the sack of Lawrence, Brown organized a small band of men to take revenge on the proslavery settlers of Kansas. Among his seven-man legion were four of his own sons and a son-in-law. Armed with finely honed swords and even sharper zeal, Brown's troops went into battle late in the evening on May 24. At their first stop they shot James Doyle in the head, split open the skulls of two of his sons, and then hacked up the bodies. An hour later they entered Allen Wilkinson's cabin and, in the face of his pleading wife, split open his skull and stabbed him with their swords. Shortly thereafter they did the same thing to William Sherman, splitting his skull, hacking his body, and this time chopping off his hand. Then Brown and his men went back to their camp, having stolen several horses along the way. Brown never admitted his involvement in the so-called Pottawatomie Massacre, but the evidence against him was overwhelming.

As the blood was flowing in the western territories, another battle erupted on the floor of Congress. Prompted by the sack of Lawrence, abolitionist Senator Charles Sumner of Massachusetts delivered a two-day speech exposing the "Crime Against Kansas." A harangue as much as an oration, the speech was filled with overheated sexual metaphors. Proslavery forces, Sumner declared, had set out to "rape" the virgin territory of Kansas. He accused Senator Andrew Butler of South Carolina of consorting with a "polluted . . . harlot, Slavery." And he made a particularly vulgar reference to Butler's speech defect. Two days later Congressman Preston S. Brooks, a distant relative of Butler's, walked into a nearly empty Senate chamber and brutally attacked Sumner with his cane. Trapped in his seat, Sumner ripped the desk from the bolts that fastened it to the floor and then collapsed, his head covered with blood. It was several years before he returned to the Senate.

Across the South, Brooks was hailed as a hero. Southern congressmen prevented his expulsion from the House. Northerners, already horrified by the Kansas-Nebraska Act, by the "border ruffians" from Missouri, and by Brooks' assault on Sumner, were shocked yet again by the South's reaction to the Sumner-Brooks affair. In astonishing numbers, northern voters responded by casting their ballots for a new Republican Party dedicated to halting the expansion of the so-called "slave power."

A New Political Party Takes Shape

The election of 1856 presented American voters with an unusually clear choice. Where a candidate stood on the Kansas-Nebraska Act betrayed a larger set of convictions about the expansion of slavery. And the expansion of slavery in turn raised a series of questions about the relative benefits of wage labor and slave labor. What was at stake in the presidential election, in other words, was the fundamental conflict between the political economy of slavery and the political economy of freedom. In the past the Whigs and Democrats had avoided such blatantly sectional issues by running candidates who appealed to both the North and the South. What was different in 1856 was the presence of a new major party, the Republicans, that appealed exclusively to northern voters.

The First Sectional Election

In 1856 antislavery became the umbrella under which the Democratic Party's opponents in the North could gather. The name of that new umbrella was the Republican Party, and the name of its first presidential candidate was John C. Frémont.

The Republican Party platform reiterated the principle embedded in the Wilmot Proviso by calling for a prohibition on the expansion of slavery into any western territories, but Fremont was pledged to a larger vision of political economy as well. The Republicans presented themselves to voters as the party of active government on behalf of economic progress. They wanted the federal government to sponsor the construction of a transcontinental railroad. They advocated high tariffs to protect young industries. They proposed a homestead act that would encourage small farmers to settle the West. And they supported the creation of land grant colleges to encourage technological innovation in American agriculture. For Republicans, government activism on behalf of a free labor economy went hand in hand with the withdrawal of government support for the political economy of slavery.

The Republicans were unified because they did not have to appeal to the South. In contrast the Democrats faced the difficult task of finding a candidate acceptable to both the northern and southern wings of the party. Franklin Pierce and Stephen Douglas, tainted by their association with the Kansas-Nebraska Act, were unacceptable to the northern Democrats. In fact, anyone associated in any way with the Kansas debacle could not be nominated. So the Democrats turned to James Buchanan of Pennsylvania, "a northern man with southern principles." Buchanan's chief asset was the fact that he was out of the country during the uproar over the Kansas-Nebraska Act. Free of those battle scars, he became the last major candidate for decades to run a successful campaign that appealed to both sections.

Where the Republicans promised to interfere with slavery in the territories, the Democrats pledged "noninterference by Congress with slavery." This wording kept the principle of popular sovereignty alive without actually endorsing it. Northern Democrats could thus unite with southern Democrats around a candidate committed, above all else, to bringing an end to public discussion of the slavery question.

The Democratic candidate could thus claim to be the only truly national candidate, the only one who could prevent the breakup of the Union. Southern leaders made it easy for Buchanan to make this argument by repeatedly warning that if Fremont and the Republicans won the presidency, the South would secede. "The election of Fremont," Robert Toombs of Georgia warned, "would be the end of the Union, and ought to be." The Democrats played on this widespread fear of disunion. The "grand and appalling issue" of the campaign, Buchanan wrote, is "Union or Disunion." Southern voters who might have gone with the Whigs instead supported Buchanan in order to thwart Fremont.

For the first time in their history, Americans were being asked to decide in a presidential election whether the Union was worth preserving. That decision might have been easy to make a generation earlier, but by 1856 it had become terribly complicated. The worth of the Union now depended on the kind of society that Union would embrace in the future. Would it be a society whose wealth was based on the labor of slaves or one that staked its prosperity on the progress of free labor? The future of the Union had become bound up with the problem of labor.

The Labor Problem and the Politics of Slavery

Northern Democrats warned that a Republican victory would flood the North with hundreds of thousands of emancipated slaves, placing them "side by side in competition with white men." The interest of northern workers therefore required the preservation of southern slavery within the Union. The most articulate spokesman for this view was Stephen Douglas. He believed that under the principle of popular sovereignty voting majorities in the territories would prevent the expansion of slavery and preserve the West for the exclusive settlement of white people.

Southern Democrats argued that white men who worked hard to get ahead had earned the right to accumulate slaves. Slavery, in this view, was the reward for free labor that was well done. "The nonslaveholder of the South preserves the status of the white man," J. D. B. DeBow explained, "and is not regarded as an inferior or a dependent." On the contrary, the southern labor system provided a poor white with the opportunity to rise up the social ladder by acquiring slaves "as soon as his savings will admit." Thus, southern Democrats claimed, slavery solved the labor problem by preserving the independence of free whites.

By contrast, Republicans insisted that slavery degraded all labor, black and white, and that the expansion of slavery was a particular threat to the economic well-being of free labor in the North. Slavery required an ignorant work force, Republicans argued. It destroyed the work ethic by depriving slaves of any incentive to get ahead. Among the masters, slavery allegedly bred a haughty disdain for hard work and self-discipline. And by stifling the economic progress of the entire South, Republicans charged, slavery denied poor whites opportunities for advancement. Hobbled by an inefficient work force and an aristocratic ruling class, the South was said to be doomed to economic backwardness, forever deprived of the benefits of progress. Having thus attacked the South, Republicans in turn defended the North as a society in which labor was free and hard work was amply rewarded. The Protestant virtues of thrift, sobriety, and diligence were systematically cultivated. Away from the stifling influence of slavery, opportunities for upward mobility were abundant, and progress was manifest. Cities thrived; industry grew; farmers prospered; and workers climbed from rags to respectability.

The fact that the southern economy was booming presented a theoretical problem for Republicans. To explain slavery's strength they asserted the existence of an increasingly aggressive **slave power**. Fears of a slave power had been circulating along the fringes of northern politics for at least a decade before the Republicans took up the theme. The slave power, they argued, had taken control of the federal government and used its position to keep a backward system alive. In a fair race slavery could never survive against free labor. To compensate for slavery's intrinsic weaknesses the slave power grew ever more arrogant until at last it was prepared to undermine the freedom of northern whites in order to perpetuate the enslavement of southern African Americans.

A potent mixture of ideological fury, paranoia, and realism, the slave power theory captured the imagination of a growing number of northern voters. Among other things, it allowed whites to feel threatened by slavery without having to sympathize with the plight of the slaves. The greater evil was not the oppression of the slave but the power of the slaveholder. "With the negroes I have nothing to do," one Massachusetts Republican explained. "But with their masters I propose to try conclusions as to our respective political rights." The same logic helped override the nativist claim that foreigners were the chief source of the nation's woes.

The Republicans did not succeed in the short run. Buchanan won five northern states and all but one of the slave states. Fremont swept the upper North and Ohio (see Map 14-5). No one was surprised that Fremont lost; what startled observers was that he did so well. All the Republicans needed to win four years later was Pennsylvania and either Illinois or Indiana. Fremont's strength in the upper North was so strong, his showing in the lower North so impressive, that the new Republican Party emerged from

the election as the "victorious loser." Never before had a clearly sectional party made so strong a showing in a presidential election. By bringing antislavery sentiment into the mainstream, the Republicans overturned a long and powerful tradition of bi-sectional politics. The slavery issue would not disappear until slavery itself did.

An "Irrepressible" Conflict?

In 1857 Democrat James Buchanan was inaugurated as president. He would preside over the last proslavery administration in American history. His efforts to silence the slavery issue once and for all proved a disastrous failure. By the end of 1858 the most prominent Republican politician in America, William Seward, had declared that the sectional conflict between North and South was "irrepressible." When Buchanan left office in 1861 his own party was in disarray, a Republican had been elected his successor, and the Union had collapsed.

The Slavery Issue Persists

In 1857 the Supreme Court handed down a controversial decision that inflamed the nation over the slavery issue. That same year an angry southern author published a notorious attack on southern slavery that led to another nationwide debate. Thus the slavery issue persisted despite the Buchanan administration's efforts to put it to rest.

Within days of Buchanan's inauguration the Supreme Court, dominated by southern Democrats, issued one of the most controversial decisions in American history. The case stretched all the way back to 1833, the year John Emerson was commissioned for duty at Fort Armstrong, Illinois, and took a slave named Dred Scott with him from Missouri. A surgeon in the U.S. Army, Emerson spent two years stationed in Illinois and two more years at Fort Snelling in Wisconsin Territory (now Minnesota). Slavery was illegal under Illinois law, and the Missouri Compromise prohibited slavery in Wisconsin Territory. In 1846, some years after Scott had been brought back to Missouri, he sued his owners claiming that several years of residence on free soil made him legally free. Having lost his suit in 1854 after a long and complicated series of moves through the Missouri courts and the federal district court, Scott appealed to the U.S. Supreme Court. By then two questions stood out: First, was Dred Scott a citizen, such that his suit had standing in a court of law? Second, did the laws of the free state of Illinois or the free territory of Wisconsin prevail over the master's property right?

The justices could have avoided controversy by issuing a narrow ruling that merely upheld the lower court's decision against Scott. But instead the majority decided, with some inappropriate coaxing from President-elect

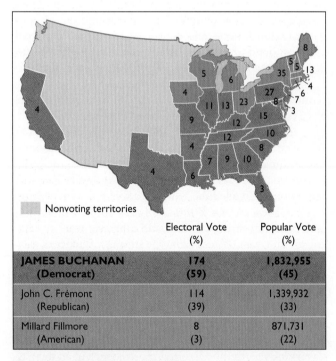

	Electoral Vote (%)	Popular Vote (%)
JAMES BUCHANAN (Democrat)	**174** **(59)**	**1,832,955** **(45)**
John C. Frémont (Republican)	114 (39)	1,339,932 (33)
Millard Fillmore (American)	8 (3)	871,731 (22)

Nonvoting territories

Map 14-5   The Election of 1856.
The presidential electoral map of 1856 reveals the growing sectional division. Although he lost the election, the Republican Fremont won a string of victories across the upper North and lost narrowly in Pennsylvania, Indiana, and Illinois. By winning those states four years later, the openly antislavery Abraham Lincoln could be elected president simply by winning the North.

Buchanan, to render a sweeping decision covering some of the most explosive issues of the day. The chief justice was Roger Taney, a Democrat of long standing who had nevertheless freed his own slaves. Like so many Democrats, he wanted to find a way to silence public debate over slavery once and for all. Instead, he ignited a firestorm.

It was not the majority decision against Scott that created the uproar. The problem was Taney's provocative and highly partisan opinion. Taney argued, first, that Dred Scott was not a citizen because he was black. Since before the republic had been founded, the chief justice reasoned, African Americans had "been regarded as beings of an inferior order . . . so far inferior that they had no rights which the white man was bound to respect." If this was true in 1776, Taney reasoned, it was true in 1857. (The problem is that it was clearly not true, in 1857 or in 1776.) Free African Americans were discriminated against throughout America, but nowhere were they denied all the rights that constituted citizenship. They held property, entered into contracts, brought suits in court, and vigorously exercised their rights of speech, press, and assembly. Furthermore, many of the discriminations to which free African Americans were subjected had only recently been enacted into law in many northern states. They were not in place when the nation was founded. Thus Taney's declaration that African Americans were not and never had been citizens was devoid of both legal and historical merit.

Second, Taney argued that Dred Scott's residence in Wisconsin Territory did not make him a free man, because the Missouri Compromise, by which Congress excluded slavery from the territory, was unconstitutional. This ruling gave legal sanction to the most extreme prosouthern position. In effect, Taney declared, Congress had no power to regulate slavery in the territories, even though Congress had been doing so since before the Constitution was written. Finally, Taney declared that two years' residence in Illinois constituted only a temporary "sojourn" and did not, therefore, invalidate a master's right to travel with his slave property in a free state. But if a master could hold a slave in a free state for two years, abolitionists asked, why not five, ten, or twenty years? By defining slave ownership as a constitutional right, Taney's decision threatened to restrict even the power of states to abolish slavery within their borders.

Republicans were infuriated by the decision, but they were put in an awkward position. If they questioned the legitimacy of a Supreme Court decision, they skirted dangerously close to Calhoun's old argument for the right of the states to nullify federal law. But the Dred Scott decision also hurt the Democrats, even though it was handed down by a Democratic majority of justices, and even though its proslavery logic was consistent with the party's rhetoric. For Taney's decision implicitly undermined the doctrine of popular sovereignty, the position advocated by most northern Democrats. Thus while Republicans fumed, Democrats in the North were left scrambling to salvage what they could from the Dred Scott decision.

Sectional tensions were fueled even further by the publication, also in 1857, of Hinton Rowan Helper's *The Impending Crisis of the South*. A modest farmer from North Carolina, Helper savagely attacked the entire political economy of slavery, especially the ruling class of slaveholders it produced. He argued that small southern farmers had no chance of achieving the kind of prosperity common to the free labor economy of the North. In 400 pages of slashing rhetoric, Helper insisted that "slavery, and nothing but slavery, has retarded the progress and prosperity of our portion of the Union." Still more provocative was Helper's ominous warning that if the slaveholders did not voluntarily dismantle their unproductive labor system, then slavery would be overthrown by revolutionary violence.

The Impending Crisis provoked a huge reaction. A condensed version was widely distributed in the North and endorsed by numerous antislavery politicians. Their endorsement in turn led to a prolonged debate between northern and southern representatives on the floor of Congress in 1858. In the South, journalists and critics were left to contemplate the possibility that slaveless farmers in their very midst might be moved by the force of Helper's logic. "Even now the arguments of Helper's infamous book have been reproduced in the South," a New Orleans newspaper declared in 1860. The "slavery question" thus threatened to erupt *within* the South, where the "armies of our enemies shall be recruited from our own forces." In this atmosphere of panic and paranoia, the Democratic Party began to split apart.

The Lecompton Constitution Splits the Democratic Party

The cause of the Democratic rupture was, once again, Kansas. In 1858 Congress had to choose between two different constitutions accompanying the territory's petition for admission to the Union. The so-called Lecompton Constitution was drawn up by proslavery partisans, who by that time represented a distinct minority of Kansas residents. Free-staters, knowing they were in the majority, submitted their own constitution to a popular referendum. Supporters of the Lecompton Constitution sent their document directly to Congress without letting Kansans vote on it. President Buchanan, surrounded by southern advisers and beholden to the southern wing of the Democratic Party, supported the proslavery minority. But the leading Democrat in the Senate, Stephen Douglas, had no choice but to reject the Lecompton Constitution, since it clearly violated his principle of popular sovereignty. Southerners had enough votes to push Lecompton through the Senate. In the House, where northern Democrats held the balance of power, the suspect constitution was rejected.

Douglas was in a difficult position. Southern Democrats assailed popular sovereignty as an antislavery ruse. Northern critics pointed out that the Dred Scott decision had rendered popular sovereignty meaningless. Shaky as it was, Douglas stood his ground. He insisted that if the people of a territory refused to pass the laws necessary to protect slavery, no master would dare go there with his human property. Douglas' logic infuriated southern Democrats, who promptly denounced him as a traitor. They demanded a federal slave code enforcing the rights of slave ownership in all the territories, a position long associated with the most extreme proslavery partisans. Once again Douglas had no choice but to oppose them, aware that in doing so the Democratic Party would split irrevocably along sectional lines.

Lincoln and Douglas Debate

Campaigning for re-election to the Senate in 1858, Douglas was forced to spell out his position in a series of extraordinary debates with a little-known Republican adversary named Abraham Lincoln. Even at the time observers recognized the significance of these seven debates. Douglas was one of the most powerful politicians in America, and the new Republican Party was forcing him to fight for his political life. In Douglas' hands rested the viability of the Democratic Party in the North. Lincoln's performance tested the popular appeal of the young Republican Party in the face of sustained assault from the North's most formidable Democrat. The Lincoln-Douglas debates spelled out clearly, and at times brilliantly, the fundamental differences between Democrats and Republicans on the issue of slavery.

Lincoln's argument was a familiar one in antislavery circles. The Founding Fathers recognized that slavery was inconsistent with the principles of the Declaration of Independence, Lincoln argued. They had refused to put the word "slave" or "slavery" into the Constitution. They had provided for the nation's withdrawal from the Atlantic slave trade. They had abolished slavery in every northern state. They had restricted the expansion of slavery into western territories. In short, Lincoln argued, the Founders had put slavery on the "course of ultimate extinction." But now the Democrats had repudiated the Founders' intentions. They invented a constitutional right to slave ownership that the Founders had never dreamed of. They denied Congress' right to regulate slavery in the territories, though the Founders themselves had done so. A Democratic Supreme Court had declared that a majority of voters in any territory could not prohibit the importation of slaves. Now the Democrats were demanding a federal slave code to *protect* slavery in all the territories. By all these means, Lincoln charged, the Democratic Party had repudiated the intentions of those who brought the nation into existence.

This situation could not continue much longer, Lincoln concluded. In a controversial speech just prior to his debates with Douglas, Lincoln warned that "A house di-

In 1858 a little-known Illinois Republican, Abraham Lincoln, ran against Stephen A. Douglas for the U.S. Senate. Their seven campaign debates, one of them pictured above, brilliantly spelled out the differences between Democrats and Republicans over slavery. Though Lincoln lost the election, he did so well in the debates that his party nominated him for the presidency two years later.

vided against itself cannot stand." The government could not continue to survive "half slave and half free." Lincoln could see only two alternatives. "Either the opponents of slavery will arrest the further spread of it, and place it where the public mind shall rest in the belief that it is in the course of ultimate extinction; or its advocates will push it forward, till it shall become alike lawful in all the States, old as well as new—North as well as South." These words became a major point of contention during the Lincoln-Douglas debates.

Douglas dismissed Lincoln's "House Divided" speech as absurd. The Union had survived for generations "half slave and half free," and there was no reason it should not continue to do so. The Founders had recognized that slavery was a local institution, Douglas argued. They let it be in the southern states, where the climate and the crops made slavery profitable. At the same time, they let the northern states alone in their decisions to abolish slavery. By allowing each state to decide on slavery for itself, Douglas argued, the Founders implicitly endorsed his own policy of popular sovereignty. However, the Supreme Court had dismissed popular sovereignty in the territories, and Lincoln repeatedly challenged Douglas to explain how the people of a territory could now exclude slavery if they chose to do so. Douglas responded that because slavery could not survive without positive laws to protect it, the people of a territory could effectively exclude slavery simply by refusing to enact a slave code. This was the famous Freeport Doctrine.

But Douglas' most consistent tactic was to confuse the question of slavery with the question of race relations. He claimed that there was little difference between the northern states that discriminated against African Americans and the southern states where most African Americans were enslaved. And he argued that by opposing slavery Lincoln was claiming that African Americans and whites should be politically and socially equal. Douglas taunted his audience with the spectacle of widespread interracial marriage and of African Americans pouring into Illinois by the tens of thousands and demanding the right to work and to vote on the same terms as whites.

Lincoln answered that his not wanting an African-American woman as his slave did not mean that he wanted her as his wife. Like Jefferson, Lincoln believed that all men and women were equally entitled to their freedom but not that freed blacks should live in the United States as the social and political equals of whites. And so Lincoln, again like Jefferson, advocated the colonization of freed slaves somewhere outside the United States. "I am not, nor ever have been in favor of bringing about in any way the social and political equality of the white and black races," Lincoln protested. He was not in favor of granting African Americans the right to vote, to sit on juries, to hold public office, or to intermarry with whites. Even Lincoln's words echoed Thomas Jefferson. "There is a physical difference

between the races," Lincoln argued, "which I believe will for ever forbid the two races living together on terms of social and political equality."

Though upsetting to modern ears, Lincoln's views on African Americans were rather moderate for his time. Most of his statements about race were defensive in tone and tentative in their claims. Unlike Douglas, who took every opportunity to parade his virulent racism, Lincoln was plainly uncomfortable with the subject. In later years he would abandon his commitment to colonization, invite leading blacks to the White House, and offer support for a limited suffrage for African Americans. Even in 1858, in the face of Douglas' relentless race-baiting, Lincoln grew firmer and more eloquent in his insistence that African Americans were fully entitled to the basic rights of life, liberty, and the pursuit of happiness. Blacks may be unequal to whites in certain respects, Lincoln argued, "but in the right to the bread which his own hand earns, he is my own equal and Judge Douglas's equal, and the equal of every living man." Here was the fundamental difference between Lincoln and Douglas in their famous debates. Douglas was openly indifferent to slavery and was prepared to see it expand wherever whites wanted it. Lincoln believed slavery was fundamentally wrong and should be put back on a course of ultimate extinction.

Lincoln narrowly lost the 1858 Senate election, but his epic battle with the Little Giant (as Douglas was known) transformed him into a leading spokesman for the Republican Party. Elsewhere in the North, the Republicans were victorious. The southern demand for a federal slave code had proved a disaster for northern Democrats. Their problems persisted even after the elections. Southern Democrats formed an obstructionist block in Congress, successfully thwarting the passage of several bills dear to the hearts of many northerners. Southerners stalled a homestead law designed to encourage the settlement of the West by small farmers. They blocked passage of a bill to facilitate the construction of a transcontinental railway. In each case the unanimous southern Democrats were joined by about half the Democrats from the North. The same thing happened with a bill to establish land grant colleges. As in the late 1840s, Congress was paralyzed by entrenched sectional animosities. And once again a congressional stalemate transformed every vote into a test of sectional loyalty.

The Retreat From Union

Between 1858 and 1860 both the North and the South rejected the sanctity of the Union. In the South the retreat from unionism was in reaction to John Brown's raid on Harpers Ferry. Brown's death was greeted as a martyr's execution throughout much of the North, leading many southerners to conclude that a union of the North and the

South was no longer viable. In 1860 northerners cast a strong majority of their votes for a sectional candidate who did not even place his name on the ballot in the South. With the election of Abraham Lincoln, the North abandoned a long-standing pattern of compromising with slavery for the sake of maintaining the Union.

John Brown's War Against Slavery

In the fall of 1858 the mysterious John Brown re-emerged to launch another battle in his private war against slavery. In the years since the massacre at Pottawatomie Creek, Brown's movements had been obscure. He traveled back and forth between Canada and Kansas, New England and Ohio. By the late 1850s he had concocted a plan to invade Virginia and free the slaves. Friends told Brown his plan was unworkable; Frederick Douglass advised him to give it up. But in Boston Brown found support from a group of well-connected intellectuals, philanthropists, and clergymen. Known as the "Secret Six," these Bostonians were dazzled by Brown's appeal to action rather than words, and while they promised more money than they delivered, they delivered enough.

After months of delay Brown finally launched his invasion. He had rented a farm in Maryland, about five miles from the town of Harpers Ferry in Virginia, where a small federal arsenal was located. Brown apparently planned to capture the arsenal and distribute the guns to slaves from the surrounding area, thereby inciting a full-scale slave rebellion. On the evening of October 16, 1859, Brown and 18 followers crossed the Potomac with a wagonload of guns, cut the telegraph wires leading into Harpers Ferry, overwhelmed a guard, and seized the armory. Brown ordered several of his men to scour the surrounding countryside in search of slaves to liberate and slaveholders to take as prisoners. They found Colonel Lewis Washington, a descendant of the first president, and carried him back to Harpers Ferry as a hostage. Brown's mission was accomplished. He sat back and waited for the slaves to rise.

The slaves did not rise, but the armed forces did. Marines were sent from Washington, D. C., led by a lieutenant colonel from the U.S. Army, named Robert E. Lee and his assistant, Lieutenant J. E. B. Stuart, both of whom would go on to become leading Confederate generals. Having arrived the morning after Brown took control of Harpers Ferry, the militia surrounded the arsenal and sized up the situation. The next day Stuart found Brown hidden in the engine room and ordered him to surrender. When Brown refused, twelve marines charged the room with bayonets. Two of Brown's men and one marine were killed, but Brown himself was only wounded. The rebellion was over less then two days after it began.

The entire raid was "absurd," Abraham Lincoln later said. "It was not a slave insurrection," he added. "It was an attempt by white men to get up a revolt among slaves, in

Artist John Curry's painting of John Brown brilliantly captures Brown's larger-than-life personality. The biblical imagery is reminiscent of Moses and suggests Brown's charismatic capacity to attract followers.

which the slaves refused to participate." All but one of Brown's "Secret Six" supporters either fled the country or disavowed any knowledge of Brown's plans. The condemnation of Brown by responsible northerners and the embarrassment of Brown's supporters initially calmed southern outrage over the invasion.

Over the next several weeks, however, northern opinion seemed to change from contempt to admiration for Brown. It was not the raid itself that caused this shift of opinion. It was Brown's calm and dignified behavior in prison, at his trial, and at his own hanging. Even Virginia's governor, Henry A. Wise, was impressed by Brown's behavior as a prisoner. "He is a bundle of the best nerves I ever saw," Wise commented. "He is a man of clear head, of courage, fortitude, and simple ingenuousness," none of which stopped the governor from ordering that Brown be tried swiftly in the Virginia courts.

Brown's calm and eloquent statements to the court and on the gallows moved northerners in vast numbers to extraordinary demonstrations of sympathy. On the day Brown was hanged, northern churches tolled their bells. Militia companies fired salutes. Public buildings across the North were draped in black. There were prayer meetings, memorials, and resolutions of all sorts. No matter how clearly mainstream politicians like Lincoln and William H. Seward disavowed Brown and his raid, white southerners saw still more clearly that John Brown had become a hero among large numbers of northerners.

Northern sympathy for John Brown shocked the white South even more than the actual raid. "Every village bell which tolled its solemn note at the execution of Brown," one South Carolinian declared, "proclaims to the South the approbation of that village of insurrection

ON TRIAL

John Brown

"Let them hang me!" John Brown declared defiantly after his capture. Brown thus put Virginia authorities in the uncomfortable position of giving the zealous abolitionist exactly what he wanted. Ten days after he launched his raid on Harpers Ferry Brown was indicted for murder, conspiracy to incite slave rebellion, and treason against the commonwealth of Virginia.

Even as he was being charged, Brown made clear that he intended to use his trial to dramatize his cause. "I do not care anything about counsel," Brown declared when the court asked if he had a lawyer. So the court appointed counsel for him. One of the lawyers, Lawson Botts, opened the trial with an attempt to introduce evidence suggesting that his client was insane. "Insanity is hereditary in that family," a telegram from Ohio explained. But just as quickly John Brown shot his lawyer down. The insanity defense was "a miserable artifice," he announced to the court. The court agreed and rejected Botts' motion to delay the trial.

As he lay wounded on his cot listening to a series of witnesses, Brown decided that his lawyers were inadequate after all and asked the court for a delay. Botts and another lawyer thereupon resigned from the case. Without skipping a beat, Judge Richard Parker promptly assigned two new attorneys and ordered that the proceeding continue. "The trial must go on," the judge declared.

On October 31, 1859, six days after the trial began, Brown's attorneys were summing up their case to the court. They argued persuasively that because Brown was not a Virginian he could hardly be guilty of treason against that state. They argued that Brown's raid on Harpers Ferry was a pathetic affair, that it had not incited a slave rebellion, and that it never really threatened the state. The prosecutor came right back: The citizens of Virginia could not be expected to sit back and allow a man like Brown to "usurp the government, manumit our slaves, confiscate the property of slaveholders,

and . . . take possession of the Commonwealth." The jury agreed with the prosecutor and pronounced Brown guilty after forty-five minutes of deliberation.

On November 2, Brown was carried back into the courtroom to face sentencing. The defendant rose from his cot and announced to the court that he had "a few words to say." The words Brown then spoke were among the most dramatic and eloquent ever uttered in an American courtroom. "It is unjust that I should suffer such a penalty," Brown declared. If he had raided Harpers Ferry "in behalf of the rich, the powerful, the intelligent, the so-called great . . . it would have been all right." He would be facing reward rather than punishment. He had learned from the Bible "that all things whatsoever I would that men should do to me, I should do even so to them. . . . I endeavored to act up to that instruction." Although Brown was approaching sixty years of age he was "yet too young to understand that God is any respecter of persons." Brown freely admitted that he had "interfered" with slavery. And "if it is deemed necessary" that he should forfeit his life and mingle his blood "with the blood of millions in this slave country . . . I say, let it be done." When his speech ended, Brown was sentenced to hang on December 2, 1859.

Brown's statement was published throughout the North, and it ensured his reputation as a martyr to the antislavery cause. But so did his behavior during the month he awaited his execution. In letters to his friends and family, Brown showed a dignity in the face of death that impressed countless Americans who read his notes in their daily newspapers. Equally impressive was the final statement he gave to his jailers as he approached the gallows on December 2. "I John Brown am now quite *certain*," the statement read, "that the crimes of this *guilty, land: will* never be purged *away*; but with Blood." Many northerners concluded that although John Brown had lived poorly, he had certainly died well.

and servile war." Across the South, newspapers and politicians responded to Harpers Ferry by questioning the value of the Union itself. If the North was prepared to sanction slave rebellion, many southerners asked, how can the North and South remain bound within the same nation? The question persisted long after Brown's execu-

tion. The Baltimore *Sun* announced that the South could not "live under a government, the majority of whose subjects or citizens regard John Brown as a martyr and a Christian hero, rather than a murderer and robber."

At a critical moment in the nation's history, Brown's trial and execution galvanized northern public opinion against slavery and southern opinion against the Union. His spirit hovered over the 1860 presidential election, long after his body was laid to rest at an abolitionist community in upstate New York.

Northerners Elect a President

In the space of a decade the entire party structure of American politics had undergone a revolution. In 1860, for the first time in history, no major party presented voters with a candidate who could appeal to both the North and the South. For all practical purposes there were two different presidential elections that year. In the slave states a southern Democrat ran against a Constitutional Unionist. In the free states a northern Democrat ran against a Republican. On the surface slavery in the territories remained the dominant issue. Below the surface, scarcely acknowledged by three of the four candidates, the future of the Union was about to be determined.

The Democratic Party met in April in Charleston, South Carolina, the center of extreme secessionist sentiment. Southern fire-eaters demanded federal recognition of slavery in all the territories as part of the Democratic Party platform. As he had done in years past, William Lowndes Yancey vowed to walk out of the convention with his Alabama delegation unless he got what he wanted. But Stephen Douglas, the leading candidate for the party's nomination, insisted on a reaffirmation of popular sovereignty. Douglas had a bare majority of the delegates supporting him, enough to push his platform through but not enough to win the party's nomination. When Douglas' plank was passed, 49 delegates from eight southern states walked out. The convention was deadlocked. Douglas could not get the two-thirds vote he needed for nomination. After 57 ballots, the Democrats adjourned, agreeing to reconvene in Baltimore a month and a half later.

But the delay only made matters worse. In Baltimore, 110 southerners bolted, nominating their own candidate. Thus the Democrats put up two presidential aspirants in 1860. Stephen Douglas ran in the North advocating popular sovereignty and insisting that the Union itself hung in the balance of the election. John Breckinridge, the southern Democratic candidate, ran on a platform calling for federal recognition of slavery in all the territories. Another candidate, John Bell of Tennessee, tried unsuccessfully to revive the Whig Party by running on a Constitutional Unionist ticket. Neither Douglas, Breckinridge, nor Bell had much chance of winning. But together they might have thrown the election into the House of Representatives by depriving the Republicans of the electoral votes necessary to win the presidency,

The Republicans were far more united. With the scent of victory in their nostrils, tens of thousands of Republicans poured into Chicago. They jammed themselves into the Wigwam, a hall built specifically to accommodate the Republican convention. Thousands more crowded around outside the hall. Inside and out the huge crowds roared their approval at the passing events. The leading candidate for the Republican nomination was William H. Seward of New York. But Seward's strength, though considerable, was also limited to the uppermost states in the North. In the border states such as Pennsylvania, Indiana, and Illinois, Seward's antislavery politics were seen as too radical. What the party needed was a candidate whose antislavery credentials were unquestioned, but whose moderation could carry the critical states of the lower North. That candidate was Abraham Lincoln. Not only was Lincoln from Illinois, he was also a moderate within the Republican Party. Unlike conservative Republicans, Lincoln did not race-bait very much, and he opposed nativist restrictions on immigration. Unlike the party's radicals, Lincoln had supported the enforcement of the Fugitive Slave Act, denounced John Brown's raid on Harpers Ferry, and insisted that the federal government had no right to interfere in the states where slavery already existed. Still, Lincoln made clear his view that slavery was immoral, that Congress had the right to restrict slavery's expansion into the territories, and that the entire slave system should be placed "in the course of ultimate extinction." No major party had ever run a candidate dedicated to such a proposition.

The Republican platform reflected the moderation of its candidate. It contained fewer antislavery planks than the 1856 platform, and it made no reference to slavery as a "relic of barbarism." In addition, Democratic intransigence in Congress had lent legitimacy to the Republicans' larger vision of political economy. Their platform called for a homestead act, protective tariffs for American industries, and federal support for a transcontinental railroad. Finally, the Republicans repudiated the extreme nativist wing of their party by asserting that the constitutional rights of legal immigrants should be protected and explicitly guaranteeing legal immigrants access to western lands opened up by the proposed homestead act.

Throughout the campaign Lincoln and the Republicans scoffed at secessionist threats coming from the South. They had heard such "old Mumbo Jumbo" before, but the southerners had never made good on their threats. Breckinridge the Democrat and Bell the Constitutional Unionist also played down the possibility of disunion. But Stephen Douglas was so convinced that the election of Lincoln would result in secession and war that he broke with precedent and actively campaigned as the only candidate who could hold the Union together. When it became clear that Lincoln was going to win anyway, Douglas rearranged his campaign schedule to make a series of speeches in the slave states. He went South "not to ask for your votes for the Presidency," he told his audiences, "but to make an appeal to you on behalf of the Union." Hard drinking and hard politicking had made an old man out of the 47-year-old Douglas. A year away from his early death, the Little Giant threw himself into a desperate battle to save the Union from falling apart.

Lincoln won every free state except New Jersey, where he took the majority of electoral votes anyway. He ran stronger in the rural districts than in the cities, thanks in large part to the party's inability to capture much of the immigrant vote. Douglas got the second largest number of votes but took only one state, Missouri. Breckinridge, the southern Democrat, took 11 slave states, though his support within those states was concentrated in the districts with the lowest proportions of slaves. The slaveholders continued to vote their traditional Whig sympathies, supporting John Bell's Constitutional Unionist candidacy but only enough for him to win three states in the upper South.

Lincoln did not campaign in the South. His name was not even on the ballot in most of the slave states. Nevertheless, by 1860, he was able to win a presidential election by appealing exclusively to voters in the North (see Map 14-6). This in turn allowed Lincoln to run on a platform dedicated to bringing slavery to an end. Here was a double vindication for antislavery forces in the North. Not only did the Republican victory show wide appeal for an antislavery platform, it also suggested that a dynamic political economy based on free labor was bound to grow faster than even a prosperous slave society. If the North could win a presidential election all by itself, it was only because it had attracted far more free men than the South. In their own way, white southerners agreed. When they looked at the election returns they concluded that no matter what assurances Lincoln gave them, the future of slavery in the Union was doomed.

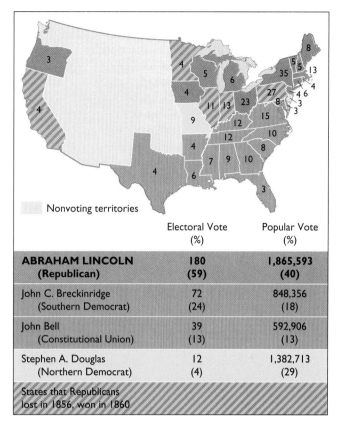

	Electoral Vote (%)	Popular Vote (%)
ABRAHAM LINCOLN (Republican)	**180 (59)**	**1,865,593 (40)**
John C. Breckinridge (Southern Democrat)	72 (24)	848,356 (18)
John Bell (Constitutional Union)	39 (13)	592,906 (13)
Stephen A. Douglas (Northern Democrat)	12 (4)	1,382,713 (29)

Nonvoting territories

States that Republicans lost in 1856, won in 1860

Map 14-6 The Election of 1860.
By 1860, no presidential candidate could appeal to voters in both the North and the South. By then the northern population had grown so rapidly that a united North could elect Lincoln to the presidency without any southern support.

Conclusion

Frederick Douglass personally hoped that Abraham Lincoln would win the election. "Slavery is the issue—the single bone of contention between all parties and sections," he insisted. "All other issues died ten years ago." The political economies of slavery and freedom had guided the nation onto two different historical pathways. The North was developing an urban, industrial economy based on the productive energy of wage labor.

In the South, a prosperous slave economy fastened in place an agricultural way of life and an older social order. The political tensions that arose from these differences finally pushed the nation into civil war. And as the war progressed, the same differences in political economy would shape the destiny of the Union and Confederate forces.

CHRONOLOGY

1838	Frederick Douglass escapes from slavery
1844	Samuel F. B. Morse invents the telegraph
1846	David Wilmot introduces his "proviso"
1847	Treaty of Guadalupe Hidalgo
1848	Zachary Taylor elected president
1850	Taylor dies; Millard Fillmore becomes president "Compromise of 1850"
1851	The "Maine Law" enacts temperance reform
1852	*Uncle Tom's Cabin* published in book form Franklin Pierce elected president
1854	Gadsden Purchase Ratified Kansas-Nebraska Act Ostend Manifesto
1856	"Bleeding Kansas" Sumner-Brooks affair James Buchanan elected president
1857	Dred Scott decision Hinton Rowan Helper publishes *The Impending Crisis of the South*
1858	Lincoln-Douglas debates
1859	John Brown's raid on Harpers Ferry
1860	Abraham Lincoln elected first Republican president
1861	First transcontinental telegraph completed

Review Questions

1. What were the major economic and social differences between the North and the South during the 1850s?

2. What is the significance of the Wilmot Proviso?

3. What were the major terms of the Compromise of 1850?

4. What is nativism, and what did it have in common with antislavery sentiment?

5. Why did the Kansas-Nebraska Act provoke so much controversy?

6. Explain the different positions taken by Stephen A. Douglas and Abraham Lincoln in the Illinois election for the U.S. Senate in 1858.

Further Readings

Tyler Anbinder, *Nativism and Slavery: The Northern Know-Nothings and the Politics of the 1850s* (1992). Anbinder demonstrates the close ties between opposition to immigration and opposition to slavery in the North.

Don E. Fehrenbacher, *The Dred Scott Case: Its Significance in American Law and Politics* (1978). This is a lucid, exhaustive account. There is an abbreviated paperback edition titled *Slavery, Law, and Politics.*

Eric Foner, *Free Soil, Free Labor, Free Men: The Ideology of the Republican Party Before the Civil War* (1970). The standard interpretation emphasizing the centrality of the labor issue and the fundamental conflict over slavery.

William W. Freehling, *The Road to Disunion: Secessionists at Bay, 1776–1854* (1990). The best treatment of the southern road to secession.

William E. Gienapp, *The Origins of the Republican Party, 1852–1856* (1987). This book is the definitive study, encompassing local as well as national issues.

Michael Holt, *The Political Crisis of the 1850s* (1978). The most astute alternative to Foner. Holt stresses the way politicians made calculated use of the slavery issue, but he doubts that the issue itself was fundamental.

Bruce Levine, *Half Slave, Half Free: The Roots of the Civil War* (1992). A good brief overview emphasizing social differences between the North and the South.

William McFeely, *Frederick Douglass* (1991). McFeely's book is the best biography of the most important black abolitionist.

Stephen B. Oates, *To Purge This Land With Blood: A Biography of John Brown* (1970). This is an outstanding account of the life of a highly controversial figure.

David Potter, *The Impending Crisis, 1848–1861* (1976). A masterpiece; perhaps the most profound one-volume examination of the political crisis of the 1850s.

History on the Internet

"Politics and Sectionalism in the 1850s"
http://odur.let.rug.nl/~usa/E/1850s/polixx.htm

This site contains interpretations of and excerpts from the Fugitive Slave Act and the Kansas-Nebraska Act. It also details the political debate over slavery in Congress and the influence of abolitionist leaders such as Frederick Douglass.

"The Dred Scott Case: A Summary"
http://www.umsl.edu/~virtualstl/dred_Scott_case/dred_button.html/summary.html

This site provides the background on the case and a discussion of the case and its impact. To read the full text version of the Supreme Court decision, see http://odur.let.rug.nl/~usa/E/1850s/polixx.htm.

"Lincoln-Douglas Debates"
http://www.umsl.edu/~virtualstl/dred_scott_case/texts/lindoug.htm

On this website, read the actual text of these famed debates between presidential candidates Abraham Lincoln and Stephen Douglas. These debates cast into sharp relief the growing differences between the North and the South.

"SCARTOONS: Racial Satire and the Civil War"
http://xroads.virginia.edu/~CAP/SCARTOONS/cartoons.html

On this site, explore the growing sectionalism, the Civil War years, and the aftermath of the War through political cartoons of the era.

"Secession Era Editorials"
http://history.furman.edu/~benson/docs/index.htm

Read about perspectives of both the North and the South through hundreds of contemporary newspaper editorials that address issues such as John Brown's raid and the Nebraska Bill.

15

A WAR FOR UNION AND EMANCIPATION

1861-1865

OUTLINE

Edmund Ruffin

From Union to Emancipation
The South Secedes
Civilians Demand a Total War
Slaves Take Advantage of the War
First Bull Run and the Shift in War Aims

Mobilizing for War
Southern Political Weaknesses
Union Naval Supremacy
Southern Military Advantages
The Political Economy of
Slavery Inhibits the Confederacy
What Were Soldiers Fighting For?

The Civil War Becomes
a Social Revolution
Union Victories in the West

Southern Military Strength in the East
Emancipation as a "Military Necessity"
The Moment of Truth

The War at Home
The Care of Casualties
Northern Reverses and Antiwar Sentiment
Gettysburg and the Justification of the War
Discontent in the Confederacy

The War Comes to a
Bloody End
Grant Takes Command
The Theory and Practice of Hard War
Sherman Marches, and Lee Surrenders
The Meaning of the Civil War

Conclusion

Edmund Ruffin

Edmund Ruffin was determined to watch John Brown die. Although in his mid-sixties, Ruffin arranged through a friend to become a cadet at Virginia Military Institute for a single day. On December 2, 1859, the elderly Ruffin donned a cadet's uniform and took his place with the color guard that attended Brown's hanging. He stared intently as "the atrocious criminal" was escorted to the scaffold. He listened in silence as Brown cursed the nation that tolerated human slavery. But when it was over Ruffin confessed to a grudging admiration for the "complete fearlessness" with which John Brown approached his own death.

Born in 1794 into one of the wealthiest planter families in eastern Virginia, Ruffin had grown up a child of privilege. By the age of twenty he was the master of a substantial plantation on the James River. Yet from his youth Edmund Ruffin was a discontented and angry man. He coveted a political career but his contempt for democracy thwarted him. In 1823 he managed to win election to a four-year term in the Virginia State Senate, but he was unwilling to forge the alliances and make the compromises that would bring him political influence. Before his term expired, Ruffin resigned his seat, "tired and disgusted with being a servant of the people." He never held public office again.

During the 1830s and 1840s Ruffin retreated to his plantations, publishing the results of his experiments in crop rotation, drainage techniques, and various new fertil-izers. His work paid off in improved productivity, higher profits, and growing public esteem. But Ruffin was always more interested in politics than farming. So he used his fame as an agricultural reformer to spread his proslavery message. By 1850 Ruffin was urging his fellow Virginians to secede from the Union in order to preserve slavery.

Ruffin made his intellectual journey from agricultural reformer to secessionist through the logic of political economy. A more productive slave economy, he reasoned, would protect the South from the growing power of the industrializing North. But as Ruffin read more thoroughly in the writings of other proslavery authors his defense of slavery grew more sophisticated. He ended up placing all the world's peoples on a sliding scale that rose from the most savage to the most civilized. Savages, Ruffin asserted, were concerned with nothing more than meeting their bare physical needs. By contrast, civilized peoples sought to raise the standard of living by indulging in more sophisti-cated physical pleasures and by cultivating the mind as well as the body. The only way for barbaric peoples to rise above savagery, Ruffin claimed, was for the powerful and industrious to force shiftless and lazy people to work, usually by enslaving them. "By this aid only," Ruffin concluded, "could leisure be afforded to the master class to cultivate mental improvement and refinement of manners." Slavery thus spurred both civilization and prosperity.

417

But Ruffin's general defense of slavery left several important questions unanswered. Who, for example, should be enslaved? Equals could not enslave equals, for that was both morally objectionable and socially disruptive. Southern slavery escaped this problem, Ruffin believed, because whites only enslaved racially inferior blacks. Left to themselves, African Americans displayed an "aversion . . . to regular and laborious toil." The only thing that could bring them out of savagery and into civilization, Ruffin concluded, was "the direction and control of a superior race." And what of the abolitionist claim that slavery was less efficient than wage labor? Ruffin agreed that in principle slaves lacked the motive of self-interest that made wage laborers more efficient, but he pointed to the exceptional conditions that tipped the balance in the United States. As long as western lands were available to absorb the surplus labor of the North, he argued, free laborers would remain content to work on their own farms at their own pace. But slaves were compelled to labor constantly on precious cash crops that could be produced in climates where, Ruffin believed, only African Americans could work. As long as these exceptional conditions prevailed, slavery would be as efficient as free labor, Ruffin concluded.

Over time the West was sure to fill up, and when that happened, Ruffin argued, free men and women would have no choice but to sell their labor at miserably low wages. Eventually the cost of free labor would sink so low that it could outperform slavery. At that point, Ruffin predicted, the misery of free laborers would give rise to socialism and anarchy. Thus perpetual social unrest was the price northerners would have to pay for their wealth and prosperity. The South, by contrast, had struck the perfect balance between material well-being and social peace. By enslaving an "inferior" race of African Americans, Ruffin argued, southern whites were able to raise the general level of civilization without the disruptions associated with wage labor.

At first Ruffin's extreme views did not sit well with his fellow Virginians. Ordinary white southerners could accept Ruffin's racism, but not his elitism. They might admire his

Edmund Ruffin, shown here in his Palmetto Guard Uniform, at the outset of the Civil War.

defense of the South, but not his attacks on democracy, yet Ruffin only grew more extreme. He supported southern conquest of the "mongrel and semi-barbarous" peoples of Latin America and the Caribbean. He began to consider the benefits of reopening the Atlantic slave trade. He complained that in Virginia "talk of secession would ruin any man with political aims."

Then, on the evening of October 16, 1859, John Brown invaded Harpers Ferry, and Ruffin's spirits soared. He circulated petitions, wrote inflammatory articles, and gave fire-breathing speeches arguing that John Brown's raid was the first of many impending attacks from the North. The election of an antislavery president, Abraham Lincoln, seemed to confirm Ruffin's predictions. Southerners at last seemed to appreciate what Ruffin had long been arguing.

Edmund Ruffin had always believed that slavery was the issue dividing the North from the South. Ironically, as the two sections approached war, it was the northerners who still clung to the belief that the Union could be held together with slavery intact. Most northerners started out thinking that the war could be fought only to restore the Union. Over time, they came to see it as a struggle to rid the nation of slavery as well. Abraham Lincoln moved with northern public opinion, eventually coming to the conclusion that only the abolition of slavery could justify so much bloodshed. Edmund Ruffin was not surprised that the northern crusade to preserve the Union eventually became a crusade for the abolition of slavery as well.

What continued to disturb Ruffin was the behavior of his fellow southerners. His prewar experience should have prepared him for the divisions among southern whites. More surprising to Ruffin was the disloyalty of the southern slaves. Nothing in his complex vision of slavery's political economy prepared Ruffin for the flood of slaves who ran to Union lines claiming their freedom. The slaves transformed a sectional conflict into a genuine civil war. In so doing they helped force the North to shift its war aim from the mere restoration of the Union to the restoration of a Union without slavery. ▪

• The shift from limited to "hard" war

• The comparative military advantages and disadvantages of the North and the South

• Social and political divisions in the Confederacy

• The role of the slaves in the process of emancipation

From Union to Emancipation

Southerners made it clear that they were going to war to preserve the political economy of slavery. In 1861 Confederate President Jefferson Davis justified secession on the grounds that northern Republican rule would make "property in slaves so insecure as to be comparatively worthless." Confederate Vice President Alexander Stephens declared that the "cornerstone" of the Confederate constitution rested "upon the great truth that the negro is not equal to the white man; that slavery, subordination to the superior race, is his natural and moral condition." Southerners talked in general about defending "states' rights" or "property rights." But they were referring specifically to the right of the states to maintain slavery and the right of individuals to hold property in slaves.

Northerners made it equally clear that they were *not* going to war to destroy slavery. It was true that many northerners thought slavery was wrong. Many more had come to believe that a "slave power" had caused the war, but few cared enough about the plight of African Americans to support a war aimed at securing their freedom. In his 1858 debates with Stephen Douglas, Abraham Lincoln had insisted that the Republican Party had no intention of interfering with slavery where it already existed. In his inaugural address of March, 1861, Lincoln reasserted this promise. "I have no purpose," he said "directly or indirectly, to interfere with slavery where it exists. I believe I have no lawful right to do so,

and I have no inclination to do so." Lincoln claimed to be fighting for nothing more than the restoration of the Union. Within the next few years, under the pressures of war, Lincoln's position would change dramatically.

The South Secedes

As the news of Lincoln's presidential election flashed across the telegraph wires, the South Carolina state legislature called a secession convention into existence. On December 20, 1860, the state withdrew from the Union on the grounds that northerners had denied to southerners their "rights of property" in slaves. "They have encouraged and assisted thousands of slaves to leave their homes," South Carolina declared, "and those who remain have been incited . . . to servile insurrection." A few weeks later, on January 9, 1861, Mississippi seceded. Florida seceded the next day and Alabama the day after that. Georgia, Louisiana, and Texas swiftly followed suit. And then, as quickly as it began, the secession movement came to a halt. The slave states of the upper South refused to leave the Union simply because Lincoln was elected. Ardent secessionists began to suspect that the South was not unified in its opposition to the North.

When Lincoln took office in early March of 1861, the entire upper South was dominated by cooperationists rather than secessionists. **Cooperationists** were committed to remaining in the Union, provided the Lincoln administration "cooperated" with southern demands. Thus even after Lincoln's inauguration Virginia would not secede and neither would Arkansas or Missouri. The state legislatures of Kentucky and Delaware refused to convene secession conventions, and in Tennessee and North

Crowds thronged the streets of Savannah to celebrate when the first confederate flag was raised.

Carolina the voters refused as well. Lincoln and many Republicans hoped that if they moved cautiously they could keep the upper South in the Union and thereby derail the entire secession movement. But cooperationism in the upper South turned out to be a weak foundation upon which to rebuild the Union. Most cooperationists believed in the right to secede and objected to any federal effort to coerce the lower South back into the United States. Cooperationists pledged their loyalty to the Union only if the federal government met certain demands for the protection of slavery.

Cooperationist demands formed the basis of several last-minute attempts at sectional compromise. The most famous was a series of constitutional amendments proposed by Senator John J. Crittenden of Kentucky. The Crittenden Compromise included several important concessions to the South. It would have restored the Missouri Compromise line and guaranteed federal protection of slavery south of that line in all territories currently held or thereafter acquired by the United States. It would have virtually prohibited Congress from abolishing slavery in Washington, D. C. and from regulating the interstate slave trade. Finally, it required the federal government to compensate masters who were unable to recover fugitive slaves from the North.

Each of these concessions was unacceptable to the Republicans, especially the one protecting slavery in all territories *acquired in the future.* This struck Republicans as an open invitation for southerners to expand the "slave power" into Central America, South America, and the Caribbean. Republican stalwarts could not accept such a compromise without repudiating everything the party stood for. In any case, once the lower South seceded, the sanctity of the Union replaced the expansion of slavery as the chief concern of most northerners. By early 1861 northern Democrats who cared little about slavery were nevertheless unwilling to compromise with any southern state that had left the Union. For this reason the Crittenden proposals, which focused on slavery rather than the Union, fell on deaf ears throughout the North.

Furthermore, by the Spring of 1861 most southerners agreed with Edmund Ruffin that there should be no more compromise with the North. Out of respect for his long years of service to the cause, southern fire-eaters invited Ruffin to South Carolina where he was given the privilege of firing one of the first shots of the Civil War. At 4:30 in the morning on April 12, 1861, Ruffin aimed a rifle at Fort Sumter and began shooting. For 33 hours Confederates subjected the fort, on an island in the middle of Charleston harbor, to relentless bombardment. The southerners wanted to prevent the U. S. government from fortifying its troops with nonmilitary supplies. They succeeded. With no alternative, the Union commander raised the white flag of surrender. Fort Sumter fell to the Confederates, and the Civil War began.

Lincoln probably understood that his attempt to resupply Fort Sumter would provoke an armed assault. He had given up hope for a peaceful resolution of the secession crisis. By publicly announcing that he would send no weapons on the resupply mission to Fort Sumter, Lincoln had skillfully maneuvered the South into firing the first shot. That was all the pretext Lincoln needed. The next day he issued a call to the states for 75,000 militiamen to report for duty within 90 days. The governors of Tennessee, Virginia, North Carolina, Arkansas, Kentucky, and Missouri refused to comply with Lincoln's request. Two days later Virginia seceded, and within a month Arkansas, Tennessee, and North Carolina did the same. Northern hopes of holding on to the upper South had vanished (see Map 15-1).

But the South remained divided. Four slave states (Kentucky, Maryland, Delaware, and Missouri) never joined the Confederacy. In the mountains of western North Carolina and eastern Tennessee, Unionist sentiment remained strong throughout the war years, even in the face of violent repression by Confederate armed forces. Virginia was literally torn apart. The western third of the state voted overwhelmingly against secession and then refused to accept the decision of the eastern slaveholders to leave the Union. Some fifty western counties promptly formed their own state government, and the new government just as promptly recognized the westerners' petition to secede from Virginia. (In 1863 the state of West Virginia was admitted to the Union.) These were among the earliest indications that southern whites were not united in the desire to secede. Where slavery was weak, in the border states and the mountains, support for secession was weak also. Where slavery thrived, so did secession. Yet despite these internal divisions, white southerners put up a long, hard fight to sustain the independence of the Confederacy.

Civilians Demand a Total War

Most Americans expected the war to last only a few months. Lincoln's first call for troops asked volunteers to enlist for 90 days. Confederate soldiers initially enlisted for 12 months. A year later Union troops were signing up for three years, and Confederates were required to serve "for the duration" of the war. Although both sides commenced the fighting with relatively limited military and political goals, the conflict steadily descended into a "hard" war. Hard war meant unconditional surrender rather than a negotiated settlement. It meant the demolition of the enemy's army rather than simple victory on the battlefield. It meant destruction of the enemy's capacity to fight, which in turn meant bringing the war to civilians. In the end it would mean the destruction of slavery.

Hard war stopped short of making civilians themselves into military targets, a practice associated with the "total" wars of the twentieth century. Yet many civilians called for total war right from the start. In the weeks fol-

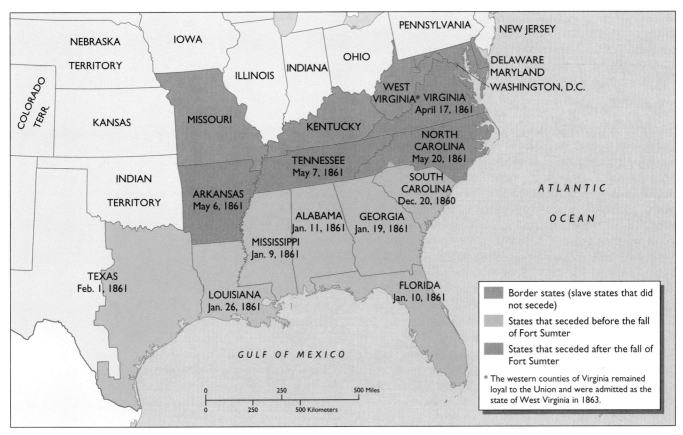

Map 15-1   The Secession of the Southern States.
The South seceded in two stages. During the "secession winter" of 1860–1861, the lower South states seceded in reaction to the election of Abraham Lincoln. The following spring the upper South seceded in response to Lincoln's attempt to resupply Fort Sumter. The border slave states of Maryland, Delaware, Kentucky, and Missouri never left the Union.

lowing the Sumter crisis enthusiasm for war overflowed in both the Union and the Confederacy. Mere military victory was not enough. In the spring of 1861 one southern woman prayed that "God may be with us to give us strength to conquer them, to exterminate *them,* to lay waste to every Northern city, town and village, to destroy them utterly." A year later, looking forward to Lee's invasion of Pennsylvania, the *Richmond* (Va.) *Dispatch* urged southern troops to "turn the whole country into a desert." Given the chance, that is precisely what the Confederates would have done. While in Pennsylvania, they burned the town of Chambersburg to the ground. In late 1864 Jefferson Davis sent Confederate agents to New York City, where they set fire to ten hotels at once, hoping to send the city up in flames.

Northerners felt no differently toward southerners. Even before the fighting began, in December 1860, Ohio Senator Benjamin Wade talked of "*making the south a desert.*" In the wake of Fort Sumter one northern judge argued that if the war persisted, the North should "restore New Orleans to its native marshes, then march across the country, burn Montgomery to ashes, and serve Charleston in the same way. . . . We must starve, drown, burn, shoot

the traitors." The war had barely begun and the civilians in the North and the South were already pressuring their political leaders to get on with the destruction of the enemy. By mid-1862, when it was clear that the war would be long and bloody, northern Senator John Sherman explained that "you cannot conduct warfare against savages unless you become half savage yourself." He therefore recommended that the North practice "every mode of warfare" known to ancient and modern history.

The military was more hesitant. For several months after the war began both the Union and Confederate commanders concentrated on building up their armies. Neither side was prepared for battle and neither sought it. Under the direction of the aged war hero, General Winfield Scott, Union military strategy was initially designed to take advantage of the North's naval superiority by blockading the entire South. This was called the Anaconda strategy, named after the snake that surrounds its prey and slowly squeezes it into submission. Confederate strategists hoped to maintain a defensive posture. The North would have to attack, but the South needed only to hold its ground.

As spring became summer, however, civilians in both the North and the South demanded something more dramatic than a long slow siege or a patient defense. "Forward to Richmond!" cried Horace Greeley, echoing northern sentiment for a swift capture of the new Confederate capital.

Slaves Take Advantage of the War

In the South the enthusiasm for battle was compounded by fantasies of a race war between African Americans and whites. "If things go on as they now are," one Georgian declared at the height of the secession crisis, "it is certain that slavery is to be abolished. . . . and then we will have black governors, black legislatures, black juries, black everything. . . . We will be completely exterminated." The lower South seceded while still in the grip of the insurrection panics that followed John Brown's raid on Harpers Ferry. Few slaves actually joined with Brown, but that did little to calm the fears of southern whites. Although the Old South had never been completely free of such fears, they were usually exaggerated. In 1861 this was no longer the case.

Shortly after Lincoln was inaugurated several slaves in Florida escaped to Fort Pickens claiming their freedom. In Virginia, scarcely a month after Fort Sumter, Union commander Benjamin F. Butler refused to return three run-

away slaves to their master on the grounds that they would have been put to work on Confederate military fortifications. Butler called the runaways "contrabands" of war, and the label stuck. Before a single major battle had taken place, Union officers in Maryland, Washington, D. C., and as far away as Missouri, were already sending reports of runaway slaves to their superiors. As the number of contrabands mounted, Butler began demanding that his superiors clarify Union policy. "As a military question it would seem to be a measure of necessity to deprive their masters of their services," he wrote on May 27, 1861. A week later Secretary of War Simon Cameron approved Butler's policy of refusing to return contraband slaves to their masters.

These were not random actions on the part of a tiny handful of slaves. As soon as the war began masters across the South discovered slaves "talking" about their freedom and making strenuous efforts to collect war news. House servants listened in on conversations at the masters' residences and reported the news to field hands in the slave quarters. One slave hid under the master's house listening to whites read newspapers aloud. Another climbed a tree to overhear conversations at parties. An illiterate slave memorized the letters her master spelled out in her presence hoping she would not understand, but she had the letters translated in the slave quarters. Whites became para-

Designated "contrabands" of war, these Virginia slaves are escaping to Union lines in August 1862. The Lincoln administration took office with a promise not to interfere with southern slavery, but runaways like those pictured here helped push the Union toward a policy of emancipation.

noid about how much their slaves knew. "Every servant is a spy upon us," one Mississippi planter complained. "They know everything." Every neighborhood had one or two literate slaves who got hold of a newspaper. News of the war's progress spread along what the slaves called the "grapevine telegraph."

The slaveholders were frustrated, but it was northern officials who were forced to take official notice of the slave's disruptive behavior. Butler's contraband policy was the first tangible result. Nevertheless, the Republicans were still pledged to leave slavery undisturbed. In July 1861 Congress passed a resolution reaffirming that the war was aimed at nothing more than the restoration of the Union. Even radical Republicans held their tongues, despite their growing conviction that the war could not be prosecuted without an attack on slavery itself. After the first major battle of the war in the summer of 1861, the radicals broke their silence.

First Bull Run and the Shift in War Aims

On July 21 inadequately trained Union and Confederate forces fought each other by a creek called Bull Run at the town of Manassas Junction, Virginia, 25 miles from Washington. Everyone knew the battle was coming. Spectators with picnic baskets followed the Union Army out of Washington to watch the events from the surrounding hillsides. Among the southerners who came to watch was Edmund Ruffin.

The Confederates took up a defensive line stretching eight miles along Bull Run and waited for the enemy to attack. Union troops had failed to keep Confederate reinforcements bottled up in the Shenandoah Valley. A flanking maneuver by Union commander Irvin McDowell nearly succeeded in dislodging the Confederate forces atop Henry House Hill, but southern officer Thomas J. Jackson, perched on his horse "like a stone wall," inspired his men to drive back the Union advance. (It would not be the last time "Stonewall Jackson" would give the Union Army grief.) The green Union troops, unaccustomed to the confusion of the battlefield, turned back in retreat (see Map 15-2). As they headed east toward Washington frightened spectators clogged the road in panic. The retreat turned into a rout.

Edmund Ruffin stood atop a nearby hill watching as Union soldiers fled. Anxious to join in the action, Ruffin commandeered a cannon, aimed, and fired, scoring a direct hit on a bridge the northern troops were running across as they escaped from the battlefield. Thrilled by his success, Ruffin made his way down the hill and through the wounded soldiers until he reached the bridge he had recently struck. He found only three bodies. "This was a great disappointment to me," Ruffin wrote. "I should have liked not only to have killed the greatest possible number but also to know if possible which I had killed and see and

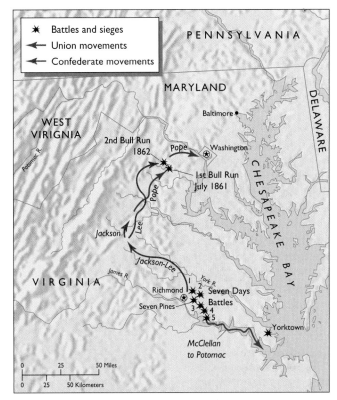

Map 15-2   The Virginia Campaigns of 1861–1862.
Between the First and Second Battles of Bull Run, the Confederate armies in Virginia consistently frustrated northern attempts to capture Richmond, the capital of the Confederate States of America. Superior southern generalship was largely responsible for the northern defeats.

count the bodies." Despite Ruffin's personal disappointment, most southerners were ecstatic, and perhaps somewhat overconfident, as a result of their victory at the first of two battles at Bull Run.

By contrast, the chaos in the Union ranks shocked the North into the realization that this would be no ninety-day war. To discipline the Union troops, Lincoln put George B. McClellan in command of the Army of the Potomac. Ninety-day volunteers gave way to three-year enlistments. The defeat also prompted northerners to rethink their war aims. Radicals broke their silence and began arguing that emancipation was a "military necessity." Republicans would support no more resolutions declaring that the restoration of the Union was the only aim of the war. Signaling this shift, the Republican-dominated Congress passed a Confiscation Act within weeks of the battle of Bull Run. For the first time, the federal government committed itself to confiscating any property, including slaves, used to prosecute the war against the United States. Benjamin Butler's contraband policy now had the status of law.

Senator Crittenden denounced the Confiscation Act as "revolutionary," but Lincoln signed it anyway. Some northern military commanders began enforcing the law somewhat liberally. By the fall of 1861 the Union Army was relying on the labor of fugitive slaves to support the northern military effort, thus stretching the definition of "military necessity" beyond what was contemplated in the Confiscation Act. By the end of 1861 the nature of the Civil War was already changing.

Also prodding the shift in war aims was the North's determination to keep England and France from recognizing the Confederate government. The Confederacy hoped to keep Europeans from respecting the Union blockade of southern ports. A diplomatic crisis loomed in late 1861 when an overly aggressive Union Navy captain intercepted a British ship, the *Trent*, in Havana. He forced two Confederate commissioners, John Slidell and James Mason, to disembark before allowing the *Trent* to sail on. The commissioners had slipped through the Union blockade and were headed for Europe, hoping to secure diplomatic recognition of the Confederacy. When the British protested, the Lincoln administration wisely backed down and released Slidell and Mason. "One war at a time," Lincoln said.

Mobilizing for War

By the end of the first summer both sides realized that the conflict would last for more than a few months and that it would involve far more than a few swift victories on the battlefield. Instead, the Civil War would demand all the resources the North and South could command. But, in 1860, neither side had many military resources to command. When Lincoln was elected president, the U. S. Army had 16,000 men. By the end of the war approximately 2,100,000 men had served in the Union armed forces. Another 900,000 served the Confederacy. To raise and sustain such numbers was an immense political and social problem. To feed, clothe, and especially to arm such numbers was an equally immense technological problem. To pay for such armed forces was an immense economic problem. As the Civil War progressed, it therefore became a test of the competing political economies of the North and the South (see Figure 15-1).

Thomas Nast's painting Seventh Regiment Departing for the War from New York City, April, 1861. *The enthusiasm on display was typical of popular sentiment in both the North and the South at the very beginning of the war. Neither side was prepared for the long and bloody war that followed.*

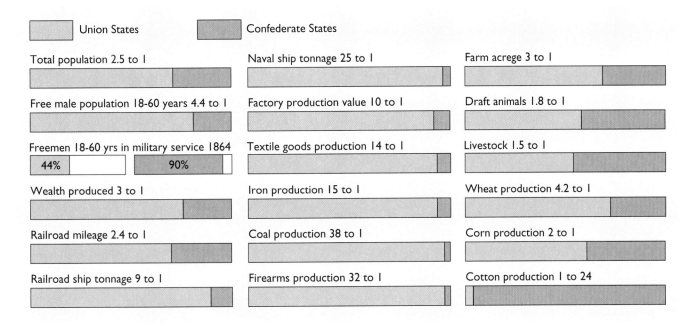

Figure 15-1 The Productive Capacities of the Union and Confederacy.

Southern Political Weaknesses

By the spring of 1861 the secessionists had constructed an impressive political apparatus. They had persuaded eleven states to leave the Union. They had convened a constitutional convention in Montgomery, Alabama. They had successfully drafted a basic charter for their new government, the Confederate States of America. They had proclaimed Richmond, Virginia, their nation's capital. And they had selected as president an experienced politician and Mississippi planter named Jefferson Davis.

The Confederate constitution varied in only minor ways from the U. S. Constitution. True to the South's Jacksonian tradition, the Confederacy banned protective tariffs and congressional appropriations for internal improvements. The Confederate president served only a single, six-year term and was given a line-item veto. The Confederate constitution explicitly protected slavery, whereas the U. S. Constitution did so implicitly. Otherwise southerners used the U. S. Constitution as a model for their own.

But these minor constitutional differences masked larger political differences that eventually favored the northern war effort. The most important was the absence of a two-party system in the South. The Whig Party had collapsed in the North during the early 1850s, and the Republican Party took its place a few years later. Throughout the war the northern Democrats represented a strong but "loyal opposition" to the Lincoln administration. In the South, by contrast, the Democratic Party ruled without serious opposition after the Whigs collapsed. As a result, in-ternal dissent within the Confederacy had no legitimate in-stitutional base. Furthermore, the white South's commit-ment to states' rights conflicted with the Confederacy's need to mount a concerted defense of the new southern na-tion. Political opposition therefore bred bitter personal feuds, often provoked by the competing wishes of state and national officials.

Union Naval Supremacy

The North was blessed with superior naval forces. From the outset northern strategists hoped to use their command of the seas to prevent the Confederacy from selling its cot-ton abroad. Ironically the Confederacy initially complied with northern strategy. Much of the industrial world de-pended on slave-produced cotton, and southern leaders sought to take advantage of this by withholding cotton from the market. They hoped to cripple northern industry while forcing England into diplomatic recognition of the Confederacy. This was the first test of the political econ-omy of slavery.

In the early months of the war, when the South em-bargoed its own cotton, the Union controlled only two bases from which to patrol thousands of miles of southern coastline. That changed in the closing months of 1861. In-genious engineering and skillful seamanship combined to give the Union Navy control of vast stretches of the At-lantic and Gulf coasts. By early 1862 Union forces were in a position to enforce their blockade, except for one thing.

The Confederacy had a magnificent new weapon designed to thwart Union naval supremacy. The South refitted an old Union ship, the *Merrimac*, with thick iron plates that rendered it all but impervious to conventional weapons. Rechristened the *Virginia*, the Confederate ironclad sailed into Union-controlled waters at Hampton Roads, Virginia, on March 8, 1862, and proceeded to wreak havoc on helpless northern ships. But that night the Union's own ironclad, the *Monitor*, arrived from New York. For most of the following day the "battle of the ironclads" raged on, with neither vessel dominating. The *Virginia* slipped up the James River to assist in the defense of Richmond, but in May the Confederates destroyed the vessel rather than allow it to be captured by approaching Union forces.

In the long run every navy in the world was rendered obsolete by the development of ironclad ships. But in the short run a standoff between the *Monitor* and the *Virginia* was as good as a loss for the Confederacy, for it left the Union Navy in substantial control of the coast and better able to enforce its blockade. And as long as the North could sustain a credible blockade, European powers kept a respectful distance from the Confederacy.

Southern Military Advantages

On land, however, the southern military probably had an important edge over the northern. Both armies had virtually identical lines of command. Each was democratic by modern standards, with enlisted men electing their own officers. On the other hand, more southerners went to military academies than did northerners. In the early years of the war these graduates brought skill and discipline to the Confederate Army that the Union could not yet match. The South's greatest advantage, however, was that it was defending its own territory. It did not have to invade the North, destroy the Union Army, or wipe out the North's industrial capacity. Southern armies fought on familiar territory, virtually in defense of their own homes. They required no occupation forces to hold captured northern territory. Closer to their sources of supply, the southern armies operated in the midst of a friendly civilian population, except for the slaves.

By contrast, the North had to fight an offensive war. It had to invade the South, destroy the Confederate armies, capture and retain a huge Confederate territory, and wipe out the South's capacity to fight. Northern soldiers fought on unfamiliar ground surrounded by a hostile civilian population, not counting the slaves. They were unaccustomed to the heat, the bad roads, and the swamps. And they lacked the motivation that comes from defending one's home turf.

The larger number of Union troops was eaten up by the fact that the North was fighting an offensive war. The Union required longer lines of supply and much larger provisions. An invading northern army of 100,000 men had to carry with it 2,500 wagons and 35,000 animals. It consumed 600 tons of supplies a day. The further it penetrated into southern territory, the more its ranks were thinned by the need to maintain increasingly tenuous supply lines. The more territory the Union troops conquered the more they were shifted from battle duty to occupation forces. As a result, many of the major battles of the Civil War were fought by roughly even numbers of Union and Confederate troops.

Even in battle the defensive posture of the Confederate Army was something of an advantage. Forts and cities on high ground (like Vicksburg and Fredericksburg) could maintain themselves against seemingly overwhelming numbers of invading troops. In the Union invasion of northern Virginia in 1864, Confederate General Robert E. Lee repeatedly held off much larger Union forces. His semicircular defensive posture made it easier for southern troops to maneuver against the northern offensive.

The Political Economy of Slavery Inhibits the Confederacy

Secessionists argued that slavery gave the South several clear military assets. The industrial world's dependence on cotton, they believed, would soon cripple northern textile mills and bring diplomatic recognition from England. In addition, a very high proportion of white men were able to serve in the southern military because slaves stayed home and performed much of the South's productive labor. This helped balance out the North's advantage in the number of military-age men. As the war dragged on, even northern Democrats sometimes pointed to the strength of slavery. "African slavery," Clement L. Vallandigham declared in January of 1863, "instead of being a source of weakness to the South, is one of her main elements of strength."

In certain ways, the relative backwardness of the slave economy had its military advantages. Because of slavery the South had remained a largely rural society. Southern men therefore knew how to shoot guns and how to ride and treat horses. Hence the Confederate cavalry during the first years of the war was far superior to the North's. It was easier for a southern farm boy to ride through mud on horseback than it was for a northern city boy to trudge through it on foot. On more than one occasion Union supply wagons found themselves bogged down by the inferior southern roads. Over time this advantage disappeared, as the Union cavalry improved and as the development of the rifle made traditional cavalry charges deadly. When the war started, however, many white southerners optimistically assumed that the average Confederate could easily whip two Yankees.

But the southerners assumed incorrectly. They overestimated England's dependence on American cotton and underestimated the strength of Britain's economic ties to the North. The English refused to break the Union blockade of the South and never granted diplomatic recognition to the Confederacy. King Cotton diplomacy failed, as did the political economy of slavery. By inhibiting immigration and the growth of cities, slavery reduced the overall population of the South leaving it with fewer fighting-age men. The Confederate Army therefore relied much more heavily on draftees than did the Union Army. If slavery freed 60 percent of southern men for military service, it eliminated from military service the 40 percent of the population that was enslaved. Leaving slaves at home while white men went off to war only made it easier for thousands of southern blacks to claim their freedom by running to Union lines.

Above all, slavery diminished the South's industrial strength. Ninety percent of the nation's factories were located in the North. Furthermore, the bulk of the Confederacy's industrial capacity was located in the upper South, which was over-run by Union forces early in the war. The South's ability to arm and supply its military was therefore severely restricted. Under the circumstances the Confederacy did surprisingly well. The South could produce most of its own artillery by 1863 but could not produce nearly as much as the North. For rifles the South relied heavily on the capture of Union supplies or on imports, an inefficient and expensive way to supply an army. Nevertheless, the South did manage to find enough rifles. The Confederacy also did a remarkable job of producing gunpowder and ammunition. As a result, the Confederate soldier was generally well armed. But he was not well fed or well clothed. The South simply could not provide its Army with food enough to keep its soldiers adequately nourished. Confederates often fought in rags, their uniforms poorly manufactured from inferior materials. In thousands of cases, southern soldiers went into battle barefoot.

Slavery also crippled the South's ability to finance its war adequately. The cotton crop was systematically embargoed. Because slaves earned no money, they could not be tapped for income taxes the way northern workers were. In any case white southerners remained true to the Jacksonian tradition of resistance to taxation. So to finance its military campaign the South began to print money in huge quantities. By 1863, with inflation raging out of control, the Confederate congress at last enacted comprehensive tax legislation. But it was too late: What little southerners paid in these new taxes they paid in depreciated Confederate currency. Trapped in its own vice, the southern government responded by speeding up the printing presses. By 1865 a Confederate dollar had the purchasing power that one Confederate cent had in 1861. Well before Lee's army surrendered, the Confederate financial structure had collapsed.

In the North, prospering farms and growing factories generated substantial liquid assets and, therefore, taxable income. In addition to the $600 million generated by taxes on incomes and personal property, the Union government eventually raised $1.5 billion from the sale of government bonds. The North also supplemented its tax revenues by printing money, the famous "greenbacks." But the North did not rely as heavily on paper money as did the South. Thanks to the Legal Tender Act, northern greenbacks became legally acceptable as currency everywhere in the country. Even southerners preferred greenbacks to Confederate dollars. Finally, the Union government floated war bonds. To ease the flow of so many dollars, the Republicans passed the National Bank Act in 1863. This law rationalized the monetary system, making the federal government what it remains today, the only printer of money and the arbiter of the rules governing the banking structure of the entire nation.

What Were Soldiers Fighting For?

Political, military, and economic differences are the tangible reasons that armies win or lose wars, but there are also important psychological reasons. Southern soldiers fought from a variety of motives. Many were simply caught up in the initial outburst of enthusiasm, enlisting for the sheer adventure of it. Most took for granted that in fighting for the South they were fighting to keep African Americans enslaved, but because they took slavery for granted, southern soldiers emphasized other motives, especially patriotism.

"The Spirit of '76" reflected the motives of many Yankee soldiers. Few went to war to free southern slaves. Rather, most were moved by a patriotic commitment to the sanctity of the Union and the legacy of the American Revolution.

Among southerners the "spirit of 1776" loomed large. In letters and diaries, Confederate soldiers declared that they were struggling to preserve the liberty and independence that their forefathers had won from Great Britain. We are fighting, an Alabama corporal explained, for "the same principles which fired the hearts of our ancestors in the revolutionary struggle." Confederate soldiers often warned that northern power was threatening southern freedom. This war, a Virginia soldier explained to his father, was "a struggle between Liberty on one side, and Tyranny on the other."

Besides the patriotic struggle to preserve their liberty and independence, southern soldiers were motivated by the defense of their homes and families. The protection of southern womanhood was a particularly potent theme in the soldiers' letters. "So long as we have such wives, mothers, and sisters to fight for," a North Carolina colonel wrote, "for so long will this struggle continue until finally our freedom will be acknowledged." Such sentiments were hardly surprising since most of the fighting was done on southern soil. Confederate troops fought with the strong conviction that they were, quite literally, defending their homes against a northern invasion.

Nevertheless, class distinctions affected the levels of patriotism in the Confederate armed forces. Slaveholders and their sons were far more likely to express patriotic sentiments than were soldiers from yeoman families. Troops from states where slavery was relatively unimportant, such as North Carolina, were markedly less enthusiastic about the war than were troops from states like South Carolina, where slavery was strong.

Class divisions were less severe in the Union Army. Impoverished immigrants sometimes joined the military to secure a steady source of income and, in later years, a substantial bounty. But Catholic immigrants were actually less likely to fight than native-born Protestants. As with their southern counterparts, the most common motivation among northern soldiers was patriotism. They, too, thought of themselves as the proud protectors of America's revolutionary heritage. Union troops compared the miseries of camp life to the sufferings of their forefathers at Valley Forge. But where southern soldiers emphasized independence and the eternal struggle between liberty and tyranny, northern troops equated freedom with the preservation of the Union. "Without Union & peace our freedom is worthless," one Ohio lieutenant declared. The Union as a "beacon of liberty" throughout the world was a common theme in the letters and diaries of northern soldiers, as was the simple preservation of law and order.

At the outset a small number of northern soldiers were motivated by antislavery principles. "I have no heart in this war if the slaves cannot be free," one young soldier from Wisconsin wrote. But many more were offended by the idea that they were risking their lives to free slaves. As the editors of one Union soldiers' newspaper put it in 1862, "We do not wish it even insinuated that we have any sym-

pathy with abolition." But as the war aims changed, so did the sentiments expressed by Union soldiers. By the end of the conflict most had accepted that emancipation was a legitimate goal of the war.

The Civil War Becomes a Social Revolution

By 1862 the North and the South had built up powerful military machines. Both sides were ready to fight a long war. This combination of will and might inevitably made the war more destructive. At the same time, the North's war aims were shifting to include the abolition of slavery, which meant the destruction of the southern social system.

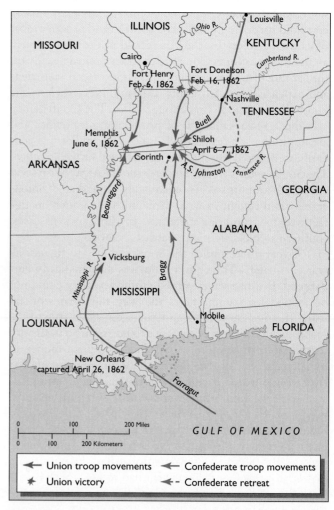

Map 15-3   The War in the West in 1862.
As Union armies floundered in the East, northern troops in the West won a decisive series of battles. Here the nature of the war changed. First, General Ulysses S. Grant demanded "unconditional surrender" of the southern troops at Forts Henry and Donelson. Then a bloody battle at Shiloh foreshadowed the increasing brutality of the war. Finally, the western theater produced two of the Union's most effective generals, Grant and William Tecumseh Sherman.

In the summer of 1862 the Lincoln administration adopted the radical Republican position that emancipation was a military necessity. Within a year Lincoln himself would be pointing to the abolition of slavery to justify the increasingly bloody war. Edmund Ruffin and his fellow planters had predicted that this would happen, but they were nevertheless shocked when it did. Throughout the South the moment of truth had arrived. Would the slaves remain loyal, as their masters had so often proclaimed? Or would the slaves continue to seek their freedom by running to Union lines, as the Lincoln administration hoped? The answers to these questions depended on the fate of the two armies on the field of battle.

Union Victories in the West

In early February, 1862, the Union Army and Navy displayed unprecedented cooperation as they joined in an aggressive strike deep into Confederate Tennessee. Led by Ulysses S. Grant, the Union Army captured Fort Henry on the Tennessee River and, shortly thereafter, Fort Donelson on the Cumberland (see Map 15-3). To the shock of Confederate officers at Fort Donelson, Grant insisted upon "unconditional and immediate surrender." The Tennessee campaign also showed some Union commanders that they could free up their armies by supplying them from the goods owned by local civilians. These two new developments, the principle of unconditional surrender and the confiscation of supplies from southern civilians, indicated the "hard" direction the war was taking.

The war's growing ferocity also became clear eight weeks later, at the battle of Shiloh. Southern General P. G. T. Beauregard, the hero of Manassas, caught Grant's troops off guard while camped at a peach orchard in southern Tennessee. The Confederate's surprise attack on April 6 forced the Union lines steadily backward, although the line did not break. By the end of the day Beauregard was telegraphing Richmond with news of his victory. But on the morning of April 7 Confederate troops were stunned by a counterattack from Union forces. Grant's troops pushed Beauregard's army back over the ground it had taken the day before. As they recrossed the battlefield soldiers passed over the bloodied, swollen bodies of the thousands of men who had fallen 24 hours earlier. When the Confederates finally retreated from Shiloh in defeat, the two armies had suffered an astounding 23,741 casualties. No battle in all of American history had ever come close to killing and wounding so many soldiers, and the worst was yet to come. The Civil War was quickly becoming a fight for the total

destruction of the enemy's forces. "At Shiloh," Ulysses Grant later wrote, "I gave up all idea of saving the Union except by complete conquest."

With Confederate forces busy at Shiloh, New Orleans was left with few defenses beyond two forts that sat astride the Mississippi River 75 miles south of the city. But they were impressive forts. It took six days of Yankee bombardment before Union commander David Glasgow Farragut attempted to break through. In the middle of the night of April 24, Farragut forced his Union fleet upriver through a blaze of burning rafts and Confederate gunfire that lit up the sky. Within a few days the Confederates evacuated both forts, and the city of New Orleans fell to Union forces. The South's largest city was occupied by Union troops under the stern command of Benjamin Butler.

Union victories in the West gave rise to northern optimism that war would be over by summer. Republicans took advantage of the mood of optimism to enact a bold legislative agenda. During the first half of 1862 both Congress and President Lincoln virtually reorganized the structure of national government in the North. Early in the year Lincoln replaced Simon Cameron, his corrupt and incompetent secretary of war, with the ruthlessly efficient Edwin M. Stanton. Stanton quickly set out to build a powerful and scrupulously honest war-making bureaucracy. Congress was even more aggressive. For years Democratic majorities had blocked passage of a number of laws that Republicans considered essential to their vision of the American political economy. Now, at last, the Republicans

The dramatic nighttime Battle of New Orleans. Union gunboats successfully slipped past heavy Confederate fortifications on the Mississippi River south of the city. With the Union capture of New Orleans, much of the lower Mississippi valley, with its large slave plantations, came under direct northern control.

had the votes and the popular support to push their agenda through Congress.

They began with a critical financial reform. To sustain the integrity of the currency, the Republicans passed a Legal Tender Act protecting northern greenbacks from inflationary pressure. To maintain the manpower of the armed forces, the Republicans instituted the first military draft in United States history. In addition, in 1862 the Republicans passed a crucial set of laws that they had advocated since their party was founded. They established a system of land-grant colleges designed to promote the scientific development of American agriculture. They passed a homestead act that promised a plot of land to free settlers in the West. Finally, the Republicans enacted their long-promised bill to finance the construction of the nation's first transcontinental railroad. Together these laws reflected the Republican Party's powerful commitment to the active use of the central government for the preservation of the Union and the promotion of capitalist development.

During the same months the Confederate government also moved to reform its bureaucracy in ways that would help sustain its military struggle. Southern leaders realized that they had made a mistake by withholding the region's cotton from the world market. The Confederate economy was already showing signs of the weakness that would lead to its financial collapse. To remedy the situation, the Confederate congress passed a comprehensive tax code that produced only disappointing revenues. In April 1862 the Confederacy established a national military draft. By centralizing taxation and conscription, however, Jefferson Davis' government at Richmond ran up against powerful resistance among the advocates of states' rights, particularly in Georgia and North Carolina. Thus where military victories in the West allowed Republicans in the North to enact an expansive legislative agenda, the Confederate government had trouble winning popular support for its own centralizing measures, despite the success with which southern troops turned back a massive northern offensive in Virginia.

Southern Military Strength in the East

The Peninsula Campaign of 1862 crushed the North's earlier optimism. The goal of the Union Army had been to capture the Confederate capital. Richmond was both the political and industrial center of the southern war for independence. Jefferson Davis and his government conducted their war from Richmond. Richmond was also the home of the huge Tredegar iron works, the largest industrial plant in the South. A disproportionate number of Confederate officers were Virginians. Many of them, like Robert E. Lee, chose to side with the South out of loyalty to their home state. Indeed, Lee was criticized for devoting too much of the Confederacy's strength to the narrow defense of Virginia. From the very beginning of the war Union strategists were determined to capture Richmond,

The Tredegar Iron Works in Richmond, Virginia, was the South's largest industrial plant. Because the South lagged so far behind the North in industrial capacity, protecting the Tredegar works was essential to the Confederate war effort.

and that was what Lincoln expected George B. McClellan to do as commander of the Army of the Potomac.

McClellan's great strength was his ability to administer and train a huge army. He instituted systematic drills and careful discipline and saw to it that his soldiers were well supplied. In the wake of their defeat at Bull Run, McClellan successfully restored his soldiers' morale and trained an army that was ready to fight. Unfortunately, McClellan was reluctant to fight. He was forever exaggerating the size of his opponents' forces. He repeatedly demanded more troops before he would take the offensive. Throughout the fall and winter of 1861–1862, McClellan stubbornly resisted Lincoln's suggestions that he attack. McClellan held all politicians in contempt, none more so than the president. He referred to Lincoln as "the original Gorilla" while styling himself after Napoleon. He sent insulting dispatches to his superiors and wrote pompous letters to his wife declaring himself the savior of the republic.

Only under intense pressure, and not until his own reputation was at stake did McClellan devise an exceedingly elaborate strategy to capture Richmond. Rather than march directly over ground McClellan very slowly moved his huge army of 112,000 men up the peninsula between the York River and the James River. Instead of directly attacking Richmond, however, McClellan dug in place at Yorktown. As usual, he allowed himself to be fooled into thinking that he faced a more formidable enemy than he actually did. The Confederates quickly became skilled at manipulating McClellan's weakness. They moved small numbers of soldiers back and forth to make him think there were more enemy troops than there really were. They planted fake cannons called "Quaker guns" along their lines to further mislead McClellan and other Union commanders. Then, in the middle of the night of May 4, 1862, the outnumbered Confederates withdrew toward Richmond. When McClellan discovered their escape, he declared it a Union victory.

The Army of the Potomac inched its way up the peninsula toward Richmond, but it never really took the offensive. Instead, Union troops were forced into battle by Confederates fighting under Robert E. Lee. Confederate General Joseph E. Johnston attacked the divided Union forces at Seven Pines on May 31, and both sides took heavy losses. Far more serious were the brutal battles of the Seven Days beginning in late June. Notwithstanding heavy Confederate losses, Lee repulsed McClellan's larger army. Lee had saved Richmond and sent the Army of the Potomac lumbering back to the fortifications around Washington, D. C. There McClellan did what he did best: He revived his soldiers' sagging morale and whipped the Army of the Potomac back into fighting shape. But he still would not do the fighting. McClellan let Union General John Pope take the offensive alone, but Pope's aggressiveness surpassed his tactical skills. He led his troops to a disastrous defeat at the Second Battle of Bull Run (August 29–30), while McClellan's huge army stood by offering no reinforcements.

By the Fall of 1862, the Union and Confederate forces had reached something of a military stalemate. The North had scored tremendous victories in the West. New Orleans was in Union hands. Grant had captured Forts Henry and Donelson. He had defeated the Confederates at Shiloh. The impressive Union Army of the Cumberland was heading toward Vicksburg, Mississippi. In the East, however, Robert E. Lee turned out to be one of the most skillful and daring commanders of the war. Stonewall Jackson, Lee's "right arm," had likewise proven himself a brilliantly aggressive soldier, and a frightening religious fanatic as well. Having kept much larger Union forces busy chasing him unsuccessfully up and down the Shenandoah Valley, Jackson had gained a reputation for invincibility among his Union enemies.

With his victory at Second Bull Run, Lee turned his army toward Maryland and launched his first invasion of the North. He hoped the Confederacy could win the war in the East before losing it in the West. A decisive strike into Pennsylvania would bolster antiwar forces in the North and impress the British and French with the Con-

federacy's strength. Lee therefore marched his confident troops across the Potomac into Maryland. Before Lee reached Pennsylvania, however, Union forces discovered the details of his planned invasion. McClellan squandered much of this advantage readying his troops for battle, but at last he met Lee's army at Sharpsburg, Maryland, beside Antietam Creek, on September 17 (see Map 15-4).

By launching his forces in three consecutive assaults rather than a single simultaneous maneuver, McClellan nearly lost Antietam. His tactics allowed the Confederates to shift their men around the battlefield whenever the

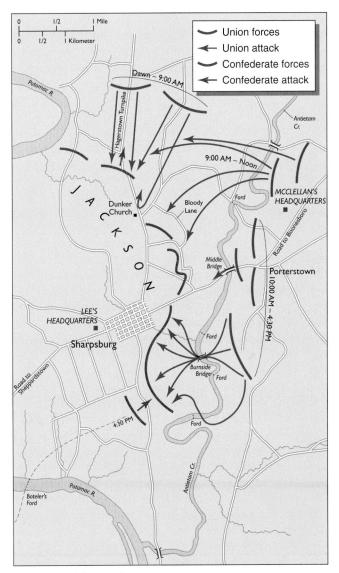

Map 15-4   The Battle of Antietam.
In September 1862 southern General Robert E. Lee led the Confederacy's first invasion of the North. He was stopped at Sharpsburg, Maryland, by Union troops under the command of George B. McClellan. Antietam was the bloodiest single day of the war, but it was an important turning point for the North. It gave Lincoln the victory he was waiting for to announce the preliminary Emancipation Proclamation.

Source: Adapted from J. G. Randall and David Donald, Civil War and Reconstruction, 2d. ed., p. 222.

fighting moved to a different location. By failing to deploy his reinforcements, McClellan missed a chance to break the center of the Confederate line. By delaying, McClellan gave Confederate reinforcements time to arrive on the scene and turn back a brutal Union attack on Lee's right. Nevertheless, Lee's men suffered staggering casualties and were unable to maintain their invasion of the North. It might have been even worse for the South, but despite intense pressure from Washington, McClellan refused to use the thousands of fresh troops at his disposal to pursue the disoriented southern army as it retreated across the Potomac. 4,800 soldiers died and 18,000 more were wounded at Antietam. It was the single bloodiest day of the war. Nevertheless, Antietam was a Union victory, and Lincoln took advantage of it to announce an important shift in northern war aims.

Emancipation as a "Military Necessity"

By the summer of 1862 President Lincoln was searching for some dramatic gesture that would break the military stalemate and convince European powers to side with the Union. He decided to issue the Emancipation Proclamation. Northern public opinion was shifting rapidly in favor of such a move. Union military advances in the plantation South in early 1862 had produced a flood of runaway slaves pouring into northern lines. Grant's sweep through western Tennessee, Farragut's capture of New Orleans and the lower Mississippi, and the Peninsula Campaign had brought Union military forces into some of the most densely populated slave regions of the South. As slaves took advantage of the opportunity to escape from their masters, Union commanders responded in a variety of ways. Some put the contrabands to work behind Union lines. Others sent the runaways back into slavery, to the horror of African Americans and the dismay of northern radicals. To clarify the situation, in March of 1862 Congress prohibited the use of Union troops to return fugitives to the South. Once again the North moved a step closer to a policy of emancipation. Citing this movement, Lincoln tried to persuade the border states to enact a policy of compensated emancipation. If you wait, Lincoln warned them, northern public opinion will push the government further toward uncompensated emancipation, leaving loyal slaveholders with nothing.

In April Congress did indeed move further by abolishing slavery in Washington, D. C. By that time so many slaves had run to the nation's capital claiming their freedom that the congressional action amounted to a belated recognition of the status quo. Nevertheless, for the first time the federal government exercised the power to emancipate slaves. Swept along by the surging tide, General David Hunter, commander of Union forces in lowcountry South Carolina and Georgia, issued a proclamation abolishing slavery in the entire area. Lincoln revoked the order because he did not think Hunter had the legal authority to issue it. But Lincoln himself was moving quickly in the direction of emancipation, and Congress was moving even faster. In June 1862 Congress prohibited slavery in all the western territories. The following month a second Confiscation Act was passed, this one declaring "forever free" the slaves of any "traitors" engaged in rebellion against the United States. At the same time Congress passed a militia act making it possible for "persons of African descent" to join the Union Army.

By mid-July of 1862 Lincoln had privately decided to issue an Emancipation Proclamation. Five days later the president announced his intentions to his cabinet. For Lincoln emancipation had become an inescapable reality. To deny the many slaves who had run to Union lines the freedom they claimed would have been unthinkable. "I do not believe it would be physically possible to return persons so circumstanced to actual slavery," the president conceded. "I believe there would be physical resistance to it which could neither be turned aside by argument nor driven away by force." Even conservative Republicans had come around to supporting a policy of emancipation. A year after radicals had first made the argument, Lincoln was prepared to issue a proclamation declaring the emancipation of the slaves. Like the radicals, he justified his move as a "military necessity" even though most of his generals opposed emancipation on the ground that it would bog the Union Army down with a mass of runaway slaves. In fact "military necessity" was Lincoln's pretext more than his motive for proclaiming emancipation. On the advice of his cabinet, however, the president waited for a battlefield victory to make his proclamation public.

Antietam provided Lincoln with that victory. On September 22, five days after Lee's invasion of Maryland was turned back, Lincoln issued his preliminary Emancipation Proclamation. Citing his war powers as commander in chief, Lincoln vowed to declare "free" all slaves held by masters in areas still in rebellion against the Union on January 1, 1863. One month before the proclamation took effect Lincoln proposed a plan of gradual emancipation in all areas under Union control. When the New Year arrived, Lincoln's final proclamation added another twist by sanctioning the enlistment of African Americans in the Union Army. Critics sniffed that the proclamation did not free a single slave, since it emancipated only those in areas controlled by Confederate forces. In fact, the proclamation transformed Union soldiers into an army of liberation. It was an open invitation for slaves to run away to Union lines, disrupting the Confederacy still further. No wonder Jefferson Davis denounced the proclamation as "the most execrable in the history of guilty man."

In the North the proclamation provoked intense criticism from the increasingly vocal peace wing of the Democratic Party. Many northern whites were enraged by the idea that the war was being fought to free the slaves. In the

African Americans serving in the Union Army symbolized the revolutionary turn the Civil War took once emancipation became the policy of the North. This scene depicts the nearly suicidal attack by the Massachusetts 54th regiment on Fort Wagner on the South Carolina coast in July 1863. Despite overwhelming loss of life by the African American troops, their bravery impressed many northerners and helped change white attitudes about the goals of the Civil War.

When Lincoln issued the Emancipation Proclamation on January 1, 1863, African Americans celebrated their freedom all across the country, even in those parts of the South that were technically unaffected by the proclamation. By assuming their freedom in this way, the former slaves gave a far broader meaning to the proclamation than the law formally allowed.

restoration of the Union and to keep slavery as it is without going into the territories," one northern soldier wrote, "not to free the niggers." But most Union troops had reached the conclusion that for the war to end the South had to be destroyed and that meant the destruction of slavery. Not even Lincoln would argue that emancipation was an end in itself. He realized that the war had become a revolution, especially with enlistment of African-American troops. But Lincoln's primary goal was still the restoration of the Union.

The Moment of Truth

The effectiveness of the Emancipation Proclamation depended in good part on the willingness of slaves to take matters into their own hands. Lincoln seemed to understand this. "How do we get the slaves to run away?" the president asked Frederick Douglass. But slaves across the South had been running to their freedom long before the federal Congress or the Lincoln administration made it a policy to accept them. Now, with emancipation as a war aim, slaves pushed still further beyond the limits of official policy. In low-country South Carolina and New Orleans slaves celebrated their freedom on January 1, 1863, even though those areas were under Union occupation and were therefore technically unaffected by the proclamation.

On plantations across the South this was the moment of truth. Would the slaves prove as faithful as their masters hoped, or as faithless as many masters feared? As the war progressed, more and more openings for the slaves to act were created. Plantation routine was severely disrupted by military activity and by the economic hardships caused by the war. In many cases the master and his sons were away in the army. Edmund Ruffin, for example, frequently left his plantation to lend his assistance to the Confederate defense of Virginia. He returned from one such expedition in July 1862, only to find his plantation ransacked, his fields destroyed, and all of his "faithful" slaves gone. The master's fears were vindicated.

White southerners were astonished by how quickly the slaves learned about the Emancipation Proclamation and other war news. "Damn niggers," a Louisiana planter complained, "they know more about politics than most of

words of one northern Democrat, we stand for "the Constitution as it is, the Union as it was, *and the Niggers where they are.*" Many northern soldiers were embittered by the Emancipation Proclamation. "I came out to fight for the

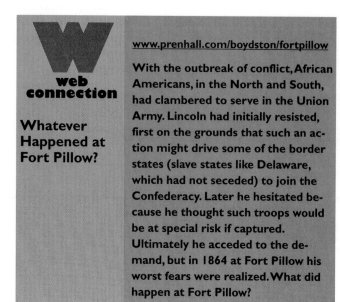

www.prenhall.com/boydston/fortpillow

web connection

Whatever Happened at Fort Pillow?

With the outbreak of conflict, African Americans, in the North and South, had clambered to serve in the Union Army. Lincoln had initially resisted, first on the grounds that such an action might drive some of the border states (slave states like Delaware, which had not seceded) to join the Confederacy. Later he hesitated because he thought such troops would be at special risk if captured. Ultimately he acceded to the demand, but in 1864 at Fort Pillow his worst fears were realized. What did happen at Fort Pillow?

the white men." The Union Army was now an army of liberation. Its mere approach, the mere rumor of its approach, sent terror through the white community. Sometimes slaves left without warning. "They have shown no signs of insubordination," one observer noted. "Down to the last moment they cultivate their maize and eat their corn cake with their old docility—then they suddenly disappear." It made no difference whether a master had been kind or cruel. The slaves left anyway. "We were all laboring under a delusion," one South Carolina planter confessed. "I believed that these people were content, happy, and attached to their masters. But events and reflection have caused me to change these opinions." Nothing, however, so angered southern whites as the appearance of African Americans in uniform.

African-American Union troops were conclusive evidence that the Civil War had become a social revolution. Although they had fought in the American Revolution and the War of 1812, before 1862 African Americans had never been allowed in the regular Army. They were banned from state militia by a 1792 statute. And although African Americans served in the Navy from the beginning of the war, northerners initially resisted the idea of an African-American infantry. The Militia Act of 1862 finally allowed African-American troops, but Lincoln remained reluctant to enlist them. In the summer of 1862, he was still trying to persuade the border states to accept compensated emancipation, and he feared that African-American troops would provoke a backlash in those areas. By the end of the year Lincoln had given up on the border states, and within a few months he became an active supporter of African-American enlistment. "The bare sight of 50,000 armed and drilled black soldiers upon the banks of the Mississippi," he said in March 1863, "would end the rebellion at once."

By the war's end 186,000 African Americans had enlisted, 134,111 of them recruited in the South. Although they made up nearly ten percent of the Union Army, African-American soldiers were never treated as the equals of white soldiers. Few African-American officers were commissioned, even from troops composed of elite, educated northern blacks. Black soldiers were paid less than whites. They were often relegated to garrison and labor duties rather than combat. African Americans were often held back from combat for fear that Confederates would kill such men if captured. But when they went into combat blacks performed respectably, and in so doing they changed the minds of many northern whites. "I have not been much in favor of colored soldiers," Elisha Hunt Rhodes admitted to his diary on June 19, 1864, but after seeing them in battle he became "convinced . . . that they will fight. So Hurrah for the colored troops!"

For African Americans themselves, especially for former slaves, the experience of joining the military to fight a war for emancipation was exhilarating. In a society that drew increasingly sharp distinctions between men and women, slaves who became soldiers often felt as though they were, in the process, becoming men. "Now we sogers are men," one African-American sergeant explained, "men the first time in our lives." As slaves they could not look their masters in the face, he added. "They used to sell and whip us, and we did not dare say one word. Now we ain't afraid, if they meet us, to run the bayonet through them."

African-American Union troops were an exhilarating spectacle for those still enslaved. "The black soldier is so presumptuous," one slave noted in amazement as he watched African-American troops land in the rice district along Georgia's coast. "They come right ashore, hold up their head. First thing I know, there was a barn, then [a] thousand bushels [of] rough rice, all in a blaze, then mas'r's great house, all cracklin' up the roof." But to white southerners, this was the "world turned upside down." As African-American troops marched through the streets of southern cities, whites shrieked in horror. They shook their fists at them, spit at them from behind windows, and found it all but impossible to control their rage and indignation. "There's my Tom," one planter muttered toward the passing regiment, "How I'd like to cut the throat of the dirty, impudent, good-for-nothing." But southern whites were not alone in their opposition to the revolutionary turn the Civil War had taken.

The War at Home

African-American troops could not end the rebellion "at once," as Lincoln hoped. Instead the war persisted for more than two years beyond the Emancipation Proclamation. As body counts rose and the economic hardships mounted, civilians in both the North and South began to register their discontent. Military setbacks lowered morale and encouraged antiwar sentiment in both sections. For northerners and southerners alike, the struggle on the home front was intensifying.

The Care of Casualties

Twenty-four thousand men had fallen at Shiloh. More than that fell during a single day of fighting at Antietam. The following year 50,000 men would die or suffer wounds at Gettysburg. At the battles of Chickamauga and Franklin, Tennessee, Confederate troops would suffer appalling losses. And in Grant's struggle against Lee in the spring of 1864 both sides would lose 100,000 men in the space of seven weeks. Casualties of this magnitude were unprecedented in American history. They were partly the consequence of inept leadership and inadequately prepared troops. But mostly they were caused by the fact that military technology had outpaced battlefield tactics. Generals continued to order traditional assaults on enemy lines even though newly developed rifles and repeating carbines made such assaults almost suicidal.

If advances in military technology multiplied the casualties, primitive medical practices did even more damage. Of the 620,000 soldiers who died in the war, two out of three were felled not by bullets but by sickness and disease. Thousands of soldiers were killed by contaminated water, spoiled food, inadequate clothing and shelter, mosquitoes, and vermin. Crowded military camps were breeding grounds for dysentery, diarrhea, malaria, and typhoid fever. Young men who had grown up in rural isolation succumbed to childhood diseases when they came into contact with their fellow soldiers. Doctors had never heard of "germs" and so had no idea that sterilization made any difference. No one knew what caused typhoid fever or malaria. There were no antibiotics, and for many surgeries liquor was the only anesthesia available. Nobody knew how to prevent gangrene and other infections caused by bullet wounds, so the field hospitals of both armies were littered with piles of amputated arms and legs.

In one area, nursing, the Civil War advanced the practice of medicine and may have prevented thousands of additional deaths. When the Civil War broke out Florence Nightingale's achievements for the British Army during the Crimean War had already inspired countless American women. Nightingale successfully transformed nursing into a respectable occupation in England. Similarly, the Civil War overturned long-standing prejudices

against the presence of women in military hospitals. The Confederacy lagged behind in institutional developments, but hundreds of southern women volunteered their services to the southern forces. As she nursed the Confederate wounded Alabamian Kate Cumming invoked the example of Florence Nightingale to counteract traditional southern stereotypes about the proper place of respectable women. Even in the North the thousands of women who volunteered their services to the Union Army had to overcome institutional barriers against them. In mid-1861, however, a

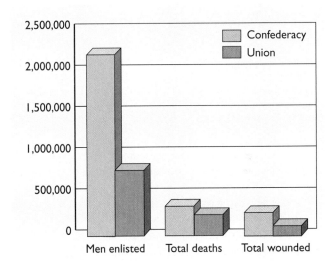

Figure 15-2 Casualties of War.

More Americans lost their lives in the Civil War than in all the nation's other wars combined. The primitive state of medical care, depicted in this gruesome scene from a military hospital, would have produced still more casualties had it not been for important advances in nursing.

powerful lobby of northern reformers persuaded Lincoln to establish the United States Sanitary Commission. Led by men but staffed by thousands of women, the "Sanitary" became a model of bureaucratic efficiency and a potent force for reform of the Army Medical Bureau. It established the first ambulance corps for the swift removal of wounded soldiers from the battlefield. It pioneered in the use of ships and railroad cars as mobile hospital units. The Sanitary Commission, together with inspiring examples of courageous service by Dorothea Dix, Clara Barton, and others, made nursing a respectable profession for thousands of women long after the war ended.

But the heroic efforts of the Sanitary Commission could not undo the fact that the Civil War had brought Americans face to face with unprecedented bloodshed. As the war dragged on, and as the aims of the war shifted, more and more Americans raised their voices in opposition to the policies of the Lincoln and Davis administrations.

Northern Reverses and Antiwar Sentiment

Lincoln struggled for years to find a commander who could stand up to great southern generals like Robert E. Lee and Stonewall Jackson. For failing to crush Lee's army after Antietam, Lincoln at last fired McClellan. The president gave command of the Army of the Potomac to a reluctant Ambrose Burnside. But Burnside could not hope to match Lee's brilliant, unorthodox approach to strategy. At Fredericksburg, Virginia, on December 13, 1862, Lee's army assumed a virtually impregnable position and subjected Burnside's men to a calamitous slaughter. Lincoln quickly replaced Burnside with "Fighting Joe" Hooker, who did a good job of restoring the fighting spirit of Union troops in the wake of the disaster at Fredericksburg. As a general, however, Hooker was a swaggering braggart who was no better at fighting than Burnside had been. At Chancellorsville, Virginia, at the beginning of May 1863, Lee violated all the rules of traditional warfare by dividing his army in two and overwhelming Hooker's forces. It was one of the bloodiest Union defeats of the war. Every commander Lincoln had put in charge of Union forces in Virginia proved more disastrous than the last. In the West Grant was bogged down outside of Vicksburg, Mississippi. The Confederacy now had a string of military victories under its belt.

These northern military reverses sustained a wave of political opposition to the Lincoln administration's emancipation policy. Northern Democrats had always favored compromise with the South on the slavery issue. They continued to argue that the only legitimate aim of the war was the restoration of the Union. Congressional Democrats had voted almost unanimously against the abolition of slavery in the District of Columbia and the ban on slavery in the territories. In the elections of 1862 Peace Democrats (known as **Copperheads**) took control of the legislatures

in Illinois and Indiana and threatened to withhold troops from the national war effort. Troops raised from the so-called "butternut" areas of southern Illinois deserted in droves in early 1863, after the Emancipation Proclamation was issued. Democrats were scandalized when the War Department authorized the formation of African-American regiments in early 1863. "This is a government of white men, made by white men and for white men, to be administered, protected, defended, and maintained by white men," one Democratic congressman insisted.

With the beginning of military conscription in March 1863, northern Democrats added the draft to the list of atrocities they attributed to the Republicans. Because northern draftees could escape conscription by paying a $300 **commutation** fee, many working-class men, especially Irish immigrants, complained that the rich could buy their way out of combat. In fact, the Irish were underrepresented in the Union Army, and there were a number of means by which working men could pay the commutation fee. But the taint of inequity remained so strong that after 20 months Congress abolished commutation.

Despite this congressional retreat, drafting white men to fight a war for African-American emancipation continued to provoke anger. Dissent became so widespread in many parts of the North that Lincoln claimed the constitutional authority to suspend *habeas corpus*. To Peace Democrats all of this looked like the destruction of white liberty for the sake of African Americans. Their leading spokesman, Clement L. Vallandigham, repeatedly attacked the president's "despotic" measures. If forced to choose between the loss of freedom for whites and the continued enslavement of African Americans, he told his fellow congressmen, "I shall not hesitate one moment to choose the latter alternative."

Vallandigham warned that antiwar sentiment was so strong that the western states might make a separate peace with the South. But it was the East that witnessed the most spectacular demonstration of antiwar feelings. In 1862 whites protesting the drift toward emancipation rioted in several northern cities. By mid-1863 Peace Democrats stepped up their antiwar rhetoric. In New York City, Irish Democrats responded to the opening of the local draft office by rioting through the streets of Manhattan. Working-class immigrants had suffered most from wartime inflation, and were most susceptible to economic competition from African Americans. Their frustration exploded into the venomous rage of the great New York City draft riots, which began on July 13, 1863, and continued for several days.

Rioters attacked the homes of leading Republicans and assaulted well-dressed men on the streets. But mostly they attacked blacks. White mobs lynched a dozen African Americans and set fire to the Colored Orphan Asylum. By the time troops arrived to suppress the disorder, more than a hundred people had died, most of them rioters killed by police and soldiers. From that point on violent northern opposition to the war subsided, in part because the draft riots had discredited the Copperheads. But northern morale was also lifted by the improving military fortunes of the Union Army.

Gettysburg and the Justification of the War

As criticism of the Lincoln administration swelled in the summer of 1863, Lee sensed an opportunity to launch a second invasion of the North. But the luck that had for so long visited the Army of Northern Virginia was finally spent. As Lee pushed his troops up through the Shenandoah valley into Pennsylvania, he lost touch with his cavalry and could not tell where Union forces were. By contrast, Union scouts kept their commanders aware of Lee's movement. On July 1 the armies converged on the small town of Gettysburg, Pennsylvania (see Map 15-5). For three days they fought the most decisive battle of the war. On the first day it looked as though the South was on its way to another victory. Confederate troops pushed the

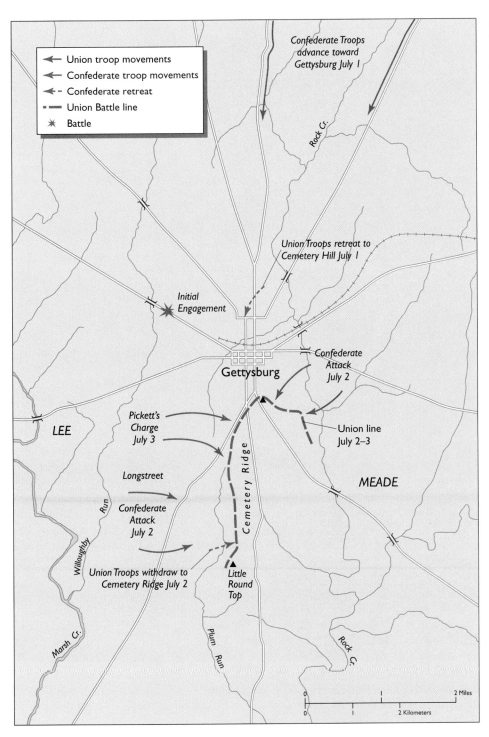

Map 15-5   The Battle of Gettysburg, July 1–3, 1863.
In three extraordinary days in Gettysburg, Pennsylvania, the Union Army turned back Lee's second invasion of the North. The Union victory, combined with equally important successes in the West at the same time, turned the tide of war in the North's favor. At the dedication of a military cemetery at Gettysburg a few months later, Lincoln articulated his most profound justification for waging war against the South.

Source: Adapted from Hammond, Inc., Maplewood, NJ.

Legend:
- Union troop movements
- Confederate troop movements
- Confederate retreat
- Union Battle line
- Battle

Confederate Troops advance toward Gettysburg July 1

Union Troops retreat to Cemetery Hill July 1

Initial Engagement

Rock Cr.

Gettysburg

Confederate Attack July 2

Union line July 2–3

LEE

Pickett's Charge July 3

Cemetery Ridge

Longstreet

MEADE

Willoughby Run

Confederate Attack July 2

Union Troops withdraw to Cemetery Ridge July 2

Little Round Top

Marsh Cr.

Plum Run

Rock Cr.

0   2 Miles
0   2 Kilometers

GROWING UP IN AMERICA

Litt Young

Litt Young was only ten years old when the Civil War began. He was born a slave to Martha Gibbs of Vicksburg, Mississippi. Gibbs provided the young Litt with adequate food and shelter, but she did not hesitate to whip her slaves into submission. She sold away Litt's sister and two brothers, and he never saw them again. The preacher Gibbs hired taught Litt and his fellow slaves "to obey our master and missy if we want to go to heaven." Even as a child Litt was put to work. "When that big bell rung at four o'clock you'd better get up," Young remembered, "'cause the overseer was standin' there with a whippin' strap if you was late." He saw his father whipped repeatedly for not getting into the field on time.

When the war broke out Litt was able to observe some of the most important military actions in the West. "I seed the Yankee gunboats when they come to Vicksburg." Then, when Grant won control of the city, Litt's mistress tried desperately to prevent her slaves from being freed. She locked young Litt and the rest of her slaves in a church for three days until forced to let them go free. Spotting a chance to escape, Gibbs seized Litt and several others and took them to Texas at gunpoint. He remained enslaved for another year in Texas, until the war ended. At the age of fifteen, Litt Young was emancipated, having spent most of his childhood in slavery.

The bodies of dead soldiers litter the battlefield at Gettysburg. Shortly thereafter workers rushed to bury the corpses in time for the dedication of the battlefield as a military cemetery. Lincoln's powerful dedication address promised "a new birth of freedom—and that government of the people, by the people, for the people, shall not perish from the earth."

Union enemy steadily backward through the streets of Gettysburg and onto the hills south of the town. But as evening fell the Union Army commanded the heights. Through the night General George Gordon Meade (who had been given command of the Union Army only days before) secured a two-mile line of high ground stretching from Cemetery Hill at the north, down along Cemetery Ridge to Little Round Top at the far south. On the second day, Lee ordered two flanking attacks and a third assault on the Union center, but at each point the Union line held. The second day at Gettysburg saw some of the most dramatic fighting of the war, particularly the extraordinary Union defense of Little Round Top. On the third day, against the strong advice of his trusted General James Longstreet, Lee ordered a direct attack by George Pickett's troops on the strongly fortified Union center. Pickett's Charge was a devastating loss for the southern troops. On July 4 the Confederates began their retreat back toward the Potomac. Pickett never forgave Lee for ordering the suicidal attack, and Lee himself offered to resign a month later.

As northerners were celebrating Lee's defeat, news came of another astonishing Union victory in the West. For months the town of Vicksburg, Mississippi, had proved invincible, to the endless frustration of General Grant. After a succession of failed strategies, Grant had decided to lay siege to the town (see Map 15-6). He cut Vicksburg off from all supplies and waited until the soldiers and civilians in the town were starved into submission. For six weeks the people of Vicksburg lived in caves, bombarded during the day by expert sharpshooters and by relentless cannon-fire at night. Consuming all of their provisions, the southerners subsisted on mules and rats. Eventually the Confederate soldiers threatened mutiny. "If you can't feed us, you had better surrender," they informed their commander on June 28. Less than a week later, after nearly two months of deprivation, Vicksburg surrendered. The Confederate commander at Port Hudson read the writing on the wall and surrendered his town as well. The Mississippi River was now completely opened to Union navigation and the Confederacy itself was split in two. Vicksburg and Gettysburg, together, were the greatest Union victories of the war.

Lincoln seemed to think so. In November, the president went to Gettysburg to speak at the dedication of a military cemetery at the battlefield. He took the opportunity to articulate a profound justification of the Union war effort. The Civil War, Lincoln said, had become a great test of democracy itself and of the principle of human equality upon which democracy was based. The soldiers who died at Gettysburg had dedicated their lives to those principles, the president noted. It remained only "for us the living" to similarly "resolve that these dead shall not have died in vain—that this nation, under God, shall have a new birth of freedom—and that government of the people, by the people, for the people, shall not perish from the earth."

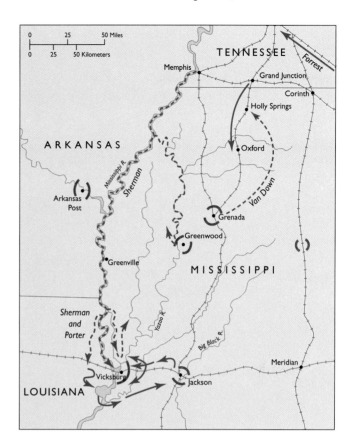

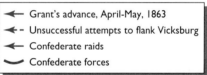

← Grant's advance, April–May, 1863
←- Unsuccessful attempts to flank Vicksburg
← Confederate raids
⌐ Confederate forces

Map 15-6   The Siege of Vicksburg, 1862–1863.
After a series of unsuccessful efforts to capture Vicksburg, Mississippi, from the Confederates, Grant settled down for a long siege. When the southern troops surrendered, in July 1863, the Union gained complete control of the Mississippi River and in so doing split the Confederacy in two. With the fall of Vicksburg, the Confederacy all but lost the war in the West.

With the Gettysburg Address Lincoln not only produced one of the greatest of American speeches, he also took brilliant advantage of the North's improving military fortunes to elevate the meaning of the war beyond the simple restoration of the Union. After 1863 antiwar sentiment in the North diminished substantially. In the South it exploded.

Discontent in the Confederacy

Southerners, both military and civilian, suffered proportionally far more casualties than did northerners. Day-to-day deprivation and physical destruction were common experiences in the Civil War South. This alone provoked resistance to Confederate war measures. But the slave states were divided over secession from the very beginning, and as the war became more relentless the divisions grew more disruptive. Whites in eastern Tennessee and western North Carolina were violently opposed to the war, and their opposition was violently suppressed by the Confederate government. Long after West Virginia declared its independence the southern armies subjected the area to repeated military assaults.

Although most whites in the seceded states remained loyal to the Confederacy, many of them bitterly attacked the government of Jefferson Davis. In the wake of Lee's defeat at Gettysburg, for example, Edmund Ruffin littered his diary with vituperative assaults on the character and competence of the Confederate president. Although formed in the name of states' rights, the Confederate government became a huge centralized bureaucracy. This was a most unpleasant irony for many white southerners. The Confederacy taxed them far beyond anything in their prewar experience.

Early in the war the government in Richmond took control of the military draft away from the states. The South relied much more heavily on draftees than did the North. A "planter's exemption" allowed the sons of wealthy slaveholders to purchase replacements, which generated tremendous hostility. Ordinary southerners complained of a "rich man's war but a poor man's fight." Opposition to taxes and to the draft led North Carolina Governor Zebulon Vance into repeated conflicts with the Davis administration. But the most important resistance came from Georgia, where a trio of powerful politicians (Governor Joseph Brown, Vice President Alexander Stephens, and Senator Robert Toombs) launched an increasingly vitriolic assault on the Confederate government. They attacked Davis as a "despot" who trampled on the rights of states. Faced with swelling internal opposition, Davis followed Lincoln's course and suspended *habeas corpus* in many parts of the Confederacy.

The South experienced none of the race riots that shook the North and no draft riot comparable to the one that rocked New York City. But the North suffered none of the bread riots that erupted in a dozen southern cities in 1863. On April 2, a thousand hungry citizens, mostly women, rampaged through the streets of Richmond, Virginia, shouting "Bread, Bread" as they ransacked local stores for food and clothing. By then life for millions of southerners had become miserable and desperate. Confederate money was becoming worthless. Devastating military campaigns swallowed up much of the precious food supply and destroyed many of the facilities for marketing the food that was produced.

As the Confederate economy collapsed, severe wartime shortages provoked bread riots by desperate women in many southern cities. Most of these women remained loyal to the Confederate cause, but their protests revealed severe strains in southern society.

In the summer of 1863 drought added to the distress. From farms across the South women wrote imploring letters begging their husbands to return. In the face of starvation, southern troops often "voted with their feet," leaving their comrades to return home to their distressed families. Although most of these desertions were temporary, they nonetheless weakened the southern nation's ability to counter the renewed vigor of Union armed forces.

The failure of the southern political economy and the wholesale destruction of southern property sent Edmund Ruffin into a profound depression. All of his money was invested in worthless Confederate war bonds. He could not understand why northerners had not risen in rebellion against their dictatorial, tyrannical president. Yet Ruffin himself was shocked by the disloyalty of ordinary whites, and he called for a dictator to take control of the Confederate cause. In May of 1864 Ruffin's son was killed in battle at Drewry's Bluff, and his plantation was occupied by Union troops. Yet neither Ruffin nor his fellow Confederates abandoned their commitment to a separate southern nation.

The War Comes to a Bloody End

In the face of civilian bread riots, war weariness, and disloyal slaves, the South persisted on the battlefield. Indeed, the last year of the war was by far the most brutal and destructive. A crippled Confederacy fought all the more desperately to maintain itself in the face of domestic collapse.

At the same time, northern society seemed stronger than ever. Amidst the most ferocious fighting ever witnessed on North American soil, the commander in chief submitted himself for re-election to the presidency and won.

Grant Takes Command

During the summer of 1863 Union forces under the command of William S. Rosecrans succeeded in pushing Braxton Bragg's Confederate troops out of central Tennessee. Bragg retreated all the way to Chattanooga, a critical rail terminal for the South. After some prodding from Washington, D. C., Rosecrans began moving his army toward Chattanooga in mid-August. By early September he was joined by Ambrose Burnside, who had just chased the Confederates out of Knoxville. Outnumbered and almost surrounded, Bragg and the Confederates abandoned Chattanooga and retreated into Georgia.

But Jefferson Davis would not give up the West without a fight. He sent reinforcements to Georgia and then ordered Bragg to return to the offensive. At the same time, Union General George Thomas pushed his troops hard so that they could reinforce Rosecrans and Burnside. On September 19 the two armies discovered each other at Chickamauga Creek in eastern Tennessee. The bloodiest battle of the western theater was about to begin.

It lasted two days. On the first day, General Thomas' troops struggled successfully to hold back a relentless Confederate assault. But on the second day, Confederates under General Longstreet discovered an opening at the center of the Union line. The southerners poured through the breach, overwhelming the Union right. A stunned Rosecrans hurriedly retreated eight miles back to Chattanooga, leaving Thomas to hold the Confederates off on his own. Luckily, Thomas' men were reinforced by the timely arrival of Gordon Granger's troops, which allowed the Union forces to beat back Longstreet's continued attacks. Thomas thus prevented a Confederate victory from becoming a complete Union rout. Nevertheless, when night fell on September 20, Thomas also retreated to Chattanooga where he and the remaining Union troops found themselves trapped by the Confederates.

Weeks after their defeat at Chickamauga, Union armies were still stuck in Chattanooga unable to feed themselves. General Rosecrans seemed paralyzed by the disaster. A frustrated President Lincoln swiftly reorganized the military structure of the western theater. He put General Grant in charge of all Union military activities between the Mississippi River and the Appalachian Mountains. In November 1863 Grant and William Tecumseh Sherman came to the rescue of the Union troops trapped at Chattanooga. Together with General Thomas, they executed a bold series of moves that effectively dislodged the Confederates from the railroad terminal in eastern Tennessee. Two days later Union forces routed the enemy at

Lookout Mountain, driving Confederate troops deep into Georgia. The war in the West was nearly over.

Lincoln at last had a general who would fight. In March of 1864 he put Ulysses Grant in charge of the entire Union Army. Grant decided on a simple two-pronged strategy: He would take effective control of the Army of the Potomac and confront Lee's Army of Northern Virginia while Sherman would hunt down and destroy Joseph E. Johnston's troops in Georgia. In these two engagements the Civil War reached its destructive heights. "From the summer of 1862, the war became a war of wholesale devastation," John Esten Cooke explained. "From the spring of 1864, it seems to have become nearly a war of extermination."

The Theory and Practice of Hard War

McClellan, Burnside, and Hooker had all withered under Lee's assaults. Grant did not. The two generals—Lee and Grant—hurled their men into battle, often directly into the lines of enemy fire. Rebuffed at one spot, they relentlessly turned and hurled men right back somewhere else. The immediate result of this titanic struggle was a month-long series of unspeakably bloody encounters beginning in the spring of 1864. The first battle took place on May 5 and 6, in a largely uninhabited stretch of woods, thick with underbrush and criss-crossed with streams. Appropriately called the Wilderness, the dense terrain made it difficult to see for any distance and all but impossible for armies to maintain strict lines. Soldiers and commanders alike were confused by the blinding woods and smoke, by the deafening roar of gunfire, and by the wailing of thousands of wounded. Men got lost; entire brigades got lost. Soldiers began shooting at flashes from nearby rifles, and their shots hit comrades as well as enemies. The flashes sparked the underbrush, setting the forest on fire. Flaming trees fell on wounded soldiers, burning them to death. In two days of fighting the Union Army suffered 17,000 casualties, the Confederates 11,000, and there was more to come.

Grant's goal was to break through Lee's defensive line and capture Richmond. But despite Grant's aggressive maneuvering, Lee always kept a step ahead, always managed to take the defensive position. With the smoke still billowing in the Wilderness, Grant marched his army south hoping to outflank Lee at Spottsylvania Court House. As usual Lee kept one step ahead and resumed his defensive posture. From May 10 to May 12 the bloodbath was repeated. Another 18,000 Union casualties; another 12,000 Confederates lost. Still Grant persisted, pushing his men further south. Determined to break through Lee's defenses, Grant waged a series of deadly skirmishes culminating in a frightful assault at Cold Harbor on June 3. In this last futile attempt to break the southern line, Union soldiers were mowed down like blades of grass. Bodies piled on top of bodies until finally Grant realized the hopelessness of the exercise and called a halt. Seven thousand Union men were killed or wounded at Cold Harbor, most of them in the first 60 minutes of fighting. The armies moved south yet again, but when Lee secured the rail link at Petersburg (a link that was critical to the defense of Richmond) Grant settled down for a prolonged siege. Northerners were shocked that so much blood had been shed to secure so little. The brutal Virginia campaign had not ended the war (see Map 15-7). More than 50,000 Union men were killed or wounded, yet Grant had not destroyed Lee's army. He had not taken Richmond. The Army of Northern Virginia and the Army of the Potomac were at a standoff, and Lincoln was up for re-election in November.

Two other military achievements saved the election of 1864 for the Republicans. The first was General Philip Sheridan's Union cavalry raid through the Shenandoah Valley in the summer of 1864 followed by his defeat of the Confederate cavalry's raid into Maryland. Ordered by Grant to wipe out the source of supplies for Lee's army, Sheridan's men blazed an astonishing path of destruction. In one sweep through the Shenandoah valley northern soldiers burned 2,000 barns and killed or chased off 7,000

animals. Sheridan's Valley Campaign demonstrated that the Union Army now had a cavalry that could match and defeat the Confederacy's.

Meanwhile General Sherman provided Lincoln with a second piece of good news prior to the November election. All through the spring and into the summer of 1864, Confederate General Joseph E. Johnston's tactical retreats frustrated Sherman's efforts to engage him. Union troops launched a brutal but unsuccessful effort to break the Confederate lines at Kennesaw Mountain, Georgia. Once again Sherman was forced to chase Johnston down rather than confront him on the battlefield. Jefferson Davis was equally frustrated. He wanted his general to stand and fight. But when Johnston fortified his army in Atlanta, the Confederate president relieved him of command and ordered John Bell Hood to attack Sherman's army directly. Hood did, and he failed. The Confederate position in Atlanta was hopeless. Hood was forced to accede to Sherman's terms of evacuation. On September 1, as the election campaign was heating up in the North, Sherman telegraphed Lincoln: "Atlanta is ours, and fairly won."

Atlanta was a Union victory, and both northerners and southerners recognized it as such. But it was not the victory Lincoln and Grant had been looking for. Sherman's charge was to engage and defeat Hood's army. Sherman accepted that charge, and he continued to believe that the war could not be won by conquering land and cities instead of enemy armies. But after Atlanta Sherman came to believe that southern civilians also had to be subdued. Sherman stopped short of "total" war, however. He never attacked civilians themselves. Instead, Sherman destroyed the homes and farms, indeed the towns and cities, upon which southern civilians depended. The white South had sustained the rebellion, Sherman concluded, and it would remain rebellious until forced to taste the bitter reality of civil war. "War is cruelty," he told the citizens of Atlanta who petitioned him for mercy. The "terrible hardships of war" are inevitable, "and the only way the people of Atlanta can hope once more to live in peace and quiet at home, is to stop the war." Sherman had become a theorist of "hard" war (see Map 15-8).

Northern Democrats were horrified by the destructive turn the war had taken. In 1864 they nominated George McClellan, the general Lincoln had fired, for president on a platform advocating compromise, a swift end to the war, and a negotiated settlement with the South. Lee and Davis hoped that by stalling Union forces northern war weariness would give the Democrats the upper hand in the coming elections. The horrors of the Wilderness Campaign were fresh in the voters' minds. Inevitably, Lincoln's policy of hard war became the major issue of the campaign. The fact that McClellan won 45 percent of the votes suggested that a substantial portion of the northern electorate disapproved of the administration's aggressive policy. But by election day Sheridan had laid waste to the Shenandoah valley, and Sherman had taken Atlanta. The majority of northern

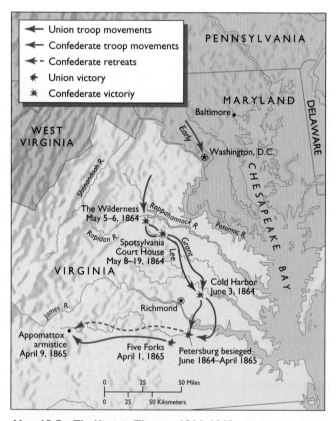

Map 15-7 The Virginia Theater, 1864–1865.
In May and June of 1864, Grant and Lee confronted each other directly in a bloody series of battles in Virginia. The indecisive outcome was a Vicksburg-like siege by Grant, this time of the city of Petersburg, where Lee dug in with his fortified troops. The shockingly high number of casualties, with no clear winner, nearly cost Lincoln his re-election to the presidency in November.

Much of Atlanta lay in ruins after General Sherman captured and burned the city. The northern general had made a conscious decision to make war "hell" for the southern civilians who supported the war.

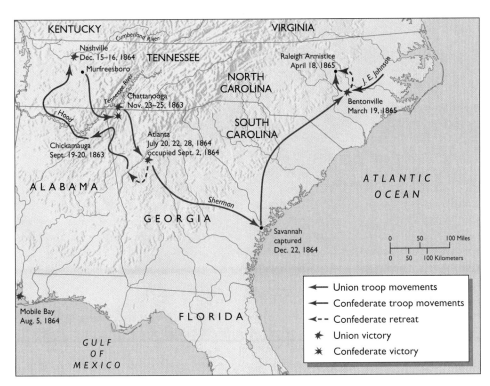

Map 15-8   The Atlanta Campaign and Sherman's March, 1864–1865.
Lincoln's re-election was saved in part by Sherman's capture of Atlanta. It was here that Sherman spelled out his theory that war must be made unbearable to southern civilians if the North was to win. From Atlanta he went on to capture Savannah after his famed "march to the sea." Sherman then turned his troops northward to cut an even greater path of destruction through South Carolina.

voters could smell a Union victory and were not about to let go of the scent. Lincoln won convincingly. The Democrats' alternative to hard war was rebuffed by 55 percent of the electorate. Only unconditional surrender was acceptable. All Confederate attempts to offer peace on lesser terms were rejected. Lee's hopes were dashed, and the siege of Petersburg continued.

Sherman Marches, and Lee Surrenders

A week after Lincoln's re-election, Sherman's men burned half of Atlanta to the ground, turned east, and marched toward the sea. Hood tried to distract Sherman by moving west toward Alabama and then up into Tennessee. But half of Sherman's army outnumbered Hood's entire force, and half is what Sherman sent to chase Hood down. In two devastating battles, at Franklin and Nashville, Tennessee, Union troops led by George Thomas destroyed all that was left of Hood's Army.

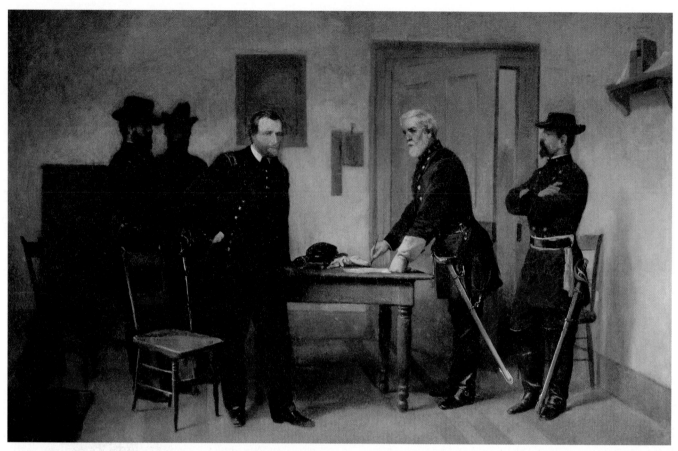

With Lee's surrender to Grant at Appomattox, the Civil War came to an end.

Meanwhile Sherman's troops were unleashing their destructive energies on farms and villages through hundreds of miles of Georgia countryside. In late December, just after General Thomas launched his final assault on the Confederate Army at Nashville, Sherman telegraphed Lincoln and offered him the city of Savannah as a Christmas present. From Savannah Sherman's men marched northward. As they crossed into South Carolina, the birthplace of secession, Union soldiers brought the practice of hard war to its ferocious climax. Northern troops torched homes and barns, destroyed crops and slaughtered livestock. They cut a path of destruction far worse than anything seen in Georgia. With Charleston in Union hands and the state capital of Columbia up in flames, Sherman continued his movement northward. Once they left South Carolina, however, Union soldiers were much better behaved.

By then events in Virginia were bringing the war to a somewhat less destructive conclusion. Lee's army was fatally weakened when Union forces took Five Forks, closing off Petersburg's last line of supply. With Lee's lines extended to the breaking point, Grant launched the final assault. On April 2, 1865, the Army of the Potomac broke through the Confederate defenses and forced Lee to abandon Petersburg. The next day Jefferson Davis and the Confederate leaders fled from Richmond. Lee moved his

tired and hungry troops westward in one last attempt to elude Grant's force. But when he reached Appomattox Court House, Lee surrendered the Army of Northern Virginia to the Union. The war was over.

With the death of the Confederacy, Edmund Ruffin lost his own will to live. In the final entry of his diary Ruffin proclaimed his "unmitigated hatred" of "the perfidious, malignant and vile Yankee race." When he had finished writing he put down his pen, picked up his gun, and fired a bullet through his brain.

The Meaning of the Civil War

The Civil War was a vindication of the northern political economy based on free labor. Despite the draft riots, Copperheads, wartime inflation, and the terrible loss of life, the Civil War years had been good for the North's economy. Mechanization allowed northern farmers to increase the nation's wheat production, despite the fact that the Union Army had drained off one-third of the farm labor force. Huge orders for military rations propelled the growth of the canned food industry. The railroad boom of the 1850s might have crashed but instead persisted through the war. By contrast, the political economy of slavery was convincingly defeated. Much of the South lay in ruins. Thousands of miles of railroad track had been destroyed. One-third of the South's livestock had been killed; one-fourth of the young white men of the South were dead. The southern social order, grounded on the enslavement of millions of African Americans, had been completely destroyed.

Northern prosperity and southern devastation implied a dramatic reconfiguring of the national political economy. In 1860 the North and the South had identical per capita incomes and nearly identical per capita wealth. By 1870 the North was 50 percent more wealthy than the South. Per capita commodity output, also identical in 1860, was 56 percent higher in the North than in the South a decade later. The redistribution of political power was equally dramatic. From the Constitutional Convention of 1787 until the secession winter of 1860–1861, the history of national politics could be written as a series of compromises with the slaveholding interest of the South. Until 1860 slaveholders and their allies had controlled the Supreme Court, dominated the presidency, and exercised disproportionate influence in Congress. But the Civil War destroyed the slaveholding class and with it the slaveholders' political power. In 1861 Republicans took control of the national government away from the southern bloc. Emancipation made that transfer of power permanent. For the rest of the century the North and the West would dominate national politics.

Union victory strengthened the advocates of a stronger, more centralized national government. "The policy of this country," declared Senator John Sherman "ought to be to make everything national as far as possible; to nationalize our country so that we shall love our country." The growth of this "nationalist" sentiment can be traced in the speeches of Abraham Lincoln. When the Civil War began he emphasized the restoration of the "Union." By the end of the war Lincoln was more likely to talk of saving the "nation." Until 1860 it was common to refer to *these* United States. Since the Civil War Americans refer to *the* United States. An influential new magazine entitled, significantly, the *Nation* was founded in 1865 on the principle that the Civil War had established, finally and forever, the supremacy and indivisibility of the nation-state.

The war itself propelled the growth of the central government, beginning with unprecedented control of the economy. Both the Union and Confederate governments directly ordered the construction of railroads, and both regulated their operation. The Confederacy demanded vast quantities of supplies for its war effort. The Union confiscated hundreds of thousands of acres of southern land and emancipated millions of slaves. Both the North and the South instituted new taxes on income, property, and consumption. The North and the South is-

sued paper money on a scale previously unimaginable; both went deeply into debt by issuing massive numbers of government bonds. Driven by wartime demands for military mobilization, most of these central state activities disappeared when the fighting stopped.

But some of the changes were permanent, and they altered the nation's political economy forever. By implementing a homestead policy, establishing land-grant colleges, and subsidizing the transcontinental railroad, Congress intervened directly to facilitate national economic development. Financial reforms designed to assist the Union war effort became a permanent part of the nation's regulatory system. The commissioner of internal revenue, created during the war, became a fixed institution in the federal bureaucracy, and greenbacks became "legal tender." The National Banking Act set rules for state and local banks that effectively forced them into a standardized national system by the end of the decade. By the time the war was over, millions of Americans found their economic interests were directly dependent on the institutions and policies of the federal government. Anyone who relied on a private bank, who traded in greenbacks, or who held government bonds had a stake in the security of the United States Treasury.

But the most dramatic consequence of the war was the emancipation of over four million slaves and the destruction of southern slave society. Was it worth 600,000 lives to destroy what Republicans called the "slave power"? No one was more tortured by the question than Abraham Lincoln. For him the Civil War had begun as a struggle to restore the Union. By late 1862 it had also become a war to destroy slavery. A year after that, at Gettysburg, it had become a crusade to renew the promise of freedom and equality held out in the Declaration of Independence. By

In his Second Inaugural Address of March 4, 1865, Lincoln suggested that four years of terrible war was the price the nation had to pay for the sin of slavery.

1865 Lincoln was more committed than ever to the permanent abolition of slavery. He wanted to insure that an emancipation justified as a "military necessity" would not be overturned when peace was restored. He and his cabinet lobbied furiously for passage of the Thirteenth Amendment abolishing slavery in the United States. On January 31, 1865, the House of Representatives approved it with only two votes to spare.

Yet even Lincoln was stunned by the price the nation had paid for emancipation. He wondered whether the bloodshed was a form of divine retribution for the unpardonable sin of slavery. In his Second Inaugural Address, in March of 1865, he prayed that the "mighty scourge of war may speedily pass away." But, Lincoln added, "if God wills that it continue, until all the wealth piled up by the bond-man's two hundred and fifty years of unrequited toil shall be sunk, and until every drop of blood drawn with the lash, shall be paid by another drawn with the sword, as was said three thousand years ago, so still it must be said, 'the judgments of the Lord, are true and righteous altogether.' "

The bloody war had ended, but there was more blood to be shed. On the evening of April 14, 1865, a disgruntled southern actor named John Wilkes Booth assassinated Abraham Lincoln at Ford's Theatre in Washington, D. C.

Conclusion

The president who had led the nation through the Civil War would not oversee the nation's reconstruction. Lincoln had given some thought to the question of how to incorporate the defeated southern states into the Union, but at the time he died neither he nor his fellow Republicans in Congress had agreed on any particular plan. Would the Union simply be *restored*, as swiftly as possible? Or would the South be *reconstructed*, continuing the revolution begun during the Civil War? At the moment Lincoln died, nobody was sure of the answer to these questions. They would emerge over the next several months and years, as the freed people in the South pressed to expand the meaning of their freedom.

CHRONOLOGY

1860	South Carolina secedes
1861	Lower South secedes
	Abraham Lincoln inaugurated
	First shots fired at Fort Sumter
	Upper South secedes
	North declares runaway slaves "contraband"
	First Battle of Bull Run
	McClellan takes command of Army of the Potomac
	First Confiscation Act
	Trent affair
1862	Battles of Fort Henry and Fort Donelson
	"Battle of the ironclads"
	Battle of Shiloh
	Union capture of New Orleans
	Slavery abolished in Washington, D. C.
	Homestead Act
	Confederacy establishes military draft
	Peninsula Campaign
	Slavery prohibited in western territories
	Second Confiscation Act; Militia Act; Morrill Land Grant College Act; Internal Revenue Act. All passed by northern Congress.
	Second Battle of Bull Run
	Battle of Antietam
	Preliminary Emancipation Proclamation
	Battle of Fredericksburg
1863	Emancipation Proclamation
	Union establishes military draft
	Battle of Chancellorsville
	Battle of Gettysburg
	Vicksburg surrenders
	New York City draft riots
	Battle of Chickamauga
	Gettysburg Address
	Battle of Lookout Mountain
1864	Wilderness Campaign
	Battle of Cold Harbor
	Siege of Petersburg begins
	Sherman captures Atlanta
	Philip Sheridan raids Shenandoah Valley
	Lincoln re-elected
	Sherman burns Atlanta and marches to the sea
	Battles of Franklin and Nashville
1864–1865	Sherman's march through the Carolinas
1865	House of Representatives approves thirteenth Amendment
	Lincoln's second inauguration
	Lee surrenders to Grant at Appomattox
	Lincoln assassinated

Review Questions

1. Define "hard war" and trace its development from 1861 to 1865.

2. What caused the North to shift to a policy of emancipation?

3. What were the political differences between the Union and the Confederacy?

4. What were the differences between northern and southern military strategies?

5. What were the major consequences of the Civil War?

6. Compare the effects of social divisions on the northern and southern war efforts.

Further Readings

Ira Berlin, et al., *Slaves No More: Three Essays on Emancipation and the Civil War* (1992). This collection gives a well-researched account of the process of emancipation.

David Herbert Donald, *Lincoln* (1995). This is the best modern biography by a master of the genre.

Shelby Foote, *The Civil War: A Narrative*, 3 volumes (1958–1974). *The Civil War* is the most thorough narrative of the military history of the war.

John Hope Franklin, *The Emancipation Proclamation* (1963). This minor classic captures the active role of the slaves in the process of emancipation.

Gary W. Gallagher, *The Confederate War* (1997). A pugnacious study arguing that southern whites were overwhelmingly loyal to the Confederacy.

Mark Grimsley, *The Hard Hand of War: Union Military Policy Toward Southern Civilians, 1861–1865* (1995). This text argues persuasively that Union military policy stopped significantly short of "total" war, an unusually thoughtful study.

Leon Litwack, *Been in the Storm So Long* (1979). An evocative account of the end of slavery as the slaves themselves experienced it.

James McPherson, *The Battle Cry of Freedom: The Civil War Era* (1988). A superb one-volume history of the war.

Philip Shaw Paludan, *A People's Contest: The Union and the Civil War, 1861–1865* (1988). *A People's Contest* covers the northern home front.

Charles Royster, *The Destructive War: William Tecumseh Sherman, Stonewall Jackson, and the Americans* (1991). A beautifully rendered account written in the tragic mode.

Kenneth M. Stampp, *And the War Came: The North and the Secession Crisis, 1860–1861* (1950 and 1965). The best treatment of Lincoln and the secession crisis.

Emory Thomas, *The Confederate Nation, 1861–1865* (1979). A fine modern treatment of the Confederacy.

Garry Wills, *Lincoln at Gettysburg: The Words that Remade America* (1992). A brilliant study of a brilliant speech.

History on the Internet

"The Civil War and Emancipation"
http://www.pbs.org/wgbh/aia/part4/4p2967.html

On this site, read about the plight of slaves and African-American freed people, the impact of the Emancipation Proclamation, and the experiences of African-American Civil War soldiers. On the "related entries" section is a link to the full text of the Emancipation Proclamation and a personal account of a former slave in an Army camp.

"Selected Civil War Photos"
http://lcweb2.loc.gov/ammem/cwphome.html

Over 1,100 photos of the Civil War fill this website. These photos depict military units, battle preparation, and the aftermath of warfare.

"Civil War Women: Primary Sources on the Internet"
http://scriptorium.lib.duke.edu/women/cwdocs.html#1

This site contains a wealth of primary-source documents that address women's experiences during the Civil War. These documents include diaries, letters, memoirs, photos, and prints.

"The Emancipation Proclamation"
http://www.nara.gov/exhall

See the original document and read the full text transcript of this important document. Also, this site contains one scholar's view on the proclamation's meaning and significance.

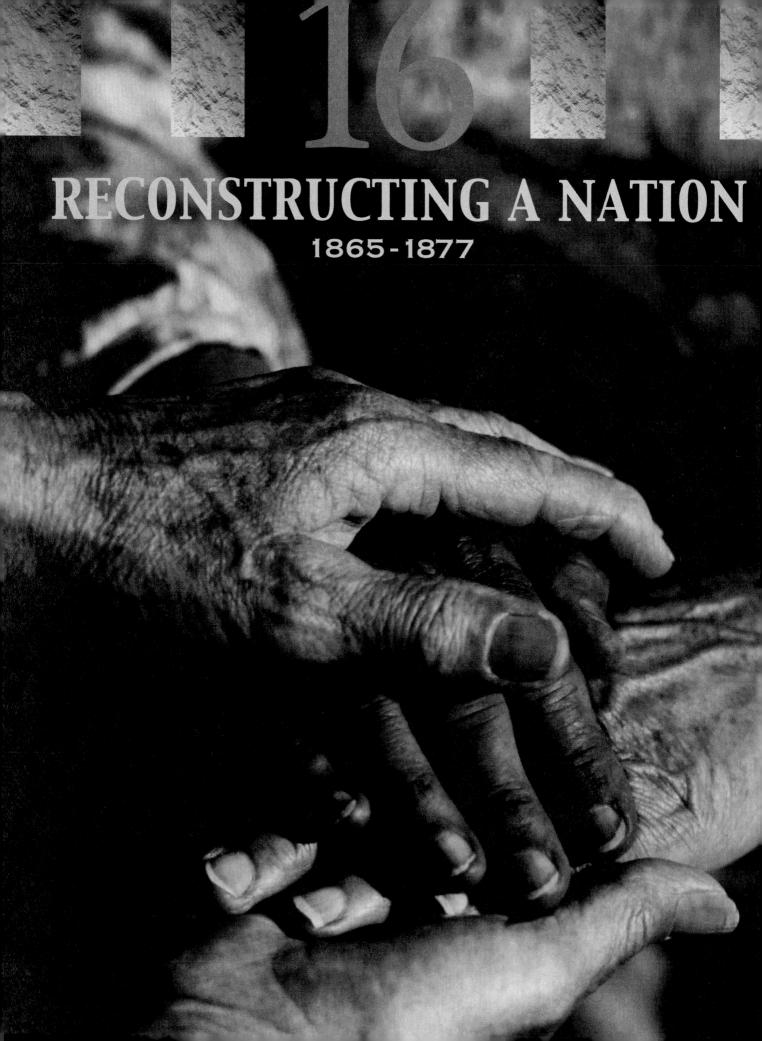

16

RECONSTRUCTING A NATION

1865-1877

O U T L I N E

John Dennett Visits a Freedmen's Bureau Court

Wartime Reconstruction

Experiments With Free Labor

Lincoln's Ten-Percent Plan *versus* the Wade-Davis Bill

The Freed People's Dream of Owning Land

Presidential Reconstruction, 1865–1867

The Political Economy of Contract Labor

Resistance to Presidential Reconstruction

Congress Clashes With the President

Origins of the Fourteenth Amendment

Race Riots and the Election of 1866

Congressional Reconstruction

Origins of the African-American Vote

Radical Reconstruction in the South

Achievements and Failures of Radical Government

The Political Economy of Sharecropping

The Retreat From Republican Radicalism

The Impeachment and Trial of Andrew Johnson

Republicans Become the Party of Moderation

The Grant Administration and Moderate Republicanism

Reconstruction in the North

The Fifteenth Amendment and Nationwide African-American Suffrage

Women and Suffrage

The Rise and Fall of the National Labor Union

The End of Reconstruction

Corruption as a National Problem

Liberal Republicans Revolt

A Depression and a Deal "Redeem" the South

Conclusion

John Dennett Visits a Freedmen's Bureau Court

John Richard Dennett arrived in Liberty, Virginia, on August 17, 1865 as part of a tour of the South during which he sent back weekly reports for publication in a new magazine called *The Nation.* The editors wanted accurate accounts of conditions in the recently defeated Confederate states and Dennett was the kind of man they could trust. He grew up in Massachusetts, graduated from Harvard, and became a firm believer in the sanctity of the Union. Dennett moved comfortably within a class of elite Yankees who thought of themselves as the "best men" the country had to offer.

After he stepped from the train at Liberty, Dennett was accompanied by a Freedmen's Bureau agent. The Freedmen's Bureau was a branch of the U. S. Army that had been established by Congress to assist the freed people in the transition from slavery to freedom. Dennett and the agent were going to the courthouse because one of the Freedmen's Bureau's functions was to adjudicate disputes between the freed people and southern whites. Dennett listened to the cases that came to the agent that day.

The first to arrive was an old white farmer who complained that two of the African Americans who worked on his farm were "roamin' about and refusin' to work in any shape or manner." He wanted the agent to help find the men and bring them back. Both men had wives and children living on his farm and eating his corn, the old man complained.

"Have you been paying any wages?" the Freedmen's Bureau agent asked. "Well, they get what the other niggers get," the farmer answered. "I a'n't payin' great wages this year," he went on, "makin' a little corn's about all." There was not much the agent could do. He had no horses and very few men, but one of his soldiers volunteered to go back to the farm with the old man and tell the blacks that "they ought to be at home supporting their wives and children."

After the farmer left, a well-to-do planter came in to see if he could fire the African Americans who had been working on his plantation since the beginning of the year. The planter complained that his workers were unmanageable now that they were free and he could no longer punish them. The sergeant warned the planter that he could not beat his workers as if they were still slaves. In that case, the planter responded, "will the Government take them off our hands? I'm sure I don't want mine any longer. They are free, and the Government ought to take them, or it ought to give the employers such power as would enable them to control the Negroes and make them work." The Freedmen's Bureau agent suspected that the planter was looking for an excuse to discharge his laborers at the end of the growing season, after they had finished most of the work but before they had been paid their wages. "If they've worked on your crops all the year so far," the agent told the planter, "I guess they've got a claim on you to keep them a while longer." When the planter left the agent told Dennett that there were lots of those cases now.

Next came a "good-looking mulatto man" representing a number of African Americans living in the countryside. They were worried by rumors that they would be forced to sign five-year contracts with their employers. "No, it a'n't true," the agent said. "You can hire yourselves out for as long as you want to." They also wanted to know if they would be allowed to rent or buy land so that they could work for themselves. "Yes, rent or buy," the agent said. But the African Americans had no horses, mules, or ploughs to work the land. So they wanted to know "if the Government would help us out after we get the land. We could rent a place up here if we had some horses to plough, and so on." But the agent had no help to offer. "The Government hasn't any ploughs or mules to give you," he said. In the end the African Americans settled for a piece of paper from the Freedmen's Bureau authorizing them to rent or buy their own farms.

This engraving shows a typical trial in a Freedmen's Bureau Courtroom.

The last case involved a field hand who came to the agent to complain that his master was beating him with a stick. "What did you do to him? You've been sassy?" the agent asked. But the field hand insisted that he had done nothing. "Well, I suppose you were lazy," the agent said. "Boss, I been working all de time," the man answered. The agent was unsympathetic. He told the field hand to go back to work. "Don't be sassy, don't be lazy when you've got work to do; and I guess he won't trouble you." The field hand left "very reluctantly," but came back a minute later and asked for a letter to his master "enjoining him to keep the peace, as he feared the man would shoot him, he having on two or three occasions threatened to do so." The agent sent him away and then told Dennett that there were "any quantity of those cases," but that his office was scarcely equipped to hear a quarter of them.

It is not surprising that most of the cases Dennett witnessed centered around labor relations. The southern economy had been devastated by the war, and everyone agreed that a successful reunion depended on the swift creation of a new political economy based on free labor. There was, however, little agreement about what kind of free labor system should replace slavery in the postwar South. What John Dennett saw in the courthouse in Liberty, Virginia, was a good indication of how difficult the labor problem was. The freed people preferred to work their own land, but they lacked the resources to rent or buy farms for themselves. Black workers and white owners who had negotiated wage contracts had trouble figuring out the limits of each other's rights and responsibilities. The former masters wanted to retain as much of their old authority as possible, including the right to physically punish their workers. The former slaves wanted as much

autonomy as possible and clearly resented the continued use of physical punishment.

The Freedmen's Bureau was placed in the middle of these conflicts. Most agents thought it was their job to get the freed people back to work, much to the dismay of many of the former slaves. But the agents also tried to ensure that the freed people were paid for the labor they performed and that they were not brutalized the way they had been as slaves. Southern whites resented this intrusion, and their resentment filtered all the way up to sympathetic politicians in Washington, D. C. As a result, the Freedmen's Bureau became a lightning rod for the political conflicts of the years immediately following the Civil War, a period known as Reconstruction.

Reconstruction raised a number of challenging questions for Americans. What conditions should the federal government impose on the southern states before they could be readmitted to the Union? Should these conditions be set by the president or by Congress? How far should the federal government go to protect the economic well-being and civil rights of the freed people? Politicians in Washington disagreed violently on these questions. At one extreme was Andrew Johnson who, as president, thought it was his responsibility to shape Reconstruction policy. Because he believed in small government and a speedy readmission of the southern states, Johnson looked upon the Freedmen's Bureau with deep suspicion. At the other extreme were the Radical Republicans, men like Congressman Thaddeus Stevens and Senator Charles Sumner. The Radicals believed that the federal government should redistribute confiscated land to the former slaves, guarantee their civil rights, and give African-American men the power of the vote. They viewed the Freedmen's Bureau as too small and weak to do the necessary job. Between the Radicals and the president's supporters were the moderate Republicans who controlled Congress. The moderates tried to work with the president, but when the president became obstreperous they shifted toward the Radical position.

Regardless of where they fell on the political spectrum, however, policymakers in the nation's capital were always responding to what went on in the South. Events in the South were shaped in turn by the policies emanating from Washington. What John Dennett saw in Liberty, Virginia, was a good example of this. The Freedmen's Bureau agent listened to the urgent requests of former masters and their former slaves, of small white farmers and wealthy planters. His responses were shaped in part by the policies established by his superiors in Washington. But his superiors shaped their policies in response to reports on conditions in the South sent back by Freedmen's Bureau agents like him and by journalists like John Dennett. From this interaction the political economy of the "New South" slowly emerged. ∎

KEY TOPICS

• Wartime approaches to Reconstruction

• The failure of President Johnson's plan for Reconstruction

• The transformation of the southern labor system

• The nature of Congressional Reconstruction

• Declining national interest in Reconstruction

Wartime Reconstruction

Long before the Civil War was over Republicans in Congress and the White House had already considered a number of questions concerning the reconstruction of the southern states. What system of free labor would replace slavery? What were the political conditions under which the southern states would be readmitted to the Union? What civil and political rights should the freed people receive? Such questions were inescapable once emancipation became Union policy. Until the southern armies actually surrendered, however, politicians in Washington put most of their energies into winning the war. As a result, no official reconstruction policy emerged before 1865. Instead, Congress and the Lincoln administration responded piecemeal to developments in those regions of the South under Union control. From these experiences a variety of approaches to the political and social reconstruction of the South emerged. Some were utopian experiments confined to particular regions or specific plantations. But other approaches, notably those developed in Louisiana, established precedents that shaped Reconstruction for many years.

Experiments With Free Labor

Classical theories of political economy taught the Republicans to believe that once the benefits of free labor were unleashed the South was bound to prosper. But two interesting wartime experiments left very differ-

ent clues about what African-American workers would do after emancipation. At Davis Bend, Mississippi, a group of highly motivated slaves established a wage labor system on the lands they purchased from Confederate president Jefferson Davis and his brother Joseph. Once in control of production, the freed people produced a highly profitable cotton crop, even before the war was over. The Davis Bend experience suggested that if left to their own devices, and given autonomy over their own lands, the freed people would produce cotton for the market. But on the Sea Islands off South Carolina, the former slaves behaved very differently. Early in the war the masters had abandoned their low-country plantations to the slaves and the Union Army. With the owners gone, the freed people abandoned the production of cash crops and focused almost exclusively on subsistence agriculture. They showed little interest in producing cotton for the market. Neither the Sea Island experience nor the community at Davis Bend established a pattern for Reconstruction across the South. Far more important were events in Louisiana.

Southern Louisiana came under Union control early in the war. The sugar and cotton plantations of the low country around New Orleans therefore provided a site for the first major experiments in the transition from slave to free labor. The Union commander of the area, General Nathaniel Banks, hoped to stem the flow of African-

Slaves in parts of coastal South Carolina were freed early in the Civil War. Here the freed people on Edisto Island in 1862 are shown planting sweet potatoes rather than cotton. In other parts of the South the former slaves returned to the cultivation of cash crops.

Charlotte Forten, born to a prominent African-American family in Philadelphia, was one of many northern women who went to the South to become a teacher of the freed slaves. Forten helped found the Penn School on St. Helena's Island in South Carolina.

Before the Civil War it was illegal in most southern states to teach a slave how to read. With emancipation, the freed people clamored for schools and teachers, such as the one pictured here. Within a few years hundreds of thousands of former slaves became literate.

American refugees running to Union lines. Unsympathetic to the wishes of the former slaves, Banks issued a series of harsh labor regulations designed to put the freed people back to work as quickly as possible. The Banks Plan required African Americans to sign year-long contracts to work on their former plantations, often for their former owners. Workers would be paid either five percent of the proceeds of the crop or three dollars per month. The former masters would provide the freed people with food and shelter. Once they signed their contracts, African-American workers were forbidden to leave the plantations without permission. So stringent were these regulations that to many critics Banks had simply replaced one form of slavery with another. "Our freedmen, on the plantations, at the present time, could more properly be called, mock freedmen," a black newspaper in New Orleans complained. Nevertheless, the Banks Plan was implemented throughout much of the lower Mississippi Valley, especially after the fall of Vicksburg in the summer of 1863. Eventually, Banks' labor regulations were applied to tens of thousands of freed people and hundreds of plantations in Louisiana and Mississippi.

The Banks Plan touched off a political controversy that stretched from New Orleans to Washington, D. C. Established planters had the most to gain from the general's plan. It allowed them to acknowledge the abolition of slavery while preserving as much as possible of the prewar labor system. But Louisiana Unionists, who had remained loyal to the government in Washington, formed a Free State Association to press for more substantial changes. In August 1863 Lincoln publicly supported the Free State movement. Five months later, hoping to speed

things along in Louisiana, the president issued a Proclamation of Amnesty and Reconstruction. With the war still going on, Lincoln issued the proclamation in an effort to undermine the Confederacy by cultivating the support of southern Unionists. It contained the outline of the so-called Ten-Percent Plan, which turned out to be not much of a plan at all.

Lincoln's Ten-Percent Plan *Versus* the Wade-Davis Bill

The Ten-Percent Plan promised full pardons and the restoration of civil rights to all those who swore their loyalty to the Union. It excluded from amnesty only a few high-ranking Confederate military and political leaders. When the number of loyal whites in any of the former Confederate states reached 10 percent of the 1860 voting population, they could organize a new state constitution and set up a new government. The only stipulation was that they recognize the abolition of slavery. Abiding by these conditions, Free State whites met in Louisiana in the spring of 1864 and produced a new constitution for the state. By traditional standards it was a progressive charter: It provided for a free system of public education, a minimum wage, a nine-hour day on public works projects, and a graduated income tax. However, although it abolished slavery in Louisiana, it also denied all African Americans the right to vote.

By the spring of 1864 such denials were no longer acceptable to Radical Republicans, either in Louisiana or in Congress. The Radicals were a small but vocal wing of the Republican Party. They were active in many parts of the

South immediately after the war, and they developed strong ties to leading Radicals in Congress such as Thaddeus Stevens of Pennsylvania and Charles Sumner of Massachusetts. Despite their differences, most Radicals favored some plan for distributing land to the former slaves. Most of them also favored federal guarantees of the civil rights of the former slaves, as well as the right to vote. All Radicals were prepared to use the full force of the federal government to enforce congressional policy in the South. Although the Radicals never formed a majority in Congress, they gradually succeeded in winning over the moderates to many of their positions. As a result, when Congress took control of Reconstruction away from the president after the elections in 1866, the process became known as Radical Reconstruction.

The Radicals were particularly strong in New Orleans thanks to the city's large and articulate community of African Americans who had been free before the Civil War. In the spring of 1864 they sent a delegation to Washington, D. C. to meet with President Lincoln and press the case for voting rights. The day after their visit Lincoln wrote a letter to the acting governor of Louisiana suggesting a limited suffrage for the most intelligent blacks and for those who

had served in the Union Army. The delegates to Louisiana's constitutional convention completely ignored Lincoln's suggestion. Shortly thereafter free African Americans in New Orleans organized a coalition with the former slaves demanding civil and political rights and the abolition of the Banks labor regulations. Radicals complained that Lincoln's Ten-Percent Plan was too kind to former Confederates and that the Banks Plan was too harsh on former slaves.

Moved largely by events in Louisiana, congressional Radicals rejected the Ten-Percent Plan. In July 1864 Congressmen Benjamin F. Wade and Henry Winter Davis proposed a different plan for reconstructing the southern states. Under the terms of the Wade-Davis Bill, Reconstruction could not begin until a majority of a state's white men swore an oath of allegiance to the Union. This "Iron-clad Oath" was far more restrictive than Lincoln's Ten-Percent Plan. In addition, the Wade-Davis Bill guaranteed full legal and civil rights to African Americans, but not the right to vote. Lincoln pocket vetoed the bill, less because he disagreed with it than because the war was going on and he was still interested in cultivating southern Unionists. By the spring of 1865, however, Lincoln had shifted toward

Because slave marriages had no legal standing, many freed people got married as soon as they could. Pictured here is one such wedding, performed at the Freedmen's Bureau.

the Radical position. In his last speech Lincoln publicly supported voting rights for some freedmen as part of the Reconstruction process.

The Louisiana experience had made several things clear. The radical wing of the Republican Party was determined to press for more civil and political rights for African Americans than moderates were initially willing to support; however, the moderates showed a willingness to move in a more radical direction. Equally important, the Louisiana experience showed that any Reconstruction policy, whether congressional or presidential, would have to consider the wishes of southern blacks.

The Freed People's Dream of Owning Land

Freedom meant many things to the millions of former slaves. It meant they could move about their neighborhoods without passes. It meant they did not have to step aside to let whites pass them on the street. It meant that their marriages would be secured by the law, without fear that a master could separate husbands from wives or parents from children. Following emancipation southern African Americans almost immediately withdrew from

white churches and established congregations with their own ministers. During Reconstruction the church emerged as a central institution in the southern African-American community. Freedom also meant literacy. Even before the war ended northern teachers poured into the South to set up makeshift schools for the freed people. The American Missionary Association organized hundreds of such northern teachers. When the fighting stopped, the U. S. Army helped recruit and organize thousands more northern women who volunteered their services as teachers. "So anxious are they to learn," Edmonia Highgate reported from Lafayette Parish, Louisiana, that children from as far as eight miles away walk to school early each morning determined "never to be tardy." The graduates of the missionary schools sometimes became teachers themselves, setting up classrooms in rundown churches and dilapidated barns, if necessary. As a result, hundreds of thousands of southern blacks became literate in the space of a few years.

But even more than churches of their own and schools for their children, the freed people wanted land. Without land, the former slaves saw no choice but to return to work for their old masters on their old farms and plantations.

An African-American church in Virginia in 1880. With emancipation, the former slaves withdrew from their masters' churches and formed their own congregations.

"The sole ambition of the freedmen at the present time appears to be to become the owner of a little piece of land," one northerner observed, "there to erect a humble home, and to dwell in peace and security at his own free will and pleasure." As the war ended many African Americans had reason to believe that the government would assist them in their quest for independent landownership.

Marching through the Carolinas in early 1865, Union General William Tecumseh Sherman discovered how important land was to the freed people on the Sea Islands. They did not want to go to work for the speculators who paid fire-sale prices to scoop up the plantations of their runaway masters. A delegation of local blacks went to Sherman to express their wishes. "The way we can best take care of ourselves is to have land," they declared, "and turn it out and till it by our own labor." Persuaded by their arguments, Sherman issued Special Field Order No. 15 granting captured land to the freed people. By June of 1865, 400,000 acres had been distributed to 40,000 former slaves.

Congress seemed to be moving in a similar direction. In March 1865, the Republicans established the Bureau of Refugees, Freedmen and Abandoned Lands, commonly known as the Freedmen's Bureau. Although designed as an emergency measure to provide newly freed slaves with food and clothing at the end of the war, the Freedmen's Bureau quickly became involved in the politics of land redistribution. As part of its mandate, the Freedmen's Bureau controlled the disposition of 850,000 acres of confiscated and abandoned Confederate lands. In July 1865, General Oliver Otis Howard, the head of the Bureau, issued Circular 13, directing his agents to rent the land to the freed people in forty-acre plots that they could eventually purchase. Some Bureau agents believed firmly that the land should be distributed to the former slaves, but more were either uncertain about the idea or openly hostile. These agents believed that slavery had taught African Americans to avoid work and ignore the future. To re-educate them in the values of thrift and hard work, the freed people should be encouraged to save up their wages and buy land for themselves. From the perspective of most Freedmen's Bureau agents, redistributing land was like giving it away to people who had not actually paid for it.

From the perspective of the former slaves, however, black workers had more than earned a right to the land. "The labor of these people had for two hundred years cleared away the forests and produced crops that brought millions of dollars annually," H. C. Bruce explained, remembering his first months of freedom. "It does seem to me that a Christian Nation would, at least, have given them one year's support, forty acres of land and a mule each." Even Abraham Lincoln seemed to agree. In March 1865 he declared in his second inaugural address that all of the South's wealth had come from the slaves' two hundred and fifty years of unrequited toil. But a month later Lincoln was dead and Andrew Johnson became president of the United States.

Presidential Reconstruction, 1865–1867

When Andrew Johnson took the oath of office in April 1865, it was still unclear whether Congress or the president would control Reconstruction policy, and whether that policy would be lenient or harsh. To the delight of Radical Republicans, Johnson had spoken sharply of punishing southern "traitors." His political roots lay in the old Jacksonian Democratic Party. He blamed the Civil War on aristocratic planters and viewed their defeat as a victory for the common people of the South. But it turned out that the new president disliked Radical Republicans as much as planter aristocrats. As a Jacksonian he was committed to limited government and therefore resisted Republican plans to use federal power to help the freed people. Like so many Democrats, Johnson's sympathy for the common man did not extend to African Americans. As a politician, Johnson lacked the flexibility and good humor that had allowed Lincoln to work constructively with his political opponents. Determined to reconstruct the South in his

AWKWARD COLLISION ON THE GRAND TRUNK COLUMBIA R. R.

In this satirical cartoon, Andrew Johnson and Congress square off against one another. The political struggle over who should control Reconstruction policy led to Congress' impeachment and trial of the president.

own way and blind to the interests of the freed people, Johnson grew increasingly bitter and resentful of the Republicans who controlled Congress. As a result, Presidential Reconstruction was a monumental failure.

The Political Economy of Contract Labor

In the mid-nineteenth century Congress was normally out of session from March until December. Having assumed the presidency in April 1865 Johnson hoped to take advantage of the long congressional recess to complete the entire Reconstruction process and present the finished product to the lawmakers when they returned in December. At the end of May the president offered amnesty and the restoration of property to white southerners who swore an oath of loyalty to the Union. He excluded only high-ranking Confederate military and political leaders and very rich planters, whom he despised. At the same time Johnson named provisional governors to the seceded states and instructed them to organize constitutional conventions elected from all those who took the loyalty oaths. To earn readmission to the Union, the seceded states were required to nullify their secession ordinances, repudiate their Confederate war debts, and ratify the Thirteenth Amendment abolishing slavery. These terms were far more lenient than Lincoln and the congressional Republicans had contemplated. They did nothing to protect the civil rights of the former slaves.

Johnson's leniency encouraged a mood of defiance among white southerners. Although they had been willing to succumb to northern directives in the spring, they were no longer willing to do so by the fall of 1865. Secessionists had been barred from participating in the states' constitutional conventions. But they participated openly in the first elections held late in the year because Johnson issued thousands of pardons to ex-Confederates and the wealthy planters he claimed to despise. Leading Confederates were thus able to assume public office in the southern states. Restored to power, white southerners promptly demanded the restoration of all properties confiscated or abandoned during the war. President Johnson quickly obliged their request. In September 1865 he ordered the Freedmen's Bureau to return all confiscated and abandoned lands to their former owners.

A few Bureau agents tried to stall the evictions until Congress came back into session in December, but when white southerners complained Johnson had the agents removed. In late 1865 thousands of African-American families were ordered to give up their plots of land. On Edisto Island off South Carolina, for example, the freed people had carved farms of their own out of the former plantations. But in January 1866 General Rufus Saxton restored the farms to their previous owners and encouraged the freed people to sign wage contracts with their old masters. "I told the people that they could take it or leave it," Sax-

ton reported, "and that if they declined to work the plantation the houses must be vacated." The blacks unanimously rejected his offer, whereupon the general ordered them to evacuate their farms within two weeks. By the end of 1865 former slaves were being forcibly evicted from the forty-acre plots they had been given by the Union Army or the Freedmen's Bureau. With this crucial turning point in the evolution of a new political economy in the South, the freed people's hopes of independent landownership were dashed. Thereafter, they would be compelled to sign contracts to work for the whites who still owned the land (see Map 16-1).

Besides ending all hopes of land redistribution, the Johnsonian state governments enacted a series of "Black Codes" severely restricting the civil rights of freed people. The Black Codes were often thinly disguised attempts to coerce African Americans to sign labor contracts with white landowners. Vagrancy statutes, for example, allowed local police to arrest and fine virtually any African-American man. If he could not pay the fine, as was the case with most recently emancipated slaves, the "vagrant" was put to work on a farm, often the one owned and operated by his former master. Even more disturbing to the former slaves were the apprenticeship clauses of the Black Codes. These laws allowed local white officials to remove children from their homes, against their parents' will, and put them to work as "apprentices" on nearby farms.

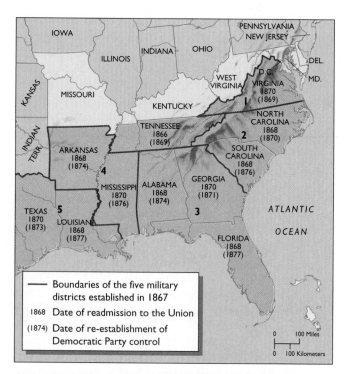

Map 16-1   Reconstruction and Redemption.
By 1870 Congress readmitted every southern state to the Union. In most cases the Republican Party retained control of the "reconstructed" state governments for only a few years.

TABLE 16-1

Cotton Prices in New York (cents per pound)

Year	Real Price (1880 $)
1864	52.59
1865	45.07
1866	24.83
1867	19.50
1868	15.73
1869	19.21
1870	17.76
1871	13.04
1872	15.06
1873	13.65
1874	13.49
1875	12.71
1876	11.82
1877	11.07

The price of cotton fell sharply and almost continuously between 1864 and 1879. But this masks the fact that the purchasing power of a pound of cotton was about the same in the 1870s and 1880s as it had been in the boom years of the 1850s.
Source: M. B. Hammond, The Cotton Industry (Macmillan, 1897), reproduced in Gavin Wright, "Cotton Competition and the Post Bellum Recovery of the American South," Journal of Economic History, 34 (Sept., 1974), p. 611.

Presidential Reconstruction left the freed people with no choice but to sign labor contracts with white landlords. The contracts restricted the personal as well as the working lives of the freed people, and employers still provided their black workers with food and shelter. In one case, a South Carolina planter contractually obliged his African-American workers to "go by his direction the same as in slavery time." In the cotton South contracts often required blacks to work in gangs, just as they had before the war. Owners sometimes prohibited their workers from leaving the plantation without permission. Former masters often continued the practice of whipping and brutalizing their workers. Contracts required African Americans to work for wages as low as one-tenth of the crop, and cotton prices were steadily falling (see Table 16-1). Even those meager wages would be forfeited by anyone who changed jobs before the end of the year. Blacks who moved into towns and cities in search of alternative employment discovered that the tax laws were designed to send them back onto farms and plantations. It is no wonder that contract labor struck the freed people as little different from slavery.

Resistance to Presidential Reconstruction

In September 1865 a group of African Americans in Virginia issued a public appeal for assistance. They began by declaring that they lacked the means to make and enforce legal contracts. The Black Codes denied African Americans the right to testify in court in any case involving a white person. "So far as legal safeguards of our rights are concerned, we are defenseless before our enemies." Their former masters had returned to their homes "with all their old pride and contempt for the Negro transformed into bitter hate for the new made freeman." In many areas organized planters blocked the development of a free labor market by agreeing among themselves to hire only their former slaves and by fixing wages at a low level. In the more remote regions, the freedmen went on, planters "still refuse to recognize their Negroes as free, forcibly retaining the wives and children of their late escaped slaves." Finally, there were numerous incidents in which black workers who had faithfully obeyed the terms of their contracts were "met by a contemptuous refusal of the stipulated compensation." As the first year of freedom drew to an end, the complaints mounted. Across the South whites reported a growing number of recalcitrant freed people who would not abide by the humiliating conditions of the contract labor system. Some African Americans refused to perform specific tasks while others were accused of being "disrespectful" to their employers or to whites in general. Some African Americans refused to answer to their slave names or insisted that they be addressed as Mr. or Mrs. As 1865 came to a close thousands of freedmen declined to renew their contracts for another year.

As black defiance spread, reports of a violent white backlash flooded into Washington in late 1865 and 1866. A former slave named Henry Adams claimed that "over two thousand colored people" were murdered around Shreveport, Louisiana, in 1865. Near Pine Bluff, Arkansas, in 1866 a visitor arrived at an African-American community the morning after whites had burned it to the ground. "24 Negro men woman and children were hanging to trees all around the cabins." African Americans were assaulted for not speaking to whites with the proper tone of submission, for disputing the terms of labor contracts, or for failing to work up to the standards white employers expected. Through relentless intimidation, whites prevented blacks from buying their own land or attending political meetings to press for civil rights. "With us the death of slavery is recognized," a former master explained, "but we don't believe that because the nigger is free he ought to be saucy; and we don't mean to have any such nonsense as letting him vote. He's helpless and ignorant, and dependent, and the old masters will still control him."

Northerners read these reports as evidence that "rebel" sentiment was reviving in the South. When Congress came back into session in December 1865, moderate Republicans were already suspicious of Presidential Reconstruction. The Radicals were the most upset. They pointed to the number of defiant secessionists in the Johnsonian governments. They argued that the contract system made a mockery of their party's commitment to free labor. They claimed that by denying basic civil rights to the freed people the Black Codes made emancipation meaningless. Finally, the

Radicals insisted that the only way to protect the interests of the freed people was to grant them the right to vote.

Congress Clashes With the President

Increasingly distressed by events in the South, Republican moderates in Congress moved toward the Radical position of active government force in the South and of voting rights for African-American men. President Johnson, meanwhile, abandoned all thought of using Reconstruction to empower ordinary southern whites at the expense of the planter aristocracy. Instead Johnson became obsessed with fears of "negro rule" in the South. When he insisted on the swift readmission of southern states that were clearly controlled by unrepentant Confederates, Congress refused. Instead, the Republicans formed a Joint Committee on Reconstruction to review conditions in the South and propose the terms for the readmission of the seceded states. Established in December of 1865, the Joint Committee reflected Congress' determination to follow its own course on Reconstruction. A sharp break between Congress and the president came a few months later.

In February 1866 Congress voted to extend the life of the Freedmen's Bureau. Concerned by widespread reports that blacks could not get justice in the South, Congress also empowered the Bureau to set up its own courts, which would supersede local jurisdictions. The Bureau's record during its first year had been mixed. It provided immediate relief to thousands of individual freed people, and it assisted in the creation of schools that taught basic literacy skills to thousands more. But in the crucial area of labor relations, the Bureau too often sided with the landowners and against the interests of the freed people. Many agents were concerned that the labor contracts were unfair or that landowners themselves showed little inclination to abide by their terms, but those same agents were usually more concerned with getting the former slaves back to work, even if that meant making them sign contracts with their former masters. "It is therefore perfectly useless for the poor laborer to look at the Freedmen's Bureau for relief," an African-American newspaper editor concluded. "He will not be assisted to get his pay or to get redress but will be told to go back and do his work."

Nevertheless the understaffed and overworked Bureau agents often acted under very difficult circumstances to protect the freed people from racist violence, unfair employers, and biased law-enforcement officials. For this reason, thousands of freedmen and freedwomen looked to the Bureau as their only hope for justice. For the same reason, however, thousands of southern whites resented the Bureau's presence, and they let Andrew Johnson know it.

To the amazement of moderate Republicans, Johnson vetoed the Freedmen's Bureau Bill. In his veto message the president complained that the legislation would increase the power of the central government at the expense of the states. By interfering in the process of Reconstruction, he claimed, Congress kept African Americans "in a state of uncertain expectation and restlessness." He invoked the Jacksonian political economy of the free market, insisting that the "laws that regulate supply and demand" were the best way to resolve the labor problem. Republicans fell just short of the two-thirds vote they needed to override the president's veto. Johnson reacted to his narrow victory with an intemperate public speech attacking the Republicans in Congress and questioning the legitimacy of the Joint Committee on Reconstruction.

Origins of the Fourteenth Amendment

A few weeks later, in March of 1866, Congress passed a landmark Civil Rights Act. It overturned the Dred Scott decision by granting United States citizenship to Americans regardless of race. This marked the first time in American history that the federal government intervened in the states to guarantee due process and basic civil rights. But as he had with the Freedmen's Bureau renewal, President Johnson vetoed the Civil Rights Act of 1866. In addition to the usual Jacksonian rhetoric about limited government, Johnson made an overtly racist argument to justify his veto. He doubted that African Americans "possess the requisite qualifications to entitle them to all the privileges and immunities of citizens of the United States." He hinted darkly that the civil rights bill would invalidate southern laws against racial intermarriage, thus legalizing sexual relations between whites and African Americans.

Johnson's two veto messages, plus his unrestrained public remarks, forced the moderate Republicans to confront the president. In short order the Republican Congress overrode the president's veto of the Civil Rights Act. At the same time the Republicans passed another Freedmen's Bureau bill. Once again Johnson vetoed it, but this time Congress overrode his veto.

To ensure that the civil rights of the freed people would be impervious to future presidential or congressional interference, the Joint Committee on Reconstruction proposed a Fourteenth Amendment to the United States Constitution. The most powerful and controversial of all the Constitution's amendments, the fourteenth guaranteed national citizenship to all males born in the United States, regardless of color. Although the amendment did not guarantee African Americans the right to vote, it based representation in Congress on the voting population of the state. This effectively punished southern states by reducing their representation if they did not allow blacks to vote.

By the summer of 1866, Congress had refused to recognize the state governments established under Johnson's plan, and it had authorized the Freedmen's Bureau to create a military justice system in the South to supersede the local courts. Congress thereby guaranteed the former slaves the basic rights of due process. Finally, it made rati-

Led by President Andrew Johnson, attacks on the Freedmen's Bureau became more and more openly racist in late 1865 and 1866. This Democratic Party broadside was circulated during the 1866 election.

fication of the Fourteenth Amendment by the former Confederate states a requirement for their readmission to the Union. Congress and the president were now at war, and Andrew Johnson went on a rampage.

Race Riots and the Election of 1866

A few weeks after Congress passed the Civil Rights Act white mobs in Memphis rioted in the streets for three days. They burned hundreds of homes, destroyed churches, and attacked schools of the city's African Americans. When the rioters finished, five women had been raped and 46 blacks were dead. "Thank heaven the white race are once more rulers in Memphis," a local newspaper declared. Three months later, white mobs in New Orleans rioted in the streets as well. Unlike the Memphis riot, however, the New Orleans massacre appears to have been an organized affair. The rioters focused their fury on a convention of Radical leaders who were demanding constitutional changes that would give African-American men in Louisiana the right to vote. Disciplined squads of white police and firemen marched to the Mechanics' Institute where the convention was in session and proceeded to slaughter the delegates. Thirty-four blacks and three whites were killed. The massacre made front-page news in papers across America, just as the 1866 election campaign was getting underway.

The Memphis and New Orleans massacres quickly became political issues in the North, thanks in large part to

Andrew Johnson's disturbing reaction to them. In late August the president undertook an unprecedented campaign tour designed to stir up the voters' hostility to Congress, but this "swing around the circle," as Johnson's tour was called, backfired. Unable to control his temper, the president blasted congressional Republicans, blaming them for the riots. At one point he suggested that Radical Congressman Thaddeus Stevens should be hanged. Republicans charged in turn that Johnson's own policies had revived the rebellious sentiments in the South that led directly to the massacres at Memphis and New Orleans.

The elections of 1866 became a popular referendum on Presidential Reconstruction. The results were "overwhelmingly against the President," the *New York Times* noted, "clearly, unmistakably, decisively in favor of Congress and its policy." Johnson's supporters suffered humiliating losses. The Republicans gained a veto-proof hold on Congress. Republican moderates were pushed further to the Radical position by the spectacle of defiant white southerners goaded by an intemperate president. Congressional Reconstruction was about to begin.

Congressional Reconstruction

Johnson's outrageous behavior during the 1866 campaign, capped by a Republican sweep of the elections, brought Presidential Reconstruction to an end. Congressional Reconstruction would be a far different affair. The Republican Congress threw out the state constitutions drawn up under the president's guidelines and replaced them with an entirely new set of state charters. Congress placed the South under direct military rule. For the first time in American history, the Senate put the president on trial. Two more amendments were added to the Constitution. African-American men finally won the right to vote, and hundreds of them assumed public office across the South. It was an extraordinary series of events, second only to emancipation in its revolutionary impact on the history of the United States.

Origins of the African-American Vote

The Congress that reconvened in December 1866 was far more Radical than the Congress that had adjourned earlier in the year. Nothing demonstrated this as clearly as the emerging consensus among moderate Republicans that southern blacks should be allowed to vote. Radical Republicans and African-American leaders had been calling for such a policy for two years. Shortly after the war ended, black men in North Carolina, some of them veterans of the Union Army, petitioned the president for "the privilege of voting." When the white backlash began in late 1865, Virginia blacks argued that if they were given the right to vote "you may rely upon us to secure justice for ourselves."

Moderate Republicans initially resisted the idea. They had hoped to build a Republican Party in the postwar South by courting the loyalty of white Unionists. At most, moderates like Abraham Lincoln contemplated granting the vote to black veterans and to educated African Americans who had been free before the war. As late as the summer of 1866 the Republican majority was prepared to do no more than punish southern states that excluded black voters. Not until early 1867 did moderates conclude that the only way to avoid a lengthy military occupation of the South was to put political power into the hands of all male freedmen. This was an extraordinary decision: Slavery was abolished everywhere in the hemisphere during the nineteenth century, but only in the United States was emancipation followed by full legal and political rights for the freedmen.

It was none other than Andrew Johnson who finally pushed the moderate Republicans over the line. All but ignoring the results of the 1866 elections, Johnson urged the southern states to defy Congress by rejecting the Fourteenth Amendment. Frustrated moderates thereupon joined with Radicals and repudiated Presidential Reconstruction. On March 2, 1867, Congress assumed control of the entire process by passing the First Reconstruction Act. It reduced the southern states to the status of territories and divided the South into five military districts directly controlled by the U. S. Army. Before the southern states could be readmitted to the Union they had to draw up new "republican" constitutions and ratify the Fourteenth Amendment. In addition, they had to allow African-American men to vote. The Second Reconstruction Act, passed a few weeks later, established the procedures to enforce African-American suffrage by placing the military in charge of voter registration. Johnson vetoed both acts, and in both cases Congress immediately overrode the president. "Congress has finally given us the means of relief," an African-American newspaper in Louisiana declared. "After governments of minorities, we are at last enabled to organize a government of the people." This was Congressional Reconstruction at its most radical, and for this reason it is often referred to as Radical Reconstruction.

Radical Reconstruction in the South

Beginning in 1867, the constitutions of the southern states were completely rewritten, thousands of African Americans began to vote, and hundreds of them assumed public office (see Table 16-2). Within six months 735,000 blacks and 635,000 whites had registered to vote across the South. "We'd walk fifteen miles in wartime to find out about the battle," a prospective black voter in Alabama explained in the spring of 1867. "We can walk fifteen miles and more to find out how to vote." African Americans formed electoral majorities in South Carolina, Florida, Mississippi, Alabama, and Louisiana. In the fall these new voters elected delegates to conventions that drew up some of the most progressive state constitutions in America. They guaran-

TABLE 16-2

Reconstruction Amendments, 1865–1870			
Amendment	Main Provisions	Congressional Passage (2/3 majority in each house required)	Ratification Process (3/4 of all states including ex-Confederate states required)
13	Slavery prohibited in United States	January 1865	December 1865 (twenty-seven states, including eight southern states)
14	1. National citizenship 2. State representation in Congress reduced proportionally to number of voters disfranchised 3. Former Confederates denied right to hold office 4. Confederate debt repudiated	June 1866	Rejected by twelve southern and border states, February 1867 Radicals make readmission of southern states hinge on ratification Ratified July 1868
15	Denial of franchise because of race, color, or past servitude explicitly prohibited	February 1869	Ratification required for readmission of Virginia, Texas, Mississippi, Georgia Ratified March 1870

teed universal manhood suffrage, mandated public-education systems, and established progressive tax structures.

The Republican governments elected under congressional authority were based on a new and unstable political coalition. Northern whites occupied a prominent place in the southern Republican Party. Stereotyped as greedy **carpetbaggers,** they were in fact a varied group that included Union veterans who stayed in the South when the war ended, idealistic reformers, well-meaning capitalists, and opportunistic Americans on the make. More important to the Republican coalition were southern whites. Derided as **scalawags** by their opponents, white Republicans in the South supported their party for many reasons. Some of them lived in upcountry regions where slavery had been unimportant and where resistance to secession and the Confederacy had been strongest. Other white Republicans had been Whigs before the war and hoped to regain some of the influence they had lost in the sectional crisis. But new African-American voters were the Republican Party's core constituency in the South. Like the Carpetbaggers and Scalawags, African-American voters were a varied lot. There were important differences between those who had been free before the war and those who had been slaves. Elite black artisans and professionals did not always share the same interests as poor black farmers and farm laborers (see Figure 16-1). Nevertheless, most African Americans were drawn together by a shared interest in securing their basic civil rights.

In the long run the class and race divisions within the southern Republican coalition would weaken the party's ability to resist the powerful forces arrayed against it. But

for a brief moment in the late 1860s and early 1870s the southern Republicans launched an impressive experiment in interracial democracy in the South. Racist legend paints these years as a dark period of "negro rule" and military domination. In fact, military rule rarely lasted more than a year or two in most places. In only one state, South Carolina, did African Americans ever control a majority of seats in the legislature. Whites outnumbered blacks in every other Republican government elected in the South during Congressional Reconstruction. Those blacks who did hold office came largely from the ranks of the prewar free African-American elite. Teachers, ministers, and small businessmen were far more common among black elected officials than were field hands and farmers. Nevertheless, these Reconstruction legislatures were more democratic, more representative of their constituents, than most legislatures in nineteenth-century America.

Achievements and Failures of Radical Government

Once in office, southern Republicans had to cultivate a white constituency and at the same time serve the interests of the African Americans who were the party's main supporters. In an effort to strengthen this bi-racial coalition in

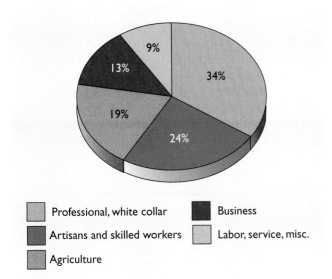

Figure 16-1 Occupations of African-American Officeholders During Reconstruction.

Source: Eric Foner, Freedom's Lawmakers: A Directory of Black Officeholders during Reconstruction, *2d. ed. (Baton Rouge, LA), p. xxi.*

RADICAL MEMBERS OF THE So. CA. LEGISLATURE.

One of the greatest achievements of Congressional Reconstruction was the election of a significant number of African Americans to public office. Only in South Carolina, however, did African Americans ever form a legislative majority.

the late 1860s, white Republican leaders emphasized a policy of active government support for economic development. Republican legislatures granted generous tax abatements for corporations and spent vast sums to encourage the construction of railroads. They preached a "Gospel of Prosperity" that promised to bring the benefits of economic development to ordinary white southerners who had been held back by the slaveholders' regime. Return the South to the Union, one Republican editor predicted, and "her levees will be rebuilt, her railroad grants restored, the mouths of the Mississippi opened, sandbars and snags removed, canals dug, marshes drained, taxes taken off cotton and sugar, emigration directed southward instead of westward, and all the material interests of the state spring into robust vigor and healthful activity." It was an exciting vision of a new political economy, but it never materialized.

In the long run the "Gospel of Prosperity" did not hold the Republican coalition together. Outside investors were unwilling to risk their capital on a region marked by so much political instability. As long as Congress and the president were at war, investment in the South was too risky. By the early 1870s, African-American politicians questioned the diversion of scarce revenues to railroads and tax breaks for corporations. Instead, they demanded more public services, especially universal education. But more government services meant higher property taxes at a time of severe economic hardship for most ordinary southerners. Many small white farmers had been devastated by the Civil War. Unaccustomed to paying high taxes and strong believers in limited government, they grew increasingly receptive to Democratic appeals for the restoration of "white man's government." Thus southern Republicans failed to develop a program around which to unite the diverse interests of their party's constituents.

Despite such powerful opposition from white majorities at home and lukewarm support from Washington, D. C., Radical governments in the South boasted several important achievements. They funded the construction of hospitals, insane asylums, prisons, and roads. They introduced homestead exemptions that protected the property of poor farmers. One of their top priorities was the establishment of universal public education. In the short time since the war ended the importance of basic literacy became clear to poor southern blacks. They had entered a world of contracts and calculations, a world where the ability to read English and add up figures was critical to a farmer's livelihood. Motivated by such concerns, Republican legislatures established public school systems that were a major improvement over their antebellum counterparts. The literacy rate among southern blacks rose steadily, thanks in large part to a cadre of newly trained African-American teachers who began staffing the classrooms within a few years of their establishment.

Nevertheless, public schools for African Americans remained inadequately funded and sharply segregated. In Savannah, Georgia, for example, the school board allocated less than five percent of its 1873 budget to support the African-American schools, although white children were in the minority in the district. Pointing to similar inequities in his own state of Florida, Congressman Josiah T. Walls called for the federal government to create a nationwide system of public schools, but there was virtually no chance that the Congress would undertake such a measure. As a result, in states like South Carolina, fewer than one in three school-age children were being educated in 1872.

The Political Economy of Sharecropping

Congressional Reconstruction made it a little easier for the former slaves to negotiate the terms of their labor contracts. Republican state legislatures in the South abolished the Black Codes, for example. By 1868 they had also passed "lien" laws, statutes giving African-American workers more control over the crops they grew. Workers with grievances had a better chance of securing justice, as southern Republicans became sheriffs, justices of the peace, and county clerks, and as southern courts accepted the testimony of African-American witnesses and allowed blacks to sit on juries.

The strongest card in the hands of the freed people was a severe shortage of agricultural workers throughout the South. After their emancipation thousands of African Americans left the countryside looking for better opportunities in towns and cities. Others left the South entirely. And even though most African Americans remained as farmers when the war ended, they reduced their working hours in several ways. African-American women withdrew from field work in significant numbers, for example. At the same time public education drew thousands of black children away from agricultural work. The resulting labor shortage forced white landlords to renegotiate their labor arrangements with the freed people.

The contract labor system that had developed during the war and under Presidential Reconstruction collapsed. It was replaced with a variety of arrangements that differed from region to region. On the sugar plantations of southern Louisiana the freed people became wage laborers. In low country South Carolina, by contrast, a large number of former slaves became independent farmers. But across the tobacco and cotton regions of the South, where the vast majority of freed people lived and worked, negotiations between workers and landlords gradually led to a new system of labor called sharecropping. The sharecropping system had a number of variations, but in most cases an agricultural worker and his family agreed to work for one year on a particular plot of land. The landowner often provided the tools, seed, and the work animals. At the end of the year the sharecropper and the landlord split the crop, perhaps one-third going to the

The free labor system that replaced slavery took different forms in different parts of the South. On the Grove plantation, in South Carolina, the freed slaves were required to sign the contracts being read to them in the picture above. In most cases, the freed people were eventually paid wages in the form of a share of the crop they produced.

sharecropper and two-thirds to the owner. If the "crop-per" had his own animals and tools he might negotiate to keep a larger share.

Sharecropping shaped the political economy of the postwar South by transforming the way cash crops were produced and marketed in much of the region. Most dra-matically, it required landowners to break up their planta-tions into family-sized plots. Under slavery, most African Americans worked in gangs under the direct supervision of a master, an overseer, or a driver. By contrast, sharecrop-pers worked in family units with no direct supervision. Be-fore the Civil War, slaveholders relied on "factors" (agents in port cities) to sell their crops and supply their planta-tions. With the breakup of the plantations after the war, each sharecropping family established its own relationship with local merchants and creditors. Merchants became crucial to the southern credit system because during the Civil War the Congress had established nationwide bank-ing standards that most southern banks could not meet. Local storekeepers were usually the only people who could extend credit to sharecroppers. The result was a dra-matic proliferation of merchants within the South. In the 1870s the number of stores grew by perhaps 300 percent. Local merchants soon became essential to the postwar southern economy. They provided sharecroppers with food, fertilizer, animal feed, and other provisions over the course of the year, until the crop was harvested.

These same developments had important consequences for small white farmers in many parts of the South. As the number of merchants grew, they fanned out into "upcoun-try" areas inhabited mostly by ordinary whites. Recon-

web connection

Did Reconstruction Work for the Freed People?

www.prenhall.com/boydston/reconstruction

Lincoln's assassination led to a power struggle between President Andrew Johnson, former Democratic senator from Tennessee, and the Republican Congress over how to "reconstruct" the South. The two sides agreed on the abolition of slavery but on little else. Often overlooked in the strug-gles over national policy were the everyday experiences of the newly freed slaves. How did they attempt to build lives for themselves? What were the principal obstacles they faced?

struction legislatures meanwhile sponsored the construc-tion of railroads in many of those same upcountry districts. The combination of merchants offering credit and railroads offering transportation made it easier than ever for small farmers to focus on the production of cash crops. Thus Re-construction accelerated the process by which the southern yeomen abandoned self-sufficient farming in favor of cash crops. Up through the 1870s, however, most white farmers continued to own their own land.

By contrast, sharecropping spread quickly among African-American farmers in the cotton South. By 1880 80 percent of cotton farms had fewer than 50 acres, the

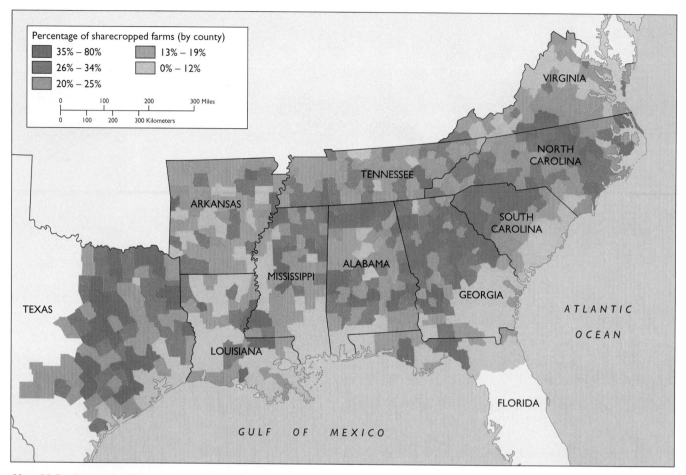

Map 16-2   Sharecropping.
By 1880 the sharecropping system had spread across the South. It was most common in the inland areas where cotton and tobacco plantations were most common before the Civil War.

majority of which were operated by croppers (see Map 16-2). A white landowner in the South complained that sharecropping was "the universal plan; negroes prefer it and I am forced to adopt it. Can't choose your system. Have to do what negroes want. They control this matter entirely." In fact, sharecropping had several advantages for landlords. It reduced their risk when cotton prices were low, it encouraged workers to increase production without costly supervision, and if sharecroppers changed jobs before the crop was harvested they would lose a whole year's pay. But the system also had advantages for the workers. For freed people who had no hope of owning their own farms, sharecropping was the next best thing. In principle it rewarded those who worked hard. The bigger the crop, the more they earned. It gave the former slaves more independence than contract labor.

Sharecropping also allowed the freed people to work in families rather than in gangs. Freedom alone had rearranged the powers of men, women, and children within the families of former slaves. Parents gained newfound control over the lives of their children. They could send sons and daughters to school; they could put their sons to work in the fields and

their daughters to work in the house. Successful parents could give their children an important head start in "the race of life." Similarly, African-American husbands gained new powers that shaped the lives of their wives. Slave marriages had no legal standing, so when the former slaves got married their relationships changed. The laws of marriage in the mid-nineteenth century defined the husband as the head of the household. Once married, women often found that their property belonged to their husbands.

The sharecropping system also assumed that the husband was the head of the household and that he made the economic decisions for the entire family. Men signed most labor contracts, and most landlords assumed that the husband would take his family to work with him. Shortly after the war Laura Towne, a teacher from the North, observed that African-American men in the South Carolina low country were claiming "the right . . . to have their own way in their families and rule their wives."

Sharecropping thereby shaped the entire political economy of the postwar South: It influenced the balance of power between men and women within cropper families; it established the balance of power between landowners

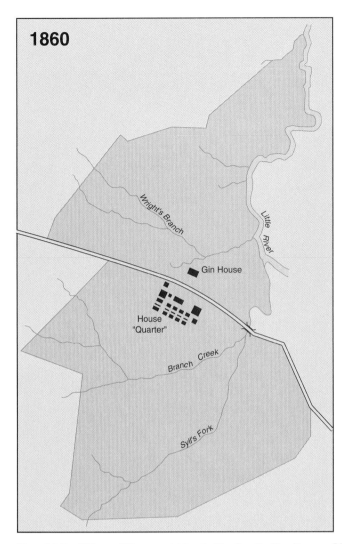

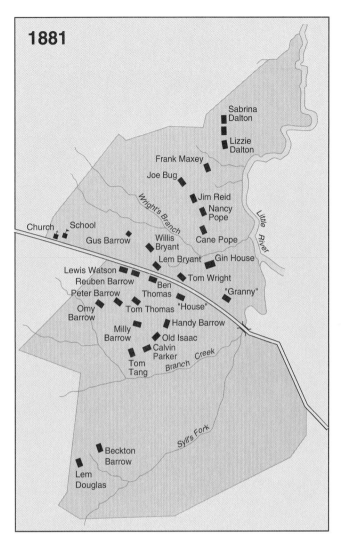

Map 16-3   *Effect of Sharecropping in the South: The Barrow Plantaton in Oglethorpe County, Georgia.*
Sharecropping cut large estates into small landholdings worked by sharecroppers and tenants, changing the landscape of the South.

and sharecroppers; and it tied the southern economy to agriculture, in particular to cotton production, in a way that seriously impeded the region's overall economic development (see Map 16-3). Yet even as this new way of life was taking shape, the Republican Party was retreating from its commitment to the freed people.

The Retreat From Republican Radicalism

By the late 1860s the Republican coalition was splintering in ways that weakened the party's continued commitment to Radical Reconstruction. In 1867 the Radicals led a drive to impeach President Johnson, but they failed to remove him from office. The fall elections suggested that northern voters were already tiring of Radical Reconstruction. By

1868 the Republicans were presenting themselves to voters as the party of moderation. They pointed out that the Democrats represented extremism and continued disruption of the southern political system and that the Democrats relied on terrorist organizations such as the Ku Klux Klan. The Republican appeal to moderation succeeded, bringing in its wake the last major achievements of Reconstruction.

The Impeachment and Trial of Andrew Johnson

Throughout 1866 and much of 1867 President Johnson waged a relentless campaign against Congress and the Radicals. When Congress began to override the president's repeated vetoes, Johnson stepped up his campaign. The conflict between Congress and the president led to a struggle over control of the military in the South. The First Reconstruction Act placed the entire South under direct military control, and the Freedmen's Bureau was a branch of the

ON TRIAL

Andrew Johnson

"Didn't I tell you so?" Thaddeus Stevens asked upon hearing the news that Johnson had ordered Stanton's dismissal. "If you don't kill the beast, it will kill you." But Radicals like Stevens had been prepared for some time to "kill the beast" by removing Andrew Johnson from office. More telling was the reluctant conclusion among moderate Republicans that the president had to be put on trial for a positive violation of the law. On February 24, 1868, the House Judiciary Committee voted nearly a dozen articles of impeachment against the president. They charged him with violating the Tenure of Office Act, of replacing a cabinet officer without the advice and consent of the Senate even though Congress was in session, of devising means to obstruct the execution of various Reconstruction laws, and of ridiculing and disrespecting Congress. The strongest case for a technical breach of the law was Johnson's attempted removal of Stanton in violation of the Tenure of Office Act, but behind that charge lay widespread disgust with the president's undignified behavior, his abusive public pronouncements, and his obstreperous interference with Congressional Reconstruction.

It was an extraordinary thing to put a president on trial. No Congress had ever done so before. By March 4, when the Senate presented the articles of impeachment, the atmosphere in Washington, D. C. was understandably agitated. Congressmen were besieged with requests for tickets to the Senate gallery. It was reported that Stanton

Court proceedings were held in the Senate chambers during the impeachment trial of President Andrew Johnson. It was an extraordinary thing to put a president on trial.

Congressmen were besieged with requests for these tickets to the Senate Gallery by constituents who wanted to observe the impeachment proceedings.

had barricaded himself in his office and was sleeping on a sofa, protected by armed guards. Yet for all the electricity surrounding the impeachment, the trial itself turned out to be a rather dull affair. For a moment Republican Senator Ben Butler lost his reserve and, citing the horror stories pouring out of the South, announced in heated tones that "We want these things stopped!" Stevens at one point referred to the president as "this offspring of assassination." For the most part, however, the participants maintained the dignity befitting so solemn an occasion.

There were, after all, serious legal questions that had to be considered. The House managers argued that a president could be removed not only for violating the Constitution or the law, but also for abusing his powers, breaking his oath of office, or neglecting his duties "without violating a positive law." In response, Johnson's lawyers argued that a president had to actually violate the law. Indeed, one of the president's attorneys went so far as to claim that the violation had to be especially severe before he could be removed. Thus even if Johnson did violate the Tenure of Office Act, it was not a serious enough breach of the law to justify removal from office. In any case the Tenure of Office Act was unconstitutional, Johnson's lawyers argued, making his violation of it

meaningless. To this argument Johnson's accusers shot right back that only the Supreme Court could decide whether or not a law was constitutional. Otherwise the president would be free to break any laws he felt like breaking.

Still, some of Johnson's sharpest critics wondered about the constitutionality of the Tenure of Office Act. They wondered whether the standards for conviction by the Senate had to be as strict as those for conviction in a court of law. And they were not sure whether the Tenure of Office Act even applied to Secretary of War Stanton, since he had been appointed by President Lincoln rather than President Johnson. Nor were constitutional questions and legal technicalities the only issues to consider. Several senators were wary of the man who stood next in line to replace Johnson in the event of a conviction. That man was Benjamin Wade, president *pro tem* of the Senate and an outspoken Radical from Ohio. The prospect of a Wade presidency disturbed both Republican moderates and the New York financial markets. Finally, Johnson behaved himself during the trial, and his lawyers quietly hinted that if the president was acquitted he would continue his good behavior. In the end, thanks to the votes of seven Republicans who sided with the president, the Senate fell one vote short of the two-thirds required to remove Johnson from office.

The Radicals were thwarted in their efforts to convict Johnson, but in other ways they had gained a victory. Hoping to avoid conviction, President Johnson had promised to abide by the law. On the advice of his supporters, Johnson at last forwarded to the Congress the new state constitutions submitted by Arkansas and South Carolina. Finally, the president stopped interfering with the Reconstruction Acts by removing Army officers who enforced the law in the South. "Andrew Johnson has been a changed man," the *Chicago Tribune* declared during the impeachment trial. "The great obstruction to the law has been virtually suspended; the President . . . has been on his good behavior." Thus Johnson was acquitted, but the Reconstruction of the South went forward anyway.

U. S. Army. Judicial authority was vested in the provost marshals. The military also oversaw the process of voter registration. But the president was the commander in chief of the military, and Andrew Johnson made clear his determination to interfere with Congress' wishes as much as he possibly could. Exercising his authority over the military, Johnson removed dozens of Freedmen's Bureau officials who acted to protect the freed people by enforcing the Civil Rights Act of 1866. He replaced Republican provost marshals with men who were hostile to Congress and contemptuous of the former slaves. In short, President Johnson went out of his way to undermine the law.

Radicals called for Johnson's impeachment, but Republican moderates and conservatives resisted such a move. Instead, the Congress hoped to restrain the president in two ways—first by refining the Reconstruction Acts, and then through the Tenure of Office Act of March 2, 1867. This act prohibited the president from removing any official whose appointment required congressional approval. One purpose of the law was to prevent Johnson from firing Secretary of War Edwin M. Stanton, who was sympathetic to the Republicans. A related statute required that all presidential orders to the military pass through General Ulysses S. Grant. Republicans hoped that this would prevent the president from systematically removing military officials who enforced the Reconstruction Acts in the South.

Congress' actions only served to provoke the president. In his veto messages and in his public pronouncements, Johnson indulged in some of the most blatant racist pandering in the history of the executive office. He played on fears of "amalgamation," "miscegenation," and racial "degeneration." He claimed that the Republicans were attempting to "Africanize" the South. He expressed fear for the safety of white womanhood. In the off-year elections of 1867 northern Democrats played the race card relentlessly and with considerable success. Democratic victories erased many of the huge Republican gains of 1866 and inspired the president to defy the restraints Congress had imposed upon him. As a test of his power, and as a deliberate provocation, Johnson asked Secretary of War Stanton to resign on August 5, 1867. Stanton refused, and a week later the president appointed General Grant as interim secretary of war. Still Stanton would not budge, so in February 1868 Johnson at last fired him outright.

Republicans Become the Party of Moderation

While Andrew Johnson was on trial in the Senate, voters in Michigan went to the polls and overwhelmingly rejected a new state constitution that granted African Americans the right to vote. Coming on the heels of Democratic victories in late 1867, Republicans read the Michigan results as another rejection of Radical Reconstruction. When Senator Charles Sumner submitted a bill confiscating the land of ex-Confederates, his fellow Republicans rebuffed him. Congressman Thaddeus Stevens was similarly thwarted when he proposed the distribution of 40 acres and a mule to the families of freed slaves. Republican moderates also rejected Radical proposals to guarantee educational opportunities for freed people and to deny voting privileges to large numbers of ex-Confederates. The Republican Party was backing away from radicalism.

During the 1868 elections Republicans continued to cultivate a moderate image. They rejected the Radicals' demand that the party platform endorse nationwide African-American suffrage. Moderates argued that African-American suffrage was a uniquely southern solution to a uniquely southern problem. The northern states should be free to decide for themselves whether to grant African-American men the vote. With plenty of time before election day, Congress readmitted six southern states to the Union, thereby demonstrating that Republican policies had successfully restored law and order to the South. By nominating General Ulysses Grant as their presidential candidate, the Republicans confirmed their retreat from radicalism. "Let Us Have Peace," was Grant's campaign slogan.

In sharp contrast, the Democrats nominated Horatio Seymour, who had been New York's governor during the Civil War. Seymour ran a vicious campaign of relentless race baiting. The Democratic platform denounced the Reconstruction Acts and promised to restore white rule to the South. The loose-tongued Seymour openly suggested that a Democratic president might nullify the governments organized under Congressional Reconstruction. Where the Republicans ran on a platform promising order and stability, the Democrats seemed to promise only continued disruption. Northern fears were confirmed by the horrendous violence that swept through the South during the election.

Southern Democrats relied on such violence to keep African-American voters from the polls on election day. At the height of the 1868 campaign an Alabama sharecropper named William Ford was visited by several members of the Ku Klux Klan. The Klansmen whipped Ford in an effort to "convince" him to vote for the Democratic presidential candidate. "They asked me who I was going to vote for: Grant or Seymour." Knowing that the Klan had whipped one of his neighbors "for talking politics," Ford claimed to be ignorant of the campaign. The Klan visit had the desired effect. "When the election came off I didn't vote," Ford testified. "I was afraid to. I thought if I couldn't vote the Republican ticket I would not vote at all." Vigilantes made similar visits in many parts of the South during the 1868 election campaign.

The Ku Klux Klan was only one of several secretive organizations dedicated to the violent overthrow of Radical Reconstruction and the restoration of white supremacy. They went by various names, including the Knights of the White Camelia, Red Shirts, and Night Riders. Some of these white vigilantes tried to force African Americans to

The Ku Klux Klan was one of a number of racist vigilante groups trying to restore the Democratic Party to power in the postwar South.

go back to work for white landlords. Some attacked African Americans who refused to abide by traditional codes of racial etiquette. But in the main, organizations such as the Klan worked to restore the political power of the Democratic Party in the South. They rampaged through the countryside intimidating white Republicans, burning African-American homes and lynching blacks who showed signs of political activism. In Arkansas alone there were 200 murders. It is fair to say that in 1868 the Ku Klux Klan served as the paramilitary arm of the southern Democratic Party.

But as a means of restoring white supremacy, the Klan's strategy of violence backfired. A wave of disgust swept across the North in late 1868. The Republicans regained control of the White House, along with 25 of the nation's 33 state legislatures. The victorious Republicans quickly seized the opportunity to preserve the achievements of Reconstruction.

The Grant Administration and Moderate Republicanism

The Republicans reinforced their moderate image by attempting to restore law and order in the South. A lengthy series of dramatic congressional hearings produced vivid evidence of the Klan's violent efforts to suppress the African-American vote in the South. Congress responded with a series of Enforcement Acts, designed to "enforce" the recently enacted Fifteenth Amendment (see the fol-

lowing section for more information). After some initial hesitation, the Grant administration used the new laws to suppress Klan violence. By the end of 1871, the anti-Klan prosecutions had effectively diminished political violence throughout the South. As a result the 1872 presidential elections were relatively free of disruption. The successful prosecution of the Ku Klux Klan helped reinforce the Republican Party's image as the voice of moderation.

Further evidence of this moderate trend was the Republican shift to an aggressive foreign policy. Before the Civil War, Republicans associated expansionism with the "slave power" and the Democratic Party. But with the triumph of nationalism, the Republicans equated American overseas expansion with the spread of liberty. They went on the offensive: In 1867 Secretary of State William Seward successfully negotiated the purchase of Alaska from Russia. For the first time, the United States claimed territory that did not border on any other state. The administration was equally adroit in its negotiations with Great Britain over the settlement of the so-called *Alabama* claims. In 1872 the English accepted responsibility for having helped equip the Confederate Navy during the Civil War. They agreed to pay over 15 million dollars in claims for damage done to American shipping by the *Alabama* and other southern warships built in England.

But Grant's aggressive foreign policy did not go uncontested. In 1869 the president set his sights on Santo Domingo (now the Dominican Republic), but the administration bungled the entire effort. Grant's private secretary negotiated a treaty without letting the cabinet, including the secretary of state, know what he was doing. Once Grant sent the treaty to Congress in 1870 it aroused the suspicions of several prominent Republican senators, including Charles Sumner and Carl Schurz. Grant then tried to bulldoze the treaty through Congress, but succeeded only in alienating more members of his own party. The Senate rejected the annexation of Santo Domingo, and the Republicans were weakened still further by the debacle.

Reconstruction in the North

Although Reconstruction was aimed primarily at shaping the transition from slavery to freedom in the South, the North was affected by the process as well. Because most northern states restricted voting to whites, the struggle over the black vote spilled beyond the borders of the defeated Confederacy. As Republicans moved toward prohibiting the use of race as a qualification for voting rights, for example, northern feminists began to raise objections. Why should African-American men recently released from slavery be guaranteed the right to vote, feminists asked, when educated northern women were still denied the privilege? Thus Reconstruction politics disrupted a long-standing alliance between abolitionists and feminists in the North. At the same time, northern workers were inspired by the radical promises of Reconstruction to launch a new wave of organized protest. Although not as dramatic as developments in the South, the transformation of the North was still an important chapter in the history of Reconstruction.

The Fifteenth Amendment and Nationwide African-American Suffrage

Before the Civil War African Americans in the North were segregated in theaters, restaurants, cemeteries, hotels, streetcars, ferries, and schools. Most northern blacks lived in states that denied them the vote. The Civil War galvanized the northern black community to launch a full-scale assault on racial discrimination, with some success. In 1863 California removed the ban on African-American testimony in the criminal courts. Two years later Illinois did the same. During the war, many northern cities abolished streetcar segregation. But when they considered black voting, northern whites retained their traditional racial prejudices. In 1865 voters in three northern states (Connecticut, Wisconsin, and Minnesota) soundly rejected constitutional amendments to enfranchise African-American men. "Slavery is dead, the negro is not, there is the misfortune," the Democratic *Cincinnati Enquirer* declared. "For the sake of all parties, would that he were." Two years of Presidential Reconstruction changed little. In 1867, even as the Republican Congress was imposing the black vote on the South, African-American suffrage was defeated by voters in Ohio, Minnesota, and Kansas.

But the shocking electoral violence of 1868 persuaded many northerners that, given the chance, southern whites would quickly strip African Americans of the right to vote. This latest shift in northern public opinion was expressed most dramatically in Iowa and Minnesota, where voters finally approved black suffrage. Emboldened by their victory in the 1868 elections, the following year Republicans took one last, deep breath and exhaled a Fifteenth Amendment to the Constitution. It prohibited the use of "race, color, or previous condition of servitude" to disqualify voters anywhere in the United States. This was nationwide black suffrage, just as the Radicals had asked for in 1868. But by 1869 the Radicals wanted more. They complained that the Fifteenth Amendment did not guarantee the vote to all adult males in the United States. Nor did it ban literacy tests and educational requirements for voting. Yet by outlawing voter discrimination on the basis of race, the Fifteenth Amendment protected the most radical achievement of Congressional Reconstruction.

The Fifteenth Amendment brought Reconstruction directly into the North by overturning the state laws that still discriminated against African-American voters. The Republicans could pass the amendment after the 1868 elections because they now controlled three-fourths of the state legislatures, allowing the Republicans to ratify the Fifteenth Amendment without popular referendums. In addition, Congress required ratification of the amendment in those southern states still to be readmitted to the Union. Virginia, Mississippi, and Texas did so and were restored to the Union in early 1870. After several irregularities were cleared up, Georgia followed suit. On March 30, 1870, the Fifteenth Amendment became part of the Constitution. For the first time in American history, racial criteria for voting were banned everywhere in the United States, North as well as South.

Women and Suffrage

The issue of African-American voting divided northern Radicals who had long been allies in the struggle for emancipation. Before the Civil War, feminists and abolitionists had forged a strong progressive coalition. They appeared on each other's platforms and gave speeches advocating both abolition and women's equality. But signs of trouble appeared as early as May 1863 when a dispute broke out at the National Convention of the Woman's National Loyal League in New York City. One of the convention's resolutions declared that "there never can be a true peace in this Republic until the civil and political rights of all citizens of African descent and all women are practically established." For some of the delegates, this resolution went too far. The Loyal League had been organized to assist in bringing about northern victory in the war against the slave South. Some delegates argued that it was inappropriate to inject the issue of women's rights into the struggle to restore the Union.

By the end of the war, Radicals were pressing for African-American suffrage in addition to emancipation. This precipitated an increasingly rancorous debate among reformers. Abolitionists argued that while they continued to support women's suffrage, the critical issue at that moment was the immediate protection of the freed people of the South. This, abolitionist Wendell Phillips argued, was "the Negro's Hour." As he explained to Elizabeth Cady Stanton in May 1865, "I would not mix the movements. . . . I think such a mixture would lose for the negro far more than we should gain for the woman." Phillips' position sparked a powerful sense of betrayal among leading women's rights activists. For 20 years they had pressed their claims for the right to vote. They had organized to support the Union in the struggle for emancipation. They were loyal allies of the Republican Party, and now the Republicans abandoned them. "Some say, 'Be still, wait, this is the negro's hour,' " Stanton complained in December 1865. It would be better, she argued, to press for "a vote based on intelligence and education for black and white,

Elizabeth Cady Stanton, a leading advocate of women's rights, was angered when Congress gave African-American men the vote without also giving it to women.

Not all feminists agreed with Stanton. Abby Kelley Foster pointed to the urgent needs of African Americans in the South at that moment. "He is treated as a slave today in the several districts of the South. Without wages, without family rights, whipped and beaten by thousands, given up to the most horrible outrages, without that protection which his value as property formerly gave him. . . . Have we any true sense of justice, are we not dead to the sentiment of humanity if we shall wish to postpone his security against present woes and future enslavement till woman shall obtain political rights?" As racist violence erupted in the postwar South, abolitionists argued that African-American suffrage was simply more urgent than women's suffrage. The African-American vote "is with us a matter of life and death, and therefore can not be postponed," Frederick Douglass argued. "I have always championed women's right to vote; but it will be seen that the present claim for the negro is one of the most *urgent* necessity. . . . The negro needs suffrage to protect his life and property."

Stanton was unmoved by such arguments. For her the Fifteenth Amendment barring racial qualifications for voting was the last straw. She complained that by granting African-American men the right to vote Republicans had subjected African-American women to a new and oppressive form of male domination. Supporters of women's suffrage therefore opposed the Fifteenth Amendment on the ground that it subjected elite, educated women to the rule of base and illiterate males, especially immigrants and African Americans. "Think of Patrick and Sambo and Hans and Yung Tung who do not know the difference between a Monarchy and a Republic," Stanton declared, "who never read the Declaration of Independence or Webster's spelling book, making laws for Lydia Maria Child, Lucretia Mott, or Fanny Kemble." Abolitionists were shocked by such remarks. They favored universal suffrage, not the "educated" suffrage that Stanton was calling for. The breach among reformers weakened the coalition of Radicals pushing to maintain a vigorous Reconstruction policy in the South.

The Rise and Fall of the National Labor Union

In the late 1860s the Boston Labor Reform Association called for a dramatic change of "the whole Social System." Just as southern society was being transformed, "so too must our dinner tables be reconstructed." Inspired by the radicalism of the Civil War and Reconstruction, industrial workers across the North organized dozens of craft unions, Eight-Hour Leagues, and workingmen's associations. The general goal of these associations was to protect northern workers who were overworked and underpaid. They called strikes, initiated consumer boycotts, and formed consumer cooperatives. In 1867 and 1868 workers in New York and Massachusetts launched impressive cam-

man and woman." Voting rights based on "intelligence and education" amounted to literacy tests that would have excluded virtually all the freed slaves as well as many immigrants, particularly the working-class Irish, Germans, and Chinese. Thus, Stanton's remarks revealed a strain of elitism that would further alienate abolitionists.

In 1866 the struggle for the Fourteenth Amendment widened the rift between feminists and abolitionists. The amendment reduced a state's congressional representation in proportion to the number of *males* who were denied the ballot. Indeed, with the passage of the Fourteenth Amendment the word "male" appeared in the Constitution for the first time. In the same year conservative Democrats cynically added women's suffrage amendments to congressional legislation securing the African-American vote, knowing that the amendments would thereby fail. But women's rights advocates sided with the conservatives. Stanton argued in May 1867 that the voting power of "unlettered" and "unwashed" men threatened the interests of women. The only thing that could "outweigh this incoming tide of ignorance, poverty and vice," she concluded, was "the virtue, wealth and education of the women of the country."

paigns to enact laws restricting the workday to eight hours. Shortly thereafter workers began electing their own candidates to state legislatures. The Knights of St. Crispin sent two dozen of its candidates to the Massachusetts state legislature in 1869.

The National Labor Union (NLU) was the first significant postwar effort to organize all "working people" into a national union. William Sylvis, an iron molder, founded the NLU in 1866 and became its president in 1868. Like most of the worker organizations of the time, the NLU subscribed to "producers ideology." It sought to unify all those who produced wealth through their own labor and skill. Hostile to anyone who made money from money, the NLU targeted bankers, financiers, and stockbrokers as the enemies of the producing classes. These sentiments were most powerful among farmers, craftsmen, and small shopkeepers, but the NLU welcomed a broader range of working people including women's rights advocates and wage earners.

Under Sylvis' direction the National Labor Union advocated a wide range of political reforms, not just bread-and-butter issues of interest to working people. Nevertheless, the NLU was thwarted by the limits of producer ideology. Sylvis believed that through successful organization American workers could take the "first step toward competence and independence." Thus Sylvis' NLU clung to the Jeffersonian vision of a society of independent petty producers. By the 1860s this vision was an outdated relic of an earlier age. Many small businessmen and factory owners took pride in their own "independence" and still considered themselves "producers." Meanwhile wage labor rather than economic independence had become the permanent condition for the majority of American workers. Sylvis showed little interest in organizing women, African Americans, rural workers, and most unskilled wage laborers. Sylvis died in 1869 and, after a miserable showing in the elections of 1872, the NLU fell apart. By then Reconstruction in the South was also coming to an end.

The End of Reconstruction

National events had as much to do with the end of Reconstruction as did events in the South. A nationwide outbreak of political corruption in the late 1860s and 1870s provoked a sharp reaction everywhere. When the corruption was exposed in the South, however, it diminished popular support for continuing Reconstruction. A group of influential northern "Liberals," previously known for their support for Reconstruction, abandoned the Republican Party in disgust in 1872. The following year a major depression turned the nation's attention away from the social and political problems of the South. The end of Reconstruction finally came after a new round of electoral vi-

olence corrupted the results of the 1876 elections. Republican politicians in Washington, D. C., responded not with renewed determination to enforce Reconstruction but with a sordid political bargain that came to symbolize the end of an era.

Corruption as a National Problem

Postwar Americans witnessed an extraordinary display of public dishonesty, from the scandals in the Grant administration to the notorious swindles of the Tweed Ring in New York City. Democrats were as prone to thievery as Republicans. Northern swindlers looted the public treasuries from Boston to San Francisco. In the South black legislators took bribes, but so did whites. Indeed, some of the most prominent whites in the South paid some of the most spectacular bribes. Corruption, it seemed, was endemic to postwar American politics.

Few Americans stopped to recall the corruption scandals of the 1850s. Nor did the opponents of Reconstruction bother to notice that the corruption of the Republican legislatures in the South was part of a nationwide trend. If corruption was everywhere to be seen in the late 1860s and 1870s, it was largely because there were more opportunities for it than ever before. The Civil War and Reconstruction had swollen government budgets at the state and national levels. Never before was government so active in collecting taxes and disbursing vast sums for the public good. Under the circumstances, many government officials proved unable to refrain from accepting bribes for votes, embezzling public funds, or using insider knowledge to defraud the taxpayers.

The federal government set the tone. In the most notorious case, the directors of the Union Pacific Railroad set up a dummy corporation called the Credit Mobilier, awarded it phony contracts, and protected it from inquiry by bribing several influential congressmen. The Grant administration was eventually smeared with scandal as well. Though personally honest, the president surrounded himself with rich nobodies and army buddies rather than respected statesmen. Grant's own private secretary was exposed as a member of the "Whiskey Ring," a cabal of midwestern distillers and revenue agents who cheated the government out of millions of tax dollars every year.

State and city governments in the North were no less corrupt. Wealthy businessmen and local elites curried favor with politicians whose votes would determine where a railroad would be built, which land would be allocated for rights of way, and how many government bonds had to be floated to pay for such projects. Henry Demarest Lloyd, a prominent social critic, declared that Standard Oil could do anything with the Pennsylvania legislature except refine it. State officials regularly accepted gifts, received salaries, and sat on the boards of corporations whose fortunes were directly affected by their votes. Cities were

William Marcy Tweed, the boss of New York's notoriously corrupt, "Tweed Ring" was parodied by the great cartoonist, William Nast. Nast's portrayal of the bloated public official became an enduring symbol of governmental corruption.

rocked by scandal as well. The spectacular growth of urban centers created a huge new demand for public services. Municipalities awarded lucrative contracts for the construction of schools, parks, libraries, water and sewer systems, and mass-transportation networks. Every such contract created apparently irresistible temptations for corruption. The Tweed Ring alone bilked New York City out of tens of millions of dollars. By these standards the corruption of the southern Reconstruction legislatures was relatively small.

But corruption in the South was real enough, and it had particular significance for the politics of Reconstruction. Southern Republicans of modest means depended heavily on the money they earned as public officials. These same men found themselves responsible for the collection of unusually high taxes; the construction of schools, hospitals, and prisons; and the award of land grants and bond issues for railroads, river improvements, and other economic-development projects. As elsewhere in industrializing America, the lure of corruption proved overwhelming. The Republican governor of Louisiana grew rich while in office by "exacting tribute" from railroads seeking state favors. The Littlefield "ring" in North Carolina spent hundreds of thousands of dollars in bribes to win huge state appropriations for a railroad that was

never built. Corruption on a vast scale implied petty corruption as well. Individual legislators sold their votes for as little as 200 dollars.

Nevertheless, the charges of corruption leveled against southern Republican governments were often unfair. As Reconstruction legislatures established basic public services, they were forced to impose taxes at far higher rates than anything antebellum voters were accustomed to. Simply extending public-school education to African Americans would have been an enormous burden on the devastated southern economy. But several Republican governments also had to build entirely new public-school systems, not to mention hospitals, roads, canals, and rail lines. Had they done all of this without so much as a dime's worth of corruption, the Reconstruction governments still would have created a tax burden that would have caused white voters to shudder in horror. Inevitably, the whites blamed their woes on corruption.

In many cases opponents of Reconstruction used attacks on corruption to mask their contempt for Republican policies. Their strategy helped galvanize opposition to the Republican Party, destroying its hopes of attracting a loyal core of white voters. Realizing that corruption only weakened their cause, black Republicans grew increasingly critical of the politics of economic development.

Finally, corruption in the South helped provoke a backlash against active government nationwide, weakening northern support for Reconstruction. The intellectual substance of this backlash was provided by a group of influential Liberal Republicans many of whom had once been ardent supporters of Radical Reconstruction.

Liberal Republicans Revolt

The term "Liberal Republicans" embraced a loosely knit group of intellectuals, politicians, publishers, and businessmen from the northern elite. These "best men" of American society were discouraged by the failure of Radical Reconstruction to bring peace to the southern states. They were even more disgusted by the pervasive corruption of postwar politics. Although small in number, Liberals exercised important influence in northern politics. They spoke through the pages of magazines like *The Nation* and newspapers such as the Springfield *Republican*. As Liberals tired of the seemingly perpetual strife aroused by Reconstruction they increasingly urged resistance to growing demands by women, African Americans, and workers.

At the heart of Liberal philosophy was a deep suspicion of democracy itself. Liberals argued that any government beholden to the interests of the ignorant masses was doomed to corruption. They did not oppose active government in general; rather, Liberals worried that democracy threatened to undermine "good" government. Public servants should be chosen on the basis of intelligence, as measured by civil-service examinations, rather than by patronage appointments that sustained corrupt party machines. Indeed, party politics itself was the enemy of good government, Liberal reformers believed.

Liberals therefore grew increasingly alienated from the Republican Party in general and from President Grant in particular. Above all they resented the fact that the Republican Party had changed. Its idealistic commitment to free labor was waning by the 1870s. Its Radical vanguard was fast disappearing. The rising generation of Republican leaders was committed primarily to keeping the party machinery well oiled. Getting and holding office had become an end in itself for Republican stalwarts.

As Republicans lost their identity as moral crusaders, Liberal reformers proposed a new vision of their own. In 1872 they left their party to support Horace Greeley, who took up the Liberal banner as the Democratic presidential candidate. The Liberal plank in the Democratic platform proclaimed the party's commitment to the principles of universal equality before the law, the integrity of the Union, and support for the Thirteenth, Fourteenth, and Fifteenth Amendments to the Constitution. At the same time, however, Liberals demanded "the immediate and absolute removal of all disabilities" imposed on the South as well as a "universal amnesty" for all ex-Confederates. Finally, the Liberals declared their belief that "local self-government" would "guard the rights of all citizens more securely than any centralized power." In effect, the Liberals were demanding the immediate end of all federal efforts to protect the former slaves.

In the long run, the Liberal view would prevail, but in 1872 it did not go over well with the voters. The Liberals' biggest liability was their own presidential candidate. Horace Greeley's erratic reputation and Republican background were too much for Democrats to swallow. In record numbers Democrats refused to go to the polls and vote for him. Grant was easily re-elected, but he and his fellow Republicans saw the returns as evidence that Reconstruction was becoming a political liability for the Republican Party.

The 1874 elections confirmed the lesson. Democrats made sweeping gains all across the North, and they maintained their electoral strength for decades. An ideological stalemate developed. For a generation, neither party would clearly dominate American politics. The Republicans would take no more risks in support of Reconstruction.

During his second term, therefore, Grant did little to protect African-American voters from the revival of violence during elections in the South. Not even the Civil Rights Act of 1875 undid the impression of waning Republican zeal. Ostensibly designed to prohibit racial discrimination in public places, the Civil Rights Act was a toothless law that had no meaningful enforcement provisions. The bill's most important clause, prohibiting segregated schools, was eliminated from the final version. Southern states ignored even this watered-down statute, and in 1883 the Supreme Court declared it unconstitutional. Thus the Civil Rights Act of 1875, the last significant piece of Reconstruction legislation, was an ironic testament to the Republican Party's declining commitment to equal rights.

A Depression and a Deal "Redeem" the South

Angered by corruption and high taxes, white Republicans across the South succumbed in growing numbers to the Democratic Party's appeal for a restoration of white supremacy. As the number of white Republicans fell, the number of black Republicans holding office in the South actually increased, even as the Grant administration backed away from the active defense of African-American civil rights. But the persistence of African-American officeholders only reinforced the Democrats' determination to "redeem" their states from Republican rule. In fact, Democrats had taken control of Virginia in 1869, sparing the state from any experience of Republican rule. North Carolina was redeemed in 1870, Georgia in 1871, and Texas two years after that. Then depression struck.

In September 1873 America's premier financial institution, Jay Cooke, went bankrupt after wildly overextend-

The severe depression that followed the financial panic of 1873 drew the nation's attention away from the problems of Reconstruction.

ing itself on investments in a second railroad to the West Coast, the Northern Pacific. Within weeks hundreds of banks and thousands of businesses, including 89 railroads, went bankrupt as well. The country sank into a depression that lasted five years and saw unemployment rise to 14 percent. Corporations responded to hard times and growing competition by slashing wages. To protect their incomes, railroad workers tried to organize a nationwide union and attempted to strike in protest several times. Their employers, however (armed with spies and court orders and backed up by an army of private policemen as well as government troops), repeatedly thwarted such efforts. A series of railroad strikes in the early and middle 1870s failed.

As the nation turned its attention to labor unrest and economic depression, the Republican Party's commitment to Reconstruction all but disappeared. By the middle of the 1870s, the Republican Party in most parts of the South was almost exclusively African American. Democrats regained control of the governments of Alabama and Arkansas in 1874. In the few southern states where black Republicans clung tenaciously to their political power, white "redeemers" turned to violent methods to overthrow the last remnants of Reconstruction.

Mississippi established the model in 1875. Confident that authorities in Washington, D.C., would no longer interfere in the South, Democrats launched an all-out campaign to regain control of the state government by any means necessary. The Democratic campaign was double edged. Crude appeals to white supremacy further reduced the dwindling number of scalawags. But the redeemers launched more powerful weapons against black Republicans. White Leagues organized a blatant campaign of violence and intimidation designed to keep African Ameri-

cans away from the polls on election day, 1875. Republicans were beaten, forced to flee the state, and in several cases murdered. Washington turned a deaf ear to African-American pleas for military protection. In the end enough blacks were kept from the polls and enough scalawags voted their racial prejudices to put the Democrats in power. Mississippi was redeemed.

The tactics tried out in Mississippi were repeated elsewhere the following year, only this time they had dramatic consequences for the presidential election of 1876. Amidst a serious economic depression, and with an electorate tired of the politics of Reconstruction, the Democrats stood a good chance of taking the presidency away from the Republicans. In fact, the Democratic candidate, Samuel J. Tilden, won 250,000 more votes than his Republican rival Rutherford B. Hayes (see Map 16-4). But outrageous electoral fraud

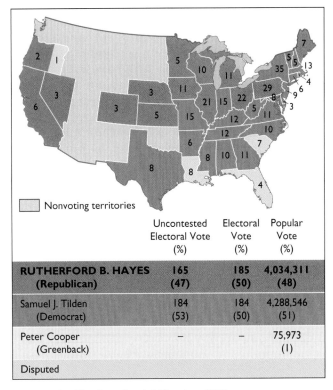

	Uncontested Electoral Vote (%)	Electoral Vote (%)	Popular Vote (%)
RUTHERFORD B. HAYES (Republican)	**165** **(47)**	**185** **(50)**	**4,034,311** **(48)**
Samuel J. Tilden (Democrat)	184 (53)	184 (50)	4,288,546 (51)
Peter Cooper (Greenback)	–	–	75,973 (1)
Disputed			

Legend: ☐ Nonvoting territories

Map 16-4 The Presidential Election, 1876.
In 1876 the Democratic presidential candidate, Samuel Tilden, won the popular vote but was denied the presidency because the Republicans who controlled Congress chose to interpret voting irregularities in Louisiana, South Carolina, Oregon, and Florida in a way that gave their candidate, Rutherford B. Hayes, all of the disputed electoral votes.

in South Carolina, Louisiana, Florida, and Oregon threw the results into doubt.

If all of the electoral votes from those states had gone to Hayes, he would have won. But if even a single electoral vote had gone to Tilden, a Democrat would have won election to the presidency for the first time in 20 years. The outcome was determined by an electoral commission with a Republican majority, and the commission awarded every one of the disputed electoral votes to the Republican candidate. Ever since then the odor of corruption has hovered about the 1876 presidential election. When Hayes was inaugurated on March 4, 1877, the legitimacy of his presidency was already in doubt. But what he did shortly after taking office made it appear as though he had won the presidency thanks to a sordid "compromise" with the Democrats to bring an end to Reconstruction in the South. There is no solid evidence that such a deal was ever actually made. Nevertheless, the new president almost immediately ordered the federal troops guarding the Republican statehouses in South Carolina and Louisiana to return to their barracks. This order marked the formal end of military occupation of the South and the symbolic end of the Reconstruction process. By late 1877, every southern state had been redeemed by the Democrats.

The following year the Supreme Court began to issue a series of rulings that further undermined the achievements of Reconstruction. In *Hall v. DeCuir* (1878) the Supreme Court invalidated a Louisiana law that prohibited racial segregation on railroads, steamboats, streetcars and other "common carriers." In 1882, the justices declared unconstitutional a federal criminal statute that was most often used to protect southern African Americans against racially motivated murders and assaults. More importantly, in the Civil Rights Cases of 1883, the Supreme Court sharply narrowed the significance of the Fourteenth Amendment by declaring that it did not pertain to discriminatory practices by private persons. This series of decisions paved the way for the Court's landmark ruling, in *Plessy v. Ferguson* (1896), that the Constitution permitted

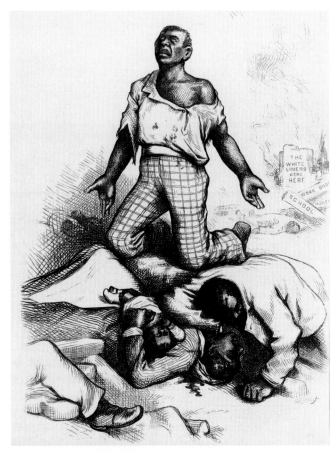

By the mid-1870s the Republican Party lost its zeal to sustain Reconstruction. In many parts of the South, violent repression left African Americans feeling abandoned by the Republican Party to which they had been so loyal.

"separate but equal" facilities for African Americans and whites on America's railroads. The Supreme Court thus put the finishing touches on the national retreat from Reconstruction.

Conclusion

Inspired by an idealized vision of a political economy based on free labor, Republicans expected emancipation to bring about a dramatic transformation of the South. Freed from the shackles of the "slave power," they thought, the entire region would soon become a shining example of democracy and prosperity. If the results were less than Republicans expected, the achievements of Reconstruction were nonetheless impressive. Across the South, African-American men and women carved out a space in which their families could live more freely than

CHRONOLOGY

1863   Lincoln's Proclamation of Amnesty and
        Reconstruction

1864   Wade-Davis Bill

1865   General Sherman's Special Field Order No. 15
        Freedmen's Bureau established
        Lincoln's second inaugural
        Lincoln assassinated. Andrew Johnson
        becomes president.
        General Howard's Circular 13
        President Johnson orders the Freedmen's
        Bureau to return confiscated lands to
        former owners
        Joint Committee on Reconstruction established
        by Congress.

1866   Congress renews Freedmen's Bureau; Johnson
        vetoes renewal bill
        Civil Rights Act vetoed by Johnson
        Congress overrides presidential veto of Civil
        Rights Act
        Congress passes Fourteenth Amendment
        Congress passes another Freedmen's Bureau Bill
        over Johnson's veto
        Johnson begins "swing around the circle"
        Republicans sweep midterm elections

1867   First and Second Reconstruction Acts
        Tenure of Office Act

1868   Johnson fires Secretary of War Stanton
        House of Representatives impeaches Johnson
        Senate trial of Johnson begins
        Acquittal of Johnson
        Fourteenth Amendment ratified
        Ulysses S. Grant wins presidential election

1869   Congress passes Fifteenth Amendment

1870   Fifteenth Amendment ratified

1872   "Liberal Republicans" leave their party
        Grant re-elected

1873   Financial "panic" sets off depression

1875   "Mississippi Plan" succeeds
        Civil Rights Act of 1875 enacted

1876   Disputed presidential election

1877   Electoral commission awards presidency to
        Rutherford B. Hayes

ever before. They established their own churches, sanctified their marriages by law, and educated their children. African-American men by the tens of thousands registered to vote and elected to office some of the most Democratic state legislatures of the nineteenth century. Voting with their feet, thousands more African-American workers repudiated an objectionable contract labor system in favor of an innovative compromise known as sharecropping. Furthermore, Reconstruction added three important amendments to the Constitution, amendments that transformed civil rights and electoral laws not only in the South but throughout the nation.

Nevertheless, the Republicans washed their hands of Reconstruction with unseemly haste. Instead of a shining example of prosperity, the political economy of sharecropping held the South in poverty and colonial dependency. Unable to attract capital investment from without, the "New South" was too poor to sustain an economic boom on its own. The Republicans also left the former slaves unprotected in a hostile world. Sharecropping offered them a degree of personal autonomy but little hope of real economic independence. Democratic redeemers excluded African Americans from the substance of power. Tired of the whole Reconstruction process, Americans turned their attention to the new and difficult problems of urban and industrial America.

Review Questions

1. Why was the "Banks Plan" in Louisiana so controversial?

2. What was the fate of the various efforts to redistribute southern land among the freed people?

3. What was so "radical" about Radical Reconstruction?

4. Why was Andrew Johnson impeached?

5. How did Reconstruction affect the North?

6. What were the major causes for the decline of Radical Reconstruction?

Further Readings

Michael Les Benedict, *The Impeachment and Trial of Andrew Johnson* (1973). Especially strong on the constitutional issues and highly critical of Andrew Johnson.

Dan T. Carter, *When the War Was Over: The Failure of Self-Reconstruction in the West* (1985). Reveals the weaknesses of Presidential Reconstruction.

W. E. B. DuBois, *Black Reconstruction in America, 1860–1880* (1935). This classic is one of the greatest American history books ever written.

Eric Foner, *Reconstruction: America's Unfinished Revolution.* The best one-volume treatment of the period.

John Hope Franklin, *Reconstruction: After the Civil War* (1961). The first modern treatment of African-American politics in the South.

Jacqueline Jones, *Labor of Love, Labor of Sorrow: Black Women, Work, and the Family from Slavery to the Present* (1985). This text includes a pioneering treatment of women's experience of Reconstruction.

Leon Litwack, *Been in the Storm So Long* (1979). This is a detailed and poignant treatment of the former slaves' first experience of freedom.

Roger Ransom and Richard Sutch, *One Kind of Freedom* (1977). The authors provide a clear picture of the breakup of the plantation system and the emergence of sharecropping.

Kenneth M. Stampp, *The Era of Reconstruction* (1965). Stampp gives a lucid overview of events in Washington, D.C.

Mark W. Summers, *The Era of Good Stealings* (1993). *Good Stealings* is a lively treatment of the corruption issue.

History on the Internet

"Finding Precedent: The Impeachment of Andrew Johnson"

http://www.andrewjohnson.com/

By examining the impeachment of President Andrew Johnson, this website explores the major issues behind the impeachment debate and describes the political factions vying to determine Reconstruction policy. The site employs the use of Reconstruction-era editorials and provides biographical sketches and portraits of many of the key figures involved.

"The Black Codes and Reaction to Reconstruction"

http://chnm.gmu.edu/courses/122/recon/code.html

This site contains the text of the Mississippi Black Code and other Reconstruction policies. The site also chronicles citizens' reactions to these policies through contemporary newspaper editorials, magazine articles, and congressional testimony, and it discusses the impact of these reforms on African Americans.

"Civil War and Reconstruction, 1861–1877: Reconstruction and Rights"

http://lcweb2.loc.gov/ammem/ndlpedu/features/timeline/civilwar/civilwar.html/recontwo/recontwo.html

In addition to a good overview of the Civil War and Reconstruction eras, read transcripts of oral histories from whites who actually experienced Reconstruction in the South. Their stories include eyewitness accounts of racially motivated violence in regard to African-American voting.

THE DECLARATION OF INDEPENDENCE

When in the course of human events it becomes necessary for one people to dissolve the political bands which have connected them with another and to assume, among the powers of the earth, the separate and equal station to which the laws of nature and of nature's God entitle them, a decent respect to the opinions of mankind requires that they should declare the causes which impel them to the separation.

We hold these truths to be self-evident, that all men are created equal; that they are endowed by their Creator with certain unalienable rights; that among these are life, liberty, and the pursuit of happiness. That, to secure these rights, governments are instituted among men, deriving their just powers from the consent of the governed; that, whenever any form of government becomes destructive of these ends, it is the right of the people to alter or to abolish it, and to institute a new government, laying its foundation on such principles, and organizing its powers in such form, as to them shall seem most likely to effect their safety and happiness. Prudence, indeed, will dictate that governments long established should not be changed for light and transient causes; and, accordingly, all experience hath shown that mankind are more disposed to suffer, while evils are sufferable, than to right themselves by abolishing the forms to which they are accustomed. But when a long train of abuses and usurpations, pursuing invariably the same object, evinces a design to reduce them under absolute despotism, it is their right, it is their duty, to throw off such government and to provide new guards for their future security. Such has been the patient sufferance of these colonies, and such is now the necessity which constrains them to alter their former systems of government. The history of the present King of Great Britain is a history of repeated injuries and usurpations, all having, in direct object, the establishment of an absolute tyranny over these States. To prove this, let facts be submitted to a candid world:

He has refused his assent to laws the most wholesome and necessary for the public good.

He has forbidden his governors to pass laws of immediate and pressing importance, unless suspended in their operation till his assent should be obtained; and, when so suspended, he has utterly neglected to attend to them.

He has refused to pass other laws for the accommodation of large districts of people, unless those people would relinquish the right of representation in the legislature, a right inestimable to them and formidable to tyrants only.

He has called together legislative bodies at places unusual, uncomfortable, and distant from the depository of their public records, for the sole purpose of fatiguing them into compliance with his measures.

He has dissolved representative houses, repeatedly for opposing, with manly firmness, his invasions on the rights of the people.

He has refused, for a long time after such dissolutions, to cause others to be elected; whereby the legislative powers, incapable of annihilation, have returned to the people at large for their exercise; the state remaining, in the meantime, exposed to all the danger of invasion from without and convulsions within.

He has endeavored to prevent the population of these States; for that purpose, obstructing the laws for naturalization of foreigners, refusing to pass others to encourage their migration hither, and raising the conditions of new appropriations of lands.

He has obstructed the administration of justice by refusing his assent to laws for establishing judiciary powers.

He has made judges dependent on his will alone for the tenure of their offices and the amount and payment of their salaries.

He has erected a multitude of new offices and sent hither swarms of officers to harass our people and eat out their substance.

He has kept among us, in time of peace, standing armies, without the consent of our legislatures.

He has affected to render the military independent of, and superior to, the civil power.

He has combined with others to subject us to a jurisdiction foreign to our Constitution and unacknowledged by our laws, giving his assent to their acts of pretended legislation—

For quartering large bodies of armed troops among us;

For protecting them, by mock trial, from punishment for any murders which they should commit on the inhabitants of these States;

For cutting off our trade with all parts of the world;

For imposing taxes on us without our consent;

For depriving us, in many cases, of the benefit of trial by jury;

For transporting us beyond seas to be tried for pretended offences;

For abolishing the free system of English laws in a neighboring province, establishing therein an arbitrary government, and enlarging its boundaries, so as to render it at once an example and fit instrument for introducing the same absolute rule into these colonies;

For taking away our charters, abolishing our most valuable laws, and altering, fundamentally, the powers of our governments.

For suspending our own legislatures and declaring themselves invested with power to legislate for us in all cases whatsoever.

He has abdicated government here by declaring us out of his protection and waging war against us.

He has plundered our seas, ravaged our coasts, burnt our towns, and destroyed the lives of our people.

He is, at this time, transporting large armies of foreign mercenaries to complete the works of death, desolation, and tyranny already begun with circumstances of cruelty and perfidy scarcely paralleled in the most barbarous ages, and totally unworthy the head of a civilized nation.

He has constrained our fellow citizens, taken captive on the high seas, to bear arms against their country, to become the executioners of their friends and brethren, or to fall themselves by their hands.

He has excited domestic insurrections amongst us and has endeavored to bring on the inhabitants of our frontiers, the merciless Indian savages, whose known rule of warfare is an undistinguished destruction of all ages, sexes, and conditions.

In every stage of these oppressions, we have petitioned for redress in the most humble terms; our repeated petitions have been answered only by repeated injury. A prince whose character is thus marked by every act which may define a tyrant is unfit to be the ruler of a free people.

Nor have we been wanting in attention to our British brethren. We have warned them, from time to time, of attempts made by their legislature to extend an unwarrantable jurisdiction over us. We have reminded them of the circumstances of our emigration and settlement here. We have appealed to their native justice and magnanimity, and we have conjured them, by the ties of our common kindred, to disavow these usurpations, which would inevitably interrupt our connections and correspondence. They, too, have been deaf to the voice of justice and consanguinity. We must, therefore, acquiesce in the necessity which denounces our separation, and hold them, as we hold the rest of mankind, enemies in war, in peace, friends.

We, therefore, the representatives of the United States of America, in general Congress assembled, appealing to the Supreme Judge of the world for the rectitude of our intentions, do, in the name and by the authority of the good people of these colonies, solemnly publish and declare, that these united colonies are, and of right ought to be, free and independent states: that they are absolved from all allegiance to the British Crown, and that all political connection between them and the state of Great Britain is, and ought to be, totally dissolved; and that, as free and independent states, they have full power to levy war, conclude peace, contract alliances, establish commerce, and to do all other acts and things which independent states may of right do. And, for the support of this declaration, with a firm reliance on the protection of Divine Providence, we mutually pledge to each other our lives, our fortunes, and our sacred honor.

THE CONSTITUTION OF THE UNITED STATES OF AMERICA

We the people of the United States, in order to form a more perfect union, establish justice, insure domestic tranquillity, provide for the common defense, promote the general welfare, and secure the blessings of liberty to ourselves and our posterity, do ordain and establish this Constitution for the United States of America.

Article I

SECTION 1. All legislative powers herein granted shall be vested in a Congress of the United States, which shall consist of a Senate and House of Representatives.

SECTION 2. 1. The House of Representatives shall be composed of members chosen every second year by the people of the several States, and the electors in each State shall have the qualifications requisite for electors of the most numerous branch of the State legislature.

2. No person shall be a representative who shall not have attained to the age of twenty-five years, and been seven years a citizen of the United States, and who shall not, when elected, be an inhabitant of that State in which he shall be chosen.

3. Representatives and direct taxes[1] shall be apportioned among the several States which may be included within this Union, according to their respective numbers, which shall be determined by adding to the whole number of free persons, including those bound to service for a term of years, and excluding Indians not taxed, three fifths of all other persons.[2] The actual enumeration shall be made within three years after the first meeting of the Congress of the United States, and within every subsequent term of ten years, in such manner as they shall be law direct. The number of representatives shall not exceed one for every thirty thousand, but each State shall have at least one representative; and until such enumeration shall be made, the State of New Hampshire shall be entitled to choose three, Massachusetts eight, Rhode Island and Providence Plantations one, Connecticut five, New York six, New Jersey four, Pennsylvania eight, Delaware one, Maryland six, Virginia ten, North Carolina five, South Carolina five, and Georgia three.

4. When vacancies happen in the representation from any State, the executive authority thereof shall issue writs of election to fill such vacancies.

5. The House of Representatives shall choose their speaker and other officers; and shall have the sole power of impeachment. → *comes from Eng*

SECTION 3. 1. The Senate of the United States shall be composed of two senators from each State, chosen by the legislature thereof,[3] for six years; and each senator shall have one vote.

2. Immediately after they shall be assembled in consequence of the first election, they shall be divided as equally as may be into three classes. The seats of the senators of the first class shall be vacated at the expiration of the second year, of the second class at the expiration of the fourth year, and of the third class at the expiration of the sixth year, so that one third may be chosen every second year; and if vacancies happen by resignation, or otherwise, during the recess of the legislature of any State, the executive thereof may make temporary appointments until the next meeting of the legislature, which shall then fill such vacancies.[4]

3. No person shall be a senator who shall not have attained to the age of thirty years, and been nine years a citizen of the United States, and who shall not, when elected, be an inhabitant of that State for which he shall be chosen.

4. The Vice President of the United States shall be President of the Senate, but shall have no vote, unless they be equally divided.

5. The Senate shall choose their other officers, and also a president pro tempore, in the absence of the Vice President, or when he shall exercise the office of the President of the United States.

6. The Senate shall have the sole power to try all impeachments. When sitting for that purpose, they shall be on oath or affirmation. When the president of the United States is tried, the chief justice shall preside: and no person shall be convicted without the concurrence of two thirds of the members present.

7. Judgment in cases of impeachment shall not extend further than to removal from office, and disqualification to hold and enjoy any office of honor, trust or profit under the United States: but the party convicted shall nevertheless be liable and subject to indictment, trial, judgment and punishment, according to law.

SECTION 4. 1. The times, places, and manner of holding elections for senators and representatives, shall be prescribed in each State by the legislature thereof; but the Congress may at any time by law make or alter such regulations, except as to the places of choosing senators.

2. The Congress shall assemble at least once in every year, and such meeting shall be on the first Monday in December, unless they shall by law appoint a different day.

SECTION 5. 1. Each House shall be the judge of the elections, returns and qualifications of its own members, and a majority of each shall constitute a quorum to do business; but a smaller number may adjourn from day to day, and may be authorized to compel the attendance of absent members, in such manner, and under such penalties as each House may provide.

2. Each House may determine the rules of its proceedings, punish its members for disorderly behavior, and, with the concurrence of two thirds, expel a member.

3. Each House shall keep a journal of its proceedings, and from time to time publish the same, excepting such parts as may in their judgment require secrecy; and the yeas and nays of the members of either house on any question shall, at the desire of one fifth of those present, be entered on the journal.

4. Neither House, during the session of Congress, shall, without the consent of the other, adjourn for more than three days, nor to any other place than that in which the two Houses shall be sitting.

[1]See the Sixteenth Amendment.
[2]See the Fourteenth Amendment.
[3]See the Seventeenth Amendment.
[4]See the Seventeenth Amendment.

Confederation Congressmen had been paid by indivi. states, some paid new, some didn't

SECTION 6. 1. The senators and representatives shall receive a compensation for their services, to be ascertained by law, and paid out of the Treasury of the United States. They shall in all cases, except treason, felony, and breach of the peace, be privileged from arrest during their attendance at the session of their respective Houses, and in going to and returning from the same; and for any speech or debate in either House, they shall not be questioned in any other place.

2. No senator or representative shall, during the time for which he was elected, be appointed to any civil office under the authority of the United States, which shall have been created, or the emoluments whereof shall have been increased, during such time; and no person holding any office under the United States shall be a member of either House during his continuance in office.

SECTION 7. 1. All bills for raising revenue shall originate in the House of Representatives; but the Senate may purpose or concur with amendments as on other bills.

2. Every bill which shall have passed the House of Representatives and the Senate, shall, before it become a law, be presented to the President of the United States; if he approves he shall sign it, but if not he shall return it, with his objections, to that House in which it shall have originated, who shall enter the objections at large on their journal, and proceed to reconsider it. If after such reconsideration two thirds of that House shall agree to pass the bill, it shall be sent, together with the objections, to the other House, by which it shall likewise be reconsidered, and if approved by two thirds of that House, it shall become a law. But in all such cases the votes of both Houses shall be determined by yeas and nays, and the names of the persons voting for and against the bill shall be entered on the journal of each House respectively. If any bill shall not be returned by the President within ten days (Sundays excepted) after it shall have been presented to him, the same shall be a law, in like manner as if he had signed it, unless the Congress by their adjournment prevent its return, in which case it shall not be a law.

3. Every order, resolution, or vote to which the concurrence of the Senate and the House of Representatives may be necessary (except on a question of adjournment) shall be presented to the President of the United States; and before the same shall take effect, shall be approved by him, or being disapproved by him, shall be repassed by two thirds of the Senate and House of Representatives, according to the rules and limitations prescribed in the case of a bill.

cong. has right to pass resolutions that have force of law, some don't have to have Pres. approval

SECTION 8. The Congress shall have the power

very imp

1. To lay and collect taxes, duties, imposts, and excises, to pay the debts and provide for the common defense and general welfare of the United States; but all duties, imposts, and excises shall be uniform throughout the United States.

2. To borrow money on the credit of the United States; *bonds*

3. To regulate commerce with foreign nations, and among the several States, and with the Indian tribes; *domestic foreign nations*

4. To establish a uniform rule of naturalization, and uniform laws on the subject of bankruptcies throughout the United States;

5. To coin money, regulate the value thereof, and of foreign coin, and fix the standard of weights and measures;

6. To provide for the punishment of counterfeiting the securities and current coin of the United States;

7. To establish post offices and post roads;

8. To promote the progress of science and useful arts, by securing for limited times to authors and inventors the exclusive right to their respective writings and discoveries;

9. To constitute tribunals inferior to the Supreme Court;

10. To define and punish piracies and felonies committed on the high seas, and offenses against the law of nations; *before 1857*

11. To declare war, grant letters of marque and reprisal, and make rules concerning captures on land and water;

12. To raise and support armies, but no appropriation of money to that use shall be for a longer term than two years; *power of purse*

13. To provide and maintain a navy;

14. To make rules for the government and regulation of the land and naval forces; *National Guard*

15. To provide for calling forth the militia to execute the laws of the Union, suppress insurrections and repel invasions;

16. To provide for organizing, arming, and disciplining the militia, and for governing such part of them as may be employed in the service of the United States, reserving to the States respectively, the appointment of the officers, and the authority of training the militia according to the discipline prescribed by Congress;

17. To exercise exclusive legislation in all cases whatsoever, over such district (not exceeding ten miles square) as may, by cession of particular States, and the acceptance of Congress, become the seat of the government of the United States, and to exercise like authority over all places purchased by the consent of

bill → Act or law when Pres. signs it
veto - refuse to sign 2/3 vote → override veto
not possible in Eng.

the legislature of the State in which the same shall be, for the erection of forts, magazines, arsenals, dock-yards, and other needful buildings; and

18. To make all laws which shall be <u>necessary and proper</u> for carrying into execution the foregoing powers, and all other powers vested by this Constitution in the government of the United States, or any department or officer thereof. *elastic clause*

SECTION 9. 1. The migration or importation of such persons as any of the States now existing shall think proper to admit, shall not be prohibited by the Congress prior to the year one thousand eight hundred and eight, but a tax or duty may be imposed on such importation, not exceeding ten dollars for each person. *foreign slave trade*

2. The privilege of the writ of habeas corpus shall not be suspended, unless when in cases of rebellion or invasion the public safety may require it.

3. No bill of attainder or ex post facto law shall be passed.

4. No capitation, or other direct, tax shall be laid, unless in proportion to the census or enumeration herein-before directed to be taken.[5]

5. No tax or duty shall be laid on articles exported from any State.

6. No preference shall be given by any regulation of commerce or revenue to the ports of one State over those of another: nor shall vessels bound to, or from, one State be obliged to enter, clear, or pay duties in another.

7. No money shall be drawn from the treasury, but in consequence of appropriations made by law; and a regular statement and account of the receipts and expenditures of all public money shall be published from time to time.

8. No title of nobility shall be granted by the United States: and no person holding any office of profit or trust under them, shall, without the consent of the Congress, accept of any present, emolument, office, or title, of any kind whatever, from any king, prince, or foreign State. *threshhold is $100,00*

SECTION 10. 1. No State shall enter into any treaty, alliance, or confederation; grant letters of marque and reprisal; coin money; emit bills of credit; make any thing but gold and silver coin a tender in payment of debts; pass any bill of attainder, ex post facto law, or law impairing the obligation of contracts, or grant, any title of nobility. *creditors afraid some*

2. No State shall, without the consent of Congress, lay any imposts or duties on imports or *would be excused for debtors, until depression*

[5]See the Sixteenth Amendment.

owe expressions of cons

exports, except what may be absolutely necessary for executing its inspection laws: and the net produce of all duties and imposts laid by any State on imports or exports, shall be for the use of the treasury of the United States; and all such laws shall be subject to the revision and control of the Congress.

3. No State shall, without the consent of the Congress, lay any duty of tonnage, keep troops, or ships of war in time of peace, enter into any agreement or compact with another State, or with a foreign power, or engage in war, unless actually invaded, or in such imminent danger as will not admit of delay. *War of 1812*

thought slavery would eventually die out

Article II

SECTION 1. 1. The executive power shall be vested in a President of the United States of America. He shall hold his office during the term of four years, and, together with the Vice President, chosen for the same term, be elected, as follows:

2. Each State shall appoint, in such manner as the legislature thereof may direct, a number of electors, equal to the whole number of senators and representatives to which the State may be entitled in the Congress: but no senator or representative, or person holding any office of trust or profit under the United States, shall be appointed an elector.

The electors shall meet in their respective States, and vote by ballot for two persons, of whom one at least shall not be an inhabitant of the same State with themselves. And they shall make a list of all the persons voted for, and of the number of votes for each; which list they shall sign and certify, and transmit sealed to the seat of the government of the United States, directed to the president of the Senate. The president of the Senate shall, in the presence of the Senate and House of Representatives, open all the certificates, and the votes shall then be counted. The person having the greatest number of votes shall be the President, if such number be a majority of the whole number of electors appointed; and if there be more than one who have such majority, and have an equal number of votes, then the House of Representatives shall immediately choose by ballot one of them for President; and if no person have a majority, then from the five highest on the list the said House shall in like manner choose the President. But in choosing the President, the votes shall be taken by States, the representation from each State having one vote; a quorum for this purpose shall consist of a member or members from two thirds of the States, and a majority of all the States shall be necessary to a choice. In every case after the choice of the President, the person having the greatest number of votes of the electors shall be the

until 1800 didn't vote for vice pres. 2nd highest in running for pres. was vice pres.

[handwritten: will not find in original const. words either of these]

Vice President. But if there should remain two or more who have equal votes, the Senate shall choose from them by ballot the Vice President.[6]

3. The Congress may determine the time of choosing the electors, and the day on which they shall give their votes; which day shall be the same throughout the United States.

4. No person except a natural born citizen, or a citizen of the United States, at the time of the adoption of this Constitution, shall be eligible to the office of President; neither shall any person be eligible to the office who shall not have attained to the age of thirty-five years, and been fourteen years a resident within the United States.

5. In case of the removal of the President from office, or of his death, resignation, or inability to discharge the powers and duties of the said office, the same shall devolve on the Vice President, and the Congress may by law provide for the case of removal, death, resignation or inability, both of the President and Vice President, declaring what officer shall then act as President, and such officer shall act accordingly until the disability be removed, or a President shall be elected.

6. The President shall, at stated times, receive for his services a compensation which shall neither be increased nor diminished during the period for which he shall have been elected, and he shall not receive within that period any other emolument from the United States, or any of them.

7. Before he enter on the execution of his office, he shall take the following oath or affirmation:—"I do solemnly swear (or affirm) that I will faithfully execute the office of president of the United States, and will to the best of my ability, preserve, protect and defend the Constitution of the United States."

SECTION 2. 1. The President shall be commander in chief of the army and navy of the United States, and of the militia of the several States, when called into the actual service of the United States; he may require the opinion in writing, of the principal officer in each of the executive departments, upon any subject relating to the duties of their respective offices, and he shall have power to grant reprieves and pardons for offenses against the United States, except in cases of impeachment.

2. He shall have power, by and with the advice and consent of the Senate, to make treaties, provided two thirds of the senators present concur; and he shall nominate, and by and with the advice and consent of

the Senate, shall appoint ambassadors, other public ministers and consuls, judges of the Supreme Court, and all other officers of the United States, whose appointments are not herein otherwise provided for, and which shall be established by law; but the Congress may by law vest the appointment of such inferior officers, as they think proper, in the President alone, in the courts of laws, or in the heads of departments.

3. The President shall have power to fill up all vacancies that may happen during the recess of the Senate, by granting commissions which shall expire at the end of their next session. *[handwritten: recess appointments]*

SECTION 3. He shall from time to time give to the Congress information of the state of the Union, and recommend to their consideration such measures as he shall judge necessary and expedient; he may, on extraordinary occasions, convene both houses, or either of them, and in case of disagreement between them with respect to the time of adjournment, he may adjourn them to such time as he shall think proper; he shall receive ambassadors and other public ministers; he shall take care that the laws be faithfully executed, and shall commission all the officers of the United States. *[handwritten: → declaring govt. is legitimate]*

SECTION 4. The President, Vice President, and all civil officers of the United States, shall be removed from office on impeachment for, and conviction of, treason, bribery, or other high crimes and misdemeanors.

Article III

SECTION 1. The judicial power of the United States shall be vested in one Supreme Court, and in such inferior courts as the Congress may from time to time ordain and establish. The judges, both of the Supreme and inferior courts, shall hold their offices during good behavior, and shall, at stated times, receive for their services, a compensation, which shall not be diminished during their continuance in office.

SECTION 2. 1. The judicial power shall extend to all cases, in law and equity, arising under this Constitution, the laws of the United States, and treaties made, or which shall be made, under their authority;—to all cases of admiralty and maritime jurisdiction;—to controversies to which the United States shall be a party;[7]—to controversies between two or more States;—between a State and citizens of another State;—between citizens of different States;—between citizens of the same State claiming lands under grants of different States, and between a State, or the citizens thereof, and foreign States, citizens or subjects.

---

[6]Superseded by the Twelfth Amendment.

[7]See the Eleventh Amendment.

[handwritten: Sen. was supposed to be like councils]

2. In all cases affecting ambassadors, other public ministers and consuls, and those in which a State shall be party, the Supreme Court shall have original jurisdiction. In all the other cases before mentioned, the Supreme Court shall have appellate jurisdiction, both as to law and fact, with such exceptions, and under such regulations as the Congress shall make.

3. The trial of all crimes, except in cases of impeachment, shall be by jury; and such trial shall be held in the State where the said crimes shall have been committed; but when not committed within any State, the trial shall be such place or places as the Congress may by law have directed.

SECTION 3. 1. Treason against the United States shall consist only in levying war against them, or in adhering to their enemies, giving them aid and comfort. No person shall be convicted of treason unless on the testimony of two witnesses to the same overt act, or on confession in open court.

2. The Congress shall have power to declare the punishment of treason, but no attainder of treason shall work corruption of blood, or forfeiture except during the life of the person attained.

Article IV

SECTION 1. Full faith and credit shall be given in each State to the public acts, records, and judicial proceedings of every other State. And the Congress may by general laws prescribe the manner in which such acts, records and proceedings shall be proved, and the effect thereof.

SECTION 2. 1. The citizens of each State shall be entitled to all privileges and immunities of citizens in the several States.[8]

2. A person charged in any State with treason, felony, or other crime, who shall flee from justice, and be found in another State, shall on demand of the executive authority of the State from which he fled, be delivered up to be removed to the State having jurisdiction of the crime.

3. No person held to service or labor in one State under the laws thereof, escaping into another, shall, in consequence of any law or regulation therein, be discharged from such service or labor, but shall be delivered up on claim of the party to whom such service or labor may be due.[9]

SECTION 3. 1. New States may be admitted by the Congress into this Union; but no new State shall be formed or erected within the jurisdiction of any other

State, nor any State be formed by the junction of two or more States, or parts of States, without the consent of the legislatures of the States concerned as well as of the Congress.

2. The Congress shall have power to dispose of and make all needful rules and regulations respecting the territory or other property belonging to the United States; and nothing in this Constitution shall be so construed as to prejudice any claims of the United States, or of any particular State.

SECTION 4. The United States shall guarantee to every State in this Union a republican form of government, and shall protect each of them against invasion; and on application of the legislature, or of the executive (when the legislature cannot be convened) against domestic violence.

Article V

The Congress, whenever two thirds of both Houses shall deem it necessary, shall propose amendments to this Constitution, or, on the application of the legislatures of two thirds of the several States, shall call a convention for proposing amendments, which in either case shall be valid to all intents and purposes, as part of this Constitution, when ratified by the legislatures of three fourths of the several States, or by conventions in three fourths thereof, as the one or the other mode of ratification may be proposed by the Congress; Provided that no amendment which may be made prior to the year one thousand eight hundred and eight shall in any manner affect the first and fourth clauses in the ninth section of the first article; and that no State, without its consent, shall be deprived of its equal suffrage in the Senate.

Article VI

1. All debts contracted and engagements entered into, before the adoption of this Constitution, shall be as valid against the United States under this Constitution, as under the Confederation.[10]

2. This Constitution, and the laws of the United States which shall be made in pursuance thereof; and all treaties made, or which shall be made, under the authority of the United States, shall be the supreme law of the land; and the judges in every State shall be bound thereby, any thing in the Constitution or laws of any State to the contrary notwithstanding.

3. The senators and representatives before mentioned, and the members of the several State legislatures, and all executive and judicial officers, both

---

[8]See the Fourteenth Amendment, Sec. 1.
[9]See the Thirteenth Amendment.

[10]See the Fourteenth Amendment, Sec. 4.

George Mason was Anglican → didn't want sects taking over

of the United States and of the several States, shall be bound by oath or affirmation to support this Constitution; but no religious test shall ever be required as a qualification to any office or public trust under the United States.

Article VII

The ratification of the conventions of nine States shall be sufficient for the establishment of this Constitution between the States so ratifying the same.

Done in Convention by the unanimous consent of the States present the seventeenth day of September in the year of our Lord one thousand seven hundred and eighty-seven, and of the independence of the United States of America the twelfth. In witness whereof we have hereunto subscribed our names.

Articles in addition to, and amendment of, the Constitution of the United States of America, proposed by Congress, and ratified by the legislatures of the several States, pursuant to the fifth article of the original Constitution.

Amendment I

[First ten amendments ratified December 15, 1791]
Congress shall make no law respecting an establishment of religion, or prohibiting the free exercise thereof; or abridging the freedom of speech, or of the press; or the right of the people peaceably to assemble, and to petition the government for a redress of grievances.

Amendment II

A well regulated militia, being necessary to the security of a free State, the right of the people to keep and bear arms, shall not be infringed.

Amendment III *response to Quartering Act*

No soldier shall, in time of peace be quartered in any house, without the consent of the owner, nor in time of war, but in a manner to be prescribed by law.

Amendment IV

The right of the people to be secure in their persons, houses, papers, and effects, against unreasonable searches and seizures, shall not be violated, and no warrants shall issue, but upon probable cause, supported by oath or affirmation, and particularly describing the place to be searched, and the persons or things to be seized. *Writs of Assistance*

Amendment V *Navigation Acts*

No person shall be held to answer for a capital or otherwise infamous crime, unless on a presentment or indictment of a grand jury, except in cases arising in the land or naval forces, or in the militia, when in actual service in time of war or public danger; nor shall any

you have a right to hide from govt.

person be subject for the same offense to be twice put in jeopardy of life or limb; nor shall be compelled in any criminal case to be a witness against himself, nor be deprived of life, liberty, or property, without due process of law; nor shall private property be taken for public use, without just compensation.

Amendment VI *courts have never defined speedy*

In all criminal prosecutions, the accused shall enjoy the right to a speedy and public trial, by an impartial jury of the State and district wherein the crime shall have been committed, which district shall have been previously ascertained by law, and to be informed of the nature and cause of the accusation; to be confronted with the witnesses against him; to have compulsory process for obtaining witnesses in his favor, and to have the assistance of counsel for his defense.

Amendment VII

In suits at common law, where the value in controversy shall exceed twenty dollars, the right of trial by jury shall be preserved, and no fact tried by a jury shall be otherwise reexamined in any court of the United States, than according to the rules of the common law.

Amendment VIII

Excessive bail shall not be required, nor excessive fines imposed, nor cruel and unusual punishments inflicted.

Amendment IX

The enumeration in the Constitution of certain rights shall not be construed to deny or disparage others retained by the people.

Amendment X

The powers not delegated to the United States by the Constitution, nor prohibited by it to the States, are reserved to the States respectively, or to the people.

Amendment XI [January 8, 1798]

The judicial power of the United States shall not be construed to extend to any suit in law or equity, commenced or prosecuted against one of the United States by citizens of another State, or by citizens or subjects of any foreign State.

Amendment XII [September 25, 1804]

The electors shall meet in their respective States, and vote by ballot for President and Vice President, one of whom, at least, shall not be an inhabitant of the same State with themselves; they shall name in their ballots the person voted for as President, and in distinct ballots the person voted for as Vice President, and they shall make distinct lists of all persons voted for as President and of all persons voted for as Vice President, and of the number of votes for each, which lists they shall sign and certify, and transmit sealed to the seat of the government of the United States, directed to the President of the Senate;—The President of the Senate shall, in the presence of the Senate and House of Representatives, open all the certificates and the votes shall then be counted;—The person having the greatest number of votes for President, shall be the President, if such number be a majority of the whole number of electors appointed; and if no person have such majority, then from the persons having the highest numbers not exceeding three on the list of those voted for as President, the House of Representatives shall choose immediately, by ballot, the President. But in choosing the President, the votes shall be taken by States, the representation from each State having one vote; a quorum for this purpose shall consist of a member or members from two thirds of the States, and a majority of all the States shall be necessary to a choice. And if the House of Representatives shall not choose a President whenever the right of choice shall devolve upon them, before the fourth day of March next following, then the Vice President shall act as President, as in the case of the death or other constitutional disability of the President. The person having the greatest number of votes as Vice President shall be the Vice President, if such number be a majority of the whole number of electors appointed, and if no person have a majority, then from the two highest numbers on the list, the Senate shall choose the Vice President; a quorum for the purpose shall consist of two thirds of the whole number of Senators, and a majority of the whole number shall be necessary to a choice. But no person constitutionally ineligible to the office of president shall be eligible to that of Vice President of the United States.

Amendment XIII [December 18, 1865]

SECTION 1. Neither slavery nor involuntary servitude, except as punishment for crime whereof the party shall have been duly convicted, shall exist within the United States, or any place subject to their jurisdiction.

SECTION 2. Congress shall have power to enforce this article by appropriate legislation.

Amendment XIV [July 28, 1868]

SECTION 1. All persons born or naturalized in the United States, and subject to the jurisdiction thereof, are citizens of the United States and of the State wherein they reside. No State shall make or enforce any law which shall abridge the privileges or immunities of citizens of the United States; nor shall any State deprive any person of life, liberty, or property, without due process of law; nor deny to any person within its jurisdiction the equal protection of the laws.

SECTION 2. Representatives shall be apportioned among the several States according to their respective numbers, counting the whole number of persons in each State, excluding Indians not taxed. But when the right to vote at any election for the choice of electors for President and Vice President of the United States, representatives in Congress, the executive and judicial officers of a State, or the members of the legislature thereof, is denied to any of the male inhabitants of such State, being twenty-one years of age, and citizens of the United States, or in any way abridged, except for participating in rebellion, or other crime, the basis of representation there shall be reduced in the proportion which the number of such male citizens shall bear to the whole number of male citizens twenty-one years of age in such State.

SECTION 3. No person shall be a senator or representative in Congress, or elector of President and Vice President, or hold any office, civil or military, under the United States, or under any State, who having previously taken an oath, as a member of Congress, or as an officer of the United States, or as a member of any State legislature, or as an executive or judicial officer of any State, to support the Constitution of the United States, shall have engaged in insurrection or rebellion against the same, or given aid or comfort to the enemies thereof. But Congress may by a vote of two thirds of each House, remove such disability.

SECTION 4. The validity of the public debt of the United States, authorized by law, including debts incurred for payment of pensions and bounties for services in suppressing insurrection or rebellion; shall not be questioned. But neither the United States nor any State shall assume or pay any debt or obligation incurred in aid of insurrection or rebellion against the United States, or any claim for the loss or emancipation of any slave; but all such debts, obligations, and claims shall be held illegal and void.

SECTION 5. The Congress shall have the power to enforce, by appropriate legislation, the provisions of this article.

Amendment XV [March 30, 1870]

SECTION 1. The right of citizens of the United States to vote shall not be denied or abridged by the United States or by any State on account of race, color, or previous condition of servitude.

SECTION 2. The Congress shall have power to enforce this article by appropriate legislation.

Amendment XVI [February 25, 1913]
The Congress shall have power to lay and collect taxes on incomes, from whatever source derived, without apportionment among the several States, and without regard to any census or enumeration.

Amendment XVII [May 31, 1913]
The Senate of the United States shall be composed of two senators from each State, elected by the people thereof, for six years; and each senator shall have one vote. The electors in each State shall have the qualifications requisite for electors of the most numerous branch of the State legislature.

When vacancies happen in the representation of any State in the Senate, the executive authority of such State shall issue writs of election to fill such vacancies: *Provided,* That the legislature of any State may empower the executive thereof to make temporary appointments until the people fill the vacancies by election as the legislature may direct.

This amendment shall not be so construed as to affect the election or term of any senator chosen before it becomes valid as part of the Constitution.

Amendment XVIII[11] [January 29, 1919]
After one year from the ratification of this article, the manufacture, sale, or transportation of intoxicating liquors within, the importation thereof into, or the exportation thereof from the United States and all territory subject to the jurisdiction thereof for beverage purposes is thereby prohibited.

The Congress and the several States shall have concurrent power to enforce this article by appropriate legislation.

This article shall be inoperative unless it shall have been ratified as an amendment to the Constitution by the legislatures of the several States, as provided in the Constitution, within seven years from the date of the submission hereof to the States by Congress.

Amendment XIX [August 26, 1920]
The right of citizens of the United States to vote shall not be denied or abridged by the United States or by any State on account of sex.

Congress shall have the power to enforce this article by appropriate legislation.

Amendment XX [January 23, 1933]
SECTION 1. The terms of the President and Vice President shall end at noon on the 20th day of January and the terms of Senators and Representatives at noon on the 3d day of January, of the years in which such terms would have ended if this article had not been ratified; and the terms of their successors shall then begin.

SECTION 2. The Congress shall assemble at least once in every year, and such meeting shall begin at noon on the 3d day of January, unless they shall by law appoint a different day.

SECTION 3. If, at the time fixed for the beginning of the term of president, the President-elect shall have died, the Vice President-elect shall become President. If a President shall not have been chosen before the time fixed for the beginning of his term, or if the President-elect shall have failed to qualify, then the Vice President-elect shall act as president until a President shall have qualified; and the Congress may by law provide for the case wherein neither a President-elect nor a Vice President-elect shall have qualified, declaring who shall then act as President, or the manner in which one who is to act shall be selected, and such person shall act accordingly until a President or Vice President shall have qualified.

SECTION 4. The Congress may by law provide for the case of the death of any of the persons from whom, the House of Representatives may choose a President whenever the right of choice shall have devolved upon them, and for the case of the death of any of the persons from whom the Senate may choose a Vice President whenever the right of choice shall have devolved upon them.

SECTION 5. Sections 1 and 2 shall take effect on the 15th day of October following the ratification of this article.

SECTION 6. This article shall be inoperative unless it shall have been ratified as an amendment to the Constitution by the legislatures of three-fourths of the several States within seven years from the date of its submission.

Amendment XXI [December 5, 1933]
SECTION 1. The Eighteenth Article of amendment to the Constitution of the United States is hereby repealed.

SECTION 2. The transportation or importation into any State, Territory, or possession of the United States for delivery or use therein of intoxicating liquors in violation of the laws thereof, is hereby prohibited.

SECTION 3. This article shall be inoperative unless it shall have been ratified as an amendment to the Constitution by conventions in the several States, as provided in the Constitution, within seven years from the date of the submission thereof to the States by the Congress.

[11]Repealed by the Twenty-first Amendment.

Amendment XXII [March 1, 1951]

No person shall be elected to the office of the President more than twice, and no person who has held the office of President, or acted as President, for more than two years of a term to which some other person was elected President shall be elected to the office of the President more than once.

But this article shall not apply to any person holding the office of President when this article was proposed by the Congress, and shall not prevent any person who may be holding the office of President, or acting as President, during the term within which this article becomes operative from holding the office of President or acting as President during the remainder of such term.

This article shall be inoperative unless it shall have been ratified as an amendment to the Constitution by the legislatures of three-fourths of the several States within seven years from the date of its submission to the States by the Congress.

Amendment XXIII [March 29, 1961]

SECTION 1. The District constituting the seat of Government of the United States shall appoint in such manner as the Congress may direct.

A number of electors of President and Vice President equal to the whole number of Senators and Representatives in Congress to which the District would be entitled if it were a State, but in no event more than the least populous State; they shall be in addition to those appointed by the States, but they shall be considered, for the purposes of the election of President and Vice Present, to be electors appointed by a State; and they shall meet in the District and perform such duties as provided by the twelfth article of amendment.

SECTION 2. The Congress shall have power to enforce this article by appropriate legislation.

Amendment XXIV [January 23, 1964]

SECTION 1. The right of citizens of the United States to vote in any primary or other election for President or Vice President, for electors for President or Vice President, or for Senator or Representative in Congress, shall not be denied or abridged by the United States or any State by reason of failure to pay any poll tax or other tax.

SECTION 2. The Congress shall have power to enforce this article by appropriate legislation.

Amendment XXV [February 10, 1967]

SECTION 1. In case of the removal of the President from office or of his death or resignation, the Vice President shall become President.

SECTION 2. Whenever there is a vacancy in the office of the Vice President, the President shall nominate a Vice President who shall take office upon confirmation by a majority of both Houses of Congress.

SECTION 3. Whenever the President transmits to the President pro tempore of the Senate and the Speaker of the House of Representatives his written declaration that he is unable to discharge the powers and duties of his office, and until he transmits to them a written declaration to the contrary, such powers and duties shall be discharged by the Vice President as Acting President.

SECTION 4. Whenever the Vice President and a majority of either the principal officers of the executive departments or of such other body as Congress may by law provide, transmit to the President pro tempore of the Senate and the Speaker of the House of Representatives their written declaration that the President is unable to discharge the powers and duties of his office, the Vice President shall immediately assume the powers and duties of the office as Acting President.

Thereafter, when the President transmits to the President pro tempore of the Senate and the Speaker of the House of Representatives his written declaration that no inability exists, he shall resume the powers and duties of his office unless the Vice President and a majority of either the principal officers of the executive departments or of such other body as Congress may by law provide, transmit within four days to the President pro tempore of the Senate and the Speaker of the House of Representatives their written declaration that the President is unable to discharge the powers and duties of his office. Thereupon Congress shall decide the issue, assembling within forty-eight hours for that purpose if not in session. If the Congress, within twenty-one days after receipt of the latter written declaration, or, if Congress is not in session, within twenty-one days after Congress is required to assemble, determines by two-thirds vote of both houses that the President is unable to discharge the powers and duties of his office, the Vice President shall continue to discharge the same as Acting President; otherwise, the President shall resume the powers and duties of his office.

Amendment XXVI [June 30, 1971]

SECTION 1. The right of citizens of the United States who are eighteen years of age or older to vote shall not be denied or abridged by the United States or by any State on account of age.

SECTION 2. The Congress shall have power to enforce this article by appropriate legislation.

Presidents and Vice Presidents

1. George Washington (1789)
   John Adams (1789)
2. John Adams (1797)
   Thomas Jefferson (1797)
3. Thomas Jefferson (1801)
   Aaron Burr (1801)
   George Clinton (1805)
4. James Madison (1809)
   George Clinton (1809)
   Elbridge Gerry (1813)
5. James Monroe (1817)
   Daniel D. Tompkins (1817)
6. John Quincy Adams (1825)
   John C. Calhoun (1825)
7. Andrew Jackson (1829)
   John C. Calhoun (1829)
   Martin Van Buren (1833)
8. Martin Van Buren (1837)
   Richard M. Johnson (1837)
9. William H. Harrison (1841)
   John Tyler (1841)
10. John Tyler (1841)
11. James K. Polk (1845)
    George M. Dallas (1845)
12. Zachary Taylor (1849)
    Millard Fillmore (1849)
13. Millard Fillmore (1850)
14. Franklin Pierce (1853)
    William R. King (1853)
15. James Buchanan (1857)
    John C. Breckinridge (1857)
16. Abraham Lincoln (1861)
    Hannibal Hamlin (1861)
    Andrew Johnson (1865)
17. Andrew Johnson (1865)
18. Ulysses S. Grant (1869)
    Schuyler Colfax (1869)
    Henry Wilson (1873)
19. Rutherford B. Hayes (1877)
    William A. Wheeler (1877)
20. James A. Garfield (1881)
    Chester A. Arthur (1881)
21. Chester A. Arthur (1881)
22. Grover Cleveland (1885)
    T. A. Hendricks (1885)

23. Benjamin Harrison (1889)
    Levi P. Morton (1889)
24. Grover Cleveland (1893)
    Adlai E. Stevenson (1893)
25. William McKinley (1897)
    Garret A. Hobart (1897)
    Theodore Roosevelt (1901)
26. Theodore Roosevelt (1901)
    Charles Fairbanks (1905)
27. William H. Taft (1909)
    James S. Sherman (1909)
28. Woodrow Wilson (1913)
    Thomas R. Marshall (1913)
29. Warren G. Harding (1921)
    Calvin Coolidge (1921)
30. Calvin Coolidge (1923)
    Charles G. Dawes (1925)
31. Herbert C. Hoover (1929)
    Charles Curtis (1929)
32. Franklin D. Roosevelt (1933)
    John Nance Garner (1933)
    Henry A. Wallace (1941)
    Harry S Truman (1945)
33. Harry S Truman (1945)
    Alben W. Barkley (1949)
34. Dwight D. Eisenhower (1953)
    Richard M. Nixon (1953)
35. John F. Kennedy (1961)
    Lyndon B. Johnson (1961)
36. Lyndon B. Johnson (1963)
    Hubert H. Humphrey (1965)
37. Richard M. Nixon (1969)
    Spiro T. Agnew (1969)
    Gerald R. Ford (1973)
38. Gerald R. Ford (1974)
    Nelson A. Rockefeller (1974)
39. James E. Carter Jr. (1977)
    Walter F. Mondale (1977)
40. Ronald W. Reagan (1981)
    George H. W. Bush (1981)
41. George H. W. Bush (1989)
    James D. Quayle III (1989)
42. William J. B. Clinton (1993)
    Albert Gore (1993)
43. George W. Bush (2001)
    Richard Cheney (2001)

Presidential Elections

Year	Number of States	Candidates	Party	Popular Vote*	Electoral Vote†	Percent- age of Popular Vote
1789	11	GEORGE WASHINGTON	No party designations		69	
		John Adams			34	
		Other Candidates			35	
1792	15	GEORGE WASHINGTON	No party designations		132	
		John Adams			77	
		George Clinton			50	
		Other Candidates			5	
1796	16	JOHN ADAMS	Federalist		71	
		Thomas Jefferson	Democratic Republican		68	
		Thomas Pinckney	Federalist		59	
		Aaron Burr	Democratic Republican		30	
		Other Candidates			48	
1800	16	THOMAS JEFFERSON	Democratic Republican		73	
		Aaron Burr	Democratic Republican		73	
		John Adams	Federalist		65	
		Charles C. Pinckney	Federalist		64	
		John Jay	Federalist		1	
1804	17	THOMAS JEFFERSON	Democratic Republican		162	
		Charles C. Pinckney	Federalist		14	
1808	17	JAMES MADISON	Democratic Republican		122	
		Charles C. Pinckney	Federalist		47	
		George Clinton	Democratic Republican		6	
1812	18	JAMES MADISON	Democratic Republican		128	
		DeWitt Clinton	Federalist		89	
1816	19	JAMES MONROE	Democratic Republican		183	
		Rufus King	Federalist		34	
1820	24	JAMES MONROE	Democratic Republican		231	
		John Quincy Adams	Independent Republican		1	
1824	24	JOHN QUINCY ADAMS		108,740	84	30.5
		Andrew Jackson		153,544	99	43.1
		William H. Crawford		46,618	41	13.1
		Henry Clay		47,136	37	13.2
1828	24	ANDREW JACKSON	Democrat	647,286	178	56.0
		John Quincy Adams	National Republican	508,064	83	44.0
1832	24	ANDREW JACKSON	Democrat	687,502	219	55.0
		Henry Clay	National Republican	530,189	49	42.4
		William Wirt	Anti-Masonic	} 33,108	7	} 2.6
		John Floyd	National Republican		11	

*Percentage of popular vote given for any election year may not total 100 percent because candidates receiving less than 1 percent of the popular vote have been omitted.

†Prior to the passage of the Twelfth Amendment in 1904, the electoral college voted for two presidential candidates; the runner-up became Vice-President. Data from Historical Statistics of the United States, Colonial Times to 1957 (1961), pp. 682–683, and The World Almanac.

Presidential Elections
(continued)

Year	Number of States	Candidates	Party	Popular Vote	Electoral Vote	Percentage of Popular Vote
1836	26	MARTIN VAN BUREN	Democrat	765,483	170	50.9
		William H. Harrison	Whig		73	
		Hugh L. White	Whig	739,795	26	49.1
		Daniel Webster	Whig		14	
		W. P. Mangum	Whig		11	
1840	26	WILLIAM H. HARRISON	Whig	1,274,624	234	53.1
		Martin Van Buren	Democrat	1,127,781	60	46.9
1844	26	JAMES K. POLK	Democrat	1,338,464	170	49.6
		Henry Clay	Whig	1,300,097	105	48.1
		James G. Birney	Liberty	62,300		2.3
1848	30	ZACHARY TAYLOR	Whig	1,360,967	163	47.4
		Lewis Cass	Democrat	1,222,342	127	42.5
		Martin Van Buren	Free Soil	291,263		10.1
1852	31	FRANKLIN PIERCE	Democrat	1,601,117	254	50.9
		Winfield Scott	Whig	1,385,453	42	44.1
		John P. Hale	Free Soil	155,825		5.0
1856	31	JAMES BUCHANAN	Democrat	1,832,955	174	45.3
		John C. Frémont	Republican	1,339,932	114	33.1
		Millard Fillmore	American ("Know Nothing")	871,731	8	21.6
1860	33	ABRAHAM LINCOLN	Republican	1,865,593	180	39.8
		Stephen A. Douglas	Democrat	1,382,713	12	29.5
		John C. Breckinridge	Democrat	848,356	72	18.1
		John Bell	Constitutional Union	592,906	39	12.6
1864	36	ABRAHAM LINCOLN	Republican	2,206,938	212	55.0
		George B. McClellan	Democrat	1,803,787	21	45.0
1868	37	ULYSSES S. GRANT	Republican	3,013,421	214	52.7
		Horatio Seymour	Democrat	2,706,829	80	47.3
1872	37	ULYSSES S. GRANT	Republican	3,596,745	286	55.6
		Horace Greeley	Democrat	2,843,446	*	43.9
1876	38	RUTHERFORD B. HAYES	Republican	4,036,572	185	48.0
		Samuel J. Tilden	Democrat	4,284,020	184	51.0
1880	38	JAMES A. GARFIELD	Republican	4,453,295	214	48.5
		Winfield S. Hancock	Democrat	4,414,082	155	48.1
		James B. Weaver	Greenback-Labor	308,578		3.4
1884	38	GROVER CLEVELAND	Democrat	4,879,507	219	48.5
		James G. Blaine	Republican	4,850,293	182	48.2
		Benjamin F. Butler	Greenback-Labor	175,370		1.8
		John P. St. John	Prohibition	150,369		1.5
1888	38	BENJAMIN HARRISON	Republican	5,447,129	233	47.9
		Grover Cleveland	Democrat	5,537,857	168	48.6
		Clinton B. Fisk	Prohibition	249,506		2.2
		Alson J. Streeter	Union Labor	146,935		1.3

*Because of the death of Greeley, Democratic electors scattered their votes.

Presidential Elections
(continued)

Year	Number of States	Candidates	Party	Popular Vote	Electoral Vote	Percentage of Popular Vote
1892	44	GROVER CLEVELAND	Democrat	5,555,426	277	46.1
		Benjamin Harrison	Republican	5,182,690	145	43.0
		James B. Weaver	People's	1,029,846	22	8.5
		John Bidwell	Prohibition	264,133		2.2
1896	45	WILLIAM MCKINLEY	Republican	7,102,246	271	51.1
		William J. Bryan	Democrat	6,492,559	176	47.7
1900	45	WILLIAM MCKINLEY	Republican	7,218,491	292	51.7
		William J. Bryan	Democrat; Populist	6,356,734	155	45.5
		John C. Woolley	Prohibition	208,914		1.5
1904	45	THEODORE ROOSEVELT	Republican	7,628,461	336	57.4
		Alton B. Parker	Democrat	5,084,223	140	37.6
		Eugene V. Debs	Socialist	402,283		3.0
		Silas C. Swallow	Prohibition	258,536		1.9
1908	46	WILLIAM H. TAFT	Republican	7,675,320	321	51.6
		William J. Bryan	Democrat	6,412,294	162	43.1
		Eugene V. Debs	Socialist	420,793		2.8
		Eugene W. Chafin	Prohibition	253,840		1.7
1912	48	WOODROW WILSON	Democrat	6,296,547	435	41.9
		Theodore Roosevelt	Progressive	4,118,571	88	27.4
		William H. Taft	Republican	3,486,720	8	23.2
		Eugene V. Debs	Socialist	900,672		6.0
		Eugene W. Chafin	Prohibition	206,275		1.4
1916	48	WOODROW WILSON	Democrat	9,127,695	277	49.4
		Charles E. Hughes	Republican	8,533,507	254	46.2
		A. L. Benson	Socialist	585,113		3.2
		J. Frank Hanly	Prohibition	220,506		1.2
1920	48	WARREN G. HARDING	Republican	16,143,407	404	60.4
		James M. Cox	Democrat	9,130,328	127	34.2
		Eugene V. Debs	Socialist	919,799		3.4
		P. P. Christensen	Farmer-Labor	265,411		1.0
1924	48	CALVIN COOLIDGE	Republican	15,718,211	382	54.0
		John W. Davis	Democrat	8,385,283	136	28.8
		Robert M. La Follette	Progressive	4,831,289	13	16.6
1928	48	HERBERT C. HOOVER	Republican	21,391,993	444	58.2
		Alfred E. Smith	Democrat	15,016,169	87	40.9
1932	48	FRANKLIN D. ROOSEVELT	Democrat	22,809,638	472	57.4
		Herbert C. Hoover	Republican	15,758,901	59	39.7
		Norman Thomas	Socialist	881,951		2.2
1936	48	FRANKLIN D. ROOSEVELT	Democrat	27,752,869	523	60.8
		Alfred M. Landon	Republican	16,674,665	8	36.5
		William Lemke	Union	882,479		1.9
1940	48	FRANKLIN D. ROOSEVELT	Democrat	27,307,819	449	54.8
		Wendell L. Willkie	Republican	22,321,018	82	44.8
1944	48	FRANKLIN D. ROOSEVELT	Democrat	25,606,585	432	53.5
		Thomas E. Dewey	Republican	22,014,745	99	46.0

Presidential Elections
(continued)

Year	Number of States	Candidates	Party	Popular Vote	Electoral Vote	Percentage of Popular Vote
1948	48	HARRY S TRUMAN	Democrat	24,105,812	303	49.5
		Thomas E. Dewey	Republican	21,970,065	189	45.1
		J. Strom Thurmond	States' Rights	1,169,063	39	2.4
		Henry A. Wallace	Progressive	1,157,172		2.4
1952	48	DWIGHT D. EISENHOWER	Republican	33,936,234	442	55.1
		Adlai E. Stevenson	Democrat	27,314,992	89	44.4
1956	48	DWIGHT D. EISENHOWER	Republican	35,590,472	457*	57.6
		Adlai E. Stevenson	Democrat	26,022,752	73	42.1
1960	50	JOHN F. KENNEDY	Democrat	34,227,096	303†	49.9
		Richard M. Nixon	Republican	34,108,546	219	49.6
1964	50	LYNDON B. JOHNSON	Democrat	42,676,220	486	61.3
		Barry M. Goldwater	Republican	26,860,314	52	38.5
1968	50	RICHARD M. NIXON	Republican	31,785,480	301	43.4
		Hubert H. Humphrey	Democrat	31,275,165	191	42.7
		George C. Wallace	American Independent	9,906,473	46	13.5
1972	50	RICHARD M. NIXON‡	Republican	47,165,234	520	60.6
		George S. McGovern	Democrat	29,168,110	17	37.5
1976	50	JIMMY CARTER	Democrat	40,828,929	297	50.1
		Gerald R. Ford	Republican	39,148,940	240	47.9
		Eugene McCarthy	Independent	739,256		0.9
1980	50	RONALD REAGAN	Republican	43,201,220	489	50.9
		Jimmy Carter	Democrat	34,913,332	49	41.2
		John B. Anderson	Independent	5,581,379		6.6
1984	50	RONALD REAGAN	Republican	53,428,357	525	59.0
		Walter F. Mondale	Democrat	36,930,923	13	41.0
1988	50	GEORGE H. W. BUSH	Republican	48,901,046	426	53.4
		Michael Dukakis	Democrat	41,809,030	111	45.6
1992	50	BILL CLINTON	Democrat	43,728,275	370	43.2
		George Bush	Republican	38,167,416	168	37.7
		H. Ross Perot	United We Stand, America	19,237,247		19.0
1996	50	BILL CLINTON	Democrat	45,590,703	379	49.0
		Bob Dole	Republican	37,816,307	159	41.0
		H. Ross Perot	Reform	7,866,284		8.0
2000	50	GEORGE W. BUSH	Republican	50,456,169	271	48.0
		Al Gore	Democrat	50,996,116	266	48.0
		Ralph Nader	Green	2,767,176	0	3.0

*Walter B. Jones received 1 electoral vote.

†Harry F. Byrd received 15 electoral votes.

‡Resigned August 9, 1974: Vice President Gerald R. Ford became President.

Admission of States into the Union

State	Date of Admission	State	Date of Admission
1. Delaware	December 7, 1787	26. Michigan	January 26, 1837
2. Pennsylvania	December 12, 1787	27. Florida	March 3, 1845
3. New Jersey	December 18, 1787	28. Texas	December 29, 1845
4. Georgia	January 2, 1788	29. Iowa	December 28, 1846
5. Connecticut	January 9, 1788	30. Wisconsin	May 29, 1848
6. Massachusetts	February 6, 1788	31. California	September 9, 1850
7. Maryland	April 28, 1788	32. Minnesota	May 11, 1858
8. South Carolina	May 23, 1788	33. Oregon	February 14, 1859
9. New Hampshire	June 21, 1788	34. Kansas	January 29, 1861
10. Virginia	June 25, 1788	35. West Virginia	June 20, 1863
11. New York	July 26, 1788	36. Nevada	October 31, 1864
12. North Carolina	November 21, 1789	37. Nebraska	March 1, 1867
13. Rhode Island	May 29, 1790	38. Colorado	August 1, 1876
14. Vermont	March 4, 1791	39. North Dakota	November 2, 1889
15. Kentucky	June 1, 1792	40. South Dakota	November 2, 1889
16. Tennessee	June 1, 1796	41. Montana	November 8, 1889
17. Ohio	March 1, 1803	42. Washington	November 11, 1889
18. Louisiana	April 30, 1812	43. Idaho	July 3, 1890
19. Indiana	December 11, 1816	44. Wyoming	July 10, 1890
20. Mississippi	December 10, 1817	45. Utah	January 4, 1896
21. Illinois	December 3, 1818	46. Oklahoma	November 16, 1907
22. Alabama	December 14, 1819	47. New Mexico	January 6, 1912
23. Maine	March 15, 1820	48. Arizona	February 14, 1912
24. Missouri	August 10, 1821	49. Alaska	January 3, 1959
25. Arkansas	June 15, 1836	50. Hawaii	August 21, 1959

DEMOGRAPHICS OF THE UNITED STATES

Population Growth

Year	Population	Percent Increase
1630	4,600	
1640	26,600	478.3
1650	50,400	90.8
1660	75,100	49.0
1670	111,900	49.0
1680	151,500	35.4
1690	210,400	38.9
1700	250,900	19.2
1710	331,700	32.2
1720	466,200	40.5
1730	629,400	35.0
1740	905,600	43.9
1750	1,170,800	29.3
1760	1,593,600	36.1
1770	2,148,100	34.8
1780	2,780,400	29.4
1790	3,929,214	41.3
1800	5,308,483	35.1
1810	7,239,881	36.4
1820	9,638,453	33.1
1830	12,866,020	33.5
1840	17,069,453	32.7
1850	23,191,876	35.9
1860	31,443,321	35.6
1870	39,818,449	26.6
1880	50,155,783	26.0
1890	62,947,714	25.5
1900	75,994,575	20.7
1910	91,972,266	21.0
1920	105,710,620	14.9
1930	122,775,046	16.1
1940	131,669,275	7.2
1950	150,697,361	14.5
1960	179,323,175	19.0
1970	203,235,298	13.3
1980	226,545,805	11.5
1990	248,709,873	9.8
2000	281,421,906	9.0

Source: *Historical Statistics of the United States* (1975); *Statistical Abstract of the United States* (1991); Population Estimates Program, Population Division, U.S. Census Bureau, April 2001. Note: Figures for 1630–1780 include British colonies within limits of present United States only; Native-American population included only in 1930 and thereafter.

Immigration, by origin
(in thousands)

Period	Europe	Americas	Asia
1820–30	106	12	—
1831–40	496	33	—
1841–50	1,597	62	—
1851–60	2,453	75	42
1861–70	2,065	167	65
1871–80	2,272	404	70
1881–90	4,735	427	70
1891–1900	3,555	39	75
1901–10	8,065	362	324
1911–20	4,322	1,144	247
1921–30	2,463	1,517	112
1931–40	348	160	16
1941–50	621	355	32
1951–60	1,326	997	150
1961–70	1,123	1,716	590
1971–80	800	1,983	1,588
1981–90	762	3,616	2,738
1991–2000	1,100	3,800	2,200

Source: *Historical Statistics of the United States* (1975); *Statistical Abstract of the United States* (1991); Population Estimates Program, Population Division, U.S. Census Bureau, April 2001.

Racial Composition of the Population
(in thousands)

Year	White	Black	Indian	Hispanic	Asian
1790	3,172	757	(NA)	(NA)	(NA)
1800	4,306	1,002	(NA)	(NA)	(NA)
1820	7,867	1,772	(NA)	(NA)	(NA)
1840	14,196	2,874	(NA)	(NA)	(NA)
1860	26,923	4,442	(NA)	(NA)	(NA)
1880	43,403	6,581	(NA)	(NA)	(NA)
1900	66,809	8,834	(NA)	(NA)	(NA)
1910	81,732	9,828	(NA)	(NA)	(NA)
1920	94,821	10,463	(NA)	(NA)	(NA)
1930	110,287	11,891	(NA)	(NA)	(NA)
1940	118,215	12,866	(NA)	(NA)	(NA)
1950	134,942	15,042	(NA)	(NA)	(NA)
1960	158,832	18,872	(NA)	(NA)	(NA)
1970	178,098	22,581	(NA)	(NA)	(NA)
1980	194,713	26,683	1,420	14,609	3,729
1990	208,704	30,483	2,065	22,354	7,458
2000	226,861	35,470	2,448	31,387	11,279

Source: *U.S. Bureau of the Census, U.S. Census of Population: 1940, vol. II, part 1, and vol. IV, part 1; 1950, vol. II, part 1; 1960, vol. I, part 1; 1970, vol. I, part B; and Current Population Reports, P25-1095 and P25-1104; and unpublished data*; Population Estimates Program, Population Division, U.S. Census Bureau, January 2001.

Work Force

Year	Total Number Workers (1000s)	Farmers as % of Total	Women as % of Total	% Workers in Unions
1810	2,330	84	(NA)	(NA)
1840	5,660	75	(NA)	(NA)
1860	11,110	53	(NA)	(NA)
1870	12,506	53	15	(NA)
1880	17,392	52	15	(NA)
1890	23,318	43	17	(NA)
1900	29,073	40	18	3
1910	38,167	31	21	6
1920	41,614	26	21	12
1930	48,830	22	22	7
1940	53,011	17	24	27
1950	59,643	12	28	25
1960	69,877	8	32	26
1970	82,049	4	37	25
1980	108,544	3	42	23
1990	117,914	3	45	16
2000	140,900	5.5	47	18.6

Source: *Historical Statistics of the United States* (1975); *Statistical Abstract of the United States* (1991 and 1996); Population Estimates Program, Population Division, U.S. Census Bureau, April 2001.

Vital Statistics
(in thousands)

Year	Births	Deaths	Marriages	Divorces
1800	55	(NA)	(NA)	(NA)
1810	54.3	(NA)	(NA)	(NA)
1820	55.2	(NA)	(NA)	(NA)
1830	51.4	(NA)	(NA)	(NA)
1840	51.8	(NA)	(NA)	(NA)
1850	43.3	(NA)	(NA)	(NA)
1860	44.3	(NA)	(NA)	(NA)
1870	38.3	(NA)	9.6 (1867)	0.3 (1867)
1880	39.8	(NA)	9.1 (1875)	0.3 (1875)
1890	31.5	(NA)	9.0	0.5
1900	32.3	17.2	9.3	0.7
1910	30.1	14.7	10.3	0.9
1920	27.7	13.0	12.0	1.6
1930	21.3	11.3	9.2	1.6
1940	19.4	10.8	12.1	2.0
1950	24.1	9.6	11.1	2.6
1960	23.7	9.5	8.5	2.2
1970	18.4	9.5	10.6	3.5
1980	15.9	8.8	10.6	5.2
1990	16.7	8.6	9.8	4.7
2000	14.8	8.8	8.5	4.1

Source: *Historical Statistics of the United States* (1975); *Statistical Abstract of the United States* (1999) CDC 2000 National Vital Statistics Report, Vol. 49, No. 6, 8/22/01.

The Economy and Federal Spending

Year	Gross National Product (GNP) (in billions)	Foreign Trade (in millions)			Federal Budget (in billions)	Federal Surplus/Deficit (in billions)	Federal Debt (in billions)
		Exports	Imports	Balance of Trade			
1790	(NA)	$ 20	$ 23	$ −3	$ 0.004	$+0.00015	$ 0.076
1800	(NA)	71	91	−20	0.011	+0.0006	0.083
1810	(NA)	67	85	−18	0.008	+0.0012	0.053
1820	(NA)	70	74	−4	0.018	−0.0004	0.091
1830	(NA)	74	71	+3	0.015	+0.100	0.049
1840	(NA)	132	107	+25	0.024	−0.005	0.004
1850	(NA)	152	178	−26	0.040	+0.004	0.064
1860	(NA)	400	362	+38	0.063	−0.01	0.065
1870	$ 7.4	451	462	−11	0.310	+0.10	2.4
1880	11.2	853	761	+92	0.268	+0.07	2.1
1890	13.1	910	823	+87	0.318	+0.09	1.2
1900	18.7	1,499	930	+569	0.521	+0.05	1.2
1910	35.3	1,919	1,646	+273	0.694	−0.02	1.1
1920	91.5	8,664	5,784	+2,880	6.357	+0.3	24.3
1930	90.7	4,013	3,500	+513	3.320	+0.7	16.3
1940	100.0	4,030	7,433	−3,403	9.6	−2.7	43.0
1950	286.5	10,816	9,125	+1,691	43.1	−2.2	257.4
1960	506.5	19,600	15,046	+4,554	92.2	+0.3	286.3
1970	992.7	42,700	40,189	+2,511	195.6	−2.8	371.0
1980	2,631.7	220,783	244,871	−24,088	590.9	−73.8	907.7
1990	5,524.5	394,030	494,042	−100,012	1,251.8	−220.5	3,233.3
2000	9,860.8	773,304	1,222,772	−449,468	1,765.7	+117.3	5,686.0

Source: *U.S. Office of Management and Budget, Budget of the United States Government, annual; Statistical Abstract of the United States, 2000.*

GLOSSARY

Arminianism Religious doctrine developed by the Dutch theologian Jacobus Arminius that argued that men and women had free will and suggested that hence they could earn their way into heaven by good works.

Armistice A cessation of hostilities by agreement among the opposing sides; a cease-fire.

Associationalism President Herbert Hoover's preferred method of responding to the depression. Rather than have the government directly involve itself in the economy, Hoover hoped to use the government to bring together "associations" of businessmen to cooperate with one another in responding to the economic crisis.

Autarky At the height of the world depression, industrial powers sought to isolate their economies within self-contained spheres, generally governed by rigid national (or imperial) economic planning. Japan's Co-Prosperity Sphere, the Soviet Union, and the British Empire each comprised a more or less closed economic unit. The goal of these autarkies was to build an internal market while reducing trade with the outside world.

Benevolent Empire The loosely affiliated network of charitable reform associations that emerged in the United States (especially in urban areas) in response to widespread revivalism of the early nineteenth century.

Berdache In Indian societies, a man who dressed and adopted the mannerisms of women and had sex only with other men. In Native American culture, the *berdache,* half man and half woman, symbolized cosmic harmony.

Budget deficit The failure of tax revenues to pay for annual federal spending on military, welfare, and other programs. The resulting budget deficits forced Washington to borrow money to cover its costs. The growing budget deficits were controversial, in part because the government's borrowing increased both its long-term debt and the amount of money it had to spend each year to pay for the interest on loans.

Busing The controversial, court-ordered practice of sending children by bus to public schools outside their neighborhoods in order to promote racial integration in the schools.

Calvinism Religious doctrine developed by the theologian John Calvin that argued that God alone determines who will receive salvation and hence, men and women cannot earn their own salvation or even be certain about their final destinies.

Carpetbagger A derogatory term referring to northern whites who moved to the South after the Civil War. Stereotyped as corrupt and unprincipled, "carpetbaggers" were in fact a diverse group motivated by a variety of interests and beliefs.

Charter colony Colony established by a trading company or other group of private entrepreneurs who received a grant of land and the right to govern it from the king. The charter colonies included Virginia, Plymouth, Massachusetts Bay, Rhode Island, and Connecticut.

City busting As late as the 1930s, President Roosevelt and most Americans regarded attacking civilians from the air as an atrocity, but during World War II cities became a primary target for U.S. warplanes. The imprecise nature of bombardment, combined with racism and the belief that Japanese and German actions justified retaliation, led American air commanders to follow a policy of systematically destroying urban areas, particularly in Japan.

Communist Member of the Communist Party or follower of the doctrines of Karl Marx. The term (or accusation) was applied more broadly in the twentieth century to brand labor unionists, progressives, civil rights workers, and other reformers as agents of a foreign ideology.

Communitarians Individuals who supported and/or took up residence in separate communities created to embody improved plans of social, religious, and/or economic life.

Commutation The controversial policy of allowing potential draftees to pay for a replacement to serve in the Army. The policy was adopted by both the Union and Confederate governments during the Civil War, and in both cases opposition to commutation was so intense that the policy was abandoned.

Consent One of the key principles of liberalism, which held that people could not be subject to laws to which they had not given their consent. This principle is reflected in both the Declaration of Independence and the preamble to the Constitution, which begins with the famous words, "We the people of the United States, in order to form a more perfect union."

Constitutionalism A loose body of thought that developed in Britain and the colonies and was used by the colonists to justify the Revolution by claiming that it was in accord with the principles of the British Constitution. Constitutionalism had two main elements. One was the rule of law, and the other, the principle of consent, that one cannot be subjected to laws or taxation except by duly elected representatives. Both were rights that had been won through struggle with the monarch.

Consumer revolution A slow and steady increase over the course of the eighteenth century in the demand for, and purchase of, consumer goods. The consumer revolution of the eighteenth century was closely related to the *industrious revolution.*

Consumerism The emerging ideology that defined the purchase of goods and services as basic to individual identity and essential to the national economy. Increasingly powerful by the 1920s and dominant by the 1950s, consumerism urged people to find happiness in the pursuit of leisure and pleasure more than in the work ethic.

Containment The basic U.S. strategy for fighting the cold war. Used by diplomat George Kennan in a 1947 magazine article, "containment" referred to the combination of diplomatic, economic, and military programs necessary to hold back Soviet expansionism after World War II.

Cooperationists Those southerners who opposed immediate secession after the election of Abraham Lincoln in 1860. Cooperationists argued instead that secessionists should wait to see if the new president was willing to "cooperate" with the South's demands.

Copperhead A northerner who sympathized with the South during the Civil War.

Deindustrialization The reverse of industrialization, as factory shutdowns decreased the size of the manufacturing sector. Plant closings began to plague the American economy in the 1970s, prompting fears that the nation would lose its industrial base.

Democratic Republicans One of the two parties to make up the first American party system. Following the fiscal and political views of Jefferson and Madison, Democratic Republicans generally advocated a weak federal government and opposed federal intervention in the economy of the nation.

Détente This French term for the relaxation of tensions was used to describe the central foreign policy innovation of the Nixon administration—a new, less-confrontational relationship with Communism. In addition to opening a dialogue with the People's Republic of China, Nixon sought a more stable, less confrontational relationship with the Soviet Union.

Diffusion The controversial theory that the problem of slavery would be resolved if the slave economy was allowed to expand, or "diffuse," into the western territories. Southerners developed this theory as early as the 1820s in response to northerners who hoped to restrict slavery's expansion.

Disfranchisement   The act of depriving a person or group of voting rights. In the nineteenth century the right to vote was popularly known as the franchise. The Fourteenth Amendment of the Constitution affirmed the right of adult male citizens to vote, but state-imposed restrictions and taxes deprived large numbers of Americans—particularly African Americans—of the vote from the 1890s until the passage of the Voting Rights Act of 1964.

Downsizing   American corporations' layoffs of both blue- and white-collar workers in an attempt to become more efficient and competitive. Downsizing was one of the factors that made Americans uneasy about the economy, despite the impressive surge of the stock market in the 1990s.

Dust Bowl   Across much of the Great Plains decades of wasteful farming practices combined with several years of drought in the early 1930s to produce a series of massive dust storms that blew the topsoil across hundreds of miles. The expansive area afflicted by these storms became known as the Dust Bowl.

E-commerce   Short for "electronic commerce," this was the term for the internet-based buying and selling that was one of the key hopes for the computer-driven postindustrial economy. The promise of e-commerce was still unfulfilled at the start of the twenty-first century.

Encomienda   A new system of labor developed by the Spanish in the New World in which Spanish settlers (*encomenderos*) compelled groups of Native Americans to work for them. The *encomendero* owned neither the land nor the Indians who worked for him, but had the unlimited right to compel a particular group of Indians to work for him. This system was unique to the New World; nothing precisely like it had existed in Spain or elsewhere in Europe.

"Establishment"   The elite of mainly Ivy-League educated, Anglo-Saxon Protestant, male, liberal, northeasterners that supposedly dominated Wall Street and Washington after World War II. The Establishment's support for corporations, activist government, and containment engendered hostility from opposite poles of the political spectrum—from conservatives and Republicans like Richard Nixon at one end and from the New Left and the Movement at the other. Although many of the post-World War II leaders of the United States did tend to share common origins and ideologies, this elite was never as powerful, self-conscious, or unified as its opponents believed.

Eugenics   The practice of attempting to solve social problems through the control of human reproduction. Drawing on the authority of evolutionary biology, eugenists enjoyed considerable influence in the United States, especially on issues of corrections and public health, from the turn of the century through World War II. Applications of this pseudoscience included the identification of "born" criminals by physical characteristics and "better baby" contests at county fairs.

Federalists   One of the two parties to make up the first American party system. Following the fiscal and political policies proposed by Alexander Hamilton, Federalists generally advocated the importance of a strong federal government, including federal intervention in the economy of the new nation.

Feminism   An ideology insisting on the fundamental equality of women and men. The feminists of the 1960s differed over how to achieve that equality: While liberal feminists mostly demanded equal rights for women in the workplace and in politics, radical feminists more thoroughly condemned the capitalist system and male oppression and demanded equality in both private and public life.

Feudalism   A social and political system that developed in Europe in the Middle Ages under which powerful lords offered less powerful noblemen protection in return for their loyalty. Feudalism also included the economic system of *manorialism,* under which dependent serfs worked on the manors controlled by those lords.

Fire-eaters   Militant southerners who pushed for secession in the 1850s.

Flexible Response   The defense doctrine of the Kennedy and Johnson administrations. Abandoning the Eisenhower administration's heavy emphasis on nuclear weapons, Flexible Response stressed the buildup of the nation's conventional and special forces so that the president had a range of military options in response to communist aggression.

Front   Early twentieth-century mechanized wars were fought along a battle line or "front" separating the opposing sides. By World War II, tactical innovations—*blitzkreig,* parachute troops, gliders, and amphibious landings—aimed to break through, disrupt, or bypass the front, which became a more fluid boundary than the fortified trench lines of World War I. The term also acquired a political meaning, particularly for labor and the left. A coalition of parties supporting (or opposing) an agreed-upon line could be called a "popular front."

Gentility   A term without a precise meaning that represented all that was polite, civilized, refined, and fashionable. It was everything that vulgarity, its opposite, was not. Because the term had no precise meaning, it was always subject to negotiation, striving, and anxiety as Americans, beginning in the eighteenth century, tried to show others that they were *genteel* through their manners, their appearance, and their styles of life.

"Glass ceiling"   The invisible barrier of discrimination that prevented female white-collar workers from rising to top executive positions in corporations.

Greenbackers   Those who advocated currency inflation by keeping the money printed during the Civil War, known as "greenbacks," in circulation.

Gridlock   The political traffic jam that tied up the federal government in the late 1980s and 1990s. Gridlock developed from the inability of either major party to control both the presidency and Congress for any extended period of time. More fundamentally, gridlock reflected the inability of any party or president to win a popular mandate for a bold legislative program.

Horizontal integration   More commonly known as "monopoly." An industry was "horizontally integrated" when a single company took control of virtually the entire market for a specific product. John D. Rockefeller's Standard Oil came close to doing this.

Humanism   A Renaissance intellectual movement that focused upon the intellectual and artistic capacities and achievements of humankind. Under the patronage of Queen Isabel, Spain became a center of European humanism.

Immediatism   The variant of antislavery sentiment that demanded immediate (as opposed to gradual) personal and federal action against the institution of slavery. This approach is most closely associated with William Lloyd Garrison and is dated from the publication of Garrison's newspaper, the *Liberator,* in January 1831.

Imperialism   A process of extending dominion over territories beyond the national boundaries of a state. In the eighteenth century, Britain extended imperial control over North America through settlement, but in the 1890s imperial influence was generally exercised through indirect rule. Subject peoples retained some local authority while the imperial power controlled commerce and defense. Few Americans went to the Philippines as settlers, but many passed through as tourists, missionaries, business executives, officials, and soldiers.

Individualism   The social and political philosophy celebrating the central importance of the individual human being in society. Insisting on the rights of the individual in relationship to the group, individualism was one of the intellectual bases of capitalism and democracy. The resurgent individualism of the 1920s, with its emphasis on each American's freedom and fulfillment, was a critical element of the decade's emergent consumerism and Republican dominance.

Industrious revolution   Beginning in the late seventeenth century in Western Europe and extending to the North American colonies in the eighteenth century, a fundamental change in the way that people worked, as they worked harder and organized their households to produce goods that could be sold, so that they would have money to pay for the new consumer goods that they wanted.

Initiative, recall, and referendum First proposed by the People's Party's Omaha platform (1892), along with the direct election of senators and the secret ballot, as measures to subject corporate capitalism to democratic controls. Progressives, chiefly in western and midwestern states, favored them as a check on the power of state officials. The *initiative* allows legislation to be proposed by petition. The *recall* allows voters to remove public officials, and the *referendum* places new laws or constitutional amendments on the ballot for the direct approval of the voters.

Interest group An association whose members organize to exert political pressure on officials or the public. Unlike political parties, whose platforms and slates cover nearly every issue and office, an interest group focuses on a narrower list of concerns reflecting the shared outlook of its members. With the decline of popular politics around the turn of the twentieth century, business, religious, agricultural, women's, professional, neighborhood, and reform associations created a new form of political participation.

Isolationist Between World War I and World War II, the United States refused to join the League of Nations, scaled back its military commitments abroad, and sought to maintain its independence of action on foreign affairs. These policies were called isolationist, although some historians prefer the term "independent internationalist" in recognition of the United States's continuing global influence. In the late 1930s, isolationists favored policies aimed at distancing the United States from European affairs and building a national defense based on air power and hemispheric security.

Joint-stock company a form of business organization that was the forerunner to the modern corporation. The joint-stock company was used to raise both capital and labor for New World ventures. Shareholders contributed either capital or their labor for a period of years.

Judicial nationalism The use of the judiciary to assert the primacy of the national government over state and local government and the legal principle of contract over principles of local custom.

Keynesian Economics The theory, named after the great English economist John Maynard Keynes, that advocated the use of "countercyclical" fiscal policy. This meant that during good times the government should pay down the debt so that, during bad times, it could afford to stimulate the economy with deficit spending.

Liberalism A body of political thought that traces its origins to John Locke and whose chief principles are consent, freedom of conscience, and property. Liberalism held that people could not be governed except by their own consent and that the purpose of government was to protect people, as well as their property.

Linked economic development A form of economic development that ties together a variety of enterprises so that development in one stimulates development in others, for example those that provide raw materials, parts, or transportation.

Manifest Destiny A term first coined in 1845 by journalist John O'Sullivan to express the belief, widespread among antebellum Americans, that the United States was destined to expand across the North American continent to the Pacific and had an irrefutable right to the lands involved in this expansion. This belief was frequently justified on the grounds of claims to political and racial superiority.

Market revolution The term used to designate the period of the early nineteenth century, roughly 1815–1830, during which internal dependence on cash markets and wages became widespread.

Mass production A system of efficient, high volume manufacturing based on division of labor into repetitive tasks, simplification and standardization of parts, increasing use of specialized machinery, and careful supervision. Emerging since the nineteenth century, mass production

reached a critical stage of development with Henry Ford's introduction of the moving assembly line at his Highland Park automobile factory. Mass production drove the prosperity of the 1920s and helped make consumerism possible.

Massive resistance The rallying cry of southern segregationists who pledged to oppose the integration of the schools ordered by the U.S. Supreme Court in *Brown v. Board of Education* in 1954. The tactics of massive resistance included legislation, demonstrations, and violence.

Massive retaliation The defense doctrine of the Eisenhower administration, which promised "instant, massive retaliation" with nuclear weapons in response to Soviet aggression.

McCarthyism The hunt for communist subversion in the United States in the first years of the cold war. Democrats in particular used the term, a reference to the sometimes disreputable tactics of Republican Senator Joseph R. McCarthy of Wisconsin, in order to question the legitimacy of the conservative anti-Communist crusade.

Mercantilism An economic theory developed in early-modern Europe to explain and guide the growth of European nation-states. Its goal was to strengthen the state by making the economy serve its interests. According to the theory of mercantilism, the world's wealth, measured in gold and silver, was fixed; that is, it could never be increased. As a result, each nation's chief economic objective must be to secure as much of the world's wealth as possible. One nation's gain was necessarily another's loss. Colonies played an important part in the theory of mercantilism. Their role was to serve as sources of raw materials and as markets for manufactured goods for the mother country alone.

Middle ground The region between European and Indian settlements in North America that was neither fully European nor fully Indian, but rather a new world created out of two different traditions. The middle ground came into being every time Europeans and Indians met, needed each other, and could not (or would not) achieve what they wanted through the use of force.

Millennialism A strain of Protestant belief that holds that history will end with the thousand-year reign of Christ (the millennium). Some Americans saw the Great Awakening, the French and Indian War, and the Revolution as signs that the millennium was about to begin in America, and this belief infused Revolutionary thought with an element of optimism. Millennialism was also one aspect of a broad drive for social perfection in nineteenth-century America.

Modernization The process by which developing countries in the Third World were to become more like the United States—i.e., capitalist, independent, and anti-Communist. Confidence about the prospects for modernization was one of the cornerstones of liberal foreign policy in the 1960s.

Moral suasion The strategy of using persuasion (as opposed to legal coercion) to convince individuals to alter their behavior. In the antebellum years, moral suasion generally implied an appeal to religious values.

Mutual Aid Societies Organizations through which people of relatively meager means pooled their resources for emergencies. Usually, individuals paid small amounts in dues and were able to borrow larger amounts in times of need. In the early nineteenth century, mutual aid societies were especially common among workers and in free African-American communities.

National Republicans Over the first twenty years of the nineteenth century, the Republican Party gradually abandoned its Jeffersonian animosity toward an activist federal government and industrial development and became a strong proponent of both of these positions. Embodied in the American system, these new views were fully captured in the party's designation of itself as National Republicans by 1824.

Nativism A bias against anyone not born in the United States and in favor of native-born Americans. This attitude assumes the superior culture and political virtue of white Americans of Anglo-Saxon descent, or of individuals assumed to have this lineage. During the period 1820–1850, Irish immigrants became the particular targets of nativist attitudes.

New Left The radical student movement that emerged in opposition to the new liberalism in the 1960s. The New Left condemned the cold war and corporate power and called for the creation of a true "participatory democracy" in the United States. Placing its faith in the radical potential of young, middle-class students, the New Left differed from the "Old Left" of the late nineteenth and early twentieth centuries, which believed workers would lead the way to socialism.

Patriotism Love of country. Ways of declaring and displaying national devotion underwent a change from the nineteenth to the twentieth century. Whereas politicians were once unblushingly called patriotic, after World War I the title was appropriated to describe the sacrifices of war veterans. Patriotic spectacle in the form of public oration and electoral rallies gave way to military-style commemorations of Armistice Day and the nation's martial heritage.

Political virtue In the political thought of the early republic, the personal qualities required in citizens if the republic was to survive.

Polygyny Taking more than one wife. Indian tribes such as the Hurons practiced polygyny, and hence they did not object when French traders who already had wives in Europe took Indian women as additional wives.

Popular sovereignty A solution to the slavery controversy espoused by leading northern Democrats in the 1850s. It held that the inhabitants of western territories should be free to decide for themselves whether or not they wanted to have slavery. In principle, popular sovereignty would prevent Congress from either enforcing or restricting slavery's expansion into the western territories.

Postindustrial economy The service- and computer-based economy that was succeeding the industrial economy, which had been dominated by manufacturing, at the end of the twentieth century.

Principle of Judicial Review The principle of law that recognizes in the judiciary the power to review and rule on the constitutionality of laws. First established in *Marbury v. Madison* (1803) under Chief Justice John Marshall.

Producers ideology The belief that all those who lived by producing goods shared a common political identity in opposition to those who lived off financial speculation, rent, or interest.

Proprietary colony Colony established by a royal grant to an individual or family. The proprietary colonies included Maryland, New York, New Jersey, Pennsylvania, and the Carolinas.

Public opinion Not quite democracy or consent, public opinion was a new way of understanding the influence of the citizenry on political calculations. Freudian psychology and the new mass media encouraged a view of the public as both fickle and powerful. Whereas the popular will (a nineteenth-century concept) was steady and rooted in national traditions, public opinion was variable and based on attitudes that could be aroused or manipulated by advertising.

Realism A major artistic movement of the late nineteenth century that embraced writers, painters, critics and photographers. Realists strove to avoid sentimentality and to depict human life "realistically."

Reconversion The economic and social transition from the war effort to peacetime. Americans feared that reconversion might bring a return to the depression conditions of the 1930s.

Re-export trade Maritime trade between two foreign ports, with an intermediate stop in a port of the ship's home nation. United States shippers commonly engaged in the re-export trade during the European wars of the late eighteenth and early nineteenth centuries, when England and France tried to prevent each other from shipping or receiving goods. United States shippers claimed that the intermediate stop in the United States made their cargoes neutral.

Republicanism A set of doctrines rooted in classical antiquity that held that power is always grasping and dangerous and presents a threat to liberty. Republicanism supplied constitutionalism with a motive by explaining how a balanced constitution could be transformed into tyranny as grasping men used their power to encroach upon the liberty of the citizens. In addition, republicanism held that people achieved fulfillment only through participation in public life, as citizens in a republic. Republicanism required the individual to display *virtue* by sacrificing his (or her) private interest for the good of the republic.

Requerimiento (the Requirement) A document issued by the Spanish Crown in 1513 in order to clarify the legal bases for the enslavement of hostile Indians. Each *conquistador* was required to read a copy of the *Requerimiento* to each group of Indians he encountered. The *Requerimiento* promised friendship to all Indians who accepted Christianity, but threatened war and enslavement for all those who resisted.

Safety-valve theory An argument commonly made in the nineteenth century that the abundance of western land spared the United States from the social upheavals common to capitalist societies in Europe. In theory, as long as eastern workers had the option of migrating west and becoming independent farmers they could not be subjected to European levels of exploitation. Thus the West was said to provide a "safety-valve" against the social pressures caused by capitalist development.

Scalawag A derogatory term referring to southern whites who sympathized with the Republicans during Reconstruction.

Second-wave feminism The reborn women's movement of the 1960s and 1970s that reinterpreted the first wave of nineteenth- and early twentieth-century feminists' insistence.

Separation of powers One of the chief innovations of the Constitution and a distinguishing mark of the American form of democracy, in which the executive, legislative, and judicial branches of government are separated so that they can check and balance each other.

Slave power In the 1850s northern Republicans explained the continued economic and political strength of slavery by claiming that a "slave power" had taken control of the federal government and used its authority to artificially keep slavery alive.

Slave society A society in which slavery is central to the economy and political structure, in contrast to a *society with slaves,* in which the presence of slaves does not alter the fundamental structures of the society.

Social Darwinism Darwin's theory of natural selection transferred from biological evolution to human history. Social Darwinists argued that some individuals and groups, particularly racial groups, were better able to survive in the "race of life."

Stagflation The unusual combination of stagnant growth and high inflation that plagued the American economy in the 1970s.

Strict constructionism The view that the Constitution has a fixed, explicit meaning which can be altered only through formal amendment. Loose constructionism is the view that the Constitution is a broad framework within which various specific interpretations and applications are possible without formal amendment.

Suburbanization The spread of suburban housing developments and, more broadly, of the suburban ideal.

Supply-side economics The controversial theory, associated with economist Arthur Laffer, that drove "Reaganomics," the conservative economic policy of the Reagan administration. In contrast to liberal economic theory, supply-side economics emphasized that producers—the "supply side" of the economic equation—drove economic growth, rather than consumers—the "demand side." To encourage producers to invest more in new production, Laffer and other supply-siders called for massive tax cuts.

Tariff   A tax on goods moving across an international boundary. Because the Constitution allows tariffs only on imports, as a political issue the tariff question has chiefly concerned the protection of domestic manufactures from foreign competition. Industries producing mainly for American consumers have preferred a higher tarriff, while farmers and industries aimed at global markets have typically favored reduced tariffs. Prior to the Civil War, the tariff was a symbol of diverging political economies in the North and South. The North advocated high tariffs to protect growing domestic manufacturing ("protective tariffs") and the South opposed high tariffs on the grounds that they increased the cost of imported manufactured goods.

Taylorism   A method for maximizing industrial efficiency by systematically reducing the time and motion involved in each step of the production process. This "scientific" system was designed by Frederick Taylor and explained in his book *The Principles of Scientific Management* (1911).

Universalism   Enlightenment belief that all people are by their nature essentially the same.

Vertical integration   The practice of taking control of every aspect of the production, distribution and sale of a commodity. For example, Andrew Carnegie vertically integrated his steel operations by purchasing the mines that produced the ore, the railroads that carried the ore to the steel mills, the mills themselves, and the distribution system that carried the finished steel to customers.

Virtual representation   British doctrine that said that all Britons, even those who did not vote, were represented by Parliament, if not "actually," by representatives they had chosen, then "virtually," because each member of Parliament was supposed to act on behalf of the entire realm, not only his constituents or even those who had voted for him.

Voluntarism   A style of political activism that took place largely outside of electoral politics. Voluntarism emerged in the nineteenth century, particularly among those Americans who were not allowed to vote. Thus women formed voluntary associations that pressed for social and political reforms, even though women were excluded from electoral politics.

Waltham System   Named after the system used in early textile mills in Waltham, Massachusetts, the term refers to the practice of bringing all elements of production together in a single factory setting with the application of nonhuman powered machinery.

Watergate   The name of the Washington, D.C., office and apartment complex where five men with ties to the presidential campaign of Richard Nixon were caught breaking into the headquarters of the Democratic National Committee in June 1972. "Watergate" became the catchall term for the wide range of illegal practices of Nixon and his followers that were uncovered in the aftermath of the break-in.

Whig Party   The political party founded by Henry Clay in the mid-1830s. The name derived from the seventeenth- and eighteenth-century British anti-monarch position and was intended to suggest that the Jacksonian Democrats (and Jackson in particular) sought despotic powers. In many ways the heirs of National Republicans, the Whigs supported economic expansion, but they also believed in a strong federal government to control the dynamism of the market. The Whig Party attracted many moral reformers.

Whitewater   With its echo of Richard Nixon's "Watergate" scandals in the 1970s, "Whitewater" became the catchall term for the scandals that plagued Bill Clinton's presidency in the 1990s. The term came from the name of a real estate development company in Arkansas. Clinton and his wife Hillary supposedly had corrupt dealings with the Whitewater Development Corporation in the 1970s and 1980s that they purportedly attempted to cover up in the 1990s.

Woman's Rights Movement   The antebellum organizing efforts of women on their own behalf, in the attempt to secure a broad range of social, civic, and political rights. This movement is generally dated from the convention at Seneca Falls in 1848. Only after the Civil War would woman's rights activism begin to confine its efforts to suffrage.

BIBLIOGRAPHY

This Bibliography contains a selected listing of the extensive body of literature available on American History. It is compiled chapter-by-chapter, enabling the reader to easily find additional references in a given area, and offers an expanded compilation of literature for students who wish to explore topics in fuller detail.

CHAPTER I

Blackburn, Robin, *The Making of New World Slavery: From the Baroque to the Modern 1492–1800* (1997). Bethell, Leslie, ed., *The Cambridge History of Latin America, Vol. I* (1984). Boucher, Philip P., *Cannibal Encounters: Europeans and Island Caribs, 1492–1763* (1992). Boxer, Charles, *The Portuguese Seaborne Empire: 1415–1825* (1969). Bray, Warwick, ed., *The Meeting of Two Worlds: Europe and the Americas, 1492–1650* (1993). Burkholder, Mark A., and Lyman Johnson, *Colonial Latin America* (2000). Canny, Nicholas, and Anthony Pagden, *Colonial Identity in the Atlantic World, 1500–1800* (1987). Casas, Bartolome de las, *A Short Account of the Destruction of the Indies,* with an introduction by Anthony Pagden (1992). Chaplin, Joyce E., *Subject Matter: Technology, The Body, and Science on the Anglo-Amercian Frontier, 1500–1676.* (2001). Clayton, Lawrence A., et al., eds., *The De Soto Chronicles: The Expedition of Hernando de Soto to North America in 1539–1543,* 2 vols. (1993). Coe, Michael, Dean Snow, and Elizabeth Benson, *Atlas of Ancient America* (1986). Crosby, Alfred W., Jr., *Ecological Imperialism: The Biological Expansion of Europe, 900–1900* (1986). Denevan, William M., ed., *The Native Population of the Americas in 1492* (1992). Diaz, Bernal, *The Conquest of New Spain* (1963). Dobyns, Henry F., *Their Number Become Thinned: Native American Population Dynamics in Eastern North America* (1983). Dunn, Oliver, and James E. Kelley, Jr., eds., *The Diario of Christopher Columbus's First Voyage to America, 1492–1493* (1989). Elliott, J. H., *Spain and Its World, 1500–1700* (1989). Fagan, Brian M., *Ancient North America: The Archeology of a Continent* (1991). Fage, J. D., *A History of Africa* (1988). Fernandez-Armesto, Felipe, *Columbus* (1991).

Gibson, Charles, *Spain in America* (1966). Gutierrez, Ramon, *When Jesus Came the Corn Mothers Went Away: Marriage, Sexuality, and Power in New Mexico, 1500–1846* (1991). Hanke, Lewis, *The Spanish Struggle for Justice in the Conquest of America* (1965). Hoffman, Paul, *A New Andalucia and a Way to the Orient* (1990). Hulme, Peter, and Neil L. Whitehead, eds., *Wild Majesty* (1992). Jennings, Francis, *The Founders of America* (1993). Kartunnen, Frances, *Between Worlds: Interpreters, Guides, and Survivors* (1994). Klein, Herbert S., *African Slavery in Latin America and the Caribbean* (1986). Kupperman, Karen O., ed., *America in European Consciousness, 1493–1750* (1995). Leon-Portilla, Miguel, ed., *The Broken Spears: The Aztec Account of the Conquest of Mexico* (1990). Liss, Peggy K., *Isabel: The Queen* (1992). Lockhart, James, and Stuart B. Schwartz, *Early Latin America* (1983). Lunenfeld, Marvin, ed., *1492: Discovery, Invasion, Encounter* (1991).

Milanich, Jerald T., and Susan Milanich, eds., *First Encounters: Spanish Explorations in the Caribbean and the United States, 1492–1570* (1989). _____, and Charles Hudson, *Hernando de Soto and the Indians of Florida* (1993). Morison, Samuel Eliot, *The European Discovery of America: The Southern Voyages, 1492–1616* (1974). _____, *Journals and Other Documents on the Life and Voyages of Christopher Columbus* (1963). Nabokov, Peter, ed., *Native American Testimony, 1492–1992* (1999). Oliver, Roland, *The African Experience: Major Themes in African History from Earliest Times to the Present* (1991). Pagden, Anthony, ed., *European Encounters with the New World* (1993). _____, *Lords of All the World: Ideologies of Empire in Spain, Britain and France, c. 1500–1800* (1995). Parry, J. H., *The Age of Reconnaissance: Discovery, Exploration and Settlement 1450–1650* (1963). _____, *The Spanish Seaborne Empire* (1966). Peters, Edward, *Inquisition* (1988). Phillips, J. R. S., *The Medieval Expansion of Europe* (1988). Quinn, David B., *North America From Earliest Discovery to First Settlements* (1975). Rouse, Irving, *The Tainos* (1992). Ruiz, Ramon Eduardo, *Triumphs and Tragedy: A History of the Mexican People* (1992).

Scammell, G. V., *The World Encompassed: The First European Maritime Empires, c. 800–1650* (1981). Solow, Barbara L., *Slavery and the Rise of the Atlantic System* (1991). Trigger, Bruce G., and Wilcomb Washburn, eds., *The Cambridge History of the Native Peoples of the Americas, Vol. 1* (1996).

CHAPTER 2

Allen, John Logan, ed., *North American Exploration: A New World* (1997). Anderson, Karen, *Chain Her by One Foot: The Subjugation of Native Women in Seventeenth-Century New France* (1991). Canny, Nicholas P., *The Elizabethan Conquest of Ireland: A Pattern Established, 1565–1576* (1976). Dechêne, Louise, *Habitants and Merchants in Seventeenth-Century Montreal* (1992). Delâge, Denys, *Bitter Feast: Amerindians and Europeans in Northeastern America, 1600–1664* (1993). Dennis, Matthew, *Cultivating a Landscape of Peace: Iroquois-European Encounters in Seventeenth-Century America* (1993). Dickason, Olive Patricia, *Canada's First Nations: A History of Founding Peoples from Earliest Times* (1992). Eccles, W. J., *The Canadian Frontier* (1974). _____, *Essays on New France* (1987).

Gleach, Frederic W., *Powhatan's World and Colonial Virginia: A Conflict of Cultures* (1997). Hoffman, Paul, *A New Andalucia and a Way to the Orient* (1990). Humc, Ivor Noël, *The Virginia Adventure: Roanoke to James Towne: An Archaeological and Historical Odyssey* (1994). Inikori, Joseph, and Stanley L.

Engerman, eds., *The Atlantic Slave Trade: Effects on Economies, Societies, and Peoples in Africa, The Americas, and Europe* (1992). Jaenen, Cornelius J., *Friend and Foe: Aspects of French-Amerindian Cultural Contact in the Sixteenth and Seventeenth Centuries* (1976). Jennings, Francis, *The Ambiguous Iroquois Empire: The Covenant Chain Confederation of Indian Tribes with English Colonies* (1984). Klein, Herbert, *African Slavery in Latin America and the Caribbean* (1986). Kupperman, Karen Ordahl, *Settling with the Indians: The Meeting of English and Indian Cultures in America, 1580–1640* (1980).

Merwick, Donna, *Possessing Albany, 1630–1710: The Dutch and English Experience* (1990). Morgan, Edmund S., *American Slavery, American Freedom: The Ordeal of Colonial Virginia* (1975). Morison, Samuel Eliot, *Samuel de Champlain: Father of New France* (1972). Peckham, Howard, and Charles Gibson, eds., *Attitudes of Colonial Powers Toward the American Indian* (1969). Quinn, David B., ed., *America From Concept to Discovery: Early Explorations of North America* (1979). _____, *North America From Earliest Discovery to First Settlements: The Norse Voyages to 1612* (1977). _____, *Set Fair for Roanoke: Voyages and Colonies, 1584–1606* (1995). Richter, Daniel K., and James H. Merrell, *Beyond the Covenant Chain: The Iroquois and Their Neighbors in Indian North America, 1600–1800* (1987). Rink, Oliver A., *Holland on the Hudson: An Economic and Social History of Dutch New York* (1986). Rountree, Helen C., ed., *Powhatan Foreign Relations* (1993).

Scammell, G. V., *The World Encompassed: The First European Maritime Empires* (1981). Trigger, Bruce, *Natives and Newcomers: Canada's "Heroic Age" Reconsidered* (1985). _____, and Wilcomb E. Washburn, eds., *The Cambridge History of the Native Peoples of the Americas, Vol. I* (1996). Wallace, Anthony F. C., *The Death and Rebirth of the Seneca* (1970). Weber, David, *The Spanish Frontier in North America* (1992). White, Richard, *The Middle Ground: Indians, Empires, and Republics in the Great Lakes Region, 1650–1815* (1991). White, Shane, *Somewhat More Independent: The End of Slavery in New York City, 1770–1810* (1991).

CHAPTER 3

Allen, David Grayson, *In English Ways: The Movement of Societies and the Transferral of English Local Law and Custom to Massachusetts Bay in the Seventeenth Century* (1981). Anderson, Virginia DeJohn, *New England's Generation: The Great Migration and the Formation of Society and Culture in the Seventeenth Century* (1991). Barbour, Philip L., ed., *The Complete Works of John Smith* (1986). _____, *Pocahontas and Her World* (1969). Bernhard, Virginia, "Men, Women and Children at Jamestown: Population and Gender in Early Virginia, 1607–1610," *Journal of Southern History*, LVIII (1992). Blackburn, Robin, *The Making of New World Slavery: From the Baroque to the Modern, 1402–1800* (1997). Bradford, William, *Of Plymouth Plantation, 1620–1647*, ed. Samuel Eliot Morison (1952). Breen, Timothy H., and Stephen Innes, *"Myne Owne Ground": Race and Freedom on Virginia's Eastern Shore, 1640–1676* (1980). Bremer, Francis J., *The Puritan Experiment: New England Society from Bradford to Edwards* (1976). Carr, Lois Green, et al., eds., *Colonial Chesapeake Society* (1988). Delbanco, Andrew, *The Puritan Ordeal* (1989). Demos, John,

ed., *Remarkable Providences: Readings on Early American History* (1991). Foster, Stephen, *The Long Argument: English Puritanism and the Shaping of New England Culture, 1570–1700* (1991). _____, *Their Solitary Way: The Puritan Social Ethic in the First Century of Settlement in New England* (1971). Freedman, Estelle B., and John D'Emilio, *Intimate Matters: A History of Sexuality in America* (1988).

Gleach, Frederic W., *Powhatan's World and Colonial Virginia: A Conflict of Cultures* (1997). Greene, Jack P., *Pursuits of Happiness: The Social Development of Early Modern British Colonies and the Formation of American Culture* (1988). Greven, Philip J., *Four Generations: Population, Land, and Family in Colonial Andover, Massachusetts* (1970). _____, *The Protestant Temperament: Patterns of Childrearing, Religious Experience, and the Self in Early America* (1977). Hambrick-Stowe, Charles, *The Practice of Piety: Puritan Devotional Disciplines in Seventeenth-century New England* (1982). Horn, James, *Adapting to a New World: English Society in the Seventeenth-Century Chesapeake* (1994). Jordan, Winthrop D., *White over Black: American Attitudes Toward the Negro, 1550–1812* (1968). Karlsen, Carol, *The Devil in the Shape of a Woman: Witchcraft in Colonial New England* (1987). Kolchin, Peter, *American Slavery, 1619–1877* (1993). Kupperman, Karen Ordahl, *Providence Island, 1630–1641: The Other Puritan Colony* (1993). _____, *Settling with the Indians: The Meeting of English and Indian Cultures in America, 1580–1640* (1980). Langdon, George D., Jr., *Pilgrim Colony: A History of New Plymouth, 1620–1691* (1966). Lockridge, Kenneth A., *A New England Town, The First Hundred Years: Dedham, Massachusetts 1636–1736* (rev. ed., 1985).

McCusker, John J., and Russell R. Menard, *The Economy of British America, 1607–1789* (1991). McGiffert, Michael, ed., "Constructing Race," *William and Mary Quarterly*, 3d Ser., LIV (1997). Miller, Perry, ed., *The American Puritans: Their Prose and Poetry* (1956). _____, *The New England Mind: The Seventeenth Century* (1939). Morgan, Edmund S., *The Puritan Dilemma: The Story of John Winthrop* (1958). _____, *Visible Saints: The History of a Puritan Idea* (1963). Norton, Mary Beth, *Founding Mothers and Fathers: Gendered Power and the Forming of American Society* (1996). Potter, Stephen R., *Commoners, Tribute, and Chiefs: The Development of Algonquian Culture in the Potomac Valley* (1993). Powell, Sumner Chilton, *Puritan Village: The Formation of a New England Town* (1963). Quinn, David Beers, *North America From Earliest Discovery to First Settlements: The Norse Voyages to 1612* (1975). Rountree, Helen, *Pocahontas's People: The Powhatan Indians of Virginia Through Four Centuries* (1990). _____, ed., *Powhatan Foreign Relations, 1500–1722* (1993). _____, *The Powhatan Indians of Virginia: Their Traditional Culture* (1989). Rutman, Darrett B., *Winthrop's Boston: A Portrait of a Puritan Town* (1965).

Salisbury, Neal, *Manitou and Providence: Indians, Europeans, and the Making of New England, 1500–1643* (1982). _____, "Squanto: Last of the Patuxets," in Gary B. Nash and David W. Sweet, eds., *Struggle and Survival in Colonial America* (1981). Stannard, David E., *The Puritan Way of Death: A Study in Religion, Culture, and Social Change* (1977). Stone, Lawrence, *The Family, Sex, and Marriage in England, 1500–1800* (1977). Stout, Harry S., *The New England Soul: Preaching and*

Religious Culture in Colonial New England (1986). Tate, Thad, and David Ammerman, eds., *The Chesapeake in the Seventeenth Century: Essays on Anglo-American Society and Politics* (1979). Thomas, M. Halsey, ed., *The Diary of Samuel Sewall, 1674–1708* (1973.) Ulrich, Laurel Thatcher, *Good Wives: Image and Reality in the Lives of Women in Northern New England, 1650–1750* (1982). Vaughan, Alden T., *New England Frontier: Puritans and Indians, 1620–1675* (1994). _____, ed., *The Puritan Tradition in America, 1620–1730* (1972). Wood, Peter H., Gregory A. Waselkov, and M. Thomas Halsey, eds., *Powhatan's Mantle: Indians in the Colonial Southeast* (1989). Woodward, Grace Steele, *Pocahontas* (1969). Zuckerman, Michael, *Peaceable Kingdoms: New England Towns in the Eighteenth Century* (1970). _____, "Pilgrims in the Wilderness: Community, Modernity, and the Maypole at Merry Mount," *New England Quarterly*, L (1977).

CHAPTER 4

Appleby, Joyce, *Economic Thought and Ideology in Seventeenth-Century England* (1978). _____, *Liberalism and Republicanism in the Historical Imagination* (1992). Bailyn, Bernard, and Philip D. Morgan, eds., *Strangers Within the Realm: Cultural Margins of the First British Empire* (1991). Berlin, Ira D., *Many Thousands Gone: The First Two Centuries of Slavery in North America* (1998). Bonomi, Patricia U., *A Factious People: Politics and Society in Colonial New York* (1971). Boyer, Paul, and Stephen Nissenbaum, *Salem Possessed: The Social Origins of Witchcraft* (1972). _____, ed. *Salem Village Witchcraft: A Documentary Record of Local Conflict in Colonial New England* (1972). Breen, T. H., *Puritans and Adventurers: Change and Persistence in Early America* (1980). Breslaw, Elaine G., *Tituba, Reluctant Witch of Salem: Devilish Indians and Puritan Fantasies* (1996). Crane, Verner, *The Southern Frontier, 1670–1732*, with a new preface by Peter H. Wood (1981). Craven, Wesley Frank, *White, Red, and Black: The Seventeenth-Century Virginian* (1971). Degler, Carl N., *Out of Our Past: The Forces that Shaped Modern America*, 3rd. ed. (1984). Dunn, Richard S., *Sugar and Slaves: The Rise of the Planter Class in the English West Indies* (1972). Eccles, W. J., *France in America* (1990). Eltis, David, *The Rise of African Slavery in the Americas* (2000). Espinosa, J. Manuel, *The Pueblo Indian Revolt of 1696 and the Franciscan Mission in New Mexico* (1988).

Goodfriend, Joyce, *Before the Melting Pot: Society and Culture in Colonial New York City, 1664–1692* (1992). Greene, Jack P., ed., *Great Britain and the American Colonies, 1606–1763* (1970). Hall, David D., ed., *Witch-Hunting in Seventeenth-Century New England: A Documentary History, 1638–1692* (1991). _____, *Worlds of Wonder, Days of Judgment: Popular Religious Belief in Early New England* (1989). Hall, Gwendolyn Midlo, *Africans in Colonial Louisiana: The Development of Afro-Creole Culture in the Eighteenth Century* (1992). Hammond, George P., and Agapito Reys, eds., *Don Juan de Oñate: Colonizer of New Mexico, 1595–1628* (1953). Hoffer, Peter Charles, *The Devil's Disciples: Makers of the Salem Witchcraft Trials* (1996). Illick, Joseph, *Colonial Pennsylvania: A History* (1976). Jennings, Francis, *The Ambiguous Iroquois Empire: The Covenant Chain Confederation of Indian Tribes with English Colonies* (1984). Johnson, Richard R., *Adjustment*

to Empire: The New England Colonies, 1665–1715 (1981). Kammen, Michael, *Colonial New York: A History* (1975). Karlsen, Carol, *The Devil in the Shape of a Woman: Witchcraft in Colonial New England* (1987). Klein, Herbert S., *African Slavery in Latin America and the Caribbean* (1986). Kishlansky, Mark, *A Monarchy Transformed: Britain, 1603–1714* (1996). Knaut, Andrew L., *The Pueblo Revolt of 1680: Conquest and Resistance in Seventeenth–Century New Mexico* (1995). Kolchin, Peter, *American Slavery, 1619–1877* (1993). Konig, David Thomas, *Law and Society in Puritan Massachusetts: Essex County, 1629–1692* (1979). Kupperman, Karen Ordahl, ed., *Major Problems in American Colonial History* (2000). Landers, Jane, *Black Society in Spanish Florida* (1999). Leach, Douglas Edward, *Arms for Empire: A Military History of the British Colonies of North America, 1607–1763* (1973). Lefler, Hugh T., and William S. Powell, *Colonial North Carolina: A History* (1973). Locke, John, *Two Treatises of Government; A Critical Edition with an Introduction,* ed., Peter Laslett (1960). Lovejoy, David S., *The Glorious Revolution in America* (1972).

Malone, Patrick M., *The Skulking Way of War: Technology and Tactics Among the New England Indians* (1991). Melvoin, Richard I., *The New England Outpost: War and Society in Colonial Deerfield* (1989). Merrell, James H., *The Indians' New World: Catawbas and their Neighbors from European Contact Through the Era of Removal* (1989). Merwick, Donna, *Possessing Albany, 1630–1710: The Dutch and English Experiences* (1990). Middlekauff, Robert, *The Mathers: Three Generations of Puritan Intellectual, 1596–1728* (1971). Middleton, Richard, *Colonial America: A History, 1585–1776* (1996). Miller, Perry, *Errand into the Wilderness* (1956). Nash, Gary B., *Quakers and Politics: Pennsylvania, 1681–1726* (1996). _____, *Red, White, and Black: The Peoples of Early America*, 2nd ed. (1982). _____, *Urban Crucible: Social Change, Political Consciousness, and the Origins of the American Revolution* (1979). _____ and Jean Soderlund, *Freedom by Degrees: Emancipation in Pennsylvania and Its Aftermath* (1991). Nobles, Gregory H., *American Frontiers: Cultural Encounters and Continental Conquest* (1997). Nylander, Jane, *Our Own Snug Firesides: Images of the New England Home, 1760–1860* (1993). Oakes, James, *Slavery and Freedom: An Interpretation of the Old South* (1990). Patterson, Orlando, *Slavery and Social Death: A Comparative Study* (1982). Pope, Robert G., *The Half-Way Covenant: Church Membership in Puritan New England* (1986). Quinn, David B., ed., *Early Maryland in a Wider World* (1982). Richter, Daniel K., *The Ordeal of the Longhouse: The Peoples of the Iroquois League in the Era of European Colonization* (1992). Ritchie, Robert C., *The Duke's Province: A Study of New York Politics and Society, 1664–1691* (1977). Robinson, W. Stitt, *The Southern Colonial Frontier, 1607–1763* (1979). Rose, Willie Lee, ed., *A Documentary History of Slavery in North America* (1976). Rosenthal, Bernard, *Salem Story: Reading the Witch Trials of 1692* (1993). Rountree, Helen, *Pocahontas's People: The Powhatan Indians of Virginia Through Four Centuries* (1990).

Simmons, Marc, *The Last Conquistador: Juan de Oñate and the Settling of the Far Southwest* (1991). Sirmans, M. Eugene, *Colonial South Carolina: A Political History, 1663–1763* (1966). Slotkin, Richard, and James K. Folson, eds., *So Dreadfull a Judgment: Puritan Responses to King Philip's War, 1676–1677*

(1978). Usner, Daniel H., Jr., *Indians, Settlers, and Slaves in a Frontier Exchange Economy: The Lower Mississippi Valley before 1783* (1992). Vaughan, Alden T., ed., *The Puritan Tradition in America, 1620–1730* (1972). Webb, Stephen Saunders, *1676: The End of American Independence* (1984). Weber, David, *The Spanish Frontier in North America* (1992). White, Richard, *The Middle Ground: Indians, Empires, and Republics in the Great Lakes Region, 1650–1815* (1991). Wooten, David, ed., *The Political Writings of John Locke* (1993). Wright, J. Leitch, Jr., *The Only Land They Knew: The Tragic Story of the American Indians in the Old South* (1981).

CHAPTER 5

Ahlstrom, Sydney E., *A Religious History of the American People* (1972). Allison, Robert J., ed., *The Interesting Narrative of the Life of Olaudah Equiano* (1995). Bailyn, Bernard, "The Peopling of British North America: An Introduction," in *Perspectives in American History,* Vol. 2 (1985). _____, *Voyagers to the West: A Passage in the Peopling of America on the Eve of the Revolution* (1986). _____, and Philip D. Morgan, eds., *Strangers within the Realm: Cultural Margins of the First British Empire* (1991). Berlin, Ira, *Many Thousands Gone: The First Two Centuries of Slavery in North America* (1998). _____, and Philip D. Morgan, eds., *Cultivation and Culture: Labor and the Shaping of Slave Life in the Americas* (1993). Bonomi, Patricia, *Under the Cope of Heaven: Religion, Society, and Politics in Colonial America* (1986). Boorstin, Daniel J., *The Lost World of Thomas Jefferson* (1948). Boydston, Jeanne, *Home and Work: Housework, Wages, and the Ideology of Labor in the Early Republic* (1990). Breen, T. H., *Puritans and Adventurers: Change and Persistence in Early America* (1980). Brewer, John, and Roy Porter, eds., *Consumption and the World of Goods* (1993). Bullock, Steven C., *Revolutionary Brotherhood: Freemasonry and the Transformation of the American Social Order, 1730–1840,* (1996). Bushman, Richard, *The Refinement of America: Persons, Houses, Cities* (1992). Butler, Jon, *Awash in a Sea of Faith: Christianizing the American People* (1990). _____, *Becoming American: The Revolution before 1776* (2000). Coleman, Kenneth, *Colonial Georgia: A History* (1976). Conroy, David W., *In Public Houses: Drink and the Revolution of Authority in Colonial Massachusetts* (1987). Cott, Nancy F., et al., eds., *Root of Bitterness: Documents of the Social History of American Women* (1996). Davis, Harold E., *The Fledgling Province: Social and Cultural Life in Colonial Georgia* (1976). Duffy, John, *Epidemics in Colonial America* (1971). Engerman, Stanley L., and Robert E. Gallman, eds., *The Cambridge Economic History of the United States* (1996). Fiering, Norman S., *Jonathan Edwards's Moral Thought and Its British Context* (1981). Franklin, Benjamin, *Writings* (1987).

Gallay, Alan, *The Formation of a Planter Elite: Jonathan Bryan and the Southern Colonial Frontier* (1989). Gilje, Paul A., *The Road to Mobocracy: Popular Disorder in New York City, 1763–1834* (1987). Gordon, Michael, ed., *The American Family in Social-Historical Perspective* (1983). Greene, Jack P., *Pursuits of Happiness: The Social Development of Early Modern British Colonies and the Formation of American Culture* (1988). _____, *The Quest for Power: The Lower Houses of Assembly in the Southern Royal Colonies, 1689–1776* (1976). _____, and

J. R. Pole, eds., *Colonial British America: Essays in the New History of the Early Modern Era* (1984). Gross, Robert A. *The Minutemen and Their World* (1976). Hancock, David, *Citizens of the World: London Merchants and the Integration of the British Atlantic Community, 1735–1785* (1995). Heimert, Alan, *Religion and the American Mind, from the Great Awakening to the Revolution* (1968). _____, and Perry Miller, eds., *The Great Awakening: Documents Illustrating the Crisis and Its Consequences* (1967). Henretta, James A., and Gregory H. Nobles, *Evolution and Revolution: American Society, 1600–1820* (1987). Hoffman, Ronald, et al., eds., *Through a Glass Darkly: Reflections on Personal Identity in Early America* (1997). Innes, Stephen A., *Creating the Commonwealth: The Economic Culture of Puritan New England* (1995). _____, ed., *Work and Labor in Early America* (1988). Kammen, Michael, *Colonial New York: A History* (1975). Klein, Herbert, *The Atlantic Slave Trade* (1999). Koch, Adrienne, and William Peden, eds., *The Life and Selected Writings of Thomas Jefferson* (1944). Kulikoff, Allan, *Tobacco and Slaves: The Development of Southern Cultures in the Chesapeake, 1680–1800* (1986). Lambert, Frank, *"Pedlar in Divinity": George Whitefield and the Transatlantic Revivals* (1994). Landers, Jane, "El Gracia de Santa Teresa de Mose: A Free Black Town in Spanish Colonial Florida," *American Historical Review,* 95 (1991). Lewis, Jan, *The Pursuit of Happiness: Family and Values in Jefferson's Virginia* (1983).

Mancall, Peter, *Deadly Medicine: Indians and Alcohol in Early America* (1995). May, Henry F., *The Enlightenment in America* (1976). Matson, Cathy, *Merchants and Empire: Trading in Colonial New York* (1998). McCusker, John J., and Russell R. Menard, *The Economy of British America, 1607–1789* (1985). Middlekauff, Robert, *The Mathers: Three Generations of Puritan Intellectuals* (1971). Middleton, Richard, *Colonial America: A History, 1585–1776* (1996). Morgan, Philip D., "Slave Life in Eighteenth-Century Charleston," *Perspectives in American History,* Vol. I (1984). _____, "Work and Culture: The Task System and the World of Lowcountry Blacks, 1700–1800," *William and Mary Quarterly,* 3d Ser., XXXIX (1982). Mullin, Michael, *Africa in America: Slave Acculturation and Resistance in the American South and the British Caribbean, 1736–1831* (1992). Oberg, Barbara B., and Harry S. Stout, eds., *Benjamin Franklin, Jonathan Edwards, and the Representation of American Culture* (1993). Olwell, Robert, *Masters, Slaves, and Subjects: The Culture of Power in the South Carolina Low Country, 1740–1790* (1998). Paine, Thomas, *Collected Writings* (1995). Rawley, James A., *The Transatlantic Slave Trade: A History* (1981). Rediker, Marcus B., *Between the Devil and the Deep Blue Sea: Merchant Seamen, Pirates, and the Anglo-American Maritime World, 1700–1750* (1987).

Sobel, Mechal, *The World they Made Together: Black and White Values in Eighteenth-Century Virginia* (1987). Spalding, Phinizy, *Oglethorpe in America* (1977). Stout, Harry S., *The Divine Dramatist: George Whitefield and the Rise of Modern Evangelicalism* (1991). Thornton, John K., "African Dimensions of the Stono Rebellion," *American Historical Review,* 91 (1994). Ulrich, Laurel Thatcher, *Good Wives; Image and Reality in the Lives of Women in Northern New England, 1650–1750* (1980). Vickers, Daniel, *Farmers and Fishermen: Two Centuries of Work in Essex County, Massachusetts, 1630–1850* (1994). Warner,

Michael, *The Letters of the Republic: Publication and the Public Sphere in Eighteenth-Century America* (1990). Whitefield, George, *Sketches of the Life and Labors of the Rev. George Whitefield* (n.d.). Wolf, Stephanie Grauman, *As Various as Their Land: The Everyday Lives of Eighteenth-Century Americans* (1993). Wright, Esmond, *Franklin of Philadelphia* (1986). Zabin, Serena, "Places of Exchange: New York City, 1700–1763," Ph.D. diss., Rutgers University (2000).

CHAPTER 6

Anderson, Fred, *A People's Army: Massachusetts Soldiers and Society in the Seven Years' War* (1984). Bailyn, Bernard, *The Origins of American Politics* (1968). Barrow, Thomas C., *Trade and Empire: The British Customs Service in Colonial America, 1660–1775* (1967). Braund, Kathleen E. Holland, *Deerskins and Duffels: Creek Indian Trade with Anglo-America, 1685–1815* (1993). Breen, T. H., "Narrative of Commercial Life: Consumption, Ideology, and Community on the Eve of the American Revolution," *William and Mary Quarterly*, 3rd Ser., L (1993). Brewer, John, *Party, Ideology, and Popular Politics at the Accession of George II* (1976). Bushman, Richard, *King and People in Provincial Massachusetts* (1985). Dowd, Gregory E., *A Spirited Resistance: The North American Indian Struggle for Unity, 1745–1815* (1992). Draper, Theodore, *A Struggle for Power: The American Revolution* (1996). Eccles, W. J., *France in America* (1990). Ferling, John E., *A Wilderness of Miseries: War and Warriors in Early America* (1980). Flexner, James Thomas, *George Washington: The Forge of Experience, 1732–1775* (1965). _____, *Lord of the Mohawks: A Biography of Sir William Johnson* (1979). Franklin, Benjamin, *Benjamin Franklin: Writings* (1987).

Gilje, Paul A., *Rioting in America* (1996). _____, *The Road to Mobocracy: Popular Disorder in New York City, 1763–1834* (1987). Gipson, Lawrence H., *The British Empire before the American Revolution*, 15 vols (1936–1972). Greene, Jack P., *Peripheries and Center: Constitutional Development in the Extended Policies of the British Empire and the United States* (1987). _____, *The Quest for Power: The Lower Houses of Assembly in the Southern Royal Colonies* (1963). Hamilton, Milton W., *Sir William Johnson: Colonial American, 1715–1763* (1976). Hinderacker, Eric, *Elusive Empires: Constructing Colonialism in the Ohio Valley, 1673–1800* (1997). Hoerder, Dirk, *Crowd Action in Revolutionary Massachusetts, 1765–1780* (1977). Holton, Woody, *Forced Founders: Indians, Debtors, Slaves & the Making of the American Revolution in Virginia* (1999). Jefferson, Thomas, *Thomas Jefferson: Writings* (1984). Jennings, Francis, *The Ambiguous Iroquois Empire: The Covenant Chain Confederation of Indian Tribes with English Colonies* (1984.) _____, *Empire of Fortune: Crowns, Colonies, and Tribes in the Seven Years War in America* (1988). Johnson, Susannah Willard, *A Narrative of the Captivity of Mrs. Johnson* (1990). Labaree, Benjamin Woods, *The Boston Tea Party* (1964). Leach, Douglas Edward, *Roots of Conflict: British Armed Forces and Colonial Americans, 1677–1763* (1986).

Maier, Pauline, *From Resistance to Revolution: Colonial Radicals and the Development of American Opposition to Britain, 1765–1776* (1972). McConnell, Michael N., *A Country Between:*

The Upper Ohio Valley and Its Peoples, 1724–1774 (1992). Melvoin, Richard I., *New England Outpost: War and Society in Colonial Deerfield* (1989). Middlekauff, Robert, *Benjamin Franklin and His Enemies* (1996). _____, *The Glorious Cause: The American Revolution, 1763–1789* (1982). Morgan, Edmund S. and Helen M., *The Stamp Act Crisis: Prologue to Revolution* (1953). Nash, Gary, *The Urban Crucible: Social Change, Political Consciousness, and the Origins of the American Revolution* (1979). Nobles, Gregory H., *American Frontiers: Cultural Encounters and Continental Conquest* (1997). Peckham, Howard H., *Pontiac and the Indian Uprising* (1947). Pencak, William, *War, Politics, and Revolution in Provincial Massachusetts* (1981). _____, "Warfare and Political Change in Mid-Eighteenth-Century Massachusetts," *The Journal of Imperial and Commonwealth History*, 8 (1980), 51–73. Robinson, W. Stitt, *The Southern Frontier, 1607–1763* (1979).

Sosin, Jack M., *The Revolutionary Frontier, 1763–1783* (1967). Steele, Ian K., *Warpaths: Invasions of North America* (1994). Ulrich, Laurel Thatcher, *Good Wives: Image and Reality in the Lives of Women in Northern New England, 1650–1750* (1982). Vaughan, Alden T., *Roots of American Racism: Essays on the Colonial Experience* (1995). Walton, Gary M., and James F. Shepherd, *The Economic Rise of Early America* (1979). Warden, G. B., *Boston, 1689–1776* (1970). Wood, Gordon S., *The Creation of the American Republic, 1776–1787* (1966). _____, *The Rising Glory of America, 1760–1820* (1990). Wright, Esmond, *Franklin of Philadelphia* (1986). Zobel, Hiller, *The Boston Massacre* (1970).

CHAPTER 7

Alden, John R., *A History of the American Revolution* (1975). Aron, Stephen, *How the West Was Lost: The Transformation of Kentucky from Daniel Boone to Henry Clay* (1996). Bailyn, Bernard, *Faces of Revolution: Personalities and Times in the Struggle for American Independence* (1990). Bailyn, Bernard, ed., *The Debate on the Constitution*, 2 vols (1993). Beeman, Richard, Stephen Botein, and Edward C. Carter II, *Beyond Confederation: Origins of the Constitution and American National Identity* (1987). Berlin, Ira, and Ronald Hoffman, eds., *Slavery and Freedom in the Age of the American Revolution* (1983). Bernstein, Richard, *Are We to Be a Nation? The Making of the Constitution* (1987). Bloch, Ruth, "The Gendered Meanings of Virtue in Revolutionary America," *Signs*, 13 (1987), 37–58. Bonwick, Colin, *The American Revolution* (1991). Calloway, Colin, *The American Revolution in Indian Country: Crisis and Diversity in Native American Communities* (1995). Carp, E. Wayne, *To Starve the Army at Pleasure: Continental Army Administration and American Political Culture, 1775–1783* (1984). Cooke, Jacob E., ed., *The Federalist* (1961). Countryman, Edward, *The American Revolution* (1985). _____, *A People in Revolution: The American Revolution and Political Society in New York, 1760–1790* (1981). Crow, Jeffrey, and Larry Tise, eds., *The Southern Experience in the American Revolution* (1978). Doerflinger, Thomas M., *A Vigorous Spirit of Enterprise: Merchants and Economic Development in Revolutionary Philadelphia* (1986). Egnal, Marc, *A Mighty Empire: The Origins of the American Revolution* (1988). Engerman, Stanley L., and Robert Gallman, eds., *The*

Cambridge Economic History of the United States, Vol I (1996). Farrand, Max, ed., *The Records of the Federal Convention of 1787*, 4 vols (1966). Fischer, David Hackett, *Paul Revere's Ride* (1994). Flexner, James Thomas, *George Washington and the New Nation (1783–1793)* (1970). _____, *George Washington in the American Revolution (1775–1783)* (1968). Fliegelman, Jay, *Declaring Independence: Jefferson, Natural Language, and the Culture of Performance* (1993). Foner, Eric, *Tom Paine and Revolutionary America* (1976).

Greene, Jack P., *Colonies to Nation, 1763–1789* (1967). _____, and J. R. Pole, eds., *The Blackwell Encyclopedia of the American Revolution* (1991). Gross, Robert A., ed., *In Debt to Shays: The Bicentennial of an Agrarian Rebellion* (1993). _____, *The Minutemen and Their World* (1976). Gruber, Ira D., *The Howe Brothers and the American Revolution* (1972). Higginbotham, Don, *The War of American Independence: Military Attitudes, Policies, and Practice, 1763–1789* (1971). Hoffman, Ronald, and Peter J. Albert, eds., *The Transforming Hand of Revolution: Reconsidering the American Revolution as a Social Movement* (1995). _____, *Women in the Age of the American Revolution* (1989). Hoffman, Ronald, et al., eds., *The Economy of Early America: The Revolutionary Period, 1763–1790* (1988). Jensen, Merrill, *The Articles of Confederation: An Interpretation of the Social-Constitutional History of the American Revolution, 1774–1781* (1970). Jordan, Winthrop D., *White Over Black: American Attitudes Toward the Negro, 1550–1812* (1968). Kaminski, John, and Richard Leffler, eds., *Federalists and Antifederalists: The Debate Over the Ratification of the Constitution* (1989). Ketcham, Ralph, *James Madison: A Biography* (1971). Klein, Rachel N., *Unification of a Slave State: Planter Class in the South Carolina Backcountry, 1760–1808* (1990). Koistinen, Paul A. C., *Beating Plowshares into Swords: The Political Economy of American Warfare, 1606–1865* (1996). Konig, David Thomas, ed., *Devising Liberty: Preserving and Creating Freedom in the New American Republic* (1995). Kurtz, Stephen G., and James H. Hudson, eds., *Essays on the American Revolution* (1973). Lee, Jean B., *The Price of Nationhood: The American Revolution in Charles County* (1994). Lewis, Jan, "The Republican Wife: Virtue and Seduction in the Early Republic," *William and Mary Quarterly*, 3d Ser., XLIV (1987), 689–721. Lockridge, Kenneth A. "Social Change and the Meaning of the American Revolution," *Journal of Social History*, 6 (1973), 403–39.

Mackesy, Piers, *The War for America, 1775–1783* (1965). Maier, Pauline, *American Scripture: Making the Declaration of Independence* (1997). _____, *The Old Revolutionaries: Political Lives in the Age of Samuel Adams* (1980). Main, Jackson Turner, *The Sovereign States* (1973). Martin, Joseph Plumb, *Private Yankee Doodle Dandy* (1962). Matson, Cathy D., and Peter S. Onuf, *A Union of Interests: Political and Economic Thought in Revolutionary America* (1990). Merrell, James H., "Declarations of Independence: Indian-White Relations in the New Nation," in Jack P. Greene, ed., *The American Revolution: Its Character and Limits* (1987), 197–223. Middlekauff, Robert, *The Glorious Cause: The American Revolution, 1763–1789* (1982). Miller, Perry, "From the Covenant to the Revival," in James Ward Smith and A. Leland Jamison, eds., *The Shaping of American Religion* (1961), 322–68.

Morris, Richard B., *The Forging of the Union, 1781–1789* (1987). _____, *Seven Who Shaped Our Destiny: The Founding Fathers as Revolutionaries* (1973). Nash, Gary B., *Race and Revolution* (1990). _____, *The Urban Crucible: Social Change, Political Consciousness, and the Origins of the American Revolution* (1979). Norton, Mary Beth, *The British-Americans: The Loyalist Exiles in England, 1774–1789* (1972). _____, *Liberty's Daughters: The Revolutionary Experience of American Women, 1750–1800* (1980). Onuf, Peter S., "The Origins and Early Development of State Legislatures," in Joel H. Silbey, ed., *Encyclopedia of the American Legislative System* (1994), 175–94. _____, *The Origins of the Federal Republic: Jurisdictional Controversies in the United States, 1775–1787* (1983). _____, *Statehood and Union: A History of the Northwest Ordinance* (1987). Paine, Thomas, *Collected Writings* (1995). Perkins, Bradford, *The Cambridge History of American Foreign Relations, Vol I: The Creation of a Republican Empire, 1776–1865* (1993). Rakove, Jack N., *The Beginnings of National Politics: An Interpretive History of the Continental Congress* (1979).

Smith, Barbara Clark, "Food Rioters and the American Revolution," *William and Mary Quarterly*, 3d Ser., LI (1994), 3–38. Storing, Herbert J., *The Complete Antifederalist*, 7 vols (1981). Syrett, Harold C., ed., *The Papers of Alexander Hamilton*, 27 vols (1961–1987). Szatmary, David P., *Shays' Rebellion: The Making of an Agrarian Insurrection* (1980). Taylor, Alan, *William Cooper's Town: Power and Persuasion on the Frontier of the Early American Republic* (1995). Wallace, Anthony F. C., *The Death and Rebirth of the Seneca* (1969). Washburn, Wilcomb E., ed., *History of Indian-White Relations* (1988). Weigley, Russell F., *Morristown: Official National Park Handbook* (1983). _____, *The Partisan War: The South Carolina Campaign of 1780–1782* (1970). Wills, Garry, *Inventing America: Jefferson's Declaration of Independence* (1978). Wood, Gordon S., *The Radicalism of the American Revolution* (1992). Young, Alfred F., ed., *The American Revolution* (1976). _____, *Beyond the American Revolution: Explorations in the History of American Radicalism* (1993).

CHAPTER 8

Appleby, Joyce Oldham, *Capitalism and a New Social Order: The Republican Vision of the 1790s* (1983). Banning, Lance, *The Jeffersonian Persuasion: Evolution of a Party Ideology* (1978). _____, *The Sacred Fire of Liberty: James Madison and the Founding of the Federal Republic* (1995). Beeman, Richard B., *The Evolution of the Southern Backcountry: A Case Study of Lunenburg County, Virginia, 1746–1832* (1984). Bemis, Samuel F., *Jay's Treaty: A Study in Commerce and Diplomacy* (1962). Berkhofer, Robert F., Jr., *Salvation and the Savage: An Analysis of Protestant Missions and American Indian Response, 1787–1862* (1965). Berlin, Ira, *Many Thousands Gone: The First Two Centuries of Slavery in North America* (1998). Buel, Richard, Jr., *Securing the Revolution: Ideology in American Politics, 1789–1815* (1972). Calloway, Colin G., *Crown and Calumet: British-Indian Relations, 1783–1815* (1987). Cole, Arthur H., ed., *Industrial and Commercial Correspondence of Alexander Hamilton* (1928). Cox, Tench, *A View of the United States of America* (1794). Cunningham, Noble E., *The*

Jeffersonian Republicans: The Formation of Party Organization, 1789–1801 (1957). Dillon, Merton L., *Slavery Attacked: Southern Slaves and their Allies, 1619–1865* (1990). Dorfman, Joseph, *The Economic Mind in American Civilization*, 2 vols (1946). Edmunds, R. David, *Tecumseh: The Quest for Indian Leadership* (1984). Elkins, Stanley, and Eric McKitrick, *The Age of Federalism: The Early American Republic, 1788–1800* (1993).

Hamilton, Alexander, *The Papers of Alexander Hamilton*, ed. Harold C. Syrett et al. 27 vols (1961–67). _____, *The Reports of Alexander Hamilton*, ed. Jacob E. Cooke (1964). Hartz, Louis, *The Liberal Tradition in America: An Interpretation of American Political Thought since the Revolution* (1955). Henretta, James A., *The Evolution of American Society, 1700–1815: An Interdisciplinary Analysis* (1973). Heyrman, Christine Leigh, *Southern Cross: The Beginnings of the Bible Belt* (1997). Hoffman, Ronald, and Peter J. Albert, eds., *Women in the Age of the American Revolution* (1989). Horsman, Reginald, *Expansionism and American Indian Policy* (1967). Jefferson, Thomas, *Notes on the State of Virginia* (1964). _____, *The Papers of Thomas Jefferson*, ed. Julian P. Boyd, 20 vols (1950). Jordan, Winthrop D., *White Over Black: American Attitudes Toward the Negro, 1550–1812* (1968). Kerber, Linda, *Women of the Republic: Intellect and Ideology in Revolutionary America* (1980). Ketcham, Ralph L., *James Madison: A Biography* (1971). Lee, Jean B., *The Price of Nationhood: The American Revolution in Charles County* (1994).

Malone, Dumas, *Jefferson and His Time* (1948–1981). Marris, Kenneth C., *The Historical Atlas of Political Parties in the United States, 1789–1989* (1988). McCoy, Drew, *The Elusive Republic: Political Economy in Jeffersonian America* (1984). Miller, John C., *The Federalist Era, 1789–1801* (1960). Mittell, Sherman F., ed., *The Federalist: A Commentary on the Constitution of the United States being a Collection of Essays Written in Support of the Constitution agreed upon September 17, 1787, by The Federal Convention* (1937). Nabakov, Peter, ed., *Native American Testimony: I Chronicle of Indian-White Relations from Prophecy to the Present, 1492–1992* (1991). Nelson, John R., Jr., *Liberty and Property: Political Economy and Policy Making, 1789–1812* (1987). Nettels, Curtis P., *The Emergence of a National Economy, 1775–1815* (1962). North, Douglass C., *The Economic Growth of the United States, 1790–1860* (1966). Norton, Mary Beth, *Liberty's Daughters: The Revolutionary Experience of American Women, 1750–1800* (1980). Perdue, Theda, *Slavery and the Evolution of Cherokee Society, 1540–1866* (1979). Peterson, Merrill D., *Thomas Jefferson and the New Nation* (1970). Risjord, Norman K., *Thomas Jefferson* (1994). Rorabaugh, W. J., *The Craft Apprentice, from Franklin to the Machine Age in America* (1986).

Shalhope, Robert E., "Toward a Republican Synthesis: The Emergence of an Understanding of Republicanism in American Historiography," *William and Mary Quarterly*, 3rd Ser. XXXIX (April 1982), 334–56. Sharp, James Roger, *American Politics in the Early Republic: The New Nation in Crisis* (1993). Sheehan, Bernard W., *Seeds of Extinction: Jeffersonian Philanthropy and the American Indian* (1973). Skemp, Sheila L., *Judith Sargent*

Murray: A Brief Biography with Documents (1988). Sloan, Herbert, *Principle and Interest: Thomas Jefferson and the Problem of Debt* (1994). Smyth, Albert Henry, ed., *The Writings of Benjamin Franklin* (1907). Sword, Wiley, *President Washington's Indian War* (1985). Taylor, Alan, *Liberty Men and Great Proprietors: The Revolutionary Settlement on the Maine Frontier, 1760–1820* (1990). Ulrich, Laurel Thatcher, *A Midwife's Tale: The Life of Martha Ballard, Based on her Diary, 1785–1812* (1990). Wallace, Anthony F. C., *The Death and Rebirth of the Seneca* (1970). Watts, Stephen, *The Republic Reborn: War and the Making of Liberal America, 1790–1820* (1987). White, Richard, *The Middle Ground: Indians, Empires, and Republics in the Great Lakes Region, 1650–1815* (1991). Wood, Gordon, *The Creation of the American Republic 1776–1787* (1969). Wright, Donald R., *African Americans in the Early Republic, 1789–1831* (1993). Wright, J. Leitch, Jr., *Creeks and Seminoles: The Destruction and Regeneration of the Muscogulge People* (1986). Yenne, Bill, *The Encyclopedia of North American Indian Tribes: A Comprehensive Study of Tribes from the Abitibi to the Zuni* (1986). Young, Alfred E., *The Democratic Republicans of New York: The Origins, 1763–1797* (1967). Zagarri, Rosemarie, *A Woman's Dilemma: Mercy Otis Warren and the American Revolution* (1995). Zverper, John, *Political Philosophy and Rhetoric: A Study of the Origins of American Party Politics* (1977).

CHAPTER 9

Ambrose, Stephen, *Undaunted Courage: Meriwether Lewis, Thomas Jefferson and the Opening of the American West* (1996). Banning, Lance, *The Jeffersonian Persuasion: Evolution of a Party Ideology* (1978). Beeman, Richard B., *The Evolution of the Southern Backcountry: A Case Study of Lunenburg County, Virginia, 1746–1832* (1984). Bergon, Frank, ed., *The Journals of Lewis and Clark* (1989). Berkhofer, Robert F., Jr., *Salvation and the Savage: An Analysis of Protestant Missions and American Indian Response, 1787–1862* (1965). Berlin, Ira, "Time, Space, and the Transformation of Afro-American Society in the United States: 1770–1820" in Elise Marienstras and Barbara Karsky, eds., *Autre Temps, Autre Espace/An Other Time, An Other Place: Études sur l'Amérique pré-Industrielle* (1986). Boles, John B., *Black Southerners, 1619–1869* (1983). _____, *The Great Revival, 1787–1805: The Origins of the Southern Evangelical Mind* (1972). Boyd, Julian P., ed., *The Papers of Thomas Jefferson* (1950). Bruce, Dickson D., Jr., *And They All Sang Hallelujah: Plain-Folk Camp-Meeting Religion, 1800–1845* (1974). Butler, Jon, *Awash in a Sea of Faith: Christianizing the American People* (1972). Cawelti, John G., *Apostles of the Self-Made Man: Changing Concepts of Success in America* (1965). Conklin, Paul K., *Cane Ridge: America's Pentecost* (1990). Curry, Leonard P., *The Free Black in Urban America, 1800–1850: The Shadow of a Dream* (1981). Dillon, Merton L., *Slavery Attacked: Southern Slaves and their Allies, 1619–1865* (1990). Dowd, Gregory Evans, *A Spirited Resistance: The North American Indian Struggle for Unity, 1745–1815* (1992). Edmunds, R. David, *Tecumseh: The Quest for Indian Leadership* (1984). Egerton, Douglas R., *Gabriel's Rebellion: The Virginia Slave Conspiracies* (1993). Foner, Philip S., *History of Black Americans: Volume One: From Africa to the Emergence of the Cotton Kingdom* (1975).

Henretta, James A., *The Evolution of American Society, 1700–1815: An Interdisciplinary Analysis* (1973). Horsman, Reginald, *Expansionism and American Indian Policy* (1967). Horton, James Oliver, and Lois E. Horton, *In Hope of Liberty: Culture, Community, and Protest among Northern Free Blacks, 1700–1860* (1997). Jordan, Winthrop D., *White Over Black: American Attitudes Toward the Negro, 1550–1812* (1968). Litwack, Leon F., *North of Slavery: The Negro in the Free States, 1790–1860* (1961).

Mahon, John K., *The War of 1812* (1972). Malone, Dumas, *Jefferson and His Time* (1948–1981). Marris, Kenneth C., *The Historical Atlas of Political Parties in the United States, 1789–1989* (1988). McCoy, Drew, *The Elusive Republic: Political Economy in Jeffersonian America* (1984). McLoughlin, William G., *Cherokee Renascence in the New Republic* (1986). _____, "Thomas Jefferson and the Beginning of Cherokee Nationalism, 1806–1809," *William and Mary Quarterly*, 3rd Ser., XXXII (1975), 547–80. Melish, Joanne Pope, *Disowning Slavery: Gradual Emancipation and "Race" in New England, 1780–1860* (1998). Nash, Gary B., *Forging Freedom: The Formation of Philadelphia's Black Community, 1720–1840* (1988). Nelson, John R., Jr., *Liberty and Property: Political Economy and Policy Making, 1789–1812* (1987). Nettels, Curtis P., *The Emergence of a National Economy, 1775–1815* (1962). North, Douglass C., *The Economic Growth of the United States, 1790–1860* (1966; First published 1961). Peterson, Merrill D., *Thomas Jefferson and the New Nation* (1970). Risjord, Norman K., *Thomas Jefferson* (1994). Rock, Howard B., *Artisans of the New Republic: the Tradesmen of New York City in the Age of Jefferson* (1984). Rorabaugh, W. J., *The Craft Apprentice, from Franklin to the Machine Age in America* (1986). Ryan, Mary P., *Cradle of the Middle Class: The Family in Oneida County, New York, 1790–1865* (1981).

Scott, Anne Firor, *Natural Allies: Women's Associations in American History* (1992). Shalhope, Robert E., "Toward a Republican Synthesis: The Emergence of an Understanding of Republicanism in American Historiography," *William and Mary Quarterly*, 3rd Ser., XXXIX (1982), 334–56. Sharp, James Roger, *American Politics in the Early Republic: The New Nation in Crisis* (1993). Sheehan, Bernard W., *Seeds of Extinction: Jeffersonian Philanthropy and the American Indian* (1973). Sidbury, James, *Ploughshares into Swords: Race, Rebellion, and Identity in Gabriel's Virginia, 1730–1810* (1997). Sloan, Herbert, *Principle and Interest: Thomas Jefferson and the Problem of Debt* (1994). Smelser, Marshall, *The Democratic Republic, 1801–1815* (1968). Smith, Rogers M., *Civic Ideals: Conflicting Visions of Citizenship in U. S. History* (1997). Stansell, Christine, *City of Women: Sex and Class in New York, 1780–1860* (1986). Stone, Barton W., "A Short History of the Life of Barton W. Stone," in James R. Rogers, *The Cane Ridge Meeting House, to which is Appended the Autobiography of B. W. Stone* (1910). Taylor, Alan, *Liberty Men and Great Proprietors: The Revolutionary Settlement on the Maine Frontier, 1760–1820* (1990). Tucker, Robert W., and David C. Hendrickson, *Empire of Liberty: the Statecraft of Thomas Jefferson* (1990). Ulrich, Laurel Thatcher, *A Midwife's Tale: The Life of Martha Ballard, Based on her Diary, 1785–1812* (1990). Wallace, Anthony F. C., *Jefferson and the Indians: The Tragic Fate of the First Americans*

(1999). Watts, Stephen, *The Republic Reborn: War and the Making of Liberal America, 1790–1820* (1987). White, Shane, *Somewhat More Independent: The End of Slavery in New York City* (1991). Wiebe, Robert H., *The Opening of American Society: From the Adoption of the Constitution to the Eve of Disunion* (1984). Wilentz, Sean, *Chants Democratic: New York City and the Rise of the American Working Class, 1788–1850* (1984). Wright, Donald R., *African Americans in the Early Republic, 1789–1831* (1993).

CHAPTER 10

Aaron, Daniel, *Cincinnati, Queen City of the West, 1819–1838* (1992). Ashworth, John, *Slavery, Capitalism, and Politics in the Antebellum Republic, Vol. 1: Commerce and Compromise, 1820–1850* (1995). Berlin, Ira, *Slaves without Masters: The Free Negro in the Antebellum South* (1974). Blackmar, Elizabeth, *Manhattan for Rent, 1785–1850* (1989). Blassingame, John W., *The Slave Community: Plantation Life in the Antebellum South* (1972). Bleser, Carol, *In Joy and Sorrow: Women, Family, and Marriage in the Victorian South, 1830–1900* (1991). Bolton, Charles C., *Poor Whites of the Antebellum South: Tenants and Laborers in Central North Carolina and Northeastern Mississippi* (1994). Brent, Linda [Harriet Jacobs], *Incidents in the Life of a Slave Girl*, ed. L. Maria Child (1973). Butler, Jon, *Awash in a Sea of Faith: Christianizing the American People* (1990). Carby, Hazel V., *Reconstructing Womanhood: The Emergence of the Afro-American Woman Novelist* (1987). Clark, Christopher, *The Roots of Rural Capitalism: Western Massachusetts, 1780–1860* (1990). Clinton, Catherine, *The Plantation Mistress: Woman's World in the Old South* (1982). Collins, Bruce, *White Society in the Antebellum South* (1985). Conklin, Paul K., *The Uneasy Center: Reformed Christianity in Antebellum America* (1995). Curry, Leonard P., *The Free Black in Urban America, 1800–1850: The Shadow of the Dream* (1981). Dangerfield, George, *The Era of Good Feelings* (1952). Davis, David Brion, *The Problem of Slavery in the Age of Revolution, 1770–1823* (1975). Douglass, Frederick, *Narrative of the Life of Frederick Douglass, an American Slave, Written by Himself*, ed. Benjamin Quarles (1960). Dowd, Gregory, *A Spirited Resistance: The North American Indian Struggle for Unity* (1992). Dublin, Thomas, *Farm to Factory: Women's Letters, 1830–1860*, 2nd ed. (1993). Duncan, John M., *Travels through Part of the United States and Canada in 1818 and 1819*, 2 vols (1823). Escott, Paul D., *Slavery Remembered: A Record of Twentieth-Century Slave Narratives* (1979). Faust, Drew, *James Henry Hammond and the Old South* (1982). Fields, Barbara Jeanne, *Slavery and Freedom on the Middle Ground: Maryland During the Nineteenth Century* (1985). Fox-Genovese, Elizabeth, *Within the Plantation Household: Black and White Women in the Old South* (1988).

Gates, Paul W., *The Farmer's Age: Agriculture, 1815–1860* (1960). Gutman, Herbert G., *The Black Family in Slavery and Freedom, 1750–1925* (1976). Hahn, Steven, and Jonathan Prude, eds., *The Countryside in the Age of Capitalist Transformation: Essays in the Social History of Rural America* (1985). Harris, J. William, ed., *Society and Culture in the Slave South* (1992). Hudson, Winthrop S., *Religion in America: An Historical Account of the Development of American Religious Life* (1965). Jones, Jacqueline, *Labor of Love, Labor of Sorrow: Black*

Women, Work, and the Family from Slavery to the Present (1985). Kolchin, Peter, *American Slavery, 1619–1877* (1993). *Letters of John Pintard to his Daughter Eliza Noel Pontard Davidson, 1816–1833,* 4 vols (1940). Licht, Walter, *Industrializing America: The Nineteenth Century* (1995). Loewenberg, Bert James, and Ruth Bogin, eds., *Black Women in Nineteenth-Century American Life: Their Words, Their Thoughts, Their Feelings* (1976).

McCurry, Stephanie, *Masters of Small Worlds: Yeoman Households, Gender Relations, and the Political Culture of the Antebellum South Carolina Low Country* (1995). Morris, Christopher, *Becoming Southern: The Evolution of a Way of Life, Warren County and Vicksburg, Mississippi, 1770–1860* (1995). Morrison, John H., *History of American Steam Navigation* (1958). Oakes, James, *The Ruling Race: A History of American Slaveholders* (1982). Riley, Glenda, *The Female Frontier: A Comparative View of Women on the Prairie and the Plains* (1988). Rock, Howard B., *Artisans of the New Republic: The Tradesmen of New York in the Age of Jefferson* (1979).

Sellers, Charles, *The Market Revolution: Jacksonian America, 1815–1846* (1991). Shammas, Carole, "Black Women's Work and the Evolution of Plantation Society in Virginia," *Labor History*, 26/1 (Winter 1985), 5–28. Sheriff, Carol, *The Artificial River: The Erie Canal and the Paradox of Progress, 1817–1862* (1996). Stansell, Christine, *City of Women: Sex and Class in New York, 1780–1860* (1986). Tadman, Michael, *Speculators and Slaves: Masters, Traders and Slaves in the Old South* (1989). White, Deborah Gray, *Ar'n't I a Woman? Female Slaves in the Plantation South* (1985). Wilentz, Sean, *Chants Democratic: New York City and the Rise of the American Working Class, 1788–1850* (1984). Wishart, David J., *The Fur Trade of the American West, 1807–1840: A Geographical Synthesis* (1979).

CHAPTER 11

Address of the Republican General Committee of Young Men of the City and County of New-York Friendly to the Election of Gen: Andrew Jackson to the Presidency to The Republican Electors of the State of New-York (1828). Baxter, Maurice G., *Henry Clay and the American System* (1995). Bellows, Barbara L., *Benevolence Among Slaveholders: Assisting the Poor in Charleston, 1670–1860* (1993). Benson, Lee, *The Concept of Jacksonian Democracy* (1961). Bestor, Arthur, *Backwoods Utopias: The Sectarian Origins and the Owenite Phase of Communitarian Socialism in America, 1663–1829*, 2nd ed. (1970). Butler, Diana Hochstedt, *Standing Against the Whirlwind: Evangelical Episcopalians in Nineteenth-Century America* (1995). Cawelti, John G., *Apostles of the Self-Made Man: Changing Concepts of Success in America* (1965). Clay, Henry, *An Address of Henry Clay, to the Public; Containing Certain Testimony in Refutation of the Charges Against Him, Made by Gen. Andrew Jackson, Touching the Last Presidential Election* (1818). Cole, Donald B., *The Presidency of Andrew Jackson* (1993). Conklin, Paul K., *The Uneasy Center: Reformed Christianity in Antebellum America* (1995). Cott, Nancy F., *The Bonds of Womanhood: "Woman's Sphere" in New England, 1780–1835* (1977). Cross, Whitney, *The Burned-Over District* (1950). Curry, Leonard P., *The Free Black in Urban America, 1800–1850: the Shadow of a Dream* (1981). Feller, Daniel, *The Jacksonian Promise: America, 1815–1840* (1995). _____, *The Public Lands in Jacksonian Politics* (1984). Finney, Charles G[randison], *Autobiography* [Originally Entitled *Memoirs of Charles Grandison Finney*] (1876). Formisano, Ronald P., *The Birth of Mass Political Parties* (1971). Foster, Lawrence, *Women, Family, and Utopia: Communal Experiments of the Shakers, the Oneida Community, and the Mormons* (1991).

Gaustad, Edwin Scott, *A Religious History of America*, Rev. ed. (1966). Ginzberg, Lori D., *Women and the Work of Benevolence: Morality, Politics, and Class in the Nineteenth–Century United States* (1991). Goodrich, Carter, *Government Promotion of American Canals and Railroads, 1800–1890* (1960). Hagan, William T., *The Sac and Fox Indians* (1958). Hall, Thomas Cuming, *The Religious Background of American Culture* (1930). Holt, Michael F., "The Anti-Masonic and Know Nothing Parties," in Arthur M. Schlesinger, Jr., ed., *History of United States Political Parties*, 4 vols (1973). _____, *The Political Crisis of the 1850s* (1978). Horsman, Reginald, *Race and Manifest Destiny: The Origins of American Racial Anglo-Saxonism* (1981). Jackson, Donald, ed., *Black Hawk: An Autobiography* (1955). Johnson, Paul E., *A Shopkeeper's Millennium* (1978). _____, and Sean Wilentz, *The Kingdom of Matthias: The Story of Sex and Salvation in Nineteenth-Century America* (1994). Licht, Walter, *Industrialization in America: The Nineteenth Century* (1995). Litwack, Leon F., *North of Slavery: The Negro in the Free States, 1790–1860* (1961). Loewenberg, Bert James, and Ruth Bogin, eds., *Black Women in Nineteenth-Century American Life: Their Words, Their Thoughts, Their Feelings* (1976).

Matthews, Donald G., "The Second Great Awakening as an Organizing Process, 1780–1830," *American Quarterly*, XXI (1969), 23–43. McCormick, Richard P., *The Second American Party System* (1966). McLoughlin, William G., *Cherokee Renascence in the New Republic* (1986). Mintz, Stephen, *Moralizers and Modernizers: America's Pre-Civil War Reformers* (1995). Nash, Gary B., *Forging Freedom: The Formation of Philadelphia's Black Community, 1720–1840* (1988). Nordhoff, Charles, *The Communistic Societies of the United States: From Personal Observations* (1966). Pollack, Queena, *Peggy Eaton: Democracy's Mistress* (1931). Prucha, Francis P., *The Great Father: The United States Government and the Indians*, 2 vols (1984). _____, *Sword of the Republic: The United States Army on the Frontier, 1783–1846* (1969). Remini, Robert V., *Andrew Jackson and the Course of American Democracy, 1833–1845* (1984). _____, *Andrew Jackson and the Course of American Empire, 1767–1821* (1977). _____, *Andrew Jackson and the Course of American Freedom, 1822–1832* (1981). Roediger, David, *The Wages of Whiteness: Race and the Making of the American Working Class* (1991). Rosenberg, Carroll Smith, *Religion and the Rise of the American City: The New York City Mission Movement, 1812–1870* (1971). Rowe, David, *Thunder and Trumpets: Millerites and Dissenting Religion in Upstate New York, 1800–1850* (1985). Rugoff, Milton, *The Beechers: An American Family of the Nineteenth Century* (1981). Ryan, Mary P., *Cradle of the Middle Class: The Family in Oneida County, New York, 1790–1865* (1981).

Satz, Ronald D., *American Indian Policy in the Jacksonian Era* (1977). Saxton, Alexander, *The Rise and Fall of the White Republic: Class Politics and Mass Culture in Nineteenth-Century America* (1990). Schlesinger, Arthur M., Jr., *The Age of Jackson* (1947). Sellers, Charles, *The Market Revolution: Jacksonian America, 1815–1846* (1991). Smith, Sam B., and Harriet Chappell Owsley, eds., *The Papers of Andrew Jackson,* 6 vols (1980). Spellman, Peter W., and Thomas A. Askew, *The Churches and the American Experience: Ideals and Institutions* (1984). Stansell, Christine, *City of Women: Sex and Class in New York, 1789–1860* (1986). Tanner, Helen Hornbeck, ed., *Atlas of Great Lakes Indian History* (1987). Taylor, George Rogers, ed., *Jackson Versus Biddle: The Struggle over the Second Bank of the United States* (1949). Van Deusen, Glendon G., *The Jacksonian Era, 1828–1848* (1959). Wallace, Anthony F. C., "Prelude to Disaster: The Course of Indian-White Relations Which Led to the Black Hawk War of 1832," in Ellen M. Whitney, ed., *The Black Hawk War, 1831–1832* (Published as vols 35–38, *Collections of the Illinois State Historical Library* 1970–1978.) I, 1–51. Walter, Ronald G., *American Reformers, 1815–1860* (1978). Ward, John William, *Andrew Jackson—Symbol for an Age* (1953). Watson, Harry L., *Liberty and Power: The Politics of Jacksonian America* (1990). Weddle, David L., *The Law as Gospel: Revival and Reform in the Theology of Charles G. Finney* (1985). Wilburn, Jean Alexander, *Biddle's Bank: The Crucial Years* (1967). Wilentz, Sean, *Chants Democratic: New York City and the Rise of the American Working Class, 1788–1850.* New York, 1984.

CHAPTER 12

Billington, Ray Allen, *The Protestant Crusade, 1800–1860: A Study of the Origins of American Nativism* (1938). Blackmar, Elizabeth, *Manhattan for Rent, 1785–1850* (1989). Blumin, Stuart M., *The Emergence of the Middle Class: Social Experience in the American City, 1760–1900* (1989). Boydston, Jeanne, *Home and Work: Housework, Wages, and the Ideology of Labor in the Early Republic* (1990). Carlton, Frank Tracy, *Economic Influences upon Educational Progress in the United States, 1820–1850* (1965). Cawelti, John G., *Apostles of the Self-Made Man: Changing Concepts of Success in America* (1965). Child, Mrs. [Lydia Maria], *The American Frugal Housewife,* 12th ed., (1833). Cole, Donald B., *The Presidency of Andrew Jackson* (1993). Cott, Nancy F., *The Bonds of Womanhood: "Woman's Sphere" in New England, 1780–1835* (1977). Curry, Leonard P., *The Free Black in Urban America, 1800–1850: The Shadow of a Dream* (1981). Davis, David Brion, "The Emergence of Immediatism in British and American Antislavery Thought," *Mississippi Valley Historical Review,* XLIX (September 1962), 209–30. Dew, Thomas R., *Review of the Debate in the Virginia Legislature of 1831 and 1832* (1832). Duberman, Martin, ed., *The Antislavery Vanguard: New Essays on the Abolitionists* (1965). Dudley, William, ed., *Slavery: Opposing Views* (1992). Feller, Daniel, *The Jacksonian Promise: America, 1815–1840* (1995). Foner, Philip S., *From Colonial Times to the Founding of the American Federation of Labor. Volume One: History of the Labor Movement in the United States* (1947). _____, *Women and the American Labor Movement: From the First Trade Unions to the Present* (1979). Freyer, Tony A., *Producers versus Capitalists: Constitutional Conflict in Antebellum America*

(1994). Friedman, Lawrence J., *Gregarious Saints: Self and Community in American Abolitionism, 1830–1870* (1982).

Ginzberg, Lori D., "'The Hearts of Your Readers Will Shudder': Fanny Wright, Infidelity, and American Free Thought," *American Quarterly,* Vol 46, No. 2 (June 1994), 195–226. Griffin, Clifford S., *Their Brothers' Keepers: Moral Stewardship in the United States, 1800–1865* (1960). Jackson, Sidney L., *America's Struggle for Free Schools: Social Tension and Education in New England and New York, 1827–42* (1965). Kaestle, Carl F., *Pillars of the Republic: Common Schools and American Society, 1780–1860* (1983). Katz, Michael B., *The Irony of Early School Reform: Educational Innovation in Mid-Nineteenth Century Massachusetts* (1968). Lazerow, Jama, *Religion and the Working Class in Antebellum America* (1995).

Mintz, Stephen, *Moralizers and Modernizers: America's Pre-Civil War Reformers* (1995). North, Douglass C., *The Economic Growth of the United States, 1790–1860* (1966. First published 1961). Pease, William H., and Jane H. Pease, *The Web of Progress: Private Values and Public Styles in Boston and Charleston, 1828–1843* (1985). Remini, Robert V., *Andrew Jackson and the Course of American Democracy, 1833–1845* (1984). _____, *Andrew Jackson and the Course of American Empire, 1767–1821* (1977). _____, *Andrew Jackson and the Course of American Freedom, 1822–1832* (1981). _____, *The Election of Andrew Jackson* (1963). Roediger, David R., *Towards the Abolition of Whiteness: Essays on Race, Politics, and Working Class History* (1994). _____, *The Wages of Whiteness: Race and the Making of the American Working Class* (1991). Rosenberg, Carroll Smith, *Religion and the Rise of the American City: The New York City Mission Movement, 1812–1870* (1971). Rudolph, Frederick, ed., *Essays on Education in the Early Republic* (1965). Ryan, Mary P., *Cradle of the Middle Class: The Family in Oneida County, New York, 1790–1865* (1981).

Saxton, Alexander, *The Rise and Fall of the White Republic: Class Politics and Mass Culture in Nineteenth-Century America* (1990). Schlesinger, Arthur M., Jr., *The Age of Jackson* (1947). Scott, Anne Firor, *Natural Allies: Women's Associations in American History* (1992). Smith, Sam B., and Harriet Chappell Owsley, eds., *The Papers of Andrew Jackson,* 6 vols (1980). Stansell, Christine, *City of Women: Sex and Class in New York, 1789–1860* (1986). Vassar, Rena L., ed., *Social History of American Education: Volume One: Colonial Times to 1860* (1965). Walker, David, *David Walker's Appeal to the Coloured Citizens of the World* (1995). Walters, Ron, *American Reformers, 1815–1860* (1978). Welter, Rush, *Popular Education and Democratic Thought in America* (1962). Wilentz, Sean, *Chants Democratic: New York City and the Rise of the American Working Class, 1788–1850* (1984). Yellin, Jean Fagan, and John C. Van Horne, eds., *The Abolitionist Sisterhood: Women's Political Culture in Antebellum America* (1994).

CHAPTER 13

Ballantine, Betty, and Ian Ballantine, eds., *The Native Americans: An Illustrated History* (1993). Bauer, K. Jack, *The Mexican War, 1846–1848* (1974). Bergeron, Paul H., *The Presidency of James K. Polk* (1987). Binkley, William C., *The Texas Revolution* (1952). Blue, Frederick J., *The Free Soilers:*

Third Party Politics (1973). Brack, Gene M., *Mexico Views Manifest Destiny* (1976). Butruille, Susan G., *Women's Voices from the Oregon Trail* (1993). Campbell, Randolph B., *An Empire for Slavery: The Peculiar Institution in Texas* (1989). Clark, Christopher, *The Communitarian Moment: the Radical Challenge of the Northampton Association* (1995). Clark, Malcolm, Jr., *Eden Seekers: The Settlement of Oregon, 1818–1862* (1981). Clayton, Lawrence R., and Joseph E. Chance, eds., *The March to Monterrey: The Diary of Lt. Rankin Dilworth* (1966). Dawley, Alan, *Class and Community: The Industrial Revolution in Lynn* (1976). Dillon, Merton L., *Slavery Attacked: Southern Slaves and Their Allies, 1618–1685* (1990). Faragher, John Mack, *Women and Men on the Overland Trail* (1979). Faust, Drew Gilpin, ed., *The Ideology of Slavery: Proslavery Thought in the Antebellum South, 1830–1860* (1981). Foster, Lawrence, *Women, Family, and Utopia: Communal Experiments of the Shakers, the Oneida Community, and the Mormons* (1991).

Ginzberg, Lori D., *Women and the Work of Benevolence: Morality, Politics, and Class in the Nineteenth-Century United States* (1990). Graebner, Norman A., *Empire on the Pacific: A Study in American Continental Expansion* (1955). Holloway, Mark, *Heavens on Earth: Utopian Communities in America, 1680–1880*, 2nd ed. (1966). Horsman, Reginald, *Race and Manifest Destiny: The Origins of American Racial Anglo-Saxonism* (1981). Isenberg, Nancy, *Sex and Citizenship in Antebellum America* (1998). Jeffrey, Julie Roy, *Converting the West: A Biography of Narcissa Whitman* (1991). Johannsen, Robert W., *To the Halls of Montezumas: The Mexican War in the American Imagination* (1985). Johnson, Paul E., and Sean Wilentz, *The Kingdom of Matthias: A Story of Sex and Salvation in Nineteenth-Century America* (1994). Kohl, Lawrence Frederick, *The Politics of Individualism: Parties and the American Character in the Jacksonian Era* (1989).

Maffly-Kipp, Laurie F., *Religion and Society in Frontier California* (1994). Marquis, Thomas B., *The Cheyennes of Montana*, ed. Thomas D. Weist (1978). Matovina, Timothy M., *Tejano Religion and Ethnicity: San Antonio, 1821–1860* (1995). McCaffrey, James M., *Army of Manifest Destiny: The American Soldier in the Mexican War, 1846–1848* (1992). Miller, Robert Ryan, ed., *The Mexican War Journal and Letters of Ralph W. Kirkham* (1991). Mintz, Steven, *Moralists and Modernizers: America's Pre-Civil War Reformers* (1995). Monaghan, Jay, *The Overland Trail* (1971). Montejano, David, *Anglos and Mexicans in the Making of Texas, 1836–1986* (1987). Morrison, Michael A., *Slavery and the American West: The Eclipse of Manifest Destiny and the Coming of the Civil War* (1997). Parker, Theodore, *The Slave Power* (1969). Peterson, Norma Lois, *The Presidencies of William Henry Harrison and John Tyler* (1989). Prude, Jonathan, *The Coming of the Industrial Order: Town and Factory Life in Rural Massachusetts, 1810–1860* (1983). Reidy, Joseph, *From Slavery to Agrarian Capitalism in the Cotton Plantation South: Central Georgia, 1800–1880* (1992). Remini, Robert, *Martin Van Buren and the Making of the Democratic Party* (1959).

Schroeder, John H., *Mr. Polk's War: American Opposition and Dissent, 1846–1848* (1973). Seager, Robert, II, *And Tyler Too: A Biography of John and Julia Gardiner Tyler* (1963). Sellers,

Charles, *James K. Polk, Continentalist: 1843–1846* (1966). _____, *James K. Polk, Jacksonian: 1795–1843* (1957). Sloan, Irving J., ed., *Martin van Buren, 1782–1862* (1969). Smith-Rosenberg, Carroll, *Disorderly Conduct: Visions of Gender in Victorian America* (1985). Stansell, Christine, *City of Women: Sex and Class in New York, 1789–1860* (1986). Stephanson, Anders, *Manifest Destiny: American Expansion and the Empire of Right* (1995). Tijerina, Andrés, *Tejanos and Texas under the Mexican Flag, 1821–1836* (1994). Weber, David, *The Mexican Frontier, 1821–1846. The American Southwest under Mexico* (1982). White, Richard, *"It's Your Misfortune and None of My Own"; A History of the American West* (1991). Wilentz, Sean, *Chants Democratic: New York City and the Rise of the American Working Class, 1788–1850* (1984). Wilson, Major L., *The Presidency of Martin Van Buren* (1984).

CHAPTER 14

Barney, William, *The Road to Secession: A New Perspective on the Old South* (1972). Blumin, Stuart, *The Emergence of the Middle Class: Social Experience in the American City, 1790–1900* (1989). Campbell, Stanley, *The Slave Catchers* (1970). Cooper, William J., Jr., *The South and the Politics of Slavery, 1828–1856* (1978). Craven, Avery, *The Coming of the Civil War*, 2nd ed. (1957). Fehrenbacher, Don E., *Prelude to Greatness: Lincoln in the 1850s* (1952). Fehrenbacher, Don, *The Slaveholding Republic: An Account of the United States Government's Relations to Slavery* (2001). Fishlow, Albert, *American Railroads and the Transformation of the Antebellum Economy* (1965). Fogel, Robert, *Without Consent or Contract: The Rise and Fall of American Slavery* (1989).

Genovese, Eugene D., *The Political Economy of Slavery: Studies in the Economy and Society of the Slave South* (1965). Greenstone, David J., *The Lincoln Persuasion: Remaking American Liberalism* (1993). Hamilton, Holman, *Prologue to Conflict: The Crisis and Compromise of 1850* (1970). Holt, Michael F., *The Rise and Fall of the American Whig Party: Jacksonian Politics and the Onset of the Civil War* (1999). Huston, James, *The Panic of 1857 and the Coming of the Civil War* (1987). Jaffa, Harry V., *Crisis of the House Divided: An Interpretation of the Lincoln-Douglas Debates* (1959). Johannsen, Robert W., *Stephen A. Douglas* (1973). Johnson, Walter, *Soul By Soul: Life Inside the Antebellum Slave Market* (1999).

May, Robert E., *The Southern Dream of a Caribbean Empire, 1854–1861* (1973). McCardell, John, *The Idea of a Southern Nation: Southern Nationalists and Southern Nationalism, 1830–1860* (1979). Morrison, Chaplain W., *Democratic Politics and Sectionalism: The Wilmot Proviso Controversy* (1967). Nevins, Allan, *Ordeal of the Union*, 4 vols (1947–1950). Nichols, Roy F., *The Disruption of American Democracy* (1948). Niven, John, *The Coming of the Civil War, 1837–1861* (1990). Oakes, James, *Slavery and Freedom: An Interpretation of the Old South* (1990). Potter, David M., *The South and the Sectional Conflict* (1969).

Sewell, Richard B., *Ballots for Freedom: Antislavery Politics in the United States, 1837–1860* (1976). Stampp, Kenneth M., *America in 1857: A Nation on the Brink* (1990). Summers, Mark W., *The*

Plundering Generation: Corruption and the Crisis of the Union, 1849–1861 (1987). Tadman, Michael, *Speculators and Slaves: Masters, Traders, and Slaves in the Old South* (1996 ed.). Takaki, Ronald, *A Pro-Slavery Crusade: The Agitation to Reopen the African Slave Trade* (1971). Wright, Gavin, *The Political Economy of the Cotton South: Households, Markets and Wealth in the Nineteenth Century* (1978). Zarefsky, David, *Lincoln, Douglas, and Slavery: The Crucible of Public Debate* (1990).

CHAPTER 15

Ball, Douglas B., *Financial Failure and Confederate Defeat* (1990). Barney, William L., *The Secessionist Impulse: Alabama and Mississippi in 1860* (1974). Bernstein, Iver, *The New York City Draft Riots: Their Significance for American Society and Politics in the Age of the Civil War* (1990). Catton, Bruce, *This Hallowed Ground* (1956). _____, *Glory Road* (1952). _____, *Mr. Lincoln's Army* (1951). _____, *A Stillness at Appomattox* (1953). Channing, Steven A., *Crisis of Fear: Secession in South Carolina* (1970). Clinton, Catherine, and Nina Silber, eds., *Divided Houses: Gender and the Civil War* (1992). Connelly, Thomas L., *The Marble Man: Robert E. Lee and His Image in American Society* (1977). Cooper, William J., Jr. *Jefferson Davis: American* (2000). Cornish, Dudley T., *The Sable Arm: Negro Troops in the Union Army* (1977). Current, Richard, *Lincoln and the First Shot* (1963). _____, ed., *Why the North Won the Civil War* (1960). Eaton, Clement, *A History of the Southern Confederacy* (1954). Escott, Paul D., *After Secession: Jefferson Davis and the Failure of Confederate Nationalism* (1978). Faust, Drew Gilpin, *The Creation of Confederate Nationalism* (1988). _____, *Mothers of Invention: Women of the Slaveholding South in the American Civil War* (1996). Fredrickson, George M., *The Inner Civil War: Northern Intellectuals and the Crisis of the Union* (1965).

Glatthaar, Joseph T., *Forged in Battle: the Civil War Alliance of Black Soldiers and White Officers* (1990). Guelzo, Allen C., *Abraham Lincoln: Redeemer President* (1999). Hettle, Wallace, *The Peculiar Democracy: Southern Democrats in Peace and Civil War* (2001). Jaffa, Harry V., *A New Birth of Freedom: Abraham Lincoln and the Coming of the Civil War* (2000). Jones, Howard, *The Union in Peril: The Crisis over British Intervention in the Civil War* (1992). Linderman, Gerald, *Embattled Courage: The Experience of Combat in the American Civil War* (1987).

McPherson, James M., *For Cause and Comrades: Why Men Fought in the Civil War* (1997). _____, *The Negro's Civil War: How American Negroes Felt and Acted During the War for the Union* (1965). _____, *The Struggle for Equality: Abolitionists and the Negro in the Civil War and Reconstruction* (1964). _____, *What They Fought For, 1861–1865* (1994). Mitchell, Reid, *Civil War Soldiers* (1988). _____, *The Vacant Chair: The Northern Soldier Leaves Home* (1993). Neely, Mark E., Jr., *The Fate of Liberty: Abraham Lincoln and Civil Liberties* (1990). Nevins, Allan, *The War for the Union*, 4 vols (1959–1971). Nolan, Alan T., *Lee Considered: General Robert E. Lee and Civil War History* (1991). Oates, Steven B., *A Woman of Valor: Clara Barton and the Civil War* (1994). Paludan, Phillip S., *Victims: A True Story of the Civil War* (1981). Potter, David M.,

Lincoln and His Party in the Secession Crisis (1942). Quarles, Benjamin, *The Negro in the Civil War* (1953). Rable, George C., *Civil Wars: Women and the Crisis of Southern Nationalism* (1989). Roark, James L., *Masters Without Slaves: Southern Planters in the Civil War and Reconstruction* (1977).

Thomas, Emory, *Robert E. Lee: A Biography* (1995). Vinovskis, Maris A., ed., *Toward a Social History of the American Civil War* (1990). Voegli, V. Jacques, *Free But Not Equal: The Midwest and the Negro during the Civil War* (1967). Wiley, Bell Irwin, *The Life of Billy Yank* (1952). _____, *The Life of Johnny Reb* (1943). Wilson, Douglas, *Honor's Voice: The Transformation of Abraham Lincoln* (1998).

CHAPTER 16

Belz, Herman, *Emancipation and Equal Rights: Politics and Constitutionalism in the Civil War Era* (1978). _____, *Reconstructing the Union: Theory and Policy during the Civil War* (1969). Benedict, Michael Les, *A Compromise of Principle: Congressional Republicans and Reconstruction* (1974). Brock, W. R., *An American Crisis: Congress and Reconstruction, 1865–1867* (1963). Cox, LaWanda, *Lincoln and Black Freedom: A Study in Presidential Leadership* (1981). Current, Richard, *Those Terrible Carpetbaggers* (1988). Donald, David, *The Politics of Reconstruction, 1864–1867* (1967). DuBois, Ellen Carol, *Feminism and Suffrage: The Emergence of an Independent Women's Movement in America, 1848–1869* (1978). Edwards, Laura, *Gendered Strife and Confusion: The Political Culture of Reconstruction* (1977). Fields, Barbara Jeanne, *Slavery and Freedom on the Middle Ground: Maryland during the Nineteenth Century* (1985). Foner, Eric, *Freedom's Lawmakers: A Directory of Black Officeholders during Reconstruction* (1993). _____, *Nothing But Freedom: Emancipation and Its Legacy* (1983).

Gillette, William, *Retreat from Reconstruction, 1869–1879* (1979). Hermann, Janet Sharp, *The Pursuit of a Dream* (1981). Holt, Thomas G., *Black over White: Negro Political Leadership in South Carolina during Reconstruction* (1977). Hyman, Harold, *A More Perfect Union: The Impact of the Civil War and Reconstruction on the Constitution* (1973). Jaynes, Gerald David, *Branches Without Roots: Genesis of the Black Working Class in the American South, 1862–1882* (1986).

McCrary, Peyton, *Abraham Lincoln and Reconstruction: The Louisiana Experiment* (1978). McFeely, William S., *Grant: A Biography* (1981). _____, *Yankee Stepfather: General O. O. Howard and the Freedmen* (1968). McGerr, Michael, *The Decline of Popular Politics: The American North, 1865–1928* (1986). McKitrick, Eric L., *Andrew Johnson and Reconstruction* (1960). Montgomery, David, *Beyond Equality: Labor and the Radical Republicans, 1861–1872* (1967). Morgan, Lynda J., *Emancipation in Virginia's Tobacco Belt, 1850–1870* (1992). Nieman, Donald L., *To Set the Law in Motion: The Freedmen's Bureau and Legal Rights for Blacks, 1865–1869* (1979). Perman, Michael, *Reunion Without Compromise: The South and Reconstruction, 1865–1879* (1973). _____, *The Road to Redemption: Southern Politics, 1868–1879* (1984). Powell, Lawrence N., *New Masters: Northern Planters during the Civil War and Reconstruction* (1980).

Rabinowitz, Howard N., *Race Relations in the Urban South, 1865–1890* (1978). Rose, Willie Lee, *Rehearsal for Reconstruction: The Port Royal Experiment* (1964). Royce, Edward, *The Origins of Southern Sharecropping* (1993).

Saville, Julie, *The Work of Reconstruction: From Slave to Wage Laborer in South Carolina, 1860–1870* (1994). Sproat, John G., *"The Best Men": Liberal Reformers in a Gilded Age* (1968). Summers, Mark, *Railroads, Reconstruction and the Gospel of Prosperity: Aid Under the Radical Republicans, 1865–1877* (1984). Trelease, Allen W., *White Terror: The Ku Klux Klan Conspiracy and Southern Reconstruction* (1971). Wayne, Michael, *The Reshaping of Plantation Society: The Natchez District, 1860–1880* (1983). Wiener, Jonathan, *Social Origins of the New South: Alabama, 1860–1885* (1978). Williamson, Joel, *After Slavery: The Negro in South Carolina during Reconstruction, 1861–1877* (1965). Wright, Gavin, *Old South, New South: Revolutions in the Southern Economy Since the Civil War* (1986).

CHAPTER 17

Ayres, Edward L., *The Promise of the New South: Life after Reconstruction* (1992). Bledstein, Burton J., *The Culture of Professionalism: The Middle Class and the Development of Higher Education in America* (1976). Bodnar, John E., *The Transplanted: A History of Immigrants in Urban America* (1985). Brody, David, *Steelworkers in America: The Nonunion Era* (1960). Cochran, Thomas, and William Miller, *The Age of Enterprise: A Social History of Industrial America* (1942). Dubofsky, Melvin, *Industrialism and the American Worker* (1975). Dykstra, Robert R., *The Cattle Towns* (1968). Fite, Gilbert C., *The Farmer's Frontier* (1963).

Goldfield, David, and Blaine Brownell, *Urban America: A History*, 2d. ed. (1990). Gutman, Herbert G., *Work, Culture and Society in Industrialising America* (1976). Handlin, Oscar, *The Uprooted: The Epic Story of the Great Migrations that Made the American People* (1951, 1973). Hearnden, Patrick H., *Independence and Empire: The New South's Cotton Mill Campaign, 1865–1901* (1982). Jackson, Kenneth T., *Crabgrass Frontier: The Suburbanization of the United States* (1985). Jeffrey, Julie Roy, *Frontier Women* (1979). Johnson, Susan Lee, *Roaring Camp: The Social World of the California Gold Rush* (2000). Josephson, Matthew, *The Robber Barons: The Great American Capitalists, 1861–1901* (1934). Limerick, Patricia Nelson, *Legacy of Conquest: The Unbroken Past of the American West* (1987). Lingenfelter, Richard, *The Hardrock Miners: A History of the Mining Labor Movement in the American West, 1863–1893* (1974).

Montgomery, David, *Workers' Control in America: Studies in the History of Work, Technology, and Labor Struggles* (1979). Rabinowitz, Howard, *Race Relations in the Urban South, 1865–1890* (1978).

Slotkin, Richard, *The Fatal Environment: The Myth of the Frontier in the Age of Industrialization* (1985). Taylor, Philip A. M., *The Distant Magnet: European Emigration to the U.S.A.* (1971). Teaford, Jon C., *City and Suburb: The Political Fragmentation of Metropolitan America, 1850–1970* (1979). Thernstrom, Stephen, *The Other Bostonians: Poverty and Progress in the American Metropolis, 1880–1970* (1973). Utley, Robert M., *The Indian Frontier of the American West, 1846–1890* (1984). Wiebe, Robert, *The Search for Order, 1877–1920* (1967). Wyman, Mark, *Hard Rock Epic: Western Miners and the Industrial Revolution, 1860–1910* (1979).

CHAPTER 18

Addams, Jane, *Twenty Years at Hull House* (1910). Archdeacon, Thomas, *Becoming American: An Ethnic History* (1981). Banner, Lois, *American Beauty* (1981). Barth, Gunther, *City People: The Rise of Modern City Culture in Nineteenth Century America* (1980). Beisel, Nicola Kay, *Imperiled Innocents: Anthony Comstock and Family Reproduction in Victorian America* (1997). Bodnar, John, *The Transplanted: A History of Immigrants in Urban America* (1985). Boorstin, Daniel J., *The Americans: The Democratic Experience* (1973). Boyer, Paul S., *Purity in Print: The Vice-society Movement and Book Censorship in America* (1968). Danly, Susan, and Cheryl Leibold, et al., *Eakins and the Photograph* (1994). Fabian, Ann, *Card Sharps and Bucket Shops: Gambling in Nineteenth-Century America* (1999). Fredrickson, George, *The Black Image in the White Mind: The Debate on Afro-American Character and Destiny, 1817–1914* (1971).

Gilfoyle, Timothy, *City of Eros: New York City, Prostitution, and the Commercialization of Sex, 1820–1920* (1992). Gorn, Elliot J., *The Manly Art: Bare-knuckle Prize Fighting in America* (1986). Graff, Gerald, *Professing Literature: An Institutional History* (1987). Green, Harvey, *Fit for America: Health, Fitness, Sport, and American Society* (1986). Harris, Neil, *Cultural Excursions: Marketing Appetites and Cultural Tastes in Modern America* (1990). Hawkins, Mike, *Social Darwinism in European and American Thought, 1860–1945: Nature as Model and Nature as Threat* (1997). Higham, John, *Send These To Me: Jews and Other Immigrants in Urban America* (1984). Hofstadter, Richard, *Social Darwinism in American Thought* (1992). Lears, T. J. Jackson, *No Place of Grace: Antimodernism and the Transformation of American Culture, 1880–1920* (1981). Lott, Eric, *Love and Theft: Blackface Minstrelsy and the American Working Class* (1993). Lucie-Smith, Edward, *American Realism* (1994).

May, Henry, *Protestant Churches and Industrial America* (1949 and 1963). Mintz, Steven, *A Prison of Expectations: The Family in Victorian Culture* (1983). Nasaw, David, *Going Out: The Rise and Fall of Public Amusements* (1993). Novak, Barbara, *American Painting of the Nineteenth Century: Realism, Idealism, and the American Experience*, 2nd ed. (1979). Rodgers, Daniel, *The Work Ethic in Industrial America, 1850–1920* (1970). Rothman, Sheila M., *Woman's Proper Place: A History of Changing Ideals and Practices, 1870 to the Present* (1978). Rydell, Robert, *All the World's A Fair: Visions of Empire at American International Expositions, 1876–1916* (1984).

Sollors, Werner, *Beyond Ethnicity: Consent and Descent in American Culture* (1986). Toll, Robert, *On With The Show: The First Century of Show Business in America* (1976). Trachtenberg, Alan, *Reading American Photographs: Images as History, Mathew Brady to Walker Evans* (1989).

CHAPTER 19

Baker, Paula C., *The Moral Frameworks of Public Life: Gender, Politics, and the State in Rural New York, 1870–1930* (1991). Beatty, Bess, *A Revolution Gone Backward: The Black Response to National Politics, 1876–1896* (1987). Beisner, Robert L., *From the Old Diplomacy to the New, 1865–1900* (1975). Bordin, Ruth, *Frances Willard: A Biography* (1986). Brock, William R., *Investigation and Responsibility: Public Responsibility in the United States, 1865–1900* (1984). Buhle, Mary Jo, *Women and American Socialism, 1870–1920* (1981). Campbell, Ballard, *Representative Democracy: Public Policy and Midwestern Legislatures in the Late Nineteenth Century* (1980). Campbell, Charles S., *The Transformation of American Foreign Relations, 1865–1900* (1976).

Garraty, John A., *The New Commonwealth, 1877–1890* (1968). Gould, Lewis L., *The Presidency of William McKinley* (1980). Hays, Samuel P., *The Response to Industrialism, 1885–1914*, 2nd ed. (1995). Jensen, Richard J., *The Winning of the Midwest: Social and Political Conflict, 1888–1896* (1971). Keller, Morton, *Affairs of State: Public Life in Late Nineteenth Century America* (1977). Kleppner, Paul J., *The Cross of Culture: A Social Analysis of Midwestern Politics, 1850–1900* (1970).

McCormick, Richard L., *The Party Period and Public Policy: American Politics from the Age of Jackson to the Progressive Era* (1986). McMath, Robert C., Jr., *The Populist Vanguard: A History of the Southern Farmers' Alliance* (1975). Mink, Gwendolyn, *Old Labor and New Immigrants in American Political Development: Union, Party, and the State, 1875–1920* (1986). Morgan, H. Wayne, *From Hayes to McKinley: National Politics, 1877–1896* (1969). Nugent, Walter T. K., *Money and American Society, 1865–1880,* (1968). Orren, Karen, *Belated Feudalism: Labor, the Law, and Liberal Development in the United States* (1991). Painter, Nell Irvin, *Standing at Armageddon: The United States, 1877–1919* (1987). Peskin, Allan, *Garfield: A Biography* (1978). Reeves, Thomas C., *Gentleman Boss: The Life of Chester Alan Arthur* (1975).

Skowronek, Stephen, *Building A New American State: The Expansion of National Administration Capacities, 1877–1920* (1982). Socolofsky, Homer Edward, and Allan B. Spetter, *The Presidency of Benjamin Harrison* (1987). Teaford, Jon C., *The Unheralded Triumph: City Government in America, 1870–1900* (1984). Terrill, Tom E., *The Tariff, Politics and American Foreign Policy, 1874–1900* (1973). Tomsich, John, *A Genteel Endeavor: American Culture and Politics in the Gilded Age* (1971). Unger, Irwin, *The Greenback Era: A Social and Political History of American Finance, 1865–1879* (1964). Weinstein, Allen, *Prelude to Populism: Origins of the Silver Issue, 1867–1878* (1970). Welch, Richard E., Jr., *The Presidencies of Grover Cleveland* (1988). Wiebe, Robert H., *The Search for Order, 1877–1920* (1967).

CHAPTER 20

Adams, Henry, *The Education of Henry Adams* (1918). Ayers, Edward L., *The Promise of the New South: Life After Reconstruction* (1992). Bailey, Thomas A., *A Diplomatic History of the American People* (1958). Brands, H. W., *The Reckless Decade: America in the 1890s* (1995). Chernow, Ron, *The House of Morgan: An American Banking Dynasty and the Rise of Modern Finance* (1990). Cochran, Thomas C., and William Miller, *The Age of Enterprise: A Social History of Industrial America* (1961). Dulles, Foster Rhea, *Labor in America: A History* (1960).

Gilbert, James B., *Perfect Cities: Chicago's Utopias of 1893* (1991). Ginger, Ray, *Age of Excess: The United States from 1877 to 1914* (1965). _____, *Altgeld's America: The Lincoln Ideal Versus Changing Realities* (1958). Kanigel, Robert, *The One Best Way: Frederick Winslow Taylor and the Enigma of Efficiency* (1997). Karnow, Stanley, *In Our Image: America's Empire in the Philippines* (1989). Lewis, David L., *W. E. B. Du Bois: Biography of a Race, 1868–1919* (1993).

McCloskey, Robert Green, *American Conservatism in the Age of Enterprise, 1865–1910* (1951). McCormick, Richard L., *The Party Period and Public Policy* (1986). McCormick, Thomas J., *China Market: America's Quest for Informal Empire, 1893–1901* (1967). McDougall, Walter A., *Let the Sea Make a Noise: A History of the North Pacific From Magellan to MacArthur* (1993). McGerr, Michael E., *The Decline of Popular Politics: The American North, 1865–1928* (1986). Montgomery, David, *The Fall of the House of Labor: The Workplace, the State, and American Labor Activism, 1865–1925* (1987). Musicant, Ivan, *Empire by Default: The Spanish American War and the Dawn of the American Century* (1998). Richardson, Dorothy, *The Long Day: The Story of a New York Working Girl* (1990). Rosenberg, Emily S., *Spreading the American Dream: American Economic and Cultural Expansion, 1890–1945* (1982).

Salvatore, Nick, *Eugene V. Debs: Citizen and Socialist* (1982). Schirmer, Daniel B., *Republic or Empire: American Resistance to the Philippine War* (1972). Slotkin, Richard, *Gunfighter Nation: The Myth of the Frontier in Twentieth Century America* (1993). Strouse, Jean, *Morgan: American Financier* (1999). Trask, David F., *The War with Spain in 1898* (1981).

CHAPTER 21

Brands, H. W., *T. R.: The Last Romantic* (1997). Bringhurst, Bruce, *Antitrust and the Oil Monopoly: The Standard Oil Cases, 1890–1911* (1979). Clark, Norman H., *Deliver Us From Evil: An Interpretation of American Prohibition* (1976). Cooper, John Milton, Jr., *The Warrior and the Priest: Theodore Roosevelt and Woodrow Wilson in American Politics* (1983). Crichon, Judy, *America 1900: The Turning Point* (1998). Diner, Steven J., *A Very Different Age: Americans in the Progressive Era* (1998). Dulles, Foster Rhea, *Labor in America* (1955). Faulkner, Harold Underwood, *The Quest for Social Justice, 1898–1914* (1931). Filene, Peter G., "Narrating Progressivism: Unitarians v. Pluralists v. Students," *Journal of American History*, 79 (1993) 4, 1546–61.

Gould, Lewis L., *The Presidency of Theodore Roosevelt* (1991). Harbaugh, William H., *Power and Responsibility: The Life and Times of Theodore Roosevelt* (1961). Kessler-Harris, Alice, *Out to Work: A History of Wage Earning Women* (1982). Lewis, David Levering, *W. E. B. Du Bois: Biography of a Race,*

1868–1919 (1993). Lukas, J. Anthony, *Big Trouble: A Murder in a Small Western Town Sets Off a Struggle for the Soul of America* (1997).

McGerr, Michael E., *The Decline of Popular Politics* (1986). McMurry, Linda O., *To Keep the Waters Troubled: The Life of Ida B. Wells* (1998). Ninkovich, Frank, *Modernity and Power: A History of the Domino Theory in the Twentieth Century* (1994). Rodgers, Daniel T., "In Search of Progressivism," *Reviews in American History,* 10 (1982) 4, 113–32. Rosen, Ruth, *The Lost Sisterhood: Prostitution in America, 1900–1918* (1982).

Salvatore, Nick, *Eugene V. Debs: Citizen and Socialist* (1982). Schiesl, Martin J., *The Politics of Efficiency: Municipal Administration and Reform in America, 1800–1920* (1977). Scully, Eileen P., "Taking the Low Road to Sino-American Relations: 'Open Door' Expansionists and the Two China Markets," *Journal of American History,* 82 (1995) 1, 62–83. Shannon, David A., *The Socialist Party of America: A History* (1955). Sklar, Kathryn Kish, *Florence Kelley and the Nation's Work: The Rise of Women's Political Culture, 1830–1900* (1995). Starr, Kevin, *Inventing the Dream: California Through the Progressive Era* (1985). Thelen, David, *Robert M. La Follette and the Insurgent Spirit* (1976). Weibe, Robert H., "The Anthracite Strike of 1902: A Record of Confusion," *Mississippi Valley Historical Review,* 48 (1961) 2, 229–51. _____, *The Search for Order, 1877–1920* (1967).

CHAPTER 22

Bailey, Thomas A., "The Sinking of the Lusitania," *The American Historical Review,* 41 (1935) 1, 54–73. Bird, Kai, *The Chairman: John J. McCloy, The Making of the American Establishment* (1992). Butler, Gregory S., "Visions of a Nation Transformed: Modernity and Ideology in Wilson's Political Thought," *Journal of Church and State,* 39 (Winter 1997) 1, 37–51. Chatfield, Charles, "World War I and the Liberal Pacifist in the United States," *American Historical Review,* 75 (1970) 7, 1920–37. Clark, Norman H., *Deliver Us From Evil: An Interpretation of American Prohibition* (1976). Clifford, John Garry, *The Citizen Soldiers: The Plattsburg Training Camp Movement, 1919–1920* (1972). Davis, Richard Harding, "The Plattsburg Idea," *Collier's* (October 9, 1915) 7–9. Ferrell, Robert H., *Woodrow Wilson and World War I, 1917–1921* (1985).

Horne, Alistair, *The Price of Glory* (1964). Katz, Freidrich, "Pancho Villa and the Attack on Columbus, New Mexico," *American Historical Review,* 83 (1978) 1, 101–30. _____, *The Secret War in Mexico: Europe, the United States, and the Mexican Revolution* (1981). Levin, N. Gordon, Jr., *Woodrow Wilson and World Politics* (1968).

Miles, Lewis W., "Plattsburgh," *Sewanee Review,* 24 (January 1916) 1, 19–23. Miller, William D., *Pretty Bubbles in the Air: America in 1919* (1991). Page, Ralph W., "What I Learned at Plattsburg," *World's Work* (November 1915), 105–08. Perry, Ralph Barton, "Impressions of a Plattsburg Recruit," *New Republic* (October 2, 1915), 229–31. Rudwick, Elliott M., *Race Riot in East Saint Louis, July 2, 1917* (1964). Russell, Francis, *Tragedy in Dedham: The Story of the Sacco-Vanzetti Case* (1962).

Schaffer, Ronald, *America in the Great War: The Rise of the War Welfare State* (1991). Schoonover, Thomas D., "To End All Social Reform: A Progressive's Search for International Order," *Reviews in American History,* 21 (1993), 647–54. Tuchman, Barbara, *The Guns of August* (1976). Ward, Robert D., "The Origin and Activities of the National Security League, 1914–1919," *Mississippi Valley Historical Review,* 47 (January 1960) 1, 51–65. Wynn, Neil A., *From Progressivism to Prosperity: World War I and American Society* (1986).

CHAPTER 23

Barron, Hal S., *Mixed Harvest: The Second Great Transformation in the Rural North, 1870–1930* (1997). Blee, Kathleen M., *Women of the Klan: Racism and Gender in the 1920s* (1991). Burner, David, *Herbert Hoover: A Public Life* (1979). _____, *The Politics of Provincialism: The Democratic Party in Transition, 1918–1932* (1968). Chandler, Alfred D., Jr., *Strategy and Structure* (1962). Coben, Stanley, *Rebellion Against Victorianism: The Impetus for Change in 1920s America* (1991). Cohen, Warren I., *Empire Without Tears: America's Foreign Relations, 1921–1933* (1987). De Benedetti, Charles, *Origins of the Modern American Peace Movement: 1915–1929* (1978). D'Emilio, John, and Estelle Freedman, *Intimate Matters: A History of Sexuality in America* (1988). Douglas, Ann, *Terrible Honesty: Mongrel Manhattan in the 1920s* (1995). Douglas, Susan J., *Inventing American Broadcasting, 1899–1922* (1987).

Gordon, Linda, *Woman's Body, Woman's Right: A Social History of Birth Control in America* (1977). Griswold, Robert, *Fatherhood in America: A History* (1993). Gutierrez, David, *Walls and Mirrors: Mexican Americans, Mexican Immigrants, and the Politics of Ethnicity* (1995). Hawley, Ellis W., *The Great War and the Search for a Modern Order: A History of the American People and Their Institutions, 1917–1933* (1992). _____, ed., *Herbert Hoover as Secretary of Commerce: Studies in New Era Thought and Practice* (1981). Hogan, Michael J., *Informal Entente: The Private Structure of Cooperation in Anglo-American Economy, 1918–1929* (1977). Hounshell, David A., *From the American System to Mass Production, 1800–1932: The Development of Manufacturing Technology in the United States* (1984). Huggins, Nathan I., *Harlem Renaissance* (1971). Jackson, Kenneth T., *The Ku Klux Klan in the City, 1915–1930* (1967). Kennedy, J. Gerald, *Imagining Paris: Exile, Writing and American Identity* (1993). Kern, Stephen, *The Culture of Time and Space, 1880–1918* (1983). Koszarski, Richard, *An Evening's Entertainment: The Age of the Silent Feature Picture, 1915–1928* (1990). Ladd-Taylor, Molly, *Mother-Work: Women, Child Welfare, and the State, 1890–1930* (1994). Lears, Jackson, *Fables of Abundance: A Cultural History of Advertising in America* (1994). Leffler, Melvyn P., *The Elusive Quest: America's Pursuit of European Stability and French Security, 1919–1933* (1979). Lemons, J. Stanley, *The Woman Citizen: Social Feminism in the 1920s* (1973). Lichtman, Alan J., *Prejudice and the Old Politics: The Presidential Election of 1928* (1979).

Marsden, George M., *Fundamentalism and American Culture: The Shaping of Twentieth-Century Evangelicalism, 1870–1925* (1980). Meyerowitz, Joanne J., *Women Adrift: Independent Wage Earners in Chicago, 1880–1930* (1988). Montgomery,

David, *The Fall of the House of Labor: The Workplace, the State, and American Labor Activism, 1865–1925* (1987). Moore, Leonard J., *Citizen Klansmen: The Ku Klux Klan in Indiana, 1921–1928* (1991). Peretti, Burton W., *The Creation of Jazz: Music, Race, and Culture in Urban America* (1992).

Schlesinger, Arthur M., Jr., *The Crisis of the Old Order: 1919–1933* (1957). Seymour, Harold, *Baseball: The Golden Age* (1971). Singal, Daniel Joseph, *The War Within: From Victorian to Modernist Thought in the South, 1919–1945* (1982). Trani, Eugene P., and David L. Wilson, *The Presidency of Warren G. Harding* (1977). Zunz, Olivier, *Making America Corporate, 1870–1920* (1990).

CHAPTER 24

Badger, Anthony J., *The New Deal: The Depression Years, 1933–1940* (1989). Bernstein, Irving, *The Lean Years* (1960). _____, *The Turbulent Years* (1970). Bernstein, Michael A., *The Great Depression: Delayed Recovery and Economic Change in America, 1929–1939* (1987). Bird, Caroline, *The Invisible Scar* (1966). Brinkley, Alan, *Liberalism and Its Discontents* (1998). _____, *Voices of Protest* (1982). Burns, James MacGregor, *Roosevelt: The Lion and the Fox* (1956). Carnegie, Dale, "Grab Your Bootstraps," *Colliers*, March 5, 1938, 14–15. Carter, Dan T., *Scottsboro: A Tragedy of the American South* Rev ed (1979). Cooke, Blanche Wiesen, *Eleanor Roosevelt* 2 vol (1992–1999). Daniels, Roger, *The Bonus March* (1971). Denning, Michael, *The Cultural Front: The Laboring of American Culture in the Twentieth Century* (1997). Edwards, Anne, *Road to Tara* (1983). Eichengreen, Barry, *Golden Fetters: The Gold Standard and the Great Depression, 1919–1939* (1995). Ellis, Edward Robb, *A Nation in Torment: The Great American Depression, 1929–1939* (1970). Fraser, Steve, *Labor Will Rule: Sidney Hillman and the Rise of American Labor* (1991). _____, and Gary Gerstle, *The Rise and Fall of the New Deal Order, 1930–1980* (1989).

Galbraith, John Kenneth, *The Great Crash: 1929* (1961). Gourevitch, Peter, *Politics in Hard Times: Comparative Responses to International Economic Crises* (1986). Granberry, Edward, "The Private Life of Margaret Mitchell," *Colliers*, March 13, 1937, 22–24. Greenberg, Cheryl Lynn, *"Or Does it Explode?": Black Harlem in the Great Depression* (1991). Gregory, James, *American Exodus: The Dust Bowl Migration and Okie Culture in California* (1989). Harriman, Margaret Case, "He Sells Hope," *Saturday Evening Post*, August 14, 1937, 12–34. Hofstadter, Richard, *The Age of Reform* (1956). Kelley, Robin D. G., *Hammer and Hoe: Alabama Communists During the Great Depression* (1990). Kennedy, David M., *Freedom From Fear: The American People in Depression and War* (1999). Kindelberger, Charles, *The World in Depression* (1973). Kirby, John B., *Black Americans in the Roosevelt Era* (1980). Klehr, Harvey, *The Heyday of American Communism: The Depression Decade* (1984). Leuchtenberg, William E., *Franklin D. Roosevelt and the New Deal* (1963).

Manchester, William, *The Glory and the Dream* (1973). McElvaine, Robert S., *The Great Depression: America, 1929–1941* (1984). Nelson, Bruce, *Workers on the Waterfront: Seamen, Longshoremen, and Unionism in the 1930s* (1988).

Patterson, James, *Congressional Conservatism and the New Deal* (1967). _____, *The New Deal and the States* (1969). Pells, Richard, *Radical Visions and American Dreams: Culture and Social Thought in the Depression Years* (1973). Plotke, David, *Building a Democratic Political Order: Reshaping American Liberalism in the 1930s and 1940s* (1996). Pyron, Darden Asbury, *Southern Daughter* (1991).

Schulman, Bruce J., *From Cotton Belt to Sunbelt: Federal Policy, Economic Development, and the Transformation of the South, 1938–1980* (1991). Sitkoff, Harvard, *A New Deal for Blacks* (1978). Temin, Peter, *Lessons from the Great Depression* (1996). Watkins, T. H., *The Hungry Years* (1999). Williams, T. Harry, *Huey Long: A Biography* (1969). Wilson, Joan Hoff, *Herbert Hoover: Forgotten Progressive* (1975). Worster, Donald, *The Dust Bowl: The Southern Plains in the 1930s* (1979).

CHAPTER 25

Adams, Michael C. C., *The Best War Ever: America and World War II* (1994). Alperovitz, Gar, *The Decision to Use the Atomic Bomb and the Architecture of an American Myth* (1995). Ambrose, Stephen, *American Heritage New History of World War II* (1997). _____, *Citizen Soldiers* (1997). Bendiner, Elmer, *The Fall of Fortresses* (1980). Bergerud, Eric, *Touched With Fire: The Land War in the South Pacific* (1996). Blum, John Morton, *V Was for Victory* (1976). Blumenson, Martin, *Kasserine Pass* (1966). Deighton, Len, *Blood, Tears and Folly: An Objective Look at World War II* (1993). Dower, John W., *War Without Mercy* (1986). Feingold, Henry L., *The Politics of Rescue: The Roosevelt Administration and the Holocaust, 1938–1945* (1970). Finkle, Lee, "The Conservative Aims of Militant Rhetoric: Black Protest During World War II," *Journal of American History*, 60 (December 1973) 3, 692–713. Flower, Desmond, and James Reeves, eds., *The War, 1939–1945: A Documentary History* (1997). Fussell, Paul, *Wartime* (1989).

Harris, William H., "A. Philip Randolph as a Charismatic Leader, 1925–1941," *Journal of Negro History*, 64 (Autumn 1979) 4, 301–315. Heinrichs, Waldo, *Threshold of War* (1988). Hobsbawm, Eric, *The Age of Extremes* (1994). Houston, Jeanne Wakatsuki, and James D. Houston, *Farewell to Manzanar* (1973). Hynes, Samuel, *Flights of Passage* (1988). Kennedy, Paul, *The Rise and Fall of the Great Powers* (1987). Kimball, Warren F., *The Juggler: Franklin Roosevelt as Wartime Statesman* (1991). Leffler, Melvyn P., *The Specter of Communism* (1994).

Manchester, William, *The Glory and the Dream: A Narrative History of America, 1932–1972* (1973). Milward, Alan S., *War, Economy and Society 1939–1945* (1977). Morison, Samuel Eliot, *Coral Sea, Midway and Submarine Actions* (1949). _____, *The Two-Ocean War* (1963). O'Neill, William L., *A Democracy at War* (1993). Perrett, Geoffrey, *Days of Sadness, Years of Triumph* (1973). Pogue, Forrest C., *George C. Marshall: Ordeal and Hope, 1939–1942* (1965). Prange, Gordon W., *Miracle at Midway* (1982). Rosenberg, Emily S., *Spreading the American Dream: American Economic and Cultural Expansion, 1890–1945* (1982).

Sitkoff, Harvard, "Racial Militancy and Interracial Violence in the Second World War," *Journal of American History*, 58

(December 1971) 3, 661–81. Spickard, Paul R., *Japanese Americans: The Formation and Transformations of an Ethnic Group* (1996). United States, Federal Bureau of Investigation, "FBI File: A. Philip Randolph" (1990). Weighley, Russell F., *Eisenhower's Lieutenants* (1981). Wright, Gordon, *The Ordeal of Total War, 1939–1945* (1997).

CHAPTER 26

Blackwelder, Julia Kirk, *Now Hiring: The Feminization of Work in the United States, 1900–1995* (1997). Boyer, Paul, *By the Bomb's Early Light: American Thought and Culture at the Dawn of the Atomic Age* (1985). Cumings, Bruce, *The Origins of the Korean War*, 2 vols (1981–1990). Dalfiume, Richard, *Desegregation of the U.S. Armed Forces: Fighting on Two Fronts, 1939–1953* (1969). Donovan, Robert J., *Conflict and Crisis: The Presidency of Harry S Truman, 1945–1948* (1977). _____, *Tumultuous Years: The Presidency of Harry S Truman, 1948–1953* (1982). Egerton, John, *Speak Now Against the Day: The Generation Before the Civil Rights Movement in the South* (1994). Fried, Richard M., *The Russians Are Coming! the Russians Are Coming!: Pageantry and Patriotism in Cold-War America* (1999).

Gaddis, John Lewis, *The United States and the Origins of the Cold War, 1941–1947* (1972). _____, *We Now Know: Rethinking Cold War History* (1997). Hamby, Alonzo L., *Beyond the New Deal: Harry S. Truman and American Liberalism* (1973). Hartmann, Susan M., *The Home Front and Beyond: American Women in the 1940s* (1982). _____, *Truman and the 80th Congress* (1971). Heller, Francis H., ed., *Economics and the Truman Administration* (1981). Hogan, Michael J., *The Marshall Plan: America, Britain, and the Reconstruction of Western Europe, 1947–1952* (1987). Knox, Donald, *The Korean War: An Oral History*, 2 vols (1985–1988). Lacey, Michael J., ed., *The Truman Presidency* (1989). LaFeber, Walter, *America, Russia, and the Cold War, 1945–1992* (1993). Lawson, Steven M., *Black Ballots: Voting Rights in the South, 1944–1969* (1976).

May, Lary, ed., *Recasting America: Culture and Politics in the Age of Cold War* (1989). McCoy, Donald, and Richard Ruetten, *Quest and Response: Minority Rights and the Truman Administration* (1973). Meier, August, and Elliott Rudwick, *CORE: A Study in the Civil Rights Movement, 1942–1968* (1973). Merrill, Dennis, ed., *Documentary History of the Truman Presidency*, 20 vols (1995–1997). Nadel, Alan, *Containment Culture: American Narratives, Postmodernism, and the Atomic Age* (1995). Navasky, Victor S., *Naming Names* (1989). Patterson, James T., *Mr. Republican: A Biography of Robert A. Taft* (1972). Poen, Monte M., *Harry S. Truman Versus the Medical Lobby: The Genesis of Medicare* (1979). Polan, Dana, *Power and Paranoia: History, Narrative, and the American Cinema, 1940–1950* (1986). Radosh, Ronald, and Joyce Milton, *The Rosenberg File: A Search for the Truth* (1984). Renshaw, Patrick, *American Labor and Consensus Capitalism, 1935–1990* (1991).

Stueck, William, *The Korean War: An International History* (1995). Sugrue, Thomas J., *The Origins of the Urban Crisis: Race and Inequality in Postwar Detroit* (1996). Weiner, Lynn Y., *From Working Girl to Working Mother: The Female Labor Force in the United States, 1820–1980* (1985). Whitfield, Stephen J., *The Culture of the Cold War* (1991).

CHAPTER 27

Baughman, James L., *The Republic of Mass Culture: Journalism, Filmmaking and Broadcasting in America since 1941* (1991). Beschloss, Michael R., *Mayday: Eisenhower, Khrushchev and the U-2 Affair* (1991). Bowie, Robert R., and Richard H. Immerman, *Waging Peace: How Eisenhower Shaped an Enduring Cold War Strategy* (2000). Breines, Wini, *Young, White, and Miserable: Growing Up Female in the Fifties* (1992). Broadwater, Jeff, *Eisenhower and the Anti-Communist Crusade* (1992). Burk, Robert Fredrick, *The Eisenhower Administration and Black Civil Rights, 1953–1961* (1984). Cullather, Nick, *Illusions of Influence: The Political Economy of United States-Philippines Relations, 1942–1960* (1994). Divine, Robert, *The Sputnik Challenge* (1993). Dockrill, Saki, *Eisenhower's New-Look National Security Policy, 1953–1961* (1996). Dudziak, Mary, *Cold War Civil Rights: Race and the Image of American Democracy* (2000). Foreman, Joel, ed., *The Other Fifties: Interrogating Midcentury American Icons* (1997). Fried, Richard M., *Nightmare in Red: The McCarthy Era in Perspective* (1990).

Gardner, Lloyd C., *Approaching Vietnam: From World War II through Dienbienphu* (1988). Gartman, David, *Auto Opium: A Social History of American Automobile Design* (1994). Graebner, William, *Coming of Age in Buffalo: Youth and Authority in the Postwar Era* (1990). Guralnick, Peter, *Last Train to Memphis: The Rise of Elvis Presley* (1994). Gutierrez, David, *Walls and Mirrors: Mexican Americans, Mexican Immigrants, and the Politics of Ethnicity* (1995). Horowitz, Daniel, ed., *American Social Classes in the 1950s: Selections from Vance Packard's The Status Seekers* (1995). Jackson, Kenneth, *Crabgrass Frontier: The Suburbanization of the United States* (1985). Jones, Gerard, *Honey, I'm Home! Sitcoms: Selling the American Dream* (1992). Karabell, Zachary, *Architects of Intervention: The United States, the Third World, and the Cold War, 1946–1962* (1999). Kluger, Richard, *Simple Justice: The History of Brown v. Board of Education and Black America's Struggle for Equality* (1977). Korrol, Virginia Sanchez, *From Colonia to Community: The History of Puerto Ricans in New York City* (1994). Kunz, Diane B., *The Economic Diplomacy of the Suez Crisis* (1991). Lhamon, Ward T., *Deliberate Speed: The Origins of a Cultural Style in the American 1950s* (1990).

May, Elaine Tyler, *Homeward Bound: American Families in the Cold War Era* (1988). Meier, Matt S., and Feliciano Ribera, *Mexican Americans, American Mexicans: from Conquistadors to Chicanos* (1993). O'Neill, William L., *American High: The Years of Confidence, 1945–1960* (1986). Pach, Chester J., and Elmo Richardson, *The Presidency of Dwight D. Eisenhower* (1991). Raines, Howell, *My Soul Is Rested: Movement Days in the Deep South Remembered* (1977). Ramos, Henry A. J., *The American G.I. Forum: In Pursuit of the Dream, 1948–1993* (1998). Rawls, James J., *Chief Red Fox Is Dead: A History of Native Americans Since 1945* (1996). Rupp, Leila J., *Survival in the Doldrums: The American Women's Rights Movement, 1945 to the 1960s* (1987).

Takeyh, Ray, *The Origins of the Eisenhower Doctrine: The US, Britain, and Nasser's Egypt, 1953–57* (2000). Watson, Steven, *The Birth of the Beat Generation: Visionaries, Rebels, and Hipsters, 1944–1960* (1995).

CHAPTER 28

Appy, Christian G., *Working-Class War: American Combat Soldiers & Vietnam* (1993). Beschloss, Michael, *The Crisis Years: Kennedy and Khrushchev, 1960–1963* (1991). Blum, John Morton, *Years of Discord: American Politics and Society, 1961–1974* (1991). Brands, H. W., *The Wages of Globalism: Lyndon Johnson and the Limits of American Power* (1995). Brick, Howard, *Age of Contradiction: American Thought and Culture in the 1960s* (2000). Burner, David, *John F. Kennedy and a New Generation* (1988). Carson, Clayborne, *In Struggle: SNCC and the Black Awakening of the 1960s* (1981). Chafe, William H., *Civilities and Civil Rights: Greensboro, North Carolina, and the Black Struggle for Freedom* (1980). Dallek, Robert, *Flawed Giant: Lyndon Johnson and His Times, 1961–1973* (1991). Davies, Gareth, *From Opportunity to Entitlement: The Transformation and Decline of Great Society Liberalism* (1996). Dickstein, Morris, *Gates of Eden: American Culture in the Sixties* (1977). Dittmer, John, *Local People: The Struggle for Civil Rights in Mississippi* (1994). Douglas, Susan J., *Where the Girls Are: Growing Up Female with the Mass Media* (1994). Downs, Frederick, *The Killing Zone: My Life in the Vietnam War* (1978). Evans, Sara, *Personal Politics: The Roots of Women's Liberation in the Civil Rights Movement & the New Left* (1979). Farber, David, ed., *The Sixties: From Memory to History* (1994).

Garrow, David J., *Bearing the Cross: Martin Luther King, Jr., and the Southern Christian Leadership Conference* (1986). Giglio, James N., *The Presidency of John F. Kennedy* (1991). Halberstam, David, *The Best and the Brightest* (1972). Haley, Alex, *The Autobiography of Malcolm X* (1966). Harrison, Cynthia, *On Account of Sex: The Politics of Women's Issues, 1945–1968* (1988). Harvey, Mark W. T., *A Symbol of Wilderness: Echo Park and the American Conservation Movement* (1994). Hodgson, Godfrey, *America in Our Time: From World War II to Nixon* (1976). Hoffman, Elizabeth Cobbs, *All You Need Is Love: The Peace Corps and the Spirit of the 1960s* (1998). Horne, Gerald, *Fire This Time: The Watts Uprising and the 1960s* (1996). Horowitz, Daniel, *Betty Friedan and the Making of the Feminine Mystique: The American Left, the Cold War, and Modern Feminism* (1998). Jeffreys-Jones, Rhodri, *Peace Now!: American Society and the Ending of the Vietnam War* (1999). Kahin, George McT., *Intervention: How America Became Involved in Vietnam* (1986). Kaiser, David E., *American Tragedy: Kennedy, Johnson, and the Origins of the Vietnam War* (2000). Krepinevich, Andrew F., Jr., *The Army and Vietnam* (1986). Linden-Ward, Blanche, & Carol Hurd Green, *Changing the Future: American Women in the 1960s* (1993).

Macedo, Stephen, ed., *Reassessing the Sixties: Debating the Political and Cultural Legacy* (1997). McAdam, Doug, *Freedom Summer* (1988). McDougall, Walter A., . . . *the Heavens and the Earth: A Political History of the Space Age* (1985). Moïse, Edwin E., *Tonkin Gulf and the Escalation of the Vietnam War* (1996).

Paterson, Thomas G., ed., *Kennedy's Quest for Victory: American Foreign Policy, 1961–1963* (1989). Payne, Charles M., *I've Got the Light of Freedom: The Organizing Tradition and the Mississippi Freedom Struggle* (1995). Pearson, Hugh, *The Shadow of the Panther: Huey Newton and the Price of Black Power in America* (1994). Ralph, James R., Jr., *Northern Protest: Martin Luther King, Jr., Chicago, and the Civil Rights Movement* (1993). Rorabaugh, W. J., *Berkeley at War: The 1960s* (1989). Rothman, Hal K., *The Greening of a Nation: Environmentalism in the United States Since 1945* (1998).

Schlesinger, Arthur M., Jr., *Robert Kennedy and His Times* (1978). Schwartz, Bernard, *Super Chief: Earl Warren and His Supreme Court* (1983). Steigerwald, David, *The Sixties and the End of Modern America* (1995). Summer, Harry G., Jr., *On Strategy: A Critical Analysis of the Vietnam War* (1982). Szatmary, David P., *Rockin' in Time: A Social History of Rock-and-Roll* (1997). Van Deburg, William L., *New Day in Babylon: The Black Power Movement and American Culture, 1965–1975* (1992). Wells, Tom, *The War Within: America's Battle Over Vietnam* (1996).

CHAPTER 29

Adam, Barry D., *The Rise of a Gay and Lesbian Movement*, Rev. ed. (1995). Barnet, Richard J., and Ronald E. Müller, *Global Reach: The Power of the Multinational Corporations* (1974). Bartley, Numan V., *The New South, 1945–1980: The Story of the South's Modernization, 1945–1980* (1995). Bernstein, Carl, and Bob Woodward, *All the President's Men* (1974). Bernstein, Michael A., and David E. Adler, eds., *Understanding American Economic Decline* (1994). Bill, James A., *The Eagle and the Lion: The Tragedy of American-Iranian Relations* (1988). Brands, H. W., *Since Vietnam: The United States in World Affairs, 1973–1995* (1996). Campisi, Jack, *The Mashpee Indians: Tribe on Trial* (1991). Carter, Dan T., *The Politics of Rage: George Wallace, the Origins of the New Conservatism, and the Transformation of American Politics* (1995). Chan, Sucheng, *Asian Americans: An Interpretive History* (1990). D'Emilio, John, *Sexual Politics, Sexual Communities: The Making of a Homosexual Minority in the United States, 1940–1970* (1983). Duberman, Martin, *Stonewall* (1993). Engelhardt, Tom, *The End of Victory Culture: Cold War America and the Disillusioning of a Generation* (1995). Espiritu, Yen Le, *Asian American Panethnicity: Bridging Institutions and Identities* (1992). Ford, Daniel F., *Three Mile Island: Thirty Minutes to Meltdown* (1982). Frye, Gaillard, *The Dream Long Deferred* (1988).

Garrow, David J., *Liberty and Sexuality: The Right to Privacy and the Making of* Roe v. Wade (1994). Garthoff, Raymond L., *Détente and Confrontation: American-Soviet Relations from Nixon to Reagan* (1994). Gartman, David, *Auto Opium: A Social History of American Automobile Design* (1994). Greene, John Robert, *The Limits of Power: The Nixon and Ford Administrations* (1992). Isaacs, Arnold R., *Without Honor: Defeat in Vietnam and Cambodia* (1983). Isaacson, Walter, *Kissinger: A Biography* (1992). Jones, Charles O., *The Trusteeship Presidency: Jimmy Carter and the United States Congress* (1988). Kimball, Jeffrey P., *Nixon's Vietnam War* (1998). LaFeber, Walter, *The Panama Canal Crisis in Historical*

Perspective (1989). Lasch, Christopher, *The Culture of Narcissism: American Life in an Age of Diminishing Expectations* (1979). Lawson, Steven F., *Running for Freedom: Civil Rights and Black Politics in America Since 1941* (1997).

Marin, Marguerite V., *Social Protest in an Urban Barrio: A Study of the Chicano Movement, 1966–1974* (1991). Nagel, Joanne, *American Indian Ethnic Renewal: Red Power and the Resurgence of Identity and Culture* (1996). Rieder, Jonathan, *Canarsie: The Jews and Italians of Brooklyn Against Liberalism* (1985). Rosen, Ellen Israel, *Bitter Choices: Blue-Collar Women in and out of Work* (1987). Ryan, Paul B., *The Iranian Rescue Mission and Why It Failed* (1986).

Sale, Kirkpatrick, *Power Shift: The Rise of the Southern Rim and Its Challenge to the Eastern Establishment* (1975). Schlesinger, Arthur M., Jr., *The Imperial Presidency* (1973). Schulman, Bruce J., *From Cotton Belt to Sun Belt: Federal Policy, Economic Development, and the Transformation of the South, 1938–1980* (1991). Schur, Edwin, *The Awareness Trap: Self-Absorption instead of Social Change* (1976). Small, Melvin, *The Presidency of Richard Nixon* (1999). Smith, Gaddis, *Morality, Reason, and Power: American Diplomacy in the Carter Years* (1986). Stern, Kenneth S., *Loud Hawk: The United States versus the American Indian Movement* (1994). Szasz, Andrew, *EcoPopulism: Toxic Waste and the Movement for Environmental Justice* (1994). Takaki, Ronald, *Strangers from a Different Shore: A History of Asian Americans* (1989). Thurow, Lester, *The Zero-Sum Society: Distribution and the Possibilities for Economic Change* (1980). Vigil, Ernesto, *The Crusade for Justice: Chicano Militancy and the Government's War on Dissent*. Wei, William, *The Asian American Movement* (1993). Wicker, Tom, *One of Us: Richard Nixon and the American Dream* (1991). Wilkinson, J. Harvie, III, *From Brown to Bakke: The Supreme Court and School Integration, 1954–1978* (1979). Wolfe, Alan, *America's Impasse: The Rise and Fall of the Politics of Growth* (1981).

CHAPTER 30

Adam, Barry D., *The Rise of a Gay and Lesbian Movement Rev. ed.* (1995). Anderson, Martin, *Revolution: The Reagan Legacy* (1988). Berman, William C., *America's Right Turn: From Nixon to Bush* (1994). Blumenthal, Sidney, *The Rise of the Counter-Establishment: From Conservative Ideology to Political Power* (1986). Campbell-Kelly, Martin, and William Aspray, *Computer: A History of the Information Machine* (1996). Cannon, Lou, *Ronald Reagan: The Role of a Lifetime* (1991). Davis, Flora, *Moving the Mountain: The Women's Movement in America since 1960* (1991). Ferree, Myra Marx, and Beth B. Hess, *Controversy and Coalition: The New Feminist Movement Across Three Decades of Change* (1994). Friedman, Benjamin M., *Day of Reckoning: The Consequences of American Economic Policy under Reagan and After* (1988).

Gallagher, John, *Perfect Enemies: The Religious Right, the Gay Movement, and the Politics of the 1990s* (1996). Garthoff, Raymond L., *Détente and Confrontation: American-Soviet Relations from Nixon to Reagan* (1994). _____, *The Great Transition: American-Soviet Relations and the End of the Cold War* (1994). Gillon, Steven M., *The Democrats' Dilemma: Walter*

F. Mondale and the Liberal Legacy (1992). Hill, Dilys M., et al., *The Reagan Presidency: An Incomplete Revolution?* (1990). Hodgson, Godfrey, *The World Turned Right Side Up: A History of the Conservative Ascendancy in America* (1996). Hoeveler, J. David, *Watch on the Right: Conservative Intellectuals in the Reagan Era* (1991). Hurt, Harry, *The Lost Tycoon: The Many Lives of Donald J. Trump* (1993). Jaynes, Gerald David, and Robin M. Williams, Jr., eds., *A Common Destiny: Blacks and American Society* (1989). Fitzgerald, Frances, *Way Out There in the Blue: Reagan and Star Wars and the End of the Cold War* (2000). Jeffords, Susan, *Hard Bodies: Hollywood Masculinity in the Reagan Era* (1994). Jorstad, Erling, *Holding Fast/Pressing On: Religion in America in the 1980s* (1990). Lewis, Michael, *Liar's Poker: Rising Through the Wreckage on Wall Street* (1989). Lofland, John, *Polite Protesters: The American Peace Movement of the 1980s* (1993).

Martin, William C., *With God on Our Side: The Rise of the Religious Right in America* (1996). McGirr, Lisa, *Suburban Warriors: The Origins of the New American Right* (2001). Meyer, Jane, and Doyle McManus, *Landslide: The Unmaking of the President, 1984–1988* (1988). Murray, Charles, *Losing Ground: American Social Policy, 1950–1980* (1984). Noonan, Peggy, *What I Saw at the Revolution: A Political Life in the Reagan Era* (1990). Phillips, Kevin P., *The Politics of Rich and Poor: Wealth and the American Electorate in the Reagan Aftermath* (1990). Rayack, Elton, *Not So Free to Choose: The Political Economy of Milton Friedman and Ronald Reagan* (1987). Reed, Adolph L., *The Jesse Jackson Phenomenon: The Crisis of Purpose in Afro-American Politics* (1986).

Schaller, Michael, *Reckoning with Reagan: America and Its President in the 1980s* (1992). Scheer, Robert, *With Enough Shovels: Reagan, Bush, and Nuclear War* (1982). Taylor, John, *Circus of Ambition: The Culture of Wealth and Power in the Eighties* (1989). Thelen, David P., *Becoming Citizens in the Age of Television: How Americans Challenged the Media and Seized Political Initiative During the Iran-Contra Debate* (1996). Thompson, Mark, ed., *Long Road to Freedom: The Advocate History of the Gay and Lesbian Movement* (1994). Wolters, Raymond, *Right Turn: William Bradford Reynolds, the Reagan Administration, and Black Civil Rights* (1996).

CHAPTER 31

Abramson, Jeffrey, ed., *Postmortem: The O. J. Simpson Case: Justice Confronts Race, Domestic Violence, Lawyers, Money, and the Media* (1996). Beschloss, Michael R., and Strobe Talbott, *At the Highest Levels: The Inside Story of the End of the Cold War* (1993). Bingham, Clara, *Women on the Hill: Challenging the Culture of Congress* (1997). Button, James W., et al., *Private Lives, Public Conflicts: Battles Over Gay Rights in American Communities* (1997). Campbell, Colin, and Bert A. Rockman, eds., *The Clinton Presidency: First Appraisals* (1996). Dertouzos, Michael L., *What Will Be: How the New World of Information Will Change Our Lives* (1998). Drew, Elizabeth, *Showdown: The Struggle Between the Gingrich Congress and the Clinton White House* (1996). Duignan, Peter, and L. H. Gann, eds., *The Debate in the United States Over Immigration* (1998). Dunnigan, James F., and Austin Bay, *From Shield to Storm:*

High-Tech Weapons, Military Strategy, & Coalition Warfare in the Persian Gulf (1992).

Gitlin, Todd, *The Twilight of Common Dreams: Why America Is Wracked by Culture Wars* (1995). Gordon, Avery, and Christopher Newfield, eds., *Mapping Multiculturalism* (1996). Green, John C., et al., eds., *Religion and the Culture Wars: Dispatches from the Front* (1996). Greenberg, Stanley B., *Middle Class Dreams: The Politics and Power of the New American Majority* (1995). Greene, John Robert, *The Presidency of George Bush* (2000). Haas, Richard N., *The Reluctant Sheriff: The United States After the Cold War* (1997). Hafner, Katie, and Matthew Lyon, *Where Wizards Stay Up Late: The Origins of the Internet* (1998). Hogan, Michael, ed., *The End of the Cold War: Its Meanings and Implications* (1992). Lind, Michael, *The Next American Nation: The New Nationalism and the Fourth American Revolution* (1995). Lowi, Theodore J., and Benjamin Ginsberg, *Embattled Democracy: Politics and Policy in the Clinton Era* (1995).

Maraniss, David, *First in His Class: A Biography of Bill Clinton* (1995). Matteo, Sherri, ed., *American Women in the Nineties: Today's Critical Issues* (1993). McGuckin, Frank, ed., *Terrorism in the United States* (1997). Morris, Roger, *Partners in Power: The Clintons and Their America* (1996). Newman, Katherine S., *Declining Fortunes: The Withering of the American Dream* (1993). Nolan, James L., Jr., ed., *The American Culture Wars: Current Contests and Future Prospects* (1996). Phillips, Kevin P., *The Politics of Rich and Poor: Wealth and the American Electorate in the Reagan Aftermath* (1990). Posner, Gerald L., *Citizen Perot: His Life and Times* (1996). Ripley, Randall B., and James M. Lindsay, eds., *U.S. Foreign Policy After the Cold War* (1997). Rivlin, Gary, *The Plot to Get Bill Gates* (1999). Rubin, Lillian B., *Families on the Fault Line: America's Working Class Speaks about the Family, the Economy, Race, and Ethnicity* (1994).

Skocpol, Theda, *Boomerang: Clinton's Health Security Effort and the Turn Against Government in U. S. Politics* (1996). Slessarev, Helene, *The Betrayal of the Urban Poor* (1991). Spain, Daphne, and Suzanne M. Bianchi, *Balancing Act: Motherhood, Marriage, and Employment Among American Women* (1996). Stern, Kenneth S., *A Force Upon the Plain: The American Militia Movement and the Politics of Hate* (1996). Stewart, James B., *Blood Sport: The President and His Adversaries* (1996). Thomas, Evan, et al., *Back from the Dead: How Clinton Survived the Republican Revolution* (1997). Toobin, Jeffrey, *A Vast Conspiracy: The Real Story of the Sex Scandal That Nearly Brought Down a President* (2000). Wray, Matt, and Annalee Newitz, eds., *White Trash: Race and Class in America* (1997).

PHOTO CREDITS

396; Liaison Agency, Inc. 398; © CORBIS, 399; The New York Public Library Prints Division, 402; Ilinois State Historical Library, 408; John S. Curry/Mrs. John Steuart Curry, 410.

Chapter 15: FPG International LLC, 416; National Archives and Records Administration, 418; The Boston Athenaeum, 419; Timothy H. O'Sullivan/The Granger Collection, 422; Seventh Regiment Fund, Inc., 424; Courtesy of the Library of Congress, 427; Chicago Historical Society, J. Joffray, P&S-1932.0027, 429; Courtesy of the Library of Congress, 430; Culver Pictures, Inc., 433 (top), Chicago Historical Society, (bottom); Culver Pictures, Inc., 435; © CORBIS, 438; CORBIS, 440; Kean Archive, 443; Smithsonian American Art Museum, Washington, D.C., 444; © CORBIS, 445.

Chapter 16: Scott Barrow/International Stock Photography Ltd., 448; The Granger Collection, New York, 450; Moorland Spingham Research Center, 452 (left), Library of Congress, (right); © CORBIS, 453; CORBIS, 454; Library of Congress, 455; Courtesy of the Library of Congress, 459; The Museum of the Confederacy, Richmond, Virginia, Photography by Katherine Wetzel, 461; The South Carolina Historical Society, 463; Thomas Nast/Courtesy of the Library of Congress, 469; Napoleon Sarony/Art Resource, N.Y., 471; Courtesy of the New-York Historical Society, New York City, 473; Collection of The New-York Historical Society, New York City, 475; Thomas Nast/Library of Congress, 476; © CORBIS, 466; © CORBIS, 467.

Chapter 17: Mark Bolster/International Stock Photography Ltd., 480; The Granger Collection, 482; © Bettmann/CORBIS, 487; Culver Pictures, Inc., 490; The Denver Public Library, Western History Collection, 491; Walter Bibikow/Picturesque Stock Photo, 494; National Archives and Records Administration, 495; The Granger Collection, 496; National Archives Records Administration, 497; Courtesy of the Library of Congress, 500; The Granger Collection, 502; American Museum of Natural History, 504; Courtesy of the Library of Congress, 505; Walker, James, Vanqueros in a Horse Corral, 0126.1480, "From the Collection of Gilcrease Museum, Tulsa", 506; CORBIS, 508.

Chapter 18: Hulton/Archive, 512; Stock Montage, Inc./Historical Pictures Collection, 514; Courtesy of the New York Public Library, 516; The Granger Collection, 519; Chicago Historical Society, 520; Black and Tan Dive, Circa 1890, Museum of the City of New York, The Jacob A. Riis Collection, 523; The Granger Collection, 527 (top), The Granger Collection, (bottom); The Granger Collection, 529; Kaufmann & Fabry/Chicago Historical Society, 1CHi-32364, 530; Jane Addams Memorial Collection (JAMC neg. 20), Special Collections, The University Library, University of Illinois at Chicago, 532; Library of Congress, 535; Thomas Eakins, American, (1844-1916). The Agnew Clinic. University of Pennsylvania Museum, 536 (left), David Wharton/Thomas Eakins, American, (1844-1916). The Swimming Hole, c. 1883-85. Oil on Canvas, 27 x 36 in. The Fort Worth Art Association, 1925; acquired by the Amon Carter Museum of Fort Worth, 1990 from the Modern Art Museum of Fort Worth through grants and donations from the Aron G. Carter Foundation, the Sid E. Richardson Foundation, the Anne Burnett and Charles Tandy Foundation, Capital Cities/ABC Foundation, Fort Worth Star-Telegram, The R.D. and Joan Dale Hubbard Foundation and the People of Fort Worth, (right); CORBIS, 537.

Chapter 19: The New York Public Library, Rare Book Division, 540; The Granger Collection, 542; The Granger Collection, New York, 545; The Granger Colleciton, 548; The Granger Collection, 549; The Granger Collection, New York, 550; © Bellew/Stock Montage, 552; The Granger Collection, 554; © B.L. Singley/CORBIS, 556; The Metropolitan Museum of Art, Purchase, Lyman G. Bloomingdale Gift, 1901. (01.7.1), 537; © Bettman/CORBIS, 560; The Granger Collection, New York, 561; The Kansas State Historical Society, Topeka, Kansas, 563.

Chapter 20: Wallace Garrison/Index Stock Imagery, Inc., 566; Edward Steichen/The Metropolitan Museum of Art, Alfred Stieglitz Collection, 1949. (49.55.167), 568; Library of Congress, 569; Duke University John W. Hartman Center, 571; Smithsonian Institution/Office of Imaging, Printing, and Photographic Services, 572; The Granger Collection, New York, 574; Berry-Hill Galleries, Inc. 576; Courtesy of the Library of Congress, 579; Courtesy of the Library of Congress, 580; North Wind Picture Archives, 581; Courtesy of the Divinity School, Yale University, 585; The William L. Clements Library, 587; Stock Montage, Inc./Historical Pictures Collection, 589.

Chapter 21: Aiello Productions, Inc., 596; Jane Addams Memorial Collection (JAMC neg. 400), Special Collections, The University Library, University of Illinois at Chicago, 598; Brown Brothers, 600; © Hulton Getty/Archive Photos, 602; Library of Congress, 603; © Bettmann/Corbis, 605; © Hulton Getty/Archive Photos, 606; © Bettmann/Corbis, 608; The Granger Collection, 609; Schomburg Center for Research in Black Culture, 610; © Collection of the New York Historical Society, 612; State Historical Society of Wisconsin, 613; © Lewis W. Hine, CORBIS, 615; Theodore Roosevelt Collection, Harvard College Library, 618.

Chapter 22: CORBIS, 626; Brown Brothers, 628; © Vera Cruz/CORBIS, 630; Jane Addams Memorial Collection (JAMC neg. 64). Special Collections. The University of Illinois at Chicago, 632; Theodore Roosevelt Collection, Harvard College Library, 634; © Hulton Getty/Archive Photos, 636; Erik Overbey Collection/University of South Alabama Archives, 637; THE GRANGER COLLECTION, New York, 640; Archibald Motley, Jr., BLACK BELT (1934) Oil on Canvas. Hampton University Museum, Hampton, Virginia, 642; Library of Congress, 644; Brown Brothers, 649; The Granger Collection, 651; Shahn, Ben. Bartolomeo Vanzetti and Nicola Sacco from the Sacco-Vanzetti series of twenty-three paintings. (1931-32). Tempera on paper over composition board, 10 1/2 x 14 1/2 (26.7 x 36.8 cm). The Museum of Modern Art, New York. Gift of Abby Aldrich Rockefeller. Digital image. © 2001 The Museum of Modern Art, New York, 652.

Chapter 23: © Minnesota Historical Society/CORBIS, 656; UPI/CORBIS, 658; © Hulton Getty/Archive Photos, 660; Charles R. Child/Chicago Historical Society, 1CHi-29202, 662; Gaslight Advertising Archives, Inc. N.Y., 663; Collection of Duncan Schiedt, 664; Courtesy of the Library of Congress, 666; Courtesy of the Library of Congress, 667; © Hulton Getty/Archive Photos, 668; Library of Congress, 670; © Bettmann/CORBIS, 671; The UT Institute of Texas Cultures, No. 99-573, 672; National Portrait Gallery/Smithsonian Institution, 674; © Bettmann/CORBIS, 676; © Hulton Getty/Archive Photos, 678.

Chapter 24: © Minnesota Historical Society/CORBIS, 682; Hulton Getty/Archive Photos, 684; Hulton Getty/Archive Photos, 685; Brown Brothers, 687; Brown Brothers, 688; Hulton Getty/Archive Photos, 690; Brown Brothers, 693; The Granger Collection, 694; Courtesy of the Library of Congress, 696; UPI/CORBIS, 697; Brown Brothers, 699; Hulton/Archive, 701; Hulton/Archive, 703; Brown Brothers, 704.

Chapter 25: © Minnesota Historical Society/CORBIS, 710; The Granger Collection, 712; THE GRANGER COLLECTION, New York, 714; THE GRANGER COLLECTION, New York, 715; The Granger Collection, 718; Culver Pictures, Inc.,(top), Hulton/Archive (bottom); Robert F. Greenhalgh, 723; Brown Brothers, 729; Hulton /Archive (left), Brown Brothers (right), 732; Anthony Potter Collection/Hulton/Archive, 733; Naval Historical Foundation, 735; PA/AP/Wide World Photos, 737; Hulton/Archive, 739.

Chapter 26: Peter Langone/International Stock Photography Ltd., 742; Harris and Ewing Photos Courtesy Harry S Truman Library, 744; © CORBIS, 747; Terry Savage Courtesy Harry S Truman Library, 748; Charles Fenno Jacobs/TimePix, 751; © Bettmann/CORBIS, 753; Courtesy: I.U. Archives and Photographic Services (#47-1082), 755; © Bettmann/CORBIS, 757; Joseph Scherschel/TimePix, 758; © Bettmann/CORBIS, 759; Brown Brothers, 760; Brown Brothers, 762; Brown Brothers, 763; Southern California Library for Social Studies and Research, 765; Hank Walker/TimePix, 767.

Chapter 27: © CORBIS, 770; Ben Martin/TimePix, 772; DuPont, 773; AP/Wide World Photos, 775; Courtesy of the New York Historical Society, New York City, 776; Bernard Hoffman/Life Magazine/© 1950 TimePix, 777; Cindy Lewis Photography, 779; © Bettmann/CORBIS, 783; Brown Brothers, 785; National Archives and Records Administration, 788; Kobel Collection, 791; AP/Wide World Photos, 792; AP/Wide World Photos, 794; The Helicopter Era, from Herblock's special for Today (Simon and Schuster, 1958) © The Washington Post, 795.

Chapter 28: Leonard Freed/Magnum Photos, Inc., 800; The Granger Collection, 802; Erich Hartmann/Magnum Photos, Inc., 804; The Granger Collection, 807; Hulton/Archive, 808; UPI/CORBIS, 811; Hulton Getty/Archive Photos, 812; Cecil Stoughton/TimePix, 817; John Launois/TimePix, 822; Ron Heflin/AP/Wide World Photos, 823; Ron Crane/TimePix, 825; Courtesy: I.U. Archives and Photographic Services, 826; Courtesy: I.U.Archives and Photographic Services, 827; AP/Wide World Photos, 828; Bill Eppridge/TimePix, 829.

Chapter 29: © Bettmann/CORBIS, 834; Fred Ward/Black Star, 836; © Bettmann/CORBIS, 840; Magnum Photos, Inc., 841; © Bettmann/CORBIS. 842; CORBIS, 843; Jason Laure/Woodfin Camp & Associates, 846; AP/Wide World Photos, 847; George Ballis/Take Stock-Images of Change, 850; Paramount/Kobal Collection, 855; Dirck Halstead/Liaison, 857; © Bettmann/CORBIS, 858; © 1979 Abbas/Magnum Photos, Inc., 861.

Chapter 30: Aiello Productions, Inc., 864; Sonia Moskowitz/Hulton/Archive, 866; Donna Day/Stone, 869; Eve Arnold/Magnum Photos, Inc., 871; Diana Walker/Liaison Agency, Inc., 872; UPI/CORBIS, 873; © Wally McNamee/CORBIS, 875; Christopher Morris/Black Star, 876; Donald Dietz/Stock Boston, 877; Cindy Karp/TimePix, 878; Karen Su/Stock Boston, 883; Chuck Nacke/Woodfin Camp & Associates, 884; Chris Brown/Stock Boston, 886; © Bettmann/CORBIS, 887; AP/Wide World Photos, 888; Reuters/Steve Jaffe/Archive Photos, 890; AP/Wide World Photos, 892.

Chapter 31: © Zen Icknow/CORBIS, 896; Paul David Mozell/Stock Boston, 898; © Premium Stock/CORBIS, 899; Doug Mills/AP/Wide World Photois, 900; Mark Richards/PhotoEdit, 902; Barry Thumma/AP/Wide World Photos, 905; © Glenn James/CORBIS SYGMA, 906; Greg Gibson/AP/Wide World Photos, 907; Robert Trippett/SIPA Press, 908; AFP/CORBIS, 909; Alexandra Avakian/TimePix, 910; Christopher Morris/Black Star, 913; Carmen Taylor/AP/Wide World Photos, 915; Mick Hutson/Retna Ltd. USA, 916; © Kulish L.A. Daily News/CORBIS SYGMA, 919; Myung J Chun/AP/Wide World Photos, 920; Brad Markel/Liaison Agency, Inc., 921; Doug Mills/AP/Wide World Photos (center), Jessica Persson/Reuters/TimePix, (left); © Gary Hershom/Reuters/ CORBIS (top right), Ruth Fremson/AP/Wide World Photos (bottom right), 922; Ken Ige/AP/Wide World Photos, 923; Kevin Fuji/SIPA Press, 924.

INDEX

A

Abenaki Indians, 40, 155-57
Abolition, 341-47
  early movement, 228
  election of 1856 issue, 404-6
  Emancipation Proclamation, 432-35
  first abolitionist, 208
  free African-American activism, 342
  Fugitive Slave Act, reaction to, 398-99
  gag rule on petitions, 346, 368-69, 396
  immediatist activism, 343, 346
  John Brown's activities, 404, 409-12
  literature related to, 343-44, 346, 399
  and Missouri Compromise, 297
  New York City, 337
  and North, 342-43
  and Northwest Ordinance of 1787, 208, 211
  post-Revolution, North versus South, 208, 228
  and Republican Party, 404-9
  slave power concept, 405-6
  violence by anti-abolitionists, 344-45
  women activists, 342, 343, 346, 369
  See also African Americans, free slaves
Acadians, 164
Acoma pueblo, 117
Act of Toleration of 1649, 70
Adams, Abigail, 258
  on women's rights, 207
Adams, Henry, 457
Adams, John
  and American Revolution, 188
  and Declaration of Independence, 190
  as Federalist, 243
  France-America relations, 243-44
  pre-Revolution, 174
  presidency of, 243-45
  presidential election (1796), 243
  as vice president, 232
  XYZ Affair, 244
Adams, John Quincy
  election of 1824 controversy, 321-22
  as National Republican, 290-91, 291
  presidency of, 323
  as secretary of state, 293, 321
Adams, Samuel
  and American Revolution, 188
  pre-Revolution, 174, 177
"Address to the Wealthy of the Land" (Carey), 347
"Address to Workingmen" (Luther), 349, 357
Adena Indians, 13
Administration of Justice Act of 1774, 180
Africa
  African control of slavery, 9, 128-29
  political economy, 7
  slavery practiced in, 7, 9, 11
African-American discrimination/seg-regation
  free African Americans, 228, 253-55
  and Ku Klux Klan, 468-69
  military, 434

schools, 359
  separate but equal ruling, 476
African Americans
  Fifteenth Amendment, 460, 469-71
  Fourteenth Amendment, 458-60, 471
  political positions of, 461, 474-75
  in Republican Party, 475
  schooling of, 454
  Thirteenth Amendment, 456, 460
  voting rights, 458-60, 470
African Americans, free slaves
  as abolitionists, 342
  black church, 253-54, 454-55
  Black Codes, 297, 456-57, 462
  in Civil War, 432-34
  communities of, 116, 143, 253-54
  family structure, 464
  Freedmen's Bureau, 449-50, 455, 458
  labor arrangements, Reconstruction era, 451-52, 456-57, 462
  land distribution to, 455
  legal status, 297
  massacre of African Americans, 457, 459, 469
  mutual aid societies of, 253
  population in 1830, 346
  as sailors, 262
  segregation, 253-55, 359
  sharecropping, 462-65
  voting restrictions, 255, 319, 453-54
  work/jobs of, 254, 256, 461
African Church of Philadelphia, 254
African Methodist Episcopal Church, 255, 256
African slaves
  African customs, practice of, 143, 144
  bi-racial relationships, 258, 303
  as crafts persons, 301
  family life, 129-30, 303
  gender roles, 102, 133
  master-slave relationship, 302-3
  plantation life, 144, 300-303, 340-41
  punishment of, 98, 143, 302, 303
  racism, 72, 98, 143, 228
  religious beliefs/practices, 144, 151, 303
  religious groups. See Black church
  task system of work, 133, 301, 340
African slaves, age of discovery
  plantation labor, 7, 9, 18, 26, 47, 49, 62
  slave trade, 7-9
African slaves, colonial era
  and American Revolution, 197, 199
  Carolina colony, 98-100
  in cities, 141-42
  Constitutional Convention on, 215
  and Dutch, 48-49, 71, 94
  and English, 52, 55-56, 71, 97-100
  free black community, Florida, 116, 143
  and French, 114-16
  fugitive slaves, 72, 197, 208
  and Great Awakening, 150-51
  importation of 1700s, 128-29
  manumissions, 102
  middle passage, 128-29

plantation labor, 71-72, 91, 98-100, 132-33
  and political economy, 70-71, 98-100, 132-34
  slave codes, 102-3, 142
  slave revolts, 141-43
  slave trade, 128-29
  and Spanish, 116
  Virginia colony, 100, 102-3, 132-34
  in West Indies, 71-72, 91, 98-99, 116, 197
African slaves, nineteenth century
  abolition movement, 341-47
  Amistad incident, 379
  Compromise of 1850, 397-98
  diffusion of slavery, 393-94
  Dred Scott decision, 406-7
  freedom for. See Abolition; African Americans; African Americans, free slaves
  Fugitive Slave Act of 1850, 398-99
  internal slave trade, 283, 302, 393-94
  Kansas-Nebraska Act, 401-4
  in Mexican territory, 371-72
  Missouri Compromise, 296-97
  Omnibus Bill, 397
  Ostend Manifesto, 403
  plantation labor, 301-2
  and political economy, 301-3, 391-95
  popular sovereignty concept, 396
  population in 1830, 346
  slave revolts, 338, 340
  Southern economy, negative impact, 302, 393, 407, 426-27
  Wilmot Proviso, 396-97
African slaves, after Revolutionary War
  and cotton boom, 261
  free African Americans, 253-55
  fugitive slaves, 228
  increase in slavery, 252-53
  and political economy, 252-53
  post-Revolution status, 208, 227-28
  slave revolts, 249-50
  slaves smuggled into U.S., 261
  Three-Fifths compromise, 215, 274
  See also African slaves, nineteenth century
Age of discovery
  Africa, 7-9
  chronology of, 30
  Columbus exploration, 3-5, 16-19
  England, 5
  Native American peoples, 11-23
  political economy. See Age of dis-covery political economy
  Portugal, 7-9, 18, 29
  Spain, 3-5, 9-11, 16-20
Age of discovery political economy
  of Africa, 7-8
  encomienda system, 19-21
  of Europe, 5-7
  European financial objectives, 4, 6, 17-18
  global trade, 5-9
  and Native Americans, 13-14, 18-20
  plantation slave labor, 7, 9, 18
  slave trade, 7-9
Agriculture
  colonial era, 130, 132-33
  and Columbian exchange, 22-23
  inventions related to, 262, 291

Native Americans, domesticated crops, 11, 14, 17, 23
  Northern boom (1820-1860), 391
  Old World plants, 22-23
  post-Revolution era, 204
  See also Farming; Plantations
Ais Indians, 38
Alabama, 469
Alabama, statehood, 282
Albany
  Dutch settlement, 47-48, 50
  and Native American trade, 107
Albany Plan of Union, 163
Alcohol consumption
  colonial era, 140
  New Netherland, 49
  temperance movement, 356-57, 400
Alcott, William, 356
Alcuin (Brown), 229, 235
Alexander IV, Pope, 18
Algonquian Indians
  agricultural practices, 14
  and French, 40, 43, 114
  Manhattan purchased from, 48
  Pontiac's Rebellion, 170-71
  wampum trade, 50-51
  as warlike people, 14, 40
Alien and Sedition Acts, 244-45
Allen, Ethan, and American Revolution, 188
Allen, Richard, 254, 256, 279
Almshouses, 141, 313
Almy and Brown, 262
American Anti-Slavery Society, 343-46, 369, 390
American Bible Society, 315, 352
American Board of Commissioners for Foreign Missions, 315, 326
American Colonization Society, 255, 342
American Frugal Housewife, The (Child), 350
American Missionary Association, 454
American Party (Know-Nothings), 400-401
American Phrenological Association, 355
American republic political economy
  and African slaves, 227-28, 261
  cotton in, 260-61
  elite control of, 224-25, 227
  exports, 205, 224-25, 261-62
  invention/technology, 262-63
  law and lawyers, 264
  and Native Americans, 229-30
  and political parties, 232-34
  post-war economy, aspects of, 203-6
  property ownership, 223-24
  re-export trade, 225
  and republicanism, 223-27, 264
  tariffs, 232-33
  women, exclusion from, 228-29
  See also Nineteenth century politi-cal economy
American Revolution
  British political objectives, 192-95
  Continental Army, 189, 193-94
  end of, 199-202
  financing of, 204-5
  France in, 195, 199, 201
  Lexington and Concord, battles of, 187-88

military actions, 187-89, 193-99
political economy, post-war, 203-6
post-war America. *See* American
  republic political economy;
  Expansionism
republicanism as ideal, 176-77
Second Continental Congress,
  188-91
women's activities, 207
American Revolution, causes
  Boston Massacre, 178, 187
  Boston Tea Party, 179-80
  British imperialism, 169-70
  Coercive Acts/Intolerable Acts,
    180-81
  Currency Act of 1764, 171
  First Continental Congress, 181
  Liberty riot, 178
  Quartering Acts, 172, 176, 178, 180
  Revenue Act of 1766, 176
  rights of colonists issue, 173
  Stamp Act of 1765, 171-76
  Stamp Act protests, 173-76
  Sugar Act of 1764, 171
  Tea Act of 1773, 178, 179
  Townshend Revenue Act
    of 1767, 176
American Society for the Promotion of
  Temperance, 357
American System, 291
Amherst, Jeffrey, 165
Amistad, 379
Anaconda strategy, Civil War, 421
Anasazi Indians, 14-15
Andros, Edmund, 106-8
Anglican Church
  in America, 251
  in England, 52, 53, 74, 93
  and Enlightenment, 147
Anglo-Dutch Wars, 94
Anglo-Powhattan Wars, 67, 69
Animals
  buffalo, 14, 23
  horses and Native Americans, 14,
    23, 363
  imported from Old World, 14,
    22-23
Antietam, battle of, 431-32, 435
Antifederalists, concept of
  Constitution, 216-17
Antimason Party, 320
Apache Indians
  horses, use of, 23
  and Spanish, 118, 119, 371
  and western migration, 375-76
Apalachee Indians, 98
Apalachicola Indians, 97
Apollo Magazine, 229
*Appeal to the Colored Citizens of the World,
  An* (Walker), 342
*Appeal to the People of the United States,
  An* (American Anti-Slavery
  Society), 346
Appleton, Nathan, 286
Appomattox, battle of, 444
Arana, Hernández, 21
Arapaho Indians, 375
Arawak Indians, 91
Arbella, 78
Archaic Indians, 11-13
Archibald, Mary Ann, 298
Arizona, U.S. claim to, 384
Armada, 53, 56, 57
Arminianism, 75, 85, 147
Armory, first armories, 262-63
Arms production, post-Revolution,
  262-63

Army
  post-Revolution, 263
  See also Defense and military
Army Medical Bureau, 436
Arnold, Benedict, and American
  Revolution, 188, 193, 198
Art
  of Africans, 7
  of Native Americans, 11, 15
Articles of Confederation, 191, 213, 217
*Associations of Adults for Mutual
  Education* (Holbrook), 355
Assumption Act of 1790, 233
Astor, John Jacob, 262
Atchison, David, 404
Atlanta Campaign, Civil War, 442-43
Attucks, Crispus, 178
Auburn State Prison, 359
Austin, Stephen F., 371, 372
Ayllón, Vázquez de, 27
Azores, 18
Aztecs
  civilization of, 15, 25-26
  Spanish conquest of, 17, 23,
    25-26, 116

B

Bacon, Elizabeth, 101
Bacon, Nathaniel, 101-2, 106
Bacon's Rebellion, 100-102
Badger, George, 402
Bagot, Charles, 292
Baley, William, 279
Ballard, Martha, 224
Baltimore
  free African-Americans, 253
  growth in 1820s, 298-300
  as port city, 133
Bambaras, 115
Bank of the United States, First, 233-34
Bank of the United States, Second,
  291-92, 294, 295
  dissolution of, 330-31, 366
Banking, national banks, 233-34, 291-92
Banks, Nathaniel, 451-52
Banks Plan, 452, 453
Baptists
  African influence, 144, 151
  colonial era, 151
  growth of congregation, 252
Barbados, 72, 91
  as slave society, 98-100
Barnes, Lucy, 142
Barton, Clara, 436
Beaumont, Gustave, 359
Beauregard, P.G.T., 429
Beaver, 262
Beaver Wars, 51
Beecher, Catharine
  on abolitionists, 345, 369
  on female self-reliance, 356, 357
Beecher, Charles, 398
Beecher, Lyman
  on American West, 314, 353
  anti-Catholicism, 352
  pro-slavery position of, 343, 345
  Protestant view of, 314, 316
  on temperance, 357
Belknap, Kit, 374
Bell, John, 412, 413
Benevolent Empire, 314-16
  on Indian removal, 326
  societies and works of, 314-16
  women in, 315-16
Benin, 7, 128
Benton, Thomas Hart, 365, 372, 382

Berdaches, 117
Berkeley, Frances, 102
Berkeley, John, 94, 101-2
Bernard, Francis, 177, 178
Best, Robert, 279
Beverley, Robert, 102
Bible Society, 316
Bible and Tract Society, 304
Biddle, Nicholas, 330-31
Bill of Rights
  amendments of, 231-32
  and Constitutional Convention,
    216, 217
Birney, James G., 343, 369, 382
Black church
  denominations, 255, 256
  free African-Americans, 253-54, 454
  plantation slaves, 150, 303
Black Codes, 297, 456-57, 462
Black Death, 6, 21
Black Hawk's War, 330
Blackfoot Indians, 375
Blatchly, Cornelius, 317
Board of Education, creation of, 358
Board for the Emigration,
  Preservation, and Improvement of
  the Aborigines of America, 326
Boise, Alice, 73
Boleyn, Anne, 74
Bonaparte, Napoleon
  attack of U.S. ships, 270, 271
  growth of power, 270
  and Louisiana Purchase, 265-66
Book of Martyrs (Foxe), 53
Book of Mormon (Smith), 312
Boone, Daniel, 264
Booth, John Wilkes, 446
Boston
  abolitionist activities, 343
  and American Revolution, 193
  anti-abolitionist violence, 344
  growth in 1820s, 298-300
  as port city, 134
  settlement of, 77
  See also American Revolution, causes
Boston Labor Reform Association, 471
Boston Manufacturing Company, 286
Boston Massacre, 178, 187
Boston News-Letter, 140
Boston Port Bill of 1774, 180
Boston Tea Party, 179-80
Botts, Lawson, 411
Boylston, Dr. Zabdiel, 146
Braddock, Edward, 163-64, 166
Bradford, William, 76, 77, 82
Bradstreet, Anne, 82, 83
Bragg, Braxton, 441
Brant, Joseph, 209, 211
Brant, Molly, 209
Brant, Sally, 226
Brazil
  Dutch in, 49
  Portuguese in, 18, 49
Breckinridge, John, 412
Breed's Hill, battle of, 188, 189
British East India Company, 178-79
Brooklyn, and American
  Revolution, 193
Brooks Brothers, 392
Brooks, Preston S., 404
Brotherton Indians, 377
Brow, William Hill, 235
Brown, Charles Brockden, 229, 235
Brown, John, 409-12
  Harpers Ferry raid, 410-11
  Pottawatomie Massacre, 404, 410
  trial of, 411

Brown, Joseph, 440
Brown University, founding of, 151
Bruce, H.C., 455
Bryan, Andrew, 151
Bryant, Edwin, 376
Bubonic plague, 6
Buchanan, James, presidency of, 405-7
Buchanan's Station, battle of, 239
Buffalo
  hunting by white Americans, 377-78
  and Native Americans, 14, 23
Bull Run, battles of, 423-24, 431
Bunker Hill, battle of, 188
Burgoyne, John, 195
Burke, Edmund, 93
Burke, Emily, 301
Burnside, Ambrose, 436, 441
Burr, Aaron
  as Democratic-Republican, 243
  -Hamilton dispute, 267
Bushnell, Horace, 371
Bustill, Cyrus, 253
Butler, Andrew, 404
Butler, Benjamin F., 422, 429, 467
Byllesby, Langton, 348-49
Byrd, William II, 143

C

Cabot, John, 35
Cacique, 17
Cajuns, 164
Cakchiquel Indians, 21
Calhoun, John C.
  on abolition, 346, 396
  as National Republican, 291
  Omnibus Bill, 397-98
  as secretary of state, 381
  as secretary of war, 322
  on Tariff of 1828, 338-39
  as vice president, 323
  and War of 1812, 272
California
  gold rush, 396
  statehood, 397
  U.S. claim to, 383, 384
Calusa Indians, 24-25, 38-39
Calvert, Charles, 108
Calvert, Sir George, 70
Calvin, John, 74
Calvinism
  beliefs of, 74
  Dutch, 47, 49
  Puritans, 74-75
Cameron, Simon, 422, 429
Canada
  and American Revolution, 189, 193
  French and Indian War, 168
  French territories, 36-46, 109-10
  fur trade, 36, 40, 43, 46, 97, 114,
    133-34
  Native Americans of, 40-46
  -U.S. dispute (1830s), 367
Canals
  Erie Canal, 285-86
  regional areas (1830), 287
Canary Islands
  Columbus exploration, 3, 16
  sugar plantations, 7, 9, 18
Cane Ridge, religious revival, 252
Cantelo, Mrs. J., 300
Cape Breton Island, 167
Capitalism, colonial era, 134-35
Capitol, construction of, 258
Carey, Mathew, 347
Carib Indians, 17-18, 23
Caribbean, *See also* West Indies

Carolina colony, 96-100
  governance of, 97
  and Native Americans, 97-98, 157
  as proprietary colony, 97
  rice cultivation, 100
  slavery in, 97-100
  and Spain, 97-98
  See also North Carolina; South
    Carolina
Caroline, 367
Carpetbaggers, 461
Carrier, Andrew, 112
Carrier, Martha, 112
Carrier, Richard, 112
Carrington, Edward, 233
Carter, Richard, 137
Carter, Robert, 137
Carteret, George, 94
Cartier, Jacques, 38, 40
Casas, Bartolomé de las, 20
Cass, Lewis, 377, 381, 396
Castle William, 174, 175, 178
Catherine of Aragon, 52, 74
Catholicism
  anti-Catholic sentiment, 351-52,
    400-401
  ban in England, 52, 74, 94
  Inquisition, 10
  Maryland colony, 70, 108
  on slavery, 18
Cayuse Indians, 373, 375
Celibacy, Shakers, 312
Central America, Native Americans of,
  15, 21
Chaco Canyon, 15
Champlain, Samuel de, 40, 42-43
Chancellorsville, battle of, 436
Channing, William Ellery, 356
Chapman, Henry, 343
Chapman, Maria Weston, 343
Charbonneau, 266
Charles I, king of England, 70, 77, 93,
  96, 173
Charles II, king of England, 93, 95,
  96, 104
Charles Town, 97
Charleston
  African slaves in, 143
  and American Revolution, 193, 195
  and Civil War, 420, 444
  colonial era, 97
  as port city, 134
  pre-Revolution, 179
Charlottesville, and American
  Revolution, 199
Charter colony
  meaning of, 70
  Virginia as, 63, 70
Charter of Libertyes and Priviledges, 95
Chase, Samuel, 259
Chattanooga, battle of, 441
Chauncy, Charles, 148, 151
Cherokee Indians
  ancestors of, 328
  culture of, 328
  governing body of, 267-68
  land deals of, 281
  and Northwest Territory, 239-40
  removal from homelands, 326-30
  revitalization movement, 269
Cherokee Nation v. Georgia, 326
Chesapeake, 270
Chesapeake Indians, 57
Cheves, Langdon, 295, 319
Cheyenne Indians, removal from
  homelands, 364-65
Chickamauga Creek, battle of, 435, 441

Chickamauga Indians, and Northwest
  Territory, 239-40
Chickasaw Indians, 114, 267
  removal from homelands, 327
Child, Lydia Marie, 343, 350, 351,
  356, 471
Children
  of Native Americans, 45
  of Puritans, 81, 82, 83
China, Marco Polo exploration of, 4, 6
Chinook Indians, 375
Chippewa Indians, 161, 239
Choctaw Indians, 28, 114, 267
  removal from homelands, 327
Christian Advocate and Herald, 373
Christiana, Battle of, 399
Christianity
  and African slaves, 150, 303
  holy wars, 10
  and Native Americans, 18-20, 33-
    35, 46, 117-18, 267, 373
  spread in age of discovery, 10-11,
    15-16, 18-20, 49
  See also Missionaries
Church of Jesus Christ of the Latter-
  day Saints. *See* Mormons
Church and state separation
  colonial ideal, 83
  and political parties, 252
Cíbola, 28
Cincinnati
  anti-abolition violence, 344
  growth of, 279-80, 304
Cipango (Japan), 4
Cities and urban growth
  African slave population, 141-42
  colonial America, 138-42
  evangelical missionary societies,
    313-14
  expansionist era, 298-300
  and family size, 299
  housing, 300
  and immigration, 298
  and internal migrants, 353
  learning societies, 235
  manufacturing centers, 298, 304
  middle class, 350-51
  pace of city, 140, 298
  and poor, 347-48
  social life, 138-40
  societies and institutions, 138-39,
    299-300
  wage dependency of workers, 347-48
  of western cities, 304
  working class, 347-48
Civic culture, post-Revolution, 235
Civil Rights Act of 1866, 458-59, 468
Civil Rights Act of 1875, 474
Civil War, 420-46
  African-American troops, 432-34
  antiwar sentiment of North, 436-37
  antiwar sentiment of South, 440
  beginning of, 420
  civilian reaction to, 420-22
  Confederate advantages, 426,
    430-32
  Confederate weaknesses, 425-26
  Confiscation Acts, 342, 423-34, 431
  consequences of, 444-46
  contraband slaves, 422-23
  Emancipation Proclamation, 432-34
  events leading to. *See* Civil War,
    causes
  Gettysburg Address, 439
  Grant's command, 429, 441-42
  Lee's command, 426, 430-32, 437,
    439, 441, 443-44

McClellan's command, 423,
  430-32, 436
medical/nursing care, 435-36
motives for soldiers, 427-28
naval resources, 425-26
Peninsula Campaign of 1862, 430-32
and political economy. *See* Civil
  War political economy
Sherman's command, 442-44
slavery, negative effects for South,
  426-27
as social revolution, 434
soldiers, motives of, 427-28
Union strengths, 425
Western victories, 429-30
  See also Reconstruction
Civil War battles
  Anaconda strategy, 421
  Antietam, 431-32, 435
  Appomattox, 444
  Atlanta Campaign, 442-43
  Bull Run, 423-24
  Chancellorsville, 436
  Chattanooga, 441
  Chickamauga Creek, 435, 441
  Cold Harbor, 441-42
  Five Forks, 444
  Franklin, 435, 443
  Fredericksburg, 436
  Gettysburg, 435, 437-39
  Nashville, 443-44
  New Orleans, 429, 432
  Second Bull Run, 431
  Seven Days, 431
  Shenandoah Valley Campaign, 442
  Shiloh, 429, 435
  Vicksburg, 436, 439
  Wilderness Campaign, 441
Civil War, causes
  anti-slavery Republicans, 404-6,
    408-9, 412-13
  cooperationist proposals, 419-20
  Dred Scott decision, 406-7
  Fugitive Slave Act, 398-99
  Harpers Ferry raid, 410-12
  John Brown's raids, 404, 409-12
  Kansas-Nebraska Act, 402-4
  Lincoln-Douglas debate, 408-9
  Lincoln, election of, 412-13
  pro-slavery Democrats, 404-9, 412-13
  Southern secession, 419-20, 421
  Union, North/South rejection of,
    409-10
  See also Abolition
Civil War political economy
  African slaves, 426-27
  northern prosperity, 444-45
  post-war federal intervention, 445
  Southern economic decline,
    426-27, 445
Clark, George Rogers, 209
Clark, William, survey of Louisiana
  Territory, 266-67
Clay, Henry
  on entrepreneurship, 354
  on Indian removal, 326
  and Missouri Compromise, 297
  as National Republican, 291
  Omnibus Bill, 397-98
  as secretary of state, 322-23
  as speaker of house, 322
  and War of 1812, 272
  and Whig Party, 331, 365-66, 379-82
Clinton, DeWitt, 279
  and Erie Canal, 285-86
Clinton, George, 269, 271
Clinton, Henry, 195

Clothing, colonial America, 136-37
Coercive Acts, 180-81
Colbert, Jean Baptiste, 114
Cold Harbor, battle of, 441-42
College of New Jersey, 151
Colleges. *See* Universities and colleges
Colonial America
  African slaves, 128-29, 132-33, 141-42
  cities and urban life, 138-42
  Dutch colony, 47-52
  elite of, 138-39, 142-43
  English colonies, 63-67, 70, 94-95,
    96-100
  and Enlightenment, 146-47
  expansion of settlements (1720-
    1760), 126
  French and Indian War, 160-69
  French territories, 106, 114-15
  gentility, rise of, 137
  and Great Awakening, 147-51
  immigration (1770s), 125-27
  political economy. *See* Colonial era
    political economy
  population growth (1700s), 125, 129
  rural society, 142
  social stratification, 137, 138, 141
  Spanish territories, 23-29,
    38-39, 116
  See also American Revolution;
    American Revolution, causes
Colonial era political economy, 130-38
  British revenues from colonies,
    169-77
  capitalism, 134-35
  consumerism, 130, 135-38
  defining factors, 130
  and Enlightenment ideals, 146-47
  European financial objectives,
    35-36, 52
  exports, 132-35
  family economy, 81-82, 130-33
  industrious revolution, 130
  land grants, 64, 68
  mercantilism, 46, 94, 134-35
  merchant activities, 134-35, 227
  and Native Americans, 40-43, 46, 97
  plantations, 47, 49, 62, 132-33, 142-45
  post-Revolutionary War. *See*
    American republic political
    economy
  private sponsorship of colonies,
    47-49, 62-64, 76, 77
  of Puritans, 80-81
  regional output and prosperity,
    132-34
  shipping, 134-35
  and slavery, 49, 70-71, 98-100, 132-34
  and war, 158-59
Colorado, U.S. claim to, 384
Colored Orphan Asylum, 436
Columbia University, founding of, 151
Columbian exchange, 22-23
Columbus, Christopher
  biographical information, 16
  explorations of, 3-5, 16-19
  and Native Americans, 3
Comanche Indians, 23, 119, 371,
  375, 376
Common school movement, 357-59
Common Sense (Paine), 137, 189-90, 229
Communitarians, 311
  See also Millennialism
Commutation fee, and Civil War
  conscription, 436
Compromise of 1850, 397-98
Concord, battle of, 188
Conestoga Indians, 127

Conestoga Manor, 170
Confederacy
    capital of, 425
    formation of, 419-20, 419-21
    president and vice president of,
        419, 425
    See also Civil War
Confiscation Acts, 423-34, 431, 432
Congregational Clergy of
    Massachusetts, 352
Congregationalism, 104, 251-52
    and abolition, 343
Congress
    lawyers as members, 264
    Reconstruction actions, 460-65
Connecticut
    Congregationalism, 252
    white male suffrage, 318
Connecticut colony
    as charter colony, 108
    founding of, 85-87
    seizure by England, 94
Connecticut Compromise, 214-15
    Three-Fifths Compromise, 215
Connecticut River, 85-86, 94
Conquistadors, 19-20, 23, 26, 27, 35
Conscription
    Civil War, 436
    commutation fee, 436
Constitution
    Bill of Rights, 216, 231-32
    ratification process, 215-17
Constitutional Convention, 213-18
    Bill of Rights, 216, 217
    Connecticut Compromise, 214-15
    Federalist versus Antifederalist
        views, 215-17
    New Jersey Plan, 214, 215
    ratification of Constitution,
        process of, 215-17
    on slavery, 215
    Virginia Plan, 214, 215
Constitutional ideals, separation of
    powers, 217
Constitutionalism, elements of, 173
Consumerism
    colonial America, 135-38
    consumer revolution, meaning
        of, 130
    meaning of, 138
Continental Army, 189, 193, 194
Contraband and Relief
    Organization, 302
Convention of 1818, 292
Coode, John, 108
Coode's Rebellion, 108
Cooke, Jay, 474-75
Cooke, John Esten, 441
Cooper, Anthony Ashley, 97
Cooper, James Fenimore, 355
Cooper, William, 224
Cooperationists, pre-Civil War propos-
    als, 419-20
Copperheads, 436-37
Corbin, Hannah Lee, 207
Corey, Giles, 112
Cornish, Samuel E., 342
Cornwallis, Lord, 196, 199
Coronado, Francisco Vázquez de, 28-29
Corporations, specially chartered
    corporations, 319
Corruption
    machine politics, 472-73
    Reconstruction era, 472-74
Cortés, Hernando, 25, 116
Corwin, Jonathan, 111
Cottagers, 133

Cotton, 260-61
    and African slaves, 261, 301
    price decline by 1880s, 457
    production decline, 337
    profitability of, 260-61, 392
Cotton gin, 260, 262
Cotton, John, 84-85
Cove Ferry, 279
Coverture, principle of, 228
Cowetas, 230
Coxe, Tench, 236
Craft associations, post-Revolution, 236
Crafts persons
    African slaves, 301
    colonists, 64, 127
    craft shops, 255-57, 300
    mutual aid societies of, 257
    of western lands, 304
Crandall, Prudence, 344
Crawford, William H., 281, 366
    as secretary of Treasury, 322
Credit' Mobilier, 472
Creek Indians, 28, 97, 114, 267
    and Northwest Territory, 239-40
    on property ownership, 230
    removal from homelands, 325,
        327, 330
    in War of 1812, 273-74
Creole, 380
Crevecoeur, J. Hector St. John de, 223
Crittenden Compromise, 420
Crittenden, John J., 420, 423
Croatoan, 56, 57
Cromwell, Oliver, 93
Crow Indians, 375
Crowninshield, Jacob, 262
Crusades, 10
Cuba
    and French and Indian War, 168
    Ostend Manifesto, 403
    Spanish territory, 4, 17, 21, 22
Culture, learning societies, 235
Cumberland Gap, 204
Cumming, Kate, 435
Cummins, Sally, 373-74
Currency
    Civil War era, 331, 366
    greenbacks, 427, 430, 445
    post-Revolution era, 204-5, 213
Currency Act of 1764, 171, 178

D

Daily Sentinel, 349
Dallas, George Mifflin, 382
Dancing Assembly, 253
Dartmouth, 179
Dartmouth, founding of, 151
Dartmouth v. Woodward, 291, 294
Davenport, James, 151
Davis, Henry Winter, 453
Davis, Jefferson
    and Civil War, 430, 442
    on Emancipation Proclamation, 432
    president of Confederacy, 419, 425
    on secession, 419
Dawes, William, and American
    Revolution, 187
De La Warr, Lord, 66-67
DeBow, J.D.B., 405
Decatur, Stephen, 260
Declaration of Independence, 190-91
    ideals of, 190-91
Declaration of Sentiments, 370
Declaratory Act of 1766, 176
Defense and military
    African Americans in, 432-34

African slaves in, 227-28, 261
    armories, 262-63
    Continental Army, 189, 193, 194
    Navy, Civil War, 259, 425-26
    post-Revolution, 262-63
    racial segregation/
        discrimination, 434
Deflation, post-Revolution, 205
Deganawidah Epic, 40, 50
Delaware Indians, 95-96, 160, 239
Delaware River, 94
Democratic Party
    and Civil War, 425-26, 429, 436,
        442-43
    first national presidential cam-
        paign, 324
    Irish vote (1850s), 400
    Jacksonian Democrats, 325, 335-36
    pro-slavery position of, 400, 404-9,
        412-13
Democratic Republican Societies,
    234, 242
Democratic Republicans
    on political economy, 250
    and presidential election
        of 1796, 243
    views of, 234, 241, 250
Dennett, John Richard, 449-50
Depressions
    depression of 1870s, 474-76
    Panic of 1819, 295, 317
    Panic of 1837, 331, 365, 366-67
Dias, Bartolomeo, 15
Dickinson, John, 177, 266
    and Articles of Confederation, 191
Dilworth, Rankin, 385
Disease
    death of Native Americans, 21-22,
        25, 46
    syphilis, 21-22
    voyage to America, 127, 129
Dix, Dorothea, 436
Doeg Indians, 101
Domestic workers, Irish immigrants, 392
Dominican Republic, 469
Dorr, Thomas, 319, 380
Douglas, Stephen A.
    and Kansas-Nebraska Act, 401-2, 405
    -Lincoln debate, 408-9
    on popular sovereignty, 396, 401-2,
        405, 408
    presidential candidate (1860),
        412-13
Douglass, Frederick
    antislavery activities, 390, 393
    biographical information, 389-90
    as slave, 283, 303, 389-90
    and woman's movement, 370, 471
Doyle, James, 404
Drake, Sir Francis, 39, 52-53, 55-56
Dred Scott case, 406-7, 458
Drinker, Elizabeth, 226
Drinker, Henry, 226
Du Pont de Nemours, E.I., 295
Duane, William J., 330
Dublin Society, 147
Dunmore, Lord, 171, 189
Durham, Bishop of, 70
Duston, Hannah, 159
Dutch colonies, 47-52
    incentives for settlers, 47-50
    New Netherland, 47-52, 94-95
    slave trade, 47, 49, 71, 94
    sugar plantations, 49
    and wampum trade, 50-51
    West Indies, 49
    See also New Netherland

Dutch East India Company, 47
Dutch Reformed Church, 49
Dutch West India Company, 47, 49
Dyer, Mary, 104

E

Eastern State Mental Hospital, 147
Eastern Woodlands tribes. See
    Woodlands Indians
Easton, Treaty of, 167
Eaton, John, 325
Eaton, Theophilus, 85
Economic growth. See Political economy
Edict of Nantes, 40
Edisto Island, 456
Education
    common school movement, 357-59
    of elite, 357
    of middle class, 357-58
    public schools, creation of, 358-59
    self-education, 354
    and social stratification, 357-58
    See also Schools; Universities and
        colleges
Edwards, Jonathan, 148, 151, 267, 314
Eighth Amendment, rights of, 232
El Paso, 118
Electoral College
    Jackson/Adams election, 322
    procedures of (1796), 243, 259
Elite
    African Americans, 461, 474-75
    colonial era, 138-39, 142-43
    control of land, 225, 227
    Democratic Republicans as, 234
    early settlers, 64, 102
    education of, 357
    insider advantage and wealth, 319
    post-Revolutionary War, 225, 227
    and republicanism, 331
    secret societies, 319-20
    social associations, colonial era, 139
    specially chartered corporations
        of, 319
    view of rural settlers, 227
Elizabeth I, queen of England, 52, 54,
    74, 93
Elkinson, Harry, 338
Ely, Ezra Stiles, 313
Ely, Samuel, 225
Emancipation Proclamation, 432-33
    African American reaction to, 433
Embargo Act of 1807, 270-71, 317-18
Embargo Act of 1809, 270-71
Emerson, John, 406
Emerson, Ralph Waldo, 355, 356
Employment discrimination
    free African Americans, 255
    women, 228-29, 347-48
Employment standards, length of
    workday, 349
Empresario, 371
Encomenderos, 118
Encomienda system, 19-21, 118-19
Enforcement Acts, 469
England
    African slaves in, 72
    in age of discovery, 5
    and American Civil War, 424, 426
    Anglican Church, 52, 53, 74, 93
    Anglo-Dutch Wars, 94
    Civil War of 1642, 93-94
    empire. See English colonies
    Glorious Revolution, 94, 107-8
    imperialism, origins of, 52
    Ireland, conquest of, 53-54

King George's War, 158, 160
Parliament, 173
Restoration, 95, 104
See also Great Britain
English colonies
Carolina colony, 96-100
colonial population (1660-
1710), 99
Connecticut colony, 94
financial incentives for settlers, 64,
68, 70, 76
financing of settlements, 53, 63, 68
French and Indian War, 160-69
Georgia colony, 145
Glorious Revolution, effects of, 107-8
indentured servants, 17, 63-64, 68
Jamestown, 63-69
King George's War, 116
King William's War, 109
Maryland colony, 70
and mercantilism, 46, 94
and Native Americans, 55-57, 62-
63, 66-69, 76-77, 80-81, 105-7
New Jersey colony, 94
New Netherland, 94-95
Pennsylvania colony, 95-96
Pilgrim and Puritan settlements,
73-87
Pontiac's Rebellion, 170-71
Queen Anne's War, 109-10, 116
religious impetus of settlers, 70,
73-74, 84
rights of colonists as issue, 108-9
Roanoke colony, 54-57
and slavery, 52, 55-56, 71
taxation and political economy,
171-72
tobacco plantations, 61-62,
71-72, 133
trade regulations, 94
Virginia colony, 63-73, 100-103
West Indies, 72, 91, 98-100
See also American Revolution;
American Revolution, causes
Enlightenment, 145-47
application to political economy,
146-47
ideals of, 146
institutions of, 147
Entertainment, social activities, colo-
nial era, 137-40
Epes, William, 73
Episcopal Church, 74
Equal Rights Party, 368
Equiano, Olaudah, 129
Erasmus, 47
Erie Canal, 285-86
Essay on Slavery and Abolitionism
(Beecher), 369
Essex, 270
Estevanico, 28
Ethnic population. *See* specific ethnic
groups
Evangelical Protestantism
millennialism, 190, 312-13
post-Revolution, 251
temperance movement, 356-57
urban missionary societies, 313-16
See also Revivalism
Evans, Oliver, 262, 284
Excise taxes
purpose of, 240
and Whiskey Rebellion, 240-41
Expansionism
Florida, 292-93
Louisiana Purchase, 263, 265-67
manifest destiny, 364, 370-71
Missouri Compromise, 296-97

Monroe presidency, 290-305
Native American reservations,
325-30, 364-65
Oregon Territory, 381-82
and political economy. *See*
Expansionism and political
economy
popular sovereignty, 396, 401-2
population increases, 282
Texas, 371-73
trans-Appalachian West, 303-5
trans-Mississippi West, 373-78
and transportation, 283-86, 394, 395
after Treaty of Ghent, 281-83, 292
War with Mexico, lands gained
in, 384
See also African Americans, nineteenth century; Native Americans,
nineteenth century; Northwest
territory; Western territory
Expansionism and political economy
African slaves, in 301-3
commercial farming, 298
manufacturing centers, 304
Northeast economic activities,
297-300
plantations, 301
rural household production, 298-99
shipping by river, 304
Southern economic activities,
300-303
urban growth, 297-300
western territory, 303-5, 393-94
See also Nineteenth century political
economy
Exported goods
colonial era, 132-35
cotton, 260-61, 337
post-Revolution, 205, 224-25, 242

F

Fallen Timbers, Battle of, 239, 242
Family economy
colonial era, 81-82, 130-33
rural families, 298
Family structure
African slaves, 129-30, 303
Africans, 7
free African Americans, 464
Native Americans, 14, 44, 45
Puritans, 81-82
and urban growth, 299
Farming
commercial farming, 298
western settlers, 305
yeoman households, 302
See also Agriculture
Farragut, David Glasgow, 429, 432
Federal debt, after Revolutionary War,
211, 233
Federal government, -state relationship.
See States and federal government
Federalist, The
No 10, (Madison, Hamilton, and
Jay), 217, 231, 234
No 84, 231
Federalists
and Adams election, 243
concept of Constitution, 215-17
Hartford Convention, 274, 275
views of, 234
Felipe II, king of Spain, 38
Female Anti-Slavery Society, 343
Female Missionary Society for the Poor
of the City of New York, 313
Female Moral Reform Society, 315, 368
Fenno, John, 234

Fernando, king of Spain, 10, 16, 23, 74
Festivals, colonial era, 140
Feudalism
and Maryland colony, 70
meaning of, 70
Fifteenth Amendment, 469-71
rights of, 460
Fifth Amendment, rights of, 232, 297
Filibusters, invasion of Cuba, 403
Fillmore, Millard
Compromise of 1850, 397-98
Fugitive Slave Act of 1850, 398-99
as president, 397-98
Finney, Charles Grandison, 313-14
Fire-eaters, 396, 420
First Amendment, rights of, 232
First Continental Congress, 181
Declaration of Rights of 1774, 181
Fishing
by French, 36, 40
Native Americans, 12-13
Fitch, John, 284
Fithian, Philip, 137
Five Forks, battle of, 444
Five Nations, of Iroquois, 40, 41, 50
Florida
ceded to United States, 292-93
free black community, 116, 143
French outposts, 38
Native Americans of, 24-25, 27-28,
38-39
Spanish conquest, 23-25, 27-28,
38-39, 116
Flour milling, inventions related to, 262
Foot, Samuel A., 339
Forbes, John, 166
Force Bill, 341
Ford, William, 468
Ford's Theatre, 446
Fort Armstrong, 406
Fort Beauséjour, 163
Fort Biloxi, 106, 114
Fort Bull, 165
Fort Cahokia, 13, 106, 114
Fort Carillon, 164, 167
Fort Caroline, 38, 40, 52
Fort Donelson, 429
Fort Duquesne, 163, 166, 167
Fort Frontenac, 167
Fort Henry, 429, 431
Fort Kaskaskia, 106, 114
Fort Louisbourg, 157, 158
Fort McHenry, 272
Fort Necessity, 161-62, 163
Fort Niagra, 157, 163, 164
Fort Orange, 05, 48
Fort Oswego, 165
Fort Pickens, 422
Fort Pill, 167
Fort St. Frédéric, 157, 163, 164
Fort Snelling, 406
Fort Stanwix, 171
Fort Stanwix, Treaty of, 171
Fort Sumter, 420, 421, 422
Fort Ticonderoga, 164, 188, 193
Fort Toulouse, 114, 145, 157
Fort Walla Walla, 373
Fort Washington, 193
Fort William Henry, 164, 165, 167
Forten, James, 254
Foster, Abby Kelley, 471
Fourteenth Amendment, 458-60, 471
rights of, 460
Fourth Amendment, rights of, 232
Fox Indians, 239, 267, 283
removal from homelands, 327, 330
Foxe, George, 53
France

in age of discovery, 5
in American Revolution, 195,
199, 201
empire. *See* French colonies
French Revolution, 241, 242
Jay's Treaty, 242, 243
Louisiana Purchase, 246-67, 263
piracy of, 38
and Proclamation of Neutrality,
241-42
XYZ Affair, 244
Franciscan missionaries, in New
Mexico, 117-18
Franklin, battle of, 435, 443
Franklin, Benjamin
and Constitutional Convention, 214
and Declaration of
Independence, 190
Enlightenment thinking of, 146
envoy to France and Revolution,
195, 201-2
institutions founded by, 147
pre-Revolution, 140, 180
on slavery, 228
Franklin, James, 140
Fredericksburg, battle of, 436
Free African Society, 236
Free slaves. *See* African Americans,
free slaves
Free Society of Traders, 95
Free-Soil Party, 396, 397, 400
Free State Association, 452
Free State Hotel, 404
Freedmen's Bureau, 449-50, 455, 458
Freedom's Journal, 342
Frémont, John C., 263, 383, 404-6
French colonies, 36-46
and African slaves, 114-16
Canadian territories, 36-46, 109-10
Florida, 38
French and Indian War, 160-69
fur trade, 36, 40, 43, 46, 97, 114
Louisiana, 106, 114-15
and Native Americans, 40-46, 106,
109-10, 157
Newfoundland, 36, 40
-Spanish conflict, 38
West Indies, 115-16, 168
French and Indian War, 160-69
end of, 168-69
events leading to, 160-61
scope of, 163-68
transfer of territory after, 168-69
and Virginia colony, 161-62
Freneau, Philip, 234
Frethorn, Richard, 71
Fugitive Slave Act of 1793, 228
Fugitive Slave Act of 1850, 398-99, 402
Fuller, Margaret, 356
Fuller, Thomas, 228
Fulton, Robert, 284-85, 294
Fundamental Constitutions, 97, 108
Fur trade
age of discovery, 36, 40, 43, 46
colonial era, 97, 114, 133-34, 230
Dutch, 47, 48
French, 36, 40, 43, 46, 97, 114
Native Americans, 36, 40, 43, 46,
114, 133-34, 230

G

Gadsden, James, 402
Gadsden Purchase, 402-3
Gag rule, on abolitionist petitions, 346,
368-69, 396
Gage, Thomas
and American Revolution, 187-88

pre-Revolution, 180-81
Gallatin, Albert, 259-60
Da Gama, Vasco, 15
Garden, Alexander, 148
Garrison, William Lloyd, 342-44, 368-69, 390
Gazette of the United States, 234
Gender roles
    African slaves, 102, 133
    Africans, 7
    Aztecs, 25
    family economy, 130-32
    matrilineal/matrilocal societies, 14, 45
    middle class, 351
    and missionaries, 117
    Native Americans, 11, 14, 45
    in plantation society, 72-73
    Puritans, 81-82, 84-85
General Colored Association of Massachusetts, 342
Genêt, Edmond Charles, 241
Genius of Universal Emancipation, The, 342
Gentility, colonial America, 137
George III, king of England, 169, 190, 294
Georgia, and Civil War, 442-43
Georgia colony
    and American Revolution, 195
    founding of, 145
    as plantation society, 145
German immigrants
    colonial era, 127
    eighteenth century, 298, 391
    Hessians in Revolution, 189, 193
Geronimo, 29
Gerry, Elbridge, 244
Gettysburg, battle of, 435, 437-39
Ghana, 7
Ghent, Treaty of 1814, 274, 279
    and westward expansion, 281-83
Gibbons, Thomas, 294
Gibbs, Martha, 438
Gilbert, Sir Humphrey, 54
"Gleaner, The" (Murray), 229, 235
Global trade
    in age of discovery, 5-9
    and merchantilist doctrine, 94
    as republican virtue, 224-25
Glorious Revolution, 94, 107, 147, 173
Godey's Lady's Book, 356
Gold, Columbus search for, 4, 17, 18
Gold rush, 396
Good, Sarah, 92, 111
Goodloe, Daniel R., 393
Goodrich, Samuel, 224
Government Act of 1774, 180
Government bonds, Civil War, 427, 445
Gowrie plantation, 340-41
Gracia Real de Santa Teresa de Mose, 116, 143
Graham cracker, 355
Graham, Sylvester, 355
Granada, conquest of Moors, 10
Granger, Gordon, 441
Grant, Ulysses S.
    Civil War, 429, 441-42
    as president, 468-75
    as secretary of war, 468
Grant, Zilpah, 357
Great Awakening, 147-51
    effects of, 149-51
    impetus for, 147-48
    and Whitfield, 148-50
Great Britain
    after Revolutionary War, 241-42

seizure of American ships, 262, 270, 272
    War of 1812, 271-74
Great United States Exploring Expedition, 380
Greeley, Horace, 394, 474
Green Corn Ceremony, 269, 328
Green Mountain Boys, 188
Green, Nathaniel, 196
Greenbacks, 427, 430, 445
Greenville, Treaty of 1795, 239, 267
Grenville, George, 171, 173, 175
Grenville, Sir Richard, 54-56
Grimké, Angelina, 369
Grimké, Sarah, 369
Guadalupe Hidalgo, Treaty of, 384
Guadeloupe, 116
Guanahaní, 3, 4
Guinea, 7
Gulick, Rachel, 279
Gullah language, 143

H

Hafen, Mary Ann, 375
Hakluyt, Richard, 52, 63
Hale, Sarah Josepha, 356
Half-faced camps, 305
Hall of Science, 354
Hall v. DeCuir, 476
Hallowell, 224
Halve Maen (Half Moon), 47
Hamilton, Alexander
    biographical information, 225
    -Burr dispute, 267
    as Federalist, 234, 243
    and *Federalist, The*, 217
    land purchase, 237
    national bank proposal, 233-34
    on political economy, 206
    and presidential election of 1796, 243
    as secretary of treasury, 232-33
    view of merchant class, 225, 227
    Zenger case, 140
Hammond, James Henry, 392-93
Hancock, John
    and American Revolution, 188
    pre-Revolution, 178
Handsome Lake (Ganioda'yo), revitalization movement, 268-69
Hanover Street Presbyterian Church, 314
Hariot, Thomas, 55
Harmer, Josiah, 239
Harmony, Pennsylvania, 312
Harpers Ferry, John Brown's raid, 409-12
Harrison, William Henry
    as president, 379-80
    and War of 1812, 272
    and western territory, 269, 282
    as Whig, 365, 379
Hartford Convention, 274, 275, 339
Hartford Female Seminary, 357
Hartford Wits, 235
Harvard University
    and Enlightenment, 147
    founding of, 81
Harvey, Thomas A., 377
Hathorne, John, 111
Haun, Catherine, 374
Hawkins, Benjamin, 230
Hawkins, John, 52-53
Hayes, Rutherford B., as president, 475-76
Hayne, Robert Y., 339

Head-Smashed-In cliff, 14
Headright, 68
Health care reform, self-care, 354, 355
Helper, Hilton Rowan, 407
Hemmings, Sally, 258
Henry of Navarre, 40
Henry, Patrick
    and Constitutional Convention, 216
    pre-Revolution, 174
Henry VII, king of England, 52
Henry VIII, king of England, 52, 74
Hessians, 189, 193
Hiawatha, 40
Hidalgo, 10, 20
Hidatsa Indians, 266
Highgate, Edmonia, 454
Hillsborough, Lord, 177
Hispaniola
    Native Americans of, 17
    Spanish territory, 17, 18
Hochelaga, 38
Hodgson, Sarah, 288-89
Holbrook, Joshiah, 355
Holy wars, *reconquista*, 9-10
Homelessness, homes for (1800s), 315-16
Homosexuality, colonial era, 73
Hood, John Bell, 442
Hooker, Fighting Joe, 436
Hooker, Thomas, 86
Hopewell Indians, 13, 14
Horses
    and Native Americans, 23, 363
    in New World, 14
Horseshoe Bend, Battle of, 274
House of Commons, 173
House of Lords, 173
Housing
    mansions of elite, 94-95
    urban, 300
Houston, Sam, 372
Howard, Oliver Otis, 455
Howe, William, 193
Hudson, Henry, 47
Hudson River valley
    Dutch settlement, 47, 94
    manors along river, 94-95
Huguenots, in New World, 38, 40
Huitzilopochtli, 25
Hull, William, 272
Human sacrifice, of Aztecs, 25
Humanism
    and religious toleration, 47
    and Spain, 10-11
Humanitarian organizations, post-Revolution, 236
Hunter, David, 432
Hunting, Native Americans, 11, 13, 14
Huron Indians
    Beaver Wars, 51
    and French, 40, 43-46
    village life and customs, 44-45
Huronia, 44-45
Hutchinson, Anne, 84-85, 104
Hutchinson, Francis, 147
Hutchinson, Thomas, 174, 179

I

Iberian Peninsula
    in age of exploration, 9-10
    Muslim domination, 5, 7, 9-10
    See also Portugal; Spain
Ice Age, and Paleo-Indians, 11
Illinois, statehood, 282, 297
Illustrations of Masonry (Morgan), 320
Immediatist activism, abolition, 343, 346

Immigrant Americans
    in cities, 298
    nativist attack, 351-52, 400-401
    work of, 352, 392
Immigration, 351-53
    immigrants of 1700s, 125-27
    immigrants of 1820s, 298
    immigrants of 1840-50s, 391-92
    restriction of. *See* Immigration laws
    See also specific ethnic groups
Immigration laws, Alien and Sedition Acts, 244-45
Impeachment, Andrew Johnson, 465-68
Impending Crisis of the South, The (Helper), 407
Imported goods
    from Africa, 7
    post-Revolution, 205
    tariffs, 232-33, 337-39
Inca, 15, 17, 23
    Spanish conquest of, 26
Incidents in the Life of a Slave Girl (Jacobs), 303
Indentured servants
    plantation labor, 17, 63-64, 68, 71, 101
    treatment of, 71, 226
India
    British empire, 178
    European exploration of, 6, 15
Indian, John, 92
Indian Territory. *See* Native American reservations
Indiana, statehood, 282
Indies. See West Indies
Indigo, as export, 130, 132, 260
Industrious revolution, meaning of, 130
Inés, Doña, 116
Infant mortality, colonial era, 73, 129
Inflation, Revolutionary War era, 204-6
Inquisition, 10
International commerce. *See* Global trade
Intolerable Acts, 180-81
Inuit, 38
Inventions
    agricultural-related, 262, 391
    of Shakers, 312
    steamboat, 284-85
    telegraph, 391
Investment vehicles, post-Revolution, 236
Ipswich Female Academy, 357
Ireland
    British conquest of, 53-54
    potato famine, 352, 391
Irish immigrants, 298, 351-53, 391-92
    anti-Catholic sentiment, 352
    jobs of, 352, 392
Ironclad ships, 426
Iroquois Indians
    agricultural practices, 14
    Beaver Wars, 41, 51
    and Covenant Chain, 107
    Five Nations, 40, 50
    French and Indian War, 161, 164
    as warlike people, 14, 40
Isabel, queen of Spain, 10-11, 16
Islam. *See* Muslims
Isleta, 118
Isthmus of Panama, 42, 52
Italy, in age of discovery, 6
Itinerant preachers
    colonial era, 123-24, 148-49
    post-Revolution, 251-52, 313

J

Jackson, Andrew
  on abolition movement, 344-46
  anti-Jackson Republicans, 365-66
  "common man" image, 310, 324, 325, 331
  conquest of Florida, 292, 321
  corruption accusation, 321-22
  first national presidential campaign, 324
  Indian removal policy, 325-30, 363-64
  presidency of, 309-10, 323-31, 335-60
  Second Bank dissolution, 330-31, 366
  tariff nullification issue, 339-41
  on Texas independence, 372
  and War of 1812, 273-75, 279, 321
Jackson, Rachel, 323, 325
Jackson, Thomas J. (Stonewall), 423, 431
Jacobs, Harriet, 303
Jamaica
  in age of discovery, 21
  colonial era, 98
James, Duke of York, 94-95
James , king of England, 95
James I, king of England, 56, 63, 68, 74, 93, 94, 95
James II, king of England, 107
James River, 63, 65, 68
Jamestown, 63-69
  settlement of, 56-57
  slavery in, 49
  starvation and death in, 65-66
Jay, John
  as chief justice, 232
  and *Federalist, The*, 217
Jay's Treaty, 242, 243
Jefferson, Thomas
  and American Revolution, 189
  British relations, 270-71
  Burr-Hamilton duel, 267
  and Declaration of Independence, 190, 258
  as Democratic-Republican, 234, 243, 250, 258
  Embargo Acts, 270-71
  Louisiana Purchase, 265-67
  on mercantilism and commerce, 258-59
  Native American policy, 267-69
  on Native Americans, 229
  political economy during presidency, 260-64
  presidency of, 257-71
  as Republican, 259, 271
  as secretary of state, 232
  on slavery, 133, 228, 258
  Tripoli War, 259-60
  as vice president, 243
  world view of, 258
Jenkins, Robert, 158
Jeremiad, 104, 148, 150
Jews
  expulsion from Spain (1492), 10
  expulsion from England (1290), 99
  Inquisition, 10
  in Netherlands, 47
  in New Netherland, 49
  organizations for, 236
Jockey Hollow, Continental Army winter quarters, 196-97
Johnson, Andrew
  impeachment of, 465-68
  presidency of, 450, 455-69

and Reconstruction, 455-59
Johnson, Anthony, 72
Johnson, Sir William, 171, 209
Johnson, Susannah Willard, 155-56, 159
Johnson, Sylvanus, 162
Johnson, William, 164
Johnston, Joseph E., 431, 441, 442
Joint-stock company
  of Alexander Hamilton, 236
  English colonies, 53, 63
  functions of, 53
Joliet, Louis, 106
Jones, Absalom, 253
Jones, Owen, 134
Jones, William, 295
Journeymen
  in crafts shops, 255-57
  trade associations of, 320
Judicial review, establishment of, 259
Judiciary Act of 1789, 232, 259
Judiciary Act of 1801, 245, 259

K

Kana'ti peoples, 328
Kansas
  bleeding Kansas, 403-4
  Kansas-Nebraska Act, 401-4
  Lecompton Constitution, 407-8
Kearny, Stephen, 383
Keckley, Elizabeth, 302
Kekionga, 230
Kelley, Abby, 369
Kelpius, Johann, 96
Kemble, Fanny, 471
Kendall, Amos, 330
Kennebec River, 76
Kentucky
  settlement of, 204
  statehood, 318
Key, Francis Scott, 272-73
Kickapoo Indians, 160, 267, 283
Kidd, Samuel, 279
King George's War, 116, 158, 160
King Philip's War, 105-6
King, Rufus, 290
King William's War, 109
Kiowa Indians, 375
Kirkland, Ohio, 313
Kivas, 15
Knights of St. Crispin, 472
Knights of the White Camelia, 468
Know-Nothing Party, 400-401
Knowles, Charles, 159
Knox, Henry
  land purchase, 237
  as secretary of war, 232
Konkow Indians, 375
Ku Klux Klan, Reconstruction era, 465, 468-69

L

La Demoiselle, Miami chieftan, 160-61
Labor unions, 348-50
  demands of (1820-30s), 349-50
  National Labor Union (NLU), 471-72
  precursors to, 255-56
  See also Strikes
Ladies Magazine, 356
Land Act of 1800, 282
Land grants, to colonists, 64, 68, 371
Land Ordinance of 1785, 211
Land pressure, meaning of, 142
Land rights, Puritans, 80

Land riots, 133
Lane, Ralph, 54-55
Lane Theological Seminary, 314, 343
Larkin, Thomas, 383
Laud, William, 93
Lawrence, 272
Laws of Burgos of 1513, 20
Lawyers, as members of Congress, 264
Leatherstocking Tales (Cooper), 355
Lecompton Constitution, 407
Lee, Ann, 311
Lee, Charles, 193
  biographical information, 256
Lee, Jarena, 251-52
Lee, Jason, 373
Lee, Richard Henry
  and American Revolution, 109, 188-89
  and Declaration of Independence, 190, 191
  on women's rights, 207
Lee, Robert E., Civil War, 426, 430-32, 437, 439, 441, 443-44
Leeward Islands, 98
Legal Tender Act, 427, 430
Leggett, William, 319
Leisler, Jacob, 108
L'Enfant, Pierre Charles, 258
León, Ponce de, 23-24
Leopold, 270
Letters from an American Farmer (Crevecoeur), 223
"Letters from a Farmer in Pennsylvania" (Dickinson), 177
Lewis, Meriwether, 263
  survey of Louisiana Territory, 266-67
Lexington, battle of, 187-88
Libel laws, colonial era, 140
Liberal Republicans, and Reconstruction, 472, 474
Liberalism
  abolitionists, 343
  and Locke's treatise, 108
  meaning of, 95
  view of government, 474
Liberator, 342-43, 390
Liberia, free African-Americans deportation, 255, 342
Liberty, 178
Liberty Party, 343, 369, 379, 382
Library
  colonial era, 147
  of new government, 235
Library Company of Philadelphia, 147
Library of Congress, 235
Life and Memorable Actions of George Washington, The (Weems), 235
Lincoln, Abraham
  assassination of, 446
  Civil War, 420-46
  -Douglas debate, 408-9
  Emancipation Proclamation, 432-34
  Gettysburg Address, 439
  presidential elections, 412-13, 419
  Reconstruction, 452-55
  Ten-Percent Plan, 452-53
  youth of, 305
Linked economic development, meaning of, 134
Liquor. *See* Alcohol consumption
Litchfield Academy, 236
Literature
  nineteenth century, 355
  post-Revolution, 235
Little Turtle, 239
Littlefield ring, 473
Livingston, Robert, 284-85, 294

and Louisiana Purchase, 265
Lloyd, Henry Demarest, 472
Locke, John, 97
  on political economy, 108, 146-47
Logan, James, 147
Logan, John, 171
Long Island
  and Dutch, 48
  and English, 94
Long, Stephen, 263
Longhouses, 44-45
Longstreet, James, 439
Lord & Taylor, 392
Lord Dunmore's War, 171
Louis XIV, king of France, 106, 107
Louisiana, statehood, 282
Louisiana colony, and French, 106, 114-15
Louisiana Purchase, 263, 265-67
  Lewis and Clark expedition, 266-67
L'Ouverture, Toussaint, 338
Lovejoy, Elija, 344
Lowell, Francis Cabot, 292
Lowell, Massachusetts
  textile mills, 286, 288-90
  worker strikes, 349-50
Loyalists, in American Revolution, 194, 195, 199, 202, 203
Lundy, Benjamin, 342
Luther, Seth, 335-36, 347, 349, 350, 354, 357
Lutherans, colonial era, 148
Luxury items
  in age of discovery, 6, 7
  colonial America, 135-37
Lyceum movement, 355

M

McClelland, George B., and Civil War, 423, 430-32, 436, 442
McCulloch, James W., 294
McCulloch v. Maryland, 294
McDowell, Irvin, 423
McGillivray, Alexander, 209, 239
Machine politics, 472-73
MacIntosh, Ebenezer, 174
Mackenzie, Alexander, 266
McLane, Louis, 330
McLeod, Alexander, 367
Macomb Purchase, 237
Macon, Nathaniel, 271, 297
Madeira
  Columbus exploration, 16
  sugar plantations, 9
Madison, Dolley, 272
Madison, James
  and Bill of Rights, 231-32
  biographical information, 185-86
  and Constitutional Convention, 213-14, 216
  as Democratic-Republican, 234, 242
  and *Federalist, The*, 217, 231, 234
  Non-Intercourse Act, 271-72
  on political economy, 206
  on political parties, 234
  pre-Revolution, 186
  presidency of, 271-75
  War of 1812, 271-74
Magazines
  nineteenth century, 356
  post-Civil War, 445, 449, 474
  post-Revolution, 235
Magellan, Ferdinand, 15, 36-37
Magna Carta, 173
Mahican Indians, and Dutch, 50
Maine, statehood, 297

Maine colony, 107
  founding of, 85
Maize, 11, 14, 23
Mali, 7
Mandan Indians, 266
Mangum, Willie P., as Whig, 365
Manhattan
  Dutch purchase, 48
  See also New York City
Manifest destiny, 364, 370-71
  meaning of, 370
  See also Expansionism
Manigault, Charles, 340-41
Mann, Horace, 358-59
Manning, William, 225, 235, 250
Mansions, Hudson River, 94-95
Manteo, 54, 56
Manufacturing
  craft shops, 255-57, 300
  growth of workers, 257
  mercantilist view, 94
  outworkers, 347-48
  textile industry, 262-63, 288-90
  urban manufacturing centers,
    298, 304
  Waltham system, 286, 288-90
Manumissions, 102
Marbury v. Madison, 259
Marbury, William, 259
Marcy, William L., 403
Marquette, Jacques, 106
Marriage
  African slaves, 129-30, 464
  colonial era, 73, 142
Marshall, John, 293-94
  Burr treason trial, 267
  Dartmouth v. Woodward, 294
  Gibbons v. Ogden, 294
  on Indian removal, 326
  McCulloch v. Maryland, 294
  Marbury v. Madison, 259
Martha Washington Temperance
    Societies, 357
Martin, Joseph Plumb, 197
Martinique, 115-16
Mary, queen of England, 52, 53
Maryland, and Civil War, 431-32, 442
Maryland colony
  and American Revolution, 193
  governance, 70, 108
  as proprietary colony, 70
  religious toleration, 70
  as royal colony, 108
  slavery in, 72
Mason, James, 424
Mason, John, 87
Masons
  African-American lodges, 253
  Antimason Party, 320
  beliefs of, 139, 147
  elite members, 320
  Order of Freemasons, 319-20
Massachusetts
  public schools, creation of, 358-59
  See also Boston
Massachusetts Bay Colony, 73-87
  as royal colony, 108
  See also Puritans
Massachusetts Bay Company, 77
Massachusetts Constitution of 1780, 206
Massachusetts General Court, 79
Massachusetts Historical Society, 235
Massasoit, 76, 105
Mather, Increase, 107, 108, 111, 146
Matrilineal/matrilocal society, Native
    Americans, 14, 45
Mavila, 28

May, Samuel J., 347
Maya, 15
Mayflower, 76
Mayflower Compact, 76
Meade, George Gordon, 439
Mechanics' Free Press, 349
Mechanics' Institute, 459
Mechanics' Library Company, 349
Mechanics' Union of Trade
    Associations, 320
Meigs, Jonathan, 269
Menéndez de Avilés, Pedro, 38-39
Menéndez, Francisco, 116
Menominee Indians, 267
Mercantile fairs, post-Revolution, 235
Mercantilism
  colonial America, 134-35
  meaning of, 46, 94, 135
Merchant class
  colonial America, 134-35
  Hamilton's view of, 225, 227
  Netherlands, 47
  post-Revolution, 224-25, 227
  and republican ideals, 227
  view of rural population, 227
Merrimac, 426
Merrimack Manufacturing Company, 294
Merry Mount, 77
Mesa Verde, 15
Mestizos, 119
Methodists, 124
  African Methodists, 144, 151,
    254-55
  beliefs of, 251
  post-Revolution growth, 252
  publishing by, 252
  temperance movement, 356
Mexico
  African slaves (1830s), 371-72
  Aztec empire, 15, 25-26
  Gadsden Purchase, 402-3
  Mayan empire, 15
  Spanish conquest of, 25-26
  Texas independence, 364, 371-73
  war with U.S. (1845-47), 382-84
Miami Indians, 160, 239
Middle class
  colonial era, 133
  education of, 357-58
  gender roles, 351
  lifestyle and aspirations of, 351
  nineteenth century, 350-51
  self-improvement, 354-56
Middle ground, meaning of, 43
Middle passage, 128-29
Military. *See* Defense and military
Militia Act of 1862, 434
Millenialism
  beliefs related to, 190, 311, 312
  Mormons, 312-13
  Rappites, 312
  Shakers, 311-12
Millennial Church, 311
Mingo Indians, 171, 239
Minnetaree Indians, 266
Missionaries
  evangelical missionary societies,
    313-14
  Franciscans, in New Mexico, 117-18
  See also Christianity
Mississippi
  and Civil War, 439
  statehood, 282
Mississippi River
  as commercial asset, 280
  steamboats, 285
Mississippian Indians, 13-14, 27-28

Missouri, statehood, 296, 297
Missouri Compromise, 296-97, 401, 406
Mittleberger, Gottfried, 127, 133
Miwok Indians, 375
Mobilian Indians, 114
Moctezuma, 25-26
Moctezuma, Isabel Cortés, 116
Mohawk Indians, as colonial allies, 50,
    106, 107
Molasses Act of 1733, 171
Monitor, 426
Monroe Doctrine, 293
Monroe, James
  Florida acquisition, 292-93
  Missouri Compromise, 296-97
  Monroe Doctrine, 293
  presidency of, 290-305
Monroe, Sally, 349
Montagnais Indians, 42
Montcalm, Louis-Joseph de, 165,
    167, 168
Montgomery, Richard, 189
Moody, Paul, 286
Moors, 5, 10
Moral suasion
  and abolition movement, 343
  reform approach, 135
Morgan, William, 320
Mormons, 312-13, 319, 396
Morris, Gouverneur, 241
  on political economy, 206
Morris, Robert, on political economy, 206
Morse, Samuel F.B., 391
Morton, Thomas, 77, 85
Mose, freed slave community, 116
Mother Bethel, 254
Mother at Home, The (Child), 356
Mott, Lucretia, 343, 369-70, 471
Mounds, Native Americans, 13-14
Moundville, 13
Mount Vernon, 213-14
Mourning wars, 40, 45, 159
Murray, Judith Sargent, 207, 229, 235
Muslims
  African, 8, 9
  Iberian Peninsula, 5, 7, 9-10
  reconquista, 9-10
  slave trade, 9
  as slaves, 18
Mutiny Act, 166
Mutual aid societies
  of crafts persons, 257
  free African Americans, 253
  Jewish, 236
Mystic Fort, 86-87

N

Narragansett Bay, 84
Narragansett Indians, 76
  and Pequot War, 86-87
Narváez, Pànfílo de, 27, 28
Nashville, battle of, 443-44
Natchez Indians, 114, 115, 157
Nation, The, 445, 449, 474
National bank. *See* Bank of the United
    States
National Bank Act of 1863, 427
National Banking Act, 445
National Convention of the Woman's
    National Loyal League, 470
National Labor Union (NLU), 471-72
National Negro Convention, 342
National Republicans, platform of,
    291, 363, 365, 380
National Road, 292
National Trades' Union, 350

Nationalism
  judicial nationalism, cases related
    to, 293-94
  and Monroe Doctrine, 293
Native American reservations
  colonial era, 69
  Indian Territory, Oklahoma, 327,
    328, 329
  map of (1835), 327
  removal of Indians to, 325-30, 364-65
Native Americans
  Anasazi Indians, 14-15
  berdache, 117
  Cherokees, 328
  domesticated crops of, 11, 14, 23
  Eastern Woodland Indians, 13-14
  gender roles, 11, 14, 45
  and horse, 23, 363
  land as property, view of, 80, 230
  languages of, 12
  lodgings of, 11, 14-15
  matrilineal/matrilocal societies,
    14, 45
  of Mexico, 15, 25-26
  migration to Americas, 11
  mound-building, 13-14
  mourning wars, 40, 45, 159
  as nomads, 11, 14, 377
  Northwest Coast Indians, 15
  Paleo-Indians, 11-13
  Plains Indians, 14
  population loss, causes of, 14, 15,
    21-22
  Pueblo Indians, 28-29, 116-18
  racism, 209, 229-30, 325
  shamans, 269
  of South America, 15, 17
  torture, purpose of, 42-43
  trade, 13-14, 15
  of West Indies, 3, 17-18, 21
  See also specific tribes
Native Americans, colonial era
  attacks by colonists, 67, 117, 209
  attacks on colonists, 66, 115, 118,
    143, 157, 159
  captivity of settlers, 155-56, 159, 162
  and Christianity, 117-18
  and Dutch, 49-52
  and English, 55-57, 62, 66-69,
    76-77, 80-81, 95-96, 105-7
  and French, 106, 109-10, 157
  French and Indian War, 45, 156,
    160-69
  fur trade, 114, 133-34, 230
  intermarriage with Europeans,
    43-44, 62, 67
  land taking by colonists, 62, 69
  Pequot War, 85-87
  and political economy, 97
  Pontiac's Rebellion, 170-71
  post-Revolution status, 209-11, 229-30
  reservations, 69
  and Revolutionary War, 202, 209, 210
  as slaves, 87, 91, 97-98, 105
  wars among tribes, 51, 86-87, 97
  wars with colonists, 67-69, 105-6,
    157, 170-71
Native Americans, New World, 11-23
  attacks on explorers, 24, 29, 39
  and Christianity, 18-20, 33-35, 43-46
  death from European disease,
    21-22, 25, 46
  European trade items, 43, 46
  and French, 40-46
  fur trade, 36, 40, 43, 46
  and political economy, 13-14,
    40-43, 46

slaughter by explorers, 17-18, 26, 28, 29
  as slaves, 18-19, 26, 30
  and Spanish, 17-29
  wars among tribes, 40, 45-46
Native Americans, nineteenth century
  attacks by white Americans, 292, 330, 376
  Black Hawk's War, 330
  Christian missionaries, 373, 377
  death from white disease, 373, 377
  Indian removal to reservations, 325-30, 375-77
  land deals, 281
  landless transients, 283
  survival/customs, disruption of, 377-78
  Treaty of Ghent, 281
  westward white migration, effects of, 375-78
Native Americans, after
    Revolutionary War
  attacks on Americans, 239, 273-74
  attacks by white Americans, 209, 237, 239, 269
  and Christianity, 267
  governing councils of, 230
  Handsome Lake revitalization movement, 268-69
  land deals, 209, 239, 267, 274
  landless transients, 283
  and Lewis and Clark expedition, 266
  Northwest Territory, 237-40
  pan-Indian alliance, 269
  and political economy, 230
  racism, 209, 229-30
  resistance to white culture, 267-69
  Treaty of Ghent, 281
  War of 1812, 273-74, 325
Nativism
  Anglo-Saxon Protestant views, 400-401
  anti-Catholic sentiment, 351-52, 400-401
  political parties of, 400-401
Nauvoo, Illinois, 313
Navajo Indians, 23, 118, 375
Navigation Acts, 94, 107
Navy
  Civil War, 425-26
  creation of, 259
  and War of 1812, 272
Nebraska Territory, Kansas-Nebraska Act, 401-2
Netherlands. See Dutch colonies; New Netherland
New Amsterdam
  Dutch settlement, 48
  See also New York City; New York colony
New Echota, Treaty of, 328
New England
  agriculture, 133, 134
  British objectives during Revolution, 192-95
  colonial exports of, 133
  Dominion of New England, 107
  King Philip's War, 105-6
  quality of life (1660s), 104
  textile manufacturing, 286, 288-90
  See also individual colonies and individual states
New England Artisan, 349
New England Association of Farmers, Mechanics, and Other Workingmen, 349
New-England Courant, 140

New England Emigrant Aid Company, 403
New England Presbyterian Church, 314
New-England Tale (Sedgwick), 356
New France. See Canada
New Guide to Health (Thomson), 354
New Hampshire, statehood, 318
New Hampshire colony
  founding of, 85
  as royal colony, 108
New Harmony, Pennsylvania, 312, 317
New Jersey colony
  and American Revolution, 193, 194, 196-97
  and Dutch, 48
  seizure by England, 94
New Jersey Plan, 214, 215
New Laws of 1542, 20
New Mexico, 116-20
  Anasazi Indians, 14-15
  encomienda system, 118, 119
  Pueblo Indians, 28-29, 116-18
  social groups of (1700s), 119
  Spanish settlement, 26, 28-29, 116-19
New Netherland, 47-52
  African slaves in, 49
  alcohol consumption, 49
  as Dutch settlement, 48-52
  English takeover, 52, 94-95
  ethnic diversity of, 48
  and Native Americans, 49-52, 106
  religious toleration, 49-50, 85, 95
  See also New York City
New Orleans
  and French and Indian War, 168
  French settlement, 114, 115, 145, 157, 265
New Orleans, Battle of, 274, 321, 324, 429, 432
New Sweden, 48
New World
  England in, 54-57, 63-69
  France in, 36-46
  Netherlands in, 47-52
  Spain in, 15-29, 23-28
  See also Colonial America; Dutch colonies; English colonies; French colonies; Spanish colonies
New World political economy
  encomienda system, 19-21, 118, 119
  European financial objectives, 23-26
  and Native Americans, 19
  origins of, 18-19
  plantations, 26
  See also specific colonies, ie. English colonies
New York City
  abolition of slavery, 337, 344
  and Civil War, 421
  growth in 1820s, 298-300
  inauguration of Washington, 221-22
  Irish immigrants in, 352, 392
  working class poverty, 347-48
New York City, colonial era
  and American Revolution, 188, 189, 193-94, 195, 198
  British takeover, 94-95
  free African-Americans, 253
  governance of, 94-95, 108
  Native American-British alliance, 106-7
  New Netherland of Dutch, 48-52
  as port city, 133, 134
  reform societies, 315
  resistance to British laws, 176, 179
  slave revolt, 141-42

urban life, 138-42
New York Evangelical Missionary Society of Young Men, 313
New York General Trades Union, 350
New York Protestant Association, 352
New York state
  Erie Canal, 285-87
  prison system, 359
New York, Treaty of 1790, 239
New-York Weekly Journal, 140
Newfoundland, French in, 36, 40
Newport, and American Revolution, 193
Newport, Christopher, 63
Newspapers
  abolitionist, 342, 344, 390
  anti-Catholic, 352
  colonial era, 140
  and Federalist, The, 234
  post-Revolution, 235
  of workers, 320, 349
Newton, Isaac, 146
Nez Percés Indians, 373, 375
Niagara, 272
Night Riders, 468
Nightingale, Florence, 435
Niles, Hezekiah, 316
Nineteenth century political economy
  and African slaves, 301-3, 391-95
  free labor in, 316-17
  and immigration, 351-53, 391-92
  middle class, 350-51
  Northern boom, 391-93
  organized labor, 348-50
  wage labor, 347-48, 391-92
  white-collar workers, 392
  working class, 347-48
  See also American republic political economy; Expansionism and political economy
Ninth Amendment, rights of, 232
Noble, Harriet, 283, 305
Nomads, Native Americans, 11, 14, 377
Non-Intercourse Act of 1809, 271-72
North Bridge, 188
North Carolina, and American Revolution, 196, 199
North, Lord, 187
North River Steamboat of Clermont, 284-85
North, Simeon, 262
Northern Pacific Railroad, 475
Northern states
  antislavery position, 337, 342-343, 398-399. See also Abolition; Civil War; Civil War, causes
  nineteenth century economic activities, 297-300, 391-92
  See also New England; specific Northern colonies and specific Northern states
Northwest, states of, 303
Northwest Coast Indians, 15
Northwest Ordinance of 1787
  cession of western lands, 211, 212
  slavery prohibition, 208, 211, 258
Northwest Passage, 36, 40, 47
Northwest Territory, 208-13, 237-42
  British evacuation of, 242
  Congress sale of land, 211
  national policy, limitations of, 209, 211, 213, 237-38, 240-41
  Native American-British alliance, 208-9
  and Native American lands, 237-40, 267
  Northwest Ordinance of 1787, 211, 212

scope of, 236-37
  Whiskey Rebellion, 240-41
Notes on the State of Virginia (Jefferson), 223-24, 228, 258, 267

Oberlin College, 343
Observation on the Sources and Effects of Unequal Wealth (Byllesby), 348-49
Occaneecchee Indians, 101
Ogden, Aaron, 294
Oglethorpe, James, 145, 146, 158
Ohio, statehood, 282
Ohio Company, 161
Ohio River Valley
  Cincinnati, growth of, 279-80
  steamboat, 285
Ojibwa Indians, 267, 283
Oklahoma, Indian Territory, 327, 328, 329
Old Spanish Trail, 374
Oliver, Andrew, 175
Oñate, Juan de, 116-17
Onesimus, 146
Opechancanough, 68-69
Oregon Territory, 381-82
Oregon Trail, 374
Organized labor. See Labor unions
Orista Indians, 39
Orphan asylums, 315
Orphan House, 316
Osborne, Sarah, 92, 150
Osgood, Samuel, as postmaster general, 232
O'Sullivan, John, 370-71
Otis, James, Jr., 174
Otis, James, Sr., 174
Ottowa Indians, 161, 239
Outworkers, wage dependency, 347-48
Overland Trail, wagon trains westward, 373-74
Owen, John, 283
Owen, Robert, 312, 317

Paine, Thomas, 137, 146, 189-90, 217, 229
Paleo-Indians, 11-13
Palmer v. Mulligan, 264
Panic of 1819, 295, 317, 337, 347
Panic of 1837, 331, 365, 366-67
Paquiquineo, 33-34
Paris, Treaty of 1763, 168
Paris, Treaty of 1783, 200, 201-2, 236-37
Parker, Richard, 411
Parliament, British, 173
Parris, Samuel, 91-92, 112
Partisanship, new republic, 234
Patroons, 48
Patuxet Indians, 76
Pawnee Indians, 119, 375
Paxton Boys, 170-71
Peace Democrats, 436
Peale, Charles Willson, 235
Penn, William, 95-96
Pennsylvania, and Civil War, 421, 437, 439
Pennsylvania colony, 95-96
  Germans in, 127
  Philadelphia, 95
  and Quakers, 95-96
  religious toleration, 96
  seizure by England, 94
  and slavery, 96
Pennsylvania Hospital, 147

Pennsylvania Society for the Abolition of Slavery, 228
People's Constitution movement, 380
People's Convention, 319
Pequot Indians, 86-87
Pequot War, 85-87
Perry, Commodore, 272
Peru, Inca, 15, 17, 23, 26
Pet banks, 330-31, 366
Petition of Right, 93
Philadelphia, 260
Philadelphia
   and American Revolution, 193
   free African Americans, 253-54
   growth in 1820s, 298-300
   Penn's plan for, 95
   as port city, 133, 134
   resistance to British laws, 179
   as temporary capital, 233
Philadelphia College, 151
Philadelphia Convention. *See* Constitutional Convention
Philadelphia Young Ladies Academy, 235-36
Phillips, Wendell, 343, 470
Phips, Lady, 111
Phips, Sir William, 109
Phrenology, 355
Pickawillany, 160, 161
Pickett, George, 439
Pierce, Franklin
   Kansas-Nebraska Act, 401-4
   as president, 399, 402-4
Pierce, Sarah, 236
Pike, Zebulon, 263
Pilgrims, 73, 75-77
   Mayflower voyage, 76
   and Native Americans, 76-77
   Plymouth colony, 75-77
Pinckney, Charles Cotesworth, 244, 269, 271
Pinckney, Eliza Lucas, 132
Pinckney, Thomas, 242
   as Federalist, 243
Pinckney Treaty, 242, 261, 265
Pinkster Day, 140
Piñon, 14
Piracy
   English, 52-53
   French, 38
Pithouses, 14
Pitt, William, 167, 168, 176
Plains Indians, 14, 23
Plan of Union, 252
Plantations
   and African culture, 144
   colonial America, 142-45
   cotton, 260-61, 301
   in expansionary era, 301-2
   indentured servants, 17, 63-64, 68, 71
   negative effects on labor-wage market, 302
   plantation village, life for slaves, 144, 301-3, 340-41
   rice, 100, 133, 260, 301, 340-41
   slave labor, 9, 26, 49, 71-72, 98-100, 132-33, 301-2, 340-41
   sugar, 9, 49, 91, 98, 99, 116, 301
   task system of labor, 133, 301, 340
   tobacco, 61-62, 71-72, 132-33, 301
Plea for the West, A (Beecher), 314, 353
Plessy v. Ferguson, 476
Plymouth colony, 73, 75-77
   See also Pilgrims
Plymouth Company, 63, 76, 77
Pocahontas, 62, 67-68

Pokanoket Indians, 76
Political campaigns, first national campaign, 324
Political economy
   capitalism, 134-35
   consumer revolution, 130
   economic revolutions, 130
   Enlightenment ideals, 146-47
   feudalism, 70
   industrious revolution, 130
   linked economic development, 134
   Locke as first theorist, 108
   mercantilism, 46, 94
   prosperity and religious beliefs, 49-50
   and war, 158-59, 203
   See also Age of discovery political economy; American republic political economy; Civil War political economy; Colonial era political economy; Expansionism and political economy; New World political economy; Nineteenth century political economy
Political parties
   American Party (Know-Nothings), 400-401
   Antimason Party, 320
   Democratic Republicans, 234, 241, 250
   Equal Rights Party, 368
   Federalists, 234
   Free-Soil Party, 396, 397, 400
   Liberty Party, 343, 369, 379, 382
   Madison's criticism of, 234
   and political economy, 232-34
   Whig Party, 331, 365-66
   workers, 320-21
   Working Men's Party, 320
   See also Democratic Party; Republican Party
Political virtue, meaning of, 223
Polk, James K.
   and national bank, 386
   presidency of, 381-86
   War with Mexico, 382-84
Polo, Marco, 4, 6, 16, 17
Polygyny, Native Americans, 44, 68
Pontiac's Rebellion, 170-71
Poor and poverty
   in colonial cities, 141
   and evangelical missionaries, 313-14
   homelessness, 315-16
   housing of, 468
   relief to needy, 141, 236, 313
   working class, 347-48
Popé, 118
Pope Day, 140
Pope, John, 431
Popular sovereignty
   Douglas on, 396, 401-2, 405, 408
   meaning of, 396
Population growth
   African slaves (1700s), 128-29
   colonial era (1700s), 65, 125-29
Portugal, age of discovery
   New World empires, 18, 29
   plantations, 7, 9, 18
   slave trade, 7, 9
   trade with Africa, 7, 9
Potato famine, Ireland, 352, 391
Potatoes, 23
Potawatomi Indians, 239, 283
Potlatch ceremony, 15
Potomac River, plans for capital, 233
Pottawatomie Massacre, 404, 410
Poverty. *See* Poor and poverty

Poverty Point, Louisiana, 11
Power of Sympathy, The (Brow), 235
Powhatan, chief, 57, 66-68
Powhatan Indians, 33-34, 57
   Anglo-Powhattan Wars, 67, 69
   and Virginia colonists, 62, 63, 66-69
Pregnancy, premarital, 142, 226
Presbyterians
   African Presbyterians, 254
   colonial era, 148, 151
   Finney's unorthodoxy, 313-14
   New Lights and Old Lights, 151, 252
   Scotland, 93, 127
Priestly, Joseph, 146
Primogeniture, 228
Princeton University, 185
   founding of, 151
Prisons
   post-Revolution, 236
   state prison system, 359-60
Privateering, English, 52-53
Proclamation of 1763, 171
Proclamation of Amnesty and Reconstruction, 452
Proclamation of Neutrality, 241-42
Property ownership
   as American ideal, 223-24
   colonial era, 64, 68, 80
   elite control of land, 225, 227
   free African Americans, 455
   Native American view, 80, 230
   Specie Circular and purchase, 331
   and voting rights, 317-18
   and women, 207, 228
Proprietary colony, meaning of, 70
Prostitution, reform associations, 368
Protestant Episcopalian Church, 251
Protestants
   anti-Catholic sentiment, 352, 400-401
   beliefs of, 74
   in England, 52, 53, 74, 93-94
   nativism, 400-401
   in Netherlands, 47
   See also Evangelical Protestantism
Providence Island, 72
Public education, colonial era, 81
Pueblo Indians
   revolts of, 29, 118
   Spanish rule, 28-29, 116-18
Pueblos, 15
Puerto Rico, Spanish territory, 17, 21, 23
Punch, John, 72
Puritans, 73-87
   beliefs of, 74-75, 78-80, 85
   commodification of environment, 80-81
   dissenters, 83-85
   English origins, 74
   family life, 81-88
   gender roles, 81-82, 84-85
   governance of, 79-80
   and Native Americans, 80-81, 85-87
   and political economy, 80-81
   prosperity as dilemma, 104
   and republicanism, 177
   witchcraft trials, 91-92, 110-12
Putnam, Ann, 112

Quakers
   as abolitionists, 343
   beliefs of, 95
   and Native Americans, 95-96
   and Pennsylvania colony, 95-96
   persecution of, 95, 104

radical, Shakers, 311-12
   and slavery, 96
   temperance movement, 356
Quartering of soldiers
   Mutiny Act, 166
   Quartering Act of 1765, 172, 176, 178
   Quartering Act of 1774, 180
Quebec
   and American Revolution, 189, 193
   French and Indian War, 168
   French settlement of, 40-43, 114
Quebec Act of 1774, 180
Queen Anne's War, 109-10, 116, 157
Quitman, John A., 403

R

Rachel and Reuben (Rowson), 235
Racism
   African slaves, 72, 98, 143, 228
   European Jews, 10, 99
   and manifest destiny, 371
   Native Americans, 209, 229-30, 325
Radical Republicans, 452-53, 457-58, 465-68
Railroads
   beginning of, 284
   expansion of (1850s), 394-95
Raleigh, Sir Walter, 35
   and Roanoke, 54-56
Ramsey, Elizabeth, 283
Randolf, Edmund
   as attorney general, 232
   and Constitutional Convention, 214
Randolph, John, 271
Rapp, George, 312
Rappites, 312
Re-export-trade
   meaning of, 262
   post-Revolution, 225
Recession, and dissolution of Second Bank, 331
Reconquista, 9-10
Reconstruction
   Congressional control of, 460-65
   corruption problem, 472-74
   depression of 1870s, 474-76
   and Johnson, 455-59
   labor unions, 471-72
   and Liberal Republicans, 474
   and Radical Republicans, 452-53, 457-58, 465-68
   Ten-Percent Plan, 452-53
   Wade-Davis Bill, 453-54
   white supremacy groups, 468-69, 475
   See also African Americans, free slaves
Reconstruction Acts, 460, 465, 468
Red Shirts, 468
Red Sticks, 273, 330
Redemptioners, 96, 103, 127
Reform activism
   Benevolent Empire, 314-16
   educational reform, 357-59
   involvement with politics, 367-69
   moral suasion approach, 315
   penal reform, 359-60
   self-reform, 354-56
   temperance movement, 356-57
   urban evangelical societies, 313-14
   woman's rights movement, 369-70
   women's participation, 299-300, 315-16
Religious groups
   African Americans. *See* Black church
   African slaves, 144, 151
   Africans, 7, 8

Aztecs, 25
and Enlightenment, 147
evangelical Protestants, 190, 312-16
Great Awakening, 147-51
as impetus for colonization, 70, 73-74, 84
itinerant preachers, 123-24, 148-49, 251-52
millennial communities, 311-13
Native Americans, 15
Protestants, 74
Puritans, 74-75, 78-80, 85
Quakers, 95-96
revivalism, 147-51, 251-52
See also individual religious groups and religious denominations
Religious toleration
in colonies, 49-50, 70, 84-85, 96
and commercial prosperity, 49-50
and humanism, 47
Removal Act of 1830, 327-30
Rensselaer, Kiliaen von, 50
Report on the Encouragement of Manufacturers, 234
Report on Public Credit, 233
"Repository for National Curiosities" (Peale), 235
Republican, 474
Republican Party
African Americans in, 475
anti-slavery position, 400, 404-9, 412-13
first presidential candidate (1856), 404-5
Liberal Republicans, 472, 474
National Republicans, 291, 363, 365, 380
origins of, 400, 404-6
Radical Republicans, 450, 452-53, 457-58, 465-68
split in 1808, 271
Whig Party, 365-66
Republicanism
as colonial ideal, 176-77
elitist connection, 331
meaning of, 176
and political economy, 223-27, 264
and slavery, 208, 302
and women, 207, 229
Requerimiento, 19
Reservations. See Native American reservations
Restoration, 95, 104
Revenue Act of 1766, 176
Revere, Paul
and American Revolution, 187
pre-Revolution, 140
Revivalism
Congregationalism, 251-52
Great Awakening, 147-51
urban revivals, 313-14
Revolutionary War. See American Revolution
Rhode Island, white male suffrage, 319
Rhode Island colony
as charter colony, 84, 108
founding of, 84
Quakers in, 104
religious toleration, 84-85
Rhodes, Elisha Hunt, 434
Rice cultivation
and African slaves, 100, 133, 301
Carolina colony, 100, 130
expense of, 260
Rich Man, Poor Man (Sedgwick), 355
Richmond
and American Revolution, 199

capital of Confederacy, 425
and Civil War, 425, 430-31, 440, 444
Richmond Dispatch, 421
Riots
Civil War draft riots, 436-37
colonial era, 140-41
of workers, 257
Road building
National Road, 292
regional areas (1830), 287
Roanoke, 54-57
as failed colony, 55-56
Roanoke Indians, 55, 56
Robards, Lewis, 323
Robbins, Thomas, 252
Rockingham, Marquess of, 175-76
Rodney, Caesar, 181
Rolfe, John, 61-62, 67-68
Roman Empire, slavery in, 9
Roosevelt, Nicholas, 285
Rosecrans, William S., 441
Rowson, Susanna, 235, 236
Royal colony
Maryland colony as, 108
Massachusetts as, 108
meaning of, 68
New Hampshire as, 108
Virginia as, 68
Royal Council, 63, 65
Royal Society of London, 147
Ruffin, Edmund, 417-18, 420, 423, 429, 433, 440, 443
Rumsey, John, 284
Rural areas
colonial America, 142
debt/credit system, 227
elite view of, 227
household production, 298-99
post-Revolution, 223-25, 227
Rush, Benjamin, 292
as Democratic-Republican, 234
Russwurm, John, 342
Rutgers University, founding of, 151

S

Sacagawea, 266
Safety valve theory, of western expansion, 394
Sagamité, 43
St. Augustine, Spanish settlement, 26, 28, 54, 56, 116
St. Clair, Arthur, 239
Saint Dominque, 116
revolution for freedom, 265
slave revolt, 249-50, 252, 338
St. Elena, 38
St. Lawrence River, 36, 38, 40, 43
Salem witchcraft trials, 91-92, 110-12
Salt Lake City, Mormon community, 313
Samoset, 77
San Antonio, 28
San Francisco, 28
San Juan de Ulúa, 52, 53
San Salvador, 3
Sanctification, Puritans, 85
Sanitary Commission, 436
Santa Anna, Antonio Lopez de, 372, 382-83, 402
Santa Fe, 28, 117
Santa Fe Trail, 374
Santo Domingo, 469
Saratoga, battle of, 195
Sauk Indians, 239, 267, 283
removal from homelands, 327, 330
Savannah
and American Revolution, 193

and Civil War, 444
Savannah Indians, 97
Saxton, Rufus, 456
Scalawags, 461, 475
Scandals. See Corruption
Scandinavian immigrants, 1800s, 298
School segregation, free African-Americans, 359
Schools
and free African Americans, 454
post-Revolution, 235-36
universities, 81, 147, 151
for women, 235-36, 357
See also Education; Universities and colleges
Schurz, Carl, 469
Scotch-Irish, in colonial America, 127
Scotland, Presbyterians in, 93, 127
Scott, Dred, 406-7
Scott, Winfield, 328, 367, 383-84, 399
Sea Islands, 143, 451, 455
Seamstresses, wage exploitation of, 347-48
Second Bull Run, battle of, 431
Second Continental Congress, 188-91
Articles of Confederation, 191
Declaration of Independence, 190-91
limitations of, 213
Secret societies, Order of Freemasons, 319-20
Sedgwick, Catherine Maria, 355
Segregation, racial. See African American discrimination/segregation
Selectmen, 80
Self-improvement, 354-56
self-care, 354, 355
self-culture, 355-56
self-education, 354
"Self-Reliance" (Emerson), 356
Self-sufficiency, as American ideal, 223-24, 316
Selu peoples, 328
Seminole Indians, 267
conquest by Jackson, 292
resistance to removal, 330
Seneca County Courier, 370
Seneca Falls Conference, 369-70
Seneca Indians, 267
Separate but equal, African Americans, 476
Separation of powers, meaning of, 217
Separatists, 75, 83, 311
Sepúlveda, Juan Ginés de, 20
Seven Days, battle of, 431
Seven Years' War, 162
Seventh Amendment, rights of, 232
Sewall, Samuel, 343
Seward, William Henry, 406, 410, 412, 469
Sexuality
premarital pregnancy, 142, 226
same-sex preference. See Homosexuality
self-discipline movement, 355
Seymour, Horatio, 468
Shakers, 311-12
gender roles, 312
inventions of, 312
Shamans, Native American, 269
Sharecropping, free African Americans, 462-65
Shawnee Indians, and Northwest Territory, 239-40
Shays' Rebellion, 206, 213
Shenandoah Valley Campaign, 442
Sherman, John, 445

Sherman, Roger, and Constitutional Convention, 214-15
Sherman, William Tecumseh, 404, 441, 444, 455
Shiloh, battle of, 429, 435
Shipbuilding
colonial era, 134
post-Revolution, 242
Shipping
British seizure of ships, 262, 270, 272
colonial era, 134-35
flatboats, 304
prosperity related to, 261-62
re-export-trade, 261
seamen, ethnic profile, 262
steamboats, 284-85
Shirley, William, 163-64
Shoshone Indians, 266, 375
Simpson, Stephen, 357
Sing-Sing, 359
Sioux Indians, 23, 375, 378
Sixth Amendment, rights of, 232
Slash-and-burn method, 14
Slater, Samuel, 262, 263, 286
Slave power, 405-6
Slave society
Carolina colony as, 97-100
meaning of, 100, 102
Virginia colony as, 100, 102-3
Slavery
in Africa, 7-9
ancient Rome, 9
characteristics of, 102
in Europe, 9, 18
Native Americans slaves, 18-19, 26, 87, 91, 97-98, 105
See also entries under African slaves
Slidell, John, 424
Smallpox, death of Native Americans, 21-22, 46
Smith, Adam, 147
Smith, John, 63, 65, 66-67, 69
Smith, Joseph, Jr., 312-13, 319
Social class. See Social stratification
Social life, colonial era, 137-40
Social stratification
and Civil War soldiers, 428
colonial America, 137, 138, 141
and education, 357-58
middle class, 350-51
post-Revolution, 225-27
working class, 347-48
See also Elite; Poor and Poverty
Societies and institutions
of African Americans, 253
colonial era, 139, 147
of elite, 139
of Enlightenment era, 147
reformers. See Reform activism
western cities, 304
of workers, 255-56
Society for the Advancement of Christianity, 316
Society of Agriculture, 258
Society for Establishing Useful Manufacturers, 236
Society of Free People of Color for Promoting the Instruction and School education of Children of African Descent, 253
Society for the Protection of Aged Seamen, 316
Society for the Relief of Aged and Indigent Respectable Females, 316
Society for Supporting the Gospel, 313
Some Causes of Popular Poverty (Blatchly), 317

Songhay, 7
Sons of Liberty, 179
Soto, Hernando de, 27-28
Soulé, Pierre, 403
South America
    in age of discovery, 17
    Dutch in, 49, 91
    Native American cultures of, 15
    Portuguese in, 29, 49
    revolt of colonies (1815), 293
    Spanish in, 15, 17, 23, 26, 29
South Carolina
    anti-abolitionist violence, 344
    and Civil War, 420, 444
South Carolina Association, 338
South Carolina colony
    and American Revolution,
        195-97, 199
    as proprietary colony, 97
    slavery in, 261
South Carolina Exposition and Protest,
    338-39
Southern states
    colonial era exports, 132
    economic stagnation and slavery,
        302, 393, 407, 426-27
    expansionary era economic activi-
        ties, 282-83, 300-303
    proslavery position, 417-418, 344-
        346. *See also* Civil War; Civil War,
        causes
    rural white underclass, 302
    tariff policy, negative aspects, 337-41
    See also specific Southern colonies
        and specific Southern states
Southwestern lands
    Native Americans of, 14-15, 28-29
    Spanish settlement, 26, 28-29, 116-19
Southwestern states, states of, 303-4
Spain
    Florida ceded to U.S., 292-93
    Ostand Manifesto, 403
    Pinckney's Treaty, 242
    See also Mexico; Spain, age of dis-
        covery; Spanish colonies
Spain, age of discovery, 9-11
    Columbus exploration, 3-5, 16-19
    empire. *See* Spanish colonies
    explorations (1492-1542), 24
    expulsion of Jews (1492), 10
    humanism, 10-11
    Inquisition, 10
    reconquista, 9-10
    rulers in, 10-11, 16, 23, 74
Spalding, Eliza Hart, 373
Spalding, Henry, 373
Spanish colonies, 15-29
    Aztecs, conquest of, 15, 17, 23, 25-
        26, 116
    Carolina territory, 97-98
    Columbian exchange, 22-23
    conquistadors, 19-20, 23, 26, 27, 35
    encomienda system, 19-21, 118-19
    Florida, 23-25, 27-28, 38-39, 116
    free black community, 116
    Inca, conquest of, 26
    Mexico, 25-26
    and Native Americans, 17-29
    Requerimiento, 19
    Southwestern lands, 26, 28-29
    West Indies, 17-18, 21-23
Specie Circular, 331, 366
Speedwell, 67
Spies. *See* Espionage
Squanto, 76-77, 85
Squatters, 304
Stamp Act of 1765, 171-72

    resistance to, 173-76
Stamp Act Congress, 175
Standard Oil corporation, 472
Stanton, Edwin M., 429, 466-68
Stanton, Elizabeth Cady, 369-70, 470-71
"Star-Spangled Banner, The" (Key), 273
State governments, creation of (1775-
    1780), 191-92
Staten Island, and American
    Revolution, 193
States and federal government
    and Articles of Confederation, 191
    nationalist versus localist views,
        212-13
Steam-power
    agriculture-related technology, 262
    steam engine, 284
    steamboat, 280, 284-85
Stephens, Alexander, 419, 440
Stevens, Thaddeus, 450, 453, 466, 468
Stewart, A.T., 392
Stewart, Maria, 342
Stone, Barton, 252, 313
Stono Bridge, 143
Stowe, Harriet Beecher, 351, 399
Strikes
    nineteenth century, 349-50, 368
    as restraint of trade, 264
Stuart, J.E.B., 410
Stuyvesant, Peter, 48-49
Suffolk Resolves, 181
Suffrage. *See* Voting rights; Woman's
    suffrage movement
Sugar
    demand in colonial era, 26, 135-36
    refining, inventions related to, 262
Sugar Act of 1764, 171, 178
Sugar plantations
    in American South, 301
    of Dutch, 49
    of English, 91, 98-99
    of French, 116
    of Portuguese, 7, 9, 18
    in West Indies, 91, 98, 99, 116
Sullivan, John L., 209
Sumner, Charles, 404, 450, 453, 469
Sunday school movement, 315
Sunday School Union, 252, 316
Supreme Court
    establishment of, 232
    first justice, 232
    judicial nationalism, 293-94
    judicial review, 259
    Marshall decisions, 293-94
Susquehannock Indians, 70, 101
Swansea, 105
Swartwout, Samuel, 325
Sweat houses, 45
Sylvis, William, 472
Syphilis, in era of exploration, 21-22

T

Tabasco Indians, 25, 116
Taino Indians, 3, 4, 17, 19, 21, 23
Talleyrand, Charles Maurice de, 244
Tallmadge, James, 297
Tanacharison, Iroquois chieftan, 161
Taney, Roger, 407
Taos, 118
Tappan, Arthur, 344, 369
Tappan, Lewis, 344, 369
Tariffs, 232-33
    Force Bill, 341
    negative effects, 337-41
    purpose of, 232
    revenues (1790-1799), 233

Tariff of 1828, 323, 337-41
Tariff of 1832, 339-41
Tariff Act of 1789, 232
Tascaluzan Indians, 28
Taverns, colonial era, 140
Taxation
    excise taxes, 240-41
    post-Revolution era, 204-5, 213
    on traded goods. *See* Tariffs
Taylor, Zachary
    as president, 396-97
    in War with Mexico, 383-84
Tea, demand in colonial era, 135-36
Tea Act of 1773, 178, 179
Tecumseh, resistance to white
    culture, 269
Telegraph, invention of, 391
Temperance movement, 356-57, 368
    and nativists, 400
Temperance Society, 316
Ten-Percent Plan, 452-53
Tennent, Gilbert, 148, 151
Tennessee
    and Civil War, 429, 441, 443-44
    settlement of, 204
    statehood, 318
Tennessee Indians, 239
Tenochtitlan, 25-26
Tenskwatawa (The Prophet), 240
    resistance to white culture, 269
Tenth Amendment, rights of, 232, 234
Tenure of Office Act, 466-67
Term limits, first state constitutions,
    191-92, 213
Tertium Quid, 271
Texas
    annexation of, 381-82, 384
    independence from Mexico, 364,
        371-73
    slavery issue, 371-73, 381, 397
Textiles
    of Africa, 7
    Lowell mills, 286, 288-90
    Slater mills, 262-63
Thatcher, Dr. James, 196
Theater, colonial era, 140
Thirteenth Amendment, 456
    rights of, 460
Thomas, George, 441, 443-44
Thompson, George, 344
Thompson, Samuel, 354, 355
Thoroughgood, Adam, 71
Three-Fifths Compromise, 215, 274, 296
Tilden, Samuel J., 475-76
Tillotson, John, 147, 148
Timberlake, Margaret O'Neale, 325
Timucua Indians, 27
Tipis, 14
Tippecanoe River, Battle of, 269
Tituba, 91-92, 110, 111
Tobacco plantations
    slave labor, 132-34, 301
    Virginia colony, 61-62, 70-73, 132-33
Tocqueville, Alexis de
    on American associationism, 314-15
    on reformers, 359-60
    on westward migration, 376
Toltecs, 15
Tomatoes, 23
Toombs, Robert, 405, 440
Tordesillas, Treaty of 1494, 18
Totem poles, 15
Town meeting, New England, 80
Townshend, Charles, 176
Townshend Revenue Act of 1767, 176
    resistance and repeal of, 176-77

Trade. *See* Exported goods; Global
    trade; Imported goods
Trail of Tears, 327, 329
Trans-Appalachian West. *See* Western
    territory
Transcendentalists, 356
Transcontinental Treaty of 1819, 292-
    93, 371
Transportation and expansionism,
    283-86
    bridges, 284
    Erie Canal, 285-86
    railroads, 284, 394-95
    regional development (1830), 287
    road building (1810-1820), 284
    steam engine, 284
    steamboat, 284-85
Tredegar Iron Works, 430
Trent, 424
Tripoli War, 259-60
Trist, John, 384
Troup, Michael, 325
Troy Female Academy, 357
Turner, Nat, 340
Tuscarora Indians, 157
Tweed, Boss, 472-73
Twelfth Amendment, provisions of, 259
Twentieth century political economy,
    World War I, 64
Twenty-Seventh Amendment, 232
Two Treatises of Government (Locke), 108
Tyler, John
    Native American policy, 330
    as president, 380-82
    and Texas annexation, 381
*Tyrannical Libertymen: A Discourse on
    Negro-Slavery in the United States,* 228

U

Uncle Tom's Cabin (Stowe), 399
Union-Pacific Railroad, 472
Unions. *See* Labor unions
Unitarian Book and Tract Society, 316
Unitarians, 252
United States, assertion as nation, 292-
    93, 445
United States Gazette, 309
Universalism, meaning of, 139
Universalists, 252
Universities and colleges, colonial era,
    81, 147, 151
University of Pennsylvania, founding
    of, 151
Upshur, Abel, 381
Urban culture
    learning organizations, 235
    social life, colonial era, 138-40
Urban growth. *See* Cities and urban
    growth
Utah, U.S. claim to, 384
Utopian communities, New
    Harmony, 317

V

Vaccination, colonial era, 146
Vallandigham, Clement L., 426, 436
Van Buren, Martin
    and depression of 1837, 366-67
    and first national campaign, 324
    on Indian removal, 326
    as president, 365-79
    as secretary of state, 325
    as vice president, 366
Vance, Zebulon, 440
Vane, Henry, 85

Vargas, Diego de, 118
Velasco, Don Luís de, 33-34, 38
Vermont, statehood, 318
Verrazano, Giovanni de, 37
Vesey, Denmark, 338
Vice reform, 368
Vicksburg, battle of, 436, 439
Vikings, 4
Vindication of the Rights of Women
   (Wollstonecraft), 229
Virginia, 426
Virginia
   and American Revolution, 199
   and Civil War, 423, 426, 430-31,
      436, 440-42, 444
   Richmond as Confederate capital,
      425, 430
   Turner slave rebellion, 340
Virginia colony, 63-73, 100-103
   and American Revolution, 189,
      196, 199
   Bacon's Rebellion, 100-102
   as charter colony, 63, 70
   French and Indian War, 161-62
   governance, 63, 65-66, 68
   House of Burgesses, 181
   indentured servants in, 63-64, 68, 71
   Jamestown, 63-69
   land grants, 64, 68
   and Native Americans, 62, 63, 66-69
   political economy of, 68
   population (1607-1699), 65
   as royal colony, 68
   settlers, diversity of, 63-65, 71
   slavery in, 71-72, 100, 102-3
   starvation and death, 65-66
   tobacco growing, 61-62, 68, 70-73
Virginia Company, 62-64, 68, 76
Virginia Plan, 214
Virginia Resolves, 174
Virtual representation, of colonists in
   Parliament, 173
Voodun, 303
Voting restrictions
   free African-Americans, 255, 319,
      453-54
   rationale for, 318-19
   women, 229, 470-71
Voting rights
   African Americans, 458-60, 470
   and property ownership, 317-18
   white male suffrage, 317-19
   women's suffrage, 470-71
Voyages (Mackenzie), 266

W

Wade, Benjamin, 402, 421, 453, 467
Wade-Davis Bill, 453-54
Wage labor, wage dependency, working
   class, 347-48, 391-92
Wagon trains, 373-75
Walker, David, 342
Walker, Robert, 382
Walls, Josiah T., 462
Waltham system, 286, 288-90
Wampanoag Indians, 105, 106
Wampum trade
   and Dutch, 50-51
   and French, 43
Wanchese, 54, 56
War, and political economy, 158-59, 203
War of 1812
   battles and campaigns of, 273

declaration of war, 272
   pre-War events, 259-60, 271-72
War Hawks, 272
War of Jenkins' Ear, 158
War of the Roses, 52
Ward, Nathaniel, 85
Washington, 379
Washington, D.C.
   abolition of slavery, 432
   as capital, 258
   slavery in, 344, 397, 420
Washington, George
   and American Revolution, 189,
      193, 196-97, 199
   and Constitutional Convention,
      213-14
   farewell address, 243
   as Federalist, 234
   French and Indian War, 161-63
   inauguration of, 221-22
   Native American policy, 238-40
   and Northwest Territory, 237-42
   plantation of, 132-33
   pre-Revolution position, 171
   presidency of, 232, 234
   Proclamation of Neutrality, 241-42
   Whiskey Rebellion, 241
Washington, Lewis, 410
Water power, textile manufacturing,
   262-63
Wayne, Anthony, 239, 242
Wea Indians, 160
Wealth of Nations, The (Smith), 147
Weapons. See Defense and military
Webster, Daniel
   as National Republican, 291
   Omnibus Bill, 397-98
   on states' rights, 339
   as Whig, 365
Weems, Mason Locke "Parson," 235
Weiland (Brown), 235
Weld, Theodore Dwight, 343
Welde, Thomas, 82
Werowance, 68, 69
Wesley, Charles, 124
Wesley, John, 124
West Indies
   African slavery in, 71-72, 91, 98-99,
      116, 197
   American exports to, 133
   Columbus voyage to, 3-5
   Native Americans of, 3, 17-18, 21
   sugar plantations, 91, 98, 99, 116
West Point, U.S. Military Academy, 263
West Virginia, statehood, 420
Western Spy, The, 279, 280
Western states
   Civil War, 428, 429-30
   slavery abolished, 432
Western territory
   and African slaves, 371-73, 393-94
   cities, growth of, 304
   homes/lodging, 305
   internal migration to, 353, 373-75
   land claims, 304, 305
   land parcels, purchase of, 282, 295
   and manifest destiny, 364
   migrants, varieties of, 282-83, 373-74
   of Native Americans, 376-78
   Overland Trail, 373-74
   population increase (1830), 304
   safety valve theory, 394
   settlement patterns, 304-5
   universal male suffrage, 318

wagon trains, 373-74
   See also Expansionism; Northwest
      Territory
Westo War, 97
Wheat, as export, 132-33
Wheelwright, John, 85
Whig Party (American)
   anti-Jacksonians, 365-66
   decline and end of, 399, 402, 425
   Harrison as, 379-80
   origins of, 331
   pro-slavery position, 396-97, 399,
      412, 413
Whiskey Rebellion, 240-41
Whiskey Ring, 472
White, Amos, 253
White Cloud, 330
White-collar workers, nineteenth cen-
   tury, 392
White, Hugh Lawson, as Whig, 365
White, John, 55, 56, 57
White supremacy, Reconstruction era
   groups, 468-69, 475
Whitefield, George, 123-24, 148-49
Whitman, Marcus, 373
Whitman, Narcissa Prentiss, 373, 374
Whitman, Walt, 377
Whitney, Eli, 260, 262-63
Wilberforce, William, 337
Wilderness Campaign, Civil War,
   441, 442
Wilkes, Charles, 380
Willamette Valley, 374
Willard, Emma, 357
William and Mary, founding of, 151
William of Orange, 94
Williams, Abigail, 91, 112
Williams, Ann, 253
Williams, Betty, 91, 112
Williams, Eunice, 162
Williams, Richard, 256
Williams, Roger, 83-85
Wilmington, as port city, 133
Wilmot, David, 396
Wilmot Proviso, 396-97, 402, 404
Wingfield, Edward Maria, 63
Wingina, 55
Winnebagoe Indians, 267
Winthrop, John, 78-79, 82, 84, 85
Wirt, William, 320
Wisconsin Territory, *Dred Scott* case, 406-7
Wise, Henry A., 410
Wise, John, 147
Wister, Daniel, 134
Witchcraft trials, 91-92, 110-12
Wolfe, James, 166, 168
Wollstonecraft, Mary, 229
Women, colonial era
   African-American women, 342
   and American Revolution, 207
   gender roles, 131-32
   Hutchinson, Anne, 84-85
   in plantation society, 72-73
   Salem witchcraft trials, 110-12
Women, nineteenth century
   abolitionists, 342, 343, 346, 369
   African slaves, 303
   authors, 351, 356, 399
   Civil War nurses, 435-36
   domestic workers, 392
   magazine editors, 356
   reform activism, 299-300, 315-16
   schools for women, 354
   textile workers, 288-90

urban workers, 299-300
   wage exploitation of, 347-48
   wagon train journey, 374-75
   workers' rights organizers, 349, 354
Women, after Revolutionary War, 206-8
   employment restrictions, 228-29
   gender roles, 206-8
   in labor force, 228-29
   legal status, 228
   property ownership, denial of,
      207, 228
   and republican ideals, 207, 229
   schools for women, 235-36
   voting restrictions, 229
Women's rights movement, 369-70
   Declaration of Sentiments, 370
   Seneca Falls Conference, 369-70
women's suffrage, 470-71
Woodlands Indians, 13-14, 40, 44
Woolman, John, 208
Worcester v. Georgia, 326
Work
   as American ideal, 223
   workplace discrimination. See
      Employment discrimination
Workday, ten-hour day demand, 349
Worker activism, labor unions, 349-50
Workers
   common laws applied to, 264
   labor unions, 348-50
   political parties of, 320-21
   status decline, nineteenth century,
      316-17
   white-collar workers, 392
Working class, 347-48
   immigrants as, 351-53, 391-92
   living conditions of, 348
   schooling of, 357
   wage dependency of, 347-48, 391-92
Working Man's Manual, A (Simpson), 357
Working Men's Advocate, The, 320
Working Men's Association of New
   York, 357
Working Men's Party, 320
World War I, financing war, 64
Wright, Frances, 349, 354, 369
Wright, Martha Coffin, 350
Writs of Assistance, 174
Wyandots, 239
Wyoming, U.S. claim to, 384

X

XYZ Affair, 244

Y

Yakima Indians, 375
Yale University, founding of, 147
Yamasee Indians, 97, 157
Yamasee War, 116, 143, 157
Yana Indians, 375
Yancey, William Lowndes, 412
Yeoman households, 302
Yorba, 7
Young, Brigham, 313
Young Ladies Academy, 236
Young, Litt, 438
Young Mother, The (Alcott), 356

Z

Zenger, John Peter, 140
Zuni pueblo, 28